LATIN AMERICA

BLAIR P. TURNER

THE WORLD TODAY SERIES

2015–2016

49TH EDITION

Blair P. Turner . . .

is Professor of History and Professor of International Studies and Political Science at the Virginia Military Institute. He earned his Ph.D. in Latin American History from the University of Florida and holds the Certificate in Latin American Studies from the renowned Center for Latin American Studies at that university. He is a two-time Fulbright scholar and has served as visiting professor at the Universidad del Sur in Argentina, the Universidad Nacional in Uruguay, and the École Politechnique in France. For the past twenty-five years, he has been an editor of *The Journal of Military History*, published jointly by the George C. Marshall Foundation and the Virginia Military Institute for the Society for Military History. He assumed authorship of *Latin America* in 2015.

The World Today Series has thousands of subscribers across the U.S. and Canada. A sample list of users who annually rely on this most up-to-date material includes:

Public library systems
Universities and colleges
High schools
Federal and state agencies
All branches of the armed forces & war colleges
National Geographic Society
National Democratic Institute
Agricultural Education Foundation
Exxon Corporation
Chevron Corporation
CNN

Adapted, rewritten and revised annually
from a book entitled *Latin America 1967*,
published in 1967 and succeeding years by

Rowman & Littlefield
An imprint of The Rowman & Littlefield Publishing Group, Inc.
4501 Forbes Blvd., Suite 200, Lanham, MD 20706
www.rowman.com

International Standard Book Number: 978-1-4758-1870-3

International Standard Serial Number: 0092-4148

Library of Congress Catalog Number 2015945682

Cover design by nvision graphic design

Cartographer: William L. Nelson

Typography by Barton Matheson Willse & Worthington
Baltimore, MD 21244

ACKNOWLEDGMENTS

This volume is the cumulative product of almost a half-century of dedicated and scholarly effort by numerous persons in all the Americas. The present author hopes to continue their good work.

São Paulo, Brazil, in 1930 . . .

. . . and today

CONTENTS

Stone piece, Tiahuanaco culture, Bolivia

The UN has received into its ranks many small countries, such as those of the Caribbean region. The purpose of this series is to reflect *modern world dynamics.* Thus, we mention only briefly the beautiful nations of the Lesser Antilles and concentrate our attention on the growth of the larger, developing countries.

Latin America Today

Latin America, always a land of color and conflict, is undergoing the most dramatic changes of its post-colonial history. These changes—political, economic, technological and cultural—are accelerating as the 21st century progresses. Latin America in 2000 bore little resemblance to the Latin America of 1900. Despite some notable exceptions, Latin America gave rise to a stereotype that persists to this day of tropical republics mired in squalor, ruled by self-serving autocrats and lagging decades if not centuries behind the economically advanced societies of Europe and North America.

Such a view ignores the fact that Argentina at the turn of the 20th century was an industrialized and agriculturally rich society boasting a higher per capita income than that of the United States or France. Sadly, as is true of many stereotypes, there was enough element of truth throughout the rest of the region to reinforce the perception of dictators, destitution and depression. Since World War II, this picture has been slowly, painfully, and sometimes violently evolving into a collection of societies entering the modern world. Some have evolved more than others, but the trend is inexorable. This evolution involves four discrete elements: a democratic revolution; economic diversification and expansion; technological acceleration; and cultural growth and projection.

DEMOCRATIC REVOLUTION

The sudden collapse of communism and the emergence of democracy in Eastern Europe at the beginning of the 1990s was one of the watershed events of world history. Less dramatic but no less historic was the slow, inexorable shift of Latin America away from its past of *caudillo* strongmen, military juntas and revolving-door regimes and toward constitutionally elected civilian governments. As recently as 1977, only three of the 20 true "Latin" American republics had genuinely democratic systems with free elections involving two or more political parties and peaceful trans-

fers of power from one to another: Colombia, Costa Rica and Venezuela.

Two other nations had what could be charitably described as imperfect civilian democracies. Mexico had enjoyed civilian rule since the promulgation of its 1917 constitution and peacefully transferred power from one president to another like clockwork every six years, with re-election strictly forbidden. But until 2000, all those presidents were of one party, the *Partido Revolucionario Institucional (PRI)*, which held government at all levels in a vise-grip and was not above rigging elections to quash the aspirations of upstart opposition parties. In the Dominican Republic, the late President Joaquín Balaguer was elected in 1966, 1970 and 1974 and attempted to hang onto power indefinitely through extra-constitutional means.

Fourteen other republics were governed by military juntas or strongmen. The longest-ruling despot was Paraguay's Gen. Alfredo Stroessner, who kept himself in power through rigged "elections" from 1954 until overthrown by one of his own generals in 1989. Even the once-envied democracies of Chile and Uruguay opted for order over chaos in 1973.

Finally, Cuba was—and still is—distinguished by the peculiar totalitarian experiment of Fidel Castro, a model that was once viewed as a beacon by guerrilla movements and left-wing political parties throughout the region. The model has been embraced by newer left-wing leaders, like Bolivia's Evo Morales, Nicaragua's Daniel Ortega and the late Hugo Chávez of Venezuela.

Democracy in Latin America, it seemed, was a concept that was unfeasible at best and unwanted at worst. But in 1978, the tide slowly began to turn, until by the late 1980s it had become a tidal wave in favor of duly elected civilian government. This transition to democracy in all but one of the Latin American Republics is described in detail in the sections on each nation, together with an indication of things to come.

Lest this picture of emerging democracy be misconstrued as overly rosy, it must be noted that two or more consecutive elections, no matter how honest in the eyes of international observers, do not in and of themselves guarantee that the mortar of democratic institutions will set properly. It often takes generations before adherence to liberal principles becomes woven into a nation's social fabric. True democracy flowers best in a climate characterized by such principles as co-equal executive, legislative and judicial branches; tolerance of opposition parties and viewpoints, whether expressed on the floor of a congress, in free and independent mass media or peacefully in the streets; unquestioned civilian control over the military; workable constitutions that endure more than a decade or two; eschewal of the temptation to resort to political violence;

Latin America Today

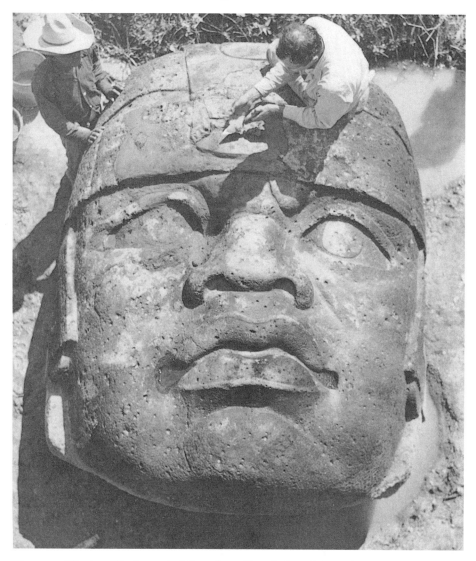

Veracruz, Mexico: The largest of the colossal heads found from the Olmec civilization

accountability for official wrongdoing; and public confidence in the integrity of governmental institutions and leaders. Most Latin American countries are still lacking in this regard.

In fairness, Latin America should be cut some slack. There is not yet a Utopian society anywhere on Earth. Even in the United States, which has long held a paternal attitude toward its wayward Latin American neighbors, political assassinations and attempted assassinations have occurred with alarming frequency, and local pockets of political corruption, complete with vote fraud, influence peddling and kickbacks, are legendary.

But the United States, Canada and the English-speaking states of the Caribbean enjoyed an advantage over their Latin American neighbors in having had a colonial master that had experienced its Glorious Revolution in 1688. The Enlighten-ment came late, if at all, to Spain, Portugal and France. The abuses of George III that Jefferson enumerated in the Declaration of Independence seem little more than nit-picks in contrast to the absolute power wielded by divine right by the monarchs of the other colonial powers. When Great Britain granted independence to its colonies, whether voluntarily or involuntarily, it left in place viable political institutions rooted in parliamentary democracy and common law upon which they could build. Washington and Jefferson learned much in the House of Burgesses of colonial Virginia. The press was privately owned. Spain, Portugal and France, by contrast, bequeathed a legacy of power concentrated in the hands of one man.

To put it another way, no Spanish king ever signed a Magna Carta.

Although the newly independent Latin America emulated the U.S. Constitution with its three branches of government with checks and balances, in practice the executive branches enjoyed disproportionate power. Latin America became the living embodiment of the adage that absolute power corrupts absolutely, and such traditions are not easily discarded. In just the past few years, despite the aforementioned advances in Latin American democracy, several elected presidents have played fast and loose with constitutional rights in the name of expediency. Prominent political activists have been assassinated in Colombia, Mexico, Brazil, Paraguay and elsewhere.

Threats Against the Press

Another troubling factor is the willingness of democratically elected presidents to employ legal and extralegal measures once employed by their dictatorial predecessors to curtail freedom of the press, especially critical editorials and investigative reporting.

Under the Spanish legal system, the principle of *desacato*, or criminal libel, is often used as a cudgel against journalists by thin-skinned public officials offended by critical reporting or editorials; truth is not a defense. Other methods that have been frequently employed to intimidate the press include tax audits, licensing of journalists, alleged labor code violations, the withdrawal of advertising by government-owned utility or transportation companies, revocation of broadcast licenses for opposition stations or revocation of work visas for aggressive foreign journalists.

As just three recent examples: Venezuela's Chávez refused to renew broadcast licenses of radio and television stations that had been critical of his government; Argentine President Cristina Fernández de Kirchner forced through Congress a bill in 2009 that ostensibly curbs media monopolies but in reality is aimed at Grupo Clarín, one of the most outspoken media voices against her; and an Ecuadorean court fined the newspaper *El Universo* $40 million in 2011 and sentenced two directors and the opinion editor to three years in prison for calling Ecuadorean Rafael Correa a "dictator" in an opinion column. Under international pressure, Correa issued a last-minute pardon and canceled the fines.

Another tactic for dealing with nettlesome journalists remains widespread in Latin America: murder. According to the Inter American Press Association (IAPA), 434 journalists were martyred in the performance of their duties in the Americas from 1987 to April 2013, including 128 in Colombia, 100 in Mexico, 51 in Brazil, 28 in Honduras, 25 in Guatemala and Peru and

18 in El Salvador. Another 25 journalists disappeared during that time, 23 of them in Mexico.

Twenty-three journalists were murdered in 2012 alone, fewer than the 31 in 2010, the deadliest year since 1991; six more were slain in 2013. Of the 29 killed in 2012 and 2013, 16 were in Mexico, nine in Honduras, three in Brazil and one in Paraguay.

Many of the murders can be linked to drug traffickers or guerrillas, but a suspicious number—many of them still unsolved and unpunished—were of journalists who were investigating official corruption or who had written critical editorials or exposés. Independent journalism in Latin America remains a high-risk occupation, and until it can be practiced without fear, true democracy cannot take root.

The Declaration of Chapultepec, promoted by the IAPA and signed in Mexico City in 1994 by representatives of 22 nations of the hemisphere, acknowledges the importance of freedom of the press and freedom of expression for democratic societies and denounces acts of violence against journalists. Yet, abuses continued to occur—and still do—even in the signatory countries.

The plight of the media was serious enough that it appeared on the agenda of the Second Summit of the Americas in Santiago, Chile, in 1998. The 34 hemispheric leaders (Castro was not invited) agreed to establish an office within the Inter-American Commission for Human Rights to investigate attacks against journalists. As of 2011, 58 successive heads of government from 32 countries and Puerto Rico had endorsed the Declaration of Chapultepec; Cuba, Haiti and Venezuela were not among them. Moreover, 106 people had been convicted and imprisoned of crimes against journalists as of February 2011.

In its annual rating of press freedom around the world, New York-based Freedom House rated the press of only three Latin American countries as "free" in 2011: Chile, Costa Rica and Uruguay. In 2012, 2013 and 2014, only Costa Rica and Uruguay were still rated as "free." It is probably not a coincidence that Transparency International perennially rates Chile, Uruguay and Costa Rica as the least corrupt of Latin America. Chile dropped to "partly free" in 2012 because of restrictions on media coverage of the sometimes-violent education demonstrations that year and because of increased media concentration in a few hands. Among those hands were those of the president from 2010–14, Sebastián Piñera, a billionaire who owns one of the private television channels.

Freedom House continues to rate the press in Cuba and Venezuela as "not free" for political restrictions on the media and for the past three years has rated Mexico and Honduras as "not free" because of the threats against journalists from criminal elements. In 2013, Freedom House downgraded the press in Ecuador and Paraguay from "partly free" to "not free," Ecuador because of President Correa's attempts to curtail media ownership and judicial harassment of opposition media, Paraguay because of the firing of journalists loyal to President Fernando Lugo at the state-owned television channel following his impeachment; the other media nonetheless reported and editorialized on events freely, and in 2014 Paraguay was again moved into the "partly free" category. Ecuador remains "not free."

The remaining Latin republics are rated as "partly free" this year. The presses of the English-speaking Caribbean countries and Suriname are rated as "free."

Auspicious and Ominous Trends

There have been encouraging signs during the past few years that executive branches, and the once-omnipotent military establishments, no longer wield unchecked power. Two presidents, Brazil's Fernando Collor and Venezuela's Carlos Andres Pérez, were impeached and removed from office by their congresses for political corruption. In Paraguay, President Raúl Cubas was impeached by the Chamber of Deputies for abuse of power in 1999 and resigned and went into exile in the face of certain conviction and removal by the Senate.

Jorge Serrano's attempt to stage a Fujimori-style self-coup in Guatemala in 1993 failed because the army remained loyal to the constitution, and he fled into exile. A coup attempt by a Paraguayan army general, Lino Oviedo, also fizzled out for lack of support in 1996.

Moreover, justice has finally been meted out for human rights abuses of past military dictatorships, despite amnesty laws. Chile's Augusto Pinochet was arrested for human rights violations on a Spanish warrant during a visit to Britain in 1998 and spent the remaining nine years of his life resisting efforts to bring him to trial in Chile. The leaders of the former Argentine junta have been prosecuted and sentenced for human rights abuses during the "dirty war" of 1976–83. Former President Jorge Rafael Videla died in a prison cell in May 2013. Former Uruguayan President Juan María Bordaberry was convicted in 2010 of a double homicide committed during the 1973–85 military dictatorship and died under house arrest the following year. Former Guatemalan strongman Efraín Ríos Montt was convicted of genocide in May 2013 and sentenced to 80 years, although nine days later the Constitutional Court overturned the conviction on procedural grounds and said the closing arguments phase would have to be repeated (see Guatemala).

Not all signs have been encouraging. There were the 1991 military coup that toppled the elected government of Jean-Bertrand Aristide in Haiti; the temporary suspension of constitutional guarantees in 1992 by Peru's Fujimori for reasons of expediency, and his shamelessly rigged "re-election" in 2000; the constitutionally questionable removal by Congress of Ecuador's Bucaram in 1998 on the ostensibly justifiable (but unproven) charge of "mental incompetence;" the unquestionably unconstitutional barracks revolt in Ecuador that overthrew President Jamil Mahuad in 2000 for the unjustifiable reason that his public popularity was too low; the rigged election in Haiti in 2000 that brought Aristide back to power; and the almost successful military coup in Venezuela in 2002 that had President Chávez under house arrest for 24 hours.

Two questionable impeachments in recent years were more like "constitutional coups." In 2009, Honduran President Manuel Zalaya was ousted in a combined congressional-military maneuver, but Congress chose its president rather than the constitutional vice president to succeed him. In 2012, Paraguayan President Fernando Lugo was impeached and removed from office for alleged malfeasance, but it sped through both houses of Congress in just two days and Lugo was given no time to mount a defense. He was succeeded by the constitutional vice president. Both the Honduran and Paraguayan power plays met severe international condemnation, including Honduras' expulsion from the Organization of American States; Paraguay was temporarily suspended from the *Mercosur* trading bloc, and both were barred from the Ibero-American Summits (see Latin America and the World).

An ominous trend has been the employment of heavy-handed, antidemocratic tactics by several elected left-wing presidents in recent years to intimidate the political opposition and media, most notably Hugo Chávez in Venezuela, Evo Morales in Bolivia, Rafael Correa in Ecuador and Daniel Ortega in Nicaragua. These tactics include outright rigged elections, denying legitimate candidates places on ballots, court-packing, tax audits or the filing of frivolous criminal charges against opposition politicians, some of whom go to jail and others into exile. These regimes have forced opposition broadcasters off the air by refusing to renew their licenses and have punished opposition newspapers by

Latin America Today

withholding government advertising or filing frivolous defamation charges.

Other left-of-center presidents have eschewed such Marxist tactics and respected democratic institutions and freedom of expression, including Ricardo Lagos and Michelle Bachelet in Chile, Tabaré Vázquez and José Mujica in Uruguay, Álvaro Colom in Guatemala, Mauricio Funes in El Salvador and Ollanta Humala in Peru.

Another disturbing antidemocratic trend has been the use of mob violence to force the resignations of democratically elected presidents who have subsequently become unpopular. Violent street protests in Argentina led to the resignation of the elected president, Fernando de la Rua, in 2001 and his eventual replacement with the man he had defeated, Eduardo Duhalde; violent demonstrations in Bolivia forced President Gonzalo Sánchez de Lozada from office in 2003 after 14 months in office, and forced his successor, Carlos Mesa, to step down in 2005 after 19 months; and street protests in Ecuador forced Congress to remove President Lucio Gutiérrez in 2005 after 27 months in office.

Two other presidents forced from office by public protests evoke less sympathy: Fujimori of Peru in 2000 and Aristide in Haiti in 2004. Both had been re-elected fraudulently.

Almost all the new Latin American democracies initially prohibited re-election, or at least immediate re-election, of presidents in an attempt to prevent future Stroessners and Balaguers, who remained in control for decades through orchestrated elections. Since then, Peru, Argentina, Brazil, Venezuela, Colombia, the Dominican Republic, Bolivia, Ecuador and Nicaragua amended their constitutions—or wrote new ones—to permit immediate re-election.

The Dominican Republic now permits a third, non-consecutive term, while Venezuela, Bolivia, Ecuador and Nicaragua now allow indefinite re-election, raising the old fears of *continuismo*.

Yet, in Panama, when President Pérez Balladares called a referendum in 1998 to seek approval for a second term, a resounding 64% of the voters rejected the idea. The Colombian Supreme Court overturned a third-term law that Congress passed in 2010 that would have permitted President Álvaro Uribe to run a third time.

A related trend is the return to power of former presidents after one or more intervening terms. Sánchez de Lozada of Bolivia did so in 2003. After the Dominican Republic lifted its ban on re-election, former President Leonel Fernández returned to power in 2004; in 2008, he was elected to a *third* term. In 2006 alone, Oscar Arias of Costa Rica, René Préval of Haiti, Alan García of Peru, Daniel Ortega of Nicaragua (after three unsuccessful re-election bids), and Michelle Bachelet of Chile all staged comebacks to reclaim the presidencies of their countries. It doesn't always work. Eduardo Frei of Chile attempted a comeback in 2010 but lost; the same happened with Alejandro Toledo of Peru in 2011 and Hipólito Mejía of the Dominican Republic in 2012.

Still another peculiarity is the number of presidents in recent years elected on their second or subsequent attempt. Presidents Álvaro Colom of Guatemala and Tabaré Vázquez of Uruguay were both elected on their third attempts, Brazil's Lula da Silva on his fourth and Uruguay's Jorge Batlle on his *fifth*. Panama's Martín Torrijos and Ricardo Martinelli, Bolivia's Morales, Honduras' Porfirio Lobo Sosa, Chile's Sebastián Piñera, Peru's Ollanta Humala, Guatemala's Otto Pérez Molina and the Dominican Republic's Danilo Medina all had run once unsuccessfully. In Latin American democracy, persistence is rewarded.

All the democracies except four require a segunda vuelta, or runoff election, to ensure the winning presidential candidate has a majority. In Honduras, Mexico, Panama and Paraguay, a simple plurality wins. In Argentina and Nicaragua, a plurality is sufficient if the winning candidate has at least a 10 percentage point lead over the candidate who runs second.

An encouraging trend in Latin American democracy that cannot be ignored is the increasing influence of women in a region once characterized by its *machismo*. Voters in six countries have elevated women to their presidencies: Violeta Barrios de Chamorro in Nicaragua (1990), Mireya Moscoso de Arias in Panama (1999), Michelle Bachelet in Chile (2006 and 2014), Cristina Fernández de Kirchner in Argentina (2007), and Laura Chinchilla in Costa Rica and Dilma Rousseff in Brazil (2010). Keiko Fujimori narrowly lost the 2011 presidential runoff in Peru.

In the English-speaking Caribbean countries, Portia Simpson Miller became the first female prime minister of Jamaica in 2006. Her party was voted out in 2007, but she returned to power in January 2012. *Time* magazine named her one of the world's 100 most influential people for 2012. Kamla Persad-Bessessar became the first female prime minister of Trinidad and Tobago in 2010.

Coupled with the acceptance of women presidents is a growing phenomenon: Male presidents barred from seeking another term are fielding their wives as surrogate candidates. It worked for Argentine President Néstor Kirchner, who saw his wife, Cristina Fernández, elected to succeed him in 2007 after serving only one term, with the expectation that he could then run for two consecutive terms in 2011 and 2015. Death upset his plans in 2010, but his wife was re-elected the following year. Presidents Leonel Fernández of the Dominican Republic, Álvaro Colom of Guatemala and Manuel Zelaya of Honduras unsuccessfully attempted to elevate their wives to the presidential chairs there, although Fernández's wife, Margarita Cedeño, was elected vice president. A curious trend has been the public's fascination in several countries with former strongmen or charismatic military figures, like the traditional *caudillos* of yore, who have entered politics. In Bo-

The Tikal Altar Stone, Guatemala

livia, former strongman Hugo Banzer was elected to the presidency by the Congress in 1997 after he won a plurality of the popular vote. He resigned after four years because of cancer, but he respected democratic institutions while in power.

In Guatemala, opinion polls once showed that the most popular political figure in the country was former military dictator Efraín Ríos Montt, a pariah in human rights circles for his alleged massacre of thousands of Indian peasants during his 1982–83 regime. He was barred by the constitution from serving again as head of state, but he successfully appealed that restriction and ran for president in 2003, at the age of 77. When push came to shove, however, the Guatemalan people decided they weren't all that nostalgic for his jack-booted rule, and he ran a poor third. He was convicted of genocide charges in May 2013.

A similar situation occurred in Paraguay. Former General Lino Oviedo, who had attempted a coup in 1996 and who was convicted and placed under house arrest, won the Colorado Party nomination for president over the opposition of incumbent civilian President Juan Carlos Wasmosy—himself of the Colorado Party. Polls favored Oviedo, who could not even leave his quarters to campaign, to win the 1998 election hands-down, causing Wasmosy to threaten to postpone the vote. The Supreme Court declared Oviedo's candidacy illegal, so his running mate, Raúl Cubas, was elected president. Cubas then ordered the release of Oviedo, the power behind the throne, sparking a governmental crisis.

Oviedo's luster dimmed after the 1999 assassination of Vice President Luis María Argaña, Oviedo's leading opponent within the Colorado Party. The day after President Cubas' resignation under threat of impeachment, Oviedo fled to Argentina, then to Brazil, where he was arrested in 2000. The Supreme Court ordered his release in 2001, and he vowed to return to Paraguay and run for the presidency. He remained in Brazil and again ran a surrogate candidate in 2003, who received only 13.5% of the vote, finishing fourth. Oviedo eventually returned to Paraguay, served his time in a military prison and at last ran for president in the 2008 election. Like Ríos Montt in Guatemala, he ran a distant third. He was planning to run again in 2013, but was killed in a helicopter crash. It was apparently accidental, but there were the inevitable conspiracy theories.

The most dramatic case of a modern-day *caudillo* occurred in Venezuela. Former Lieutenant Colonel Hugo Chávez, who spent two years in prison for leading a failed attempt to overthrow President Carlos Andres Pérez in 1992, capitalized on public disgust with the corruption of the two traditional parties to run for presi-

dent in 1998 as an independent populist. Chávez won a landslide victory. Upon assuming office in February 1999, he expressed his contempt for the legislative and judicial branches, then called for an election for a constituent assembly to rewrite the 1962 constitution. His adherents won 90% of the seats in that assembly, which then forged a new organic law that allowed Chávez to serve for two consecutive six-year terms, besides granting him broad new powers. Voters overwhelmingly approved the new constitution, whereupon Chávez called for a new presidential election in 2000. Chávez won with 59% of the vote, an even greater landslide than in 1998. An open admirer of Cuba's Fidel Castro, Chávez openly expressed contempt for freedom of the press and the voices of dissent. He has voiced the familiar siren song of *caudillos* past who assume dictatorial powers: It is the only way to solve the country's problems.

Mounting opposition to Chávez's heavy-handed methods erupted into violence in 2002, which led to an abortive military coup. Within 48 hours, additional violence by pro-Chávez mobs effected his return to power. In 2004, Chávez's opponents collected more than the 2.4 million signatures for a recall election, but Chávez emerged stronger than ever when 59% of the voters chose not to remove him. In 2006, he won another six-year term with 63%, showing just how polarized Venezuela was between pro- and anti-Chávez camps. He was re-elected again in 2012 with a much-reduced 53%, but died of cancer weeks after an inauguration he was too ill to attend. Ironically, Like Argentina's Juan Perón, Chávez was an elected autocrat, a political oxymoron if there ever was one.

A Chávez-like phenomenon occurred in troubled Ecuador, where Lucio Gutiérrez, a flamboyant colonel who spent six months in jail for his role in overthrowing Mahuad in 2000, was elected president in 2002 on a platform to clean up corruption and effect social justice. But Gutiérrez fell from grace when he himself came under suspicion for corruption. In the face of mounting street protests demanding Gutiérrez's resignation, Congress removed him from office in 2005 and sent him into exile in Brazil, the third Ecuadorean president to be removed either by Congress or the military within eight years.

In Peru, a left-wing former lieutenant colonel, Ollanta Humala, who pledged the same type of radical reforms as Chávez, made it into the 2006 presidential runoff and was narrowly defeated by former President García, but he was elected in 2011.

Finally, in Suriname, former military strongman Dési Bouterse was elected president by the country's parliament in 2010, even though he was an international fugi-

tive wanted for drug trafficking and was facing trial in Suriname for the killings of 15 opponents in 1982. In April 2012, the National Assembly granted him immunity.

There is nothing new about people in struggling societies turning to a strong-willed, charismatic leader who promises to bring order out of chaos, in Latin America or elsewhere. It evokes memories of the infamous explanation by an Italian woman for why Mussolini remained popular for so long: "Because he made the trains run on time." The fact that a former strongman is elected president in a free, honest popular vote does not in and of itself represent a threat to democracy; Brazil's Getulio Vargas (a civilian) and Chile's Carlos Ibáñez (a soldier) both were returned to power in free elections. Indeed, it is the very manifestation of the people's will. It can be argued that the United States has elevated a number of military heroes to the presidency—most recently in 1952 and 1956—without undermining its democracy. But the United States and Latin America have vastly different traditions where military presidents are concerned, and the question that remains unanswered at this juncture is whether military men who win power through the ballot box are committed democrats or Trojan horses who will disregard the democratic process if it becomes inconvenient to them, as Chávez has done.

Public Perceptions of Democracy

Thus, how "free" is Latin America? In its 2013 report on overall freedom, in which it rates political rights and civil liberties on seven-point scales, Freedom House rated nine of the 20 Latin American republics and all the English-speaking Caribbean as "free," 10 Latin American countries as "partly free" and just one—Cuba—as "not free" (see "Freedom Rankings" table). A dramatic change in 2011 was Mexico dropping from "free" to "partly free" because of drug-related violence and corruption.

Even when civilians are elected, Latin Americans have shown themselves incredibly impatient with new presidents who do not prove themselves to be Supermen (or women) who can solve all their countries' problems quickly.

For 16 years, an important barometer of Latin American public opinion was the ambitious periodic 17 nation survey begun in 1996 by the Chilean polling firm *Latinobarómetro* for the British newsmagazine *The Economist* on Latin Americans' attitudes toward their young democracies. The Dominican Republic became the 18th nation in the survey in 2004. Only Cuba and Haiti were excluded.

Respondents were asked each year whether they agree with the statements, "Democracy is preferable to any other kind

Latin America Today

of government," and "In certain circumstances, an authoritarian government can be preferable to a democratic one." In the 2009 and 2010 surveys, support for democracy had increased in seven of 17 countries since 1996. Yet, in 2007, support for democracy was below 50% in *nine* countries; in 2011, it was below 50% in only four: Guatemala, Honduras and, somewhat surprisingly, Brazil and Mexico.

Interestingly, the highest support for democracy in 2009, 2010 and 2011 was in Chávez's Venezuela, at 84% the first two years and 77% in 2011. The lowest support in is Guatemala, 46% in 2010 and 36% in 2011. Overall, 58% of Latin Americans said they prefer a democratic form of government.

In 2011, just 17% of Latin Americans said authoritarian government is sometimes justified. The lowest percentage was 11% in Uruguay, where democracy is strongly rooted. The highest was 27% in violence-racked Honduras, followed by 22% in corruption-plagued Paraguay.

When asked simply, "How satisfied are you with the way democracy works in your country," the percentage responding "somewhat satisfied" or "very satisfied" was higher in 2010 than in 2001 in 16 of the 18 countries; Honduras and Peru showed no change. The three countries with the highest percentages of satisfaction in 2010 were the same three that Freedom House rated as the "freest" and Transparency International rated the least corrupt: Uruguay, Costa Rica and Chile. That question was not included in the 2011 survey.

Overall, when the Latin America of 2014 is compared with the Latin America of 1977, there can be no disputing the advances that have been made toward democracy, so in fairness, the Latin American glass should be viewed as four-fifths full rather than one-fifth empty. The long-range prospects for democracy in Latin America appear guarded, and ultimately will depend on economic stability and development—and on the patience and determination of the Latin Americans themselves.

ECONOMIC DIVFERSIFICATION AND FREE TRADE

For more than a hundred years, most of the post-colonial Latin American countries languished in the economic doldrums while North America experienced robust economic growth and prosperity. Only Argentina experienced growth similar to that of the United States and Canada. Several factors condemned Latin America to the poverty from which it is only now beginning to emerge.

Just as Spain, Portugal and France failed to bequeath a democratic tradition to their former colonies, neither did they leave behind sound economic infrastructures. Sadly, these colonial powers were more concerned with exploitation than with development. Spain in particular was obsessed with how much precious metal could be extracted from the ground, not with agriculture or with building roads, schools or financial institutions.

Granted, the Jamestown colonists had come in search of gold, but when it became apparent that there was no gold in Virginia, the English recognized that the fecund soil offered other opportunities. The demand created for tobacco and later cotton generated the wealth that gold did not. Subsequent English and Scottish immigrants to the New World, whether to escape debtors' prison or religious persecution, came prepared to exploit the wealth of the soil or to engage in mercantilism. This fostered an independent, entrepreneurial spirit that was carried over into the post-independence period.

In addition, the Industrial Revolution was exported successfully from Britain to America. Industry, agriculture and the advent of public education led in the 19th century to the rise of a literate middle class of independent farmers and merchants with political rights sandwiched between those who amassed great wealth and those left behind in destitution. The unique concept of homesteading, providing free title to land in return for working it, further broadened the base of the independent-minded middle class in the English colonies and later the United States. The opportunities it offered for self-advancement also sparked a wave of immigration that brought with it new zeal and new ideas.

There was no corresponding industrialization, democratization or mass education in Spain, Portugal and France or in most of their erstwhile colonies in the 19th century. The result was a dual class structure in which a tiny, educated, wealthy elite, a disproportionate number of them Caucasian, held absolute economic and political power over a mass of desperately poor, illiterate Indian and *mestizo* peons or, in Brazil and Haiti, black slaves. This structure was enforced in some countries for decades by a lone dictator, such as Paraguay's Rodrigo Gaspar de Francia or Mexico's Porfirio Díaz. Thus, social inequality enforced at bayonet point, and usually condoned by the Catholic Church, became the second major obstacle to Latin American development. Industrial growth requires a literate workforce.

The third major obstacle was monocultural dependency, the reliance of a country's economy on a single resource for export. This handicap persisted throughout the late 19th century and in some cases well into the 20th. Thus, Brazil and Colombia depended on coffee, Bolivia on tin, Chile on copper, Peru on guano fertilizer, Cuba, the Dominican Republic and Haiti on sugar, Venezuela on petroleum and Ecuador and the Central American republics on bananas. The derogatory term "banana republic" is another unfortunate Latin American stereotype, but again, it had some basis in fact. The products upon which these countries depended for foreign exchange were at the mercy of the world market. To use an old analogy, when the world tin market sneezed, Bolivia caught pneumonia.

Compounding this situation was a fourth obstacle, undercapitalization, which could only be overcome by surrendering control of the nation's one valuable resource to those who *did* have capital: foreign investors. Consequently, foreign-owned companies, mostly British and U.S., came to dominate these underdeveloped economies, exercising considerable political influence over their host governments. Probably the most egregious example was that of the United Fruit Company of the United States, which treated the Central American countries as private fiefs.

PER CAPITA GDP, 2012	
United States	$52,340
Canada	$51,570
Bahamas	$20,600
Puerto Rico	$18,000
Barbados	$15,080
Trinidad & Tobago	$14,710
Chile	$14,310
Uruguay	$13,580
Argentina	$12,475*
Venezuela	$12,460
Brazil	$11,630
Mexico	$9,640
Costa Rica	$8,820
Suriname	$8,680
Panama	$8,510
Grenada	$7,220
Colombia	$7,020
Peru	$6,060
Cuba	$5,890*
Dominican Rep.	$5,470
Ecuador	$5,170
Jamaica	$5,130
Belize	$4,490*
El Salvador	$3,590
Guyana	$3,410
Paraguay	$3,400
Guatemala	$3,120
Bolivia	$2,220
Honduras	$2,120
Nicaragua	$1,650
Haiti	$760

*2011

SOURCE: World Bank, Atlas method

These deplorable conditions persisted decade after decade, as those with the power and money were able to maintain the status quo through force if necessary. Those lacking power could only submit. In those countries where democracy did manage to gain a temporary foothold in the late 19th and early 20th centuries—Argentina, Brazil, Chile and Uruguay—it is not surprising that socialist, communist and anarchist movements won adherents, much as they did in the United States during the same era. If misery existed under a capitalist system, the logic went, capitalism must be the enemy. Foreign capitalists were especially popular whipping boys. Expropriation of foreign holdings came into vogue, beginning with Mexico's nationalization of the oil industry in 1938. Guerrilla movements also targeted foreign companies.

Latin American intellectuals, from the 1960s until the early '90s, almost universally followed like sheep a school of thinking known as "dependency theory," which held that Latin America was economically and culturally "dependent" upon the developed countries, especially the United States. Occasionally even reform-minded military officers would seize power with a promise to redress social wrongs, such as the military government in Peru from 1968–80 that sought to impose a socialist system based on the Yugoslav model. Marxism came to power by force of arms in Cuba in 1959 and in Nicaragua in 1979 and through the ballot box in Chile in 1970. Fidel Castro became an enticing role model.

Even conservative military regimes created state-owned corporations to run utilities, airlines, railroads, ports, mines and oil refineries. The realization that a cumbersome bureaucracy was a woefully inefficient way to provide reliable telephone or electrical service came slowly.

Other economic experiments like high protective tariffs and regional trade blocs were aimed at what were seen as sinister outside forces. Alas, these also proved a disappointment. Tariffs designed to protect fledgling local industries often created bloated monopolies that produced substandard and overpriced products. Trade blocs such as the Central American Common Market and the Andean Pact proved ineffectual because the member countries were not producing products for export that the other members wanted to import.

The right-wing Pinochet government in Chile became the regional maverick when it withdrew from the Andean Pact and scuttled its protective tariffs to create a free-market economy based on the theories of Nobel Prize-winning U.S. economist Milton Friedman. Many of Pinochet's economic brain trust studied under Friedman at the University of Chicago, earning them the sobriquet, "Chicago Boys." The initial result was a disastrous recession as local businesses proved unable to compete with better and cheaper foreign imports. But gradually the economy equalized, showing real growth with single-digit inflation, something unattainable under the Marxist government of Salvador Allende. Pinochet also broke Chile's dependency on copper exports, promoting the export of fresh fruits. Chile's free-market strategy proved so successful that Pinochet's civilian successors have left it in place and it has been emulated by its neighbors. Alas, the Pinochet's regime's record in human rights is far less admirable.

According to *The Economist*, economic growth in Latin America was a robust 6% in 2010, fueled by world demand for such commodities as petroleum, minerals and soybeans but it dropped to 3.5% in 2011.

Two presidents who were the very embodiments of Latin America's conversion from public sector to private sector dominance were Brazil's Fernando Henrique Cardoso (1995–2003), an erstwhile Marxist economist and leading dependency theorist, and Argentina's Carlos Saúl Menem (1989–99), a Peronist who steered the country on a course 180 degrees from that set by his patron saint, Juan Perón.

In the 1990s, Latin America experienced an economic boom that had U.S. and European economists predicting that the region could repeat the success story of the robust export-oriented economies of Asia. This expectation was heightened by the catastrophic collapse of the Asian stock markets in late 1997. Mexico joined the North American Free Trade Agreement (NAFTA) in 1993, while Argentina, Brazil, Paraguay and Uruguay formed *Mercosur,* a trade bloc that showed moderate signs of success. The bloc almost collapsed in the wake of the economic crises in Argentina and Brazil, then showed signs of revitalization. So has the Andean Pact, composed of Bolivia, Colombia, Ecuador, Peru and Venezuela. In mid-2004, the two blocs discussed creating a South American free-trade area. In 2006, Venezuela became a member of *Mercosur,* but it seceded from the Andean Pact because Colombia and Peru signed bilateral trade agreements with the United States.

By the late '90s, Latin America was experiencing regional economic growth that averaged a healthy 3% per year, but in 1998, uncertainty over the Russian ruble caused a chain-reaction market panic that hit the United States, the major Asian stock markets, and then Brazil, Argentina and Mexico. The crisis worsened in January 1999 when the bottom dropped out of the Brazilian stock market. The panic spread to neighboring stock markets, and for a time it appeared a massive regional recession was likely. The market crisis coincided with a dramatic drop in the world

Quinceañera, **a special 15th birthday celebration**

Photo by Gary Seldomridge

Latin America Today

market price of petroleum, which affected the economies of Venezuela, Ecuador and Mexico. The situation eventually stabilized.

No longer seen as bogeymen, foreign investors were not only welcome but openly courted, and the political stability spreading through the region made it an attractive target for investment. In addition, tourism continued to expand, providing jobs and a pollution-free source of foreign exchange.

Following up on the concept of NAFTA and *Mercosur*, U.S. President Bill Clinton invited the Western Hemisphere's heads of state, minus Cuba's Fidel Castro, to Miami in 1993 for the First Summit of the Americas. There, the idea of establishing a hemisphere-wide Free Trade Area of the Americas (FTAA), with membership limited to democratic countries, was first advanced.

At the Second Summit of the Americas in Santiago, Chile, in 1998, the 34 heads of state (once again, Castro was not invited), approved blueprints to establish the FTAA by 2005. Also recognizing that true economic development is dependent upon an educated workforce, the summit's communiqué called for the expenditure of $6.1 billion over three years to improve educa-

tion. It also set a goal that 100% of the hemisphere's children would have access to elementary education and 75% would have access to secondary education by 2010.

The Third Summit of the Americas was held in Quebec City, Canada, in 2001, and once again the FTAA was the top agenda item. The new U.S. president, George W. Bush, was an even more enthusiastic advocate of the FTAA than Clinton. The heads of state set a target date of January 1, 2005, for establishment of what would become the world's largest free-trade bloc, encompassing 800 million people and accounting for an estimated $15 trillion in trade. The concept was not without its nay-sayers. In the streets of Quebec, protesters representing labor unions, environmental groups and various anti-capitalist organizations engaged in violent protests in an attempt to break up the summit. Inside the summit, Venezuela's Chávez charged that the lofty goals of the Miami and Santiago summits of reducing poverty had not been met, while Brazilian President Cardoso complained about U.S. anti-dumping laws.

A harbinger of doom for the FTAA came at a 2003 meeting of the World Trade Or-

ganization in Cancun, Mexico, which collapsed largely because of the opposition of Latin American members. At a "mini" Summit of the Americas in Monterrey, Mexico, in 2004, Chávez was joined by two powerful new anti-FTAA allies, Luiz Inácio "Lula" da Silva of Brazil and Néstor Kirchner of Argentina. Besides the anti-dumping issue, they demanded a reduction in U.S. agricultural subsidies so their exports could compete. The United States, meanwhile, pressed for greater protection for intellectual property.

Mercosur embarked on concluding free-trade pacts with the Andean Pact, Mexico, and the European Union, though the talks with the EU broke down and remain stalled. The target date for the FTAA quietly passed, and even Bush acknowledged the FTAA was moribund when the Fourth Summit of the Americas convened in Mar del Plata, Argentina in 2005. The summit accomplished nothing of substance.

At the Fifth Summit of the Americas in Port-of-Spain, Trinidad in 2009, the climate was even more hostile to the FTAA, and the new U.S. president, Barack Obama, prudently avoided the subject. It was avoided again at the Sixth Summit in Cartagena, Colombia, in 2012, and no consensus was reached on any other issue. The next summit is scheduled for Panama in 2015.

As with the trend toward democracy, the dramatic improvement in the Latin American economy has had its negative aspects, as well as nagging, unremedied problems: the continued gap between the very wealthy and the very poor; endemic corruption; environmental pollution; urban overpopulation; and an underground economy based on the illegal traffic of drugs.

According to a report released in 1996 by the U.N. Economic Commission for Latin America and the Caribbean, now named the Economic Commission for Latin America and the Caribbean (ECLAC), one third of Latin Americans lived in poverty and 18 percent of them lived in dire poverty, earning less than $1 a day. Even in comparatively affluent countries such as Uruguay, the wealthiest 10 percent of the population had access to 15 times the resources of the poorest 10 percent; in Honduras and Peru, the figure was 80 times.

Ten years later, the overall economic picture had improved dramatically. In 2006, according to ECLAC, regional economic growth was a healthy 5.3%, the third consecutive year of strong growth, while once-feared inflation was only 4.8%; per capita income had risen 11.7% since 2003. The 2008–09 global recession slowed Latin American economic growth but in 2010 it rebounded to 5.9%; it was still 4.5% in 2011 and 3.2 % in 2012 (see table). The International Monetary Fund estimated growth in 2013 slowed to 2.7%.

Latin America Today

The percentage of Latin Americans living in poverty has steadily declined, from 48% in 1990 to 38.5% in 2006 and to 28.8% in 2012. At the same time, the middle class, depending on a variety of definitions, has steadily expanded, and according to the World Bank the rate of those considered middle class reached 30% in 2012, eclipsing those living in poverty for the first time. However, the fact that poverty still afflicts more than a fourth of the population, while 13% remain in extreme poverty, remains a nagging social, economic and political issue.

Because of steady economic growth and expansion of the middle class in Latin America, the past two years have seen a dramatic phenomenon: the return of tens of thousands of Latin American expatriate workers from Spain and Portugal, whose own economies have shown negative growth for three of the past four years.

In these emerging democracies, the impatient masses now have access to the ballot box, and they have been using it. Latin America has seen a rebirth of the once-discredited movements of the left, with their siren song of help for the underprivileged.

Such newly industrialized countries as Mexico, Argentina, Brazil and Chile are learning quickly what it took the United States and other developed economies more than a century to discover: that industrialization carries an expensive environmental price tag. The air pollution in Mexico City, Santiago and São Paulo is notorious, as well as a serious health hazard. Rivers and coastlines have become dumping grounds for the toxic waste by-products of heavy industry. Brazil did not begin to take action until 1998 to slow the destruction of the vast Amazon rain forests in the name of agriculture, an environmental rape that had raised international concerns for its exacerbation of global warming.

In most of these still-underprivileged countries, this is a price they have been willing to pay in order to provide jobs for growing urban populations. But unless some solutions are found soon, those who are "lucky" enough to find work in the major cities may find that they have condemned themselves and their children to early graves.

An encouraging economic and environmental trend is the growth of ethanol plants in sugar-producing countries to meet the world's growing demand for the alternative fuel in the face of escalating petroleum prices. Brazil pioneered the manufacture of ethanol from sugar cane and of ethanol-powered vehicles in the 1970s to reduce its dependence on imported petroleum, and other tropical countries have begun to realize the potential of the fuel, which burns cleaner than gasoline. Moreover, ethanol made from sugar cane has a greater yield

A street-corner guitarist ekes out a living in Quito, Ecuador. *Photo by Zachary LaSalle; all rights reserved*

per acre and is less expensive to produce than the corn-based ethanol produced in the United States. Latin America stands to be a major exporter, as well as consumer, of ethanol, in the coming years, although critics, such as Venezuela's Chávez, warn that diverting food crops to ethanol will worsen world-wide hunger.

Unchecked population growth has been problematical in countries ranging from industrial giants such as Mexico and Brazil to desperately poor agrarian Haiti. Too often social scientists in developed countries, many of whom apparently never visit Latin America, are too quick to single out the Roman Catholic Church's ban on contraception as the primary culprit. Although this is a factor, the urban middle classes in Latin America have proven just as willing to practice birth control in defiance of the pope as Roman Catholics in North America or Europe. Most of the population growth occurs in the lower economic strata, but not because they are more devout Catholics.

There are long-standing cultural factors at play as well. The *macho* ethic holds that the number of children a man sires is an outward manifestation of his virility, his very manhood. Moreover, as is the case in Africa and Asia, poor Latin Americans dependent upon agriculture for their existence see children as future field hands, someone to help carry their burdens as they themselves age. Such traditions cannot be overcome by government decree, but until some way is found to ensure that the number of new job-seekers does not exceed supply, Latin America's newly affluent cities will continue to be ringed by slums populated by those with high expectations, waiting their turn for a better life that may never come.

The drug trade has created in some areas the illusion of prosperity. In reality, it has brought back the monocultural dependence of poor farmers on a single cash crop. In the cities, it has brought fabulous wealth to a tiny cadre of drug lords, wealth that has trickled down in droplets to the veritable army of lab processors, transporters, security personnel and others who have been enticed away from legitimate pursuits by the promise of quick, if venal, wealth.

It has been estimated that the Rodríguez Orijuela brothers, Gilberto and Miguel, the leaders of the Cali Cartel of Colombia who were extradited to the United States in 2004, are worth $250 billion. But the wealth drugs generate is illusionary—there is so much of it there is nothing left on which to spend it. Further, the real economies within which the drug trade operates cannot officially incorporate it. Governments cannot tax billions in revenue that is not legal and not claimed. Moreover, it proves a drain on the economy because governments must spend millions on enforcement that proves futile, while the very governmental institutions that seek vainly to bring this illicit industry to bay are themselves corrupted from the top down by the drug barons.

The futility is exacerbated by the rather naive counter-narcotics policies of the consuming countries of the north. For years, the hope has been that somehow impoverished peasants can be made to see that they are endangering lives in Los Angeles or Chicago and that they can be persuaded to substitute cultivating coca with another cash crop—whose yield per hectare may be one tenth as much. Unless the insatiable demand for narcotics can be curbed in the consuming countries, there will be poor Latin Americans willing to run the risks to cultivate, process and transport drugs.

TECHNOLOGICAL EMERGENCE

Yet another stereotype of Latin America, persistently reinforced by Hollywood, is of a backward region with muddy streets

9

Latin America Today

and antiquated technology. In the rural areas, that is still too often the case. But in the major cities, the economic boom has led inevitably to investment in modernizing the technological infrastructures. The impetus is the very essence of free-market capitalism: the necessity to compete. Visitors to even the poorer capital cities of most Latin American capitals will find computers literally everywhere, in hotels, banks, newspapers, universities and even small businesses. Internet cafés are trendy. To ignore computerization is to fall behind the competition.

The communications revolution also has pervaded Latin America. For example, the tallest structure on the Santiago, Chile, skyline, just two blocks from the Moneda (presidential) Palace along Avenida Bernardo O'Higgins, is the Entel Tower, bristling with antennas and satellite dishes linking Santiago with the interior and with the rest of the world. Guests at even mid-priced hotels in a country like Guatemala may be surprised to find CNN and HBO on their television sets. Again, competition demands this. Cell phone use exploded in Latin America in the 1990s, largely because it was quicker and cheaper to subscribe to cell phone service that to wait for weeks

or months to have a more expensive conventional telephone installed by a cumbersome state-owned utility.

As is the case in developed countries, the technological revolution has been an upward spiral, with innovation breeding innovation. Some of these countries, such as Brazil and Chile, now manufacture their own computer hardware and software. Free-trade agreements facilitate the transfer of technology across international boundaries.

If there is a negative picture at all in the technological emergence of Latin America, it is that there is still a long way to go. If public investment is made in upgrading public transportation, perhaps with modern subway systems such as Santiago's, it could help lessen the air pollution crises in the capital cities; as bad as Santiago's air quality is, it would be worse if the subway had not supplanted hundreds of buses belching oily exhaust from the combustion of cheap fuel. Despite advances in medical technology, more funds need to be invested in that sector to acquire state-of-the-art equipment. If the current economic expansion continues, it is inevitable that technological expansion will continue in its wake.

CULTURAL GROWTH AND PROJECTION

There is no more a "Latin American culture" than there is a homogenous U.S. or European culture. Which music, for example, is indicative of U.S. culture: jazz, blues, country-western, bluegrass, rock 'n' roll, rap, or grunge rock? The answer, of course, is all of the above. Is there a typically European art, literary style, music, architecture, fashion or cuisine? They vary, of course, from country to country. Today, there is cultural "borrowing" between North America and Europe, and now Latin America is joining in.

Latin American culture—or better described, cultures—also are regionalized. The stereotype of the Latin American as a devout Catholic *mestizo* who speaks Spanish, wears white *campesino* cotton clothing, listens to mariachi music and eats spicy food is as far from reality as the Latin American stereotype of the "typical" gringo as a rich, Anglo-Saxon Protestant who wears Calvin Klein jeans, listens to rock music and eats nothing but steak or hamburgers. (All right, maybe there's a kernel of truth to the rock and hamburger part.)

The face of the Andes

The North American view of Latin America understandably has been geographically influenced by neighboring Mexico. As Don Podesta of the *Washington Post* once wrote, Mexico is "a prism through which all Latin culture is viewed." But it is a woefully distorted view. In reality, the majority of South Americans are Portuguese-speaking Brazilians. Chile has a Lutheran minority of more than 10% stemming from German immigration in the 19th century, while nearly 40% of Guatemalans are converts to evangelical Protestantism. Mariachi music is no more, nor less, representative of Latin America than are Argentina's tango, Brazil's samba, the salsa of the Caribbean countries, the flute music of the Andean highlands, Chile's *huaso* music or the harp-based folk music of Paraguay. An Argentine accustomed to his bland meat-and-pasta diet would probably gag on chili-pepper-laced *ceviche*, a concoction of raw fish and lime juice peculiar to the Pacific coast countries.

Ethnic Diversity

Ethnically, the Hispanic colonies evolved far differently from their counterparts in North America, or for that matter, in Brazil. The English colonizers pushed the Indian tribes back beyond the ever-expanding frontier, or simply exterminated them, while for manual labor in the fields they imported black slaves from West Africa. The Portuguese followed a roughly similar policy in Brazil. The Spanish, meanwhile, enslaved the Indian populations they found there, pressing them into service in the mines and on the *haciendas*. But while miscegenation was limited between the English on the one hand and the Indians and black slaves on the other, it was widespread in Brazil and the Spanish colonies, producing a mixed race of *mestizos* in the Hispanic realm, and of *mulattos* in Brazil.

This ethnic mosaic was not woven evenly, which resulted in the cultural discreteness of today. The Argentines, like their counterparts in the United States, followed a shameless policy of genocide against the indigenous inhabitants, with the result that its culture is preponderantly Caucasian-European. So is that of Costa Rica, but there the white settlers found the land largely uninhabited. In Guatemala, Peru and Bolivia, the undiluted Indian races are in the majority, and their languages and cultures persist. Perhaps the most diversified cultural tapestry is that of Panama, where apart from whites, *mestizos* and Indians there are the descendants of black laborers brought from the Caribbean early in this century to construct the canal, and the Orientals who came later.

Just as the Anglo-Saxon stereotype is fading in the United States, so is the Hispanic stereotype no longer *apropriado* in Latin America, and for the same reason: successive waves of massive immigration beginning in the late 19th century and continuing to the present. Roughly half of all Argentines and Uruguayans, for example, are of Italian lineage, descendants of migrant farm workers who came to harvest grapes because of the reversed seasons and decided to stay. Germans, British and other Europeans also flocked to Argentina, Uruguay and Chile, as did European Jews seeking escape from persecution. Spanish Republicans seeking asylum after their defeat in the 1936–39 civil war settled throughout the region. Most Latin American countries also have unassimilated colonies of Arabs, Gypsies, blacks, and Orientals.

To underscore just how much of a melting pot Latin America has become, we have only to consider the surnames of some of the recent elected presidents in more than half of the former Spanish and Portuguese colonies over the past two decades: Sanguinetti in Uruguay and Martinelli in Panama (Italian); Fujimori in Peru (Japanese); Aylwin in Chile (Welsh); Frei in Chile (Swiss); Wasmosy in Paraguay (Hungarian); Menem in Argentina, Bucaram and Mahaud in Ecuador and Saca in El Salvador (Arab); Fox in Mexico (English), Kirchner in Argentina (German), Berger in Guatemala (Belgian), Bachelet in Chile (French) and Rousseff in Brazil (Bulgarian).

By contrast, of its 43 presidents, the United States has had but seven without Anglo-Saxon surnames: Van Buren and the two Roosevelts (Dutch), Kennedy and Reagan (Irish), Eisenhower (German) and Obama (Kenyan).

Literature, Cinema, TV and Music

Language, religion and ethnicity may be the roots of a culture, but its flowers are thoughts, ideas and expressions. In this regard, Latin America represents a veritable cultural nursery, one that finally has begun achieving recognition from the rest of the world. To be sure, U.S. and European cultural influences are much in evidence, ranging from Coca-Cola, McDonald's and Calvin Klein to the *plan europeo* practiced by the hotels and the architecture that makes cities like Buenos Aires, Rio de Janeiro and Santiago appear like New World copies of Madrid, Milan or Lisbon.

The dependency theorists who warned that Latin America was economically subjugated by the United States also wrung their hands over perceived U.S. cultural intrusion; for some reason, they never seemed threatened by European influences. Despite Coca-Cola, McDonald's, Calvin Klein, Rambo, rock music and the once-ubiquitous "I Love Lucy" reruns, the *dependentistas* wasted a great deal of bile for nothing. The Latin American cultures not only were not supplanted, but Latin American art, music, literature, cinema and television have grown into distinctive genres in their own right, and these cultural expressions have been projected to the developed world.

Six Latin Americans have received the Nobel Prize for Literature: Gabriela Mistral of Chile (1945), Miguel Ángel Asturias of Guatemala (1967), Pablo Neruda of Chile (1971), Gabriel García Márquez of Colombia (1982), Octavio Paz of Mexico (1990) and Mario Vargas Llosa of Peru (2010), all of whose works have been translated into several languages. Two other giants of 20th century Latin American literature, the blind Argentine poet Jorge Luis Borges and the Mexican novelist Carlos Fuentes, were perennial prospects for the Nobel but both died still waiting. They did receive Spain's prestigious Miguel de Cervantes Prize, the highest honor for Spanish-language literature, Borges in 1979 and Fuentes in 1987. Nineteen Latin American writers have received the Cervantes Prize since its inception in 1976, most recently Mexico's Elena Poniatowska in 2014.

Latin American cinema sprouted in the 1930s and flourished in the 1940s, especially in Argentina, Brazil and Mexico. But creative expression on film was hampered by decades of dictatorships throughout the region, of both left and right. Talented directors, actors and screenwriters often fled into exile to Europe, the United States or another Latin American country—if they were not were jailed.

It wasn't until 1960 that a Latin American film, Mexico's *Macario*, received a nomination for the Academy Award for Best Foreign Film in the United States. By 2013, 21 Latin American films had been nominated for that Oscar, eight from Mexico, six from Argentina, four from Brazil and one each from Nicaragua, Peru and Chile. Two won the Oscar, *La historia official (The Official Story)* in 1986 and *El secreto de sus ojos (The Secret in Their Eyes)* in 2009, both from Argentina. Only one Latin American film has won the Palme d'Or at the Cannes Film Festival since its inception in 1955: Brazil's *O Pagador de Promesas (Keeper of Promises)* in 1962; *Keeper of Promises* also received an Oscar nomination that year. Two Brazilian and one Peruvian films have won the Golden Bear in the Berlin International Film festival.

Both Brazil and France claim the legendary film *Orfeu Negro (Black Orpheus)*, directed by Marcel Camus of France but filmed in Portuguese in Brazil and based on the play, *Orfeu da Conceição* by Brazil-

Latin America Today

ian playwright Vinicius de Moraes, which was his adaptation of the Greek legend. The score is by Brazilian composer Carlos Antonio Jobim. It won both the Oscar for Best Foreign Film and the Palme d'Or in 1959. Most, but not all, official lists regard it as French.

Among the Latin American directors whose films have achieved cross-cultural acclaim in U.S. and European competitions in recent years are Mexico's Alejandro González Iñárritu (*Babel, Biutiful*) and Alfonso Cuarón (*Gravity*), Argentina's Juan José Campanella (*The Secret in Their Eyes*), Peru's Claudia Llosa (*The Milk of Sorrow*) and Chile's Pablo Larraín (*No*). *The Secret in Their Eyes* (*El Secreto de sus Ojos*) received the U.S. Academy Award in 2009 for Best Foreign Film, while Cuarón won the Oscar for Best Director in 2014 for *Gravity. Biutiful, The Milk of Sorrow* (*La Teta Asustada*) and *No* all were nominated for Best Foreign Film.

Because Latin American art, music, literature and cinema are so individualistic according to nation, they are examined more fully under the "Culture" section of each chapter in this book.

Latin American television development lagged well behind that of the United States and Europe, and because of its higher price tag it was usually the governments that led the way. This made television, like radio, an important political tool and a pawn in the quest for power. An exception was in Chile, where the first three stations were licensed to major universities. In recent years, state-owned television stations have yielded increasingly to privatization; in several countries, as in Britain, privately owned stations compete with the government station or network. In its early days, television programming in Latin America was crude, unreliable and heavily dependent on translated imported programs from the United States, which were cheaper than producing programs locally. This reality lent grist to the argument of the cultural dependency theorists.

That has changed dramatically since the 1970s, with Mexico, Brazil, Argentina, Venezuela, Colombia and Chile all producing that uniquely Latin American soap opera, the *telenovela*, both for domestic consumption and for export. Variety shows are reminiscent of those of the United States in the 1950s and 1960s. One that reaches a hemispheric audience is *Sábado Gigante*, begun in 1962 and now transmitted every Saturday from Miami but emceed by a Chilean, Mario Krutzberger, better known by the stage name Don Francisco.

Latin America has embraced U.S.-style sitcoms and news magazine shows, and some U.S. imports are still in evidence, but the dependency theorists' fears that they would outpace demand for programs produced in the native language have not been realized.

Latin American high culture and pop culture have received increasing acceptance in the United States and Europe. Novelists like García Márquez, Vargas Llosa, Carlos Fuentes of Mexico and Isabel Allende of Chile are widely translated into English and other languages. Fuentes died in 2012 and García Márquez in 2014, but their literary legacies endure. Film stars like Salma Hayek of Mexico regularly are cast in U.S. films. Pop singers like Colombia's Shakira and Juanes, the Dominican Republic's Juan Luis Guerra and Guatemala's Ricardo Arcona are winning Grammy Awards. U.S. baseball has witnessed a huge infusion of Latin American talent, like Sammy Sosa of the Dominican Republic and "El Duque" Hernández of Cuba.

GROWING INDEPENDENCE AND INTEGRATION

Most Latin American nations have abandoned the attitude of paranoia vis-à-vis their neighbor to the north, although mistrust lingers. The elected presidents of Bolivia, Ecuador, Nicaragua and Venezuela are openly antagonistic to the United States and maintain close ties to Cuba. Granted, the United States did much to warrant paranoia with its policy of gunboat diplomacy and CIA-sponsored intrigue. A sardonic joke underscored the Latin American view of the United States: Why are there never military coups in the United States? Because they don't have an American Embassy!

The most recent U.S. military intervention in the region, in Haiti in 1994, however well intentioned it may have been, inevitably raised eyebrows anew in Latin American capitals. For that reason, virtually all Latin American governments opposed in principle the U.S. invasion of far-off Iraq in 2003. Still, the United States is not seen quite as the bogeyman it once was, and country after country has elected presidents who earned undergraduate or graduate degrees in the United States, something that is no longer a political stigma.

Meanwhile, the relationship of old that bordered on paternalism has yielded to one of a more equitable partnership in terms of trade. The failure of the FTAA underscores the region's growing independence. But even leftist presidents who opposed the FTAA have welcomed bilateral trade with the U.S. and, of course, U.S. investments. Trade with Europe, China and the Middle East has increased exponentially in the past decade, and China has supplanted the United States as the lead-

ing trading partner of several countries (see next chapter).

Another encouraging sign of growing Latin American independence from the United States since the advent of democracy has been the trend toward regional cooperation and integration. In 1986, 19 democratic countries established the so-called Rio Group—17 of the Spanish-speaking republics (less Cuba), Brazil and Guyana. Unlike the Organization of American States (see U.S.-Latin American Relations), the United States is not a signatory. The Rio Group was created to promote democracy within the region, but its annual summits provide the heads of state of these nations an opportunity to discuss issues of mutual concern, including regional trade, drug trafficking, terrorism and political unrest.

An even newer organization, the South American Union of Nations, or *UNASUR* in Spanish and *USASUL* in Portuguese, was established in Cuzco, Peru, in 2004. The presidents of six countries and foreign ministers of six others signed the accord: the 10 Spanish- or Portuguese-speaking countries of South America, plus Guyana and Suriname. The group was the outgrowth of talks between South America's two free-trade blocs, *Mercosur* and the Andean Pact, to create a continent-wide free-trade zone, which has a combined gross domestic product of more than $1 trillion. The presidents of Brazil and Peru also announced their countries would collaborate to construct the first east-west highway across the continent from ocean to ocean, which they said would further integration even more. Argentina and Chile are currently at work on a $3.5 billion rail and highway tunnel through the Andes that will greatly facilitate the flow of cargo between Atlantic and Pacific ports.

The new community was largely the brainchild of Brazilian President da Silva. Citing the European Union as a model, da Silva said he envisioned, eventually, a unified continent with a central government, one foreign policy and a common currency. At a summit in Buenos Aires in 2010, attended by 10 of the 12 presidents, former Argentine President Kirchner was unanimously elected *USASUR*'s secretary-general, and the organization was to be headquartered temporarily in Buenos Aires. Kirchner died suddenly five months later and was succeeded by former Colombian Foreign Minister María Emma Mejía. She was succeeded in 2012 by fellow Colombian Alí Rodríguez Araque. The chairmanship rotates each year.

Emerging from a Rio Group summit in 2010 is an even newer experiment in regional integration, the 33-nation Community of Latin American and Caribbean States, known by its Spanish acronym

CORRUPTION PERCEPTIONS INDEX 2013		
Country	Score	World Rank
Denmark	91	1
Canada	81	9
Barbados	75	15
United States	73	19
Uruguay	73	19
Bahamas	71	22
Chile	71	22
Puerto Rico	62	33
Costa Rica	53	49
Cuba	46	63
Brazil	42	72
El Salvador	38	83
Jamaica	38	83
Peru	38	83
Trinidad & Tobago	38	83
Colombia	36	94
Suriname	36	94
Ecuador	35	102
Panama	35	102
Argentina	34	106
Bolivia	34	106
Mexico	34	106
Dominican Rep.	29	123
Guatemala	29	123
Nicaragua	28	127
Guyana	27	136
Honduras	26	140
Paraguay	24	150
Venezuela	20	160
Haiti	19	165
Sudan	11	174

Not rated: Belize, Grenada

SOURCE: Transparency International

CELAC. Instigated by Venezuela's Chávez, *CELAC* had its first summit meeting in Caracas, Venezuela, on December 2–3, 2011. It excludes the United States and Canada, which was widely interpreted as Chávez's effort to supplant the OAS. Yet, the center-right, pro-U.S. presidents of Mexico, Honduras, Panama, Colombia and Chile attended the summit. Chile hosted the next summit in January 2013, in conjunction with the periodic European Union-Latin America-Caribbean Summit (see Latin America Today). At the most recent *CELAC* summit in Havana, Cuba, in January 2014, the 30 heads of state declared their countries a "zone of peace" and pledged to work toward eliminating inequality.

Time will tell whether *CELAC* is a meaningful step toward regional integration, or whether it is a duplication of effort by groups like *UNASUR* that could ultimately founder because of ideological differences and old nationalistic antagonisms among the members. For example, its most recent president was Cuba's Raúl Castro, a Marxist and the only non-elected chief of state in the group, who is poles apart from leaders like Chile's Sebastián Piñera or Panama's Ricardo Martinelli, both wealthy, conservative businessmen. Chile and Peru, Colombia and Nicaragua and Venezuela and Guyana have unresolved territorial disputes. The presidency is now held by Costa Rica.

In May 2011, Chile, Colombia and Peru established the Integrated Market of Latin America, in effect merging their *bolsas,* or stock markets, with $600 billion in capitalization. It became the second-largest stock market after Brazil's. Mexico quickly joined as well. The four countries are all pro-U.S. and pro-free market, and most already had FTAs with each other. These four countries now constitute a free-trade bloc called the Pacific Alliance, and *Mercosur* members Paraguay and Uruguay have requested observer status.

LOOKING FORWARD . . .

In attempting to digest this description of the political, economic, technological and cultural realities of Latin America today, one must invariably return to the analogous glass that is half full rather than half empty. Unquestionably, advances have been made, but other issues must be addressed if Latin America is to continue to develop democratically, socially and economically.

Mob rule to force out duly elected presidents must be eschewed. Otherwise, political anarchy will lead to the type of instability that invites a return to authoritarianism. Press freedom must be respected as an independent check on would-be autocrats. Environmental pollution, that inevitable by-product of development, threatens the health of the next generation. Institutionalized corruption is still a political and economic leech on the lifeblood of almost all the countries of the region (see Corruption Perceptions Index). Hygiene and health care still lag far behind those of the developed world. Most importantly, that next generation needs to be provided with better education. Latin America continues to trail the developed world and the emerging countries of Asia in educational quality. The next generation must be more than merely literate; it must join the digital age.

The hemisphere's greatest remaining blight, the anachronistic totalitarian system in Cuba, appears to be acquiescing to the weight of history. In 2008, in failing health, Fidel Castro resigned as president and relinquished most of his power to his brother, Raúl. There are encouraging signs that Raúl Castro is open to new ideas. He has released virtually all the prisoners of conscience. Free-market reforms have been initiated and he has lifted travel restrictions. Yet, there is still no talk of free and contested elections or a free and independent press, and Cuba remains the least-free nation of the hemisphere.

The overall trend in Latin America toward greater political freedom, economic development, technological expansion, cultural individuality and regional integration is evident. There have inevitably been setbacks. There will be more. But for the moment, Latin America appears to be investing in its future, it has assumed its place on the world stage and its stock is clearly on the rise.

The Early Americans

THE GEOGRAPHICAL FACTOR

Few civilizations have been so influenced by geographical factors as those in Latin America. Contrary to long-held beliefs, the lands of Central and South America are neither young nor generally fertile. Old and trampled by several civilizations, large territories had already been abandoned by the Indians, even before the arrival of the Spanish and Portuguese. The Mayas probably exhausted their initial homeland, and the Incas called the vast desert regions between Peru and Chile "the land of hunger and death." Furthermore, the continent had few and scattered ports and is internally divided by rugged mountains, jungles, turbulent rivers and arid zones, which constitute formidable obstacles for communication or exploitation of natural resources.

Thus, since pre-Columbian times, societies developed in isolated clusters, having little contact with other communities. The Spanish policy of building cities as centers of political power increased this basic pattern of concentration and regionalism. Consequently, once the unifying authority of the Spanish king collapsed, it was impossible to keep all those remote and distant cities under a common authority. Immediately, almost every important urban center felt capable of demanding and asserting its own independence.

Geography not only contributed to this fragmentation, but also greatly determined the acceleration of two negative social trends that continue to hinder Latin American progress: (1) the abnormal growth of cities, especially capitals, constantly attracting masses of impoverished peasants—Mexico City's population jumped from less than 5 million in 1963 to 13.1 million in 2000—and (2) the lack of balance in the national population distribution. In almost every Latin country, the population is concentrated in one third to one half of its territory, leaving large zones almost uninhabited. Such conditions make the exploitation of the hinterland's resources a difficult and costly enterprise.

Indian Civilizations

When the Spaniards and other Europeans reached the New World, they found the native Americans in various stages of cultural development. Thinly scattered nomadic tribes of hunters and fishermen who also practiced simple farming populated much of the region. In contrast, three groups of natives—the Mayas, the Aztecs and the Incas—developed comparatively sophisticated and complex civilizations. They constructed large cities with imposing architectural styling, organized empires, acquired a knowledge of mathematics and astronomy and worked in precious stones and metals. The majority of these Indian civilizations had a fatalistic concept of life and the universe; their worship halls and temples were full of terrifying gods who incessantly demanded sacrifices, usually human. Their societies were stratified by class divisions and were based more on communal interest and units than on individual achievements. Furthermore, vast distances and geographical obstacles hindered enlightening inter-cultural relations, while the absence of wheeled vehicles or horses, cows or oxen limited their economic expansion or mass mobility. Perhaps because of such limitations, only one of these civilizations, the Mayas, developed some form of primitive writing, while none discovered the practical use of the wheel. In spite of intense research by scientists and archaeologists, we don't have yet a clear picture of the intricate aspects of the social systems and collective beliefs of pre-Columbian Indian societies because the Catholic Church, in the throes of the Spanish Inquisition, destroyed any vestiges of "heathen" knowledge. Many questions remain to be answered.

The Mayas (Guatemala, Mexico, Belize, Honduras, El Salvador)

As the most advanced and sophisticated of the early American civilizations, Mayan culture flourished for more than 1,000 years, reaching the peak of its development in the 7th and 8th centuries A.D. Mayan life was sustained by a single basic crop: corn, which grew in such abundance that it allowed them time to engage in a multitude of activities other than raising

The Early Americans

food, thus raising their lifestyle above that of the other Indian societies that remained tied to the soil for subsistence. Apparently the Mayas lived mostly in Greek-style independent city-states, tied together by an extensive road system and a common culture. A warlike people, the Mayas placed most political power in the hands of an extended royal family and priests. Mayan religion was based on the worship of many gods, but the practice declined with the growing sophistication of the society. Initially, religious ceremonies called for frequent human sacrifices. Art and architecture were not inferior to that of Europe at the time. As pioneers in the use of mathematics and astronomy, the Mayas refined an advanced calendar as early as the 4th century B.C. They also devised the mathematical concept of *zero* and developed a highly complex form of writing based on hieroglyphics (picture writing), which until today remains partially undeciphered. They had a surprisingly advanced knowledge of medicine as well.

Among the greatest achievements of the Mayas was art, including sculpture, pottery and textiles. Foremost was architecture. Major reminders of the Mayan civilization survive today in the form of thousands of monumental temples, soaring pyramids and majestic palaces. Many of these impressive structures have been discovered only in the past century, enveloped in the lush, tropical jungles of Central America and southern Mexico.

These vestiges of the past have yet to reveal why the Mayas suddenly abandoned their great cities long before the arrival of the Spaniards. Was it due to massive crop failure? Pestilence? Military defeat? Rebellion by slaves? The answer to this question is slowly being revealed; it probably involved the split-up of a large empire because of rivalries and a limited food supply, followed by succession of unnumbered small states each with its own fortification and the fascination of the people with constant warfare. The techniques of siege were probably perfected, and they killed each other off to an extent that those remaining simply disappeared into the thick foliage to live as primitives.

The Aztecs (Mexico)

When Hernán Cortés landed on the Mexican coast in 1519, the Aztec empire was at the very height of its power and development. Assimilating the knowledge

Aztec goddess *Coatlicue*

and achievements of previous civilizations such as the Olmecs and the Toltecs, the Aztecs developed into a harsh and efficient military society that allowed them to conquer and enslave all of central Mexico from the Atlantic to the Pacific. This brutal form of domination provoked constant rebellions among the tribes they subjugated, from whom they extracted slaves, concubines and human victims for sacrifice to their gods. In one especially dry season, Montezuma I, claiming that "the gods are thirsty," sacrificed 20,000 human beings on Aztec altars.

The Aztec social system rested on a rigid class structure with most manual work being performed by slaves captured during military campaigns. The economy was based on corn. Aztec architecture was impressive and their capital city of Tenochtitlán, now the site of Mexico City, was described by the conquering Spaniards as being equal to any in Europe. Although not as advanced as the Mayas had been in the use of science, mathematics or writing, the Aztecs did develop a more cohesive empire, even though it was based on force. The widespread resentment among enslaved neighboring groups was shrewdly exploited by Cortés to topple the Aztec empire.

Incas (Peru, Ecuador, Bolivia)

The empire carved out of the rugged Andes by the Incas reached its greatest level of development about a century before the arrival of the Spaniards. Through conquest of weaker Indian tribes in the region, the Incas expanded their realm from Peru through southern Colombia, Ecuador and Bolivia, and northern Chile—a combined area of more than 350,000 square miles. Facilitated by an ef-

Mayan ruins at Tikal, Guatemala

15

The Early Americans

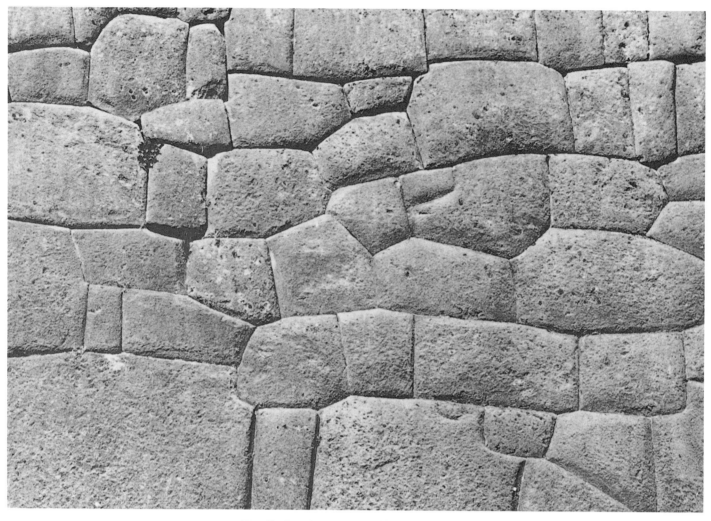

Detail of an Inca stone wall in Cuzco, Peru

ficient administrative command, a courier communications network and an impressive road system rivaling that of the Roman Empire, the Incas were able to weave their vast domain into the most highly organized and efficient civilization of all the native Americans. They developed an intricate form of writing through the use of coded knots on strings attached to a baton, called *quipus.*

At the head of the entire system was the ruling god-emperor called Inca. Under him was a highly structured noble class and priests, followed by lower level officials. The rigid chain of command permeated every corner of the empire. The Incas integrated newly conquered tribes into the realm by imposing a single language, *Quechua,* religion and social structure. Except for the highly rigid caste system of the ruling elite, the Inca state came close to being a totalitarian socialist state. All property was owned by the state and all work was organized on a communal basis. Through a system called *"mita"* (which the Spaniards later immediately adopted in the re-

gion) all members of the lower classes were obliged to work free for the empire for a period of four months every year. In return, the empire provided for the needs of its citizens. The result was a rather dull life for the masses—with little incentive, capability or effort to rebel. They dulled their misery and their hunger with a fermented beverage called *chicha,* still consumed today, and from chewing coca leaves.

The heart of the empire was the capital of Cuzco (literally "navel" in Quechua). A magnificent city by almost any standard, Cuzco glistened with enormous palaces and temples (many of which were lavishly decorated with gold) and other imposing dwellings that housed the elite. Even today, some of these structures are still in use, having withstood for centuries the abuses of man and the elements.

Although the Incas were less developed than the Mayas in the skills of writing, mathematics and astronomy, they surpassed the Mayas in architecture, water works, stonework and engineering. Indeed, some lengthy Inca suspension

bridges were found when the Europeans reached the area and remained in use until the middle of the 19th century. Inca systems of irrigation, pottery, textiles, medicines and even surgical techniques were remarkable.

The Incas' greatest gift to the world, however, was the potato, which in time would save tens of thousands of Europeans from starvation.

Despite its vast power, the Inca empire quickly fell to the *conquistadores.* The reasons for the sudden collapse of America's greatest Indian civilization were numerous: the Spaniards possessed superiority in firearms, employed advanced military tactics, exploited the advantage of horses and were relentlessly driven onward by the lure of gold. In contrast, the Inca empire was mortally weakened by a rigid social system in which the vital administrative structure was paralyzed once the top Inca was captured. In addition, a devastating war of succession between two royal Inca brothers had left the empire exhausted and divided. As a result, the Incas fell easy prey

Major Native Cultures About 1500

to a band of only 184 conquerors, led by a cunning Francisco Pizarro.

Other Indian civilizations that reached a high level of development were the Chibchas of northern Colombia, the Pueblo Indians of New Mexico and the Araucanas in what is now southern Chile. The fierce Araucanas resisted conquest and assimilation until well after Chile's independence from Spain. Indeed, the 16th century Spanish conquerors of Latin America—in contrast to the 17th century English, French and Dutch settlers in North America—encountered civilized natives whose social level was not greatly inferior to their own.

The impact of the conquest destroyed the Indian civilizations and looted their priceless treasures. To this was added the seizure of their valuable lands, forced labor and the spread of diseases unknown to the Indians, which decimated their population. The Spanish intermarried with the women of the former Indian ruling classes and built their empire on the social and economic foundations of the vanquished civilizations, giving rise to a new *mestizo* race. Unsuited to plantation labor, especially in the tropics, the Indians were replaced in Brazil and other areas by slaves imported from Africa and indentured laborers from Asia.

One of the most lasting achievements of the Spaniards was the conversion of the Indians to Catholicism. Devoted missionaries, still imbued with the religious fervor of the "glorious crusade" of the Inquisition, which had expelled the Arabs from Spain, risked their lives to preach the new faith among the Indians. Many of them learned their subjects' languages and defended them from the greed of the *conquistadores* and even the Spanish crown. Thanks to their examples and sacrifices,

the Catholic religion, or at least some variation of Catholicism, penetrated deeply among the Indian masses, transforming the Church into a powerful and influential institution in Latin America from the colonial period; its influence is waning as Indians migrate to the larger cities.

Scattered remnants of Indian civilization retreated from Spanish influence to the mountains of Guatemala, Ecuador, Peru and Bolivia, while the majority remained under Spanish rule. In Brazil, the Portuguese drove the indigenous tribes deep into the vast interior, much as happened in British North America. Until recent times, many of the local tribes succeeded in preserving their ancient communal life, languages and customs. Today, the Quechua-speaking Indians still number some 6 million in Bolivia and 2 million in Ecuador. Although their living conditions have scarcely improved since Pizarro's time, Andean Indians have remained detached and suspicious of meager government efforts to incorporate these survivors of the Inca Empire into a modern social and economic structure.

Efforts to modernize traditional Indian lifestyles have also been painfully slow in Central America and Mexico. In Guatemala, the descendants of the Mayas have continued to cling to their traditional customs despite government programs to en-

courage change. Even in Mexico, the most *mestizo* country in Latin America, many of Aztec and Mayan ancestry, particularly in the southern area, still have only marginal contact with the 21st century—even though modernization of Indian lifestyles has been a nominal objective of the Mexican government.

The process of social change accelerated after World War II with the aid of modern communications—particularly the transistor radio—which helped to penetrate the isolation that has allowed outmoded social, economic and political conditions to persist in the remote hinterlands.

Recently, some Latin American governments, particularly those of Mexico and Peru, have begun to show an increasing appreciation of the contributions and heritage of the early American civilizations. This growing interest has not been without cost. The rising appeal for Indian art has led to large-scale looting of ancient monuments and graves. In Central America and in the Andes, art thieves have stolen priceless stonework, jewelry and pottery—irreparably damaging some of it in the process—in an effort to satisfy the modern demand for genuine ancient art. In that sense, today's art thieves are continuing the same traditions of the *conquistadores* who plundered the early American Indian civilizations.

The ruins of Machu Picchu, the remote mountainous retreat of the Inca rulers, so well hidden that it was not until discovered in 1911.

Conquest, Colonization, and the Challenge of Independence

Cortés and the ambassadors of Moctezuma

Cortés began his conquest of Mexico in 1519. Pizarro invaded Peru in 1531 and Quesada and others began the conquest of Colombia in 1536. The Spaniards' superiority in weaponry and cavalry does not fully explain the victory of so few over so many. The decisive factor was the different character of the contending armies. Based on individual initiative, the Spanish regiments could face and fight formidable odds no matter what the losses. Based on strict authority and command, the Indian armies usually disintegrated when the general or high priest was captured or killed. In the battle of Otumba, Cortés had no gunpowder and only 16 horsemen, while the Aztecs were 20,000 strong. When a desperate Spanish charge killed the Aztec commander, the Indian army remained paralyzed while Cortés and his small group marched toward the safety of Tlaxcala, the capital of a powerful Indian tribe that had become Cortés' ally.

The conquest and colonization of Brazil followed a different pattern. By the Treaty of Tordesillas of 1494, Spain and Portugal divided South America between them along the 45th Meridian—Spain to the west, Portugal to the east. As early as April 22, 1500, Admiral Pedro Alvares Cabral established Portugal's authority over the region, but as further explorations found no traces of gold and silver, and since Portugal was then fully engaged in its profitable Asian trade, Brazil received scant attention. For many years, colonists occupied only a narrow belt of coastal land. The *"bandeirantes,"* rough adventurers and *mestizos* organized in groups called *"bandeiras,"* were the ones who in their search for wealth slowly opened the interior of Brazil, pushing the nomadic Indian tribes into remote areas. Portugal's declining Asian trade ultimately stimulated emigration to Brazil. In 1549, after the appointment of the first royal governors, a better system of land distribution was established and the Jesuits opened their first schools.

The strategic position and potential of Brazil attracted foreign attacks. French and Dutch attempts to hold Brazilian territories failed, however, and by 1645 the expanding colony was under Portugal's firm control. Initially sugar production flourished in the north, but the discovery of gold in what is today the state of Minas Gerais made the south the economic and political center of the colony, a position consolidated by subsequent discoveries of diamonds and precious stones. At the beginning of the 19th century, Brazil was a growing but still basically rural colony, with a vast and untouched hinterland.

During the colonial period, Spain created a highly centralized government, with most power concentrated in the monarch, and an internal balance of power that functioned remarkably well for three centuries. The region was divided into four viceroyalties: New Spain (capital, Mexico City), New Granada (capital, Bogotá), Peru (capital, Lima), and Rio de la Plata (capital, Buenos Aires). Several captains-general ruled less important territories. All judicial matters were dealt with by the *audiencias,* and the designation of ecclesiastical posts remained in the king's hands. At the end of his term, every viceroy had to submit to a *juicio de residencia,* a sort of trial where everyone could accuse him of improprieties or abuses of power. Although initially some authority had been granted to city councils *(cabildos),* eventually their autonomy was greatly reduced by royal control. Consequently, the colonies gained little experience in self-government or administration of public affairs.

Conquest, Colonization, and the Challenge of Independence

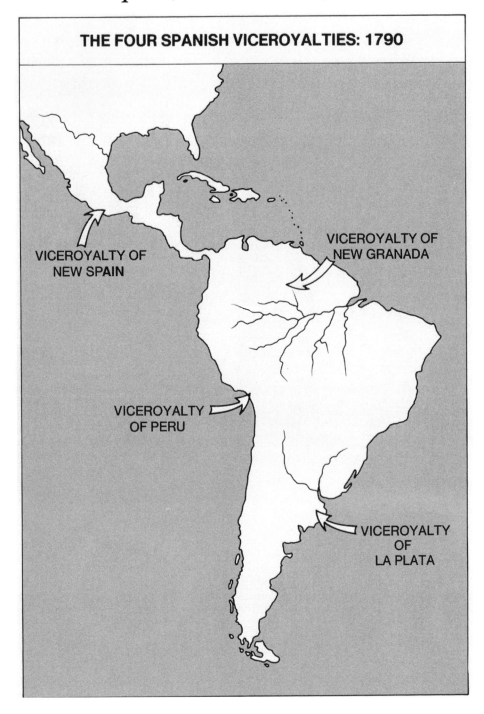

THE FOUR SPANISH VICEROYALTIES: 1790

VICEROYALTY OF NEW SPAIN

VICEROYALTY OF NEW GRANADA

VICEROYALTY OF PERU

VICEROYALTY OF LA PLATA

wielded political power. The aspiration of the *criollos* to be treated as equals and to share political power with the European-born intensified the friction. Aware of Spain's and Portugal's decline as European powers, the *criollos* turned to the French Enlightenment, and later to the new United States, for cultural and philosophical guidance.

The French Revolution had more impact in Latin America than did the American one. In Haiti, the division of the French white ruling elite brought about by France's political turmoil, sparked a rebellion of the black slaves under Toussaint L'Overture, which after a bloody and devastating war, ended with the liberation of the island. In the rest of Latin America, though, the creoles were far from being *Jacobins* (revolutionaries). A minority sympathized with the Declaration of Human Rights, but the majority was aware of the dangers which an open rebellion against Spain and Portugal could bring. Fearful of the surrounding masses of Indians and *mestizos*, most of the creoles wanted reforms, not revolution. Only the collapse of the Iberian monarchies could prompt them into action.

In 1808, Napoleon gave them the opportunity. Invading the Iberian peninsula, he imprisoned the new Spanish king, Fernando VII, whom he had lured to Paris, and placed his brother, Joseph Bonaparte, on the Spanish throne. In Portugal, Napoleon forced the Braganças, the royal family, to escape to Rio de Janeiro. Confronted with this political crisis, the *criollos* were free to act.

Independence and Its Aftermath

While the Spanish people rebelled against the Napoleonic armies, and the

The Church was in charge of education, but private religious orders, especially the Jesuits, made determined efforts to modernize learning. Education was largely confined, however, to the sons—not daughters—of the ruling class. A humanistic, non-scientific type of education became traditional in Ibero-America. Under the patronage of the Church and the Crown, architecture and schools of painting flourished, and the Baroque style, perfectly suited to dazzle the masses, became dominant in all artistic expression. By the middle of the 18th century, Hispanic America displayed important cities like Mexico and Lima, impressive cathedrals, a few universities and even famous writers like Sor Juana Inés de la Cruz and Carlos de Siguenza y Gongora.

Brazil's development was much slower, and it still had only scattered rural towns.

At the beginning of the 18th century, the ruling elite became increasingly divided between the *criollos*, or Creoles (those born in America) and the *peninsulares* (mainly functionaries recently arrived from Spain or Portugal). The *criollos* generally controlled the land, while the *peninsulares*

Cathedral of Cuzco, built about 1535

19

Conquest, Colonization, and the Challenge of Independence

General José de San Martín proclaims Peru's independence, July 1821

Brazilians proudly received their sovereigns, Hispano-Americans were left in a political vacuum. Their initial reaction was to swear fidelity to the imprisoned King Fernando. Soon, however, they realized *their* power. Deprived of legitimacy and without hope of receiving reinforcements from Spain, colonial authorities were practically paralyzed. By 1810, the *criollos* had moved from tentative autonomy to openly declaring independence. Significantly, Mexico and Peru, the two viceroyalties where Indian population was in greater proportion, initially remained under Spanish control. Immediately, regionalism and individualism began to fragment colonial unity. In the principal cities of the continent, hastily formed governments adopted republican constitutions and strove to extend their shaky authority over the surrounding territories.

In 1814, Napoleon's defeat brought the absolutist Fernando back to the Spanish throne. The prestige of the restored king, and some military reinforcements, gave the colonial authorities the upper hand. By 1816, with the exception of Buenos Aires, including the Viceroyalty of Rio de la Plata, Spanish rule had been re-established over most of the empire.

Absolutism, however, no longer appealed to the *criollos*, who had been "con-

taminated" by the ideas of Voltaire, Locke and Jefferson. Furthermore, Spain's political troubles had not ended. In 1820, a poorly equipped army destined to fight in America rebelled against the king, occupied Madrid and imposed a liberal constitution. In the meantime, inspired by the leadership of Simón Bolívar and José de San Martín, the *criollos* renewed their war for independence. After organizing an army in Argentina, San Martín crossed the Andes and defeated the Spaniards in Chile. Bolívar obtained similar victories in Venezuela and Colombia. After invading Peru and meeting Bolívar, San Martín abandoned the struggle and retired to France, the first in a long list of disillusioned liberators. Bolívar marched into Peru and on December 9, 1824, his best commander, Antonio José de Sucre, defeated the last royalist army in the battle of Ayacucho.

Two years before that decisive battle, with less violence, Mexico and Brazil achieved independence. In Mexico, the successive rebellions of two priests, Father Miguel Hidalgo and Father José María Morelos, backed mostly by Indians and *mestizos*, had been defeated by an alliance of conservative *criollos* and Spanish forces. In 1820, the proclamation of a liberal constitution in Spain induced those conservative allies to seek independence.

Their instrument was a Creole army officer, Agustín de Iturbide, whose mission was to defeat the remaining republican guerrillas and to proclaim a conservative empire. Instead, Iturbide gained popularity by appealing to *all* factions, entered Mexico City in triumph in 1821 and proclaimed himself Emperor Agustín I. He ruled little more than a year before being overthrown and sent into exile. When he returned uninvited, he was captured and shot, paving the way for Mexico's first liberal constitution in 1824.

In Brazil, Portugal's liberal revolution produced similar consequences. The new government in Lisbon recalled the king, and tried to reduce Brazil back to a colonial status. Before departing Brazil, the king designated his son Pedro as regent and gave him sound advice: if the Brazilians want independence, don't *oppose* them, *lead* them. Shortly after his father's departure, Pedro received a peremptory summons from the Lisbon parliament. Encouraged and supported by the Brazilians, he refused to go. When Portugal sent him a rash ultimatum, Pedro answered by proclaiming Brazil's independence. On December 1, 1822, he was crowned emperor of Brazil.

Portugal had lost its American colony and only Cuba and Puerto Rico remained

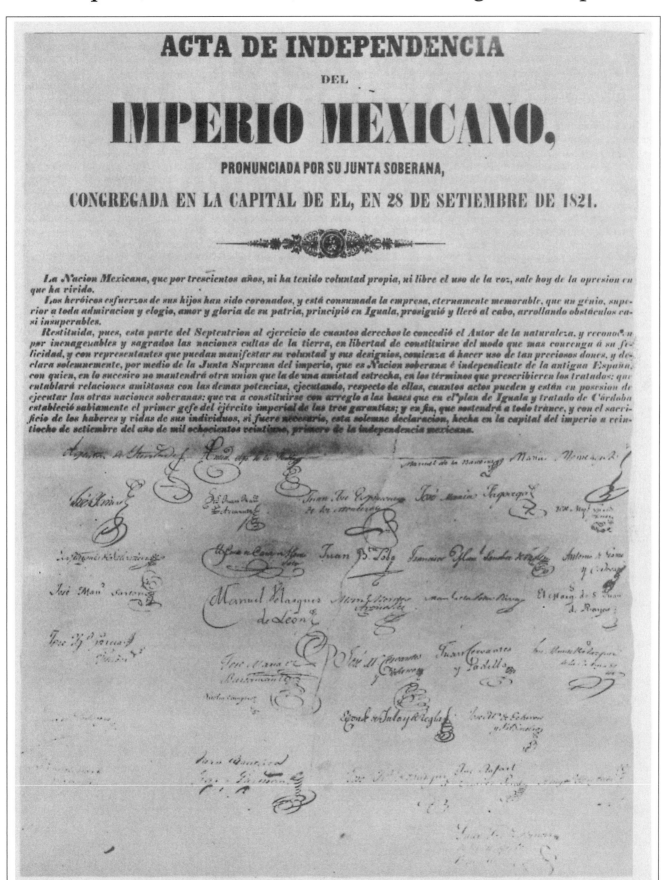

Mexico's Declaration of Independence with Iturbide's signature, top left-hand corner

Conquest, Colonization, and the Challenge of Independence

under Spanish rule. Britain had wrested control of Jamaica and other Caribbean islands from Spain in the mid-17th century. Spain had ceded Louisiana in 1802 to Napoleon, who quickly sold it to the United States for $15 million. Spain ceded Florida to the United States in 1819 and the island of Chiloe to Chile in 1826. The last vestiges of European colonialism in Central and South America and the Caribbean then were British Honduras (now Belize), British Guiana (now Guyana), Dutch Guiana (now Suriname), French Guiana and various islands held by Britain, France, the Netherlands and even tiny Denmark.

The Challenge of Independence

The first 50 years of independence were marked by political turmoil, dictatorships, regional confrontations and economic decline. The only exceptions to this were Chile, where a small territory and a rather homogenous population allowed the Creole elite to develop a strong and stable government, and Brazil, where the monarchy provided a moderate unifying force.

In the rest of Latin America, the lack of consensus on who should rule, massive ignorance, racial differences and a tradition of authoritarianism, opened the doors for *caudillos*, strong leaders who temporarily commanded the loyalty of armed groups and imposed their authority over congresses and constitutions. There were *caudillos* of all sorts: enigmatic men like Gaspar Rodríguez de Francia, who closed Paraguay to foreign influences; barbarians like Bolivian Mariano Melgarejo, who "executed" his uniform for hurting his neck; ultra-Catholics like Ecuadorian García Moreno and liberals like Venezuelan Gusmán Blanco. But almost all of them, even Argentine Juan Manuel de Rosas, represented more a consequence than a cause. They filled a political vacuum and, to a certain extent, contributed to uniting the nations they ruled.

Around 1870, Latin America entered a period of political stability and economic progress. In Argentina, Buenos Aires' liberal oligarchy finally imposed its authority over the provinces. Brazil became a republic in 1889 and even Mexico, a land plagued by internal dissension and foreign military interventions, attained political stability under the firm control of dictator Porfirio Díaz. Almost simultaneously, expanding European markets, especially Britain's, which had become the dominant economic power in Latin America, increased the demands for Latin American products, ushering in a period of growth and economic dependence.

During this period, waves of European immigrants poured into Argentina, Brazil, Chile and, in lesser numbers, into other Latin American nations. Political parties appeared, government control over the remote territories expanded thanks to better communication and the creation of professional armies, and towns like Buenos Aires, Rio de Janeiro and México became burgeoning cities.

In 1898, the United States intervened in the Cuban war of independence, defeated Spain and occupied Cuba and Puerto Rico. Cuba became "independent" in 1902, while the following year, Panama severed itself from Colombia (an event orchestrated by the United States) and signed a

U.S. troops camp in front of the Presidential Palace in Havana, 1898

Conquest, Colonization, and the Challenge of Independence

View of the Zócalo, Mexico City's main square

treaty with Washington authorizing the construction of a canal in an "American" territorial zone that was to extend from the Caribbean to the Pacific, physically dividing Panama. In spite of those ominous notes, which sent a wave of anti-imperialism throughout Latin America, at the beginning of the 20th century a mood of optimism reigned in the hemisphere.

Many of the old problems, though, remained unsolved. Unequal distribution of wealth, economic dependence, landless peasants and regional concentration of power all hampered genuine development. Very soon, hemispheric and international events demonstrated the fragility of Latin American political stability. In 1910, the Mexican Revolution began. Four years later, World War I exposed the vulnerability of some Latin American economies, while the demand for Chilean nitrates and Argentine beef benefited those countries. After the Russian Revolution of 1917, Communist parties appeared in almost every Latin American country. Another economic crisis shook the continent

in 1919; thus, the 1920s were years of political turmoil crowned by the devastating economic crisis of the worldwide depression of 1929–1939.

Few Latin American governments survived the impact of the Great Depression. Only World War II and the emergence of the United States as a global power temporarily revitalized the economy of the hemisphere. But the period after the war also brought the economic competition of new underdeveloped nations, the decline of Latin exports, and, finally, with Cuba's revolution, the entrance of Latin America into the ideological struggle between the U.S. and the Soviet Union.

In 1961, Castro's Cuba, the first socialist regime in the Western Hemisphere, launched a continental offensive under Marxist banners. The emergence of pro-Castro guerrilla movements throughout the region disrupted the slow but steady progress toward democracy experienced in the 1950s, when military regimes were toppled in Argentina, Venezuela, Colombia, Brazil, Guatemala and Peru. Threatened by this new enemy, Latin American armies, occasionally backed or tacitly supported by equally alarmed civilians, responded with a series of military coups in the 1960s and early 1970s, which reduced the number of truly democratic governments to only three: Colombia, Costa Rica, and Venezuela.

Simultaneously, Washington initiated an ambitious "Alliance for Progress" to lessen Latin American economic and social problems, and increased its military aid to the armies. By 1975, most of the guerrillas had been defeated, but dictatorial regimes dominated most of the continent. Under new authoritarian economic guidelines, there was some progress toward industri-

alization and agricultural development. In the 1970s Latin America spent more money on education (in relative terms of national budgets) than any other region in the world.

The stormy economic winds of the early 1980s brought a sudden halt to that effort. The oil crisis, accompanied by the subsequent economic recession in the United States and Western Europe, hit Latin America hard. With astronomical external public debts, plummeting prices for its products and sources for further loans drying up, Latin America plunged into its worst economic crisis of the last five decades. While austerity measures triggered popular protests in several countries, the emergence of the Marxist-oriented *Sandinista* regime in Nicaragua brought forth an oblique U.S. intervention. The *Sandinistas* were voted out in a 1990 election.

By the end of the 1980s, military regimes had yielded to elected civilian governments in Argentina, Bolivia, Brazil, Chile, Ecuador, El Salvador, Guatemala, Haiti, Honduras, Paraguay, Peru and Uruguay, while Mexico initiated political reforms that led to a pluralist party system in place of one-party dominance. The Dominican Republic elected presidents other than Joaquín Balaguer. Only Cuba remained authoritarian.

Latin America entered the 21st century in the midst of impressive economic expansion that was giving rise at long last to a middle class. But it also was experiencing political growing pains as the young democracies sought to cope with perennial woes such as widespread poverty, drug trafficking and institutionalized corruption. Developing strong, viable democratic institutions for the future remains the challenge for the present.

U.S.-Latin American Relations

The history of the relationship between the United States and Latin America can be divided into five relatively distinct periods: **1820–80**, the era of the Monroe Doctrine and U.S. paternalism; **1880–1934**, the era of open U.S. imperialism, intervention, and the policies of gunboat diplomacy and the "big stick;" **1934–45**, the "Good Neighbor Policy;" **1945–90**, the Cold War, the Alliance for Progress, the Cuban and Nicaraguan revolutions and U.S. support for anti-communist dictators; and **1990–present**, the post Cold War era, the emergence of democracy in Latin America and a growing U.S.-Latin American trade partnership.

U.S. PATERNALISM

The example of U.S. independence from Britain stirred rebellious ideas among the Creole elites in colonial Latin America. Actually, geographical, cultural and political barriers greatly reduced the impact of American "revolutionary" wars in the southern hemisphere. Only the tiny minority of cultivated Creoles had some notion of what had happened in North America.

Following President Washington's isolationist policy, the United States for years remained indifferent to the affairs of the southern neighboring nations. While Latin America struggled and achieved independence, the United States concentrated on purchasing Florida from Spain in 1821 and avoided any act or declaration that could endanger those negotiations.

In 1823, President James Monroe delivered his famous message to Congress, quickly raised to the rank of a "doctrine," warning European powers that any attempt to extend their system to any portion of this hemisphere would be considered as a threat to the United States.

Despite its significance, the Monroe Doctrine was a U.S. unilateral declaration that did not imply any concern or interest in Latin American problems. When Simón Bolívar, dreaming of unifying the newly born Latin American states, convened the ill-fated first Pan-American Congress three years later, the United States reacted with little enthusiasm. The United States did not invoke the Monroe Doctrine in 1833 when Britain occupied the Falkland Islands claimed by Argentina, nor in 1838–40, when France took military actions against Mexico and Buenos Aires. In 1848, its victory in the war with Mexico allowed the United States to acquire vast territories from that country and to extend its territory to the Pacific Ocean.

Historical circumstances prevented Latin America from expressing any strong criticism of the United States during Mexico's debacle. Fragmented into several fledgling states, facing almost continuous internal political turmoil and poorly informed of international events, Latin America was not ready for continental solidarity.

France's Napoleon III took advantage of the U.S. Civil War to invade Mexico in 1862 and put the Austrian Archduke Maximilian on the throne of a supposed empire. The United States was in no position to enforce the Monroe Doctrine, but following the defeat of the Confederacy the United States threatened to intervene militarily if Napoleon did not withdraw French troops. The United States also recognized the republican government of Benito Juárez. France withdrew, leaving Maximilian to face a *juarista* firing squad.

During almost the entire 19th century, the dominant power in Latin America was Great Britain, not the United States. By 1880, however, the situation had changed. Political stability and economic progress in Latin America coincided with the emergence of expansionist or imperialist trends in the United States.

GUNBOAT DIPLOMACY AND THE 'BIG STICK'

In 1889, the United States showed its growing economic interest in the southern regions by holding in Washington the first Pan-American Conference and establishing the basis for an inter-American regional system under U.S. domination. Shortly after that conference, American expansionism transformed the image of the United States from a "model" to be copied by Latin America into an aggressive "Colossus of the North," bent on dominating the entire hemisphere. The Pan-American Union later evolved in 1948 into the Organization of American States (OAS).

In 1898, the United States intervened in the Cuban rebellion against Spain, defeated Spain and occupied Cuba, Puerto Rico and the Philippines. Cuba proclaimed its independence in 1902 only after accepting an amendment in its constitution (the Platt Amendment) that gave the United States the right to intervene in Cuban affairs under certain conditions (determined by the United States). The United States also leased the naval base at Guantanamo, which it still occupies.

Meanwhile, President Theodore Roosevelt, famed for his motto "speak softly but carry a big stick," utilized intrigue and the threat of military intervention to help Panama gain its independence from Colombia in 1903. The acquisition of rights to build the Panama Canal and the Roosevelt Corollary to the Monroe Doctrine, by which the United States maintained the right to decide when a "flagrant wrongdoing" had occurred in a Latin America state that merited "preventive intervention," defined a new imperialist U.S. policy nicknamed "gunboat diplomacy."

Woodrow Wilson, a self-professed progressive on domestic policy, soon proved that he could be as jingoistic as Roosevelt in the name of imposing his vision of democratic morality on the nations to the south. After the odious Victoriano Huerta overthrew and murdered the democratic reformer Francisco Madero in Mexico just days before Wilson's inauguration in 1913, Wilson soon signaled that it would be U.S. policy to promote democracy in Mexico and elsewhere. When U.S. intelligence determined that a shipment of German arms was bound for Veracruz, Wilson ordered U.S. Marines to seize the Mexican port in 1914 to prevent the guns from reaching Huerta, a move that backfired by causing Mexican public opinion to rally around the dictator.

After Huerta was toppled in 1915, Wilson threw his support behind the new president, Venustiano Carranza, who was opposed by such rebel leaders as Emiliano Zapata in the south and Francisco "Pan-

International Conference of American States, Washington, D.C., 1889

cho" Villa in the north. Wilson could do little in the south, but he allowed Carranza's troops to use U.S. railroads to outflank Villa. Enraged, Villa attacked the town of Columbus, New Mexico, in 1916, killing 19 Americans and prompting Wilson to dispatch Gen. John J. Pershing on a "punitive expedition" into Mexico to pursue Villa. Once again, the U.S. intervention had the effect only of galvanizing the various Mexican warring factions against the *gringo* invaders. The expedition was a total failure, and even long after the end of the Mexican Revolution, Mexico's distrust of its triggerhappy northern neighbor lingered.

Also during his first term, before he became more preoccupied with the threat from Germany that led to U.S. entry into World War I, Wilson sent the Marines at one time or another to occupy Nicaragua, Honduras, Costa Rica, the Dominican Republic and Haiti. The Marines remained in Nicaragua throughout much of the 1920s, battling a rebel leader who was to become a martyr and would lend his name to a Marxist movement 50 years later: Augusto César Sandino. The occupation of Haiti endured for 19 years, under five presidents of both parties, until 1934.

World War I diminished Great Britain's influence and facilitated U.S. economic expansion in the hemisphere. Between 1913 and 1920, U.S. commerce with Latin America increased by 400%. In 1929, U.S. investment in the region amounted to more than $5 billion, exceeding Britain's by almost $1 billion. Latin American bitterness, however, worried Washington. By the sixth Conference of American States in Havana in 1928, Nicaraguan guerrilla leader Sandino, fighting the Marines in his country, had become a Latin hero and the United States began to reconsider the wisdom of the "big stick" policy. The economic crash of 1929 increased interest in a policy change.

GOOD NEIGHBOR POLICY AND THE COLD WAR

In 1933, President Franklin Roosevelt proclaimed the Good Neighbor Policy.

From 1933–45, U.S.-Latin relations experienced a considerable improvement. Economic recovery and better trade agreements, the rise of fascism, adoption by the Communist parties of a conciliatory tactic known as the "popular front" and the spirit of solidarity provoked by World War II, contributed to raising the Good Neighbor Policy and Panamericanism to a real level of continental unity.

Roosevelt died in 1945, the war ended, and the United States once more relegated Latin America to a secondary position. From the end of World War II to the Cuban Revolution, U.S.-Latin American relations steadily declined. While Washington

The President of Colombia addresses the OAS conference, Bogotá, March 1948.

concentrated its attention on Europe and Korea to confront the Soviet global challenge, Latin America confronted old and pressing economic, political and social problems: Population growth, unstable economies, populist movements and military interventions. Latin America soon became a pawn in the Cold War, as the United States sought to create a solid anticommunist bloc in the hemisphere.

In 1954, when the elected leftist government of President Jacobo Arbenz in Guatemala posed a perceived threat to the unity of the bloc, the United States used the first conference of the new Organization of American States (OAS), created in Bogotá in 1948, to pressure Latin delegates into an anti-Guatemalan declaration. A few months later, Arbenz was toppled by a U.S.-backed invasion from Honduras.

Democratic leaders and parties in Latin America denounced what they considered U.S. favoritism toward anti-communist dictators. This criticism found a favorable echo when a powerful upsurge of democratic movements swept the continent. The *MNR (Movimiento Nacionalísta Revolucionario)* came to power in Bolivia in 1952; in 1955, Juan Perón fell in Argentina, and in the following years, Generals Odría, Rojas Pinilla and Pérez Jiménez were toppled in Peru, Colombia and Venezuela, respectively. "Democracy is on the march," proclaimed Costa Rican leader José Figueres in 1959. That year, General Fulgencio Batista was forced to abandon Cuba as Fidel Castro entered Havana in triumph, hailed as a democratic hero. Contrary to general expectations in and outside the island, the Cuban revolution moved radically to the left, creating an entirely new situation in Latin American history.

Immediately after seizing power, Castro sought to revolutionize Latin America by

U.S.-Latin American Relations

encouraging and aiding guerrilla groups in several countries. This policy, the rapid socialization of the revolutionary regime and increasing anti-American propaganda, strained relations with the United States. In 1960, when President Dwight Eisenhower reduced the quota of Cuban sugar allowed to enter the United States, the Soviet Union announced it would purchase the total amount of the reduction, and arms from the communist bloc began pouring into Cuba. In January 1961, after much mutual recrimination, Eisenhower broke diplomatic relations with Cuba; they have never been restored.

John F. Kennedy, inaugurated just days later, inherited from Eisenhower a CIA plan for an invasion of Cuba by anti-Castro exiles. The force of 1,200 men had been training clandestinely in Guatemala, again governed by a president friendly to the United States. At the last minute, however, Kennedy withdrew crucial air support for the operation, fearing a Soviet response. The Bay of Pigs (Playa Girón) invasion was a disaster, raising Castro to the level of an international hero in the eyes of some, and damaging the United States' reputation as a military power.

Emboldened by this U.S. failure, the Soviets secretly began placing nuclear missiles in Cuba capable of striking deep inside the continental United States. A dangerous Soviet-American confrontation followed. In October 1962, the United States imposed a naval "quarantine" around Cuba to prevent the delivery of more missiles, and demanded the removal of those already there. The world teetered closer to the brink of nuclear war than at any time during the Cold War. After a tense standoff, the Soviets pulled the missiles out of Cuba, but at the same time, obtained a guarantee from Washington that no further aggressive action would be taken against Castro. The anti-communist bloc in the Western Hemisphere seemingly had been broken.

Protected by the U.S.-Soviet pact, Castro increased his guerrilla campaign in Latin America. The United States, which had managed to isolate Cuba diplomatically in 1961, answered with the Alliance for Progress, to promote economic progress in Latin America, and with renewed military aid to friendly Latin American countries. The second aspect of the strategy proved more successful than the first. Although few economic advantages were accomplished by the Alliance for Progress, Latin American armies defeated the guerrillas everywhere in the region. Unfortunately, victory was usually preceded or followed by military coups. By the end of the 1960s, only a few democracies had survived the military onslaught.

The guerrillas' defeat, and the deterioration of Cuba's economy, rescued by Soviet aid, forced Castro to abandon his independent guerrilla path and to accept tacit Soviet control of Cuba. Yet, from 1973–75, U.S.-Cuban relations improved slightly. Many Latin American nations re-established relations with Cuba, while several influential voices in the United States asked for an end to the commercial embargo imposed on the island. In 1975, the conciliatory trend was halted when Castro sent troops to Angola to aid a faltering socialist regime, and publicly denounced U.S. "colonialism" in Puerto Rico.

Castro was not the only crisis facing the United States in Latin America during the 1960s. In January 1964, less than two months after Lyndon Johnson succeeded the assassinated Kennedy, riots erupted in Panama when foolhardy American high school students in the U.S.-controlled Canal Zone tore down the Panamanian flag which, under a decree from President Eisenhower, flew beside the U.S. flag in the Zone. U.S. troops opened fire on the rioters as they spilled over into the Zone; a total of 22 Panamanians and six Americans were killed in the bloodshed. Panama still honors its slain citizens on every anniversary of the riots, and Fourth of July Avenue in Panama City was renamed "Avenue of the Martyrs."

The following year, the left-wing Juan Bosch came to power in the Dominican Republic, sparking civil unrest, and an alarmed Johnson feared that the country would become "another Cuba." He dispatched the 82nd Airborne Division to restore order, but not before there was considerable fighting and loss of life. When an adviser suggested that the OAS assume the peace-making role in the Dominican Republic, the earthy LBJ was reported to have commented, "Those people couldn't pour piss out of a boot if they had instructions written on the heel." True or not, it epitomized what Latin Americans regarded as U.S. arrogance and condescension.

The back-to-back incidents of U.S. military force in Panama and the Dominican Republic reinforced Latin America's distrust of its powerful neighbor, and greatly enhanced Castro's prestige among left-leaning, anti-U.S. movements in the region.

In 1967, Johnson enjoyed a modest triumph with a CIA operation to train a Bolivian ranger battalion that ultimately tracked down and killed the legendary revolutionary Ernesto "Che" Guevara.

Republican President Richard Nixon did little to dissipate Latin American distrust in 1970 when the CIA made a clumsy attempt to bribe Chilean congressmen into blocking the election of the Marxist Salvador Allende as president after he had received a narrow plurality, but not a majority, of the popular vote. As another example of both the prevailing Cold War mentality and traditional U.S. arrogance toward Latin America, National Security Adviser Henry Kissinger reportedly said, "I see no reason to allow a country to go communist because of the irresponsibility of its own people."

Allende was elected, and he promptly nationalized most U.S. businesses. Nixon responded with an economic embargo against Chile, which brought Allende sympathy even from non-Marxist Latin Americans. Like Castro, he was viewed as a heroic David standing up to the American Goliath. It wasn't revealed until 1975 that Nixon's CIA also waged a clandestine effort to destabilize the Allende government by instigating public protests and strikes by independent truck drivers. The CIA also was tangentially involved in the military coup that overthrew Allende in September 1973. Allende died in the bloody coup, and although it is still debated whether it was by his own hand or the hands of the military, another anti-U.S. martyr had been created.

That same year, the Uruguayan military overthrew that country's long-standing democracy, which had proven incapable of dealing with the *Tupamaros*, an urban revolutionary movement. U.S. complicity was also suspected in the Uruguayan coup. The military regime succeeded in crushing the *Tupamaros*—along with Uruguayan democracy for the next 12 years.

Democratic President Jimmy Carter reversed long-standing U.S. policy of supporting military dictatorships in the name of anti-communism and embarked on a moralistic crusade reminiscent of Woodrow Wilson's. He appointed ambassadors who aggressively confronted the right-wing generals in Brazil, Chile, Argentina, Uruguay, El Salvador, Nicaragua and Paraguay for alleged human rights violations and curtailed or cut military aid to those countries. He also strained relations with Brazil just weeks into his presidency in 1977 by condemning its nuclear program, which provoked Brazil into canceling its mutual-defense treaty with the United States.

At the same time, Carter sought to ameliorate long-standing distrust of the United States by signing the historic Panama Canal treaties—somewhat hypocritically—with a left-wing dictator, Omar Torrijos. The signing ceremony at OAS headquarters in Washington in 1977 was a major hemispheric event, with all the Latin American heads of state except Castro in attendance.

The *Sandinistas* toppled strongman Anastasio Somoza—a West Point graduate—in Nicaragua on Carter's watch in 1979, but they exhibited little gratitude to the United States for withdrawing its traditional support for Somoza. They vilified the United States, turned to Cuba and the Soviet Union for support and began establishing a Marxist state with little regard for the human rights that Carter professed to cherish.

Carter faced another Latin American crisis in 1980 with the so-called Mariel boatlift, named for a small Cuban port. When Castro declared that anyone who wished to leave Cuba was free to do so, thousands of boats owned by Cuban-American expatriates in Florida sailed to Mariel in a Dunkirk-like evacuation and carried about 125,000 Cubans to the United States. Too late was it discovered that thousands of them were common criminals and lunatics Castro had removed from prisons and asylums and forced onto the boats. Carter's inept handling of the crisis was a major issue in the 1980 election.

In that election, Republican Ronald Reagan defeated Carter in a landslide and immediately ordered a 180-degree course change in Latin American policy. He reversed Carter's human-rights policy and began patching up relations with the military strongmen. He restored military aid and enlarged the training programs for Latin American officers and non-commissioned officers at the U.S. Army's School of the Americas (which Carter had relocated from Panama to Georgia) to combat Marxist insurgencies. Despite congressional objections, he lavished military aid on the military regime in El Salvador to combat that insurgency, and he fired the Carter-appointed ambassador there who had the audacity to criticize the regime after four American nuns were raped and murdered by right-wing death squads.

Reagan's unequivocal support for Britain in its war with Argentina over the Falkland Islands in May 1982 strained relations with Latin America. So did his invasion of the Caribbean island nation of Grenada in October 1983, after its Marxist president, Maurice Bishop, was overthrown and murdered by a cabal of pro-Cuban, Marxist-Leninist soldiers. The invasion, all too reminiscent of the era of gunboat diplomacy, was denounced even by the anti-communist strongmen Reagan had been courting.

Reagan also provided military and financial aid to the Nicaraguan *Contras*, who were battling to topple the *Sandinistas* and whom Reagan praised as "the moral equivalent of our founding fathers." All this was part of Reagan's overall strategy of defeating the Soviet Union and winning the Cold War with a massive military buildup and confronting the Soviets vicariously with surrogate warriors on such far-flung battlefields as Afghanistan, Angola and Central America.

Reagan's support for the *Contras* almost proved the undoing of his presidency. When the Democratic-controlled Congress prohibited any further aid to the *Contras*, Reagan's minions made an end-run around Congress by secretly selling arms to Iran, then at war with Iraq, and diverting the profits to the *Contras*. When the deal became public in late 1986, a major scandal erupted that lingered until Reagan left office in 1989. By then, however, Reagan's strategy of out-spending the Soviet Union into oblivion was well on its way to success.

A NEW BUT DIFFICULT PARTNERSHIP

With the collapse of the Soviet Union, Reagan's successor, Republican George H. W. Bush, had the opportunity to usher in a new era of mutual understanding and cooperation between the United States and Latin America without the old issue of communism vs. anticommunism hanging over both parties. He attended an anti-drug summit in Cartagena, Colombia, and promised closer ties with Latin America in return for its cooperation on drug control.

However, Bush's military intervention in Panama in December 1989, no matter how justifiable in light of strongman Manuel Noriega's provocations, was denounced throughout the hemisphere as just another example of the naked application of U.S. power to enforce its will in Latin America.

Another obstacle in U.S.-Latin American relations left over from the Reagan era was effectively eliminated when the *Sandinistas* finally were removed from power—by free election—in 1990.

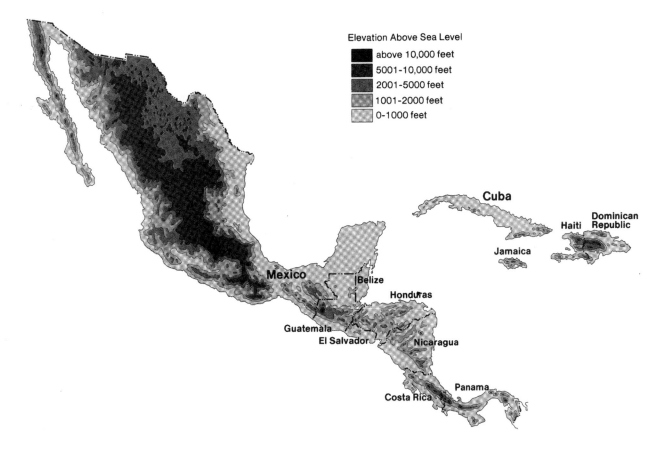

Elevation Above Sea Level

- above 10,000 feet
- 5001-10,000 feet
- 2001-5000 feet
- 1001-2000 feet
- 0-1000 feet

U.S.-Latin American Relations

Elevation Above Sea Level

■	above 10,000 feet
■	5001-10,000 feet
■	2001-5000 feet
■	1001-2000 feet
□	0-1000 feet

Toward the end of his single term in office, Bush negotiated the North American Free Trade Agreement (NAFTA) with Canada and Mexico, and he openly advocated a hemisphere-wide free trade zone.

By the time Democrat Bill Clinton took office in 1993, virtually all the dictatorships had been replaced by democratically elected civilian governments. He had to contend neither with gross abuses of human rights, as Carter had, nor with the problem of communist insurgencies, as Reagan had. In his second year in office, Clinton invited the heads of state of all the nations of the hemisphere except Cuba to a Summit of the Americas in Miami in December 1994. There, he resurrected Bush's proposal for a Free Trade Area of the Americas (FTAA), open to any country with a democratic form of government. Toward that end, he made a state visit to Brazil, Uruguay, Argentina and Chile in 1997.

Nonetheless, Clinton found himself resorting to armed intervention just as his two Republican predecessors had. After the military strongmen who had overthrown the democratically elected Haitian President Jean-Bertrand Aristide refused to acquiesce to international pressure to restore Aristide, Clinton ordered the 82nd Airborne Division to Haiti in September 1994 to keep order and to effect the transition back to democracy. Although this invasion was a benevolent one and there was minimal loss of life, the televised images of American paratroopers landing in Haiti in full battle dress evoked the old specter of Theodore Roosevelt's "big stick." The Americans withdrew in 1995 and were replaced by U.N. peacekeepers, who remain there today two decades hence.

At the Second Summit of the Americas in Santiago, Chile, in 1998, the 34 hemispheric leaders (once again, Castro had been excluded) issued a communiqué that

called for establishment of the FTAA by 2005. Clinton praised Latin America's advances in democracy, but called for "a second generation of reforms" to consolidate the region's fragile democracies.

Although the Santiago summit was marked by unprecedented good will between the U.S. president and his Latin American counterparts, there were still nagging complaints about U.S. hegemony. Among these were the continued U.S. embargo against Cuba, with which nearly all the Latin American countries by then had diplomatic and trade relations, and the U.S. policy of "certifying" countries as cooperating allies in the war against drugs as a condition for financial aid, which the Latin Americans saw as demeaning.

The drug issue as a whole continues to strain North-South relations today, with the United States pushing for support at eradicating coca, marijuana and heroin poppy cultivation at their sources, while Latin America argues that there would be no market for illegal drugs if the United States would curb the demand for them at home. Both sides, of course, have a point.

Clinton's successor in 2001, Republican George W. Bush, at first showed a greater interest in, and sensitivity toward, Latin America than had most of his predecessors, including his father. In fact, he declared the 21st century "the century of the Americas." A former governor of Texas, he was fluent in Spanish and openly courted Hispanic votes in the 2000 presidential race. Indeed, the Cuban-American vote in Florida provided the narrow victory in that state that gave him an Electoral College victory over the Democratic candidate, Al Gore.

Accustomed to dealing with Mexican authorities as governor, Bush made a state visit to Mexico weeks after his inauguration to meet with the newly inaugurated President Vicente Fox; in the past, new U.S. presidents had made their first trip abroad to Western Europe. Both conservatives, Bush and Fox got on well. Bush also hosted Chilean President Ricardo Lagos and Brazilian President Fernando Henrique Cardoso at the White House soon after the visit to Mexico.

In April 2001, Bush attended the Third Summit of the Americas in Quebec, where he voiced his strong commitment to the FTAA. The leaders agreed to a target date of January 1, 2005, and made adherence to representative democracy a condition for participation. The only major opposition came from Cardoso, who accused the United States of protectionism, and Venezuela's Hugo Chávez, who said the FTAA would do nothing to alleviate poverty.

Bush concluded a bilateral free-trade pact with Chile in 2003, which was seen as a precursor to the FTAA. He also pushed for a free trade agreement with Central

America and the Dominican Republic; in 2009, Costa Rica became the final country to sign on.

Five months after Quebec, U.S. Secretary of State Colin Powell flew to Lima, Peru, to attend the periodic summit of OAS foreign ministers, ostensibly to emphasize again the Bush administration's commitment to regional integration and democracy.

The date: September 11, 2001.

Within hours of his arrival, Powell hastily returned to Washington to deal with the terrorist attacks on New York and Washington. Although his Latin American colleagues were sympathetic and understanding, there could have been no more symbolic reminder that U.S. priorities in the world lay elsewhere.

Perhaps mindful of the need to mend fences in the wake of the shift of global priorities after 9/11, Bush made a four-day tour of Mexico, El Salvador and Peru in 2002. In Mexico, he attended a U.N. summit on poverty in Monterrey, to assure Latin America and other developing regions that the U.S. was concerned with more than the war on terror. In El Salvador, he held a summit with several Central American presidents to assure them of his commitment to a U.S.-Central American-Dominican Republic free trade pact. In Lima, Bush told his Andean counterparts that he was trying to persuade a recalcitrant Democratic-controlled Senate to reinstate preferential tariffs, and he urged continued cooperation on combating terrorism and drug trafficking. On all three stops, he reiterated his support for democracy.

Despite Bush's wooing, more and more newly elected leaders began echoing skepticism toward the FTAA. In December 2001, Argentine President Fernando de la Rua, an FTAA advocate, was forced to resign because of an economic crisis and deadly riots. He was replaced by Eduardo Duhalde, who was cool to the FTAA; Duhalde's elected successor, Néstor Kirchner, was hostile to it. Brazil's president, Luiz Inácio da Silva, elected in 2002, was a longtime critic of the FTAA, more so even than his predecessor, Cardoso. Da Silva and Kirchner instead called for strengthening the *Mercosur* trade bloc (Argentina, Brazil, Uruguay and Paraguay) and for increased regional economic integration in preference to the FTAA, which they argued would be dominated by the United States.

Mexico's Fox, despite his conservatism and warm relations with Bush, met with da Silva at the Rio Group summit in Peru in 2002 and came away committed to greater Mexican trade with *Mercosur.*

Opposition to the FTAA grew steadily, with the elections of Nicanor Duarte Frutos, and later Fernando Lugo, in Paraguay; Tabaré Vázquez and later José Mujica in Uruguay; Evo Morales in Bolivia; Rafael

Correa in Ecuador; Manuel Zelaya in Honduras; Daniel Ortega in Nicaragua; and Mauricio Funes in El Salvador.

In 2002, the 10 presidents from South America's two major trading blocs, *Mercosur* and the Andean Pact, (Bolivia, Colombia, Ecuador, Peru and Venezuela) met in Guayaquil, Ecuador; the president of Chile, an associate member of *Mercosur*, also attended. In the so-called "Guayaquil Consensus," the presidents agreed that strengthened trade between the two South American blocs must precede implementation of the FTAA, and there was more grumbling that the U.S. preached free trade while practicing protectionism. In 2003, Peru joined Bolivia and Chile as associate members of *Mercosur*, and Venezuela applied for full membership in 2006 but the Paraguayan Senate blocked it.

The January 1, 2005 deadline for establishing the FTAA came and went, and when the Fourth Summit of the Americas was held in Mar del Plata, Argentina, in November 2005, even Bush acknowledged the idea was stalled. A total of 29 of the 34 nations still favored an FTAA, but Argentina, Brazil, Paraguay, Uruguay and Venezuela effectively blocked it. Mexico's Fox suggested the 29 countries move ahead on their own, but without the participation of major economies like Brazil and Argentina, it would have served little purpose. As usual, the summit was made contentious by violent anti-Bush demonstrations and by Chávez's strident anti-U.S. comments. The summit accomplished nothing other than a photo opportunity; the leaders did not even see the need to issue a communiqué.

Meanwhile, Castro and Chávez began lobbying for what they call the "Bolivarian Alternative for Latin America;" its Spanish acronym, *ALBA*, also means "dawn." They envision Latin American integration that excludes the United States. President Morales of Bolivia, elected in 2005, eagerly signed on to the idea, as did Correa of Ecuador, Ortega of Nicaragua, Zelaya of Honduras and Lugo of Paraguay. Honduras was expelled after Zelaya was forced from office in 2009 (see Honduras).

Despite Bush's declaration of "the century of the Americas," drug certification and four other practices or incidents strained U.S.-Latin American relations on his watch and called into question the depth of his administration's commitment to Latin America in general or to its democratization in particular.

The first was the abortive military coup in Venezuela in 2002 that had Chávez under house arrest for 48 hours. Chávez had long been—and remains today—a thorn in the side of the United States because of his close ties to Cuba, Iran, Saddam Hussein's Iraq and Moammar Gadhafi's Libya as well as for his opposition to the FTAA. State Depart-

ment statements issued within hours of the coup clearly conveyed the idea that the Bush administration regarded the overthrow of Chávez, who had twice been elected by overwhelming majorities, as the will of the Venezuelan people. The administration said, essentially, that Chávez had it coming. When Chávez was reinstalled two days later, President Bush's then-national security adviser, Condoleezza Rice, said she hoped Chávez had learned something from his experience. The message regarding U.S. policy toward Latin America was unmistakable: We're all for democracy—as long as you don't elect someone we don't like.

The second was the Bush administration having its ambassadors openly electioneer for presidential candidates it favored, a stunning breach of diplomatic protocol. The first such instance came in the 2001 Nicaraguan campaign, when the U.S. ambassador appeared at functions for the Liberal candidate, Enrique Bolaños, whose opponent was the former *Sandinista* president, Daniel Ortega. Bolaños won.

A few months later, the U.S. ambassador used the same tactics in Bolivia, where one of the candidates was Morales, leader of the coca farmers, who had pledged to reverse the incumbent administration's coca-eradication policy. This time, this blatant interference almost backfired. Morales, whom polls had predicted would receive no more than 12% of the vote, was catapulted into second place, with about 21% (see Bolivia). Congress then had to choose between Morales and former President Sánchez de Losada, and the ambassador lobbied members of Congress to vote for Sánchez, who ultimately won, but U.S. interference left a bitter taste in the mouths of Bolivians.

In the 2005 elections, Morales won a first-round victory in Bolivia, while in October 2006, Ortega was elected in Nicaragua. Both have since been re-elected.

The third unpopular episode was the U.S. intervention in Iraq in 2003, which for many Latin American countries was just too reminiscent of U.S. gunboat diplomacy. Even those countries morally opposed to Saddam Hussein's regime and generally friendly to the United States, such as Mexico and Chile, publicly criticized the war. Chile's opposition on the U.N. Security Council briefly delayed the U.S.-Chilean free-trade agreement. Four countries—the Dominican Republic, El Salvador, Honduras and Nicaragua—did send contingents of several hundred troops each to participate in the allied coalition in Iraq. All but El Salvador decided to pull their troops out, however, after Spain withdrew its troops from Iraq in the wake of the Madrid terrorist bombings in 2004. El Salvador kept a contingent in Iraq until early 2009.

The fourth has been the practice—which in fairness did not originate with Bush

U.S.-Latin American Relations

and has continued under Obama—to send lower-echelon representatives to the inaugurations of democratically elected presidents. When a dozen or more heads of state from Latin America, and sometimes elsewhere, attend an inauguration and the United States sends a mere cabinet secretary, and sometimes undersecretary, the contrast does not go unnoticed and can only be seen as offensive. Fidel Castro regularly attended inaugurations before age and illness kept him at home.

This souring of U.S.-Latin American relations was acutely evident when Powell attended the OAS foreign ministers' summit in Santiago, Chile, in 2003. He urged his 33 colleagues to denounce Cuba's crackdown on dissent that April (see Cuba) and to support the transition to a democratic Cuba. Powell's plea met an icy reception. Just a month earlier, the United States had failed to persuade the OAS to adopt a resolution condemning the crackdown, winning support from only 17 of the 34 members. Even countries opposed to Castro also oppose the U.S. trade embargo. The rejection of the U.S. position against Cuba appeared to be a case of Latin American blood being thicker than Western Hemisphere water and general resentment against a paternalistic U.S. attitude.

In 2004, the pro-U.S. Miguel Angel Rodríguez, who served as president of Costa Rica from 1998–2002, was elected secretary-general of the OAS. Just two weeks later, Rodríguez resigned amid allegations that as president he received $900,000 in foreign payoffs or kickbacks. The jockeying for the OAS leadership lasted six months. The United States' preferred candidate was Mexican Foreign Secretary José Luis Derbez—which may have doomed his candidacy. When the first vote in 2005 ended in a 17–17 tie between Derbez and Chilean Interior Minister José Miguel Insulza, Derbez dropped out in the interest of unity.

The 2005 annual meeting of the OAS foreign ministers was held in Fort Lauderdale, Florida, the first time the meeting had been held on U.S. soil since 1971. Both Bush and Rice addressed the meeting, urging the OAS to grant the secretary-general greater power to deal with countries drifting back toward authoritarianism. Venezuela responded that the idea was obviously directed at it. Most members agreed the language had Venezuela in mind, and in a major rebuff of the United States, the final resolution was a watered-down version that stressed "the right of self-determination and the principle of non-intervention" over worries about would-be dictators.

Apparently in response to growing anti-U.S. sentiment, Bush made a goodwill visit in 2007 to Brazil, Uruguay, Colombia, Guatemala and Mexico, but he was met with anything but goodwill. His stops in each country were met by large, sometimes violent protests, and Chávez made rival visits to Argentina and Bolivia, where he addressed large, enthusiastic anti-Bush rallies. In Guatemala, Mayan Indians performed an "exorcism" after Bush's visit to an archeological site to rid it of evil spirits. About the only substantive accomplishment of the visit was an ethanol-promotion agreement Bush signed with Brazil's da Silva. Even that was marked by discord when da Silva publicly called on the U.S. Congress to repeal the 54-cent-a-gallon tariff on Brazilian ethanol, which is designed to protect U.S. corn-based ethanol. Bush responded bluntly that the law would not be repealed before it expired in 2009.

Democrat Barack Obama succeeded Bush in 2009, and his appearance at the Fifth Summit of the Americas in Trinidad and Tobago that April served as his much-anticipated debut on the hemispheric stage. Even before then, Obama sent Vice President Joseph Biden to Santiago for a mini-summit with the center-left presidents of Chile, Brazil, Argentina and Uruguay and the prime ministers of Britain and Spain to discuss the international financial crisis and environmental issues as a precursor to the G-20 Summit in London. Biden also visited Peru and Costa Rica.

On the eve of his departure to Port-of-Spain, Trinidad, Obama fulfilled a campaign promise—which helped him carry the key state of Florida—to rescind the Bush Administration's restrictions on Cuban Americans traveling to Cuba and on the amount of money they could remit to families in Cuba. Fidel Castro grumbled that this wasn't enough, that Obama should lift the trade embargo, but Obama said the next move was up to Cuba.

The day before the summit, Cuban President Raúl Castro—ironically while attending a summit of the left-wing *ALBA* countries in Caracas—reversed decades of Cuban policy by saying, "We are prepared, wherever they want, to discuss everything—human rights, freedom of the press, political prisoners—everything, everything, everything that they want to discuss." Obama replied cautiously that "the United States seeks a new beginning with Cuba," but suggested that Cuba demonstrate its willingness by releasing political prisoners. Within days, Fidel Castro threw cold water on his brother's dramatic overture, saying in his newspaper column that Raúl didn't really mean "everything" was open to discussion. Fidel said Raúl only meant Cuba was willing to talk but that it would not compromise the principles of the Revolution—such as suppressing freedom of thought. Raúl quickly clarified his remarks, removing any doubt over who was still in charge.

Obama made his first state visit to Mexico en route to the Trinidad summit, promising President Felipe Calderón he would do more to stop the traffic of weapons to Mexico in an effort to curtail the alarming rise in drug-related violence, but he said immigration reform would not be on his agenda until the end of 2009. (He later moved it back to the end of 2010). Simultaneously, Secretary of State Hillary Clinton visited Haiti and the Dominican Republic on her way to the summit.

At the summit, Obama listened indulgently as Nicaragua's Ortega delivered a 50-minute anti-U.S. harangue straight out of the Cold War. Obama countered that he had not come to rehash "stale debates" but to look to the future, and he quipped that at least Ortega "did not blame me for things that happened when I was three months old."

The greatest anticipation centered on how Chávez would behave toward the new U.S. president, whom he had already called an "ignoramus" who had "the same stench" as Bush. The two leaders perfunctorily shook hands, and during a business session, the grandstanding Chávez approached a surprised Obama to present him a copy of a leftist book, *Latin America's Open Veins—Five Hundred Years of the Pillage of a Continent* by Uruguayan author Eduardo Galeano. They shook hands again, as the TV cameras rolled. At both encounters, Chávez told Obama in English, "I want to be your friend." Toward the end of the summit, Chávez approached Hillary Clinton to voice his willingness to restore ambassadorial-level relations, which he had disrupted the previous September by expelling the U.S. ambassador; the United States responded by booting out the Venezuelan ambassador. Ambassadors were exchanged again in June.

Obama called the summit "very productive," and assured Latin America that he wanted to be equal partners. He said he had been struck by how many of his counterparts had mentioned the role that Cuban doctors have played in their countries, while U.S. involvement had been in the form of drug interdiction or military aid. "If our only interaction with many of these countries is drug interdiction—if our only interaction is military—then we may not be developing the connections that can over time increase our influence and have a beneficial effect," Obama said. However, he also chided Chávez for his tendency to play to the TV cameras and for years of "inflammatory" rhetoric toward the United States. Ultimately, he said, "The test for all of us is not simply words but also deeds."

Clinton later said at the State Department that the Obama administration would not continue Bush policy of attempting to isolate hostile nations like Cuba and Venezuela, a policy she said had failed, but would seek dialogue with even its harshest critics. At the same time, she said the United States expects reciprocal gestures from Cuba. She also called the growing Chinese, Russian and Iranian influence in the region "quite disturbing."

Since then, her meetings with Latin American leaders *did* appear aimed at isolating Chávez. When Uruguayan President Vázquez visited Washington in 2009, Clinton expressed her concern that Russia's $2.2 billion arms credit to Venezuela could provoke an "arms race" in the region.

Just two months after the Trinidad summit, Obama found himself at odds with most of the countries in Latin America—and the OAS—over the Honduran Congress' forced removal of President Manuel Zelaya, ostensibly for abuse of authority. Obama issued a lukewarm condemnation of Zelaya's removal, while a chorus arose in Latin America demanding his reinstatement. The OAS expelled Honduras. When Honduras proceeded with its regularly scheduled elections that November and the pro-U.S. Porfirio Lobo Sosa was elected in a fair vote, the United States recognized his government, but at first only Costa Rica, Panama, Colombia and Peru followed suit. The *ALBA* countries still refuse to recognize Lobo Sosa's government.

Obama did not replace Bush's assistant secretary of state for Western Hemisphere affairs, Thomas A. Shannon Jr., for 10 months. Obama appointed Chilean-born Arturo Valenzuela and named Shannon ambassador to Brazil. Valenzuela served until 2011 and was succeeded by Roberta Jacobson, a career State Department employee.

Obama was preoccupied with events in the Middle East during the first two years of his presidency, and it wasn't until March 2011 that he made his first goodwill visit to Latin America, accompanied by first lady Michelle Obama and their two daughters. Included on the five-day itinerary were Brazil, Chile and El Salvador.

Despite his seeming neglect of the region, he was better received by Latin Americans than Bush had been. Indeed, they seemed to be more enthralled with him than they had for any U.S. president since Kennedy. Just as Kennedy had struck a positive chord as the first Catholic president, it is possible that black and *mestizo* Latin Americans identify with Obama as the first member of his race to achieve the presidency.

In all three countries, goodwill shared the front seat with hard policy matters. Indeed, his tour was overshadowed by U.S. airstrikes against Libya, conjuring up again memories of the "big stick." In Brazil, Obama was met with cheering crowds. He and President Dilma Rousseff and their top advisers discussed nagging trade issues. The visit was seen as positive, with

Rousseff insisting she wants a new strategic partnership with the United States and a better relationship than existed under her predecessor, da Silva. Obama hosted Rousseff at the White House in April 2012.

In Chile, which has a free trade agreement with the United States, Presidents Obama and Sebastián Piñera signed a nuclear cooperation agreement, but protesters recalled CIA involvement against the Allende regime.

In El Salvador, which also has a FTA with the United States, Obama did something Bush hadn't done: visited the tomb of Archbishop Oscar Romero, assassinated by right-wing death squads in 1980 (see El Salvador). He and President Mauricio Funes, the first president elected under the banner of the *FMLN* and himself a former guerrilla, had amicable but frank talks about the three major issues affecting the bilateral relationship: immigration, violent crime and trade.

The Sixth Summit of the Americas in Cartagena, Colombia, in April 2012 can only be called a flop. It was overshadowed from the beginning by a scandal in which several members of Obama's Secret Service detail were sent home and later dismissed for heavy drinking and cavorting with prostitutes the night before the president's arrival, which diverted media attention from the summit itself.

Obama found himself on the defensive more than ever over Cuba's exclusion from the summit. Ecuador's Rafael Correa refused to attend because of it, and Venezuela's Chávez and Nicaragua's Ortega said they would boycott the next summit in Panama in 2015 unless Cuba were included (Chávez died in March 2013). Argentine President Fernández also used the summit as a forum to press Argentina's claims against Britain over the Falklands Islands, putting Britain's staunch allies, the United States and Canada, in an awk-ward spot, hemispherically speaking. Once again, there was no final communiqué.

Obama made his second Latin American goodwill visit early in his second term, May 2–5, 2013, to Mexico and Costa Rica. In Mexico City, he held his first meeting with the new president, Enrique Peña Nieto. The two presidents had the same general agenda as both of their predecessors: drugs, immigration, trade and security. Obama said in a speech to young people at the National Museum of Anthropology that each country should abandon old stereotypes of the other, and he recognized Mexico's emergence as a major player on the global stage.

In Costa Rica, Obama met with representatives of the eight-nation Central American Integration System (*SICA*). The leaders discussed drug- and gang-related violence in the region and Obama stressed the need for economic development, but he offered no dramatic new initiatives.

Just three weeks after Obama's visit to Latin America, Vice President Joe Biden made a six-day tour that included Colombia, Trinidad and Tobago and Brazil. In Colombia, he and President Juan Manuel Santos heralded the year-old FTA and pledged continued cooperation. In Port-of-Spain, Trinidad, Biden met with 15 Caribbean leaders and signed an agreement aimed at increasing trade and economic cooperation. Prime Minister Kamla Persad-Bissesar said the closed-door talks were both "frank" and "brutal." Biden's last stop was Brazil, with which the U.S. now enjoys a trade surplus because of Brazil's purchases of oil-drilling equipment. Biden visited a *Petrobras* research facility and met with President Rousseff, who is scheduled to visit the White House again in October.

Significantly, Biden left Trinidad the same day Chinese President Xi Jinping arrived for talks with those same Caribbean leaders. From there Xi went to Costa Rica and Mexico. China has undertaken a major rivalry with the U.S. in Latin America for trade and influence (see Latin America and the World).

The new U.S. secretary of state, John Kerry, got off to an awkward start with Latin America because of a seemingly innocuous offhand remark. During an appearance before the House Foreign Affairs Committee in April 2013, he referred to the Western Hemisphere as "our back yard." Although the context of his remarks was that the region is "vital" to U.S. interests, the media of the anti-U.S. countries like Venezuela and Bolivia seized upon the remark as a continued example of U.S. condescension.

Things did not improve in June and July 2013 when Edward Snowden, the fugitive former employee of the U.S. National Security Agency who had leaked sensitive information, was reportedly considering requesting asylum from several countries, including Bolivia, Cuba, Ecuador, Nicaragua and Venezuela. Vice President Biden telephoned Ecuador's Correa directly to ask that Snowden not be given refuge there. Correa was non-committal, at least publicly. When Morales' plane was grounded overnight in Vienna en route back to Bolivia from Moscow on suspicion that Snowden was aboard, it provoked a diplomatic crisis between Latin America and Europe (see Latin America and the World). Snowden requested asylum in Russia, apparently because there was no way to fly from Moscow to any of the Latin American countries without crossing the airspace of a U.S. ally. Russia eventually granted the request, after allowing Snowden to stew in the Moscow airport for weeks, and he remains in Russia.

U.S.-Latin American relations deteriorated further with the revelation in September 2013 that the NSA has tapped the private telephone conversations of various

U.S.-Latin American Relations

world leaders *allied* with the U.S., including Brazil's President Rousseff. President Obama had invited her to a state dinner at the White House in October, the only world leader to have been accorded a state dinner that year. After the eavesdropping revelation broke, she canceled the planned visit. Three months later, however, they kissed each other on the cheek at the memorial service in South Africa for Nelson Mandela. Obama was also photographed shaking hands with Raúl Castro, which made news around the world.

Vice President Joe Biden discussed the NSA matter with Rousseff when he went to Brazil in June to cheer for Team USA in the World Cup. He assured Rousseff there would be no repetition of eavesdropping, but he stopped short of apologizing.

At the same time, a potential humanitarian disaster has been unfolding along the U.S.-Mexican border as tens of thousands of children from violence-racked Central America, as young as four years old and unaccompanied by adults, suddenly began crossing the U.S. border illegally and have been placed in makeshift detention facilities. The reason for the sudden surge

in child migration may be a memo Obama signed in 2012 called the Deferred Action for Childhood Arrivals, which defers deportation for illegal immigrants who were brought to the United States as children. The erroneous rumor spread in Central America that if children crossed the border alone and surrendered, they would be allowed to stay. The "Dream Surge" apparently is being orchestrated by the notorious "coyotes" who profit in human smuggling.

Secretary of Homeland Security Jeh Johnson warned that only children with at least one parent in the United States would be allowed to stay; the rest would be deported. As of June, 47,000 children had entered the country illegally in 2014, and it was estimated the figure would reach 70,000 to 90,000 by the end of the year. The children have been placed under the care of the Department of Health and Human Services and were being housed at various military bases and in impromptu detention centers, such as a Border Patrol warehouse in Nogales, Arizona, where 1,100 children were housed in cramped conditions, raising international concerns for their welfare.

The crisis caused Biden to stop in Guatemala on his way home from Brazil on June 20 to meet with Guatemalan President Otto Pérez Molina, Salvadoran President Salvador Sánchez Cerén, Mexican Interior Secretary Miguel Ángel Osorio and Honduran President Juan Orlando Hernández's cabinet chief of staff to discuss the situation (see Guatemala). Biden bluntly told them the children would be deported and that their countries bore a responsibility at their ends to prevent their children from being placed in such dangerous circumstances. He pledged tens of millions of dollars in aid to Guatemala, El Salvador and Honduras, from which most of the children came, to enhance security and to provide youth centers.

The Latin American representatives just as bluntly pressed back by blaming the United States for not coming up with a coherent immigration policy and urged Biden to extend temporary protective status (TPS) to the children because of the violent conditions in their countries of origin. Biden pressed right back by conditioning the granting of TPS to migration reforms adopted by the Guatemalan Congress, as

The leaders of 33 hemispheric counries pose for an official portrait at the First Summit of the Community of Latin American and Caribbean States, known by its Spanish acronym *CELAC*, in Caracas, Venezuela in 2011. *CELAC*, which excludes the United States and Canada, was designed as a counterweight to the U.S.-dominated Organization of American States (OAS).

Photo by Nelson González Leal

Hondurans and Salvadorans must transit Guatemala. The atmosphere of the meeting was reportedly testy.

Obama also telephoned Mexican President Enrique Peña Nieto on June 19 to urge him to tighten Mexico's border with Guatemala and to crack down on the *"coyotes."*

The immigration issue had already become a major domestic political issue in the United States. A tentative compromise between Democrats and Republicans had been reached but appeared dead with the primary defeat in June of House Majority Leader Eric Cantor of Virginia, who lost to a tea party candidate who had criticized Cantor for compromising on immigration. As this book went to press, Republicans were blaming Obama for the child migration crisis, and immigration appeared to be a political football heading into the November mid-term elections.

REGIONAL INTEGRATION?

When the First Summit of the Americas convened in Miami in 1994, it was during an atmosphere of enthusiasm for emerging democracy and the prospect of hemispheric free trade. Over the following 18 years, the FTAA idea died and there is now growing tolerance of Cuba's totalitarian regime, especially by Venezuela, Bolivia, Ecuador and Nicaragua, which are increasingly authoritarian themselves. The usefulness of future summits is in grave doubt.

The same may now be true of the OAS, which is criticized by the left as being a U.S. lapdog and by the right as being pro-Cuba. After the OAS expelled Honduras but voted to reinstate Cuba (which Cuba has refused to do), the Republican-controlled House Appropriations Committee in 2011 voted to delete the OAS' $42 million U.S. contribution from the budget. The Democratic-controlled Senate did not go along. Republicans are displeased with Insulza's leadership. Leftist leaders like Chávez and Ecuador's Correa, meanwhile, chafed at being condemned for human rights abuses by the OAS' Inter-American Commission on Human Rights.

Whatever its shortcomings, the OAS remains a potentially constructive force for hemispheric dialogue and human rights. It also interjected itself into the drug dialogue with a study released in May 2013 that calls for legalization of marijuana, something advocated by both pro- and anti-U.S. leaders.

As an outgrowth of the old Rio Pact (see Latin America Today), and at the initiative of da Silva, the 12 South American countries, including Guyana and Suriname, signed an accord in Cuzco, Peru, in December 2004 creating the South American Union of Nations (*UNASUR* in Spanish and *UNASUL* in Portuguese). It was ratified in 2008, and in 2010, former Argentine President Kirchner was elected secretary-general. He died of a heart attack that October and was succeeded by former Colombian Foreign Minister María Emma Mejía. The organization was rent by internal discord when it expelled Paraguay in 2012 following the rapid and questionable impeachment and removal of President Fernando Lugo. Paraguay was welcomed back at the most recent summit in Paramaribo, Suriname, in August 2013, following the inauguration of the new, legitimately elected President Horacio Cartes. *USASUR* has also been in a quandary over what position to take regarding Venezuela's heavy-handed treatment of dissenters.

The newly created, 33-member Community of Latin American and Caribbean States, or *CELAC*, was designed as a meaningful substitute to the OAS—but without the United States and Canada. It was established in 2010 with the left-wing Chávez and the right-wing Chilean President Piñera as co-chairs. The first summit was held in Caracas in December 2011 and the second in Havana, Cuba, in January 2014. In Havana, the assembled leaders declared their countries a "zone of peace" and pledged themselves to combat inequality, poverty and hunger. The attendance of OAS Secretary-General Insulza, as well as U.N. Secretary-General Ban Ki Moon, lent the new organization prestige and credibility. Ultimately, however, a hemispheric organization that excludes the United States makes as much sense as the American League excluding the New York Yankees. A *Latinobarómetro* poll conducted by *The Economist* in 18 Latin American countries in 2013 showed that 49% of respondents were not in favor of a hemispheric organization that excludes the U.S., down from 56% in 2011.

In sum, if U.S. policy toward Latin America seems paradoxical and pendular, so do Latin American attitudes toward the United States. Despite the election of a succession of pro-Chávez, anti-U.S. presidents in the region, even such left-wing presidents as da Silva, Vázquez of Uruguay, Morales of Bolivia and Humala of Peru demonstrated they realize their countries' economic well-being depends in no small part on access of their goods to U.S. markets. Even as they echoed Chávez's anti-imperialist rhetoric, they eagerly sought bilateral trade agreements with the United States or pleaded with the U.S. Congress to extend the preferential tariffs on their non-traditional products, which represent billions of dollars in sales and hundreds of thousands of jobs.

In other words, Latin Americans are saying, we detest your paternalistic attitude, your trade embargo of Cuba, your drug certification, your restrictive immigration quotas and your intervention in Iraq and elsewhere, but business is business.

One of the most dramatic changes taking place in Latin America is its progressive integration into the rest of the world. Almost totally isolated during most of the 19th century and until World War II, first under the tutelage of Britain and then of the United States, Latin America has since then experienced a progressive "opening to the world."

Canada and Europe

After 1960, Canada increased its economic and cultural ties with Latin countries, principally Brazil, Cuba and, with NAFTA in 1994, Mexico. Canada didn't become a member of the OAS until 1990, and like the United States, it was excluded from the newly formed Community of Latin American and Caribbean States (*CELAC*).

By 2011, Canada also had bilateral free-trade agreements (FTAs) with Costa Rica, Panama, Peru and Chile and was pursuing one with Colombia. Prime Minister Stephen Harper made a six-day tour of Brazil, Colombia, Costa Rica and Honduras that year, aimed at expanding trade even further. Harper attended the summit of the new four-nation Pacific Alliance (Chile, Colombia, Mexico and Peru) in Cali, Colombia, in May 2013 as an observer; Canada could become a full member of the free-trade bloc. Canada has been engaged for a decade in free-trade talks with El Salvador, Guatemala, Honduras and Nicaragua as a bloc. Canada also is negotiating a FTA with the 15-nation Caribbean Common Market, or CARICOM. Mexico is Canada's third-largest trading partner after the U.S. and China.

Canadian companies have invested heavily in the region, especially mineral companies.

The most important nations of Western Europe, especially Germany, Italy and Spain, reinforced their influence in the hemisphere through economic aid, cultural programs and support for political groups or parties attuned to their predominant ideologies. Since 1990, European countries have invested heavily in Latin America; Spain invests more in its former colonies than anywhere else. The European Union has FTAs with Chile, Colombia, Mexico and Peru, the new Pacific Alliance countries.

In 1999, the EU and the *Mercosur* trade bloc—Argentina, Brazil, Paraguay and Uruguay—began talks for a FTA. The talks stalled in 2004 over the EU's reluctance to flood its market with cheaper agricultural products, while the *Mercosur* countries worried about European manu-

Latin America and the World

factured goods threatening local industries. The talks resumed in 2013 after both sides appeared ready to compromise, but stalled again over Argentina's continued protectionist stance. Brazil threatened to seek a separate FTA if Argentina failed to compromise, and when this book went to press in mid-2014 there were signs that the deal may finally go through. Also in early 2014, Venezuela became a full member of *Mercosur.*

An unexpected crisis in Latin American-European relations exploded in 2013. Edward Snowden, the former U.S. National Security Agency employee wanted on an arrest warrant for leaking sensitive classified information, fled to Hong Kong, then to Moscow, where he was stuck in an airport transit lounge as a stateless person with a revoked U.S. passport and no country to go to. He listed several countries where he was considering seeking asylum, including Bolivia, Cuba, Ecuador, Nicaragua and Venezuela, all anti-U.S.

Coincidentally, Bolivia's Morales was in Moscow to attend a summit of gas-exporting countries. He coyly said he would give Snowden's request "serious consideration" if he made it. When Morales left Moscow, France, Spain, Italy and Portugal, all U.S. NATO allies, refused to allow Morales' plane to use their airspace, forcing it to land in Vienna to refuel, where it remained overnight. While Morales was literally trapped there, the Spanish ambassador asked permission to inspect the plane to see if Snowden was aboard; Morales refused, but insisted Snowden was not on board.

Morales was cleared to leave, and when he returned to Bolivia he denounced what he called Europe's "act of aggression." He summoned an emergency meeting of *UNASUR* presidents in Cochabamba, but only the presidents of Argentina, Ecuador, Suriname, Uruguay and Venezuela joined him. The more pro-U.S. presidents of Chile, Colombia and Peru voiced their solidarity with Morales, but did not attend. Colombia's Juan Manuel Santos said the grounding of the plane of the president of a sovereign country was "unheard of," but he warned, "let's not turn this into a diplomatic crisis for Latin America and the EU."

Argentina's Fernández demanded an apology from Europe for the incident, but when France apologized to the Bolivian government, Morales responded, "Apologies are not enough." The OAS also condemned the grounding on July 8. It turned out Snowden had never left Russia, and remains there under temporary asylum.

Russia and Japan

During the Cold War, the Soviet Union eagerly sought to extend its influence, and enjoyed some degree of success. The Castro regime, which transformed Cuba into a formidable military base, opened the door for further Soviet influence in Latin America. The Peruvian military regime of 1968–80 enjoyed close ties with the Soviet Union, which re-equipped the Peruvian army with T-62 tanks and its air force with MiGs. The Nicaraguan army under the *Sandinistas* also received Soviet weapons, including tanks, helicopter gunships, surface-to-air missiles and other modern armaments. Every year, thousands of Latin American students received grants to study in Moscow, and Marxist publications multiplied on the continent. Latin America, a region once relegated by the Kremlin to a secondary position, became one of its top priorities (as foretold by Lenin before his death).

With the fall of communism, Russia has maintained warm relations with Latin America—the warmest with Cuba and Venezuela. President Dmitry Medvedev visited Peru, Brazil, Venezuela and Cuba in 2008. In 2010, he visited Argentina, while Prime Minister Vladimir Putin visited Venezuela.

Russian-Latin American trade is growing, with Russian weapons, ships and aircraft its most popular commodities. Venezuela has been a major buyer, but in 2013 Brazil concluded a $150 million helicopter deal with Russia, and Russia was seeking to sell Brazil $1 billion worth of missiles.

In recent decades, there has been increased Japanese interest in investment in Latin America. With its huge surplus from a favorable balance of foreign trade for years, the supply of money was ample. Japanese investment in Latin America peaked at $29.6 billion in 2008, but in part because of the global recession they dropped to $17.4 billion in 2009 and only $5.3 billion in 2010.

Japan was the first Asian country to join the Inter-American Development Bank, in 1976, and has invested more that $5.6 billion.

Between 1990 and 2011, Japan accounted for 24.5% of Latin America's total trade with Asia, second to 32.5% with China. Just between 2005 and 2009, Japanese exports to Latin America increased 34%, from $23.3 billion to $31.4 billion, more than to any other region, while imports from Latin America increased 26%, from $14.8 billion to $18.7 billion.

In 2012, Peru became the third Latin American to conclude a FTA with Japan, after Chile and Peru, and Japan was negotiating a fourth with Colombia.

China's Growing Influence

During much of the Cold War, Latin American countries other than Cuba joined

the United States in recognizing the Nationalist Chinese government on Taiwan as the legitimate government of China. Mexico recognized the communist regime in Beijing in 1971, seven years before the United States did. One by one, most other Latin American countries followed suit. However, of the 22 nations that still maintain full diplomatic relations with Taiwan, 12 are developing nations of the Western Hemisphere that have benefited greatly from Taiwan's generosity with foreign aid: Belize, the Dominican Republic, El Salvador, Guatemala, Haiti, Honduras, Nicaragua, Panama, Paraguay, St. Kitts and Nevis, St. Lucia, and St. Vincent and the Grenadines. The fact that the leftist governments of Nicaragua and El Salvador still recognize Taiwan is especially curious.

Over the past decade, however, the economically resilient People's Republic of China has greatly expanded its political and economic influence among the other Latin American nations. Chinese President Hu Jintao made an unprecedented state visit to Chile, Argentina and Brazil in 2004, signing letters of intent to invest tens of billions of dollars in those countries' infrastructures and to greatly expand trade. China, meanwhile, has great demand for Chilean copper and South American agricultural products, especially soybeans. Venezuela's Chávez visited Beijing in 2004; China pledged to invest in Venezuela's oil industry and to double bilateral trade. Chile and China concluded a FTA in 2005

Hu returned to Latin America in 2008 to sign a $70 million investment agreement with Cuba and to sign a FTA with Peru on the eve of the APEC summit (see below). China has extended billions of dollars worth of loans to Argentina, Brazil and Ecuador, among others. China has now launched two satellites for Venezuela, one observation and one telecommunications. Direct Chinese investment in Latin America totaled more than $150 billion in 2011. In March 2013, China announced it was investing $2 billion in the Inter-American Development Bank.

China's trade with Latin America mushroomed from $10 billion in 2000 to $178.6 billion in 2010, almost evenly balanced between imports and exports. Since then it has exploded to $255.5 billion in 2012, with a $6.6 billion surplus in favor of China. Since 2009, China has replaced the United States as the major trading partner of Brazil, Chile and Peru. Hu visited Brazil in 2010 but was forced to cancel stops in Venezuela and Chile because of an earthquake in China. New Brazilian President Rousseff visited China in 2011. The U.N. Economic Commission for Latin America and the Caribbean (ECLAC) predicted that China would surpass the EU as Latin

America's second-largest trading partner and would eclipse the United States in 15 years.

China has also become a major source of loans to Latin America, an estimated $100 billion, mostly for infrastructure development. Half that amount has gone just to Venezuela. Brazil accounts for about $13 billion, Argentina for $12 billion and Ecuador for $10 billion. The loans to Venezuela and Ecuador are largely repaid with oil, those to Argentina and Brazil with soybeans and other agricultural products.

Significantly, the new Chinese President, Xi Jinping, made a state visit to Latin America in May 2013, just six months after assuming leadership, much earlier than Hu's first visit. Xi arrived in Port-of-Spain, Trinidad and Tobago, for talks with 15 Caribbean leaders the same day Vice President Joe Biden concluded talks with those same leaders. Xi then visited Costa Rica and Mexico, the same countries President Obama had just visited weeks before, and only then did he fly to California for his first-ever meeting with Obama. There could have been no more dramatic demonstration of the importance China places on Latin America. By the same token, the new Mexican president, Enrique Peña Nieto, visited China in April 2013, four months after taking office and one month before *his* first meeting with Obama as president.

China's growing influence in Latin America is the focus of the book *The Dragon in the Room* (see Bibliography).

India and Iran

India also has begun to represent a lucrative market for Latin American commodities. Trade between India and Latin America has skyrocketed from $2.1 billion in 2000 to $17.2 billion in 2009, $25 billion in 2011and $30 billion in 2012. The Indian government predicted it could reach $50 billion by 2014. Brazil is now India's major trading partner.

Iran has begun making a concerted effort to gain influence in Latin America, stemming from the friendship between Chávez and Iranian President Mahmoud Ahmadinejad. Brazil also ingratiated itself to Iran in 2010 when President da Silva rejected the United States' call for U.N. sanctions against Iran over its nuclear enrichment program and joined with the Turkish premier in brokering a compromise. Ahmadinejad visited Brazil and Venezuela in 2009, and in January 2012 he visited Venezuela, Cuba, Ecuador and Nicaragua (for the second inaugural of President Ortega). The current governments of all four countries, like Iran's, are ardently anti-U.S.

Iran provides technical assistance to Latin American petroleum companies. Its leading trading partner in the region is Brazil, with bilateral trade totaling $2.6 billion in 2011. Brazilian-Iranian relations have been cooler under da Silva's successor, Dilma Rousseff. Total Iranian-Latin American trade tripled just from 2008 to 2009, to $2.9 billion. By 2012 it was $4 billion.

Iran's growing influence in Latin America had not extended to Argentina, which is still seeking justice for the bombings of the Israeli Embassy in Buenos Aires in 1992 that killed 29 people and the 1994 bombing of the Israeli-Argentine Mutual Association, a Jewish community center in Buenos Aires, that killed 85 and injured more than 300. Both bombings were linked to the Iranian-backed terrorist organization Hezbollah. Iran steadfastly denied complicity for two decades, despite Argentine intelligence to the contrary. Bilateral relations soured even more in 2009 when Ahmadinejad appointed as defense minister a man Argentina contends masterminded the 1994 bombing. President Cristina Fernández sent Ahmadinejad a sharply worded protest. A major breakthrough came in February when the Argentine Congress approved an agreement with Iran to create a five-member commission to investigate the 1994 bombing. Despite bilateral tensions, trade between Iran and Argentina skyrocketed from $84 million in 2008 to $1.2 billion in 2011.

To counter what is seen as hostile Iranian influence in the region, U.S. President Barack Obama signed the Countering Iran in the Western Hemisphere Act in December 2012.

International Organizations

Latin America has two rotating seats on the 15-member U.N. Security Council, but in 2005 Brazil joined with Germany, Japan and India in sponsoring a resolution to expand the council to 25 members and make those four countries permanent members along with the United States, Russia, Britain, France and China. Permanent members have veto power. Their petition still has not been approved, however, in part because of Mexican and Argentine resentment of Brazil's ambition. President Rousseff pushed Brazil's ambitions during her White House meeting with President Obama in April 2012.

Latin America's two rotating seats have sometimes placed Latin America in the forefront of world events, as when Chile and Mexico voted to oppose the U.S. resolution authorizing its invasion of Iraq in 2003. The two-year seats have since become coveted political prizes, leading to intra-regional contention. In 2006, Venezuela's Chávez made a controversial speech before the U.N. General Assembly equating President Bush with the devil, and he announced Venezuela would bid for one of the Security Council seats to advance his anti-U.S. agenda. Guatemala, with U.S. backing, also bid for the seat, but neither country could obtain the two-thirds majority of the General Assembly. After more than 20 ballots, the 32 Latin American and Caribbean ambassadors compromised on Panama.

Latin America's current members are Argentina, through 2014, and Chile, through 2015.

Latin America also has played a leading role in the so-called G-15, a group of developing countries, most of them rich in natural resources or with large industrial bases, which was organized in Belgrade, Yugoslavia in 1989 as a counterpart to the G-7 (later G-8) group of highly industrialized countries. Originally the bloc had 15 members, but expanded to 18; Peru has since withdrawn. Six Latin American or Caribbean countries belong to the G-15: Argentina, Brazil, Chile, Jamaica, Mexico and Venezuela. The other members are Algeria, Egypt, India, Indonesia, Iran, Kenya, Malaysia, Nigeria, Senegal, Sri Lanka and Zimbabwe. Venezuela hosted the 12th G-15 summit in 2004 and Cuba, which is not a member, hosted the 13th in 2006 to coincide with a meeting of the 118-nation Non-Aligned Movement.

Overlapping with the G-15 is the G-21, an organization of developing countries designed to present a unified stance in trade negotiations with the developed countries, particularly over the thorny issue of agricultural subsidies in the developed countries, which developing countries complain is hypocritical and makes their agricultural exports uncompetitive. The organization's 22 countries encompass half the globe's population and most of its farmers. Thirteen of those countries are Latin American: Argentina, Bolivia, Brazil, Chile, Colombia, Costa Rica, Cuba, Ecuador, Guatemala, Mexico, Paraguay, Peru and Venezuela. The others are China, Egypt, India, Indonesia, Nigeria, Pakistan, the Philippines, South Africa and Thailand.

At the G-8 summit of the world's leading economies in France in 2002, the leaders of Latin America's two largest economies—Brazil's da Silva and Mexico's Fox—attended for the first time. At the expanded G-20 summit in London in 2009, the presidents of Brazil, Mexico and Argentina participated, as they did in the 2010 summit in Toronto and the Cannes, France, summit in November 2011, at which Mexico assumed the chairmanship. Mexico's President Calderón hosted the 2012 G-20 summit in Los Cabos, Baja California Sur, June 18–19. The next G-20 summit is scheduled for St. Petersburg, Russia, in September 2013.

Latin America and the World

Mexico, Peru and Chile are among the 21 countries with robust economies around the Pacific Rim that comprise the so-called Asia-Pacific Economic Cooperation (APEC) group. Other members include the United States, Canada, Japan, China, South Korea, Thailand, Malaysia and Australia. Chile hosted the annual summit in 2004, where the United States proposed a free-trade zone that would dwarf the European Union or the ill-fated FTAA. Such a bloc is far in the future, however. Peru hosted the 2008 summit, where the members condemned trade protectionism. In 2010, Colombia applied for APEC membership, which has not yet been approved. Panama and Costa Rica also have expressed interest.

In 1994, Mexico became the first Latin American country admitted to the Organization of Economic Cooperation and Development (OECD), composed of the world's major economies. Chile was admitted in 2010.

The Ibero-American Summits

Beginning with the first meeting in Guadalajara, Mexico, in 1991, the heads of government and key ministers of Spain, Portugal and the 19 Latin American countries they once colonized have convened every October or November for the Ibero-American Summit. Tiny Andorra is also a member. Unlike the OAS and the Summits of the Americas, the United States is not included but Cuba is. Equatorial Guinea, the Philippines and Puerto Rico are associate members. The agendas initially included such topics as trade and human rights. Although these summits have accomplished little of substance, such as persuading Cuba to clean up its human rights act, they have provided a forum for a healthful exchange of ideas of mutual importance to the Latin American leaders and their Iberian counterparts, such as health, education and the environment. They also have helped give Latin America a toehold in European trade, as Spain and Portugal are both members of the European Union.

With the election of more and more left-wing leaders in Spain and Latin America, the summits have been less critical of Cuba's human rights record and more critical of the United States. At the 15th summit in Salamanca, Spain, in 2005, a resolution called on the United States to ease its economic embargo against Cuba. That summit also approved the establishment of the group's first permanent general secretariat.

U.N. Secretary-General Kofi Annan attended that summit for the first time, as well as the 16th summit in Montevideo, Uruguay, in 2006. That summit dealt largely with migration issues, and the leaders condemned U.S. plans to build a security fence along the Mexican border. Attendance at that summit was unusually poor; six presidents were absent, which upset the summit's host, Uruguay's Tabaré Vázquez.

The Ibero-American summits usually attract little attention outside the member countries, but the 2007 summit in Santiago, Chile, splashed into world headlines when Venezuela's Chávez used his allotted time for a diatribe against former conservative Spanish President José María Aznar, calling him a "fascist" and accusing him of complicity in the 2002 coup attempt against him. His tirade proved too much even for Spanish President José Luis Rodríguez Zapatero, Aznar's political archrival, who used his allotted time to rebut Chávez's attack on a duly elected Spanish chief of government and to admonish Chávez for his undiplomatic language. Chávez, not known for his tolerance of criticism at home, repeatedly tried to interrupt Zapatero, a violation of the summit's parliamentary procedure. Finally, Spain's King Juan Carlos leaned forward and told Chávez, *Por qué no te callas?* (Why don't you shut up?). Chávez briefly threatened to sever diplomatic relations with Spain, which up until then had been friendly to him under Zapatero; meanwhile, the king became an overnight hero in Spain. (Chávez later reconciled with the king on a visit to Spain.)

The 19th summit in Estoril, Portugal, in 2009, was supposed to deal primarily with technological innovation and advancement, but degenerated into a squabble over the presidential election held in Honduras the day before. The representatives unanimously passed a resolution condemning the ouster of Honduran President Manuel Zelaya that June, but they were divided over whether to recognize his duly elected successor, Porfirio Lobo Sosa. Honduras' interim president did not attend the summit.

Argentine President Cristina Fernández did not invite Honduran President Lobo to the 20th summit in Mar del Plata in 2010, still calling his election illegitimate. A resolution was approved stating that by unanimous vote, a country could be expelled from the organization if it does not have a democratic government—without explaining how Cuba could remain a member. The theme of the summit was education, and the delegates approved a 57-point declaration that called for investing $100 billion to eradicate illiteracy in the region by 2015. Costa Rica denounced Nicaragua's incursion into its territory (see Costa Rica and Nicaragua), while the delegates endorsed Fernández's call for a new dialogue with Britain over the sovereignty of the Falklands (Malvinas) Islands.

The 21st summit in Asunción, Paraguay, in October 2011 was even more poorly attended than the one in 2006, with only 12 of the 22 chiefs of state attending. Even Rousseff and Fernández of neighboring Brazil and Argentina stayed away, lamely claiming they had to prepare for the G-20 summit in Cannes, France, a few days later.

The diminishing interest raised speculation whether the 22nd summit in Cádiz, Spain, in 2012 might be the last. It, too, was poorly attended, with even many of the usual left-wing grandstanders absent: Castro's Raúl Castro, Nicaragua's Daniel Ortega and Venezuela's Chávez, who was debilitated by cancer and died four months later. As a replay of the 2009 Honduran controversy, Paraguay's participation was blocked because of the lightning impeachment of President Fernando Lugo, deemed undemocratic by several presidents who threatened to stay away if interim President Federico Franco were allowed to attend. But an even more important development of the summit was the dramatic role reversal of Spain and Portugal, whose economies were in a tailspin while those of most Latin American countries were enjoying healthy expansion. Reminding their former colonies of the aid and investment they had bestowed on them in the past, Spain and Portugal now humbly pleaded with Latin America to reciprocate. Another new twist at this summit was the participation of José Ángel Gurría, a Mexican economist and secretary-general of the OECD, composed of the world's 34 major economies. Spain, Portugal, Mexico and Chile are members.

The 23rd summit in Panama, October 18–19, 2013, was no better attended, and the organization seemed at a lost to redefine itself. The absence for the first time of Spain's King Juan Carlos was especially ominous. There wasn't even a final declaration. By contrast, the *CELAC* summit in Havana three months later had only three of its 33 countries not represented.

EU-Latin American-Caribbean Summits

As an outgrowth of the Ibero-American summits, the first summit of leaders of the European Union, Latin America and the Caribbean was held in Rio de Janeiro, Brazil, in 1999. Spain hosted another two-day summit in Madrid in 2002, which was attended by about 50 heads of government and their foreign and economy ministers. Trade and terrorism dominated the agenda. The EU and Chile ended their "association" agreement, the first step to beginning a FTA signed later that year; Mexico already had such an agreement, and its trade with Europe had grown from $19 billion to more than $48 billion. The EU pledged to initiate separate free-trade talks with the Andean, Caribbean and Central American trade blocs. *Mercosur* then entered into an "association" agreement with the EU like Chile had. The EU also acceded to a request from the Colombian president to add the Revolutionary Armed Forces of Colombia (*FARC*) to its list of terrorist organizations.

The Third EU-Latin American-Caribbean summit, held in Guadalajara, Mexico, in 2004, proved more political and more contentious. The major agreement was a resolution calling for a strengthening of the United Nations, which the delegates said should be the sole entity to resolve international conflicts. It was seen as an oblique criticism of U.S. intervention in Iraq. Less obliquely, the delegates condemned the abuse of Iraqi prisoners by U.S. forces. Cuba attacked the EU for allegedly blocking a resolution against the U.S. economic embargo and was the only nation of the 58 represented to withhold approval of the summit's final declaration. The Cuban government called the EU "a flock of sheep" that follows the U.S. lead. EU President Romano Prodi chided Cuba for its confrontational attitude.

Also at the summit, representatives of the EU and *Mercosur* fine-tuned some of the points for a FTA, which would have represented $40 billion in trade. The EU and *Mercosur* had concluded a FTA earlier that year, but it soon became unraveled as the two blocs quibbled over a wide array of issues. *Mercosur* wanted greater access to Europe for its agricultural products, while the EU wanted greater access for its industrial goods. The deal went nowhere.

The Fourth EU-Latin America-Caribbean Summit in Vienna in 2006 opened under a cloud because the new Bolivian President, Evo Morales, had just nationalized the natural gas operations of several foreign companies, including British, French, Spanish, U.S. and Brazilian. The developed countries warned Morales and Venezuela's Chávez that such nationalizations discourage investment and in the end harm the developing countries. The other agenda items for the 58 leaders were trade and energy. By 2005, trade among the 58 countries had increased 13%, to $152 billion.

The Fifth Summit was held in Lima, Peru, in 2008, attended by representatives of 60 countries, including 37 heads of state. The two primary agenda items were poverty and the environment and climate change, but the leaders' attention also turned to the stalled FTAs between the EU and *Mercosur* and Andean Pact blocs. The EU opted instead for bilateral trade deals with individual countries. In the final declaration, the leaders expressed concern for skyrocketing world food prices, with particular attention to Haiti, which had just experienced food riots.

The Sixth Summit, held in Madrid in May 2010, appeared doomed before it started when 12 South American countries announced they would boycott it over the invitation to Honduran President Lobo, whom they deemed as illegitimate even though elected by a landslide in a fair election. The 12 leaders continued to demand the reinstatement of Zelaya. In the end, Lobo declined to attend, but Venezuela's Chávez and Cuba's Raúl Castro still stayed away. The summit went ahead with leaders or representatives of 60 nations. The global recession and the devastating earthquake in Haiti were major topics, as were technology, innovation, trade and immigration. Among the positive results of the summit was the creating of the EU-LAC Foundation, designed to promote bi-regional understanding and development, and the creation of a fund, initially with $150 million, for infrastructure projects in Latin America.

Also noteworthy were the holding of numerous "mini-summits," in which trade between individual nations or blocs was discussed. As a result, the EU entered into a trade association agreement with Central America and agreed to resume the long-delayed FTA talks with *Mercosur*. The EU also signed a trilateral trade agreement with Colombia and Peru. The EU-*Mercosur* talks were expected to conclude in July 2011, but they dragged on into 2012, at which time Spain asked the EU to exclude Argentina from any deal because of Argentina's decision to renationalize its oil company *YPF*, targeting the 51% owned by the Spanish oil company Repsol (see Argentina). Argentina's *Mercosur* partners, which now include Venezuela, were threatening in 2014 to conclude separate FTAs with the EU.

The Seventh Summit in Santiago, Chile, was postponed from 2012 until January 26–27, 2013, to avoid scheduling conflicts with other international summits, including the G-20. Four members of the EU-LAC Foundation had attended the Ibero-American Summit in Spain as observers for the first time. Sixty nations were represented, and they reached a consensus on providing legal guarantees for investors and on reducing trade barriers. But the long-stalled EU-*Mercosur* FTA still failed to materialize. The EU, however, did express interest in a FTA with Central America. The summit segued into a regular meeting of *CELAC*, which proved to be little more than a photo op of handshakes between leaders, like German Chancellor Angela Merkel and Cuba's Raúl Castro.

South American-Arab Summits

Even as the trade deal between *Mercosur* and the EU stalled, a new window of opportunity opened with the First South American-Arab Countries Summit (*ASPA* in Spanish and Portuguese) in Brasilia, Brazil, in 2005. Heretofore, trade between Latin America and the Middle East had been meager, despite the blood ties that date back to the Moorish occupation of the Iberian Peninsula before 1492 and, more recently, to 19th and 20th century Arab emigration to Latin America (see Latin America Today). An estimated 20 million Latin Americans are of Arab descent, and they have achieved economic success and influence disproportionate to their numbers. Arab-American presidents have been elected in Argentina, Ecuador and El Salvador.

The first summit, organized and hosted by Brazil's da Silva, brought together representatives of 12 South American and 22 Arab countries of the Middle East and North Africa. Many of those were heads of state, including new presidents Mahmoud Abbas of the Palestinian Authority and Jalal Talabani of Iraq (in reality a Kurd, not an Arab).

A tangible result of the summit was an agreement between *Mercosur* and the six nation Gulf Cooperation Council (Bahrain, Kuwait, Oman, Qatar, Saudi Arabia and the United Arab Emirates) to initiate negotiations for a FTA. But the summit had more far-reaching results as a forum for the disdain both regions harbor toward U.S. economic and military hegemony. Da Silva, in fact, rejected a U.S. request for observer status at the summit. The Declaration of Brasilia did denounce terrorism and expressed support for Iraq's battle against insurgents, but it also endorsed resistance to "foreign occupation." The declaration called for a sovereign Palestinian state and called on Israel to withdraw to its pre-1967 borders and to dismantle its settlements in Palestinian territory, including East Jerusalem. The declaration embraced the concept of free trade, but said it should be geared toward the benefit of the world's poor and should not widen the gap between developed and developing nations.

Trade between the two regions almost tripled, from $8 billion to $21 billion, by the time the Second *ASPA* Summit was held in Doha, Qatar, in 2009, on the heels of an Arab League meeting there and on the eve of the G-20 Summit in London. Three of the summit participants—Argentina, Brazil and Saudi Arabia—also attended the G-20. Once again, 22 Arab and 12 South American countries attended, including 16 Arab and eight South American heads of state. And once again, the summit declara-

Latin America and the World

tion called for creation of an independent Palestinian state, while condemning Israel for its invasion of Gaza. Venezuela and Bolivia had severed diplomatic relations with Israel over the invasion.

The international financial crisis also was a major agenda item, and Venezuela's Chávez suggested replacing the U.S. dollar as an international currency with an oil-based "petro-currency." The final communiqué called for the "necessity of establishing an international financial system that prevents financial speculation and takes into account adequate regulations." The participants sidestepped the thorny issue of Sudan's alleged genocide in Darfur, although Argentine President Fernández avoided being photographed with Sudanese President Omar al-Bashir, subject

of an international arrest warrant. The two regions agreed to continue their cooperation in international forums.

The Third *ASPA* Summit was supposed to be held in Lima, Peru, in April 2011, after only two years instead of four, but it was postponed because of the ongoing Arab Spring uprisings in Tunisia, Egypt, Libya, Syria, Yemen and Bahrain. It was finally held in October 2012, with the participation of representatives of 21 Arab and 11 South American countries. Among the heads of state attending were Jordan's King Abdullah, the Palestinian Authority's Mahmoud Abbas, and the presidents of Tunisia, Lebanon, Argentina, Chile, Colombia, Ecuador and, of course, Peru's host, Ollanta Humala. The Arab members blocked Syria's participation be-

cause of President Basdhar Asad's atrocities against his own people, while the Latin Americans blackballed Paraguay for the allegedly undemocratic impeachment of President Fernando Lugo. Besides the usual platitudes praising bilateral cooperation, the 70-point Lima Declaration reaffirmed the call for a sovereign Palestinian state and called for nuclear weapons-free zones "everywhere," perhaps a reflection of Arab concerns about Iran.

The potential for trade agreements between Latin America, on the one hand, and the EU, the Middle East, China or India, on the other, remains enormous. It signals a lessening of Latin America's traditional dependence on the United States. Meanwhile, Latin America is playing increasingly important roles on the global stage.

The Republic of Argentina

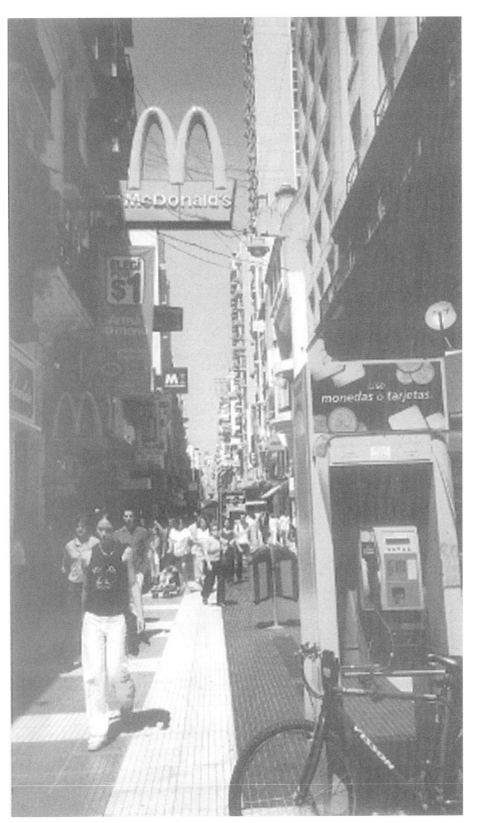

Downtown Buenos Aires

Capital City: Buenos Aires (Pop. 15.2 million in Buenos Aires Province, 2010.)

Climate: The northern *Chaco* region is wet and hot; the central plains, or *Pampas*, are temperate with moderate rainfall; southern Patagonia is arid, becoming wet and cold in the southernmost part

Neighboring Countries: Uruguay and Brazil (East); Paraguay and Bolivia (North); Chile (West)

Official Language: Spanish

Other Principal Tongues: English, German, Italian

Ethnic Background: European (predominantly Spanish and Italian) 98%; *Mestizo* (mixed Spanish and Indian ancestry) 2%

Principal Religion: Roman Catholicism

Chief Commercial Products: Meat, grain, oilseed, hides, wool

Currency: Peso

Gross Domestic Product: U.S. $484.6 billion in 2013, est., ($11,263 per capita)

Former Colonial Status: Spanish Crown Colony (1580–1816)

Independence Date: July 9, 1816

Chief of State: Cristina Elisabet Fernández Wilhelm viuda de Kirchner (b. February 19, 1953), president (since December 10, 2007)

National Flag: Sky blue, white and sky blue equal horizontal stripes with "the sun of May" centered in the white stripe.

Argentina varies widely in terrain and climate. Four main regions are generally recognized. The northern region (*Chaco*) is heavily forested, low, wet and hot; the central plains (*Pampas*) are flat, fertile and temperate, well watered along the coast and increasingly dry to the west; the southern region (*Patagonia*) is an arid, windswept plateau, cut through by grassy valleys; the fourth region (Andes) runs the length of the Argentine-Chilean frontier—the mountains are low and glaciated in the south, high and dry in the central part and gradually widen into the high plateau of Bolivia in the north.

Argentina's most important river is the Paraná, with tributaries that flow into the Río de la Plata estuary north of Buenos Aires. Three-quarters of Argentina's land is too dry for cultivation without irrigation. The capital city and adjoining *Pampas* have 98% of the population. Temperatures vary from the hot, humid *Chaco* to the cold and damp Patagonia in the south.

HISTORY: The Río de la Plata estuary was first visited in 1516 by Spanish explorers who were driven off by hostile Indians. Magellan visited the region in 1520 and Spain made unsuccessful efforts to establish colonies on the Paraná River in 1527 and 1536. The Spanish moved up river to the Paraná's junction with the Paraguay River, where they founded Asunción, the

Area: 1,072,745 square miles (2,771,300 sq. km.) Argentina claims 1,084,120 square miles, including the Falkland Islands, in dispute with Great Britain, and other territories claimed by Chile. Its claims in Argentina total 373,774 square miles (965,597 sq. km.)

Population: 43,024,374 (2014 est.)

Argentina

center of Spanish operations in southeastern South America for the succeeding 50 years. In 1573, an expedition from Asunción established a settlement in the vicinity of modern Buenos Aires and subsequently Spain transferred its base of colonial government from Asunción to the new town.

Argentina was settled by two main streams of colonists: one crossed the Andes from Peru and occupied the fertile oases along the areas on the eastern slopes of the Andes, founding Córdoba and Tucumán; the other arrived directly from Europe and settled in and around the port of Buenos Aires. Thus, from the start, two distinct groups of Argentine people developed. The people of the interior, a mixture of Spanish and Indian heritage, were dependent on the grazing of cattle on the plains of the central *Pampas* and upon small home manufactures. These isolated people developed a rude, self-sufficient civilization fiercely resistant to encroachment and disdainful of the ruling authority established in Buenos Aires by urban intellectuals.

The people of Buenos Aires, a mixture of Europeans (Spanish, French, English, Italian and German) who came to the port for trade, to defend the region or to govern it, had little interest in the Latin Americans and re-created in Buenos Aires the standards of living of the European cities from which they originated. The nobility, which governed the defending military, and the

clergy, retained special privileges; they could neither be tried in the local courts nor be held accountable to the people for their actions.

Under the Spanish colonial system, Latin America was held by a few people who administered their grants as feudal holdings. Far removed from the restraints of the Spanish court, the Argentine people evolved into a somewhat wild and free civilization that allowed the development of community and regional pride. In 1806

and 1807, British expeditions attacked and temporarily occupied Buenos Aires; in both cases, almost without Spanish aid, the Creoles rallied and defeated the British. The following year, Napoleon's invasion of Spain turned the British into allies, but the exhilaration of those victories did much to imbue self-confidence among the Creoles.

On May 25, 1810, the *cabildo* of Buenos Aires declared it would govern the viceroyalty of La Plata in the name of the deposed King Fernando VII; rebel envoys

and armies were sent to the provinces to forge national unity, but, as in the rest of Hispanic America, attempts to hold the former viceroyalty's territories under Buenos Aires' control were far from successful. A provincial assembly eventually declared independence on July 9, 1816. Paraguay proclaimed its own independence and Uruguay, under the guidance of its popular hero José Manuel Artígas, insisted on autonomy, ushering in a long period of Brazilian-Argentine conflict over the region, which culminated in a

City Hall in Buenos Aires, 1846

precarious Uruguayan independence in the 1840s. Even in the interior of what is today Argentina, the provinces constantly rebelled against Buenos Aires. The first 50 years of Argentine history is the history of the struggle between Buenos Aires and the provinces, and of political turmoil in the capital, where different types of government were tried in a desperate search for stability.

Argentina's greatest hero, General José de San Martín, refused to be dragged into such internecine disputes and concentrated on organizing an army to invade and liberate Chile. Like Bolívar in the north, San Martín was convinced that independence could not be assured until no Spanish stronghold remained in South America. Subsequently he crossed the Andes with his army, battling the Spanish into submission in Chile. He then turned to Peru, where he linked up with the liberator of northern South America, Simón Bolívar. Disappointed by Bolívar's refusal to take command of the two armies, San Martín, feeling that his presence as a military man might adversely affect the Peruvian revolution, retired and left for France, where he remained for the rest of his life.

Argentina started its independent history with great territorial losses and a division between its social groups—those of the port and the interior, the metropolis and the countryside. The elimination of Spanish control created a series of conflicts among the regional contenders for power. There was immediate strife between the ranchers controlling large estates on the coast and the merchants in Buenos Aires, who insisted that all trade pass through

the port, with duties and taxes used for the capital city rather than for the country. The interior provinces in turn demanded a federal form of government, with autonomous sovereign states and a national capital outside Buenos Aires.

To foster economic development, the leaders of Buenos Aires wanted to promote agriculture and expand European immigration to farm the land as was being done in the United States. The coastal ranchers, knowing that small farms would destroy their great *estancias*, made common cause with the interior to overthrow the Buenos Aires leaders and installed their own leader in 1835, Juan Manuel de Rosas. In the name of federalism, he brutally imposed "national unity" and stubbornly opposed French and British intervention in Río de la Plata, preserving Argentina for future generations. Unfortunately, his enemies belonged to one of the most brilliant generations in Argentine history, one that produced quantities of great literature. These eminent writers included Domingo Faustino Sarmiento and Bartolomé Mitre, both destined to become presidents of the republic (see Culture). A combination of Brazilian forces and Argentine caudillos finally overthrew Rosas' government in 1852.

The constitution of 1853 provided for a federal system and moved the seat of government to Paraná, 150 miles north of Buenos Aires. The former capital seceded from the union, was defeated, renewed the war and was again defeated by national forces. In 1861, the provinces accepted Buenos Aires' supremacy and the first constitutional president, Mitre, assumed office. During

the years of the non-urban leadership, the fertile *Pampas* lands were seized and distributed to large estate holders, a policy that continued for several years; the governments used the army "to open" the interior of Argentina, which meant eliminating the Indians. Argentina became a cattle-raising country, while importing all manufactured goods and even food from Europe.

In the late 19th century, the demand for chilled beef led to changes in the meat industry, requiring better cattle and grains for both cattle-feeding and human consumption. Despite the changes in production, Argentine economic and political power remained in the hands of a small group of planters, ranchers and the merchants in Buenos Aires.

Contemptuous of the cattle-herding *gauchos*, the *porteños*, as residents of Buenos Aires are called, opened Argentina to European immigrants. From 1852 to 1895, hundreds of thousands of Italians, Spanish, Germans and British poured in. In 1852, of a total population of 1.2 million, non-Argentines were less than 5%, but by 1895, of almost 4 million inhabitants, more than 1 million were foreigners.

By the beginning of the 20th century, the demands for political equality by this mass of immigrants transformed the political scene. The Radical Party had become the most popular among the immigrants and emerged into the first really populist party of Argentina. Organized by an enigmatic leader, Hipólito Irigoyen, the Radical Party has maintained its influence, in one form or another, up to the present day.

Industrialization came late to Argentina and was largely due to British investment during the last half of the 19th century. Concentrated in Buenos Aires and in the

General José de San Martín

Argentina

General Bartolomé Mitre

hands of a few large investors, industry centered on the supply of local needs and the transportation and processing of Argentina's export commodities. Although industrialization changed the ratio of national earnings from agriculture and cattle raising to include industrial products, it provided little increase in total earnings.

The formation of labor unions, largely through the efforts of immigrants, posed the first threat to the historic domination of the country by landed interests and industrialists, both Argentine and foreign. The unions also included displaced agricultural laborers and were initially disorganized and effectively excluded from participation in political or economic power until the first decades of the 20th century.

Hipólito Yrigoyen

The ruling elite chose compromise. In 1912, electoral laws were liberalized, providing for a secret ballot and minority party representation. The first elections held under this system in 1916 resulted in a Radical Party victory under Irigoyen and the defeat of the large landowners' and industrialists' Conservative Party. The Radical Party governed from 1916–30. Its programs included expansion of the democratic system and social reforms to benefit workers, but these fell short of expectations.

Political and social unrest soon appeared. In 1918 there was a student rebellion at the University of Córdoba; a year later, widespread strikes provoked bloody confrontations with the police. Social unrest soon caused the downfall of the Radical Party. A restless army, weary of turmoil and fascinated by Italian dictator Benito Mussolini and his totalitarian efficiency, found its opportunity in 1930 when the international depression gripped the country. An elderly Irigoyen was deposed and the armed forces seized the government "to save the nation from chaos." These "saviors" remained in or behind power for more than five decades and remain a force to be reckoned with to this day.

The Conservative Party was restored to power. For the next 13 years, a combination of landowners, bankers, merchants and generals controlled the government. But in 1943, a group of pseudo-fascist army officers, who feared the government's progressive inclinations toward the Allied powers, used "official corruption" as a pretext to seize power. Lacking a program, and with limited leadership abilities, the government failed to cope with internal problems and mismanaged foreign relations.

The Perón Eras

From the rubble of political confusion there emerged a new leader, Colonel Juan Domingo Perón, a classic charismatic *caudillo* who, wittingly or unwittingly, united forces that had resisted conservative efforts to reestablish political dominance. He brilliantly saw that no government could exist without the support of the middle class, which had grown substantially, and, more important, the laboring class.

Named labor minister under the conservative military government, Perón devoted his efforts toward seizing control of the labor unions from the Radical and Conservative parties. Tremendous assistance came from popular radio personality María Eva Duarte. The military-conservative element sensed too late that he had acquired an immense power base. When an attempt was made to remove Perón in 1945, masses rallied to his support and forced the gov-

ernment to desist. In the elections of 1946, Perón became president with a substantial majority.

Perón married the glamorous and even more charismatic Duarte, popularly called "Evita," and they used their abilities well, gaining firm control of labor and creating a popular mass organization called the *descamisados* ("shirtless ones"). Despite the fact that Perón threatened conservative interests, he was able to gain and hold vital army support through pay raises and military expenditures. He also received support of the clergy through advocacy of programs for religious education and by adopting a moderate position on church-state relations.

Perón and Evita built their strength through propaganda and blatant patronage, but some of their accomplishments were significant. The working class was brought into the political arena and made aware of its massive power. Evita's charitable social works provided health and welfare benefits to the poor (all, of course, widely publicized). The increased wages paid to labor and the practice of "featherbedding" in the government of Buenos Aires was deceiving, as rising prices canceled increased earnings. Mass housing, schools and hospitals and a flood of labor laws favorable to the workers dominated Perón's programs.

There was a dark side to this seeming largesse. The regime used various forms of intimidation against real or perceived opponents. Businessmen who failed to toe the line found themselves threatened with tax audits or health and safety inspections. Outspoken opponents were jailed on one pretext or another or forced into exile. The influential and nettlesome opposition newspaper *La Prensa* was expropriated in 1951. Good squads regularly resorted to physical violence to stifle opposition. Argentina was, in effect, an elected dictatorship. Just as Perón's idol, Mussolini, had proclaimed himself *Il Duce,* Perón became *El Líder* (The Leader).

Costly and often inefficient industries were created to provide jobs for the thousands streaming into the cities. Agriculture, the backbone of the economy, was taxed heavily to pay for ill-planned industrialization. The natural result was a drop in farm output, which in turn caused a drop in exports and foreign trade. Trade deficits have been perennial in Argentina.

Perón's handling of foreign relations was astute and restored Argentina's international prestige. However, his efforts to establish Argentine political leadership in Latin America were resented and resisted by most of the other nations of the continent.

The death of Evita in 1952 from cancer marked the beginning of the decline of

President and Mrs. Perón

Perón's power. Within a short time, the bankrupt state of the economy became apparent and thereafter the moral bankruptcy was difficult to hide. Popular unrest and increasing economic problems gave the armed forces, which had resisted Perón's attempts to control them, an opportunity to intervene. In September 1955, a military insurrection ended his rule, and Perón went into exile in Spain. *La Prensa* was reported to its rightful owners.

The army installed an honest but timid provisional president, who proved unable to cope with the overwhelming problems inherited from Perón. After two months, he was replaced by another general who was able to restore civil order and hold elections in 1958.

Arturo Frondizi, a civilian elected in 1958, was capable, but also a stern disciplinarian who sought to repair the damage created by Perón. He lasted until 1962, when he was overthrown by the military and replaced by Dr. Arturo Illia, who lasted until 1966 when he, too, was deposed by another military coup.

Lieutenant General Carlos Ongania was installed as the next president. He was nicknamed *"El Caño"* (The Pipe), because he was said to be straight on the outside but hollow within. His solution for Argentina's problems was to ban political parties, dismiss the Congress and neutralize the courts. It was not long before he envisioned another regime modeled after that of Mussolini with himself (of course) as permanent head. By 1969, however, his dream turned into a nightmare, replete with riots, strikes and general unrest, and he was overthrown.

Three years of near-anarchy and frequent changes in military government leadership ensued. The generals ordered elections for March 1973, and most political parties were legalized, including Perón's *Justicialista* movement. Long-standing criminal charges against Perón were dropped to permit his return from Spain. He had maintained control of his movement by balancing one rival faction against another and issuing vague political statements.

When the military refused to permit Perón to run for the presidency, he instructed his party to nominate Héctor J. Cámpora, a colorless party worker. Campaigning on the slogan "Cámpora to the presidency, Perón to power," the *Justicialistas* gained 49.5% of the vote, plus large majorities in congressional and provincial races.

Inaugurated in May 1973, Cámpora pledged to revitalize the economy, increase benefits for labor and seek closer ties with "neutralist" countries. However, Cámpora's efforts to cooperate with the restive leftists within the party quickly alienated its conservative members. Street fighting between rival factions became common; when one bloody shootout left 25 dead and hundreds wounded at an airport reception for Perón, Cámpora and his entire Cabinet were forced to resign after only 49 days in power. New elections were set for September. With anti-Perón military leaders having been forced into retirement, Perón, then 77, was free to run for president.

Ironically, many of those who supported *El Líder* included such former enemies as the military, the large landowners and business leaders—all of whom welcomed his increased conservatism. Perón's main support, however, came from his traditional base of power: organized labor. As his running mate, Perón chose his wife, Isabel, a 42-year-old former cabaret dancer. Certain of victory, he ran a leisurely campaign based on vague promises of national unity. He received 61.9% of the vote, while the candidate of the opposition Radical Civic Union received 24.3%. A third center-right coalition candidate won less than 15%.

The problems facing Perón were immense. The economy was plagued with low growth and high inflation; leftist terrorism was rampant and his own political movement was badly divided. Perón concocted an unrealistic mixture of a leftist foreign policy and a conservative domestic program. He sought closer economic and political ties with Marxist and Third World countries. Huge credits ($1.2 billion) were offered to Cuba; at the same time, greater restrictions were placed on foreign private investments in Argentina.

Perón's domestic policies, however, were staunchly conservative. He openly courted right-wing union and political leaders. At his direction, left-wing government and school officials were dismissed and leftist publications closed. He publicly berated leftist *Peronista* youths as "mercenaries at the service of foreign forces." These conservative policies merely widened the rift within his movement. Having played an important role in bringing Perón back to power through their struggles with the military government, the leftists now refused to be pushed out. Left-wing guerrillas continued their attacks against conservative union leaders, right-wing government officials and foreign businessmen. Conservatives responded with counter-terror. The basic functions of the government ground to a halt as the rift between the right and the left, as well as between *Peronistas* and anti-*Peronistas*, fragmented the nation.

Perón's hapless plight was perhaps best seen in his 1974 May Day speech: while he was calling for "peace and conciliation" among his followers, rival *Peronista* factions broke into bloody street fighting even before his speech ended. The continued jockeying for position became even more intense as Perón's health began to fail; in hindsight, he was senile when he returned from Spanish exile. Each faction

Argentina

hoped to be able to seize control of the party should *El Líder* die in office.

The aging Perón tired easily and had difficulty concentrating for more than brief periods. In November, he suffered a mild heart attack from which he never recovered; death came from heart failure on July 1, 1974.

With Perón's passing, most national leaders quickly pledged their *oral* support for constitutional government and the new president, María Estela Martínez de Perón, widely known simply as "Isabel" or "Isabelita." However, a crucial difference existed between the loyalty the people showed toward *El Presidente Perón* on the one hand and *La Presidente Perón* on the other. She lacked his personal magnetism and the immense power base he had held, and she was totally unimaginative. Moreover, Argentines could not help but draw unfavorable references between her and the much more popular and charismatic Evita. Actually, Perón reportedly had selected her as his running mate only to allow him additional time to choose a more likely successor.

Occupying the highest office ever held by a woman in the Western Hemisphere, Isabel held conservative views that were bitterly opposed by leftists, while old-line *Peronistas* resented her because she was not Evita. More ominous, the old guard regarded her background as a nightclub dancer with a sixth-grade education as woefully inadequate—which it was. The upper classes dismissed her as a commoner, as they had Evita. Feeling herself

La Presidente **Isabela Perón**

thus isolated from traditional sources of power, Isabel began to rely heavily on the advice and counsel of José López Rega, minister of social welfare, a close confidant of the late president and somewhat mysterious practitioner of the occult. He, too, favored staunch conservative measures which, needless to say, were opposed by moderates and bitterly resisted by leftists.

Frail and reclusive, Isabel delegated broad power to López Rega and other key officials in the hope of pulling the nation out of an economic nosedive caused by runaway inflation, growing shortages of industrial and consumer goods, a thriving black market, huge budget and foreign trade deficits, declining domestic and foreign investments and a disastrous drop in farm output. Isabel worsened the fiscal plight by permitting large wage increases in violation of an earlier wage-price freeze. Although the move was popular with the large labor movement, it triggered widespread business losses which, in turn, led to a further escalation of inflation, which by 1975 was at an annual rate of 330%.

Meanwhile, the policy of overtaxing farmers to subsidize the immense urban population had caused a major decline in farm exports, which traditionally furnished the bulk of Argentina's foreign exchange earnings. As a result, the nation faced a trade deficit of $600 million in 1975. Worse, some $2 billion in foreign debts were due the same year; although foreign reserves stood at $1 billion when the *Peronistas* took office in 1973, they plummeted to an all-time low of only $2 million by early 1976. To finance the government, the money supply was expanded by 200%.

In spite of further attempts at austerity (which failed), the economic picture worsened until there was virtual paralysis. Political conditions also declined—violence became the worst in the nation's history. Assassinations by left-wing and right-wing terrorists claimed 1,100 lives during 1975. One leftist group, the *Montanaros*, collected huge fees by kidnapping business leaders. One kidnapping netted the guerrillas $60 million.

During the 21 months she was in office, Isabel reorganized the Cabinet 10 times. The conservative labor movement—long a pillar of support for Perón—continued to increase the distance between itself and Isabel. The loss of this vital support paved the way for the collapse of the Perón presidency. Increasingly erratic, *La Presidente* took a leave of absence from her job in late 1975.

Compounding the economic and political malaise was a growing public resentment against increasing reports of widespread political corruption. Among those implicated was Isabel, who was accused of transferring half a million dollars from

Lt. Gen. Jorge Rafael Videla

a public charity to her own bank account. The *Peronista*-controlled Congress voted along strict party lines to block an inquiry. At the same time, López Rega's Rasputin-like influence over the president was the subject of widespread gossip.

Government corruption, rising terrorism, a reeling economy and disintegrating government control of national affairs prompted a long expected military coup on March 24, 1976—the sixth within the prior 21 years. Isabel was whisked away from the roof of the presidential palace by helicopter—under military arrest. Army Lieutenant General Jorge Rafael Videla, 50, was named president and head of the three-man junta.

The "Dirty War"

To combat Argentina's mounting problems, the generals vowed to fight for three key goals: an end to political terrorism, a drastic cut in the inflation rate and economic development.

To control inflation, wages were frozen, taxes were increased and prices were allowed to rise to their natural levels. Also, the peso was devalued by 70%, government spending was reduced and farm prices were raised to stimulate agricultural growth. These measures helped cut inflation from 35% *a month* to about 10% by early 1978. Political corruption was a special target, and the *junta* moved swiftly to prosecute those who profited illegally under the *Peronista* government; Isabel Perón was so charged and remained under house arrest.

The junta was able to boast of some dramatic improvements in the economy. Foreign reserves jumped from $20 million in 1976 to $10 *billion* by mid-1980. Farm output also grew, paced by a 52% rise in wheat production during the 1978–79 season over the previous harvest. Oil and natural gas exploration was increased as the government sought to attain self-sufficiency in energy. Nonetheless, the liberalization of monetary policy helped to undermine confidence in the peso.

The cost in human lives was even greater. Hoping to improve domestic stability—and thereby stimulate economic investments—the government unleashed a terror campaign against the leftists. Between 1976 and 1981, some 6,000 to 15,000 persons simply "disappeared" after having been arrested by security forces. To protest these human rights abuses, the Carter administration suspended military aid to Argentina.

For their part, however, the leftists didn't have the words "human rights" in their vocabulary. Summary executions of military personnel using clandestine, terrorist and guerrilla tactics were ordinary occurrences at the time. Terrorist bombings claimed many innocent lives.

Retaliation by the military was equally grisly. It was revealed in 1995 that a naval mechanics school converted into a prison was the destination for many of those arrested by the military. A prison guard wielding a hypodermic loaded with a hypnotic drug would inject a shackled prisoner. When he became unconscious, he was loaded aboard an airplane that flew over the Atlantic for an appropriate distance. The unconscious (but not dead) prisoner would be unceremoniously dumped overboard. Dissidents thus did indeed disappear, without a trace. The school also served as a torture center.

Economic Woes

The nation's economic boom proved short-lived, and by 1981 the country was mired in a recession and disenchanted with military rule. To enhance its public

ARGENTINAZO: ¡LAS MALVINAS RECUPERADAS!

ACCION CONJUNTA DE NUESTRAS FUERZAS ARMADAS; MARCHAN AVIONES Y BARCOS EN GRAN OPERATIVO; EL TIEMPO CONSPIRA

¡Las Malvinas están incorporadas, definitivamente, a nuestro territorio! La frase y la fecha, ya históricas, fueron escuchadas esta madrugada en círculos oficiales y políticos, mientras todo el país, sin distinción de banderías, grita, más que nunca ¡Argentina! ¡Argentina!
La esperada resolución de las Fuerzas Armadas Argentinas

del uso de la fuerza" y la "indiferencia" del gobierno del Reino Unido frente a las propuestas argentinas para considerar por vías pacíficas y de negociación el diferendo. En su presentación ante la OEA, la Argentina denunció que los actos del gobierno británico han creado una "situación de grave tensión que podría llegar a poner en peligro el mantea

Buenos Aires' *Cronica* (April 2, 1982) hails Argentina's "recovery" of the Malvinas (Falkland Islands)

image, the junta tried several moves. In 1981, Videla was replaced by a more moderate general, Roberto Viola. The government bowed to the demands of the *Peronistas* and freed Isabel; she promptly took up a luxurious and quiet exile in Spain.

Still, the opposition to military rule persisted. In December 1981 the junta fired Viola, replacing him with hardline Army Commander Leopoldo F. Galtieri. In contrast to Viola, who attempted to deal with the banned political parties, the new president sought to reaffirm the military's control of the government and its commitment to free-market economic policies.

Although Galtieri pledged to deal more firmly with the nation's economic problems, the recession intensified, driving inflation to 130% and unemployment to 13–16%. By March 1982, labor unrest was spreading and the outlawed political parties were agitating for a return to constitutional government.

The Falkland Islands War

At that point, Galtieri and some top military commanders made a momentous decision. Taking advantage of a dispute between Argentina and Britain over the

General Leopoldo F. Galtieri   **Argentine troops man the Falkland beaches**

Argentina

sparsely populated but British-held Falkland Islands (*Malvinas* to the Argentines), the president ordered the armed forces to seize them in April 1982. After an absence of 149 years, the Argentine flag once again flew over this disputed territory. Overnight, Galtieri and his military conquerors were the heroes of Argentina. For the next 74 days, Argentina and Britain were at war.

The dispute over the Falklands started in the 1500s. On the basis of initial occupation, the Argentine historical claim did seem to have somewhat greater validity.

Despite treaties, the British established colonies on the islands in the 1770s, but they were soon abandoned. The Spanish claims to the islands were transferred to Argentina when it achieved independence in 1816. Four years later, Argentina reaffirmed its sovereignty over the archipelago as parts of the islands were settled and land grants were awarded.

At the urging of the U.S. consulate in Buenos Aires, the British forcibly occupied the islands in 1833 and all Argentine residents were deported. For the next 149 years, Argentines were prevented from living on the islands, and until 1999 Argentine citizens had to buy a round-trip ticket before they were even allowed to *visit* the islands. Since 1851 the islands had been largely controlled by the Falkland Islands Company, a London-based firm that owns 40% of the main two islands.

Economically, the Falklands have little to offer except offshore oil deposits. Charles Darwin called them "the miserable islands" when he visited them in 1833. Most of the residents today are engaged in sheep ranching and wool production.

The Argentine invasion of 1982 *did* violate two basic principles of international law: use of force to settle international disputes and the right of self-determination. As a result, the U.N. Security Council voted to demand that they withdraw. There was widespread sentiment in Latin America in favor of returning the islands to Argentina, and the United Nations had voted overwhelmingly in the 1960s and 1970s to ask Great Britain to negotiate on the islands' "decolonization." The British position in 1982 was for 25 more years of control over the islands. Argentina warned that it might seek "other means" to resolve the dispute.

It was this frustration with diplomacy that set the stage for the invasion. The conflict quickly escalated. The Argentine air force crippled a British destroyer with an Exocet missile and sank a conveyer ship, while a British submarine torpedoed and sank the Argentine battleship Belgrano, with a loss of more than 300 lives. The British army landed in the Falklands, quickly defeating the Argentine defenders, most of them poorly trained conscripts.

After 10 weeks, there were 1,700 Argentine casualties, including 650 dead or missing. The beaten Argentines left enormous amounts of military equipment worth millions of dollars. The British held 11,000 POWs. After a lengthy delay, they were returned to remote ports in Argentina where they were received amid great security (in part to prevent media coverage) and with little fanfare. The battle cost the British $2 billion—$1 million for each Falklander.

For Argentina, the war was a disaster. The army was humiliated, the military dictatorship was discredited and the economy was pushed toward bankruptcy. In Buenos Aires, fickle, angry crowds marched on the Plaza de Mayo demanding to nail "Galtieri to the wall!" In order to prevent elimination of its power, the *junta* promptly fired him.

For the next week, the government remained virtually paralyzed while the three armed forces quarreled over a successor. Having just lost on the battlefield, the army—the largest of the three services—had no intention of going down in defeat on the home front as well. Unable to reach an agreement, it named retired Major General Reynaldo Benito Antonio Bignone as president. In dismay, the navy and air force said they would not actively participate in the new government.

The United States was put in an awkward position by the conflict. Its endorsement of a 1947 Inter-American Treaty of Mutual Defense (better known as the Rio Treaty) was questioned when it refused to side with Argentina, but Secretary of State Al Haig that the Rio Treaty did not apply because the first use of force had not come from outside the hemisphere. Argentina's support of President Reagan's efforts against communists in Nicaragua and El Salvador was terminated.

Return to Democracy

Demoralized by defeat and besieged by monumental social and economic problems, the military government allowed the electoral process to run as fast and smoothly as possible while attempting a rear-guard action to protect the armed forces from future prosecution. Encouraged by political freedom, human rights activists demanded more information about the *desaparecidos* (disappeared ones) during the "Dirty War" and stern punishment for those responsible. The *junta* answered with a declaration that the *desaparecidos* should be considered dead and with a law granting amnesty to military security personnel involved in the anti-terrorist campaign of 1976–1982. Outraged public opinion forced the presidential candidates to announce they would repeal the law as soon as civilian authority was re-established.

On October 30, 1983, general elections were held. The winner, Raúl Alfonsín of the Radical Civic Union (*UCR*), represented a more moderate tendency in the Argentine political spectrum. The *Peronistas*, poorly organized, had hoped for Isabel to return, but she preferred her more peaceful life in Spain.

The new democratic government faced a multitude of urgent problems, but three were especially pressing: control of the armed forces, labor demands and a depressed economy. The full extent of the military's crackdown became clear in 1985 when nine military leaders, including Videla, Viola, Galtieri and Admiral Emilio Massera were placed on trial. Furious over the military's attempt to whitewash the gruesome activities of elite military and paramilitary units, the civilian courts assumed jurisdiction. The trial furnished lively media material, describing in detail methods of torture and execution. The officers' defense was predictable: they were fighting a war against subversives financed from abroad, and they did not know the extent of the excesses being perpetrated by their subordinates. In typical Nurenburg fashion, those subordinates claimed they were simply following orders.

Videla and Massera (the Navy member of the Videla *junta*) were sentenced to life for 62 murders; three others were given nominal sentences. Galtieri and two other principals were acquitted, but Galtieri was sentenced by a court martial to 12 years imprisonment for "negligence" in directing the armed forces during the Malvinas war. His son, killed in the conflict, was buried on one of the islands.

Thousands of human rights activists, led by the Mothers of the Plaza de Mayo, who sought information as to their absent loved ones, paraded to protest the leniency of the sentences. This illustrated a well-known fact about the military in Argentina—the country cannot exist without it and cannot stand living with it. Nevertheless, prosecution of thousands of former military and police strongmen began in 1986, with orders that they be expedited. This led to extreme unrest within the ranks and, in 1987, a serious threat of military revolt. To dispel this, Alfonsín asked Congress to grant amnesty to all military personnel below the rank of colonel. The net result was that of 7,000 potential defendants who could have been tried for atrocities, perhaps 50 actually were charged; there were few convictions. The quest for justice continues to haunt Argentina (see Ghosts of the Past).

In 1985, there began action as well against former *Montanaro* leaders who had touched off the "Dirty War" of the 1970s. The defense to charges of murder and kidnapping was also predictable: the organization was only exercising political rights and responsibilities.

It was on the international economic front that Argentina scored its most impressive, if indecisive, success. Under the burden of a public debt estimated at about $48 billion, Argentina threatened to ignore a 1984 deadline for paying $500 million in interest to creditors around the world. The alarmed creditor bankers agreed to new terms and better payment conditions. Argentina temporarily gained a respite and showed other debtor nations they were not without bargaining power.

The austerity program, necessary to support economic reorganization on even a modest level, sharply lowered living standards. A basic problem involved investment funds. The trade surplus was eaten up by the need to pay interest. It was necessary to borrow additional funds to pay that interest, pushing the external debt to $64 billion.

Although Alfonsín initially appeared to be an astute politician, his knowledge of

Raúl Alfonsín

economic policy was meager, and he had no competent advisers. The result was hyperinflation caused by spiraling wages and prices (as much as 400% per month!). He introduced a new currency, the *austral*, but it was devalued so many times it became worthless.

Alfonsín tried repeated wage-price freezes that didn't work. Strikes became commonplace. Although the country could have been self-sufficient in oil production, he demanded 50% of production from potential foreign producers as the price of exploration.

The *Peronista* movement splintered into two factions, but in 1988 they agreed on the nomination of Carlos Saúl Menem, popular governor of the impoverished

northwestern province of La Rioja, for president. His running mate was Eduardo Duhalde, from Buenos Aires. Years later, they would become bitter rivals for control of the party.

Menem, of Syrian descent, was colorful and charismatic, promising everything to everybody. He was known for his love of movie starlets and fast cars. He trounced his opponent from Alfonsín's *UCR*, receiving 47.4% of the vote to 32.5%. Alfonsín had vowed to serve until the end of his term in November 1989, but, beset with riots and a host of unsolvable problems, he stepped down in July; Menem was sworn in. He was faced with a debt of $69 billion.

The Menem Presidency

What those attending the inaugural heard was quite different from that which they heard before the election. "I do not bring easy or immediate promises . . . I can only offer my people work, sacrifice and hope," he said, sounding rather Churchillian. "We must tell the truth, once and for all: Argentina has broken down." He announced a number of controversial measures calculated to restore order.

The early days of Menem's presidency were stormy. Prices rose, restaurants emptied and pasta became a disliked meat substitute. By the end of 1989, all military were pardoned, including Galtieri and later, Videla, infuriating many; 1 million signed a resolution of protest. Menem normalized relations with Britain. His popularity plummeted. He took an ominous step in 1990, signing a decree authorizing the military to act in the event of "social upheaval." Further, it would command all state and local police in such an event. The economy continued its downward spiral and the middle class became poor.

In an ingenious move, Menem privatized about 90 state monopolies. Part of the purchase price was the purchase of a portion of Argentina's external debt, worth about 30 cents to the dollar. The first to go was the antiquated telephone system, which fetched more than $1.8 billion in hard currency. In 1992, Menem effectively tied the latest Argentine currency, again called the peso, to the U.S. dollar to slow inflation and to encourage North American and European investment.

The economy turned sharply upward, at least on the surface, but the improvement did not affect all sectors. In a hurry to placate union workers and the economic elite, the government neglected the small business sector and the white-collar workers. Privatization took its toll among relatives and party favorites—or as economists call them, "redundancies." In other words, unless a person actually did something pro-

Carlos Saúl Menem

ductive, he or she was fired. In the past, this was unheard of. Favoritism had not been limited to the elite; unions also had benefited. The result was the same: low productivity.

Foreign investors remained wary, so Menem energetically set about changing age-old employment patterns. The result spoke for itself. Both the GDP and the annual per capita income more than *doubled* after 1990, while inflation was in single digits.

Meanwhile, scandals and corruption involving Menem's in-laws tarnished his image (although he never pretended to be an angel). When a dispute arose with his wife in 1990, he threw her out of the presidential palace. She provided exciting copy for the media, particularly the tabloids.

Menem moved to repeal the constitutional limitation that forbade a president more than one consecutive term. His constitutional six-year term was to end in 1995. To do this, it was necessary to have the cooperation of the *UCR*. A deal was made (the Olivos Pact) between Menem's *Justicialista* Party and the *UCR* for a constituent assembly, the prime purpose of which was to enable Menem to run for a second term. The two parties had the two-thirds majority (211 of 305 seats) adequate to adopt the constitutional amendment. The bill also reduced the presidential term to four years, created the office of prime minister and gave the president the power to nominate Supreme Court justices, subject to a two-thirds vote in the Senate.

Menem easily won re-election in May 1995 with about 50 percent of the vote, thus avoiding a runoff. Duhalde left the ticket to win the governorship of Buenos Aires Province. No sooner did Menem win his second term than the effects of

Argentina

Edición
Internacional
Vía Aérea

LA NACION

Una selección
de la semana

Año 120 - Nros. 42.255 al 42.281 - Ed. Int. Nº 1502 - Año 28   Buenos Aires, lunes 3 de julio de 1989   Bouchard 557, C. P. 1106. Tel. 313-1003, 1453 y 312-3021/9

Menem dispondría la libertad de militares

Lo reveló implícitamente, al sostener que no puede ver encerrados "ni a los pájaros"; viajará a los EE. UU., en septiembre, por el problema de la deuda externa

Por César Ivancovich

(Enviado especial de LA NACION)

Jueves 29

LA RIOJA.- El presidente electo, Carlos Menem, reiteró que hay que cerrar las heridas entre militares y civiles y reveló implícitamente que todos los hombres de armas condenados por la Justicia recuperarán su libertad, al utilizar la expresión: "Yo no puedo ver encerrados ni a los pájaros".

También anunció que viajará en septiembre próximo a los Estados Unidos, en un intento por revertir la "extrema dureza" advertida en los medios financieros internacionales respecto de la Argentina.

"No hay vuelta que darle, todo pasa por allí", comentó el todavía gobernador riojano al justificar la aceptación del convite formulado por el presidente norteamericano, Georges Bush,

Menem no sólo se refirió a las dificultades que enfrenta la economía en el plano externo –en su reciente viaje a Washington, el canciller-designado, Domingo Cavallo, se estrelló contra una dura muralla construida por los centros financieros–, sino también en el ámbito local.

Admitió, por ejemplo, que esos 2500 millones de dólares que según versiones aportarían empresas locales para el arranque de su plan económico son, por ahora, algo así como un espejismo en el medio del desierto. Nadie sabe, empero, si al seguir avanzando la imagen corresponderá efectivamente a un oasis.

Por lo que dicen los allegados de

Lo que sí dijo ayer el presidente electo es que la dureza que implica va a ser mayor después de los cien días que al comienzo de su gestión. Cree que las medidas de shock por aplicarse de entrada según efectivas para bajar la inflación, pero que las requeridas para mantenerla en ese nivel, después de los tres primeros meses, podrían llegar a ser mucho más duras.

Este enviado le preguntó si creía que los operadores retirarían su capital del circuito financiero para invertirlo en la producción. "Sí. Los especuladores deberán replegarse, pues habrá créditos baratos para la producción. Las mesas de dinero tendrán que adaptarse o desaparecer", sentenció.

Formalizaron sus renuncias Alfonsín y Víctor Martínez

Las presentaron en el Congreso; serán aceptadas el 8, antes de que jure Menem

Sábado 1

El presidente Raúl Alfonsín y el vicepresidente Víctor Martínez presentaron ayer al Parlamento sus renuncias, para que la Asamblea Legislativa del 8 del actual las acepte momentos antes de que preste juramento como nuevo mandatario el doctor Carlos Saúl Menem.

Se formalizaron así las dimisiones anunciadas por Alfonsín en su discurso del 12 de junio, cuando anticipó su decisión de resignar el cargo a partir de ayer.

El sobre lacrado con la renuncia del jefe del Estado llegó al Congreso en manos del secretario general de la Presidencia, Carlos Becerra, quien lo entregó a Víctor Martínez en su carácter de titular del Senado.

Al recibir la renuncia –en una breve ceremonia realizada en su despacho– Martínez sumó la suya, también en sobre cerrado. Ambos fueron entregados al secretario parlamentario de la Cámara alta, Antonio Macris, y sólo serán

a la formalidad o un mensaje extenso con consideraciones o pronunciamientos políticos.

"Misión histórica"

"Presentar la renuncia me apena un poco, pero nos complace saber que esto lo hacemos en beneficio del país", dijo Víctor Martínez a los periodistas tras el acto en su despacho.

Becerra, por su parte, declaró que se sentía "muy honrado por esta misión histórica que me encomendó el Presidente: este acto cierra el capítulo de la consolidación de la democracia".

Agregó que el radicalismo acompañará "con alta responsabilidad" la nueva etapa política que comienza el 8 del actual.

Alfonsín en el Congreso

Martínez confirmó, asimismo, que pasado mañana Alfonsín concurrirá al Congreso, a las 17, para saludar protocolarmente al nuevo titular provisional

La Nación headlines two watershed events on July 3, 1989: President–elect Menem's declaration that he would release jailed military officers as a gesture of reconciliation, and the resignations of President Alfonsín and Vice President Martínez, which allowed Menem to take office five months early.

---

the Mexican peso devaluation struck Argentina, plunging it into recession. Unemployment soared to 18%.

Menem kept his promises to modernize the economy through privatization and other free-market reforms, and he accomplished the unthinkable by keeping inflation to single digits. Still, the painful remedies cost Menem his popularity. In 1996, the *Peronistas* were dealt a severe blow when Fernando de la Rua, the *UCR* candidate for mayor of Buenos Aires, won a decisive victory in that *Peronista* stronghold.

In 1997, the Radicals entered into an opposition alliance with *Frepaso*, a *Peronist* splinter group, to contest the October congressional elections. The Alliance wisely chose not to attack Menem's successful free-market policies, because the economy was growing at a robust 8%. Instead, the Alliance hit the president where he was most vulnerable: the rampant corruption within his administration, which had grown so bad that Economy Minister Domingo Cavallo, the architect of the new economic miracle, resigned in disgust in 1996. In the elections for 127 of the 257 seats in the lower house, the *Peronistas* suffered another serious setback by losing their absolute majority, dropping from 131 seats to 119; their share of the popular vote plummeted from 43% in 1995 to 36%. The Alliance won 106 seats, while other parties held 32 and the balance of power.

There was a hostile relationship between Menem and the press. By then,

Argentine media enjoyed unprecedented freedom and they dutifully exposed scandal after scandal in the Menem government. In January 1997, José Luis Cabezas, an investigative photographer who was probing alleged police corruption, was found beaten, shot and burned to a cinder in his car. The crime shocked the nation and brought international pressure on Menem to bring the killers to justice. The scandal reached a head in 1998 when the wife of one of two policemen arrested in connection with Cabezas' murder publicly revealed that they had been hired by Alfredo Yabrán, a powerful, influential and secretive tycoon rumored to have Mafia ties and who for good measure was a close friend of Menem's. Cabezas had surreptitiously taken the first published photographs of the reclusive Yabrán, who, like Menem, was of Arab descent. As police closed in on Yabrán's *estancia* to arrest him for Cabezas' murder, the tycoon apparently shot himself to death. There was no autopsy, and rumors circulated that the Mafia had silenced him. Quipped the U.S. ambassador: "Yabrán committed suicide, but we don't know who did it yet."

The Elections of 1999

Duhalde, as governor of Buenos Aires Province, regarded himself as the logical heir apparent to Menem. But Menem shocked the country—and infuriated Duhalde—by hinting in 1998 that he would be

amenable to a constitutional amendment permitting him to run for a *third* term. For most it seemed a moot point; the Peronists had lost their majority in the Chamber of Deputies. and opinion polls showed him running in the single digits.

Tension between Menem and Duhalde mounted, and Duhalde pulled off an astute political maneuver: a referendum in Buenos Aires Province on whether or not the constitution should be amended to allow Menem to run again. It was a classic poker player's bluff; it could have backfired if the vote were yes, but Duhalde was confident the vote would go against Menem. Menem realized it, too, and folded. He withdrew from the race, but boasted he would return to power in 2003. Duhalde easily won the party primary.

The Alliance, meanwhile, had a schism of its own between the *UCR*'s Fernando de la Rua, mayor of Buenos Aires, and *Frepaso*'s Senator Graciela Fernández Meijide, mother of one of the "desaparacidos" of the Dirty War. In the Alliance's primary, de la Rua handily defeated her 63% to 36%. De la Rua chose as his running mate a *Frepaso* strategist, Carlos Alvarez. As a consolation, Fernández Meijide became the Alliance's candidate to succeed Duhalde as governor of Buenos Aires Province. Her opponent was Menem's retiring vice president, Carlos Ruckauf.

The disgruntled Domingo Cavallo, Menem's erstwhile economic adviser, launched an independent candidacy for president.

48

A gaucho on the Pampa and the socially elite at the glittering Teatro Colón in Buenos Aires.

The ensuing campaign was the most dramatic the country had seen since the restoration of democracy. But 10 years of Peronist rule, coupled with nagging public concerns over official corruption and an alarming 14.5% unemployment, proved too much of an encumbrance for Duhalde. In the balloting in October 1999, de la Rua scored a decisive first round victory, receiving 48.5% of the vote to Duhalde's 38% and Cavallo's 10.2%. With characteristic bombast, Menem declared on election night, "I could have won easily," a highly debatable claim.

The Alliance increased its number of seats in the Chamber of Deputies from 106 to 123, six short of a majority, while the *Justicialistas* fell from 122 seats to 101, their worst showing since 1985. The *Justicialistas* did win a number of governorships, among them Buenos Aires, where Ruckauf defeated Fernández Meijide. Moreover, they still controlled the Senate, forcing de la Rua to govern by consensus.

In July 1999, Foreign Minister Guido di Tella and British Foreign Secretary Robin Cook signed a bilateral agreement that in effect ended the diplomatic hostilities over the Falkland Islands. Argentine nationals were once again permitted to visit the islands.

Even before he took office, de la Rua also found himself involved in foreign affairs.

He and Menem both denounced Spanish Judge Garzón's charges against 98 former Argentine officers (see Ghosts from the Past) as an infringement on Argentine sovereignty and refused to recognize them.

Faced with a strained relationship with an old European friend, de la Rua made an effort to further improve relations with a long-time European foe. While in Paris in November to represent the Alliance in the Socialist International convention, he met with British Prime Minister Tony Blair. The two men agreed in principle to expand upon the bilateral agreement reached in July on the Falkland Islands. Prince Andrew, a Falklands War veteran, represented Britain at de la Rua's inauguration.

De la Rua's Aborted Presidency

De la Rua was sworn in on December 10, 1999. The new president soon demonstrated he represented not merely a change in parties and personalities but in style. He sold Tango 1, the presidential jet, a Boeing 757 that cost Argentine taxpayers $66 million and a small fortune to fly and maintain. De la Rua flew by commercial jet.

De la Rua advocated a $2.5 billion tax increase to reduce the $7.1 billion budget deficit. The IMF responded with a $7.4 billion loan, but the tax increase was un-

popular with the public. Nonetheless, polls showed that while his government had only a 42% approval rating, the president's was 63%. That would soon change.

De la Rua introduced a controversial labor reform bill to allow more flexibility in labor contracts, a gesture to wary foreign investors and to the IMF. The still-powerful unions took to the streets after it passed the Chamber of Deputies. In April 2000, union militants surrounded the Congress and clashed with police. It was merely a taste of what was to come.

The Senate passed, 57–4, a compromise version. De la Rua slyly promised entrenched labor bosses that he would not probe their operations if they would support it. The Chamber of Deputies passed it 121–84.

Fissures appeared in the Radical-*Frepaso* Alliance after de la Rua announced $938 million in budget cuts and reductions of up to 15% in civil service salaries. *Frepaso* members of Congress revolted, as did Fernández Meijide, who was social development minister. Left-wing members of the Alliance also grumbled over what they regarded as undue influence on de la Rua by his close friend Fernando de Santibañes, a prominent and conservative banker de la Rua had named head of the National Intelligence Service (*SIDE*).

De la Rua shuffled his Cabinet in October 2000. But when he retained Santibañes, Vice President Alvarez resigned in protest, which proved a fateful decision. Fernández Meijide remained in the Cabinet. Alvarez's resignation would confront Argentina with a constitutional crisis 14 months later.

At year's end, de la Rua admitted that the country's economic performance had been disappointing in 2000, with GDP down by 5% and unemployment remaining around 15%. About the only bright spot was a $40 billion IMF economic rescue package. Among the terms: Argentina had to reduce its budget deficit from more than $9 billion to $6.5 billion by the end of 2001.

In March 2001, de la Rua appointed as economy minister a conservative technocrat, Ricardo López Murphy, trusted by investors but detested by the Peronists and *Frepaso*. He lasted only two weeks, but he provoked the last remaining *Frepaso* Cabinet members, including Fernández Meijide, to resign by announcing $4.5 billion in budget cuts. De la Rua stunned the country—but delighted international financial markets—by resurrecting Domingo Cavallo to replace López.

Cavallo came up with a series of offbeat ideas designed to placate the IMF and, in theory, to jumpstart the flagging economy. One proposal: Granting emergency powers for one year to the president—in real-

Argentina

ity, to Cavallo—to deal with the crisis by decree. Congress and the IMF approved these "superpowers." Cavallo then offered another offbeat idea: Instead of pegging the peso solely to the dollar, the inflation-busting technique he had fathered a decade earlier, he proposed pegging the peso to the average of the dollar and the Euro, the European Union's new monetary unit.

In a separate development, a federal prosecutor accused Menem of being the intellectual author of illegal arms sales in 1991 to Ecuador, then in a virtual state of war with Peru, and to Croatia, then under a U.N. arms embargo. Menem denied it.

Always flamboyant, the 70-year-old Menem splashed back into the international headlines in 2001 by marrying Cecilia Bolocco, a 36-year-old former Miss Universe from Chile. He made headlines again when he was placed under house arrest on the arms sale charges. He was indicted, but the Supreme Court threw out the charges.

In July 2001, de la Rua announced another austerity plan that included a 13% pay cut for civil servants, which sparked labor protests. Argentina's country risk indicator jumped to 1,616 points—worse than troubled Ecuador's. By October, de la Rua's approval rating was 18% and Cavallo's was 16%.

In the October elections for the entire Senate and half the Chamber of Deputies, the Peronists strengthened their majority in the Senate and increased from 102 to 116 in the lower chamber, becoming the largest bloc. The *UCR* dropped from 84 seats to 71, while *Frepaso* dropped from 23 to 17. In the popular vote, the Peronists received 40%, the Alliance only 23%. Duhalde won a Senate seat from Buenos Aires. But 30% of Argentines angrily cast blank ballots or nullified them. The public mood was dangerously ugly.

De la Rua and Cavallo desperately tried to deal with the deepening crisis and to avoid default on the national debt, which had increased to $132 billion; it would be the largest default in history, one that threatened to generate global shock waves. In November, he announced a "debt swap," that traded $95 billion worth of existing bonds that paid 11% for longer-term bonds that paid only 7%; for investors, it was a no-brainer. Then the Peronist governors rejected his proposed reduction in federal remittances to the state governments, something he needed to meet the terms for a $22 billion international rescue plan.

Descent into Chaos

By December 2001, fears of an imminent default and economic meltdown had Argentines in a near-panic. De la Rua infuriated them by reducing the monthly limit on savings withdrawals from $1,500 to

Fernando de la Rua

$1,000. The IMF did not help by freezing a $1.3 billion installment on its $22 billion line of credit because of the government's lack of progress in meeting demands on deficit reduction and because it felt the peso had become overvalued.

Events then exploded in chain reaction. On December 11, the government pleaded for consensus with the Peronists to cut the budget 14% to obtain the desperately needed IMF help. The deficit was $11 billion, double what de la Rua had assured the IMF it would be by year's end. The Peronists demanded de la Rua's resignation as their price for cooperation. On December 13, there was a massive general strike to protest the 18.3% unemployment. The next day, the government announced it had allayed defaulting on the debt by making a loan payment of more than $700 million.

For the next six days, Argentina was a powder keg. On December 19, it exploded. The spark was a demonstration by mostly middle-class Argentines, frustrated over the decline in their living standards and weary of their financial insecurity. The demonstrations began with the traditional *cacerolazo*, the banging on pots and pans, but soon there were violent clashes with police. Full-scale rioting erupted in the capital and other cities. Rioters looted grocery stores. Five people were killed that first day, and de la Rua declared a 30-day state of siege—the first since the 1989 riots that shortened the Alfonsín presidency. The riots continued on December 20. Demonstrators tried to storm de la Rua's office. More people were killed, as de la Rua pleaded for calm. With the republic literally falling apart, the entire cabinet, including Cavallo, resigned in a vain attempt to quell the violence. The number of rioters in Buenos Aires alone was estimated at 20,000. Thou-

sands of people rushed to banks to withdraw their monthly limit.

That evening, de la Rua resigned, two years and 10 days after he was inaugurated, and at sunset he was ignominiously whisked away from the Casa Rosada by helicopter, a scene eerily like that in 1976 when the military overthrew Isabel Perón. The mobs cheered, but it was a hollow celebration; the death toll had climbed to 22.

Despite de la Rua's resignation, the rioting continued, as a leaderless government tried to cope with the violence as well as with a constitutional crisis. With the vacancy in the vice presidency caused by Alvarez's resignation, de la Rua's constitutional successor was the Senate president, Ramón Puerta, a Peronist. But Puerta eschewed his constitutional mandate, which he said made him president for only 48 hours.

Thus, Argentina was literally on the brink of anarchy by December 22, when Congress called new elections for March and the Peronists tapped their governor of San Luis, Adolfo Rodríguez Sáa, as their choice for interim president until then. He was elected on a 169–138 vote in a joint session of Congress and sworn in on December 23. Rodríguez Sáa lifted the state of siege, suspended payment on the foreign debt, and channeled the money into the creation of 1 million new jobs, the first 24,000 to be public service jobs.

It seemed that the country at least was no longer rudderless, as calm temporarily returned; the final death toll from the riots was 27, with hundreds more injured or arrested.

On December 29, pot-banging protesters took to the streets again to protest Rodríguez Sáa's decision to continue the limit on savings withdrawals. Again, the protests turned violent, although not deadly. Protesters coined a new slogan that summed up the national mood: *Que se vayan todos!* (Throw all of them out!) They tried to storm the Casa Rosada and the Congress, but were expelled by riot police.

If Rodríguez Sáa had thought he would have more success than de la Rua at achieving a consensus, he was soon disappointed. He urged the Peronist leaders to offer solutions that might quell the popular uprising without worsening the economic crisis and to reach a consensus on how to select the Peronist candidate for the March election. They could not—or would not.

On December 30, after exactly one week in office, Rodríguez Sáa resigned in disgust, bitterly lashing out at the members of his own party for failing to support him. Mob rule, it seemed, was close to prevailing in Argentina.

The next hapless interim president was Eduardo Carmoña, speaker of the Chamber of Deputies, who like Puerta would

Rounding up sheep for market

keep the presidential chair warm for 48 hours until a joint session of Congress met on New Year's Day 2002 to select the nation's fifth president in 12 days. Meanwhile, on New Year's Eve, Congress canceled the March election and decided to appoint an interim president. The initial plan was for the interim president to fill out de la Rua's term, which would have expired on December 10, 2003.

Caretaker Government

The unfortunate "winner" of the January 1 balloting: Duhalde, the losing presidential candidate in 1999. He was sworn in on January 2, 2002. He told Congress and the nation that he was scrapping the "exhausted model" of free markets and neoliberal economic policies that he blamed for the country's plight and that he would "recreate the conditions" to attract investors. "Argentina is bankrupt," he bluntly told his countrymen, "Argentina is destroyed. This model destroyed everything." He called for a return to the pre-Menem Peronist ideals of populism and protectionism. He promised to guarantee deposits and continued the moratorium on foreign debt payments. But he avoided mention of the two most sensitive topics—a possible peso devaluation and whether he would lift the detested restriction on bank withdrawals, which Argentines had nicknamed *"el corralito,"* or little corral.

Duhalde appointed a bipartisan cabinet, but the key posts went to Peronists. As economy minister, he named Jorge Remes Lenicov, an internationally respected economist. Duhalde and Remes proposed an emergency economic plan that granted them *carte blanche,* authorized devaluation

of the peso and froze job layoffs for six months.

On January 3, Argentina missed an interest payment on a $28 billion loan; the country was officially in default. Congress quickly approved the plan. Remes ended the decade-old peg of the peso to the dollar and devalued the peso 40%, saying it would be allowed to float freely.

The IMF denounced Duhalde's economic plan as incoherent, while U.S. President George W. Bush told the OAS in Washington that Argentina would face a "bleak and stagnant future" if it returned to protectionism.

The Supreme Court declared the restrictions on savings unconstitutional. Remes responded with another bank holiday, as depositors armed themselves with court orders directing the banks to give them their money. Remes declared that bank withdrawals and government transactions would be in pesos, sparking more violent demonstrations. (A year later, the Supreme Court ruled the conversion of bank accounts from dollars to pesos was an unconstitutional infringement of private property rights.)

Duhalde finally persuaded the Peronist governors to agree to a revenue-sharing plan the IMF demanded. Still, unemployment increased to an alarming 23.8% in April 2002—about what it was in the United States during the depths of the

Great Depression. The peso hit an all-time low of 4.00 to the dollar. The percentage of Argentines living below the $200-a-month poverty line mushroomed to 57%. Suddenly, another old enemy returned: inflation. In April 2002 alone, prices rose 10%. The combination of double-digit unemployment and double-digit inflation defied the laws of economics and renewed a climate of desperation. The government devised a scheme requiring depositors to accept five- and 10-year bonds in exchange for some accounts. Depositors reacted with fury.

In April, Remes resigned after Congress rejected a bank reform plan. Duhalde appointed Roberto Lavagna, a trade expert and former ambassador to the European Union and the World Trade Organization, as economy minister—the country's sixth in 14 months.

In a separate, unrelated development, Cavallo was arrested in connection with the alleged sale of illegal arms to Ecuador and Croatia that had implicated Menem. At the same time, an appeals court ordered the presiding judge in the case to reopen the investigation of Menem and several others.

In January 2003, the IMF agreed to a $6.8 billion loan to prevent a default on the $141 billion debt, which would have had global financial repercussions that nobody wanted.

An Argentine classic: a gaucho and his mount

Argentina

The Election of 2003

A frustrated Duhalde advanced the presidential elections by six months, then moved them back again to April 27. For the first time, a runoff would be held if no candidate received a majority.

A new intra-party turf battle erupted between the Menem and Duhalde factions over who the Peronist candidate would be. Duhalde received backing to scrap the Peronist primary altogether, obviously because he knew Menem might win. Instead, the election became a free-for-all, with rival Peronists, Radicals and independents winding up on the same ballot, Louisiana-style.

Rodríguez Sáa declared his candidacy, as did a dark horse, Néstor Kirchner, the populist Peronist governor of Santa Cruz Province in remote, sparsely populated Patagonia. Duhalde endorsed Kirchner, infuriating both Menem and Rodríguez Sáa. Kirchner astutely promised to retain the popular Lavagna as economy minister. With three strong candidates slinging mud at each other, the Peronists appeared to be disemboweling themselves.

The opposition was fragmented, too. Former Economy Minister López Murphy, a Radical who survived his association with de la Rua with his reputation intact, announced as an independent and became the preferred choice of the country's business sector. Another new face, Elisa Carrió, elected to Congress as a Radical, launched a new movement with an anti-corruption platform. The poor, discredited *UCR* offered up a political lightweight, Leopoldo Moreau, as its sacrificial lamb.

The vote totals stunned everyone:

Menem	4,686,646	24.36%
Kirchner	4,232,052	22.0%
López Murphy	3,144,528	16.34%
Carrió	2,720,692	14.14%
Rodríguez Sáa	2,715,799	14.12%
Moreau	450,489	2.34%

Far from feeling elated over his first-place showing, the once-popular Menem was shocked that he had failed to poll even a fourth of the vote. He was shocked even more when polls showed Kirchner would humiliate him by more than 2–1 in the runoff. Faced with his first-ever electoral defeat, what Menem did next was generated by pure ego: Four days before the runoff, he withdrew, making Kirchner president by default. It was more than just an egotistical move designed to avoid humiliation; it was pure Machiavellian politics, Menem-style. Kirchner would have to govern—if he lasted—on a shaky mandate from only 22% of the voters. Menem, meanwhile, would be reminding Argentines of that every step of the way.

Kirchner Shakes Up the System

Kirchner, 53, a lawyer, was sworn in on May 25, 2003. Shaky mandate or not, he began rattling the country's institutions and its foreign policy. At least 12 Latin American presidents attended the inauguration, including Cuba's Fidel Castro, Venezuela's Hugo Chávez and Brazil's Luiz Inácio da Silva—all critics of the U.S.-supported Free Trade Area of the Americas. Kirchner repeated his opposition to the FTAA, and the inauguration became a festival of the Latin American left. Kirchner also declared he sided with da Silva in stressing regional Latin American integration, touting a concept he called "national capitalism." The Bush administration snubbed Kirchner by sending only the secretary of housing and urban development, Mel Martínez.

Just three days into his term, Kirchner forced 27 army generals and 13 navy admirals into retirement. The upper echelons of the armed forces reacted angrily, but meekly complied. What else could they do? They obtained little sympathy from the senior field-grade officers who stood in line for promotion to general and admiral. Then Kirchner began cashiering top-ranking federal police officers as well.

Kirchner next asked Congress to impeach "some" of the nine Supreme Court justices, whom Kirchner accused of corruption and cronyism and of holding the nation "hostage" by decisions that had hamstrung many of Duhalde's economic reforms. Kirchner focused on justices appointed by, and still loyal to, Menem, especially Supreme Court President Julio Nazareno. He and four more Menem appointees resigned in the face of likely impeachment.

Kirchner then shook up taxpayers by announcing a crackdown on tax evasion—a time-honored tradition in Argentina. Reliable estimates indicate that revenue could be increased by 50% if all the tax cheaters paid what they owe.

Kirchner simultaneously made a splash in international circles. When U.S. Secretary of State Powell belatedly visited Argentina, Kirchner assured him he wanted amicable relations, but insisted that Washington maintain a respectful distance. The next day, Kirchner flew to Brasilia, where he and da Silva repeated their call for greater Latin American integration. Kirchner also reiterated Argentina's claim of sovereignty over the Malvinas (Falkland Islands), and called on Britain to resume talks on the islands' future. Britain summarily rejected the suggestion.

Horst Köhler, managing director of the IMF, came to Buenos Aires to meet with Kirchner and Lavagna on the conditions for debt restructuring. Kirchner bluntly

Eduardo Duhalde

told Köhler that he would not agree to any further conditions that would cause more suffering, and Köhler just as bluntly replied that the suffering would end only if there were an economic climate that again attracted foreign investors and encouraged Argentines to bring their money back from foreign accounts. The two sides agreed to negotiate a three-year plan to repay the $13.5 billion that would be coming due between 2003 and 2006. Köhler left saying he was "impressed" with Kirchner.

Nonetheless, in September 2003, Argentina defaulted on a $3 billion payment to the IMF on its $90 billion debt, the largest single missed payment in IMF history. A day later, Kirchner negotiated a deal with the IMF that allowed Argentina to restructure payment of $21 billion of the debt over three years. Kirchner addressed the United Nations in New York, where he laid part of the blame at the feet of the IMF and of developed nations that block the exports of developing nations.

In January 2004, the IMF announced it was satisfied with Argentine compliance with the 2003 agreement. But in August, Kirchner suddenly and inexplicably canceled the agreement, even defiantly informed the holders of the $102.6 billion in outstanding Argentine bonds that he would exchange them for new bonds worth only about 30–35% of the value of the originals, in essence, telling them to take it or leave it. Creditors screamed foul and demanded that Kirchner compromise, but faced with recovering 30 cents on the dollar or nothing, more than 70% of the bondholders decided to take it. Officially, the world's largest debt default in modern history was over, but Argentina had no international credit.

Ironically, one effect of the reneging on debt obligations was a huge budget surplus, which Kirchner invested in infrastructure and social programs. Thus,

Ghosts from the Past

The past came back to haunt Argentina in 1998 when two former naval officers made statements that scraped open the still-healing wounds of the Dirty War. One, Adolfo Scilingo, voluntarily traveled to Spain, where he was wanted for human rights violations against Spanish citizens in Argentina, and served three months in jail. Upon his release, he openly expressed remorse in a press interview that he had participated in the so-called "death flights," in which an estimated 1,000 naked prisoners were thrown to their deaths into the ocean from aircraft. He called for war-crimes trials for his fellow officers. He collaborated with investigative journalist Horacio Verbitsky to publish the memoir, *The Flight*, in 1996.

The other officer, Alfredo Astiz, known by the sobriquet "the Blond Angel of Death," was arrogant and unrepentant. Astiz had been sentenced *in absentia* to life in prison by France in 1990 for the murder of two nuns, and he was also wanted by Spain and Italy for Dirty War atrocities against nationals of those countries. He, too, admitted in a magazine interview that he had killed prisoners, but justified it as necessary. His remarks sparked an outcry. Jailed briefly, he remained defiant. President Carlos Menem stripped him of his rank. In 2001, Astiz was arrested at the request of Sweden, which wanted him to try him for the death of a Swedish girl during the Dirty War. He was later released.

The Astiz case prompted a move to repeal the amnesty granted to military officers after the return to civilian rule. In the end, Congress passed a watered-down version.

Almost simultaneously, the public expressed outrage over Menem's plan to raze the Navy Mechanics School, the most notorious of the military's torture centers during the Dirty War, and replace it with a park containing a memorial to the victims. Most Argentines preferred to convert the school into a museum, like those dedicated to Holocaust victims. A judge issued an injunction against the demolition, not on sentimental grounds but because it might destroy criminal evidence.

Former President Videla was rearrested in 1998, on charges he participated in selling the babies of "disappeared" dissidents to adoptive parents. Videla's 1990 pardon on war crimes charges did not cover these new allegations. The so-called "baby-stealing" probe widened after Videla's arrest. Former Admiral Emilio Massera, navy chief during the Dirty War, was rearrested after DNA tests showed that two women adopted as babies were children of parents who had disappeared after being arrested; one of them was adopted and raised by an aide of Massera. Massera suffered a debilitating stroke in 2004 and the next year was ruled mentally incompetent to stand trial. In 2006, federal judges nullified the pardons Alfonsín had granted to Videla and Massera in 1990. Massera died in 2010.

Videla, who turned 85 in 2010, went on trial that September, not only on the baby kidnapping charges but for the kidnapping and torture of 40 prisoners. He was convicted and sentenced to life imprisonment.

Former President Reynaldo Bignone was arrested in 1999 for possible involvement in the baby-kidnapping scheme but was not charged with a specific crime. Several more officers were detained in the baby-stealing investigation. His case, too, languished until 2009, when he and six other elderly former officers finally went on trial, not on the old baby-stealing allegations,

but for the kidnapping and torture of 56 prisoners at the Campo de Mayo detention center in Buenos Aires. More than 100 people testified in the five-month trial. In 2010, the defendants were convicted and sentenced to 25 years in prison—not house arrest, as had been requested because of their age. Bignone was then tried for a separate case, of operating a secret torture center in a hospital. In December 2011, when he was 83, he was convicted and sentenced to another 15 years.

On July 5, 2012, Videla was sentenced to an additional 50 years and Bignone another 15. Nine other defendants also received prison terms for baby-stealing.

In March 2013, Videla and Bignone went on trial again, along with 23 other defendants, in connection with their alleged roles in Operation Condor, the multi-national plan to eliminate leftist dissidents. But two months later, Videla died in his jail cell on May 17 at age 87. Bignone, aged 86, was sentenced to a further 23 years in prison in October 2014.

Spanish Judge Baltasar Garzón, the same judge who had requested the arrest of former Chilean strongman Augusto Pinochet by the British in 1998, charged 98 former Argentine officers with alleged human rights abuses in 1999.

In 2001, a federal judge ruled that the amnesty laws absolving the military of wrongdoing in human rights cases were unconstitutional. A judge then ordered the arrests of 12 former military men and six civilians at the request of Judge Garzón. In 2002, former President Galtieri and 41 others were detained in connection with the disappearance of 20 *Montanaro* suspects during his presidency. Galtieri died in 2003.

President Néstor Kirchner (2003–07), accelerated investigations into, and arrests for, human rights abuses. At his urging, Congress repealed two of Alfonsín's amnesty laws that had blocked further prosecutions of military officers.

A federal judge ordered the arrests of 45 former officers. Forty of them had been charged by Garzón and Spain sought their extradition, but Kirchner insisted on bringing them to justice in Argentina The notorious Astiz was arrested. France sought his extradition for the murder of the two French nuns, but his indictment in Argentina in 2004 served notice that he would face an Argentine court. Eventually, an Argentine court convicted Artiz of various crimes in October 2011 and sentenced him to life imprisonment.

Kirchner then recalled the Argentine attaché to Italy, Horacio Losito, in connection with the massacre of 22 dissidents in Chacó in 1976. A retired brigadier general and two retired colonels were arrested as part of the investigation into torture centers operated in Buenos Aires during the Dirty War, including the Navy Mechanics School. Kirchner also ordered police files opened and an investigation into whether the army was still abusing prisoners three years after the return to democracy.

Scilingo, the navy captain who had voluntarily surrendered to Spanish authorities and had admitted participation in the "death flights," finally went on trial in Madrid in 2005. Scilingo abruptly recanted his confession, but the court found him guilty of 30 counts of murder and of torture and illegal detentions. He was sentenced to 640 years. In 2007, the Spanish Supreme Court increased the sentence to 1,084 years.

In 2005, the Argentine Supreme Court declared an amnesty granted to lower-level police officials unconstitutional, making possible the prosecutions of nearly 800 people.

Another Argentine officer Spain actually had behind bars was Ricardo Miguel Cavallo, a former lieutenant at the Navy Mechanics School, who was arrested in 2003. Spain extradited him to Argentina in 2008 and sentenced him to life in prison in October 2011.

Other ghosts pre-date the Dirty War. In 2007, former President Isabel Perón was arrested in her exile in Spain in connection with the disappearance of a Peronist activist during her presidency in 1976. She was released, but Argentina subsequently sought her extradition. In a court appearance in 2008, Perón, then 77, argued that she is immune from extradition because she has Spanish as well as Argentine citizenship; her attorneys also argued she is in poor health. Two weeks later, the Spanish court rejected the extradition request on the curious grounds that the allegations did not constitute an abuse of human rights.

In 2008, two retired generals, Antonio Bussi and Luciano Menendez, were sentenced to life imprisonment—both were in their 80s—for the kidnap-murder of Senator Guillermo Vargas on the day of the 1976 military coup. Both were unrepentant. Menendez already had been sentenced to life for the murder of four activists in 1977. He went on trial again in 2009 for illegal detentions, torture and homicide. But a key witness, a former detention camp guard, was found stabbed to death in his bathtub in Cordoba. Numerous other witnesses in human rights trials have died under mysterious circumstances. Nonetheless, Menendez was convicted and given another life sentence on in December 2010.

Two former navy pilots were arrested in in 2009 in connection with the "death flights." Captain Emir Sisul Hess was arrested in Bariloche for the deaths of 56 prisoners, while Lieutenant Julio Alberto Poch was arrested in Spain, accused of piloting flights from which 950 prisoners may have been thrown to their deaths. Poch was extradited to Argentina in 2010, but a judge dismissed the charges for lack of evidence. Still, he was indicted in 2011 and his trial is still ongoing.

The abuses of the Dirty War have inspired novels and motion pictures in Argentina and abroad. The illegal adoptions of babies of murdered dissidents were the focus of the acclaimed Argentine movie *La historia official (The Official Story)*, which won the U.S. Academy Award for Best Foreign Film in 1985. The infamous Navy Mechanics School inspired Lawrence Thornton's award-winning U.S. novel *Imagining Argentina*, which was made into a motion picture in 2003 starring Antonio Banderas and Emma Thompson. An Argentine novel, Eduardo Sacheri's *El secreto de sus ojos (The Secret in Their Eyes)*, was made into a movie by Argentine director Juan José Campanella in 2009 It, too, won the Oscar for Best Foreign Film (see Culture).

Estimates of the numbers of "disappeared" range from 9,000 to 30,000, although the official number is 13,000. Their families continue to seek answers and justice, and sometimes find them. In May 2012, CNN reported the story of Victoria Montenegro, who through DNA analysis was able to confirm that the human remains in an Uruguayan cemetery were those of her father, who disappeared in 1976 when she was a newborn. She was abducted and adopted by a military family. Montenegro, 36, learned when she was 24 that the couple who raised her were not her biological parents and began a search for her true identity. More such stories will inevitably surface, and the ghosts from the past will continue to haunt Argentina for years to come.

Argentina

although his actions and his rhetoric made Kirchner a pariah to the IMF, he became enormously popular with Argentines. He became the first president since Menem who could boast of an *improving* economy.

An acute energy shortage was blamed on frozen electricity rates that led to increased demand. The foreign-owned utility companies complained that inflation made the current rates unrealistic and prevented further investment, but Kirchner refused to raise rates on residential customers. Some local blackouts occurred. Energy shortages remain a nagging issue.

In 2004, an Argentine judge issued an arrest warrant for Menem, who was living in Chile with his Chilean wife and their baby, for allegedly embezzling $60 million from two prison construction projects. A Chilean judge rejected Argentina's extradition petition because Menem's failure to appear in court is not an extraditable offense. Two Argentine judges rescinded the warrant, and the flamboyant Menem triumphantly and with media fanfare returned to Argentina, vowing to unseat Kirchner in 2007.

Kirchner experienced the same kind of break with his mentor Duhalde that Duhalde had had earlier with his mentor Menem, as both grappled for control of the *Peronista* movement. The crucial test of their strength came in the 2005 mid-term congressional elections for a third of the 72 Senate seats and almost half the seats in the 257-member Chamber of Deputies.

The most symbolic showdown came in the Senate race in Buenos Aires Province, which pitted the two rivals' wives against each other. It turned into the political equivalent of a female mud-wrestling match. Cristina Fernández de Kirchner soundly defeated Hilda González de Duhalde, 46% to 20%. Kirchner's allies also won 15 of the 16 Senate seats, giving the Kirchner faction a majority. His faction also emerged as the largest in the Chamber of Deputies. Kirchner had finally received the electoral mandate Menem had denied him in 2003.

Emboldened, Kirchner announced a cabinet shakeup, stunning the country by removing Lavagna, who was largely credited for Argentina's near-miraculous economic recovery. Probably the most controversial new face was that of Defense Minister Nilda Garré, who had been involved with the leftist *Montanaro* guerrillas during the Dirty War.

In a dramatic development, Kirchner announced in December 2005 that Argentina was repaying its entire $9.8 billion debt to the IMF, using currency reserves that had accumulated during the economic recovery. The repayment saved Argentina 4.5% interest payments, further fattening the budget surplus for domestic programs

that had made Kirchner so popular. The announcement came two days after Brazilian President da Silva made a similar announcement—and almost four years to the day after the riots that precipitated de la Rua's resignation. Argentina had come a long way back from the brink of the abyss. However, Kirchner paid nothing toward a $6.7 billion debt owed to the so-called Paris Club of creditor countries, including the United States, Japan, Germany and Italy.

Congress granted Kirchner virtual *carte blanche* in 2006 to reallocate spending, causing concern in some circles over such a concentration of power. Kirchner also began re-nationalizing some companies, including the postal service, the Buenos Aires water system and an airline.

A Dynastic Power Play

The economy grew by 9.2% in 2006 and remained robust as the country prepared for the presidential election in October 2007. The man Menem had thought would collapse from his shaky 22% mandate in 2003 enjoyed a 70% approval rating, phenomenal for Latin America—or any democracy. He coyly insisted, as he had from the beginning, that he would not seek a second term, although few believed him.

Lavagna announced his candidacy, hoping voters would credit him with Argentina's economic miracle. He was endorsed by former presidents Alfonsín and Duhalde, for whatever that was worth. Elisa Carrió ran again; anti-corruption remained her theme. Former interim President Rodríguez Sáa also ran, as did 10 lesser candidates. Still, polls showed Kirchner unbeatable.

Then, the always enigmatic president did something every bit as Machiavellian as Menem had done in 2003: He announced he was yielding the Peronist presidential nomination to his wife, Cristina, 54. The apparent motive: If elected to a second term, he would have to yield power in 2011; if his wife could keep the presidential chair warm for four years, he could run again in 2011 and stretch their rule to 12 years—or longer. Political pundits immediately began comparing Senator Fernández de Kirchner to Senator Hillary Rodham Clinton in the United States. Because of her stylish manner, others compared her to Eva Perón. Indeed, Fernández herself publicly stated she identified with Evita.

This nepotistic power play would have offended voters in most countries, but it was indicative of Kirchner's popularity for taking Argentina from economic bust to boom and from chaos to confidence that Argentines enthusiastically rallied around his wife.

Although the Peronists were split between Fernández and Lavagna, the *UCR* had virtually ceased to exist as a viable political force, as some Radicals supported Carrió, others backed Lavagna, while one, Julio Cobos, the governor of Mendoza, became Fernández's running mate.

More than 19 million Argentines voted, a turnout of 74.14%. Fernández received 8.2 million votes, or 44.9%, to 4.2 million, or 23%, for Carrió. Because the difference was greater than 10 percentage points, Fernández was elected without a runoff. The once-popular Lavagna was a distant third with 3.1 million votes, or 16.9%.

Argentina's first elected woman president—and Latin America's fourth—was sworn in on December 10, 2007.

Any hope that relations with the U.S. would improve under Fernández were dashed when the U.S. Justice Department in Miami arrested and indicted two Venezuelan businessmen for allegedly funneling $800,000 in illegal campaign contributions to Fernández's campaign in a suitcase. The money reportedly originated with the state-owned Venezuelan oil company, *Petroven*. Fernández denounced the allegations as "garbage," but became reticent as evidence mounted. Two Venezuelans and an Uruguayan pleaded guilty in federal court in Miami in 2008 of failing to register as foreign agents. Another went on trial, while a fifth testified that another suitcase containing $4.2 million from the Venezuelan government made it through customs to Fernández's campaign. The Argentine media labeled the scandal "Suitcasegate."

Fernández found herself faced with a more serious challenge close to home in 2008 after she abruptly and drastically raised the export tariffs on agricultural products; the tax on soybeans alone was hiked from 27% to 44%. Farmers went on strike and blockaded roads leading into the capital, and grocery store shelves emptied. The beef-loving Argentine middle class resorted to the traditional form of protest, the *cacerolazo*, the pounding on pots and pans. Protests erupted throughout the country, including in the Plaza de Mayo, the first *cacerolazo* there since the economic meltdown of 2001. Fernández denounced the farmers' strike as "extortion."

After 21 days, the farmers voluntarily suspended their strike, apparently fearful the privation it created could backfire on their cause. The crisis forced the resignation of Fernández's economy minister. After talks with the government failed, the farmers announced another eight-day stoppage. The public generally sympathized with the farmers, and Fernández's approval rating plummeted to 20%.

The farmers took the tax to court, and the Supreme Court agreed to rule on the

Argentina

Former President Néstor Kirchner

President Cristina Fernández de Kirchner

Former President Alfonsín died on March 31, 2009, at the age of 82. The accolades from all political parties and the outpouring of public grief at his state funeral for the man who brought Argentina from dictatorship to democracy in 1983 was in sharp contrast to the denunciations and riots that forced him to leave office early in 1989.

In the latest of their Machiavellian power plays, the Kirchners pushed Congress to advance the date of the 2009 mid-term congressional elections, from October to June. The president's popularity was 30%, and the couple evidently feared it would sink even lower by October. In addition, the global recession caused the economy to slow dramatically after the boom years, and the Kirchner faction of the *Justicialista* Party feared voter reprisals.

Kirchner himself ran for the Chamber of Deputies to head his faction's ticket in Buenos Aires, putting his political future on the line. The anti-Kirchner faction nominated wealthy businessman Francisco de Narváez. The erstwhile president who had boasted a 70% approval rating, narrowly lost to de Narváez, although he was awarded a seat through proportional representation.

The pro-Kirchner faction lost its majority in both houses. Kirchner resigned as party president the next day. His Peronist faction won just 35 Senate seats to 37 for the opposition alliance. In the Chamber of Deputies, the Kirchners' Front for Victory won only 87 of the 257 seats. The resurgent *UCR* won 42, the anti-Kirchner Peronist faction (Federal Peronism) won 29 and the rest were fragmented among 31 other movements.

Instead of being humiliated, the Kirchners grew more combative. In August 2009, President Fernández introduced the controversial Audio-Visual Communication Bill, ostensibly designed to diversify the country's broadcast outlets. In reality, it seemed aimed directly at breaking up the powerful Grupo Clarín, a media conglomerate that owns the influential newspaper of the same name and controls two thirds of the country's cable television market. The newspaper has been one of the Kirchners' most nettlesome critics; probably not coincidentally, de Narváez is a member of its board of directors. "Freedom of expression cannot turn into freedom of extortion," she rationalized in a speech. Tax auditors raided the newspaper's offices, but found nothing incriminating.

The media bill mandated that the nation's radio and television outlets would be divided into thirds among the government, private companies and "nonprofit" organizations. In the lower house, the president won the support of enough independent deputies to ensure passage.

Opponents walked out in protest, and it passed 147–4. It passed the Senate 44–24. International journalism organizations denounced it as a Chávez-like measure to intimidate opposition media and to extend government control over mass communication. The law was set to go into effect in December 2012, but Grupo Clarín won an injunction that put the cable TV divestiture on hold. The Supreme Court ultimately upheld the law in late 2013.

By 2010, the once-plump budget surplus had become a yawning deficit. To alleviate it, Fernández ordered the Central Bank to transfer $6.6 billion in foreign reserves to a special fund for debt service. The bank's director protested that the Central Bank was independent of presidential mandates and that only Congress could authorize such a transfer. Fernández replaced him with a director who complied with her order, but then the opposition-controlled Congress stymied her.

Nonetheless, Congress granted her authorization to lift the ban her husband had imposed on debt restructuring and she began to try to mend fences with foreign—and domestic—holders of Argentine bonds. With the sour economy, she needed to make Argentine bonds attractive again by lowering their risk factor. Eventually, a compromise was effected.

Even as their popularity plummeted at home, the Kirchners enhanced their stature on the world stage. Fernández delivered the closing address at the 2009 Ibero-American Summit in Estoril, Portugal. In 2010, she attended President Barack Obama's Nuclear Security Summit in Washington, where she and Obama engaged in bilateral talks on non-proliferation and apparently came away in agreement. A month later,

constitutionality of the president's imposing a tax by decree instead of by statute. Apparently sensing she would lose, she introduced the legislation to Congress. It narrowly passed in the Chamber of Deputies and the Senate vote ended in a 36–36 tie. Vice President Cobos, the Radical whom Fernández had chosen in the interest of unity, cast the tie-breaking vote— *against* the bill. A furious Fernández retaliated by sacking six of Cobos' loyalists from their government posts.

Fernández turned her attention to the economy, which was impacted by the worldwide market slump in late 2008 and went into recession. In a dramatic reversal of her husband's policy, she announced she would repay the $6.7 billion owed to the Paris Club. This not only saved money on interest payments, but made Argentina eligible for new loans for infrastructure improvements at reduced interest rates. This in turn lessened Argentina's growing dependence on Venezuela, to which Argentina was paying a usurious 15% interest rate on bonds.

Fernández made another dramatic announcement in 2008: the re-nationalization of the unpopular private pension system, which amounted to $23 billion. Critics accused her of raiding the pension system to meet a budget deficit caused by the falling price of soybeans. The move negatively affected private investment.

In 2009, Fernández and the farmers seemed to reach an agreement to end their tax standoff, but when Congress failed to obtain a quorum to reduce the taxes, the farmers blockaded highways throughout the country. Vice President Cobos again broke with the president.

Argentina

Fernández took center stage at the Sixth EU-Latin American-Caribbean Summit in Madrid. She received Russian President Dmitry Medvedev on his first state visit to Argentina in 2010. She hosted the Ibero-American Summit in Mar del Plata in 2010, which she used as a forum to renew Argentina's claim to the Falklands.

In 2009, her foreign ministry issued a sharply worded protest to Iran when President Mahmoud Ahmadinejad appointed as defense minister Ahmad Vahidi, whom Argentina believes masterminded the 1994 terrorist bombing of the Israeli-Argentina Mutual Association in Buenos Aires that killed 87 people. This issue is another that distanced Fernández from her one-time ally and benefactor, Chávez, who enjoyed close ties with Iran. In 2013, Argentina and Iran agreed to a special commission to investigate the bombing.

In May 2010, Kirchner was elected the first secretary-general of the six-year-old South American Union of Nations *(UNASUR)*. Until the organization set up its permanent headquarters in Quito, Ecuador, it was seated in Buenos Aires. Kirchner's acceptance of the *USASUR* post seemed peculiar, as he had publicly indicated he intended to stand for president again in 2011.

Widowhood and Re-Election

Whatever the Kirchners' plans were in domestic politics and on the international stage came to a sudden end on October 27, 2010, when Kirchner suffered a fatal heart attack at his home in Santa Cruz. He was only 60. He had undergone two procedures to clear arterial blockages that year, but had ignored his doctors' warnings to follow a less hectic schedule. The country and its president were plunged into mourning, and even the Kirchners' opponents were gracious in their accolades. A month later, a tearful Fernández addressed the nation, thanked Argentines for their support and insisted she would continue shouldering her responsibilities.

Until Kirchner's death, polls had shown his wife's approval rating as low as 23%, and an opposition victory in 2011 appeared probable. But suddenly public sympathy for a grieving widow accelerated her standing in the polls. She also was aided by an economic growth rate of 9% in 2010, spurred by the soybean bonanza, and it was running about the same in 2011, making her an even more difficult target. A third factor in her favor was a disunited opposition.

Ten candidates appeared on the ballot in the first-ever open presidential primary on August 14, 2011. Both the Peronists and the opposition were fragmented, with former President Duhalde serving as standard-bearer for the anti-Kirchner Peronists while Raúl Alfonsín, son and namesake of the late former president, was the most prominent of several candidates for the *UCR* and other non-Peronist parties. To appear on the October 23 presidential ballot, a candidate had to poll at least 1.5% in the primary.

The turnout in the primary was 21.4 million, a remarkable turnout for a primary of 81.4%. Fernández's Front for Victory *(FPV)* received a bare but absolute majority, 50.2%. Alfonsín and Duhalde were virtually tied for a distant second, with 12.2% each, while a Socialist, Hermes Binner, received 10.2%. Three other candidates made the cut for the October ballot: Carrió, former President Rodríguez Saá and Jorge Altamira of the Workers Left Front. But the Fernández juggernaut was a political reality.

Fernández had dumped the disloyal Cobos from her ticket and replaced him with Economy Minister Amado Boudou—a choice she came to regret. Her real running mate, however, was her dead husband. She was still dressed in black at campaign appearances and invoked his memory constantly, in effect transforming him into a political saint.

The strategy worked. On October 23, the turnout was just a few thousand more than it had been in the primary. The results:

Fernández	11,864,456	54.1%
Binner	3,684,595	16.8%
Alfonsín	2,442,880	11.1%
Rodríguez Saá	1,745,303	8.0%
Duhalde	1,285,783	5.9%
Altamira	503,342	2.3%
Carrió	399,641	1.8%

In the congressional balloting, her *FPV* faction increased its majority in the Senate and once again emerged as the largest bloc in the lower house.

Within two weeks of her victory, Fernández made two bold but practical economic decisions that would have been imprudent before voters cast their ballots. She eased subsidies that had kept the cost of such essentials as utilities and transportation artificially low for years but which were becoming an economic liability, and by executive order she required justification for Argentines to exchange pesos for foreign currency at money exchange firms.

By the time Fernández was inaugurated for her second term on December 10, 2011, the economy was showing definite signs of a slowdown, and the budget surplus turned into a deficit. Coupled with this was increasing evidence that her government had been falsifying the official inflation figures through statistical gimmickry for four years. At year's end, the government insisted it was 9.7%, while private economists put the figure closer to 25%. The president's response was to threaten to prosecute economists who published unofficial inflation figures, which raised serious questions about freedom of expression.

By executive decree, she essentially stripped the Central Bank of its remaining autonomy and tapped its resources.

In an even more controversial move in May 2012, she ordered the renationalization of the oil company YPF, which Memem had privatized in 1994, by targeting the 51% ownership in YPF that the Spanish company Repsol had purchased in 1999. Fernández claimed that too much of *YPF's* profits were going to Spain and not being reinvested in exploration. Argentina had become a net importer of petroleum, eliminating one of the country's traditional sources of foreign exchange. Spain reacted angrily to the takeover, and threatened to scuttle the long-going talks between the EU and *Mercosur* for a free-trade agreement unless Argentina were excluded.

Even before the *YPF* takeover, Fernández resorted to a time-tested technique for diverting the public's attention from the worsening economy: She raised the level of rhetoric with Britain over the Falkland Islands as the 30th anniversary of the 1982 war approached. She had been raising the issue at international summits, and she had persuaded her three *Mercosur* partners not to permit the 30-odd vessels flying the Falklands flag from docking in their ports. When the news broke in 2012 that Prince William, a Royal Air Force helicopter pilot, would serve a tour of duty in the Falklands, Fernández denounced "this militarization of the South Atlantic." In reality, an enlarged British garrison of 1,700 had defended the islands since the war. She hinted she would deny permission for commercial flights to the islands from Chile to pass through Argentine airspace. The industry minister urged Argentine companies to boycott British imports.

British Prime Minister David Cameron rejected Argentina's renewed claims to the islands, saying he would agree to it only of the islanders approved it in a referendum—knowing they would not. In effect, he accused Fernández of advocating reverse colonialism, which did not play well in Argentina. Protesters burned Union Jacks outside the British Embassy in Buenos Aires. (The climate did not improve after an editorial on the website of the Falklands newspaper *Penguin News* referred to Fernández as a "bitch.") In unusually inflammatory language against another head of government, she said Cameron's remarks were "mediocre and almost stupid." She raised the issue again at the Summit of the Americas in Cartagena, Colombia, in April 2012, where she discussed the matter directly with President Obama. Secretary of State Hillary Clinton suggested bilateral talks, seen as a U.S. withdrawal from its unqualified support for Britain on the Falklands issue.

The embattled president encountered a new headache in 2012 when a federal prosecutor announced that Vice President Boudou, 48, was under investigation for influence peddling, specifically that he benefited from a $55 million contract to the Ciccione Co. for printing the country's currency. In May, the prosecutor broadened the investigation to allegations of illegal enrichment while he was economy minister. Boudou denied the allegations, and the government appeared to be using judicial roadblocks to stymie the inquiry. In 2013, the prosecutor dropped the investigation for lack of evidence.

Fernández's long-running battle to break up Grupo Clarín (but not media conglomerates that support her) came to a head in December 2012 as the government was about to carry out the forced divestiture of Clarín's cable TV channels. They were to be parceled up among the state and private concerns—owned, of course, by her allies. But Clarín fought back and won an injunction against the divestiture; an appeals court quickly threw out the injunction. Clarín appealed to the Supreme Court, which dealt the president a setback by reinstating the injunction. But in October 2013, the Supreme Court upheld the new media law, which was a major victory for her.

Congress approved a controversial presidential initiative in 2013, one seen as increasing her influence over the judiciary. It increased the membership of the Council of Magistrates, which appoints judges, from 13 to 19. Twelve will be elected, six will be members of Congress and one will represent the executive branch. Fernández no doubt expects to appoint her loyalists to those six seats.

Fernández consequently has faced mounting unrest from her own people, both because of the souring economy and her often heavy-handed measures, such as unleashing the national tax agency to harass her critics—but not her friends. The audits have seldom turned up anything incriminating. In September 2012, tens of thousands of middle-class protesters took to the streets banging pots and pans, the traditional *cacerolazo.* In December, violent protests and looting erupted, reminiscent of December 2001, which left two people dead.

Some unions, part of the Peronists' core constituency, have turned against her, and transit, banking and hospital workers went on strike. Other Peronist insiders resent Fernández's son, Máximo Kirchner, leader of a left-wing Peronist movement, whom critics see as wielding a Rasputin-like influence over his mother.

An Argentine Pope

Virtually all Argentines, whether Catholic, non-Catholic or not even religious, were electrified on March 16, 2013, when Cardinal Jorge Mario Bergoglio, the former archbishop of Buenos Aires, was elected the first pope from the New World and the first Jesuit. Almost immediately, however, the new Pope Francis came under a cloud when critics raised old allegations, first raised in investigative journalist Horacio Verbitsky's 2005 book *The Silence,* that he had turned a blind eye and deaf ear to the human rights abuses of the Dirty War. His conservative positions as archbishop also had brought him into headlong conflict with Fernández.

Francis' defenders countered, with documented evidence and witnesses, that he had quietly provided sanctuary to a number of dissidents, and noted that despite his social conservatism on such issues as abortion and same-sex marriage, he had always been an advocate for the poor and had lived in a humble apartment instead of the archbishop's opulent residence. He also rode public transport to work. He has continued that ascetic lifestyle as pope.

Shortly after Bergoglio was elected pope, Fernández flew to the Vatican and had lunch with her old nemesis. Their past hostility was not in evidence; he even gave her a kiss. They also found common cause on one issue: Argentina's claims to the Falklands, although as pope he is unlikely to put pressure on Britain.

Recent Developments

In March 2013, the Falkland Islanders returned to the polls in the latest referendum on their status and voted to remain under the British Crown—by 1,513 votes to four! Fernández denounced the vote as a "parody." Fernández alleged in April 2014 the Falklands were a secret NATO nuclear base, a charge Cameron brushed off as "wholly false."

One of the controversial economic decisions taken by the Kirchner and Fernández administrations finally boomeranged—the take-it-or-leave-it debt swaps of 2005 and 2010. A group of U.S. hedge funds, which held more than $1 billion worth of Argentine bonds and had refused the deal to receive 35% of the value of the bonds or nothing, sued Argentina in federal court in New York. The judge ordered Argentina to pay $1.33 billion in restitution.

As a semi-comical consequence, the Argentine navy's three-masted frigate, Libertad, used to train cadets, was seized on October 1 when it docked in Ghana, which acted on a legal international injunction brought by one of the creditor hedge funds, Elliot Management. Elliot threatened to sell the ship as partial payment for what Argentina owes. Fernández denounced Elliot as a "vulture."

Argentina appealed the judgment to the 2nd U.S. Circuit Court of Appeals, arguing the ship has diplomatic immunity. In August 2013, the court ruled in favor of Elliot, and Argentina appealed to the U.S. Supreme Court. On June 16, 2014, in an 8-1 vote, the Supreme Court refused to review Argentina's appeal. In a separate case, the court ruled that Argentina's creditors were legally entitled to seek restitution anywhere in the world, a ruling that the U.S. State Department had warned could ricochet on the United States.

After the Supreme Court refused to hear Argentina's appeal, the trial judge gave Argentina until June 30 to pay $1.65 billion to the hedge funds or be in default. But under U.S. law, Argentina cannot pay its debts to one group of creditors without paying them all, which would total about $15 billion, roughly half of Argentina's foreign reserves. Negotiations with Elliott and the other creditor plaintiffs broke down on June 19, and Argentina stubbornly refused to pay as the deadline lapsed. It took out ads in *The New York Times* and the *Financial Times* assailing the hedge funds, and it threatened to "charge" the judge before the International Court of Justice in The Hague.

Argentina had a 30-day grace period before officially undergoing its second default in 13 years, and when this book went to press it had agreed to send a negotiating team to New York on July 7. Meanwhile, world financial markets were nervously watching the developments. Even if Argentina settles and pays up, that would likely open the door for more lawsuits by creditors who caved in and accepted Kirchner's 35% offer.

Fernández's notorious practice of falsifying inflation also finally backfired. On February 1, 2013, the IMF censured Argentina for this violation of IMF rules and gave it until September 29 to comply or be barred from borrowing money; outright expulsion was a possibility. Fernández grudgingly complied, even as she continued to deny cooking the books. Meanwhile, the unofficial value of the peso against the dollar plummeted, fueling inflation even more. Independent economists are still skeptical of the somewhat more realistic inflation figures, estimated at 20.8% in 2013.

Her and her husband's refusal to increase subsidized electric rates for 11 years or to invest in new equipment or energy sources led to more and more serious blackouts. Faced with reality, Fernández announced an inevitable and painful rate increase of 72%.

In May 2013, Fernández sought to avoid a peso devaluation by offering a three-

Argentina

month amnesty to Argentines who had been converting pesos to foreign currencies and stashing them abroad—or in their mattresses. By April 2013, the peso had slid to 8.75 to the dollar, about 42% below the government's make-believe exchange rate. She offered tax-free bonds in return, a sucker's deal if there ever was one.

In another desperate attempt to shore up her sagging popularity, which had dropped 30 percentage points in 15 months, she agreed to a 24% wage increase to 2 million members of labor unions that were still loyal to her. Such an increase, of course, is proving as inflationary as the peso devaluation she is trying to avoid. In January 2013, she also had declared a 15.8% increase in public pension payments, the Argentine equivalent of Social Security. Instead of boosting her popularity, the increase was ridiculed by pensioners who complained that it didn't come close to keeping up with the actual inflation rate.

A year after it strained relations with Spain by renationalizing *YPF*, Argentina, strapped for capital to explore the vast Vaca Muerta shale oil field, was forced to swallow its nationalist pride and sign a $1.24 billion deal with the *U.S.* oil firm, Chevron.

Argentines went to the polls in August 2013 for the peculiar primary elections, which are designed to winnow out small, frivolous parties in advance of a general election, in this case the mid-term congressional elections. Both were seen as a bellwether of the president's popularity, which by October was 26%, the third-lowest in Latin America. In the primary, her *FPV* faction was the only one well organized enough to run a national slate, and so it finished first with 26% of the vote, a dramatic drop from her winning majority in 2011; it lost in Buenos Aires and in 14 other provinces, including her home province of Santa Cruz. Especially galling for her was the victory in Buenos Aires of a *FPV* defector, Sergio Massa, the mayor of Tigre and her former cabinet chief, who bested the *FPV* candidate by five points.

The day after the primary, unbeknownst to the public, Fernández suffered a head injury in a fall and was secretly hospitalized. Supporters and opponents alike were puzzled why she didn't take to the campaign trail in support of her faction's candidates. It wasn't until October 8, when she underwent emergency surgery to relieve bleeding from a hematoma inside her skull, that the public was made aware of her condition.

Perhaps the absence of the increasingly unpopular president actually benefited the *FPV*. In the October 27 congressional elections, the *FPV* claimed a muted victory by winning essentially the same number of

seats it already had, retaining its bare majority in both houses; it could have fared much worse. It won only 33% of the vote. It lost in the five largest provinces and Santa Cruz, plus six other provinces. In Buenos Aires, Massa's Renewal Front trounced the *FPV* 44% to 32%. Massa now heads a 16-member delegation in the Chamber of Deputies, and his victory automatically makes him a leading contender to succeed Fernández in 2015 (see The Future).

Civil unrest broke out again in December 2013, this time in Córdoba, an opposition-controlled province. When police went on strike for higher wages (supposedly because bribe money dried up from a crackdown on prostitution), looting ensued. Shop owners used violence to combat violence. The provincial governor called on federal authorities to restore order, and faulted the president for what he called a deliberately delayed response. Fernández blamed the governor for mismanaging the police. Police then went on strike in 15 more provinces, leading to more looting. In the unrest, 10 people died and 130 were injured.

At about the same time, Fernández disappeared again from public view for more than a month, fueling more speculation about her health. She finally made a public appearance in late January 2014, with no explanation for the lengthy disappearance. Concerns linger about her fitness to govern.

After six years of stalemate between *Mercosur* and the EU over a free-trade agreement, the two sides suddenly showed willingness to compromise in late 2013. But then Fernández refused to go along with *Mercosur's* concessions, saying they would threaten Argentine industry. Spain, meanwhile, remains miffed over Argentina's nationalization of Repsol's share in *YPF*. Fernández's Brazilian counterpart, Dilma Rousseff, is threatening to conclude a bilateral FTA with the EU if Fernández remains intransigent.

CULTURE: The 16th century Spanish conquerors transplanted their language, religion and architecture to the lands along the Río Plata and Paraná River. The colonial-era Jesuit ruins of San Ignacio Mini, Santa Ana, Nuestra Señora de Loreto and Santa María Mayor are UNESCO World Heritage Sites, as are the Jesuit Block and Estancias of Córdoba.

Unlike most of the South American colonies, Argentina did not develop a *mestizo* race (European-Indian) because the indigenous inhabitants were driven ever westward beyond the expanding frontier or were exterminated outright. This genocidal military policy extended into the late 19th century. While the United States and neighboring Brazil imported African

slaves, what was to become the laboring class in Argentina stemmed from a wave of European immigrants, chiefly from Spain and Italy, who were attracted during the 19th century by work on the cattle ranches and in the wheat fields, vineyards and emerging industries.

Consequently, Argentina's ethnic make-up today is almost wholly European, with Italian descendants accounting for nearly half the population. This also has given Argentine Spanish a distinctly Italian inflection, an unmistakable accent that is the butt of jokes in other Latin American countries. Lesser influxes of British and German settlers, many of them well-to-do investors, also have colored Argentina's social fabric, as have Jews, Arabs and Gypsies.

Which is not to say that Argentina lacks a rich cultural heritage of its own. As occurred in the United States, the romanticism associated with the conquest of the frontier and the development of vast stretches of rich farming and grazing lands of the *Pampas* gave rise to a uniquely Argentine folk hero: the *gaucho*, or cowboy. As with the North American cowboy, it is difficult to separate myth from reality, but unquestionably the raw-boned *gauchos* with their baggy cotton pants, sheepskin chaps and *bolas*, (the device used to ensnare the legs of running calves) greatly shaped Argentine culture and folklore. Their drum-based music, *malambo*, is as identifiable with Argentine culture as the tango.

One of the great works of the so-called golden age of Argentine literature of the late 19th and early 20th centuries was the epic poem *El gaucho Martín Fierro*, written by José Hernández in two installments in 1872 and 1879. Martín Fierro occupies much the same place in Argentine folklore as do Paul Bunyan or Pecos Bill in the United States. It is not uncommon to see truck stops in northern Argentina today named for this folk hero. The legacy of the *gauchos* also is exploited today for tourist purposes in such Buenos Aires steakhouses as *La Estancia*, where waiters dress in traditional *gaucho* garb and *malambo* groups provide live music.

The wealth of the *estancias*, or ranches, also shaped Argentines' meat-based diets. The most popular eating places in Argentina, except perhaps for the ubiquitous pasta bars, are *parrilladas*, which specialize in assorted meats grilled over wood embers; often an entire goat is staked out on a metal frame and roasted in front of a *fogón*, or bonfire. The most common social gathering is the *asado*, a barbecue on a massive scale in which sometimes dozens of guests consume a variety of meats and wash them down with copious amounts of domestic wine, which can be excellent.

The relative enlightenment that followed the Rosas dictatorship in the mid-19th century allowed a rich literary tradition to take root. Two of the greatest writers of this period also were leaders in the struggle for democracy. Bartolomé Mitre served as president of the republic during the pivotal period of 1862–68, and two years after leaving the presidency he founded the daily newspaper *La Nación,* still published by his descendants today and regarded as one of the world's great newspapers.

Domingo Faustino Sarmiento was forced into exile during the Rosas era and nettled the dictatorship from neighboring Chile, where he edited *El Mercurio,* then based in Valparaiso. Sarmiento's writings proved inspirational not only for Argentines but for other Latin Americans saddled with dictatorship, and he is revered as one of the premier figures of Latin American letters. He succeeded Mitre in the presidency, serving from 1868–74.

Another great newspaper of record, *La Prensa,* was established in 1869; it served as a conduit for the poems, stories and essays of the great writers of the golden age. Both it and *La Nación* also developed a reputation for resisting the will of dictators; *La Prensa,* published by several generations of the Gainza and Paz families, was closed by Perón from 1951–55.

This tradition continued into the 20th century, when *La Nación* made space available for the verse of a blind man acknowledged as Argentina's greatest poet: Jorge Luis Borges (1899–1986). His reputation was global, although the Nobel Prize eluded him all his life. Like many of Latin America's great writers, artists and musicians, he spent much of his career in Europe, in part because of Argentina's periodic reversions to dictatorship and the chilling effect that invariably had on the arts. He received Spain's Miguel de Cervantes Prize in 1979 and died in Switzerland in 1986.

Other notable 20th century Argentine writers include Julio Cortázar (1914–84), a novelist, playwright and poet, perhaps best remembered for the plays *Los reyes* (1949) and *Bestiario* (1951) and the novels *Los premios* (1960), *Rayuela* (1963), *62/Modelo para armar* (1968), and *Libro de Manuel* (1973); and Ernesto Sábato (1911–2011), a renowned essayist and author of three memorable novels: *El túnel* (1948), *Sobre héroes y tumbas* (1961), and *Abbadón el exterminador* (1974).

Both Cortázar and Sábato achieved recognition throughout the Spanish-speaking— and reading—world, and their works have been translated into numerous other languages. Sábato received the Cervantes Prize for 1984.

Manuel Puig (1932–90), wrote a tale of two political prisoners sharing a cell that was adapted to the stage and the screen: *El beso de la mujer araña* ("The Kiss of the Spi-

Carlos Gardel

der Woman.") Another Argentine writer, Adolfo Pérez Esquivel, received the Nobel Peace Prize in 1980 for his courageous opposition to military rule.

Two other Argentines have received the Cervantes Prize: Adolfo Bioy Casares (1914–99) in 1990 and the poet Juan Gelman (b. 1930) in 2007. Bioy, a friend and collaborator of Borges, was a novelist and journalist best remembered for the 1940 science fiction novel, *La invención de Morel (The Invention of Morel).*

In music, Argentina has produced its share of classical composers, the most renowned being Alberto Ginastera (1916–83). Argentina also has partial claim to Carlos Kleiber (1930–2004), one of the world's most eminent 20th century composers. His father, Erich Kleiber, also a noted composer, emigrated from Austria to Argentina in 1935 to escape the Nazis. Carlos Kleiber divided his career between Argentina and Europe, where he died and is buried.

A contemporary classical composer of international renown, if sometimes controversial, is Osvaldo Golijov (b. 1960), who was born in La Plata of Jewish-Russian-Romanian ancestry. He won two U.S. Grammy Awards in 2007 for his operatic composition *Aindamar: Fountain of Tears:* Best Opera Recording and Best Classical Contemporary Composition. He was nominated for a Grammy in 2002 for *Yiddishbbuk.*

But when one thinks of Argentine music, one thinks of the tango. The dance and music that has become synonymous with Argentina emerged as an erotic art form

in the sleazy nightclubs and brothels of La Boca, the port district of Buenos Aires. Its contagious rhythm and sexual innuendo won it ready acceptance in the *avant-garde* circles of Paris during the 1920s, and from the Left Bank its popularity spread throughout the bistros and cabarets of Europe and the Prohibition-era U.S. nightclubs and speak-easies.

Ironically, the tango composer and singer who came to be most identified with the genre was an immigrant from France at age 3: Carlos Gardel (1890–1935). Killed in a plane crash in Colombia at age 45, Gardel even today is the center of an Elvis-like cult following in Argentina. Posters of the forever-young Gardel, his slick black hair parted in the middle, or wearing a fedora, are a ubiquitous symbol of the nation's cultural identity.

Eventually, through the talents of the internationally renowned composer Astor Piazzolla (1921–92), the tango emerged into a classical form acceptable in polite society. One literally cannot escape the sounds of the tango in Argentine restaurants, so ingrained is it in the life of the nation. Two U.S.-made movies, *Scent of a Woman* and *Evita,* have revived interest in the tango abroad. The tango performed in *Scent of a Woman* was *Por una cabeza,* written by Gardel and Alfredo Le Pera shortly before they perished together in Colombia.

In contemporary popular music, Argentina's Mercedes Sosa (1935–2009) was known as "The Voice of Latin America." A folksinger who used the sobriquet *La Negra* (the Black One), she performed with Joan Baez, among other luminaries, and was a goodwill ambassador for Argentina. She received Latin Grammys for Best Folk Album for *Misa criolla* (2000), *Acústico* (2003) and *Corazón libre* (2006). Her song *Balderrama* was in the score of the 2008 U.S. movie *Ché,* starring Benicio del Toro. Her final album, *Cantora 1,* posthumously won the Latin Grammy for Best Folk Album and Best Recording Package; it was also nominated for Album of the Year.

Argentina collected 47 Latin Grammy Awards in the United States between 2001 and 2011.

Argentine cinema, established in the 1930s, enjoyed something of a boom during the first Perón era, but lapsed into mediocrity during subsequent military regimes, particularly that of 1976–83, when political repression and artistic censorship forced many leading actors and directors into exile. Since 1983 it has enjoyed a renaissance and has won some international accolades.

Luis Puenzo's *La historia oficial, (The Official Story),* the account of a middle-aged housewife who comes to realize that her adopted daughter was taken from two slain dissidents during the "Dirty War,"

Argentina

became the first Argentine film to win the U.S. Academy Award for Best Foreign Film in 1985 and a Golden Globe in 1986. Norma Aleandro won Best Actress in the Cannes Film Festival and the New York Film Critics Award.

Argentina's second Oscar came in 2010 for Juan José Campanella's *El secreto de sus ojos (The Secret in Their Eyes)*, which also won Spain's Goya Award for Best Spanish Language Foreign Film for 2009. Based on a novel by Eduardo Sacheri, it involves a detective in 1999 who tries to solve the rape and murder of a dissident in 1974. In Argentina, it became the second-greatest box office success since Leonardo Favio's *Nazareno Cruz y el lobo (Nazareno Cruz and the Wolf)* in 1975.

Another noted director was María Luisa Bemberg (1946–94), whose films that achieved acclaim abroad included *Miss Mary*, with Julie Christie, a story set in the 1930s, which Bemberg both wrote and directed; and *Camila*, the true story of a girl and her lover priest who were executed for their forbidden love during the Rosas regime in the 1840s. It was nominated for the Best Foreign Film Oscar in 1984.

The other Argentine films to be nominated for Best Foreign Film were Sergio Renán's *La tregua (The Truce)* in 1974, the Spaniard Carlos Saura's *Tango, no me dejas nunca (Tango)* in 1998 and Campanella's *El hijo de la novia (Son of the Bride)* in 2001.

Thirteen Argentine films have won Spain's Goya Award for Best Spanish Language Foreign Film since its inception in 1986.

Radio in Argentina enjoyed a golden age in the 1920s and '30s, just as it had in the United States, the exception being that tango enjoyed equal billing with that of the Big Band sounds. Soap operas were popular, and provided the boost to stardom of an ambitious young actress named Eva Duarte—later Eva Perón.

Television began as a state venture and wallowed in mediocrity for decades for much the same reason as did the cinema: the flight of talent from the censorship of military regimes. The result was a dependence on dubbed imported programs, mostly from the United States. Today's less-encumbered Argentine television has seen a boom in locally produced programs, many of them the ever-popular *telenovelas*, which often are exported.

Argentine journalism remains highly developed, but also highly politicized. There are about 40 dailies in the country, divided fairly evenly between the capital and the provinces. A growing number are online only.

The venerable *La Prensa* and *La Nación* remain the country's most prestigious dailies, if not the most widely read. The circulation leader is *Crónica* (founded 1963),

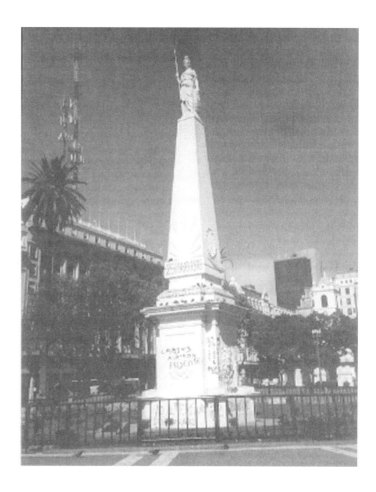

a working class tabloid that specializes in sports, followed by *Clarín* (1945), which now controls the media conglomerate Grupo Clarín, a nettlesome critic of the late President Néstor Kirchner and his wife and successor, Cristina Fernández. The company was the target of a new media law in 2009 designed to "diversify" mass communication by divesting Grupo Clarín of its cable television channels. The company won an injunction against the government in late 2012, but in October 2013 the Supreme Court upheld the breakup (see History). In part because of the government pressure on Grupo Clarín, New York-based Freedom House rates the Argentine press as only "partly free."

A younger paper that has become increasingly influential as the voice of the left is *Página/12* (1987), which was co-founded by the noted author and investigative journalist Horacio Verbitsky, who was once a *Montanaro* guerrilla. He remains a contributor and columnist, and although he was a critic of President Carlos Menem, he has avidly supported Kirchner and Fernández. Verbitsky also has contributed to *The Daily Beast* in the U.S. Verbitsky has achieved international notoriety for his books on the Dirty War, including *Flight*, about the infamous death flights, and *The*

Silence, published in 2005, which accused then-Archbishop Jorge Mario Bergoglio, now Pope Francis, of indifference at best and complicity at worst regarding the military regime's human rights abuses.

ECONOMY: Argentina is well-endowed with some of the richest farmland in the world and as a result, the economy has traditionally been based on agriculture, primarily cattle, wheat and wine. A favorable balance of trade led to industrialization as well, and at the turn of the 20th century, Argentina was one of the four wealthiest nations in the world.

After World War II, the economy was plagued by the fiscal policies of the first Perón administration. When he took office in 1946, reserves stood at a respectable $1.5 billion. By 1955 that surplus had vanished and the nation was deeply in the red. Every government since then has added to the debt. Agriculture was penalized in order to promote industrialization. Food prices were held artificially low and taxes were placed on farm exports in order to finance the construction of factories.

The government role in the economy also expanded. The state controlled more than half of all heavy industry—most of which has been inefficient, overstaffed and unprofitable. Because of a lack of capital investment in newer techniques, it became the equivalent of the "rust belt" industry of the northeast United States, which has been undergoing replacement by facilities erected in the southern United States because of onerous taxes, wages and workers' benefits in the North.

Argentina for more than half a century enjoyed the most evenly distributed and largest per capita income in Latin America. Much of this wealth, however, was eroded by runaway inflation, particularly during the 1980s. Perón taught the nation to live beyond its means, printing more and more pesos, establishing a precedent which was repeated over and over.

Once the *Peronistas* returned to power in 1973, the economy was harassed by widespread strikes, a shortage of consumer goods and high job absenteeism. Even more damaging was the disastrous drop in farm exports, which usually had counted for 70% of the nation's foreign earnings. Although poor weather was a contributing factor, most farm problems stemmed from government policies that maintained low food prices for the people of Buenos Aires and the cities, where 80% of the nation lives. Beef exports dropped to their lowest level of the century when the European Common Market reduced Argentine meat imports. At the same time, beef consumption rose because of lowered prices. By 1975 Argentines consumed 220 pounds of beef per person annually, twice the U.S. figure.

Industrial output fell, partially due to a shortage of parts, frequent strikes and low capital reinvestment. The nation's once-mighty auto industry also broke down, with eight foreign-owned assembly plants losing $160 million on their Argentine operations in 1975. During that period, the growth in the nation's gross national product dropped to zero. It went as low as –9% in the late 1980s.

The military rulers in power from 1976–83 sought to return Argentina to a free-market system—a dramatic about-face from the state planning that had dominated the economy since Perón first took office. The impact of the changes was limited—partly because 60% of the economy was under government control or ownership.

The worst depression, coupled with hyper-inflation, corruption, overspending, a bulging bureaucracy in Buenos Aires and the provinces, and the excessive demands of labor unions, all took the starch out of the economy during the presidency of Raúl Alfonsín, of the Radical Civil Union (1983–89). One observer noted, "In the U.S. and Europe, things are either automatic or predictable. Here, nothing is automatic or predictable." Riots forced Alfonsín to relinquish power to his successor several months early.

Under Peronist President Carlos Menem (1989–99), things at last began changing (although a bitter pill for many). In 1992, he announced he was pegging the peso to the U.S. dollar, one-to-one. The effect was almost immediate. Inflation dropped from 40% per month to less than 10% per year, which enabled Argentina at last to engage in intelligent financial planning. It also attracted foreign investment in quantities necessary for renewed growth. Menem also abandoned protectionism and embraced free-market economics, which for a Peronist was heretical. But there was no questioning its success.

Capital that used to migrate abroad began staying within Argentina, and funds began returning there from overseas. The return on investment was attractive in the 1990s, and Argentina imposed fewer and fewer restrictions on withdrawal of profits by investors, in stark contrast to much of the rest of Latin America.

The devaluation of the Mexican peso in 1994 presented a major threat to Argentine economic stability since it, just as Mexico, had been presumed to be a place for safe investment. Menem responded energetically to preserve Argentina's reputation, and did so successfully. He almost immediately instituted an austerity program to reduce imports and wages, two unpopular moves which had to be made just before the May 1995 elections. The program enabled Argentina's banking system to defend its currency.

By 1998, Argentina had successfully overcome the effects of the 1994–95 Mexican peso crisis, only to begin feeling the effects of the crisis in the Asian markets. Growth was still in the neighborhood of 8%, and though unemployment was down it was still an uncomfortable 13%. Inflation for 1998 was a mere 1%. Overall, these were the best economic times Argentina had seen in decades. But it was not to last.

Foreseeing a coming slump, the IMF approved a three-year, $2.8 billion loan for Argentina in February 1998. Nonetheless, the country slid into recession. Meanwhile, in a surprise move apparently aimed at shoring up his traditional support among the once-powerful labor unions, Menem swung the pendulum back from his policy of appeasing the needs of big business by proposing new labor regulations that essentially left in place the *Peronistas*' liberal severance benefits

Year-end figures for 1999 graphically demonstrated the severity of the recession incoming Radical President Fernando de la Rua had inherited from Menem. Real GDP declined by 3.5%, and unemployment was 14.5%. About the only good news was that inflation *declined* by 2%. De la Rua's painful austerity measures and the labor reform bill were needed to obtain funds from the

IMF, but experts warned that it could be some time before the benefits were felt. Those experts proved correct. De la Rua made an ill-advised prediction that Argentina would end 2000 with positive growth of 3.5% to 4%, a prediction that returned to haunt him. The economy *shrank* another 0.5%. Unemployment was still a troubling 14.7% and it grew steadily worse.

De la Rua publicly called for *Mercosur* to emulate the European Union by adopting a common currency for the trade bloc. He predicted monetary union could be in place within three years, but financial experts said it could take 10. De la Rua also was an advocate of the Free Trade Area of the Americas (FTAA).

In late 2001, the recession deepened as unemployment grew to 18.3% and de la Rua sought desperately to meet the deficit-reduction goals he had set to ensure continued IMF support so Argentina could avoid default on its $132 billion foreign debt. When he imposed strict limits of $1,000 a month on savings withdrawals, angry Argentines took to the streets. The demonstrations erupted in violence that left 27 people dead and forced de la Rua to resign (see Descent into Chaos).

The new interim president, Eduardo Duhalde, pushed an emergency economic reform package through Congress, after which he revoked Menem's 10-year-old dollar-parity plan.

The crisis had plunged more and more Argentines into poverty. A 2000 study by the Social Development Ministry had reported that 37% of Argentines lived below the poverty line of $200 a month. By 2002, that figure was a staggering 57%, and in mid-2003 it had increased to 58.5%; 28% were classified as living in extreme poverty, double the percentage from before the meltdown. Bartering became commonplace, as did eking a living by scavenging from garbage dumps.

GDP growth was down 1% in 2001 and a near-cataclysmic 13.6% in 2002 before it finally bottomed out. Unemployment abated to 18%, and the peso rebounded from 4.0 to about 2.8 to the dollar.

Néstor Kirchner, who took office on May 25, 2003, still had an economic nightmare to deal with. He rejected Menem's free-market approach and returned to the populism of Juan Perón. He also joined forces with Brazil's new center-left president, Luiz Inácio da Silva, in calling for a revival of the *Mercosur* trade bloc.

Kirchner's hard-ball tactics in negotiating with the IMF bore fruit with an agreement reached in 2004, but Kirchner later canceled the agreement. In a bold maneuver, he bluntly made a take-it-or-leave it offer to creditors to exchange $102.6 billion in Argentine bonds for new ones worth only about 35% of the origi-

Argentina

nal indebtedness, and he gave them a deadline of February 25, 2005, to decide. Unhappy creditors had little choice but to accept and take the loss; those who did accounted for 76% of the debt. In December 2005, Argentina repaid its entire remaining debt to the IMF of almost $9.8 billion.

Without a doubt, the diversion of resources from debt servicing led to a dramatic resurgence in the economy. Argentina showed growth in 2003 for the first time in five years, a robust 8.7%, and averaged 8.6% for the next five years, something Argentina has not experienced since its Golden Age at the turn of the 20th century. In 2006, growth was 9.2%, third-highest in Latin America, behind the Dominican Republic and Venezuela, and in 2007 it was 8.7%. The poverty rate also dropped from 58% in 2002 to 27% in 2007. Unemployment, still about 16% for both 2003 and 2004, dropped to 11% at the end of 2005 and to 10% in 2006 and 2007. On the other hand, inflation was 12%, the highest since 1992 if the 2002 peso devaluation is discounted.

Much of the improvement could be attributed to high market prices for agricultural products, Argentina's traditional export, especially corn and soybeans, which have joined wheat as the major cash crops. Argentina is currently the world's second-largest exporter of corn and the third-largest of soybeans.

In December 2007, Kirchner turned the reins of government over to his wife, Cristina Fernández de Kirchner, who was faced with the uncharacteristic problem for Argentina of trying to moderate an overheated economy. In 2008, she attempted to increase export tariffs on agricultural products by more than 50%, provoking a serious strike by farmers and a tax crackdown on major grain export companies (see History).

In 2008, the government claimed inflation was 9%, but experts accused the government of "cooking" inflation figures by eliminating products that were rising in price the steepest, on the dubious premise that people would put their spending priorities on other products. More reliable estimates put the rate for 2008 at 25%. In 2009 it was reliably estimated at 16%, and in 2010 it soared to 22%. Private economists estimated it at 25.3% in 2012. In Feburary 2013, the IMF sanctioned Argentina and gave it a deadline of September 29 to report accurate statistics. Fernández grudgingly complied. Private sources estimated inflation for 2013 at 20.8%.

The pressure on the peso caused it to drop to 8.75 to the dollar on the unofficial market in April 2013, forcing Fernández to offer an amnesty to Argentines who had been converting their pesos to foreign currencies and depositing them abroad.

Economic growth remained a robust 7.1% in 2008, but a 40% drop in the international price of soybeans, coupled with the international market crisis, led to a –2.5% drop in 2009. It rebounded in 2010 to a respectable 9.2% and by another 8.9% in 2011, both years the second-highest in Latin America. It slowed to only 2.6% in 2012 because a drought devastated the soybean crop. Growth in 2013 was 3.5%.

Unemployment was 7.8% in 2010, 7.2% in 2011 and 2012 and 7.5% in 2013. The gap between rich and poor remains a nagging social and economic problem. An estimated 30% of the population in this relatively affluent country still lives below the poverty line.

THE FUTURE: There is no doubt that President Cristina Fernández owed her dramatic come-from-behind re-election victory in 2011 to the unexpected death of her husband and mentor. Her strategy of appealing to public sympathy by literally draping herself in mourning and campaigning on her husband's memory was dazzlingly successful.

However, the once-booming economy, wrought by her husband's decision to default on international loans and by unrealistic subsidies on utilities and transportation, has turned to bust and blackouts. Growth plummeted from 8.9% in 2011 to 2.6% in 2012 and 3.5% in 2013. Her practice of cooking the books to conceal the true inflation rate also backfired, resulting in sanctions from the IMF. She has used the Central Bank and the newly renationalized oil company *YPF* as cash cows for quick fixes, but now she needs international credit to bail the country out and Argentina remains a pariah in global lending circles.

With the loss of its appeal to the U.S. Supreme Court, Argentina is now facing another default because of its failure to pay the $1.65 billion to the U.S. hedge funds that refused to accept the 35% payment for its bonds in 2005 by the June 30 deadline. The result of that default could be disastrous for Argentina. It was still involved in legal wrangling during the 30-day grace period when this book went to press.

She alienated Spain over the *YPF* takeover and even members of her own party with her imperious attitude.

Finally, she has alienated her own people with her haughty attitude; her seeming deference to her son, Máximo, leader of a left-wing Peronist faction; her efforts to use a new media law as a cudgel against Grupo Clarín, but not against friendly media; and a 72% electrical rate hike, inevitable after she and her husband refused to raise rates for more than a decade.

She has adroitly sought once again to distract her people's attention from the economy and the scandals by provoking a new dispute with Britain over the Falklands. The nationalist fervor she has re-aroused served her purpose for the short term, but as prices climbed 25.6% in 2012 and 20.8% in 2013 in real, not fanciful, terms and unemployment lines remain lengthy, her popularity has inevitably suffered. Her public approval rating plummeted from 69% at the beginning of 2012 to 26% on the eve of the congressional elections in October 2013. Among Latin American presidents, only Juan Manuel Santos of Colombia (25%) and Laura Chinchilla of Costa Rica (9%) were less popular.

Adios, public sympathy for the grieving widow.

Her Front for Victory *(FPV)* faction retained its bare majorities in both houses in the October 27, 2013, mid-term elections, but its percentage of the popular vote shrank. Gone is any possibility of a constitutional amendment that would permit her to seek a third term in 2015—assuming she could even win.

Several names already have emerged as potential candidates to succeed her in 2015, chief among them the Peronist renegade Sergio Massa, 41, her onetime cabinet chief, who defected from her *FPV* to form his own Renewal Front. It won 16 seats in the mid-term voting. The non-Peronist opposition, meanwhile, remains fragmented and disorganized. Probably the most credible candidate among them is the popular mayor of Buenos Aires, Mauricio Macri, 55, a member of a conservative group called Republican Proposal *(PRO)*.

Who is Fernández's own choice to succeed her? Good question. She has shown no inclination to groom, much less anoint, a successor, apparently because her vanity precludes her from sharing the spotlight with an understudy. It would not be surprising if she suddenly throws her support behind Máximo, 37, to perpetuate the dynasty, but with just a year to go, it may be too late for her to promote anyone. The only thing predictable about Argentine politics is that it is unpredictable.

A more immediate question concerns the president's precarious health and how effectively she will be able to govern for her remaining two years, especially after brain surgery in October 2013 and two mysterious, month-long absences from the public eye within three months.

Belize

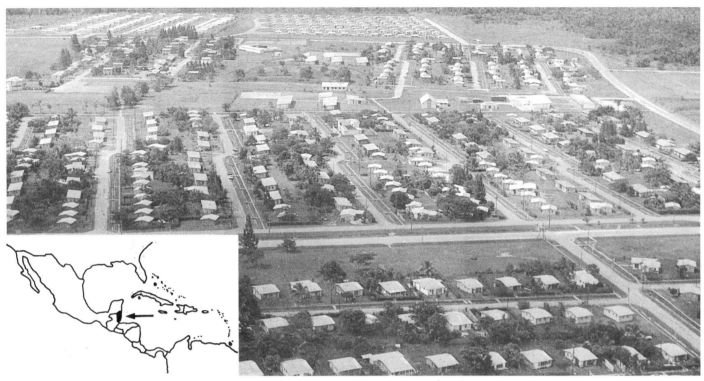

Aerial view of Belmopan

(pronouced Beh-lees)

Area: 8,866 sq. mi., somewhat larger than Massachusetts.
Population: 340,844 (2014 est.).
Capital City: Belmopan (Pop. 13,500).
Climate: Hot and humid.
Neighboring Countries: Mexico (North); Guatemala (West); Honduras lies 50 miles to the southeast across the Gulf of Honduras.
Official Language: English.
Other Principal Tongues: Spanish and some Indian dialects.
Ethnic Background: African (65%); Mestizo, Creole and those of Mayan ancestry, European.
Principal Religions: Roman Catholicism, Anglican Protestant Christianity.
Chief Commercial Products: Sugar, citrus fruit, lobster, shrimp, forest products.
Currency: Belize Dollar.
Gross Domestic Product: U.S. $1.637 billion (est.) in 2013 ($4,803 per capita)
Former Colonial Status: British Colony (1862–1981).
National Day: September 21 (Independence Day).
Chief of State: Queen Elizabeth II of Great Britain, represented by Sir Colville Young, governor general.
Head of Government: Dean Barrow (born March 2, 1951), prime minister (since February 8, 2008).

National Flag: A white circle on a blue field, with red horizontal bars at top and bottom. The circle shows two workers and symbols of agriculture, industry and maritime activity.

Wedged between Mexico's Yucatán Peninsula to the north and Guatemala to the west and south, and calmed by placid waters of the Caribbean Sea on its eastern coastline, Belize is a warm to hot and humid country about 174 miles long and 69 miles wide at its widest point. Flat and swampy on the coast, but mercifully relieved by pleasant sea breezes, the beaches are unspoiled and beautiful. The terrain slowly rises toward the interior to about 3,000 feet above sea level into pine forests and pasturelands. At lower altitudes, tropical growth predominates.

Some 15 miles offshore there is the longest barrier reef in the Western Hemisphere, stretching 190 miles, offering a spectacular variety of tropical fish and coral formations, a delight for the experienced snorkel diver. The land is thinly inhabited; the largest town is Belize City with a population of about 50,000—which, however, has an international airport.

HISTORY: Belize was part of the Mayan domain, which declined about 1000 A.D. It was settled about 1638 by bands of British woodcutters illegally harvesting the timber in Spanish domains. These settlers

managed their own affairs and government, although the Spanish tried many times to eject them. In 1786 Britain finally appointed a superintendent for the territory; in 1840 it was termed a colony, called British Honduras, although it was not officially a colony until 1862 when it was made subordinate to Jamaica. In 1884 it was made a separate crown colony.

Colonial status continued until 1964 when the colony was granted full internal

Belize

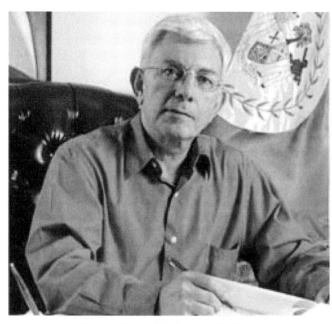

Former Prime Minister Said Musa

self-government. In June 1973, its name was changed to Belize. Following an outbreak of rioting, the colony was given its independence in September 1981.

Guatemala long had claimed Belize as an integral part of its territory. It protested the granting of independence and refused to recognize it. Britain maintained a force of some 1,800 troops to maintain Belize's security. Guatemalan President Vinicio Cerezo generally conceded that Belize's independence was negotiable, provided Guatemala obtained access to the Atlantic via one or more of its ports. The dispute was settled in late 1992 when such rights were granted, and Guatemala formally recognized Belize.

Government consists of a 31-member House of Representatives, expanded from 29 in 2008, and an eight-member Senate; in a 2008 referendum, voters changed it from appointed to elected.

The People's United Party (PUP) of George Price held power from independence until 1984, when it was defeated by the United Democratic Party (UDP) led by Manuel Esquivel, running on a free-trade platform. But in late 1989, the Price and the PUP returned to power by a narrow majority of 15–14, later increased to 16–13 when a UDP member deserted his party.

Price introduced the "clinic day" on Wednesdays, whereby any Belizean could drop in his office in Belize City and tell him of his concerns. His successors have continued this popular tradition.

In early 1993 Britain announced that it would withdraw its force from Belize within 15 months. Price, hoping to gain from the recent years of prosperity, held elections in June 1993, 15 months before they were due. Security was the main is-

sue. Guatemala had repudiated the treaty recognizing Belize. The UDP seized the issue, typified by a song: "We don't want no Guatemala!" It won narrowly, 16–13 seats, and Esquivel again became prime minister.

Belize repudiated the treaty with Guatemala. British troops departed on January 1, 1994, and security became the responsibility of the Belize Defense Force.

The UDP government, alleging mismanagement by the PUP, raised taxes early in its five-year mandate. Most controversial was a 15% value-added tax; the government also raised utility rates. These unpopular measures returned to haunt Esquivel, and in the general election in August 1998, the pendulum swung sharply back to the PUP, which had chosen Said Musa, a former attorney general under Price, as its standard bearer. Musa is of Palestinian descent.

In the campaign, Musa denounced Esquivel's "killa taxes," which he said were frightening away foreign investors. He pledged to cut utility rates and to create 15,000 new jobs. The appeal paid off; the PUP won in a landslide, taking 23 of the 29 seats in the lower house. Esquivel was defeated in his own district by the mayor of Belize City. He was replaced as opposition leader by Dean Barrow, who is of African descent and had served as deputy prime minister and foreign minister.

The PUP became the first party since independence to win two consecutive mandates, albeit with a slightly reduced majority, winning 22 of the 29 seats in the general elections in March 2003.

Musa's popularity waned because of alleged corruption. In 2004, it was disclosed that $3 million had been taken from the country's social security fund to cover

the debts of a company owned by the finance minister. Seven cabinet ministers resigned, demanding that Musa fire the finance minister, which he did. Musa then assumed the finance portfolio himself.

In 2005, Musa did what he had denounced Esquivel for doing in 1998—proposed a dramatic tax increase, as well as a cut in services. He said the measures were necessary to service the country's staggering debt, one of the highest in the world as a percentage of GDP (see Economy). Under Musa alone, the debt rose to 90.4% of GDP in 2007. Demonstrations outside the House of Representatives during the tax debate turned violent, a rarity in Belize.

The violence intensified in 2005 when Musa announced plans to sell the government's shares in the telephone company, BTL, to U.S. interests. Saboteurs, apparently union workers, cut down telephone poles and severed power lines, disrupting the power and communications grids. Looting broke out in Belize City that left one dead, 27 injured and 100 arrested. Teachers and civil servants staged strikes. Three UDP leaders were arrested in confrontations with police. The UDP demanded that Musa resign, but he steadfastly refused.

In 2006, the government announced it could not service its debt. On January 31, 2007, a historic agreement was reached with Belize's foreign creditors to swap 98% of the existing debt for bonds that will mature in 2029. Belize paid 4.5% to service the bonds for the first three years, 6% for the next two years, then 8.5% per year until maturity.

Musa called new elections for the House of Representatives, which had been expanded by two seats, on February 7, 2008. He simultaneously called a referendum on changing the Senate from an appointed to an elected body, which the UDP denounced as a gimmick to help the PUP in the parliamentary election. If so, it failed, because the UDP scored a landslide victory, winning 25 of the 31 seats; voters also approved an elected Senate by a margin of 61%–39%. The following day, Dean Barrow, 56, who holds a law degree from the University of Miami, became Belize's first black prime minister. He also assumed the finance portfolio.

One issue that has preoccupied the Barrow government has been its nationalization of Belize Telemedia, the country's largest telephone company, in 2009. Barrow alleged that Telemedia and other companies had benefited from a "sweetheart deal" under Musa's PUP government. Barrow said he intended the takeover to be only temporary until a new buyer can be found. The takeover put Barrow at odds with Lord Michael Ashcroft, a member of the British House of Lords who is believed to be the largest single investor

Prime Minister Dean O. Barrow

in Belize, including of Belize Bank, which was a shareholder in Telemedia. Barrow claimed that Ashcroft's net worth was greater than Belize's GDP. Ashcroft spent part of his youth in Belize and has made no secret of his financial stake there. From 1998–2000, he served as Musa's ambassador to the United Nations, but in an interview in 2009 he claimed to be the greatest single contributor to the UDP's 2008 campaign, which brought Barrow to power. He insisted he always had regarded Barrow as a friend.

Barrow's efforts to undo the sweetheart arrangements, which he said stifled competition, landed his government in court in Belize and in arbitration in Britain. Barrow prevailed in court, but the British arbitrators levied awards of $41 million against the Belizean government, which Barrow has vowed not to pay. Meanwhile, Telemedia lost tens of thousands of subscribers under government tutelage, making it more difficult to sell. According to Belizean media, Telemedia engaged in heavy-handed tactics against its major private competitor, Smart Speednet, such as reneging on an interconnectivity agreement. In his Independence Day address in S2010, Barrow announced that Telemedia was doubling Internet bandwidth at no extra charge, evidently to lure back customers.

Barrow also generated controversy by submitting Belize's long-standing border dispute with Guatemala to the International Court of Justice in The Hague, Netherlands. In May 2011, representatives of the two nations signed an agreement at the Organization of American States in Washington agreeing to let the ICJ adjudicate the dispute, but it would still have to be ratified by referendum in both countries. Guatemala's claim of 4,900 square miles (12,700 km^2) includes more than half of Belize's territory. As of mid-2012, the referenda had not been scheduled.

Barrow called a general election for March 7, 2012. The major issue was Belize's still-crushing debt. Barrow called for yet another renegotiation of the debt, like that of 2007. The interest on the so-called "superbond" is scheduled to jump to 8.5% in 2013. The opposition leader, Francis Fonseca, argued that the obligations could be met by expanding the economy. Another issue was offshore oil drilling, a sensitive topic in tourism-dependent Belize, especially since the 2010 BP disaster off the Louisiana coast. Fonseca called for a drilling moratorium, Barrow for a referendum.

The voters narrowly gave Barrow's UDP a second mandate but with a greatly reduced majority, 17 seats to 14 for the PUP. The UDP received 50.4% of the popular vote to 47.5% for the PUP.

Belize found itself unwillingly in the international spotlight in November 2012 when John McAfee, the enigmatic millionaire founder of the U.S. anti-virus software firm that bears his name, was named a person of interest for questioning in connection with the murder of Gregory Faull, McAfee's neighbor on Ambergris Caye. McAfee went into hiding, but emailed Wired magazine's website that he was innocent. McAfee gave up control of his company in 1994 and had been living an opulent lifestyle in Belize. He turned up a month later in Guatemala, where he was detained briefly. Because no charges had been filed against him in Belize, a Guatemalan judge allowed him to return to the U.S., where he remains.

The murder mystery became a hot topic for tabloid news media and social media. McAfee, 67, did not the limelight since his return to the U.S. In interviews, he claimed Belizean police tried to shake him down for a $2 million bribe and when he refused, they tried to frame him for the murder of Faull, with whom he had quarreled over the poisoning of McAfee's dogs. McAfee praised Belize as one of the world's most beautiful countries, but ridiculed it as a "third-rate banana republic" with an alarming murder rate. Belizean authorities still have not filed formal charges, but they seized his assets.

CULTURE: Creoles, of mixed African and European blood, who speak a distinct dialect that is a mix of English, Carib and Spanish, account for one fourth of the population. Increasing immigration from war-torn and poverty-stricken Central America since the 1980s has changed the cultural mosaic, and *mestizos* now account for almost half the population. Descendants of the Mayas account for about 11%, Caucasians for about 10% and Garifunas,

unassimilated black descendants of escaped slaves, 6%. Creole is the official language, but Belize is unofficially bilingual, and Spanish instruction is now mandatory in schools.

A colony of German-speaking Mennonites produces almost all the country's dairy products. There also are colonies of Taiwanese, Sri Lankans and Arabs in this harmonious ethnic gumbo. Former Prime Minister Said Musa is of Palestinian descent, and in 2008 Dean Barrow became the first black prime minister.

Belmopan, the capital city, was built in 1971 in the center of the country about 50 miles west of Belize City, which is the largest urban area with a population of about 50,000. For the tourist, the city is not safe for a lone pedestrian, especially after dark. This also is true of those traveling alone to remote tourist facilities. Armed robbery and muggings are growing in number in spite of efforts by the government to control crime.

U.S. baseball is immensely popular; both men and women spend hours watching games.

There are roughly 700 Mayan ruins about 1,000 years old, which can be seen on guided tours, and unusual wildlife is prolific. The result has been that Belize has become a popular destination for adventuresome tourists.

Belize's best-known cultural figure in international circles was probably the Punta musician Andy Palacio (1960–2008). Punta is the genre associated with Palacio's Garifuna culture, and Palacio devoted his short life to preserving that culture and language. He recorded five albums, his last being *Watina* in 2007. He served as head of the National Institute of Culture and History for a time.

Belize's small and scattered population cannot support a daily newspaper. The most widely read independent newspaper is the biweekly *Amandala*, founded in 1969 in Belize City as a mouthpiece for the black population. Its only major competitor is the independent weekly, *The Reporter*, founded in 1967. The PUP and UDP both publish weekly newspapers, *The Belize Times* and *The Guardian*, respectively.

ECONOMY: Until recent times, forestry was the most important activity in Belize, but as the timber supply grew sparse, sugar cane growing took on more importance and now is the leading industry. Although the country has a great deal of land which is well suited for agriculture, only a small portion is farmed, and it is necessary for Belize to import millions of dollars in foodstuffs. Belize's major trading partners are the United States and the United Kingdom—about two thirds of its exports and imports are with these nations. It is

Belize

a member of the Caribbean Community (CARICOM).

The lush lower altitudes of Belize, with their tropical climate, are favorable locations for two crops: marijuana and oranges for juice. The first presented a problem both to Belize and the United States in the 1980s. Production rose quickly to more than 1,000 tons annually and Belize became the second-largest supplier to U.S. dealers. After 1984 this was curtailed and virtually eliminated by a spraying program, but not before a high government official was arrested and indicted in Miami (1985) on charges of conspiring to export 30,000 tons annually to the United States. Production is now closely monitored and is less than 100 tons per year.

Cocaine proved to be a far more serious problem. As alternative routes of transportation from Colombia to the United States were restricted, Belize took up the slack. Small airplanes would land on rural roads for refueling. In order to stop this, the government erected poles on the sides of the roads to break the wings of the craft. Local people bent the poles to eliminate their effectiveness.

Major exports are sugar, bananas, citrus fruit and clothing. The United States and Great Britain each accounted for about 30% of Belize's exports in 2009; the United States accounted for more than a third of imports, with Mexico in second place.

Belize is relatively more prosperous than its Spanish-speaking neighbors, with an estimated per capita GDP of about $4,600 in 2011 and 2012. Real GDP was estimated at $1.52 billion in 2012 and $1.637 billion in 2013.

Real economic growth was once healthy: 9.2% in 2003 and 2004, 5.1% in 2005 and 5.6% in 2006, thanks largely to tourism. The number of overnight tourists in 2006 was 247,000, roughly equal to the country's population, an increase of 4.5% over 2005. It slumped slightly to 245,000 in 2008 and 242,000 in 2009 according to the World Bank, probably because of the global recession. By 2011 it was back up to 250,000, according to the Belize Tourism Board. New hotel construction is booming, but investment in infrastructure is badly needed. Prime Minister Dean Barrow announced a $25 million road into the interior in 2010. Several cruise lines now make port calls in Belize, and its reef is a favorite spot for snorkeling. Belize also has been promoted in recent years for eco-tourism and as a retirement location.

Threatening the tourism boom is the world's third-highest murder rate per 100,000 people in 2012. The rate has climbed from 42 in 2010 and 39 in 2011 to 44.7 in 2012, the most recent year available.

GDP growth dropped to 1.6% in 2007, rebounded to 4.8% in 2008 and was zero in 2009, a reflection of the global recession and the drop in tourism. Growth has since been steady but modest: 2.7% in 2010, 2.0% in 2011, 2.3% in 2012 and 2.5% in 2013.

Unemployment dropped from 9.4% in 2006 to 8.1% in 2008 but shot up to 13.1% in 2010. By 2012 it was down to 11.3% but shot back up to 15.5% in 2013.

Inflation was 1.3% in both 2012 and 2013.

A succession of governments has sought to boost the economy with drunken-sailor spending and heavy borrowing. The public debt by 2007 was $1.17 billion, nearly 100% of GDP, among the highest in the world. Standard & Poor's downgraded Belize's bonds in 2006 and called the country's financial situation "dire." The debt restructuring agreement announced in 2007 (see History) did little more than buy time. The debt was down to $954.1 million in 2008, or 67% of GDP. But in 2009 it was back up to $1.01 billion, or 71% of GDP. By 2012 it was $1.497 billion, officially 90.8% of GDP, the 16th highest of the world's roughly 180 nations. In 2013, Belize restructured its debt, which by year's end had dropped to 75.1% of GDP.

THE FUTURE: It is tempting to draw an analogy between Belize and the American frontier of the 19th century. Belize harks back to an earlier, less hurried time, a place where "civilization" has not yet taken over with fast-food chains and computers. Tourists and immigrants have flocked here to take advantage of the legendary scuba diving in the longest coral reef in the Western Hemisphere, one of UNESCO's World Heritage Sites; to enjoy the unspoiled beaches; to soak up the culture of the Mayan ruins; and to experience the unique ecological wonders. But the real allure is that Belize is an anachronism, a laid-back, English-speaking enclave in the tropics just two hours by air from Houston, a place that has eschewed the frenetic pace of the 21st century, where visitors can "get away from it all" for a few days and settlers can find a new life in an unspoiled, underpopulated paradise.

But there is trouble in paradise. Corruption, drug trafficking, banditry in the rural areas, the world's third-highest murder rate (44.7 per 100,000 people in 2012) and a crushing public debt threaten Belize's greatest asset: its peacefulness. Greater transparency would go a long way toward establishing confidence in governmental institutions, but political cronyism is entrenched in both parties. A poll in 2005 suggested that 49% of Belizeans would be willing to vote for a third party, but in the general elections of 2008 and 2012, when there were three new alternative parties, they collected only 2% of the vote among them.

Ironically, Belize is hampered by the very thing that has made it so appealing: resistance to change. Thus far, Prime Minister Dean Barrow has had no more success than his predecessors. Voters gave him a new mandate on March 7, 2012, but his plans to deal with the country's crushing public debt, still 75%% of GDP, 34th highest in the world, is to renegotiate it rather than to engage in belt-tightening. That's a good way to win votes, but a questionable way to run a country.

Plurinational State of Bolivia

Nestled in the rugged mountains is a shimmering Andean lake

Area: 424,052 sq. mi.
Population: 10,631,486 (2014 est.)
Capital Cities: La Paz (Pop. 812,000 est. in 2012), seat of the executive and legislative branches; and Sucre (224,838 est. in 2010), the judicial seat.
Climate: The eastern lowlands are hot all year round; they are wet from November through March, dry from May through September. The highland climate varies greatly with the altitude. The high plateau, or *altiplano*, is dry and cold all year round.
Neighboring Countries: Brazil (North and East); Paraguay (Southeast); Argentina (South); Chile (Southwest); Peru (Northwest).

Official Language: Spanish
Other Principal Tongues: Quechua, Aymara and Guaraní
Ethnic Background: Indian (70%); *mestizo* (mixed European and Indian (25%); European (5%)
Principal Religion: Roman Catholic Christianity
Chief Commercial Products: Tin, lead, zinc, silver, tungsten, gold, natural gas, agricultural products. Coca production, used to make cocaine, is a major source of income.
Currency: Bolivian Peso
Gross Domestic Product: U.S. $29.81 billion in 2013 ($2,804 per capita, official exchange rate).

Former Colonial Status: Spanish colony known as Upper Peru (1538–1825)
Independence Date: August 6, 1825
Chief of State: Juan Evo Morales Ayma (b. October 26, 1959), president (since January 22, 2006).
National Flag: Equal red, yellow and green horizontal stripes.

Bolivia, the fifth-largest nation in South America, is landlocked. Stretching 1,000 miles from north to south and 800 miles east to west, it is divided into two highly contrasting regions—the *altiplano* (a high mountain plateau) and the eastern lowlands. The Andean mountain range reaches its greatest width—some 400 miles—in Bo-

Bolivia

livia. The *Western Cordillera*, which separates Bolivia from Chile and Peru, contains snowy peaks of 19,000 to 21,240 feet, with numerous rough volcanoes along the crest. The narrow passes to the Pacific coast exceed 13,000 feet in altitude. The *altiplano*, lying to the east of the *Western Cordillera*, is an arid, windswept, treeless plateau some 85 miles wide and 520 miles in length and much of it is above 13,000 feet.

Split into basins by spurs from the *Western Cordillera*, the southern portion is parched desert, uninhabited except for mining camps; the northern portion, containing chilly Lake Titicaca (3,400 square miles at 12,500 feet), has many small settlements along the river flowing into the lake, and around the shore there is a large and prosperous Indian farming population. The eastern *cordillera*, separating the *altiplano* from the lowlands, reaches 20,000 feet in the north, but is much lower in the south.

The mountains drop sharply to the northeast and the hot, humid Amazon basin. Further to the south they form a stepped descent to a region called the *Puno* and then into the *Chaco* plains of Paraguay and Argentina. The valleys that cut into the eastern slopes of the mountains are fertile, semi-tropical and densely inhabited. These valleys, called *yungas*, produce a wide variety of cereals and fruits, but the task of transporting them to the cities of the *altiplano* is formidable. The lowland tropical plains of the northeast, once heavily populated, are now largely abandoned because of their inaccessibility.

HISTORY: The Aymara Indians of the Lake Titicaca region had a relatively high level of development between 500 and 900 A.D., but archeologists believe indigenous people inhabited the area as early as 1500 B.C. This civilization disappeared from some undetermined disaster and the Quechua-speaking Inca invaders found the surviving Aymaras living among ancient monuments and ruins they could not explain. The well-preserved pre-Incan ruins of Tiahuanaco (Tiwanaku) was made a UNESCO World Heritage Site in 2000. Bolivia was still in Inca hands when the Spaniards arrived from Peru in 1538.

The Spanish development of Bolivia began with the discovery of a silver mountain at Potosí in 1545, followed by additional discoveries at Oruro. The capital, Sucre, was founded in 1539. La Paz, founded in 1548, was an important terminal for treasure convoys preparing for the difficult passage to Peru; it became the seat of government in 1898 after the silver played out near Sucre, which remains the judicial seat.

The Inca social and economic organizations were abandoned in a mad effort to extract and process the metallic wealth of the mountains—tin, silver, lead and zinc. Jesuit missionaries penetrated the tropical lowlands, gathering the Indians into prosperous farming communities that endured into the 18th century. However, they aroused little interest on the part of the Spanish authorities and had even less influence on the social and political development of the country. The Spaniards intermarried with the Indians, producing a large group of multi-ethnic *mestizos* that would affect the course of Bolivian history.

Revolutionary movements against Spanish rule began early in Bolivia; revolts by *mestizos* broke out in La Paz in 1661 and at Cochabamba in 1730. Indian revolts occurred in Sucre, Cochabamba, Oruro and La Paz from 1776 to 1780. The University of San Francisco Xavier in Sucre issued a call in 1809 for the liberation of all colonies from Spain. Although several attempts were made to free Bolivia, they were unsuccessful until 1825, when Simón Bolívar

Exacting Inca stonework

68

Bolivia

sent General Antonio José de Sucre to free Upper Peru. Independence was declared on August 6 of that year.

Few South American nations faced greater initial handicaps than Bolivia. There were few competent patriotic leaders among the landed aristocracy, and there was no middle class. The apathetic Indians and the *mestizos* were simply pawns in a game they did not understand. The military, which had been trained in the campaigns of San Martín and Bolívar, seized power. The history of independent Bolivia's first 50 years is a dismal recitation of misrule and violence as jealous rivals struggled for power. Following its defeat in The War of the Pacific (1879–83), Bolivia lost its Pacific provinces to Chile and became a landlocked nation.

During the 1880s and 1890s, several able men occupied the presidency. Silver mining was revived, a few schools were opened and political parties were established. Traditional Liberal and Conservative titles were adopted, but their memberships represented little more than opposing factions of the nation's ruling elite. One of the principal Liberal demands was for the transfer of the capital from Sucre to La Paz. After seizing the presidency by revolt, a Liberal regime made La Paz the seat of government.

Under Liberal leadership, Bolivia achieved a degree of stability in the first two decades of the 20th century. Economic reforms were undertaken, disputes with Chile and Brazil were resolved—with losses of territory but with receipt of indemnities—mining was expanded and roads and railroads were built. The motive behind this limited "modernization" was the increasing world demand for tin, a mineral that quickly became Bolivia's basic export, transforming the small group that controlled its extraction—the "tin barons"—into powerful international millionaires. In the 1920s, a party carrying the Republican label came to power, and it sought foreign capital for mining and petroleum interests, attracting U.S. investors.

By the 1930s, U.S. interests controlled most of Bolivia's mineral concessions. Although some of the investment capital went into roads, railroads and agriculture, much of it was wasted by irresponsible spending. When the world depression of the 1930s hit Bolivia, its economy collapsed, the treasury defaulted on its bonds and the Republican president was ousted.

In 1931 elections, Daniel Salamanca, a competent businessman, became president amid hopes that he could bring order out of chaos. This optimistic mood was shattered the following year with the outbreak of the Chaco War with Paraguay. Blame for this senseless conflict lies with the miscalculation of the leadership of both countries. Humiliated by a long series of military disasters, both nations overestimated their own capabilities and underestimated those of the other. Though ostensibly more powerful than Paraguay, Bolivia, in a monumental display of military incompetence, suffered a crushing defeat in which 52,000 of its soldiers were killed. Fought to exhaustion on both sides, the war ended with Paraguay in possession of the disputed Chaco region in 1935. Soldiers returning home, angered by their shabby treatment during the war, joined with university students and labor agitators in demanding social reforms.

In 1936, a group of socially conscious military officers led by Colonel David Toro overthrew the civilian government and proclaimed Bolivia a "socialist republic." This short-lived government established the first labor ministry and expropriated the holdings of Standard Oil. After only a year and a half, Toro was overthrown by an even more radical officer, Colonel Germán Busch, a hero of the Chaco War. He implemented the first labor code, encouraged organization of the tin miners and imposed governmental control over the tin companies. Busch died suddenly in 1939, and it remains a mystery whether he died by his own hand or those of conservative economic interests alarmed by the pace of his reforms. At any rate, his death temporarily halted social reform.

Conservative military elements took control of the ballot boxes in 1940 elections and installed their man as president. For the next three years, the country was ruled by these right-wing elements, but there arose a number of civilian-based political parties and movements, ranging from Trotskyite on the left to the Bolivian Falange, modeled after the movement of Spain's Generalissimo Francisco Franco, on the right.

The one that was to have the most profound impact on the country, however, one that endures to this day, was the Revolutionary Nationalist Movement, or *MNR*, led by Víctor Paz Estenssoro, who had been an economic adviser to Busch. When another group of military reformers overthrew the conservatives in 1943 and installed Major Gualberto Villarroel as president, they invited the *MNR* to participate in the new government. Although Villarroel was enlightened in his treatment of the Indian population and was sympathetic to the miners, he proved too conservative for ultra-leftwing elements that overthrew him and publicly hanged him in 1946.

The 1952 Revolution

The following six years were marked by exceptional political turbulence and instability, even for Bolivia. The end of this vol-

A Bolivian miner gazes into the icicled entrance of a tin mine near La Paz

Bolivia

View of La Paz

atile period, in which Bolivia was ruled by a wearisome series of military *juntas*, was marked by the beginning of what scholars regard as one of Latin America's four genuine social revolutions, along with those of Mexico, Cuba and Nicaragua.

In 1952, the *MNR* led a revolt that left about 3,000 dead and led to the installation of Paz Estenssoro as president. His revolutionary government took three remarkable steps: it temporarily abolished the army and replaced it with armed militias of Indians and tin miners; it extended universal suffrage to the illiterate masses, giving them genuine political power for the first time; and it implemented true land reform, breaking up huge estates and giving Indian peasants title to their own plots. The *MNR* also established itself within the unions and Indian communities, making it then the country's premier civilian political force for decades.

The revolution was hampered by a lack of trained administrators, by inadequate financial resources, by opposition from both internal and external elements and, above all, by a steady decline in tin prices that put Bolivia in chronic economic crisis. Nonetheless, for its first 12 years the revolution gave power to the powerless and brought an end to revolving-door governments. When Paz Estenssoro's four-year term expired in 1956, he was succeeded by another *MNR* leader, Hernán Siles Suazo. Paz Estenssoro returned to power in the 1960 election, but when he made overtures toward re-election in 1964, the newly organized revolutionary army proved as skillful at staging a *coup d'etat* as had its

predecessors. The vice president and former air force commander, General René Barrientos, came to power in November 1964 and forced Paz Estenssoro into exile. Despite the *MNR's* failure to retain power, its 12 years of revolution proved to be a *fait accompli* from which there was no turning back to the "old order."

The flamboyant and charismatic Barrientos, a moderate conservative, proved a highly popular president, and he was given a resounding mandate in a 1966 election. In 1967, he promulgated a new constitution that would last for 42 years, venerable for a Bolivian organic law. That same year, a U.S.-trained counter-insurgency battalion captured and executed the legendary Argentine-born revolutionary, Ernesto "Che" Guevara, who had attempted to launch a Cuban-style revolution among Bolivia's rural Indians. Barrientos was fond of making personal visits to the interior by helicopter, and on one such trip, in April 1969, he died in a helicopter crash.

Military Rule, 1969–82

Barrientos was succeeded by his vice president, who was quickly overthrown by General Alfredo Ovando, a leftist and nationalist who expropriated the holdings of Gulf Oil Co. He was in turn overthrown by the even more left-wing General Juan José Torres in 1970. Torres replaced the Congress with a Soviet-style "People's Assembly" and forged a coalition of Marxist intellectuals and tin miners. However, he failed to win the support of the peasants,

as Barrientos had, or most workers. Even worse, he alienated the U.S. Embassy.

Coup No. 187 (the best estimate) in 145 years of independence came in 1971, bringing to power a more conservative military strongman, Colonel Hugo Banzer Suárez. By 1975, Banzer had fended off 13 coup attempts, and by 1978, after seven years, he had held power continuously longer than any Bolivian president of the 20th century. The formula for his longevity was a three-point strategy: elimination of major political opposition, economic improvement and increased emphasis on foreign affairs to divert popular attention from unsolved domestic problems. Perhaps the best example of this last strategy was Bolivia's renewed demand for access to the sea through Chile.

In July 1978 Banzer called for an open presidential election in which he had intended to relinquish power to his hand-picked successor, Colonel Juan Pereda Asbún. But in the balloting, former President Siles Suazo won a plurality, while Pereda ran a poor third. Congress was to decide the outcome, but rather than risk the anti-military Siles Suazo coming to power, Banzer suddenly resigned and Pereda proclaimed himself president. Banzer's departure thus created a power vacuum that was to return Bolivia to political turmoil for two years.

The usurpation of power lasted only four months. General David Padilla, the latest reform-minded officer, overthrew Pereda in November and pledged to pave the way for yet another free election in July 1979. In that contest, Siles Suazo again polled a plurality but not a majority, throwing the decision to Congress. Under the ever-watchful eye of the jittery military, Congress opted for a compromise choice for president: Walter Guevara Arce, a civilian leader of the 1952 revolution who later split from the *MNR* and therefore was acceptable to conservative military elements. This good-faith effort at restoring civilian rule also would last only four months, when an overly ambitious colonel, Alberto Natusch Busch, led a successful coup.

Busch, whose only apparent motive was personal gain, immediately found himself faced with overwhelming domestic and international opposition to his naked power play. After only 19 days in power, he was forced to resign and he fled into exile, taking an undetermined amount of cash from the national treasury with him. Congress then chose Lidia Gueiler as Bolivia's first woman president. She had no sooner taken office, of course, before speculation began as to when she would be overthrown and by which officer. She called still another election in June 1980 to choose a president, and once again the victor was Siles Suazo. Coup No. 191

General García Meza

took place and General Luis García Meza seized control of the government.

Thus, in the 24 months between Banzer's resignation in July 1978 and García Meza's coup in July 1980, Bolivia had a total of seven presidents.

García Meza's 13 months in power marked the harshest crackdown on personal freedom in Bolivia's modern history. Hundreds were arrested, some labor leaders were murdered and strict censorship was imposed on the press. The new military regime seemed determined to muzzle—and if possible to exterminate—the opposition in the labor movement. Reports held that 500 to 2,000 political prisoners were jailed. The Carter Administration suspended all aid and Bolivia had to turn to neighboring military governments for assistance.

Seeking to consolidate his control, García Meza jailed his opponents and allegedly bribed key members of the armed forces with payoff money from drug traffickers. Such heavy-handed tactics, combined with depressed economic conditions, fomented widespread opposition to the military. In August 1981, reformist military officers forced García Meza to resign.

Named as the new head of the three-man military *junta* was General Celso Torrelio Villa. Political conditions remained unstable as the nation chafed under harsh military rule. Tin workers mounted widespread strikes to demand a return of their union and political rights which the *junta* suspended in 1980. Hoping to ease criticism of the regime, Torrelio promised to reduce human rights violations, to slow the rampant flow of illegal cocaine out of the country and to reduce the state's role in the economy while expanding the opportunities for private enterprise.

Although such policies pleased the United States, which resumed full diplomatic ties after a 16-month delay, the promises prompted skepticism at home. Efforts to impose austerity measures

touched off widespread strikes. When the peso was allowed to float, it promptly fell 76% in value. This was only a precursor of that which was to come.

Return to Democracy

To reduce growing criticism, the *junta* promised to lift its ban on political activity and to hold elections for a constituent assembly early in 1983, but as the economic crisis worsened and popular agitation spread, the government was forced to lift the ban on the activities of parties and unions. Torrelio resigned in mid-1982 and the remainder of the democratically elected Congress of 1980 confirmed Siles Suazo's 1980 election victory; in late 1982 he and Jaime Paz Zamora, a Socialist and the nephew of Paz Estenssoro, were installed as president and vice president.

The situation inherited by the civilian government bordered on total chaos. The public debt amounted to about $3 billion, inflation was out of control, unemployment was rampant and the corruptive influence of the drug traffic had reached alarming proportions. The government made valiant, but disorganized, attempts to impose a program of economic austerity and public honesty. Its partial success provoked opposition and social unrest.

Battered by strikes and coup rumors, the civilian government survived against formidable odds. Exemplifying the extent of the regime's troubles, in 1984 Siles Suazo encouraged private sectors to invest in the country, rejected a demand for a 500% rise in workers' wages, proclaimed a new war against drug dealers, promised to reduce inflation to 45%, reaffirmed his confidence in the loyalty of the armed forces and appealed to international institutions to lend more money to Bolivia to save the nation from a "desperate economic situation."

The president was abducted one month later and held for some hours before being released in what appeared to be a clumsy attempt to stage a military coup.

Social unrest, several more strikes and inflation, which at the beginning of 1985 was running at an astronomical annual rate of 24,000%, led Siles Suazo to advance presidential elections to 1985. It appeared that General Hugo Banzer would win, and he actually received more votes than the runner–up in an election riddled with corruption, particularly in the La Paz area. Although former President Paz Estenssoro, age 77, received 26.4% of the vote, about 2% less than Banzer, he was elected president by the new Congress, in which Paz Estenssoro's party received more seats Banzer's. He was sworn in in August 1985.

Paz Estenssoro successfully renegotiated Bolivia's foreign debt. He also promised decentralization of the economy, par-

ticularly the state mining and petroleum monopolies. These moves and others increased food prices ten-fold and provoked strikes and violence that led to the declaration of a state of siege. Surprisingly, Banzer and his supporters joined Paz Estenssoro's efforts for economic reform. As a result of the dramatic changes, the IMF, the World Bank, the United States, Japan, China and European countries resumed loans to Bolivia.

The 1985–88 period was not kind to Bolivia. The bottom dropped out of world tin prices in 1985. Further complicating Bolivia's problems was the discovery of Brazilian deposits that were mined much more easily. Bolivia wound up in the position of marketing tin for less than one third the price of production. The government had no choice but to close the most inefficient mines, causing unemployment to rise to 32%, sparking protests.

Finally, the United States decided to tackle its growing cocaine problem by eliminating the source—coca leaf cultivation. At first, it offered $350 for every hectare of coca leaf taken out of production. Because coca growers, mostly peasants, can make up to $10,000 per hectare, the plan was poorly received and actively resisted by farmers. Then, in "Operation Blast Furnace," the United States persuaded the Bolivian government to cooperate, with the assistance of U.S. helicopters and armaments, in destroying facilities used to process coca into cocaine. The result: crowds demonstrated in front of the U.S. Embassy shouting *"Viva coca!"*

U.S. anti-coca efforts from 1986–97 were hampered for several reasons. First, there was the demand for cocaine. If Bolivian coca production went down, it rose in neighboring nations. Second, coca production was an informal government industry, an elaborate, ever-changing system of bribery that had invaded even the Supreme Court. Third, paid informants were useless because drug figureheads had counter-informants up to the highest level of the military and police.

The 1989 presidential elections produced two top candidates out of nine—Gonzalo Sánchez de Lozada, candidate of the *MNR*, received 23% of the vote and Banzer received 22%. Jaime Paz Zamora, a leftist, received 19.5%. Three months of meetings in smoke-filled rooms ensued. Finally, in August, the third-place Paz Zamora was declared the new president. Why? Banzer, who while in power had jailed and exiled Paz Zamora in the 1970s, threw his support behind his former arch foe in exchange for 10 out of 17 cabinet posts that virtually assured his control of the government.

Paz Zamora pledged to continue his uncle's style of government and did so.

Bolivia

Unrest did not cease; his term was marred by a nationwide teacher's strike and a murky plot to assassinate him, the chief drug enforcement officer and the U.S. ambassador in 1990. Drug raids with U.S. assistance were only moderately successful and highly resented.

In the 1993 elections, Cabinet ministers resigned to support Banzer. In spite of this, Sánchez de Lozada won a plurality of 36%; Banzer then threw his support to his rival, and Congress decreed Sánchez de Lozada president.

Like many other Latin American presidents of the 1990s, Sánchez de Lozada, popularly—and unpopularly—known as "Goni," undertook a pragmatic program of privatizing cumbersome state-owned enterprises, including the national airline, the oil company and the telecommunications infrastructure. He also sought to decentralize power, placing unprecedented control in the hands of the departments. He also welcomed foreign investors with red-carpet incentives.

Faced with strikes and protests by the majority Indian community for this seeming betrayal of the 1952 revolution, Sánchez reached a new land-reform agreement with Indian leaders in 1996, the most significant such law since the transcendental land-reform law of 1952. Unlike the earlier law, the new statute not only gave peasants title to their land but also permitted them to sell it. Previously, they could only bequeath it to their children, with the result that individual plots became too small to be economically viable.

Banzer Returns to Power

The reforms were the leading issue of the 1997 elections, which drew 10 candidates. All the major candidates embraced Sánchez's reforms, but Banzer capitalized on the discontent among the poor by running on a foggy populist platform that included his promise to "humanize" the reforms. The ploy worked, and Banzer, now a zealous democrat who pledged to respect human rights, emerged as the frontrunner with 22% of the vote. The *MNR* candidate was second with 18% and former President Paz Zamora was third with 17%. There was a 70% turnout of 3.2 million voters.

Congress again was required to select the president, but this time Banzer's right-wing Nationalist Democratic Alliance (*ADN*) forged an unusual alliance with populist and left-wing parties to assure him of victory. Banzer, then 71, received the necessary majority of 79 of the 157 deputies after only two thirds of them had voted. The new vice president was Jorge Quiroga, 37, a previous finance minister under Paz Zamora, a former IBM executive and an engineering graduate of Texas A&M who was married to a Texan. They were sworn in the next day, August 6, Independence Day, for a term that had been constitutionally extended from four to five years.

Banzer issued a controversial pledge to eradicate Bolivia's coca production before the end of his term in 2002, news that gladdened the Clinton administration.

The powerful Confederation of Bolivian Workers (*COB*) soon began engaging in the country's second most popular pastime after soccer: general strikes. The *COB* demanded an increase in the monthly minimum wage from $45 to an unreasonable and inflationary $667. The government counter-offered $54, which the *COB* rejected. It called three 48-hour general strikes in 1997 and 1998. When the government refused to budge, an open-ended strike began in April 1998. Coca-growing peasants in the Chapare region joined the strike by setting up roadblocks on the Santa Cruz-Cochabamba highway. Hundreds of troops and police were dispatched to disperse them, and violence erupted.

Negotiations between the government and the *COB* broke down when the government refused to accept the participation of Evo Morales, the leader of the coca growers, who had been elected to Congress in 1997. Morales proposed that the government offer incentives for the peasants to switch to alternative crops, which, in fact, already had been done; non-traditional crops in Chapare by then outnumbered coca acreage 3–1. The government also had paid farmers up to $2,500 per hectare—almost all of it provided by the United States—to uproot coca plants, but the incentive program was not to be extended beyond 1998. Cooperate now and get paid, or be an outlaw, was the strategy.

Miffed, Morales accused Banzer of having had ties to drug traffickers, which the president denied. The strike turned violent, with 18 fatalities. But in the test of wills, Banzer prevailed. He reported to Congress that of the estimated 40,000 hectares of coca cultivation, 7,000 were eradicated in 1997 and 11,620 in 1998. Critics maintained that new cultivation reduced the net eradication in those years to only 2,000 and 8,000, respectively. Morales and younger, less moderate spokesmen for the growers complained that the ostensible markets for the alternative crops did not exist.

Banzer faced another challenge in 1998 when former President Sánchez de Lozada called for an investigation into Banzer's role in the human rights abuses committed during his military regime, when an estimated 200 people were killed. The call no doubt was inspired by the arrest

Hugo Banzer Suárez

in London days earlier of former Chilean strongman Augusto Pinochet and by the ongoing investigation of Argentine military men for atrocities committed during the "Dirty War." Banzer accused the *MNR* of hypocrisy and called on the opposition party to examine its own complicity with military regimes.

In 1999, the government announced even more impressive figures in the coca-eradication program: 14,000 hectares removed that year, compared with 11,670 in 1998, which left only 16,000 hectares under cultivation.

General strikes continued to plague the country. In April 2000, a seemingly routine local protest in Cochabamba against an increase in water prices turned violent and presented Banzer with his gravest domestic crisis yet. The protests spread to five of the nine departments; five people were killed and 40 injured, dozens were arrested, and the president issued a 90-day state of siege, the seventh since the restoration of democracy. The unrest quickly spread, as angry farmers erected roadblocks in five departments. The Catholic Church defused that crisis by mediating a settlement.

In late 2000, Banzer declared the successful culmination of the coca eradication program, claiming 40,000 hectares had been removed from cultivation; 12,000 hectares in Yungas were allowed to be cultivated for "traditional" purposes, a concession to the sentiments of local Indians. Still, the peasants complained that other crops, such as coffee, would earn them only a fraction of what they made from coca.

A new variable was added into the Bolivian political equation in November 2000, when a new Indian-based political party, *Movimiento Indígeno Pachacuti* (the Aymara word for "revival"), was established by

Bolivia

Felipe Quispe, the head of a peasant labor confederation.

Banzer pushed through Congress in 2001 an ambitious, 50-point constitutional reform to broaden, in principle at least, Bolivian democracy. The reforms targeted election fraud by removing local elections from the control of local kingpins, providing for referenda, and by empowering the Supreme Court rather than Congress with the decision to revoke congressional immunity in corruption investigations. The opposition *MNR* grudgingly supported the plan.

A political era came to an end in Bolivia on June 7, 2001, when four-time former president Paz Estenssoro, the intellectual author of the 1952 revolution, died at 93 on the 59th anniversary of the founding of the *MNR*. His funeral in Tarija attracted thousands of peasants, who mingled with the elite of various parties who came to pay tribute to the man and his legacy.

The incumbent president would soon follow him. Banzer, a heavy smoker, was diagnosed with lung and liver cancer. He resigned effective August 6, 2001, Independence Day and the fourth anniversary of his inauguration, and Vice President Quiroga was sworn in the following day for the remaining year of his term. Banzer, 75, died nine months later. Thousands filled the streets to pay homage to this dictator-turned-democrat.

A lame duck from the start, Quiroga seemed determined to make a mark during his brief occupancy of the presidential palace. He pledged to continue Banzer's coca eradication policy, and he pushed several reform measures through Congress, including a civil service, non-partisan electoral courts, expanded powers for the comptroller-general and financial accountability for public officials. Armed with his new power, the comptroller-general began investigating other congressmen and other public officials without regard to party. One problem that still went unaddressed, however, was the rampant corruption in the national police.

When Quiroga issued a decree that outlawed the drying, shipping or sale of coca leaves in open markets, Morales denounced the decree as unconstitutional. When police attempted to close such a market near Cochabamba in January 2002, the protests flared into violence that left nine people, including four policemen, dead. A congressional panel sought to strip Morales of his seat for allegedly inciting the violence, but Quiroga and Morales compromised.

The Cliffhanger of 2002

The 2002 presidential race was the usual free-for-all. Two former presidents,

Sánchez de Lozada of the *MNR* and Paz Zamora of the Movement of the Revolutionary Left (*MIR*) entered the race. Quiroga's *ADN* nominated Ronald MacLean. Morales entered the race as the candidate of the Movement to Socialism (*MAS*), while Felipe Quispe stood for the Pachacuti Indigenous Movement (*MIP*). Rounding out the cluttered field of major contenders was the long-time mayor of Cochabamba and a former army captain, Manfred Villa Reyes, standard-bearer of the populist-oriented New Republican Force (*NFR*).

Sánchez, then 72, pledged to continue free-market reforms and to make Bolivia more attractive to investors, initiatives he had taken as president. Paz and Morales both denounced free-market capitalism. Paz said he would return some of the country's vast natural gas wealth to state control, while Morales, who chewed coca leaves at his rallies as a political statement, vowed to discontinue the coca eradication program and bombastically declared he would expel the *"yanquis."* Reyes offered only vague generalities.

U.S. Ambassador Manuel Rocha, in a stunning breach of diplomatic protocol, warned during a ceremony he attended with President Quiroga that voting for Morales could jeopardize continued U.S. aid. Bolivians of all political stripes denounced this U.S. intrusion into domestic politics. (Many Bolivians already were sensitive to U.S. intrusion, as the first lady still held U.S. citizenship.)

Sánchez took an early lead on June 30, with Reyes Villa close behind. But to everyone's surprise, Morales surged into third place. For nine days, the country—and the Bush administration—held their breaths. After the votes trickled in from the remote altiplano—coca-growing country—Morales finished in second place just 721 votes ahead of Reyes! A total of 2,993,708 Bolivians had voted, a respectable turnout of 72.04%. The complete official count:

Sánchez de Lozada	624,126	22.46%
Morales	581,884	20.94%
Reyes	581,163	20.91%
Paz	453,375	16.31%

Sánchez and Morales each carried four of the nine departments; Paz carried one.

Congress then had to choose from between Sánchez and Morales, and frantic jockeying began. The press reported again that Ambassador Rocha was thrusting himself into domestic politics by participating in an inter-party meeting and that he was applying "pressure" on behalf of Sánchez and against Morales.

For his part, Morales suddenly began sounding conciliatory. He insisted there

Former President Jorge Quiroga

was a difference between coca cultivation and narcotrafficking, which he said he had always opposed, but he blamed the problem on the demand for cocaine in the developed countries. He also made conciliatory remarks about the World Bank and the IMF.

Yet, on August 4, Congress elected Sánchez de Lozada, over Morales, 84–43.

An Abortive Presidency

Sánchez and Vice President Carlos Mesa were inaugurated on August 6, 2002. In his address, Sánchez made conciliatory overtures to the Indian-based movements that constituted much of the congressional opposition for the first time, promised to launch massive public works projects to create jobs and warned his countrymen that they "must choose between progress and collapse."

With his shaky 22% mandate, there was little Sánchez could accomplish, and even that meager base of support quickly eroded. Long-simmering tensions over the coca eradication program erupted into violence again in 2003, when troops sought to clear roadblocks that angry farmers had erected. The farmers kept the La Paz-Cochabamba highway closed for two weeks, and the resulting violence left 10 civilians and two soldiers dead before the government and the farmers agreed to negotiate. The worst was yet to come.

Sánchez announced plans for a new progressive income tax of up to 12.5% to augment the value-added tax, in order to meet IMF demands to reduce the budget deficit from 8.5% to 5.5%. The reaction was immediate, and violent. First, 7,000 La Paz police officers, who were demand-

73

Bolivia

**Former President
Gonzalo Sánchez de Lozada**

ing a 40% salary increase, went on strike to protest the new tax. They were joined by thousands of other protesters, who besieged the presidential palace. Protesters chanted, "Resign or die, those are your choices," apparently a parody of Sánchez's inaugural address.

Sánchez called out the troops. Policemen and soldiers confronted each other. In the ensuing exchange of gunfire, 14 people died. Chaos erupted as mobs looted and burned department stores; others occupied or set fire to 12 government buildings, including the vice president's office. Fires raged out of control as firefighters joined the striking policemen. Other riots broke out in Cochabamba and other cities.

Sánchez himself escaped from the presidential palace in an ambulance. Shaken, he agreed to rescind the income tax. Policemen returned to work and order was restored. The final toll was 32 dead and at least 102 injured, the worst civil violence since the implementation of democracy. A peaceful mass protest demanded Sánchez's resignation, and the president responded two days later by purging his cabinet of his most unpopular ministers and reduced the number of ministries from 18 to 13 to reduce expenditures. The IMF moderated its budget deficit demand to 6.5%.

By mid-2003, Sánchez's approval rating was 19%, second-lowest of any Latin American leader; it would plummet still lower. Bolivia remained a powder keg, which exploded again in September 2003. The spark was something that should have been heralded as a major boost to the economy: a $5 billion pipeline to Chile by which natural gas could be sold for export to the western United States. Nationalists were furious that the pipeline would pass through the territory that Bolivia lost to Chile in the War of the Pacific of 1879–84, and Morales and other peasant leaders objected to selling Bolivia's natural resources to the hated *yanquis*. Clashes between peasants and security forces left seven dead, and angry peasants once again blockaded La Paz. Teachers and street vendors in La Paz joined the protests, followed by the miners. Their demand: Sánchez's resignation.

Another 16 people died over the next two weeks; the El Alto suburb of La Paz was placed under martial law. A desperate Sánchez agreed to cancel the pipeline project, which would have created hundreds of badly needed jobs and brought in $1.5 billion a year in foreign exchange. The cancellation failed to placate the protesters, however, and on October 13 La Paz was paralyzed by a transportation strike. Fifteen people died in clashes in La Paz, El Alto and Santa Cruz, two of them soldiers. Morales joined those demanding that Sánchez resign, and in a stunning development, Vice President Mesa withdrew his support for the president because of the use of deadly force against the protesters and urged him to change course.

The embattled president, whose approval rating had dropped to a pitiful 9%, addressed the nation, but in unconciliatory language he refused to resign and blamed the unrest on "foreign" elements, apparently a reference to Venezuela's Hugo Chávez and Libya's Muammar Qadhafi, with whom Morales has close ties. The speech only inflamed the situation.

Thousands of miners marched on La Paz to join protesters who had besieged the capital with burning tires and rock barricades; the death toll mounted. On October 17, with his allies abandoning him, the death toll at 74 and the country on the brink of chaos, Sánchez bitterly submitted his resignation to Congress. He and his wife flew to Miami. The violent street protests were transformed immediately into mass celebrations.

Mesa Seeks Consensus

Hours later, Mesa, a 50-year-old historian and a respected journalist, was sworn in as Bolivia's 82nd president, providing some constitutional trappings to the third overthrow by mob rule of an elected South American president in less than four years. Addressing Congress, Mesa pledged a "period of historic transition" and promised a non-partisan cabinet. He advocated resolving the gas pipeline issue by referendum; the gas-producing areas that stood to benefit from it were solidly in favor of its construction.

Morales, widely seen as the man who orchestrated Sánchez's downfall, suddenly became statesmanlike and pledged to give Mesa a grace period to restore order.

By mid-2004, Mesa's approval ratings were above 70%, a dramatic contrast to the detested Sánchez. He held the promised referendum on the gas pipeline in July 2004. Voters approved all five issues on the ballot, one of them by 92%, handing the president a major vote of confidence. The referendum, a new experience for Bolivians, increased taxes at the wellhead on the foreign companies and trimmed some of their rights.

But that did not defuse the gas issue. The left pushed for either renationalization of oil and gas companies or at least greater state control. The gas-producing provinces of Santa Cruz and Tarija, however, had stood to benefit greatly from the pipeline deal. There was a 24-hour general strike in the two departments to demand autonomy from La Paz so they could close the deal themselves, the beginning of a separatist movement that still threatens to tear Bolivia in two.

A town-hall meeting was held in Santa Cruz, Bolivia's largest city with 1.4 million people, in January 2005 to demand popular election of the local governor; the president still appointed departmental governors. Tarija Department, where 85% of the gas reserves are located, also backed the separatist movement. Mesa acceded to the *cruzeños'* demand rather than risk bloodshed. He agreed to elections for all nine departmental governors in 2005, and he said he would call another referendum to decide the autonomy issue.

The next flash point was a controversial energy bill. Morales advocated raising the royalty on oil and gas extraction from 18% to 50%. Mesa sought a compromise that would put a 32% maximum tax on top of the 18% royalty. Morales and the various indigenous groups rejected the compromise, erected roadblocks and precipitated yet another crisis that came to a head in March 2005, when Mesa threatened to resign unless the demonstrations ended. Morales refused, and Mesa submitted his resignation to Congress. His bluff worked. Thousands of pro-Mesa demonstrators converged on the Congress, which unanimously rejected the resignation. Even Morales admitted he did not want Mesa to quit—yet.

Congress passed a compromise energy bill. Mesa stunned the country by refusing to either sign or veto it. The indigenous movements reacted with more protests. Mesa had kept his promise not to use deadly force, but he threatened again to resign if the protests turned violent.

The Senate president signed the bill into law. Morales continued to demand a 50% tax, and an "indefinite" strike began in El Alto to demand outright nationalization and even the dissolution of Congress. Tens of thousands of protesters besieged La Paz. Police fired tear gas and rubber bullets, but not live ammunition. Mesa abruptly proclaimed he would serve out the remainder of his term and not cave in to pressure. It was ominously reminiscent of October 2003.

In Santa Cruz, the autonomy movement was revived when Congress failed to call for a referendum. Leaders of the movement called a referendum themselves.

With Congress deadlocked, Mesa signed a decree for an election in October for members of a constituent assembly that would rewrite the constitution to give more power to the Indian communities, one of the militants' key demands. Mesa set the same day for a referendum on departmental autonomy. Neither side was placated. Both U.N. Secretary-General Kofi Annan and Pope Benedict XVI urged Bolivians to resolve the crisis peacefully.

On June 6, 2005, Mesa resigned a second time. He suggested that neither of the presidents of the Senate or Chamber of Deputies, who were next in the line of succession, should accept the presidency, which would require a new election within 150 days. Only the electoral process, Mesa warned, could save the nation, which he said was "on the brink of civil war."

The Congress abandoned La Paz for an emergency session in the judicial capital of Sucre. Protests quickly erupted there as well. On June 9, Congress voted to accept Mesa's resignation. Morales said his party would refuse to recognize either the Senate president or the Chamber president; consequently, both men refused to accept the presidency. Under the constitution, that left Supreme Court Chief Justice Eduardo Rodríguez next in line. He was sworn in late that night as Bolivia's 83rd president—and the fourth in less than two years. Clearly, Morales had become the new power in Bolivia. That same day, the so-called "Paris Club," composed of the eight largest creditor nations, announced it was canceling $40 billion in Bolivian debt.

Morales Achieves Power

The various factions in Congress set December 18, 2005, as the date for new elections for president, Congress and, for the first time, the departmental governors, and July 2, 2006, as the date for elections for the constituent assembly. Morales stood again as the *MAS* candidate. The other now-discredited established parties all but disappeared. A total of seven other candidates entered the fray, but the conservative, pro-free trade forces eventually coalesced around the candidacy of former interim President Jorge Quiroga and a hastily assembled electoral vehicle, Podemos (We Can). .

Morales was even more bombastic than in 2002, vowing to become the "nightmare" of the United States. He made ambiguous declarations, saying he would nationalize oil and gas but honor contracts with foreign-owned firms, and vowing to end the coca eradication program while promising to work with the United States against cocaine production. His motto was "zero cocaine, but not zero coca." He also pledged to implement a "democratic revolution" along the lines of that of Venezuela's Chávez and embraced what he called "21st century socialism."

Former President Carlos Mesa

Almost 2.8 million Bolivians went to the polls, a turnout of 84.5%. The final tally stunned the nation and the world:

Morales	1,544,374	53.7%
Quiroga	821,745	28.6%

The vote was truly historic. For the first time in their 23-year-old democracy, Bolivians had given a president a majority mandate, and for the first time in Bolivia's 180 years of independence, a member of the indigenous majority had been elevated to the presidential palace.

The *MAS* won 64 of the 130 seats in the Chamber of Deputies, just two short of an absolute majority, to 44 seats for Quiroga's *Podemos*. In the Senate, however, *Podemos* won 13 of the 27 seats to 12 for the *MAS*. Pro-Morales governors won in only three of the nine departments.

President-elect Morales embarked on a whirlwind 10-day world tour, first to Havana and Caracas to celebrate his win with his ideological heroes, Castro and Chávez. From there he went to Europe, South Africa, China and Brazil. In Brazil, he promised President da Silva, his friend and, like him, a socialist and former union leader, that he would not nationalize the holdings of *Petrobras*, Brazil's state-owned oil and gas firms, which had been one of the four companies responsible for discovering and exploiting Bolivia's rich gas deposits. Washington was pointedly excluded from Morales' itinerary.

On January 22, 2006, Washington's "nightmare" came true as Evo Morales, 46, assumed the presidential sash. Álvaro García was sworn in as vice president. Morales wore an open-necked jacket, and thousands of Indians attended the inauguration. So did Chávez and 10 other Latin American presidents (Castro was uncharacteristically absent), while the United States was represented only by Bush's assistant secretary of state for Western Hemisphere affairs.

The world waited to see whether Morales would pragmatically abandon his fiery leftist rhetoric once in office, like Brazil's da Silva, or become another loose cannon like Chávez. He chose the loose cannon option.

First, he loaded his cabinet with left-wing members of his indigenous movement and a handful of left-wing intellectuals with little or no administrative experience. Next, he tripled the minimum wage, which threatened to cripple small businesses and return Bolivia to the hyperinflation of the 1980s. At the same time, he slashed his own salary and those of even mid-level government bureaucrats, sparking mass resignations.

Morales saved his 100th day in office for his greatest bombshell. On May 1, 2006, International Labor Day, Morales declared Bolivia's gas deposits under state control and dispatched troops to seize the fields being exploited by French, British, Brazilian and Spanish-Argentine firms. Morales, clad in a hard hat, went to the largest gas field, operated by *Petrobras*, to read the decree; so much for his promise to da Silva. He declared that the firms would have to sign new contracts within six months or forfeit their property, a Mafia-like ultimatum.

He also increased the government's take of gas revenue from the 50% agreed to the year before to 82%, and declared that *YPFB*, Bolivia's state-owned oil company, would have majority control not only of the companies drilling for oil and gas in Bolivia but of refineries and pipelines as well. The heretofore friendly governments of Brazil, Spain and Argentina were stunned. Ironically, those socialist leaders were now on the receiving end of a nationalization. One of da Silva's responses was to begin expansion of Brazil's hydroelectric potential to reduce the dependence on Bolivian gas for electricity generation.

Morales returned to Havana, where he, Castro and Chávez signed a pact declaring the Bolivarian Alternative for Latin America, or *ALBA*, which is also the Spanish word for "dawn." *ALBA* was designed

Bolivia

as an alternative to the Free Trade Area of the Americas (FTAA) advocated by the United States.

Morales' natural gas power play cast a pall over the Fourth European Union-Latin American-Caribbean Summit in Vienna a few days later. Morales was warned that such draconian actions would serve only to discourage further foreign investment. Morales continued to insist in Vienna, not very convincingly, that he would respect investors' rights.

Morales further emulated Chávez's Bolivarian Revolution by decreeing re-distribution of 9,600 square miles of state-owned land to peasant farmers, mostly in the agriculture-rich east, as part of his "agrarian revolution." The plots are about 124 acres and titles were to be guaranteed. Morales said he planned to distribute 77,000 square miles during his five-year term, raising fears among agricultural business interests.

Just as it was with Chávez in 1999, the next step for Morales was the election in July for the 255 members of the constitu-

ent assembly, who drew up a new constitution revamping Bolivian institutions to guarantee the rights of the indigenous majority, and the concurrent referendum on regional autonomy. Unlike Cháves, Morales was dealt a muted victory. His *MAS* won a majority of 137 seats in the assembly to 65 for *Podemos,* but that was well short of the two-thirds he needed for his rubber-stamped revolutionary constitution. A majority of 55% of the voters opposed regional autonomy, but it carried handily in the four eastern departments, putting them on a collision course with La Paz.

Lacking the needed two-thirds majority, Morales decided in good Marxist fashion to change the rules. His delegates to the constituent assembly insisted that articles to the new constitution could be approved by a simple majority, although the final document would require a two-thirds vote and ratification by the voters. Squabbling between the pro- and anti-Morales factions led to fistfights in the assembly. The new constitution lengthened the pres-

idential term to five years and permitted immediate re-election, but set a two-term limit.

Meanwhile, Morales discovered that nationalizing oil and gas fields was one thing, operating them was something else. By August 2006, he admitted that the state-owned firm, *YPFB,* was desperately short of operating capital and was on the brink of shutting down. As the six-month deadline he had given the foreign companies approached, he pragmatically compromised. To appease the Brazilians, he fired his energy minister and reduced the taxes and royalties on *Petrobras'* two largest fields from 82% to 50%—still more than it had paid before. He reached agreements with the other companies that were essentially the same as the deal Mesa had struck that Morales had opposed so vigorously. *YPFB* has a majority 51% stake in the firms' operations, far from the full nationalization Morales had promised.

Morales suddenly ceased his anti-*yanqui* rhetoric when the realized that the preferential tariff the United States had granted

Bolivian textiles was due to expire in December 2006. Hat in hand, the Bolivians lobbied the new Democratic-controlled Congress to renew the accords. The pro-union by the deputy trade and exports minister was back in Washington to plead for another extension. The textile agreement brought in so much foreign exchange and created so many jobs in Morales' core constituency that he was forced to swallow his pride.

Morales resorted to decidedly undemocratic tactics to ramrod his constitution through the assembly. Pro-Morales demonstrators in Sucre blocked access to the assembly of anti-Morales delegates. The Morales faction quickly passed a constitution that, among other things, imposed heavy new taxes on the four wealthy eastern provinces, gave new powers to the indigenous majority at the expense of the Caucasian and *mestizo* minorities and lifted the ban on re-election that would allow Morales to run again. The assembly set May 4, 2008, as the date for the referendum on the new organic law.

The governors of Santa Cruz, Beni, Panda and Tarija responded by declaring their autonomy. Santa Cruz went a step further by scheduling a referendum on autonomy for May 4, the same day as the national referendum on the constitution.

The government postponed the May 4 referendum, but Santa Cruz proceeded with its autonomy referendum, which Morales angrily declared to be illegitimate and said La Paz would not recognize the results. Congress passed a resolution to that effect, with the government employing the same mob-rule tactics to prevent opposition members from entering.

In the referendum, 86% of *cruzeños* voted in favor of autonomy. Morales declared the vote a failure.

Morales next called a peculiar referendum in August on whether he, Vice President García and eight departmental governors would remain in office. In a twist of Chávez's victory in the recall election in Venezuela, Morales called this recall election on *himself*. With a turnout of 84%, Morales received a convincing vote of confidence with 67.4%, 13 percentage points higher than his 2005 election victory. Two anti-Morales governors, including former presidential candidate Manfred Reyes Villa of Cochabamba, were ousted and replaced by Morales appointees. The vote intensified the country's growing polarization. The anti-Morales governors of the four eastern departments were retained with strengthened majorities.

This emboldened the government to move forward on the new constitution in a heavy-handed manner. Morales announced yet *another* referendum, this time on his new constitution, in December 2008.

The four anti-Morales governors who had survived recall called for civil disobedience, including a general strike, in the so-called *"Media Luna"* departments (for their crescent-moon shape) to demand their share of oil and gas revenues that Morales had diverted to his social programs. Hundreds of opposition protesters seized a major gas field. One pipeline exploded, cutting off lucrative gas exports to Brazil. On September 11–12, 2008, anti-government and pro-government demonstrators fired on each other in Pando. In a separate incident in El Porvenir, Pando, as many as 19 peasants died in an ambush and about 50 were wounded.

Morales, again finding himself on the other side of the barricades, dispatched troops, declared martial law and arrested Pando Governor Leopoldo Fernández despite his constitutional immunity. Troops killed two protesters.

Fernández has been held ever since and has become an international *cause célèbre*. He faces a litany of charges, including treason and "genocide" for the "Porvenir Massacre." The trial finally got underway in August 2010 against Fernández and 24 other defendants; the prosecution had a list of 314 witnesses. Fernández was transferred to a maximum-security prison in 2011 even as the trial dragged on, with frequent delays. Fernández was hospitalized with what was described as arterial hypertension and cardiac arrhythmia. Then, in February 2013, he underwent surgery for kidney cancer. A court ordered him released from prison and placed under house arrest, and the trial drags on. He is now 62.

The violence flared for three weeks, leaving an estimated 30 dead. U.S. Ambassador Philip Goldberg met with the regional governors, prompting Morales to declare him *persona non grata* and expel him from Bolivia. The Bush administration responded by expelling the Bolivian ambassador and declaring Bolivia "non-compliant" in the war on drugs, threatening the cutoff of $30 million in aid. Morales later expelled U.S. Drug Enforcement Agency (DEA) agents.

Both sides prudently backed away from the brink of civil war, which neither really needed nor wanted. Mediators from neighboring nations were called in. Some compromises were reached on the new constitution, but in the end, the 411-article document gave Morales most of what he wanted: The right to run for re-election, greater state control over the economy and enhanced rights for the indigenous majority. The various Indian "nations" would be granted greater control over their own natural resources. The opposition, weakened by the president's two-thirds mandate on August 10 and frightened by the arrest of the Pando governor, could do little but howl in protest.

The outcome of the constitutional referendum was a foregone conclusion. The turnout was 3.5 million voters, or 90.3%, 61.4% of whom voted for the new organic law. Voters also approved limiting landholdings to 5,000 hectares.

U.S.-Bolivian relations went from deplorable to abysmal. After expelling the U.S. ambassador and visiting Libya and Iran, Morales displayed the height of diplomatic *chutzpah* by sending a delegation to Washington to plead for continuation of the preferential tariffs for Bolivian goods! Even as the Bolivians arrived, Secretary of State Condoleezza Rica announced the preferences would be allowed to expire on December 31, 2008. The move was expected to cost Bolivia an estimated 30,000 jobs and to price an estimated $300 million in Bolivian goods off the U.S. market. Morales bombastically declared that Bolivia did not need the drug aid or the preferential tariffs, apparently in the belief that his friend in Caracas would come to his rescue.

In 2008, Bolivia demanded the extradition of former President Sánchez de Lozada for "genocide" in the violence of 2003. In 2009, a district court in Miami rejected extradition but permitted civil actions against Sánchez to proceed in the U.S.

Morales expelled another U.S. diplomat in March 2009 for allegedly conspiring with opposition groups, and in April he accused the DEA of conspiring to assassinate him, but produced no convincing evidence.

To further annoy Washington, Morales hosted another visit by Iranian President Mahmoud Ahmadinejad. They signed a "mutual cooperation" agreement and made it a media event. In reality, the agreement served no purpose other than to irritate the U.S., and it certainly did little to make up for the loss of Bolivia's preferential tariffs with the U.S.. Female members of the Bolivian Congress objected to an earlier treaty signed by the two presidents in 2007 because of Iran's treatment of women.

In March 2009, Morales went on a hunger strike to intimidate Congress into setting the date for the election in which he expected to coast to a second term. Congress acquiesced and set December 6 for the presidential election and April 4, 2010, as the date for regional and municipal elections.

Second Term, Heavier Hand

The anti-Morales forces feebly coalesced around a new alliance, the Plan Progress for Bolivia. It nominated former Cochabamba Governor Reyes Villa, whom Morales had nudged out of second place in the 2002 cliffhanger. Six other candidates appeared on the ballot. But the opposition knew from the start that mathematics was against them.

Bolivia

Morales received 2,943,209 votes, or 64.2%, to only 1,212,795, or 26.5%, for Reyes Villa. Morales' *MAS* received 88 of the 130 seats in the Chamber of Deputies and 26 of the 36 Senate seats. The Plan Progress for Bolivia won 37 seats in the lower house and 10 in the Senate.

The departmental elections in April reinforced Bolivia's growing polarization. The *MAS* won the governorships of Chuquisaca, Cochabamba, La Paz, Oruro, Pando and Potosí. The opposition won in the eastern *"Media Luna"* departments of Beni, Santa Cruz and Tarija.

Since his second inauguration in January 2010 for the expanded five-year term, Morales has used his power as a cudgel to intimidate his opponents under the rubric of judicial reform and anti-corruption. His leading presidential opponent, Reyes Villa, was accused of fraud and fled to the United States, saying he could not get a fair trial in Bolivia. Four former presidents also are facing various charges. Sánchez de Lozada, still in the United States, is being tried *in absentia* on the genocide charges, but in 2012 Bolivia was still seeking his extradition from the United States.

Morales' new judicial reform, which provides for popular election of judges, also places the burden of proof on the defendant in corruption cases. The opposition charged that the so-called reform was a thinly veiled effort by Morales to pack the judiciary with his loyalists. Opponents of his reform orchestrated a vote boycott when the judges were elected in October 2011. Only 40.3% of the votes were valid, 41% of the ballots were defaced and 18.5% were blank. Morales swore in the 56 new judges in January 2012.

Another ominous feature of his "reform" is a new law that permits removal of public officials who have been merely charged with crimes, not convicted. Thus far, it has been used exclusively against officials critical of Morales.

More mass protests, the kind Morales himself used to lead against sitting presidents, erupted in December 2010. The day after Christmas, Morales announced that the subsidies on gasoline and diesel fuel, implemented six years earlier under Mesa, were no longer economically viable and would be allowed to expire. The subsidies cost the government $360 million in 2010 and with the skyrocketing price of crude oil it rose even further in 2011. The subsidies made Bolivian gasoline and diesel half the price it is in Brazil and Peru, sparking lucrative bootlegging operations. The effect of lifting the subsidies was an immediate increase of 73% in the price of gasoline and 84% for diesel, but taxi and bus owners were not allowed to make corresponding increases in fares. The announcement was made not very courageously on a Sunday,

President Evo Morales

while Morales was on one of his regular visits to Venezuela.

Private transport workers went on strike, and protesters took to the streets. On New Year's Eve, a chastened Morales rescinded the lifting of subsidies, but the problems they created remain. Meanwhile, Morales' approval rating in major cities dropped to 32%.

Morales next found himself at odds with some of his erstwhile supporters among the indigenous Indians. In September 2011, three tribes marched on La Paz to protest Morales' plan to build a road through a national park and Indian reserve, which the president claimed was necessary for development. The Indians were miffed that they had been informed of the road only after contracts were signed. Morales supporters blocked the marchers, and a standoff ensued. Foreign Minister David Choquehuanca went to the site to negotiate, but the protesters took him hostage. Morales then dispatched police to arrest the Indians.

The images in the media of armed police arresting primitive Indians conjured up memories of Morales' predecessors. His defense and justice ministers and other officials resigned in protest. He postponed plans for the road until after—what else?—a referendum in Bení and Cochabamba departments. But the Indians denounced the referendum idea as divisive and argued that the road threatens their way of life. Morales' handling of the pro-

test alienated many of his indigenous supporters. Various polling organizations in the first half of 2012 put his approval rating at about 32–35%—the third-lowest in the Western Hemisphere.

As another example of the government's lack of tolerance for criticism, Vice President Álvaro García Linera issued a blunt warning in October 2012 that he was taking names and would hold people accountable for criticizing Morales on Facebook or Twitter. Morales' allies in Congress threatened to pass legislation regulating social media.

Bolivians, and the world, were shocked by a brazen daylight attack on popular radio journalist Fernando Vidal in the southern city of Yacuiba in October 2012. Four masked men invaded Vidal's Radio Popular as he was on the air interviewing a guest about alleged corruption in the customs police in that area. Yocuiba is on a cocaine smuggling route. The attackers entered the studio, fired shots in the air, splashed gasoline on Vidal and a station employee and set them afire. Vidal was critically injured with second- and third-degree burns; he spent two months in an Argentine hospital. The employee was less critically injured.

Four men were arrested within days as they tried to enter Argentina. Denunciations poured in from press freedom groups around the world. The motive remains unclear; Vidal, 70, a former mayor, is a former supporter of Morales who broke with the president over what Vidal called his increasing authoritarianism. But Vidal also angered right-wing political groups, local officials and smugglers with his accusations of corruption. Authorities do not seem to be in a hurry to uncover the motive or the mastermind.

In November 2012, Morales nationalized two Spanish-owned electricity companies. He argued that the state could provide electricity at cheaper rates. Unlike Bolivia's previous experience with state-owned utilities, Morales recognized that they require capital investment. He dedicated $3.3 billion in 2012 from the natural resources windfall that has heated up the economy to expand and improve the state-controlled water system; he planned to invest another $3.8 billion in 2013. It was not clear whether he planned to do the same with electricity to increase the percentage of Bolivians with access to power from the current 78%.

Recent Developments

Just as it seemed Bolivian-U.S. relations couldn't get worse, they did. On May 1, 2013, Morales expelled the U.S. aid organization, the Agency for International Development, accusing it of seeking to undermine his government by infiltrating peasant unions and other groups. As usual, he offered no tangible evidence. There wasn't much left to expel; the U.S. had cut foreign aid to Bolivia from $100 million in 2008—the year Morales expelled the U.S. ambassador and the DEA—to $28 million in 2012.

Bolivia was one of about 20 countries to which Edward Snowden, the U.S. fugitive wanted for leaking classified information from his former job with the National Security Agency, had requested asylum in mid-2013. He eventually accepted asylum in Russia.

Morales was in Moscow to attend a summit of gas-exporting countries while Snowden was holed up in a transit lounge of the Moscow airport. He coyly said he would give Snowden's request "serious consideration" if he made it. When Morales left Moscow on July 3, France, Spain, Italy and Portugal reportedly refused to allow Morales' plane to use their airspace, forcing the plane to land in Vienna to refuel, where it remained overnight. While Morales was literally trapped there, the Spanish ambassador asked permission to inspect the plane to see if Snowden was aboard; Morales refused, but insisted Snowden was not on board.

Morales was cleared to leave, and when he returned to Bolivia he denounced what he called Europe's "act of aggression." He summoned an emergency meeting of *UNASUR* presidents in Cochabamba on July 4, but only the presidents of Argentina, Ecuador, Suriname, Uruguay and Venezuela attended (see Latin America and the World). He also threatened to close the U.S. Embassy.

Morales raised the rhetoric in his annual address to the U.N. General Assembly in September 2013, calling for the creation of an international "people's tribunal" for the purpose of bringing a lawsuit against the Obama administration for "crimes against humanity."

Morales also worsened already deplorable relations with Chile in late 2012 by suddenly diverting the water of a stream that had historically followed a natural drainage pattern into Chile. Chileans in that arid region depend on the water for their very survival. The Morales government issued only a lame rationale that the water was needed for irrigation and electricity generation in Bolivia, even though there is no agriculture in the area and the stream is too small to generate economically viable amounts of electricity.

Tensions were also strained with Brazil in August 2013 when a Brazilian diplomat helped an opposition senator, Roger Pinto, who had been living in the Brazilian Embassy more than a year after accusing members of Morales' government of corruption and drug trafficking, escape to Brazil in a diplomatic car. The Brazilian foreign minister was forced to resign over the incident.

In a stunning development, the Morales-packed Supreme Court ruled on May 20, 2013, that Morales could seek another term in 2014 because he was elected to his first term under the old constitution; thus, it ruled, the two-term limit began with his 2009 election. The opposition vowed to contest the court's ruling, but Congress has already amended the constitution to permit Morales to run again.

Eyes are now on the October 12 election. The question is, can he win again? Morales' popularity has followed a roller-coaster course. The Mitofsky poll of the approval ratings of 20 hemispheric leaders in September 2012 put Morales in 13th place with 41%. A Bolivian poll in January 2013 put his approval at 30%, his all-time low. But by October 2013, a new Mitofsky poll showed he had rebounded to 59%, probably because of a spurt of economic growth from the export of commodities and increased social spending.

More recent polling has been sketchy and of questionable reliability, but Morales is generally shown with a strong lead over his leading opponent, Samuel Doria Medina of the Broad Front, which is allied with the old *MNR*. Medina received 69% of the vote in a primary in April. Other candidates include former La Paz Mayor Juan del Granado of the Without Fear Movement and Santa Cruz Governor Rubén Costas of the Social Democratic Movement. The Green Party may still field a token candidate. If necessary, a runoff will be held on December 7.

In what may or may not have been an election-year gimmick, Morales, 54, signed up in May 2014 to play midfield on the Sport Boys professional soccer team beginning in August, at a minimum-wage salary of $213 a month.

CULTURE: The Spanish conquerors and settlers of Bolivia built new cities and tended to concentrate there, leaving the interior to the indigenous Aymara Indians. Today, the majority of Bolivians still speak Aymara as their first language, learning Spanish as a necessity to conduct official business. A substantial minority of the population also speaks Quéchua, the ancient tongue of the Incas. The populations of the cities of La Paz and Potosí are about 70% indigenous Indian, 25% *mestizo* and only 5% European.

Bolivian culture, consequently, remains essentially Indian with only a thin veneer of European Christianity superimposed upon it. Both cultures are represented as UNESCO World Heritage Sites: the ancient city of Tiahuanaco (Tiwanaku), which dates to 500 A.D.; the archeological site of Samaipata with its huge inscripted stone, which was built in the 14th century; the Jesuit missions of Chiquitos, begun in 1696; and the colonial-era cities of Potosí and Sucre.

Bolivia has produced few cultural figures of international note, although the flute–based folk music of the *altiplano* has become internationally popular abroad. It is not unusual to see *altiplano* flute bands in colorful Indian dress playing on street corners from New Orleans to New York to Paris to Venice. Bolivians insist that the Brazilians "stole" the music for the megahit dance *Lambada* in the 1990s from Bolivia. No Bolivian singers have ever won a Latin Grammy Award.

Because of the abysmally low literacy rate, Bolivia never developed a strong literary tradition. There were two newspapers of note, however, both published in *La Paz: El Diario*, founded in 1904, and *Presencia*, established by the Catholic Church during the revolutionary year 1952. *Presencia* ceased publication in 2001. Other current independent dailies now include *Los Tiempos, El Deber, La Prensa* and *La Razón*. The government of Evo Morales began publishing the daily newspaper *Cambio* in 2008. Freedom House rates the Bolivian press as only "partly free."

There are only 12 state-run or Catholic institutions of higher learning scattered about Bolivia, including the military engineering school, and three private universities. The Pontifical University of St. Francis Xavier in Sucre was founded in 1624 and is the second-oldest university in Latin America. Also prestigious is the Higher University of San Andrés (UMSA) in La Paz, founded in 1830.

ECONOMY: Bolivia's economy has been based on the extraction of its mineral wealth for more than 400 years. The vast sums produced were exported, with little or no benefit accruing to the Bolivian people. Mismanagement and the decline of world demands for its minerals resulted in the *de facto* bankruptcy of the Bolivian government. While the 1952 revolution largely ended serfdom, a lack of technical and financial resources limited a more even distribution of wealth and income. The nation's major source of income, the tin mines, are largely a thing of the past and has been replaced at least in part by exports of petroleum and natural gas. Hydrocarbons now account for 30% of government revenues, and natural gas accounts for 50% of export revenue.

The other mainstay of the Bolivian economy is coca leaf. President Banzer's program to eradicate coca cultivation between 1997 and 2002 was largely successful, but it created social unrest among the impoverished peasants who depend on it for

Bolivia

their livelihood. This program ceased with the election of the coca growers' leader, Evo Morales, as president in 2005.

Bolivia remains one of the hemisphere's poorest nations. GDP growth was 5% or less for a decade, but has since been stimulated by sales of natural gas and other natural resources. Growth was 4.6% in 2007, 2.8% in 2009, 4.1% in 2010 and 5.1% in 2011. In 2012 it was 5.2%, fourth-highest in the hemisphere, and in 2013 it was 6.5%, the third-highest.

But the boom is trickling down slowly. Per capita income in 2010 was $1,810, still the third-poorest in the hemisphere, ahead of only Haiti and Nicaragua. In 2011, Bolivia moved ahead of Honduras to become the fourth-poorest, with PCI of $2,020. It remained in fourth place in 2013, at $2,220. An estimated 49.6% of Bolivians still live on less than $2 a day.

President Sánchez de Lozada sought to boost the economy with the potentially lucrative sale of natural gas to the United States. Bolivia then had estimated gas reserves of 53.4 trillion cubic feet, second only to Venezuela in South America. This move encountered furious opposition from the left. Public protests against the planned construction of a $5 billion gas pipeline to a Chilean port led to Sánchez's resignation in October 2003 and to the resignation of his successor, Carlos Mesa, in June 2005 (see History). In 2007, Bolivia's natural gas production was an estimated 14.7 billion cubic feet, of which it exported 11.7 bcf. Brazil is its major customer.

On May 1, 2006, President Evo Morales, elected on the campaign slogan of "21st century socialism," decreed the nationalization of oil and gas deposits, which affected the holdings of Brazil's *Petrobras*, France's Total and the Spanish-Argentine firm Repsol S.A., among others, which had invested $5 billion in exploration and in developing Bolivia's natural gas industry (see History). Morales found himself forced to compromise with the foreign companies when the new state-owned firm, *YPFB*, found itself in need of $180 million in operating capital, as well as technological expertise.

The estimates of Bolivian gas reserves by domestic and foreign sources have been estimated at between 11.2 trillion and 24 trillion cubic feet, making them now the continent's second-largest. Gas production plummeted by 14% in 2009, to 445.7 bcf, both because of mismanagement and the dearth of new foreign investment. In 2010 it rose 14% to 507.5 bcf, still 10 bcf less than in 2008. In 2011 it was up by 9.9%, to 557.6 bcf. Figures for 2012 and were not available. YPFB, the state-owned hydrocarbons company, is investing $4 billion in the gas sector through 2015 and announced it expects to maintain current production levels through 2015.

In addition to its natural gas wealth, Bolivia suddenly finds itself sitting atop another potential windfall: lithium. Estimates of Bolivia's reserves of lithium in the salt flats of Uyuni range from 20 million to 100 million tons, which would be the world's largest. World demand for lithium has mushroomed because it is a key ingredient for the batteries used to power hybrid and electric cars. Bolivia's deposits represent just over half the world's known reserves; Chile is a distant second. Several Japanese and European companies expressed interest in mining the deposits, but the Morales government resisted foreign exploitation. The state-owned firm *COMIBOL* invested $19 million in a lithium plant in Llipi, which opened in January 2013. It is expected to produce 40 tons a year to start, but the government's goal is 30,000 tons, about 20% of global demand. Morales has declared that Bolivia can one day produce its own batteries and battery-powered cars, and proclaimed Bolivia the "Saudi Arabia of lithium."

A trade preference accord Bolivia had enjoyed under the U.S. Andean Trade Protection and Drug Eradication Act of 1991 was allowed to expire on December 31, 2008, representing a potential loss of $300 million in annual exports to the U.S., mostly textiles, and 30,000 jobs. Most of them were in factories in the impoverished El Alto suburb of La Paz, one of Morales' core constituencies. The U.S. Congress did not renew them in retaliation for Morales' expulsion of the U.S. ambassador in 2008 (see History).

THE FUTURE: Evo Morales' election in 2005 was analogous to the ascension to power of Nelson Mandela in South Africa after decades of apartheid. Alas, Morales has shown himself to be no Nelson Mandela. Mandela effected reconciliation between the black majority and white minority, which was, and still is, the country's economic powerhouse. The same is true of Bolivia's Caucasian minority. Unlike Mandela, Morales has set about to create a "tyranny of the majority" on the model of his mentor, Venezuela's Hugo Chávez. Moreover, the white population of South Africa is diffused throughout the country, while Bolivia is regionally polarized between the indigenous western departments and the Caucasian- and *mestizo*-dominated eastern departments. Instead of effecting reconciliation, Morales has chosen to bleed the affluent eastern departments of the income from their natural gas resources and alienate their people.

Morales' lack of statesmanship and vision has also unnecessarily earned Bolivia enemies abroad, alienating not only the United States, which responded by suspending Bolivia's preferential tariffs at the end of 2008, but even erstwhile friends like Brazil and Spain, whose companies he has nationalized. He seemed to be banking on the largess of Chávez to keep his economy afloat in the wake of the loss of the U.S. market. But Chávez died in March 2013. For the time being, the Bolivian economy is riding high thanks to world demand for its natural gas, lithium and other natural resources. If the world markets soften, what will he do to prop up his socialist model?

The outbreak of violence in September 2008 brought Bolivia perilously close to outright civil war. That possibility persists. The unknown variable in this complex equation is the officer and NCO corps in the Bolivian military. If the eastern departments secede, will these soldiers or former soldiers then choose sides, as happened at the outbreak of the U.S. Civil War? Such a civil war could result in appalling bloodshed if both sides have professional military leadership and weaponry.

Yet, despite his divisiveness and heavy-handedness, Morales' rise to power, his constant holding of referenda (which he knows he has the votes to win) and his landslide re-election victory in 2009, seemed to elevate his countrymen's faith in democracy. According to the annual *Latinobarómetro* surveys published by the British newsmagazine *The Economist,* the percentage of Bolivians who believe that democracy is preferable to any other form of government plummeted from 64% in 1996 to 50% in 2003 (when Sánchez fell) to just 45% in chaotic 2004. In 2006, Morales' first year in office, it was back up to 62%; in 2008, it was 68% and in 2009, it was 71%, fourth-highest in Latin America. It dropped back to 64% in 2011, still above the Latin American average of 58%. But in a new 2013 *Latinobarómetro* survey, when asked "how satisfied with the way democracy works in your country?" only about 39% of Bolivians responded they are very satisfied or somewhat satisfied—one point below the Latin American average.

Unfortunately, democracy Morales-style has proved to be an emulation of the dictatorship of the proletariat his friend Chávez implanted in Venezuela. The filing of criminal charges against four of Morales' presidential predecessors, his 2009 opponent and the former governor of Panda; his so-called judicial "reforms," which appear to be designed to effect retribution rather than justice; and his vice president's threat to regulate social media and punish those who criticize Morales, are not encouraging. Neither is the ruling by the Supreme Court, packed with his loyal minions, which has allowed him to run for another five-year term in the October 12, 2014, election. Polls show he will likely win again, allowing him to further consolidate his Chávez-style revolution.

Brazil

Iguazu Falls (Brazil, Argentina, Paraguay)

Area: 3,286,500 square miles
Population: 202,656,788 (2014 est.).
Capital City: Brasilia (Pop. 2.5 million in 2010).
Climate: The northern lowlands are hot, with heavy rainfall; the central plateau and northeastern regions are subtropical and dry; the southern regions are temperate with moderate rainfall.
Neighboring Countries: French Guiana, Suriname, Guyana, Venezuela, Colombia (North); Peru, Bolivia (West); Paraguay, Argentina, Uruguay (Southwest).
Official Language: Portuguese.
Other Principal Tongues: English, French, German and other European languages.
Ethnic Background: Black African/Mulatto (48%), European White (48%); Other (3%); Native Indian (1%).
Principal Religion: Christianity (Roman Catholic 75%, Protestant Evangelical 20%).
Chief Commercial Products: Coffee, refined metal ores, chemicals, cacao, soybeans, sugar, cotton, wood, automobiles and parts, shoes.
Currency: Real (established July 1, 1994).
Gross Domestic Product: U.S. $2.19 trillion in 2013 (est.) ($10,806 per capita, official exchange rate);
Former Colonial Status: Colony of Portugal (1500–1815); Kingdom of the Portuguese Empire (1815–1822).
Independence Date: September 7, 1822.

Chief of State: Dilma Vana Rousseff (b. December 14, 1947), president (since January 1, 2011).
National Flag: Green, with a yellow lozenge enclosing a blue sphere with 21 stars, five of which form the Southern Cross, and the motto *Ordem e Progresso* (Order and Progress).

Brazil occupies almost half of the South American continent and is almost as large as the continental United States. It stretches some 2,700 miles from the Guiana highlands in the North to the plains of Uruguay in the South and an equal distance from the "hump" on the Atlantic Coast to the jungles of Bolivia and Peru in the West. Almost half of this area is the hot, humid basin of the mighty Amazon River and its thousands of winding tributaries.

The northeast Bahia region, the interior of the "hump," is a semi-arid region; to the south and inland is a plateau drained to the northeast by the São Francisco River. This is a region of forests and plains which attracts migrants from other parts of Brazil and from abroad. The plains of the extreme south drain into the Paraná River valley. The southern states from Minas Gerais to Rio Grande do Sul comprise the effective Brazil, where approximately 90% of the population lives on less than 30% of the land. In an effort to draw settlers into other areas of the interior, the capital was moved in 1960 from pleasant and coastal Rio de Ja-

neiro to inland and not so pleasant Brasilia. A modern city as planned, the capital is now surrounded by outlying shantytowns with almost one million people within 12 miles of the central area.

HISTORY: Pedro Alvares Cabral first raised the Portuguese flag in Brazil on April 22, 1500 after having been blown off course while en route (he thought) from Portugal to India. The Portuguese government, preoccupied with its India trade, took little interest in the American claim until 1530, when it established a colony at Rio de Janeiro and in 1532 founded São Vincente. The land was quickly divided into vast estates with frontages on the Atlantic Ocean and ran west to the line of demarcation between Spanish and Portuguese areas for discovery and colonization—approximately the 45th meridian west, set by the Treaty of Tordesillas in 1494. These estates, called *capitanias*, were granted as feudal holdings to the nobles who were to build towns and forts, explore, settle colonists and enrich the mother country. Thirteen estates were laid out, but the poor quality of the colonists sent out and the oppressive climate gave them a poor start.

In spite of this, several towns were founded—Olinda in 1535, Santo Amaro, Itamarca and Pernambuco in 1536, Bahia in 1549—and from these towns expeditions explored the interior.

Brazil

From 1580 to 1640, Brazil was under Spanish control—Philip II of Spain had inherited the Portuguese throne. During this period, explorations were pushed beyond the demarcation line, but few towns were established in the dense interior. From 1630 to 1654, the Dutch briefly held the northeast coast from Pernambuco to Parnaiba. During most of its colonial period, Brazil was in reality a coastal colony with an immense, unexplored interior. That the colonies prospered and remained under Portuguese control was largely due to the politics of Europe and to the efforts of two capable leaders—General Tomé de Souza and General Mem de Sá—and to the efforts of a few Jesuit missionaries.

For almost one and a half centuries following Spanish rule, Brazil was neglected by the Portuguese government. It did, however, benefit from the liberal policies of the Marquis of Pombal, the Portuguese prime minister under Joséph I (1749–77), who did much to improve public services. In general, Brazil's communities were ruled by municipal councils with little interference from Lisbon. By the end of the colonial period, cities had developed power and prestige reminiscent of the feudal ones of Europe. The smaller municipalities were at the mercy of the militia commanders, and the great estates were under the absolute rule of their owners.

Probably the most cohesive force in the Brazilian colonies was the Catholic Church, and the most influential of the churchmen were the Jesuits. The Portuguese church had been influenced by modifying cultures at home, both Moslem and Oriental, and was subject to still more change in Brazil because of the native Indian and imported African cultures. The Jesuits took as their first responsibility the protection of the Indians. Despite the opposition of the planters, who needed labor, they gathered their charges into fortified villages, taught them useful arts and crafts, and improved methods of agriculture simultaneously with the fundamentals of Christianity.

The ouster of the Jesuits in 1759 was simply political reaction to the fact that they were so successful in their work of protecting the native Indians that they were bad for the colony's businessmen.

The settling of Brazil's interior was the work of a few pioneers, the celebrated *bandeirantes*, the boldest of whom were the missionaries and the slave raiders of São Paulo. The latter were foremost in establishing Portuguese rule in the interior; their raids forced the remaining Indians to withdraw deeper inland and served as a counter-force against Spanish penetrations. In their wake came planters and, later, gold prospectors. As African slaves were introduced, the slave raiders turned to commerce and industry, making São Paulo the most prosperous Brazilian state. The colonial economy was based on sugar and forest products until the end of the 17th century, when the lure of gold depopulated the plantations as owners and their slaves migrated to Minas Gerais. Gold was also found in Mato Grosso and Goiás; about the same time it was learned that the bright stones found in Minas Gerais were diamonds. This wealth brought an influx of immigrants and pushed the frontier further inland. In 1763 the capital of Brazil

was transferred from the north to Rio de Janeiro.

The cities furnished only the middlemen, the brokers and the hucksters in the development of colonial Brazil. Its theoretically rigid class society was in fact for many decades a bizarre mixture of aristocracy, democracy and anarchy. At the top was the ruling class from Portugal; next came those of Portuguese origin born in Brazil—which included a majority of the estate owners; then followed in descending order mixed bloods, slaves and native Indians.

Actually, the system was elastic. The mulatto children born of the owner and his slaves might be reared equally with his legitimate children, and the Negro with the capacity to win wealth or influence took precedence with the elite. By the end of the colonial period, the whites had declined in number and influence, while those of mixed ancestry showed strength and a high degree of adaptation to the Brazilian environment. Brazil's society was tolerant, and the freedom from interference from Portugal allowed it to develop a one-class people—Brazilians.

Brazil's history as an independent state may be divided into two periods: Empire and Republic, and these in turn have their subdivisions. Certainly, loyalty to

Brazil

Rio de Janeiro about 1825

the crown kept the regional factions from creating small states, as happened in the Spanish states of Gran Colombia and Central America.

Empire and Republic

In 1822, Pedro I, crown prince of Portugal and titular prince of Brazil, refused an order to return to Portugal and on September 7 declared Brazil independent. Surviving republican and separatist movements, he was able to create a constitutional monarchy. With his father's death in 1826, he inherited the throne of Portugal, which he renounced in favor of his five-year-old daughter to appease those Brazilians who feared a reunion with Portugal. However, through mismanagement and corruption, Pedro alienated the Brazilians, who in 1831 forced his abdication in favor of his five-year-old son, Pedro II. Fortunate in his tutors and regents, Pedro II proved to be a capable leader who retained the affection of the Brazilian people for a period of 49 years.

Although the abdication of Pedro I left Brazil on the verge of anarchy, the regents who governed during Pedro II were able to suppress rebellions. They made many liberal changes in the constitution, and Brazil avoided the series of tyrannical dictatorships experienced by many of the former Spanish colonies.

From his coronation in 1841 until 1850, Pedro II was occupied with establishing his authority to rule. The Brazil of this era consisted of population centers at Rio de Janeiro, Minas Gerais, São Paulo and Pernambuco. The population numbered some 7 million—between 1 and 2 million whites, 3 to 4 million Negro slaves, a million free Negroes and people of mixed blood and a half million Indians. The immense Amazon River basin was largely unexplored and while the cattle-raising south and the states of São Paulo and Minas Gerais were showing progress, the remainder of Brazil was still little more than a fringe of Atlantic coast settlements.

Although Pedro II's government was patterned after that of Great Britain, it lacked the popular base of the British government; the illiterate mass of Brazilians had no vote, and effective control fell to landowners, merchants and the learned men of the cities. Pedro's government was conducted by his ministers, while he exercised the role of arbitrator. The 1840s were devoted to the suppression of separatist movements and consolidation of the nation; the 1850s and 1860s were spent in resolving Brazil's foreign disputes and in enlarging the national territory. The 1870s and 1880s were marked by much liberal legislation, the growth of republican ideas, the abolition of slavery and the end of the Empire.

From the 1850s to the 1870s, Brazil's economy expanded in a manner similar to that of the United States. Railroads, industry, agriculture and land speculation attracted large amounts of capital and a stream of immigrants who brought technical skills missing from Brazil's own population. By the mid-1870s, Brazil was earning a net profit of some $20 million from its foreign trade. During this period, Pedro II fostered education and Brazilian cultural expression developed. Through the 1860s his popularity and support were such that he could have governed under any title—king, emperor or president.

Liberal in his religious views, he respected freedom of worship; when in 1865 the pope published a ban against Freemasonry, Pedro refused to permit its adoption in Brazil. Despite his stand, the conflict between church and Masonry grew to the point that he personally became involved, losing support from the church and the clergy without satisfying the Masons. Following the Paraguayan War (1865–70), the Emperor became involved in a dispute between the army and the Liberal Party;

Dom Pedro II, Emperor of Brazil

Brazil

while keeping the army under civilian control, he insisted upon supporting its legitimate needs for maintaining professional competence. These measures satisfied neither group and cost him the support of the elements whose interests he was defending.

The support of landowners was lost when slavery was abolished in 1871; the law also safeguarded the owners' economic interests and provided for the training of the emancipated slaves. Again, neither side was satisfied with Pedro's moderation and he was forced to abdicate in 1889 in the face of an impending military coup.

General Deodoro da Fonseca announced by decree the creation of the Federative Republic of Brazil, composed of 20 states. Pledged to recognize and respect the obligations created under the empire, the new government won popular acclaim. A constitution based on that of the United States was imposed on the country by decree in 1891. Although theoretically founded under democratic principles, the constitution gave less voice to the populace than it had under Pedro II. Fonseca later proved to be an inept leader and was replaced in 1893 by Marshal Floriano Peixoto, an even more capricious figure who provoked the navy into a rebellion which was followed by a short-lived civil war.

A reign of terror, heretofore unknown in Brazil, followed the rebellion. In 1894, Peixoto peacefully turned the government over to a more moderate civilian president, Prudente de Morais Barros, the first of three consecutive presidents from São Paulo.

The government was badly demoralized and had an empty treasury, while the people were widely split during a military-civilian standoff. Further complicating the scene were the *conselheiros,* a group of fanatics in the northeast who held out against the army until the last man was killed. The president spent his last year in office in peace.

The years to 1910 saw the republic develop under a series of three capable presidents, but two decades of turmoil then ensued, testing the strength of the federal republic. Problems centered around political meddling by the military, anarchic regionalism and an ailing economy, all of which were complicated by World War I. The military-civilian division worsened and continued for some 20 years, while loyalty to individual states was greater than national loyalty and was compounded by various militia loyal to local political leaders.

The Vargas Era

Asian rubber production, the decline of coffee prices and the loss of foreign markets, rubbed salt in already sore wounds. Foreign debts and unwise fiscal policies in Brazil brought it to the verge of bankruptcy. The worldwide depression and political blunders of the government brought on military intervention in 1930 and the installation of the populist governor of Rio Grande do Sul, Getulio Vargas, who ruled as dictator for 15 years. He combined a shrewd sense of politics with managerial ability and personal honesty. Sometimes compared with the Jesuits who defended the Indians against the landlords, Vargas posed as a defender of Brazil against the military and the powerful state governors, while trying to unify the laboring classes and grant the right to vote to the entire population. He was also compared to Italy's Benito Mussolini and Portugal's dictator, Antonio de Oliveira Salazar.

Getulio Vargas, 1934

Vargas rehabilitated the economy and forced state cooperation with the new national government. A new pseudo-fascist constitution in 1934 enfranchised women and provided social legislation to protect workers. Peace endured for a year, but was followed by communist and fascist attempts to seize power. Profiting from the scare, Vargas suspended the constitution in 1937, extended his term and ruled by decree. He called his regime the *Estado Novo* (New State), after Salazar's.

An amiable but forceful dictator, he selected capable men to administer government services and accomplished much to improve the living standards of the poor. His management of the national economy was sound and Brazil made notable progress in industrialization and production. He also brought Brazil into World War II on the side of the Allies and sent troops to fight in Italy. Despite the generally popular nature of his rule, by the end of the war, opposition had developed to the point that Vargas could only retain his position by the use of force.

On October 29, 1945, a committee of military officers persuaded Vargas to resign. Vargas already had ordered free elections for December, in which General Eurico Gaspar Dutra won the presidency by a decisive margin. Colorless and inept, he was unable to control the economy. Overspending and corruption and inflation spelled the end of his career.

In the elections of 1950, Vargas entered the competition as a candidate of the Labor Party and announced himself to be the champion of democratic government. The National Democratic Union was unable to stop his demagogic appeal. But his new term in office was not impressive; his appointees were largely incompetent and many were corrupt.

By 1954, general discontent was highly apparent; both the military and civilian elements were in a mood to unseat Vargas—events were triggered by an attack on the editor of a leading Rio newspaper. Faced with the evidence that his own bodyguard was implicated, and under military pressure for his resignation, Vargas instead committed suicide in his office.

Juscelino Kubitschek was elected in 1955, and it was he who initiated work on the new capital city of Brasilia. The government formally moved from Rio de Janeiro to Brasilia in 1960. There were also a flurry of strikes and refusals of the International Monetary Fund and Washington to advance further sums to a seemingly extravagant Brazil.

Campaigning on a platform of austerity and competent government, Jãnio Quadros won the 1960 elections by the largest plurality of any president in Brazilian history. However, he was embarrassed by a last-minute round of wage increases granted by Kubitschek and the election of a controversial leftist, João Goulart, as vice president. Quadros faced staggering problems, including large foreign debts, mounting inflation, widespread opposition to his plan for trade with the communist bloc and moderation toward Cuba. This led to feelings of frustration and his sudden resignation in August 1961.

Goulart was permitted to take office the following month only after agreeing to demands by conservative military officials to a drastic limitation of presidential powers. Brazil thus became a rudderless ship, headed by a president with no authority and a congress bitterly divided among 12 political parties. Faced with a stagnant economy, inflation that had reached an annual rate of 100% by 1964 and deepening social division, Goulart fought for and obtained greater power through a plebiscite in 1963. Relying increasingly on leftist

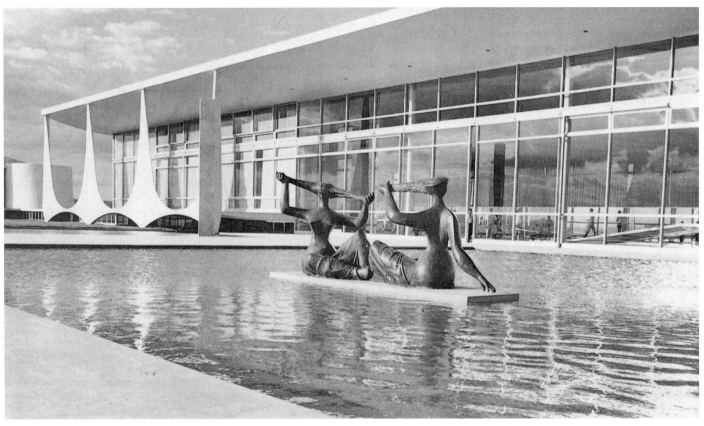

Brasilia's Alvorada Palace, the presidential residence

support, he sought to divide the military and use mass demonstrations to intimidate his opposition.

Military-*ARENA* Rule, 1964–85

Fearing the nation might be plunged into chaos, the armed forces ousted Goulart on April 1, 1964, and replaced him with General Humberto Castelo Branco. This began a series of military governments that altered the political and economic face of Brazil.

Regarding themselves as authentic "revolutionaries," the military imposed a presidential government controlled by the high command of about 12 top officers better known as the *Estado Maior* or general staff. Their basic goal was not a social revolution, but an industrial revolution to enable Brazil to become a major world power. Relying heavily on technicians, the military government was relatively honest and nonpolitical. Indeed, the traditional politicians were suspect, "social" programs had low priority and human rights were respected only when they did not interfere with the "revolution."

The military quickly imposed austere economic measures to control inflation. In addition, all political parties were disbanded and replaced by two new ones: the Alliance for National Renovation (*ARENA*), and the Brazilian Democratic Movement (*MDB*).

In theory, *ARENA* was to be the dominant, government party, while the *MDB* was to furnish token opposition. In reality, both parties were powerless to challenge the military. The military saw to it that *ARENA* won a large majority in carefully supervised 1966 elections. Following instructions, legislators then chose as the next president Marshal Arthur da Costa e Silva in 1967. In late 1968 he dissolved Congress, instituted press censorship and jailed prominent political opponents, including Kubitschek. In addition he suspended judicial "interference" with prosecution for "crimes against the state."

When Costa e Silva suffered a paralyzing stroke in mid-1969, General Emilio Garrastazu Médici was named president. Prosperity and repression were the two prominent traits of his regime, which believed that the first is possible only because of the latter. Under his tutelage, Brazil developed a prosperous economy, forcing even critics to compare the "Brazilian economic miracle" with the post-war boom in Germany and Japan, albeit at tremendous loss of liberty.

The expanding economy helped finance ambitious government projects in education, health and public works. The Trans-Amazonian highway linked Brazil's Atlantic coast with the Peruvian border, hacked 3,250 miles through vast empty stretches of the national heartland. The cost of economic boom was high; industrial growth was financed largely through exploitation of workers. During the first 10 years of military rule, the economy grew by 56% while real wages dropped by 55%. The result was a severe decrease in purchasing power for the lower classes.

In the same period, government expenditures for education were reduced by half and investments in health and social services also declined in real terms. While the upper 5% of the population saw its share of the national wealth jump to a total of 36%, the lower half's share dropped to 14%. Although Brazilian business executives were among the world's best paid, the bottom 40% of the people were underfed.

The political situation was even more rigidly controlled—the 1967 constitution, imposed by the military, provided for a strong executive and a powerless congress. Through Institutional Acts Nos. 5, 13 and 14, the regime systematically silenced its critics. Torture of political opponents was condemned by the Human Rights Commission of the Organization of American States. Prior censorship was imposed on the print media and the arts. Yet, some criticism of the regime seeped out. Most outspoken was the Catholic

Brazil

Church. The regime in turn charged that church work with the poor was communist-oriented. Paramilitary secret police frequently raided church offices, seizing property and harassing leaders. The regime conducted a major crackdown in 1973 on church activities that offended it.

A shamelessly rigged presidential election was held in early 1974. The official government candidate—selected by the military high command—was retired Army General Ernesto Geisel, a portly 68-year-old former head of the Brazilian oil monopoly, Petrobras. The only opposition candidate was denied meaningful access to the media during the campaign; he could not speak out against the regime, but he called the election a "farce." There

was no direct vote for president in Brazil; the "electoral college" formalized the selection of the new president by a vote of 400–76.

Although he promised a degree of moderation, Geisel cautioned that social reform must wait until the nation's economic problems were solved. Nevertheless, press censorship was greatly reduced, although not eliminated, and police repression was also less evident. Efforts were made to improve strained relations with the Catholic Church and organized labor; small steps were taken to increase wages for the workers.

After allowing politicians a greater voice in national affairs, despite objections from hardliners within the ruling military councils, Geisel went ahead with plans to

hold congressional elections in late 1974. The results proved to be a disaster for the regime and *ARENA*. The opposition *MDB* received twice the vote of the military-backed slate, winning 16 of 22 Senate seats and a third of the Chamber of Deputies.

Geisel tried to walk a tightrope between the two sides—he decided not to overturn the election results, but at the same time he appeared to have placated the conservative military by permitting a rise in right-wing "vigilante" acts against suspected leftists and petty criminals. Reports of torture of political opponents continued to circulate; most of this activity was conducted by the government's Intelligence Operations Detachment (*DOI*). The president revoked the political rights of three opposition leg-

STATES AND TERRITORIES

islators who charged that Brazil was being run by "an aristocracy wearing uniforms." The regime also brought charges against 21 critical journalists.

Economic decline had a dramatic impact on both Brazil's domestic and foreign policy. The quadrupling of oil prices by the Organization of Petroleum Exporting Countries (OPEC) in 1973–74 had a dramatic impact on Brazil, which then imported nearly 90% of its petroleum. Geisel's pragmatic response was to begin production of ethanol from expanded cultivation of sugar cane, and he decreed Brazilian auto manufacturers to begin producing ethanol-burning engines (see Economy). Brazil thus became a trendsetter in the production of alternative fuels, although the rest of the world did not catch on for another 30 years.

In foreign affairs, Brazil in 1975 became the first Latin American nation (aside from Cuba) to recognize the Soviet- and Cuban-backed revolutionaries in the Angolan civil war. This surprising move by the staunchly anti-communist regime was largely due to economics, as Brazil hoped to buy Angolan oil and wanted to include that country in an international coffee cartel to raise the price of that commodity. It also viewed this Portuguese-speaking African nation as a potential customer for Brazilian products.

Although Brazil always had maintained cordial relations with the United States, there was a strain in 1975. Besides recognizing Angola, Brazil voted in the UN to equate Zionism with racism. (Brazil imported much of its oil from Arab states).

Further questions centered around development of atomic power based on West German technology. Although Brazil said it would not build an atomic bomb, the United States and other countries feared Brazil's entry into the nuclear field would accelerate the race for nuclear weapons then shaping up in the Third World.

In 1977, the new Carter administration reduced military aid until Brazil showed greater respect for human rights and called on Brazil to terminate its nuclear program. Brazil's response was cancellation of the entire 25-year-old military pact with the United States.

Geisel faced a serious conflict with the business community, which openly complained that it was being elbowed aside by huge, state-run industries and fast-growing multi-national corporations. Small farmers (as in the United States) were forced off their land by huge farm combines and other modern agricultural techniques. Political tensions mounted.

After the Congress dismissed Geisel's proposal for judicial changes in 1977, the president dismissed Congress for two weeks. By decree, he ordered changes that made Brazil a one-party state. Under the plan, the president, all state governors and a third of the Senate would be elected indirectly, and in a manner so as to force them to remain under permanent control of *ARENA* and the military. The measure further gave the president another year in office.

Geisel chose his successor, announcing in early 1978 that General João Baptista de Oliveira Figueiredo, head of the national

intelligence agency, would become the next chief executive. Virtually unknown to the public at the time of his nomination, Figueiredo sought to project the image of a Harry Truman-style "man in the street"—a campaign model that sharply contrasted with Brazil's normally stern, colorless military leadership. The obedient electoral college officially named Figueiredo to a six-year term. In contrast, unusually free congressional elections were held in late 1978. To the chagrin of the military, the opposition *MDB* won a majority of the 45 million popular votes, largely because of big margins in urban areas. Nevertheless, since Brazilian law prohibited any opposition party from winning control of Congress, *ARENA* wound up with 231 of the 420 seats in the lower house and 42 of the 67 Senate seats. All 21 state governors and most city mayors were appointed directly by the military.

Installed in March 1979, Figueiredo pledged to "open this country up to democracy"—a promise that dismayed some army officers who distrusted civilian government. Under a new plan, free, direct elections were to be held for every office except president. Brazil suddenly came alive with political activity. For the first time, government opponents were allowed access to the news media, and the last political prisoner was released. At least six parties fielded candidates. The plan put all Chamber of Deputies seats and one-third of the Senate seats up for grabs.

Maintaining the government-proclaimed policy of gradually returning the country to democratic rule, on November 15, 1982, peaceful elections were held for 479 seats in the Chamber of Deputies, one third of the seats in the Senate, the state governorships and assemblies, and the municipalities. Five parties participated—one pro-government, the *Partido Democratico Social* (*PDS*), and four opposition groups, the most important of which was the *Partido Movimento Democratico Brasileiro* (*PMDB*). The *PDS* gained an overall victory, retaining vital control of Congress, but the opposition, mainly the *PMDB* and the *Partido Trabalhista Brasileiro* (*PTB*)—Brazilian Labor Party—managed to win the governorships of the three most important states: São Paulo, Rio de Janeiro and Minas Gerais.

Public attention then became focused on the presidential elections. The majority of the opposition leaders favored direct presidential elections. The military-backed *PDS* convention in Brasilia nominated Paulo Salim Maluf, a wealthy businessman of Lebanese heritage. At the same time, a coalition of the *PMDB* and dissident *PDS* delegates calling itself the Democratic Alliance met and selected a widely known and revered public figure, Dr. Tancredo Neves. This elderly gentleman had the unique ability

Cattle-drawn cart

Brazil

to attract the support of not only military elements, but communists and leftists. José Sarney, who had recently resigned as head of the *PDS*, was named his vice presidential candidate.

Figueiredo, beleaguered by both illness and the military, correctly foresaw a Neves victory. He made peace with him in an unwritten agreement. Sensing the tide running against him, Maluf attempted to make party allegiance binding on all delegates of the electoral college. The effort failed.

Return to Democracy

In January 1985, indirect presidential elections were held, and an 686-member electoral college representing most political parties elected Neves by a majority of 480–180 for Maluf.

Neves would have been sworn into office for a five-year term on March 15, officially ending a period of military rule of 21 years. Popular celebrations were cut short by the president-elect's sudden illness. Neves was rushed to the hospital the day before his inauguration; he died on April 21, 1985, plunging the country into mourning.

Vice President Sarney, who had been acting president during Neves' illness, assumed the presidency and proclaimed that he would follow "the ideas and plans of Tancredo Neves." He inherited a coalition of Neves' center-left *PMDB* and the smaller rightist Liberal Front Party (*PFL*), formed by a faction of the *PDS* of which Sarney had been president. Bickering between the two factions erupted almost immediately. Sarney initially ruled somewhat timidly and it appeared that he lacked the leadership necessary to move Brazil forward.

Labor unrest was rampant; a strike by a half million truckers, who in early 1986 blocked highways, threatened the food supply of the cities. This was topped by 1985 strikes by 2 million other workers, many under the leadership of a trade union firebrand destined to play a major role in Brazilian politics for the next two decades: Luiz Inácio da Silva, better known by his sobriquet "Lula."

Sarney did nothing to lessen corruption, that which had grown worse under the military. He spent the nation into virtual bankruptcy but did nothing for the impoverished masses.

Nature was not kind to Brazil, either. A killing frost in the 1970s destroyed millions of coffee trees; as soon as the industry had recovered, a murderous drought killed or stunted the plants, reducing production by 50%. Floods in the northeast and southeast in the 1980s followed by a five-year drought in the northeast left more than a million homeless. In late 1994,

Former President and Mrs. Figueiredo

killing frosts again hit the coffee trees, resulting in a 100% rise in the price of Brazil's favored Arabica coffee. These natural disasters increased migration of unskilled, penniless people to the cities.

Economic Reforms and External Debt

Sarney's attempt at economic reform was "The *Cruzado* Program," which froze prices and decreed wage increases of 20% in many sectors. The *cruzeiro* was abolished and the *cruzado* took its place, at a ratio of 1,000:1. An ostensible freeze on government hiring commenced at both the federal and state levels.

The staggering foreign debt (the largest in the world at $108 billion) was hesitantly rescheduled by the "Paris Club," a group of creditor nations representing commercial and national banks that had lent money to Brazil.

A watered-down land reform plan permitted the purchase only of sub-marginal land, yet landowners sometimes hired gunmen to drive out peasants who had resettled. "Liberation theology" priests and bishops of the Roman Catholic Church who supported the poor fomented unrest. Pope John Paul II reminded the National Conference of Brazilian Bishops that the clergy had to stay out of politics, although he, too, supported land reform in Brazil.

High interest rates were established to discourage capital flight. Taxes were raised, including on the purchases of U.S. dollars (25%) and cars, and on compulsory "loans" to the government. These reforms were generally greeted with acceptance by a country that had been sapped economically for so long. But the "maharajas"— persons with low or nonexistent work at government "jobs"—remained a parasite.

The *PMDB* and *PFL* increased their majority in the Chamber of Deputies in 1986 elections to a total of 374 out of 487 seats.

Because of inflation and currency instability, a vigorous black market developed. Brazil sank into actual bankruptcy. Sarney made it official in 1987: Brazil would suspend payment of principal and interest on its foreign debt indefinitely, which disrupted international credit. The moratorium worsened economic chaos within Brazil to the extent that there was a genuine threat of resumed military control.

Although heavily indebted, Brazil became the 10th-largest industrial nation in the world. It developed a lively business in aircraft and armaments worldwide, selling products of good quality and easily repairable. It surpassed Bolivia in tin production and experimented in enriched nuclear fuels, while avowing not to develop weapons. Nevertheless, it insisted on classifying itself as a Third World nation.

Former President José Sarney

Glamorous Rio de Janeiro from the ocean . . .

Supreme Court overturned him. Civil servants had tenure under the constitution and could not be fired. Collor also oversaw the sale of 4,675 government limousines.

Things began to fall apart in 1992, when Collor was caught up in an unprecedented four-part storm.

First, the righteousness he displayed in his campaign inflamed the passions of his supporters to a degree he never anticipated. Second, his loose-cannon younger brother decided to play to the tabloid media in a series of exposés that became a media frenzy. Third, Collor had virtually no support in either house of the Congress, and his Cabinet turned out to have the loyalty of hyenas. Finally, he had used about $2.5 million in campaign contributions for personal purposes.

The attacks by non-Collor-owned media were vicious. The alleged offenses he was charged with had been commonplace and overlooked in Brazil for more than a century. But incited particularly by a rival TV network, popular demonstrations against Collor became commonplace.

Congress impeached Collor in 1992, which some felt was like the pot indicting the kettle. He resigned rather than face a televised, months-long trial, but was convicted of "lack of decorum."

The Supreme Court dismissed criminal charges because of "insufficient evidence." Collor benefited from the unwritten Brazilian law that no former political leader is convicted—of anything. In 2006, he was elected to the Senate.

Fernando Collor de Mello

After five years of economic chaos under Sarney, capped by an inflation rate of 1,700% in 1989, the 1989 elections centered on the economy. Although 30 candidates entered the fray, three emerged as the frontrunners. Because candidates of the left-wing *PTB* had been so successful in municipal elections in 1988, its leader, "Lula" da Silva, was initially the frontrunner. Leonel Brizola of the also leftist Democratic Worker's Party was second. Both were quickly outpaced by Fernando Collor de Mello, of the hastily organized, right-of-center National Reconstruction Party (*PRN*).

This wealthy, tall, handsome governor of poverty-stricken Alagoas State, trained as an economist, began his career as a reporter and went on to own a number of media organizations. He contrasted sharply with da Silva, a lathe operator with a fifth-grade education. Collor made a bold promise: 7% annual economic growth. If there was anything left over, it would be used to retire foreign debt.

The campaign for the November election was dirty and spirited. When the dust

settled, Collor had 28.5% of the vote and da Silva 16%. About 17% cast blank ballots (voting is compulsory over the age of 18 in Brazil). After an equally heated runoff in December, which had a turnout of 88.1%, Collor won 50% to da Silva's 44.2%; the rest were void or blank.

Collor took office on March 15, 1990. If the people thought Collor's campaign promises were stiff medicine, they gasped when decrees started to issue from the presidential palace. Banks were closed for three days and savings accounts were limited to withdrawals of the equivalent of $1,200. Industries were allowed to withdraw only enough to pay current salaries, resulting in wholesale layoffs. Although this initially landed about $88 billion, it quickly dwindled to about $16 billion through corruption. The cruzeiro was reconstituted the national currency at a vastly increased value. Much of Brazil reverted to a barter economy because of currency shortages. Yet, 80% of the people stood solidly behind Collor despite personal sacrifices.

The president had vowed to get rid of 360,000 unneeded government workers. He reached the figure of 260,000, but the

Itamar Franco

Collor's successor, Itamar Franco, was an unintelligent, colorless, temperamen-

Brazil

tal hack who had bubbled to the top of the Brazilian political cauldron. He showed poor judgment in personal matters while in office, permitting himself to be shown on TV holding hands with and kissing a young pornography actress.

During most of Franco's 27-month tenure, Brazil went from disorganized to chaotic. Inflation neared 40% per month, devaluing the currency to the point that it was virtually worthless. About half the people lived outside the wage economy. The authority of the state virtually disappeared. Murder, which had been frequent, became ordinary. The killing of homeless "street children" in Rio and other large cities reached dreadful levels. Prostitution at age 8 was common. Shantytowns around the cities (*favelas*) were, and still are, controlled largely by drug gangs.

An effort was made in 1994 to assert control by sending the military with armored vehicles into areas close to Rio de Janeiro, which has the third-largest slums in Latin America. This was done when it became apparent that innocent people were being frequently killed during police forays in pursuit of drug dealers.

The Congress wallowed eyeball deep in its own scandals; with Collor disposed of, the media turned on it. The judiciary and police also remained openly corrupt.

After wearing out four finance ministers, Franco appointed Fernando Henrique Cardoso in 1994. It was an unlikely choice; Cardoso was a longtime Marxist economist and one of the loudest of the *dependentistas,* who viewed foreign investments as a threat to national identity. His book, *Dependency and Underdevelopment in Latin America,* was the Koran of dependency theorists. When it was published, Cardoso was exiled by the military government.

Once in office as finance minister, equipped with power rather than theories, Cardoso underwent a conversion as dramatic as that of St. Paul on the road to Damascus. He pragmatically replaced the inflation-riddled and devaluation-prone *cruzeiro* with a new currency, the *real,* which was pegged to the U.S. dollar. Cardoso also began welcoming foreign investors and dismantling inefficient and costly state-owned utilities and other enterprises. Under Cardoso's guidance, inflation plummeted from 2,500% annually to double-digits. He became a national hero, an economic David who had slain the hyperinflation Goliath.

In October 1994, Cardoso was the presidential candidate of a coalition of his own Social Democratic Party and Franco's larger *PMDB.* He handily defeated da Silva, the perennial candidate of the left, 54.3% to 27%; turnout was 82.2%.

Cardoso and Crisis

Cardoso was inaugurated in January 1995 to a reduced four-year term, and he forged a record as an able and effective president. His policies stabilized the *real* and provided real GDP growth that was a steady 3-4% throughout his first term. He also followed through with his privatization program, as billions in foreign investment flowed into the country. At the end of 1997, unemployment was a mere 4.84%. On the negative side, corruption remained ingrained, resisting attempts to combat it from the top.

An important political development in 1996 was the election of Celso Pitta as the first black mayor of São Paulo, although his administration, too, was marred by corruption.

Riding a crest of popularity, Cardoso persuaded Congress in 1997 to amend the constitution to allow him to seek a second term, arguing that no president could successfully deal with the country's prodigious problems in one four-year term. His popularity was only marginally affected by the impact of the Asian market crisis that October that caused him to impose another austerity plan. Unemployment shot up sharply in 1998.

Da Silva, again, was his only major opponent. The 1999 campaign took a nasty turn when da Silva accused Cardoso of offering to sell off the state-owned communications firm, *Telebras,* below market value: Cardoso responded by suing da Silva for defamation.

In September, the world financial jitters, stemming from the previous year's Asian market crisis and uncertainty over the Russian ruble and debt payments, came crashing down on Brazil. Rumors spread that Brazil would devalue the *real,* which

... seen from Corcovado crowned by Christ the Redeemer, and then to ...

... the city's dark side where poverty and desperation live side by side in the favelas

caused a market panic in São Paulo. On one day, the market dropped 13%, and the panic spread to Argentina, Mexico, Venezuela and Colombia; shock waves also were felt in New York, Europe and Asia.

To defend the *real*, the government sold off $30 billion of its reserves of dollars. Interest rates were raised from 29.75% to 49.75%. Cardoso announced an austerity program to reduce the huge budget deficit, a move sure to reassure the IMF and nervous foreign investors, but highly risky for a politician nine days away from an election.

Yet, voters gave Cardoso a resounding new mandate, 53% to 32%. He put off details of the austerity program until after the governor's races three weeks later. Franco, now Cardoso's bitter enemy, was elected governor of Minas Gerais.

Cardoso was inaugurated for his second term on January 1, 1999; the same day, Franco was inaugurated as governor of Minas Gerais. Cardoso's austerity plan calmed the fears of foreign investors and lending institutions. The slide of the *real* had stopped, and it was still pegged to the dollar; sanity returned to the stock market, and inflation had remained under control.

Suddenly, the willful Franco, known to be consumed with jealousy against Cardoso, tossed a boulder into this tranquil pond and precipitated a financial crisis with global repercussions. He announced a 90-day moratorium on the payment of his state's $13.5 billion debt, triggering another market panic that far surpassed the one in September. World markets nosedived, and international condemnation

was heaped upon Franco, who actually seemed to relish the attention. It backfired on him; the World Bank froze $209 million in development loans for Minas Gerais.

The central government could no longer prop up the *real* by selling dollars so it abandoned the five-year-old *Real* Plan—which Franco and Cardoso had introduced together—and announced that the *real* would float against foreign currencies. At one point, the *real* plummeted 46%, before beginning a slow climb. The devaluation made Brazilian exports more attractive.

Brazil slid into recession, but international fears that the Brazilian economy would collapse proved unfounded. Cardoso's painful austerity measures coupled with rising unemployment dragged down his approval rating.

In 1999, the economy shrank by .4%, not as bad as Cardoso had predicted, and grew by 2.6% in 2000. In April 2000, Brazil paid off the last of the $41.5 billion of the international loan package the IMF and other institutions had advanced during the 1999 market panic. Clearly, the economy was back on track.

There was a historic governmental restructuring in 1999. Cardoso created a new defense ministry, consolidating the three armed services and placing them under a civilian minister for the first time. The three chiefs of the uniformed services simultaneously were removed from the cabinet. The change showed how far the country had emerged from the 1964–85 dictatorship.

On April 22, 2000, Brazil observed the 500th anniversary of the landing of Portuguese sailor Pedro Alvares Cabral in Brazil in 1500. But what Cardoso had intended as a major celebration of national identity and unity turned ugly when nearly 200 Indian tribes protested the event in Porto Seguro as an insult to their own cultural identity. They had a point; there were 6 million indigenous inhabitants when Cabral landed, but there were only 700,000 left. One of their banners asked: "Who says Brazil was discovered?" The Indians were joined by some African Brazilians, who said to celebrate the Portuguese arrival was to celebrate the legacy of slavery. The protests turned violent as police and Indians clashed. Cardoso cut short his appearance in Porto Seguro, his carefully planned party in ruins.

A more violent confrontation occurred between authorities and landless peasants who squatted on unused lands and even forcibly occupied government buildings in Brasilia. About 30,000 peasants of the Landless Rural Workers Movement, or *MST*, took part in the protests, which left one peasant dead and 47 injured. Cardoso agreed to parcel out 5 million more acres in addition to the 40 million that he al-

Brazil

Former President Itamar Franco

ready had distributed. The landless issue remains volatile in Brazil.

Voters went to the polls in October 2000 to elect mayors and councilmen in more than 5,500 municipalities. For the first time, re-election was permitted. Da Silva's Workers Party (*PT*) increased its share of the popular vote from 10.6% in 1996 to 14.1% and the number of mayors from 112 to 174. In the 31 cities holding runoffs on October 29, the *PT* won 13 of the 16 that it contested. Marta Suplicy, a former television sex psychologist in the 1980s who later served in Congress, was elected mayor of São Paulo.

Congress approved a long-debated revision to the country's archaic 1916 civil code in 2001, legitimizing the civil status of people born out of wedlock, lowering the age of majority for marrying or signing contracts from 21 to 18, and eliminating the preferential legal status of men over women. Previously, a man could annul his marriage if he discovered his bride was not a virgin. Under the new code, neither spouse can go into debt without the consent of the other, and divorced fathers have equal custody rights.

Meanwhile, Brazil's alarming crime problem, and the methods used to deal with it, remained in the international spotlight. Reports of extrajudicial executions of criminal suspects, especially youths in the country's squalid *favelas*, were commonplace—and still are. In 2001, Amnesty International alleged that torture was still a widespread practice by Brazilian security forces.

Brazilians were reminded of the evil nature of the problem in 2002 when Tim Lopes, an award-winning investigative reporter for the *Globo* network, was murdered while conducting an undercover investigation into sex abuse and drug use

in a Rio de Janeiro *favela*. His burned and desecrated corpse was found in a cave. The killing outraged the country. Four people were arrested, including a drug lord.

Lula Finally Prevails

Da Silva declared his fourth candidacy in 2002, and this time the polls showed him leading a field of lesser-known candidates. Among those were Health Minister José Serra, of the *PSDB* and Cardoso's acknowledged choice as his successor; Rio de Janeiro State Governor Anthony Garotinho of Brazilian Socialist Party; former President Franco of the *PMDB,* then governor of Minas Gerais but still a pariah; Ciro Gomes of the moderate-left Popular Socialist Party; and Maranhão State Governor Roseana Sarney, daughter of former President José Sarney of the *PFL,* still part of the governing coalition. Sarney later dropped out because of a financing scandal.

The possibility of a da Silva victory sent a chill through international financial markets, prompting the candidate to engage in some frantic public relations maneuvering. The *PT* pointed to the sound fiscal records of the states and municipalities it controlled, and da Silva pledged to continue Cardoso's rational policies; he even began wearing suits and ties! Moreover, the *PT* entered into an alliance with the center-right Liberal Party in June, and da Silva named José Alencar, a Liberal senator, as his running mate.

Da Silva decided to play statesman, seeking to dispel his international image as a leftist bogeyman. Pundits la-

**Former President
Fernando Henrique Cardoso**

beled the new da Silva "Lula Light." Da Silva's bandwagon attracted a rush of latecomers.

On October 6, 82.2% of the 115.1 million registered voters in the world's fourth-largest democracy turned out. The results:

Da Silva	39,443,876	46.44%
Serra	19,700,470	23.20%
Garotinho	15,175,776	17.87%
Gomes	10,167,650	11.97%

The runoff was largely anticlimactic, and Da Silva's bandwagon took on the appearance of an M-1 tank. Serra bravely continued, but even Cardoso distanced himself from his own candidate.

The voters gave da Silva the expected present for his 57th birthday on October 27:

Da Silva	52,777,919	61.28%
Serra	33,354,230	38.72%

Turnout was 79.5%. Serra graciously conceded, as congratulations poured in from Cardoso, George W. Bush and other world leaders. Millions of da Silva's supporters poured into the streets for a Carnaval-like celebration.

On January 1, 2003, the one-time shoe-shine boy, metal lathe operator and trade union leader who never went beyond the fifth grade finally realized the goal that had eluded him in three previous elections as he was sworn in as president. He was the first avowed leftist to serve as president since Goulart, overthrown by the military in 1964, and the first one elected directly. Brazilians, and the world, waited anxiously to see whether he would prove to be another statesman like South Africa's Nelson Mandela—or another loose cannon like Venezuela's Hugo Chávez.

Da Silva performed a dexterous balancing act between the fire-breathing leftists in his own party on the one hand and the IMF, the Brazilian business community and the conservative opposition in Congress on the other. He had little choice but to govern by consensus; his *PT* had only 91 seats in the 513-member Chamber of Deputies, although it was the largest bloc in the lower house, and 14 in the 81-member Senate.

Da Silva struck an unlikely deal and made former President Sarney of the *PSDB*, once the target of da Silva's strikes, president of the Senate. Da Silva hammered together a coalition of nine of the 16 parties in the Congress, but the opposition still enjoyed a comfortable majority in both houses. The opposition, fortunately, opted for cooperation over confrontation.

To mollify his core constituency on the left, da Silva led his entire cabinet on a visit to one of Rio's worst *favelas*. He delayed

a contract to purchase 12 new jet fighters for the air force. He hosted the assembly of the left-wing World Social Forum in Porto Alegre. He created a Council for Economic and Social Development, a town-hall-style body the *PT* had used successfully at the local level. And he made elimination of hunger his top priority through the establishment of *Fome Zero* (Zero Hunger), an ambitious nutrition program.

Although he toned down his rhetoric against the FTAA, which he once said would amount to U.S. "annexation" of Latin America, he continued to insist on greater "reciprocity" in U.S.-Latin American trade and indicated his intention to try to reinvigorate *Mercosur* as a regional alternative.

Da Silva successfully downplayed his bogeyman image. He met with IMF representatives regarding a $30 billion loan package, and the IMF seemed pleased. As chief of staff he appointed José Dirceu, the *PT* president who engineered the party's move to the center; as finance minister he appointed Antonio Palocci, a physician, who pursued a fiscal policy that exceeded IMF expectations; as foreign minister he named a career diplomat, Celso Amorim; and as head of the Central Bank he named Henrique Meirelles, former director of global banking for FleetBoston Financial Corporation. He pragmatically undertook critically needed reforms in taxation and the cumbersome public pension system, which caused grumbling on the left but which were straining public finances. He flew to Washington to meet with President Bush, and the two leaders got on so amicably that one would never had suspected their earlier ideological antipathy.

After 100 days in office, da Silva's approval rating was 75%.

Da Silva pushed for two major reforms in 2003. One was a restructuring of the overly generous civil service pension system, which was $19 billion in debt and had become a luxury Brazilians couldn't afford. The president forged a consensus to obtain the necessary three-fifths majority in both houses of Congress, but fringe elements within da Silva's own party, and the civil service union that had long supported the *PT*, opposed it.

The other major reform was a simplification of the cumbersome and complex tax system that had confusing overlaps between the states and the federal government.

The Landless Movement *(MST)*, which had helped elect da Silva by curtailing its activities during the campaign, charged that da Silva had reneged on his promise to give titles to 60,000 families in his first year in office. The government itself admitted it had given titles to only 36,000 families. Peasants invaded more than 200 parcels of land in 2003, and 63 of them were killed in the resulting clashes with the landowners' hired militias; it was the bloodiest year since 1990.

Dancing in the streets . . . then after Carnaval

Da Silva pledged to provide land to 115,000 families in 2004 and to 400,000 before the end of his term (Cardoso resettled 526,400 families in eight years). The promise merely emboldened the peasants, and squatters invaded parcels of unused land, mostly in the impoverished northeast. The ministry in charge of the land program exacerbated the problem by giving priority to peasants in existing camps on unused land, which served as an incentive for more invasions.

By 2005, only 117,500 families had received land, and 12,000 landless farmers staged a protest march from Goiania to Brasilia that ended in violent clashes with police. The Pastoral Land Commission reported that the 1,801 violent incidents stemming from land disputes in 2004 were the highest in 20 years. The commission put the number of people killed in land disputes since democracy was restored in 1985 at 1,400. Meanwhile, the centrist parties in da Silva's coalition pressured da Silva to show more backbone against the *MST*. Clearly, the president was *entre a cruz e a espada*, as the Brazilians say.

In 2004, the *PT* found itself embroiled in a series of corruption scandals, something the self-righteous party once boasted it was above. The most serious involved Da Silva's chief of staff, José Dirceu, who had appointed the head of Rio de Janeiro's state lottery, Waldomiro Diniz, as deputy secretary of parliamentary affairs. The media aired a video showing Diniz apparently accepting campaign funds from a local numbers racketeer in exchange for favors when he headed the lottery. Diniz was fired, and Dirceu offered to resign, but da Silva rejected the offer.

In international affairs, da Silva sought to give Brazil an ever-higher profile. He visited Washington again, and he and Bush again spoke glowingly of their relationship. That was remarkable, given the on-going battle over U.S. tariffs, da Silva's close friendships with Cuba's Castro and Venezuela's Hugo Chávez, and da Silva's outspoken criticism of the U.S. invasion and occupation of Iraq.

Da Silva visited China in 2004, and the two countries announced they would launch their third joint satellite and concluded a $5 billion deal for China to purchase Brazilian iron ore.

Brazil's own fledgling space program was plagued by technical failures and, in

Brazil

2003, a disaster. A 100-foot VLS-3 rocket exploded on the launch pad at the Alcantara Launch Center on the Atlantic Coast, three days before launching, killing 21 people.

Brazil contributed a force of 1,200 troops to the U.N. peacekeeping mission in Haiti in 2004, the largest national contingent, and the peacekeeping mission was under Brazilian command.

Brazil's nuclear program sparked international controversy in 2004 when *The Washington Post* reported Brazil had denied U.N. inspectors access to a new uranium enrichment facility under construction at Resende. Brazil is the world's sixth-largest producer of uranium, but must send it abroad for enrichment. The new centrifuges would permit Brazil to enrich its own uranium for its Angra I and II nuclear power plants, which provide 4.3% of Brazil's electricity. (Work continues on Angra III, expected to be operational in 2015.)

Brazil insisted it would allow inspectors access to part of the facility, but not to the centrifuges on the grounds that it would compromise industrial secrecy. The science and technology minister struck an accord with the IAEA whereby inspectors would examine the pipes leading to the centrifuges, but would not make a visual inspection of the centrifuges. The IAEA inspection was required before enrichment could begin. The IAEA said its inspection was to ensure that no weapons-grade fuel can be produced. Brazil maintained it has no intention of producing weapons-grade fuel.

The influential newspaper *O Estado de São Paulo* then quoted a former U.S. Defense Department source saying the IAEA suspected Brazil had obtained a centrifuge on the black market from a notorious Pakistani scientist who has sold nuclear technology to rogue states like Iran, Libya and North Korea. U.S. Secretary of State Colin Powell visited Brasilia and expressed his confidence that Brazil did not intend to build nuclear weapons. Then the U.S. magazine *Science* reported that the enrichment facility would provide Brazil with enough weapons-grade fuel to produce six warheads per year and 63 per year by 2014. An IAEA team revisited the Resende plant, after which the agency gave the green light for Brazil to begin enriching fuel.

Da Silva found himself at the center of another international incident in 2004.

The New York Times' bureau chief in Rio de Janeiro, Larry Rohter, wrote an article quoting da Silva's 1998 running mate, Leonel Brizola, and others as saying da Silva had a drinking problem that could affect his performance. Da Silva denounced the article as "slander" and revoked Rohter's work visa for "offending the honor of the president." It would be the first time a foreign journalist had been expelled since the military regime was in power. The domestic and international reaction from human rights and journalism organizations was swift. Cardoso labeled da Silva's overreaction as undemocratic. The Supreme Court blocked the revocation, and a chastened da Silva rescinded it.

Da Silva again raised doubts about his commitment to press freedom after magazines reported leaked documents suggesting that Henrique Meirelles, head of the central bank, had evaded taxes. Da Silva introduced a bill to create a national press council that would require licenses to practice journalism, impose a code of conduct and have the power to punish violations. The council also would prevent leaks and require reporters to "show respect" for people they write about and to

The Cathedral, Brasilia

Fishing in the waters of the mighty Amazon River near Manaus

do nothing "contrary to human values." In short, the council would prevent the press from reporting freely, as guaranteed in the constitution. Media organs called the idea a throwback to the military regime, which had once jailed da Silva. Faced with massive domestic and international condemnation, da Silva withdrew the bill.

The 2004 quadrennial elections for the 5,562 municipalities were a muted victory for da Silva's *PT*. In the first round, the *PT* more than doubled its number of mayoralties from 187 to 389. But São Paulo Mayor Marta Suplicy lost to former presidential candidate José Serra of the *PSDB*. The *PT* won 11 of the cities contested in the runoff but lost 12, including Porto Alegre, which the *PT* had governed for 16 years.

Ghosts from the military dictatorship returned to haunt Brazil in 2004, when newspapers published gruesome pictures purported to be the body of Vladimir Herzog, a journalist accused of Communist sympathies slain by the military in a 1975 incident that garnered worldwide attention. Da Silva's government insisted pictures were not of Herzog. Seeking to maintain amicable relations with the armed forces, da Silva appointed Vice President Alencar as the new defense minister; he remained vice president. Da Silva issued a decree permitting declassification of files from the dictatorship era, when about 400 dissidents were killed. Cardoso had ordered them classified forever.

On February 12, 2005, Sister Dorothy Stang, a 73-year-old American nun who had championed the rights of Indians and landless peasants of Para state and had

opposed ranching and illegal logging in the Amazon rain forest, was shot to death following a dispute with a rancher. She became an international martyr overnight.

Da Silva ordered an investigation and dispatched 4,000 troops into the area. Three men were initially arrested and charged with killing Stang. Also charged was the rancher who allegedly ordered the murder, who surrendered six weeks later. A fourth alleged accomplice was arrested later. Two of the suspects were convicted in 2005 after recanting their original confessions. They were accused of accepting $25,000 from ranchers to kill Stang. The actual hitman admitted killing Stang, but said he did so when she reached for her Bible and he mistakenly thought she was reaching for a gun. He contended he shot her in self-defense—six times! Both men denied accepting money. One was sentenced to 28 years, the other to 17. The hitman was freed from prison after serving less than nine years. In 2007, the rancher was convicted of ordering Stang's murder and sentenced to 30 years, but in 2008 he was retried and acquitted when a witness said he had given false testimony against him. The same jury upheld one of the hitmen's conviction. In 2010, a second rancher was convicted of ordering Stang's murder and sentenced to 30 years. He, too, was given a new trial, and in 2013 was reconvicted and sentenced to 30 years. This time, an appeals court upheld the conviction.

Amnesty International issued a scathing report in 2005 accusing the government of not doing enough to protect Indian rights. In a remarkable ceremony at the presidential palace on April 19, Indian Day, the da Silva government officially apologized to the Indians for all past abuses and injustices.

In 2005, Brazil joined Germany, Japan and India in introducing a U.N. resolution that would expand the 15-member Security Council to 25 and make those four countries permanent members along with the United States, Russia, China, Britain and France. But Brazil's regional rivals, Argentina and Mexico, oppose a permanent seat for Brazil. Secretary-General Kofi Annan said the issue needed further study. Brazil has continued to press the issue.

Da Silva was instrumental in creating the IBSA (India-Brazil-South Africa) Dialogue Forum, designed to promote cooperation among Southern Hemisphere nations, and he hosted its first summit in Brasilia in 2006.

Da Silva was one of the few South American presidents whose popularity was consistently above 50%. However, new scandals involving the *PT* erupted in 2005. The respected newsmagazine *Veja*

accused a postal manager of accepting a bribe in exchange for a construction contract and accused *PT* leader Roberto Jefferson of involvement. Jefferson admitted the *PT* had paid monthly "allowances" totaling $12,000 to unnamed lawmakers in return for their participation in the shaky coalition. Jefferson offered no proof and said da Silva himself was unaware of the payments, but that Dirceu was. Dirceu denied the charges, but he resigned as chief of staff to return to his congressional seat. He was replaced as chief of staff by Dilma Rousseff, who had served as energy minister and soon became the power behind the throne in Brazil. Da Silva insisted that his government "has not swept dirt under the rug."

The vote-buying scandal, nicknamed *"mensalão"* (big monthly payment) by the media, became the subject of congressional and media scrutiny. Months later, the Chamber of Deputies expelled Dirceu and three other members after concluding they took the monthly payments; four others resigned, and eight were exonerated. Da Silva's approval rating dropped to its nadir, but it rose when the multi-party congressional investigative panel concluded in its report that he had not been implicated. The investigation dragged on for years, and 25 suspects, including Dirceu, were eventually convicted in 2012.

Finance Minister Palocci, who had won high marks for engineering steady, moderate economic growth without inflation, was accused in 2006 of collecting illegal campaign contributions for the *PT*, including one from the Cuban government, while he was mayor of Ribeirão Preto in São Paulo State. Palocci denied the accusations, as da Silva stood by him. Gradually, the evidence became more convincing and the denials more hollow. Palocci resigned after a new allegation, supported by witnesses, that he attended meetings at which lobbyists provided Palocci and others in power with prostitutes and paid them off with briefcases filled with cash.

Lula's Second Term

Da Silva did not declare his intention to seek re-election before the congressional report clearing him of wrongdoing in the *mensalão* scandal. The *PSDB* nominated São Paulo State Governor Geraldo Alckmin, a 53-year-old anesthesiologist. Serra announced he would seek to replace Alckmin as governor instead of taking on Lula again.

Five other candidates entered the race, but it soon narrowed to Lula and Alckmin.

This time, da Silva did not have to defend himself against the charges of being a left-wing boogeyman. He had strengthened his support among the poor with his anti-hunger program and by increasing

Brazil

the minimum wage by 17%, but he had not proven a loose cannon. Yet, he was encumbered by the scandals within his own party and lackluster economic growth of 2.4% in 2005, well below the Latin American and world averages, both of which Alckmin exploited.

Days before the October 1 election, *PT* operatives were caught with $780,000 in cash that was to have been used to purchase damaging information to use against Serra in his campaign for governor of São Paulo. Da Silva unwisely ignored the embarrassment. Even more unwisely, he ducked the final presidential debate, which many voters regarded as cowardly and arrogant.

They delivered a rebuke by denying him the expected first-round win:

| Da Silva | 46,662,365 | 48.61% |
| Alckmin | 39,968,369 | 41.64% |

In the four-week runoff campaign, da Silva rebounded, and he and Alckmin exchanged increasingly acrimonious charges. In the end, da Silva successfully portrayed Alckmin as too pro-business and too zealous to privatize state-owned entities. The results:

| Da Silva | 58,295,042 | 60.8% |
| Alckmin | 37,543,178 | 39.2% |

After four years in office, Lula was given a new mandate that was only half a percentage point less than his 2002 runoff victory, but he received 4.5 million more votes—a convincing vote of confidence.

Da Silva's *PT* won 83 of the 513 seats, a loss of eight from 2002, but still the second-largest bloc after the *PMDB*'s 89. The *PT* had more pragmatists than before. The *PSDB* and *PFL* each had 65, and 16 other parties comprised the remainder of the usual patchwork quilt. The Senate was almost evenly divided between supporters and opponents of the government. Once again, da Silva hammered out a fragile coalition. Serra easily won the São Paulo governorship.

He was faced almost immediately with the renewed crisis of rampant street crime, especially in Rio de Janeiro. With nearly 50 murders annually per 100,000 people, it was officially one of the world's most dangerous cities, and renegade policemen and soldiers had formed vigilante groups that murdered suspected drug dealers, reminiscent of the notorious death squads of the 1950s.

In 2006, GDP had grown by only 2.8%, well below the average for Latin America and the world. Da Silva unveiled a "growth acceleration package," which reduced interest rates to 13.25%, still higher than neighboring countries. It also called

Former President Luiz Inácio da Silva

for investing $236 billion in infrastructure projects and housing over four years, a reduction in taxes by $5.4 billion during the same period and continued reduction of the bloated public payroll.

Da Silva welcomed George W. Bush on a state visit to Brazil in 2007, which was marred by large demonstrations. The two leaders signed an accord encouraging greater worldwide production of ethanol, although da Silva failed to get Bush to agree to repeal the 54-cent-a-gallon tariff on Brazilian ethanol. Da Silva visited Bush at Camp David a month later.

Ironically, as relations grew warmer with Bush, they became strained with his erstwhile ally, Chávez. Da Silva attended a Latin American energy summit in Caracas, where Chávez lashed out at his ethanol-promotion plan, saying it would take land away from producing food for the poor. (Chávez, of course, was also concerned that his petroleum exports would be jeopardized.) Da Silva responded that Latin America still has sufficient arable land to produce both food and ethanol.

In 2007, da Silva disavowed a constitutional amendment that would allow him to seek a third term, but he said he hoped to designate his successor.

As another example of da Silva's effort to cast Brazil—and himself—in the role of an international leader, he hosted the third summit of the 12 South American presidents in Brasilia in 2008, where a new continental organization was established: the Union of South American Nations (*UNASUR* in Spanish and *UNASUL* in Portuguese). It is an outgrowth of the South American Community established in Cuzco, Peru, in 2004. Modeled after the European Union, *UNASUR* incorporates the *Mercosur* and old Andean Pact trade

blocs and established a headquarters in Quito, Ecuador, a parliament in Cochabamba, Bolivia, and a Bank of the South located in Caracas, Venezuela. The eventual goal is to have a common South American currency and passport.

Da Silva hosted Russian President Dmitry Medvedev in 2008, then hosted a summit in Salvador attended by 33 leaders of the Western Hemisphere; unlike the Summits of the Americas, Cuba was invited while the United States was not. Da Silva was adroitly statesmanlike, holding the middle ground against *yanqui*-haters like Chávez. The leaders discussed the global economic downturn and defense issues, but little of substance was achieved except a photo-op.

Da Silva had an amicable meeting with new U.S. President Barack Obama at the White House in 2009, where he restated his belief that major developing countries like Brazil, China and India should have a greater voice in world affairs. A month later, Da Silva carried that message to the G-20 Summit in London.

Although da Silva continued to enjoy approval ratings of 75–80%, his scandal-plagued *PT* scored only minor gains in the important municipal elections of October 2008. Marta Suplicy, seeking to regain the São Paulo mayoralty, lost to an ally of Governor Serra, Gilberto Kassab.

In 2008, da Silva visited an offshore oil platform in the rich new Tupi field, where he ceremoniously coated his hands with the first crude oil extracted from the field that could make Brazil a major oil exporter (see Economy).

The financial windfall from the Tupi oilfield permitted Brazil to become a serious contender to host the 2016 Olympic Games in Rio de Janeiro. Da Silva was among a host of world leaders who flew to Oslo, Norway, in October 2009 to lobby for the games. His efforts paid off, and the announcement that the International Olympic Committee had chosen Rio, despite fears over its crime rate, set off rejoicing in Brazil. It will mark the first time the Olympics have been held in South America. Brazil has pledged to spend $14.4 billion to build an Olympic village and on new infrastructure to assure access among the various sites.

Brazil also was chosen to host the World Cup in 2014.

Da Silva continued to attract world attention, not all of it favorable. In 2009, he hosted a visit by Iranian President Mahmoud Ahmadinejad, who was seeking Brazilian support in the U.N. against sanctions for Iran's uranium enrichment program. Pictures of the two smiling leaders embracing raised eyebrows around the world and sparked criticism at home. U.S. Secretary of State Hillary Clinton was concerned enough that she flew to Brasilia to discuss it with Foreign Minister Amorin. At a joint news conference, however, Amorin said Brazil "would not bend" to U.S. pressure to support sanctions against Iran.

Working with Prime Minister Recap Tayyip Erdogan of Turkey—like Brazil then a member of the U.N. Security Council—da Silva flew to Teheran for three-cornered talks with Ahmadinejad and brokered a compromise deal by which Iran would ship 1,200 kilograms of its low-grade enriched fuel to Turkey in exchange for 120 kilos of fully enriched fuel for Iran's nuclear reactor. The swap was hailed as proof that Iran was not interested in having enough enriched uranium to produce a nuclear weapon. The Obama administration and much of the world community remained skeptical.

First Woman President

In 2009, Da Silva anointed his chief of staff, Dilma Rousseff, 62, as his successor. The daughter of an affluent Bulgarian immigrant, Rousseff enjoyed a privileged upbringing and a private education in a French-language school in Belo Horizonte. Yet, she joined a guerrilla movement during the early days of the military regime and married a guerrilla leader, Carlos Araújo, her second husband, by whom she had a daughter in 1976. They divorced in 2000.

Rousseff was imprisoned from 1970–72 and subjected to 22 days of torture, leading some people later to compare her with Joan of Arc. She went on to earn an economics degree and after the return to democracy became involved in public administration. She served as municipal treasury secretary of Porto Alegre and energy minister of Rio Grande do Sul state. She served as da Silva's energy minister until he appointed her chief of staff.

She seemed an unlikely choice even apart from her guerrilla background, never having run for elective office. She had just been treated for lymphatic cancer and was pronounced cured. Rousseff chose Marcel Temer of the *PMDB* as her running mate, though there was reported to be friction between the two.

In August, her campaign, and the *PT*, were dealt a seeming setback when Senator Marina Silva of the Green Party, a longtime *PT* loyalist, defected over dissatisfaction with da Silva's centrist domestic policy abnd announced her own presidential candidacy.

São Paulo Governor Serra was regarded as the logical opposition candidate. For almost a year polls showed him leading Rousseff by as much as 20 percentage points. But he vacillated over resigning as governor, while da Silva campaigned vigorously for his chosen candidate, equating her with Nelson Mandela. She edged ahead in the polls, aided by a now-booming economy and a 7% unemployment rate. Her lackluster performance in a televised debate did not seem to affect her.

Six other candidates besides Rousseff, Serra and Silva entered the race, but they received less than 1% each. On October 3, for the first time, more than 100 million Brazilians voted, a turnout of 91.4%. The results:

Rousseff	47,651,434	46.9%
Serra	33,132,289	32.6%
Silva	19,636,389	19.3%

Serra and Rousseff had two debates before the runoff. Silva's supporters were logically closer philosophically to Rousseff than to Serra, but Silva and Rousseff had clashed over Rousseff's enthusiasm for development when Silva was environ-

mental minister. Silva endorsed neither candidate, but in the end, the math was against Serra:

Rousseff	55,572,529	56.05%
Serra	43,711,388	43.95%

A tearful Rousseff told cheering supporters that she was proud to be Brazil's first woman president and would champion women's issues, but she surprised feminists by saying she personally opposes abortion although she would not restrict access to it.

In Congress, Rousseff had a stronger hand than Lula did. Her patchwork coalition had 359 of the 519 seats in the Chamber of Deputies and 54 of 81 in the Senate. The opposition *PSDB* did retain the governorships of São Paulo and Minas Gerais.

Continuity and Scandals

Rousseff's inauguration on January 1, 2011, was attended by 23 heads of state. Secretary of State Hillary Clinton represented the United States, but the two women did little more than shake hands, while Rousseff had private meetings with Chávez and other Latin American left-wing presidents. Rousseff pledged to continue da Silva's pragmatic economic policies that had resulted in GDP growth of 7.5% in 2010, among the fastest in Latin America.

Continuity seemed to be Rousseff's goal. She retained da Silva's finance minister, Guido Manteca, and unwisely appointed his first, scandal-tainted finance minister, Antonio Palocci, as chief of staff. But she replaced the prickly foreign minister, Celso Amorim, with Antonio Patriota, a former ambassador to the U.S.

She told Congress that eradication of poverty would be her primary domestic concern. Yet, she resisted a move by the trade unions for an inflationary increase in the minimum wage, agreeing to a much pared-down hike. She also revealed she would be fiscally conservative, calling for a 2.5% reduction in the budget.

Rousseff also continued da Silva's ambidextrous foreign policy, cementing close ties with Iran and with China, which had eclipsed the United States as Brazil's leading trade partner (see Economy) and was now Brazil's largest investor. Like her two predecessors, she criticized the United States and the EU for their alleged trade protectionism. Yet, she extended an offer of dialogue with the developed countries, and she was more critical than Lula of Iran's human rights record.

She hosted President Obama in March 2011 and offered a "new era" in U.S.-Brazilian relations. A month later, she made a state visit to China, where she and Hu

A rural church in Curitiba World Bank Photo

Brazil

Destruction of the Amazon: A global catastrophe

During the 1990s, Brazil finally began to deal with a problem that had brought it international condemnation for more than a decade: the destruction of the Amazon rain forest, which encompasses 1.6 million square miles and is believed to be home to 30% of the world's plant and animal species. The wholesale destruction of this priceless resource continues at a much reduced but still alarming pace.

In their zeal to foster growth, a succession of Brazilian presidents, both military and civilian, gave agricultural development of the vast, virgin Amazon Basin a high priority. Developers were given *carte blanche* to use slash-and-burn methods to cut away trees to make room for cultivation, despite protests by national and international ecologists that such destruction could have a global impact. The clearing of vast areas of oxygen-producing trees, they argued, would contribute to the world-wide buildup of greenhouse gases and contribute to global warming, as would the carbon dioxide produced by the fires.

Brazilian environmental activist Chico Mendes was murdered in 1988 for his high-profile efforts to save the forest, while president after president ignored the issue in the name of development.

In 1998, the Cardoso government released a report with the bittersweet finding that deforestation had reached its peak in 1994–95 of 11,621 square miles, double the 5,958 square miles cleared in 1993–94, and had begun tapering off. The rate in 1995–96 was down to 7,200 square miles, and 5,200 in 1996–97. Since 1978, the report said, 200,000 square miles, or one eighth of the forest, had been lost.

Congress approved legislation giving the federal environmental agency power to enforce protective laws and providing criminal penalties for violators. Ironically, a devastating fire in Roraima state, exacerbated by a drought, destroyed the forest at a pace even more rapid than man's.

In 2001, another 7,014 square miles was lost through logging or fires. The government banned mahogany logging altogether, and in 2002 it made operational a huge, $1.4 billion radar network, called the System for the Vigilance of the Amazon, or *SIVAM*, designed to maintain surveillance to thwart drug trafficking and illegal logging and mining.

Nonetheless, a report released by a group of environmental experts stated that deforestation accelerated by an alarming 40% in 2002, to 9,840 square miles, the worst year since 1995. The government's own official figures were 8,983 square miles. The loss slowed dramatically in 2002–03, according to the government, to 2.1%, still a loss of 9,496 square miles.

The government's figures for 2003–04 were grimmer: 10,088 square miles, an accelerated increase of 6.2%, the second-worst loss on record. That meant an area larger than New Jersey had been lost each year for three years. The government acknowledged in 2004 that burning of the rain forest accounted for three fourths of Brazil's greenhouse gas emissions, while Brazil accounted for 3% of the world's greenhouse gases.

The seven members of the Green Party in the lower house of Congress withdrew from the governing coalition of President da Silva in 2005 to protest his government's failure to stop the destruction. The party complained that while the government has set aside preserves, it also had promoted dams, roads and farming.

Despite the criticism, the situation began to improve dramatically. In 2005, the loss was 7,256 square miles, a 31% decrease; in 2006, it was 5,421 square miles, a 49% decrease; and in 2007 it was 3,865 square miles, another 47% decrease.

Yet, according to the World Wildlife Fund, more than 17% of the Amazon rain forest had been destroyed. A report released by the International Center for Forestry Research in Indonesia in 2004 blamed much of the increased deforestation on cattle ranching, while a report by the group Friends of the Earth cited construction of a highway through the Amazon, BR-163, which illegal loggers were using to gain access. Still others blamed soybean farming; Blairo Maggi, then governor of Mato Grosso state, where three fourths of the destruction has taken place, is the world's largest soybean producer.

Environmentalists had another martyr in 2005 when Dorothy Stang, a 73-year-old American nun who agitated against ranching and illegal logging in the rain forest, was murdered in a dispute with a rancher in Para state (see History). It wasn't until 2013 that the rancher was convicted and sentenced to 30 years.

Largely in response to Stang's murder, the da Silva government mandated a reserve of 32,000 square miles of rain forest in Para, Mato Grosso and Roraima that would be off-limits to illegal loggers and ranchers; controlled logging would be strictly monitored. An estimated 350 logging companies operate in the Amazon. The international environmental organization Greenpeace hailed the move as historic, but also faulted the government for failing to do more. In 2005 it whimsically named Maggi the winner of its first annual "Golden Chainsaw" award.

Federal investigators arrested 90 people, about half of them officials of the federal environmental protection ministry, *Ibama*, and the rest businessmen, in a crackdown on bribery by illegal logging companies in 2005. The officials were accused of accepting bribes in return for documents certifying that trees had been cut legally. Much of the illegal logging took place on Indian enclaves and in national parks. Such corruption is understandable; the value of wood harvested illegally since the early 1990s is estimated at $370 million.

A federal law enacted in 2006 set aside—over 10 years—3% of empty rainforest as "public forest" in which logging is strictly controlled. The da Silva government set aside about 60,000 square miles of conservation area, and 57,915 square miles of the Guyana Shield, dense forest bordering Guyana, Suriname and French Guiana, was put under protection.

Da Silva's environment minister, Marina Silva, resigned in 2008 in frustration over what she said was the president's lack of commitment. Her successor was Carlos Minc, like her an environmental activist, who accepted on the condition that his efforts would be taken seriously. On his watch, the Brazilian government, acting on evidence supplied by Greenpeace, sued three British supermarket chains in 2009 for selling meat allegedly from illegal ranching operations in the Amazon.

Silva later defected from the president's political party and ran as the Green Party candidate for president in 2010, running third and garnering 19.3% of the vote. The winner was da Silva's hand-picked successor, Dilma Rousseff, his chief of staff, who had clashed frequently with Silva on the issue of development vs. conservation.

Brazil's hunger for energy now threatens the Amazon, not from burning, but from flooding by four new hydroelectric dams on the upper Amazon along the borders with Peru and Bolivia. The National Institute for Amazon Research said the dams would flood twice the area of 200 square miles the government claims. In January 2011, 29 days after Rousseff's inauguration, the government announced plans for yet another dam, the Belo Monte, on the Xingu River in Para state. Belo Monte would be Brazil's second-largest dam and will inundate approximately 200 square miles of forest and displace 20,000 people, mostly indigenous. A federal judge ordered a halt to the project in August 2012, until its full impact on indigenous communities could be determined.

According to Brazil's National Institute for Space Research (*INPE*), the deforestation rate accelerated by 11% in 2008, to 4,984 square miles. At the end of 2008, the government set new goals to dramatically reduce rainforest destruction 70% by 2017—a 40% reduction in 2009 alone, another 30% from 2010-13 and 30% from 2014-17. If the *INPE* figures are accurate, the plan is on track; 2,882 square miles were destroyed in 2009, a 42% decrease from 2008. In 2010, the destruction decreased another 14%, to 2,491 square miles. In 2011, it was a record low 2,410 square miles, still the size of Delaware, but deforestation in Mata Grosso jumped 20% that year. In 2012, destruction was down to "only" 1,798 square miles, a 27% reduction.

A devastating drought in 2010 had a greater impact than the 2005 drought, the worst on record. Brazilian and British scientists concluded in a report published in the journal *Science* that instead of the rainforest absorbing much of the world's carbon dioxide, the emission of CO_2 from decomposing vegetation killed by the drought could exceed 5 billion tons.

Two more rainforest activists became martyrs in 2011. José Claudio Ribeiro da Silva and his wife, María, had reported illegal logging to prosecutors in Para state and had fought clearing rainforest to plant soybeans. They were shot to death in an ambush.

In December 2011, the Senate passed, 59–7, controversial revisions to the Forest Code supported by farmers and the agricultural industry that would allow them to clear 50% of the land they own in environmentally sensitive areas instead of the current 20%. Greenpeace Brasil called it a "day of shame" and lobbied against it in the lower house, which nonetheless passed it in April 274–184. Rousseff used her line-item veto to kill 12 of the provisions, including some of the most objectionable to environmentalists, but she reduced the amount of forest that small farmers are required to retain and she did not veto the amnesty for illegal logging committed before 2008.

Greens denounced it as a betrayal. The bill was returned to Congress, which had 30 days to override the vetoes or agree to the changes. A somewhat watered-down version, which reduced the mandatory belt of vegetation along riverbanks from 30 to 15 meters among other changes, went into effect in August. In January 2013, federal attorneys challenged some of the new provisions before the Supreme Court, saying they undermine the protection of the forest.

The naysayers may have been correct. In 2012–13, deforestation jumped 28%, to 2,255 square miles, ending a decade-long decline. Greenpeace and Brazilian environmentalists placed the blame squarely at Rousseff's door.

Jintao signed more than 20 agreements. China bought 35 Embraer E190 commercial jets worth an estimated $1.4 billion, while China made a $300 million investment in a telecommunications center in São Paulo.

Although poverty was her main domestic issue, she could not ignore the specter of violent crime any more than Lula could, not with the World Cup and the Olympics coming. In November 2010, Lula had dispatched 2,600 troops and police backed by armored vehicles into Complexo de Alemão, a Rio *favela* controlled by drug traffickers; 37 people died. In February, Rousseff ordered another raid in which nearly 1,000 military and police personnel, using armored vehicles, peacefully occupied the crime-ridden Morro dos Prazeres *favela*.

Such crackdowns in the name of guaranteeing security for the two sports events drew a rebuke from Amnesty International, which condemned what it called the forcible removal of people from their homes in *favelas* near the complex where both events will be held. Local authorities said the removals were necessary for the greater good of the community.

A watershed event for Brazil—and Latin America—came in 2011 when the Brazilian Supreme Court ruled 10-1 that same-sex civil unions must be recognized. The da Silva administration had tried unsuccessfully for two years to persuade Congress to legalize civil unions.

In May 2011, a media exposé accused Chief of Staff Palocci of increasing his personal wealth 20-fold through influence peddling for businesses while a member of Congress, similar to the type of activities that led to his resignation as finance minister in 2006. This sparked an audit and calls from the opposition for a congressional inquiry. With her huge majority in Congress, Rousseff blocked the inquiry, and she publicly declared she was standing by Palocci—just as da Silva had done at first. But in June, Palocci resigned, throwing the government into turmoil. Rousseff named a new *PT* senator, Gleisi Hoffman, 45, a protégé of Rousseff's rather than da Silva's, as his successor.

More scandals erupted involving the Lula holdovers. By February 2012, no fewer than seven of Rousseff's cabinet ministers had resigned because of different accusations of corruption. She sacked Defense Minister Nelson Jobim in August 2011 for criticizing other officials, replacing him with Celso Amorim.

The chain of resignations caused some doubts about her ability to govern, but in the long run they proved fortuitous in that they allowed her to appoint her own people. Gradually, she has recast the government in her image, and by early 2012 her approval rating was 70%.

President Dilma Rousseff

However, when she attempted to follow up her anti-corruption campaign by attacking Brazil's notorious pork-barrel system, she found herself stymied by entrenched interests within her own governing coalition. Some parties pulled out in protest, and she was forced to slow down the pace of the reforms. She also to come to grips with the still-overburdened, overgenerous civil service pension system, which is unsustainable.

President Obama hosted Rousseff at the White House in April 2012. As usual, the talks focused on trade, but Rousseff also pressed Brazil's ambition to become a permanent member of the U.N. Security Council. Obama declined to endorse the idea.

On May 25, 2012, Rousseff vetoed 12 provisions of a controversial revision of the Forest Code, ostensibly to enhance preservation of the Amazon rainforest, but environmentalists were still critical of the changes (see Destruction of the Amazon: A Global Catastrophe).

Following the lead of Argentina, Chile and Uruguay, which have sought to come to terms with the memories of their military regimes, Rousseff swore in a "truth commission" in June 2012 that was given two years to investigate abuses committed back to 1946, which predates the most recent military regime. In a formal ceremony, the government apologized to 120 former political prisoners—including Rousseff herself, who did not attend the ceremony.

In Brazil, justice is often delayed, and consequently denied, especially for venal politicians. It is still delayed, but no longer denied. After seven years of investigations and delays in the 2005 *mensalão* scandal, 38 defendants finally went on

trial before the Supreme Court in August 2012 for allegedly sending or receiving monthly payments as bribes for supporting da Silva's congressional coalition. The biggest fish among them was José Dirceu, Lula's former chief of staff. On December 17, 2012, the Supreme Court announced 25 convictions, including Dirceu, who was sentenced to 10 years and 10 months. Also convicted were José Genoino, former head of the *PT,* and Delubio Soares, former *PT* treasurer. One defendant was sentenced to 40 years.

Brazil was near the bottom in Latin America in economic growth in 2012, just 1.3%, the worst performance in a decade. Only Paraguay had slower growth. A drought affected both soybean exports and hydroelectric output, forcing industry to pay for more costly gas-generated electricity. To make matters worse for Rousseff, inflation rose to 6.6%. Unemployment nudged up slightly, from 6% to 6.2%. The economy was also buffeted by striking public sector workers in the second half of the year. In the end, government workers received an inflation-linked raise of 15.8%, which further fueled inflation.

Rousseff announced a major new initiative in late 2012 to lure private investors into a badly needed upgrading of the country's infrastructure, especially roads, bridges, railways, airports and ports. Delays in exports were making Brazilian goods less competitive.

The unfolding *mensalão* trial and the dismal economic figures normally would have affected the ruling party in the quadrennial municipal election in October 2012. But Rousseff continued to enjoy phenomenal popularity. The Mitofsky poll of Mexico gave her a 62% approval rating, fifth highest of 20 Western Hemisphere leaders. Her popularity was the likely reason the *PT* fared as well as it did. On October 7, the *PT* won 628 mayoral contests, up from 550 in 2008. The *PMDB*, allied with the government, dropped from 1,193 mayors to 1,025 and the opposition *PSDB* dropped from 787 mayors to 693. In the runoff elections of October 28, the *PT*'s Fernando Haddad defeated two-time presidential candidate José Serra of the *PSDB*, 56% to 44%, for mayor of São Paulo.

Recent Developments

Popularity in Brazil can prove fleeting. Public protests broke out in June 2013 against a 50-cent increase in bus fares, and the protests quickly escalated into a nationwide public manifestation against government in general, with millions of people taking to the streets. The protests continued in July, attracting members of both the middle and lower classes. The protesters complained most loudly against

Brazil

higher prices, corruption and poorly managed public services. It was the most widespread protest since the demonstrations against Collor de Mello in 1992, but with a modern twist: the use of social media was a crucial element. Fringe anarchist groups attempted to exploit the protests, which turned violent. A policeman was killed, and police retaliation against the alleged perpetrators left nine more people dead.

Rousseff's approval rating took a decided dip, and there were fears that the protests could disrupt the World Cup games in June and July 2014. There were more violent protests in late 2013 by people displaced by the destruction of *favelas* to make way for the Olympics in 2016. Although the protests had died down by June 2014, the public's mood remained ugly.

U.S.-Brazilian relations soured noticeably in September 2013 with media reports that the U.S. National Security Agency had tapped the telephone conversations of world leaders allied with the U.S., including Rousseff. Brazilian media had a field day with the revelations, and Rousseff demanded an explanation and an apology—which were not forthcoming. President Obama had invited Rousseff for a state dinner at the White House in October, the first Brazilian president to have been accorded a state dinner since Cardoso in 1995. Not surprisingly, Rousseff "postponed" her visit, but it was obvious it was an outright cancellation. Obama and Rousseff kissed each other on the cheek at Nelson Mandela's funeral service in South Africa that December, but relations have not fully recovered.

Vice President Joe Biden met with Rousseff in June when he attended one of the Team USA's matches in the World Cup. Biden assured Rousseff that there would be no repetition of the eavesdropping—but stopped short of an apology.

In a stunning development, the truth commission concluded in December 2013 that former President Juscelino Kubitschek did not die accidentally in an automobile accident in Resende in 1976 but was murdered by the military government. A bullet fragment was found in the skull of Kubitschek's limousine driver. The limo had collided with a bus. A month earlier, the body of former President João Goulart was exhumed to verify a report by a former Uruguayan intelligence officer that he had been poisoned in exile in Argentina in 1976; no autopsy had been performed in either Argentina or Brazil, both under right-wing military dictatorships. Goulart's death had been attributed to a heart attack. The results of the belated autopsy had not been released by mid-2014.

Besides the World Cup, Brazilians' attention in mid-2014 was focused on the upcoming October 5 presidential election. Public protests are not a welcome harbinger of a president's chances for re-election. Mid-way through her term in early 2013, Rousseff was riding a crest of popularity and appeared unbeatable. A Datafolha poll showed her approval rating still above 50% in June 2013, before the protests broke out. By the end of that month, it had plummeted to 30%. By October, the Mitofsky poll of the popularity of Western Hemisphere leaders put her popularity at 37 percent, 12th out of 19 leaders, a stark decline from the year before.

Three candidates declared in 2013 they were interested in challenging Rousseff. Aécio Neves of the *PTSB* initially appeared the strongest candidate, but his party is plagued by corruption woes in São Paulo State.

Polls showed the strongest potential challenger to Rousseff in a hypothetical runoff to be Marina Silva, the environmental activist who ran third in 2010 and who enjoys wide public respect for her honesty. She sought to found a new party called the Sustainability Network, but in October 2013, the Electoral Court ruled that her party had fallen almost half a million signatures short of the number required to appear on the ballot. She was then forced to "shop around" for a party to call home. She chose the small Socialist Party, but she had to settle for being the running mate of the party's nominee, Eduardo Campos, 49, governor of Pernambuco. His party had been a member of Rousseff's coalition. Despite the party's name, he is regarded as a centrist. As expected, the *PSDB* nominated Neves, 54, former governor of Minas Gerais and grandson of the ill-fated President-elect Tancredo Neves.

Complicating Rousseff's chances, the biggest scandal since the *mensalão* scandal erupted in February 2014 when the CEO of *Petrobras* announced she was concluding an investigation into allegations that *Petrobras* officials had accepted $139.2 million in bribes from a Dutch offshore firm. In March, the Senate demanded its own investigation, and members of Rousseff's governing coalition, especially the *PMDB*, joined the chorus demanding answers.

Rousseff also is handicapped by a faltering economy. Growth in 2013 remained a lackluster 2.5%, while inflation increased to 6.2%.

By April 2014, polls showed Rousseff being forced into a runoff. In May, Datafolha showed the government's approval rating at 35%. A CNT/MDA poll showed Rousseff in the lead with 37% to 21% for Neves and 11% for Campos. But "don't know" was a strong second place with 30%. The question is which way the undecides will go by October 5 (see The Future).

CULTURE: Brazil is culturally unique among the Latin American republics, with its mix of Portuguese and African accents in religion, music, architecture and food. There was little interplay between the invading Portuguese colonizers and the indigenous Indians, and what scattered tribes remain are isolated and unassimilated in the vast interior Amazon rain forest. It was the influx of African slaves that shaped modern Brazil's ethnic and cultural composition.

It can be argued that Brazilian culture today is tripartite. In the far southern temperate zone, characterized by wheat farming, cattle ranching and coffee production, the population is predominantly Caucasian, a cross-current of European immigration. As in Argentina, the cattle culture produced a distinct sub-culture with a meat-based diet. The Brazilian equivalent of the Argentine *asado* is the *churrasco*, a variety of grilled meats and sausages. This region is the home of Brazil's national dish, *feijoada*, a culinary orgy traditionally served on Wednesdays and Saturdays and consisting of various smoked meats and sausages, black beans (*feijão*), rice, greens and orange slices.

In the northeast, on the "hump" of Brazil, the population is predominantly black and the culture has its roots in Africa, a mere 1,000 miles across the Atlantic. Despite the ostensible dominance of the Roman Catholic Church in Brazil, blacks still practice *macumba*, a voodoo-like tribal religion based on black magic. In this equatorial climate, there is little cattle ranching, and the diet is based more on seafood and the universal Brazilian staples, black beans and rice. The Bahian style of cooking is characterized by stewing fish, shellfish or chicken in dende oil, derived from a palm nut, and coconut milk. Perhaps the region's greatest contribution to Brazilian culture, however, is its music. Here is where the samba was born, and like Argentina's tango it began in the slums and won mainstream acceptance and an international following.

The third element of Brazilian culture is in the cosmopolitan and industrial urban centers, chiefly Rio de Janeiro and São Paulo, where the other two cultures converge. Here, Catholicism and *macumba* have intertwined to give the world one of its most distinctive cultural offerings: *Carnaval*, the Brazilian version of *Mardi Gras*, the great explosion of revelry and hedonism before the onset of the somber season of Lent.

Officially, Brazil is the largest Roman Catholic country in the world, and there was speculation that a Brazilian cardinal, Claudio Hummes, would be elected pope when Pope John Paul II died in April 2005. However, census figures show that the number of practicing Catholics has declined from 84 million in 1991 to 74 million in 2000, while the number of evangelical

Protestants has soared from 9 million to 15 million in the same period. Recent polls indicate that 125 million Brazilians still consider themselves Catholic, even though they do not attend Mass, but an overwhelming majority of them disagree with the church on contraception and abortion.

Perhaps in response to this, Pope Benedict XVI visited Brazil in May 2007, one of his few foreign trips. He canonized Brazil's first native-born saint, Friar Antonio de Sant'Anna Galvão, a Franciscan monk who lived in the 18th and 19th centuries and is credited with 5,000 miracle cures.

One of Brazil's great social and cultural anomalies is that although racial tolerance has been practiced for generations and intermarriage between whites and blacks is relatively commonplace, the country's social elite and its political power structure remain virtually entirely Caucasian, while blacks still occupy a disproportionate share of the bottommost rung of Brazil's social and economic ladder. Mulattos are caught somewhere in between.

While the Portuguese influence is most keenly felt in Brazil's architecture and literature, the African contribution has been greatest to Brazilian folklore, art and music. Moreover, there was considerable French influence during the immediate post-independence period. During the reign of Emperor Dom Pedro I (1825–31), the French-founded Royal School of Science, Arts and Crafts was incorporated into the Academy of Fine Arts. French influence on Brazilian art was especially strong.

Nineteenth century Brazilian literature also was influenced by French naturalism. The two leading Brazilian representatives of this style were Aluísio de Azevedo (1857-1913), author of the novels *Ó mulato* and *O Cortiço (The Slum)*; and the mulatto novelist, poet, playwright and story writer Joaquim Maria Machado de Assis (1839-1908). In the early 20th century were published two novels that remain classics of Brazilian—and Latin American—literature: *Os sertões*, by Eucliudes da Cunha (1866-1909), and *Canaã*, by José Pereira de Graça Aranha (1868-1931), for whom one of Brazil's modern literature prizes is named.

Arguably the country's most internationally renowned writer of the 20th century was Jorge Amado, (1912–2001), whose novels *Terra do sem fin, Dona Flor e seus dois maridos* and *Gabriela, cravo e canela*, have been translated and marketed worldwide. His death in 2001, four days before his 89th birthday, was a cause for national mourning, and his passing was noted around the world. Other noteworthy contemporary writers include the poet and essayist Carlos Drummond de Andrade (1902-87) and playwright Nelson Rodrigues (1912-80).

In music, the samba and other styles of African origin bridge the gap between folk and popular. Brazilian classical composers whose works incorporated Brazilian folk styles included Claudio Santoro and the better-known, and internationally renowned, Heitor Villa-Lobos (1887–1959). Villa-Lobos is best remembered for his 14 *Chôros*, composed while working in *avant-garde* Paris from 1925–30. *Chôros* were popular street serenades in Rio de Janeiro in the early 20th century, and they inspired Villa-Lobos' classical compositions much the way the tango inspired those of Astor Piazzolla in neighboring Argentina or jazz influenced those of George Gershwin in the United States.

Brazilian popular music, or *MPB* as it is called in the press, is a major domestic industry. Perhaps the best known abroad were Sergio Mendes (b. 1941), whose group Brasil 66 was especially popular in the United States in the 1960s during the *Bossa Nova* craze, and Antonio Carlos Jobim (1927–94), who wrote such internationally popular tunes as *Desafinado, Meditacão, Insensatez (End of a Love Affair), Garota de Ipanema (Girl from Ipanema)* and *The One-Note Samba*.

Brazilian pop singers whose popularity spread throughout Latin America include Roberto Carlos (b. 1941) and Elis Regina (1945–82). Regina's daughter, Maria Rita, splashed onto the international scene in 2005 when she was named Best New Artist at the Latin Grammy Awards ceremony in Los Angeles. Another young Brazilian, Gaby Amarantos (b. 1978), from Belém, Para, won the Latin Grammy for Best New Artist in Las Vegas in 2012. She specializes in a style called *tecno brega*. Her album *Treme* was also nominated for Best Brazilian Roots Album.

The *sertanejo* genre is the Brazilian equivalent of country music, a hybrid of pop and traditional *caipira*. The duo Chitãozinho & Xororó, whose real names are José Lima Sobrinho and Durval de Lima, who are brothers, are credited as the creators of *sertanejo*. They have sold 30 million albums since 1970. They won a Latin Grammy in 2012. A rising *sertanejo* star who has achieved acclaim abroad is Michel Telo (b. 1981).

The Latin Grammys now have seven Brazilian categories, including Best Samba and Best Sertanejo. From 2001 to 2012, Brazil won 125 Latin Grammys, just one behind the leader, Mexico.

Internationally known Brazilian artists included Waldemar Cordeiro, sculptor Mario Carvo Jr., and the naturalist painter Candido Portinari. In the field of architecture Brazil boasts the internationally famous Oscar Niemeyer (1907–2012), whose most enduring creation is Brazil's futuristic capital city, Brasilia, constructed in the 1950s during the presidency of Juscelino Kubitschek. The city is a UNESCO World Heritage Site.

The Brazilian film industry, one of the region's oldest, received an impetus in the 1960s and 1970s through the creative genius of director Glauber Rocha (1939–81) and his *Cinema Novo* movement. He is best remembered for his trilogy, *Deus e o Diabo na Terra do Sol (God and the Devil in the Land of the Sun)* in 1964, *Terra em Transe (Land in Transition)* in 1967 and *O Dragão da Maldade Contra o Santo Guerreiro (The Dragon of Evil vs. The Holy Warrior)* in 1969. *Deus e o Diabo* was nominated for the *Palme d'Or* at the Cannes Film Festival, while Rocha was named best director at Cannes for *O Dragão da Maldade*.

Brazilian films, long exported to other Latin American countries and to Portugal, have won increasing critical acclaim elsewhere. Two Brazilian films have won the *Palme d'Or, Orfeu Negro (Black Orpheus)* in 1959 and Anselmo Duarte's *O Pagador de Promesas (The Keeper of Promises,* also titled *The Given Word)* in 1962. Both films also were nominated for the U.S. Academy Award for Best Foreign Film, and *Black Orpheus* won the Oscar. There is some dispute whether *Black Orpheus* should be rated Brazilian or French because it was directed by Marcel Camus, but it was filmed in Portuguese in Brazil and based on the play, *Orfeu da Conceição* by Brazilian playwright Vinicius de Moraes, which was his adaptation of the Greek legend. The score is by Brazilian composer Carlos Antonio Jobim (see above).

Two other internationally acclaimed Brazilian films from that period were the comedy *Dona Flor e seus dois maridos* (1976), adapted from the Jorge Amado novel and directed by Bruno Barreto, and *Pixote* (1981), a dark film directed by the Argentine exile Héctor Babenco (b. 1946) about the lives of Brazil's street children, which won actress Marilia Pera the New York Film Critics' Award for best actress in 1982. Babenco also directed the English-language *Kiss of the Spider Woman* (1985), based on the Argentine novel by Manuel Puig and starring U.S. actor William Hurt and Puerto Rican Raúl Julia but set in Brazil during the military regime.

After that, Brazilian cinematic creativity went into a decade-long slump. After the state-owned firm *Embrafilme* was abolished in 1990, ending government subsidies, only a handful of films was produced each year in the 1990s and only 1% of the films shown in Brazil were domestically produced, compared with 40% during the era of *Cinema Novo*. But in the late 1990s, a new law allowed film companies a tax write-off if they invested up to 3% in new films.

The incentive helped spark a revival, and Brazilian films again achieved international acclaim. Three Brazilian films were nominated for best Foreign Film in the United States in the 1990s: *O Quatrilho*

Brazil

(1995), a story about Italian immigrants to Brazil, directed by Bruno Barreto's brother, Fábio; *O Que E Isso Companheiro* (*Four Days in September*), the true story of the kidnapping of a U.S. ambassador, directed by Bruno Barreto, (1997); and Walter Selles' *Central do Brasil* (*Central Station*), a story of an elderly woman who befriends an orphan boy (1998). Fernanda Montenegro was nominated for a Best Actress Oscar for *Central Station.*

Eu, Tu, Eles (*Me, You, Them*), a true story of polygamy in the Brazilian outback directed by Andrucha Waddington, received widespread acclaim at the 2001 Cannes Film Festival and won prizes at festivals in Cuba and the Czech Republic.

In 2002–03, another Brazilian film that won box office success at home and critical acclaim abroad was *Cidade de Deus* (*City of God*), the name of an infamous Rio de Janeiro *favela*, or slum. Adapted from a novel by Paulo Lins and directed by Fernando Meirelles, the film examines the drug gang culture there. It received four Oscar nominations in the United States in 2004.

The Brazilian Culture Ministry selected the film *Olga*, by Jayme Monjardi, as Brazil's entry for best foreign film in the 2005 Oscars, but it was not nominated. It is the true story of Olga Benario, a German Jew who emigrated to Brazil, married a Communist activist and was deported back to Germany, where she died in a concentration camp in 1942.

A different sort of phenomenon was the 2004 film *Mary, Mother of the Son of God,* directed by the charismatic Catholic priest and pop music sensation Marcelo Rossi. It had the same sort of impact as Mel Gibson's *The Passion of the Christ* in the United States.

Brazilian radio and television developed along U.S. lines, though in its early days Brazilian television depended heavily on U.S. imports. That has changed, and Brazil now exports its translated *telenovelas* throughout Latin America. The mammoth *Globo* Network, with 75 million viewers, claims the largest audience of any network in the world.

Educational reform was late in coming to Brazil, and it lags behind some of its neighbors in literacy and newspaper readership per 1,000 people. For decades Brazil's most respected daily has been *O Estado de São Paulo*, owned by the Mesquita family, which resisted the press controls imposed by both Getulio Vargas and the military regimes of 1964–85. Rio's two elite newspapers are *Jornal do Brasil*, founded in 1891, and the circulation leader, *O Globo*, which also owns the like-named television network. Numerous tabloid newspapers boast large circulations throughout the country. There are several high-quality magazines, including *Manchete, Veja* and *Isto É*. The Brazilian media, especially *Veja,* have played a crucial role in exposing government corruption, but because of the government's traditional hostility to the press, Freedom House rates Brazil's media as "partly free."

UNESCO has designated 12 Brazilian locations as World Heritage Sites, ranging from the colonial-era sections of the cities of Diamantina, Goiás, Olinda, Ouro Preto, Salvador de Bahia and São Luis, to the futuristic capital city of Brasilia, designed in the 1950s by Lucio Costa and Oscar Niemeyer.

Brazil has more than 2,300 institutions of higher learning. Probably the most prestigious is the University of São Paulo, founded in 1827.

ECONOMY: In 2009, Brazil boasted the world's eighth-largest economy. Occupying half the continent, Brazil has immense natural wealth, including a diverse agricultural sector in which tropical and subtropical products flourish. A significant cattle industry in the south provides meat for domestic consumption and leather for export. The country also has been blessed with mineral wealth, including gold, iron, manganese, chromium, tin and in recent years, petroleum. Brazil also is the world's third-leading producer of bauxite, the raw material from which aluminum is refined.

Manufacturing began early in the 20th century, but domestic industry, protected from imports by high tariffs, failed to match that of neighboring Argentina. Like many Latin American countries, Brazil adopted a quasi-socialist mixed economy, characterized by public sector control of utilities and transportation. Brazil's economic growth has long been hamstrung by one of the world's highest birthrates, which largely accounts for the high percentage of people living below the poverty line.

The military governments that ruled from 1964–85 reversed policy in the late 1960s by inviting foreign investors into Brazil, offering attractive tax incentives. The resulting capitalization led to a boom that international economists referred to as the "Brazilian economic miracle." Foreign automobile manufacturers put Brazil on wheels, and Volkswagen and General Motors remain major manufacturers today. An aggressive effort was made to increase nontraditional exports, including automobiles, tractors, military vehicles, weapons, aircraft and shoes. In 1967 the government declared the port of Manaus near the mouth of the Amazon a free-trade zone, which still produces consumer items for export.

The miracle abruptly halted in 1974–75 because of a dual blow: OPEC's quadrupling of petroleum prices, which sparked a worldwide recession that was felt especially keenly in Brazil, which then imported 90% of its oil; and a devastating frost in the south that virtually destroyed Brazil's coffee crop, the leading export item. The military rulers sought a twofold solution. Because coffee trees require seven years to produce marketable beans, farmers were encouraged to replant much of the destroyed coffee acreage with soybeans, an annual crop that provided immediate export earnings. The second was to begin manufacturing automobiles designed to burn pure alcohol, distilled from domestically grown sugar cane. Ethanol production fell to *Petrobras*, the state-owned oil firm. Exploitation of newly discovered offshore oil deposits, coupled with the ethanol program, eventually led to independence from oil imports.

Also in response to energy needs, Brazil joined with Paraguay to build the Itaipu dam, the world's second-largest, in the late 1970s.

As in Argentina, efforts by the military to deal with the recession sparked hyperinflation, which continued into the democratic period. Inflation peaked in 1994, when then-Finance Minister Cardoso implemented the *"Real* Plan," named for the new currency unit. Inflation dropped to double-digit, then single-digit levels by 1997, when the Asian economic crisis forced President Cardoso to adopt a drastic austerity plan that included a 40% increase in interest rates and $18 billion worth of public savings, paid for through a combination of spending cuts and tax increases. Still, unemployment jumped to 7.25%, the highest in 13 years. In order to further shore up the *real* and prevent a flight of foreign capital, Cardoso streamlined the civil service and made social security cuts, which sparked violent protests.

By mid-2000, there were clear signs that Brazil had weathered the crisis. It finished 1999 with a slight GDP growth of about 1%. The growth rate for 2000 was an encouraging 4.5%, but in 2001 in dropped back to 3% and in 2002 it fell even further to 1.5%, barely enough to keep up with the growth in the workforce. The *real* stabilized, though it experienced fluctuations. As another positive indicator, the Central Bank announced in 2000 that it was repaying $10.5 billion of the $41.5 billion emergency loan package the IMF had extended in 1999 to rescue the economy, bringing to $18.2 billion the amount that had been repaid.

Unemployment remained about 8% from 1999–2002, although urban unemployment still was only half that of Argentina.

Cardoso met with U.S. President George W. Bush at the White House in 2001. Bush proposed a U.S.-Brazilian free-trade pact, but a skeptical Cardoso questioned Bush's sincerity by pointing out protectionist U.S.

Brazil

anti-dumping measures aimed at Brazilian steel and produce. Cardoso repeated his criticism at the Third Summit of the Americas in Quebec. The steel dispute worsened in 2002 when Bush, yielding to demands from domestic steelmakers, imposed a 30% tariff on most steel imports. Brazil protested the U.S. tariff before the World Trade Organization.

The predicted election of the socialist former union leader Lula da Silva as president in 2002 caused jitters in world financial markets. Da Silva met with the IMF to dispel the notion he was a reckless left-wing firebrand. The IMF took da Silva at his word and approved a new $30 billion loan package shortly before the election. He was re-elected in 2006. He carefully followed a pragmatic economic policy not unlike that of Cardoso's, which was ironic given that he twice ran against Cardoso and vilified his policies.

Da Silva had little to boast about on the economy at the end of his first term. GDP, which had increased by 1.9% in 2002, declined by –0.2% in 2003, the economy's worst showing in a decade. Moreover, unemployment at year-end stood at 12.2%, while inflation was 9%. Inflation dropped to 3% by 2006.

GDP growth for 2004 rebounded to 5.2%, which temporarily boosted da Silva's popularity. He also enjoyed a huge budget surplus, much of which was used to create dead-end public service jobs. GDP growth in 2005 slid back to 2.4%, but inflation remained in the single digits and unemployment continued to decline.

Brazil attained two significant economic milestones in 2005 and 2006. In December 2005, Brazil announced it was repaying its entire $15.5 billion debt to the IMF in full, which saved on interest payments and freed up revenue for da Silva's promised domestic programs. The early repayment was ironic considering the fears the IMF and foreign banks had of a da Silva presidency.

In April 2006, Brazil announced it had achieved petroleum self-sufficiency, through a combination of new offshore discoveries and the 30-year-old ethanol substitution program.

Petrobras produced 15 billion liters of ethanol in 2005, 17 billion in 2007 and 24.9 billion in 2009, but frosts affected the 2011 sugar crop and a high world price for sugar diverted production, resulting in a 17.7% decrease in ethanol production, to 21.1 billion liters. *Petrobras* has a 50–50 partnership with the Japanese firm Nippon Alcohol Hanbai to produce 1.8 billion liters of ethanol annually for the Japanese market. By 2013, ethanol production had risen back to 23.7 billion liters.

The 54-cent-per-gallon U.S. tariff on Brazilian ethanol remains a bone of contention between the two countries. U.S.

agribusiness, which receives billions of dollars in subsidies to produce corn-based ethanol, does not want competition from the cheaper, sugar-based Brazilian fuel. Currently, about 3.5 million hectares are devoted to sugar cultivation devoted to ethanol, and experiments are underway to develop cane with higher sucrose yields and that require less water. Brazil has indeed come a long way since the 1970s, when it imported 90% of its petroleum.

GDP growth in 2006 was a still-lackluster 3.7%, and the average for da Silva's first term was 2.6%. Da Silva made economic growth a major priority as he began his second term in 2007. Growth was a healthy 6.1% in 2007, one of the highest in Latin America, and 5.1% in 2008, but it declined –0.2% in 2009 because of the global recession. Despite the recession, unemployment declined from 7.9% in 2008 to 7.4% in 2009. Inflation was 4.2% in 2009.

Petrobras announced another exciting offshore discovery in November 2007, a deep field called Tupi that it said could contain 5–8 billion barrels of oil and that would give Brazil the world's eighth-largest oil and gas reserves. Brazil may for the first time become an oil *exporter*. In 2009, *Petrobras* signed a $10 billion contract with China's oil company to provide 200,000 barrels per day from the Tupi field for 10 years. Yet, Brazil turned down Saudi Arabia's invitation to join OPEC. Da Silva was present for the extraction of the first crude oil from the Tupi field. He has since upset private shareholders who control 60% of *Petrobras* by proposing legislation to create a new state-owned company, *Petrosal,* that would be devoted exclusively to the Tupi exploitation; half the revenue would go to the government. Coastal states had benefited greatly from the oil windfall, but in 2009 non-coastal states successfully lobbied Congress for a greater share.

The decision by Bolivian President Evo Morales in May 2006 to nationalize that country's natural gas fields—in which *Petrobras* had invested heavily and from which Brazil imports much of its natural gas—and to increase the tax from 50% to 82% strained relations between the two previously friendly governments and greatly increased the cost of gas for Brazilian consumers. To meet rising energy demands, the government in 2007 announced plans for a third Angra nuclear generating plant.

Work also has begun two new dams on the Madeira River in Rondonia state to be completed by 2012 and for a third dam, Belo Monte, on the Xingu River, which would become the world's third largest. It would produce up to 11.2 billion kilowatt hours during the rainy season, but a judge delayed construction in 2013 until its impact on indigenous communities could be determined.

Internationally, da Silva placed greater emphasis on the *Mercosur* trade bloc and sought to forge a merger of *Mercosur* with the Andean Pact and a free-trade agreement with the European Union. Negotiations for the latter collapsed in 2004 but were revived in 2010.

By the end of da Silva's second term, Brazil was an economic powerhouse. The rising world price for petroleum and demand for Brazilian agricultural products and manufacturing goods sparked a 7.5% growth in GDP in 2010, again one of the highest in the region and the highest since 1986. Unemployment was only 6.7% at the end of 2010, compared with 9% in the United States. Inflation was 4.9%, unchanged from 2009. Brazil's GDP of $2.02 trillion was the seventh-largest in the world in 2010, surpassing G-8 members Italy, Canada and Russia. *Petrobras* posted a $20 billion profit for 2010, while the giant Brazilian mining firm Vale announced profits of $17.3 billion, three times higher than 2009. Embraer, the aircraft manufacturer, was third largest in the world behind Boeing in the United States and Airbus in Europe.

Da Silva's successor in 2011, Dilma Rousseff, pledged to continue da Silva's pragmatic, and successful, economic policies. She is emphasizing trade with China, especially iron ore, soybeans and aircraft. Bilateral trade increased from $2.3 billion in 2000 to $564 billion in 2010; between 2009 and 2010 alone, Brazilian-Chinese trade increased 52%, and China surpassed the United States as Brazil's leading trade partner. Rousseff signed more than 20 new trade and investment agreements with Hu Jintao during her state visit to China in April 2011.

Rousseff directed *Petrobras* to invest $3.5 billion over four years to double ethanol production.

In October 2013, *Petrobras* joined Shell, Total and two Chinese companied in a consortium that won the bid to develop the vast Libra offshore oil deposits, one the world's largest fields, estimated to contain 8-12 billion barrels. Only 11 companies submitted bids, far fewer than anticipated. Their bid was $7 billion up front, and they plan to spend $185 billion in development over 35 years. *Petrobras* holds a 40% interest in the consortium, Shell and Total 20% each and the Chinese companies 10% each.

GDP growth slowed to 2.7% in 2011, Rousseff's first full year, but unemployment also dropped from 6.7% to 6%. Growth in 2012 was a disappointing .9% (officially 1.3%), lower than any Latin American country except Paraguay. Unemployment edged back up to 6.2%. In 2013 growth was back up to 2.5%, still below the Latin American average.

Although inflation rose from 5% in 2010 to 6.5% in 2011, the Central Bank shocked

Brazil

the world in 2011 by drastically lowering interest rates, some by as much as two thirds. They are still the highest in Latin America or of any of the world's major economies, a legacy of the fear of the hyperinflation of the 1980s. Even so, inflation was still 6.6% in 2012 and 6.2% in 2013 and helped fuel the public protests in June and July 2013 (see History).

THE FUTURE: "Lula" da Silva's eight-year stewardship of the world's fourth-largest democracy and seventh-largest economy was impressive, far exceeding expectations. He successfully performed a delicate highwire act, placating his natural constituency on the left with ambitious social programs while reassuring the right and center by keeping the shaky economy on at least an even keel. He succeeded in accomplishing something peacefully that Latin American leftists have long dreamed of: a redistribution of wealth. The Brazilian middle class grew dramatically on his watch.

In the process, he made enemies on both sides—something that statesmen sometimes must do. He left office with an approval rating of 80%, phenomenal for a Latin American president after eight years.

It is indicative of his popularity that voters elected his anointed successor, Dilma Rousseff, Latin America's sixth elected woman president and Brazil's first. She inherited a booming economy, and did little to upset that apple cart. In 2011, Brazil's GDP of $2.5 trillion eclipsed Britain's to become the world's sixth-largest. According to current projections, Brazil's economy will be the fourth-largest by 2030, behind China, the United States and India. Brazil was in the global spotlight when it hosted the 2014 World Cup and will be again with the 2016 Olympics, which could be advantageous if she hopes to continue Lula's aspirations to make Brazil one of the premier powers of the world, with a permanent seat on the UN Security Council.

But the economy has since soured and *Petrobras* officials have been accused of massive bribery. Rousseff's popularity plummeted from more than 60% in 2012 to less than 40% in mid-2014. Consequently, she faces a tougher-than-expected re-election battle on October 5. She once looked unbeatable, but polls now show that although she is leading her two serious contenders, Aécio Neves, 54, of the *PSDB* and Eduardo Campos, 49, of the Socialist

Party (whose running mate is the highly respected Marina Silva), she may well be forced into a runoff on October 26. Pollsters who have queried voters' attitudes have detected another important variable: After 12 years of *PT* rule, millions of Brazilians are simply ready for a change.

The ultimate outcome may depend on whether she faces Neves or Campos in the runoff. Campos is a defector from Rousseff's ruling coalition, but would he throw his support behind the far more conservative Neves? That seems a long shot. Silva may prove to be the wild card. She, too, is philosophically closer to Rousseff than to Neves, but she and Rousseff have bad blood dating to their time in Lula's cabinet. Moreover, deforestation of the Amazon rain forest jumped 28% in 2012-13, ending a decade-long decline, and environmentalists blame Rousseff and the watered down 2012 Forest Code (See Destruction of the Amazon: A Global Catastrophe). The math still favors Rousseff, but even if she prevails, she can expect a much rockier second term. The *PMDB*, the largest party in Congress and the linchpin of her governing coalition, has already hinted it may quit after the election.

Grinding corn to be used for Pamonha, a typical dish in Minas Gerais.   Clotilde Soares Guilbeau

104

Chile

La Moneda (presidential palace) in Santiago

Area: 286,322 square miles; Chile also claims sovereignty over a tract in Antarctica totaling 478,444 square miles.

Population: 17,363,894 (2014 est.)

Capital City: Santiago (Pop. 6 million in 2012).

Climate: Northern coastal lowlands are very hot and dry; the central valley is warm and dry from October through April and mild and damp through September; the southern regions are wet and cold.

Neighboring Countries: Peru (Northwest); Bolivia (Northeast); Argentina (East).

Official Language: Spanish

Other Principal Tongues: German, Quechua and Araucana.

Ethnic Background: The majority are mestizo (mixed European and Indian).

Principal Religion: Roman Catholic Christianity.

Chief Commercial Products: Copper, nitrates, iron, steel, foodstuffs, processed fish, wine, fresh produce, wood.

Currency: Peso.

Gross Domestic Product: U.S. $281.7 billion in 2013 ($16,223 per capita, official exchange rate).

Former Colonial Status: Spanish Crown Colony (1541–1818).

Independence Day: September 18, 1810.

Chief of State: Dr. Veronica Michelle Bachelet Jeria (born September 29, 1951), president (since March 11, 2014).

National Flag: White, blue and red, with a white star in the blue stripe.

Chile, a name derived from an old Indian word meaning "land's end," sixth in size among the South American countries, is a strip of land 2,600 miles long and averaging 110 miles wide, lying between the Andes and the Pacific Ocean. Nearly one-half of this territory is occupied by the Andes Mountains and a coastal range of peaks. Because of its north-south length, Chile has a wide range of soils and climates; the country's frontier with Peru runs from Arica on the Pacific coast east to the crest of the Andes. The frontier with Bolivia and Argentina follows the crest of the Andes—18,000 feet high in the north, rising to 23,000 feet in the center and dropping to 13,000 feet in the south. The coastal range runs from the north to deep south, dropping abruptly into the sea with few ports. The heartland of Chile is the central valley between the two ranges.

Chile is divided into five natural regions. The northern, extending 600 miles south from the Peruvian border to Copiapo, is one of the driest regions of the world. Here are found rich nitrate deposits and major copper mines for which Chile has been famous. From Copiapo 400 miles south to Illapel, there is a semi-arid region; however, there is sufficient rainfall to permit the raising of crops in the valleys. Chile's iron ore is found in this region. From Illapel 500 miles south to Concepción is the fertile area of the lush, green central valley. With adequate rainfall in the winter (May to August) the valley is intensively cultivated. Here also are the three principal cities and the major portion of the population. From Concepción to Puerto Montt there is a forest region, with large, sparkling lakes and rivers where rainfall is oppressively heavy during the fall and winter. The fifth and last zone stretches south 1,000 miles from Puerto Montt. This is an almost uninhabited wild region of cold mountains, glaciers and small islands. Rainfall is torrential and the climate stormy, wet and chilling.

HISTORY: Prior to the arrival of the Spaniards, Chile was the home from time immemorial of the Araucanas, a loosely grouped civilization that was completely isolated from the rest of mankind. Their origins remain a mystery.

In the early 15th century, the Incas pushed across the desert and conquered the tribes of Mapuche Indians in the north-

105

Chile

ern half of the fertile valley where present-day Santiago is located. However, they were unable to penetrate south of the river Maule because of Araucana resistance. The Spaniards founded Santiago in 1541. About a century later, the Indians entered into a treaty with the Spanish to retain the land south of Concepción. Despite the treaty, war continued between the Araucanas and their would-be conquerors until late in the 19th century.

During the conquest, the land was divided into great estates among the army officers; soldiers and settlers married Indian women captives, producing a *mestizo* population with qualities of both conquerors and the conquered. The colonial period was one of savage warfare and internal dissension. Particularly sharp were clashes between landowners and the clergy over the practice of holding Indians in slavery. During the 17th century, slavery was replaced by a system of sharecropping which prevailed until the late 20th century.

To the wars and dissensions that marked Chile's history must be added a long list of natural disasters. Earthquakes and tidal waves have repeatedly destroyed its cities. Moreover, from the end of the 16th century until final independence in 1818, Chile's coasts were infested with British and French pirates.

For the entire Spanish period, Chile was part of the Viceroyalty of Peru, governed from Lima; trade with areas other than the colony was forbidden, which led to wholesale smuggling. Reports in the early 18th century indicated some 40 French ships engaged in illegal trade with Chile. Not until 1778 was trade permitted between Chile and Spain. Neglected by both Spain and Lima, the landowning aristocracy felt

little loyalty to their own overlords and developed their estates as semi-independent fiefs.

Chile declared its independence from Spain on September 18, 1810, while Spain was occupied by the French under Napoleon. That is Chile's official independence day, but it took eight years of bitter war between the Chileans and Spanish forces before independence became a reality. General José de San Martín led an army from Argentina across the Andes to support the Chilean forces under General Bernardo O'Higgins. They defeated the Spanish at the battles of Chacabuco in 1817. Formal independence was declared again on February 12, 1818, and final victory came when San Martín defeated the Spanish at the battle of Maipú on April 5.

O'Higgins, became the first president of the republic with dictatorial powers, and under his leadership the first consti-

Punta Arenas, the only city on the Strait of Magellan

Courtesy: Mr. & Mrs. Schuyler Lowe

General Bernardo O'Higgins

tution was drafted. Almost revolutionary in its liberal democratic ideas, it served as a model for the famous constitution adopted in 1833.

Opposition of the landowners to O'Higgins' efforts to redistribute land to small farmers, to separate church and state and to encourage free education resulted in his ouster in 1823. For nearly 100 years, the country was ruled by a small oligarchy of landowners, or *latifundistas* who owned the major share of valuable land for two more centuries. Conservatives, advocating a strong central government, dominated the political scene until 1861. Their autocratic rule enlarged the economy and united the country, but the repression of the Liberal Party laid the basis for years of bitter conflict.

Liberals came to power in 1861 and were successful in modifying some of the more restrictive measures of the conservative regime. However, they made little progress against the landowners or the church.

Liberals ruled until 1891, during which time longstanding disputes with Peru and Bolivia led to the War of the Pacific (1879–1884). Although unprepared for war, Chile quickly defeated Bolivia, overran the disputed nitrate fields and occupied Lima from 1881 to 1884. Dictating the victor's terms, Chile took possession of both Bolivian and Peruvian provinces and the ports of Arica and Antofagasta.

Liberal José Balmaceda, elected to the presidency in 1886, decided the time was ripe for major reforms to improve the lot of the poor and to curb the power of the landlords and the church. By 1890, he had created a crisis in urging these programs and in 1891 the Congress voted to depose him and installed a naval officer to head a provisional government. With the support of the army, Balmaceda resisted the action; the result was a civil war resulting in the deaths of some 10,000, with widespread damage. Balmaceda was ultimately forced

to seek asylum in the Argentine Embassy, where he committed suicide.

Balmaceda's death also marked the death of the Liberal era and ushered in the phenomenon of congressional rule that predominated over the executive—definitely an anomaly for Latin America. The conservative oligarchy wielded virtually unchecked control for the next three decades through a political machine known as *La Fronda*. This same period witnessed a proliferation of political parties that supplanted the traditional Liberals and Conservatives: Radical, National, Democratic, Socialist and Communist, among others. Moreover, there was an industrial revolution that led to greater agitation for reform by organized labor movements. World War I saw a boom in the demand for Chilean nitrates, although the wealth that flowed into the country, as usual, failed to trickle down to the lower economic strata. At the end of the war, the same social ferment that led to the Bolshevik Revolution in Russia erupted in Chile in the form of strikes. Revolution seemed imminent.

Alessandri and Ibáñez

In 1920, a so-called Liberal Alliance of Radicals, Democrats, some Liberals and other factions, coalesced behind the nomination of Arturo Alessandri Palma for president. Like Franklin D. Roosevelt and John F. Kennedy, Alessandri was a handsome, wealthy patrician with a charismatic personality who convinced the working classes that he had their interests at heart. His message paralleled that of President Hipólito Irigoyen in neighboring Argentina, whose social reforms had defused a revolution there and caught the fancy of Chileans. Alessandri advocated separation of church and state, women's suffrage and increased taxes on the wealthy, including an income tax, to fund social welfare programs. Alessandri's popular appeal was such that he eked out a narrow plurality despite the *latifundistas*' control of the rural vote. Faced with the prospect of a genuine revolution, such as the one that had just unfolded in Mexico, the oligarchy's representatives in Congress pragmatically realized that Alessandri represented the lesser of two evils and voted to ratify his victory.

It was a largely hollow victory, because although the Liberal Alliance controlled the Chamber of Deputies, the right still controlled the Senate and frustrated virtually all of Alessandri's reform measures save the income tax. Congress' obstinance, however, was to prove its undoing, because one of the measures that was tied up was the army's appropriation, always a mistake in Latin America. In September 1924, a band of officers invaded Congress

and demanded that it approve Alessandri's reform package (as well as their back pay). The officers then demanded that the president sign the measures. He complied, but to protest this undemocratic intervention, he resigned and left for self-imposed exile, first to Argentina, then to his parents' native Italy.

A power vacuum resulted, into which stepped in January 1925 a young colonel who would have a direct or indirect influence on Chilean government for more than 30 years: Carlos Ibáñez del Campo. Ironically, it was this military man who would implement much of the remainder of the reforms Alessandri had called for in 1920, and he somehow did so without alarming the oligarchy. Moreover, he promulgated the 1925 constitution, largely inspired by Alessandri, which returned power to the executive and served as the cornerstone for a reborn but shaky democracy that would last until 1973. Hardly a democrat himself, however, Ibáñez ruled from behind the throne for two years until he was "elected" in a highly suspect election in 1927. Although he enjoyed widespread public approval for a time, not even this military strongman could control events in New York. With the Stock Market Crash of 1929, the world price of copper plummeted, dragging Chile into the Great Depression. Ibáñez was overthrown in 1931, and there was a bewildering succession of revolving-door governments, including a socialist one, for the next 15 months. During this period of chaos, Alessandri returned from Italy and his leadership-starved countrymen returned him to the presidency for a six-year term in October 1932.

The Alessandri of the 1930s, however, was a changed man from the fiery reformer of the 1920s. His exile in Mussolini's Italy had taught him the value of order and stability. He skillfully placated the discrete elements of the power structure—the military, the church, the wealthy landowners and industrialists, the middle class—when necessary; he resorted to a heavy hand to keep the social ferment from exploding. Yet, he gave women the right to vote in 1935. He once dissolved Congress, and he threw strike leaders in jail, causing the Socialists and Communists to break away and form a European-style Popular Front then in vogue.

The Popular Front's presidential candidate in 1938, Pedro Aguirre Cerda, an intellectual, won by a narrow plurality. His government was responsible for the creation of Latin America's most comprehensive social welfare program, made possible largely by the jump in copper and nitrate prices caused by the outbreak of World War II, and it became something of a model for the left-wing reformers in

Chile

Latin America and Europe. It also proved a training ground for a generation of left-wing politicians at home; Aguirre Cerda's minister of health, for example, was a young physician named Salvador Allende. The war also caused a breakup of the Popular Front because of the nonaggression pact between Hitler and Stalin.

President Aguirre died in 1941 and a Radical, Juan Antonio Ríos, defeated Ibáñez, the candidate of the right, in the ensuing election. Ríos, who was considerably to the right of his predecessor, oversaw a booming wartime economy and, largely because of German influence, maintained a neutral course until just before the end of the war, when Chile declared war on the all-but-defeated Axis.

Ríos, too, died in office, and in the election to choose a successor in 1946 the vote was fragmented among several candidates. Congress then selected another Radical, Gabriel González Videla, who formed a coalition government that included Socialists and Communists. Not only did the United States exert pressure on González Videla because of the Communist influence, but the Communists began engaging in intrigues aimed at seizing absolute power. In 1948, González Videla purged the Communists not only from his cabinet but from Congress, including the world-renowned poet and future Nobel Laureate, Pablo Neruda.

Chile swung even farther to the right in the election of 1952 when Ibáñez, then 75, finally succeeded in finishing in first place in another fragmented election. Labeling himself above politics, this quasi-fascist managed to draw votes from poor laborers and farm workers. Congress, following its tradition to ratify the top vote-getter, returned him to power. Despite fears that he would seek to become another Juan Perón, whom he admired, Ibáñez presided over a largely do-nothing government for six years. When he failed to take strong action to deal with spiraling inflation, the populace became bitterly disillusioned with this once-dynamic leader.

In 1958, the Socialists and Communists united behind the candidacy of Salvador Allende, a Marxist. The Liberals and Conservatives rallied behind a moderate, Jorge Alessandri, son of Arturo, while a new force, the Christian Democrats, nominated Eduardo Frei Montalva. Alessandri finished just 1% ahead of Allende, giving the establishment a scare. Alessandri proved quite conservative, and although he helped stabilize the economy, he failed to address the perennial social ills that were providing grist for the far left.

By 1964, it seemed the impatience of the lower classes for some remedies to their plight could well give Allende a plurality of the popular vote and, if Congress followed tradition, the presidency. Fearing that eventuality, the rightists gradually abandoned their own candidate and rallied behind the Christian Democrats' Frei, who represented a middle course of reform without revolution. Frei easily defeated Allende with 55% of the vote, the first time in decades that a candidate had won with an absolute majority. Frei made good on many of his promises, initiating land reform and making the first steps toward nationalization of the foreign-owned copper mines. But he found himself in a damned-if-you-do-damned-if-you-don't dilemma. The right vilified him for going too far, the left for not going far enough.

Allende and Pinochet

In 1970, Allende was again a candidate, this time of a Socialist-Communist-Radical coalition called Popular Unity. But this time the right split with the Christian Democrats and nominated former President Alessandri, by then quite elderly, while the Christian Democrats nominated a left-of-center candidate, Rodomiro Tomic, who tried unsuccessfully to steal Allende's thunder. Polls showed the race a tossup between Allende and Alessandri, and the world watched with expectation to see if Allende would usher in the world's first democratically elected Marxist government. Ironically, only 29% of the electorate turned out for what would become the most fateful election in Chile's history. Allende won by an eyelash, 36.4% to Alessandri's 35.2%. Under the 1925 constitution, the choice fell again to Congress. Despite a clumsy attempt by the CIA to bribe Christian Democratic congressmen to vote for Alessandri, Congress confirmed Allende, and Frei placed the presidential sash over the shoulders of his Marxist successor on November 3, 1970.

The victory of Popular Unity caught even Allende and his supporters by surprise. Despite their shaky mandate, they set off to turn Chile into a Marxist state, gradually alienating the centrist Christian Democrats who initially provided them with the congressional votes they needed to pass legislation. The government implemented a hastily devised economic program that nationalized the U.S.-owned copper mines and telephone system. Virtually no compensation was offered, which resulted in economic sanctions by the Nixon Administration. The Soviet Union and China, for a time, willingly came to Chile's economic rescue. In other action, the government increased wages and froze prices, which temporarily created the illusion of prosperity; Chileans went on a spending spree, and in 1971 municipal elections voters expressed their

View of downtown Santiago

108

Salvador Allende

General Augusto Pinochet Ugarte

gratitude by giving Popular Unity 49% of the vote.

The Soviet Union started to worry about being burdened with supporting a second Latin American nation. Fidel Castro warned Allende in 1973 during a state visit that Chile's economic plans were the opposite of Marxism, in which consumption is held to a minimum. Allende replied that he was working in a system where he had to win re-election until a "dictatorship of the proletariat" could be established, and rejected Castro's advice.

Although general disintegration of the economy was well underway by the time of 1973 congressional elections, thirst for continued consumerism resulted in an increased share of the vote for Allende's coalition to 44%. Voter enthusiasm could not save the economy, which was experiencing a "domino" style collapse in which one sector brought down others. First to fall were the retail stores. With prices fixed and wages raised, stores could not afford to restock sold items; when everything on the shelves was gone, the stores closed, idling thousands.

The result in agriculture was the same. Instead of orderly land redistribution, Allende simply broke up plantations of wealthy persons regardless of productivity. Owners refused to plant crops which would be harvested by others. Political cronies were appointed to administer the nationalized farms. As production dropped 20%, it became necessary for Chile to increase food imports.

Spurred on by widespread public support for his expropriation of the copper mines, Allende ordered the nationalization of other key industries—including those owned by Chileans. Taking their cues from the government, workers (and outside agitators) began seizing farms and factories throughout the country. To the great dismay of Allende's economic planners, workers did not hesitate to strike against newly expropriated state industries. These work stoppages—combined with inept management of nationalized firms, led to a catastrophic decline in economic output.

Allende isolated Chile in foreign affairs and trade. The availability of loans from non-communist nations and institutions predictably disappeared. The Soviets and Chinese heaped praise on Chile, but offered little monetary support. The United States even declined Chilean offers to buy food for cash.

The people found themselves standing for hours in lines to buy what few consumer goods were left. As the government continued to "finance" itself by printing more money, inflation ran wild. Food was scarce; spare parts for machinery were nonexistent; only the black market flourished. Strikes and street fights between rival political factions became common. Political bickering in the Congress froze all constructive activity.

As things crumbled, the opposition became more unified. The right-wing National Party and the fascist Fatherland and Freedom Party began to sabotage operations of the government. The culmination of resistance came when a two-month strike by the nation's truck owners opposing nationalization—a strike a U.S. congressional inquiry later determined to have been partly financed by the CIA—virtually cleared the roads at the same time protesting housewives were filling the streets banging pots and pans.

With civil war imminent, the military staged its long-expected coup on September 11, 1973. Quickly seizing control, they announced that Allende had killed himself with a machine gun given to him as a gift by Castro.

During his brief but stormy term as president, Allende left a lasting mark on the nation. He sought to increase the living standards of the poor, to distribute farms to those who worked the land and to provide a full spectrum of social and economic benefits. He might possibly have succeeded if a unified, workable plan had first been developed and if at the same time he had been given enough time and had control of his followers.

Although Allende was unable to control his supporters, civil liberties were largely respected. A small number of political opponents was sent into exile, but none was killed. The vigorous opposition press (two-thirds of the total) remained free, but endured government harassment. Opposition parties thrived while critics of the government spoke out without fear of reprisal. Congress and the courts continued to function normally. Yet his administration was a disaster. When the Congress and courts opposed his policies, Allende felt free to ignore them.

Allende never received a majority of votes in any election, thus he lacked the necessary public support for changes that were so radical. He came to power because of a divided opposition rather than because of his own popularity.

Once it decided to move against the Allende government, the *junta* left no holds barred. Leftists and suspected opponents of the *junta* were promptly exterminated or rounded up in huge detention centers. Catholic Church officials in Chile estimated that one out of every 100 Chileans was arrested at least once during the 16 1/2 years the military held power. Many, according to the government, were "shot while trying to escape." Others simply disappeared while under detention. Other opponents of the regime were exiled. By 1980, the government allowed many to return.

General Carlos Prats, Pinochet's predecessor as army commander, who had opposed the coup, went into self-imposed exile in Argentina. A year later, he and his wife were killed in a car bombing that two decades later was linked to Pinochet's infamous National Intelligence Directorate, or *DINA*. Another prominent exile, Orlando Letelier, who had served as Allende's defense and foreign ministers, was killed in an almost identical car bombing in Washington, D.C. in 1976. That assassination, also linked to *DINA*, strained relations with the United States because it occurred in Washington and because Letelier's American secretary also was killed in the bombing. Four men, including one American, ultimately were convicted of Letelier's death.

Chile

A major victim of military repression was Chile's long-standing tradition as a pioneering Latin American democracy. Upon seizing power the *junta* immediately closed Congress and pointedly used its chambers to store records of political prisoners. The constitution was suspended and the courts neutralized. Freedom of the press disappeared and suspected books and publications were destroyed. Schools, factories and the nation itself were placed under rigid control to discourage dissent and—most importantly—to "root out Marxism."

Political parties (except selected right-wing groups) were placed "in suspension." The Christian Democratic Party newspaper was closed and its leader, former President Frei, was forced to muzzle his biting criticism. Not surprisingly, Marxists suffered most. Socialist and Communist leaders were arrested, killed, exiled or forced into hiding.

The only group that continually dared to speak out against the generals was the Catholic clergy. The *junta* responded by banning some religious festivals and arresting priests and nuns suspected of leftist sympathies. When the Catholic Church published a book by former President Frei in 1976 calling for a return to democracy, the government quickly outlawed public discussion of it. In his sermons, Raúl Cardinal Silva Henríquez condemned the regime's austerity program, which he said was pushing the nation's poor to the edge of starvation.

A major goal of the military rulers had been to pull Chile out of an economic tailspin caused by the Allende administration. Skilled managers were sent to farms and factories while property seized by the previous government was returned. Taxes and interest rates were increased and the amount of currency in circulation was reduced by cuts in government spending of 15% to 20%. Strikes were strongly "discouraged," while the nation's high unemployment rate in the months following the coup forced wage levels downward.

To increase farm output and industrial production, prices of consumer goods—including food—were allowed to rise to their natural levels. Soaring food costs, however, threatened fully a third of the nation with hunger. To prevent starvation, the government provided the most destitute with limited food handouts and low-paying public works jobs.

Although the *junta* consisted of four military men, real power was in the hands of General Augusto Pinochet Ugarte. Pinochet initially said democracy could not be restored during his lifetime or the lifetime of his successor. Military rule, he had insisted, could not be lifted until "the ills of democracy" had been erased. On freedom of expression, Pinochet was once quoted

as saying, "We're not against ideas; we're just against people spreading them."

Still, his economic program was a tremendous success. Pinochet surrounded himself with a clique of civilian economic technocrats, many of whom had studied under free-market guru Milton Friedman at the University of Chicago, and who quickly won the monicker, "*los* Chicago Boys" (see Economy).

Chileans surged to the polls in 1978 to give a simple "*sí*" or "*no*" vote in a plebiscite testing support for the military rulers. The *junta* received a lopsided 75% approval.

Even as Pinochet savored his electoral triumph, however, he was confronted with a serious threat from abroad. Neighboring Argentina suddenly revived an old territorial claim over three rocky, uninhabited islands at the mouth of the Beagle Channel in faraway Tierra del Fuego. At Argentina's suggestion, the two countries submitted their competing claims to the islands—Lennox, Picton and Nueva—to the British Crown for arbitration. The British ruled that Chile had legitimate sovereignty over all three islands, whereupon the Argentine military government of General Jorge Rafael Videla renounced the decision it itself had sought and threatened to seize the islands by force.

By December 1978, both countries were on a war footing, and hostilities appeared imminent. Literally at the 11th hour, the two right-wing military strongmen agreed to a second arbitration, this time by the Vatican. The Italian cardinal assigned to review the matter also concluded that Chile had the stronger claim. Despite occasional saber-rattling, Argentina eventually dropped the matter. But Pinochet had the last laugh. When Argentina foolishly invaded the Falkland Islands in 1982, precipitating war with Britain, Pinochet secretly allowed the Royal Navy to use Chilean territorial waters and islands, even as Chile was echoing the denunciation of other Latin American countries of the perceived British aggression against their sister republic.

Despite widespread national and international criticism of its harsh political and rigid economic policies, the *junta* could point to some dramatic successes: the inflation rate dropped from 600% per year in 1973 to just under 10% in 1981—one of the lowest in Latin America. In addition, foreign investment rose rapidly.

The regime became increasingly tolerant of public criticism, and arrests of political opponents declined. At the same time, a limited number of Chileans sent into exile following the coup were allowed to return home.

Another "*sí*" or "*no*" plebiscite was put before the voters in September 1980. By a

2–1 margin, they approved Pinochet's desire to remain in power for another eight years. His term was technically scheduled to end in 1990 after an election to choose his successor. But the strongman still enjoyed an added insurance policy: the *junta* had the power to reappoint him for *another* eight years—which in theory could stretch his term until 1997.

Human rights violations by Chile's military rulers touched off widespread international protests and complicated relations with the United States. After Chilean secret police were linked to the 1976 assassination of Letelier, the Carter administration cut off most military aid in 1979. When a member of the military involved in the murder identified the masterminds of the plot in 1986, the United States demanded their extradition; Pinochet ignored the demand.

By then the Reagan administration, favorably impressed with the *junta*'s anticommunist leanings, had sought to improve ties between the two countries. In 1981, some trade barriers were removed and the United States invited Chile to participate in joint naval exercises. The U.S. Senate voted in 1981 to resume military aid to Chile—on the condition that Santiago comply with "internationally recognized standards of human rights."

Entrance of La Moneda, the presidential palace

110

Chile suffered a severe recession in 1981–83, resulting in a reduction of about 13% in GDP and forcing the government to intervene in private enterprise to prevent an increasing number of bankruptcies. By May 1983, it was estimated that 21% of the urban force was unemployed. The following month, a strike of truck drivers and copper miners—the first important labor challenge to the military government since 1973—appeared to be the beginning of a deep social crisis. The government's swift reaction, combining repression with conciliation, defused the danger.

In September 1986, Pinochet narrowly escaped death in an ambush by left-wing terrorists on his motorcade that left five of his bodyguards dead. The radical Manuel Rodríguez Patriotic Front (*FPMR*) claimed responsibility; predictably, Pinochet responded with a new 90-day state of siege and announced he would "expel or lock up all those people talking about human rights and all those things."

Pinochet announced the legalization of political parties in March 1987 (except Marxists). But there was a catch: no party could be affiliated with one that had existed before. A visit by Pope John Paul II in 1987 was marred by clashes between dissidents and forces of the regime.

Return to Democracy

Pinochet made his intentions known in 1986 when he scheduled another plebiscite for October 7, 1988. A yes vote would have returned him to power for another eight years. As the plebiscite drew near, Pinochet underwent a marked change. Instead of his former elitist, aloof style, he promoted the image of a kindly old grandfather. He counted on the division of the opposition (17 parties) and confidently predicted he would win. But the various parties formed a coalition called the Command for No that had a single ambition: to oust Pinochet.

The voting was relatively close because of a single reason: economic prosperity. By 1988, inflation had descended to 8% and Chile enjoyed a trade surplus of more than $1.5 billion. The outcome was 54% to 43% against Pinochet. The country held its breath, wondering what he would do. Somewhat hesitantly, he announced that as provided for by law, elections would be held in December 1989.

Patricio Aylwin, a centrist Christian Democrat who had been a senator when the 1973 coup occurred, was the presidential candidate of a coalition of 17 center-left parties called the *Concertación*. The Communists were not part of the coalition but gave tacit support to Aylwin. In a three-way contest, Aylwin received 55%

against Pinochet's hand-picked candidate, who received only 29%, and a tycoon who polled 15% as an independent. This author covered the election as a freelance journalist, and when Aylwin's victory became clear there was an outpouring of jubilation as *Concertación* supporters filled the streets to celebrate the end of 17 years of authoritarian rule.

On March 11, 1990, Pinochet placed the presidential sash on the shoulders of his civilian successor, marking a major milestone in the life of the country.

Not surprisingly, friction soon developed between the two over the issue of civilian control. Aylwin asked Pinochet to resign as army commander, but the general refused, saying his presence provided stability for the transition to democracy. There was little Aylwin could do, as the 1980 constitution permitted Pinochet to remain in command until the end of 1997, and the *Concertación* lacked the votes in Congress to amend the constitution.

In fact, the constitution also allowed Pinochet to name nine permanent "institutional" senators to the 47-member upper house of Congress when he left office, which gave the conservative opposition a narrow majority and effective veto power over legislation passed by the *Concertación*-controlled Chamber of Deputies. The opposition also enjoyed a disproportionate number of elected seats in both houses because of the peculiar double-member districts, in which the top two vote-getters are both elected. It created gridlock. Among other things, the opposition-con-

Fish market in Puerto Montt

Chile's favorite poet and Nobel Prize winner Pablo Neruda

trolled Senate repeatedly blocked executive branch efforts to abolish the national holiday for September 11, the anniversary of the coup. The holiday wasn't abolished until 1999.

Aylwin was pressured to try all major military figures responsible for disappearances. In the style of a skilled politician, he appointed a commission to investigate and study the matter. The commission found that 3,197 people had been killed outright or disappeared at the hands of the military following the coup, but in the midst of prosperity, most Chileans seemed to prefer to let the past rest in peace.

Chile prospered under Aylwin, and its economy expanded at a rate approaching an average of 10% per year. It still had a thorny problem with the perpetually poor, but the government attempted to tackle that problem, too. Prosperity and growth were the products of free trade (few, if any tariffs); foreign investment, the latter flowing in at a rate of more than U.S. $1 billion a year; and booming exports of Chilean agricultural products.

Another Frei Presidency

In December 1993, voters affirmed their satisfaction with the status quo by electing Eduardo Frei Ruiz-Tagle, son of the president who preceded Allende, to the presidency by a resounding 59 percent of the vote against five opponents. Arturo Alessandri, grandson and namesake of the president of the 1920s and 1930s and nephew of the late President Jorge Alessandri, was second with 29 percent. The once-mighty Communist Party received only about 3 percent.

Congress extended the presidential term from four to six years, as it was before the military coup. Like Aylwin, Frei was a Christian Democrat who was the candidate of the *Concertación*.

Chile

La Moneda, the Presidential Palace in Santiago and site of the 1973 coup of Allende

The *Concertación* retained its majority in the lower house, but the eight remaining "institutional senators" named by Pinochet (one had died) allowed the conservative opposition to keep control of the upper chamber and serve as a brake on the majority.

Following the counsel of a group of influential advisers, Frei wisely kept the successful economic policies in effect, and Chile's economic growth remained the envy of Latin America. The combination of stable civilian government and free-market economics made Chile a favorite target of foreign investors, who increasingly sought new opportunities in the region as they once did in the Pacific Rim countries of Asia. Frei also emerged as a leader of regional importance, hosting the Second Summit of the Americas in 1998.

Like Aylwin, Frei experienced friction with Pinochet, who successfully resisted efforts to curtail the extraordinary authority granted to him in his personalized 1980 constitution. Pinochet finally retired as army commander, at age 82, in 1998.

But Pinochet's long-awaited retirement did not mean he was withdrawing from public life—or from controversy. The day after his retirement ceremony, and still adhering to a right given to him in the constitution as a former head of state, he assumed a lifetime seat in the Senate, joining the other non-elected "institutional senators" who gave the conservative opposition a majority. Pinochet's transfer to the Senate angered left-wing lawmakers, and there were demonstrations to protest such an antidemocratic measure. Efforts to

block Pinochet by judicial means failed, as did an impeachment motion in the Chamber of Deputies, which was rejected in an unusual secret ballot 62–52. Once again, the aging general demonstrated he was still a force to contend with.

Congressional elections in 1997 failed to alter the balance of power, but voters sent some confusing signals. The lineup in the Chamber of Deputies remained 70–50 in favor of the *Concertación*, but it lost one Senate seat, giving it 20 of the elected seats to 18 for the conservatives. With the "institutional" senators, including Pinochet, the opposition held a majority. There were two major surprises: the ultra-rightwing (Independent Democratic Union (*UDI*) became the second ranking party in the Senate, moving ahead of its opposition partner, the National Renewal (*RN*).

'El Caso Pinochet'

Chilean government and society were thrust into turmoil in October 1998 when Pinochet flew to London for back surgery. As he was recuperating in a clinic, the British government formally arrested him, acting on an extradition request from Spain.

A Spanish judge, Baltasar Garzón, on his own initiative, requested the extradition to account for Spanish citizens tortured and killed during the military regime. Garzón eventually cited the 1988 U.N. International Convention Against Torture, by which a country can seek the arrest in a second country of someone accused of torture committed in a third country. Judges in Switzerland and France soon submitted

similar extradition requests for Pinochet, while Chilean exiles-by-choice in France, Denmark, Italy and Belgium also filed petitions against him.

News of the arrest made headlines around the world. In Chile, the news was greeted with glee by Pinochet's detractors and with outrage by his supporters. But the Spanish warrant and the British arrest also struck at the core of Chilean nationalism, and moderate Chileans, even some Pinochet-haters, denounced the action as a violation of Chilean sovereignty.

President Frei, despite his own personal animosity to the general, dutifully urged Pinochet's release on the grounds that as a member of the Chilean Senate he enjoyed diplomatic immunity. In a case of delicious irony, Foreign Minister José Miguel Insulza, who himself was arrested after the coup and spent years in exile, went to London to plead Pinochet's cause.

The Pinochet case then began a torturous (no pun intended) 16-month journey through the British court system. The case was heard before a panel of five Law Lords, jurists who are members of the House of Lords, Britain's court of last resort. On November 25—Pinochet's 83rd birthday—the Law Lords voted 3–2 that Pinochet's arrest was legal.

The proud general was required to undergo the ignominy of appearing in court for a bail hearing. He huffily declared in Spanish that he did not recognize the jurisdiction of a non-Chilean court, and the judge remanded him on bail. The House of Lords agreed that Pinochet was entitled to a new hearing before a seven-judge panel.

In March 1999, the Law Lords ruled 6–1 that Pinochet's arrest was legal and that the extradition request could proceed, but they agreed with Pinochet's lawyers that he could not be held accountable for any crime allegedly committed before September 29, 1988—the date that Britain incorporated the international torture convention into its criminal laws. This effectively dismissed 29 of the 32 charges in the Spanish warrant. The general remained under arrest on the other three counts. Garzón began raising new allegations of cases committed after 1988.

In April 1999, Home Secretary Jack Straw proceeded with the extradition request. That September, Pinochet's lawyers argued that Spain lacked jurisdiction to try the general for alleged crimes that occurred in Chile and also that he was too ill to stand trial. A magistrate rejected Pinochet's arguments and declared that he could be extradited. Once again, the decision fell upon Straw, who vacillated three months before ordering that Pinochet undergo a series of medical examinations to determine whether he were too ill to be extradited. The general, by then 84, un-

**Former President
Eduardo Frei Ruiz-Tagle**

derwent the exams in January 2000, after which Straw decided that Pinochet was indeed too ill to be extradited, setting off a torrent of outrage by human rights groups.

A Chilean air force plane was dispatched to Britain, and in March 2000, the once-proud Pinochet returned to his native soil—in a wheelchair.

His travails continued, however. In May 2000 the Santiago Court of Appeals voted 13–9 to strip him of his legislative immunity as senator-for-life to allow him to stand trial. Pinochet's lawyers appealed to the Supreme Court, arguing again that he was too frail. The Supreme Court voted 14–6 to uphold the decision to strip Pinochet of his immunity. Simultaneously, the U.S. government announced it planned to investigate whether Pinochet were the intellectual author of the 1976 Letelier assassination.

Judge Juan Guzmán found a loophole around the amnesty law that protected members of the military from being tried for atrocities committed following the coup. He decided to try him for the *kidnappings,* not murders, of 18 prisoners who disappeared and were never accounted for during the infamous "Caravan of Death," a helicopter-borne squad of soldiers that scoured the country after the coup and carried dissidents away to their deaths.

Guzmán generated world headlines by announcing that Pinochet would stand trial and placed him under house arrest. An appeals court overturned his order, on the grounds that Guzmán never interrogated Pinochet before arresting him. Pinochet ignored his lawyers and agreed to let Guzmán interrogate him in his seaside home. As a result, the judge declared Pinochet mentally competent to stand trial and issued an arrest warrant. An appeals court

ruled that Pinochet was mentally incompetent, but the Supreme Court overturned that decision.

The lawyers wrangled until the Supreme Court ruled 4–1 in July 2002 that Pinochet was mentally incompetent. Three days later, Pinochet resigned his lifetime Senate seat. His 29-year political career and an era in Chilean history were over.

But Pinochet's legal problems persisted. Argentina requested his extradition in connection with the 1974 car bomb assassination there of the exiled General Carlos Prats and his wife. The Supreme Court, citing its incompetence ruling, blocked the request.

In November 2003, Pinochet granted an interview to a Spanish-language network in Miami, in which he laid the blame on the human rights abuses on his subordinates. In the interview, Pinochet came across as quite lucid. Suddenly, he was facing charges again, not only for the Prats assassination, but for nine kidnappings and one murder committed as part of the so-called "Operation Condor," a joint effort by South American military regimes of the 1970s to kill or imprison leftists.

In a 14–9 decision in 2004 that stunned both sides, the Santiago Court of Appeals stripped Pinochet of his immunity, leaving him vulnerable not only to prosecution but to about 200 civil lawsuits. The Supreme Court upheld the appeals court. His lawyers again appealed on the grounds that Pinochet was incompetent, and he was examined by three doctors: one appointed by Pinochet's lawyers, one by the families of victims, one by Guzmán. In their report, the doctors appointed by the judge and the defense agreed Pinochet was incompetent, while the third said he was competent. Guzmán went with the doctor who said he was competent and issued an indictment in the Condor case. Five days later, Pinochet

was hospitalized with a stroke. In January 2005, a panel of the Supreme Court upheld the indictment 3–2.

As if Pinochet did not have enough legal problems with the human rights charges, in 2004 a U.S. Senate committee report alleged that the Washington-based Riggs Bank had allowed Pinochet and his wife to illegally stash $8 million in accounts there from 1994–2002. Although most Chileans had come to accept that Pinochet was the intellectual author of human rights abuses, it was widely believed, even by some of his opponents, that he was personally honest.

The Chilean government compared the amount of money Pinochet had stashed abroad and the amount he claimed for taxes; they didn't add up, and the government sued him for back taxes. Pinochet's long-time nemesis, Spanish Judge Garzón, charged the Pinochets and eight others with money laundering. The Chilean government froze $5 million of Pinochet's assets. Two days before Pinochet's 90th birthday in November 2005, a judge placed him under house arrest for the fraud and tax evasion charges; he was later fingerprinted and mugshots were taken at his house. In January 2006, Pinochet, his wife and four of their children were indicted. The case dragged on until the feeble old general finally died on December 10, 2006, at age 91.

The armed forces were caught in a dilemma with Pinochet's arrest. Although the military protested vigorously, it seemed to realize that it is a new day in Chile, and that it would be bad public relations to undermine a duly elected government. Moreover, the military felt compelled to own up to the whereabouts of the bodies of many of the "disappeared." Once a death is confirmed, it is covered by the amnesty law and can no longer be treated as a kidnapping. Alas, the military

Torres del Paine

Chile

acknowledged that many victims were dumped at sea.

The Lagos Presidency

As the Pinochet drama unfolded in 1999, Chileans elected their third president since the restoration of democracy. In a coalition primary, the *PPD*'s Ricardo Lagos, 61, a neo-socialist economist, defeated Andrés Zaldivar, a moderate Christian Democrat, with 70% of the vote. The two right-wing opposition parties, *RN* and the *UDI*, also held a joint primary, and the overwhelming winner was the *UDI*'s Joaquín Lavín, also an economist and a former mayor of the affluent Santiago suburb of Los Condes. During the Pinochet regime, Lavín had been one of the "Chicago Boys," the University of Chicago-educated economists who engineered Chile's free-market economic miracle. The Communist Party leader Gladys Marín mounted a separate candidacy, while three lesser candidates completed the field.

The results of the first round on December 12 were breathtakingly close: 3,359,679, or 47.96 percent, for Lagos, to 3,328,652, or 47.52 percent, for Lavín. Marín received only 223,000 votes, or 3.2 percent, but those votes would prove crucial in the January 16, 2000 runoff.

By then, Lagos had heeded the advice of his advisers and was beginning to campaign in a more laid-back style, addressing crowds without a coat, although he still wore a tie. Both candidates tried to outdo each other with lavish, U.S.-style campaign promises that left analysts wondering how they expected to pay for them.

The runoff was almost as dramatic as the first round: 3,677,968 or 51.31% for Lagos, to 3,490,561, or 48.69% for Lavín. Lavín winner by coming went personally to Lagos' hotel to congratulate him, then the two of them went to the balcony together where, to the delight of the cheering Lagos supporters, Lavín magnanimously pledged his support to the president-elect. Lagos was inaugurated on March 11, 2000.

In the municipal elections in October 2000 for 341 local governments, the *Concertación* polled 52% of the popular vote nationwide, down from 56% in the 1996 municipal elections. Moreover, it lost about 40 cities and towns to the opposition. In the Santiago mayor's race, Lavín was elected with 62%.

The next major showdown came in the congressional elections in December 2001. The *Concertación* received 51.4% of the 1.7 million votes cast, compared with 44% for the conservative coalition *Alianza para Chile* and 2.6% for the Communists. But in the tabulation of seats, the *Concertación* lost ground. Even with former President Frei assuming a lifetime Senate seat, and the continued absence of Pinochet, the elec-

The front page of the Santiago daily *La Tercera* the morning after the January 16, 2000, presidential runoff shows the victorious Ricardo Lagos, right, with his defeated opponent, Joaquín Lavín, in a display of gracious goodwill.

tion resulted in a tie in the upper chamber. In the Chamber of Deputies, the *Concertación* dropped from 70 to 63 deputies.

Chile suddenly found itself in the world spotlight in 2003 when it assumed one of the rotating seats on the 15-member U.N. Security Council just as debate began over the proposed U.S. resolution to authorize the use of force against Iraq. Chile opposed the war resolution, straining relations with the United States, with which it had just concluded a long-sought free-trade agreement (see Economy).

An uncharacteristic political sex scandal involving pedophile charges against a wealthy politically connected businessmen and three senators from both major coalitions created a media circus in late 2003. Two of the senators were from the *UDI*, which caused a rift between the *RN*'s president, Sebastián Piñera, and Pablo Longueira, the *UDI* president. Their squabbling became so caustic that Lavín declared he would pursue a presidential candidacy independent of the two parties.

Two institutional changes of historic proportions were implemented in 2004 and 2005. In 2004, Lagos signed into law a bill legalizing divorce in Chile, the last Latin American country do so. Then the opposition-controlled Senate agreed to reform Pinochet's 1980 constitution to abolish the eight appointed senators, to repeal the provision giving former presidents Senate seats for life and to give the president the power enjoyed in other democracies to remove the heads of the armed forces. Still in place, however, is the double-member district system that guarantees the opposition virtual parity in both houses. In 2005, the two chambers finally agreed on the amendment, which also shortened the presidential term back to four years. The change left the Senate with 38 members, all elected.

Virtually as historic was the statement issued in 2004 by General Juan Emilio Cheyre, commander of the army, acknowledging for the first time the army's institutional responsibility for the "morally unacceptable actions of the past." Lagos praised the army's decision, and said it represented the army's "integration into today's democratic Chile." Lagos appointed the Valech Commission to come up with a definitive number of people tortured during the military regime. It interviewed 35,000 people and issued its report in 2004, in which the government admitted that torture was state policy during the military regime and that 28,000 people had been tortured. In 2011, another the commission added 9,800 more to that number (see below).

Lagos hosted the annual summit of the Asia-Pacific Economic Cooperation (APEC) group in 2004, and he called for a free-trade agreement by 2020 of the 21 signatories, which represent 60% of the world's economy.

Bachelet Makes History

Responding to opposition complaints that Foreign Minister Soledad Alvear and Defense Minister Michelle Bachelet were campaigning for president on company time, Lagos replaced both of them in 2004.

The *Concertación* made its poorest showing to date in the 2004 municipal elections. In the popular vote, it led the opposition coalition *Alianza* 45% to 39%, and it won 199 of the 345 municipal governments. It was the first time the *Concertación* had failed to poll a majority in municipal elections. The *Alianza* retained the mayoralty of Santiago. Lavín decided not to run so he could focus on his presidential candidacy.

Two major developments in 2005 changed the electoral landscape. First, the long-simmering opposition rivalry between the *UDI* and *RN* came to a head. Instead of endorsing Lavín's candidacy again as expected, *RN* abruptly voted to run its leader, Sebastián Piñera, as its candidate. Days later, Alvear dropped out of the race, assuring that Bachelet would be the *Concertación* candidate.

The only drama for the December 11, 2005 election was whether Bachelet would win outright and, if not, whether she would face Lavín or Piñera in the runoff. She was an unlikely frontrunner in a conservative, devoutly Catholic country, an agnostic who separated from her husband and bore a child by a lover. She also had had an extra-marital affair with a leader of the notorious Manuel Rodríguez Revolutionary Front, a left-wing terrorist group responsible for the 1986 assassination attempt on Pinochet, which became a campaign issue.

Voter turnout was 87.7%. The results:

Bachelet	3,190,691	46%
Piñera	1,763,964	25.4%
Lavín	1,612,608	23.2%

Lavín graciously pledged his support to Piñera for the January 15, 2006 runoff, and Piñera quixotically campaigned to try to overtake Bachelet's huge lead. The runoff, which had a turnout of 87.1%, was closer than some had predicted, but Bachelet's mandate was convincing:

Bachelet	3,723,019	53.5%
Piñera	3,236,394	46.5%

On March 11, 2006, Bachelet, 54, made history not only as Chile's first woman president, but unlike Nicaragua's Violeta Chamorro and Panama's Mireya Moscoso, she was the first elected Latin American female president who was not the widow of a prominent political figure. With the changes to the constitution, the *Concertación* also won a majority in both houses of Congress.

Bachelet captured the fancy of the global media because of her peculiar, mixed background. She is the daughter of an air force general and attended school in Washington when her father was assigned

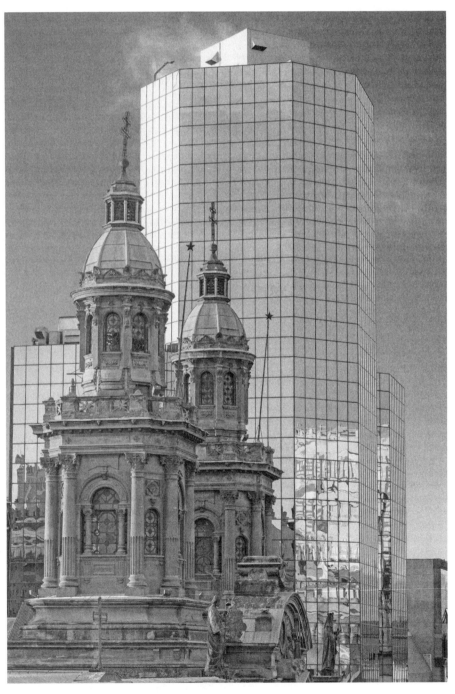

A mix of colonial and modern in Santiago

Chile

to Chile's military mission there in the 1960s. Following the 1973 coup, which her father refused to support, he was arrested for treason and died in prison of a heart attack. Bachelet and her mother were also arrested and tortured. Bachelet went into exile in Communist East Germany, where she studied pediatrics and married her husband, also a Chilean exile, by whom she had two children. She completed her medical degree after she returned to Chile in 1979.

Despite her leftist background and her medical training, Bachelet also studied military strategy and graduated from the Inter-American Defense College in Washington in 1998. She later earned the praise of armed forces officers during her tenure as Lagos' defense minister. She earlier had served as his health minister.

Bachelet pledged to continue the moderate, free-market economic policies of her three predecessors and met with President Bush at the White House.

The End of an Era

On Pinochet's 91st birthday on November 25, 2006, the ever-unpredictable general had his wife read a prepared statement in which he suddenly acknowledged the human rights abuses committed during his years in power.

"Today, near the end of my days, I want to say that I harbor no rancor against anybody, that I love my fatherland above all and that I take political responsibility for everything that was done, which had no other goal than making Chile greater and avoiding its disintegration," the statement read. "I assume full political responsibility for what happened."

Two days later, he was again arrested, but the general apparently knew he would elude further prosecution. On December 3, he suffered an acute heart attack; on December 10, his wife's 84th birthday, he died.

Even in death, Pinochet proved a polarizing figure for his countrymen; some mourned and praised him, others rejoiced. Bachelet denied him a state funeral, although he was accorded full military honors at the Military Academy; Bachelet declined to attend, saying it would be "a violation of my conscience." At his request, he was cremated so that vandals could not desecrate his tomb. An era in Chilean—and world—history was finally at an end.

But the legal battle surrounding his wealth did not die with him. In 2007, Pinochet's widow, Lucia, his five children and several of his former associates were detained for two days and indicted on embezzlement charges. The Supreme Court later threw out the charges against his widow and four of the children on the grounds that they had not been government employees and could not have committed embezzlement. Charges against eight associates also were dismissed, but the court upheld the indictments against Pinochet's oldest son, Augusto, and two associates. The court also ordered an investigation of the Pinochets' assets. A study by the University of Chile concluded that almost $18 million of Pinochet's personal wealth was not justified by his work for the state. In 2012, the government also ordered his will opened to determine how he acquired his wealth, but the will offered no clues. The case is still ongoing. Lucia Pinochet turns 91 in December 2013.

Protests and Peru

Bachelet found herself contending with a crippling strike at a copper mine, street protests by students and teachers demanding to know why the boom in revenue from high copper prices was not being channeled into education, and commuters' anger over a newly reorganized but poorly planned bus system in Santiago that turned into a nightmare. She also rankled men in this *macho* country by arbitrarily appointing half the Cabinet posts to women, regardless of merit, and introducing legislation that would mandate all parties to designate 30% of their candidates for Congress as women. A poll in 2007 showed that 61% of respondents lacked confidence in her ability to handle a crisis.

She reshuffled her Cabinet and made a remarkable, televised apology for her performance. Yet, hundreds of high school students went on a rampage in Santiago, erecting burning barricades and looting supermarkets. Thirty-two policemen were injured and more than 800 people were arrested. Exactly what the students were protesting was unclear, other than their general dissatisfaction with the status quo in Latin America's strongest economy. There were more violent outbursts on September 11, 2007, the 34th anniversary of the coup. Stores were looted and burned, a policeman was killed, 41 people were injured and 216 were detained.

As if she didn't have enough problems at home, Bachelet suddenly had one with Peru. The two countries' long-standing animosity, dating to Chile's annexation of Peruvian territory after the War of the Pacific of 1879–84, was strained further by Chile's delay in extraditing former Peruvian President Alberto Fujimori, wanted in Peru for a host of charges (see Peru).

It seemed relations had improved with the signing of a bilateral free-trade agreement in 2006, but then, in 2007, Peru abruptly renounced a maritime boundary agreement dating to the 1950s. It had extended due west into the Pacific from the point where their land border reaches the coast. Peru now claimed the maritime boundary is an extension of the land border, which points southwesterly. In January 2008, Peru published a map claiming a 14,630-square-mile tract of Chilean waters that is rich in fish.

Chile withdrew its ambassador from Lima and said it would exercise its territorial rights over the area. Peruvian President Alan García said Peru would take its claim to the International Court of Justice in the Hague, Netherlands, which can take years to rule. Relations worsened further in 2009 when Peru announced it had arrested an air force officer for spying for Chile. Ironically, Bachelet and García were both in Singapore for the annual APEC summit when the news broke. García canceled a scheduled workshop with Bachelet and flew back to Lima. The IJC pondered Peru's claim for almost seven years before issuing a decision in January 2014 that gave each side some of what it wanted.

By 2008, in part because of an economic boom fueled by record high prices for copper on the world market, Bachelet's esteem in the eyes of her countrymen suddenly soared, with an approval rating of 75%. Nonetheless, in the closely watched bellwether municipal elections in 2008, the conservative opposition *Alianza* won 144 mayor's races to only 101 for the *Concertación,* including Santiago, Valparaiso and Concepción. The *Alianza* received 40.7% of the popular vote to only 28.7% for the *Concertación.* Broken down by party, the *PDC* won 59 mayoralties, the *UDI* 58, *RN* 55 and Bachelet's *PS,* only 30. It was an ominous harbinger for the *Concertación* going into the 2009 presidential campaign.

Political and Geological Earthquakes

Bachelet and the *Concertación* had hoped to parlay her new popularity into a fifth consecutive victory, but after 20 years of center-left presidents, voters seemed ready for a change. Also, the booming economy went into a slump in 2009 because of the global recession. The ruling alliance made two fatal errors: first, not holding an open primary as in the past, and second, by turning to the past rather than to the future by nominating former President Frei, 67. In protest, Socialist Deputy Marco Enríquez-Ominani, 36, bolted from the *Concertación* and launched an independent candidacy.

The conservative opposition, now under the banner Coalition for Change, again nominated Piñera, 59, a billionaire whose business interests include the *Chilevisión* TV channel and a fourth of LAN Chile, the formerly state-owned airline. He holds a master's degree and a doctorate in economics from Harvard.

The Communist Party nominated Jorge Arrate.

Piñera pledged to restofre 6% economic growth and to make Chile a First World developed country by 2018. He downplayed his wealth and adroitly promised to continue the social welfare programs of the *Concertación* that Chileans had come to expect. He came across well in televised debates, while Frei appeared dour and uninspiring. Enríquez-Ominami also came across as more charismatic than Frei, and he cut deeply into the *Concertación*'s base.

Dredging up ghosts from the past, a judge concluded days before the election that the death of the first President Eduardo Frei in 1982 was a murder, and issued indictments against six people, including two doctors. The elder Frei, who was becoming vocal in his opposition to the Pinochet regime, is widely believed to have been poisoned during a routine hospital stay for stomach surgery. The judge cited evidence that Frei had been given low doses of mustard gas and thallium over a period of time, weakening his immune system. But scientists questioned the validity of the evidence, and an appeals court freed the suspects on bail and removed the judge from the case. The suspicious timing just before the election also caused skepticism.

If the judge intended to generate sympathy for the younger Frei, he failed. The results of the first round on December 13:

Piñera	3,074,164	44.1%
Frei	2,065,061	29.6%
Enríquez-Ominami	1,405,124	20.1%
Arrate	433,195	6.2%

The Alliance for Change won 58 seats in the Chamber of Deputies to 57 for the *Concertación*. They tied at nine each for the 18 Senate seats at stake. In the new Senate, the *Concertación* had 19 of the 38 seats, the Alliance 16.

Enríquez-Ominami could have played kingmaker in the January 2010 runoff, but he refused to endorse either Piñera or Frei. Exit polls showed that 36% of Enríquez-Ominami's voters opted for change over ideology and voted for Piñera. The runoff results:

Piñera	3,591,182	51.6%
Frei	3,367,790	48.4%

After 20 years of wandering in the political wilderness, the conservative opposition was finally given a chance to show it was ready to move from its Pinochet-tainted past and to lead Chile into the future. It was the first time the right had won the presidency since Jorge Alessandri in 1958.

Bachelet, who left office with an 84% approval rating, bequeathed to Piñera an

Former President Sebastián Piñera

improving economy and a discretionary fund of $1.1. billion that she had wisely set aside from the copper windfall. It would prove vital to face a challenge neither Piñera nor his countrymen anticipated.

On February 27, 2010, just 12 days before the transfer of power, central Chile was struck by a magnitude 8.8 earthquake that killed 500 people and inflicted $15–30 billion in damage to the infrastructure. A tsunami washed away entire villages. It was reminiscent of the earthquake and tsunami of comparable historic magnitude that destroyed Puerto Montt in 1960. Concepción sustained major damage. An estimated 400,000-500,000 homes were totally destroyed or seriously damaged, leaving 2 million people homeless—almost one eighth of the country's population. It was indicative of Chilean engineering that the percentage of homes and office buildings destroyed, and the death toll, were not higher, a sharp contrast to the Haitian earthquake the month before (see Haiti).

Several presidents came to Santiago for Piñera's inauguration on March 11. The ceremony was jolted by a severe aftershock and the newly installed president eschewed post-inaugural festivities to tour devastated areas by helicopter.

Piñera demonstrated a take-charge approach, mandating that schools re-open within a week at temporary facilities. He decided to use $400 million of the discretionary fund for reconstruction, but imposed a $2 billion corporate tax increase to help pay the rest, a move that did not go over well with his core constituency. Fortunately, the vital copper mines are well to the north of the affected zone.

Overshadowed by the transfer of power and the earthquake was an equally historic event. Chile became the 34th member of the Organization of Economic Cooperation and Development (OECD), a group

of the world's most developed countries. It was the second Latin American country, after Mexico, to be admitted. Chile had to revise its tax structure and lessen the degree of state participation in *CODELCO*, the state-owned copper company, as conditions for membership. The accession agreement was signed in Santiago on January 11, 2010, and on May 7, Chile signed the OECD Charter.

Chile was in the world spotlight again from August to October 2010, when the San José gold and silver mine near Copiapó in the Atacama Desert collapsed, trapping 33 miners more than 2,000 feet underground. After it was determined the miners were alive, media from around the world descended on Copiapó to cover the desperate, seemingly quixotic rescue effort. But engineers from Chile and other countries drilled a rescue shaft, first providing light, water, food, even televised soccer games, to the trapped miners. After 69 days, the miners were extracted one by one through the narrow shaft in an ingenious capsule, all watched on live TV around the world. Piñera came to offer encouragement to the miners' families and to provide government support. The euphoria over the rescue soon gave way to some hard questions about mine safety in Chile. The San José mine, accused of ignoring safety regulations, closed.

The Student Revolt

After his decisive handling of the earthquake and mine rescue, Piñera enjoyed an approval rating of 70%. But a new crisis sent it plummeting.

In May 2011, secondary school students went on strike and seized about 100 schools. Unlike the 2006 student protests, the so-called "penguin revolution," this movement spread, encompassing university students and other sectors of the population. By June, there were mass protests in the Alameda in Santiago, including the traditional *cacerolazos*, the beating of pots and pans, something the capital hadn't seen since the return to democracy 21 years earlier. The protests became a daily occurrence, and some fringe elements—probably not even students but delinquents—clashed with riot police and looted stores. In a case of *déjà vu* that the students were too young to appreciate, tear gas and water cannons were used to disperse the protests, something else not seen since the days of dictatorship.

The issue had been long simmering. Despite Chile's advances in democracy and economic growth, social classes in Chile remain rigidly stratified. There has been upward social mobility; the number of students enrolled at university level has increased five-fold since 1990. But educa-

Chile

tion in Chile remains largely private, with the state providing only 20% of funding even for tax-supported schools like the University of Chile, the lowest percentage in the OECD; student tuition provides the remainder. Moreover, many new universities and even secondary schools are profit-making institutions, although for-profit schools were outlawed by Pinochet; they take advantage of a loophole and call themselves "real estate companies," which lease the facilities to the schools! Thus, to obtain a university education, lower-income students and their families must go deeply into debt, paying tuition with variable loans at interest rates of up to 5.8%.

Finally, the quality of schools and curriculum in economically disadvantaged areas is inferior to those in more affluent areas.

The protesters demanded a free education, paid by the state, and an end to for-profit schools. Sensing an opportunity to gain political capital, the *Concertación* sided with the protesters, as did the Chilean Labor Confederation (CTC).

Piñera responded clumsily, sending confusing, ambiguous signals of acquiescence and defiance. On the one hand, he agreed to negotiate, and pledged to divert $4 billion from the copper windfall contingency fund to improve existing schools. He sacked the education minister, former presidential candidate and Santiago mayor Joaquín Lavín, who had proposed increasing government support for the non-traditional, profit-making schools. The president also proposed legislation making the interest on all student loans a uniform 2%. But he refused to agree to tuition-free education, claiming it would disproportionately benefit the wealthy, or to abolish profit-making schools. And he infuriated the protesters—and many other Chileans—by attempting to ban protests in the Alameda, a definite throwback to Pinochet. The protesters defied the ban.

Opinion polls showed 70% of the public siding with the students on most issues, although later polls showed support for tuition-free schooling dropped to 45%; the taxpayers apparently realized who would be replacing the tuition.

Talks between the government and the students broke down in October. The protests entered their second academic year in March 2012. Piñera's approval rating was 33%—tying with Panama's President Roberto Martinelli for the second-lowest in the Western Hemisphere. By September he had "improved" to 36%; only Honduras' Porfirio Lobo Sosa and Costa Rica's Laura Chinchilla were less popular.

Piñera's sagging popularity no doubt played a role in the October 28 municipal elections, which saw a dramatic comeback for the left and served as a bellwether of

public opinion on the student protests. Voter registration had been made automatic, adding about 5 million new voters, but voting was no longer mandatory, so turnout declined to 41%. The *Concertación* and other opposition parties received 43% of the vote to 37% for the parties of the ruling coalition. The left's biggest prize was Santiago, where the *PPD*'s Carolina Tohá unseated Mayor Pablo Zalaquett of the *UDI*. Zalaquett had ordered police to crack down on protesters; Tohá declared her sympathy for the students. Her father, José Tohá, was Allende's vice president and was tortured to death in detention. Allende's granddaughter, Maya Fernández Allende, narrowly lost her bid for mayor of the Santiago suburb of Ñuñoa. But the opposition did capture the longtime conservative stronghold of Providencia, as well as Concepción. The right retained control of Valparaíso.

The education stalemate continued peacefully for a year, until the protests erupted again, first on April 11, 2013, when protesters took to the streets in several cities, an estimated 80,000 in Santiago. That protest was loud but relatively peaceful. But the next one, on May 9, resulted in clashes between demonstrators and police. Students hurled stones and firebombs, and police responded with tear gas and water cannons. About 130 people were arrested. There were about 37,000 protesters in Santiago, while thousands more demonstrated outside the Congress building in Valparaiso.

Piñera addressed Congress as hundreds of students loudly but peacefully demonstrated outside. He refused to budge on free or even lower-priced education or on eliminating profit-making schools, offering only free kindergarten and a commission to investigate education quality.

Chile's economy grew by 5% in 2012, the fifth-fastest growth in the Western Hemisphere.

More ghosts from the past returned to haunt Chile in May 2011. A judge ordered President Allende's body exhumed for an independent autopsy in hopes of solving the lingering controversy over whether he committed suicide or was slain by the military. After two months, the team of Chilean and independent forensics experts in São Paulo, Brazil, confirmed Allende killed himself. A judge officially closed the case in September 2012. During the same period, Bachelet reopened the Valech Commission's investigation from the Lagos presidency. In August 2011, it presented its report to Piñera, increasing the confirmed number of people tortured from 28,000 to 37,800.

Another ghost literally rose from the grave in April 2013 after a judge, acting on a request from the Communist Party, or-

dered the exhumation of Nobel Laureate poet Pablo Neruda (see Culture) to determine whether he may have been poisoned by *DINA*, Pinochet's intelligence agency. Neruda, a member of the Communist Party, died just 12 days after the 1973 coup, reportedly of prostate cancer. His former chauffeur charged that Neruda had been administered a lethal injection by a *DINA* agent posing as a doctor at the clinic where Neruda was being treated for the cancer. He died the day before he had planned to go into exile. Why the chauffeur waited 40 years to make such an electrifying revelation about the death of an internationally renowned figure was not clear. In November, the findings of domestic and foreign forensics experts concluded that there was no evidence of poisoning and that Neruda died of natural causes.

In January 2014, the International Court of Justice finally reached a decision the maritime claim Peru had filed in 2007. By a 10-6 vote, the IJC reached what can best be called an arbitrary compromise, granting Peru most of the area it had sought but allowing Chile to retain sovereignty over its fish-rich coastal waters. The Peruvians were happier than the Chileans, but the two countries appear agreeable to work out the arrangements.

Bachelet Returns

Shortly before the student protests re-erupted, Bachelet completed a two-year stint as head of the U.N. Organization for Women and returned to Chile to announce she would seek a second term in the 2013 presidential election. She pledged to abolish for-profit education—something she didn't attempt to do during the 2006 student protests.

By October 2013, Piñera's popularity in the Mitofsky poll was still 36%, 13th out of 19 hemispheric leaders, despite a relatively robust economy and low inflation. Although he could not run for immediate re-election, his dismal approval rating tainted his Alliance coalition (the "for Change" had been dropped). After 20 years in opposition, the right finally had received its chance to prove how well it could govern—and flubbed that chance.

Bachelet received 73% of the vote in a primary for the *Concertación*, now called the New Majority, composed of Bachelet's Socialist Party, the Christian Democrats, the *PPD* and, for the first time, the Communist Party.

Former Economy Minister Pablo Longuera, 55, of the *UDI* won the Alliance's primary in June 2013 with 51% of the vote over former Defense Minister Andrés Allamand of the *RN*. But just a month later, Longuera suddenly shook up the race by dropping out, explaining he

President Michelle Bachelet

was suffering from depression. The badly shaken Alliance chose as his replacement Evelyn Matthei, 60, of the *UDI*, who had served as Piñera's labor and social security minister.

Ironically, Matthei's father served as air force commander during the Pinochet era, and before the 1973 coup he had been a close friend of Bachelet's father, also an air force general. Bachelet and Matthei had played together as girls.

Seven other candidates were on the ballot, including Enríquez-Ominami, the renegade Socialist who received 20% of the vote in 2009, and Franco Parisi, 46, an economist and high-profile TV commentator who ran as an independent. Polls showed Bachelet with a wide lead over Matthei, even after Bachelet failed to participate with the other eight candidates in a televised debate on October 9. All nine candidates participated in a radio debate on October 25, and they all participated in two remaining TV debates.

Bachelet campaigned on a three-plank platform. First, public education would be free, including higher education, beginning with the poorest 70% of students; for-profit schools would be outlawed. Second, to help pay for the education reform, Bachelet proposed a tax reform plan that would raise the corporate income tax from 20% to 25% over five years, while lowering the top rate of personal income tax from 40% to 35%. She also proposed eliminating the controversial *Fondo Utilitad Tributaria* (*FUT*), which provided tax breaks for reinvested profits. The *FUT* was widely credited with fueling the reinvestment that had spurred Chile's robust economic growth, but it was also riddled with loopholes that allowed the rich to evade personal income taxes. Third, she advocated a constitutional convention to replace Pino-

chet's 1980 constitution and bring Chile in line with other modern democracies.

Matthei, who had a respectable record as a legislator and cabinet minister, was nonetheless handicapped by having campaigned for a *"Sí"* vote in the 1988 referendum that would have kept Pinochet in power another eight years.

The only suspense in the first round on November 17 was whether Bachelet could win without a runoff. Not quite:

Bachelet	3,075,839	46.7%
Matthei	1,648,481	25.0%
Enríquez-Ominami	732,542	11.0%
Parisi	666,015	10.1%
Others	471,931	7.2%
Null	66.935	1.0%
Blank	46,268	0.7%

Because mandatory voting had been repealed, turnout in the *primaera vuelta* was only 49.35%. Bachelet's New Majority lived up to its name, winning 67 of the 120 seats in the Chamber of Deputies to 49 for the Alliance, one for Enríquez-Ominami's party and three independents. Half the 38 Senate seats were contested, and the New Majority now holds a total of 21 seats to 16 for the Alliance and one independent.

With her 2-1 lead over Matthei and the Socialist leanings of Enríquez-Ominami and his followers, there was no suspense at all in the *segunda vuelta* on December 15; there was merely the novelty of Chileans choosing between two women for the first time. The two candidates debated once on radio and once on television. Turnout was a disappointing 42%. The results:

Bachelet	3,470,379	62.2%
Matthei	2,111,891	37.8%

Bachelet was sworn in for her second term on March 11, 2014. "Chile has only one great enemy: inequality," she declared. Most of Latin America's presidents attended the inauguration, as did U.S. Vice President Joe Biden, but Venezuela's Nicolás Maduro canceled because of criticism by Biden of Maduro's heavy-handed response to political dissent in Venezuela. Bachelet's inauguration segued into a summit of *UNASUR* leaders to discuss the street protests in Venezuela.

Keeping a campaign promise, Bachelet submitted her tax reform proposal to Congress before March was out. It would raise $8.2 billion to help finance the projected $15 billion education reform. The Chamber of Deputies approved it in April, but it was still being hotly debated in the Senate when this book went to press. Small businessmen joined their richer counterparts in opposing the abolition of the *FUT*, warning that it would pose a severe burden on them, while conservative econo-

mists warned that it would cause Chile's already cooling economy to slow even more. Bachelet's new finance minister, Alberto Arenas, rejected that notion during grilling before the Senate's finance committee in June. But even the Central Bank admitted in May that growth in the first quarter had slowed to 2.4% and growth for the year was projected at 3%, the slowest in four years. (See The Future)

CULTURE: One of Spain's least-developed colonies, since independence Chile has made cultural contributions far out of proportion to its size, particularly in literature. During the 19th century, Chile's intellectual climate produced not only outstanding writers but attracted others seeking greater freedom of expression.

Two outstanding examples are Venezuela's Andrés Bello, whose statue stands in front of the University of Chile, which he founded, and Argentina's Domingo Faustino Sarmiento, who spent several years in exile as editor of *El Mercurio* during the dictatorship of Juan Manuel de Rosas in his native land.

During this era Chile produced a number of its own realist prose writers, the best known of whom was probably the novelist Alberto Blest Gana, author of such enduring classics as *El niño que enloqueció de amor*. The late 19th century also produced a golden age in art, though it was heavily influenced by contemporary French impressionism.

In the 20th century, Chile enjoyed the distinction of being the only Latin American country to have produced two Nobel Prize-winning poets, Lucía Godoy Alcayaga (1886–1957) and Naftalí Reyes (1904–73). But the world does not remember them by those names; it remembers them as Gabriela Mistral and Pablo Neruda. Both achieved international acclaim, and both represented Chile abroad for a time as diplomats. Mistral taught for several years in the United States. Their verse has been translated into several languages, and Neruda especially has become a global icon. Probably his most revered work is *Canto general* (1950), a series of 10 books of poetry. The centennial of his birth on July 12, 2004, was marked by observances in Chile and throughout the Spanish-speaking world. His home overlooking the Pacific at Isla Negra is a popular pilgrimage destination for his admirers. His exile to Italy in the 1940s inspired the 1994 Italian film, *Il Postino*.

Another poet, Gonzalo Rojas (1917–2011), a contemporary of Neruda's, received Spain's prestigious Cervantes Prize for Spanish-language literature in 2003. He had spent the Pinochet era in exile.

Jorge Edwards (b. 1931), a novelist, journalist and diplomat, received the

Chile

Cervantes Prize in 1999. His best-known novel is *Persona non grata*, inspired by his expulsion from Cuba in 1971.

The most recent Chilean recipient of the Cervantes Prize is the poet Nicanor Parra (b. 1914), who received the award in 2011 at age 97. He is regularly considered a possible recipient for the Nobel. He is the brother of the late folksinger Violeta Parra (see below).

Two of Chile's best-known popular fiction writers today are the novelist Isabel Allende, a distant cousin of the Marxist president, who now lives in California, and Ariel Dorfman. Two of Allende's novels, *La casa de los espíritus,* and *De amor y sombras,* were adapted for the English-language films *The House of the Spirits* and *Of Love and Shadows.* Dorfman's play, *La muerte y la doncella,* was adapted for the U.S. movie *Death and the Maiden,* starring Sigourney Weaver and Ben Kingsley.

The premier figure in classical music in the 20th century was the internationally renowned concert pianist Claudio Arrau (1903–91), who spent most of his career in Europe.

In popular music, a folk singer who achieved cult-legend status much as Elvis Presley did in the United States was Violeta Parra (1917–67), like Arrau born in Chillán but who remained in Chile. Probably best remembered for the song, *Gracias a la vida,* Parra committed suicide over an unhappy love affair in 1967. Like Neruda, her likeness is still seen everywhere in Chile, and her voice or her songs remain popular throughout the Hispanic world.

Chile's folklore is grounded in the tradition of the *huaso,* a trans-Andean version of Argentina's gaucho. Its guitar-based music is similar to Mexican *ranchero.* Distinctly Chilean, however, is the national folk dance, the *cueca,* which traditionally is performed in conjunction with Chilean independence day on September 18 but is performed in touristy cafes year-round.

Chile's reputation as a haven for political and artistic expression disappeared during the 1973–90 military regime. Many of its own artistic, literary and musical figures were either killed or exiled. One of Chile's best-known popular singers, Victor Jara, was killed in the Santiago stadium after the 1973 coup.

In contemporary popular music, the former rock band La Ley, which recorded from 1989 to 2003, won a U.S. Grammy Award in 2001 for its album on its performance on *MTV Unplugged.* It also won two Latin Grammys, for its albums *Uno* in 2000 and *Libertad* in 2003. Some of the band members formed a new group, Los Niñitos Azules.

Among the cinema figures who fled the dictatorship was film director Miguel Littín (b. 1942), the first Chilean director to achieve international renown, whose films have twice been nominated for the U.S. Academy Award for Best Foreign Film. He settled first in Cuba, then in Spain, and worked in Mexico, Europe and elsewhere before returning to Chile after Pinochet stepped down. He first achieved international recognition for his 1969 film, *El chacal de Nahueltoro (The Jackal of Nahueltoto),* the true story of a man executed for the murder of a woman and her five children, a crime that riveted Chileans' attention in the 1960s. In Mexico he directed *Actas de Marusia (Letters from Marusia),* nominated for Best Foreign Film in 1976, and *Recursos del método (Reasons of State),* a Cuban-French-Mexican production in 1978 that was an adaptation of the Cuban novel by Alejo Carpentier (see Cuba). He directed *Alsino y el condor (Alsino and the Condor)* in Nicaragua, which also was nominated for Best Foreign Film in 1982. Since his return to Chile, his credits have included *Los náufragos (The Shipwrecked)* in 1994, *Tierra del Fuego* (2000) and his most recent, *Dawson Isla 10* (2009), about the island where members of Allende's cabinet were incarcerated after the coup.

After 1990, many film artists returned, and a new cinematic generation emerged in Chile, less tied to the Marxist traditions of the past but which still draws inspiration from Chile's traditional class divisions and from the Pinochet dictatorship.

Among the new directors is Ricardo Larraín (b. 1957), whose 1991 movie, *La frontera,* about a man sentenced to internal exile under Pinochet, won international acclaim, including a Silver Bear at the Berlin Film Festival.

Another is Marcelo Ferrari (b. 1962), whose critically acclaimed 2003 film *Sub terra* focused on the plight of miners in 1897 and has been widely distributed abroad. His fifth and most recent film is *Bombal* (2012), a biopic about Chilean writer María Luisa Bombal. He already had directed a biopic about Pablo Neruda, *De Neftalí a Pablo* (2004).

Still another up-and-coming young director is Andrés Wood (b. 1965) whose semi-autobiographical drama *Machuca* (2004), set in the weeks before the 1973 coup, won an Ariel Award in Mexico and was named Most Popular International Film at the 2004 Vancouver Film Festival. His latest, *Violeta se fue a los cielos (Violeta),* a biopic about folksinger Violeta Parra (see above), was Chile's 2011 candidate for Best Foreign Film in the United States. It was not selected, but it did win the Grand Jury Prize for Drama at the 2012 Sundance Film Festival in Utah. Wood also co-wrote the screenplay.

Chile's selection in 2012 *was* nominated for Best Foreign Film: *No,* directed by Pablo Larraín. It is based on the 1988 referendum in which voters rejected (by voting *no*) another eight years in power for Pinochet. It stars the renowned Mexican actor Gael García Bernal (see Mexico).

Gabriela Mistral

Among the most prominent Chilean actors, in film and television, is Fernando Reyes (b. 1954), who appeared in both *Sub terra* and *Machuca.*

Television came to Chile in 1960, but rather than the first stations being private or government-owned as in other Latin American countries, the first three stations were put on the air by the University of Chile, Catholic University of Santiago and Catholic University of Valparaíso; these universities still operate the stations today. The government launched *TV Nacional* in 1967. It wasn't until the early 1990s that the first two private franchises were awarded. Chilean television has become increasingly less dependent on foreign programming and has produced a number of creditable programs of its own, some of which are exported to other Latin American countries.

Chile was the birthplace of the Latin American press. The region's first regularly published newspaper, *La Aurora de Chile,* appeared in 1810 and lasted nearly a decade. The press used to print it is on display in the National Library. Chile also is the home of the oldest continually published newspaper in Latin America, *El Mercurio,* which began as a weekly in Valparaíso in 1837, became a daily a few years later, and began publishing in Santiago in 1900.

Today six dailies are published in the capital, including the government's *La Nación.* The other five are in the hands of two newspaper conglomerates, including *El Mercurio,* which also publishes *La Segunda* and *Las Últimas Noticias.* Their main rival is *La Tercera,* long the country's circulation leader, which also publishes *La Cuarta,* a working-class tabloid. Two free-circulation newspapers are published in the capital, *La Hora* and *El Publimetro,* popular with subway commuters. There are 23 provincial dailies, including two

Lake of Yeso in the Andes

owned by *El Mercurio* in Valparaíso and Antofagasta.

Chile was traditionally a beacon for press freedom in Latin America, but the Pinochet government imposed prior censorship and jailed journalists suspected of leftist sympathies. After the return to democracy in 1990, Freedom House perennially ranked the Chilean press as among the three freest in Latin America, along with those of Uruguay and Costa Rica, But in 2011, Chile was downgraded to "partly free" because of restrictions imposed on media covering the violent student demonstrations (see History) and because of lack of diversity of media ownership.

Chile boasts six of UNESCO's World Heritage Sites: Rapa Nui National Park on Easter Island, with its famous *moai* heads; the architecturally intriguing wooden churches of the island of Chiloé; the historic seaport quarter of Valparaíso; the Humberstone and Santa Laura saltpeter works; and the early 20th century mining town of Sewell, near Rancagua.

ECONOMY: Few countries in the world have been whipsawed as violently from one political or economic extreme to another as has Chile. The country was long dependent on copper for foreign exchange, which as late as the 1970s still accounted for 60 percent of exports. It is still the leading export. As with Bolivia's dependence on tin, fluctuations in the world copper market often led to recessions in Chile. Moreover, the copper mines, as well as many of the country's utilities, were owned by foreign corporations, a fact that provided the Communist and Socialist

parties with election-year ammunition. The elder Eduardo Frei tried to steer Chile on a middle course between Marxism and capitalism in the 1960s, an effort rewarded by President Lyndon Johnson, who lent Chile substantial foreign aid. Frei's halfway economic and social reforms proved of limited success, however, and in the end were criticized by the right as too radical and by the left as inadequate.

The result was the narrow minority victory of Salvador Allende's Popular Unity coalition in 1970, which jerked the country abruptly to the left. Allende nationalized the copper mines and utilities, moves that were applauded even by Allende's opponents at first because of nationalist pride. But signing a decree nationalizing an industry is one thing; running it efficiently and profitably proved quite another. The result was one of the many economic disasters of the Allende regime.

Another was land reform, through the breaking up of the huge *latifundias* of wealthy and often absentee owners. On the surface, such reform seemed a long-overdue application of social justice. In reality, it destroyed agricultural operations that often were operating well, replacing them with small communal plots that were not commercially useful and run by peasants with little or no knowledge of efficient agricultural techniques.

Marxist distribution policies also resulted in severe, Cuban-style shortages, which eroded what little confidence the regime still enjoyed. To compound its woes, the regime was beset by hyperinflation of 1,000 percent annually. The country was on the verge of social and economic chaos

when the military intervened on September 11, 1973.

The military government of General Pinochet quickly restored order and reversed virtually every policy of the Marxist experiment. Land holdings were restored to their original owners, although a new homesteading law was implemented to provide land to small farmers who were able to demonstrate they planned to make it produce something beyond the basic needs of their families. For a time, nationalized industries were run by the state, but by the 1980s they were privatized.

The Pinochet government made it clear it intended a dramatic break with the past, that it would not merely restore the *status quo ante* Allende. With the government's encouragement, Chilean entrepreneurs began to exploit the extraordinarily rich nitrate deposits. Because of the reversal of seasons in the Southern Hemisphere, Chile began exporting enormous quantities of produce to the United States, Europe and Japan during the Northern Hemisphere winter. By the time Pinochet relinquished power in 1990, agricultural exports exceeded those of copper, thus breaking the traditional dependence. Yet, even copper contributed to the Chilean economy as never before in the 1990s as exports from other copper-mining countries, such as Zaïre and Zambia, declined because of inefficiency and instability and the world market price soared.

The most dramatic economic transition of the Pinochet regime, however, was the move to almost pure free-market economics. Pinochet surrounded himself with a "kitchen cabinet" of civilian economic technocrats, many of whom had been schooled under Milton Friedman at the University of Chicago. Thus, the press quickly dubbed this team of economists "los Chicago Boys." Chile withdrew from the Andean Pact in the late 1970s and slashed its high protective tariffs, which led to a flood of cheap imported goods. At the same time, government subsidies that had kept inefficient domestic industries afloat were eliminated, forcing them to sink or swim; more than a few sank. After a brief period of seeming prosperity, the new policies plunged Chile into a severe recession in 1981. Large and small industries, unable to compete with foreign imports, foundered. So did many banks. The economic crisis lasted more than three years before the new economic realities took hold.

New Chilean industries proved capable of holding their own in the international marketplace. One such example was Chile's new arms industries, born out of necessity from the cutoff of U.S. military aid because of Pinochet's human rights violations. Chilean wineries are another

Chile

international marketing success story, and there are now computer hardware and software industries.

By 1990, when Pinochet turned over power to Patricio Aylwin, Chile was in the midst of an economic boom. Ironically, while the new civilian government publicly reviled Pinochet for his human rights abuses, it grudgingly acknowledged the success of his free-market policies by retaining them. It was an especially bitter pill for the Socialists who were part of the governing coalition. The result, however, was an economy that for several years was the envy of Latin America—and the world. Real GDP growth between 1990 and 1997 averaged a dazzling 8% annually, exceeding 12% in 1992 and 10% in 1995. Contributing to Chile's success, and to its attractiveness to foreign investors, are wage costs lower than Mexico's or South Asia's and an educated workforce; the literacy rate is 96%, compared with Brazil's 83%. In addition to robust growth, inflation was trimmed to 6% and unemployment to 4%. Chile also became widely admired for its private pension fund administrator *(AFP)* system, implemented during the Pinochet era and continued since, which provided

retirees far greater returns than the government's social security system. U.S. congressmen eyed Chile's retirement system as a possible model.

Chile is an associate member of the four-nation *Mercosur* free-trade pact (Argentina, Brazil, Uruguay and Paraguay), but because its tariff policies differ so sharply from the other four, it has opted against full membership. Chile was expected to become the fourth member of NAFTA. President Eduardo Frei discussed the issue with President Clinton during a state visit to Washington in 1997.

A major success story in recent years has been Chile's wines, long recognized for their quality. Wine exports skyrocketed 5,000%, from $10.9 million in 1985 to $526 million in 1999, accounting for 5.4% of total exports. The trend continues upward, although subject to periods of drought, as large new tracts in the central region have been planted with grapes.

In 1997, the economy became a victim of its own success. Frei was twice forced to raise interest rates to prevent the economy from overheating and to keep inflation under control. The price of copper, which despite diversification still accounted for 42%

of export earnings, dropped from $1.19 to 75 cents a pound, and the October market panic in Asia, which buys about a third of Chile's exports, had repercussions in Chile. GDP growth for 1998 was only 3.3%, compared with the steamroller of 7.1% in 1997 and 7.2% in 1996. Worse still, the economy shrank by 2.7% in 1999, while unemployment leaped from 6% to 11% and per capita income fell slightly from $5,100 to $5,000. meaning Chile officially was in recession for the first time in 15 years.

The recession almost proved the undoing of the ruling *Concertación* in the presidential elections of 1999–2000. President Ricardo Lagos of the *Concertación,* who had barely squeaked into office, saw real GDP growth snap back from the negative column to a healthy 5.4% in 2000; it was up 4.0% in 2001 but only 2.1% in 2002, reflecting the economic crisis in neighboring Argentina and the recession in the United States, the leading market for its exports.

Like Brazil's Fernando Henrique Cardoso, the Socialist Lagos underwent a dramatic conversion to free-market principles and followed an economic course that was so conservative the opposition had little to quibble with. He traveled to Quebec in 2001 for the third Summit of the Americas and embraced the concept of a Free Trade Area of the Americas. He concluded a $9 billion free-trade agreement (FTA) with the European Union in 2002. The United States and Chile resumed free-trade talks that had begun 11 years earlier. After reaching some compromises over environmental issues and capital investment out-flows among others, the two countries signed a $6 billion FTA in 2003. In 2004, Chile concluded a $1.1 billion FTA with South Korea. Since then, Chile has concluded FTAs with China, India, Japan, New Zealand, Singapore, Peru and, in 2008, with Australia.

Growth for 2003 was 3.3%, and it jumped to 6.1% in 2004—the best showing since 1997, largely because of a high international market price for copper—and 6.3% in 2005. It dropped to 4% in 2006, in part because of a strike at a copper mine and the decision of energy-starved Argentina to suspend natural gas exports to Chile, requiring more expensive fuels to generate electricity. Growth was back up to 5.1% in 2007, again due to record high copper prices. The copper windfall also gave Chile a budget surplus, and it is debt-free, a rarity in Latin America.

Growth in 2008 was down to 3.2%, reflecting the impact of the global recession on export-dependent Chile, and in 2009 the economy *shrank* by –1.5%. But in 2010 it grew by 7.5%, among the six highest in Latin America, despite the earthquake's disruption to the infrastructure. Growth

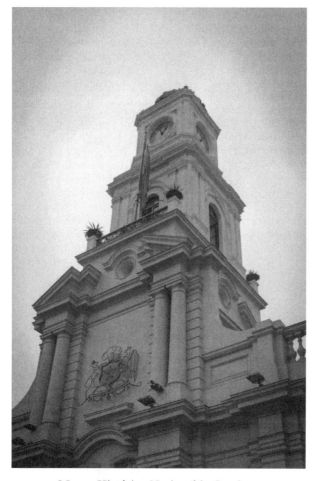

Museo Histórico Nacional in Santiago

was 6.5% in 2011, fueled in part by earthquake reconstruction and 5.0% in 2012, the fifth-fastest in the Western Hemisphere; the Economic Commission for Latin America and the Caribbean (ECLAC) put it at 5.5%. Growth slowed somewhat to 4.4% in 2013, still the fifth highest of the 20 Latin American republics and seventh in the Western hemisphere.

Inflation has remained steady, dropping from 4.5% in 2000 to only 1.1% in 2003, the lowest rate since 1935. In 2008 it was at 8%, but with the recession it dropped to 1.5% in 2009 and 1.7% in 2010. It was 3.3% in 2011, 3% in 2012 and 1.7% in 2013.

Unemployment has dropped from 9.6%% in 2009 and 7.1% in 2010 to 6.6% in 2011, 6.3% in 2012 and 6% in 2013.

The devastating earthquake that struck Chile in February 2010 caused an estimated $4 billion to $7 billion in damage and disrupted the wine industry, which suffered an estimated $250 million in damage. Ironically, however, the influx of international aid, coupled with reconstruction activity, drove down unemployment and it enhanced revenues from increased sales and income taxes.

Chile achieved a major milestone in 2010 when it became the first Latin American nation to be admitted to the Organization for Economic Cooperation and Development (OECD), a "club" of more than 30 of the world's richest and most developed countries. President Sebastián Piñera, who took office that year, has set a goal of Chile becoming a First World country by 2018, the bicentennial of Chile's achieving independence.

In May 2013, Chile's environmental regulator blocked further construction of the $8.5 billion Pascua-Lama gold mine, the world's highest, on the Chilean-Argentine border. The Diaguita Indian tribe complained that chemical by-products from the construction were contaminating its water supply, causing health problems. On May 24, the environmental superintendent levied a $16 million fine, the maximum, against Barrick Gold Corp., the Canadian firm building the mine, for "very serious" violations of its mining permit.

THE FUTURE: The army's dramatic confession of its sins during the dictatorship, the government's come-clean report on torture and Pinochet's deathbed confession have been cathartic. The historic changes to Pinochet's 1980 constitution eliminating the unelected senators have made Chile a more genuine democracy.

With Pinochet's death, the governing *Concertación* lost a unifying factor, and after 20 years in power, the coalition was showing its age. The election of billionaire businessman Sebastián Piñera in 2009 was as historic a change as when Patricio

Aylwin replaced Pinochet. He was the first conservative elected president since Jorge Alessandri in 1958, yet, Piñera was as pragmatically committed to retaining the *Concertación's* popular social welfare programs as the *Concertación* was in retaining Pinochet's successful free-market economic policies.

Piñera predicted Chile would join the ranks of First World countries by 2018. It seems to be well on its way. Chile joined the Organization for Economic Cooperation and Development in 2010, a group of the world's richest democracies. Freedom House rates Chile as among the three freest countries of Latin America, while Transparency International ranks it as the least corrupt after Uruguay; indeed, in TI's 2010 and 2011 Corruption Perceptions Index, Chile had a better score than the United States.

But there is a nagging dark cloud on Chile's bright horizon, which has already produced a thunderstorm. In 2011, this author warned that Piñera needed to focus on one of the *Concertación's* glaring failures if Chile is to join the ranks of the First World: the need to reform Chile's public education system. That festering issue exploded into violence that dragged on for three years, and Piñera's handling of the crisis was not impressive. His countrymen regarded him as arrogant and aloof, he left office with an approval rating of 36% and his unpopularity was an albatross around the neck of the ruling Alliance coalition. Small wonder that voters viewed former President Michelle Bachelet, who left office in 2010 with an 84% approval rating, with nostalgia in the 2013 election.

Thus, the pendulum has swung back, as it's designed to do in a workable democracy. Her landslide 62.2% victory in the December 15, 2013, runoff provides her with a much stronger mandate than she had in 2006. She can benefit from the mistakes she made in her first term, as well as from Piñera's. Some pundits have predicted she will make a sharper turn to the left than before, but that seems unlikely. Her moderate Christian Democratic coalition partners have 21 seats in the 120-seat Chamber of Deputies compared with 15 for her Socialist Party, and both parties have six seats in the 38-member Senate. Her majority in Congress is not as overwhelming as her percentage of the vote for president because of Chile's peculiar double-member congressional districts, a holdover from Pinochet's constitution that guarantees a seat to the second-place candidates in both houses. That feature is one of the reasons Bachelet has made a new constitution one of her goals, but talk of a constitutional convention, rather than merely amending the existing constitution, is reminiscent of what Hugo Chávez did in Venezuela to consolidate his power. The conservative opposition has more than enough votes to block that, but standing in the way of needed reforms could backfire on them.

Bachelet's immediate concern will be to make good on her promise to abolish for-profit education and to make higher education free or at least affordable for promising students, who are the key to Chile's elevation to First World status. She didn't do it in her first term. She now has the opportunity again. The opposition would be wise not to try to stymie her.

Valparaiso: Chile's second city on the beach

The Republic of Colombia

Area: 439,405 square miles.

Population: 46,245,297 (2014 est.).

Capital City: Bogotá (Pop. 8.25 million, estimate).

Climate: The lowlands are generally hot, with heavy rainfall except for the Guajira Peninsula, which is arid. Highland climate varies with altitude, becoming quite temperate and pleasant in the higher elevations.

Neighboring Countries: Venezuela (East and Northeast); Brazil (Southeast); Peru and Ecuador (South); Panama (Northwest).

Official Language: Spanish.

Other Principal Tongues: Isolated Indian dialects.

Ethnic Background: *Mestizo* (mixed European and Indian, 58%), European (20%) Mulatto (mixed Black and Caucasian, 14%), African (4%), Mixed African-Indian and Indian (4%).

Principal Religion: Roman Catholic Christianity.

Chief Commercial Products: Refined cocaine, a technically illegal export worth over $10 billion U.S., coffee, petroleum, cotton, tobacco, sugar, textiles, bananas, fresh-cut flowers.

Currency: Peso.

Gross Domestic Product: U.S. $369.2 billion in 2013, est. ($8,071 per capita, official exchange rate). This does not include money from drug trafficking, which, if included, would increase this figure by an estimated 25%.

Former Colonial Status: Spanish Crown Colony (1525–1819)

Independence Date: July 20, 1810.

Chief of State: Juan Manuel Santos Calderón (b. August 10, 1951), president (since August 7, 2010).

National Flag: Yellow, blue and red horizontal stripes.

Colombia is the fourth-largest nation in South America and the only one with both Atlantic and Pacific coasts. The high Andes mountains divide the country into four ranges and occupy about two fifths of the land. To the east of the mountains are the great plains (*llanos*) and the western tip of the Guiana Highland. The majority of Colombia's population is concentrated in the green valleys and mountain basins that lie between the ranges of the Andes.

Eleven of Colombia's 14 urban centers are in the mountain valleys; the remainder are on the Caribbean coast. The vast plains along the base of the eastern range contain cattle ranches, but the extensions of the plains into the jungle-filled Amazon Basin are almost unpopulated. The northern ends of the mountain valleys, which fan out to the Caribbean coast, are wet, hot and almost uninhabited.

Colombia's people comprise communities that vary from white, Indian and black populations to combinations of mixed ancestry. Rivers have been Colombia's most important means of communication; the Magdalena is navigable for nearly 1,000 miles and still is the principal means of transporting cargo to and from Bogotá. The second great river is the Cauca, not important for transportation but for furnishing water for irrigation and power for industry in the Cauca Valley. A major construction program, similar to that of the Tennessee Valley project, was undertaken to further develop the Cauca Valley's resources.

As in all countries near the Equator, altitude is the principal factor, modifying an otherwise oppressive climate. Throughout the country rainfall is ample. There are no seasons applicable to the whole country. Summer is generally considered the dry season and the rainy season is winter; however, in some regions along the Pacific, rains, either violent thunderstorms or warm, steady showers, fall every day of the year. From sea level to 3,000 feet the climate is tropical; from 3,000 to 6,500 feet it is temperate; above 6,500 feet it is chilly.

Crops are grown at elevations up to 10,000 feet, but above this level trees thin out and tall peaks are covered by snow year around.

HISTORY: The Spaniards discovered the coast of Colombia about 1500, but the Indians proved so hostile that the explorers quickly withdrew. The first settlement was later established at Santa Marta in 1525, and Cartagena was subsequently founded in 1533. The interior was not penetrated until 1536, when Gonzalo Jiménez de Quesada explored the Magdalena River seeking its source. Climbing the eastern range, he found the Chibcha Indians in several of the mountain valleys, conquered them and founded Bogotá, the present capital. The Chibchas were sedentary, agricultural people who had developed a fairly high level of civilization.

An expedition from Ecuador under Sebastián de Belalcazar discovered the Cauca Valley and founded Pasto, Popayán and Cali in 1536. Nicolaus de Federmann led an expedition toward the site of Bogotá from Venezuela. Belalcazar reached Bogotá in 1538 and came into contact with Federmann in 1539. Similar to other conquests, the period of settlement was marked by conflict among the various groups of conquerors. The Spaniards introduced sugarcane, wheat, cattle, sheep and horses and established a royal government at Bogotá in 1550 for the administration of most of the land in modern Colombia.

Gold was discovered in Antioquía about 1550, rapidly reducing further interest in the agricultural regions around Bogotá and Cali. Almost simultaneously with the start of gold shipments to Spain, English and Dutch pirates started their attacks on Spanish shipping and the Caribbean ports. However, the interior of the country was at peace and, unmolested, gradually developed. Descendants of the conquerors amassed large estates, worked by Indian or black slaves and established a semi-feudal system of agriculture that still persists in the remote parts of Colombia.

During the colonial period, what is modern-day Colombia was part of the viceroyalty of New Granada. The movement for independence started in the 1790s following publication of the French Revolution's Declaration of the Rights of Man. This was not a popular movement, but rather one of young intellectuals from the aristocratic families of Bogotá.

Revolts erupted in Venezuela in 1796 and 1806, followed by an abortive attempt to set up an independent government at Bogotá. However, the provinces were divided and the Spanish re-established control. When news reached New Granada in 1810 that Spain's King Fernando VII had been deposed by Napoleon, the restive creoles revolted again. This time they seized Cartagena, then town after town in the Cauca and Magdalena valleys. On July 20, 1810, today observed as independence day, the *cabildo* in Bogotá arrested the viceroy and assumed control. Independence came after eight years of see-saw warfare in which Simón Bolívar and his generals, José Antonio Páez, Francisco de Paula Santander and Antonio José de Sucre victoriously marched and countermarched across Colombia, Venezuela and Ecuador. Following the defeat of the Spanish forces at the Battle of Boyacá, the Republic of Gran Colombia was proclaimed December 17, 1819, incorporating Venezuela, Colombia and Ecuador in a political union.

The allies in the war for independence divided over the form of government that should be established for the new state. Bolívar advocated a strong central government, while Páez and Santander pressed for a federation of sovereign states. Later, this discord would lead to the establishment of two political parties that still control the country today: the Conservatives, in favor of central government and close relations with the Catholic Church, and the Liberals, favoring a federation of states and separation of church and state.

The Republic of Gran Colombia lasted only 10 years. Venezuela separated from the union in 1829 and Ecuador declared its independence a year later; the remaining provinces took the name of New Granada. The name Colombia was restored in 1861 as the United States of Colombia and became the Republic of Colombia in 1886.

From its inception, the new republic was torn with dissent. Bolívar sought to create a "Great Colombia"; Santander believed there was little hope for uniting diverse people with few common interests into an effective union. Dissent grew during the period of the wars of liberation of Peru and Bolivia (1822–24). In 1826, Bolívar assumed dictatorial power. By 1830, opposition to him led to revolt, the republic was broken up, and the *el Libertador* died on his way into exile.

Santander became the actual founder of Colombia. Recalled from exile in 1832, he brought a degree of order from the chaos of war. Despite his own championing of democratic ideas, he imposed a strict discipline, organized finances and set up central government services with an iron hand. He and his successor pursued moderate policies concerning the church and the differences between the Conservatives and Liberals on the form of government. However, the radicals of both sides, as well as regional interests, sought their goals by force of arms; from 1839 to 1842 civil war was waged intermittently by constantly changing forces.

By 1840 the gap between the Conservative and Liberal views had widened; the Liberals were characterized as blasphe-mous and disorderly, while the Conservatives gained power as defenders of order, godliness and good government. The Conservatives (as usual during this period) represented an alliance of the landowners, the church and the army.

From 1840 to 1880, the two parties alternated in power, each using its position to persecute the other and generally provoking recurrent strife bordering on civil war. In spite of this turmoil, by 1880 the economy had broadened, the population had doubled since independence, communication and trade were improved and Colombia had few international problems.

The election of Rafael Núñez in 1880 marked a major change in Colombia's history. A long-time Liberal, he united the moderates of his party with the more moderate Conservatives and formed the National Party. Surviving another Conservative-Liberal civil war in 1884–85, Núñez secured adoption of Colombia's 10th constitution and brought order to the country. The Liberal regime became progressively conservative and subsequently dictatorial. The privileges of the church were restored, peace was maintained and political dissent was suppressed. His death in 1899 left the government in the hands of Conservatives without a leader capable of avoiding the consequences of 20 years of repression. Civil war raged for three years as the Liberals sought to oust the Conservatives. The so-called Thousand Day War left more than 100,000 dead, widespread destruction, a ruined economy and a demoralized people. These losses were soon followed by the revolt of the province of Panama in 1903 (arranged by the United States; see Panama).

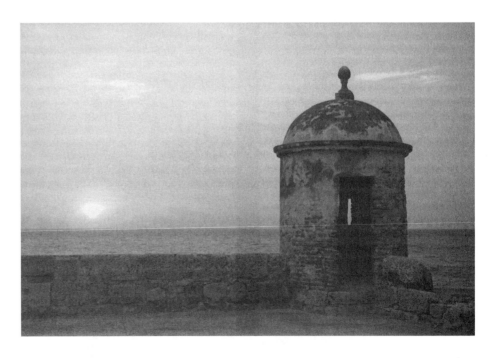

Colombia

The Colombians demanded a leader capable of reuniting the country and rebuilding the economy. A Conservative seemed to fit the bill; a proud and energetic man, Rafael Reyes assumed dictatorial powers. His five-year term was stormy—despite an empty treasury and a bitter people, he was able to reorganize the national finances, restore Colombia's credit, initiate construction of roads and railroads and encourage development of the coffee industry. Opposition forced his resignation in 1909.

Five Conservative presidents followed him (1909–1930). This era was marked by advances in political realism and cooperation. Elections became more honest, a semblance of a two-party government was developed and censorship of the press was reduced. During the same period, the economy improved, production rose, petroleum was discovered and business grew with the boom years of the 1920s. The ready money brought on an expansion of industry: railroads and power plants were built and coffee production expanded. The affluence also corrupted public officials and led to over expansion and inflation.

The Great Depression produced a financial disaster that discredited the Conservatives, and in 1930 a Liberal government came to power.

The peaceful transfer of power in 1930 was in marked contrast to the violence found in other parts of Latin America and to Colombia's own past. So, too, the Liberals of 1930 were quite distinct from their predecessors. Most of the issues that had produced the civil wars of the previous century were dead or no longer important. The Liberal Party of 1930 was interested in economic and social reforms to protect the interests of labor and of the growing middle class.

The first of three elected Liberal presidents who would govern for the next 16 years, Enrique Olaya Herrera (1930–34), satisfied reform-minded Liberals while his moderation reassured Conservatives. The second, Alfonso López (1934–38), a wealthy publisher and intellectual, was far more outspoken and dynamic. To secure needed social reforms, he implemented radical changes in the constitution that frightened Conservatives. However, he tempered their fears with more moderate legislation. His successor, Eduardo Santos (1938–42), publisher of the influential Liberal daily *El Tiempo*, moved the country sharply back to the right, bringing denunciation from López and creating the first signs of the growing schism between the left and right wings of the party.

López returned to power in the 1942 election and brought the country into World War II on the side of the Allies, much to the displeasure of pro-Axis Conservatives and neutralists within his own party. Compounding López's problems, a corruption scandal erupted during his second administration that embroiled members of his own family. Increasingly, moderate Liberals joined with Conservatives in Congress to block his proposals. There were numerous plots against him,

and he faced discontent from underpaid government employees. Under mounting pressure, he resigned in 1945 and was replaced by an interim president until the 1946 election.

La Violencia

The Liberal split led to the election of a Conservative, Mariano Ospina Pérez, in 1946 with a plurality of 42% of the vote. A timid man in the wrong job at the wrong time, he was incapable of controlling either the growing militancy of the Liberal left or the fanaticism of the crypto-fascists in his own party. Bloodshed erupted between elements of these two political extremes, and there were revolts in several departments.

The murder in April 1948 of Jorge Eliécer Gaitán, a popular leader of the Liberal left, touched off a riot in the capital of such violence that the term *Bogotazo* was coined to describe a situation in which a whole people rioted. Some 2,000 deaths resulted as mobs roamed the streets, burning, looting and shooting. The conflict spread throughout the country as Liberals and Conservatives fought for control of villages and rural communities. The president declared martial law and gradually restored an appearance of order. It was in this atmosphere that the elections of 1950 were held. The Liberal Party, badly split, expected trouble at the polls and stayed away; the Conservatives elected their candidate, Laureano Gómez.

President Gómez was an admirer of Franco and Hitler, and installed an ultra-rightist regime. Ruling as a dictator, he used the army and police to hunt down and exterminate the Liberals. From his regime there developed an undeclared civil war that caused an estimated 200,000 deaths and a way of life known as *La Violencia* (The Violence). In 1953, he was ousted by a military coup, and General Gustavo Rojas Pinilla was installed as president. The change, accompanied by an amnesty, brought a lull in the fighting. However, his administration proved cruel and incompetent. The sole redeeming feature of his rule was that he did not discriminate between Liberals and Conservatives, forcing these enemies to arrange a truce in order to oust him in 1957.

Democracy Takes Root

There followed a Liberal-Conservative coalition, known as the National Unity Agreement, which would alternate Liberal and Conservative presidents for 16 years. A Liberal, Alberto Lleras Camargo, took office on August 7, 1958. Having to cope not only with the conflict between the parties but with the equally bitter inter-

Bolívar crossing the Andes

nal party strife, Lleras Camargo nonetheless succeeded in separating the political antagonists from rural bandits who were capitalizing on a continuing reign of terror. He pursued moderate policies in social and economic matters while seeking political unity. His moderation restored a degree of stability, but the government, lacking a majority, was unable to enact any of the needed reforms.

Lleras Camargo's Conservative successor in 1962, Guillermo León Valencia, unable to obtain legislative cooperation for even the routine functions of government, was forced to rule by decree. The current guerrilla war began on his watch in 1964.

The Liberal regime that followed from 1966 to 1970 was forced to use the same system. Under President Carlos Lleras Restrepo, Colombia enjoyed a comfortable rate of economic growth and continued decline in traditional rural banditry and violence.

Misael Pastrana Borrero, a Conservative, was elected by a slim 1.5% majority over former dictator Rojas Pinilla in 1970. A politically unknown Conservative economist, Pastrana sought to diversify the farm-based economy. Although exports soared and certain sectors of the economy improved, runaway inflation and increasing unemployment became major issues in the 1974 election campaign.

With the National Unity Agreement expiring at the presidential level in 1974, Colombians voted in the nation's first open election in more than 20 years. Alfonso López Michelsen, a Liberal, was elected with 52% of the vote. In second place was the Conservative candidate, while Rojas Pinilla's daughter ran a strong third as an independent. Although the Liberals also had won large majorities in both houses of Congress, the Constitution required that all appointive offices be divided equally between the Liberals and Conservatives until 1978; this requirement was extended informally through 1986.

López Michelsen declared a "national economic emergency" just five weeks after taking office in August 1974 to bypass the slow-moving Congress and institute by decree certain economic reforms. His plan included raising the daily wage by 40% to $1.50, imposing a hefty tax increase on the wealthy and on luxury imports and instituting a special tax on idle farmland to encourage greater output. Various steps were taken to cut the inflation rate from 30% in 1974 to an estimated 20% in 1976.

These bold measures met stiff opposition. Conservatives charged that the new taxes were recessionary and discouraged investments. Leftists demanded even more radical change, particularly in the rural sector. The top 4% of the population owned 68% of the farmland while the bottom 73% of the people held just 7%, consisting of small plots that provided a living only for a small family. Two thirds of the nation's youth suffered from malnutrition.

The Liberal Party candidate, Julio César Turbay Ayala, defeated his Conservative opponent in 1978 by 140,000 votes. He immediately implemented his law-and-order promises by ordering an all-out military campaign against political violence, drug smuggling and general lawlessness.

Harsher tactics against guerrillas led to worldwide charges of human rights violations. Yet, the M-19 continued its sensational terrorism throughout 1980: seizure of 15 diplomats, murder of an American missionary and a 300-man attack on two towns. In a murderous shootout with government troops in 1981 in which much of the M-19 high command died, more than 400 people were killed.

Liberal infighting ultimately resulted in a Conservative victory in the 1982 presidential election. The new president, Belisario Betancur, adopted a populist domestic policy to help the lower classes and a foreign policy more independent of the United States. The government persuaded some guerrillas to become part of the lawful political process.

Return to *La Violencia*

The next several administrations found themselves trying to deal with escalating violence from guerrillas, drug traffickers and right-wing paramilitary elements that was to make Colombia one of the most dangerous countries on Earth. Betancur ordered a crackdown on rampant drug trafficking in 1984. The powerful drug barons retaliated against the judiciary, and contributed heavily to the various guerrilla movements active in the country. When the president in turn authorized the extradition of the drug lords to the United States for trial, the cocaine producers hired guerrillas to wipe out the judges involved.

During the 1980s, about 100 revolutionary groups or coalitions were active, all dedicated to terrorism. In 1985, the M-19 stormed the Palace of Justice using mortar fire and grenades. Betancur ordered the army to storm the building, resulting in the deaths of 11 Supreme Court justices and several other people. After the event, one Colombian judge said, "You either have the choice of accepting a $500,000 bribe from these people or be killed." In all, 350 judges and prosecutors were killed during the 1980s. The Supreme Court ruled the extradition treaty unconstitutional.

The next president, Virgilio Barco, a Liberal (1986–90), also declared war on the drug barons. Fearful of being extradited, the drug barons paralyzed efforts to control leftist guerrillas. They bribed or killed uncounted local police and eluded the national police and army. Crusading journalists also were assassinated. When a leading Liberal candidate for president, Luis Carlos Galán, was gunned down in 1989, Barco responded by reinstating the extradition laws. The terrified justice minister resigned, going into hiding in the United States with her son.

However, the lives of *Los Extraditables* also were hell on Earth. They increasingly became interested in a trial in Colombia and the possibility that bribes and favors would produce a lenient sentence in a country-club prison. In the interim, their drug business could be operated by their lieutenants.

Disillusioned by events in the former Soviet Union and Eastern Europe, M-19 guerrillas began laying down their arms in 1989. Presidential elections were held in May 1990. After the notoriously bloodthirsty Medellín Cartel of Pablo Escobar assassinated Galán, yet another candidate, Carlos Pizarro, a former guerrilla commander, was assassinated by right-wing elements. Abandoning a promise to continue the war on drug leaders, César Gaviria of the Liberal Party won with less than a majority.

The war on the cartels was costly—there were 40 or more murders a day. The cost of having a policeman killed was $4,000 and a judge was $20,000—pocket change for the drug barons. All officials traveled in armored vehicles in motorcades. The drug cartels proclaimed a unilateral truce in mid-1990 and the level of violence abated sharply. Gaviria decreed that any drug baron who surrendered and confessed would not be extradited to the United States and would have his Colombian jail sentence cut in half. These promises proved costly.

In 1991, several kingpins, including Escobar and the Ochoa brothers, surrendered. Escobar was allowed to build his own luxurious "jail" close to Medellín, his home town. It was virtually an open house. Rated as one of the wealthiest men in the world, he enjoyed the company of 11 of his associates, claiming that the walls of the "jail" were in place to keep his enemies out. A deal obviously had been struck.

But even these pleasant conditions bored Escobar. He started running his cocaine business from the "jail," and used it as a site for the execution of real and imagined rivals. This was too much for the government and, exasperated, it sent a force to seize the "jail" and its prime occupant. But Escobar was forewarned and escaped in July 1992. He was hunted not only by federal forces, but by an impromptu group of former henchmen turned into reward-seekers (the United States and Colombia had posted $8.7 million for his capture). Loosely

Colombia

organized, they were known as *"Los Pepes"* (People Persecuted by Pablo Escobar).

Weary, he offered to surrender in 1993, but the terms were impossible. He hid for several weeks in Medellín, but was located by means of a traced telephone call. He and his bodyguard "offered resistance" and were shot dead on December 2, 1993, trying to elude pursuers on the rooftop of the building in which he had hidden. His funeral was sheer pandemonium as thousands paid him tribute; he had given generously to many people and causes. The fact was, he had a huge surplus of money that *had* to be given away.

After 1990, Cali replaced Medellín as the center of the cocaine trade with its own cartel of drug overlords, chiefly the Rodríguez Orejuela brothers. It eventually controlled 80% of the world's cocaine production and trade. Its leadership has changed several times in theory. When jailed, the drug kingpins operated from cells and their orders were carried out by a constantly changing army of lieutenants. An elaborate system of distribution and money laundering remains in place and functions smoothly. The profits are enormous, and drugs are no longer being transported by small aircraft. There are many remote airports in Mexico and Central America where a 747 can land and quickly unload at night. Mexico is the route of transport of an estimated 70% of the cocaine entering the United States.

A new prosecutor general, Gustavo de Greiff, angered both U.S. Attorney General Janet Reno and many Colombian officials by suggesting that drug legalization be given serious consideration. He met with three kingpins of the Cali Cartel to discuss a plea bargain, whereby none of them would receive more than five years in a country-club prison. U.S. and Colombian officials were dismayed. De Greiff retired in 1994 and the Supreme Court named as his replacement Alfonso Valdivieso. The new special prosecutor's tenure thus began at precisely the same time as a new president's, one who was shrouded with scandal even before taking office and who never shook it off.

The Samper Presidency

Ernesto Samper, the Liberal candidate in 1994, bragged in his campaign that he bore 11 bullet wounds from an assassination attempt by drug traffickers. Indeed, he had survived an attempt on his life in 1989 by the Medellín Cartel. He was the front-runner in the first round of voting in May 1994, and he was elected president in the June runoff by a razor-thin margin over his Conservative opponent, Andrés Pastrana.

Before his inauguration in August, however, a series of audiotapes of telephone conversations between Samper or members of his campaign staff and kingpins of the Cali Cartel were leaked to the press, which quickly dubbed them the "narco-cassettes." Thus, Samper was sworn into office under a cloud. In Sampert's first year in office, his defense minister, who had been his campaign manager, was arrested and admitted that the Samper campaign had accepted about $6 million in assistance from the Cali Cartel. Samper became a pariah to the United States, and in 1996 the Clinton Administration revoked Colombia's certification as an ally in the war against drugs.

Samper also was under pressure at home to resign because of the embarrassing revelations. When he refused, the lower house of Congress brought impeachment charges. But the House of Representatives voted decisively not to impeach; even the opposition Conservatives voted 2–1 against impeachment. Why? Some observers contended that the House of Representatives was fearful of the political turmoil that would result from removing a president. Still others believed Congress wanted to send a signal to the United States not to interfere in Colombia's internal affairs.

The infuriated U.S. ambassador still waged a war of words against Samper and the Colombian government as a whole. The United States even revoked Samper's visa to visit the United States, a stunning rebuke of a sitting chief of state.

Samper was again humiliated when a stash of heroin was discovered on the presidential aircraft just as it was about to take the president to New York to address the United Nations—on the war against drugs! Authorities impounded his plane, and he had to fly to New York on a commercial aircraft. (Three Colombian Air Force soldiers were later charged with having smuggled the heroin onto the aircraft.)

In 1997, the Clinton Administration again refused to certify Colombia as an ally in the drug war. Still, Samper hung tough, and vowed to serve until the end of his term.

Meanwhile, Valdivieso enjoyed some success in his campaign against the Cali Cartel. In 1996, the Rodríguez Orejuela brothers, Gilberto and Miguel, surrendered separately to authorities and were incarcerated in La Picota, a country-club prison, to await trial. A third Cali Cartel kingpin, José Santacruz Londoño, also surrendered but later opted to escape. He subsequently was gunned down, ostensibly by a rival drug gang. A judge sentenced Gilberto Rodríguez Orejuela to 10½ years in prison; Miguel subsequently was sentenced to terms of nine and 22 years. Both the U.S. and Colombian governments expressed outrage over the light sentences, which led to the continued decertification of Colombia as an ally in the drug war.

Another major kingpin, Helmer "Pacho" Herrera, was sentenced in 1998 to six years and eight months in prison. Herrera was murdered in his jail cell seven months later, apparently in a contract killing by a rival drug gang.

In 1997, the Clinton administration lifted its ban on military aid, suspended because of alleged human rights abuses by the army and the paramilitary groups it was accused of supporting. But the United States stipulated the $37 million could be used only for operations against guerrillas suspected of dealing with narcotics traffickers, and those operations were to be confined to an area in the south referred to as "the Box." In 1998, for the first time in three years, the

A view of Medellín

Clinton administration "certified" Colombia as an ally in the drug war.

Guerrilla Warfare Stalemates

Coupled with the Colombian government's inability to come to grips with drug trafficking has been its stalemated war against the guerrilla groups, principally the Revolutionary Armed Forces of Colombia (*FARC*) and the National Liberation Army (*ELN*). Another once-nettlesome group, *M-19*, abandoned its armed struggle to participate in the electoral system, with minimal success. The *FARC* and *ELN* continued to control vast areas of the rugged interior, but with a new twist. In the wake of the collapse of the Soviet Union, the two groups appeared to become motivated less by ideology and more by greed, and they became mercenary forces in the hire of the drug traffickers. In other words, they became common outlaws, much as Jesse James and other former Confederate guerrillas did after the U.S. Civil War.

The rebels disrupted the country's vital oil pipeline to the Caribbean coast regularly, they assassinate or kidnap local, state and national officials, and still frequently kidnap domestic and foreign businessmen or politicians for astronomical ransoms that help them purchase sophisticated arms on the international black market. However, the rebels lack the military strength to take Bogotá by storm. It has been a classic military stalemate.

In 1998, the *FARC* launched a Tet-like offensive designed to disrupt the congressional elections. The rebels inflicted the worst defeat to date on the army in 30 years. At least 83 soldiers were killed and another 61 captured.

The guerrillas and the armed forces are not the only key players in this protracted guerrilla war. Another is the various right-wing paramilitary groups that have committed numerous atrocities against civilians, mostly peasants, who are suspected of rebel sympathies. International human rights groups allege that these groups have the tacit support of the army, which the army unconvincingly continues to deny. In 1997, Carlos Castaño, leader of the most notorious of these groups, brought 5,000 paramilitary fighters together under the umbrella of the so-called United Self-Defense Forces of Colombia (*AUC*). In 1997 and 1998, the *AUC* was responsible for several civilian massacres in different departments, many of which brought reprisals from the guerrillas. By 2003, the *AUC* was believed to have 10,000 fighters under arms.

Pastrana Seeks Peace

The Liberals nominated President Samper's hand-picked candidate, former Interior Minister Horacio Serpa, for president in 1998. But Serpa's nomination threatened to split the party as anti-Samper reformers, led by Representative Ingrid Betancourt of the so-called Liberal Oxygen faction, denounced him.

The Conservatives renominated Andrés Pastrana, who narrowly lost to Samper in 1994, while retired General Harold Bedoya, whom Samper had sacked, launched an independent candidacy, as did Noemí Sanín, who had served as a cabinet minister under both Betancur and Gaviria.

In the congressional elections in March, the Liberals won 53 of the 102 Senate seats to 27 for the Conservatives and about the same proportion of seats in the 161-member House of Representatives. Turnout was a higher-than-expected 44%, despite the backdrop of a guerrilla offensive and the usual voter apathy. The maverick Betancourt won her Senate seat by the largest majority of any candidate.

On election day, Serpa emerged with a razor-thin first-place finish of 34.3% to Pastrana's 34.0%. Sanín drew 26.6%, the largest vote for an independent candidate since Rojas Pinilla in 1970. The guerrillas behaved themselves, permitting a record turnout of 10.7 million.

Four days before the June runoff, the media reported that a Pastrana representative had met with Manuel "Tirofijo" Marulanda of the *FARC*, who declared that Pastrana was the candidate with the greater chance of negotiating peace. This crippled Serpa, whose slogan was "the road to peace." In a record turnout of 12 million voters, or 59%, Pastrana won with 50.4% to Serpa's 46.5%, almost the identical margin by which Pastrana had lost to

Samper. The remaining 3.1% cast blank ballots in protest.

Pastrana, 44, took office on August 7, 1998. Son of former President Misael Pastrana, he was schooled as a lawyer but eschewed that profession in favor of broadcast journalism, which he practiced until he was elected to the Bogotá city council in the 1980s. He was elected mayor in 1988 and a senator in 1991.

Shortly after his inauguration, Pastrana met again with Marulanda. Much to the army's displeasure, Pastrana agreed to the *FARC*'s demand to demilitarize an area the size of Switzerland in Caquetá as a pre-condition to peace talks. Pastrana fired the army commander because of his opposition.

Those who had hoped for a cessation of hostilities in anticipation of the peace talks were cruelly disillusioned when the *FARC* launched its biggest push since the Caguan offensive, this time in coca-rich Vaupes Department in the southeast. The rebels overran the departmental capital, Mitu, killing 60 policemen and 10 civilians; 40 policemen were taken prisoner. The army suffered heavy casualties retaking the town. Despite the rebel offensive, the army meekly completed the demilitarization in Caquetá.

In a separate development, the U.S. Congress tripled the amount of aid to the Colombian police for its drug-fighting efforts, to $289 million. In 1999, the Clinton administration, which had not requested the dramatic increase in counter-drug aid, recertified Colombia as an ally in the drug war.

The peace talks began on schedule in January 1999, but days later the *AUC*

Plaza de Bolívar, Bogotá

Colombia

killed 130 alleged guerrilla sympathizers. Pastrana flew to Havana and met with Fidel Castro and Venezuelan President-elect Hugo Chávez to solicit their intercession with the guerrillas. Nonetheless, the *FARC* broke off the talks, demanding that Pastrana clamp down on the paramilitaries.

Peace talks and warfare dragged on simultaneously. In November 1999, government and *FARC* representatives met in Sweden, and Pastrana suggested a cease-fire for the holiday season. The *FARC* responded with another major offensive, with coordinated attacks in six departments. Still, government and *FARC* representatives met again at the Vatican in February 2000 with a representative of Pope John Paul II, with inconclusive results. That November, the *FARC* suspended the talks indefinitely, ostensibly to protest the government's failure to curtail army involvement with the paramilitaries. Pastrana met Marulanda again in the jungle and agreed to an eight-month extension of the safe haven and a purging of the army's ranks of suspected collaborators with the *AUC*.

Yet, the killing continued. Although the armed forces scored a few impressive tactical victories, they also suffered humiliating setbacks. In October 2000, 800 *FARC* guerrillas attacked a town in Urubá Department. Five Blackhawk helicopters brought elite troops to the rescue. One was shot down by ground fire, killing all 22 men on board; a second was grounded by mechanical failure; the other three reached their landing zone, but the 60 troops were annihilated after they landed. In another incident, the *FARC* "executed" 13 captured policemen The *FARC* were competing with the *AUC* to seize the moral *low* ground.

A prisoner exchange occurred in June 2001, when the *FARC* released a badly wounded police colonel and three other officers. In exchange, the government released 73 ill prisoners. The *FARC* then released 242 more prisoners, leaving only an estimated 42 still in its hands. Some hailed the exchange as the most positive product of the two and a half years of "peace" talks, while some skeptics claimed the *FARC* was only ridding itself of a logistical burden.

The public had reason to be skeptical. A report by the president's human rights office showed that in the first four months of 2001, the number of killings by non-governmental forces had actually *increased* by 75% over the previous year. Of those deaths, 529 were attributed to the *AUC*, 190 to the *FARC* and 50 to the *ELN*.

For its part, the *ELN* demanded that the government create a demilitarized zone for it in the north as it had for the *FARC* in the south, although it was more modest in its demand: "only" 2,300 square miles. Amazingly, despite the failure of the concessions to the *FARC* to bring peace, Pastrana agreed to demilitarize three municipalities in Bolívar and Antioquía departments, a total of about 1,800 square miles, to appease the *ELN*.

Government and *ELN* representatives met in Geneva in 2000, but the talks failed. Pastrana at first refused to yield to the demands for a safe haven, but after the *ELN* staged some spectacular kidnappings as a show of force, the jelly-spined Pastrana acquiesced in 2001, agreeing to a reduced area of about 1,100 square miles, still larger than Rhode Island. Residents in the area, spurred in part by the *AUC*, protested their government's surrendering them and their lands to the *ELN*'s control in exchange for—nothing.

The *AUC's* strength was estimated at 8,000 in 2001. It flouted the rules of warfare by massacring civilians to achieve its nebulous goals. One such atrocity was a raid in Cauca state in 2001 in which 32 civilians were reported killed; the arms of a 17-year-old girl were severed with a chain saw. The U.S. government formally declared the *AUC* a terrorist organization.

A milestone for the *AUC* came with Castaño's supposed resignation in 2001, ostensibly because he could not control the more bloodthirsty elements. In reality he merely yielded the *AUC*'s military command to Salvatore Mancuso, perceived as more of a hardliner than Castaño. In a 2002 interview at a hideout, Mancuso boasted that the *AUC* numbered 14,000 effectives and promised even greater bloodshed.

The *FARC* broke off talks again in early 2002. Pastrana gave them 48 hours to abandon the demilitarized zone, then dispatched troops into the area. The *FARC* responded with a 14-point negotiating plan, which Pastrana at first rejected, but then acquiesced. The *FARC* responded to the president's show of good faith by setting off bombs in a town 30 miles from Bogotá and by attacking a prison and freeing 39 rebels, killing four soldiers. Yet, Pastrana caved in again and agreed to resume cease-fire negotiations, to be brokered by the United Nations.

Events then exploded in a dramatic and violent chain reaction. In February 2002, after the *FARC* hijacked a domestic airliner and forced it to land, kidnapping a prominent senator on board, Pastrana finally realized the futility of attempting to negotiate with people of bad faith and broke off the peace talks. He sent the army into the safe haven and ordered the air force to bomb and strafe *FARC* base camps and landing strips in the zone; the military met surprisingly feeble resistance.

In response, the *FARC* kidnapped independent presidential candidate Ingrid Betancourt. She remained a hostage for six years. The *FARC* then went on a rampage of assassinations, bombings and kidnappings. It made an unsuccessful attempt to assassinate the front-running presidential candidate Alvaro Uribe, who was calling for a military victory over the *FARC* (see The Elections of 2002), and it kidnapped the governor of Antioquía. But the worst was yet to come.

In May 2002, about 1,000 *FARC* and 600 *AUC* fighters engaged in a bloody battle for the village of Bella Vista in Chocó Department. More than 500 civilians were huddled in a church for safety during the battle when a *FARC* gas-cylinder mortar shell crashed through the roof and exploded, killing and dismembering 117 people, including 40 children. The *FARC* admitted firing the mortar round but claimed the church had been hit by accident. It cynically blamed the *AUC* for the appalling death toll, saying the civilians should not have been in the town—where they lived. It took the army eight days to reach the area. The Bella Vista atrocity shocked an already numbed Colombia, as well as the international community. The U.N. human rights representative to Colombia called it a "war crime."

Pastrana asked a U.N. human rights investigating team to visit the area. In a scathing report, it concluded the *FARC* were directly responsible for the deaths, but it blamed the *AUC* for putting the civilians in harm's way and it assailed the Pastrana government for ignoring warnings the United Nations had given it that a violent confrontation was imminent. It also castigated the army for its tardiness in reaching the town. The U.S. Congress, meanwhile, demanded to know why the army, the beneficiary of so much U.S. aid, had responded so slowly, while the European Union acceded to a request from Pastrana to follow the U.S. lead in declaring the *FARC* a terrorist organization.

The guerrilla war soured Colombia's relations with neighboring Venezuela. In 2001, the government of President Hugo Chávez, long suspected of abetting the Colombian guerrillas, admitted it had captured, then released, an *ELN* member suspected in a 1999 airplane hijacking. Pastrana and Chávez met at the Venezuelan town of Puerto Ordaz. By then Venezuela had rearrested the hijack suspect; Pastrana sought his extradition. The two presidents announced that Venezuela would serve as an active partner in the negotiations between the Colombian government and the guerrillas and that their two armed forces would exchange intelligence information. However, Colombian intelligence was aware that aircraft regularly flew between Venezuela's border region and the *FARC* safe haven.

A potentially important new variable was added to this already complex equation in 2002 when the Bush administration asked Congress to approve additional military aid for Colombia. In a major policy shift, Secretary of State Colin Powell said the aid should be used against the guerrillas, not just against the drug traffickers. The United States saw the *FARC* as just another international terrorist organization to be included in its war on terrorism in the wake of the September 11, 2001, attacks. The *FARC's* alleged international links had been spotlighted when three suspected members of the Irish Republican Army were arrested in Colombia, accused of providing the *FARC* with terror training. In fact, the *FARC's* bombings in Bogotá had distinct IRA fingerprints.

"Plan Colombia"

As the peace talks and the fighting both droned on, Pastrana outlined a six-year, $7.5 billion plan to destroy the drug trade. Called *"Plan Colombia,"* it included expanded enforcement as well as incentives to farmers to plant alternative crops. The Clinton administration had asked Congress in 2000 for $1.6 billion for aid to both the Colombian police and army for their counter-drug operations. Among the hardware included for *Plan Colombia* were 30 sophisticated Blackhawk helicopters. As usual, the administration insisted that the new aid money for the army would be used only against drug traffickers, not against the guerrillas, thus seeking to perpetuate the myth that the two were distinguishable and unrelated.

The U.S. Congress approved a reduced $1.3 billion aid package, which Clinton signed into law. Colombia thus became the third-largest recipient of U.S. military aid after Israel and Egypt. Clinton met with Pastrana in Cartagena.

U.S. Special Forces, or "Green Berets," trained a special counter-drug brigade of three battalions, totaling 3,000 men. The brigade received 16 Blackhawks and 25 Super Hueys. The *FARC* denounced *Plan Colombia,* using it as a convenient pretext for scuttling the peace talks. Clearly, they were feeling the pinch.

The new U.S. president, George W. Bush, upped the ante for *Plan Colombia*. In 2001, Congress approved an additional $676 million to battle the Colombian drug trade, a 50% increase. With all that money, some of it was bound to go bad. In 2002, the U.S. Congress partially suspended further aid for the drug war when Colombian media and the U.S. Embassy reported that $2 million had disappeared. Six officers of the national police's anti-drug unit were fired, and the commander himself resigned.

A major event in the drug war occurred in 2001 when Fabio Ochoa, an alleged kingpin of the old Medellín cartel, was

Former President Andrés Pastrana

extradited to the United States. It was a major departure for Colombia, which had not extradited such a notorious suspect in more than 10 years. Ochoa was convicted in Miami in 2003.

According to the U.N. Drug Control Program, the number of hectares under coca cultivation in Colombia declined by 11% from 2000 to 2001, to 145,000, and by another 30% in 2002. There were even greater inroads under the new government of President Alvaro Uribe, who took office in August 2002.

The Elections of 2002

The hapless Pastrana's Conservative Party lost badly in the departmental and municipal elections in 2000, a bellwether for the presidential contest in May 2002. The Conservatives failed to win a single governorship, while the Liberals and independents each won 15. The campaigns were marked by the usual violence and intimidation; more than 20 candidates were killed either by guerrillas or paramilitaries.

In the presidential race, the Liberals again nominated Horacio Serpa. The Conservatives nominated Juan Camilo Restrepo, who had been Pastrana's finance minister. Once again, there were several independent candidates, seemingly assuring the race would be thrown into a run-off again: Noemí Sanín, who polled over a fourth of the vote in 1998; Senator Ingrid Betancourt, a prominent Liberal renegade who had supported Pastrana in 1998; and Álvaro Uribe, a former Liberal governor of Antioquía, candidate of a movement called *Primero Colombia,* who pledged to get tough with the guerrillas. Rounding out the field was Luis Eduardo Garzón

of the far-left Social and Political Front. It looked like Colombian politics as usual—but this election would not be usual.

As the peace talks droned on and *FARC* outrages continued, Uribe suddenly broke from the pack by promising to double the size of the military and seek an all-out victory over the guerrillas. His campaign slogan was *"mano firme, corazón grande"* (firm hand, big heart). After the peace talks collapsed and Betancourt was kidnapped, he soared to 59% in the polls.

In the March congressional elections, the Liberals retained their majorities in both houses, but at least 27 new senators publicly declared their support for Uribe (the *AUC* claimed that 35% of the new Congress were its sympathizers). Voters clearly were in a get-tough mood.

Restrepo dropped out, leaving the Conservative Party without a presidential candidate for the first time since it was founded in 1849.

Uribe's tough anti-*FARC* rhetoric was not lost on the guerrillas. They attempted to assassinate him by setting off a remote-controlled bomb under a bridge on a highway near Barranquilla as his motorcade passed. He escaped unhurt, but three bystanders were killed and 15 injured. For Uribe, the attack was *déjà vu;* in 1983, his father had been killed when he resisted a *FARC* kidnap attempt.

The attempt on Uribe's life only boosted his standing in the polls. A desperate Serpa alleged that Uribe was drawing support from the right-wing paramilitaries; Uribe denied it.

The results on May 26 were a veritable landslide, not just a mandate in favor of the hawk, Uribe, over the dove, Serpa, but a repudiation of the guerrillas. A total of 11.2 million Colombians voted, a turnout of 46.3%. Uribe scored a decisive first-round victory with 5.7 million votes, or 52.9%; Serpa received 3.5 million, or 31.7%. Garzón was a distant third, followed closely by Sanín; Betancourt, still in *FARC* captivity, was a poor fifth.

The president-elect announced he still favored a U.N.-brokered peace with the guerrillas but that he was willing to engage in peace talks with the paramilitaries. He promised to continue the war against drugs, to reduce corruption and increase efficiency in government, and to increase social spending.

A Harvard-educated lawyer, Uribe, 50, had a positive record as an efficient governor of Antioquía. He met with President Bush in Washington and other senior officials and in New York with U.N. Secretary-General Kofi Annan. Back home, he advocated a constitutional amendment to allow him to declare a state of emergency to deal with the guerrillas, which gave chills to human rights advocates.

Colombia

Uribe Gets Tough

Uribe was inaugurated on August 7, 2002—indoors for security reasons. Pastrana, an Andean version of Neville Chamberlain, left office a pitiful failure, with an approval rating of 20%. The *FARC* launched a mortar attack near the National Palace in an attempt to disrupt the inauguration, killing 19 people and injuring 60.

Uribe soon proved as tough as Pastrana had spineless. He declared a 90-day state of emergency to crack down on the guerrillas, the paramilitaries and the narcotraffickers, though human rights advocates feared an erosion of civil liberties. Roadblocks, ID checks and warrantless arrests became commonplace; some areas were placed under martial law. The state of emergency was twice extended, until May 2003.

Uribe proposed equipping 1 million citizens with two-way radios so they could report guerrilla activity; recruiting for volunteers was brisk. Uribe also introduced an emergency war tax to pay for his promised military buildup. In Antioquía, he gave local military commanders a dressing down—on national television—for failing to take action against reported guerrilla activity in the area. He ordered the training of young farmers to create a rural militia that numbered 12,000.

Uribe visited Washington again to lobby for $450 million in military and counternarcotics aid, assuring liberal U.S. senators he would respect human rights. He visited again with Annan, who admonished him to clean up Colombia's human rights act. Bush's State Department certified that Colombia passed muster under a U.S. law that denies aid to countries that violate human rights, and it released the first $41.6 million in aid. Secretary of State Powell visited Bogotá in 2002 and sent mixed signals, praising Uribe's get-tough policy while warning him that the United States would not tolerate human rights abuses.

Uribe's policy was not to negotiate with the *FARC*, the *ELN* or the *AUC* as long as they engaged in combat, but he held out the promise of renewed talks to any group that declared a unilateral cease-fire. It paid off; the *AUC* declared a cease-fire in December 2002.

The *AUC* leadership felt the heat not only of the army and the *FARC*, but of the U.S. Justice Department, which unsealed indictments against Castaño and Mancuso in 2002, alleging they were instrumental in the shipment of 17 tons of cocaine to the United States since 1997 and calling them a threat to U.S. national security.

Talks between the government and the *AUC* broke down in 2003 after the *AUC* accused the army of "massacring" 12 *AUC* members. The army said they were killed in an ambush. The *AUC* suffered another blow when the army captured one of its most notorious commanders, Said Sepúlveda, believed responsible for the deaths of 450 people. Mancuso announced in July 2003 the *AUC* would lay down its arms because of the army's successes against the *FARC*, promising a complete demobilization by the end of 2005.

In February 2003, the *FARC* set off a powerful car bomb that gutted a 10-story social club in Bogotá frequented by the capital's elite. The death toll of 35 included six children; another 168 people were injured. It was the worst act of terrorism in Bogotá since the bloody days of Pablo Escobar, and it sparked national outrage.

Another *FARC* atrocity turned into an international incident when a small counterdrug aircraft carrying four American "contractors" for the U.S. Southern Command and one Colombian crashed behind *FARC* lines. The rebels apparently executed the Colombian sergeant and one American and took the other three Americans prisoner. The Colombian government bristled, however, when the Bush administration sent a reported 150 troops to search for the three Americans, calling it an interference in Colombia's internal affairs. It was an incredible windfall for the *FARC*, which announced it was holding the Americans as "prisoners of war" and said they would be released in exchange for dozens of rebel prisoners. They were eventually rescued by Colombian special forces in 2008.

In an even bolder act, the *FARC* executed 10 hostages, including former Antioquía Governor Guillermo Gaviria, who had been kidnapped in 1997, when the army attempted a rescue mission in 2003.

The government claimed a major political victory over the *FARC* in 2003 when Rafael Rojas, commander of the *FARC*'s 46th Front, surrendered and, in a nationally televised event with Uribe, urged his former comrades to do the same.

A low-ranking judge created an international incident in 2002 when he ordered the release of Gilberto and Miguel Rodríguez Orejuela, the imprisoned leaders of the Cali cocaine cartel, after they had served only about half their terms. Uribe appealed their release, and another judge ordered that Miguel, 59, be retained in prison, but agreed that Gilberto, 63, should be released for "good behavior." This infuriated Uribe—and U.S. authorities who had long sought the brothers' extradition. He was rearrested in 2003 on an outstanding charge that he shipped 330 pounds of cocaine to the United States—in 1995. Both were extradited, Gilberto in 2004 and Miguel in 2005. Both were convicted and sentenced to 30 years, which they are serving in separate prisons.

In 2004, the *FARC*'s Ricardo Palmera, alias Simón Trinidad, was arrested in Ecuador, the highest-ranking *FARC* leader to be captured up to then.

As a sign that Uribe's crackdown was having an effect, the *FARC* and the *ELN* in 2003 re-established an alliance that had dissolved nearly 20 years before and declared they would engage in joint military actions. But the army continued to win victories in the field.

Security forces also continued to inflict losses on the paramilitaries. In 2003, 800 *AUC* effectives laid down their arms in Medellín, and in 2004, the *AUC* signed an agreement with the government's negotiator to move into a 230-square-mile safe haven. The inducement was a generous amnesty and even cash rewards; human rights groups protested that some *AUC* leaders should be tried for war crimes. The U.S., meanwhile, wanted some extradited for drug trafficking. Uribe compromised and agreed that *AUC* members could be tried for atrocities before a special war crimes tribunal and would face five to 10 years in prison. He did not agree to extradite them.

Castaño mysteriously vanished in 2004 and was believed killed by a rival faction that opposed demobilization. Former *AUC* leader Carlos Mauricio García, who had opposed the *AUC*'s involvement in drug trafficking, was gunned down in Bogotá in 2004.

Defense Minister Jorge Alberto Uribe, no relation to the president, announced that 16,000 members of the *FARC*, *ELN* or *AUC* had been killed or captured or had surrendered during 2003. Moreover, the murder rate in 2003, though still high by most international standards, was the lowest since 1986. By 2006, it was lower still.

A group of 80 human rights organizations issued a scathing report in 2003 titled "The Authoritarian Curse," which accused Uribe of sanctioning human rights abuses and of undermining civil liberties. Uribe accused his critics of being sympathetic to "terrorists." He defended his approach in a speech to the U.N. General Assembly.

In its 2004 annual report, the Office of the U.N. High Commissioner for Human Rights called the human rights situation in Colombia "critical," but praised the government for restoring law and order in wide areas. It also assailed the guerrillas and the paramilitaries. Jan Egeland, U.N. under-secretary for humanitarian affairs, called the situation in Colombia a "humanitarian catastrophe." Egeland noted that the number of displaced persons had risen to 1 million, third highest in the world behind Congo and Sudan; by 2006, the number of displaced persons was second only to Sudan, some 2.5 million.

A major *FARC* leader, Ricardo Palmera, was extradited to the United States in 2005

Santuario (sanctuary) de las Lajas in Nariño State in southwestern Colombia, partially built into the rock of the mountain

Courtesy: Embassy of Colombia

Colombia

to face drug charges. In 2006, Ramón Isaza, head of the *AUC*'s Medio Magdalena Bloc, and 1,000 of his operatives laid down their arms, bringing to 22,000 the number of paramilitaries who had accepted amnesty.

Colombian authorities discovered a cache of 13.8 tons of cocaine worth $400 million in a wooden underground chamber near the Pacific coast in 2005, the largest seizure of cocaine ever on Colombian soil. Some of the cocaine belonged to the *FARC* and some to the *AUC*; the two battlefield rivals had actually contracted with the same trafficker!

The already tense relations with Venezuela over Chávez's alleged support for the guerrillas were strained further when Colombian peasants reported that Venezuelan air force jets and helicopters crossed the border in March 2003, providing close air support for *FARC* rebels battling paramilitaries in North Santander Department. Uribe confronted Venezuela with the evidence. He and Chávez met face-to-face in Puerto Ordaz, Venezuela, but the meeting produced little of substance.

Relations grew tense again in 2004 after Colombia announced the capture of Rodrigo Granda, the *FARC*'s foreign affairs representative. Colombia claimed Granda had been arrested in Cúcuta, a Colombian town near the border. Soon, however, Colombian and Venezuelan newspapers reported that Granda had, in fact, been abducted in Caracas by Colombian agents. Uribe confirmed the reports. Chávez denounced the violation of Venezuelan sovereignty, canceled bilateral trade agreements, recalled his ambassador and demanded that Uribe apologize, without offering an explanation of why or how Granda was in Venezuela in the first place and was given Venezuelan citizenship. Uribe did not apologize. The two presidents held an amiable, even jovial meeting in Santa Marta, Colombia, in December 2005, during which Uribe acknowledged that several Colombian officers had been conspiring with anti-Chávez Venezuelan officers and vowed to prevent such intrigue.

Uribe's Second Term

Uribe's approval rating soared to 80% in 2003, and he introduced a constitutional amendment that would permit him to run for re-election in 2006, but the Senate rejected it. He tried again. A poll indicated that 72% of Colombians favored it, and both major parties endorsed it. It passed and was submitted to the Constitutional Court, which approved it in 2005.

A faction of pro-Uribe Liberals defected and formed the Social National Unity Party, nicknamed the "U Party." Traditional Liberals said it smacked of *personalismo*. The old Conservative Party by then was also allied with Uribe's movement. In 2006 congressional elections, Uribe's party or its allies won roughly two thirds of the 102 Senate seats and a majority in the 163-member House. Six new members were suspected of having paramilitary links.

The pro-Uribe parties nominated him for president under an umbrella coalition called *Colombia Primero* (Colombia First). The Liberals again nominated the two-time loser, Horacio Serpa. The Democratic Pole fielded Senator Carlos Gaviria, 69, no relation to the former president. Antanas Mockus, a flamboyant former Bogotá mayor, launched an independent bid. There were three minor candidates.

There was little suspense as to the outcome. The major surprises were the size of Uribe's mandate, the strong showing by Gaviria, and the drop in support for Serpa. Voter turnout on May 28 was normal—45.1%. The results:

Santiago's outlet to the sea, the port city of Valparaiso

134

Colombia

Uribe	7,363,421	62.2%
Gaviria	2,609,412	22.0%
Serpa	1,401,173	11.8%
Mockus	146,540	1.2%
Others	87,126	.8%

Uribe's unprecedented landslide sent a clear signal to the guerrillas, the paramilitaries and the drug traffickers: Uribe had the people's support for his no-nonsense approach. His victory was also celebrated in Washington; Uribe was about the only friend the United States had left on the continent. He was inaugurated for his second term on August 7, 2006.

Uribe found himself *entre la espada y la pared,* trying to get the disbanded paramilitaries to fulfill their promises to cooperate with investigators and prosecutors in exchange for leniency and to avoid extradition to the U.S., while at the same time placating domestic and international human rights advocates who believed he was being *too* lenient with alleged war criminals.

Uribe stuck with his get-tough policy on the paramilitaries. Although 31,000 of them had laid down their arms by the end of 2006, they remained politically influential. In 2007, eight members of Congress were arrested for alleged paramilitary ties. One, Senator Alvaro Araújo, was the brother of Uribe's foreign minister, María Consuelo Araújo. She resigned. Also embarrassing to Uribe was the arrest of his intelligence chief.

But while Uribe's supporters argued that the arrests showed the government was serious about exposing the paramilitaries' connections no matter where they led, domestic and foreign skeptics, including the new Democratic-controlled U.S. Congress, countered that there were still too many unanswered questions about the president's own possible complicity.

In March 2007, President Bush visited Bogotá, the first sitting U.S. president to visit the capital since Ronald Reagan in 1982. Thousands protested the visit. Uribe visited Bush a month later at Camp David, where they discussed military aid, Senate ratification of a proposed bilateral FTA signed in 2006 and extension of the preferential tariff agreement under which Colombia has exported hundreds of millions of dollars worth of fresh flowers and other non-traditional products. But a hostile Democratic Congress, leery of both Uribe's possible ties to paramilitaries and the 1,300 trade unionists murdered in Colombia over the past 10 years, delayed action. Uribe hired a public relations firm to lobby Democratic congressmen.

After a two-year trial that riveted the attention of the country, Alberto Santofimio, a one-time Liberal Party luminary, was convicted in 2007 of conspiring with the Medellín Cartel in the 1989 assassination

Former President Álvaro Uribe Vélez

of Luis Carlos Galán, his rival for the Liberal presidential nomination. Santofimio was sentenced to 24 years.

Ecuador Raid and 'Parapolitics'

Colombian warplanes bombed a *FARC* camp just across the border in Ecuador in March 2008, killing 22 guerrillas, among them Luis Edgar Devia, better known by his *nom de guerre,* Raúl Reyes, one of the *FARC*'s seven-member general secretariat and its international press spokesman. Colombian troops entered Ecuador to recover Reyes' body and three of his laptop computers, which proved an intelligence bonanza.

Ecuadorian President Rafael Correa ordered 3,200 troops to the border and broke diplomatic relations. Chávez bombastically ordered 10 battalions to the Colombian border. He also broke diplomatic relations, as did Nicaraguan President Daniel Ortega. Open warfare appeared imminent. Correa called on the Organization of American States to condemn Colombia's raid. The OAS responded with a lukewarm resolution labeling the raid a violation of Ecuadorian sovereignty and territorial integrity. This did not mollify Correa. The OAS sent a delegation headed by Secretary-General José Miguel Insulza to Colombia and Ecuador to investigate the raid and to defuse the crisis.

Colombia then announced that the captured laptops showed Correa had received a $20,000 campaign contribution from the *FARC;* that Chávez had given the *FARC* $300 million, proving him a liar; and that the *FARC* were seeking the technology to build a radioactive "dirty bomb." Uribe vowed to take the evidence against Chávez before an international court; in Washington, Bush declared his support for Uribe and denounced Chávez's provocations.

Uribe, Correa and Chávez met in Santo Domingo, Dominican Republic. After a contentious exchange between Uribe and Correa, the three presidents signed a declaration ending the crisis. Uribe, in effect, apologized and said he would never again violate a neighbor's sovereignty; Correa and Chávez accepted the apology and agreed to work together with Colombia to control the *FARC.*

The *FARC* leadership received a series of other blows in 2008. Another member of its secretariat, Iván Ríos (real name Manuel de Jesús Muñoz) was murdered by his bodyguard, apparently to collect the $2.7 million reward; he did. It suffered a third blow when Nelly Ávila Moreno, also known as Karina, a senior *FARC* commander in Antioquia and the suspected mastermind of the murder of Uribe's father in 1983, accepted Uribe's invitation to turn herself in. She urged other rebels to follow her example.

Finally, the *FARC* announced that Marulanda (real name Pedro Antonio Marín), had died of a heart attack in a hideout in March. His successor was Guillermo León Sáez, who goes by the *nom de guerre* Alfonso Cano.

Uribe's popularity soared even higher as a result of the border incursion, but he was soon embarrassed by growing evidence of involvement by members of his party—and his family—with the paramilitaries. The media dubbed the growing scandal "parapolitics." Uribe's second cousin, Mario Uribe, resigned as Senate president in 2007; 30 other members of Congress faced charges of paramilitary links. Mario Uribe was arrested for questioning about an alleged meeting with the *AUC*'s Mancuso in 2002. He spent only four months in jail before a prosecutor released him for lack of evidence.

The "parapolitics" scandal did little to persuade the Democratic-controlled U.S. Congress to look kindly upon Uribe. The U.S. House of Representatives voted to *cut* military aid to Colombia from $590 million to $530 million. In early 2008, Secretary of State Condoleezza Rice brought a delegation of nine Democratic congressmen to Colombia in an attempt to overcome opposition to the proposed bilateral FTA. Both Democratic candidates for president, Hillary Rodham Clinton and Barack Obama, as well as House Speaker Nancy Pelosi, all said they opposed approval of the FTA. Clinton was embarrassed when it was revealed that one of her campaign staffers had been a paid lobbyist for the Colombian government.

The plight of the 750-odd hostages still held by the *FARC* garnered greater international attention in 2007 and 2008, especially the fate of Ingrid Betancourt, who holds dual Colombian and French citizen-

Colombia

ship and was reported to be gravely ill with hepatitis and suffering from chronic depression. French President Nicholas Sarkozy declared Betancourt's release a top priority. In 2007, he persuaded Uribe to release Rodrigo Granda, the *FARC* leader whose arrest in Caracas had provoked the 2004 diplomatic crisis, in an attempt to secure her release. Granda went to Cuba, but the *FARC* still did not release Betancourt. Sarkozy dispatched a humanitarian delegation to Colombia in 2008 to persuade the *FARC* to release her or to at least allow her to be treated by a physician. The mission failed.

The world was electrified on July 2, 2008, by the stunning news that Colombian intelligence agents posing as *FARC* guerrillas and as members of an international humanitarian organization had rescued Betancourt, the three American contractors captured in 2003 and 11 other hostages. The commandos flew into the *FARC* camp by helicopter with a cover story they had orders from the new *FARC* commander, Alfonso Cano, to move the hostages to another camp. The bluff worked, and once airborne the commandos overpowered the two *FARC* guards assigned to accompany the hostages. Not a shot was fired.

The 'False Positives Scandal'

The Defense Ministry did not bask for long in the international glow of the audacious rescue. In October 2008, media reports in Colombia and the U.S. alleged the army commander, General Mario Montoya, had practiced a system of officer promotions based on a unit's body counts, which in turn had led to innocent civilians being killed on the pretext that they were guerrillas.

The claiming of civilian bodies as guerrillas killed in combat became known internationally as the "false-positives scandal." In one controversial incident, 11 young unemployed men from the Bogota slum of Soacha were recruited for supposed well-paying jobs, then taken to North Santander Department and murdered. Their bodies were found in a mass grave. A U.N. investigator called the murders of civilians by the army "widespread and systematic." Amnesty International claimed security forces carried out 330 "extrajudicial executions" in 2007, a one-third increase over previous years.

Uribe sacked three generals and 24 other officers or sergeants and disavowed the promotion policy. A CIA memo leaked to the press alleged that Montoya had followed the promotion policy when he was a brigade commander. Montoya resigned and was replaced by General Freddy Padilla, who himself was tainted by suspected human rights abuses. Uribe

ordered the army and police to undertake investigations. The U.S. suspended military aid to selected brigades. (U.S. military aid to Colombia totaled $615 million in 2007.) By mid-2009, 22 soldiers had been arrested in connection with the false-positives scandal and almost 1,200 were under investigation. By mid-2012, the attorney general was investigating 1,700 cases. In 2012, Congress passed a constitutional amendment that crimes against humanity committed by members of the security forces would be tried in civilian courts, not by courts-martial.

The Administrative Directorate of Security *(DAS)*, the Colombian equivalent of the FBI, became the target of an investigation after allegations that it had illegally wiretapped politicians of both Uribe's coalition and the opposition, judges and journalists. Uribe disavowed knowledge of the wiretaps. The deputy director of the *DAS* resigned, and in 2009 Uribe transferred responsibility for legal wiretaps to the National Police.

In January 2009, the enigmatic *FARC* set off a bomb at a Blockbuster store in Bogota that killed two people, then released a total of six of their remaining 700 hostages. Among those were Alan Jara, governor of Meta Department when he was abducted in 2001.

The *FARC*'s strength was believed to have diminished from 20,000 to about 8,000.

Uribe and Obama

Uribe met with his new U.S. counterpart, Barack Obama, at the Summit of the Americas in Trinidad and Tobago in 2009, and it soon became apparent Uribe would enjoy as close a relationship with Obama as he had with Bush—despite Obama's opposition to the bilateral FTA. Uribe visited Washington, ostensibly to advance the stalled FTA, and the two countries announced they were discussing a defense cooperation agreement (DCA) giving the United States access to several Colombian bases to make up for Ecuador's termination of the base agreement at Manta (see Ecuador).

The reports created a firestorm in Colombia and abroad. Both conservative and left-wing members of the Colombian Congress voiced concern about a supposed influx of U.S. soldiers, while every president in South America expressed opposition. Chávez, of course, said "the winds of war" had been unleashed. He reduced trade with Colombia by 70% in reprisal.

The two sides announced the details of the 10-year agreement that August. There was a hastily called summit of the South American Union of Nations (*UNASUR*) in Bariloche, Argentina, which Uribe did not

attend. The DCA was signed in October. Under the terms, U.S. personnel would utilize three Colombian air bases, Palanquero, Apjay and Malambo; two naval bases, including Malaga; and two army bases. It stipulated that U.S. access would be limited to drug interdiction and support for Colombian forces against guerrillas, but that U.S. forces could not act against a third country. It continued the current cap on U.S. personnel at 600 military and 800 civilian contractors.

The base pact, among other issues, led to a shouting match between Uribe and Chávez during the periodic Rio Pact summit in 2010 in Cancun, Mexico. Chávez shouted *"Véte al carajo!"*—somewhat stronger language than "Go to hell"—at Uribe and was about to stomp out of the meeting, when Uribe shouted for Chávez to "be a man" and defend his arguments.

The issue became moot in August 2010, when the Constitutional Court ruled the base deal with the U.S. unconstitutional.

The Elections of 2010

Whether or not Uribe would be allowed to run for a third term in 2010, and if he would run if he could, was the country's major guessing game. Defense Minister Juan Manuel Santos, with Uribe's blessing, resigned to run for president in the event Uribe could not or would not. Uribe still enjoyed a phenomenal approval rating of 70%.

In August 2009, the Senate voted 56-2 to call a referendum on whether the constitution should be amended to permit a third consecutive term. The Chamber of Representatives followed suit, 85–5. The opposition boycotted both votes. In February 2010, the Constitutional Court, composed of Uribe appointees, voted 7–2 that a third term would be an unconstitutional threat to democracy. It barred Uribe and future presidents not just from a third consecutive term but from a third term, *period*.

Santos put his campaign in high gear as the candidate of Uribe's U Party. The scion of the prominent Liberal family that owns the newspaper *El Tiempo* and grand-nephew of President Eduardo Santos (1938–40), Santos studied at Harvard, Tufts, the University of Kansas and the London School of Economics.

Eight other candidates entered, but only four had a serious chance of making it into a runoff: Antanas Mockus, the flamboyant two-time mayor of Bogota, who campaigned on a moderate populist platform; Noemí Sanín, a Conservative who ran a strong independent campaign for president in 1998; Germán Vargas of the Radical Change party, which is pro-Uribe; and Gustavo Petro, a 39-year-old left-wing senator of the Alternative Pole party, who had belonged to the M-19 guerrilla group. Betancourt decided not to run. For the first time in memory, the Liberals fielded no candidate.

As always, the congressional elections in March 2010 proved a bellwether for the presidential election. The U Party won 25.2% of the votes and 27 of the 102 Senate seats, up from 20. The Conservatives, part of Uribe's coalition, finished second with 20.6% of the vote and 23 seats, a gain of four. Overall, Uribe's coalition had a strengthened Senate majority. In the Chamber of Representatives, the U Party won 47 of the 166 seats, the Conservatives 38, and Radical Change, 15, again, an absolute coalition majority. The Liberals won 37, the *PIN* 12 and Alternative Pole, only four.

The first round on May 30 quickly narrowed to Santos and Mockus. The two men, both 58, held similar beliefs except that Mockus advocated conciliation with Venezuela while Santos favored Uribe's confrontational approach. In a new twist for Colombian politics, Santos' official website had links to his Facebook and Twitter pages. Santos' strategy was to wrap himself in the mantle of the still-popular Uribe, which paid off. Polls had showed the two men in a statistical dead heat, but an unusually high turnout of 49% surprised everyone. The results:

Santos	6,802,043	46.7%
Mockus	3,134,222	21.5%
Vargas	1,473,627	10.11%
Petro	1,331,267	9.14%
Sanin	893,819	6.13%

Both major guerrilla groups endeavored to disrupt the June 20 runoff. The *FARC* killed three soldiers and the *ELN* killed seven policemen. Still, more than 13.3 million Colombians turned out, The results:

Santos	9,028,943	69.1%
Mockus	3,587,975	27.5%

Santos declared that under his administration, Colombia "will be an ally of all the countries in the world." Congratulations poured in from the presidents of Brazil, Spain, the United States and other countries—but his victory was greeted by stony silence from Venezuela and Ecuador.

Santos Changes Course

Between the election and Santos' inauguration on August 7, relations with Venezuela deteriorated further when Colombia released tangible evidence, including

The headline in *El Tiempo* on June 21, 2010, quotes President-elect Juan Manuel Santos, declaring, "The hour of unity has arrived."

Colombia

**President
Juan Manuel Santos**

videos, that 1,500 *FARC* guerrillas were housed in 87 camps in Venezuela. Chávez broke off diplomatic relations.

As the first indication that Santos' governing style would be different from Uribe's, Santos dispatched his incoming foreign minister, María Ángela Holguín—who had resigned as Uribe's ambassador to the U.N. over policy differences—to invite Ecuador's Correa to attend his inauguration as a first step toward patching up old differences. He extended a similar invitation to Chávez.

Correa accepted, and was one of 17 heads of state to attend. Several U.S. congressmen attended, significant because of the long-stalled FTA. Chávez declined, although he delegated his foreign minister, Nicolás Maduro, to represent him and to carry a "message of love and solidarity."

In his inaugural address, Santos distanced himself further from Uribe by saying his main focus would be on reducing unemployment and poverty. "I can now have different priorities, and mine are not security," Santos said. "They are more to do with jobs and the fight against poverty. We have the second highest unemployment rate in Latin America, poverty of roughly 45%, extreme poverty of around 17%. Those numbers are too high." He also boldly promised to restore land titles to small farmers who'd been forced out by guerrillas and paramilitaries, a volatile issue. He told the guerrillas, "The door to dialogue is not closed."

Santos' inauguration was held in the main plaza before 5,000 people—although 60,000 troops and police provided security. The *FARC* had plotted to disrupt the inauguration but were thwarted.

Santos and Chávez met in Santa Marta, Colombia, three days after the inauguration—Santos' 59th birthday. Chávez continued to insist he was not supporting the guerrillas, but he restored diplomatic rela-

tions and lifted the trade sanctions he had imposed over the U.S. base deal. The two presidents have met several more times over the ensuing four years, and relations have warmed.

The *FARC* responded to Santos' offer of dialogue by launching the worst series of attacks in months, which left about 40 police and soldiers dead. If it was a test of the new president's backbone, they did not have to wait long for an answer. Santos ordered a bombing raid and commando attack on a *FARC* base camp that September that killed the *FARC's* military strategist, Victor Julio Suárez, known by the *nom de guerre* Mono Jojoy, a member of the seven-member governing secretariat. He was behind some of the worst violence over the past two decades, including the kidnapping of Betancourt. His death was greeted by the same jubilation in Colombia that Osama bin Laden's death later was in the U.S. Like the 2008 raid into Ecuador, this raid also resulted in the seizure of laptops and memory sticks that proved an intelligence bonanza.

In March 2011, another high-ranking *FARC* operative, Oliver Solarte, was killed in a raid in Putumayo department. Solarte was one echelon below the secretariat and was the *FARC's* liaison with Mexican drug traffickers.

The ongoing battle against the paramilitaries also scored a major victory on Christmas Day 2010 when a police operation resulted in the death of Pedro Guerrero, alias *"El Cuchillo"* (The Knife), leader of a paramilitary group with major cocaine operations and responsible for widespread killings.

Santos visited Washington in April 2011 to make another attempt to conclude the FTA. This time, President Obama suddenly reversed the position he had taken as a candidate in 2008 and declared that approval of the FTA was "vital" for U.S. economic recovery. Yet, union organizations in both Colombia and the United States, and Obama's own party in Congress, continued to oppose it. Democrats control the Senate, while Republicans, who have long favored the FTA, had won control of the House. Obama's support proved the difference. On October 12, 2011, the FTA passed Congress with votes of 262–167 in the House and 66–33 in the Senate. It took effect on May 15, 2012—five and a half years after it had been signed. It is expected to boost bilateral trade by $1.1 billion.

In November 2011 *FARC* leader Alfonso Cano was killed in an army attack on a guerrilla base camp in Cauca department. It was the first time in the *FARC's* 47-year history that one of its leaders had died of unnatural causes. As with El Cuchillo's death, the country celebrated the news,

and Santos' approval rating jumped up from an already phenomenal 79% to 83%. The *FARC* named a hardliner, Rodrigo Londoño Echeverri, who boasts two *noms de guerre*, Timochenko and Timoleón Jiménez, to succeed Cano in January 2013. Jiménez, 54, joined the *FARC* in the early 1990s and, according to the U.S. State Department, was responsible for its lucrative cocaine operations.

Santos then found himself challenged on a different front. Hundreds, perhaps thousands of supposedly demobilized right-wing paramilitaries regrouped into an organized, well-armed criminal entity with a nebulous political message that calls itself the *Urabeños*. When one of its leaders was killed in a firefight with police on January 1, 2012, the *Urabeños* called for a two-day general strike in Santa Marta, threatening Mafia-like reprisals for businesses that didn't comply. They burned 11 commercial vehicles for violating the strike. Police reportedly arrested 1,000 *Urabeños* in 2011, but they are believed to have another 1,600 under arms. Santos has refused to negotiate with them.

He faced a potentially more serious adversary in October 2012 when he underwent surgery for prostate cancer.

After 11 years of deliberation, the International Court of Justice in The Hague shocked Colombia on November 19, 2012, by ruling in favor of Nicaragua on its maritime territorial claims that affect several uninhabited but fish-rich Colombian-held islands in the Caribbean. Although the ICJ upheld Colombian sovereignty over San Andrés and some tiny uninhabited islands, the granting of a 200-mile maritime exclusion zone effectively cut the islands off from Colombia. It also revokes Colombia's traditional rights to fish in those waters. There is no appeal from the IJC, and 82% of the Colombian public wanted Santos to refuse to accept the ruling. Santos met with his Nicaraguan counterpart Daniel Ortega in Mexico on December 1, who assured Santos he would continue to respect Colombia's historic rights of access. The two men disavowed any military action.

Santos and Chávez met again in December 2011 and signed several bilateral agreements. Chávez apparently acceded to Santos' behind-the-scenes requests, in contrast with Uribe's public demands, to expel the guerrillas from Venezuela. A new, uncertain chapter in bilateral relations began with Chávez's death in March 2013. Santos and his wife attended the funeral.

A protest by farmers demanding better price supports for their products escalated into a rampage of violence in Bogotá in August 2012 as apparent criminal elements capitalized on the protests to engage in looting and vandalism. The violence spread to other locations around the country, leaving two people dead and dozens injured. Santos ordered 50,000 troops to patrol the capital.

New Talks With the *FARC*

The *FARC*'s new commander, Timoleón Jiménez, sent two open letters to Santos offering to reopen peace talks, and in February 2012 he made the dramatic announcement that the *FARC* would abandon kidnapping and release the 10 remaining captive members of the security forces. In May, the *FARC* also released a French journalist.

Santos was cool at first to the *FARC*'s overtures, calling them "insufficient," while Jiménez scotched any suggestion that his willingness to negotiate indicated the *FARC* were about to surrender.

The army scored another well-publicized victory in an operation in Meta department in March 2012, killing 35 *FARC* guerrillas. The *FARC* were believed then to have no more than 9,200 guerrillas under arms, compared with 20,000 before Uribe's crackdown. Both the *FARC* and *ELN* were continuing to attack oil pipelines and disrupt oil production.

Then, in August 2012, Santos revealed that secret talks had been held with the *FARC* and that the first face-to-face peace negotiations since 2002 would soon commence. The two sides began talks in October in Oslo, Norway, and they have continued since then in Havana. Santos made clear from the start that he was no Pastrana, and outlined several conditions: There would be no safe haven, military operations against the *FARC* would continue, the *FARC*'s long-standing political demands would not be on the bargaining table and the talks' ultimate goal would be peace, followed by the *FARC*'s incorporation into the democratic process. The *FARC* agreed.

The two sides reached an accord in May 2013 on rural development to combat poverty. An impatient and politically nervous Santos imposed a deadline of November 2013, six months before the next presidential election, for a final agreement to be signed. But *FARC* negotiator Marco León rejected that deadline, saying Santos should place a higher priority on peace than on his personal political ambitions.

The public grew impatient with the talks, too. Tens of thousands of Colombians, representing both sides, staged street demonstrations in April 2013 to show their support for a successful outcome. Santos joined them; Uribe did not. In August, rebels killed 13 soldiers.

The two sides agreed on a second issue in November, the incorporation of the

FARC into the political process. To do this, the government agreed to gerrymander some congressional districts in *FARC* areas to give the rebels an electoral advantage. Uribe and others denounced the deal. Still being negotiated by mid-2014 were the far more difficult issues of disengaging the *FARC* from drug trafficking and whether the *FARC* leaders could be prosecuted for past crimes or would receive amnesty.

The glacial pace of the peace talks became a political football as Colombia approached the congressional and presidential elections of March and May 2014 (see The Elections of 2014). Santos had gambled his political future on the success of the peace talks. Like Pastrana before him, he placed his hopes in the good faith of the *FARC,* which demonstrated its good faith on December 7 by setting off a bomb at a farmers' market in Cauca department that killed five soldiers, a policeman and three civilians and wounded three soldiers, 12 policemen and 23 others. Santos denounced the attack as "cowardly" and said the country must remain on the offensive. Yet, he remained committed to the interminable peace talks in Havana as Colombians prepared to vote. The country also marked a grim milestone in March 2014: The 50th anniversary of the beginning of the guerrilla war, which by then had claimed more than 200,000 lives.

Days before the May 25 election, the two sides reached agreement on the drug issue.

The Elections of 2014

As Santos became cozier with Chávez, friction was inevitable between Santos and Uribe, who was known to be miffed as well by Santos' reversal of a number of his other policies, which he has taken as a personal rebuke. For example, Santos agreed to provide titles to landowners displaced not just by the guerrillas, but by the security forces. Santos revoked Uribe's tax breaks for investment and reversed his criminalization of drugs for personal use. Finally, Santos' government has prosecuted or placed under investigation several of Uribe's associates for alleged paramilitary connections, corruption or abuse of power. Probably the highest profile case was Jorge Noguera, Uribe's former *DAS* chief, who was convicted in September 2011 of providing the paramilitaries with names of student and union leaders and left-wing activists for execution. He was sentenced to 25 years in prison and ordered to pay $1.9 million in restitution.

The increasingly public animosity between Santos and Uribe split the ruling coalition asunder. Although Santos was elected under the banner of the U Party, the man for whom the U Party was named

formally organized a new party, Democratic Center *(CD),* to field a candidate against Santos and to seek seats in the March 9, 2014 congressional elections.

The president, meanwhile, watched his popularity evaporate from the second most popular leader of the Western Hemisphere to the second *least* popular. In April 2012, the Mitofsky poll of Mexico put Santos' approval rating at 67%, the second-highest behind Ecuador's Correa, but by September 2012, after the announcement of peace talks, it had slid to 54%, or eighth place. By October 2013, the Mitofsky poll put him at 25%; only Laura Chinchilla of Costa Rica was less popular. But he declared his candidacy in November.

In a controversial convention in October, marked by allegations of fraud, Óscar Iván Zuluaga, 54, a former U Party senator and finance minister in Uribe's second term, defeated former Vice President Francisco Santos (the president's cousin) for the Democratic Center nomination. Uribe's supporters coalesced around Zuluaga, who pledged to shut down the peace talks if elected.

Also entering the race were Marta Lucia Ramírez, who served as defense minister under Uribe, of the Conservative Party; former Bogotá interim Mayor Clara López Obregón of the left-wing Alternative Democratic Pole; and Enrique Peñalosa, also a former mayor of Bogotá, of the Green Party.

As always, the congressional elections on March 9 were a much-watched bellwether in advance of the first round of presidential voting on May 25, especially with Uribe's *CD* being tested for the first time. Turnout was only 43.6%, lower than 2010 or 2006, and more than 6% of voters for both houses cast blank votes. Santos' U Party and its coalition allies, the Liberals and Conservatives, retained solid majorities but lost ground to Uribe's *CD.* In the 102-member Senate, the U Party retained 21 seats, a loss of seven; the Conservatives fell from 22 seats to 19, and the Liberals were unchanged with 17. The new *CD* won 19; one of the *CD* senators is Uribe himself. In the 168-seat Chamber of Representatives, the Liberals won 39 seats, a gain of two; the U Party won 37, a loss of 10; the Conservatives won 27, a loss of 11; and the *CD* won 18.

The week after the congressional elections, voters were reminded of the state of the president's health when, during a campaign speech, Santos experienced incontinence. The video of the president and his wet trousers went viral, much to Santos' annoyance. Incontinence is a common side effect of prostate surgery.

The campaigns of both leading presidential candidates were blemished with scandal in the weeks leading up to the

Colombia

election. On May 5, Santos' main campaign strategist, Juan.José Rendón, resigned after the magazine *Semana* and the newspaper *El Espectador* reported that he accepted $12 million in exchange from several drug lords in exchange for negotiating their surrender on favorable terms. Uribe then alleged that $2 million of the bribe was channeled to help pay off Santos' 2010 campaign debt. Rendón admitted being approached by the drug lords but denied taking any money. He said he resigned not to hurt Santos' chances, which the president called "gallant."

The next day, a government prosecutor announced the arrest of Andrés Sepúlpeda, the Zuluaga campaign's social media contractor, for alleged espionage, data interception and using malicious software. Sepúlveda was accused of hacking into the communications of the government and *FARC* negotiators in Havana in an effort to damage the peace talks to the detriment of Santos. The prosecutor also claimed evidence that Sepúlveda had eavesdropped on Santos' own emails. Zuluaga's campaign manager, Luis Alfonso Hoyos, was forced to resign.

This was the poisonous atmosphere as 40.1% of eligible Colombian voters went to the polls on May 25. The stunning results:

Zuluaga	3,759,971	29.25%
Santos	3,301,815	26.7%
Ramírez	1,995,698	15.5%
López	1,958,414	15.2%
Peñalosa	1,065,142	8.3%
Blank	770,610	6.0%

Within days of the first round, Zuluaga backtracked on his long-standing campaign promise to withdraw from the peace talks, apparently realizing the mathematical necessity of the votes of Peñalosa supporters, but insisted the *FARC* cease fighting if they expected the talks to continue. He could logically count on Ramírez's voters, while López's would rally behind Santos—if they decided to vote at all.

Another round of peace talks began in Havana on June 5, but lasted only two days instead of the usual 11, because of the impending runoff. The stakes were high for both sides, and the *FARC* seemed politically savvy enough to know that continued deadlock would probably help elect Zuluaga, the last thing they needed or wanted. Thus, on June 7, the two sides overcame the fourth major stumbling block to peace by acknowledging that war victims were the responsibility of both sides and that both should help compensate the victims.

Santos received López's endorsement, plus the endorsements of 80 key business leaders. The *FARC* demonstrated good faith by calling a cease-fire for election day, June 15. These factors may have tipped the balance. The polls had indicated the runoff was too close to call, so there was high drama when the polls closed. The unofficial totals reported by *El Tiempo* the next day:

Santos	7,816,986	50.95%
Zuluaga	6,905,001	45.0%
Blank	619,396	4.03%

"I don't recognize any enemies," Santos said in his victory declaration, and he called on the *FARC* to conclude the peace process and the Uribe-Zuluaga supporters to unite with him in the quest for peace. López pledged her support for Santos' government, but said her party would not join it. Santos was inaugurated for his second term on August 7 (see The Future).

CULTURE: The blend of the European and Indian races was more thorough in Colombia than in the nations of the southern areas of Latin America. Moreover, refugee blacks from the Caribbean settled along the northern coast and, as elsewhere, have made their contribution to Colombian music and art. Two styles of folk music, *cumbia* and *vallenato*, are indigenous to Colombia's Caribbean coast but have been emulated by musicians in other Latin American countries.

Alas, the so-called Bolivarian countries of the northwestern tier of South America, those liberated by Simón Bolivar, were not characterized by the comparative freedom of expression and political stability of the countries of the southern part of the continent. Colombia's long history of dictatorship, political turmoil and domestic violence conspired to retard its cultural development until the latter half of the 20th century. The overthrow of the Rojas Pinilla dictatorship, and the truce reached between the warring Liberal and Conservative parties in 1958, marked a watershed in Colombian cultural expression. Bogotá's self-proclaimed title of "the Athens of South America" is a bit boastful, but there is no question that the country has made a regional impact.

This is especially true in the plastic arts, as a visit to the top floor of the *Museo Nacional* in Bogotá will attest. As in Chile, the influence of France on 19th century Colombian art is unmistakable, but in the late 20th century a number of talented Colombian painters and sculptors have won international reputations. Perhaps the three best known are Edgar Negret, the abstractionist Alejandro Obregón and Fernando Botero.

The premier figure of Colombian literature was Gabriel García Márquez (1927-2014), who received the Nobel Prize in 1982 and was widely hailed as the most influential Spanish-language novelist since Miguel de Cervantes. He was born in Aracataca and spent his early career as a journalist. His landmark novel was *Cien años de soledad*, but later novels that won international acclaim include *Crónica de una muerte anunciada* and *El amor en los tiempos de cólera*. His last was *Memorias de mis putas tristes* in 2004, which was not as well received. Although he won worldwide fame as a novelist, he continued to write non-fiction and was Latin America's leading practitioner of the so-called New Journalism style. In 1998, he used some of his Nobel Prize money to buy a controlling interest in the magazine *Cambio*, to which he regularly contributed articles and columns.

Despite his international prestige, García Márquez was denied a visa to visit the United States during the Reagan administration because of his leftist views. In 2002, he released the first of three installments of his memoirs, *Vivir para conratla (Live to Tell It)*. He was a close friend of Fidel Castro's and for a time maintained a residence in Havana. He also had a home in Paris, but in his last years lived in Mexico City, where he died on April 17, 2014, at the age of 87. His ashes were to be divided between Mexico and Colombia, where President Juan Manuel Santos declared him "the greatest Colombian of all time."

Another Colombian literary star was Álvaro Mutis (1923-2014), a novelist and poet who has achieved acclaim in the Spanish-speaking world with the fictitious character, Maqroll el Gaviero; such novels as *La última escala del Tramp Steamer* and *Amirbar*; and the book of poetry, *La mansión de Araucaíma*. He received Spain's coveted Cervantes Prize in 2001, becoming the first writer from any country to win all three of Spain's most prestigious literary awards.

Bogotá and the major provincial capitals of Medellín, Cartagena, Cali and Barranquilla have active theatrical and musical communities, though much is still borrowed from abroad. Colombian popular music has definite Caribbean influence.

Colombian cinema still lags behind the more established industries of Mexico, Brazil and Argentina, but a few feature-length films are produced each year. Colombia's best-known director is Víctor Gaviria (b. 1955), who won international recognition with *Rodrigo D: No futuro* in 1990 and *La vendedora de rosas* (the rose vendor girl), in 1998, both examinations of the effects of the Medellín drug culture on children. These were the first Colombian films entered in competition at the Cannes Film Festival, although they won no awards. He later directed *Su-*

mas y restas (Additions and Subtractions) in 2004, also about the Medellín drug trade. His most recent project is *Sangre Negra: La hora de los traidores* (Black Blood: The hour of the traitors), a biopic about a notorious Liberal *bandolero* during *La Violencia* of the 1950s named Jacinto Cruz Usma, known by the *nom de guerre* Sangrenegra. It is adapted from the book *La hora de los traidores: Los últimos días de Sangrenegra* by Pedro Claver Téllez.

In 2004, a joint U.S.-Colombian production, *María, llena eres de gracia (Maria Full of Grace)*, starring the Colombian actress Catalina Sandino Moreno (b. 1981) and written and directed by the American Joshua Marston, received international acclaim. Sandino was nominated for the U.S. Academy Award for Best Actress for this performance as a pregnant teenager used as a cocaine-carrying "mule," and it won her Best Actress at the Berlin Film Festival. She has since appeared with Benicio del Toro in *Ché Part One* and *Ché Part Two*; *The Twilight Saga: Eclipse*; and *For Greater Glory*.

Another production that has achieved notice abroad, if no major awards, is the comedy *Lecciones para un beso (lessons for a kiss)*, directed by Juan Pablo Bustamante and scripted in part by Nobel Laureate García Márquez (see above) in 2011.

Colombian television has become largely self-sufficient in programming, and some of its *telenovelas* are exported.

In popular music, the beautiful young singer Shakira Ripoll (b. 1977) has won international renown in recent years, including U.S. Grammy Awards for Best Latin Pop in 2001 and Best Latin Rock 2006, and eight Latin Grammys. She was named Person of the Year at the 2011 Latin Grammy Awards ceremony, was chosen to sing the Colombian national anthem at the Sixth Summit of the Americas in Cartagena in April 2012 and she also addressed the summit on the topic of education for poor children. She has sold 70 million albums and 60 million singles worldwide. There is a brain behind the beauty; according to Mensa International, her IQ of 140 makes her a genius.

Eclipsing even Shakira in the number of Grammys won is Colombia's other megastar, Juan Esteban Arristazábal (b. 1972), internationally known by the stage name Juanes. As of 2012, Juanes had a record 19 Latin Grammys, including eight in 2008, and in 2010 he shared a "mainstream" Grammy with Taylor Swift for best rap song collaboration. In 2012, his album *MTV Unplugged* was named Album of the Year and won for Best Long Video. He has sold 15 million albums worldwide. He gained notoriety as one of 12 Latin pop

singers who appeared at the "Peace Concert" in Havana in 2009, which critics said implied a lack of concern for Cuba's human rights violations.

Yet another Colombian singer of renown is Carlos Vives (b. 1961), a *telenovela* actor who became a singer in 1991 when he had to sing for a biographical film about *vallenato* composer Rafael Escalona. His 1993 album *Clásicos de la Provincia*, which fused the traditional *vallenato* sounds with rock, pop and funk, was a hit all over Latin America. In 2013, he won three Latin Grammy Awards: Song of the Year and Best Tropical Song for *Volví a Nacer* (with Andrés Castro), and Best Tropical Fusion Album, for *Corazón Profundo*.

Through 2012, Colombians had collected a total of 56 Latin Grammys.

Colombia's leading recording artist and songwriter was once Diomedes Díaz (b. 1957), popularly known as *"El Jefe"* and as *"El Cacique de la Junta."* Díaz has written and/or recorded 33 popular songs since 1976. He was convicted in 2002 of the wrongful death by cocaine overdose of his 22-year-old lover but spent only 37 months in jail. He was also banned from performing in Cali after he snorted cocaine on stage in 2005. His failure to appear for a performance in Santa Marta sparked a riot. He recorded two more songs in 2009.

The Colombian press, like so much else in the country, has been shaped by the Liberal-Conservative rivalry and in recent years has been the target of drug-related violence. Involvement of newspaper owners in politics has been commonplace, most notably former Presidents Laureano Gómez, who established the Conservative mouthpiece *El Siglo*, and Eduardo Santos, whose family still publishes the prestigious pro-Liberal daily *El Tiempo*. Ironically, these two rival newspapers both were intimidated by the Rojas Pinilla dictatorship, forcing them to collaborate editorially against the dictator. The dean of the Colombian press and its circulation leader is another pro-Liberal paper, *El Espectador*, which has won international plaudits for its courageous editorial attacks against the drug cartels. Its editor, Guillermo Cano, was murdered by the Medellín Cartel in 1986, just one of scores of Colombian journalists who have given their lives in the line of duty. *El Espectador* has since become a weekly.

Several high-quality news magazines are published, the most widely read being *Cromos, Revista Cambio* and *Semana*. Nobel laureate Gabriel García Márquez (see above) bought a controlling interest in *Cambio* in 1999.

There are 34 tax-supported institutions of higher education in Colombia,

10 national and 24 departmental. Premier among them is the National University *(UN)*, founded in 1867. It is based in Bogotá but has satellite campuses in Arauca, Leticia, Manizales, Medellín, Palmira and San Andrés. The system has more than 40,000 students. There are also 16 Catholic universities; the Pontifical Xaverian University and Our Lady of the Rosary University in Bogotá date to the 17th century, among the oldest schools in the hemisphere. There are more than 30 private non-sectarian institutions as well, the most prestigious being Externado University in Bogotá, founded in 1886.

Colombia has five historical or cultural sites that have been designated UNESCO World Heritage Sites, the best known being the beautiful colonial quarter of Cartagena with its famous fortress and yellow-domed cathedral. Others are the old quarter of Santa Cruz de Mompox, the National Archeological Park of Tierradentro and the San Augustín Archeological Park. The newest, inscribed in 2011, is the so-called Coffee Cultural Landscape of Colombia, which includes six separate sites in the historic coffee-growing region in Antioquía.

ECONOMY: The informal economy of Colombia is based on production and smuggled export of refined cocaine and far outweighs the formal economy based on agriculture. The coca leaves are not generally grown in Colombia, but come from Peru, Ecuador and Bolivia, where an acre can yield $10,000 a year. The final stage of processing takes place in Colombia, which traditionally has had but loose control over illicit activities. Small "factories" are easily moved, and with police double-agents abounding, when there is a raid on a facility, no one is home.

Most of the population, however, was employed in agriculture, which is handicapped by inefficient techniques and misuse of resources—produce and labor. Rural violence is common and has stimulated migration to the cities since 1948 where many of the newcomers are unemployable because of lack of education and skills. Now, only 1.7% of the people work the land. An estimated 60% are engaged in the cocaine traffic in one capacity or another. The resources of Colombia are capable of supporting the growing population without the cocaine industry, but numerous problems, principally poor distribution of wealth, must be resolved before there can be major economic gains.

Government programs were undertaken to end the traditional dependence on coffee exports, and by 1973 other goods and products produced more foreign income than coffee. Manufactured goods

Colombia

are slowly gaining a larger share of total exports.

The López Michelsen (1978–82) administration sought to revitalize the rural sector through agrarian reform and government investment. Tighter controls over foreign-owned firms and banks, together with new taxes on the wealthy increased government revenues 50%.

Colombia has a thriving coal industry; it is not only self-sufficient in oil, but is an exporter. Honda makes motorcycles here, with production exceeding 50,000 units per year.

Coffee has long been a mainstay of the economy, particularly the Arabica bean. Coffee output hit a 35-year low in 2011 because of heavy rains that led to a plague of leaf rust. Output partially recovered in 2012, and 40% of trees were replanted. The 2013-14 harvest showed a 34% increase over the previous year and was the best since 2007.

The overall economic picture in Colombia was bleak for several years. Chronic high unemployment, along with the endemic corruption within the Samper government, was one of the major issues in the 1998 presidential election that saw an end to 12 years of Liberal rule. The jobless rate that year was 16%, second only to Haiti among the 20 Latin republics, while inflation also was among the highest in the region at 18%. The picture did not improve much under Conservative President Pastrana, however. Real GDP growth was 3% or less between 1998 and 2002.

Growth improved under the administration of President Álvaro Uribe, both because of his hard-nosed fiscal policy and because of the dramatic improvement in public security. GDP growth was 3.2% in 2003, 4% in 2004 and 5.1% in 2005. It jumped to a robust 6.7% in 2006 and 7.7% for 2007. Then the global recession hit in late 2008, cutting growth to 2.6%. In 2009 it *shrank* by 0.1%. It rebounded to 4.4% in 2010.

In 2011, the first full year under President Juan Manuel Santos, growth was a robust 5.7%. It fell to a still-healthy 4.3% in 2012 and 4.2% in 2013.

The unemployment picture has been dismal for more than a decade: 18.1% in 1999, 19.7% in 2000 and 20.5% in 2001, the worst in Latin America. At the end of 2003, the first full year of Uribe's administration, it was down to 14%, and at the end of 2005, it was 10.2%, and it has fluctuated little since then. It was 10.8% in 2011, 10.3% in 2012 and 9.7% in 2013.

Inflation has remained manageable: 2.3% in 2010, 3.4% in 2011, 3.2% in 2012 and 2.2% in 2013.

The combination of sluggish economic growth, population increase, joblessness and inflation has affected Colombians' living standards for years. Per capita GDP declined from $2,440 in 1997 to $1,844 in 2003, but it rebounded to $3,250 in 2007. By 2011, it had doubled to $7,188, but it was inequitably distributed; 32.7% of the population was still below the poverty line in 2012.

Colombia signed two major free-trade agreements, with the *Mercosur* trade bloc in 2004 and with the United States in 2006. The *Mercosur* deal gives Colombian

Exiting Colombia on the Pan-American Highway into Ecuador, one encounters highland travelers. *Photo by Katie Thompson*

exports duty-free entry to Brazil and Argentina over eight to 10 years, while tariffs will be eliminated on those countries' exports to Colombia over a period of 12 to 15 years. The bilateral agreement with the United States made Colombia the ninth Latin American country to reach one. Peru signed one the previous month. Bilateral trade with the United States totaled $14.3 billion. However, the Democratic-controlled U.S. Senate stalled the FTA (see History) until President Barack Obama finally supported it in mid-2011. It passed that October and took effect May 15, 2012.

In 2008, Colombia signed a FTA with Canada, which went into effect in 2011. Bilateral trade in 2010 was $1.8 billion.

After bilateral tensions led Venezuela, Colombia's second-largest trading partner after the United States, to restrict Colombian imports, China became Colombia's second-largest trading partner in 2009. In 2011, the two countries had bilateral trade of $8.2 billion, a one-year increase of 39%. President Juan Manuel Santos made a five-day visit to China in May 2012.

Because of bilateral FTAs with the United States, the old Andean Pact, composed of Colombia, Venezuela, Ecuador, Peru and Bolivia, became largely irrelevant as a result. As one consequence, Colombia now buys its soybeans from the United States instead of from Bolivia.

The reduction in violence has led Colombia to promote tourism, and in 2006 tourism revenues were up almost 50% above 2005. In 2001, Colombia had 1.9 million visitors, accounting for $1.5 billion in foreign exchange. By 2010, Colombia had 2.39 million visitors, bringing in $2.8 billion. But that still ranked just 10th place in the Western Hemisphere. Tourism in 2012 increased just 1.8%, far below the regional average.

Foreign oil companies are now more willing to invest, which has borne fruit. Foreign investment in the oil industry skyrocketed from $278 million in 2003 to $4.3 billion in 2011. Colombia was to have become a net oil importer by 2007, but as of 2011 that had not yet happened. Attacks by guerrillas on pipelines and tankers were continuing in 2012. Net oil reserves in 2011 were estimated 1.9 billion barrels, and production was expected to be up to 1.5 million bpd by 2015. Natural gas reserves in 2011 were estimated at 377 billion cubic meters. It exported 1.8 billion cubic meters in 2009.

Overall, foreign direct investment in Colombia jumped from $13.2 billion in 2011 to $15.823 billion in 2012, $8.2 billion of which went to mining and oil and gas.

Colombia's economy has been hampered not just by violence but by a dilapidated infrastructure. In 2011, President Santos announced a bold 10-year, $55 billion renovation plan that will double the miles of four-lane highways, expand railways and port facilities and modernize Bogotá's airport.

THE FUTURE: The first and second rounds of the 2014 presidential election were clearly a referendum on the Havana peace talks, and their glacial pace almost caused Juan Manuel Santos to become the first incumbent Latin American president defeated for re-election since Hipólito Mejía in the Dominican Republic in 2004. But after a last-minute breakthrough on June 7 in which the two sides stopped blaming each other for atrocities that claimed civilian lives and agreed to jointly compensate victims, Colombian voters decided to reject former President Uribe's call for a return to a hardline approach and, in the words of the John Lennon song, to "give peace a chance."

The two sides must now return to the bargaining table. They've reached accords on rural development, the integration of the *FARC* into the political process and disengaging the *FARC* from the drug trade. Still remaining are the highest hurdles of all: for the *FARC* to lay down their arms, and how the peace will be ratified and implemented. Now that Santos has been re-elected, the *FARC* have no incentive to move with haste.

The Republic of Costa Rica

Ecotourism is a major industry and source of national pride in Costa Rica

Area: 19,647 square miles.

Population: 4,755,234 (2014 est.).

Capital City: San José (Pop. 288,000 in 2011).

Climate: The coastal lowlands are hot and tropical, with heavy rains from April to December. The valley of the central highlands is temperate, with moderate rains during the wet season.

Neighboring Countries: Nicaragua (North); Panama (Southeast).

Official Language: Spanish

Ethnic Background: Overwhelmingly Spanish European descent, blended with some Indian lineage. A few Indians with African heritage are found along the Atlantic coast; some pure-blood Indians live in the highlands.

Principal Religion: Roman Catholic Christianity.

Chief Commercial Products: Coffee, bananas, sugar and cacao.

Currency: Colón.

Gross Domestic Product: U.S. $48.51 billion in 2013 ($10,330 per capita, official exchange rate).

Former Colonial Status: Spanish Crown Colony (1522–1821).

Independence Date: September 15, 1821.

Chief of State: Luis Guillermo Solís Rivera (b. April 25, 1958), president (since May 8, 2014).

National Flag: Blue, white and red horizontal stripes.

Costa Rica, literally *Rich Coast*, is next to the smallest of the Central American republics. Lying between Nicaragua and Panama with coasts on both the Atlantic and Pacific oceans, the distance from ocean to ocean varies from 75 to 175 miles.

The country is divided into three distinct regions: the Atlantic coastal plains, the central highlands and the Pacific coast. The central highlands are part of a chain of scenic mountains rising in Nicaragua and running southeast through Costa Rica into Panama. They contain lofty peaks reaching 12,500 feet and several steep-sided inter-mountain valleys. The green central valley, some 40 miles wide and 50 miles long, lying between 3,000 and 6,000 feet above sea level, is the most densely populated part of Costa Rica.

The two principal cities, San José and Cartago, share the valley with four volcanoes, two of which are still violently active. Mount Irazú, close to the capital, littered the city with ashes and cinders in 1962. Arenal erupted in 1998.

Costa Rica's coffee is grown on the slopes of the hills and volcanoes which rim the valley. The Atlantic coastal plains are moist and low, heavily forested and sparsely settled. Costa Rica's main port in the east is Puerto Limón, the only city of commercial importance in the area.

The Pacific lowlands, drier than the Atlantic plains, are quite narrow except for the Nicoya and Osa peninsulas. Thinly settled, the region produces bananas and fiber on large plantations. The port of Golfito on the Pacific coast handles most of the country's exports. Lying in the tropical rainbelt, Costa Rica has more than abundant rainfall, particularly in the rainy season from April to December of each year. Some parts of the oppressive Atlantic coast region have rain during 300 days of the year.

HISTORY: The Spaniards discovered the Nicoya Peninsula in 1522, settling in the Central Valley, where a few sedentary Indian farmers were found. They organized into a hacienda system of independent farm communities. The Spaniards intermarried with the Indians, who were assimilated into the Spanish culture. Cartago was founded in 1563, but no expansion of this settlement occurred for 145 years, during which time the Costa Ricans evolved as a community of small farmers. With the assimilated Indians and a few slaves, the Costa Rican worked his own land, developing a system of small, efficient and independent landowners and a tradition of industry not usually found in colonial Hispanic society. Settlers from Cartago founded Heredia in 1717 and San José in 1737; by 1750 the population had reached approximately 2,500, divided into some 400 family groups.

Independence from Spain was achieved on September 15, 1821 as a result of actions in Guatemala, Mexico and other colonies. Costa Rica fell victim to the civil wars which followed the separation of the Central American Republics from the short-lived Mexican Empire. However, remoteness from the scene of the bitter quarrels between conservatives and liberals in Guatemala and El Salvador minimized the effects of the civil war in Costa Rica. The most significant events of Costa Rica's history as an independent state have been its efforts to develop the economy to provide the revenues required to support the people.

The government encouraged the production of coffee in 1825, offering free land for development. From 1850, the coffee trade attracted new settlers and inspired the development of roads and the settlement of areas outside the central valley. The building of railroads between the 1870s and 1890s introduced banana growing to provide traffic for the new system. At the same time, West Indians were brought in to build the railroads, clear the forests and work the Atlantic coast plantations.

Subsequently, irrigated banana plantations were developed on the Pacific coast, resulting in the building of ports at Golfito and Puntarenas. On the Nicoya Peninsula and in the northwest, cattle raising became and remains an important industry.

Politically, the Costa Rican experience was tranquil. The first experiments in government were hardly more than gentlemanly agreements among the principal families. The constitution of 1848 abolished the army and replaced it with a civil guard. Costa Rica has had only one major experience with dictatorial government.

Tomás Guardia came to power in 1870 and ruled as dictator until 1882. Exiling opposition leaders and spending money with a lavish hand, he broke up the traditional parties, installed his friends in office but also undertook to modernize the rural agricultural state. He built roads, railroads, schools and public buildings, increased the production of sugar and coffee and encouraged international trade.

Political freedom was restored by free and honest elections in 1889. Three subsequent attempts were made to seize the government: in 1917, which lasted two years; an unsuccessful attempt in 1932; and the refusal of the National Assembly to recognize the election victory of Otilio Ulate over former President Rafael Calderón in 1948. This led to a six-week civil war that left 2,000 people dead.

Showcase Democracy

José Figueres, founder of the National Liberation Party *(PLN)*, which is still one of the country's major parties, led a band of 700 revolutionaries that prevented Calderón from regaining power. Figueres, whom Calderón had sent into exile from 1942–44, served for 18 months as head of a revolutionary junta, during which time he granted women the right to vote, abolished the standing army and implemented the Uruguay-like social welfare system still in place today. He relinquished power in 1949 to the duly elected Luis Rafael Ulate, a respected journalist and member of the National Union Party, whose name has changed several times and is today the Social Christian Unity Party *(PUSC)*. This began an uninterrupted period of two-party, democratic government, peacefully alternating between the *PLN* and the Social Christians, until the scandal-plagued *PUSC* went into eclipse in 2006. It is Latin America's oldest democracy.

Figueres was elected to succeed Ulate in 1953. A successful coffee grower and businessman, he expanded public works and increased government revenues. An outspoken critic of Caribbean dictatorships, he was denounced as a "communist" and an invasion force from Nicaragua moved to unseat him. An appeal to the Organization of American States ended the conflict. Dominican dictator Rafael Trujillo plotted to assassinate him. Figueres served another term as president from 1970–74, and is still revered as the patriarch of Costa Rica's democracy. His son and namesake was president from 1994–98. He died in 1990.

Daniel Oduber of the *PLN* was elected to succeed Figueres in 1974 with 42% of the vote. Oduber promised agrarian reform and constitutional changes to increase the power of the executive branch. However, in 1978, voters ousted the *PLN*, electing

Rodrigo Carazo of the Democratic Renovation Party. He won by 50% to 49% over the *PLN* candidate, Luís Alberto Monge.

The right-of-center president soon found his administration beset by scandals and fiscal problems. For years, Costa Ricans imported more than they exported and spent more than they earned. Somehow, it worked until 1980, when the nation's imported oil bills and international interest charges skyrocketed while earnings from exports nosedived.

Rather than impose needed austerity measures (the government subsidized food, fuel and luxury imports), Carazo sought to stave off disaster by printing more paper money. International lenders responded by cutting off credit.

Carazo became the most unpopular president in recent years. In 1982, voters elected Monge, a former labor organizer, who this time took 58% of the vote. His popularity remained high in spite of an unpleasant task: austerity measures to bolster a sagging economy.

Trouble in the Neighborhood

By 1984, Costa Rica was besieged by other problems. The armed conflicts in

neighboring Nicaragua and El Salvador threatened to interfere with the national political process at a time when economic conditions in the nation reached a dangerously low level; the national public debt increased to $4.4 billion by 1986, placing the government on the brink of bankruptcy. Significantly, the government asked the United States for $7.3 million in order to improve its military capability to resist increasing *Sandinista* pressure on its Nicaraguan border. By 1985, U.S. military advisers were training the Costa Rican National Guard.

In 1986, voters elected Oscar Arias Sánchez of the *PLN* president by a majority of 52.3%. A highly educated and respected man, he performed admirably in the face of adversities affecting the country, including communist infiltration of the labor movement. His performance was mostly steady, and sometimes erratic. During a visit to Washington in 1987, he urged President Reagan to discontinue aid to the anti-communist *contras* of Nicaragua, stating that they were fomenting unrest in Central America. But a few days later, he declared that so long as the *Sandinista* regime of Nicaragua existed, there would be a danger that communism would spread throughout Central America.

Arias was the architect in 1987 of a peace plan for Central America, a scheme immediately embraced by liberals in the U.S. Congress who had been trying to end aid to the *contras*. With the demise of the Soviet Union, the *Sandinistas* found the economic rug abruptly yanked out from under their regime, and grudgingly accepted the Arias plan, which included democra-

Costa Rica

tization of Nicaragua. Arias received the Nobel Peace Price for his efforts.

Arias was succeeded in 1990 by Rafael Angelo Calderón, a lawyer from the *PUSC*. He significantly cut the number of civil employees and undertook a number of measures to modernize the economy.

In the 1994 election, the *PLN* returned to power with the candidacy of José María Figueres, son of the former president. He narrowly defeated Miguel Angel Rodríguez of the *PUSC*. Each attacked the other's allegedly shady past.

Although the Harvard-educated Figueres was elected on a promise to retain the Uruguayan-style social welfare system his father had engineered, once in office he did what so many other Latin American presidents have done in recent years. Confronted with economic reality, including a cumbersome public debt of $3.5 billion that represented 40% of GDP, he abandoned his party's idealistic social principles and sought pragmatic solutions to the country's economic woes. His greatest feat was in touting Costa Rica's low labor costs and highly literate work force to persuade transnational high-tech firms to locate assembly plants in Costa Rica. His major prize was Intel Corp., which agreed to build a $300 million assembly plant that has since exported $2–3 billion per year in Pentium processors. By 2009, Intel accounted for 20% of Costa Rica's exports.

Among Figueres' other economic successes, he lowered the unemployment rate from 6.2% in 1996 to 5.4% in 1997, cut inflation to 11.2% in 1997, the lowest in four years, and oversaw a modest GDP growth rate of 4% in 1997. Yet, Figueres proved the most unpopular president since Carazo. Despite Figueres' economic successes, Costa Ricans still grumbled that their glass was half empty rather than half full. The Figueres administration was plagued by a number of low-level scandals, hardly more than peccadillos by Latin American standards but which undermined public confidence. The public also was concerned over an alarming increase in common crime, including violent crime, once rare. Finally, Figueres was faulted for neglecting the nation's infrastructure, especially the sorry condition of streets and highways.

The time was ripe for the *PUSC*'s Rodríguez to make a comeback in 1998. The *PLN* candidate, former soccer star José Miguel Corrales, distanced himself from the unpopular Figueres sought to seize the moral high ground by purging the party of congressional and municipal candidates with allegedly questionable backgrounds, which alienated Corrales from the rank and file of his own party. Rodríguez's strategy might well have been summed up, "It's the potholes, stupid." At times, he

sounded more like a candidate for county commissioner than for president, promising to repave highways, to expand water purification systems, even to remove the hated turnstiles from buses and to allow passengers to exit from the rear. The outcome was closer than the polls had predicted, with Rodríguez winning by a 46–43% margin over Corrales.

Rodríguez did something unusual for a Latin American president: keep his promises. He expanded the San José airport and embarked on an ambitious road-building and repaving program. He was aggressive in luring more foreign investors, an initiative that appeared to pay off (see Economy). However, Rodríguez was met with street protests when he attempted to privatize state-owned companies as has been done in virtually every other Latin American country except Cuba and Uruguay.

The 2002 election reflected Costa Ricans' growing disenchantment with what they regarded as a lack of choice between the two major parties. For the first time in Costa Rica's venerable 53-year-old democ-

Former President and Mrs. Abel Pacheco

racy, a third-party candidate emerged who threatened the traditional parties' grip on power. In 2001, Ottón Solís, a 48-year-old economist and *PLN* dissident, formed the Citizen Action Party (*PAC*). The *PUSC* nominated a 68-year-old psychiatrist and congressional deputy, Abel Pacheco, while the *PLN* nominated Rolando Araya, a chemical engineer. Both Pacheco and Araya had high name recognition from having been television commentators.

Solís attacked what was widely perceived as the two main parties' corruption; Pacheco pledged to crack down on common crime, which had become a major

problem and a threat to the all-important tourist industry; Araya placed his emphasis on improving education.

Solís prevented either major party candidate from receiving the necessary 40% to avoid a runoff. Pacheco received 38.5%, Araya was second with 30.9% and Solís was a strong third with 26.3%. Besides throwing the election into a runoff for the first time, Solís' *PAC* also emerged as the kingmaker in the new Congress with 14 seats; the *PUSC* won 19 and the *PLN*, 17. Voter turnout was 69%.

In the runoff, Araya tried to win Solís' voters by pledging a crackdown on corruption, but he had little success because of the bitter attacks he had made on Solís in the first round. Pacheco won with a resounding mandate of 58%, the first time the *PUSC* had won two successive elections.

In 2004, Costa Rica belatedly agreed to join El Salvador, Guatemala, Honduras, Nicaragua and the Dominican Republic in creating a Central American Free Trade Agreement (CAFTA) with the United States. Costa Rica at first balked at opening up its state-owned insurance and telecommunications industries to competition with U.S. firms. Under a compromise reached with the United States, those two sectors would not become fully competitive until 2011. Still, the National Assembly hesitated to ratify the treaty, which was opposed by the powerful unions.

Uncharacteristic Scandals

Costa Ricans were stunned when a series of events began unfolding in 2004 that implicated the current and three former presidents, from both major parties, in alleged financial improprieties.

There were 13 days of street protests when it was reported that the lucrative contract for vehicle inspections was awarded to a Spanish firm in which a political adviser of President Pacheco had part ownership. But this relatively mild conflict of interest was nothing compared to two later bombshells.

First, prosecutors announced they were investigating two payments from the Taiwan government totaling $400,000 in 2001 and 2002 to a company controlled by former President Rodríguez, who just two weeks earlier had been elected secretary-general of the Organization of American States. At the same time, the former head of the state-owned power and telephone company, *ICE*, testified that he had accepted a $2.4 million "prize," a euphemism for kickback, from the French firm Alcatel for a $149 million cell phone contract in 2001 and that he had passed $550,000 of it to then-President Rodríguez. Rodríguez resigned his OAS post and returned to

Costa Rica

Costa Rica to answer the charges. He was briefly handcuffed and jailed, then sentenced to house arrest, then jailed again pending trial.

Then former President Calderón was also jailed, accused of taking $9 million in kickbacks from a $39 million loan from Finland for medical equipment to upgrade the state health care system. He allegedly brokered the deal in 2001, seven years after leaving office. Calderón and Rodríguez are both of the *PUSC*. He later stood accused of embezzling funds from the social security system.

Next it was the turn of former President Figueres of the *PLN*, who had become head of the World Economic Forum, a Swiss-based think tank. He was accused in Costa Rica of failing to report as income about $1 million he received from Alcatel for supposed "consulting fees." Figueres admitted receiving the money, which violated the terms of his contract with the WEF. He resigned and returned to Costa Rica to face possible tax evasion charges.

Almost simultaneously, Pacheco stood accused of illegally accepting foreign contributions for his 2002 campaign. Nine officials resigned from Pacheco's government, while the public works minister was caught running a loan-shark operation.

In 2005, judges agreed to release both Calderón and Rodríguez, who had complained of health problems, from jail and placed them under house arrest pending trial. Rodríguez had to post $430,000 in bond and Calderón, $500,000.

Figueres was exonerated by a judge in 2005 and by the attorney general in 2007. Calderón finally went on trial in November 2008. In October 2009, he was convicted of the embezzlement charges and sentenced to five years, as was the former head of the social security system.

Rodríguez went in trial in April 2010. In April 2011 he was convicted and sentenced to five years. He continued to maintain his independence, accusing the attorney general of political opportunism and vowing to appeal.

Arias Returns

At the height of the scandals, Oscar Arias, the only recent president *not* to be under investigation, announced he would run for president again in 2006 for the *PLN*. The *PUSC* had no candidate with the stature of the respected Nobel laureate and settled for a veteran party hack, Ricardo Toledo. Solís was again the candidate for the *PAC*. A new player on the field was the Libertarian Movement *(ML)*, which nominated Otto Guevara.

Besides corruption, the major issue proved to be Costa Rican ratification of CAFTA; Costa Rica's failure to do so de-

Former President Oscar Arias Sánchez

layed CAFTA's formal establishment beyond the January 1, 2006 target date. Arias and Guevara strongly supported ratification, while Solís, backed by the labor unions, opposed it.

Voter turnout was only 65.4%, the lowest in the history the 57-year-old democracy. A slow count produced a cliffhanger between Solís and Arias, prompting a manual recount. The official results were not announced for 17 days:

Arias	664,551	40.9%
Solís	646,382	39.8%
Guevara	137,710	8.5%

In the balloting for the National Assembly, Arias' *PLN* fell just short of a majority, winning 25 of the 57 seats, an increase of eight. Solís' *PAC* became the second largest bloc with 17 seats. The Libertarian Movement won six, while the *PUSC* was humiliated, dropping from first to fourth place with five seats.

CAFTA ratification remained stalled by endless legislative and judicial wrangling. CAFTA opponents tried and failed to persuade the Supreme Electoral Tribunal *(TSE)* to approve a referendum on the issue.

In 2007, tens of thousands of CAFTA opponents, mostly farmers and trade unionists, staged a peaceful protest march in San José. The *TSE* suddenly reversed itself and gave the go-ahead for a referendum, which the Assembly approved 48–5. It was held on October 7, 2007. Voter turnout was 59.2%, and the outcome, so close it wasn't validated for days, showed how sharply divided Costa Ricans were on CAFTA:

Sí	805,658	51.56%
No	756,814	48.44%

CAFTA opponents refused to recognize the results. Nonetheless, CAFTA came into existence on January 1, 2009.

As he did in the 1980s, Arias again sought to play peacemaker by brokering negotiations in 2009 between deposed Honduran President Manuel Zelaya and interim President Roberto Micheletti. The talks in San José proved futile. After the election and inauguration of Porfirio Lobo Sosa, Costa Rica became one of only four Latin American countries to join the United States in recognizing the new Honduran president; the others were Colombia, Panama and Peru.

First Woman President

Arias threw his support behind Vice President Laura Chinchilla for the *PLN* presidential nomination for 2010, and the party nominated her. She also had served as justice minister before resigning both posts to run. Ottón Solís faced a challenge for the *PAC* nomination from Epsy Campbell, a 46-year-old economist of Jamaican parentage, but the party nominated him for a third time. Otto Guevara stood again at the *ML* candidate. Former President Calderón declared his intention to run despite his pending corruption trial, but the *PUSC* eventually nominated Luis Fishman, who had little name recognition. Five minor party candidates also were on the ballot.

Despite a slight downturn in the economy from the global recession, Arias and the *PLN* enjoyed the continued goodwill of the voters, upon which Chinchilla capitalized. Moreover, gradual acceptance of CAFTA had deprived Solís of his major issue. Turnout on February 7 was up somewhat from 2006 to 69.1%, and this time there was no cliffhanger:

Chinchilla	863,803	46.8%
Solís	464,454	25.6%
Guevara	384,540	20.8%
Fishman	71,330	3.9%

Chinchilla had to govern by consensus as the *PLN* lost two of its 25 seats in the Assembly. The *CAC* won 11, the *ML* 10 and the *PUSC* six, a gain of one. Two other parties claimed the other five seats.

On May 8, 2010, Chinchilla, 51, made history as she was sworn in as Costa Rica's first woman president and as Latin America's fifth. She holds a master's degree in public policy from Georgetown University in Washington and worked as a consultant for several years on judicial and public security reform for various governmental and non-governmental organizations.

Although the *PLN* is a member of the Socialist International and she promised to continue Costa Rica's traditional welfare

Costa Rica

**Former President
Laura Chinchilla Miranda**

model, Chinchilla is a social conservative who opposes abortion and gay marriage. Nonetheless, she was divorced and bore a son out of wedlock by the Spaniard to whom she is now married. She is also environmentally conscious, and on her first day in office signed an executive order prohibiting strip-mining for gold.

Chinchilla faced a foreign crisis in October 2010 when Nicaraguans began dredging operations near the mouth of the San Juan River, which forms the border between the two countries on the Caribbean side. But then the Nicaraguan workmen, backed by a reported 20 armed soldiers, encamped on Calero Island, which Costa Rica claims. Costa Rica protested the incursion, and in a bizarre rejoinder, Nicaragua claimed the men were on Nicaraguan soil, according to Google Map. That led Google to announce that its map was wrong and that at any rate its maps should not be used to justify a border incursion.

With no army, Chinchilla turned to the OAS and to the International Court of Justice in The Hague, while Nicaraguan President Daniel Ortega continued to deny there had been an incursion. In March 2011, the ICJ issued a preliminary ruling on a 13–4 vote that barred either country from moving personnel to the disputed area in order to prevent an escalation. Relations were already strained between the two countries because of the presence of an estimated 600,000 illegal Nicaraguan immigrants in more prosperous Costa Rica and because of Ortega's behavior as Central America's neighborhood bully.

On November 21, 2013, the IJC ruled in favor of Costa Rica and mandated the removal of Nicaraguan forces from Calero Island.

Chinchilla implemented an unpopular austerity plan in 2011 to reduce a crushing $997 million deficit. Her approval rating dropped to 26% in the multinational

Mitofsky poll as a result, the lowest of any leader in the Western Hemisphere. This was despite relatively brisk economic growth of 4.8%.

The National Assembly made international news in 2012 by voting 14-5 to outlaw hunting, the first Latin American nation to do so.

President Barack Obama made a two-nation visit to Mexico and Costa Rica in May 2013. In Costa Rica, he met with the other Central American presidents and discussed a variety of topics (see U.S.-Latin American Relations).

A Shift in Power

By October 2013, Mexico's Mitofsky poll showed Chinchilla was still the least popular leader of the hemisphere, with an approval rating of only 9%. Voter disenchantment was not only with her but with the traditional party system. This time there were 13 parties that fielded candidates for the February 2, 2014, presidential election, but only five had any serious chance of making it into an expected runoff.

The *PLN* pinned its hopes on former San José Mayor Johnny Araya, 56. For the first time, the *PAC* conducted a party primary, on July 20, 2013. The narrow winner was Luis Guillermo Solís, 55, a left-wing social scientist and history professor at the University of Costa Rica and a former diplomat under Arias and the second Figueres. He bolted from the *PLN* in 2005, and had never held elected office. He is no relation to the three-time *PAC* candidate Ottón Solís.

The *PUSC* nominated Rodolfo Hernández, a former director of the national children's hospital, who withdrew and was replaced by Rodolfo Piza, an attorney; the *ML* renominated Guevara; and the left-wing Broad Front alliance coalesced around José María Villalta, an attorney and the Broad Front's only deputy in the Assembly.

Araya led in the polls until January, with Villalta in second place, when Solís, who was running fourth, made an unexpectedly strong account in a debate. He began to surge in the polls, promising to combat corruption, improve the infrastructure and eliminate inequality, although he worried businessmen with his left-wing views. Araya also hurt himself by not knowing the price of milk in an interview.

Turnout on February 2 was 68.2%, or 2.1 million voters. The breathtaking results:

Solis	629,866	30.6%
Araya	610,634	29.7%
Villalta	354,479	17.3%
Guevara	233,064	11.3%
Piza	123,653	6.0%

For only the second time in the country's history, no candidate obtained the required 40% plurality and a runoff was scheduled for April 6. But after a poll by the University of Costa Rica showed Araya trailing by 43 points, he announced on March 5 he would stop campaigning, thus conceding the election. The *segunda vuelta* thus was largely anticlimactic:

Solís	1,314,327	77.8%
Araya	374,844	22.2%

Besides being the first third-party candidate to win over the two traditional parties, Solís also made history as the first president to receive more than 1 million votes. The *PLN* still retained the largest bloc in the 57-member Assembly with 18 seats, to 13 for the *PAC*, 9 for the Broad Front, 8 for the *PUSC* and 4 for the *ML*. Solís will have to do some coalition building.

He faced his first challenge even before his inauguration when Intel, which built a microchip processing plant in Costa Rica in 1997 and was a major employer, announced two days after the runoff it was closing the plant and laying off 1,500 workers (see Economy). Bank of America also said it was laying off 1,500 workers. Solís met with Intel executives, who assured him the decision was made not because of his election but because of the need to cut costs. That was why the San Francisco-based company came to Costa Rica in the first place, but those operations are now being moved to China, Vietnam and Malaysia, where labor is even cheaper. The company said it would still have 1,000 engineers in Costa Rica for research and development.

Solís named newly elected Vice President Helio Fallas to serve as finance minister as well, charging him to reduce the huge budget deficit without raising taxes and to lure new foreign investment to make up for the departure of Intel and the Bank of America. He has announced a civil service hiring freeze, and workers who retire or quit will not be replaced.

Representatives of 80 nations attended the May 8 inauguration, including the presidents of Bolivia, the Dominican Republic, Ecuador, El Salvador, Guatemala and Honduras, —but not Nicaragua's Ortega, who was not invited, a hint that Solís is as miffed as Chinchilla over the border dispute. Nicaragua's vice president attended, as did three other vice presidents, Spain's Prince Felipe and OAS Secretary General José Miguel Insulza. The United States sent only Gina McCarthy, administrator of the Environmental Protection Agency. In his address, Solís said he hopes to balance the budget within two years and to "effectively combat poverty, not just administer it." Accomplishing

Costa Rica

President Luis Guillermo Solís
Presidencia de la República de Costa Rica

both will prove a daunting task (see The Future).

CULTURE: Costa Ricans are predominantly Roman Catholic and primarily of European, especially Spanish, ancestry; the country has the lowest percentage of Indians and *mestizos* of any Central American country. Early in the colonial era, the few Indians native to the area were assimilated into a uniform, friendly society of middle class merchants and small farmers. The pure Spanish descendants emerged as a small, rich elite controlling the wealth of Costa Rica.

Popular cultural expression is found in music and dance. The most characteristic art expression is the brilliantly decorated ox carts like those still found in rural Spain and Portugal; they are accepted as a national symbol, although they have been replaced by trucks and tractors in the national economy.

Through energetic promotion of education, Costa Rica has achieved the highest literacy rate in Central America—96%—greater than that of the United States. The country has no fewer than 48 institutions of higher learning, only four of which are state-supported. The oldest and most prestigious is the University of Costa Rica, near the capital, which traces its origins to 1832 and has 40,000 students. Newly elected President Luis Guillermo Solís was a history professor there.

Few Costa Rican writers achieved international renown, but two of the most revered nationally are the poet Robert Brenes Misén (1874–1947), remembered for *En el silencio*; and Carmen Lyra, pseudonym for María Isabel Carvajal (1887–1949), a journalist, educator, feminist activist and novelist, remembered for the 1918 novel *En una silla de ruedas* (in a wheelchair) and the short story anthology, *Cuentos de mi*

Tía Panchita (stories of my Aunt Panchita). The National Assembly posthumously garlanded both in the 1970s, and Lyra's image is on Costa Rica's 20 Colón note.

In music, Costa Rica boasts the internationally acclaimed operatic tenor Melico Salazar (1887–1950), for whom the Teatro Reventos was renamed in 1979.

A rising star in popular music is the Costa Rican-born singer-songwriter-dancer Deborah Nowalski Kader (b. 1980), known by the stage name Debi Nova, who studied at UCLA, performed with the Brazilian musician Sérgio Mendes and now works in Los Angeles. She wrote the 10 songs for her 2010 debut album *Luna Nueva*, including her single, *Drummer Boy*. Rather than strictly Latino, her music incorporates R&B and rap. She has also performed on *Dancing With the Stars*. She released her second album, *Soy*, in 2014.

Costa Rica has a vigorous free press. The country's newspaper of record is *La Nación*, founded in 1946. There are four other dailies, including the country's oldest, *La Prensa Libre*, founded in 1889. The daily with the largest circulation is the working-class tabloid, *Diario Extra*, founded in 1979. The English-language weekly *The Tico Times*, founded in 1956, is widely read by U.S., British and Canadian expatriates and by the country's intelligentsia, but it closed its print edition in 2012 and is now online only. Fifteen television stations provide a wide variety of entertainment. Costa Rica is one of only two Latin American countries since 2011 whose press is rated as "free" by Freedom House. The other is Uruguay.

Not coincidentally, Costa Rica's high literacy rate and its tradition of respect for freedom of expression have perennially placed it with Chile and Uruguay as the three least corrupt countries in Latin America, according to Transparency International. Yet, despite their national slogan, *"vida pura,"* roughly "life is great," Costa Ricans tend to complain about the institutions that have made them the envy of other Latin Americans. In the 2013 *Latinobarómetro* poll, only 38% of Costa Ricans said they were satisfied with the way their democracy works, two points below the Latin American average.

Blessed with some of the world's greatest natural beauty, and with the largest percentage of its territory in national parks of any nation, Costa Ricans are understandably environmentally conscious. Two national parks, La Amistad and Cocos Island, and the Guanacaste Conservation Area, are UNESCO World Heritage Sites. The country is in the midst of a "go green" campaign aimed at having a carbon neutral footprint.

ECONOMY: Costa Rica's main export crops are coffee and bananas. Industrial

activity once was limited to processing agricultural products for market and the production of import substitutes for domestic consumption. In recent years, foreign firms have established assembly plants.

Tourism is a rapidly growing industry, thanks to beautiful beaches on both coasts and a number of rain forest reserves, and in 1995 became the largest source of foreign exchange. Costa Rica has proportionately more land in national parks than any other country. A record 2.34 million tourists visited Costa Rica in 2012, an increase of 200,000 from 2011, bringing in more than $2.4 billion in foreign exchange. In 2013, that rose 3.6% to 2.4 million tourists. The Travel and Tourism Competitiveness Index ranked Costa Rica the third most competitive tourist destination in Latin America and 47th in the world for 2013.

Costa Rica also has proven an ideal site for a relatively luxurious retirement at a modest cost for U.S. citizens. Stability and lower prices for everything but imported goods are attractive to middle-class retirees. Costa Rica advertises itself in U.S. media as an excellent place for retirees, attracting widespread interest. About 50,000 Americans have settled here.

Motorola announced in 1998 it would begin scaling back the output of its Costa Rican plant, but the impact was more than neutralized by the opening of Intel's Pentium processor plant. The plant's $2–3 billion in exports since 1999 helped give Costa Rica trade surpluses, compared with earlier huge deficits. It accounted for about 20% of Costa Rica's exports, and Intel invested another $800 million in its Costa Rica operations. But shortly after the 2014 presidential election, Intel announced it would lay off 1,500 workers and move its operations to China, Malaysia and Vietnam.

After the initial construction was over, GDP growth for 2000 was a meager 1.4%, only .7% in 2001, and 3.0% in 2002.

Political stability, an educated labor force and the Rodríguez administration's eight-year tax exemption for manufacturers of export products, proved attractive to foreign investors. One target: the cumbersome government-owned electricity and telecommunications company, which Rodríguez attempted unsuccessfully to privatize. Costa Ricans have proven stubbornly reluctant to dismantle the quasi-socialist public sector, apparently out of fear of the unknown and despite the privatization trend that has swept Latin America. Even cellular telephone service and insurance are state-owned in Costa Rica. High-tech and ecotourism are gradually transforming the Costa Rican economy, replacing the far more market-sensitive coffee and bananas as the mainstays of the economy.

Costa Rica

Growth rose to 8.8% in 2006 and 7.8% for 2007. With the global recession, it dropped to 2.6% in 2008, the lowest since 2002, and shrank by –1.3% in 2009. Since then growth has been steady and consistent: 4.7% in 2010, 4.2% in 2011, 4.8% in 2012 and 3.5% in 2013. Growth was expected to slow to 2.2% in 2014 because of the Intel closure. The Bank of America also announced it would lay off 1,500 workers.

Despite Costa Rica's relatively high standard of living compared with most Latin American countries, 24.8% of the population was below the poverty line in 2011.

Unemployment has remained steady and quite low by Latin American standards: 6.7% in 2003, 4.6% in 2007 and 4.9% in 2008. With the recession, it jumped to 7.8% in 2009, but fell slightly to 6.9% in 2010. It was 6.5% in 2011, then climbed to 7.9% in 2012 and 2013.

Inflation has steadily declined from a high of 11.5% in 2007 to 4.5% in 2012. It rose to 5.6% in 2013.

Costa Rica became a signatory in 2004 to the Central American Free Trade Agreement with the United States, El Salvador, the Dominican Republic, Guatemala, Honduras and Nicaragua, but ratification was opposed by labor unions and some business sectors because of concerns over the state-owned insurance and telecommunications industries, which are sacred cows. Ratification became an issue in the 2006 presidential election. The winner, Oscar Arias, favored ratification, which was narrowly approved in a referendum on October 7, 2007 (see History).

In 2010, Costa Rica expressed an interest in joining the Asia-Pacific Economic Conference (APEC), but it has not been admitted.

In his second administration, President Oscar Arias oversaw a reduction in the once-crushing public debt, although in 2008 it was still 42.2% of GDP, climbing to 49.3% in 2009. Under President Laura Chinchilla, the public debt soared from 42.7% of GDP in 2010 to 51.9% in 2012.

Costa Rica enjoyed its first budget surplus in 50 years in 2007, but under Chinchilla it became a $977 million deficit, or 5% of GDP. Chinchilla imposed a painful austerity package designed to reduce the deficit, and imposed a moratorium on oil exploration in favor of promoting ecotourism. She left office with the lowest approval rating of any leader in the Western Hemisphere. The new president, Luis Guillermo Solís, who took office on May 8, 2014, called the deficit the "greatest challenge" facing his government and pledged to bring it under control within two years.

THE FUTURE: Although Costa Ricans grumbled for years about suspected corruption by their politicians, they were nonetheless boastful that their political system was still far more circumspect than those of most other Latin American countries. Indeed, Transparency International consistently rates Costa Rica in its annual Corruption Perceptions Index among the three least corrupt countries in Latin America; only Chile and Uruguay are regarded as less corrupt (see Latin America Today).

But the jailing of former Presidents Calderón and Rodríguez in 2004, and the investigations against President Pacheco and former President Figueres, shook Costa Ricans' pride in their country's perceived rectitude. They became like parents who thought their teenage daughter had done nothing worse than smoke cigarettes and drink beer, only to discover she had been smoking marijuana and charging the soccer team for sexual favors. Calderón became the first Costa Rican president to be convicted of anything; he was sentenced to five years in 2009. Rodríguez was convicted in 2011 and also sentenced to five years. Oscar Arias' second term in office, 2006–10, was the first in almost two decades that was largely untainted by scandal.

Laura Chinchilla made history in 2010 as Costa Rica's first woman president. Other than bearing a child out of wedlock—little more than a peccadillo in Latin America—she apparently was free of scandal in her public career. Chinchilla steered a moderate course in economic and diplomatic matters, and demonstrated her mettle by suing Daniel Ortega's Nicaragua, Central America's neighborhood bully, in the International Court of Justice over Nicaragua's incursion into Costa Rican territory. But she failed to come to grips with a budget deficit and a crushing national debt, and her attempts to do so drove down her popularity among her spoiled countrymen, who also expected her to do something about the growing crime problem. In 2010 the homicide rate was 11 per 100,000, among the top 26 countries in the world. In 2011, it at least had dropped to 10 per 100,000. By comparison, Uruguay's was only 6 and the United States', 5.

In 2012, her approval rating in Mexico's Mitofsky poll was 12%, and by October 2013, it was 9%, the lowest of any leader in the hemisphere.

The Costa Ricans' attitude toward their once-envied democracy has soured. The annual *Latinobarómetro* survey by *The Economist* showed the percentage of Costa Ricans who believed democracy is preferable to any other form of government dropped from 80% in 1996 to only 53% in 2013. It dropped 12 points just between 2011 and 2013, the largest drop of the 18 nations in the survey. Only 38% said in 2013 they were satisfied with the way their democracy is working, two points below the Latin American average.

Small wonder that Costa Ricans turned their backs on the two traditional parties in the 2014 presidential election and elected Luis Guillermo Solís of the 12-year-old Civic Action Party. Solís, who turned 56 on April 25, is of mixed Jamaican and Chinese ancestry. His father was a shoemaker. He served as ambassador to Panama under Arías but has more of a reputation as a left-wing academic. He earned his master's degree from Tulane University in New Orleans and taught one year at Florida International University.

Costa Rican businessmen and potential foreign investors are watching closely to see just how far left he plans to take the country. With the departure of Intel Corporation and the Bank of America, he needs to lure in new companies to replace those 3,000 jobs. He will be more successful if he proves to be a pragmatic leftist like outgoing Salvadoran President Mauricio Funes rather than a firebrand Marxist like Ecuador's Rafael Correa. Besides, the Costa Ricans are not likely to stand for an infringement on their cherished freedoms as the Ecuadorians have done. He also has promised to balance the huge budget deficit in two years without new taxes. That could require cuts to Costa Ricans' equally cherished public services and welfare state, something anathema to most leftists. He may have as short a honeymoon as Chinchilla did.

The Socialist Republic of Cuba

"*Señores* Imperialists: We are not in the least afraid of you!"

Photo by Sheila Curtin

Area: 44,217 square miles; with the Isle of Youth, 45,397 square miles.

Population: 11,047, 231 in 2014 (est.).

Capital City: Havana (Pop. 2.14 million in 2010, est.).

Climate: Tropical with little daily or seasonal change. Cuba is buffeted by occasional tropical hurricanes from July to October.

Neighboring Countries: Cuba is an island, the largest and most westerly of the Greater Antilles islands, lying 90 miles south of Florida and separated from Hispaniola by 40 miles.

Official Language: Spanish.

Ethnic Background: Mulatto (mixed black and white), 51%; white, 37%; black, 11%; other, 1%.

Principal Religion: Roman Catholic.

Chief Commercial Products: Sugar, minerals and tobacco.

Currency: Peso.

Gross Domestic Product: U.S. $72.3 billion (est.) in 2012 ($6,528 per capita in real terms).

Former Colonial Status: Spanish Crown Colony (1492–1898).

Independence Date: May 20, 1902. (Spanish rule ended on December 10, 1898).

Chief of State: Raúl Modesto Castro Ruz (b. June 3, 1931), president of the Council of State (since February 28, 2008).

National Flag: Three blue and two white horizontal stripes; a white star in a red triangle at the staff.

Cuba, an island 745 miles long and not over 90 miles wide at any point, lies east and west across the Gulf of Mexico, 90 miles south of Key West, Florida. Cuba is gifted with moderate temperatures, adequate rainfall and excellent soils. While the general impression of Cuba is one of rolling hills, it is in fact quite mountainous in parts. To the west of Havana is the Sierra de los Organos, with elevations of up to 2,500 feet; toward the center of the island are the Trinidad Mountains rising to 3,700 feet; in the east the Sierra Maestra has peaks reaching 6,500 feet. About one sixth of the land is forested. The rough, stony headlands east of Guantanamo Bay are semi-arid and the source of copper, nickel, chrome and iron ores.

HISTORY: Columbus discovered Cuba in 1492 and was conquered by the Spanish in 1511. Indians offered little resistance and, decimated by hard labor and epidemics, disappeared fairly rapidly. By the end of the 16th century only small, dwindling groups survived in the mountainous areas of the island.

The Spanish conquest of the continent relegated Cuba and the other islands in the Caribbean to a secondary position in the rapidly expanding empire. Lured by the news of gold and glory coming from Mexico and Peru, Spanish immigrants abandoned Cuba to join further exploration and conquests. Two factors, though, compelled Spain to pay special attention to Cuba: its strategic geographical location, dominating the entrance to the Gulf of Mexico, and the increasing attacks by pirates, which forced Spain to concentrate its naval resources in "convoys," or fleets, for better protection of its rich cargoes. These fleets, one departing from Veracruz, Mexico, and the other from Cartagena, Colombia, joined in Havana and then, under the protection of the Spanish navy, sailed for Europe. Consequently the port of Havana had to be extremely well fortified, and the sporadic presence of these fleets allowed for a flourishing degree of commerce.

During the 18th century the development of the island gained some momentum. The decline of gold and silver production on the continent convinced many Spaniards to remain in Cuba. Garrisons protected several ports besides Havana;

Cuba

smuggling with other islands—principally Jamaica and Haiti, by then British and French possessions—increased trade. The rising demand for the island's first valuable export, tobacco, created favorable conditions for steady economic growth. The strategic importance of Cuba was highlighted in 1762 when Havana was attacked and captured by a large British expeditionary force. The British did not expand their occupation beyond the port, and they stayed less than two years. However, the attack jolted Spain. More fortifications were built on the island, more capable officials were sent to govern the colony and a program of road construction began into the interior. Almost simultaneously, the island's sugar production began to demonstrate its rich potential.

The independence of the United States in 1783 opened a close and expanding market, and the collapse of Haiti's sugar production in 1799–1801 during its devastating war for independence gave Cuba a truly golden opportunity. In the first three decades of the 19th century, the island changed rapidly into the world's leading sugar producer. Sugar production, however, required a growing number of black slaves, who would alter Cuban culture.

Fearing a repetition of Haiti's experience, and enjoying unhindered prosperity—the Napoleonic wars and affairs in South America had kept Spain occupied in other areas—Cubans were not eager to risk all in an attempt to break with the mother country. After 1830, this situation began to change. Concentrating her attention on Cuba, Spain increased taxation, imposed arbitrary rules for its own benefit and completely alienated the creoles (native-born Cubans of Spanish ancestry), by denying them any voice in the government. Seeking annexation to the United States, many slave owners promoted armed expeditions from southern American ports, but the North's resistance to the incorporation of another slave territory

José Martí

into the Union, and the eventual defeat of the South in the American Civil War, put an end to those efforts.

By 1865, the majority of the creoles still held hopes of obtaining reforms from Madrid. Only a minority still advocated independence. But an international economic crisis in 1866 and Madrid's dismissal in 1867 of a Cuban delegation demanding reforms set the stage for the *independentistas*. In 1868, in the town of Yara, Carlos Manuel de Céspedes raised the banner of independence.

Using guerrilla tactics, and under the guidance of able military leaders, the Cubans fought valiantly against an increasing number of Spanish troops for 10 years. Their failure to invade the rich western provinces (the struggle was limited to the eastern regions), internal dissension, ex-

haustion of resources and renewed Spanish promises of reforms, brought peace in 1878. But despite the Cuban Autonomist Party's efforts, few reforms materialized. By 1890, Cuban discontent was growing and a new, exceptional leader had appeared: José Martí. Poet, essayist and patriot, Martí managed to unite almost all Cuban exiles, organized a conspiracy on the island and prepared to renew the struggle. He dreamed of a short, popular war that would avoid the destruction of wealth, the rise of military *caudillos* and U.S. intervention. In 1895 the war began and Martí was killed in one of its first skirmishes.

U.S. Domination

From 1895 until 1898, the Cubans fought Spain's military might. This time, able to carry the war throughout the entire island, the rebels torched much of Cuba's sources of wealth. Increasingly alarmed, and stimulated by imperialist groups and a "yellow" (sensationalist) press, the United States finally intervened in 1898 after the explosion of the battleship *Maine* in Havana harbor raised the clamor for war to a peak. The "splendid little war" against an exhausted Spain lasted a few months and ended with U.S. military occupation of Cuba.

After reorganizing a country ravaged by war and disease, the U.S. military forces abandoned the island in 1902. That year, the Cuban people proclaimed a constitution, although the Platt Amendment enacted by the U.S. Congress gave the United States the right to intervene in case of crisis and the use of a naval base at Guantanamo

President Batista deposits his ballot

Bay. Tomás Estrada Palma was elected the first democratic president.

Estrada Palma's honest administration was marred by political turmoil when the president sought re-election in 1906, and the United States reoccupied the island for two years. After building a Cuban army and overseeing the election of Liberal José Miguel Gómez, the United States once more pulled out its military forces.

The next 20 years witnessed rapid expansion of sugar production, increased U.S. investment, persistent political corruption and instability of a one-product economy. Nevertheless, the republic progressed in many areas. Education improved, communication was expanded and a new nationalistic awareness matured. An economic crisis in 1919–21 resulted in a rising crescendo of popular demands for the abrogation of the Platt Amendment and strong protests against official corruption.

Liberal Gerardo Machado was elected president in 1925 and initiated a vast program of national regeneration and public construction. His popularity declined in 1928 when he sought re-election. It plunged even more after the economic collapse of 1929–30. Faced with widespread misery and with violent opposition spearheaded by university students and an underground dissident group known as *ABC*, Machado responded with brutality. By 1933, despite increased terrorism on the part of the government, the struggle had reached a stalemate; the opposition had no realistic hopes of toppling Machado, and the government was unable to eliminate its opponents. Washington again intervened.

Constrained by his own "Good Neighbor Policy," which precluded the use of military force, the recently elected President Franklin Roosevelt sent his trusted aide Sumner Welles to seek a legal solution for Cuba; his mission was to prevent a revolution and avoid U.S. military intervention. Posing as a mediator, Welles pressured Machado into making concessions, encouraged the opposition and eroded the army's loyalty to the president. A general strike forced Machado to flee the island. Immediately Welles organized a provisional government with the cooperation of the *ABC* and the majority of the opposition. But the revolutionary momentum disrupted his plan.

Despite the unevenness of U.S.–Cuban relations politically, the two nations developed close economic ties during the post-independence period through the 1959 Cuban Revolution. U.S. investment was encouraged and protected, and in fact became a mainstay of the Cuban economy. In spite of domestic Cuban upheavals, there was an unwritten understanding that neither U.S. investments nor Cuban tourist facilities calculated to attract Americans would be disturbed.

Some aspects of this relationship were resented by many Cubans, particularly the common U.S. notion that Cuba was a paradise for those seeking sexual adventures not explicitly described, but well-known. Many "French" postcards (pornography, judged by then-prevailing standards in the United States) had their origin in Cuba. Numerous films "for private exhibition" were produced and made in the island nation. Tourists relished the decadence offered by the casinos and nightclubs, many controlled by organized crime figures, chief among them Meyer Lansky.

Havana and other coastal resorts and towns were favored ports of call for cruise ships and there was regular steamship service catering to vacationers. A luxurious train regularly departed from New York—"The Havana Special"—which ran down the east coast through Miami to Key West over a rail causeway. From there, the cars were loaded onto seagoing ferries that took them to their ultimate destination,

---

The U.S. and Cuba
1902–1959

Despite the unevenness of U.S.–Cuban relations politically, the two nations developed close economic ties during the post-independence period through the 1959 Cuban Revolution. U.S. investment was encouraged and protected, and in fact became a mainstay of the Cuban economy. In spite of domestic Cuban upheavals, there was an unwritten understanding that neither U.S. investments nor Cuban tourist facilities calculated to attract Americans would be disturbed.

Some aspects of this relationship were resented by many Cubans, particularly the common U.S. notion that Cuba was a paradise for those seeking sexual adventures not explicitly described, but well-known. Many "French" postcards (pornography, judged by then-prevailing standards in the United States) had their origin in Cuba. Numerous films "for private exhibition" were produced and made in the island nation. Tourists relished the decadence offered by the casinos and nightclubs, many controlled by organized crime figures, chief among them Meyer Lansky.

Havana and other coastal resorts and towns were favored ports of call for resort and cruise ships and there was regular steamship service catering to vacationers. A luxurious train regularly departed from New York—"The Havana Special"—which ran down the east coast through Miami and went on to Key West over a rail causeway. From there, the cars were loaded onto seagoing ferries which took them to their ultimate destination, loaded with fun-seeking vacationers. This ended in 1936 when a devastating hurricane wiped out the causeway.

As airline traffic came into its own after World War II, Havana was a favorite destination of tourists and vacationers. This pleasant state of affairs continued right up to 1960, with all political considerations being put aside.

Cuba

loaded with vacationers. This ended in 1936 when a devastating hurricane wiped out the causeway.

As airline traffic came into its own after World War II, Havana was a favorite destination of tourists.

The Batista Era

There followed a military insurrection of army sergeants, headed by Fulgencio Batista, which was transformed by university students into a revolutionary movement that toppled the provisional government. For four turbulent months under a temporary president, the students and the sergeants (by then *colonels*) tried to enforce a radical and ambitious program of social reforms. Sternly opposed by Welles, the government collapsed in January 1934 when Batista shifted to the opposition. As soon as a moderate president was installed, Washington abrogated the Platt Amendment. For the following decade, *real power* centered around Batista.

Batista was neither a bloodthirsty dictator nor a counter-revolutionary. A man of humble origins, both shrewd and ambitious, he preferred bribery and corruption over brutality. Well aware of the importance of the nationalistic and social forces unleashed by the revolutionary episode of 1933, he tried to use them for his own benefit.

Encouraging the emergence of political parties and the return to the island of political exiles, he quickly restored stability. Labor unions were legally protected, social legislation approved and a modest plan for national recovery announced. After Batista harshly repressed a general strike in 1935, the Cuban political atmosphere became calm. Supported by several parties, including, ironically, the Communist Party, Batista convened a constitutional assembly, and in 1940 promulgated one of the most advanced social constitutions in all of Latin America. That same year, Batista was elected president.

Rum-running out of Cuba during Prohibition in the United States became a lucrative enterprise for organized crime. After Prohibition ended, mobsters like Meyer Lansky saw the potential for U.S. tourism in Cuba. Hotels, casinos and night-clubs flourished, as did the Cuban officials who benefited from payoffs.

With the price of sugar climbing during World War II, Batista's term coincided with a return to economic prosperity. In 1944, Batista crowned his accomplishments by allowing free elections. Ramón Grau San Martín, a hero of 1933 and head of the *Auténtico* Party, obtained an overwhelming majority. The *Auténticos* ruled from 1944–48 with a positive record of benefits for workers, respect for democratic values, a more equitable distribution of wealth,

Ché Guevara, 1959

continuing economic recovery and rising living standards, but they were tarnished by public corruption on an unprecedented scale.

Grau was succeeded in 1948 by a fellow *Auténtico*, Carlos Prío Socarrás, who proved equally venal. Before the people could repudiate the *Auténticos* in 1952 elections, Batista disrupted the political process with a military coup.

Trying to keep up democratic appearances, Batista promised elections in 1954. But the illegitimacy of his government prompted political parties and numerous sectors of the population to demand a return to "true democracy." Soon more radical opponents appeared. The students organized violent acts and on July 26, 1953—now a holiday in Cuba—a group of young men under the leadership of Fidel Castro made an unsuccessful attack on the Moncada Barracks in Santiago de Cuba. The sheer brutality of its repression mobilized popular support for the rebels. With Castro and his surviving group in prison, Batista renewed his futile effort to gain legitimacy.

Batista was "elected" to the presidency in 1954 and he allowed *all* political prisoners to go free—including young Castro. But opposition to Batista increased. While a Student Revolutionary Federation resorted to terrorism to achieve Batista's overthrow, Castro, who had been in exile in Mexico, landed an expedition of 86 men in Oriente Province in December 1956—among them his brother Raúl and an Argentine Marxist named Ernesto "Che" Guevara—and took refuge in the Sierra Maestra mountains of eastern Cuba.

Weakened by adverse propaganda and its own corruption, with a demoralized army incapable of mounting any serious operation, the regime consistently lost ground. When in 1958 Washington showed its disapproval by proclaiming an arms embargo, Batista was doomed.

On December 31 he fled the island (with millions of dollars stashed safely in Swiss banks), and Castro's rebel army entered Havana in triumph on January 1, 1959.

The Cuban Revolution

For the vast majority of the Cuban people, Batista's downfall promised an end to an illegitimate and violent episode in their history and a quick return to the democratic process. Castro, and other leaders of the 26th of July Movement (named after the attack on the Moncada Barracks) had repeatedly promised the restoration of the 1940 constitution, freedom of expression, elections within 18 months and an end to political corruption. Thus, the 32-year-old leader, enhanced by his heroic image, received the almost unanimous applause of the Cuban people. Batista had fallen into such disrepute in the eyes of the world that Castro was considered a liberating hero; the Eisenhower administration hoped that firm and friendly ties with the new government on the island could be forged, together with enhanced U.S. investment. Castro, however, had other ideas.

The son of a wealthy Spanish landowner who studied for a time in a Jesuit seminary, Castro had very early shown inclinations toward violence and unlimited ambition: he wanted unrestricted, absolute power. Increasing his power with a series of laws which, at least temporarily, benefited the masses—agrarian reform, increased wages, a reduction of the cost of public services—he simultaneously

Fidel pursuing his passion for baseball, 1960

used his popularity, or his charisma, as a weapon to crush his opponents.

Dr. Manuel Urrutia, the same man he had appointed president six months before, was forced to resign under a barrage of insults. A new slogan appeared: "Revolution first, elections later!" Special tribunals dealt harshly with *Batistianos* and later with anyone accused of counter-revolution; about 550 were executed by firing squads. In late 1959, one of the heroes of the revolution, Major Huber Matos, resigned to protest an increasing communist influence in the government. He was sentenced to 20 years in prison. By the end of that year, almost all of the media were under government control. Ominously, another slogan proclaimed that "to be anti-communist is to be counter-revolutionary."

Castro also began building a formidable military apparatus, commanded by his brother, Raúl. He also appointed "Che" Guevara as minister of industry. Guevara embarked on a disastrous plan to communize Cuba's means of production. Tens of millions of dollars worth of U.S. land and business holdings were expropriated, further souring bilateral relations. In 1960, the United States retaliated with an economic embargo of the Castro regime, still in effect four decades later, and in January 1961 the outgoing Eisenhower administration severed diplomatic relations.

Meanwhile, there was widespread disillusionment in Cuba. Tens of thousands left the island (with their descendants, the figure is now more than 2 million); others organized resistance. Anti-communist guerrillas appeared in the central mountains and acts of sabotage became common.

Encouraged by this show of resistance, the U.S. CIA and Cuban exiles in Florida hatched a scheme for Cuban expatriates to invade. The people, supposedly fed up with Castro, were anticipated to join the invaders in a groundswell movement that would envelop and suffocate the newborn regime. In April 1961, an expedition of about 1,200 Cuban exiles invaded at the Playa Girón, known in English as the Bay of Pigs, on the southern coast of Cuba. The size of the force, the anticipated response by Castro's forces and the terrain involved all mandated the use of air support. Further, no coordination had been undertaken with internal Cuban resistance forces, which had little, if any, organization. When President Kennedy decided at the last minute to withhold the crucial air support, the invasion force was a sitting duck target for Castro's army. The whole plan was, in the words of Sir Winston Churchill, "a wretched half-measure." About 100 of the invaders were killed and the remainder captured.

Castro triumphantly announced that total victory had been won against "American imperialism," and he proceeded to wipe out all remaining internal resistance. Defiantly, he proclaimed Cuba a socialist state. Emboldened by what appeared to be an indication of U.S. weakness, the Soviet Union, which until then had refrained from any military commitment, began sending advisers and vast amounts of military equipment to Cuba—including intermediate-range ballistic missiles with nuclear warheads.

In October 1962, President Kennedy, still smarting from the Bay of Pigs fiasco, imposed a naval "quarantine" of Cuba, placed U.S. military forces on alert and demanded withdrawal of the missiles. For 13 days, the world teetered on the brink of thermonuclear war. Soviet Premier Nikita Khrushchëv grudgingly complied with the U.S. demands, but only after obtaining a costly oral promise from Kennedy: the U.S. would never invade Cuba. Kennedy thus verbally abrogated a cornerstone of U.S. Latin American policy—the long-standing Monroe Doctrine. Emboldened by that assurance, Castro embarked on a series of continental revolutionary adventures.

Castro's formula for revolutionary success was guerrilla warfare modeled on the Cuban experience. From 1962–68, Havana became a center of support for leftist revolutionaries who spread their activities from Mexico to Argentina. Nevertheless, the formula failed. Opposed by local communist parties that rejected *any* revolution they did not control as the "vanguard of the proletariat," and confronted by armies much better trained than Batista's, the guerrillas were defeated everywhere. In 1967, Guevara was killed in Bolivia, becoming an international Marxist icon and martyr. A dangerous deterioration of Cuba's economy forced Castro to fold the guerrilla banner and to accept the orthodox communist line demanded by the Soviet Union. Castro applauded the 1968 Soviet invasion of Czechoslovakia and publicly criticized China's Mao Tse-tung.

Consolidating Communism's Grip

Unlike the dual party-government structure of the Soviet Union, Cuba became a personality cult under Castro, much as China did under Mao. However, three stated goals of 20th century communism were achieved with remarkable success: the eradication of illiteracy, universal medical care and public housing. The centrally planned economy of the Soviet Union did not appear. Even though he had no skills in economics, Castro waded in without hesitation, wrecking the economy. Erratic planning, concentration of total power in Castro's hands and burgeoning bureaucracies, capped by the maintenance of a huge military force (once about 450,000) resulted in declining sugar productivity and failure to develop other resources for trade and income.

Increased Soviet aid became vital for the survival of the revolution. When in 1968 Moscow applied economic pressure to avoid pouring increasing amounts of economic aid into a bottomless chasm, Castro surrendered more of what had become Cuba's limited independence. He made an urgent effort in 1970 to obtain desperately needed hard currency by mobilizing urban residents, sending thousands of them into the fields to harvest sugar cane with machetes, hoping for a 10-million-ton crop. The effort failed, and it disrupted the economy for months. The next year, Castro began a process of "institutionalization" (creating organizations theoretically capable of sharing his power) while yielding increasing control over economic planning to Soviet advisers.

The Cuban debt to the Soviet Union, despite its annual purchases of the sugar crop at a level above the prevailing world price, gradually rose to more than $5 billion. In an effort to repay the Soviets, Castro was receptive to a request for the use of his troops for international communist adventures. In 1975, Castro deployed 20,000 soldiers to Angola to prop up that tottering communist regime; by 1989, that force had grown to almost 60,000. Having no stake in the outcome of Angola's ongoing struggle, the Cubans turned out to be lackluster fighters. Many returned home infected with AIDS and without a "victory,"

Cuban militia woman, 1960

Cuba

"We are dignified and revolutionary Cubans." Propaganda in Viñales

Photo by Wayne Thompson

ending an unfortunate chapter in communist adventurism. Cuban involvement in Ethiopia, Yemen, Nicaragua, El Salvador and Guatemala also occurred during the 1970s and 1980s.

Both the United States and Cuba were humiliated in early 1980. Hundreds of Cubans stormed into the compound of the Peruvian Embassy in Havana, begging for political asylum. In a bold and unprecedented move, Castro suddenly announced that any Cuban who wished to leave the country was free to do so. The result was a frantic exodus, as thousands of small privately owned boats crossed the Florida Straits to the port of Mariel to pick up refugees in a Dunkirk-like evacuation. About 125,000 so-called *Marielitos* departed the island. Most were honorable and were assimilated into the Florida Cuban community as well as in other places. But a significant number were lunatics and criminals, some forced onto the waiting boats at gunpoint, who wound up in already overcrowded U.S. federal prisons. Many others were homosexuals, considered undesirable in Cuba.

It had been a master stroke by Castro, a means of emptying his prisons and asylums as well as getting rid of potentially troublesome dissenters. But even he realized that he had overplayed his hand. After tedious indirect negotiations with the United States, Castro agreed to accept the undesirables back. Many of the prisoners rioted, however, preferring life as detainees in the United States to life in Cuba. The so-called "Mariel Boatlift" became a political issue in the 1980 U.S. presidential campaign, one of several foreign policy fiascos of President Jimmy Carter that contributed to Ronald Reagan's landslide victory.

There followed eight years of increased bilateral hostility and U.S. military opposi-

tion to Cuban adventurism in Nicaragua, El Salvador and Grenada, among other places. The U.S. invasion of Grenada in 1983 and the increasing presence of U.S. advisers and troops in Central America made Castro more cautious. As a further demonstration of its submission to the Soviets, Cuba declined to attend the 1984 Summer Olympics in Los Angeles. Relations with the United States appeared to thaw briefly in 1984, but then resumed their frozen state when "Radio Martí" started broadcasting from Miami with U.S. government support. Cuba quickly jammed it.

Fall of the Soviet Benefactor

The ascension to power of Mikhail Gorbachëv in the Soviet Union proved fateful for Cuba. In 1986, Soviet trade terms became tougher, and subsidies shrank. Soviet aid had been as much as $6 billion a year. In 1989, Gorbachëv visited the island. He had already concluded that overlaying the Castro regime with Soviet technicians and advisers had not and would not work. Moreover, the Soviets by then had to borrow money from Western banks and to import food from the United States. The deterioration accelerated rapidly, and by 1991–92 Cuba was in the grip of economic disaster.

At the 1991 Politburo meeting, Castro praised the achievements of Cuba under socialism. Then his mood turned to one of rage—he berated the assemblage, lashed out at the shortcomings of the Cuban people, vilified capitalism and vented his anger on the United States, the trade embargo in particular, Americans in general and all the presidents from Kennedy to Bush. He blamed all of Cuba's problems on these sources, not on poor Cuban leadership.

Later added to his list of pariahs was the former Soviet Union and Gorbachëv.

Cuba began wooing of capitalist nations perceived as unthreatening, such as Canada and Spain.

Between 1989 and 1992, Cuba's annual purchasing power dropped from $8.1 billion to $2.2 billion. Sugar production descended to 7 million tons, even with rationing and dispatching urban workers to harvest the cane by hand (there was no fuel).

The administration of President George H.W. Bush tightened the 1960 embargo in late 1992 with the Torricelli Amendment. No U.S. company, affiliate or subsidiary in the United States or abroad, could trade with Cuba in any form. U.S. ports are closed to any ship of any nation or registry that has, within the previous six months, called at a Cuban port. These tightened screws, together with the disappearance of $300 million a year in Soviet aid, left Cubans in near-destitution. Increasing numbers attempted to flee in flimsy boats or inner-tube rafts. There may never be an accurate accounting of how many have drowned, died of dehydration or been eaten by sharks in a desperate attempt to escape their misery.

Cuba's economic prostration brought some basic changes the 1990s. Possession of the U.S. dollar was legalized in 1993 and for 11 years was virtually the only hard currency on the island (see Economy). The peso officially traded at 1:1 with the dollar, but it took more than 100 pesos to buy a dollar on the open market. With the advent of the dollar came a system of black markets that still pervades everything.

Persons in certain trades and professions were allowed to become "self-employed" in a variety of enterprises, but only if they first secured permits. Of course, a permit that is granted can be revoked, which they later were. Small enterprises bloomed, particularly in urban areas. A large number of "mom and pop" restaurants were known for delicious food in Havana, for fees payable in U.S. dollars. Bicycle repair, plumbing, and similar services were by contract with one of the entrepreneurs. Physicians were not allowed the same freedom.

Cuba used the threat of a renewed flood of refugees to lessen or abate the U.S. embargo. Severe shortages of just about everything led to increased pressures to migrate to the United States. When these were resisted, there were anti-government riots in and near Havana. The Clinton administration, dealing with a flood of Haitian refugees, tried to discourage the Cuban refugees, but refused to alter the tight embargo. A stop-gap "solution" of interning refugees in the U.S. base at Guantanamo Bay failed. The attempts to leave Cuba for Florida resulted in the loss of many lives. Castro threatened to unleash another wave of boat people in the summer of 1995; this was averted by a U.S. plan to gradually admit the Cubans remaining at Guantanamo.

The Helms-Burton Act

On February 24, 1996, in an unexplainable and stupid act, Cuban air force jets shot down two unarmed small aircraft that were patrolling the waters off the coast of Cuba to protect the "boat people" from mishap. Three members of the Miami-based exile organization, Brothers to the Rescue, were killed. There was an immediate outcry in the U.S. Congress; the result was the Helms-Burton Act, strengthening the embargo. Any foreign firm doing business with Cuba could be penalized in the United States. The avowed purpose was to stifle even minuscule investment and loans to Cuba.

In some respects, the Helms-Burton Act backfired on the United States in that it appears to have done more to anger traditional U.S. allies, Canada in particular, than to punish Cuba.

Castro turned 70 in 1996. The once-flamboyant revolutionary toured Europe and attended the Latin American summit in Chile, dressed in stylish business suits rather than the fatigue uniform of old. In Rome, the avowed atheist visited Pope John Paul II, and the two announced that the pontiff would visit Cuba in 1998.

A visit to Havana in 1996 by Democratic U.S. Representative Bill Richardson of New Mexico succeeded in winning release of a number of political prisoners. As a further sign of an easing of tensions, the Clinton administration approved a request by 10 U.S. news organizations to establish bureaus in Cuba.

No foreign media, however, were allowed to cover Castro's seven-hour speech in October 1997 before the Fifth Communist Party Congress, the first in six years. The aging dictator squelched any hopes Cuba would deviate further from its dogmatic Marxism. He blamed the United States for a series of terrorist bombings at Cuba's tourist-oriented hotels, accusing the Clinton administration of trying to undermine the Revolution by frightening away badly needed foreign tourists (see Economy).

Castro tied the congress to the week-long ceremony to rebury the skeletal remains of Che Guevara that had been recovered from the Bolivian jungle after 30 years. On the eve of the congress, however, four dissidents, among them Vladimoro Roca, a former air force pilot and son of revolutionary hero Blas Roca, issued a document titled "Homeland for Us All," which ridiculed the congress for focusing on the past glories of the revolution without offering solutions for the problems of the present. All four were sentenced to prison.

Cuba suffered another public relations disaster with the defection to Costa Rica in 1997 of the talented pitcher Orlando "El Duque" Hernández, half-brother of the Florida Marlins' Livan Hernández. Livan Hernández had defected in Mexico in 1995, and in 1996, his half-brother was banned from playing baseball in Cuba. Orlando Hernández was given a U.S. visa and was recruited into the Majors. It was yet another humiliation for the baseball-loving Castro. So was the much-publicized

request of his 41-year-old daughter, Alina Fernández-Revuelta, for political asylum in Spain during the papal visit.

The Papal Visit of 1998

Another public relations gimmick was even more stunning: Castro's invitation to Pope John Paul II to visit Cuba, which the pope accepted. This was a major gamble for Castro, because he would not be able to censor the strong-willed pope the way he controls his own people's thinking. On the other hand, he apparently reasoned, the gesture might bring a relaxing of the U.S. trade embargo.

Enigmatic as ever, Castro declared at the 1997 Ibero-American Summit in Venezuela that Cuba would never deviate from its revolutionary course, rejecting calls from his peers for more respect for human rights. Yet, as a gesture to the pope, Castro permitted the first Christmas holiday Cubans had had since 1969 (the declaration of atheism as official state doctrine had been rescinded in 1992). He also eased restrictions on religious worship, and suddenly Catholic churches were filled for Mass; other sects received increased interest as well from a people starved for spirituality, including young people born after the Revolution.

The pope's four-day visit in January 1998 was truly historic, with hundreds of thousands of Cubans attending open-air Masses. Castro, true to his word, welcomed the pontiff at the airport and even attended a Mass; he also addressed John Paul as "holy father" and recalled that he had been schooled by Jesuits. Hundreds of exiles were granted special permission to return for the event, many of whom were reunited with loved ones they had not seen for nearly 40 years.

The pope's public declarations must have made Castro cringe. He denounced human rights violations and the denial of religious freedom, and called for the release of political prisoners. At the same time, he noted that the Vatican and the Cuban Revolution find common ground in their concern for the poor. More importantly for Fidel, he lamented the human suffering on the island and called for a lifting of the U.S. embargo. The pope privately presented Castro with the names of 270 jailed dissidents and requested their release. In February, all were released but 70, who remained jailed for "security reasons." At the same time, the government reiterated that the laws against political dissent remained in effect, raising doubts as to whether there has been any meaningful move toward greater freedom of expression.

Nonetheless, Castro's gamble at least partly paid off. After the dissidents were

Varadero Beach—a protected area that the Cuban government would like all to believe is "typical."

Photo by Sheila Curtin

157

Cuba

Transportation in Cuba: bus (left) or rare private automobile

Photo by Katherine Dickson

On a happier note, Castro approved an exhibition baseball game in Havana in 1999 between the Baltimore Orioles and the Cuban All-Stars. Castro attended the historic, invitation-only game, the first time a U.S. Major League team had played in Cuba since 1959. Some observers compared the initiative with the "ping-pong diplomacy" between the United States and China in the early 1970s. Much to Castro's chagrin, the Orioles won the game, 3–2. The All-Stars redeemed themselves in a second game in Baltimore, defeating the Orioles 12–6. The victory was muted, however, by yet another embarrassing defection; a pitching coach went to a Baltimore police station and requested asylum. The Cuban team was abruptly ordered home.

The Elián González Controversy

On November 25, 1999, a five-year-old Cuban boy, Elián González, was found clinging to an inner-tube off the east coast of Florida. In the ensuing days, the boy was turned over to an uncle in Miami, and it was learned that he was one of just three survivors of a raft that left Cuba with 11 people on board. Among those lost were the boy's mother and her boyfriend.

The case became a media sensation in the United States, while Castro exploited it for propaganda value. He declared the boy had been "kidnapped" by his mother and demanded that he be returned to his father in Cuba. He organized mass demonstrations to focus world attention on the case. Counter-demonstrations soon

freed, President Clinton resumed sales of medical goods and of airline service that had been severed after the 1996 downing of the two unarmed planes. He also renewed permission for dollars to be sent to Cuba. Since then, however, U.S.-Cuban relations resumed their usual roller-coaster course, while continued repression brought more international condemnation.

Dissent and Baseball Diplomacy

The government implemented a new sedition law in 1998, aimed primarily at independent journalists and political dissidents. One of its first victims was journalist Mario Viera, who sent abroad a column, "Morals in Underwear," that lampooned the Cuban justice system and poked fun at Foreign Minister José Peraza Chapeau. Viera was jailed for "defaming" Peraza Chapeau, and his trial drew about a dozen courageous protesters.

Still another independent journalist, Jesús Joel Díaz Hernández, was sentenced to four years in 1999 for "dangerous social behavior." The New York-based Committee to Protect Journalists named Castro as one of the world's 10 "enemies of the press."

The so-called "Group of Four" was sentenced in 1999 to jail terms ranging from three and a half to five years for issuing the 1997 document criticizing the party congress. The sentences sparked protests on the island and brought denunciations from human rights groups abroad.

The Cuban dissidents' courageous activities have been reminiscent of the nonviolent movements of Gandhi, Martin Luther King, Lech Walesa and Aung San Suu Kyi. In 1999, they opened a "school" for teaching the tactics of civil disobedience. Two opposition movements boldly delivered to the Council of State a document

that detailed plans for a peaceful transition to democracy.

Dr. Oscar Elías Biscet, a well-known physician and dissident, was sentenced to three years in prison for "public disorder and instigating crime." His offense: He hung three Cuban flags upside down as a symbol of protest!

International pressure against Castro's repression continued. The Inter American Press Association, the Committee to Protect Journalists and Reporters Sans Frontières in France all sent notes to Castro demanding he release jailed independent journalists and stop harassing others. One such independent journalist, Raúl Rivero, was named the recipient of the prestigious Maria Moors Cabot Award by Columbia University in 1999, but the government refused to grant him a visa to accept it.

Another leading dissident, Elizardo Sánchez, formed the Commission for Human Rights and National Reconciliation, which monitors dissidents' arrests and reports them to the outside world.

In 2000, the government unexpectedly granted early release to three of four dissidents imprisoned in 1997 for criticizing a Communist Party document to foreign journalists. The case had sparked international condemnation, even from Castro's friend, Colombian Nobel Laureate Garbriel García Márquez. One of those released, Marta Beatríz Roque, an economist, had staged a two-month hunger strike in 1999.

José González Bridón, leader of the dissident labor group Confederation of Democratic Workers, wrote an article in 2000 reporting that a dissident had been killed by her ex-husband, which was published on the wesite of the Miami-based Cuba Free Press. He was sentenced to two years in May 2001 for reporting "false news" about Cuba.

The bicycle is the only sure method of transportation in this gas-and-car starved nation. *Photo by Sheila Curtin*

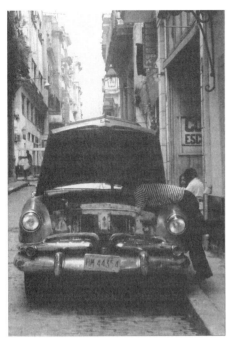

From a street scene in Old Town Havana, to . . .

occurred in the exile community in Miami to demand that the boy be granted political asylum and be allowed to stay with his Miami relatives. (The difference between the mass demonstrations, of course, was that participation at the ones in Miami was purely voluntary.) Castro also paraded the boy's tearful father, Juan Miguel González, before television cameras, to plead for his son's return.

Legally, Castro had a strong case. Under U.S. and international laws, a surviving parent is the presumptive custodian. There began a tortuous legal battle, after the Immigration and Naturalization Service declared that the boy should be returned to his father. Attorney General Janet Reno supported that position, where-upon the Miami relatives filed suit in federal court seeking an immigration hearing.

The case became a political football in the United States. The Republican-controlled Congress suggested either granting the boy U.S. citizenship so he could not be deported or granting resident alien status to the father. Juan Miguel González, a Castro loyalist, indignantly refused, and Castro gleefully milked his refusal for propaganda value. The case also became an issue in the 2000 U.S. presidential campaign when Vice President Al Gore, hoping to carry Florida, dramatically broke with the Clinton administration and advocated giving the boy resident alien status. Opinion polls, however, showed that a majority of Americans nationwide favored returning the boy to Cuba.

A U.S. district judge rejected the family's suit. The United States granted a visa to Juan Miguel González, who arrived in Washington in April. But his Miami relatives and their attorneys continued to file legal motions to delay surrendering Elián. Her patience wearing thin, Reno demanded that they surrender the boy, but still they stonewalled. Finally, in the pre-dawn hours of April 22, INS agents in SWAT gear stormed into the González house in Miami and hustled the terrified child into a waiting van.

Cuba's totalitarian leader praised Reno for the forcible seizure, praise that must have made Reno squirm. Father and son were reunited in Washington. That June, a U.S. circuit court ruled that the INS had acted properly when it had rejected an asylum hearing and that only a parent should have the right to make such a decision for a child that age. Although the decision was what Elián's father (and Castro) wanted, Castro nonetheless summoned more mass demonstrations in Cuba to protest it. Why? Because Elián and his father had to wait until the Miami relatives exhausted their appeals. On June 28, after the U.S. Supreme Court rejected the Miami relatives' appeal, Juan Miguel and Elián returned to Cuba to a heroes' welcome.

Cuba's Isolation Worsens

Cuba continued to experience diplomatic triumphs and embarrassments. In 1999, Havana hosted the Ibero-American Summit for the first time, but Castro was annoyed when some participants called for greater democratization on the island. Several leaders met with dissidents, and Castro lashed out at the international media for what he termed disproportionate coverage of the dissidents.

Whatever public relations value Castro may have gleaned from the summit was nullified in 2000 when the U.N. Commission on Human Rights in Geneva voted, 21–18 with 14 abstentions, to censure Cuba for its repression of dissent and religious freedom. Especially galling for Castro was the fact that two of Cuba's erstwhile allies, Poland and the Czech Republic, sponsored the motion.

U.S.-Cuban relations turned chillier with the election of the new U.S. president, George W. Bush, in 2000. The fact that Bush owed his razor-thin election victory to the overwhelming vote he received from the Cuban exile community in Florida, thus giving him Florida's 25 electoral votes, was not lost on the Castro brothers.

In 2001, Senators Jesse Helms—co-author of the Helms-Burton Act—and Joseph Lieberman—the losing Democratic vice presidential candidate—co-sponsored a bill to allocate $100 million to Cuban dissidents over four years. In an apparent case of reverse psychology, Cuban Foreign Minister Felipe Pérez Roque endorsed the measure, saying it would demonstrate to the world that the United States is seeking to subvert Cuba.

Despite the harder line toward Castro of the Bush administration, the president angered Cuban exiles by doing the same thing that President Clinton had done every six months for four years: He exercised the executive prerogative granted under the Helms-Burton Act to block lawsuits against foreign companies occupying expropriated U.S. property in Cuba.

. . . typical apartment housing in Havana

Photo by Sheila Curtin

Cuba

But Bush tightened enforcement of the trade embargo and showed greater support for dissenters. The United States offered scholarships to Cuban prisoners of conscience, and the U.S. Interests Section in Havana distributed radios and information about free-market capitalism.

Despite souring relations, Castro condemned the September 11, 2001, terrorist attacks on the United States and was conciliatory toward the imprisonment of al-Qaeda and Taliban prisoners at Guantanamo Bay. Castro even offered to provide medical and sanitary support, and pledged to return any prisoners who escaped. In response, Bush permitted the historic sale of food to Cuba as a humanitarian gesture in the wake of Hurricane Michelle, which caused widespread suffering. Cuba purchased $30 million worth of food.

By 2002, Cuba was increasingly isolated diplomatically and encountered serious problems in its relations with two traditional friends, Russia and Mexico. In 2001, Russian President Vladimir Putin closed an electronic surveillance station the Soviets had operated near Havana since 1964. Castro complained he had not been asked for his "permission." He accused Putin—probably correctly—of trying to curry favor with Bush, whom Putin needed far more than he needed Castro. What Castro probably lamented the most was the loss of the $200 million annual rent Russia paid.

In 2002, Mexican President Vicente Fox, the first opposition president in 70 years and a conservative businessman who enjoyed a warm working relationship with Bush, made his first state visit to Cuba. Fox and Castro engaged in cordial talks, aimed primarily at trade. During the visit, Mexican Foreign Minister Jorge Castañeda assured the Cubans that Mexico would neither "sponsor nor co-sponsor" a resolution before the U.N. Human Rights Commission in Geneva, implying that Mexico would abstain as it usually did. The visit turned sour when Fox, unlike previous visiting Mexican presidents, agreed to meet with Cuban dissidents.

Later that month, Castañeda said "the doors of the Mexican Embassy are open to all Cubans," a remark paraphrased by Radio Martí as an invitation to seek political asylum. Days later, 25 youths crashed a bus through the embassy gates. Police forcibly prevented hundreds of others from entering the embassy compound; foreign journalists were pushed back, cursed or manhandled. The Cubans inside the compound yelled anti-Castro slogans from the roof. The incident prompted a phone call from Fox to Castro. When the men did not seek asylum and refused to leave, Fox allowed Cuban security forces to enter the embassy to arrest them.

Next, Fox hosted an international poverty summit in Monterrey, which Castro decided at the last minute to attend, posing another dilemma for Fox because Bush was scheduled to attend. Castro left in a huff after his prepared speech to the conference, accusing Fox of asking him to leave; Fox denied it.

Then Mexico joined eight other Latin American nations in voting for a resolution, proposed by Uruguay, calling on Castro to permit democratic reforms; the resolution passed 23–21, with nine abstentions. Castro denounced Mexico's "betrayal." In a stunning breach of diplomatic protocol, he called Fox a liar for denying Castro had been unwelcome at the Monterrey conference, and he played for international journalists a recording of his telephone conversation with Fox, which did imply that Fox was concerned about Castro's presence. Despite the tiff, that May the two countries marked the 100th anniversary of their diplomatic relations. However, Mexico replaced its ambassador in Havana, who was seen as too friendly with Castro for Fox's taste.

Castro also antagonized Uruguay for the U.N. resolution by calling President Jorge Batlle a "lackey" of the United States. Batlle broke diplomatic relations that had been re-established in 1986 after a 25-year break, giving the Cuban ambassador 72 hours to leave the country.

Castro received another international rebuke in 2002 when the European Union balked at an aid initiative by Barbados on behalf of Cuba, which had just joined the 63-member African-Pacific-Caribbean group of former European colonies. Under the Cotonou Agreement, signed between the EU and the APC countries in 2000, the EU made a $12.7 billion aid package available to the APC over five years. But the EU demurred on speeding up Cuba's access to the funds, citing its lack of commitment to democracy and human rights. Cuba correctly labeled the EU decision a "humiliation and a slap in the face."

It was followed by another slap from the EU. The European Parliament named Cuban dissident Osvaldo Payá, organizer of the Varela Project (see next section) and founder of the Christian Liberation Movement, the recipient of the 2002 Sakharov Award for Human Rights and Freedom of Thought. Other recipients for the prestigious award have included Nobel Peace Laureates Nelson Mandela of South Africa and Aung San Suu Kyi of Myanmar.

In 2002, Cuba for the first time hosted a meeting of the 15-member Caribbean Community (CARICOM), for which Cuba has only observer status. Cuba reapplied for inclusion in the Cotonou Agreement, and the CARICOM states pledged to support Cuba. Poul Nielson, EU commissioner for development and humanitarian aid, met with Cuban authorities. Some Cuban dissidents favored Cuba's inclusion in Cotonou, believing Cuba would be under more pressure to adhere to democratic principles, while others argued that it would merely reward Castro's government for its repression. Nielson concluded that Cuba's inclusion could help bring about democratic reform. However, the EU quickly saw the prospects for Cuban democratization for what they are: an illusion (see Crackdown and Aftermath).

Perhaps in response to its growing isolation and alienation, Cuba suddenly declared it was willing to sign the Nuclear

Relaxing in Santiago *Photo by Wayne Thompson*

Cuba's three propaganda "newspapers"

Non-Proliferation Treaty, which it had always refused to do on the grounds that it somehow needed to "defend" itself.

Castro witnessed first-hand just how isolated his archaic system is when he visited another old friend, China, in 2003, his first visit in seven years. Castro confessed his amazement at the changes since his last visit, changes that had made China an economic powerhouse through market reforms. But Castro made it clear when that he did not intend to institute similar reforms.

The Varela Project

In 2002, Castro stunned the world, as he had with the invitation to the pope in 1998, by inviting former U.S. President Jimmy Carter to visit Cuba; Carter, long a champion of Latin American democracy, accepted.

Carter spent five days in Cuba, the highest-ranking American to visit Cuba since 1959. Castro kept his word to allow Carter to address the Cuban people in his unpracticed Spanish without censorship. In his live address on radio and televi-sion, which was reported verbatim in the next day's issue of the official newspaper *Granma*, Carter denounced Cuba's restrictions on human rights, and he endorsed the Varela Project, a petition drive initiated by dissidents and signed by 11,020 Cubans, for a referendum on free elections and free expression. Of course, his puzzled listeners had read or heard nothing about the Varela Project through the Cuban media. Carter also called for an end to the U.S. embargo. Castro trumpeted Carter's call for an end to the embargo, while ignoring his calls for democratization.

Almost as if in response to Carter's call for an end to the embargo, Bush flew to Miami to deliver a policy address on the 100th anniversary of Cuban independence on May 20. Bush rejected any notion of rescinding the embargo, and called on Castro to impose long-overdue reforms.

Castro cynically launched a petition drive of his own, one calling for a constitutional amendment declaring the principles of the Cuban Revolution "untouchable"—in effect, a constitutional amendment forbidding constitutional amendments. The government claimed that 8.2 million of the country's 11 million people—statistically, virtually everyone of voting age and then some—had signed the petition, which went before the National Assembly. The 557 deputies, of course, approved the amendment unanimously, without discussion. There was one major difference between the two petition drives: It did not require any courage to sign Castro's petition.

Castro's own petition drive was an indication that the dissidents' efforts were striking a raw nerve. The world soon learned how raw that nerve was.

'Primavera Negra'

Undeterred by the predictable rejection of the Varela Project, the dissident movement organized the Assembly to Promote Civil Society. Organized by economist Marta Beatríz Roque, the group comprised 321 discrete movements and touted itself as a shadow parliament. Many in the group did not support the Varela Project, arguing that it is lukewarm, the first indication of a schism within the opposition.

In 2002, Dr. Oscar Elías Biscet, the dissident sentenced to three years for hanging

Cuba

Cuban flags upside down, was released three months before his term was up, but he was rearrested in December for participating in a protest in Matanzas.

Oswaldo Payá, the organizer of the Varela Project, was granted a travel visa at the last minute to go to Europe to receive the Sakharov Award from the European Parliament (see Cuba's Isolation Worsens), but not before his home was vandalized. The visa was granted after Spain, Cuba's window to the EU, applied diplomatic pressure. Payá visited eight countries and met with Pope John Paul II, Czech President Vaclav Havel, Mexican President Fox and U.S. Secretary of State Colin Powell, which did little to endear him to the Cuban government. Neither did Payá's nomination for the Nobel Peace Prize by Havel, himself a writer who had once opposed—and help topple—a Communist government.

Cuba held its latest "election" for the real parliament and provincial assemblies in 2003. Turnout was reported to be 97.6%, which the government and party hailed as "proof" of support for the Revolution. Dissidents boycotted the election, and a few courageously put up banners ridiculing it.

The chief of the U.S. Interests Section in Havana, James Cason, visited with 20 members of the Assembly to Promote Civil Society at Roque's home, declared the Castro government was "afraid" to grant civil liberties and called for Biscet's release. Castro denounced Cason's action as a "blatant provocation."

Then, the ax fell. On March 11, 2003, Roque and other dissidents began a hunger strike. Almost simultaneously, during the visit by EU Commissioner Nielson to discuss the Cotonou Agreement, by which Cuba stood to benefit by as much as $100 million, Vladimiro Roca and other leading dissidents petitioned the EU to deny Cuba's admission. Coincidentally or not, it was the same week the United States invaded Iraq. On March 18, with the attention of the world's media focused on Iraq, authorities rounded up some of the country's best-known dissidents, whom the government labeled "mercenaries," including Roque. When the roundup was completed, 78 people had been jailed, 21 of them independent journalists, including the best-known journalist, Raúl Rivero, and Hector Palacios, who had been active in the Varela Project. The predictable charge: subversive activities. As significant as the list of those who had been arrested was the list of those who had not: Payá, Roca and Elizardo Sánchez.

Justice proved swift if not just. Trials began in April, and prosecutors indicated at first they would seek life terms for some of the dissidents. Foreign journalists were barred from the kangaroo-court

La Quinceañera—turning 15.
Photo by Gary Seldomridge

proceedings, but news quickly leaked out. Among the startling revelations was that one well-known independent journalist, Manuel David Orrío, was in fact an undercover agent who infiltratede the dissident movement. He had attended meetings at the U.S. interests section, and he testified that Rivero and other journalists were conspiring with Cason to undermine the government.

The sentences also were handed down behind closed doors, but news of them soon reached the international media: Roque and Rivero, 20 years; Palacios and Biscet, 25. The heaviest sentence, 27 years, was meted out to journalist Omar Rodrí-

guez Saludes. His crime: launching Cuba's first independent magazine! The dissidents went immediately to prison; 60 were held in solitary confinement.

Some Cuban dissidents defiantly continued to defy Castro, while as many as 40 independent journalists courageously continued to e-mail free-lance articles to foreign news organizations. They coined a term for the crackdown that stuck: *"Primavera Negra,"* or Black Spring.

Coinciding with the crackdown and the sham trials three hijackings, two of airliners and one of a ferry. Both airliners were hijacked to Key West, and 25 of the 50 passengers and crews chose to remain in the United States. Then eight hijackers commandeered a ferry with 50 passengers and attempted to take it to Florida, but low fuel forced it back to Mariel. Cuban troops stormed the ferry and arrested the hijackers, who were tried just as the trials of the dissidents were unfolding. Three were sentenced to death and executed by firing squad.

If Castro had thought that the world's preoccupation with Iraq would cause the crackdown, the trials of the dissidents and the executions of the hijackers to go unnoticed, he was quickly disillusioned and no doubt stunned by the ferocity of the reaction. All were widely reported abroad, and media groups like the Committee to Protect Journalists, Society of Professional Journalists, Inter American Press Association, American Society of Newspaper Editors and Reporters Sans Frontières all called on the Cuban government to release the independent journalists. International human rights groups like Amnesty International, Human Rights Watch and the Carter Center also denounced the arrests and stiff sentences.

The EU and Pope John Paul II also condemned the crackdown; even longtime friends Canada and Spain sternly called

Special show for children in Havana's National Museum of Fine Arts

upon Cuba to release the prisoners. The execution of the hijackers days later intensified the chorus of denunciations from countries where capital punishment is banned, like Mexico. Castro shrugged off the condemnation.

As another indication of Castro's growing isolation, Costa Rica, which in the past had supported resolutions that called only for a U.N. human rights monitor to visit Cuba, indicated it would support a U.S.-backed resolution expressing "deep concern" over the crackdown and calling on Cuba to release the dissidents. EU representatives also supported the resolution.

But the 53-member commission was still dominated by countries with despotic regimes, such as Sudan; it rejected the harsh resolution 31–15. Instead, it approved 24–20 the previous year's resolution for Cuba to allow a human rights monitor, French judge Christine Chanet, to visit the island. Castro had rejected Chanet's visit, calling her post "illegitimate," and refused to abide by the resolution. The Cuban delegate to the commission called Peru, Nicaragua, Uruguay and Costa Rica "repugnant lackeys" of the United States for voting for the resolution.

'The Cocktail War'

Days later, Cuba was awarded one of Latin America's six seats on the commission, prompting the U.S. delegate to walk out in disgust. The 15-nation EU—later increased to 25—not only unanimously rejected Cuba's participation in the Cotonou Agreement but voted to impose diplomatic sanctions that limited high-level visits to Cuba and reduced the EU's participation in Cuban cultural events. Even more galling, the EU announced it would begin inviting Cuban dissidents to receptions on European national days. The media quickly dubbed the Cuban-EU dispute the "cocktail war."

Castro defiantly labeled the EU, which buys 35% of Cuba's exports and had provided about $160 million in aid to Cuba over 10 years, as "a gang, a mafia" that had caved in to U.S. pressure. During a four-hour televised address, he called Spanish Prime Minister José María Aznar a "little Führer" and Italian Prime Minister Silvio Berlusconi a "fascist" and a "clown." Spain for years had been Cuba's leading apologist before the EU, even under conservative governments like Aznar's.

The next day, Fidel and Raúl led hundreds of thousands of people in a mass protest outside the Spanish and Italian embassies. Castro used the occasion of the 50th anniversary of the July 26, 1953, attack on the Moncada Barracks, the spark of the Cuban Revolution, to reject further aid from the EU under the Cotonou Agreement. His tirades against the EU and Cuba's mother country served only to further alienate himself from the community of nations. The European Parliament responded with a resolution formally condemning Cuba for its human rights abuses.

Another humiliation came in 2004 when the U.N. Educational, Scientific and Cultural Organization (UNESCO) awarded the Guillermo Cano World Press Freedom Award to Raúl Rivero, one of the imprisoned journalists. Cuba denounced the award as "deplorable and embarrassing." Yes, but for whom?

The regime suddenly invited a delegation of international journalists in 2004 to tour the prison where the dissidents were incarcerated, but they were allowed to speak only with inmates chosen by the government. They did not meet with Rivero.

Cuba again cast itself in the role of outcast at the third summit of 53 EU, Latin American and Caribbean countries in Guadalajara, Mexico, in 2004, which Castro did not attend. For once, Cuba was on the same side with the EU and its neighbors on a resolution condemning U.S. abuse of Iraqi prisoners. But the resolution wasn't harsh enough for Foreign Minister Pérez Roque, who accused the EU of scuttling a resolution condemning the U.S. trade embargo. Cuba was the only country not to vote for the final declaration.

Even as Castro was alienating old friends, he cultivated two new ones: newly elected presidents Luiz Inácio da Silva of Brazil and Néstor Kirchner of Argentina, who both assumed office in 2003. Castro attended both inaugurations. Kirchner re-established diplomatic relations with Cuba, which former President Fernando de la Rua had severed in 2001 because of Castro's insults. Da Silva, a longtime friend of Castro's, visited Havana to sign bilateral agreements and a deal to stretch out Cuban repayment of its $40 million debt to Brazil. Argentina and Brazil abstained on the U.N. Human Rights Commission vote condemning Cuba in 2004, and neither da Silva nor Kirchner expressed any qualms over la Primavera Negra.

In 2005, Uruguay's new left-wing president, Tabaré Vázquez, restored diplomatic relations as his first official act, although Castro did not attend the inauguration.

Cuba's relations with Spain also improved dramatically with the election victory of the Socialists in 2004. José Luis Rodríguez Zapatero replaced Aznar as prime minister, and Zapatero began interceding on Castro's behalf with the EU. He argued that the freeze in diplomatic relations was not having the desired effect. Spain, Hungary and Belgium re-established normal relations with Cuba after Castro released five dissidents, including Rivero, on health grounds; Rivero went into exile

Farm family in Viñales
Photo by Wayne Thompson

in Spain. Over the next three months, he released nine more. All the EU nations then resumed full relations. It seemed the "cocktail war" was over.

Self-Alienation Grows

Poland and the Czech Republic were the only EU members still skeptical of appeasing Castro without reciprocity; they were soon proved right. When the EU foreign ministers announced the EU would continue to monitor Cuba on human rights, Castro ridiculed the EU and said he had no intention of changing his policies. "What are they going to forgive us for?" he asked. "Cuba does not need Europe."

Britain's deputy foreign secretary for Latin America visited Havana and urged Castro to release all the jailed dissidents. Castro bluntly told him he would not release the dissidents and told the EU to stop interfering in Cuba's internal affairs. So much for Chamberlain-style appeasement of dictators.

Then EU Development Commissioner Louis Michel, a Belgian, arrived in Havana for talks with Castro as well as with Payá and other dissidents. Castro said the talks were "very frank," while Michel called them "very optimistic and positive." He proclaimed Castro "a very kind man." Michel noted that Castro had released 14 of the 75 dissidents and asked him politely to please release the remaining 61.

He did not, however, and Charet, still barred from visiting Cuba, submitted to the U.N. Human Rights Commission her scathing report on Cuba's refusal to free prisoners of conscience and its harassment of other dissidents. In 2005, for the sixth consecutive year, the commission voted to condemn Cuba, 21–17 with 15 abstentions. Castro responded that he "couldn't care less."

Meanwhile, "Cocktail War II" erupted in 2005 when Cuba expelled five European parliamentarians—three Spanish, one

Cuba

German and one Czech—who had gone there to attend a rally of the Assembly to Promote Civil Society, the dissident group. Entry was denied to two Polish members of the European Parliament and four European journalists were arrested. The EU expressed its "concern," while Italy and even Spain summoned the Cuban ambassadors to express their displeasure. Castro had alienated his best friend in Europe.

Cuban authorities permitted the rally of the Assembly to Promote Civil Society in 2005, but forbade coverage by foreign journalists. About 200 people attended, led by Roque, who had been released from prison. Not attending was Payá, now Roque's rival within the dissident movement. Payá had called for a "National Dialogue" on the transition for post-Castro Cuba that included 57 exiles, but some anti-Castro hardliners opposed Payá's offer to include members of the government in the dialogue.

Meanwhile, the wives of the jailed dissidents, nicknamed *"Las Damas en Blanco"* (The Ladies in White), staged marches and candlelight vigils to focus attention on the plight of their husbands. They continue to protest today, despite intimidation.

While relations with the EU went from bad to good to worse than ever, Castro hosted an amicable visit by his fellow autocrat, Chinese President Hu Jintao, in 2004, during which the two countries signed new trade agreements. China accounts for 10% of Cuba's trade and is Cuba's third-largest trading partner after Venezuela and Spain. China also pledged to invest $500 million in a new nickel plant, while Cuba agreed to export 4,400 tons of nickel to China for its hungry industries.

When Pope John Paul II died in April 2005, the always unpredictable Castro declared three days of mourning and even attended a memorial Mass at Havana Cathedral—the first time he had entered the building since his sister's wedding in 1959.

An amusing episode in the on-going battle for human rights was the appearance in 2005 of an underground video, titled *Monte Roque,* which satirized the government's electronic surveillance of its citizens. Other underground videos have spoofed such things as chronic shortages, but this was the first that actually poked fun at official policy.

Growing Cuban-U.S. Tension

The 2003 crackdown derailed, at least temporarily, the growing sentiment in the U.S. Congress to lift the embargo. After the easing of the embargo in 2000, Cuba imported 600,000 tons of U.S. agricultural products, paid for in cash. In 2002, Cuba bought $750,000 worth of grocery items, the first such transaction in 40 years. Despite objections from the Bush administration, U.S. agricultural executives held a food fair in Cuba in 2002, also the first in 40 years. Cuba concluded $66 million in food contracts.

Cuba was an issue again in the 2004 U.S. presidential election. Bush reiterated his hardline policy to please Cuban-American voters in Florida. Bush unveiled a 500-page report by a presidential commission he had named to study the post-Castro succession. Bush declared he would not wait for Castro's death to begin planning for a democratic transition. To tighten the economic screws, Bush changed the regulations for visits by Cuban Americans to family members in Cuba from one a year to one every three years, and he lowered the per diem allowance for expenditures during those visits from $160 to $50. He retained the current $1,200-a-year cap on remittances to the island.

To Bush's surprise, some leading dissidents, including Payá, Sánchez and Gutiérrez, denounced the report as U.S. interference and argued that Cubans and Cubans alone should decide the succession. Meanwhile, Democratic presidential contender John Kerry went to Florida to charge that Bush had given only "lip service" to Cu-

ban Americans, while he promised to work "full-time" to bring about a democratic transition in Cuba.

Castro responded by suspending sales of all but essential items at the island's 5,300 dollars-only stores, inflicting a hardship on his own people that he blamed on the United States. Castro abruptly ordered the stores reopened, but with prices about 15% higher than before, which he also blamed on the United States.

On the eve of the U.S. election, and in an apparent attempt to influence the outcome, Castro ordered the Central Bank to declare that the U.S. dollar would no longer be accepted at Cuban stores, even the so-called dollar stores. Instead, only the "convertible peso" would be accepted. Castro also told his countrymen to ask relatives living abroad to send remittances in Euros, British pounds or Swiss francs. Cubans could still exchange dollars for pesos, but with a 10% surcharge; other currencies were not subject to the surcharge.

Castro apparently hoped the measure would intimidate Cuban Americans to vote for Kerry, but Bush was re-elected, and this time he carried Florida decisively.

By 2005, according to the Cuban government, purchases of U.S. food had passed the $1 billion mark, and ever since then, the United States has been the largest source of imported food. Although the U.S. government permitted the sales as "humanitarian" exceptions to the embargo (and profitable for Republican campaign contributors), the Treasury Department made things tougher on Cuba. Effective March 31, 2005, Cuba had to pay for all shipments in cash in advance, before ships are loaded, instead of upon delivery.

The U.S. Coast Guard reported that the number of Cubans it had intercepted at sea had more than doubled from 2004 to 2005. Meanwhile, the number of Cubans who actually succeeded in reaching shore—and thus guaranteed asylum—totaled more than 2,500, compared with fewer than 1,000 in 2004. Dozens more were confirmed to have died at sea. An estimated 6,000 more entered the United States through Mexico.

In 2005, Michael Parmly replaced Cason as head of the U.S. interests section. At first, Castro heralded the change, but Parmly soon made it apparent he would continue Cason's support for the dissidents. He also erected an electronic billboard outside the interests section to post messages nettlesome to the government.

The Posada Carriles Case

The most serious U.S.-Cuban conflict since the Elián González controversy exploded in May 2005. The United States detained Luis Posada Carriles, a 77-year-

Farming in Cuba   *Photo by Katherine Dickson*

164

old anti-Castro firebrand who had bribed his way out of a Venezuelan prison in 1985 while awaiting retrial for allegedly masterminding the 1976 bombing of a Cuban airliner that killed 73 people off Barbados. Arrested in Miami, where he had supporters, Posada had been in the United States for two months, entering illegally through Mexico. Reportedly, he had intended to seek political asylum, but went into hiding. He surfaced to hold a news conference, which led to Cuban and Venezuelan demands for his arrest.

Posada spent four years in prison in Panama, where he attempted to assassinate Castro during a summit in Panama in 2000; he was pardoned in 2004 (see Panama). Cuba also accuses him of the bombings of hotels in the 1990s, one of which killed an Italian tourist. In a notorious interview with *The New York Times,* Posada admitted his involvement in the hotel bombing and lamented that the Italian had "been in the wrong place at the wrong time." Asked if he had any remorse, he replied, "I sleep like a baby." He later recanted his confession.

Venezuelan President Hugo Chávez demanded that the United States extradite Posada to Venezuela. He had already been twice acquitted of charges stemming from the airliner bombing. Posada, a renegade former CIA agent turned terrorist, holds Venezuelan citizenship, and the bombing was believed to have been planned in Caracas. Two other Venezuelans were convicted for their roles. Posada's supporters in Miami argued against extradition, saying Chávez could send him to Cuba, where he would face execution.

For his part, Castro termed Posada's arrest a "farce," questioning how such a high-profile fugitive could have entered and spent two months in the United States undetected. He also accused Bush of having a double standard toward terrorists. For once, Castro had not one but two valid points, and like the Elián González case, he milked the Posada case for its propaganda value. What especially outraged Castro and Chávez was that Posada was arrested not as a fugitive from justice, but for illegally entering the country.

The U.S. government played into Castro's hands by its clumsy handling of the case. At first, authorities said they would decide what to do with Posada within 48 hours, then began stalling. In 2007, a federal judge ruled he could be released on $250,000 bond, provoking outrage in Havana and Caracas; an appeals court upheld the granting of bail. Posada went to Miami, and in May 2007, a district judge dismissed the immigration fraud charges, saying the Justice Department had railroaded Posada. The Justice Department then obtained a perjury indictment from a federal grand

jury in El Paso in 2009, charging Posada with lying about his knowledge of the tourist hotel bombings as well as lying to immigration officials. He finally went on trial in January 2011, and in April was acquitted. Venezuela is still demanding his extradition for the airliner bombing.

Raúl and Reform?

On August 1, 2006, Castro stunned the nation and the world, announcing he had undergone surgery for intestinal bleeding and was relinquishing power "temporarily" as president of the Council of State to his brother Raúl. Fidel remained head of the party. The transition to Raúl generated headlines worldwide, as well as celebrations in Miami's exile community, as rumors spread that Fidel was actually dead or comatose. Fidel did not appear in public, but a video was released showing Chávez visiting him in his hospital room.

Fidel underwent two more operations. Another "proof of life" video was to reassure the Cuban people, but his shockingly gaunt, cadaverous appearance only fueled speculation that death was imminent. Castro's physician announced he was suffering from diverticulitis, a swelling of the intestine common among the elderly. Fidel failed to make his customary appearance at the 2007 May Day celebration.

It was widely believed in Cuba and abroad that Raúl's stewardship was largely window-dressing and that Fidel was still running things from his sickbed. He began writing a column, "Reflections by Comrade Fidel," for *Granma.*

Constitutionally, Raúl was next in the line of transition, but Fidel's duties were parceled out among six other top officials as well. Among them were Carlos Lage, the vice president, a de facto prime minister and a popular and able administrator; Felipe Pérez Roque, the foreign minister; Francisco Soberón, head of the central bank; and Ricardo Alarcón, president of the National Assembly, who was frequently interviewed by U.S. television networks. They muzzled any appearance of a power struggle, although Raúl publicly expressed an interest in Chinese-style economic reforms, while Lage publicly opposed them. (Both Lage and Alarcón were subsequently purged.)

Raúl acknowledged in 2007 that the economy was badly in need of "structural and conceptual changes." With some understatement, he said Cuba's $15 monthly wage was "insufficient" and called the state-run dairy production system "absurd." He had long been known to be impatient with the shortcomings of Cuba's bureaucracy, and he evidently listened to suggestions with an open mind. It was a

dramatic departure from his brother's single-mindedness and resistance to change. Raúl also showed an inclination to delegate responsibility, in sharp contrast to Fidel's micromanagerial style.

Raúl slowly loosened restrictions on private enterprise as Fidel had done in 1994, and paid debts to dairy farmers and others private producers. He replaced the aging, gas-guzzling Russian-built public transit buses with modern, fuel-efficient Chinese models. With Venezuelan help, he augmented the electrical system with thousands of diesel-powered generators and mandated replacing incandescent bulbs with fluorescents, reducing the endemic blackouts.

Lacking Fidel's oratorical skills, Raúl eschewed Fidel's mass rallies and long-winded speeches. Perhaps most dramatically, he reduced the number of political prisoners from roughly 300 to 240, although 61 of the 75 people jailed in the 2003 crackdown remained behind bars. Harassment of dissidents eased briefly.

A turning point in Cuban, and world, history came on February 18, 2008, when Fidel formally relinquished all power in a letter to the Cuban people published in *Granma,* which read in part:

"Dear compatriots:
"The moment has come to nominate and elect the State Council, its president, its vice presidents and secretary. . .
"My wishes have always been to discharge my duties to my last breath. That's all I can offer. . .
"It would be a betrayal to my conscience to accept a responsibility requiring more mobility and dedication than I am physically able to offer. This I say devoid of all drama. . .
"This is not my farewell to you. My only wish is to fight as a soldier in the battle of ideas. I shall continue to write under the heading of 'Reflections by Comrade Fidel.' It will be just another weapon you can count on. Perhaps my voice will be heard. I shall be careful.
"Thanks.
"Fidel Castro Ruz"

Days later, the 614-member National Assembly unanimously elected Raúl president of the Council of State, ushering in a new but uncertain era in Cuban, and Latin American, history. As his first vice president, he named José Ramón Machado, nearly a year *older* than himself, quashing expectations about grooming the next generation to take over. Few of his seven appointees to the Politburo's executive committee were under 70. Fidel remained first secretary.

Raúl continued his reform of what he called "excessive restrictions," lifting the

Cuba

prohibition against Cubans staying in hotels reserved for foreigners, a restriction most Cubans found offensive. Of course, few Cubans can afford to stay in the resort hotels on their $15 monthly salaries. He also pragmatically agreed to expand the acreage allocated to private farmers in the hopes of reducing imports.

He also announced he wanted to lift the restriction on Cubans' Internet access, but complained that the U.S. embargo prevented Cuba from tying in to U.S.-controlled undersea fiber-optic cables. Venezuela's Chávez promised to provide Cuba with access to its fiber-optic network. Like so many other things, Internet access in Cuba had become a black-market commodity. The Venezuelan cable was not activated until 2013, relying on a branch through Jamaica.

Raúl allowed Cubans to use cell phones. The Bush White House expressed skepticism toward Raúl's changes, but Bush said if Raúl were serious, he would allow Americans to send cell phones to Cuba.

Both these "reforms" proved to have strings attached. Cubans are prohibited from having Internet access on their home computers, and Internet access via smartphones also is banned. This has resulted in a "password black market," with Cubans who have lawful Internet access giving, or selling, their passwords to those who do not.

Raúl then announced he would call a party congress in 2009, the first since 1997, to discuss the eventual post-Castro—both of them—leadership. But in August 2009, he abruptly changed his mind, saying, "The party is not ready." The congress was eventually held in April 2011.

Cuba's struggling economy was dealt a dual blow by Hurricanes Gustav and Ike in 2008. The government expanded the program that permits private farming, increasing existing plots to 40 hectares (100 acres), while opening up new plots of 13 hectares on unused state land. More than 5,500 people applied.

As a sign of a possible thaw in relations between the communist government and the Catholic Church, Raúl attended the beatification ceremony in 2008 for Friar José Olallo, a 19th century monk known for his work with the poor and elderly. A miracle was credited to Olallo in 1999, qualifying him for beatification, the first step toward sainthood. It was the first beatification ceremony ever held in Cuba.

Return of the Hard Line

Cuba observed the 50th anniversary of the Revolution on January 1, 2009. International media descended on Havana in the expectation that Fidel would make a public appearance. He did not, but he continued to receive, and to be photographed with, visiting heads of state. Raúl delivered a hard-line speech for the celebration that reasserted Cuba's hostility toward the United States. Yet, just three weeks later, the enigmatic brothers began sounding conciliatory. Raúl said he would be willing to meet with President-elect Barack Obama, while Argentine President Kirchner quoted Fidel as saying that Obama is "a sincere man with good ideas."

On the eve of the Summit of the Americas in Trinidad and Tobago in 2009, Obama kept a campaign promise by lifting restrictions on travel and monetary remittances by Cuban Americans (Obama had carried Florida). Days later, in Caracas for a meeting of the left-wing *ALBA* countries, Raúl reiterated his willingness to meet with Obama, and in a stunning reversal of long-standing Cuban policy, said he was willing to discuss "everything, everything, everything," including such heretofore non-negotiable topics as release of political prisoners and freedom of the press.

Fidel quickly quashed the initiative in his newspaper column, saying the media had "misinterpreted" Raúl's words and that the basic principles of the Revolution were not negotiable. Raúl subsequently issued his own "clarification." There was no longer any doubt who was still calling the shots.

Obama stopped well short of lifting the trade embargo, saying it was up to Cuba to show good faith by releasing prisoners of conscience. A CNN poll that April said two thirds of Americans favored lifting the embargo and three fourths favor renewing diplomatic relations. Both brothers countered that the embargo should be lifted without any Cuban *quid pro quo*. Havana and Washington did resume immigration talks that Bush had been suspended five years earlier, but Obama did not lift the travel ban as many had expected.

In a dramatic development in June 2009, the OAS, meeting in Honduras, abruptly rescinded the 47-year-old expulsion of Cuba and invited Cuba to rejoin, contingent upon acquiescing on such issues as the remaining 220 prisoners of conscience. Fidel himself declared Cuba would not apply to rejoin the OAS; Raúl's opinion was not reported.

In December 2009, Cuba arrested Alan Gross, a subcontractor for the U.S. Agency for International Development, accusing him of spying and "destabilization" activities. The White House denied it, insisting Gross was helping Cuba's Jewish community with its Internet communication. The United States then angered Cuba by including it among 14 nations on a terrorist "watch list."

In this poisoned atmosphere, bilateral talks resumed in February 2010, but they broke down when Cuba refused to release Gross or to release dissidents. Secretary of State Hillary Clinton blamed Cuba for the impasse, accusing it of using the U.S. embargo as an "excuse" for its economic failures.

Gross was tried in March 2011. His wife and three U.S. government observers were allowed to attend. To no one's surprise, Gross, then 62, was found guilty and sentenced to 15 years. It is widely believed Cuba is using Gross as a bargaining chip to obtain the release of the five Cubans convicted of spying in the United States in 2001. Former New Mexico Governor and UN Ambassador Bill Richardson visited Cuba to try to effect Gross' release, but he failed and left the island angry. One of the five convicted Cuban spies completed his sentence in 2013 and another in February 2014. Both received heroes' welcomes in Cuba. Yet, Gross remained behind bars in mid-2014 and was reported in failing health.

Other issues overshadowed the talks as well. In October 2009, Cuba refused to grant an exit visa to Yoani Sánchez, who writes the controversial dissident blog *Generation Y* (see Culture), so she could fly to New York to accept the prestigious Maria Moors Cabot Award, presented each year by Columbia University to a courageous journalist. In November, she alleged that government security agents abducted and beat her.

That same month, 10 prominent dissidents, including Beatríz Roque, holed up in a Havana house and went on a hunger strike that garnered international media attention—but none at home, of course.

Then Orlando Zapata, one of the remaining prisoners from the 2003 crackdown, also went on a total hunger strike to protest his conditions. After 85 days, he died on February 23, 2010, prompting denunciations from around the world. A chastened Raúl Castro claimed he "lamented" Zapata's death, even as he continued to insist he was a "common criminal."

In 2010, Cardinal Jaime Ortega published an unusually harsh attack on the government in the church's monthly magazine, *Palabra Nueva (New Word)*, calling on it to negotiate in good faith with the United States to obtain a lifting of the embargo and alleviate the suffering of the Cuban people. In May, Raúl held a four-hour meeting with Ortega and Havana Archbishop Dionisio García. The Vatican foreign minister visited Cuba in June. Raúl agreed to allow the Ladies in White to march without harassment—for a time.

Guillermo Farinas, a 48-year-old writer and psychologist jailed in 2003, began a hunger strike after Zapata died. He was at the point of death in July when the government, terrified it would have another martyr on its hands, acceded to Cardinal Ortega's request to release the remaining 52 dissidents jailed in the 2003 *"Primavera Negra"* and allow them to go to Spain. Farinas ended his hunger strike, and was eventually released.

By October 2010, 41 of the 52 prisoners had been released and sent into exile, most to Spain and some to Chile. But the remaining 11 refused to leave prison unless they were allowed to remain in Cuba. In March 2011, the government relented, and the last of the 2003 detainees was freed. Dissident Elizardo Sánchez maintained there are still 100 prisoners of conscience, although even he admits some are common criminals.

Alas, the freeing of those dissidents did not stop the arrests of others or mean that Cubans were free to express themselves. Hunger striker Farinas was nominated for the EU's Sakharov Award for Human Rights in 2010, but the government denied him an exit visa. He was later rearrested and held briefly for participating in a protest over a dissident's eviction from his home.

As the first anniversary of Zapata's death approached in 2011, dozens of dissidents were detained, including Zapata's mother, Reina Luisa Tamayo, to discourage public demonstrations. When Tamayo and other dissidents gathered at the Havana home of dissident Laura Pollán, a leader of the Ladies in White, to commemorate Zapata's death, a crowd of pro-government thugs pelted the house with eggs and shouted insults. Tamayo was allowed to go into exile in the U.S. after the government agreed to allow Tamayo to take her son's ashes with her.

Government retribution was not limited to dissidents. Pedro Pablo Oliva, an internationally renowned artist and sculptor who was a member of the Pinar del Rio provincial legislature, posted a letter on Yoani Sánchez's *Generation Y* blog in 2011 complaining of constraints on opinion. He was promptly expelled from the legislature.

The regime continued to harass and jail dissidents. Weekend marches by the Ladies in White in eastern Cuba were harassed, sometimes with tear gas or pepper spray. In September 2011, about two dozen Ladies in White were briefly detained in Santiago, including Laura Pollán, whose Havana home had become a meeting place for dissidents (see above). The next day, two of the released *Primavera Negra* prisoners, Ángel Moya and José Daniel Ferrer, were arrested in the east as they prepared to take part in a march. A month later, Pollán was hospitalized in Havana with acute respiratory distress and died on October 14; she was 63. There was no evidence of foul play. Blogger Yoani Sánchez reported

President Raúl Castro

her death, which was picked up by media outlets around the world.

On Christmas Eve 2011, Raúl announced the unprecedented release of 2,900 prisoners—most of them jailed for common crimes. Whether it was a humanitarian gesture or a pragmatic logistical move to eliminate 2,900 mouths to feed, was not clear.

Dissidents who were not released included René Cobas, who went on a hunger strike in protest. On New Years Day 2012, he died of a heart attack, provoking the usual international condemnation. Then, on January 19, another dissident, Wilman Villar, 31, who had been on a hunger strike for 50 days and whom Amnesty International was preparing to designate a prisoner of conscience, died of pneumonia and organ failure. There were more international denunciations. The government responded the next day by releasing another hunger striker, Guillermo Farinas. Three days later, it released three AI-designated prisoners of conscience who had been held without charges for 52 days for participating in a demonstration, but threatened them with harsher sentences if they resumed their activities.

On March 18, just a week before the March 26–29 visit of Pope Benedict XVI, 70 Ladies in White were arrested but were released the next day. Even as he was leaving Rome for his visits to Mexico and Cuba, Benedict said Cuba's Marxist system "no longer corresponds to reality." In Cuba, he met with Raúl and said Mass before throngs in Santiago, where he prayed for those "deprived of freedom," and in Revolution Plaza in Havana. As did his predecessor John Paul II in 1998, Benedict also condemned the U.S. embargo. When the pope left, Marino Murillo, vice president of the Council of Ministers, bluntly averred to international journalists that "there will

not be political reform." Yet, responding to the pope's request, Raúl declared Good Friday a holiday—at least for 2012.

Major Overhaul

Besides the mounting domestic and international pressure for reform, Raúl was hamstrung by an ever-worsening economy in 2009 and 2010, including a soaring trade deficit from fuel imports, a downturn in tourism and GDP growth because of the global recession, damage from the 2008 hurricanes and the worst sugar harvest since 1905; and by revelations of corruption, which he acknowledged. He fired his education minister and the rector of the University of Havana in 2009, and the sugar and transport ministers in 2010, or for outright corruption. More firings came in 2011. Raúl mandated a new auditor general's office to probe corruption.

The government eliminated free hot lunches for workers, saving $350 million in mostly imported food, but granted workers a 15-peso-a-day (60 cents) increase as compensation. Offices were ordered to run air conditioning only five hours daily.

Raúl next allowed private barber shops and hair salons to begin operating again, as well as small cafés where workers could buy their lunches, which has stimulated tax revenue.

In September 2010, Raúl acknowledged that the socialist system as structured was unworkable and announced that 500,000 government workers would be laid off by mid-2011 and "encouraged" to go into business for themselves. Over the long term, he said 1 million state workers would be laid off, about one fifth of the total.

The government listed 178, later increased to 181, occupations deemed acceptable for the new entrepreneurs, so-called *cuentapropios*, including restaurateurs, electricians, hair stylists and clowns; doctors, lawyers, engineers and other professionals would have to continue working for the state. Cubans were allowed to own their own homes, but not sell them, and they could not "accumulate" property.

The oft-delayed Sixth Party Congress was finally held in April 2011, coinciding with the 50th anniversary of the Bay of Pigs victory. Its agenda was almost exclusively devoted to Raúl's proposed reforms; Fidel appeared at the final sessions. In his 2½-hour speech, Raúl emphasized that the reforms do not spell the end of socialism but that they are necessary to preserve the gains of the Revolution. He shocked many by proposing that government officials be limited to two five-year terms. He said that Cubans henceforth should have the right to sell as well as own their homes, and that Communist Party membership

Cuba

would no longer be required to hold government jobs. He advocated renewed dialogue with the United States, and even said it should be easier for Cubans to be allowed to travel abroad.

He also called for a "systematic rejuvenation" of the nation's leadership to prepare for a smooth transition to the post-Castro era, but he offered nothing immediately toward that end. Raúl was dutifully elected party secretary to succeed Fidel, but the No. 2 spot went to the government's first vice president, José Ramón Machado, a year older than Raúl but a loyal ally since 1952.

Raúl made no suggestion that Cuba should have free and open elections or a free and independent press.

Raúl's plan to unburden the bureaucracy by creating a new body of self-employed small businessmen, or *cuentapropios*, fell behind schedule. The list of 181 approved professions proved inadequate to absorb that many workers, and the newly installed system for levying and collecting income taxes was proving inefficient, resulting in a huge budget deficit amounting to 3.7% of GDP.

Raúl has since sent bewilderingly mixed signals on the pace of his reforms. He told the National Assembly in July 2012 that the reforms would continue, but "without haste." After permitting 181 categories of entrepreneurs, he has made it as costly as possible for them by failing to allow a system of wholesalers, forcing restaurant owners to buy food and equipment at retail prices. Then he effectively closed the tap on a current of manufactured goods, mostly U.S., that "mules" had been bringing in from abroad for resale and paying a few Cuban pesos for the excess baggage fee.

In September 2012, Raúl mandated that the fee for baggage over 66 pounds would have to be paid in the "convertible peso," pegged to the dollar, making popular luxury items like home entertainment systems and computers cost-prohibitive.

In 2011, Obama signed an executive order lifting the restriction that remittances could be sent only to family members, although non-family members receiving remittances could not include government or party officials. Obama then loosened travel restrictions, although visits to Cuba would have to be for academic, cultural or religious purposes. As usual, the Castro brothers grumbled that the changes didn't go far enough.

Cuba hosted two other high-profile visitors besides the pope in 2012—Iranian President Mahmoud Ahmadinejad in January and Brazilian President Dilma Rousseff in February. Cuba and Iran share rabidly anti-U.S. foreign policies, while Cuba has become increasingly reliant on Brazil—

along with China—for foreign investment (see Economy).

In the first hint that Raúl may be bringing younger blood into his geriatric power circle, he demoted two of Fidel's elderly henchmen in March 2012: José Ramón Fernández, vice president of the Council of Ministers, who had commanded the Bay of Pigs counterattack; and José M. Miyar, minister of science, technology and environment, once Fidel's personal secretary. Both were replaced with much younger technocrats.

Osvaldo Paya's Death

The dissidents and the international community were all shocked on July 22, 2012, when dissident activist Osvaldo Payá and another dissident, Harold Cepero, were killed in a car crash near Bayamo, Granma Province, in eastern Cuba. Payá, 60, and Cepero were traveling with two representatives of conservative European parties' youth movements, Jens Afren Modig of Sweden and Ángel Carromero of Spain; Carromero was driving the rented car. Modig and Carromero, who sustained minor injuries, were detained for questioning and admitted they had illegally brought 4,000 Euros ($4,900) from their political movements to aid the dissidents.

Dissident blogger Yoani Sánchez broke the news of the deaths, which immediately fueled suspicion that the two dissidents were targets of a government hit. Payá's daughter claimed, offering no substantiation, that their car had been run off the road. But both the Europeans testified to police that no other vehicles were involved and Carromero admitted he had lost control of the car on a sharp turn on the gravel road.

Modig confessed to bringing in the illegal contribution, contritely apologized and was allowed to leave the country. But Carromero was charged with vehicular manslaughter, putting the government in the ironic position of prosecuting someone for the death of a dissident. In October, he was convicted and sentenced to four years.

Sánchez and her husband were detained when they drove to Bayamo for her to cover the trial for the Spanish newspaper *El País*. Police quietly returned them to their home in Havana the next day, without incident. The government accused her of attempting to turn Carromero's trial into a media circus.

Surprisingly, Carromero was freed just two months later under a bilateral agreement with Spain that allows a citizen of one country convicted in the other to serve his sentence in his home country. In August 2013, Carromero alleged in an inter-

view with the Spanish newspaper *El País*, the Spanish wire service Efe and the *Nuevo Herald* of Miami that contrary to the Cuban government's account of the accident, Payá's car was forced off the road by a car bearing government license plates. He further claimed that Payá and Cepero were injured but alive when they were all taken to a hospital. He said that when he told an interrogator that a car had forced them off the road, he was slapped and told, "No, that's not what happened."

In 2014, Carromero was writing a book about the incident. It is unlikely to appear in Cuban bookstores.

Recent Developments

A potentially historic reform came in October 2012 when Raúl lifted the detested, 52-year-old requirement that Cubans obtain an exit visa for traveling abroad, effective January 14, 2013.

Putting the lifting of the exit visa to the test after 20 failed attempts, Yoaní Sánchez left Cuba for a three-month, three-continent, 13-country speaking tour. She met Obama aides, but not the president, at the White House, visited the New York offices of Google and Twitter and met with Cuban exiles in Miami. She also visited Mexico, Peru and Brazil, where rowdy pro-Castro demonstrators disrupted her appearance at the screening of a documentary about her and the quest for press freedom in Cuba. Even abroad, in ostensibly democratic countries, Cuban citizens are denied freedom of speech. In Europe, she visited the Czech Republic, Germany, Italy, the Netherlands, Norway, Poland, Spain and Sweden. There was some suspense about whether she would be allowed to return to Cuba, but she returned uneventfully in May.

The regime still makes it as difficult as possible for independent journalists to disseminate unsanctioned information. Internet access is limited to computers in governmental and some private offices, and smartphones are not allowed to pick up the Internet. Thus, enterprising dissidents use text-messaging and the new social media, like Facebook and Twitter, to thwart censorship, just as the dissidents did in the 2010 Arab Spring in Tunisia, Egypt and Libya.

Amnesty International added five new prisoners of conscience in August 2013 and called for their release. They were jailed for putting up anti-government posters in Guantanamo in 2012. Two are sons of Ladies in White.

It came as no shock in February 2013 when the National Assembly unanimously re-elected Raúl to his second five-year term, and he generated only mild surprise by insisting that he would retire at the end of it; if he lives, he will be 87. He joked to skeptical foreign journalists that, "I have the right to retire."

What did come as a surprise, and generated international headlines, was his announcement of a new, much younger first vice president in place of the 83-year-old Machado: General Miguel Díaz-Canel, 52, who effectively is Raúl's heir apparent. Little is known of his views on the reforms, and whether he will accelerate them or apply the brakes (see The Future). He is an engineer by profession and an army officer who rose through the Communist Party ranks. He has foreign policy experience and developed a relationship with Venezuelan Foreign Minister Nicolás Maduro, who succeeded Chávez as president when Chávez died in March 2013. Venezuela's oil largess remains crucial for Cuba.

Fidel, 86, spoke briefly to the Assembly, a response to rumors he had suffered a crippling stroke.

In the year since, the pace of reforms has slowed to a trickle and what changes that have been forthcoming can best be described as almost-reforms. For example, the government set up a showroom—which was nothing more than that—for new and used vehicles from Europe and China. But the prices are far beyond the reach of Cubans who make $20 a month or even of the *cuentapropios*. Some second-hand small cars were priced at $30,000, while new luxury cars sell for $250,000.

As another example, in June 2013, the government opened 118 Internet cafés around the island, which it calls "navigation centers." The catch: Access costs a prohibitive $4.50 an hour.

In October 2013, the government announced it would gradually phase out the dual currency system of the Cuban peso and the *CUC*, or convertible peso.

Although relations remain tense with the United States over the incarceration of Alan Gross, a seemingly mundane event generated photos and headlines around the world in December 2013 when Raúl and Obama unexpectedly greeted one another and shook hands during the memorial service for Nelson Mandela in South Africa. The goodwill was short-lived. In April, U.S. media reported a scheme hatched in 2010 by the Agency for International Development to create a Twitter-like social medium in Cuba designed to thwart the state-owned media and to foment dissent. The clandestine service, whimsically called ZunZuneo—Cuban slang for the tweeting a hummingbird makes—attracted an estimated 40,000 users at its peak. Besides circumventing the Cuban government's control, however, the plan also skirted U.S. law, which requires congressional approval for covert operations. Members of

Cuban state-owned media released this picture of a sweatsuit-clad Fidel Castro talking with unidentified people at the national Center for Scientific Research in Havana on July 10, 2010, apparently to dispel rumors that he was dead or incapacitated.
Photo by Alex Castro/Cubadebate

Congress reacted almost as angrily as did the Cuban government.

Relations also may be thawing with France, and consequently with the EU, strained for more than a decade (see The 'Cocktail War'). French Foreign Minister Laurent Fabius visited Havana and met with Raúl in April 2014. He was the highest-ranking French official to visit in 31 years. France is interested in increasing exports, while Cuba wants to be readmitted to the Paris Club for debt renegotiation. The EU is reportedly not as concerned about human rights in Cuba as it once was.

Blogger Yoani Sánchez attempted to create a digital newspaper in May 2014, but the government blocked access to the site (see Culture).

CULTURE: Cuba is an ethnic peculiarity in Latin America. The Spaniards largely exterminated the native Carib Indians, but the influx of blacks from the British West Indies gave Cuba a distinctive Euro-African culture. About 62% of Cubans today are black or mulatto. Although Roman Catholicism took root in colonial times and has survived the repression of the communist government, thousands of Cubans of African descent, both before and after the Revolution, practice a hybrid religion called *santería* that blends elements of Catholicism with ancient Yoruban tribal rites. Santeria rituals have actually become a lucrative tourist attraction.

The colonial-era city centers of Havana and Santiago, and its fortresses, are UNESCO World Heritage Sites, as are the old sections of Camagüey and Cienfuegos.

Although independence came to Cuba eight decades later than it did to its sister republics, some Creole writers and poets gained recognition during the 19th century. Best known of these is the poet José

Martí (1853–95), a leader in Cuba's quest for independence, who was martyred in a battle against the Spanish. Cuba's best-known 20th century poet was Nicolás Guillén (1902–87), whose verse celebrated the island's African cultural heritage.

Another celebrated 20th century Cuban writer in the Hispanic world and beyond was the novelist Guillermo Cabrera Infante (1929–2005), but the current Cuban government does not claim him because he fell out of favor with Castro in 1962 and did most of his acclaimed work after leaving Cuba in 1967. He won Spain's coveted Cervantes Prize in Literature in 1997. Most critics regard his most famous work as *Tres triste tigres* (English title *Three Trapped Tigers)*, published in 1967, which was a sketch of pre-revolutionary Havana nightlife. Also well known were the autobiographical *Habana para un infante difunto (Infante's Inferno)* in 1979 and *Mea Cuba* in 1993. He obtained British citizenship and died in London.

Two other Cubans have received the Cervantes Prize: Alejo Carpentier (1904–80) in 1977 and Dulce María Loynaz (1902–97) in 1992.

Carpentier, born in Switzerland of a French father and Russian mother, studied in Havana in the 1920s and settled there, entering journalism and helping found the Communist Party. He was jailed, then exiled by the Machado regime. He returned to Cuba when the Revolution triumphed in 1959. Among his best-remembered works is the 1974 novel *El recurso del método (Reasons of State)*, about a dictatorship in an unnamed Latin American country in the early 1900s, which was adapted into a French-Cuban-Mexican motion picture directed by the Chilean Miguel Littín (see Chile) in 1978. He was also a renowned historian of Afro-Cuban music.

Loynaz, whose father authored the lyrics of the Cuban national anthem, was a poet, remembered for the collections *Bestuarium (bestiary)* and *Poemas náufragos (shipwrecked poems)*. A posthumous English translation of selected poems was published abroad in 2002, *A Woman in Her Garden*.

Novelist, poet and essayist Cintio Vitier (1921–2009) received Mexico's coveted Juan Rulfo Literature Prize in 2002. He had received Cuba's National Literature Prize in 1988.

A young contemporary writer who has received several domestic and international literary awards is Amir Valle (b. 1967), who first gained attention in 2006 with his detective novel, *Santuario de sombras (sanctuary of shadows)*, published in Spain, and *Las palabras y los muertos* (the words and the dead). The latter won the Mario Vargas Llosa International Novel Prize. Another, non-fiction book, *Jineteras*, published in Spain, Argentina, Colombia and the United

Cuba

States in 2006, angered the Cuban government because it dealt with the sensitive topic of prostitution on the island. In 2006, while on a book tour in Europe, Valle overstayed his Cuban exit visa. He declared he had not defected but his intent was to assert his right to come and go as he pleased. He went into self-imposed exile in Berlin, where he remains. His website states: "I am a Cuban writer: this is my cross . . . I do not inhabit Cuba: Cuba inhabits me. And I love my island with the same rage that makes me suffer. I love her diversity and I suffer from her blindness." His latest novels are *Largas noches con Flavia (Long Nights With Flavia),* published in Spain in 2008; *Lust,* published in Germany in 2009; *Las raíces del odio* in Spain in 2012 and *Nunca dejes que te vean llorar* in Italy in 2012.

Cuba's leading cultural export has been its music. The African-based rhythms of *son,* the *mambo,* the *rumba* and the *cha-cha-cha* were the rage in the United States and Europe during the 1940s and 1950s, and brought stardom to such bandleaders as Xavier Cugat and Desi Arnaz. The Cuban genre *son* is the cornerstone of the Caribbean's popular *salsa.*

The Cuban Revolution proved to be a cultural tradeoff. On the one hand, the repressiveness of the totalitarian system caused many of Cuba's most talented writers, artists, singers, musicians and actors to abandon Cuba for the United States, Spain or another Latin American country to more freely express themselves.

None was better known than Celia Cruz (1925–2003), the acknowledged "queen of salsa." In prerevolutionary Cuba she won fame as the lead singer for the band, *La Sonora Matancera.* She resumed singing after she emigrated to the United States, eventually becoming a pop icon as salsa won acceptance among *anglos* as well as *latinos.* She won a Grammy Award in 1990. So great was her hemispheric recognition that when she died in New York City in 2003, thousands turned out for her funeral, and her obituary was carried all over Latin America—even, grudgingly, in the Cuban media.

Perhaps the best-known singer who has remained in Cuba is Silvio Rodríguez (b. 1946), a folk singer and songwriter known as the leader of the so-called *nueva trova* movement. He has enjoyed special privileges for traveling abroad and earning money, including a tour in the United States in 2010, his first U.S. tour since 1979; he performed at Carnegie Hall. Usually a darling of the Cuban regime and the bane of the exiles in Miami, Rodríguez performed with Colombian pop icon Juanes (see Colombia) at the "Concert for Peace" in Havana in September 2009, but in 2010 he released an album that called on the regime to free political prisoners and overhaul the way the country is run. The re-

**"Gitana Tropical"
by Victor Manuel García, 1929. In
Museo National de Bellas Artes, Cuba**

gime was not pleased. He was scheduled to sing at a "Concert for the Motherland" in April 2010, but instead he read a prepared statement defending the regime from the negative international fallout following the death of Orlando Zapata, a jailed dissident who died after an 85-day hunger strike (see History). He left the stage without singing. He may have had to cut a deal to go on the U.S. tour.

Ironically, one of the people most responsible for renewing international interest in traditional Cuban music was an American composer and guitarist, Ry Cooder, an *aficionado* of Cuban sounds. He obtained permission to travel to Cuba in 1996 in quest of some of the aging figures of prerevolutionary music. He assembled pianist Rubén González, singer Ibrahim Ferrer and singers-guitarists Eliades Ochoa and Compay Segundo for a recording session under the name, the Buena Vista Social Club. The 1997 CD became a hit and won a Grammy Award, and the group's new fame led German director Wim Wenders to make a movie, *The Buena Vista Social Club,* which received an Oscar nomination. Segundo and González died in 2003, Ferrer in 2005; their passing made headlines all over Latin America as well as the United States.

Ochoa, by far the youngest, turned 68 in 2014. He recorded *Se saltó un león* and *La colección cubana* in 2006 and *AfroCubism* in 2010. He won the Latin Grammy for

best Tropical Album in 2012 for *Un bolero para tí.* Nine of his albums are listed on Amazon.

A newer genre that has become popular in Cuba is a blend of rap and reggae known as "raggaeton." It has become something of an underground movement, as many of its songs touch upon *tabú* subjects and poke fun of the system. Probably the most popular rapper in Cuba is Aldo Rodríguez of the group, *Los Aldeanos* (The Villagers). The regime has sought unsuccessfully to control rap music, but thus far *Los Aldeanos* have not gone to jail.

Cuba had received a total of 40 Latin Grammys through 2012, proving that music can transcend politics.

While many cultural figures fled Cuba, previously banned leftist writers and other intellectuals from other countries were free to come. The Castro regimes have taken great pride in their commitment to fostering arts and preserving the indigenous culture, particularly art, music, literature, theater and cinema. Several Cuban films have achieved international recognition in highbrow circles, but naturally they convey subtle—or not so subtle—ideological messages.

Some outstanding talent remained in Cuba after the Revolution, including the composer José Ardévol and Latin America's prima ballerina, Alicia Alonso (b. 1920). But other creative minds felt the heavy hand of the communist system. At least two cases of repression brought international condemnation upon the regime, even from its sympathizers. When the writer Herberto Padilla was jailed in 1971, there was an outcry from such leftist intellectuals as Jean-Paul Sartre, Colombian novelist Gabriel García Márquez and the Mexican poet Octavio Paz. Castro ordered Padilla released, but only after the writer signed a confession of his "errors against the Revolution," which he was obligated to read before the Cuban Congress on Education and Culture.

As an indicator of postrevolutionary culture, the Congress passed a resolution that said, in part, that the mass media, writers and artists "are powerful instruments of ideological education whose utilization and development should not be left to spontaneity and improvisation." Padilla worked in obscurity as a translator before being allowed to emigrate to the United States in 1980. In 1981, the poet Armando Valladares was imprisoned, provoking more international pressure. He, too, was allowed to resettle in the United States. Several intellectuals remain imprisoned in Cuba, although a visiting U.S. congressional delegation won the release of a few in 1996.

Postrevolutionary Cuban cinema has received broad support from the state, which of course entails creative restric-

Cuba

tions. A Cuban director who received international acclaim for his mildly satirical comedies of Cuban life was Tomás Gutiérrez Alea (1928–96), who first gained recognition with the slapstick comedy *Muerte de un burócrata (Death of a Bureaucrat)* in 1966, and *Memorias del subdesarrollo (Memories of Underdevelopment)* in 1968, adapted from the Cuban novel by Edmundo Desnoes (b. 1930); it was the first Cuban film screened in the United States since the Revolution. He directed *La última cena (The Last Supper)* in 1976. Because of ill health, he co-directed *Fresas y chocolate (Strawberry and Chocolate)* in 1993 with Juan Carlos Tobía. It remains the only Cuban film nominated for the U.S. Academy Award for Best Foreign Film. His last film was a romantic comedy, *Guantanamera*, in 1994. It won a Silver Bear at the Berlin Film Festival.

A prolific and versatile director who also has been widely garlanded abroad is Fernando Pérez, known for such award-winning films as *Clandestinos (Clandestine)*, 1987; *Madagascar*, 1994; *La vida es silbar (Life is to Whistle)*, 1998; and *Suite Habana*, 2003. His latest film was a biopic, *José Martí: El ojo del canario (José Martí: The Eye of the Canary)*, in 2010. Less well received was *Hello, Hemingway* (1990).

The history of the Cuban press is not a happy one, either before or since the Revolution. There was an eight-year period of relative press freedom during the constitutional administrations of Ramón Grau San Martín and Carlos Prío Socarrás prior to Batista's imposition of dictatorship in 1952. The Cuban government subsidized the press, which placed an economic sword of Damocles over newspapers critical of Batista. There were several independent dailies before the Revolution, the most prestigious being *Diario de la Marina*.

By 1962, Castro had expropriated all the independent newspapers and magazines, and only one daily newspaper remained: *Granma*, the official *Communist Party* and government mouthpiece, named for the boat that brought Castro and his revolutionaries from Mexico in 1956. *Granma*, of course, is as much a propaganda organ as a genuinely informative newspaper. The regime retained the name of one confiscated magazine, *Bohemia*, which is somewhat less propagandistic and more of a literary and artistic review.

All things considered, the term "revolutionary journalism" is an oxymoron, because everything that appears in print or is transmitted over the airwaves is tightly controlled by the regime. Meaningful intellectual freedom and pluralism of thought expressed in opinion-editorial pieces remain non-existent, and modern Cuban cultural expression has been rendered quadriplegic for half a century. About a third of the people sentenced to prison in the crackdown on dissent in 2003 (see History) were independent journalists, such as Raúl Rivero, who was later released and is now in exile in Spain.

Cuba's most prominent independent journalist is now Yoani Sánchez (b. 1975), who in 2007 began clandestinely posting the now-popular blog, *Generación Y*, which satirizes and criticizes life in Cuba. The blog was receiving 1.2 million hits monthly in 2008, and the government blocked access to it within Cuba. Sánchez was awarded Spain's coveted Ortega y Gasset Prize in the category of digital journalism in 2008, but the government refused her permission to attend. (Rivero received an Ortega y Gasset Prize in 2007). She sent a tape recording of her acceptance speech, which read in part: "The fact that I am not there is more revealing of the Cuban reality than all of the posts I have written in my blog in all these months. But someday, it won't take courage to put down in writing all these things we are living today."

Time magazine named her one of the world's 100 most influential people in 2008, and in 2009, she scored a journalistic coup by interviewing President Obama online for her blog. *The Huffington Post* began carrying her blog in 2008, and she writes a regular column for the Madrid daily *El País*—activities that have caused other independent journalists to be imprisoned. Columbia University gave her the prestigious Maria Moors Cabot Award for courageous journalism in 2009, but again the government denied her permission to leave Cuba.

She has been detained a few times, but the government apparently fears an international backlash if she is prosecuted. Former President Jimmy Carter met with Sánchez during his 2011 visit to Cuba. *Generación Y* can be found at www. des-

Yoani Sánchez, the Cuban blogger
Photo by Generación Y

decuba.com/generaciony. It is translated into 17 languages and has millions of hits per month. The government has created a "counter-site," Yoanislandia.com, which seeks to discredit her as a U.S. instrument seeking to undermine the regime. As of 2012, Sánchez had 200,000 followers on Twitter (@14ymedio). Her husband, Reinaldo Escobar, collaborates with her. In 2013, she was finally allowed to leave and made an 80-day tour to 13 countries in North America, South America and Europe.

On May 21, 2014, she established a digital newspaper, 14ymedio.com, but the government blocked access to it, redirecting potential Cuban readers to Yoanislandia.com. Readers abroad can access the newspaper, which picked up 5,100 Twitter followers in its first three days.

ECONOMY: Like so many Latin American countries, Cuba was condemned to a mono-cultural dependency on a given commodity, in Cuba's case, sugar cane. Nickel deposits and Cuba's famous black tobacco provided some economic diversity, but for the most part Cuba's prosperity or lack of it depended largely on the world market price for sugar. Even so, Cuba enjoyed a generally higher standard of living than did most of its sister republics, and it was somewhat ironic that Marxism took root here rather than in one of the more destitute nations.

The Marxist experiment proved no more feasible in this tropical setting than it did in Eastern Europe. As industry minister in the early 1960s, the legendary Ché Guevara set out to convert Cuba into an industrialized state, with disastrous results. What Cuba became, and what it still is today, is an illusion of self-sufficiency, with housing, education and medical care all provided "free." But it was the infusion of nearly $1 million a day worth of Soviet aid for 30 years, and guaranteed Soviet purchases of Cuban sugar, that made this smoke-and-mirrors economy viable. The dependency on sugar continued, the difference being that with collectivized agriculture, crop yields dropped precipitously after the Revolution.

On paper, the Cuban peso was proclaimed to be worth more than the U.S. dollar, while in reality it was worthless. Official per capita GDP figures were disregarded by international economists, and largely still are (see below). The classic communist method of distribution of goods and services resulted in chronic food shortages, which the regime blamed solely on the U.S. embargo rather than face the reality of the system's design flaws.

When the Soviet sugar daddy (pun intended) began collapsing in the late 1980s and the aid stopped pouring in, the plight of the people became increasingly desper-

Cuba

ate. The unpredictable Castro suddenly shifted policy during what he euphemistically termed Cuba's "special period" of readjustment. In a desperate bid to alleviate the destitution, Castro decided to allow private agricultural plots and fruit markets and permitted some skilled workers, such as mechanics, to moonlight as entrepreneurs, called *cuentapropistas*. The Cubans eagerly responded. When many of these small entrepreneurs and farmers began showing signs of bourgeois prosperity, Castro just as unpredictably terminated the experiment in limited capitalism temporarily. At the Fourth Communist Party Congress in 1991, again motivated by desperation to alleviate food shortages, he resumed limited private and cooperative cultivation. He also permitted the U.S. dollar to circulate, in effect creating a dual currency system.

In 1993, Castro expanded limited entrepreneurship to 157 discrete areas of endeavor. For example, he permitted the licensing of mom-and-pop restaurants called *paladares*, and small pensions called *casas particulares*. By 1995, more than 200,000 tiny restaurants and hotels had been licensed, but they faced such stringent regulation and fees that the number dropped to 150,000 in 2001. Those that remained have proven popular with customers and modestly lucrative for their owners.

By 1997, the private agricultural plots and co-ops were providing more food than the state farms. By 2002, there were 65,000 such small farms, grouped into 1,116 co-operatives. In a remarkable concession to their success, the National Assembly voted in 2002 to increase the amount of profits rebated to member farms from 50% to 70%.

In another seemingly counterrevolutionary move in 1994 that stemmed from raw desperation, Castro ordered the old decadent hotels, casinos and nightclubs to reopen under state tutelage. Cubans were not permitted to frequent such bourgeois establishments, of course, only to work there. The fun spots are reserved for foreign tourists, Canadians mostly, who are encouraged to pay with dollars. The gimmick to bring in desperately needed foreign exchange was successful, so much so that anti-Castro dissidents—whether from Florida or Cuba has not been determined—set off bombs in three of the hotels in 1997, killing one tourist and injuring four, in an obvious attempt to frighten other tourists away.

Cuba remains the world's eighth-largest sugar producer, but the sugar industry has deteriorated dramatically in recent years, in part because of natural factors, but also because of outdated equipment and low world market prices. Hurricane Georges was a factor in the 24% drop in sugar production in 1998, from 4.2 to 3.4 million metric tons. The sugar crop was hit again in 2001 by Hurricane Michelle, which destroyed an estimated 35% of the crop.

Nonetheless, official figures released in 2002 put the harvest at 3.61 million tons, up slightly from the record low of 3.53 million in 2001, but a far cry from the record of 8.1 million in 1989. Because of lower market prices, the 2002 crop brought in about $120 million less in export earnings than the $561 million from the 2001 crop.

Faced with grim economic realities, the government grudgingly and quietly closed 71 of the island's 156 sugar mills and said it plans to modernize the remaining ones. It also announced plans to replace about half of the 3.5 million acres devoted to sugar cultivation with crops that will help feed the Cuban people, such as rice. On the remaining land, using improved techniques, the government hoped to increase the sugar yield from 16 tons per acre to 23. But the 2002–03 harvest showed a cataclysmic drop of 45%, to 2 million tons, a new record low. Still, Castro stubbornly clung to the collectivist model.

The 2003–04 harvest was up slightly to 2.5 million tons, but the worst drought in a century devastated the sugar crop of 2004–05. A glum Castro admitted the harvest would be no more than 1.7 million tons, possibly only 1.5 million, the lowest since 1909—before mechanization. The 2005–06 and 2006–07 harvests were equally disappointing, 1.2 million tons each year, due to both bad weather and mechanical breakdowns at the 39 remaining mills, although the high international price for sugar helped boost GDP growth somewhat.

Raúl took charge in 2008 and began cracking down on inefficiency. Despite increasing the number of mills to 44, the government media admitted that the 2009–10 harvest fell 850,000 tons short of its goal and that the harvest was the worst since 1905. Raúl sacked his sugar minister.

For the first time in 20 years, the 2010–11 crop met the government's quota, 1.1 million tons, bringing in $333 million. The government reported that the 2011–12 crop showed a 16% increase, or about 1.28 million tons, but admitted that was still 68,000 tons below quota. It predicted a 20% increase for 2012-13, but it increased only 12.5%, to 1.44 million tons, according to the government's own figures. The increase for 2013-14 was 20%, to 1.8 million tons..

Low sugar production prevents Cuba from capitalizing on the current international boom in ethanol. It is estimated Cuba could produce 1.6 billion gallons of ethanol from sugar cane a year, but Fidel Castro refused to divert sugar from a foodstuff to ethanol. That could change if Raúl becomes desperate enough and is willing to accept Brazilian help to set up ethanol distilleries.

Cuba is the world's sixth-largest producer of nickel and holds 30% of the world's reserves. Its exports of nickel and cobalt in 2001 exceeded $600 million. It produced 75,200 tons in 2002 and has the potential for 100 million, but because of the 2003 crackdown on dissent it has had difficulty finding European, Canadian or Australian mining firms willing to make the necessary $1.2 billion investment. In 2004, Chinese President Hu Jintao visited Cuba and agreed to invest $500 million in Cuba's nickel industry, not out of the goodness of his heart but because China's booming industries need the nickel. China is to import 4,400 tons annually. Record high nickel prices on the international market in 2007 helped boost Cuba's export revenue. In 2011, nickel brought in $1.25 billion, four times as much as sugar.

Cuba has hoped tourism would be its economic savior, and to a degree, it has been. In 1999, Vice President Carlos Lage admitted the country was relying increasingly on foreign tourism for development. He said tourism brought in $1.7 billion in badly needed foreign exchange in 1998 and that it showed a 30% increase in the first quarter of 1999. An estimated 1.8 million tourists visited Cuba in 2000, bringing in $1.9 billion, dwarfing the amount from sugar exports. In 2001, the number of tourists dropped by 5% to 1.7 million, reflecting the global drop in tourism as a consequence of the September 11, 2001 terror attacks on the United States and a devastating hurricane, and in the first quarter of 2002 it was down by 14%. During the winter of 2001–02, several Cuban hotels actually closed up for lack of business, while prices at dollar stores skyrocketed.

Most of Cuba's tourists are from Canada and Europe, and in response to that fact, Cuba officially began accepting the Euro as well as the dollar in 2002. By 2003, it seemed the crisis had been weathered, with 1.9 million tourists bringing in $2.1 billion. In 2003, Castro himself presided at the opening of a 944-room resort on Cuba's northeast coast, the largest resort yet. The total number of hotel rooms on the island is now about 40,000. The government reported that in 2004, the number of tourists hit the 2 million mark, bringing in 15% more in foreign exchange than in 2003. The reports added tourism accounted for 4% of foreign exchange in 1990 and 41% in 2004.

The number of tourists in 2005 hit 2.32 million, then declined by 4.3% in 2006; in 2007, it declined again, to 2.15 million. For 2008, the government announced a record 2.35 million visitors, who brought in a record $2.7 billion, up $326 million from 2007. Despite global recession, the figure for 2009 was 2.4 million, an increase of 3.5%. In 2010 it was 2.5 million.

Cuba

In May 2011, President Obama lifted more of the travel restrictions to Cuba. Ostensibly, U.S. citizens must be part of an academic, religious or cultural group, but they still have to stay in hotels and eat in restaurants. Not surprisingly, the number of visitors was a record 2.7 million in 2011, bringing in $2.5 billion, twice as much as nickel and eight times as much as sugar. In 2012, the year President Obama lifted remaining travel restrictions, tourist arrivals hit a new record, 2.84 million. The government is allowing foreign companies to build a new golf resort and the largest marina in the Caribbean in the beach resort of Varadero. Preliminary estimates for 2013 are that the number of tourists would be down by about 1.2%.

So desperate has Cuba been for foreign exchange that Venezuela, about the best friend Cuba still has and the source of a third of its oil, was forced to suspend oil shipments in 2002 when Cuba was unable to pay more than $63 million it owed for past shipments. The shipments resumed five months later under a deferred payments plan.

Cuba has been producing about 75,000 barrels of crude oil a day, about half its needs. Fidel Castro announced in 2004 the discovery of a deposit off the north coast containing an estimated 100 million barrels; estimates since then have placed it at perhaps 4 billion barrels. However, U.S. deep-water technology will be needed to fully exploit most of the deposits, and U.S. firms are still prohibited from drilling in Cuba. The Spanish firm Repsol began an exploratory well in January 2012, but in May it announced it was a dry hole and capped the well. Five other foreign firms have abandoned their attempts at deepwater wells because of hard rock. An Italian firm is still drilling in the Florida Strait.

Also dwarfing sugar earnings as a source of foreign exchange in recent years have been remittances from Cubans living abroad, primarily the United States, Mexico and Spain. At the beginning of the Bush administration in 2001, they totaled $1 billion. Bush limited remittances to $2,000 per year ($500 per quarter), but only to family members. By 2008, his last year in office, they had grown to $1.45 billion. In 2011, President Obama signed an executive order that permits remittances to non-family members, but not to government or party officials. Consequently, remittances have leaped from $1.65 billion in 2009 and $1.92 billion in 2010 to $2.3 billion in 2011—about 4% of the official GDP. With President Obama's lifting on restrictions, they hit $2.6 billion in 2012, eclipsing tourism as the leading source of foreign exchange, and were $2.77 billion in 2013.

Since the collapse of the Soviet Union, Cuba has come to rely on foreign—i.e.,

capitalist—investors for economic development. By 2002 there were nearly 400 joint ventures with the state, about 60% of them with Canadian, Spanish, French and Italian firms, specializing primarily in tourism, construction and biotechnology. Such investments totaled an estimated $5 billion. But the drop in tourism, coupled with an unfavorable business climate, led to a dramatic decline in foreign investments. From an annual average of $268 million from 1996–2000, including $488 million in 2000, it plunged to only 38.9 million in 2001. The number of joint ventures dropped to about 300 in 2004, in part because the government abruptly began stiffening bureaucratic rules to drive out smaller businesses. By 2009, several foreign companies were complaining that the cash-strapped government had not been paying them their share of the profits from the joint ventures. One executive who complained publicly had his contract revoked.

In October 2011, the relations between the government and foreign investors deteriorated further when two British and one Canadian managers were jailed for unspecified corruption charges. They have been held without charge for two years but their trials were scheduled to begin in July 2013.

GDP growth averaged a respectable 4.7% per year from 1998–2003, thanks almost wholly to the foreign capitalist investors, who are theoretically anathema to the Marxist-Leninist model. The government claimed growth in 2004 was 5%, while the Economist Intelligence Unit in London put it at 3%. In 2006, reliable estimates put growth at a healthy 9.5%, largely because of unusually high international prices for both sugar and nickel. In 2007 it was estimated at 7.3%, dropping to 4.3% in 2008. With the global recession, it dropped to 1.4% in 2009 and 1.5% in 2010.

On paper, the country claimed a per capita income of $2,800 in 2003, which was suspicious considering that the average monthly wage is only about $15. This is accomplished through a smoke-and-mirrors technique called "purchasing power parity," or PPP, which factors in such benefits as free rents and medical care. In 2005, the figure was raised to $3,300, even as destitute Cubans continued to flee the country, and to a questionable $9,500 in 2007. In 2009, the World Bank estimated Cuban per capita income in real terms at $5,500, while the CIA World Factbook put PPP at $9,700 in 2009 and $10,200 in 2010. More recent estimates remain unavailable.

In 2004, thanks to aid from Venezuela, Castro ordered one of his periodic crackdowns on entrepreneurship, which many Cubans rely on to survive. Among those affected were private auto mechanics and even clowns who perform at birthday parties. He also froze new licenses for the

popular *paladores,* or private restaurants, and *casas particulares,* a kind of Cuban bed-and-breakfast. He placed the existing establishments under onerous new restrictions and fees that could only be seen as disincentives. His logic was analogous to shutting off the engines once a plane had attained cruising altitude. Yet, in 2005, he confidently declared an end to the "special period" of austerity and readjustment following the Soviet collapse.

In 2008, his brother Raúl replaced him as president. In 2009, faced with a desperately troubled economy, Raúl again expanded private agricultural plots, including some close to Havana, and permitted small enterprises such as barber shops and beauty salons to start operating again. He expanded this concept further in 2010, laying off 500,000 state workers and encouraging them to engage in entrepreneurship. The government approved a list of 178 "acceptable" occupations for private enterprise. These reforms were ratified by the Sixth Party Congress in April 2011. Already the *paladares* are reappearing, and by October 2011 the government reported than 338,000 people had applied for small business licenses. Of course, if they are successful, they will be heavily taxed under the new tax code unveiled in 2011: 50% on incomes and 25% for social security. Even so, educated professionals are making more on the remaining 25% than they were making working for the state. By mid-2012, there were more than 200,000 so-called *cuentapropios,* not enough to take up the slack from the planned state layoffs.

Raúl also has been turning increasingly toward China and Brazil, and less to Canada and Europe, for desperately needed foreign investment. By 2010, China had become Cuba's second-largest trading partner after Venezuela, with about $1.8 billion in bilateral trade. Chinese Vice President Xi Jinping visited Havana in June 2011 and signed 13 economic agreements with Cuba, including interest-free loans for irrigation projects. Raúl visited China in July, 2012. Brazilian President Dilma Rousseff made a state visit to Cuba in February 2012 and renewed the pledge of cooperation made to Cuba by her predecessor, Lula da Silva. Brazil is building a $900 million port facility in Mariel and its development bank is helping upgrade Cuba's airports.

Whether because of the recovering world economy, increased foreign investment, the *cuentaproprio* program or all three, GDP growth was up 2.8% in 2011 and an estimated 3.1% in 2012. The government forecast growth of 3.0% in 2013, but figures were still unavailable in mid-2014.

For a decade, Fidel Castro pragmatically allowed U.S. dollars to be spent at certain stores, appropriately tagged "dol-

Cuba

lar stores." That ended abruptly in 2004, when Castro ordered the Central Bank to prohibit circulation of the dollar at stores and businesses. In its place, there was the so-called "convertible peso," with an exchange rate to the dollar of 1:1. For government paychecks and most everyday uses, Cubans still used the regular peso, which Castro devalued in 2005 from 27 to the dollar to 25; it is now 24:1. The Central Bank levies a 10% surcharge to convert dollars to either kind of peso, while the Euro and other hard foreign currencies are exempt. The government announced in 2013 it was foirced to end the dual-currency experiment.

In sum, Cuba today remains an economic basket case, a destitute society with an economy propped up only by a flourishing black market for almost everything, including parts for the prerevolutionary Fords and Chevrolets that still chug along on Havana's streets as in a scene from a 1950s movie. Prostitution is widespread despite revolutionary disapproval, and begging, something Fidel Castro once boasted he had eliminated, is back. A beggar, in fact, is what the entire country has become, totally reliant on pity from friendly countries.

Although the U.S. government is under increased pressure from its friends abroad and from some members of Congress and businessmen at home to lift the 1960 economic embargo—the argument being that it penalizes the average Cuban more than it does the Castro regime—an end to the embargo would not prove to be the panacea that many assume. Only thorough economic reform, such as occurred in China or in Hungary and other former East Bloc nations, will bring significant improvement. Raúl Castro's dramatic moves in 2010 and 2011 toward encouraging small-scale entrepreneurship is a positive indication that he is far more pragmatic than his brother.

The deep-water port in Mariel that Brazil is building will become a free-trade zone, something China and Vietnam have both tried. It will have a capacity of 1 million containers a year.

His reforms are an auspicious sign that the regime is finally facing hard realities, but it has a long way to go.

THE FUTURE: One of the world's great guessing games for years was: How much longer can Fidel Castro last? On February 18, 2008, he ostensibly relinquished power to his brother, Raúl, who had governed as caretaker since Fidel fell critically ill in 2006. In 2011, Fidel surprised everyone by claiming he had relinquished all power in 2006. If he did, it didn't show.

Raúl, who turned 83 on June 3, has shown some tantalizing signs that major change is in the offing. He released all 75 of the prisoners of conscience jailed in the 2003 *"Primavera Negra."* He detests bureaucratic inefficiency and took steps to combat it. The historic Sixth Party Congress in April 2011 ratified the dramatic decision to allow entrepreneurship in 181 carefully selected occupations not deemed a threat to the socialist system. He vowed to retire at the end of his second five-year term in 2018; relinquishing power voluntarily is not common among communist dictators.

The geriatric leadership of the 1950s remained largely in place, but in February 2013, Raúl anointed 52-year-old Miguel Díaz-Canel as his heir apparent. Relatively little is known of what goes on inside Díaz-Canel's head, or where he may take Cuba after 2018.

Missing thus far from the winds of change sweeping Cuba is a willingness to engage in meaningful dialogue with the dissidents. With the deaths of Laura Pollán and Osvaldo Payá, and the exile of Raúl Rivera and others, the most visible dissident on the island is now *Generation Y* blogger Yoani Sánchez, who has become a burr under Raúl's hide. The regime gritted its teeth during her three-month, 13-nation tour. The government still attempts to muzzle freedom of expression and the press by banning Internet access on home computers or smartphones, but enterprising Cubans, not just dissidents but those who simply desire greater freedom, are finding ways to circumvent the government's restrictions through social media like Twitter and Facebook and through password-swapping. The regime is learning, as did the dictators of Tunisia, Egypt and Libya during the 2010 Arab Spring, that ideas are becoming increasingly harder to stifle in the 21st century.

Also missing in these discussions of "reform" is any suggestion of contested elections. Raúl has shown no inclination to introduce a Cuban *glasnost.* Some reform. Will Díaz-Canel, who was born after the Revolution, prove more open-minded?

Meanwhile, Cubans continue to flee their Marxist "paradise;" others have been allowed to go into exile. Cuba's population declined by 12,000 between 2010 and 2011, by 14,000 between 2011 and 2012, and by another 14,000 between 2013 and 2014—the only Latin American country to actually *lose* population. Even the once-admired medical system has declined in quality, because Cuba has dispatched tens of thousands of doctors to 77 other countries, mostly to its "oil daddy" Venezuela, to boost its international prestige. Doctors who make $20 a month in Cuba are finding they can make far more as *cuentapropios,* running a small restaurant or bar.

The Obama administration, which indicated early-on it felt the time was ripe for a new era in U.S.-Cuban relations, has discovered to its dismay what 10 earlier administrations learned from bitter experience: The Castros' concept of "negotiations" means the United States lifts its embargo and Cuba yields little or nothing in return. Yet, support for the embargo appears to be waning anyway, in Congress as well as among the population. Polls show a clear majority favors normalization of relations. Former Secretary of State Hillary Clinton now claims in her memoir that she called for the lifting of the embargo because it hadn't worked and because the Castros have used it as the whipping boy for their own economic failures, but that she failed to persuade Obama. U.S. businessmen, meanwhile, don't want to miss out on the money to be made in Cuba, which Europeans, Chinese, Brazilians and others are making.

Hopefully, after both Castros are gone and relations are normalized, the inevitable transition will be peaceful rather than violent. Díaz-Canel, if he indeed does succeed to power, should pragmatically embrace something like the Uruguayan or Costa Rican models, allowing Cubans to enjoy the impressive social services that have given them the longest life expectancy and lowest infant mortality in Latin America, but at the same time to enjoy the right to freely elect their leaders, to read, watch and listen to what they choose, to surf the Internet, to practice their religion without discrimination, to pursue a profession of their choosing, to live or travel where they want—in short, to live as a *free* people at last.

A diversity of transportation in Havana. *Photo by Steven Leibo*

Dominican Republic

Panorama of Santo Domingo with the Presidential Palace in the foreground

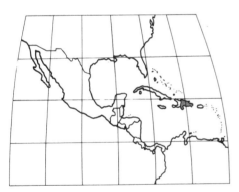

Area: 18,811 square miles

Population: 10,379,741 (2014 est.)

Capital City: Santo Domingo (Pop. 2.9 million in 2010, est.).

Climate: Tropical, tempered by sea breezes; moderate rainfall is heaviest from April to December.

Neighboring Countries: The Dominican Republic occupies the eastern two thirds of the island of Hispaniola, the second largest of the Greater Antilles; the Republic of Haiti occupies the western one-third of the island.

Official Language: Spanish.

Other Principal Tongues: There are small French and English-speaking groups.

Ethnic Background: Mixed European, African and Indian origin (73%), White (16%), Negro (11%).

Principal Religion: Roman Catholic Christianity.

Chief Commercial Products: Tourism, sugar, bananas, cacao, coffee, nickel, gold, textiles, clothing.

Currency: Peso.

Gross Domestic Product: U.S. $59.27 billion in 2013, est. ($5,800 per capita, official exchange rate).

Former Colonial Status: Spanish Crown Colony (1492–1795); French Possession (1795–1808); Spanish Control (1808–21); occupied by Haiti (1822–44).

Independence Date: February 27, 1844.

Chief of State: Danilo Medina Sánchez (b. November 10, 1951), president (since August 16, 2012).

National Flag: Blue and red, quartered by a white cross.

The Dominican Republic occupies the eastern two-thirds of the island of Hispaniola, also known by its Indian name, *Hayti*, which means place of mountains. Majestically cresting at 10,000 feet in the center of the island, mountain spurs run south to the Caribbean Sea and to the east, dropping to rolling hills before reaching the coast. A separate range, with peaks reaching 4,000 feet, runs along the north coast of the Dominican Republic. The Cibao Valley, lying between the central range and north coast hills, and the southern coastal plains, are the most productive agricultural lands of the island and the most heavily popu-

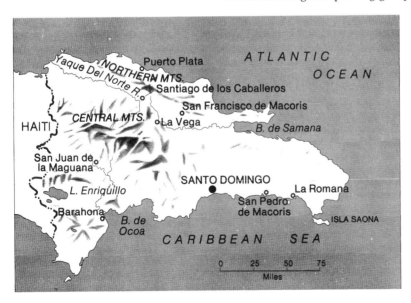

Dominican Republic

lated regions. The slopes of the mountains, green throughout the year, are forested and well watered and are the locale of most of the country's coffee production.

The climate, while tropical, is moderated by invigorating sea breezes. During the dry season, December to March, the trade winds cool the air, making the southern coast beaches a major tourist attraction.

HISTORY: The island of Hispaniola was discovered by Columbus on his first voyage and selected as the site for his first colonization effort. The city of Santo Domingo, founded in 1496, is the oldest European-established city in the Americas. The native Indians were described as peaceful by Columbus and were absorbed into the Spanish population; they became virtually extinct as a race within 30 years of the Spanish discovery. Slaves from Africa were introduced in the 1520s. The discovery of more valuable domains on the mainland and the exhaustion of gold deposits on the island caused the Spanish to lose interest in Hispaniola at an early date after it was settled by them.

The island was frequently attacked by pirates and privateers—Santo Domingo was held for ransom by the English privateer Sir Francis Drake in 1585. Buccaneers took the western part of the island in 1630, and French settlers arrived shortly thereafter. The western portion of Hispaniola was ceded to France in 1697. With the outbreak of the French Revolution in 1789, a series of rebellions occurred on the island. The French section of the island, Haiti, was overrun by British and Spanish forces in 1791; they were expelled by the French in the same year and France was given possession of the entire island by treaty in 1795. Returned to Spain in 1806, the Spanish-speaking Dominicans declared themselves independent in 1821, but were conquered by the neighboring Haitians in the following year, and did not achieve final independence until 1844.

The independent history of the Dominican Republic has been a continuation of internal war, foreign intervention and misrule. From 1844 to 1861, the country was governed by a succession of military men who were put in office by various factions of the island's upper class. Constant unrest and invasions from Haiti caused General Pedro Santana to invite the Spanish to return in 1861; however, the Spanish discipline was no more welcome than it had been earlier, and the Spaniards were again ousted in 1865. The second republic was as restless as the first, and the government passed from one dictator to another in an unbroken series of corrupt administrations which had little or no governing ability.

By 1905, the Dominican Republic was largely bankrupt and threatened with oc-

cupation by European powers seeking to collect bad debts; the United States intervened under a 50-year treaty to administer the island's finances. There were more or less continuous revolts—in 1914 the United States landed Marines to bolster the government; nevertheless, the president was ousted in 1916. From 1916 to 1922, the country was administered by the U.S. Navy.

A provisional government was re-established in 1922 and in 1924 U.S. troops were withdrawn. Following a reasonably effective administration, revolt again broke out in 1930. General Rafael Leonidas Trujillo Molina (1891–1961), commandant of the military, seized power.

The Trujillo Era

Trujillo ruthlessly suppressed all opposition, dominating the island as its absolute ruler for 31 years and creating a personality cult, calling himself *"El Jefe."* He also renamed the capital Ciudad Trujillo.

At the same time, he shoved his backward country into the 20th century, but at a price. With the treasury empty, the people poverty-stricken, the capital destroyed by a hurricane and foreign debts almost three times the total annual income, Trujillo took on the herculean task of rebuilding the country. Twenty years later, internal and foreign debts had been paid; the national income had multiplied to 40 times the level of 1930 and the nation had a balanced budget for most of the period. Schools, roads and numerous public buildings were constructed during the Trujillo years.

"El Jefe" also built a huge personal fortune, valued at an estimated $800 million and comprising 60% of all land in the nation. The cost of his rule was the total loss of personal liberty for the Dominican people, who were held in check by the bloodthirsty Trujillo's efficient and merciless

**General Rafael Leonidas
Trujillo Molina, 1930**

secret police force. An estimated 50,000 people were killed during his rule, among them three of the Mirabal sisters, left-wing dissidents who were immortalized in Julia Álvarez's 1994 novel, *In the Time of the Butterflies* (see Culture). His worst atrocity was the infamous "Parsley Massacre" of 1937, in which he ordered the slaughter of Haitian immigrants along the border he suspected were harboring his political opponents. The death toll has been estimated at from 20,000 to 30,000.

Trujillo even attempted to assassinate Venezuelan President Rómulo Betancourt, a vocal critic, in 1960 by having a bomb placed in his car. Betancourt was wounded, but survived, and international condemnation was heaped upon Trujillo over the clumsy plot.

Trujillo was himself assassinated on May 30, 1961, in an ambush outside the capital. Members of the country's elite, with CIA support, had plotted his death, fearful that unless they took action, communist insurgents could come to power as they had in Cuba. Attempts by Trujillo's son to retain control of the country were unsuccessful and the family fled the island in late 1961. They reburied his body in Paris.

The Balaguer 'Democracy'

Joaquín Balaguer, titular president at the time of the assassination, maintained a semblance of order after the flight of the Trujillo family by promising to step down when provisions for elections could be made. Balaguer was overthrown by a military coup in early 1962 and a few days later, a counter-coup installed the vice president.

The first experiment in democratic government was undertaken in late 1962; Juan Bosch, a moderate leftist, was chosen president in honest elections. He was inaugurated with feelings of optimism; honest, well-intentioned but politically inexperienced, he was overthrown by a military coup six months later as he attempted to limit the power of the armed forces.

In April 1965, civil war erupted when dissident elements in the armed forces sought to return Juan Bosch to office. As the death toll mounted (an estimated 2,000 were killed), and fearing the imminent defeat of the conservative faction and creation of a new Castro-style government, the U.S. President Lyndon Johnson intervened with 22,000 combat troops.

The Organization of American States agreed to send in additional troops and to take over the task of preserving order and conducting elections. Nevertheless, the fact that the United States intervened unilaterally—in violation of existing inter-American agreements—caused widespread anti-U.S. sentiment in Latin America.

Dominican Republic

Carefully supervised by the OAS, free elections were held in mid-1966 and Balaguer, supported by a centrist coalition, won the presidency. He followed a moderate economic policy, satisfying few of the demands of the warring factions. The U.S. intervention solved none of the social or economic problems—it merely postponed the day when these questions would be resolved.

After amending the constitution so that he could succeed himself, Balaguer was re-elected to a second term in 1970. Unable to unite, the rival candidates provided only token resistance. Bosch boycotted the elections because he knew the military would overrule his left-wing policies.

Under Balaguer, the economy achieved the most spectacular growth of any Latin American nation. Gross domestic product rose by an impressive 12.5% in 1972 and 1973—the world's highest rate in those years. Virtually every key sector of the economy set records in 1973, particularly agriculture, tourism and mining. Pacing the growth was the nation's revitalized sugar industry, where workers responded to a profit-sharing plan by increasing output.

The significant factor in the nation's economic boom was the political stability enforced by the soft-spoken Balaguer. The president's conservative Reformist Party pursued a policy called *continuísmo*, which meant a strong emphasis on law and order and economic development. However, opposition parties often received heavy-handed treatment in the name of stability. Balaguer obtained the all-important loyalty of the armed forces by granting special favors.

During 1971, the administration was linked to a right-wing vigilante group called "The Gang," which terrorized and murdered several hundred suspected and real leftists. When a tiny group of 10 Cuban-trained guerrillas entered the country in early 1973, they were quickly eliminated. Balaguer used the occasion to polish off the rest of his opposition; political opponents were jailed, the university was closed and opposition newspapers and media were seized. Major political leaders were forced into hiding or exile.

The repression of political opponents set the stage for the 1974 elections. Although the opposition was divided among about 20 small parties, the two major groups (one liberal, the other conservative) formed a coalition and nominated Silvestre Antonio Guzmán, a wealthy cattle rancher.

Although Balaguer was at first regarded as a shoo-in for re-election despite his promise during the 1970 campaign to seek a constitutional change banning the re-election of presidents, a sudden groundswell of support for Guzmán

Joaquín Balaguer

clearly alarmed the administration. When Balaguer hurriedly implemented a new voting rule, the opposition boycotted the election, charging that the new rules would permit administration supporters to vote more than once. With the opposition boycott and the military openly supporting his re-election, Balaguer coasted to an easy "victory."

Major problems facing him at the start of his third term were inflation, which had reached an annual rate of 20% by mid-1974, and high unemployment. A more fundamental problem was the fact that although the Dominican Republic was enjoying the most prosperous period in its history, the benefits of the boom were confined largely to the upper class, while fully 80% of the people remained trapped in poverty. The annual per capita income hovered at $350 while the population growth was increasing at a dangerous 3.6%.

Interregnum

Balaguer suffered a stunning upset in the 1978 presidential election when he was defeated by Guzmán of the Dominican Revolutionary Party (*PRD*). Balaguer supporters in the army temporarily halted vote tabulation when early returns showed him losing. However, strong protests at home and abroad, especially from the Carter administration, forced the military to allow the results to stand.

Guzmán's program to promote domestic peace and a strong economy was generally successful during the first three years of his term, with gains in health, education and rural development. However, a dramatic increase in the price of imported oil, plus a sharp drop in sugar export earnings as the United States and the Western Hemisphere were gripped by recession, plunged the economy into a recession by late 1980. Guzmán declined to run for re-

election in 1982—the first time a Dominican chief of state had offered to step down *voluntarily*.

The May 1982 elections saw the ruling *PRD* presidential candidate, moderate social democrat Salvador Jorge Blanco, win with 46% of the vote. His two main opponents were Balaguer (39.14%) and Bosch (9.69%). Blanco, a 55-year-old constitutional lawyer affiliated with the Socialist International, saw his *PRD* also win control of Congress and most local governments. Although 12 people died in campaign violence, the election was generally the most honest and peaceful in the nation's history. Unfortunately, the last victim proved to be President Guzmán himself, who committed suicide a month before leaving office.

At the insistence of the International Monetary Fund and creditor banks, Blanco imposed economic austerity, reducing luxury imports and limiting government expenditures. This led to a slow increase in GDP growth, still slower than that of the population growth, and the per capita income fell slightly. The situation became tense in 1984 when a series of popular demonstrations led to bloody confrontations with police. Because of the sagging economy, Blanco's popularity sagged equally in 1985.

Balaguer Returns

The elections in both 1986 and 1990 pitted an elderly Balaguer against an energetic opponent. Both campaigns were heated, replete with personal insults and slanderous statements. Notwithstanding an attempt by the military to halt ballot-counting in 1986, Balaguer won even though his opponent was considered a shoo-in and despite the fact that Balaguer was virtually blinded by glaucoma.

The contest in 1990 was between Balaguer and Bosch, only four years younger than he; Balaguer won by a margin of 22,000 votes out of 1.9 million. The reason for the two victories of the aging Balaguer was simple: relative prosperity. Both elections were tainted with the usual irregularities.

Balaguer carefully paved the way for yet another run for the presidency in 1994. This time, the favored opponent was José Francisco Peña Gómez, leader of the *PRD* and former Santo Domingo mayor. The campaign was extraordinarily dirty. Because Peña Gómez was black, and Dominicans harbor a deep fear and distrust of black Haitians, Balaguer successfully capitalized on these emotions. A video was used allegedly showing Peña Gómez practicing voodoo in Haitian style. Balaguer won by an estimated 30,000 votes amid charges of fraud.

The Clinton administration, trying to enforce an embargo of Haiti and need-

Dominican Republic

ing Dominican help, chose to ignore the irregularities. Balaguer cooperated with the embargo, with the tacit understanding that the Clinton administration would not protest the 1994 election results. The matter quietly faded, and the 87-year-old Balaguer was inaugurated in August; by then he was totally blind.

Fernández and Mejía

Tacitly acknowledging irregularities, Balaguer, then 89, agreed to step down mid-way through his term and new elections were held in 1996. Meanwhile, Congress amended the constitution in 1994 to prohibit immediate re-election for president.

In the first round of voting in May 1996, Peña Gómez of the *PRD* led with 46% of the vote to 39% for Leonel Fernández Reyna of Bosch's *PLD*. Balaguer, though the longtime rival of Bosch, disliked Peña Gómez even more, and threw his support behind Fernández, a 42-year-old lawyer who grew up in New York City. In the runoff, Fernández edged out Peña Gómez with 51.25% of the vote in a contest that international observers proclaimed fair and untainted by the traditional Balaguer trickery. The new president promised to take the Dominican Republic down a "new road."

Fernández found that "new road" a bumpy one. In the 1996 elections, his party won only one seat in the 30-member Senate and 12 of 120 seats in the lower house. In the 1998 congressional elections, the *PRD* swept all but five seats in the Senate and won an absolute majority in the Chamber

Former President Hipólito Mejía

of Deputies. Peña Gómez, however, died before he could savor his party's triumph.

A truly historic event occurred in 1998 when Fidel Castro visited the Dominican Republic for the first time, shortly after Fernández re-established diplomatic relations. Officially, Castro's visit was to attend the 14-nation Caribbean Forum summit. Few were surprised when Castro paid a call on his old ally, Bosch, then 89. But Castro astonished everyone by visiting the 92-year-old Balaguer at his home. The two aging Cold War antagonists sat side-by-side nearly an hour and engaged in a cordial, even jocular conversation.

Tension among the parties turned violent in 1999. At issue was the election of a new secretary-general of the Dominican Municipal League, the organization that distributes revenues totaling 4% of the national budget to the local governments. The *PLD* and Balaguer's newly named Social Christian Reform Party (*PRSC*) joined forces once again to elect a secretary-general, prompting the dominant *PRD* to meet separately and "elect" its own candidate. Pro-*PRD* demonstrators surrounded the headquarters of the municipal league and clashed with police. Soldiers also surrounded the Congress building; the *PRD* denounced Fernández as a would-be dictator.

By 1999, Fernández could boast a 40% increase in economic growth in his four years and Latin America's second-highest growth rate of 7% per year (see Economy). Such booms usually favor the party in power, but Fernández could not run for re-election in 2000, barred by the law aimed at Balaguer. Thus, he engineered the nomination of an economic adviser, Danilo Medina, 47, as the *PLD*'s standard bearer. A 59-year-old agricultural economist, Hipólito Mejía, became the PRD nominee. The venerable and resilient Balaguer, 93, again became the PRSC nominee.

Balaguer proved a spoiler for the *PLD*, dividing the conservative vote. Mejía, preached a populist message, vowing that the poor would begin enjoying the fruits of the burgeoning economy through expanded public works and improved education, a persuasive message to those who felt left out of the growing prosperity. He fostered his image as a simple farmer, and charmed voters with Lincolnian folk wisdom and humor.

As usual, the campaign turned violent. As Mejía's car passed the house of a local *PLD* official in Moca, gunfire erupted, and Mejía's bodyguards shot and killed the *PLD* official and another man, claiming an assassination attempt. The *PLD* maintained that the bodyguards had fired first.

In the vote results of May 16, certified as fair by more than 100 international observers, Mejía received 49.87% of the vote—

tantalizingly close to a first-round victory. Medina and Balaguer finished in a dead heat for second place—but with Medina slightly ahead, 24.94% to 24.61%. On May 18, Balaguer announced he was accepting Mejía's election, meaning he would not endorse Medina in a runoff. Medina, faced with the near-impossibility of closing a 25-point gap, withdrew.

Mejía was inaugurated on August 16, 2000. He inherited from Fernández the most robust economic growth in Latin America, which benefited Mejía's *PRD* in the mid-term congressional elections in May 2002. The party swept 29 of the 32 Senate seats, a gain of 10; strengthened its lead in the 150-member Chamber of Deputies; and won control of 104 of the 125 municipalities. Armed with these overwhelming majorities, the *PRD* amended the constitution to permit the immediate re-election of a president for a second term, largely because Mejía insisted that he was not interested in running again.

In February 2002, the *PLD* lost its patriarch when Bosch died at 92. He was buried with full state honors, and diplomatic representatives of six countries and Puerto Rico—but not the United States—attended the funeral, as did thousands of Dominicans. Bosch was followed in death five months later by his arch-rival, Balaguer, 95. A colorful era in Dominican history was over.

Mejía's popularity plummeted after the mid-term elections as the once-vibrant economy turned sour (see Economy). Power blackouts, created when the privatized power companies could not keep up with demand, led to protests in 2002 that left two people dead and 50 injured. Mejía responded by renationalizing the power companies, which cost about $600 million, causing the IMF to cancel a loan for that amount.

Mejía announced a series of austerity measures in 2003 designed to halt an alarming increase in inflation and the decline in the value of the peso, which lost 65% from 2003 to 2004. Mejía reduced the number of government jobs and of government salaries. Unlike in other Latin American countries, where the opposition launches general strikes and confrontational street demonstrations to protest austerity measures, the opposition charged that the measures did not go far enough and called for street protests to demand even greater spending cuts.

The reeling economy was dealt a knock-out blow when Banco Intercontinental, or Baninter, the country's third-largest private bank, went bankrupt in April 2003 as the result of an embezzlement and fraud scandal. The central bank was legally obligated to pay only 500,000 pesos, or $12,000, to each depositor, but it generously compensated the depositors for their entire losses, a total of $2.4 billion that the economy could not absorb. The bank's owners went to jail, but that did not prevent the ripple effects of the bailout on the economy.

By early 2004, inflation was running at 42%, and unemployment was 16%. Dominicans began joining Cubans and Haitians in trying to reach the United States—or Puerto Rico. It was a stark contrast to the boom times of the 1990s.

Fernández Makes a Comeback

Mejía made an abrupt about face and announced he planned to run again in 2004. He met with immediate opposition from within his own *PRD*, whose rules still precluded immediate re-nomination. Mejía arrogantly pressed on with his re-election plans despite polls that showed 73% of Dominicans opposed a second term.

He did not increase his popularity by contributing 370 Dominican troops to the allied coalition in Iraq. He began withdrawing them in 2004, after Spain withdrew its troops following the al-Qaeda terror attacks in Madrid.

An anti-re-election faction chose *PRD* president Hatuey de Camps as its candidate, but party regulars dutifully renominated Mejía at a convention boycotted by the de Camps faction. Mejía then attempted a Byzantine maneuver, pushing through Congress a bill that would allow each party to nominate up to five candidates, with the one receiving the most votes to receive all the party's votes. In the face of a public outcry, he declared that "power is there to be exercised." This only inflamed public opinion further.

Former President Fernández, meanwhile, announced his own comeback bid as the *PLD* candidate. Rounding out the field was Eduardo Estrella of Balaguer's *PRSC*.

Mejía was so unpopular at that point he was booed at baseball games. Businessmen staged a two-day strike, in which 20 people were injured. The IMF, meanwhile, reapproved the desperately needed loan, but parceled it out in increments. Gradually, as polls showed Mejía ahead of the other factions in the *PRD*, the party faithful gradually coalesced around his candidacy as the only way to prevent a Fernández comeback.

There was a new twist to the 2004 campaign: The three candidates campaigned in Miami and New York, because Dominicans living abroad were allowed to vote for president for the first time; more than 52,000 were registered to do so. An estimated 1 million Dominicans reside in the United States, another 100,000 in Puerto Rico. Polling centers also were estab-

Former President Leonel Fernández

lished in Montreal, Caracas, Madrid and Barcelona.

In the end, Dominicans chose between a president who had presided over a boom and another who had presided over a bust. The turnout was 72% of the 5 million registered voters, compared with 76% in 2000. The results:

Fernández	2,063,871	57.11%
Mejía	1,215,928	33.65%
Estrella	312,493	8.65%

Fernández was inaugurated for his second term on August 16, 2004. He named four men to high-level posts who were under investigation for allegedly embezzling $100 million during his first term from a fund created to establish jobs and mediate strikes. Fernández dismissed the charges as "politically motivated."

Fernández tackled the economic crisis with a series of painful austerity measures. He pushed through the *PRD*-controlled Congress increases in various taxes, including the VAT, or sales tax, from 12% to 16% to reduce a $490 million budget deficit and to prevent a default on the $7.9 billion debt. He also began ending subsidies on gas and electricity, but eased that blow by concluding an agreement for low-cost Venezuelan oil for electricity generation. Power blackouts remained a problem.

At the same time, he declared he would cut 20% from the budget and reduce the size of the bloated public payroll, which Mejía had increased by 30% to 400,000. Among those losing their jobs were 97 of the army's 202 generals; Fernández said the country didn't need, and couldn't afford, that many generals.

There was some grumbling over the austerity measures, but they began turning the economy around. At the height of the crisis, the peso dropped to 51 to the dollar; by the end of 2004, it was back up to 29. The country recorded a modest increase in the GDP for 2004 after posting a loss in 2003. Fernández reinforced his reputation as an economic wizard in 2005 with GDP growth of 9.3%. In 2006, it was 10.7%, the highest in Latin America, and in 2007 it was a still-robust 7.9%.

In 2005, the corruption investigation shoe was on the foot of the other party. Charges were filed against two of Mejía's former ministers and several businessmen in an alleged scheme to divert $60 million designated for buses and minivans for the public transportation system into their own pockets. However, Fernández was less than aggressive in dealing with alleged corruption on his predecessor's watch, apparently because he needed the *PRD*'s support in Congress.

That changed with the congressional elections of 2006, in which the *PLD* obtained 52% of the vote and won a majority in both houses. The *PLD* won 96 seats in the Chamber of Deputies to 60 for the *PRD* and 22 for the *PRSC*; in the Senate, the *PLD* won 22 seats, the *PRD* 7, the *PRSC*, 3.

In 2005, the Dominican Republic ratified the Dominican Republic-Central American Free Trade Agreement with the United States. It went into effect on March 1, 2007.

Besides having brought back the boom times of his first term, Fernández in his second term built the first subway system in the Caribbean for Santo Domingo, cost $700 million. The first 11-mile segment opened on the eve of the 2008 presidential election campaign. The subway opened in January 2009, and despite skeptics who complained it was a waste of money, it has been successful.

Third Term

Although there were still nagging problems, such as 16% unemployment, a high poverty rate and chronic blackouts, Fernández was the hands-down favorite for the May 2008 election, now that immediate re-election was permitted. First he faced a challenge from his own two-time secretary of the presidency, Danilo Medina, the unsuccessful *PLD* candidate in 2000. Medina resigned to challenge Fernández in the *PLD* primary, but Fernández crushed him, 72% to 28%.

The *PRD* unwisely nominated its leader, Miguel Vargas Maldonado, who had been Mejía's public works minister. He was still under a cloud of suspicion for alleged financial irregularities. The *PRSC* nominated a flamboyant populist, Amable Aristy Castro, former general-secretary of

Dominican Republic

the Dominican Municipal League. There were four minor candidates.

Four people were killed in the customary election-related violence. Voter turnout was 70.67%. Fernández scored a convincing first-round victory with 2.2 million votes, or 53.8%. Vargas had 1.65 million, or 40.5%, while Aristy polled only 188,000, or 4.6%, a pitiful showing for Balaguer's old party. Fernández was sworn in for his third term on August 16.

Fernández continued to enjoy respectable economic growth until the global recession hit in late 2008. In 2010, the president visited neighboring Haiti in the wake of the devastating earthquake there and pledged immediate medical and reconstruction aid. It was not out of pure benevolence; Dominicans feared a new migration of desperate Haitians.

The 2010 congressional elections were marred by the usual violence, including a clash between security forces and PRD demonstrators in San Cristobal that left a PRD partisan dead and three wounded. The PLD increased its majority, winning 54.6% of the vote and 105 seats in the Chamber of Deputies and 31 of the 32 Senate seats.

The Election of 2012

Fernández's supporters sought to amend the constitution so the president could run for a *fourth* term in 2012, and he did little to discourage them. Fernández abruptly announced he would not seek a fourth term, but considered following the lead of former Argentine President Kirchner and then-Guatemalan President Colom by running his wife, Margarita Cedeño, as the *PLD* candidate. An attorney, Cedeño filed as a pre-candidate, But in October, she bowed out in favor of Medina, 61, who had lost the 2000 presidential election to Mejía and the 2008 *PLD* nomination to Fernández. The two men had patched up their differences, and Medina named the first lady as his running mate.

The *PRD* once again nominated Mejía, now 71, setting up a rematch of the 2000 election. Polls showed the race a tossup. The *PUSC*, fearing a Mejía victory, decided not to field a candidate to avoid splitting the anti-Mejía vote. Both men campaigned in New York, especially the Washington Heights neighborhood of the Bronx, where much of the 380,000 Dominicans in New York are concentrated. Medina also was aided by an economy that grew 4.5% in 2011, a far cry from the boom days, but better than any year under Mejía. He probably also benefited from having a woman as his running mate.

Medina's persistence finally paid off. The voter turnout on May 20 was 70.2%. The results:

President Danilo Medina

Medina	2,323,150	51.2%
Mejía	2,129,997	47%

Mejía ungraciously claimed the election was fraudulent, despite the 200 international observers who declared it fair, and vowed to contest the results. Rather than congratulating Medina, he warned that the country was returning to "totalitarianism."

In his inaugural address on August 16, 2012, Medina said he wanted to "fix what's wrong and do what has never been done before," including reducing the 34% poverty rate and cracking down on the country's notorious corruption. Dominicans had heard both promises before, but just as Fernández had done in 2004, Medina kept on some shady figures from the past in his government.

Recent Developments

To his horror, Medina discovered when he took charge that the budget deficit was twice what Fernández had claimed it was, about 8% of GDP. His response was to do what both Fernández and Mejía had done—impose painful austerity measures. But he opted in favor of tax increases, as Fernández had done, instead of slashing government services, as Mejía had done. The public payroll is infamously bloated and over-generous, and waste is on a scandalous scale, so there was plenty of room for cutting. But Medina chose to raise the value-added tax from 16% to 18%, and to impose stiff tax increases on alcohol and tobacco. This could actually worsen the fiscal crisis by stifling consumer spending, thus reducing revenue from the VAT.

Public outrage led to violent demonstrations in November 2012 that left two people dead. The protests continued for weeks, with the demonstrators blaming Fernández for creating the deficit through profligate spending before leaving office. Dominicans even demonstrated against the tax increases in New York City in December. The increases took effect on January 1, 2013.

Despite the austerity measures, and a slowing of GDP growth to 3.9% in 2013, Mexico's Mitofsky poll in October 2013 gave Medina a phenomenal approval rating of 88%, the highest of any leader in the Western Hemisphere.

Relations became strained with neighboring Haiti, and with all the predominantly black member states of the Caribbean Community (CARICOM), in September 2013. The Constitutional Court made the immigration law that requires citizens to show at least one parent was a legal resident in the Dominican Republic retroactive to 2004, thereby nullifying the citizenship of at least 200,000 Dominicans of Haitian origin, rendering them stateless. Medina issued an executive decree giving them 18 months to register with the authorities. A Dominican columnist called the move "civil genocide," a term picked up by Haitian President Michel Martelly. The Dominican Republic broke off talks with Haiti. CARICOM denounced the decision as racist, and suspended the Dominican Republic's application for membership that it had been sitting on for eight years.

CULTURE: The succession of lengthy dictatorships since independence, coupled with poverty and illiteracy, was not conducive to the development of Dominican culture. Ethnically, the island is a mix of European, Indian and African, and the domestic culture is a hybridization that has influenced its music. A dance that has won popular acceptance abroad is the *merengue*, with its contagious Caribbean rhythm.

The absence of educational reform and the resulting low literacy rate crippled the Dominican Republic's literary growth. The prose fiction writer Juan Bosch, who served briefly as president in the 1960s and remained influential in Dominican politics until his death, was one of only a handful of Dominicans who obtained international recognition in literature or the arts. Among the country's most notable cultural contribution is the fashion designer, Oscar de la Renta (b. 1932).

Probably the most celebrated contemporary Dominican writer is Julia Álvarez, who was born in New York in 1950 of Dominican parents. They returned to the Dominican Republic in the early 1950s and her parents became active in the anti-

Trujillo underground founded by the four Mirabal sisters. Her parents' activities inspired Álvarez's 1994 novel, *In the Time of the Butterflies,* based on the story of the Mirabal sisters, three of whom were murdered in 1960. Álvarez and her parents returned to the U.S. that year. The book was made into a U.S.-Mexican movie in 2001, starring Salma Hayek as Minerva Mirabal, Edward James Olmos as Trujillo, and Marc Anthony. Álvarez also wrote *How the García Girls Lost Their Accents* in 1991.

The story of the Mirabal sisters also inspired the 2009 documentary film *Trópico de sangre,* by Dominican screenwriter and director Juan Delancer.

The Trujillo dictatorship is also the focus of a new museum that opened in Santo Domingo in 2011 the day before the 50th anniversary of the dictator's assassination. The museum recreates a torture chamber, complete with captured audiotapes of torture sessions.

By the late 20th century, the Dominican Republic was making up for lost cultural ground, particularly in music. It gave the world its signature sound, the *merengue.* As of 2012, Dominican recording artists had won a total of 21 Latin Grammy Awards.

Fifteen of those Latin Grammys have gone to Juan Luis Guerra (b. 1957), the singer-composer-songwriter-guitarist credited with rejuvenating *merengue* and with popularizing the so-called slum genre *bachata.* He swept five Latin Grammys in 2007 with his album, *La Llave de mi Corazón* (the key to my heart), including Album of the Year. It also won the Grammy Award that year for Best Tropical Latin Album. He won three more Latin Grammys in 2010, including Album of the Year for *A Son de Guerra.* He was nominated for six more in 2012 and won two, Album of the Year and Producer of the Year for his collaboration with the Colombian singer Juanes on the album *MTV Unplugged.* In 2013, his album *Asondeguerra Tour* won the Grammy for Best Contemporary Tropical Album. He is a celebrity throughout Latin America and a megastar at home. He has sold more than 30 million recordings of his songs.

Another well-known *merengue* performer internationally is Chichí Peralta (b. 1966), who won a Latin Grammy for Best Merengue Album in 2001 for *De Vuelta al Barrio* (back to the neighborhood). In 2007 the government named him a goodwill ambassador.

The independent Dominican press often has felt the pressure of dictators. The dean of the press is the daily *Listín Diario,* founded in 1889, which flourished until shut down by the Trujillo dictatorship. It resumed publication in 1963 and has followed a left-of-center editorial line, counterbalanced by the country's other

"respectable" newspaper, *El Caribe. Listín Diario* was taken over by the government in 2003, not for criticizing the government but because its owner, Ramón Baéz, was arrested for fraud and embezzlement following the collapse of Banco Intercontinental, of which he was an owner (see History). A judge ruled in 2004 that the newspaper was not connected to the bank collapse and ordered it returned to Baéz's family. Because hundreds of thousands of Dominicans now live abroad, especially the United States, there has been a proliferation of online newspapers that allow expatriates to keep up with events back home. Not all have remained viable.

Sports is a national obsession, particularly soccer and baseball. Numerous Dominican baseball players have gone on to play in the U.S. major leagues, most notably Sammy Sosa of the Chicago Cubs, a source of great national pride, who hit 66 home runs in 1998, five more than Roger Maris' previous record of 61 in 1961.

The historic colonial quarter of Santo Domingo is a UNESCO World Heritage Site. The cathedral there contained the bones of Columbus from 1542–1795; the Spanish removed them when the French conquered the island. The Dominican Republic still claims the "real" remains of the explorer are in an elaborate tomb in the Columbus Lighthouse in Santo Domingo, although DNA tests in 2006 verified that Columbus' remains are in the cathedral in Seville, Spain.

The Dominican Republic has 26 institutions of higher learning. The Autonomous University of Santo Domingo, founded in 1538, is one of the oldest in the New World.

ECONOMY: The Dominican economy has been traditionally based on agriculture, with sugar being the main cash crop. However, now tourism produces more income than sugar as sugar prices fell and the U.S. reduced the Dominican quota allowed for importation. New hotels and tourist facilities have sprung up throughout the nation. In 2002, tourism revenue amounted to $2 billion.

An aggressive government program to place unused farmland into production has increased the output of other cash products such as meat, coffee, tobacco and cacao. Thanks to an ambitious irrigation program centering around a four-dam system on the Nizao River, some farm regions are now producing up to three crops a year in contrast to a single crop in previous years.

Also gaining in importance is the nation's mining industry. Exports include gold, iron, nickel, bauxite, salt and gypsum. In 2009, a Canadian consortium began investing $4 billion, the largest foreign investment in the nation's history, in the Rosario gold mine, which the government abandoned in 1999. It is projected to provide the government with $10 billion in revenue over 25 years, but in 2013 it became the subject of controversy when residents near the mine began reporting health problems and complain that the discharge from the mine was killing their livestock. Cyanide is used in gold mining. The government stonewalled requests for information on its environmental impact statement for the project.

Three huge oil refineries, which re-export imported petroleum as refined fuels, also have boosted the economy. Unsuccessful efforts were made to increase the output from the nation's own small oil fields. Output rose from zero in 2008 to 392 barrels per day in 2010, then dropped back to 60 bpd in 2013.

Tourism has grown steadily in importance and is now the second-largest source of foreign exchange after exports. Tourist arrivals totaled 4.6 million in 2013, the fourth year in a row they have set a record. That capitalized into $5.1 billion in revenue, or 7.7% of GDP, the highest percentage of any nation in Latin America. Most of the tourists are drawn to the beaches of Punta Cana on the east coast. Punta Cana's international airport accounts for 63% of the arrivals, compared with 24% for the capital. Expedia.com rated the Dominican Republic as the top tourist destination in the Caribbean for 2013.

The Dominican Republic continues to attract record amounts of investment, partly because of the comparatively stable political conditions.

Foreign investment in luxury hotels and resorts, textiles, clothing and assembly-for-re-export plants, like Mexico's *maquiladoras,* created about 200,000 new jobs in the 1990s. The result was what could only be called a boom during the presidency of Leonel Fernández (1996–2000) of the conservative, business-oriented Democratic Liberation Party *(PLD).* Even as some of the major economies of the region slipped into recession after the Brazilian market meltdowns of 1998 and 1999, the Dominican Republic maintained the highest sus-

Dominican Republic

tained GDP growth in Latin America from 1997–2000, above 7% a year.

Per capita GDP has risen correspondingly, from $1,572 in 1996 to $2,486 in 2001 to $5,800 in 2013, but in 2010 34.4% of the population was still below the poverty line.

Mid-way through the presidency of Hipólito Mejía (2000–04), a populist of the Democratic Revolutionary Party *(PRD)*, the economy went into a tailspin. Unemployment jumped to 16%, inflation soared to 42% and the foreign debt more than doubled, from $3.7 billion to $7.6 billion. The value of the peso fell from 18 to the dollar to 51. The government generously paid out $2.4 billion to depositors in the bailout of Banco Intercontinental in 2003. The country's third-largest bank collapsed because of fraud and embezzlement, which exacerbated the crisis and caused an estimated $2 billion in foreign capital to be withdrawn from Dominican banks in the wake of the scandal.

Real GDP growth slumped to 3% in 2001 and 4.1% in 2002, then *declined* –0.4% in 2003. Per capita GDP dropped to $2,320 in 2002 and $1,896 in 2003. Boom had turned to bust.

The downturn was largely responsible for the return to power in 2004 of former President Fernández. He quickly imposed a number of austerity measures, which turned the economy around (see History).

GDP growth in 2004 was a meager 1.8%, a far cry from the boom years, but at least positive rather than negative. In 2005 it was back up to the boom level of 9.3%, while inflation was reduced to 7.4%. In 2006, growth was 10.7%, the highest in Latin America, while inflation was only 5%; growth in 2007 was a still-high 8.5%, and per capita income was back up to $3,850. Ironically, the strengthened peso against the dollar led to a 17% decline in textile exports and the loss of 41,000 jobs. Fernández was elected to a third term in 2008.

Growth slowed to 5.3% in 2008 and 1.8% in 2009, largely because of the global recession and growing unemployment in the United States, which has affected the ever-vital remittances from Dominicans working there. Growth was 4% or above from 2010 to 2012, dropping to 3.9% in 2013.

Unemployment has remained steady at about 14%-15% since 2008, falling to 13.3% in 2011. It was back up to 15% in 2013.

With the recession, inflation dropped from 10.6% in 2008 to 1.4% in 2009. It was 6.3% in 2010 and 8.6% in 2011, but only 2.7% in 2012. It rose to 5% in 2013.

Remittances from Dominicans living abroad, mostly the United States, leaped from $1.5 billion in 1999 to $2.7 billion in 2004, to $3.1 billion in 2008. They leveled off with the 2009–09 financial crisis and recession in the United States. In 2011 they were a record $3.3 billion, a 7.7% increase from 2010, or about 6% of GDP. It dropped slightly in 2012 to $3.2 billion. The Dominican Republic ranks in fifth place for remittances in Latin America.

The Dominican Republic ratified its membership in the U.S.-Central American Free trade Agreement (CAFTA-DR) in March 2007. The United States accounts for 47% of Dominican exports and 43% of imports.

THE FUTURE: The Dominican Republic went from boom under Leonel Fernández to bust under Hipólito Mejía back to boom under Fernández. Fernández's major shortcoming in three terms in office was his failure to channel the booming growth rate to reduce nagging unemployment or to significantly reduce the poverty rate to less than 34%. He has now passed his, and Balaguer's, mantle to his protégé, Danilo Medina, whose narrow election victory saved the country from another four years of Mejía. With Fernández's wife, Margarita Cedeño, as his vice president, it may be difficult for Medina to prove who's in charge.

The deadly street protests against Medina's tax increases in November 2012 were an ominous warning that the Dominicans demand real, not cosmetic, changes. Any attempt to reform the notoriously corrupt patronage system will likely create friction with Fernández. A power struggle between Fernández and Medina, like that between Colombian President Juan Manuel Santos and his predecessor and mentor, Álvaro Uribe, is quite possible.

Whatever he's doing, Dominicans seem to approve. In September 2013 Medina had an approval rating of 88%, the highest of any leader in the Western Hemisphere.

Partial view of the port of Santo Domingo

Ecuador

An Andean landscape

Area: 104,749 square miles.

Population: 15,654,411 (2014 est.).

Capital City: Quito (Pop. 1.6 million in 2010).

Climate: The eastern lowlands are hot and wet; the coastal plains receive seasonally heavy rainfall; the highland climate becomes increasingly temperate with altitude.

Neighboring Countries: Colombia (north); Peru (east and south).

Official Language: Spanish.

Other Principal Tongues: Quechua and Jívaro.

Ethnic Background: Predominantly Indian, with small groups of European and African origin.

Principal Religion: Roman Catholic Christianity.

183

Ecuador

Chief Commercial Products: Petroleum, coffee, bananas, cacao, shrimp, sardines.

Currency: U.S. Dollar (formerly the *sucre*).

Gross Domestic Product: U.S. $91.41 billion, 2013, est. ($5,921 per capita, official exchange rate).

Former Colonial Status: Spanish Crown Colony (1532–1821); a state of *Gran Colombia* (1822–1830).

Independence Date: May 13, 1830.

Chief of State: Rafael Vicente Correa Delgado (b. April 6, 1963), president (since January 15, 2007).

National Flag: A top yellow stripe, center blue stripe and a lower red stripe.

Because of disputes with Peru over boundaries, and territorial losses in the 1942 settlement of a war with Peru, Ecuador's area is uncertain. It has three distinct zones: the vast Andean highland, with lofty, snow-capped peaks and green valleys; the narrow coastal plain between the Andes and the Pacific, from 50 to 100 miles wide; and the *Oriente* (East), consisting of tropical jungles in the upper Amazon Basin. The high mountain valleys have a temperate climate, rich soils and moderate rainfall suitable for dairy farming and the production of cereals and vegetables. The Pacific coastal plains are tropical and devoted to plantation farming of bananas, cotton, sugar and cocoa. The *Oriente* is more than one third of the agricultural land of Ecuador and is a thick, virgin forest and jungle land containing valuable timber, although much of it cannot be transported to market at a profit.

Lying about 650 miles off the coastline are the Galapagos Islands, an archipelago situated on the Equator. Consisting of 14 islands and numerous islets, it is a haven for many species of waterfowl and giant turtles. With a population of 650, it is regularly visited by tour groups interested in its unspoiled setting.

HISTORY: Shortly before Spanish penetration of Ecuador, the ancient Inca Empire had been united under a single chief, Huayna Cápac, in 1526. Francisco Pizarro, the Spanish conquistador, touched along the coastline in 1528 at about the time Cápac died.

After returning temporarily to Spain, Pizarro came back to Ecuador with a larger force seeking the treasures he believed were in the interior. Huayna Cápac had divided his empire between two sons—Huáscar, who ruled the Cuzco area, and Atahualpa, who ruled over Quito.

After holding him for a huge ransom of gold and silver, Pizarro executed Atahualpa and mercilessly started the suppression of the Incas.

The invasion of Ecuador followed the pattern of other Spanish conquests. As the Incas and their subject tribes were defeated, the land was awarded in large grants to the successful leaders; the Indians were enslaved to work the estates and the Spaniards built strategically located cities to administer the territory. The low, unhealthy coastal plains had been shunned by the Incas, who lived in the temperate highland and valleys. The Spanish followed the same pattern building their cities of Quito, Ona, Cuenca and Loja above the 5,000-foot level.

The Spanish made little effort to improve the port of Guayaquil or to farm its valley, leaving the fever-ridden region to later arrivals and outcasts from the highlands. Thus, the colonial period continued a regionalism well established in the Inca period and which still divides the highlander from the coastal dweller.

Spanish rule was not challenged for several harsh, uneventful centuries. Antonio José de Sucre, a brilliant military leader under Simón Bolívar, united Ecuador with neighboring Colombia and Venezuela from 1822 to 1830. This union dissolved when Ecuador and Venezuela withdrew. Bolívar died at the age of 47 shortly thereafter.

Ecuador's history as an independent state has been an alternating swing from near anarchy under weak governments to the enforced peace established by dictators. The first president of Ecuador, Juan José Flores, a brave soldier but an indifferent governor, appealed to the Conservatives in Quito and aroused the opposition of the Liberals in Guayaquil. However, he worked out a scheme to alternate as president with Vicente Rocafuerte, a Guayaquil Liberal—a device that remained in effect until 1845.

In the next 15 years, Ecuador had 11 changes of administration, most of them Liberal; there were three constitutions and sporadic civil wars as well as border wars with Peru and Colombia. By 1860 there was little semblance of a central government—local strongmen ruled the communities with the support of their gunmen. Popular opposition to the cession of Guayaquil and the southern provinces to Peru in 1860 brought a Conservative to power, who established a theocratic Catholic dictatorship which lasted until his assassination in 1875. However, he did more for the unification of the country and for its economy than any other 19th century leader.

For 20 years, Ecuador returned to civil war and anarchy, banditry, and economic deterioration. Conservatives regularly won the elections and were regularly ousted by Liberals from Guayaquil until the revolution of 1895; this brought 50 years of Liberal rule to Ecuador, highlighted by three more constitutions, the passage of 28 presidents and uninterrupted political, social and eco-nomic crises. While the power of the Conservatives and the church were curtailed, the Liberal promises of free elections and honest government had little meaning, by and large. Galo Plaza Lasso (1948–52) was a notable exception. He became secretary-general of the Organization of American States in 1968.

From 1952–63, Conservatives alternated in power with Liberal José María Velasco Ibarra until a reform military government seized power; it was promptly overthrown by the Liberals it sought to assist.

A constituent assembly elected an interim president in 1966; he was succeeded by the aging Velasco, elected for a fifth time. Always controversial, he soon grew restless with his inability to win congressional approval for his economic policies. With the approval of the armed forces, he seized dictatorial power in mid-1970, dismissing the Congress and replacing the moderate constitution (Ecuador's 16th) with a more conservative 1946 version.

Velasco vowed to surrender power to his legally elected successor in 1972. But, fearing a free election would be won by Assad Bucaram, a left-leaning former mayor of Guayaquil, the armed forces seized power in early 1972 and installed General Guillermo Rodríguez Lara as president. Modeling itself after the reformist Peruvian military government, the new regime pledged its policies would be "revolutionary and nationalistic."

The regime concentrated on how best to spend the huge tax royalties pouring into the treasury from Ecuador's newly developed oil fields; most funds were spent on public works (education, highways and hospitals) and fancy military hardware.

Despite the oil boom, dissatisfaction arose against the center-right regime. Leftists denounced inaction of promised social and economic reforms, while Conservatives condemned swollen civil service rolls (one in every 10 workers) and new taxes on luxury imports. The oil revenue-fed inflation, high unemployment and continuing government corruption and repression heightened the discontent.

Democracy, Ecuadorean Style

An unsuccessful attempt by dissident soldiers to oust Rodríguez Lara in 1975 left 22 dead and 100 injured. But after widespread student and labor unrest in early 1976, the strongman was finally toppled by a *junta* headed by Admiral Alfredo Poveda. The new rulers promptly moved to restore civilian rule. In January 1978, voters approved another constitution; elections were held six months later, followed by a run-off in April 1979.

Jaime Roldós Aguilera, a mild-mannered populist attorney from Guayaquil, was elected president for a four-year term by 59% of the vote. At 38, he was the youngest chief executive in Latin America. Although his own Concentration of Popular Forces party and the allied Democratic Left party won 45 of the 69 seats in the unicameral Congress, the new president was unable to build a ruling coalition. Ironically, his bitterest rival was Assad Bucaram, his father-in-law and leader of Congress. Because Roldós rejected Bucaram's populist program in favor of a more conservative approach, the two quickly became enemies and Bucaram blocked virtually all of Roldos' proposals. Austerity measures further damaged Roldós' effectiveness, leading to widespread disorder and the threat of another coup.

A border clash with Peru in 1981 temporarily diverted attention from Ecuador's economic problems. Although the basic dispute dates back to 1830, the latest crisis centered around the 1942 border treaty between the two nations, which Ecuador later disavowed.

On May 24, 1981, Roldós, his wife and seven others were killed in a plane crash while on a trip to the troubled border region. He was succeeded by Vice President Osvaldo Hurtado. The late president's brother, León, was named vice president.

In May 1984, León Febrés Cordero, of the conservative Social Christian Party, a businessman and candidate of the Front for National Reconstruction, was elected president. His first year saw modest economic growth, but also worker unrest and often bitter friction between the president and Congress. Febrés Cordero, an energetic, free-market capitalist, provided Ecuador with strong if heavy-handed leadership. He packed a .45 automatic pistol. When the choice of 18 members of the judiciary by the opposition-controlled Congress didn't suit him, he had the Supreme Court surrounded by tanks so they could not take the oath of office. He chose 18 others, more to his liking. Opposition members were fired from government positions and critical newspapers suffered a drop in public advertising. Difficulties with the military, punctuated by two attempts at mutiny, led to an unsuccessful effort to impeach Febrés Cordero for "disgracing the national honor."

Adverse economic conditions led Ecuadorians to turn to two leftists in 1988 elections. The contest was hot, with charges such as "alcoholic atheist" and "drug-trafficking fascist" commonplace. Rodrigo Borja ultimately won. Political bickering and infighting, corruption and a stale economy were the main features of the Borja years.

Apparently tired of the "same old thing," voters turned to a conservative in 1992: Sixto Durán Ballén, a 71-year-old architect born in Boston, who promised basic reforms. He wasted no time in putting them into effect. He devalued the sucre by 27.5%, and auctioned off inefficient, money-losing state-owned enterprises. Subsidies on commodities were sharply reduced or eliminated, but to prevent hardships, Durán raised wages modestly. Ecuador dropped its membership in OPEC and announced it would establish its own quotas to market its petroleum. Production rose 18% in 1993, but lower international oil prices decreased income.

Higher fuel and electricity prices, reduced state spending and a freeze on government employment combined to create serious unrest in 1992. Payment on the $13 billion external debt was suspended, freezing international credit. Strikes and bombings by terrorist groups added to Ecuador's difficulties.

On January 29, 1995, the long-simmering border dispute with Peru finally erupted into open warfare in an isolated, mountainous area. Several times before there had been minor border clashes close to the anniversary of the January 29, 1942, Rio Accords by which Ecuador had been forced to cede nearly half its territory. This time, however, the incident quickly escalated into full-scale war with mortar attacks and airstrikes. Ecuadorian gunners shot down a Peruvian helicopter and three jet fighter-bombers. Frightened civilians fled their villages. Two tentative ceasefires in February failed to hold. The four guarantor countries—Argentina, Brazil, Chile and the United States—finally succeeded in effecting a definite cease-fire on

July 25. In the three weeks of heavy fighting at the outset of the hostilities, 73 people were killed and at least 200 wounded; each side took a number of prisoners, later expatriated.

The economy became generally better-organized during the Durán years, but scandal detracted from its successes and little attention was paid to the poor. This neglect was to influence the 1996 presidential election.

The Bucaram Fiasco

In the first round of voting in May 1996, Jaime Nebot of the Social Christian Party led Abdalá Bucaram of the *Roldosista* Party, 30% to 26%. The July runoff thus presented voters with a clear choice: Nebot, a conservative who favored continuation of privatization of key economic sectors, and Bucaram, a populist who opposed privatization or reform of the cumbersome social security system. Bucaram also displayed a flamboyance on the campaign trail that startled, and apparently amused, voters. He unabashedly proclaimed himself "*El Loco*." The unorthodox appeal worked: Bucaram defeated Nebot 54.1% to 45.9%.

What followed in the six months after Bucaram's inauguration in August 1996 marked the most bizarre episode in modern Ecuadorian political history, as the unpredictable Bucaram shocked Ecuadorians almost daily with his strange public antics and even stranger governmental measures. He made international headlines when he invited Lorena Bobbitt, the Ecuadorian-born woman infamous for sev-

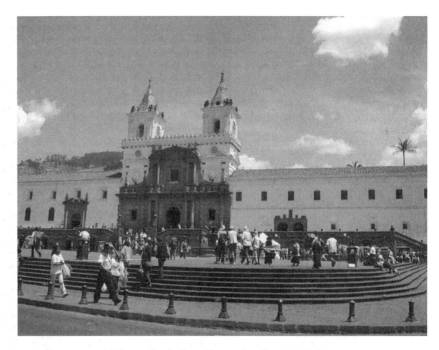

The cathedral on the main plaza in Quito

Ecuador

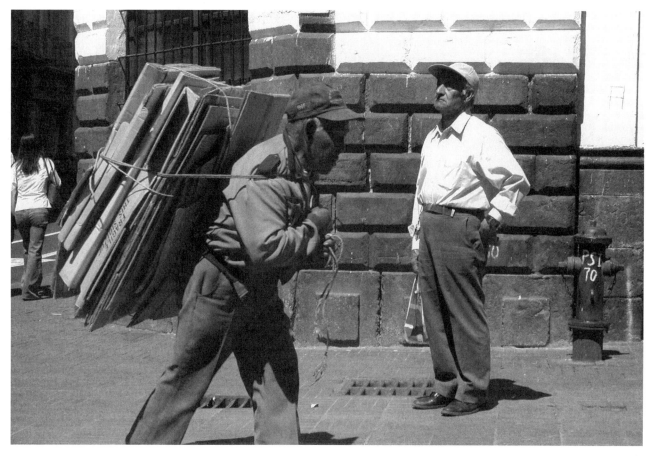

Making a living in the poorer part of Quito

ering her husband's penis in the United States, to the presidential palace for lunch. He took to singing in a rock band, and an Associated Press photo of the president, clutching a microphone and flanked by buxom, scantily clad beauties, was published all over the world. When a presidential helicopter crashed and burned, Bucaram denounced it as an assassination attempt.

He shocked almost everyone by hiring Argentina's sacked economy minister, Domingo Cavallo, to be his economic adviser. More shocking still, he discarded his populist campaign promises and imposed an austerity program that included geometric price increases for public services, such as public transport (200%), electricity (more than 100%) and natural gas (250%). Bucaram's draconian measures sparked widespread protests, some of them violent. His approval rating dropped out of sight.

In February 1997, as Bucaram came under intense pressure to resign, Ecuador plunged into semi-chaos. The beleaguered president imposed a state of emergency that allowed him to take extra-constitutional measures, such as banning demonstrations and imposing press censorship. In a move that delighted the public but which totally disregarded the constitution,

Congress removed Bucaram from office on the grounds of "mental incapacity," despite the absence of any authoritative medical or psychiatric testimony.

Bucaram's peculiar behavior proved to be the least of his transgressions. He went into self-imposed exile in Panama (long a dumping ground for deposed and disgraced rulers), denouncing Congress for its unconstitutional actions. Evidence then surfaced that he may have absconded with as much as $26 million from the treasury. Some estimates placed the total that Bucaram and his entourage withdrew illegally from the treasury during his six months in power at $80 million. The Supreme Court formally charged Bucaram and four of his aides with corruption, influence peddling, embezzlement and nepotism, and unsuccessfully sought his extradition. (Guatemala, it should be noted, has tried unsuccessfully since 1993 to extradite former President Jorge Serrano from Panama, who also allegedly stole millions from the treasury.) One of the aides was arrested in Peru, carrying $3.4 million.

Revolving-Door Presidency

The post-Bucaram transition also proved chaotic—and probably unconsti-

tutional. At first, Vice President Rosalia Arteaga was duly sworn in as Ecuador's first woman president, with the tacit blessing of the armed forces. But within days Congress "elected" one of its leaders, Fabián Alarcón, to serve as interim president until a new presidential election could be called. In a referendum in May, 74% of Ecuadorian voters "ratified" Alarcón's interim presidency until August 1998. On another of the 14 referendum issues, 65% of voters indicated that they approved of Bucaram's removal from office. In Panama, Bucaram ridiculed the plebiscite as a "political show."

Ecuadorians went to the polls in November 1997 to elect a constituent assembly charged with overhauling the 1978 organic law in the wake of the Bucaram fiasco and to prepare for the election of a new president. The Social Christian Party of former President Febrés Cordero won a plurality of 24 of the 70 seats. Former President Hurtado's Popular Christian Party was a distant second with nine seats, while 11 other parties split the remainder, ensuring that whatever emerged from the assembly would be by broad consensus.

In 1998, the assembly voted 60–7 to preclude anyone convicted of corruption, embezzlement or other misuse of public funds, from running for public office, a move aimed squarely at Bucaram, who already had announced from Panama that he planned to run in the next presidential election. He soon relinquished his candidacy and endorsed the country's leading banana exporter, Álvaro Noboa, as the *Roldosista* candidate. The first round of voting was another free-for-all, with five other candidates vying with Noboa. The frontrunner was Quito Mayor Jamil Mahuad of the Popular Democracy movement.

In the first round of balloting on May 31, 1998, Mahuad placed first with 36.6% and Noboa came in second with 29.7%. In the July 12 runoff, Mahuad pulled off a narrow victory, receiving 51% of the valid votes, or 2,242,836 to Noboa's 2,140,628. Mahuad took office on August 10.

Mahuad presented a sobering change from Bucaram; apparently the only thing they had in common was Lebanese ancestry. He was well prepared professionally, having served as labor minister under Roldós, then as a member of Congress before serving two terms as mayor of Quito. He earned a master's degree in public administration from Harvard.

Ecuadorians again were distracted from domestic concerns by renewed border tensions with Peru, which in July 1997 had begun acquiring advanced Russian MiGs. Unlike 1995, however, sanity prevailed and the two countries sent representatives to Brasilia to negotiate a timetable for demarcation of the 48-mile stretch of disputed frontier. In January 1998, the representatives signed an accord that set a deadline for reaching a final agreement. Also signing were representatives of the four peace guarantors—Brazil, Argentina, Chile and the United States.

Mahuad and Peruvian President Alberto Fujimori signed the peace accord in Brasilia in 1998, definitively delineating the disputed stretch of frontier that led to the 1995 war. The agreement was almost entirely along the lines Peru had demanded, that the border would follow the divide of the Cordillera del Condor range. As a gesture to Ecuador, however, Peru acquiesced Tiwintza Hill, which Ecuadorian soldiers had successfully defended against the Peruvians in 1995.

The next step of the peace process came in January 1999, when Mahuad and Fujimori met on the border to dedicate the first border post at Lagartococha. They met again in Washington, where they worked out the final details of the peace agreement and of a $3 billion cross-border international loan package. Fujimori pledged not to buy new weapons, while Mahuad announced he was cutting the draft by 60% and converting 8,000 soldiers—a fourth of the army—into policemen. Under the 10-year border development plan, the two

Former President Jamil Mahuad

countries were to make the border region accessible by new roads, to integrate their electrical grids and to embark on joint irrigation and resource-exploitation projects. Moreover, Peru was to allow Ecuador to use its oil pipeline. President Bill Clinton hosted the two presidents at the White House to toast them on their achievement, the peaceful resolution of the last major border conflict in Latin America.

Back at home, Mahuad had to face the ever-present economic crisis. No longer a member of OPEC, Ecuador could only watch helplessly as the price of oil on the world market plummeted in 1998, at one point diving to just over $11 a barrel. The price of Ecuador's other major export, bananas, also remained depressed. Ecuador then sustained $2.6 billion in damage from the floods of the 1997–98 *El Niño* and suffered financial fallout from Brazil's economic meltdown in 1998. Mahuad delivered grim economic news: a $1.5 billion budget deficit and a projected growth rate of 1.7 percent for 1999, with inflation estimated at 22%. Public discontent over the inevitable austerity measures erupted again into street demonstrations.

Several banks foundered. Mahuad declared a week-long bank holiday and imposed a 60-day state of emergency. The value of the *sucre* went into a free-fall, losing 60% of its value at one point. As part of a new austerity plan, Mahuad tripled the price of gasoline and raised the value-added tax from 10% to 15%. Transit workers went on strike. The Social Christian Party, the coalition partner of Mahuad's Popular Democracy party, denounced the austerity plan as "inhuman." Mahuad's public approval rating fell to 16%.

Mahuad caved in struck a deal with the left-of-center parties in Congress for a watered-down plan. The price of gasoline was rolled back, and in place of the VAT increase the Congress reinstated the income tax, with a 15% ceiling.

Yet, the political and economic situations deteriorated from bad to worse to impossible. Every time Mahuad sought to impose austerity measures to win IMF approval for desperately needed capital, street protests forced him to back down. He sought a $1.2 billion bailout of 18 defunct banks, but then the head of one bank, who had been arrested for fraud, revealed he had donated more than $3 million to Mahuad's campaign.

In 1999, Mahuad announced Ecuador could not make the $98 million interest payment on its $6 billion in Brady bonds, which the U.S. Treasury had extended to 18 countries to help them restructure their debts (Ecuador's total foreign debt by then was a ponderous $13.6 billion). A month later, Ecuador became the first nation to default on its Brady bonds. The *sucre* fell from 7,000 to 25,000 to the dollar; inflation had hit 61%; foreign creditors pounded on the door; and military officers were publicly criticizing the civilian government's inaction, prompting rumors of an imminent coup. Moreover, a poll showed that 91% disapproved of Mahuad's performance and that 53% wanted him to resign.

Dollarization and Downfall

On January 9, 2000, the desperate president unveiled a desperate plan: He would replace the *sucre* with the U.S. dollar—not merely peg the *sucre* to the dollar as the Argentines had done, but make the dollar the official currency, as it is in Panama. The dramatic proposal seemed to have a popular consensus. The Social Christians, *Roldosista* Party and Mahuad's own Popular Democracy party reached a rare agreement in support of dollarization. One poll showed that 59% of the public supported the idea.

Not so with the rural Indians who make up 40% of the population. Within days, the Ecuadorian Confederation of Indigenous Communities (*CONAIE*), reportedly the most powerful Indian-rights group in the Americas, not only declared its opposition to dollarization but demanded that Mahuad resign and mobilized thousands of peasants to march on Quito. Violence appeared imminent.

Matters came to a head on January 21, when *CONAIE* protesters stormed and occupied the Congress building. They were joined by about 150 field-grade military officers, led by Colonel Lucio Gutiérrez, who echoed the Indians' demand that the president resign. Faced with open rebel-

Ecuador

lion, Mahuad fled the presidential palace and took refuge at a military base, but he steadfastly refused to resign. His defense minister, General Carlos Mendoza, announced he was assuming power at the head of a three-man junta, which also included *CONAIE* leader Antonio Vargas.

With the backing of the military, the ouster of Mahuad became a *fait accompli.* It was Latin America's first military *coup d'etat* since the overthrow of Jean-Bertrand Aristide in Haiti in 1991. After 22 years of tenuous democracy, Ecuador's constitutional system finally had broken down, a victim of mob rule.

For 24 tense hours, the junta faced intense diplomatic pressure from the United States, Canada, the Organization of American States, the European Union, U.N. Secretary-General Kofi Annan and most Latin American presidents. Even Bucaram, who had long denounced Mahuad as a usurper, condemned his overthrow. In a stunning turnabout, Mendoza declared he would yield power to the constitutional vice president, Gustavo Noboa, apparently to maintain some semblance of constitutional niceties.

Though the transfer of power was undemocratic, the new president was at least a respectable figure. Noboa, 62, was a lawyer and former dean of Catholic University, who gained fame as one of the negotiators of the border settlement with Peru. The hapless Mahuad, who still refused to resign, lamely expressed his backing for Noboa. "A deposed president doesn't resign," he said wanly, "he's just deposed." Congress confirmed Noboa to fill out the remainder of Mahuad's term, to 2003.

Ironically, Noboa announced he would push forward with dollarization, which had precipitated Mahuad's downfall. Under pressure from the IMF and other international lending institutions, which had promised $2 billion in loans, Congress approved the plan. The IMF approved a $304 million loan package, with more contingent upon further concessions. Noboa announced that Ecuador would resume payments on its Brady bonds.

In another hypocritical attempt at constitutional window-dressing, the government moved quickly to "punish" the people who had brought about Mahuad's overthrow. The defense ministry arrested four colonels and 12 lieutenant colonels and began investigating the roles of hundreds more junior officers. The ministry narrowed the number to be court-martialed to 16 officers and one sergeant.

To bring this farce to an end, Noboa asked Congress to declare an amnesty to those who participated in the coup. The head of the Joint Chiefs of Staff and the commanders of the navy and the air force (but not the army) resigned their posts to protest the president's recommendation for amnesty. Nonetheless, Congress approved amnesty for all 117 military rebels. Public opinion polls, which seem to govern Ecuador, showed that 67% of the public supported the amnesty.

Not so with the dollarization plan. A majority, according to the polls, now opposed it. *CONAIE,* labor unions and students called a one-day strike to demand that the government revoke its agreement with the IMF, and the usual 10,000 demonstrators peacefully turned out in the streets of the capital.

Nonetheless, dollarization went into effect as planned in September 2000. The stability of the currency, coupled with the rising international price of petroleum and a $2 billion international loan package arranged by the IMF, led to a surprisingly rosy economic picture by year's end. Noboa enjoyed a relative—and rare—popularity.

But defections gave a center-left bloc a majority in Congress, which resisted Noboa's privatization plans for electricity, petroleum and telecommunications that the IMF—and foreign investors—expected. Moreover, the Constitutional Tribunal ruled 44 points of the privatization program unconstitutional. In February 2001, when Noboa acceded to IMF demands and doubled the price of cooking gas and raised the price of gasoline by 22% to offset the reduction of subsidies, *CONAIE* and other groups besieged the capital. Noboa declared a state of emergency, and in the ensuing violence four protesters were killed. Noboa caved in to demands to scale back the increases. The IMF reluctantly agreed.

Congress thumbed its nose again at the IMF by rejecting an increase in the VAT from 12% to 15%. It also rejected other revenue-raising measures, assuring a crushing budget deficit. The Constitutional Tribunal hamstrung the president's fiscal reform efforts by declaring unconstitutional a tax he had proposed to satisfy IMF demands; international financial markets reacted negatively.

To compound Noboa's domestic problems, in May 2000 members of a dissident faction of the Revolutionary Armed Forces of Colombia (*FARC*) encroached into Ecuadorian territory. Two of the rebels were killed in a firefight with the Ecuadorian army. The army beefed up its 1,500-man border forces with an additional 2,000 troops.

The Elections of 2002

The presidential and congressional campaign in October and November 2002 turned into the customary Ecuadorian donnybrook. Former President Febrés Cordero of the Social Christian Party, still the country's largest, decided against making a comeback bid because of ill health. The party nominated its congressional leader and former trade minister, Xavier Neira.

The field became crowded as former presidents Borja of the Democratic Left and Hurtado both entered the race, as did, once again, the banana millionaire Álvaro Noboa, no relation to President Noboa. León Roldós, brother of the late president, entered as a Socialist. Another former president's brother, Jacobo Bucaram, became the *Roldosista* candidate.

But the race suddenly became unconventional with the entry of two leaders of the 2000 coup: Indian activist Antonio Vargas, and cashiered army Colonel Lucio Gutiérrez, who had spent time in jail and who became the candidate of the newly organized January 21 Patriotic Society. The parallels between Gutiérrez and Venezuela's Hugo Chávez were unmistakable. The results of the first round stunned everyone and sent a chill through Ecuador's political establishment—and the U.S. State Department. About 5.1 million, or 63%, of Ecuador's registered voters turned out. The results:

Gutiérrez	943,123	02.3%
Noboa	794,614	17.4%
Roldós	703,593	15.5%
Borja	638,142	14.1%
Neira	553,106	12.2%
Bucaram	544,688	11.9%

Gutiérrez and Noboa sought to mend fences with the losers for the November runoff. Because both Noboa and Gutiérrez were political outsiders with populist messages, the political establishment was lukewarm to both of them. As the country's wealthiest man, Noboa appeared less frightening than Gutiérrez, who had the support of *CONAIE* and of Marxist-Leninist and other far-left elements.

The race came down to personalities. Noboa unconvincingly tried to persuade the country's impoverished masses that as a millionaire, he could serve their interests better than Gutiérrez by luring foreign investors to Ecuador. Like Chávez in Venezuela, Gutiérrez pledged to combat corruption as well as to increase funding for education and health.

Gutiérrez won a decisive mandate with more than 2.7 million votes, or 54.4%, to less than 2.3 million, or 45.6%, for Noboa.

Gutiérrez suddenly sounded conciliatory and toned down his leftist rhetoric; he even apologized for saying that all the former presidents deserved to be in jail. He had little choice; Ecuador still desperately needed IMF and World Bank assistance. Moreover, the Social Christians and Democratic Left formed a peculiar right-

188

left opposition bloc of 62 members of the 100-seat Congress. Gutiérrez's party and its allies had but 17 seats.

Another Abortive Presidency

Gutiérrez, 45, a civil engineer and an erstwhile pentathlete, was sworn in as Ecuador's sixth president in as many years on January 15, 2003. His vice president was Alfredo Palacio, a 64-year-old heart surgeon and a populist who had served as health minister under Durán. The new president's task was unenviable: a $300 million budget deficit, $2.6 billion in foreign debt payments, an intransigent congressional opposition, a wary IMF, a resentful military high command and a notoriously impatient and fickle electorate.

The new president bewildered his constituency by undertaking a chameleon-like ideological transformation. He made some obligatory gestures to his Indian supporters, such as appointing an Indian activist as foreign minister and reducing his own salary by 20%. But he appointed a mainstream, investor-friendly economist as finance minister.

Gutiérrez met with President Bush in Washington both before and after his inauguration and pledged Ecuador's cooperation against drug traffickers and terrorists. He also persuaded the IMF to make a $205 million loan available. Back home, he sought to placate the IMF by proposing tax increases; he increased the price of gasoline by a third and of electricity by 10%, seeking to create a $250 million budget surplus. A third of the $6.7 billion budget for 2003 was earmarked for debt reduction, only a fourth to promised social programs; it also increased military spending by 40.5%. Moreover, Gutiérrez pledged to retain the dollar, the root cause of his 2000 coup.

Vice President Palacio broke with him, but wisely did not resign. *CONAIE*'s political arm, Pachakutik, withdrew its congressional support. He turned to the conservative Social Christians. It was an unlikely match, but it held for a time. *CONAIE* and affiliated Indian groups pressured Gutiérrez to resign.

Gutiérrez also faced hostility from his generals, no doubt resentful over taking orders from a former colonel. Seventeen generals and admirals resigned, allowing Gutiérrez to appoint officers he could trust.

Five of his civilian appointees also resigned because of allegations of past unethical conduct.

As Gutiérrez's approval rating slid to 18%, he himself became embroiled in a scandal. A former governor arrested on cocaine trafficking charges reported that he gave $30 million to Gutiérrez's campaign. Gutiérrez denied involvement in drug trafficking. He also was accused of accepting illegal donations from Mexico's Labor Party.

As if he didn't have enough problems with the IMF, opposition politicians, disgruntled generals, betrayed supporters and corruption accusations, Gutiérrez found himself in a nasty public controversy with his estranged wife, Ximena Bohorquéz, a prominent physician and a member of Congress for Gutiérrez's January 21 Patriotic Society. Bohorquéz complained in a newspaper interview that her husband had not lived up to his campaign promise to appoint well-qualified and uncorrupted officials. The president accused her of engaging in "cheap politics." Bohorquéz lived in the family's home rather than the presidential palace. The couple announced a reconciliation, but then she began criticizing his economic policies. Their marriage provided Ecuadorians with a real-life *telenovela*.

In 2003, former President Noboa became the third former president to go into exile to avoid prosecution. Mahuad already had taken up residence in the United States. Bucaram was still in Panama. Noboa allegedly schemed to use government bonds to shore up state-owned banks, among other sins. He asked for and received asylum in the Dominican embassy. Gutiérrez issued a safe-conduct, and Noboa flew to the Dominican Republic.

In 2004, the Social Christian Party withdrew its support and announced it would seek impeachment proceedings against Gutiérrez for misusing public funds for political purposes in the municipal elections. The party collected the necessary 51-vote majority to begin impeachment hearings, although it was well short of the two thirds for removal. Gutiérrez forged an unusual new 52-member coalition in Congress with the *roldosistas* and the party of millionaire Alvaro Noboa. This ended the impeachment effort.

Gutiérrez should have left well enough alone. But he had Congress remove the 31 justices of the Supreme Court, most of them Social Christians, accusing them of being biased. He introduced a bill to broaden his powers, including dissolving Congress. The move was widely regarded as revenge for the impeachment effort.

That smacked too much of dictatorship for the Ecuadorians, who already had enough grievances against him. By early 2005, demonstrations demanding the president's resignation gripped the country. It was reminiscent of January 2000.

A new wrinkle developed when the head of the "temporary" Supreme Court, a *Roldosista,* suddenly declared all charges against former President Bucaram "null and void," paving the way for *"El Loco"*

Former President Lucio Gutiérrez

to return to the country. He also dropped pending charges against former President Noboa, and both exiled presidents returned to the country.

Then the mayor of Quito, a former army commander, urged the armed forces not to recognize Gutiérrez, in effect, calling for another coup. But the defense minister said the armed forces would continue to support the constitutional president.

Bucaram, a Gutiérrez ally, did his friend an unwitting disservice when in a radio interview he said cavalierly that Gutiérrez should dissolve Congress and declare a state of emergency. Rumors spread that Gutiérrez was planning to do just that, sparking a mini-panic in financial markets and causing the value of Ecuadorian bonds to drop. The interior minister frantically denied Gutiérrez planned to dissolve Congress.

But the damage was done. Gutiérrez's opponents filled the streets of Quito again, banging pots and pans and honking horns, demanding he resign. Gutiérrez declared a state of emergency, fired his hand-picked Supreme Court justices who were causing the crisis and vowed in an interview that he would not resign. After all, he said with some validity, the economy was booming compared with the crisis that led to Mahuad's ouster in 2000 (see Economy).

In an attempt to pacify the demonstrators, Gutiérrez lifted the state of emergency after less than 24 hours. He addressed the nation on television, insisted he had achieved his primary objective of removing the Supreme Court and that "tranquility is returning."

But it was not. The streets remained filled with thousands of unmollified, noisy but non-violent protesters—but no soldiers. Thousands of demonstrators also filled

Ecuador

the streets of Guayaquil. In Quito, 30,000 protesters shouted *"Fuera, Lucio!"* ("Lucio, out!"). Police fired tear gas to drive them back from the presidential palace.

On April 20, Congress voted 62–0 to remove Gutiérrez from office on the peculiar pretext that he had "abandoned his post." Gutiérrez flew from the roof of the palace by helicopter and sought asylum at the Brazilian embassy. He flew to Brazil four days later, becoming the latest of several Ecuadorian presidents forced into exile. He later obtained asylum in Colombia.

The Palacio Interregnum

Vice President Palacio, a populist who had become critical of Gutiérrez's move to the right, was sworn in. But this did not pacify some of the protesters, who trapped him in the building where he took the oath, demanding that he dissolve Congress and call new elections. Palacio said he would call a referendum on constitutional reforms before calling any election, and he received the all-important pledge of support from the armed forces.

The OAS expressed concern whether Gutiérrez's removal was constitutional, and sent a high-level delegation to investigate. After meetings with Palacio and the opposition, the OAS concluded that Palacio's government was legitimate.

Meanwhile, Bucaram, sensing the shifting political winds could be unhealthy for him, quickly fled to Peru and then back to Panama, which again granted him asylum. Noboa chose to remain in Ecuador, and was placed under house arrest on the charges that he had mishandled debt negotiations.

Palacio demonstrated his constitutional muscle by appointing new armed forces commanders.

As economy minister, Palacio named a leftist economist, Rafael Correa, who announced that the government was reversing Gutiérrez's policy and would spend more oil revenue on social programs and less on debt servicing. But Correa resigned after only four months when Palacio sought to appease the World Bank.

Palacio's shift to the left did not save him from the usual protests. Protesters shut down the vital oilfields in the Amazon region for a week, dynamiting pipelines and destroying pumps, demanding that more of the government's revenue windfall from the high price of petroleum on the world market be spent on social programs there. The disruption of the oil supply and the damage to the pipelines cost the government an estimated $400 million.

Gutiérrez gave up his asylum in Colombia and returned to Ecuador in 2005, vowing to take legal action to reclaim the presidency against what he called an il-

Former Interim President Alfredo Palacio

legal takeover. Palacio ordered Gutiérrez jailed as "a threat to national security." He remained in prison five months, when the Supreme Court ordered him released for lack of evidence. The Supreme Court also reduced the charges against former President Noboa and ordered him released from house arrest.

Palacio stunned foreign investors in 2006 by expropriating the lucrative holdings of Occidental Petroleum for alleged breach of contract. He may have been inspired by Bolivian President Evo Morales' nationalization of foreign oil companies 15 days earlier.

Palacio hosted a summit with Presidents Uribe of Colombia, Toledo of Peru and Morales of Bolivia, to reiterate the right of members of the all-but-defunct Andean Pact to negotiate bilateral free-trade agreements (FTAs) with the United States. Venezuela's Chávez, a fierce critic of such pacts, was not invited; he angrily withdrew from the Andean Pact after Colombia and Peru signed FTAs with the United States. The meeting represented an abrupt about face for Morales, who had agreed with Chávez. Uribe, a key U.S. ally, promised to urge Washington to renew free-trade talks with Ecuador and to extend the trade preferences granted Andean nations in 1991 in return for substituting coca with other crops, which were due to expire at the end of 2006. Without FTAs, Washington had indicated it would not extend the highly beneficial preferences, under which Ecuador sells avocados and artichokes to the United States. For Palacio and Morales to continue seeking FTAs after nationalizing foreign oil companies was seen as a bit erratic.

The Elections of 2006

The next presidential campaign was the usual circus, with 13 candidates. As usual, there were some old names, and as happened in 2002, a newcomer came out of nowhere to break from the back of the pack. Only this time, the new would-be *caudillo* sprang not from the barracks, but from academe.

Alvaro Noboa, the billionaire banana magnate, launched his third presidential attempt, this time as candidate of a movement with the grandiose name Institutional Renewal Party of National Action, or *PRIAN*. Gilmar Gutiérrez, brother of the deposed president, was the standard bearer of their January 21 Patriotic Society. Once again, former President Roldos' brother León was the *roldosista* candidate, while the Social Christians nominated Cynthia Viteri. Among the remaining nine candidates was former Economy Minister Rafael Correa, a left-wing economics professor who had hammered together a movement called Alliance for Change. It did not field a congressional slate, however, probably because Correa was planning to scrap the institution, which he called a "sewer of corruption."

Like Gutiérrez in 2003, Correa sounded a Chávez-like message that rejected free trade with the United States, promised to spend more oil wealth on social programs and hinted that Ecuador should default on its foreign debt. He said he disliked dollarization, but would grudgingly continue it. He echoed Chávez's anti-U.S. rhetoric, once calling President Bush "dimwitted," and he said he would not renew the lease on the U.S. counterdrug base at Manta when it expired in 2009. (Ironically, Correa earned his doctorate in economics at the University of Illinois.) Correa also pledged, like Chávez, to call a constituent assembly to revamp Ecuador through what he called a "citizens' revolution" that would rid the country of its "partyocracy." Also like Gutiérrez, Correa was young and charismatic.

The results on October 15 were:

Noboa	1,464,251	26.83%
Correa	1,246,333	22.84%
Gutiérrez	950,895	17.42%
Roldós	809,754	14.84%
Viteri	525,728	9.63%

The six-week runoff campaign was pure political theater, even by Ecuadorian standards. Correa charged that the computer breakdown on election night experienced by the Brazilian firm contracted to tabulate the results was nothing less than fraud and that he had finished ahead of Noboa. But a team from the OAS investigated the incident and declared the vote results were accurate.

Noboa, as before, used his wealth to give away presents to voters at his rallies. Like Correa, he ran on a populist platform, although unlike Correa he advocated a FTA with the United States. Both sounded messianic, with Correa declaring himself a "Christian leftist," while Noboa proclaimed himself to be "a messenger of God." Noboa was humiliated days before the runoff when the list of voters who had signed up for 1.2 million homes he had promised was discovered in the trash.

On November 26, voters spoke decisively:

Correa	3,517,635	56.67%
Noboa	2,689,418	43.33%

A disturbing factor in the election was that more than a million voters cast null or blank ballots, which are no longer included in the vote totals.

The "Citizens' Revolution" Begins

Correa, just 43, was sworn in on January 15, 2007. Although he toned down his fiery rhetoric in the runoff campaign, he soon demonstrated he intended to move full speed ahead with his "citizens' revolution," first by electing a constituent assembly that would scrap the 1998 constitution and compose a new one that would transform Ecuador's political system to create what he called "21st century socialism." It was the same course taken by Chávez in Venezuela and Morales in Bolivia.

Congress approved Correa's call for the assembly, but inserted a proviso that it could not dissolve the existing Congress. Correa turned to the Supreme Electoral Tribunal, packed with his appointees, which ruled that the constituent assembly would have absolute power, including to supersede the Congress. Congress responded by removing the president of the electoral tribunal, which responded in turn by "firing" 57 members of Congress who had approved the constituent assembly only if it did not have the authority to dissolve the existing Congress.

Although the dismissed legislators were replaced by members of their own party, the new members proved to be more compliant to Correa. Congress then approved a referendum for April 15 on the issue of calling elections for a constituent assembly, as had been done in Venezuela and in Bolivia.

A judge declared the legislators' dismissal unconstitutional and ordered they be reinstated. The president of the Congress agreed, angering the Correa backers. The case went before the Constitutional Court, which upheld the dismissal. Fifteen of them opted for exile when Correa threatened them with arrest on trumped-

up charges; he later relented. Congress voted to dismiss the judges, but without the backing of the executive, there was no way they could enforce it.

Ecuadorians went to the polls again for the *sí o no* referendum on whether to elect a 130-member constituent assembly. Correa threatened to resign if voters rejected the idea, but they approved it with a resounding 80%.

In September 2007, voters returned to the polls to elect the constituent assembly; Correa's newly renamed movement, *Acuerdo País*, won 80 of the 130 seats. Gutiérrez's faction won 18. High on Correa's agenda was the removal of the restriction of immediate re-election of the president, the dissolution of Congress and the stripping of power from the traditional elite. It appeared to be the next step toward a Venezuelan-style elected autocracy.

Meanwhile, for all his railing against corruption, Correa was acutely embarrassed when a clandestine video surfaced showing his finance minister, Ricardo Patiño, meeting with three bond investors shortly before Patiño hinted Ecuador would not meet a $135 million interest payment, which led to uncertainty in the bond market. Ecuador made the interest payment, the market stabilized, and the investors allegedly benefited to the tune of $200 million; the government reportedly made $50 million. The scandal forced Correa to cashier Patiño—to another job.

Border Incident

Correa suddenly found himself in the midst of a foreign policy crisis, which he milked for political value. On March 1, 2008, Colombian warplanes bombed a camp of the Revolutionary Armed Forces of Colombia *(FARC)* in heavy jungle a few kilometers inside Ecuador. Correa maintained later that Colombian President Álvaro Uribe had called him to say Colombian forces had entered Ecuador in hot pursuit of the rebels. Uribe later admitted that the attack was not in hot pursuit but a raid, and that Colombian ground forces had encroached on Ecuadorian territory after the airstrike to seize the camp. Twenty-two *FARC* guerrillas were killed in the operation.

Correa broke off diplomatic relations with Colombia and moved 3,200 troops to the border. His ally Chávez moved troops to the Venezuelan-Colombian border. A two-front war appeared imminent. Correa called on the OAS to condemn Colombia, but the OAS approved a watered-down resolution admonishing Colombia for violating Ecuador's sovereignty and territorial integrity and promised to investigate the incident. Uribe, meanwhile, announced that three laptop computers

confiscated at the *FARC* camp contained evidence of the complicity of both Correa and Chávez with the *FARC,* among other things, a $20,000 laundered donation to Correa's campaign from the *FARC*.

Correa, Uribe and Chávez met in the Dominican Republic, where Correa and Uribe engaged in a heated discussion. Uribe ultimately apologized for the incursion and promised not to repeat it, while Correa and Chávez pledged to cooperate with Colombia in its battle against the *FARC*.

New Constitution, New Election

Correa's steamroller was in high gear in 2008 and 2009. The constituent assembly supplanted the Congress and assumed the country's legislative function. It overwhelmingly approved the new 444-article constitution, Ecuador's 20th, which among other things permits two successive four-year presidential terms, increases the power of the executive over a 124-seat National Assembly, reduces the size of the Supreme Court from 31 to 21 justices and makes it subordinate to a new Constitutionality Court, bans foreign military bases and greatly increases state control over the economy. Voters ratified the constitution in yet another referendum on that September by 64%. It received only 45% in Guayaquil, however, which remains an anti-Correa hotbed.

Flushed with another victory, and buoyed temporarily by an economic windfall of record-high petroleum prices, Correa generated international headlines in 2008 by threatening to default on the foreign debt if an investigative commission found parts of the debt to be "illegitimate." In December, he followed through, refusing payments on $3.6 billion in bonds on the grounds that previous presidents had exceeded their authority in agreeing to the "immoral" terms. Appearing on national television, Correa declared, "We know full well who we are up against: real monsters who will not hesitate to try to crush the country and to try to make an example of Ecuador."

The impetuous move again made Ecuador a pariah in international lending circles, at a time when oil prices had dropped from $140 a barrel to $35, killing the goose that laid the golden eggs to finance Correa's ambitious social programs. He desperately turned to China for loans, and offered oil drilling rights in return for a $1.2 billion concession.

His actions only enhanced his own popularity going into the first presidential election under his new constitution. Both former President Gutiérrez and the thrice-defeated Noboa launched quixotic bids in the April 26, 2009, election, as did five can-

Ecuador

didates of the traditional parties. Former President Febres Cordero had died in December 2008. The traditional movements were so discredited that the outcome was a foregone conclusion. A total of 7.1 million voters, a turnout of 75.3%, went to the polls, but 1.2 million of them, fully 15.5% of the total, cast blank or null votes in protest. The remainder gave Correa a resounding first-round victory:

Correa	3,586,439	52.0%
Gutiérrez	1,947,830	28.4%
Noboa	786,718	11.4%

Correa's again-renamed *Alianza País* movement fell short of a majority in the National Assembly, winning 59 of the 124 seats. Gutiérrez's January 21 Patriotic Pole was second with 19 seats and the Social Christians won 11. Eight other parties or movements split the remainder. Correa warned that if the legislative branch blocked his proposals, he would dissolve it in accordance with his new constitution and call a new election.

Correa's second inaugural was on August 10, 2009. The "Chávezization" of Ecuador was well underway, with notable differences. Correa has not sought to nationalize key industries like electricity and telecommunications. He has not moved to confiscate large landholdings, although the new constitution contains language about land being used for "social" purposes. Despite his refusal to extend U.S. rights to use the base at Manta and bringing Ecuador into Chávez's *ALBA*, he has largely eschewed inflammatory anti-U.S. rhetoric and seems intent on preserving the preferential trade tariffs Ecuador enjoys.

Correa moved to resolve his differences with Colombia's Uribe and to normalize relations. Foreign Ministers Jaime Bermúdez of Colombia and Fander Falconi of Ecuador signed a pledge in 2009 not to attack across the border. But a low-ranking judge, acting on his own volition, muddied the diplomatic waters by issuing an arrest warrant for Colombian General Freddy Padilla, the armed forces commander, in connection with the 2008 border incident. An earlier arrest warrant had been issued against Juan Manuel Santos, then Colombia's defense minister, who was elected president in 2010. Colombia rejected both warrants, saying Ecuador has no jurisdiction over the actions of Colombian officials.

Santos dispatched his incoming foreign minister to Quito in 2010 with an olive branch, and personally invited Correa to attend his inauguration. Correa did, and expressed his desire for amicable relations. Santos would soon offer Correa crucial support.

Although he professes to champion Ecuador's indigenous population and speaks Quechua, Correa has had the same difficulties with Indian militants as his predecessors. In 2009, Indians blockaded a highway on the edge of the Amazon basin to protest Correa's water resources plan, which would divert water for the economically important mining in that area. Violence erupted that left a schoolteacher dead. Each side blamed the other.

At about the same time, Correa devised a controversial "carbon reduction" scheme by which developed countries would pay Ecuador *not* to develop oil deposits in the Amazon, thus reducing carbon emissions believed to contribute to global warming. With the fall of oil prices and a 5% drop in Ecuadorian oil production in 2009, Correa sought $3.6 billion from credit from China and other foreign sources to continue financing his social revolution, but his default had backfired on Ecuador—and him.

As was true with his predecessors, Correa's once phenomenal popularity began to slide, from a 72% approval rating at the time of his re-election to 42% by the end of 2009. Besides losing the support of the indigenous population, Correa alienated the middle class with his increasing emulation of Chávez's dictatorial policies. He ordered creation of Cuban-style "committees for the defense of the revolution," in effect a network to spy on opponents. In 2010, he tried to pass a Venezuelan-style media law that would greatly have restricted freedom of the press and expression, but his own party balked at the idea and came up with a watered-down version, much to the president's annoyance.

One reason Correa has called the media his "worst enemy" was because of an exposé by the venerable Guayaquil daily *Expreso* in 2009 that Correa's older brother, Fabricio, had received $167 million in construction contracts despite a law that prohibits relatives of officials from benefiting from government contracts. The president at first castigated the newspaper for spreading lies, but when the charges appeared to have validity, he disavowed his brother and called him "unbalanced by greed." Fabricio Correa countered that corruption was rife in the administration and turned over to the attorney general a "corruption file" that supposedly documented high-level wrongdoing.

The Police Revolt of 2010

Correa faced the most serious threat to his rule in September 2010 after he issued a new civil service law that adjusted pay and bonuses for state employees, including the military and national police. Two hundred angry and armed national policemen took to the streets to protest what

President Rafael Correa

they charged was a reduction of their bonuses. Correa personally confronted the rebellious policemen, reportedly opening his shirt and daring the policemen to kill him. One policeman threw a tear gas grenade at Correa, who donned a gas mask and retreated. Another policeman physically attacked Correa, trying to tear off his mask and striking him in the knee; it was public knowledge that Correa had had knee surgery the week before.

Correa was taken to the nearby police hospital. He was under veritable siege for several hours, but conducted a telephone interview with a television station, denouncing what he called a "coup attempt." He also appeared defiantly on a balcony, daring the police to come get him.

Army troops arrived at the hospital to rescue Correa, and a firefight ensued, leaving two soldiers, a policeman and a bystander dead. The soldiers hurried Correa to the presidential palace, where he railed against the ingratitude of the police, saying, "No one has done more for the police than I have." He also denied their bonuses had been reduced.

Correa called a 10-day state of emergency. Schools and airports were closed. Ten policemen and an army major were arrested and charged with treason. The national police chief resigned. There was little evidence to support Correa's charge that the police had planned a coup, because he was never asked to resign and no provisions had been made for a transition. However, the state-run radio station aired captured police radio transmissions that suggested the police debated whether or not to kill Correa.

Expressions of support for Correa poured in from his fellow presidents in the South American Union (*UNASUR*), including Santos, as well as from the

United Nations, the United States and the OAS. Correa's approval rating jumped 10 points.

Tightening His Grip

Armed with this boost in popularity, Correa announced in 2011 that he would conduct another referendum, in reality a questionnaire, asking voters to respond yes or no to 10 proposed constitutional amendments. Several dealt with changes in penal law, such as how long a person could be detained without trial. Another dealt with restructuring the judicial system. The most controversial asked whether owners of mass media should be prohibited from owning enterprises outside the communication industry. All the questions were phrased in esoteric legal language that was difficult for common citizens to understand. Critics alleged that the changes were designed solely to help Correa consolidate his power.

Nine million people went to the polls on May 7, 2011, 10% of whom cast blank or invalid ballots, so only one of the 10 items was approved by a bare majority, the one dealing with pre-trial detention. The others were approved by pluralities ranging from 44% to 48%.

Relations with the U.S. soured again unexpectedly in April 2011 when Wikileaks revealed a confidential cable from the U.S. Embassy in Quito alleging that a former police chief had been involved in acts of corruption and that Correa was aware of it. Correa expelled Ambassador Heather Hodges; the United States responded by expelling Ecuador's ambassador.

Correa next resumed his war on the media, which garnered him international

notoriety that he had not anticipated. The editorial page editor for the influential Quayaquil newspaper *El Universo*, Emilio Palacio, called Correa a "dictator" in his column and claimed he had ordered troops to open fire on the crowd outside the hospital during the 2010 police revolt. Correa sued Palacio and three of the newspaper's directors for $80 million! Palacio admitted he didn't have evidence, and *El Universo* offered to run a retraction and give Correa equal time, but he refused and personally went to court. When the defendants appeared, pro-Correa goons pelted them with eggs.

In July 2011, a judge sentenced Palacio and the directors, Carlos, César and Nicolás Pérez, to three years in prison, awarded $30 million in damages and fined the newspaper another $10 million. Correa gloated over his victory, saying it ended the media's "reign of terror." International journalism organizations like the Committee to Protect Journalists and the OAS' Inter-American Commission on Human Rights expressed dismay and warned it would result in self-censorship—which no doubt Correa intended. UNESCO issued a report in 2011 that called for repeal of the libel laws. *El Universo* appealed the judgment, arguing it would bankrupt the paper. An appeals court upheld the award in 2012. Correa also filed a $2 million libel suit against two investigative journalists who wrote an exposé book about Correa's brother, Fabricio.

In January 2012, an appeals court upheld the $40 million libel judgment against *El Universo*. Once again there was an outpouring of international indignation, from *The New York Times*, *The Washington Post*, the CPJ, the Inter-American Press

Association and other media entities and groups, which called it outright censorship. Whether or not Correa was shaken by the international criticism or was conducting a tactical withdrawal, he abruptly announced he was "forgiving" the $40 million libel award against *El Universo*.

But in January 2012, at his request, the National Assembly passed a new electoral law that severely restricts media coverage of election campaigns. One provision prohibits the media from "either directly or indirectly promoting any given candidate, proposal, options, electoral preferences or political thesis, through articles, specials or any other form of message." In other words, newspapers could not endorse a candidate, or criticize one, which are hallmarks of a free press in any democracy. Another provision bans campaign coverage for 48 hours before an election, while another prohibits private citizens or companies from buying political advertising for 90 days before an election. The law took effect in February. It violates the press freedom article of his own constitution.

Correa vowed that independent, privately owned media will become "the exception rather than the rule" in Ecuador as he establishes government-controlled media outlets. He has followed through with that threat, expropriating 19 radio stations and one television to create a state-owned media empire, as Chávez did in Venezuela. In 2012, the New York-based Freedom House lowered Ecuador's press-freedom rating from "partly free" to "not free."

The Assange Case

Correa eagerly thrust himself into the international limelight in mid-2012 after Julian Assange, the founder of Wikileaks, took refuge in the Ecuadorian Embassy in London on June 19 and asked for asylum. He was wanted in the U.S. for publishing classified documents and in Sweden for sexual assault, a charge Assange insists is trumped up to facilitate his extradition to the U.S.

A tense two-month diplomatic tug of war ensued between Ecuador and Britain. Correa claimed the British ambassador to Ecuador had threatened in a letter to storm the London embassy if Assange were not turned over; Foreign Secretary William Hague denied any such threat. Correa announced he was granting Assange asylum, but Britain refused to grant him safe-conduct out of the country. Two years later, Assange is still a "guest" of the Ecuadorian government in its tiny London embassy. Correa, ironically and hypocritically, declared he granted Assange asylum to defend freedom of speech!

Perhaps because of the Assange case, Edward Snowden, the former U.S. Na-

Giant tortoises of the Galápagos Islands

Ecuador

tional Security Agency employee who became an international fugitive for leaking highly sensitive classified information, indicated that he intended to fly from what was to be a temporary stopover in Moscow to Cuba and on to Ecuador, where he would request political asylum. There were also reports that Snowden would be a guest in the Ecuadorian Embassy in Moscow.

While President Obama was on a state visit to Africa, Vice President Joe Biden personally telephoned Correa to request that Snowden not be given asylum. Correa was non-committal publicly, but Snowden did not go to the Ecuadorian Embassy. Snowden eventually requested asylum in Russia, apparently because there was no way to fly from Moscow to Ecuador without crossing the airspace of a U.S. ally that could order his plane grounded. He remains in Russia.

Re-Election

Correa may have become a pariah in international human rights circles, but in September 2012, his approval rating among his countrymen was the highest of any leader in the Western Hemisphere. Mexico's Mitofsky poll put it at 80%.

Correa was blessed by rebounding oil prices, which despite declining production overall stimulated economic growth and allowed him to wisely channel much of the windfall into badly needed repairs to the horribly deteriorated highway infrastructure. He also provided generous welfare payments to the 28% of Ecuadorians still below the poverty line and built clinics and schools in small towns. This helped buoy his already phenomenal popularity heading toward the February 17, 2013 election, as did the stability he had brought Ecuador after years of turmoil, economic crises and a revolving-door presidency.

He was aided still further by the opposition itself, which was hopelessly fragmented. Seven candidates were on the ballot against him, none with much name recognition except for Lucio Gutiérrez. Emerging as the leading contender was a banker not affiliated with any of the traditional parties, Guillermo Lasso. Passions during the campaign erupted into violence on February 5 when two people were stabbed to death at a Correa rally.

The outcome was a foregone conclusion:

Correa	4,918,482	57.2%
Lasso	1,951,102	22.7%
Gutiérrez	578,875	6.7%

Correa's *Alianza PAIS* emerged with a supermajority of 100 of the 137 Assembly seats, with the rest fragmented among six

parties and independents. Correa was inaugurated for another four-year term on August 10.

Recent Developments

Despite his earlier vow not to initiate new drilling in the Amazon in order to reduce Ecuador's carbon footprint, Correa shocked the country, and angered environmentalists and indigenous groups, with the announcement in August 2013 that he would ask the Assembly to approve oil drilling in the Yasuní National Park, a 3,800-square-mile (9,820-square-kilometer) enclave of Amazon rainforest on the Peruvian border that is home to numerous unique species of animals and plants and to at least two indigenous tribes. Unfortunately, it is also "home" to an estimated 840 million barrels of oil, worth a potential $18 billion at current prices.

Correa justified his about-face by blaming the international community for not coughing up the $3.6 billion in credits he sought in 2009 in exchange for not drilling in the rainforest; only $116 million in pledges and $13 million in cash were forthcoming. "The world has failed us," he told his countrymen. Although his own 2008 constitution prohibits drilling in protected areas, he cited a convenient loophole that allows for exemptions if they are in the national interest. Of course, under his constitution, the national interest is whatever Correa says it is.

Environmentalists in Ecuador and abroad reacted predictably, as did indigenous organizations. A poll two months earlier showed 66% of Ecuadorians were opposed to drilling in protected areas. Suspiciously, another poll taken after his announcement, and after passage of yet another new communication law (see below), showed only 32% opposed to drilling. Correa pressed ahead, promising the indigenous tribes in the area that they would receive some of the proceeds for education and health care—something he had already been promising for years. The Assembly dutifully approved the exemption, 108-25. When this book went to press, it appeared that PetroEcuador would be contracting with two Chinese companies to exploit the Yasuní.

Public protests notwithstanding, Mexico's Mitofsky poll in October 2013 showed Correa was still the second-most popular leader in the hemisphere with an approval rating of 84%.

Correa renewed his war against the media with a controversial and dictatorial Organic Communication Law, which he said was needed to ensure "a good press." While the law purports to guarantee freedom of expression and prohibits prior censorship, it has overly broad provisions that

prohibit journalists from impugning people's reputations through what it terms "media lynching," and even dictates standards for headlines. The law holds media administrators liable for violations. It gives anyone supposedly injured by a media report equal time or space to respond. It also parcels out broadcast frequencies, one third for private stations, one third for public stations and one third for "community" stations. Most onerous, it established a *Superintendencia de Información y Comunicación,* known as *Supercom,* which has the power to assess fines for violations. Anyone can bring a grievance against the media, no matter how frivolous. With Correa's new supermajority, he steamrollered the law through the Assembly without debate in June 2013, by the same 108-25 majority it later passed the drilling bill.

Ecuadorian journalists call the new law *La Ley Morzada* (The Gag Law). The Inter American Press Association, Committee to Protect Journalists, Reporters Without Borders and even the United Nations denounced the law as the death knell for press freedom in Ecuador.

It didn't take long for the new law to have the desired effect, by stifling media reporting on public protests against the drilling law. In January 2014, police raided the home of Correa critic Fernando Villavicencio, who had vowed to go public with evidence of corruption in the government, and seized his computers. When the cartoonist for *El Universo* lampooned the raid, *Supercom* ruled that the cartoonist had impugned the honor of the police, fined the paper 2% of monthly sales and ordered the cartoonist to "correct" his cartoon! Thus, he dutifully drew a tongue-in-cheek cartoon that showed the police treating Villavicencio with exaggerated courtesy. The readers understood the biting satire.

As this book was going to press, *Supercom* notified *El Universo, El Comercio, La Hora* and *Hoy* that they were the subject of a complaint that they had given insufficient space to Correa's visit to Chile in May and had scheduled a hearing (see The Future).

Correa told the government newspaper *El Telégrafo* (which has never been the subject of a *Supercom* action) in March 2014 that he would not seek a second full term in 2017. But on May 24, he asked the Assembly to pass a constitutional amendment to permit immediate re-election, although remaining coy about whether he would seek another term.

CULTURE: Ecuador is the quintessential *mestizo* country, with pure European and Indian descendants being heavily outnumbered by their ethnic hybrid. Of the two cultures, it is the Indian that has had the greater influence on the country's cultural identity. Ecuador is a remnant of the Inca Empire, and Quéchua is still widely spoken. The 200-odd Quéchua-based dialects serve as a unifying thread among the rural people. The Indian roots are visible and audible in the country's art and traditional folk music and dances.

The capital city of Quito and the historic center of Santa Ana de los Ríos de Cuenca are UNESCO World Heritage Sites.

Like too many other Latin American countries, Ecuador has been whipsawed by dictatorship and political instability that had a negative impact on cultural growth. Juan León Mera (1832–94) is generally regarded as the first noteworthy Ecuadorian writer, best remembered for the 1879 novel *Cumandá*, set in the Ecuadorian jungle. Mera also wrote the lyrics to the national anthem.

Ecuadorian culture attracted little attention outside its borders until the 20th century. Its outstanding literary figure remains playwright and novelist Jorge Icaza (1906–78), whose 1934 novel *Huasipungo* exposed the injustices and hardships to which the Indians were subjected. It remains a Latin American classic, which inspired the so-called "Indigenist" movement in Latin American literature and which has been translated into at least 17 languages. Icaza revised it in 1953 and 1960. It has been likened to John Steinbeck's *Grapes of Wrath* for its treatment of social injustice.

Another prominent novelist, short-story writer and essayist was José de la Cuadra y Vargas (1903–41), who also wrote from the point of view of the common man—although he himself had a law degree and was a university president. His best-known works are probably the novel, *Los Sangurimas* (1934), and the story *La Tigra*; both were adapted into movies. *La Tigra* was adapted twice, once for an Argentine movie in 1954 and again in 1989 by the Ecuadorian director Camilio Luzuriaga. *Los Sangurimas* became an Ecuadorian TV movie in 1998. Cuadra was only 37 when he died.

Ecuador has produced several renowned artists, the best known of whom have been Oswaldo Guayasamín (1919–99), a revolutionary painter in the style of Mexico's Diego Rivera, and Eduardo Kingman Riofrío (1913–98), whose works stressed indigenous subjects. A museum containing Guayasamín's works was dedicated in Quito in 2002.

Ecuador's best-known folk music genres are *Sanjuanito*, the flute-based Andean sounds that have become so popular in international music festivals; and *pasillo*, which is more uniquely Ecuadorian.

Beatríz Parra Durango (b. 1940) is Ecuador's best-known classical soprano internationally. She studied in Moscow and once sang in operas all over the world, including 15 years with the Colombia Opera Theater, but is now retired and teaches voice.

Ecuador's most renowned Latin singer was Julio Jaramillo (1935–78), who performed Ecuadorian *pasillos, boleros* and other genres all over Latin America. His signature song was *Nuestro juramento* (our oath). He achieved a cult-like following, like Carlos Gardel in Argentina or Elvis Presley in the United States. Like them, he died young. A quarter of a million people paid homage at his funeral.

In contemporary popular music, Paulina Aguirre, a singer and songwriter who splices traditional Andean sounds with Latin pop-rock, became the first and only Ecuadorian to receive a Latin Grammy nomination in 2007 and to win one in 2009 for her album *Esperando tu Voz (Waiting for Your Voice.)* She received another nomination in the Christian Music category in 2012 for *Rompe el Silencio.*

The high illiteracy rate has hampered development of the printed media. There are a number of mid-sized dailies, centered in Quito and Guayaquil. The oldest is the elite *El Telégrafo*, founded in 1884 and located in Guayaquil. The government assumed control in 2007 after the conviction of its owner on various criminal charges. The nation's circulation leader with about 200,000 daily is *El Universo*, which dates to 1921 and also is published in the port city. The capital's leading paper is *El Comercio*. There also are a number of magazines. The press has been subjected to increased intimidation under President Rafael Correa with restrictive laws and libel suits. Freedom House changed its rating of the Ecuadorian media in 2012 from "partly free" to "not free." It became even less free in June 2013 with the passage of the Organic Communication Law (see History-Recent Developments).

Ecuadorian higher education is making up for lost time, with more than 60 institutions of higher learning, most of them established since the establishment of democracy in 1978. The Central University of Ecuador in Quito is the dean, founded in 1826. The University of Guayaquil and the National Polytechnic School in Quito date to the 1860s.

ECONOMY: Ecuador's economy was always dependent upon the export of agricultural products, especially bananas, and minerals, predominantly petroleum, to pay for needed imports.

Ecuador's economic future improved dramatically with the discovery of rich oil deposits, estimated at 5 billion barrels of high-grade petroleum, in the jungles east of the Andes. Oil income quadrupled government revenues with royalties reaching about $500 million by 1975, and Ecuador became a member of OPEC. Nationalistic oil policies later forced most private firms to leave the country—thereby reducing exploration for new deposits. As a result, production declined; domestic oil consumption came close to outstripping production.

In 1981, oil output rose 27% to a total of 77 million barrels. However, the country's unfriendly attitude toward foreign oil companies prior to 1984 made it difficult to obtain foreign investment for new exploration. This was remedied during the administration of Febrés Cordero, beginning in 1986.

But in 1985, Saudi Arabia increased its production because other OPEC nations were cheating on their oil quotas. This allowed the price for the product to "float," and the worldwide market went into a steep decline. The price descended to one third of its 1980 level in 1986 (less than $10 a barrel), rebounding to $17 by 1995. Ecuador withdrew from OPEC in 1992.

As of 2007 and 2008, oil production was not sufficient to capitalize on the skyrocketing price of petroleum, and ironically, the high prices actually hurt Ecuador because it lacks refining capacity and must import its fuel. In 2009, production dropped by 5%.

Ecuador, together with Peru and Bolivia, is a major producer of raw cocaine paste, which is processed into powder in Colombia. Numerous "factories" are located within Ecuador (owned by Colombian cartels) where the paste is processed because of control measures within Colombia. Distribution is still via Colombia.

The devastating effects of *El Niño* in 1997, the drastic drop in world oil prices in 1998 and the simultaneous meltdown of the Asian and Brazilian financial markets all contributed to an economic crisis that President Mahuad declared to be the worst in 70 years. But OPEC's decision in 1999 to boost the price of oil augured well for Ecuador.

Meanwhile, a panel of WTO experts sided with the United States, Ecuador, Guatemala, Honduras and Panama in their complaint that the European Union's banana import policy was discriminatory. The five plaintiff countries had charged that the EU showed favoritism to bananas imported from former Caribbean colonies and against Latin American producers and U.S. distributors, in violation of international trading regulations. Ecuador exported 16% of its bananas to the EU, more than 650,000 tons.

Mahuad and the Congress compromised on an austerity plan, which deepened the recession in 1999, leading a desperate Mahuad to recommend replacing the *sucre* with the dollar. Real GDP declined by a devastating 7.5%, unemployment jumped

Ecuador

from 11.5% in 1998 to 16.9%, per capita income fell from $1,619 to $1,164, and inflation was again the highest in Latin America: 50.4%.

The dollarization scheme led to massive protests, which in turn led to Mahuad's ouster in 2000, but his vice president and successor, Gustavo Noboa, also embraced dollarization and put it into effect (see History). The dollar replaced the *sucre* as Ecuador's legal tender that September. The resulting currency stabilization, coupled with the fortuitous rise in international oil prices, led to a growth rate for 2000 of 2.0%. Inflation, however, nearly doubled to a crippling 96.6%, again the highest in Latin America, while unemployment dropped slightly to 14.7%.

The figures for 2001 were dramatically better, although deceptive. The good news was that real GDP increased by 5.6%, the fastest growth in Latin America. In reality, this only recovered the ground lost in 1999. Inflation dropped plummeted to "only" 22.4%.

Two factors were responsible for the strong showing in 2001. Noboa signed a $1.3 billion contract for an oil pipeline that was expected to create 50,000 jobs and, when completed, to boost petroleum exports by 50%. A more important factor was a peculiar demographic phenomenon. During the 1999–2000 economic meltdown, an estimated 1 million Ecuadorians abandoned the country, legally and illegally, seeking work abroad in the United States, Spain, Italy and other countries. In 2001, the government actually created a program to expedite the exit visas of its citizens to work abroad. Year-end figures for 2001 showed that this both cut domestic unemployment almost by half to 8.8% (although 40% were still considered underemployed) and generated $1.4 billion in remittances from abroad, accounting for 8% of GDP, second only to oil exports.

By 2003, remittances totaled $1.5 billion, or 5.6% of GDP. At the end of 2008, when the global recession began, they nosedived to $700 million. In 2011, there were an estimated 2 million Ecuadorians working abroad—15% of the population. Remittances that year rose to a record $2.67 billion—4% of GDP and third-highest in South America after Colombia and Peru. In 2012 they totaled $2.68 billion.

The economy grew at a rate of 6.9% in 2004, among the highest in Latin America, while inflation was only 1.95%. The spike in international oil prices in 2004 was largely responsible for the growth. Income from oil exports totaled $2.13 billion, accounting for 43% of national revenue, definitely an over-reliance. Despite the even higher price for crude oil in 2005 and 2006, growth was only 3.9% in 2005 and 2006 and 2.5% in 2007. Growth in 2008 was a healthy 6.5%, almost exclusively because of the skyrocketing world price of oil, which reached more than $140 a barrel. Then the global recession began, oil dropped to $35, and growth declined by –1.0% in 2009. It grew 3.6% in 2010 and 7.8% in 2011, the result of higher world oil prices and $6.3 billion in Chinese loans. The dramatic drop in the market price for a barrel of oil in 2012 took a toll on Ecuador; growth dropped to 4.0% in both 2012 and 2013.

A development that could have a chilling effect on future foreign investment is a $19 billion judgment against Chevron-Texaco by an Ecuadorian court, stemming from a lawsuit brought against Chevron in 1993 on behalf of 30,000 mostly indigenous residents of the Amazon region. The plaintiffs allege that the then-Texaco dumped toxic waste into Amazon tributaries. The company maintains it cleaned up the spills. An appeals court upheld the award in January 2012 and the Supreme Court refused to consider Chevron's appeal. Chevron took the matter to the United Nations, and an arbitration panel in The Hague concluded that Texaco had settled with damages with the Mahuad administration in 1998 and that Ecuador should not seek further damages. Ecuador refused to abide by the ruling.

Correa made a surprise decision in 2013 to grant an exemption to allow oil drilling in the environmentally sensitive Yasuní National Park, which sits atop a field with an estimated 840 million barrels worth $18 billion. The decision set off a firestorm of criticism by environmenalists and indigenous peoples in the area (see History-recent Developments).

Tourism has increased, largely because of the popularity of the Galápagos Islands for foreign visitors. The Sangay National Park also attracts ecotourists. Both are UNESCO World Heritage Sites. Tourism in 2007 was the third-largest generator of foreign exchange, but Ecuador is still in the bottom third of Latin American countries for tourist arrivals, which have increased from 1 million in 2008 to 1.37 million in 2013, a 7.4% increase over 2012. Tourism generated $4.7 billion in revenue in 2013, or 5.3% of GDP.

Per capita GDP has risen steadily since the 1999 crisis, jumping from $1,450 per capita in 2002 to $2,424 in 2005 to $3,850 in 2010. Yet, 28.6% of the population was still below the poverty line at the end of 2011. In dropped to 27.3% in 2012.

Something Ecuador must address if it is ever to get a permanent handle on its economy is the entrenched corruption that costs the economy an estimated $2 billion a year—more than 10% of GDP. Tax evasion alone costs the public treasury an estimated $600–$800 million a year. In 2010, Transparency International, the corruption watchdog group, rated Ecuador the sixth most corrupt country of the 20 Latin American republics. In 2011 it had "improved" to eighth most corrupt, and in 2013 it was No. 10—right in the middle. All the presidents since 1997 have been accused of enriching themselves in one way or another. President Rafael Correa, inaugurated in 2007, promised reform through his new constitution approved by voters in 2008. But his own finance minister was

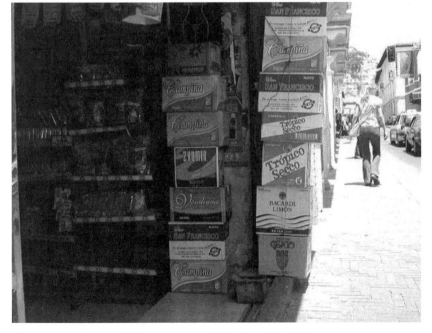

Shopping in a neighborhood in Quito

Ecuador

fired in a bond manipulation scheme (see History).

Another problem that needs to be addressed is illegal logging in Ecuador's rain forests, a precious natural resource. The government estimates that 370,000 acres of virgin forest fall to the saws each year, but environmental groups indicate it could be twice that. An estimated 70% of the lumber sold is cut illegally. In 1999, the government, unable to regulate the logging effectively itself, wisely contracted with a Swiss firm to monitor the logging and to tax legal logging. Under pressure from the logging industry, the Constitutional Tribunal overturned the outsourcing agreement in 2003, for unclear legal reasons.

Environmentalists also are concerned with illegal shark fishing and harvesting of sea cucumbers in the Galápagos Islands, considered a World Heritage Site by the United Nations. In 2007, UNESCO placed the Galapagos Islands on its list of endangered World Heritage Sites.

THE FUTURE: Three elected Ecuadorian presidents were ousted by the military, the Congress or the mobs in the streets in just eight years. Rafael Correa is the latest would-be savior to climb to the top of the greased pole that the Ecuadorian presidency had become, and he has managed to stay there for a phenomenal eight years and been re-elected twice by landslides. He promised to revamp Ecuador's notoriously corrupt system, still the sixth most corrupt in Latin America in 2012, which is an improvement from fourth worst in 2009, but down from eighth worst in 2011, according to Transparency International.

Correa's phenomenal popularity emboldened him to make war against the mass media, which, in the absence of

a meaningful political opposition, was the only institution capable of criticizing or questioning him. Unfortunately, he doesn't like to be criticized or questioned. The country's new electoral law effectively emasculates the media by forbidding it to endorse candidates—a hallowed tradition of democracy. The 2013 Organic Communication Law imposes even more restrictions on the press, rendering the watchdog toothless.

None of Correa's restrictions on freedom of expression seems to upset the Ecuadorian people, thanks to an improvement in the oil-based economy and his channeling of windfall oil revenues into public works projects and social programs. His approval rating of 84% in 2013 was the second-highest of any leader in the Western Hemisphere.

The Ecuadorian people's faith in democracy has taken a roller-coaster ride, before and after Correa. The annual *Latinobarómetro* poll by *The Economist* showed that in 1996, 52% of Ecuadorians believed that democracy was preferable to any other form of government. By 2009, when Correa's approval rating dropped to 42%, belief in democracy had dropped to 43%, a 13-point one-year drop and the second-lowest of the 18 nations in the survey. But by 2013, it was back up to 62%, the sixth-highest. Moreover, the 2013 *Latinobarómetro* survey showed that 60% of Ecuadorians are satisfied with the way democracy works in their country, the second-highest percentage in the survey; the Latin American average was only 40%.

Meanwhile, the percentage of Ecuadorians who believe authoritarianism is sometimes preferable to democracy jumped from 16% in 2008 to 25% in 2009,

the third-highest in the survey. By 2013, it was only 14%.

Yet, authoritarianism is where Correa has led his country, popular or not. Ecuadorians may have a greater faith in democracy, but it is increasingly democracy as defined by Rafael Correa. His efforts to create a state-run broadcast empire, his attacks on opposition media and his constitutional amendment allowing him to pack the courts with his appointees mirror those of his *ALBA* brothers, Bolivia's Evo Morales, Nicaragua's Daniel Ortega and his mentor, the late Hugo Chávez of Venezuela.

Correa claimed in an interview that he would not want to seek a second full term in 2017, claiming, "It's very damaging when one person becomes indispensable." Nonetheless, in May he asked the Assembly to pass a constitutional amendment to permit immediate re-election—just in case he decides he is indispensable.

To give Correa his due, there are some reasons for his popularity, besides his big, charismatic smile. He has increased needed social spending, brought down the poverty rate a bit and made Ecuador "only" the 10th most corrupt nation in Latin America; in 2006, when he was elected, Ecuador was the fifth most corrupt.

Unfortunately, like Chávez, Morales in Bolivia and Ortega, he has interpreted his winning majorities as license to run roughshod over political dissenters and freedom of the press, which left-leaning leaders like Vázquez and Mujica of Uruguay, Bachelet of Chile and Funes of El Salvador have not done.

He may change his mind and decide that he is "indispensable" after all in 2017. But even if he steps aside, will Ecuadorians get their freedoms back?

The Republic of El Salvador

Street scene in San Salvador

Area: 8,260 square miles.

Population: 6,125,512 (2014 estimate, excluding an estimated 3 million expatriates).

Capital City: San Salvador (Pop. 1.75 million, estimated).

Climate: Tropical in the coastal plain, becoming temperate at higher altitudes.

Neighboring Countries: Honduras (North and East); Guatemala (West).

Official Language: Spanish.

Ethnic Background: *Mestizo* (mixed Spanish and Indian).

Principal Religion: Roman Catholic Christianity.

Chief Commercial Products: Coffee, Cotton, Sugar.

Currency: U.S. Dollar (formerly the *Colón*).

Gross Domestic Product: U.S. $24.67 billion in 2013 ($4,027 per capita, official exchange rate).

Former Colonial Status: Spanish Crown Colony (1524–1821).

Independence Date: September 15, 1821

Chief of State: Salvador Sánchez Cerén (b. June 18, 1944), president (since June 1, 2014).

National Flag: Blue, white and blue horizontal stripes with the national coat of arms on the white stripe.

El Salvador is the smallest and most densely populated of the Central American republics. Most of the country is a volcanic upland with two parallel rows of volcanoes running east to west. Fourteen of the cones exceed 3,000 feet and three reach more than 7,000 feet. Lowlands lie north and south of the volcanic ranges. El Salvador's principal river, the Lempa, drains the northern lowlands by cutting through the volcanic region to reach the Pacific.

El Salvador's soils are rich and easily accessible from the Pacific coast; thus it is one of the few Latin American countries in which the whole of the national territory is settled. Various estimates are given for the percentages of European, Indian and African ancestry in the national population, but the most obvious facts are that there are no tribal Indians and few blacks, and that the white minority claiming pure European origins is indistinguishable from the admittedly *mestizo*, a mixture of

Spanish and Indian. Cotton and sugar are raised on the coastal plains and the Lempa River valley, while the slopes of the volcanoes produce coffee. The climate is healthful and the rainfall abundant, with the rainy season running from May through October.

HISTORY: El Salvador was conquered by Pedro de Alvarado with a force from Mexico in 1524. Defeating the Indians and capturing their capital, Cuscutlán, he joined the region to the Captaincy-General of Guatemala. The small number of Spanish settlers intermarried with the Indians and established large agricultural and cattle-raising estates in the fertile valleys of the volcanic uplands, a pattern of land holding which exists today, and the root of much of El Salvador's present-day social problems. The remnants of the Indian population still farm village-owned lands in the mountains.

El Salvador declared its independence from Spain on September 15, 1821, with the other countries of Central America. Joining in a short-lived federation until its breakup in 1838, El Salvador was a center for the liberal republican opposition to the conservatives of Guatemala. It sought admission to the United States at one time and participated in several attempts to unite with Honduras and Nicaragua. As was true in most of the Central American republics, the political history of El Salvador during the 19th century after independence was one of turbulence, revolution, dictators, military governments and civil strife. Added to the internal difficulties of the nation were frequent periods of conflict with neighboring states.

The first quarter of the 20th century was relatively peaceful, but this was followed by period of virtual anarchy until the seizure of power by an absolute ruler, Hernández Martínez, from 1931 to 1944. The low point of his regime came in 1932, when a peasant uprising in protest against the landed elite cost 20,000 lives, almost all of them peasants, an event remembered today as *"La Matanza"* (the slaughter).

Various factions have been labeled conservative (favoring central government and close church-state relations) and liberal (anti-clerical federalists); however, those represented only blocs within the elite landowning class and were not truly different political entities. A degree of political stability was existed from 1948–60, but popular opposition to the elite's domination of politics and continuing economic inequality centered around a small number of wealthy and a comparatively huge number of poor.

This led to minor change in October 1960, when a provisional military-civilian *junta* took power, promising to reform the nation's political structure and hold elections. A new constitution was adopted in 1962 and in presidential elections held the same year there was but one candidate, Adalberto Rivera of the *Partido de Conciliación Nacional (PCN)*, a movement controlled by the oligarchy and the military. Although he and his party were supposed to be "middle-of-the-road," there was no such thing in El Salvador. There were right-wing, elitist elements and communist-leftist rebels, with little in between. Providing capable and honest leadership, Rivera encouraged the development of light industry and supported the nation's participation in the Central American Common Market.

Starting about 1960, a culture of violence gripped the country. Right-wing vigilante groups, such as the White Warrior's Union, often joined with government forces—including rightist members of the army, the National Guard and the Treasury Police—to torture and execute peasant leaders and other advocates of social reform. Leftist groups—including Marxist-led guerrilla units such as the People's Revolutionary Army, the Popular Forces of Liberation, and the Armed Forces of National Resis-

tance—responded in kind with attacks against military forces and their conservative supporters. Generally, leftist groups tended to pinpoint specific targets, while right-wing terrorists employed random violence. As a result, a large percentage of the political deaths in El Salvador have been linked to conservative forces.

Another *PCN* "moderate" candidate, Colonel Fidel Sánchez Hernández, won the 1967 election. His policies included an unheard-of land ownership reform proposal that infuriated conservatives, businessmen and wealthy landowners. The brief but bitter "Soccer War" was fought with Honduras in 1969 (see Honduras).

Great controversy surrounded the presidential elections of 1972. Christian Democrat José Napoleón Duarte, a nominal moderate, apparently outpolled *PCN* candidate Colonel Arturo Armando Molina. However, a subsequent "official" count gave the ruling *PCN* party a 22,000-vote victory; Molina's "election" was confirmed by Congress, where the *PCN* enjoyed a two-thirds majority. The military used a similar tactic for the presidential elections of 1977 when the ruling *PCN* candidate, General Carlos Humberto Romero, was declared the winner by a two-to-one margin over his opponent, another right-wing officer. When riots broke out against the

rigged elections, the government imposed martial law. Before order was restored, an estimated 100 protesters were killed.

A staunch conservative, Romero was involuntarily faced immediately with urgent problems of land reform, human rights and the Catholic Church, which had become reformist. He equated change from the old order with communism. Most of the fertile farmland in the valleys and lowlands (about 60% of the total) continued to be owned by a handful of families who were closely allied to the ruling armed forces. In contrast, more than 65% of the population lived in abject poverty. Backed by the military, the conservative aristocracy had traditionally blocked disorganized peasant demands for land and reform. Wealthy landowners (including military officers who owned large estates) feared a repetition of the unsuccessful peasant uprisings against the landed elite of 1932.

The pace of fighting between rightists and leftists rose dramatically after Romero became president. Hoping to wipe out all opposition, he launched a bitter campaign against leftists and their sympathizers.

Coup and Civil War

As the nation moved toward complete chaos, a group of liberal army officers led by Colonel Adolfo Arnoldo Majano ousted Romero in a bloodless coup in November 1979. Power then shifted to a progressive five-man *junta* that included Majano and two members of the centrist Christian Democratic Party. The new rulers promised sweeping economic and social reforms that provided nationalization of key parts of foreign trade industries, including coffee marketing; nationalization of many banks, which traditionally provided loans only to the upper class; and land reform.

On paper, the land reform proposal was comparable in scope to those of Mexico,

El Salvador

Bolivia and Peru. The first phase, affecting 400 estates containing more than 1,235 acres each, would have redistributed about 600,000 acres of land (about 25% of the nation's arable land) to peasants. A second phase, planned for 1981, was to involve all farms larger than 370 acres.

A major catalyst for reform was the Carter administration in Washington, which supplied El Salvador with economic and military assistance. Washington feared that unless fundamental reforms were enacted, El Salvador would slide into a disastrous class war.

Conservative opposition to the *junta's* reforms proved overwhelming, however, and right-wing violence rose dramatically. The assassination of Archbishop Oscar Romero in 1980 shocked the nation and the world, and in 1980 conservatives murdered the head of the country's Human Rights Commission (its report had embarrassed the government). The top six leaders of a "centrist" political front that included the Christian Democratic Party were killed in late 1980, and the following month four U.S. women Catholic missionaries, including three nuns, were murdered. Two U.S. agricultural agents associated with the nation's land reform program were murdered as well.

Appalled by this violence, Carter halted all aid to El Salvador in late 1980. The Salvadoran military responded by taking aim at the *junta*, but the result was unexpected. Majano was replaced by a new four-member *junta* headed by José Napoleón Duarte of the Christian Democratic Party. A graduate of Notre Dame, the 55-year-old civil engineer pledged to move forward with social reform while taking steps to control right-wing terrorism. Duarte quietly

José Napoleón Duarte

retired some right-wing military leaders while others were reassigned to isolated posts.

Convinced the time was ripe for revolution, the guerrillas launched a full-scale "final assault" against government forces in January 1981. Although supplied with Nicaraguan and Cuban arms, the rebels found no popular support in the countryside, and the offensive foundered.

In Washington, the new Reagan administration issued a report claiming to have "concrete" evidence that the Salvadoran guerrilla front was a part of a "worldwide communist conspiracy" masterminded by the Soviet Union. Insisting that it was necessary to "draw the line" against communism, Reagan ordered a resumption of large-scale military and economic assistance to El Salvador. He also fired the Carter-appointed ambassador.

Despite such aid, Duarte's regime found itself increasingly dependent on the military for survival. To placate powerful right-wing critics, Duarte shelved many of his promised reforms. Meanwhile, the security forces continued to commit atrocities, none more heinous than the massacre of as many as 1,000 peasants in the village of El Mozote, Morazán, in December 1981.

Hoping to increase domestic support for the government and to improve El Salvador's international image, Washington pressured Duarte to hold elections for a Constituent Assembly in 1982 as the first step toward a return to constitutional government. While almost all leftists boycotted the elections—and the guerrillas sought to disrupt them—voter turnout was a heavy 1.3 million.

Duarte's center-left Christian Democratic Party (*PDC*) won 40% of the vote and 24 seats in the 60-seat Constituent Assembly, the largest total of any single party. But right-wing tickets led by the National Republican Alliance (*ARENA*) and the National Conciliation Party (*PCN*) gained nearly 60% of the vote and 34 seats.

Much to the chagrin of Duarte and his supporters in Washington, the rightists promptly formed a coalition and voted to exclude the *PDC* from participation in the new government. Named president of the Assembly was arch-conservative Roberto D'Aubuisson, an ex-army intelligence officer allegedly linked to the right-wing death squads. In 1980, he had been arrested for plotting a coup against the government.

Under strong pressure from the influential defense minister, General José Guillermo García, the Assembly elected a moderate U.S.-educated economist and banker as provisional president: Álvaro Alfredo Magaña, 56. The Assembly also named three vice presidents, one each for *ARENA*, *PCN*, and the *PDC*.

As the first democratically elected president in 50 years, Magaña was expected to have only a limited impact on the country's destiny. The rightist-controlled Assembly sought to strip the president of any real power while Assembly President D'Aubuisson tried to repeal many of the reforms planned by the Duarte regime. In one of its first acts, the Assembly dismantled Phases II and III of the land reform program longed for by the poor. (By mid-1982, provisional land titles had been given to more than 7,000 peasants under the program.) D'Aubuisson boasted he would wipe out the guerrilla movement "in no more than six months."

Salvadoran guerrillas, Usulátan Province

200

El Salvador

A young rural mother does the family wash

Although weakened by the failures of its 1981 "final assault," the guerrillas were not dislodged. The insurgents controlled most of Chalatenango and Morazán provinces in the mountainous north near the Honduran border. The five major Marxist groups quarreled among themselves, but joined under a single umbrella organization, the Farabundo Martí National Liberation Front (FMLN). Most of the groups, which traced their common roots to the communist-inspired peasant uprising in 1932, became active in the late 1960s and early 1970s. France and Mexico recognized the FMLN in 1981 as a "representative political force"—a move that only alienated the United States.

As full-scale civil war unfolded, the government began to improve its military capabilities. The United States was drawn increasingly into the war. The Reagan administration effectively wrote a blank check to those in charge, a military establishment whose loyalty was consistently identified with the elite. U.S. advisers took their place alongside the Salvadoran military, training and developing rapid-response battalions that were quite effective,

but which soon acquired a reputation as "death squads." The most notorious was the Atlacatl Battalion. The U.S. Congress, repelled by government-sponsored atrocities, rigidly limited the number of advisers to 55.

The guerrillas began receiving Soviet military and financial resources, channeled through Cuba, which buttressed Reagan's argument. Alongside the government forces were private forces that frequently perpetrated atrocities. But they were not one-sided. Both sides resorted to the worst sort of warfare, using any tactic or method necessary to instill total fear in innocent bystanders. Public torture, mutilation and murder of innocents, all became acceptable tools.

The U.S. Senate Foreign Relations Committee voted to cut $100 million from the Reagan administration's $226 million aid package in 1982. The House of Representatives passed a resolution requiring the president to certify that the Salvadoran government was making "good faith efforts" to prosecute five National Guard personnel accused of the 1980 murders of the three American nuns and a lay worker.

The war increasingly spilled over into other parts of Central America. Thousands of Salvadoran peasants fled to Honduras to escape the terror from the guerrillas and the right-wing death squads. An estimated 2 million Salvadorans lived outside the country; 1 million of them, mostly illegal immigrants, were in the United States.

Guatemala, Honduras, Costa Rica and El Salvador formed a common front to exchange intelligence and coordinate strategy against Nicaraguan and Salvadoran guerrillas. Both Honduras and Guatemala maintained large troop concentrations along their common borders with El Salvador. Honduran troops controlled a contested zone along the border of the two countries, partly to prevent the communist rebellion from spreading into its territory.

The FMLN sought to disrupt elections in 1984, but Salvadorans went to the polls under the eyes of scores of international observers. Duarte defeated D'Aubuisson for president, and immediately traveled to Washington to ask for more aid for both social programs and military assistance. In 1985 legislative and municipal elections, the PDC, in an upset, captured a majority of seats in the National Assembly and municipal councils.

The Catholic Church announced it would try to mediate in the civil war. This eased the cautious attitude of the U.S. Congress, which in 1984 appropriated additional emergency and military aid. But in 1985, the communists kidnapped Duarte's daughter at San Salvador University. The president had to agree to release 22 rebels and to grant safe passage for 96 wounded guerrillas to Cuba to win her release. He sent his family to the United States to avoid further kidnappings. The military and rightists were furious at his apparent weakness, but talk of a coup faded. He was, after all, necessary for continued U.S. military aid.

The beefed-up military achieved greater successes in 1986–87. Ultimately the conflict cost $6 billion in U.S. aid. Periodic negotiations failed, as both sides negotiated with ultimatums. In 1988 the FMLN rejected a proposal that it participate in municipal and legislative elections. When it finally tried this in 1991, in spite of successfully blocking observation at 30 polling places it controlled, only one of its candidates was sent to the National Assembly.

In 1989, the FMLN agreed to take part in and respect the outcome of presidential elections if they were postponed for six months. It demanded other conditions that made the deal impossible. Six candidates vied for president in 1989. The FMLN nominally supported one. The PDC had unwisely divided into two factions. ARENA nominated Alfredo Cristiani, far more moderate and less frightening than

El Salvador

D'Aubuisson. The guerrillas again resorted to terrorism to disrupt the electoral process, such as severing the ink-stained fingers of voters, and the right-wing death squads retaliated, committing their own atrocities. As usual, the innocent suffered.

Cristiani won with 54% of the vote.

By late 1989, it was apparent that Soviet-Cuban aid was going to dry up. Deciding that negotiations were the best course, the FMLN tried two super-offensives as last-ditch efforts in 1989 and 1990 to win as much territory as possible and thereby be in a better negotiating position. The guerrillas held parts of San Salvador for several days, but could not consolidate their gains. Nine members of a death squad murdered seven pro-guerrilla Jesuit priests in cold blood on the campus of the University of Central America, together with their servant and her daughter in the melee. Two of the soldiers later were sentenced to 30 years imprisonment for following orders. Eventually, higher-ranking officers were brought to trial.

Peace at Last

After the last-gasp rebel offensive of 1989, both sides were forced to acknowledge a stalemate. Neither could achieve full victory, and each side was willing to make peace; all that was needed was an appropriate broker. In September 1991, the U.S. ambassador and his military group commander seized that initiative by traveling boldly into guerrilla territory in a four-wheel-drive vehicle to confront an astonished FMLN leadership. Essentially, the two U.S. officials asked what it would take for the FMLN to make peace. Two of the rebels' key expectations for a post-war El Salvador were seemingly reasonable:

Former President Armando Calderón Sol

rural electrification and an end to death-squad atrocities. The ambassador brought these and other bargaining points back to the capital. On December 31, the two sides signed a truce that ended 12 years of slaughter that had claimed an estimated 75,000 lives, a grim toll in a country of only 6 million people.

The formal signing of the peace accords followed on January 16, 1992. Under the terms of the agreement, guaranteed by the United Nations, the FMLN laid down its arms and agreed to participate in the democratic process. The army ceased its sponsorship of death-squad activities. Despite an occasional low-level violation, the desire for peace superseded the deep-seated class hatreds that had led to the bloodbath.

Less realistic was the establishment of a "truth commission" to investigate the atrocities committed during the war. Among the recommendations in its 211-page report was that the entire Supreme Court be sacked. President Cristiani ignored these and other recommendations, but the country's mood was one of forgive and forget. Despite a few setbacks, the tenuous armistice took hold.

By the first postwar elections, both Duarte and D'Aubuisson had died of cancer. Armando Calderón Sol was the ARENA presidential candidate in 1994; Rubén Zamora was the choice of a leftist coalition that included the FMLN. People were incredulous at seeing once-feared guerrillas soliciting votes. In the first round, Calderón scored not quite 50% in balloting that was free of irregularities; Zamora received 25%. Calderón sailed to an easy runoff victory.

ARENA and an allied party took 43 seats in the 84-seat Assembly, while the FMLN won 21 and the PDC fell to 18. The PDC soon fragmented again.

Nagging problems remained. Former guerrillas had been promised jobs and stipends to enable them to live decently, but no one had planned where the funds would come from. Some practiced thievery, kidnapping and demolition of homes to obtain or extort money from small villages and the countryside. This illustrated an age-old problem: what is done with the revolutionaries when the revolution is over?

The lower echelon army troops also went frequently unpaid, but were promised tracts in the rich, upper highlands, to be taken from the land barons. Anticipating this, many squatted on the large *estancias*, but were driven from them. They became embittered and restive.

The political and economic elites received a scare in the municipal and congressional elections of 1997. ARENA lost its absolute majority in the Assembly, winning just 28 of the 84 seats, while the FMLN

shocked the country—and the world—by winning 27. ARENA governed in coalition with small conservative parties. Moreover, the FMLN won the mayoralties of most of the major cities, including San Salvador.

President Calderón became increasingly unpopular because of a stagnant economy, allegations of corruption and an alarming increase in violent crime that he seemed impotent to control. It seemed possible that the former guerrillas would win through the ballot box what they had failed for 12 years to win on the battlefield. But two things stymied the pro-FMLN trend.

First, ARENA cleaned up its act by nominating as its presidential candidate Francisco "Paco" Flores, an unthreatening, 39-year-old, U.S.-educated former philosophy professor with no links to the dark days of D'Aubuisson's death squads. In fact, he had taught at Central American University and became friends with the Jesuit priests slain by the army during the 1989 guerrilla offensive. He became an adviser to President Cristiani, then was elected to the National Assembly, becoming the chamber's president after the 1997 elections.

Second, the FMLN was rife with intra-party bickering between Marxist hardliners and moderates. In a party caucus, San Salvador Mayor Hector Silva, a moderate, deadlocked with another moderate, Victoria Áviles. Both acquiesced in favor of yet another moderate, Facundo Guardado, a former commander-in-chief of the rebel army, best remembered for his seizure of the Sheraton Hotel during the 1989 offensive. But the squabble within the FMLN, which at times resembled a barroom brawl, was shown to the country on television, creating grave doubts about the party's ability to govern.

The Flores Presidency

Flores avoided a runoff by receiving just under 52% of the vote, to 29% for Guardado.

The FMLN rebounded in 2000, winning 31 seats in the National Assembly, while ARENA's seats remained unchanged at 29. ARENA still enjoyed a small majority through coalitions.

Two major but unrelated events occurred in 2001. On January 1, El Salvador joined Panama and Ecuador by abandoning its currency and embracing the dollar. On January 13, the country was hit by a devastating earthquake that killed 1,200 people and caused an estimated $1 billion in damage—about half the national budget. A second quake struck exactly a month later, which added to the damage but mercifully claimed far fewer lives.

In March 2002, U.S. President George W. Bush included El Salvador on his itinerary for a three-nation visit to Latin America. He held a summit with the other presidents of Central America, at which Bush preached his gospel of free trade.

Despite an improving economy, the *FMLN* again won 31 Assembly seats to 27 for *ARENA* in 2003, recovering the six seats it had lost from defections. *ARENA* enjoyed a working majority through its alliance with the *PCN*, which won 16 seats. The *FMLN* also retained the mayoralty of San Salvador.

In 2003, Flores dispatched a contingent of 380 troops to participate in the allied coalition in Iraq, under Spanish command. El Salvador kept its troops in Iraq even after Spain withdrew its forces.

The waning days of the Flores administration were clouded by graft scandals.

The Saca Presidency

ARENA and the *FMLN* presented voters with an even sharper choice in 2004 than they had in 1999. *ARENA* again presented a youthful, post-civil war candidate by nominating Elías Antonio "Tony" Saca, 39, a former sportscaster who had become a media executive. The *FMLN*, which apparently had not learned anything about not frightening voters, chose Schafik Handal, 73, a well-known leader of the Communist faction of the guerrilla movement. About the only thing the two men had in common was that they were born of Palestinian immigrant parents.

ARENA used the usual scare tactics against the Communist Handal, hinting that the United States could begin restricting remittances by Salvadorans living in the United States, as they do with Cuban Americans, if Handal won. Handal did little to downplay his past, pledging to establish diplomatic relations with Cuba and the People's Republic of China, to pull Salvadoran troops out of Iraq, to heavily tax businesses and the wealthy, to bring back the *Colón* to circulate alongside the dollar and to oppose a Central American free-trade agreement with the United States.

On March 21, 67.3% of the Salvadoran electorate turned out to vote; the outcome was little different from that of 1999:

Saca	1,314,436	57.7%
Handal	812,519	35.7%
Others	150,518	6.6%

Handal ungraciously blamed his defeat on *ARENA*'s "lies and blackmail." He died in 2006.

Saca continued Flores' commitment to the Allied Coalition in Iraq even after Honduras, Nicaragua and the Dominican Republic brought their troops home. Saca sent new contingents of 380 troops to Iraq every six months. He ended El Salvador's

participation on December 31, 2008, the date the U.N. mandate expired.

As another indication of El Salvador's pro-U.S. policy, the National Assembly voted 49–35 in 2004 to ratify the proposed Central American Free Trade Agreement. It was the first country to do so. It went into effect on March 1, 2006, despite public protests.

A major multinational problem that Saca faced was the growing threat in El Salvador, the United States, Mexico, Guatemala and Honduras of *maras*, or street gangs. These groups, formed by Central American, mostly Salvadoran, emigrants in Los Angeles, constitute a serious form of organized crime. Perhaps the most infamous is *Mara Salvatrucha-13*, or *MS-13*, believed to have 100,000 members in 31 states and five countries, including Canada. Another is called *Mara-18*. So serious is the threat that the FBI opened a special anti-gang office in San Salvador in 2005.

El Salvador had the unfortunate distinction in 2006 of having the highest murder rate in the entire world, 55.3 per 100,000 inhabitants. In 2007 and 2008, it was second-highest after Honduras, with 49 and 52 murders per 100,000, respectively. It has remained in second place ever since.

In the 2006 legislative and municipal elections, *ARENA* and the *FMLN* were virtually tied in the popular vote with about 39% each, but *ARENA* regained a slight lead in the Assembly, 34 seats to 32. *ARENA* also fared better than the *FMLN* in the municipal races. The *FMLN* barely held on to the mayoralty of San Salvador.

A violent incident reminiscent of the dark days of civil war shocked the country in 2007. Three *ARENA* members of the Central American Parliament, which sits in Guatemala City, were abducted when their convoy was attacked between the Salvadoran-Guatemalan border and Guatemala City. They were shot and then set on fire, apparently while still alive. Their charred

Former President Francisco Flores

bodies were found on a farm. Among them were Eduardo d'Aubuisson, son of the late *ARENA* founder, and Ramón González, a co-founder. Four Guatemalan police officers were jailed on suspicion of complicity in the murders. Three days later, hitmen entered the Guatemalan jail and killed all four suspects. The motive for the *ARENA* members' assassination was unclear, but drug traffickers were believed involved.

Mauricio Funes Makes History

By 2009, *ARENA* had won four consecutive elections and had held the presidency for 20 years, unusual in any democracy. Voters were in the mood for a change, and this time the *FMLN* wised up and nominated a moderate, a television journalist named Mauricio Funes, 49. Funes, who had hosted a popular interview show in El Salvador and also worked as a freelancer for *CNN en Español*, had not fought as a guerrilla and was not an ideological hardliner, although his brother was a guerrilla who was killed in action. *ARENA* nominated Rodrigo Ávila.

The triennial legislative and municipal elections in January 2009 failed to serve as a clear bellwether for the March 15 presidential election. The *FMLN* gained three seats to again become the largest party in the Assembly with 35 seats to 32 for *ARENA*. The *FMLN* also won most of the municipalities, but *ARENA* won the mayoralty of the capital for the first time in 12 years.

Although the mild-mannered Funes was hardly the bogeyman previous *FMLN* candidates had been, *ARENA* attacked his running mate, Salvador Sánchez Cerén, a hardline former guerrilla commander, and even his wife, Vanda Pignato, a Brazilian who had been an activist in the Workers Party there. Ávila warned that Funes would become another Hugo Chávez, while Funes insisted he would not abandon the dollar and would keep El Salvador in CAFTA. About his most radical proposal was a tax increase on the rich to fund social programs.

On March 15, voters decided to finally give the former guerrillas a shot at national power:

Funes	1,349,142	51.3%
Ávila	1,280,995	48.7%

Funes was sworn in on June 1, 2009, the latest of a growing string of leftist Latin American presidents. Oddly, Chávez and Bolivia's Evo Morales did not attend the inauguration, but U.S. Secretary of State Hillary Clinton did. After the ceremony, Funes visited the tomb of the assassinated Archbishop Romero, and one of his first official acts was to

El Salvador

Former President Elias Antonio Saca

restore diplomatic relations with Cuba, the last Latin American nation to do so. He also discussed severing El Salvador's long-standing relations with Taiwan and establishing relations with the People's Republic of China, but said later he was only "exploring" that option. He never did, but said El Salvador would establish trade with the People's Republic.

Funes joined the majority of Latin American presidents in refusing to recognize the elected government of President Porfirio Lobo Sosa of neighboring Honduras as a protest against the forced removal of President Manuel Zalaya in June 2009 (see Honduras). He later relented, and even backed Honduras' readmission to the OAS.

He named his wife minister of "social inclusion," while Vice President Sánchez doubled as education minister.

The world was reminded of El Salvador's rampant gang violence when Christian Poveda, a French film director who had just released a documentary about the *Mara-18* titled *La Vida Loca*, was shot to death north of San Salvador in September 2009. A member of the national police and 11 *Mara-18* members were arrested. The *Mara-18* member who allegedly ordered the murder was already in prison. In March 2011, the 11 gang members were convicted. Two received 30-year sentences, one was sentenced to 20 years and the remaining eight received four-year sentences.

Funes has hewn a pragmatic, centrist course that has alienated some of the hard-line leftists within the *FMLN*, but it gave him a 79% approval rating at the end of 2010 and left the opposition *ARENA* fragmented over policy. He enacted badly

needed social programs that *ARENA* failed to do in 20 years, such as providing free public education, with free uniforms and shoes. The government reported that school attendance was up by 22,000. He also expanded health care.

El Salvador was the third country President Barack Obama visited during his five-day Latin American visit in March 2011. He made the dramatically symbolic gesture of visiting the tomb of Archbishop Oscar Romero two days before the anniversary of Romero's assassination by a right-wing death squad on March 24, 1980. President Bush did not visit the tomb on his 2002 visit.

El Salvador and Honduras had seesawed in recent years for the dubious distinction of having the world's highest murder rate. In 2009, El Salvador was the "winner," with 71 homicides per 100,000 people, compared with 67 in Honduras. In 2010 and 2011, Honduras regained the lead, with 77 murders to 69.9 in El Salvador in 2010; in 2011, Honduras had 86, to 71 for El Salvador.

Then, in a development potentially as significant as the 1992 peace accords, the imprisoned leaders of the two most sanguinary gangs, *Mara Salvatrucha* and *Barrio 18,* met in their maximum-security prison in March 2012 to negotiate a truce. The talks were brokered by the Catholic Church and Raúl Mijango, a former National Assembly member. The two leaders shook hands and pledged peace.

The government initially disavowed any role in the truce talks, but later admitted it had agreed to transfer the leaders to minimum-security prisons and to provide more amenities. The government also pledged aid to help gang members integrate into society as productive citizens. The truce was met by widespread skepticism of the gangs' good faith, but in the first half of 2012, murders were down 32% and kidnappings were down 50%, but extortion was down only 10%. Gang leaders even met with OAS Secretary-General José Miguel Insulza, and ceremoniously laid assault weapons at his feet as a gesture of sincerity.

El Salvador dropped to the world's fourth deadliest country in 2012, with 41.2 homicides per 100,000. By March 2013, the first anniversary of the truce, the murder rate had officially dropped 50%. However, some renegade gang members refused to honor the truce, and residents complain that the gangs continue shaking them down for protection money. There have also been disappearances, which have not been counted among the homicides because the bodies are never found. Both *FMLN* and *ARENA* mayors have complained that the promised government aid has not been forthcoming.

Former President Mauricio Funes

Besides being plagued by its own home-grown *maras,* there is evidence that the notorious Mexican drug trafficking organization, *Los Zetas,* is operating in El Salvador. In 2011, three current or former members of the Salvadoran armed forces were arrested for allegedly attempting to sell military weaponry, including 1,800 grenades, to *Los Zetas.*

A restless ghost from the civil war came back to haunt El Salvador in 2011 when a Spanish judge issued an indictment against 20 former members of the military in connection with the 1989 massacre of six Jesuit priests, their housekeeper and her daughter. Nine of them turned themselves in to Salvadoran military authorities, three of them generals, including former Defense Minister Rafael Humberto Larios. The Defense Ministry, to the surprise of many, turned them over to civilian authorities. In February 2012, the Supreme Court agreed to begin extradition proceedings for 13 of the officers. The alleged mastermind of the massacre, Inocente Montanto, now 72, is serving a sentence for immigration fraud in the United States. Three other suspects are living in the United States and face deportation.

Meanwhile, in January 2012, as part of the celebration of the 20th anniversary of the peace accords, Funes issued a formal, and emotional, apology on behalf of the government for the El Mozote Massacre in December 1981, in which as many as 1,000 peasants were believed slain by security forces. The following September, his attorney general opened an investigation into El Mozote after the Inter-American Court of Human Rights in Costa Rica ruled that

El Salvador

the 1992 amnesty does not apply to acts recognized as war crimes under international law.

Despite Funes being the third-most popular leader in the Western Hemisphere, with an approval rating of 65%, the *FMLN* lost four seats in the triennial National Assembly elections in March 2012. It now has 31, while *ARENA* has 33, a gain of one. A new group composed largely of defectors from the *FMLN*, the Grand Alliance for National Unity (*GANA*), has the balance of power in the 84-seat Assembly with 11 seats, while the National Coalition has seven and two tiny parties have one each. *ARENA* also did well in the mayoral races. In San Salvador, *ARENA*'s Norman Quijano received 63%, defeating Jorge Schafik Handal, son of the late *FMLN* presidential candidate in 2004.

The Elections of 2014

In the Mitofsky poll in September 2012, Funes had risen to second most popular president in the hemisphere, with an approval rating of 72%. A year later he was still in fifth place, with 64%, phenomenal for a Latin American president after more than four years in power. The question was, could the *FMLN* capitalize on his popularity to retain the presidency in the February 2, 2014, presidential election?

The two major parties both nominated sexagenarians: Vice President Sánchez Cerén, 69, of the *FMLN*, and San Salvador Mayor Norman Quijano, 67, of *ARENA*. But the race became complicated by the entry of former President Saca, "only" 58, who ran with the backing of a curious alliance of *GANA* and the old Christian Democratic Party. Saca's quest for a second term was challenged in the Supreme Court, but the constitution prohibits only *immediate* re-election. No other former president had sought a non-consecutive term—but then Cristiani and Flores were both tainted by scandals. The Supreme Court deftly handled the question, ruling that Saca could run, but that only party banners, not candidates' faces, could appear on the ballot. Saca's face was much better known than either Sánchez's or Quijano's, both as a former president and as a former TV journalist. Two lesser candidates also appeared on the ballot

Quijano moved *ARENA* sharply to the right, campaigning on a hard-line platform to crack down on the gangs, as he had done as mayor. He reminded voters that Sánchez had served as a guerrilla commander and portrayed him as a Marxist bogeyman who would take El Salvador down a Venezuela-like path. Sánchez vowed to continue Funes' moderate policies and called for giving the gang truce an opportunity to work, citing the dramatic drop in homicides. Saca seemed to stake out the middle ground, promising a business-friendly environment that would create jobs, yet embracing Funes' social programs. The five candidates appeared in a lackluster televised debate on January 12.

A new twist in this election was that expatriates were allowed to vote absentee for the first time, a feature that Mexico, Venezuela and the Dominican Republic had adopted because of their huge émigré populations in the United States and elsewhere. An estimated one third of Salvadorans live abroad, 2 million of them in the United States. Sánchez made a campaign visit to California, while Quijano campaigned in the large Salvadoran community in the Washington, D.C., area.

The polls all showed Sánchez with a commanding lead, but with Saca in the mix, not by enough to avoid a runoff. They were right. A respectable 55% of the 4.96 million voters cast ballots on February 2. The results:

Sánchez Cerén	1,315,768	48.93%
Quijano	1,047,592	38.96%
Saca	307,603	11.31%

Sánchez's lead looked insurmountable, but not if Saca's voters turned to *ARENA*, Saca's old party. Quijano suddenly softened his hard-line rhetoric to appeal to moderates and now promised to give the gang truce a chance. Turnout jumped to an unprecedented 60.6% in the March 9 runoff, with the total exceeding 3 million for the first time. The photo-finish result was the closest in the country's history:

Sánchez Cerén	1,495,815	50.11%
Quijano	1,489,451	49.89%

Fourteen ballot boxes were scrutinized for reported discrepancies, while the bombastic Quijano said *ARENA* was on a "war footing" to prevent fraud and demanded that the vote be nullified. But the electoral tribunal rejected his demand and on March 16 declared Sánchez the winner. He was inaugurated on June 1. Óscar Ortíz, another former guerrilla, was sworn in as vice president. Presidents Evo Morales of Bolivia and Danilo Medina attended, as did Spain's Prince Felipe and Taiwan Premier Jiang Yi-huah; the United States sent only the head of the Small Business Administration, apparently because she has a Hispanic surname. (See The Future)

El Salvador found itself in the forefront of a potential humanitarian disaster along the U.S.-Mexican border in June 2014 as tens of thousands of children as young as four years old unaccompanied by adults, most of them from Honduras, Guatemala and El Salvador, suddenly began crossing the U.S. border illegally. They were being housed at various impromptu detention centers, raising international concerns for their welfare. Sánchez met in Guatemala with U.S. Vice President Joe Biden, Guatemalan President Otto Pérez Molina and a representative of the Honduran government on June 20 to discuss the crisis (see Guatemala).

CULTURE: Ancient ruins of Mayan civilization have yielded treasures from the countryside which are being intensely studied, and there are explorations in

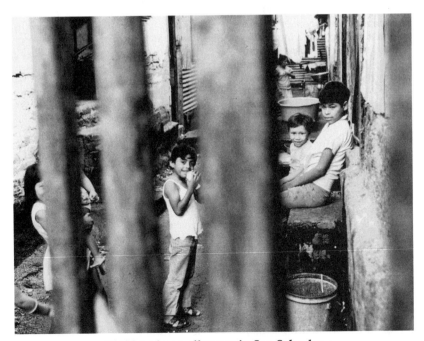
Children in an alleyway in San Salvador

El Salvador

President Salvador Sánchez Cerén
Photo by Presidency of El Salvador

progress for traces of even earlier inhabitants. One invaluable site near San Salvador was bulldozed for a housing development and the U.S. embassy. The ruins of Tazumal, San Andrés and Joya de Cerén are popular tourist attractions; Joya de Cerén is a UNESCO World Heritage Site.

Two centuries of poverty, illiteracy, dictatorships and, until 20 years ago, civil war stymied El Salvador's cultural development. Even today, many talented artists, writers, musicians and performers live abroad.

El Salvador's music, like that of Guatemala, is characterized by the xylophone-like *marimba*. Probably El Salvador's best-known musical figure was the composer and folk musician Francisco "Pancho" Lara (1900–89). His folk song *El carbonero*, about a campesino charcoal vendor, remains part of the country's national identity and is sometimes referred to as "the second national anthem."

In literature, El Salvador's best-known poet was Claudia Lars (1899–1974), pseudonym for Margarita del Carmen Brannon Vega, daughter of an Irishman, whose works have been collected into 12 volumes published between 1934 and 1972.

A rising star in contemporary Latin American—and North American—literature is the prolific Salvadoran novelist and short story writer Horacio Castellanos Moya (b. 1957), four of whose novels have been translated into English: *Baile con serpientes (Dance With Snakes*, 1996, 2009), *La diabla en el espejo (She-Devil in the Mirror*, 2000, 2009), *Insensatéz (Senselessness*, 2004, 2008) and *Tirana memoria (Tyrant Memory*, 2008, 2011). His other novels are *La diáspora* (1988), *El asco* (1997), *Donde no estén ustedes* (2003), *El arma en el hombre (2002), Desmoranamiento* (2006) and *La servienta y el luchador* (2011). *La diabla en el espejo* was a finalist for Venezuela's Romulo Gallegos Prize in 2001, while *Senselessness* received

the Northern California Book Award in 2009.

Born in Honduras but raised in El Salvador, Castellanos abandoned his university studies in El Salvador in 1979 because of the turbulence of the civil war and lived in self-imposed exile in Canada, where he resumed his studies; in Costa Rica; and 12 years in Mexico City, working as a journalist, until after the peace accords were signed in 1992. He lived in Spain from 1999–2001, then in Mexico, then in Frankfurt from 2004–06. He taught several years at the University of Pittsburgh and is currently a professor of Spanish at the University of Iowa.

El Salvador's most internationally renowned artist is Fernando Llort (b. 1949), designated "El Salvador's National Artist" by the Foundation for Self-Sufficiency in Central America. He studied art in France, Belgium and at Louisiana State University before returning to El Salvador during the civil war. He settled in the town of La Palma, in Chalatenango, which he has made famous for its identification as an artists' colony and whose economy he ignited as a result. His abstract style focuses on the lives of *campesinos* and native flora and fauna. His style has been compared to those of Pablo Picasso and Joan Miró. He still teaches art in La Palma, but his works have been exhibited in Latin America, the United States, Canada, Germany and Japan.

El Salvador is one of six Latin American countries that has yet to win a Latin Grammy Award.

Two competing daily newspapers have dominated the Salvadoran press for decades: *El Gráfico* and *El Diario de Hoy*. Because of El Salvador's huge expatriate population, they and nine other newspapers have online editions. Since the end of the civil war the press has generally been free, but dominated by economic interests that are pro-*ARENA*. An exception is the left-leaning *El Mundo*. Freedom House rates the Salvadoran press as "partly free."

El Salvador has 23 institutions of higher learning. The University of El Salvador was founded in 1841.

ECONOMY: Agriculture is the dominant factor, with the major cash crops being coffee, sugar and cotton. Despite its small size, El Salvador ranks among the top five coffee producers in the world. Farming remains largely under the control of a small group of wealthy landowners; the large peasant population lives in virtual serfdom. Serious overcrowding and limited economic opportunities in rural regions have caused many peasants to migrate to the already congested cities.

After World War II, light industry gained steadily, making El Salvador the most industrialized nation in Central America. The civil war was costly in spite of U.S.

assistance and seriously undermined economic growth.

The state banking industry was privatized after the war. A major portion of the budget formerly devoted to the military is now being used for health and welfare.

Although El Salvador is plagued by widespread poverty and its economy is far from booming, it is certainly nowhere near the basket cases of neighboring Honduras, which has slightly over half the per capita income of El Salvador, or Nicaragua, where it is one third as much. Peace brought greater foreign investment in the form of *maquiladora* assembly plants for textile products, which in turn have created jobs. Tourism has risen modestly since the killing stopped.

Real GDP growth has been sluggish for years, only 2.8% per year or less from 1997 to 2005. Part of the blame was the damage wrought by Hurricane Mitch in 1998 and the twin earthquakes of 2001. Growth was a more encouraging 4.2% in 2006 and 4.7% in 2007, but it dropped back to 2.5% in 2008. With the global recession and the consequent drop in remittances, it shrank by –3.5% in 2009. It has grown by less than 2% a year from 2010 to 2013.

Unemployment has remained about 6–7% for a decade; it was 6.3% in 2013. The poverty rate fell from 66% in 1991, the year before the civil war ended, to 30.7% in 2006. By 2009 it was back up to 37.9% and 36.5% in 2011.

Inflation was stabilized as a result of replacing the *Colón* with the dollar on January 1, 2001.

The dollarization made sound economic sense; tens of thousands of Salvadorans live and work in the United States, and the billions of dollars in remittances they send home to their families annually have become an important pillar of the economy since the exodus of refugees during the civil war. In 2006, the Central Bank placed the value of remittances at $3.3 billion; nearly a fourth of Salvadoran families received them. They fell during the 2008–09 recession, but rebounded to $3.65 billion in both 2010 and 2011. They were $3.67 billion in 2012 and a record $4.2 billion in 2013, the fourth-highest of any Latin American country and fully 16.5% of GDP.

In March 2006, El Salvador became the first country formally to be incorporated into the U.S.-Dominican Republic-Central American Free Trade Agreement (DR-CAFTA). It is expected to boost Salvadoran exports, although the *FMLN* argues that it threatens domestic manufacturers and street vendors and others with low-cost U.S. imports.

THE FUTURE: The former guerrillas of the *FMLN* finally achieved national power at the ballot box in 2009 with the election of President Mauricio Funes, and have now retained the presidency with the election of Salvador Sánchez Cerén, the first actual guerrilla combatant to hold the presidency. The new vice president, Óscar Ortíz, also is a former guerrilla.

Funes, who did not serve in combat, showed himself to be a centrist pragmatist, like the mild-mannered Álvaro Colom in neighboring Guatemala, rather than a fire-breathing Marxist, like bombastic Daniel Ortega in neighboring Nicaragua. Funes managed to assuage his core constituency of leftists in the *FMLN* with improvements in education and health care, but he eschewed radical economic changes. Dollarization has provided monetary stability, CAFTA has opened up U.S. markets to Salvadoran products and about 3 million Salvadoran expatriates in the United States remit more than $4 billion a year back home. Ideology is one thing, economic realities are another.

Salvadorans' faith in the democratic process has run hot and cold, according to the annual *Latinobarómetro* poll in *The Economist*. In 1996, the first year of the survey, 56% of Salvadorans said they agreed that democracy is preferable to any other form of government. It reached a nadir of 25% in 2001. In 2009, the year Funes was inaugurated, it jumped to 68%. The 18-point one-year increase from 2008 was the greatest of the 18 nations in the survey. But the next year it fell back to 59%, the greatest one-year *decline* of any country in the survey, and to 54% in 2011, below the regional average of 58%. By 2013, it had dropped to 49%. Only 39% said they were satisfied with the way democracy works in their country in 2013, just below the Latin American average.

Like his two predecessors, Sánchez is faced with two persistent problems: a sagging economy that has seen GDP growth below 2% each of the last four years, and still-rampant gang-related crime, which consistently has given El Salvador one of the world's highest murder rates per capita. The historic gang truce brokered by the Catholic Church in March 2012 is showing evidence two years hence of having a dramatic effect in reducing the death toll by 50%. However, kidnappings and extortion remain endemic. El Salvador is not yet a safe, peaceful country, but the truce was an auspicious start. Sánchez has pledged to continue it.

What the world—and foreign investors—are waiting to see is whether Sánchez has indeed put aside his Marxist guerrilla past and will follow Funes' pragmatic course, or will shift the country sharply to the left, in the orbits of Cuba, Venezuela and Nicaragua. Sánchez already has brought El Salvador into Petrocaribe, Venezuela's Faustian organization that offers discounted petroleum, something Funes did not do. Yet, he insists that he emulates another aging former guerrilla, Uruguayan President José Mujica, who has followed a moderate course.

With a razor-thin winning margin of only 6,400 votes and a shaky coalition in the Assembly, Sánchez lacks the mandate for anything too radical.

Guatemala

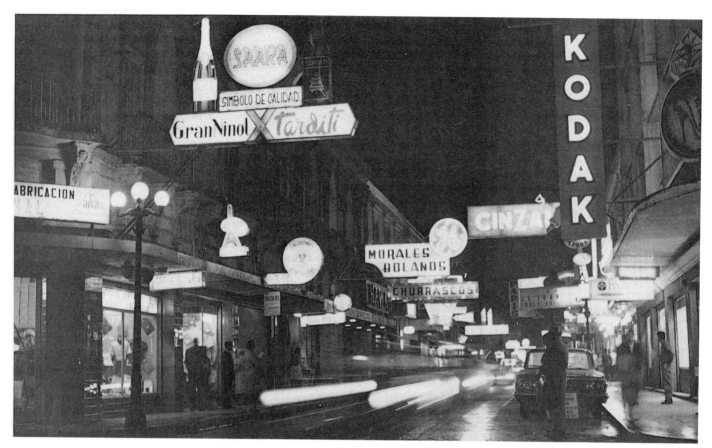

Guatemala City in the late evening

Area: 42,031 square miles.

Population: 14,647,083 (2014 est.).

Capital City: Guatemala City (Pop. 1.075 million in 2009; 2.3 million in metropolitan area).

Climate: Tropical on the coastal plains, temperate at the higher altitudes; heaviest rainfall is from May to October.

Neighboring Countries: Mexico (north and west); Belize (northeast); Honduras, El Salvador (east).

Official Language: Spanish.

Other Principal Tongues: Twenty distinct Maya-based dialects; Quiché is the most important.

Ethnic Background: Maya Indian origin (55%), *mestizo or Ladino* (mixed Spanish

Guatemala

and Indian, (42%) European or African (3%).

Principal Religion: Roman Catholic Christianity. A substantial number of people have converted to evangelical Protestantism (about 25–30%).

Chief Commercial Products: Coffee, cotton, bananas, corn and other agricultural products.

Currency: *Quetzal.*

Gross Domestic Product: U.S. $53.9 billion in 2013, est. ($3,750 per capita, official exchange rate)

Former Colonial Status: Spanish Crown Colony (1524–1821).

Independence Date: September 15, 1821.

Chief of State: Otto Fernando Pérez Molina (b. December 1, 1950), president (since January 14, 2012).

National Flag: Blue, white and blue vertical stripes with national crest in the center white stripe.

Guatemala, the most populous of the Central American republics, is a mountainous highland bordered by coastal plains in the North and South. The southern Pacific coast plain is a 200-mile ribbon of land reaching a maximum of 30 miles in width. The highland rises abruptly from this plain to an elevation of 8,000 to 10,000 feet with a string of volcanoes on the southern rim. Three of these volcanoes are above 13,000 feet and three of them are still quite active.

The highland is interspersed with basins ranging from 5,000 to 8,000 feet in elevation, which are the most heavily populated regions of Guatemala. The northeastern lowlands are more extensive than the southern, and include the valleys of the Motagua River, which originates in the southern volcanoes and flows 185 miles into the Gulf of Honduras; the Polochic River drains the more westerly mountains along a 200-mile course into Lake Izabal, a salty lagoon extending some 50 miles west from the Gulf of Honduras.

The Petén, a low, poorly drained plain, extending north 100 miles into the Yucatán Peninsula, is heavily forested and sparsely populated.

HISTORY: Guatemala was conquered by Spanish forces from Mexico in 1523 and the first Spanish settlement was established in 1524. Finding little precious metal and a land peopled by a sedentary agricultural folk, the Spanish governor rapidly lost interest in the region. Left to their own devices, the Spanish settlers intermarried with the Indians. The missionaries sought to Christianize the Mayas, whose culture began centuries before the birth of Christ. The fertile mountain valleys were developed into semi-independent estates worked by virtually enslaved Indians. The majority of the Maya, Quiché and other peoples of Mayan origin simply withdrew from the Spanish-speaking community and maintained their traditional way of life. The efforts of the missionaries to Christianize the Indians did not fully displace their pagan gods—rather, the Indians tended to add the Christian God to their own deities.

Before independence, the Captaincy-General of Guatemala included the modern Central American states and the southern provinces of present-day Mexico. Sparsely settled by the Spanish, the region contained subdued tribes in the highlands and poor settlements on the Pacific coast, while the Caribbean coast was in the hands of buccaneers, native Indians who had retained their independence and a few illegal British settlers.

Augustín de Iturbide, emperor of Mexico, invited the patriot committee of Guatemala to join Mexico in 1821. Despite considerable opposition, the Central American states were annexed in 1822; with Iturbide's abdication in 1823 they declared themselves independent. The northern state of Chiapas elected to remain with Mexico; Soconusco later joined that nation in 1842.

The independent states formed a federation known as the United Provinces of Central America. Two parties appeared in the formation of a government—the *Serviles* (conservatives) who wanted a strong central government and close ties with the Church, and the *Radicales*, who favored a federal republic and curtailment

Panorama of Guatemala City with the civic center in the foreground

209

Guatemala

of the privileges of the landowners and the clergy. A constitution based on that of the United States was adopted and a liberal president was installed. The liberal-conservative conflict resulted in a series of wars, and the confederation collapsed in 1838.

Independence and Dictatorship

From the time of dissolution of the union to 1944, Guatemala was dominated by four dictators. The first was Rafael Carrera (1838–65), who was an illiterate but popular *mestizo* leader, beloved of the Indians, but a religious fanatic of conservative persuasion. Hating liberals, he intervened in neighboring countries, seeking the overthrow of liberal presidents.

After his death, another conservative was elected, but liberal Justo Rufino Barrios gained control of the government in 1871 and ruled until his death in 1885 in the battle of Chalchuapa, El Salvador, while trying to reunite Central America

General Jorge Ubico

by military force. A man of progressive ideas, Rufino fostered public education, built railroads and achieved a measure of economic development. He also curtailed the privileges of the landowners and destroyed the political power of the clergy.

Manuel Estrada Cabrera (1897–1920), a cultured but ruthless man, ruled as a despot with no effort to conceal his absolute power. Jorge Ubico came to power in 1931 and ruled until 1944. Honest and hard-working, he suppressed the previous corruption in government, bolstered the economy and carried out many social reforms of benefit to the laboring classes.

Opposition to Ubico's strict discipline resulted in public disorder and he ultimately resigned in the so-called "October Revolution" in 1944. Following two short-lived military governments, a liberal in-

tellectual and novelist, Juan José Arévalo, was elected president in a genuinely free election, taking office in 1945. He implemented a number of reforms, including social security, university autonomy and labor laws, and is still remembered as one of Guatemala's most enlightened presidents.

In the elections of 1950, Jacobo Arbenz Guzmán won as the candidate for the Revolutionary Action and National Regeneration parties. Inexperienced, with a government infiltrated by communists, he was overthrown in 1954 by Colonel Carlos Castillo Armas in a coup promoted by the U.S. CIA. Basically corrupt and ineffective, the latter was assassinated in 1957 in the presidential residence.

Following inconclusive elections, Miguel Idígoras Fuentes was appointed president in 1958; also corrupt and arrogant, he was in turn overthrown by a military coup in 1963. Colonel Enrique Peralta Azúrdia, who assumed the power of chief of state, suspended the constitution, dismissed Congress and ruled by decree until 1966, when in free and apparently honest elections, Julio César Méndez Montenegro, a liberal, was elected. This was an effort to return constitutional government to Guatemala. In reality, it was the beginning of 20 years of military-dominated governments. It was also in the 1960s that a guerrilla insurgency began that lasted until 1996.

The single most impressive accomplishment of President Méndez Montenegro was his ability to stay in office until the end of his term. Beset by radicals and powerful conservatives, Méndez was forced to abandon reform programs and concentrate instead on pleasing traditionally powerful elements.

With virtual civil war between right-wing and leftist extremists continuing-unabated, voters turned to conservative Colonel Carlos Arana in the 1970 presidential elections. Promising "bread and peace," the noted counter-insurgency expert nearly wiped out the leftist guerrilla movement by indiscriminately repressing all opposition political groups. His term was marked by a reduction in political violence and improved economic conditions.

As the 1974 presidential election approached, the military stipulated that any candidate would be acceptable—so long as he was in the armed forces. The ruling coalition thus nominated as its candidate the moderate former defense minister, General Kjell (pronounced "shell") Eugenio Laugerud García of the *Partido Institucional Democrático (PID)*. But when the early election returns gave National Opposition Front candidate Brigadier General Efraín Ríos Montt a formidable lead, the government suddenly halted the tabulation. Several days later the regime announced

that Laugerud had won with 41% of the vote. Although such blatant fraud caused an uproar, the military refused to permit a recount.

The election also catapulted Ríos Montt into national—and international—prominence and notoriety, where he remains to this day.

Relations between the new president and ultra-conservative elements in the ruling coalition—led by former President Arana and the right-wing *Movimiento de Liberación Nacional (MLN)*—soon soured when Laugerud suggested mild reforms to ease the plight of the impoverished highland Indians. The *MLN*, representing the wealthy landowners, bitterly accused the president of being a "communist" for encouraging the formation of rural peasant cooperatives to increase production from inefficient, small peasant plots.

Guatemala was devastated in early 1976 when a violent earthquake in 17 of the 22 provinces killed 24,000 people. In addition, 76,000 were injured and 1.5 million left homeless. Although large amounts of foreign aid quickly poured into the country, little of it filtered down to the peasants because of bureaucratic bungling and political corruption.

None of the presidential candidates received a majority of votes in the 1978 election; 60% of the electorate ignored or boycotted the balloting. Congress elected the government-supported candidate, General Fernando Romeo Lucas García, but only 35 of the eligible lawmakers participated in the congressional vote. The new president promptly reversed the previous

General Fernando Romeo Lucas García

administration's policy of supporting limited reforms. Thus began an all-out campaign against both moderates and leftists.

Right-wing paramilitary "death squads," such as the Secret Anti-Communist Army, which drew most of its support from army and police units, systematically wiped out thousands of government opponents. Key targets included student, labor, peasant and political leaders. During its four years in office, Lucas García's regime was widely regarded as the most repressive and corrupt in Latin America. London-based Amnesty International accused him of operating "murder and torture" chambers in an annex of the Presidential Palace.

A 1981 report by the Human Rights Commission of the Organization of American States found the Lucas García regime responsible for the "great majority" of political murders in the country at the time. Evangelical Church officials estimated that at least 11,000 civilians died from political violence in 1981 alone. The Catholic Church reported that 200,000 Guatemalan peasants fled to neighboring Central American countries to escape the violence.

In an attempt to halt rural support for the guerrillas, Lucas García sought to wipe out key segments of the Indian population. Such repression, however, induced many peasants to join the insurgents. As a result, warfare spread to seven provinces and the number of guerrillas increased from 1,500 in 1980 to about 4,000 in 1982.

Because of Guatemala's dismal human rights record, the Carter administration in Washington halted most military and economic aid to the country in 1977. Lucas García angrily responded by rejecting all U.S. military assistance. The subsequent election of Ronald Reagan was warmly applauded by Lucas García's supporters, who hoped that Washington would resume assistance. Yet, the Reagan administration also kept its distance, although $3.2 million in military aid was provided in 1981.

Unbridled repression by the regime was not limited to its battle against peasants and leftists. When moderate Christian Democracy (DC) party members urged in late 1980 that all political groups be-allowed to participate in upcoming March 1982 elections, right-wing terrorists responded by assassinating 76 DC members.

Not surprisingly, only conservatives dared to run for president in the March 7, 1982 elections. When the balloting failed to produce a winner with a majority, Congress again voted to elect the government-supported candidate, General Angel Aníbal Guevara—who had received a bare 16% of the popular vote. The three losing candidates were arrested when they protested that the election was a fraud.

The 1982 Coup

On March 23, 1982, as the political crisis escalated, a core group of 20 junior officers in the barracks decided to vote with their guns. Early in the morning, they surrounded the Presidential Palace, forcing Lucas García to flee from a side door.

The bloodless coup was attributed to a variety of factors: the administration's heavy-handed treatment of opponents that had offended nearly all segments of the population; the perceptions of the president-elect as a clone of the unpopular Lucas García; and the rising dissatisfaction of junior officers in the army. Indeed, while these men were being sent to the field to fight against the guerrillas, senior officers were frequently given safe, cushy jobs in the rear. The widespread corruption that permeated the regime and the military high command was galling, even by Guatemalan standards. Vast public works projects initiated by the regime seemed to have been created for the sole purpose of providing a source of graft for top government officials. Of the 900 or so officers in the Guatemalan army, fully 240 were colonels or generals!

The coup created a temporary political vacuum; three different juntas were proclaimed the first day before the military finally settled on one led by Ríos Montt, then 55 and retired. His participation tended to give the junta some legitimacy, as Ríos Montt had probably won the 1974 elections, only to see the prize stolen.

Within hours of assuming power, the new junta annulled the March elections, abolished Congress, suspended the 1965 constitution, barred activities by political parties, reaffirmed Guatemala's age-old claim to Belize, arrested various civilians for corruption, ruled out elections in the

General José Efraín Ríos Montt

General Oscar Humberto Mejía Victores

near future and announced that the new government would rule by decree.

In the hope of dealing with the country's insurgency, the junta proposed an amnesty plan to leftist guerrillas. When the offer was rejected, Ríos Montt ordered an all-out "final assault" against the guerrillas in mid-1982, wiping out about 400 villages in the process.

Finding the three-member junta cumbersome, Ríos Montt fired his partners in mid-1982 and proclaimed himself president—breaking his pledge not to do so. The new president was a curiosity. A "born-again" evangelical Christian, he loved to quote the Bible to friends and foes alike when enunciating government policy. Thus, when asked about the nation's civil strife, he answered that the best way to combat it was with "love." On Sundays he gave spiritual pep-talks on national television. He was fond of saying that he "had lunch with God today."

His moralistic approach produced some positive results. He ordered a rare public campaign against corruption and cracked down on right-wing paramilitary vigilante groups. As a result, violent urban crime subsided dramatically, although political violence continued unabated in the countryside. Impressed by his efforts to reduce human rights violations, the Reagan administration offered Guatemala $4.5 million in military aid and $50 million in economic assistance in 1982.

Ríos Montt's grip on the presidency was tenuous. Some powerful elements in the military opposed his anti-corruption campaign, which reduced lucrative supplementary income sources for high-ranking officials. Others disliked his moralistic approach, dubbing him "Ayatollah." His evangelical beliefs made him extremely unpopular among the majority Catholics. General Oscar Humberto Mejía Victores overthrew Ríos Montt in mid-1983 and proclaimed himself president.

Guatemala

Democracy Returns

Mejía promised a return to democracy. Elections for a constituent assembly were held in mid-1984; 71% of the electorate voted, which remains the record voter turnout. The *DC* led by a narrow plurality. A new constitution was adopted on May 31, 1985, and congressional and presidential elections were held that November.

In honest elections, Vinicio Cerezo, a Christian Democrat who proclaimed himself "left of center," won the presidency—a dubious honor. During the military years, immense debts were run up and the treasury was empty. The International Monetary Fund suspended loan agreements. Military and state police death squads had caused the disappearance of about 100,000 people.

Victorious leftists insisted on punishing the military, but Cerezo wisely announced that although investigations would be conducted into human rights violations,

no punishments would result, infuriating many of his supporters. Mejía had decreed a general amnesty for the military during his final days in office. Underlining this, during the first three weeks of civilian government, five dozen bodies, some mutilated, were scattered throughout the country. More selective killings followed.

But "Vinicio," as the then-popular young president was known, carefully planned and executed a single raid and mass arrest of the Department of Technical Investigation, a military unit devoted to "counter-insurgency." Two hundred agents were fired and 400 were dispatched for "additional training." He also made substantial changes in the military leadership.

A committee on human rights was formed. But the civilian government had the same problems experienced in Argentina and in El Salvador: self-protection by the military. The matter was "resolved" when the Supreme Court issued more than a thousand writs of habeas corpus.

As might have been expected, no one had any genuine desire to go around digging up dead bodies.

The right-wing military, police and vigilante groups did not have a monopoly on cruel violence. Three left-wing guerrilla groups joined into the Guatemalan National Revolutionary Union (*URNG*); in 1990 they moved their operations from remote, rural areas and were operating in the more populous regions around Guatemala City. They were bold enough to stop traffic on the Pan-American Highway to collect "taxes."

Inconclusive talks were held in Madrid in 1987 and 1988 between the government and rebel representatives. The rebels were down to 1,000 men from a high of 10,000, and only operated in remote areas where they were equally despised by local Indian inhabitants, who just wanted to be left alone by both sides.

Military coups were aborted without violence in 1988 and 1989. But murders and

Woman picking corn

World Bank Photo

Guatemala

Former President Ramiro de León Carpio

disappearances at the hand of right-wing groups continued at the rate of more than 1,000 a year. Cerezo's popularity dwindled as his inability to control the military became increasingly apparent; further, he justifiably acquired the reputation as a playboy, spending much of his time during the week away from the capital or jetting abroad.

The country was in a state of nearanarchy by 1990. Countless paramilitary groups and the army operated freely, murdering at will virtually anyone suspected of being a leftist, the definition of which sometimes included anyone found outside after dark at night. In this setting, Ríos Montt campaigned in the 1990 elections on a "no-nonsense" platform; he was ruled ineligible to run under the 1986 constitution in a provision, directed against him, that forbade anyone from serving more than once as chief of state.

The Serrano Presidency

Jorge Serrano Elías, an evangelical Protestant, was elected president in a January 1991 runoff with 68% of the vote. Only about one third bothered to vote, however. He pledged to end the 30-year-old civil war.

While Cerezo had proved inept, Serrano proved venal and power-hungry. In May 1993, he attempted to effect a Fujimoristyle "self coup" that initially had the backing of the armed forces. Serrano announced that he was dissolving Congress and ruling by decree on the familiar pretext that only in this way could he come to grips with the serious socioeconomic problems facing the country. To make sure the Guatemalan people received only the information he wanted them to, he imposed prior censorship on the print and broadcast media, which immediately began collaborating with one another to outwit the censors and get information to the public.

For a week, it appeared that Guatemala would experience a throwback to the bad old days of strongman rule. But thousands of demonstrators flooded the streets of the capital to protest Serrano's power grab, among them such eminent figures as 1992 Nobel Peace Prize Laureate Rigoberta Menchú and U.N. Human Rights Ombudsman Ramiro de León Carpio. Moreover, the U.S. State Department hinted not very subtly that aid to Guatemala would likely evaporate. Simultaneously, the Constitutional Court declared Serrano's actions illegal.

The armed forces, realizing they were backing the wrong side, refused further to support the coup attempt. For a change, the military found itself hailed as a champion of democracy! Serrano fled the country to a life of luxurious exile in Panama with an estimated $25 million in "retirement funds" from the treasury. (Guatemala is still trying unsuccessfully to have Serrano extradited.)

Congress then named de León Carpio interim president, which proved to be a sound choice. As was the case with the interim presidency of Gerald Ford after the power abuses of Richard Nixon, de León Carpio proved fair and just, albeit a bit lackluster.

Legislative elections in mid-1994 (14% voted) resulted in a plurality for the Guatemalan Republican Front (*FRG*) led by Ríos Montt, who became president of the Congress. Four other parties split the remainder of the 80-seat body. The *FRG* repeatedly found itself outmaneuvered by the other parties in Congress.

Most of the next two years in Guatemala were even more turbulent than ever. The president turned to the army for support. The insurgency continued in spite of an agreement supposedly ending it. Torture and murder remained commonplace.

The Arzú Presidency and Peace

In November 1995, 12 candidates vied for president, whose term had been reduced from five to four years. The top two vote-getters were former Guatemala City Mayor Alvaro Arzú of the Party of National Advancement (*PAN*), and Alfonso Portillo of the *FRG*, the political vehicle of the still-popular Ríos Montt, whom the Constitutional Court again had ruled could not run. The court also prohibited the former strongman's wife from running, leaving Portillo as the stand-in candidate. Portillo unabashedly declared that Ríos Montt would serve in a high-level advisory capacity if he were elected.

**Former President
Alvaro Enrique Arzú Irigoyen**

In the January 1996 runoff, Arzú squeaked into office with only 52% of the vote; he lost 18 of the 21 departments outside his power base in the capital, an indicator of the lingering popular appeal of Ríos Montt. Arzú's *PAN* won 43 of the 80 seats in the unicameral Congress, though Ríos Montt's *FRG* remained a potent opposition. The *URNG*, in its first test at the polls, elected two deputies.

The new president pledged to respect human rights and insisted, not altogether convincingly, that the armed forces would be subordinate to the civilian authority. However, Arzú was mainstream enough, coming from a wealthy and prominent business family, that he posed no threat to the generals and seemed adept at working with them.

Above all else, Arzú pledged to continue the peace talks and see them through to fruition. The two sides met throughout 1996 in Mexico City and finally reached an historic truce, though some grumbled over the amnesty given to members of the security forces for past human rights abuses. On December 27, 1996, several Latin American presidents and UN Secretary-General Boutros Boutros-Ghali came to Guatemala City to witness the momentous signing of the accords that ended Central America's longest civil war. The peace took hold, with no serious violations by either side. The war-weary country at last had reason for some optimism regarding its future.

Arzú, smooth and charming while courting votes, proved ornery and arrogant as president. Days after his inauguration in January 1996, while Arzú was horseback

Guatemala

Nobel Laureate Rigoberta Menchú

riding near Antigua, a milk truck suddenly headed toward him. Halted by the bodyguards, the driver fled from the vehicle. The bodyguards then opened fire, killing him. The presidential palace described the incident as an assassination attempt. But when the media looked deeper, they concluded that the driver was a drunken milkman who had panicked.

A furious Arzú accused the media, most of which were critical of him, of attempting to discredit him. He then took measures aimed at curtailing the independent press. He used the government-subsidized television program, *Avances*, as a vehicle to vilify his editorial critics in the press and investigative reporting that had proved embarrassing to his administration. Arzú also cajoled wealthy friends to stop advertising in specified print media, particularly the country's leading daily, *Prensa Libre*, and the weekly newsmagazine *Crónica*. For business people who were not his friends, he extended a Godfather-like offer: Stop advertising, or face tax audits. *Prensa Libre* was too economically viable to be seriously hurt by the campaign, but *Crónica* was driven to the point of bankruptcy. In 1998, *Crónica* was bought out by a group of businessmen loyal to Arzú; its editorial staff was fired and its editorial tone changed overnight. It's credibility gone, it eventually folded.

On the positive side, the peace process took hold, although the public found itself polarized between those who demanded justice for past atrocities and those who preferred to forget the horrors of the past. Unfortunately, horrors kept occurring.

The Gerardi Murder

In April 1998, a Roman Catholic bishop, Juan José Gerardi Conedera, head of the church's human rights office, released a controversial report that laid the blame for most of the human rights abuses squarely at the feet of the army. Days later, Gerardi was found bludgeoned to death in his quarters. The crime stunned the country and reverberated abroad.

The official, secular investigation into the murder resembled a Keystone Kops farce. First, a local drunk who had been a laborer for Gerardi was arrested, but eventually was released for lack of evidence. Then authorities arrested a priest and accused him of killing Gerardi in a homosexual crime of passion, and the bishop's cook for complicity; both were released days later.

To make this comic-opera spectacle complete, the suspect priest's dog was "arrested" on suspicion of mauling Gerardi to death. However, Gerardi's body was exhumed for a second autopsy, which ruled out the canine theory. In a touch of irony worthy of a Greek comedy, Gerardi's successor as head of the church's human rights office was none other than Bishop Mario Ríos Montt, brother of the former strongman.

The Gerardi investigation ground on throughout 1999, largely because of intense public and media pressure, domestic and international. Authorities announced that DNA from blood samples taken at the scene matched one of the suspects. Still, there were no arrests.

Public opinion already had indicted the same culprit that Gerardi had named: the army. These suspicions intensified when the prosecutor, who had been following the military lead, fled to the U.S. because of death threats.

In 2001, police arrested army Captain Byron Lima Oliva and his father, retired Colonel Disrael Lima Estrada, in connection with the murder. Police also rearrested Gerardi's cook and issued a warrant for the priest, Mario Orantes, both of whom had been arrested and released in 1998. An intelligence NCO with the presidential guard, Sergeant Major José Obdulio Villanueva, was arrested the next day. It was Villanueva who had killed the milkman in 1996, for which he had been sentenced to five years in prison but arranged to pay a $1,500 fine instead. Orantes was arrested when he returned from the U.S. to face the charges. A judge subsequently freed Villanueva because of an apparently iron-clad alibi. He was later rearrested, and the four accused men went on trial in March 2002.

The trial absorbed Guatemala's attention—and that of human rights activists

around the world—before the historic verdicts were handed down on June 8, 2002: guilty! The judge sentenced the two Limas and Villanueva to 30 years and Orantes to 20; the cook was acquitted.

The elation of human rights groups over the conviction proved short-lived. Six weeks later, the judge fled the country because of death threats. The four convicted men appealed, and an appeals court overturned their convictions and ordered a new trial, ostensibly because of questionable testimony from one eyewitness. They were not set free, however. In February 2003, Villanueva was killed and decapitated when rival gangs of inmates at his prison north of the capital went on a rampage. It took 800 riot police to quell the disturbance.

The Gerardi case is the subject of the 2007 book, *The Art of Political Murder* (see Bibliography).

Quest for Justice

Some measure of justice for past atrocities also was meted out in 1998, when three former members of an army-organized civilian militia force were convicted and sentenced to death by lethal injection for their roles in the so-called Rio Negro Massacre in March 1982—during the first days of the Ríos Montt regime—in which 130 Indian peasants were slain. An appeals court overturned the sentences, but they were reinstated in 1999.

Guatemala moved closer to its long-sought catharsis in February 1999 when the three-member Historical Clarification Commission issued its report after 18 months of investigation into the human rights abuses committed during the civil war. Among its more controversial findings: More than 200,000 people had been killed; there had been 42,000 individual human rights violations, 29,000 of them fatal; 92% of these violations had been committed by the army; and U.S. businesses and the CIA had pressured successive Guatemalan governments into ruthlessly suppressing the guerrilla movement, particularly when Ríos Montt was in power.

When the commission presented its report at the National Theater before a crowd of 2,000 people, mostly relatives of victims, the crowd chanted, *"justicia! justicia!"* Arzú attended the ceremony and shook hands with the commission members, but studiously avoided accepting a copy of the report, citing "protocol." This led to catcalls from the crowd. Some observers concluded that Arzú's actions were intended to distance the government from the report. Days later, President Clinton visited Guatemala during his tour of countries affected by Hurricane Mitch and, while stopping short of a formal apology, expressed "regret" for the U.S. role in the human rights abuses.

The quest for justice became an international issue in December 1999 when Guatemala's most illustrious human rights champion, 1992 Nobel Peace Laureate Rigoberta Menchú, flew to Madrid to file a lawsuit before the Spanish Supreme Court against eight past military and civilian figures, including former military strongmen Ríos Montt, Lucas García and Mejía Victores. It was the same court that had requested the extradition of former Chilean dictator Augusto Pinochet from Britain for alleged rights abuses in 1998.

Menchú chose Spain because it had shown its commitment to human rights in the Pinochet case and others. (Ironically, Ríos Montt had served as Guatemala's military attaché to Spain during the 1970s, a consolation prize for having been cheated out of the presidency in the fraudulent 1974 election.)

Among Menchú's complaints was the assault by security forces on the Spanish Embassy in Guatemala in 1980 after it was seized by guerrillas. In the ensuing fire, 39 Spanish diplomats and guerrillas perished, including Menchú's father. She also cited the deaths of her mother and two brothers between 1980 and 1982, and for the deaths of four Spanish priests during the same period. Menchú's eyes filled with tears as she explained that her mother's remains were never found. "I just want to recover my mother's bones and give her a decent burial," she said. Asked if a dialogue between her and Ríos Montt were possible, she said bitterly, "I'd have to wait 2,000 years."

Another milestone in the quest for justice was reached in 2002 when Colonel Juan Valencia, a former assistant director of the presidential guard, was convicted and sentenced to 30 years for ordering the 1990 murder of U.S. anthropologist and human rights activist Myrna Mack. Two of his superiors, however, were acquitted, much to the chagrin of human rights advocates. The Guatemalan government officially acknowledged to the Inter-American Human Rights Commission in Costa Rica in 2003 that the government bore "institutional responsibility" for Mack's death. However, the country's human rights record continued to come under international scrutiny.

The Elections of 1999

The country was focused in 1999 on both a referendum, called the *"Consulta Popular,"* on the constitutional changes agreed upon in the peace agreement, and on the upcoming presidential election. About 50 complex issues were boiled down to four referendum items, including a restructuring of the armed forces' role in society and the granting of far greater cultural and political autonomy to the indigenous Mayas. Only about 18% of the electorate bothered to vote, and they rejected all the initiatives by more than a 2–1 margin. The voters seemed to be saying they were not quite ready for their society to be overhauled by politicians, but with a turnout of 18%, it was clear most didn't care one way or the other.

In the presidential race, Alfonso Portillo, the Ríos Montt stand-in who almost upset Arzú in the 1996 runoff, was renominated by the *FRG*. He had been campaigning for three years, as had Ríos Montt on his behalf.

The *PAN* dutifully nominated Arzú's hand-picked choice, Guatemala City Mayor Oscar Berger, who quickly had a falling-out with the president when he demonstrated he intended to be his own man.

The *URNG* experienced intra-party bickering between moderates and hardliners, eventually nominating a moderate, Álvaro Colom, an Indian rights advocate and nephew of a well-known leftist politician and mayor of Guatemala City who was assassinated during the presidency of Lucas García. An engineer, Colom himself is Caucasian. The *URNG* became part of a left-wing coalition called the New Nation Alliance (*ANN*).

The campaign took an interesting twist when Portillo admitted he shot two men to death in self-defense while teaching in Mexico in 1982. He said had become involved in a local political dispute and that two members of the rival faction attacked him with firearms. The Mexican authorities declined to prosecute Portillo. Berger (pronounced bear-ZHAY), who is of Belgian descent, tried to make political capital out of this confession, but the polls showed that it had no effect.

On November 7, an unexpectedly high 53% voted. Portillo almost won outright, with 48% to 30% for Berger and 12% for Colom; nine lesser candidates split the remainder. The *FRG* won an absolute majority in the newly expanded Congress, 63 of 113 seats, ensuring Ríos Montt's return to the speaker's chair. (His daughter, Zury, was No. 2 on the party's proportional representation list of deputies.) The *PAN* won 37 seats, the *ANN* nine.

The campaign for the *segunda vuelta* on December 26 was anticlimactic, as polls showed a Portillo victory inevitable.

Turnout was predictably low: 40.9%. Portillo won by the anticipated landslide: 1,184,932 of the valid votes, or 68.32%, to 549,407 votes, or 31.68% for Berger. Portillo was the first presidential candidate to poll more than 1 million votes.

The Portillo Presidency

Portillo, 48, was inaugurated on January 14, 2000. In his address, he vowed to fulfill reforms promised in the peace accords, which the Arzú government had not implemented, and he pledged to bring the Bishop Gerardi's killers to justice, calling the failure to do so after two years a "disgrace."

Portillo stunned the political and military establishments and the international community by appointing as defense minister a mere colonel, bypassing 19 generals and one admiral. He later appointed Ríos Montt's son to command the army. He introduced a military reform package allowing him to appoint a civilian defense minister. He also promised to abolish the infamous presidential guard, another promise that went unkept.

As expected, Portillo and Ríos Montt became tangled in a power struggle within the *FRG*, in both the executive and legislative branches. Ríos Montt and 22 other *FRG* deputies were caught up in a scandal involving the illegal altering of the percentage on a revenue bill on liquor from 20% to 10%—after it had passed. Ríos Montt and the other deputies denied they had changed the figure, but a reporter for the daily *Prensa Libre* produced an audiotape of a committee meeting in which the amount had been set at 10%. The press dubbed the scandal "Boozegate." Portillo apparently was not involved, but the scandal embarrassed him.

Then two newspapers reported they had documentation that Portillo and Vice President Francisco Reyes had used dummy companies to open Panamanian bank accounts in 2001 designed to receive $1.5 million monthly in deposits. Days later, 3,000 protesters banged pots and pans in front of the government palace, demanding that Portillo and Reyes resign. Portillo denied the allegations, calling them a smear campaign by "the oligarchy."

Meanwhile, past atrocities kept on surfacing—literally. In 2002, the bodies of 47 people, apparently Indian peasants massacred during the civil war, were unearthed from a mass grave found beneath a school in Rabinal, 120 miles north of the capital. In 2003, Ríos Montt traveled to Rabinal to attend an *FRG* meeting even as local Mayas were preparing to rebury the remains of 66 of the victims. When he arrived, the furious Indians began hurling rocks at him. He escaped unhurt. With a touch of bitter irony, his legislator-daughter Zury termed the incident a "violation of human rights."

Human rights advocates continued to fault Portillo for failing to keep his promise to abolish the presidential guard. In 2001, Amnesty International charged that

Guatemala

Former President Alfonso Portillo

threats against human rights workers in Guatemala had increased on Portillo's watch.

In 2002, Guillermo Ovalle, an administrator of the Rigoberta Menchú Foundation, was gunned down in broad daylight. Authorities maintained—as they had in the Gerardi murder four years earlier—that it was an apparent robbery attempt. Human rights workers excavating the mass graves of victims of army massacres in the 1980s received death threats. Then, in December 2002, two prominent Indian rights activists were abducted and murdered. According to the U.N. human rights ombudsman in Guatemala, there were 70 murders, attempted murders or death threats against human rights workers in 2002.

On a brighter note, Pope John Paul II made his third visit to Guatemala in 2002 to canonize Pedro de San José Betancur (1619–67), son of a shepherd in the Canary Islands, who lived humbly in Antigua, Guatemala, became a Franciscan brother and preached to prison inmates. He also raised money for orphans, established a hospital for the poor and founded the Antigua-based Bethlehemite Congregation. His grave in Antigua is a place of pilgrimage, and thousands have claimed miracles were granted after touching the tomb.

'Jueves Negro' and the Elections of 2003

Berger sought the *PAN* nomination again in 2003, but the party broke up into three factions, with the regulars nominating Leonel López Rodas, who had labored

to keep the party afloat after Berger's poor showing in 1999. A faction loyal to former President Arzú resurrected an old party, the Unionist Party *(PU)*, choosing as its candidate Guatemala City Mayor Fritz Garcia-Gallont. Berger became the candidate of three tiny parties that comprised the Grand National Alliance *(GANA)*. Colom entered the race again, this time as head of a coalition of left-wing parties called the National Union of Hope *(UNE)*. There were six minor candidates.

With the judicial appointments Portillo had made over three and a half years, Ríos Montt, by then 77, staged a Machiavellian maneuver to circumvent the constitution and run for president as the *FRG* candidate. The Supreme Electoral Tribunal again barred him from running. He appealed to the Supreme Court, which upheld the electoral tribunal's decision. He then appealed to the Constitutionality Court, which for the first time had a majority of *FRG* justices. In a stunning reversal, the Constitutionality Court voted 4–2 to allow his candidacy.

Ríos Montt's opponents appealed that decision back to the Supreme Court, which granted a stay. What happened next shocked the country and the world, and may have turned the tide irreversibly against Ríos Montt. In an obviously well-orchestrated show of force, hundreds of pro-*FRG* peasants were bused to the capital from the country in exchange for a promise of $40 and three meals a day for two days. They were issued clubs and ski masks.

On Thursday, July 24, they went on a rampage, erecting barricades, burning tires, smashing store windows and demonstrating outside the Supreme Court and the Constitutionality Court. They turned on journalists covering the disturbances, beating some of them or dousing them with gasoline. A 65-year-old television reporter, ironically with a pro-*FRG* station, died of a heart attack while being chased by club-wielding goons. Through it all, police failed to intervene. Portillo announced he would send in troops to maintain order; they never arrived. The disturbances, which the media named *Jueves Negro* (Black Thursday), spilled over into Friday. Then, Ríos Montt gave the order to end the demonstrations, and the goons dispersed.

Incredibly, the *FRG* insisted that it had not instigated *Jueves Negro*, even after newspaper photographs showed well-known *FRG* leaders, including Jorge Arévalo, a high-ranking congressman, and Ríos Montt's niece, involved in the disturbances. Polls for years had suggested that Ríos Montt could win the presidency if he were allowed to run. Now, faced with the reality of Ríos Montt's candidacy, voters got cold feet after *Jueves Negro*. He slipped

to third, then fourth, then fifth place in the polls.

Ríos Montt never recovered the ground he lost from *Jueves Negro* to make it into the runoff. On November 9, 55.2% of the electorate went to the polls. The results:

Berger	904,533	34.5%
Colom	694,734	26.5%
Ríos Montt	503,994	19.2%
López Rodas	218,577	8.3%
García-Gallont	79,784	3.0%
Others	222,423	8.6%

Under the complicated proportional representation formula, Berger's new *GANA* coalition emerged as the largest movement in the newly enlarged Congress, with 48 of the 158 seats. The *FRG* was still a major force, finishing second with 42 seats. Colom's *UNE* won 33, the *PAN* won 15 and five other parties won 18.

Berger and Colom embarked on what was a gentlemanly campaign for the *segunda vuelta* in December. The turnout was 46.8%. The results:

Berger	1,235,303	54.13%
Colom	1,046,868	45.87%

It was the closest the Guatemalan left had ever come to tasting victory. Berger's *GANA*, Colom's *UNE* and the *PAN* announced an unorthodox right-center-left legislative coalition, giving them a working majority of 96 seats. The *FRG* was once again in opposition, with Zury Ríos its leader in Congress. She made international headlines a year later by marrying U.S. Representative Jerry Weller, a Republican from Illinois; it was her fourth marriage.

Berger Makes Changes

Berger was sworn in on January 14, 2004, the latest in a growing list of Latin American presidents elected on their second or subsequent attempts. In his address, Berger promised to crack down on corruption and human rights abuses, something the jaded Guatemalans had heard time and again. In a gesture reminiscent of Andrew Jackson, he opened the doors of the presidential palace on inauguration day, allowing thousands of ordinary people to visit.

Berger set out to make good on his promises. He appointed Nobel Laureate Rigoberta Menchú as a "goodwill ambassador" to help monitor the 1996 peace accords, something that would have been unthinkable under Portillo. Berger seemed sensitive about his Belgian heritage and his reputation as a member of the ruling elite in the overwhelmingly Mayan country. He appointed a leftist activist as human rights commissioner.

In 2004, a court ordered Ríos Montt placed under house arrest, not for genocide, but for the death of the journalist on *Jueves Negro.* He eventually went on trial for genocide in 2013 (see Justice at Last?).

In a move that once would have provoked a military coup, Berger reduced the army almost by half, from 27,000 to 15,500; the savings went to welfare and education. Berger and members of his government received death threats over the cuts. He also did what Arzú and Portillo promised to do but didn't: He disbanded the notorious presidential guard.

Under Berger, both the executive and legislative branches declared war on the country's endemic corruption—a formidable enemy. Transparency International ranked Guatemala as the third most corrupt country in the Western Hemisphere in 2004 (only Haiti and Paraguay were worse) and one of the 23 worst in the world. By 2007, Berger's final year in office, Guatemala had "improved" to the eighth most corrupt in the Western Hemisphere and ranked as 111th most corrupt in the world out of 179 nations.

The government launched an investigation into Portillo's Panamanian bank accounts. The U.S. government revoked the former president's visa; Portillo fled the country, surfacing in Mexico on a one-year work visa. The auditor released a report stating that $600 million in public funds was unaccounted for over a 12-year period, which also implicated the presidencies of Arzú and de León Carpio, as well as Serrano, whose crookedness was well known. The auditor said about half that amount was bilked from the public health system. Mexico extradited Portillo in 2008 in connection with $15 million worth of military kickbacks to him and others while he was president. He and several associates were acquitted in May 2011. He now awaits extradition to the United States (see Colom Battles Crime, Scandal and Hunger).

Racial discrimination had been outlawed in 2002, but no one had ever been prosecuted for it until 2004. Five men with *FRG* ties, including Ríos Montt's grandson, were charged with abuse against Rigoberta Menchú in 2003 when she testified at a hearing against allowing Ríos Montt to run for president. They allegedly shoved her and said, "Go back to selling tomatoes in the market, Indian." In 2005, the five were convicted and sentenced to 38 months each.

Although U.N. Secretary-General Kofi Annan warned that the country still had a long way to go in providing rights to the Indian majority, the U.N. Verification Mission for Guatemala was closed in 2004. In its place, the U.N. established the International Commission Against Impunity in Guatemala *(CICIG)* in 2006 to investigate past or present rights violations. It has a staff of 180 and works to assist Guatemalan law enforcement and judicial institutions rather than supplant them. Its two-year mandate was later extended to 2011, then extended again.

Besides coming to terms with corruption and rights abuses, Berger faced skyrocketing street crime and an alarmingly high murder rate. In 2005, Guatemala tied with Venezuela for the world's third-highest murder rate, 42 per 100,000 inhabitants; in 2006, it increased to 45. It became so critical that Berger ordered 1,600 army troops to augment the police in patrolling the capital and fired his interior minister and police chief. Much of the crime is believed linked to the international *maras,* or street gangs, with roots in El Salvador and Los Angeles, California (see El Salvador). Drug trafficking also remains a menace. An estimated 75% of the cocaine that enters the United States passes through Guatemala.

The Congress ratified Guatemala's membership in the proposed Dominican Republic-Central America Free Trade Agreement (DR-CAFTA) with the United States in 2005. The CAFTA vote was briefly delayed when 4,000 left-wing demonstrators outside the legislative building hurled rocks and bottles at police, who responded with tear gas. Guatemalan participation in CAFTA took effect on July 1, 2006.

Guatemala was one of the stops on President Bush's five-nation tour of Latin America in 2007. The brief visit was purely of a goodwill nature, although the extraordinary security resulted in traffic jams that caused more anger than goodwill. Bush visited a Mayan archeological site, after which some Mayan shamans performed an "exorcism." The report that Bush brought his own drinking water offended Guatemalan sensibilities.

The Elections of 2007

As always, the field for the September 9, 2007 presidential and congressional elections was fragmented, with 14 candidates on the presidential ballot. President Berger threw his support behind Alejandro Giammatei, a Christian Democrat who was his prison director, for the *GANA* nomination. Retired General Otto Pérez Molina, a presidential chief of staff under De León Carpio and a negotiator for the 1996 peace accords, became the candidate of a new conservative movement called the Patriotic Party *(PP).* Colom again became the standard bearer for *UNE.* The *FRG* nominated Luis Rabbé, who was Portillo's minister of communication and had a reputation for corruption. Former Guatemala City Mayor Fritz García-Gallont was again the candidate of Arzú's Unionist Party. Nobel Laureate Rigoberta Menchú declared her candidacy, but the various Indian groups would not coalesce around her. Eduardo Suger was the candidate of the Center for Social Action.

Also as usual, the campaign was marred by violence. Over four months, 40 candidates or party officials, activists or their relatives were killed, 18 of them from Colom's *UNE.* Amnesty International called on the candidates to conduct their campaigns "in a manner consistent with respect for the rule of law and human rights standards." Colom said 14 of the *UNE* members killed were slain by "organized crime," a reference to the notorious *maras.*

The climate of fear that common crime had created was the overriding issue when five of the candidates appeared for an unprecedented televised debate, which CNN aired throughout the hemisphere. Pérez Molina, whose campaign slogan was *"mano dura"* (stern hand), promised a get-tough approach to the *maras,* the bloodthirsty gangs terrorizing the capital and other cities. Colom, whose kindler, gentler slogan was *"vida, desrarollo y paz"* (life, development and peace), argued that economic reforms and greater socioeconomic equality would help eliminate the root causes of crime.

A total of 3,280,609 valid ballots were cast in the first round, an unusually high turnout of 60.5%. The results:

Colom	926,244	28.23%
Pérez Molina	771,244	23.51%
Giammattei	565,270	17.23%
Suger	244,448	7.43%
Rabbé	239,208	7.29%

There were three notable results of the first round: the left finished in first place for the first time with the tenacious Colom; Ríos Montt's once powerful *FRG* finished a pitiful fifth; and Menchú had placed a dismal seventh with a mere 3% of the vote, 101,316.

In the simultaneous election for the 158 congressional deputies through proportional representation, Colom's *UNE* finished first with 48 seats; *GANA* received 37; Pérez Molina's *PP,* 30; the *FRG,* 15; seven other parties accounted for the remaining 28 seats.

In the runoff between Colom and Pérez Molina for two newspapers. Polls almost universally favored Pérez Molina, but two factors made the outcome uncertain. One is the reluctance of poll respondents in Guatemala to tell the truth, and Colom's voters feared retribution against *UNE.* Another was the fact that Thursday, November 1, All Saints Day, was a national holiday, and thousands of affluent residents of Guatemala City—Pérez Molina's

Guatemala

Former President Oscar Berger

core constituency—had opted to take off Friday as well and leave the capital for a four-day weekend.

The overconfident Pérez Molina, like Aesop's hare, failed to show up for a televised debate with Colom. Pérez Molina was unquestionably handsomer and more charismatic than Colom, who has gaunt, Lincolnesque features and speaks in a dull, nasal-monotone. But Pérez Molina's no-show rubbed voters the wrong way. So did his *mano dura* slogan, which conjured up memories of the military's past human rights abuses, although Pérez Molina's own hands were apparently clean.

Street crime remained the burning issue in the runoff: coils of razor wire, often electrified, topped the walls around homes, businesses, even churches. The ubiquitous small shops are now fronted with bars, and customers place their orders through them.

Army troops with automatic weapons and national policemen stood guard outside polling places to discourage electoral violence, while army helicopters patrolled overhead. A total of 2,743,798 voters cast ballots, a greatly reduced turnout of 48.3%, which, as expected, was to Colom's advantage. The historic results:

Colom	1,449,153	52.82%
Pérez Molina	1,294,645	47.18%

Colom swept 20 of the 22 departments, although Pérez Molina carried the capital handily. Pérez Molina conceded defeat, without congratulating Colom. Colom's supporters partied celebrated the end to their wandering for years in the political wilderness.

At the president-elect's traditional morning-after press conference, Colon was flanked by Vice President-elect Rafael Espada, a prominent heart surgeon in Houston, Texas. Colom bent over backward to dispel any suggestions that he is a left-wing firebrand in the style of Venezuela's Hugo Chávez. Asked whether he would be closer to Washington or to Chávez, Colom replied cautiously that relations with the U.S. "will be more or less as they are now. I hope to strengthen the relationship. We've always been good partners."

Colom added that Guatemala also enjoys friendly relations with Venezuela, which he said will continue, but he insisted, "We don't have any special connection." He said he also would maintain friendly relations with Cuba as well with conservative leaders like Colombian President Álvaro Uribe and especially with Mexican President Felipe Calderón, "because we share a common border and are brother peoples."

Colom Battles Crime, Scandal and Hunger

The 56-year-old Colom was inaugurated on January 14, 2008, ushering in what many hoped would be a new era in Guatemalan history. As Colom had suggested, both Chávez and Uribe attended. Colom promised that "today marks the beginning of privileges for the poor and those without opportunity."

The crime situation worsened, and Mexican President Calderón's crackdown on the drug cartels forced some of them to shuffle their operations into Guatemala, whose institutions are weaker. In 2009, 6,451 murders were recorded in Guatemala; by comparison, 1,951 civilians and 498 U.S. soldiers, a total of 2,449, were killed in Iraq in 2009. Anti-Colom posters showed Colom bare-chested with trademark *mara* tattoos.

But the killing that shook the Colom administration to its core was that of a prominent attorney, Rodrigo Rosenberg, gunned down by two assailants while riding a bicycle in the capital in May 2009. A security video showed two gunmen; the second one fired a *coup de grace* into Rosenberg's head. The next day, a video surfaced that Rosenberg had made three days before his death in which he declared, "Unfortunately, if you are watching this message, it is because I was assassinated by President Álvaro Colom, with help from Gustavo Alejos."

Alejos was Colom's private secretary. Rosenberg also accused the president's wife, Sandra Torres, other presidential aides and various bankers and businessmen of involvement in the April 2009 murders of businessman Khalil Musa, Rosenberg's client, and Musa's daughter, who was Rosenberg's girlfriend. Rosenberg alleged on the video the Musas were killed because they refused to participate in a corruption scheme involving the government's Rural Development Bank, which he called a "den of thieves, drug traffickers and murderers." Rosenberg said he was marked for death for alleging the government's involvement in the Musa murders.

"El caso Rosenberg" became a media sensation, picked up by international media; the video was aired on YouTube. Colom went on television to plaintively deny any complicity in Rosenberg's death by himself, his wife or others. The government website blamed Rosenberg's death on "organized crime" and accused Colom opponents of exploiting it to discredit him.

Hundreds of thousands of violence-weary Guatemalans protested in the streets. The U.N.'s International Commission Against Impunity in Guatemala (*CICIG*) began a six-month investigation into Rosenberg's death that involved more than 300 crime experts from 11 countries.

Seven men, including a policeman and several *mara* members, were arrested in September 2009 in the Rosenberg's case, but still unsolved was who hired them or why. In January 2010, the commission concluded that Rosenberg, despondent over his girlfriend's murder, his impending second divorce and his mother's death, and bitter against the Colom government for failing to apprehend the Musas' killers, engineered an elaborate suicide scheme to discredit the government. The report found he paid his own hit-men. Two brothers turned themselves in that June. Colom expressed relief over what he saw as his and his wife's exoneration, but some Guatemalans remained skeptical—and still are.

Guatemala's violent crime again made international headlines in 2009, when five policemen were killed in a shootout with drug traffickers; the police were allegedly trying to *steal*, not seize, 750 kilos of cocaine. Colom sacked his national police chief for allegedly stealing drugs and cash and appointed Baltazar Gómez. The *CICIG* investigated the deaths of the five officers, and in 2010 the jaded country was stunned again by the news that Police Chief Gómez and Nelly Bonilla, the top counter-narcotics official, had been arrested for drug trafficking and conspiring to thwart the investigation into the fatal incident.

U.S. Secretary of State Hillary Clinton visited Guatemala a few days later to discuss the drug trafficking crisis.

In other matters, Colom declared a "state of national calamity" in 2009 because of widespread malnutrition, which was exacerbated by a drought. Colom theorized that the declaration would facilitate international food aid to 300,000 needy

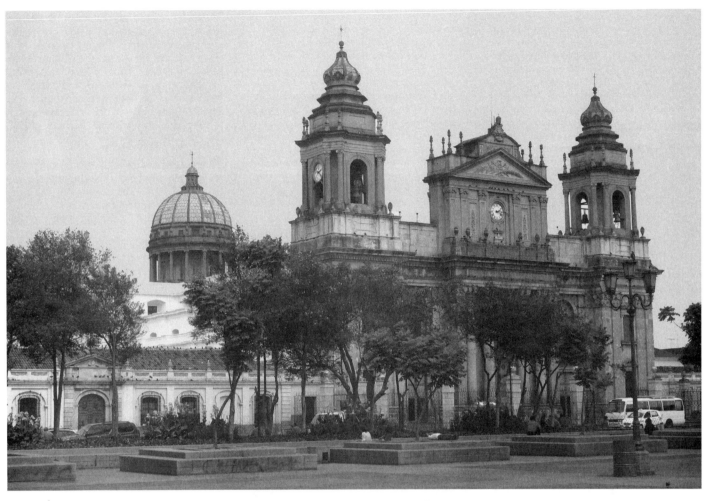

The colonial Cathedral of Guatemala City. . .

people. He cited U.N. statistics showing Guatemala with the highest rate of malnutrition in Latin America and fourth-highest in the world, although its per capita income is higher than many other countries with lower rates of malnutrition. Half of Guatemala's children under the age of 5 were undernourished, he said. UNICEF estimates that in the predominantly indigenous rural areas, child undernourishment could be as high as 80%, and stunted growth is widespread.

The government released a report in 2009 that concluded that at least 333 children had been stolen by the army during the civil war and sold through international adoption agencies, similar to what happened during the Dirty War in Argentina.

Compounding the *mara*-related violence, the notorious Mexican drug trafficking organization, *Los Zetas*, invaded the remote jungle region bordering Mexico, where cocaine from Colombia bound for the U.S. is offloaded at hidden landing strips. In 2010, heavily armed and well-equipped *Zetas* overwhelmed a police unit and engaged army soldiers in a battle that left one dead and several wounded. Colom declared a two-month state of siege in Alta Verapaz department, which permitted warrantless arrests.

In May 2011, *Los Zetas* massacred and beheaded 27 peasants, including two women, on a farm in Petén department. Colom again declared a state of siege; one Guatemalan and five Mexican members of *Los Zetas* were arrested. Colom announced that renegade former members of Guatemala's special forces may have been involved in the massacre. *Los Zetas* are composed largely of deserters from Mexico's special forces (see Mexico).

Former President Portillo and his defense and finance minister finally went on trial in January 2011 on charges they embezzled $15 million in defense funds. The country was shocked when the three-judge panel voted 2–1 to acquit them. The acquittals were widely seen as blows to the justice system and the war on corruption. Portillo's triumph was short-lived. In August 2011, the Constitutional Court ordered his extradition to the U.S. on charges of laundering $70 million through U.S. banks. Colom refused to block the extradition. Portillo was held in a military prison for almost two years before he was extradited, the first Guatemalan president to be extradited (see Justice at Last?)

The Elections of 2011

First lady Sandra Torres de Colom made international headlines when she announced in 2011 that she was divorcing her husband "so I can be married to the Guatemalan people." She declared her candidacy for president under the banner of her husband's *UNE*. A family court granted the divorce suspiciously quickly for Guatemala, five weeks. Other parties filed legal challenges to Torres' candidacy, accusing her of fraud and of attempting to subvert the constitution.

The Supreme Electoral Tribunal rejected Torres's candidacy on grounds of "supposed legal fraud." Her supporters appealed to the Constitutionality Court, which also ruled against her. It was then too late for the *UNE* to field a new candi-

Guatemala

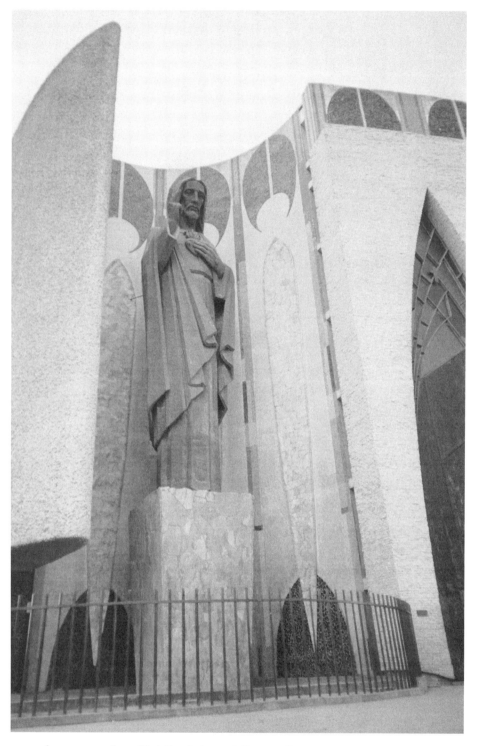

. . . and a more modern Christian interpretation nearby

date for the September 11 election. Neither did *GANA*, although the two parties forged an unlikely coalition for the congressional election.

Pérez Molina, the loser of the 2007 runoff, declared his candidacy. Other strong contenders included Eduardo Suger, the Swiss-born, U.S.-educated conservative physicist running under the banner of Commitment, Renewal and Order (*CREO*); Harold Caballeros, a Harvard-educated evangelical of the coalition Vision with Values and Encounter for Guatemala (*VV-EG*), who had the backing of the business elite; and Manuel Baldizón, of Renewed Democratic Liberty (*LIDER*). Nobel Laureate Rigoberta Menchú entered the race again.

Arzú declared his intention to seek another term in defiance of the prohibition against re-election. But he backed down and, taking a page from the Coloms' book, fielded his wife, Patricia Escobar de Arzú, as his stand-in—without a divorce. She was viewed as nothing other than Arzú's political puppet. Arzú himself then sought a third consecutive term as mayor of Guatemala City.

The old *PAN* fielded Juan Gutiérrez. Mario Estrada was the candidate of a new movement called Nationalist Change Union (*UCN*), while Giammattei ran again as candidate of the Social Action Center. In all, there were 10 candidates on the first-round ballot.

By 2011, Guatemalans were even more crime-weary than they had been in 2007. The homicide rate for 2010 was 41 per 100,000, the world's fifth highest; in 2011, it was still tied with Belize and Jamaica for fifth place with 39. Corruption had actually worsened on Colom's watch, according to Transparency International. In 2010, TI rated Guatemala the 11th most corrupt of the 20 Latin American republics; in 2011, it was seventh worst. *Los Zetas* by then were operating in 75% of the country. Armed robberies, burglaries and kidnappings for ransom were everyday occurrences. Election violence marred the campaign itself, claiming about 35 lives.

Pérez Molina resurrected his *"mano dura"* slogan from 2007, only this time he found a more receptive audience. Polls showed that 67% of voters regarded security as the most important issue facing the country, something not lost on the candidates. Pérez Molina soared to first place in the polls, and this time his opponents—except Menchú—refrained from trying to portray him as a military bogeyman, even when he promised in a debate to use elite army units to fight the *maras* and *Los Zetas*. Baldizón's slogan, for example, was "Security Now!"

Besides the crime issue, Pérez Molina had history on his side: Each of the last four presidents had run at least once unsuccessfully. Voter turnout on September 11 was a record-shattering 69.4%. The outcome:

Pérez Molina	1,611,493	36.0%
Baldizón	1,038,287	23.2%
Suger	732,842	16.4%
Estrada	383,643	8.6%
Caballeros	275,475	6.2%
Menchú	146,353	3.3%
Gutiérrez	123,648	2.8%
Escobar de Arzú	97,381	2.2%
Others	65,433	1.5%

Pérez Molina's Patriotic Party increased from 30 to 56 seats in the congressional election, the most of any party, but still

23 short of a majority in the 158-seat legislature. The *UNE-GANA* alliance was second with 48 seats, while the *UCN* and *LIDER* tied with 14 seats each and Suger's *CREO* won 12. Five other parties split the remainder. Arzú was re-elected mayor of the capital.

There was little suspense as to the outcome of the *segunda vuelta* on November 6:

Pérez Molina	2,300.979	53.74%
Baldizón	1,981,003	46.26%

Pérez Molina, 61, was inaugurated on January 14, 2012. Besides promising to "neutralize" organized crime, to bring down the murder rate to "only" 36 per 100,000 by July and to increase the size of the national police by 40%, he pledged to continue Colom's popular social programs, especially hunger reduction, without explaining how he will be able to finance both. As popular as they are, Colom's social programs came at the expense of the highway infrastructure, which is crumbling.

The new president soon made an international splash when, at a meeting of Central American leaders, he proposed decriminalizing marijuana. He raised the issue again at the Sixth Summit of the Americas in Cartagena, Colombia, a month later.

The new president surprised many by retaining Colom's popular justice minister, Claudia Paz y Paz, who has prosecuted former military figures, including some of Pérez Molina's erstwhile comrades-in-arms, for human rights abuses.

Within a few months, he showed that *mano dura* was more than a campaign slogan. In October 2012, protesters barricaded the highways around the town of Totonicapán to protest Pérez Molina's capping of electricity rates at a rate higher than they thought fair. The president sent in armed soldiers, in vehicles driven by armed security guards. According to news reports, the protesters grew menacing and a security guard opened fire. Others then opened fire, killing six protesters and wounding more than 30. Riots then erupted, with the local inhabitants demanding justice. Human rights groups condemned what they called the government's trigger-happy response.

Yet, the public seemed to approve of *la mano dura.* In September 2012, the Mitofsky poll showed Pérez Molina the third most popular president of the Western Hemisphere with an approval rating of 69%. In January 2013, the first anniversary of his inauguration, a *Prensa Libre* poll put it at 70%.

Justice at Last?

More old ghosts from the past came back in 2012. Former President Mejía, the

The military is an ever-present aspect of Guatemalan political life

general who overthrew Ríos Montt, was declared mentally and physically incompetent to stand trial for rights abuses. But five former soldiers were convicted in 2011 and 2012 of complicity in the 1982 massacre—during Ríos Montt's regime—of 250 peasants in the village of Dos Erres. All were sentenced to the same peculiar term of 6,060 years each.

More spectacularly, a prosecutor ordered Ríos Montt, then 85, to testify in a court hearing to determine whether he should stand trial for genocide and crimes against humanity. Specifically, he was accused of ordering the systematic massacres of Ixil Indians, at least 1,771 of whom were killed during his 1982-83 regime. He appeared, but refused to testify. Judge Carol Flores ruled Ríos Montt could be tried. He claimed amnesty under the 1996 peace accords, but the judge ruled the accords did not provide amnesty for human rights abuses and that Guatemala is signatory to international treaties that preclude amnesty in genocide cases.

Legal maneuvering delayed the case for a year, but the former general finally went on trial in January 2013. It is the first time a person has been tried for genocide in a national court in his own country rather than in an international court. Guatemalan public opinion was sharply divided on the genocide charges, with some, including Pérez Molina, arguing that it is airing Guatemala's dirty linen before the world. Some legal scholars questioned whether the prosecution would be able to prove intent. Others contended that it cast Guatemala in a positive light by demonstrating that there is no impunity for genocide.

For 17 weeks the court heard chilling, gruesome testimony from Ixil Indians who related tales of mass killings, rapes and torture. An unusual twist was the presence of foreign ambassadors in the audience, including the American. Suddenly, on April 19, the panel's three judges squabbled over various legal procedures submitted by the defense, including whether the head judge, Jazmín Barrios, should recuse herself. She had made no secret of her bias against Ríos Montt, and the defense was not allowed to present certain pieces of exculpatory evidence. It appeared the trial could be reset to zero, but the panel decided to continue, a decision that proved fateful.

On May 10, in a decision that made headlines around the world, the court convicted the 86-year-old Ríos Montt of genocide. Barrios sentenced him to the maximum, 80 years, then joined in the cheering with the anti-Ríos Montt spectators. Even Ríos Montt's detractors were suspicious over the sentencing document being prepared in just two days, suggesting it had been prepared well in advance of the verdict. The bar association later sanctioned Barrios for her conduct in the trial.

The U.S. State Department and international human rights groups hailed the verdict as historic and cathartic. Pérez Molina was critical, saying he personally knew of no genocide during his army service.

The jubilation was fleeting. Ten days later, the Constitutionality Court overturned the verdict and threw out everything that transpired in the trial after April 19, saying the trial should have been halted until the procedural issues over the defense's motions were resolved. The phase

Guatemala

The front page of *Prensa Libre* for November 21, 2004, was bittersweet for the Guatemalan Republican Front (*FRG*) of former strongman Efraín Ríos Montt. At right is a photo from the wedding of his daughter, Zury, the FRG's leader in Congress, who married U.S. Representative Jerry Weller of Illinois. At the left is a headline that reads, "The FRG: Divided and affected by corruption."

of the trial after April 19, largely closing arguments, must be repeated once those defense arguments are ruled upon, so Ríos Montt, who turned 88 in June, is not off the hook. The retrial is now tentatively scheduled for January 2015. He continues to maintain he never ordered the killings. The overwhelming majority of Guatemalans are too young to remember the Ríos Montt era, and they have been more apathetic about the outcome than their elders.

In yet another case of justice delayed, former President Portillo, who had been held in a military prison for almost two years, was finally extradited to the U.S. on May 24, 2013. His transfer took place in utmost secrecy, to the annoyance of journalists. Portillo was flown to New York, where he was given a medical exam. He pleaded not guilty in federal court to charges he laundered $70 million. But in March 2014 he changed his plea to guilty, and in May the judge sentenced him to five years and 120 months and fined him $2.5 million. If given credit for time served, he could be free in 18 months. The judge had not decided when this book went to press if he would serve his sentence in the United States or Guatemala.

Recent Developments

Despite *la mano dura*, Guatemala's homicide rate actually worsened slightly in 2012, to 39.9 per 100,000, still the world's fifth highest. Pérez Molina dropped from third to ninth most popular leader of the hemisphere, with an approval rating in October 2013 of 48%—still four points better than Barack Obama.

In a decision that raised fears of a step back for the justice system—if indeed it could step back further—the Constitutionality Court ruled in February that Attorney General Claudia Paz y Paz, who had been chosen by a nominating committee for attorney general and appointed by Colom to a fixed five-year term, would have to step down in May 2014, seven months early, citing a legal technicality. She has won praise for tackling organized crime and for prosecuting Ríos Montt; *Forbes* called her one of the "five most powerful women changing the world" in 2012. That may have been her undoing, and her admirers alleged that she had run afoul of the country's oligarchy by trying to change *too* much in Guatemala. She sought another term from the 11-member nominating committee, composed of the president of the Supreme Court, two bar association members and 11 law school deans. Although she received the second-highest score, she was not on the list of six nominees submitted to Pérez Molina.

A more positive development was the appointment by the United Nations of a respected Colombian judge, Iván Velásquez, to take over *CICIG* in October 2013. He publicly announced his intent to investigate links between drug cartels and Guatemala's political parties.

A humanitarian crisis was unfolding in mid-2014 along the U.S.-Mexican border as tens of thousands of children as young as four years old unaccompanied by adults, most of them from Guatemala, El Salvador and Honduras, suddenly began crossing the U.S. border illegally. The reason for the sudden surge in child migration may be a memo President Obama signed in 2012 called the Deferred Action for Childhood Arrivals, which defers deportation for illegal immigrants who were brought to the United States as children. The erroneous rumor spread in Central America that if children cross the border alone and surrender, they would be allowed to stay. When this book went to press, 47,000 children had entered the country illegally in 2014. The children have been placed in impromptu detention centers, raising international concerns for their welfare. An estimated 1,550 of the children being detained are Guatemalan.

Vice President Joe Biden came to Guatemala on June 20 to meet with Pérez Molina, Salvadoran President Salvador Sánchez Cerén, Mexican Interior Secretary Miguel Ángel Osorio and Honduran President Juan Orlando Hernández's cabinet chief of staff, Jorge Ramón Hernández Alcerro, to discuss the situation. The meetings proved contentious. Biden bluntly told them the "situation is not sustainable," that the children would be deported and that their countries bore a responsibility at their ends to prevent their children from being placed in such dangerous circumstances. He pledged $93 million in aid to Guatemala, El Salvador and Honduras, from which most of the children came. This includes $40 million to head off youths from joining gangs in Guatemala, $25 million for 77 youth outreach centers in El Salvador and $18.5 million for 77 similar centers in Honduras. The Latin American representatives just as bluntly pressed back by blaming the United States for not coming up with a coherent immigration policy and urged Biden to extend temporary protective status (TPS) to the children because of the violent conditions in their countries of origin.

Pérez Molina further proposed in his own meeting with Biden that the U.S. grant temporary work permits for Central American migrants, who would then return home. Biden pressed right back by conditioning the granting of TPS to migration reforms adopted by the Guatemalan Congress, as Hondurans and Salvadorans must transit Guatemala.

CULTURE: The culture of modern Guatemala represents a composite of traditional Mayan and colonial Spanish. Although the mixing of the two bloods has produced a *mestizo* element called by the locals *"Ladino,"* the majority of the population remains unassimilated, pure-blood Indians of Mayan descent who speak a number of dialects, the most widely spoken being Quiché. The Mayan heritage has largely shaped the country's rich folklore in art and music, much to the benefit of the country's tourist industry. Guatemalans take special pride in their *marimba* bands, which often greet arriving visitors at the capital's airport.

Both cultures are represented on UNESCO's list of World Heritage Sites: the Mayan ruins of Tikal and Quirigua, and the Spanish colonial city of Antigua.

Guatemala's religious practices are among the most curious in Latin America. Roman Catholicism never firmly took root, despite efforts by zealous colonial-era priests to force or entice the Indians away from their pagan practices. Eventually, the Church came to realize that it would have better results with a little more tolerance. Today, in towns such as Chichicastenango, visitors can see Indians practicing their tribal rites inside the Catholic cathedral. The shallow roots of Catholicism also made Guatemala a promising target for the proselytizing of U.S.-based evangeli-

President Otto Pérez Molina

cal Protestantism. Today an estimated one third of the population are zealous, "born-again" fundamentalists; among the converts were former strongman Efraín Ríos Montt and former President Jorge Serrano.

An abysmally low literacy rate, combined with chronic dictatorship and political violence, forced many of Guatemala's talented writers, artists and musicians to work abroad. But the cultural glass is far from empty. The country's most eminent writer was Miguel Ángel Asturias (1899–1974), probably best remembered for his novel, *El Señor Presidente*. In 1967, Asturias became only the second Latin American to receive the Nobel Prize for Literature.

Former President Juan José Arévalo (1904–90) was a noted literary figure as well, and also served as ambassador to Israel.

Another internationally acclaimed literary figure was short story writer Augusto Monterroso, who went into exile to Mexico in 1944 during the Ubico dictatorship and remained there until his death in 2003 at the age of 81. He received Spain's prestigious Prince of Asturias Award, and his story *El dinosaurio (The Dinosaur)* is reputed to be the shortest story in any language. It contained seven words: *"Cuando despertó, el dinosaurio todavía estaba allí."* ("When he awoke, the dinosaur was still there.")

In contemporary popular music, a Guatemalan Latin pop singer who has won widespread international fame is the flamboyant Ricardo Arjona (b. 1964), who has sold more than 20 million albums. His 2005 album *Adentro* won two Latin Grammy Awards, for Best Latin Pop Al-

bum and Best Male Pop Vocal. Two of his albums have won Latin Billboard Awards: *A tí* in 2007 and *Quinto Piso Tour* in 2010. His duet *Fuiste tú* with fellow Guatemalan singer Gaby Moreno (b. 1981) was nominated for Record of the Year and Song of the Year in the 2012 Latin Grammys, and his album *Independiente* was nominated for Album of the Year and Best Singer-Songwriter Album.

Moreno won the Latain Grammy for Best New Artist in 2013.

Illiteracy and political violence also took its toll on the development of the Guatemalan press. Dozens of journalists, from newspaper publishers to reporters, were murdered by one side or the other during the 36-year civil war that ended in December 1996. There is only a handful of daily newspapers, all of them relatively young and all published in the capital, and even fewer magazines. The oldest, most prestigious newspaper, and the circulation leader until 2000, is *Prensa Libre*, founded in 1951. *Siglo Veintiuno* began publishing in 1991 and has become the country's second prestigious daily, winning high marks for its quality and reliability. Both papers now publish sensational, working-class tabloids as well. *Nuestro Diario*, published by *Prensa Libre*, has a circulation that was once 300,000, the greatest in Central America and a phenomenal number given the high illiteracy rate. It has since dropped to 200,000, apparently because of the country's dire economic situation.

Radio is a popular, and influential, medium in Guatemala because of the poverty and illiteracy. The three privately owned over-the-air television stations are monopolized by a Mexican, Ángel González, who is married to a Guatemalan; critics charge that his ownership, and the monopoly, are illegal, but he has managed to remain friendly with all the powers that be, no matter what their political leanings. In 2003, a new cable channel, Guatevisión, broke González's television monopoly and reaches 300,000 homes. Its independent news reporting is especially popular. More than 90% of Guatemalan homes now have cable television, exceeded in Latin America only by Argentina.

Freedom House perennially rates the Guatemalan media as only "partly free."

Guatemala has 12 institutions of higher learning, the most venerable being San Carlos University, founded in 1676.

ECONOMY: Guatemala's economy is based almost entirely on agriculture. Major cash crops include coffee, bananas, beef and cotton, with coffee the main export crop. Most farmland is controlled by huge estates—the top 2% of the population owns more than 60% of the farmland. The large Indian population lives outside

Guatemala

U.S. Vice President Joe Biden and Guatemalan President Otto Pérez Molina at the 2014 conference on migrant children held in Guatemala City.

the formal economy on small plots in the highlands.

Light industry has grown, but economic development remains handicapped by the traditional, largely feudal economic system. Also impeding development are communications problems caused by the large number of Indian dialects used in Guatemala.

Although the devastating earthquake of 1976 affected the nation's productivity by damaging the infrastructure, economic output survived largely intact. Major cash crops, produced mostly along the coastal regions, were unaffected.

Efforts to root out corruption, a national pastime in Guatemala, have shown some results. Officials who heretofore would have gotten away with enriching themselves have been going to jail. In 2004, Transparency International ranked Guatemala the third most corrupt nation in the Western Hemisphere and one of the 23 most corrupt in the world; by 2008, it had "improved" to 10th most corrupt in the region, but by 2013, it had slid back to sixth place.

Guatemala was heavily affected by Hurricane Mitch in 1998. The human toll was 268 dead, 121 missing and 734,198 adversely affected. Ninety-eight bridges were destroyed, 60% of the roads were damaged and 45–60% of the corn crop, so vital for domestic consumption, was destroyed.

The hurricane could be only partially blamed for the grave downturn in the economy in 1998–99, sparked by a drop in coffee prices. Real GDP dropped by –6.2%.

GDP showed modest but steady growth of 3.3% in 2000, 2.3% in 2001 and 2.2% in 2002, which barely recovered the ground lost in 1999 and failed to keep up with population growth. Growth remained meager until 2006, when it increased by 12.1%. Growth was 6.3% in 2007 and 4% in 2008, but as elsewhere in Latin America, the global recession led to a decline in 2009 of –0.5%. In 2010 it rose a modest 2.9%, despite damage from a tropical storm, and 3.9% in 2011. It was 3.1% in 2012, below the Latin American average, and 3.3% in 2013.

Guatemala remained the fifth poorest nation in the Western Hemisphere in 2012, and it has one of the world's greatest disparities in distribution of wealth. An estimated 56.2% of the population was below the poverty line in 2004; in 2011, it was still 54%. Official statistics put the unemployment rate in 2012 at an impossibly low 4.1%; underemployment is far higher.

As with other Central American countries, poverty has forced tens of thousands to emigrate, legally or illegally, mostly to Mexico or the United States, in search of opportunity. And as with other countries, remittances from abroad have become a mainstay of the economy. In 2012, Guatemalans living abroad sent a record $4.78 billion home to their families, an 8.4% increase from 2011. This represented 9.5% of GDP. The central bank estimated they would be $5.1 billion for 2013.

Since 2003, the dollar has circulated alongside the *quetzal* and is accepted as legal tender, which has kept inflation under control. Inflation dropped from 6.2% in 2011 to 3.8% in 2012. It rose to 4.4% in 2013.

In 2005, Guatemala ratified the Dominican Republic-Central American Free Trade Agreement with the United States. Guatemala's participation went into effect on July 1, 2006. As a result, foreign direct investment increased from $353 million in 2006 to $535 million in 2007.

THE FUTURE: Guatemalans now have elected seven presidents since the restoration of democracy in 1985. They were bitterly disillusioned with the first four and blasé about the fifth and sixth. They have never returned a ruling party to power.

It is hard to blame them. The first president was a playboy who showed little interest in improving the country. The second tried to become a dictator and remains in Panama after fleeing with $25 million from the treasury. The third succeeded in ending the civil war, but was disliked for his handling of the economy and for his elitism. The fourth was the stand-in for a former dictator accused of genocide and went into self-imposed exile in Mexico, but was extradited to stand trial for corruption. He was acquitted, but he was extradited to the U.S. and convicted on money laundering charges.

Oscar Berger came the closest to overcoming his countrymen's cynicism and establishing their faith in their democracy and their institutions, although the problem of violent, organized crime worsened on his watch. Álvaro Colom, the first candidate of the left to win the presidency, steered a moderate course and, although uninspiring, at least came across as decent and addressed such social issues as children's malnutrition. Next, desperate for someone who could tackle the country's alarming crime, they turned in 2011 to Otto Pérez Molina to try out his *mano dura* solution, which they had rejected in 2007 in favor of Colom.

Not surprisingly, Guatemalans' attitudes toward democracy and authoritarianism have followed a roller-coaster course. In the periodic *Latinobarómetro* poll published in the British newsmagazine *The Economist,* the percentage of Guatemalans who see democracy as preferable to any other form of government nosedived from 50% in 1996 to just 33% in 2003, the last year of the corrupt and repressive Portillo presidency. Under Berger, support for democracy rose to 41% in 2006, but in 2007, an election year, it dropped again to 32%, the lowest of the 18 Latin American countries in the survey.

At the same time, the percentage who believe authoritarianism is sometimes preferable to democracy rose from 21% in 1996 to 33% in 2007—the second-highest after Paraguay—and 32% in 2009. Guatemala and Paraguay were the only nations in the survey where support for authoritarianism was actually *higher* than that for democracy in 2007.

Under Colom, support for democracy jumped from 34% in 2008 to 46% in 2010, while support for authoritarianism plummeted from 30% in 2009 to 17% in 2010. Support for democracy dropped back to 36% in 2011, another election year, once again the lowest in the survey, while support for authoritarianism rose to 22%. Under Pérez Molina, support for democracy jumped to 41% in 2013, but that was still the second-lowest in Latin America. Support for authoritarianism dropped to 19% in 2013.

The 2013 *Latinobarómetro* survey also showed that only about a fourth of Guatemalans were satisfied with the way democracy works in their country, well below the 18-nation average of 40%.

After two and a half years of Pérez Molina's *mano dura* approach, Guatemala still has the world's fifth-highest homicide rate and Transparency International still ranks it as the sixth most corrupt of 20 Latin American countries. Meanwhile, economic growth is stuck in the doldrums, 3.3% in 2013, 14th place in Latin America and below the hemispheric average. Pérez Molina dropped from third-most popular leader in the Western Hemisphere with an approval rating of 69% in 2012 to ninth-most popular with 48% in 2013.

The disillusioned Guatemalans go to the polls again in September 2015. History suggests the next president will be one who has run and lost before, suggesting it could be Manuel Baldizón's turn to win, but Guatemalans have pretty much exhausted their choices by experimenting with all the parties and philosophies on the country's political spectrum. What or who will they turn to next? It could be someone on the radical fringe, the only thing that hasn't been tried. Or, they could rally around the highly respected but sacked former attorney general, Claudia Paz y Paz. All she needs is a willing party—and some good bodyguards.

The Cooperative Republic of Guyana

A diver prepares to look for diamonds in the Essequibo River

Area: 82,978 square miles.

Population: 735,554 in 2014 (est.).

Capital City: Georgetown (Pop. 134,497 (2002).

Climate: Tropically hot and humid; there are heavy rains from April to August and from November to January.

Neighboring Countries: Suriname (East); Brazil (South and West); Venezuela (West).

Official Language: English.

Other Principal Tongues: Various East Indian dialects.

Ethnic Background: East Indian (about 52%), African and mulatto (about 41%), European and mixed (about 7%).

Principal Religion: Christianity (Anglican Protestant).

Other Principal Religions: Roman Catholic Christianity, Hinduism, Islam.

Chief Commercial Products: Bauxite, sugar, rice, aluminum, shrimp, molasses, timber, rum, diamonds.

Currency: Guyana Dollar.

Gross Domestic Product: U.S. $3.02 billion in 2013, est. ($4,122 per capita, official exchange rate).

Former Colonial Status: Colony of the Dutch West India Company (1616–1796); British Colony (1796–1966).

Independence Date: May 26, 1966.

Chief of State: David Granger (b. July 15, 1945), president (since May 16, 2015).

National Flag: A yellow field bordered in green with black, red and white triangles from top to bottom along the staff.

Guyana lies on the northeast coast of South America. A narrow (5 to 10 miles wide) ribbon of swampy plain extends along the 200-mile length of the coastline. Much of this land lies below sea level and is intersected by large rivers requiring a complex system of dikes and canals to protect it from both floods and drought. Annual rainfall averages 80 to 100 inches and the country is hot the year round; the daily temperature variation of 10° F is greater than the seasonal changes. This coastal region is the country's principal agricultural area and contains some 90% of the population.

Inland from the coastal plains, the land rises to natural grassy plains with poor soils and scrub bush. It is here that gold, diamonds and bauxite are found. Further inland, heavily forested hills rise to the base of the Guiana Highlands, with elevations of over 8,000 feet on the Guyana-Venezuela border, rising out of the forests in vertical red cliffs of 2,000 feet. Rivers flowing out of the highland produce spectacular falls as they drop to the lowlands.

Guyana's principal rivers, the Corantijn on the Suriname frontier, the Berbice and the Essequibo, which flow into the Atlantic at Georgetown, are navigable for only short distances because of falls and rapids—yet they are of major importance as means of communication in the roadless interior.

HISTORY: The Dutch first settled on the banks of the Essequibo River as early as 1596, but permanent settlements were not established until the Dutch West India Company started its operations about 1620. The Dutch drained the swamps and lagoons and initiated the system of dikes and canals which make the coastal plain habitable. The Spanish and Portuguese conquerors of the lands to the west and south saw no apparent value in the Guianas and did not molest the British, French and Dutch settlers of the region.

British forces captured the Dutch settlement in 1796, and the territory now incorporated into Guyana was ceded to the British in 1814. In 1831, the colony was officially named British Guiana. The British confined themselves to plantation operations along the coast and some lumbering along the rivers. Sugar, rice and cotton were the principal crops.

Forebears of the current population arrived in two different groups. Africans came in the 17th and 18th centuries to work the plantations. With the abolition of slavery in 1830, Asian peoples migrated from India, China and southeast Asia, and they now account for the largest element in the population. During the 19th century, the British further developed the drainage system and built roads and railroads in an effort to open the interior for settlement and exploitation of the mineral wealth. However, few people moved to that area. Descendants of the Africans have tended to gather in the urban areas as mechanics and tradesmen; the Asians have remained on the farms and plantations along the coast. Despite Guyana's size, the habitable land is overcrowded and the interior is uninhabited except for a few aboriginal Indians.

Politically, the British started tutoring the people of Guyana for independence after World War II. Self-government, which was planned for 1962, had to be postponed until 1966 because of bitter racial friction between the Asian and African sectors. Cheddi Jagan, leftist leader of the Asian people, was premier during most of these four years. His open sympathy with world communism and policies directed against those of African descent led to his defeat, and Forbes Burnham, of African descent, became prime minister. A constitutional change of 1965 provided for proportional representation of the two communities in the parliament, called the National Assem-

Guyana

bly, and the election of moderate leaders in 1964 made possible the granting of independence in 1966.

Under Burnham's leadership, racial tensions eased, although scattered disturbances surfaced occasionally. Burnham was re-elected in 1968, easily defeating Jagan. During his second term, he emphasized broadening the base of the economy and a neutral foreign policy. To reduce dependence on sugar exports, he gave more attention to development of other crops.

Burnham started moving toward the political left in 1970, declaring Guyana to be a "cooperative republic" and establishing 1,200 small worker cooperatives. The government began taking over the foreign-owned bauxite mining operations in 1971. Burnham was elected in 1973 to a third term, again defeating Jagan. His People's National Congress (PNC) won 37 seats in the 57-member Assembly to 14 for Jagan's People's Progressive Party (PPP).

Burnham's main strength came from blacks who live in the cities, while Jagan dominated the East Indian vote in the rural areas. Although Asians comprised 52% of the population compared to 40% who were black, Burnham skillfully garnered his winning margins through political patronage and by espousing ideas originally proposed by his opponent.

Both Burnham and Jagan were dedicated Marxists. In 1976, the government nationalized the huge British-owned sugar industry—the last remaining major foreign investment in Guyana. Steps were taken to control the insurance, banking and rum industries, so that the state ultimately controlled 85% of the economy.

With Burnham continuing his swing to the left, he gained the unexpected endorsement of Jagan for his economic programs. This political accommodation brought an unfamiliar tranquility to Guyana, which was short-lived.

World attention of an unwanted sort was focused on Guyana in November 1978 when 913 members of a bizarre religious cult from California called the People's Temple, homesteading in the isolated, newly constructed jungle commune of Jonestown named for its messianic leader, Jim Jones, committed mass suicide after drinking a concoction laced with cyanide.

Burnham decreed a new constitution in 1980 that gave him increased control over opposition political parties and the judicial system. Three months later, he won another five-year term in office.

A 140-year-old border dispute with Venezuela erupted anew in 1982 with Venezuelan incursions into Guyana. This latest dispute had been smoldering since 1962, when Venezuela suddenly declared the 1899 accords (which the United States helped to arrange between Britain and

Venezuela) void. The dispute has quietly faded into the background since 1988, which marked state visits by the heads of the respective nations to each other. It threatens to flare up again, however, because of vast untapped oil deposits believed to lie in the disputed zone.

Burnham died of heart failure in 1985 after minor throat surgery in Moscow. Although he had made plans for his family to take over Guyana, surprisingly the party endorsed his vice president, Desmond Hoyte. Balloting in a subsequent election gave the PNC 42 of the 53 seats in the National Assembly; Jagan claimed the contest was rigged.

President Hoyte, realizing that the collapsing Soviet Union offered no economic hope for Guyana, dropped all pro-Soviet rhetoric and traditional communist pronouncements and actively sought closer ties with Western nations. He personally visited the United States to encourage investment (without results). Energetic plans were initiated to get the state out of business and to drastically cut government personnel. Credit became available from the International Monetary Fund and the United States as a result. Hoyte wisely began including talented Asians at top levels within his administration.

Cheddi and Janet Jagan

Elections in October 1992, considered the fairest ever held in Guyana, ended the PNC's 28 years in power. The outcome was totally unexpected, because in

Guyana

1991–92 Guyana's economy had hummed along well, and conditions had improved considerably. Usually in times of prosperity voters settle for what they have. But Jagan led the PPP, which entered into an alliance with four small opposition groups to form the PPP-Civic alliance, to an upset victory, gaining a working majority of 35 seats in the Assembly. This was *not* the old Cheddi Jagan. He had dropped all illusions of Marxism and was able to portray himself as a moderate progressive rather than as a radical leftist.

With the typical zeal of the newly converted, Jagan implemented sweeping economic changes. From its high of 105% in 1989, inflation was reduced to 4.5% in 1996. That same year, he signed an agreement to reduce Guyana's debt to the Paris Club of creditor nations by two thirds. The erstwhile Marxist also opened Guyana's agricultural, mining and forestry sectors to foreign investors. Foreign economists praised Guyana's example as one of the most successful adjustments from a state-controlled to a free-market system.

That legacy proved to be Jagan's requiem. In February 1997, the 78-year-old president suffered a serious heart attack. He was taken to Washington, where he died on March 6. Prime Minister Samuel Hinds was sworn in to succeed Jagan. Hinds then named Jagan's widow, Chicago-born Janet Rosenberg Jagan, as Guyana's first woman and first Jewish prime minister.

For the presidential and parliamentary elections in December 1997, Hoyte again stood as presidential candidate for the PNC, but President Hinds stood aside to allow Mrs. Jagan to be the standard-bearer of the PPP. Jagan insisted she was running reluctantly to fulfill a deathbed wish of her husband. But Hoyte accused her of nepotism and of seeking to establish a nation of "Jagana." Race also played a role in the campaign, with Hoyte supporters denouncing her as "that Caucasian old lady" and alleging that she still carried a U.S. passport. In reality, her Guyanese credentials were impeccable. She had lived there for 54 years and had lost her U.S. citizenship when she voted in British Guiana in 1947. She had served time in jail with her husband during the independence struggle in the 1950s.

In balloting that the PNC immediately denounced as rigged, Jagan unofficially received 191,332 votes to 144,359 for Hoyte. She was hastily inaugurated just four days later, publicly defying a court injunction the PNC had obtained to block the ceremony. Hinds became prime minister. Although observers from the Organization of American States pronounced the elections fair, PNC loyalists embarked on a month of street protests, some quelled by army troops and police using tear gas. To help defuse the volatile situation, a negotiating team from the

Caribbean Community (Caricom), headed by former Barbados Prime Minister Henry Forde, brokered an agreement between Mrs. Jagan and Hoyte that called for an end to street demonstrations and the institution of constitutional reforms.

The deal was a remarkable concession for Mrs. Jagan's government, because it called for new elections within three years, two years short of her constitutional mandate. Under the agreement, the constitutional reforms would be worked out within 18 months, and the elections would come within 18 months after that. Although the unrest quieted down, the personal animosity between Jagan and Hoyte lingered.

Hoyte and other critics of Jagan blamed her unreconstructed Marxism for discouraging badly needed foreign investments; her government, they noted, steadfastly refused to consider tax incentives, which drove potential investors to other, more inviting countries. Despite her life-long de-votion to Marxism, however, Jagan pragmatically but grudgingly moved to privatize some cumbersome state-controlled enterprises, including the airline and a bauxite operation. Such economic reforms paid dividends in 1999, when the World Bank and the IMF granted Guyana $256 million in relief for its $1.09 billion national debt under the Heavily Indebted Poor Countries initiative that rewards countries that implement painful but needed reforms. Guyana was only the third country to receive such debt relief under this program.

The Jagdeo Era

A chronic heart condition forced Jagan to undergo treatment in the United States, and on August 11, 1999, she resigned. Although Prime Minister Hinds was in line to succeed her, he deferred in favor of the finance minister, Bharrat Jagdeo, who, at 35, became the youngest head of state in the hemisphere. The departure of Jagan did little to defuse the tense rivalry between the PNP and the PPP, however, as Hoyte refused to recognize Jagdeo's government.

But in 2000, Jagdeo's main preoccupation was the long-simmering border disputes with both Venezuela to the west and Suriname to the east. In May, Venezuela issued a formal protest over a concession that Guyana had granted to a Texas company to construct a $100 million satellite launching facility in the disputed Essequibo region. Venezuela called the concession an "unfriendly act" and called on the Guyanese government to "review" it. The site was chosen because of its proximity to the Equator, which makes it easier to launch heavy payloads into geosynchronous orbits. The European Space Agency has a similar facility in nearby French Guiana.

Former President Bharrat Jagdeo

Then, in June 2000, Suriname ordered a Canadian oil drilling company to tow its offshore platform from what it claimed was Surinamese territorial waters in the Atlantic Ocean. Like the Essequibo dispute with Venezuela, this dispute dates to colonial times. At issue is which bank of the Corantijn River forms the boundary between the two countries. The river empties into a V-shaped gulf, and the border is extended into the Atlantic Ocean. It was in that narrow disputed corridor that Guyana had granted a drilling concession to the Toronto-based company, which reluctantly towed its expensive platform into undisputed Guyanese waters and waited for the two countries to resolve the matter diplomatically.

Each country accused the other of moving troops up to their common land border. The two governments agreed to a series of talks, first in Georgetown, then in Paramaribo, which ended in failure. Another round of talks in July also failed, and further talks were put on hold because of the campaign for the 2001 election in Guyana. Meanwhile, each country made tragicomic attempts to build up its minuscule military force. Guyana, which has no navy, purchased two aging British and three U.S. warships, while Suriname beefed up its existing navy. There was far more at stake in the 7,700 square-mile disputed zone than water and fish; it sits atop an estimated 15 billion barrels of oil which, at a time of rising oil prices, could prove a jackpot for both of these impoverished nations. On September 21, 2007, a U.N. tribunal awarded most of the disputed tract to Guyana. The Canadian firm resumed operations in 2009, but in 2012 it reported that its three exploratory wells were dry.

The general elections originally were scheduled for January 2001, but an independent electoral commission concluded they could not be held before March. In December 2000, Jagdeo, after consulting with Hoyte, set them for March 19. Because of the ugliness of the disputed 1997 elections, the 2001 contest drew an

Guyana

unusual amount of international scrutiny: 170 observers from six organizations and 45 nationalities. The election was carried out with a minimum of discord.

The results were a resounding victory for Jagdeo and his PPP, which had an electoral alliance with the small Civic Party: 209,031 votes, or 53%, to 164,074, or 42%, for Hoyte's PNC. In the 65-seat Assembly, the PPP-C won an outright majority of 35 seats, the PNC won 27 and minor parties took the remaining three. Despite the clear-cut results, which the international observers termed fair and honest, the PNC filed a formal complaint with the electoral commission, claiming thousands of opposition voters had been turned away at the polls. Meanwhile, disgruntled PNC supporters went on a rampage in Georgetown, looting shops and torching a gas station. Police used tear gas to restore order. It was politics as usual in Guyana.

Not long after the election violence, the international human rights group Amnesty International accused Guyanese police of operating death squads that had allegedly summarily executed as many as 15 criminal suspects. The government denied the allegations.

Political violence erupted once again in 2002 when pro-PNC demonstrators staged protests outside Jagdeo's office, apparently to embarrass the president, who was hosting a summit of leaders of the 14 Caribbean Community countries. Two protesters were killed and six wounded. Jagdeo called the incident an assassination attempt.

The political landscape changed dramatically with Hoyte's sudden death in December 2002. The partisan tension was evident even at his funeral, when Bagdeo magnanimously delivered a eulogy to his fallen rival but was sometimes drowned out by PNP hecklers.

PNP members of Parliament staged a boycott in 2003 that lasted several months. The stalemate between the two parties ended when the PNP elected Robert Corbin as leader of the opposition. On May 2, 2003, which Bagdeo termed an "historic" day, he and Corbin sealed a pact that they termed "Constructive Engagement," by which the PNP ended its parliamentary boycott and Bagdeo appointed a nine-member Ethnic Relations Commission with powers to investigate and punish incidents of racial injustice. It was not to last, however.

In March 2004, the PNP staged a mass demonstration to investigate the mysterious killings of 40 black criminals by what was believed to be a death squad called the Phantom Gang, allegedly headed by Home Affairs Minister Ronald Gajraj. Supposedly, firearms and telephone records were traced to Gajraj's office. The United States and Canada, without explanation, revoked his visas. Gajraj denied the allega-

President David Granger

tions and offered to step aside. Bagdeo at first declined his offer. Corbin, meanwhile, withdrew from the Constructive Engagement agreement and resumed the PNP's boycott of the National Assembly.

Bagdeo appointed an investigative commission, but Corbin, still dissatisfied, refused to cooperate with it or to abide by its results. The situation became more volatile in June 2004, when George Bacchus, an Afro-Guyanese rancher who had made the initial accusation of a death squad on national television, was shot to death at his home by unknown assailants. Bacchus was about to testify in the trial of two men accused of killing Bacchus' brother. Bacchus had claimed that his brother was slain by death-squad members who mistook his brother for him. Meanwhile, the magistrate hearing the case resigned because of death threats. The PNP accused the government of complicity in Bacchus' death.

Gajraj eventually stepped down pending the outcome of the commission's inquiry. In 2005, the commission formally exonerated Gajraj of any direct complicity in the death squads, although it acknowledged he had an "unhealthy" relationship with organized crime figures and had illegally interfered with firearms licenses. He was reinstated as home affairs minister, which sparked complaints from the U.S. State Department, the European Union and the Guyana Human Rights Association.

The latest killing to shock the country was that of Bagdeo's agriculture minister, Satyadeo Sawh, in April 2006. Several gunmen burst into Sawh's home and killed him, his brother and sister and a security guard. It was not clear whether it was a common robbery or a political assassination.

Guyana achieved some international prestige in 2006 when it assumed chairmanship of the 20-member Rio Group.

After the violence of 2001, the nation braced itself for presidential-parliamentary elections of August 28, 2006. A new element was a third force, the Alliance for Change, which apparently expected to become a power broker between the two major parties. It did well, but not well enough to become a kingmaker. The results:

PPP/C	183,867	54.6%	36 seats
PNC	114,608	34.0%	21 seats
Alliance	28,366	8.4%	5 seats
Others	9,514	8%	2 seats

Lesser parties took the remaining two seats. The turnout was 70%, high by U.S. and Latin American standards, but a disappointing drop from the 92% in 2001. Contrary to expectations, the 2006 election was relatively peaceful.

Former President Janet Jagan died on March 28, 2009.

The Elections of 2011

In 2011, Jagdeo decided not to seek another term as president, and in April the PPP Central Committee unanimously nominated Donald Ramotar, the party's general secretary since 1997, as its presidential candidate. The PNC nominated retired Brigadier General David A. Granger, a former commander of the Guyana Defense Force, who turned 66 in July. He is also founder and managing editor of the *Guyana Review* newsmagazine. The PNC teamed up with another group, the Partnership for National Unity, to form the APNU.

The elections were postponed from August 12 to November 28. Voters returned the PPP to power for its fifth straight term, but for the first time it lost its parliamentary majority, dropping from 36 to 32 seats out of 65. The PNC/PNU alliance won 26. The Alliance for Change now holds the balance of power with seven seats. Two other parties hold one seat each. The APNU alleged vote fraud, which the government did not allay by delaying the final results until November 30. Hundreds of Granger supporters demonstrated outside the National Assembly. It looked like there might be a repeat of the post-electoral violence of 2001, but the ambassadors from the United States, Canada and the EU called upon the APNU to accept the results, and cooler heads prevailed.

Ramotar, a 61-year-old economist educated in Guyana, was sworn in on December 3, 2011. For three and a half years he has tried to govern by consensus with the opposition parties, which hold a one-seat majority between them. Animosities remain high.

CULTURE: Guyana is a unique cultural cross-breeding of its British colonial past, the African influence of escaped or freed slaves and the more recent influence of im-

Guyana

migrants from India, whose descendants now outnumber those of African descent and have become the dominant political force. Sadly, ethnic tension is part of the cultural fabric, and threatens to tear it.

Guyana's best-known cultural figure is writer Edward Ricardo (E.R.) Braithwaite (b. 1912), who was born in British Guiana, educated at City College in New York and at the Universities of Cambridge and London. He became an engineer but drifted into teaching, social work and writing. His autobiographical 1959 novel *To Sir, With Love* was made into a motion picture in 1967, starring Sidney Poitier as Braithwaite. His other novels include *Paid Servant* in 1962, *Choice of Straws* in 1965 and *Reluctant Neighbours* in 1972. He has spent much of his career abroad as a Guyanese diplomat, including ambassador to the United Nations, as an educational consultant for UNESCO and as a visiting professor in the United States. He observed his 100th birthday in June 2012, and President Donald Ramotar presented him with the Cacique Crown of Honour that August.

Another noted expatriate is the novelist, short story writer and actress Pauline Melville (b. 1948), daughter of a Guyanese father and British mother. She has won international awards for her novel *The Ventriloquist's Tale* (1997) and her collection of short stories, *Shape-Shifter* (1990). She also works as an actress in Britain.

Guyanese music, like its politics, is a reflection of its African and Asian-Indian roots. Shanto is a hybrid of calypso and an Afro-Caribbean sound called mento, both imported from Jamaica. Guyanese dance bands were popular abroad long before the country gained independence.

The country's only major institution of higher learning is the University of Guyana, established in 1963, three years before independence, by then-Premier Cheddi Jagan on the grounds of the colonial-era Queens College.

ECONOMY: Despite large mineral and forest resources, Guyana's economy is agricultural and severely limited to foreign markets. Much of the nation's sparsely settled but potentially rich interior is also claimed by Venezuela. Efforts to populate this inhospitable region have been unsuccessful.

Although the ambitious Burnham sought to convert Guyana into a Marxist state, change was initially gradual in an attempt to avoid the disruptions that occurred in Cuba and in Chile. But after 1982, all curbs in the march toward socialism disappeared. The result was disastrous. The purchasing power of the average citizen declined by 40% compared to 1976 figures.

The state-owned bauxite operation, called *Guybau*, showed a profit largely

because of high world prices, which have since declined. Before the romance with communism, farm output was constant; rice and sugar exports initially rose after independence. In 1977, Guyana applied for formal association with *Comecon*, the communist bloc's common market. Yet, Guyana also became a member of the Inter-American Development Bank, a Washington-based organization of the OAS.

Strikes in 1983 and 1984 resulted in a sharp decline in bauxite production. Guyana's economic situation deteriorated dreadfully in 1984–86. Negotiations with the International Monetary Fund were suspended and the IMF declared Guyana ineligible for further assistance. There initially was no improvement under Hoyte, who inherited an economy that had descended to primitive agriculture. Eventually, the Hoyte administration brought some modest prosperity. Although strict conditions imposed by the IMF were resented, they were successful.

Throughout most of the 1990s, Guyana experienced extraordinary GDP growth averaging 7% a year. Unlike many of its Latin American neighbors that were cursed by dependence on one export commodity, Guyana is blessed with diversified exports, including bauxite (aluminum ore), gold, timber, sugar, shrimp and rice. But the robust growth halted abruptly in 1998, when the Asian financial crisis and *El Niño* both hit Guyana. World market prices for timber, gold, bauxite and sugar all fell; timber exports alone dropped 35% because of the crisis in Asia, the major consumer of Guyanese wood. Only rice exports showed an increase. As a result, GDP growth for 1998 declined by 1.3% and grew only .3% in 1999 and another .5% in 2000, 2001 and 2002.

It was still a sluggish 1.9% in 2004, but in 2006 and 2007 it was 6.3%, thanks largely to favorable prices for bauxite, rice and sugar. It slowed to 4% in 2008. Because of the global recession, growth was negative for 2009, –1.7%. It grew by 4.4% in 2010, 5.44% in 2011, 3.7% in 2012. In 2013 it jumped by 5.3%, the fourth-highest in the hemisphere.

According to the World Bank, 89% of college-educated Guyanese lived and worked abroad in 2009, the highest brain drain in the entire world. Net population actually declined by 2,800 between 2010 and 2011 and by another 7,400 between 2011 and 2013. Consequently, remittances from abroad have become a vital economic ingredient, mushrooming from $27 million in 2000 to $266 million in 2009 and $374 million in 2010. They were about $400 million in both 2011 and 2012, or 17% of GDP.

For the Guyanese who remain, 35% lived below them poverty line in 2006, the most recent year available.

In 2004, Guyana had the dubious distinction of having a public debt that was 200% of GDP, the highest in the entire world. Thus, when the so-called Paris Club of the wealthiest creditor nations met in 2005 to discuss debt forgiveness, Guyana was one of the 18 countries—four of them in the Western Hemisphere—that qualified. In 2006 and 2007, the World Bank, Inter-American Development Bank and Japan forgave a total of $700 million in debt. Nonetheless, in 2013 public debt was still 59.9% of GDP, ranking 49th in the world.

Gold has been mined in Guyana since the late 19th century and has become an increasingly vital pillar of the economy, especially since the spike in international gold prices to more than $1,600 an ounce. The Natural Resources and Environment Ministry reported that gold production in 2011 was 363,083 ounces, 14% above predictions, and gold accounted for a fourth of the value of Guyana's exports in 2011. Output for 2012 was a record 460,000 ounces, worth approximately $750 million. The Guyana Gold and Diamond Miners Association was predicting 500,000 ounces for 2013. Gold mining remains the principal activity at Port Kaituma. Exploration for gold in the dense Amazon rainforest raised concerns among environmentalists, so the government stopped granting new permits in July 2012. The Canadian company Guyana Goldfields signed a $1 billion contract in 2011 to develop the Aurora Mines. It announced it hopes to pour its first gold bar in 2015.

Diamond production has tapered off, from 341,000 carats in 2006 to 144,000 in 2010. About half come from the Mazaruni River and its tributaries. Some is by commercial mining operations, but amateur prospecting is a cottage industry.

THE FUTURE: Any future for Guyana, one of the seven poorest countries in the hemisphere in 2013, depends on the PPP and PNC getting their acts together and defusing the country's long-simmering racial tension between blacks and Asians. The potential for an oil boom is there if the suspected vast deposits off the coast can be tapped—and assuming it doesn't enhance the country's already notorious corruption. Transparency International rated it the fifth most corrupt country in the hemisphere the last three years.

General elections in May 2015 pitted the incumbent PPP/C party against a new coalition (formed in in February specifically for the election) of the APNU and the AFC (Alliance for Change). The APNU/AFC squeaked out a victory by only 1 seat, 33 to 32, but this slim majority gave them the presidency. Former PNC candidate, retired General David Granger, was inaugurated on May 16, 2015.

The Republic of Haiti

Emperor Henri Christophe's *La Citadelle*, the mountaintop fortress in the north that took 13 years and the labor of 200,000 men to build.

Area: 10,711 square miles.

Population: 9,996,731 (2014 est.).

Capital City: Port-au-Prince (705,000 in 2003).

Climate: Tropical, moderate at higher elevations; rainy season from May to December.

Neighboring Countries: Haiti occupies the western third of Hispañola, the second-largest of the Greater-Antilles; the Dominican Republic occupies the eastern two thirds of the island.

Official Languages: French and Creole, a mixture of French and African origin spoken by almost all Haitians.

Other Principal Tongues: Creole, a dialect of French and African origin spoken by a majority of the rural Haitians.

Ethnic Background: African Negro (90%), mixed African and European (10%).

Principal Religion: Officially Roman Catholic Christianity, but a majority of Haitians practice *voodoo*, a variety of animism similar to African native religions, but with a greater emphasis on mysticism.

Chief Commercial Products: Coffee, light industrial products, sisal, sugar and textiles.

Currency: Gourde.

Gross Domestic Product: U.S. $8.287 billion in 2013 ($829 per capita, official exchange rate).

Former Colonial Status: Spanish Colony (1492–1697); French Colony (1697–1804).

Independence Date: January 1, 1804.

Chief of State: Michel Joseph Martelly (b. February 12, 1961), president (since May 14, 2011).

National Flag: Blue and red vertical stripes, coat of arms on white square in center.

The Haitian western one third of the island of Hispaniola is covered by tropically green mountains rising to heights of 9,000 feet. The narrow coastal plains and river valleys, one fifth of the total territory of the nation, are arable, but irrigation is necessary in many of the fields. Of these areas, the Artibonne River valley and the north coastal plains are most suited to agriculture. The mountains that divide Haiti and the Dominican Republic prevent the moisture-laden trade winds from reaching Haiti, thus its lands are generally drier than those of its neighbor.

HISTORY: Haiti was discovered by Columbus in 1492 and remained under Spanish control for the following 200 years. Because of the limited number of settlers, the Spanish exploited the eastern part of Hispaniola, neglecting the western portion, which became a popular base for French-speaking pirates. The western portion of the island was ceded to France in 1697, and ultimately became one of that country's most profitable colonies. African slaves had been brought in by the Spanish and their numbers increased during French rule. The slaves obtained their freedom during the period of the French Revolution in a confusion of slave rebellions and civil wars that involved blacks, mulattos, French, Spanish and English on the island of Hispaniola.

Toussaint L'Ouverture, a former slave, rose rapidly to the rank of general during this period. He fought with the Spanish against the French, later joined the French against the English, and ultimately forced them from the island. Napoleon sent a large force under his brother-in-law, General Victor-Emmanuel Leclerc, which captured L'Ouverture and attempted to restore slavery. Independence was finally achieved in 1804 after a dozen years of bitter bloodshed when the French forces were defeated and expelled by the Haitians.

General Jean Jacques Dessalines, commander of the black army, was named

Haiti

governor-general for life. An ex-slave, illiterate, brutal and arrogant, he lacked the qualifications for ruling his newborn nation and was unable to secure aides capable of compensating for his ignorance. The few whites left in Haiti were slaughtered by Dessalines' order—the war had been fought not only to obtain freedom, but also to destroy anything that would remind the blacks of serfdom and forced labor.

Drafting a constitution abolishing slavery, prohibiting land ownership by whites and making the term *Negro* synonymous with Haitian, Dessalines was enthroned as Emperor Jacques I. By use of conscripted labor and enforced discipline, he made some progress in restoring order and in rebuilding the economy until he was assassinated in 1806 by his two trusted military commanders, Henri Christophe and Alexandre Pétion. Haiti then split into two states—the north ruled from Cap-Haitien by Henri Christophe and the south ruled as a republic by Alexandre Pétion. Christophe styled himself emperor; he constructed a massive castle and established an elaborate circle of courtiers, dukes, duchesses and barons who were former slaves. In contrast, Pétion governed the south as an independent republic, and his rule was relatively moderate and progressive. He was at war with Henri Christophe from 1811–18, when the latter, faced with rebellion caused by his cruelty, shot himself with a silver bullet.

Haiti was reunited between 1818 and 1820 by Jean Pierre Boyer, a French-educated mulatto who was able to dominate the entire island by 1822. Initially of moderate outlook, the declining economy and disruption of society induced Boyer to resort to harsh tactics to till the land and restore governmental authority. When he was overthrown in 1844, the Spanish-speaking eastern portion of the island regained its independence and Haiti again fell into the hands of illiterate leaders.

The period from 1843 to 1915 was one of disorder, tyranny and bloodshed under 22 dictators. It was a period of economic and social deterioration. The only occupants of the presidential palace who accomplished any beneficial acts were Fabre Geffrard (1859–67), who cut the army in half, built a few schools and signed a concordat with the Vatican to revitalize the church. Lysius Salomon (1879–88) created a national bank, built rural schools and imported French school teachers. The last, Florvil Hyppolite (1889–96), built bridges, docks and public buildings and opened telephone and telegraph services.

U.S. Intervention, 1915–34

The country degenerated into anarchy in 1908, culminating in the killing and dis-

memberment of President Guillaume Sam by an angry mob on July 28, 1915. Sailors and Marines on a U.S. naval vessel offshore promptly seized Port-au-Prince to restore order. The occupation was to last for 19 years under five U.S. presidents of both parties, during which the military high commissioner, Marine Brigadier General John H. Russell, oversaw the successive "elections" of puppet presidents. The president from 1922–30 was Louis Borno, who collaborated so well with Russell that a U.S. financial adviser to Haiti called the arrangement a "joint dictatorship." The United States also imposed a new constitution on Haiti in 1918, written by the assistant secretary of the Navy—Franklin Delano Roosevelt. FDR later was to boast of its authorship. Under Russell's tutelage, there was no freedom of the press or other basic civil liberties. Several newspaper editors, in fact, were jailed in the name of establishing democracy, something that Thomas Jefferson would have frowned upon.

In 1919, the *cacos*, or peasants, under the leadership of the charismatic Charlemagne Peralte, revolted against U.S. rule. In an operation that has become part of Marine Corps folklore, Major Smedley Butler disguised himself, infiltrated Peralte's camp,

killed him with his revolver and forced the other *cacos* to flee. The revolt was crushed, with more than 3,000 Haitians killed in the process.

On the positive side, the Marines greatly improved Haiti's infrastructure. From 1919–22 they built 365 miles of roads and improved 200 miles of existing road. Irrigation systems were repaired and experimental farms set up. The Marines also established the *Garde d'Haiti*, a constabulary that had American officers, to maintain law and order. This force, however, later would become little more than the personal goon squad for a succession of dictators. Moreover, the Americans made no effort to diversify the coffee-dependent economy or to train schoolteachers, with the result that Haiti remained the poorest and least literate nation of the Americas.

When a strike led to another outbreak of violence in 1929 that the Marines ruthlessly crushed, President Herbert Hoover dispatched an investigative commission to inspect the U.S. role in Haiti. In its report, the commission concluded: "The failure of the occupation to understand the social problems of Haiti, its brusque attempt to plant democracy there by drill and harrow, its determination to set up a middle class—however wise and necessary it may seem to Americans—all these explain why, in part, the high hopes of our good works in this land have not been realized."

A new legislative assembly was elected in October 1930, General Russell resigned on November 1, and legislators chose an opposition newspaper editor, Stenio Vincent, as president. Haitians reassumed control of key public agencies a year later. On August 15, 1934, President Roosevelt, who had once boasted of writing Haiti's consti-

Dr. Francois "Papa Doc" Duvalier

tution, withdrew the Marines. It would be 60 years, one month and four days before the next U.S. military intervention.

The departure of the U.S. Marines in 1934 was hailed as Haiti's second emancipation. Haitian politicians and military officers were restored to their former privileges, and the following three decades revealed that Haiti had profited little from U.S. military rule. The Marines had sought to place the educated mulatto minority in power, but the *Garde d'Haiti,* consisting principally of mulattos, emerged as the dominant force.

The Duvalier Era

The election of Dr. Francois "Papa Doc" Duvalier as president in 1957 began a new era of dictatorial rule. A devoted voodoo practitioner, Duvalier ruled Haiti by a combination of superstition and brutality. He created an incredibly cruel and imaginative force known as the *Tonton Macoutes* (rough translation: "Uncle's Boogeymen"), which had the capability of dispensing instant justice (usually death or unbelievable torture). This force became an all-pervasive instrument of Haiti's "government."

The single most significant accomplishment of Duvalier's administration was his durability and longevity—he died apparently of natural causes in April 1971. Before his death, Duvalier named his portly, naïve, childish, fun-loving son, Jean-Claude ("Baby Doc") as Haiti's next president for life. Assuming a serious attitude not considered possible, the youthful ruler immediately began reshaping Haiti's horror-filled image with a semblance of political stability and programmed economic growth under the tutelage of his older sister Simone and his mother. New foreign investments created more than 80,000 low-paying jobs.

Although Haiti received more per capita foreign aid than any other Western Hemi-

sphere nation, most benefits were diluted by corruption. Half of all foreign loans and grants were funneled into secret accounts controlled by government leaders. The nation's stagnant economy prompted thousands to flee—often in unsafe boats—to the Bahamas and the United States in search of work. At one time, one out of every 10 persons in the Bahamas was said to be an illegal alien from Haiti.

To improve its international image, Haiti permitted limited free elections in 1979. The so-called "liberalization program" was short-lived; in November 1980 opposition political and intellectual leaders were arrested and deported in the worst government purge since 1963. Although it was not initially apparent to the outside world, "Baby Doc" apparently had become estranged from his mother and "divorced" his sister as the "first lady" of Haiti in favor of a light-skinned charmer, Michèle Bennett. Her father, on the verge of bankruptcy, quickly became the coffee export baron on Haiti and the family attached itself firmly to the inner circles of government. Michèle tried to emulate the late Evita Perón of Argentina.

To outward appearances, Michèle Duvalier was the soul of charity and kindness, opening orphanages, providing relief for the poor and tirelessly working against injustice. But the palace life she created was another story. Luxuries piled upon luxuries and she "ran" Jean-Claude with an iron fist. Worst of all, she had television sets placed in every small town and settlement to show all of her charitable works and, foolishly, to broadcast the festivities from the marble palace. Her father and family graduated from the edge of bankruptcy to rich, elite exporters and businessmen. Goose liver paté contrasted sharply with garbage, and anger started to smolder.

The Revolt of 1986

Perhaps the straw that broke Haiti's back occurred when Michèle went on a Paris shopping spree that cost more than $1 million. Among the items purchased in profusion were fur coats to be given as gifts to close friends. When this appeared on Haitian television, it proved the beginning of the end.

The final insult came with the arrival of 1,200 money-laden passengers for the inauguration of a much-celebrated (and criticized) new tourist haven on the island of Labadie at a resort developed under questionable financial circumstances. They were not to be exposed to Haiti's "backward" atmosphere, but rather, to luxury.

Rioting erupted in January 1986. Duvalier made tentative efforts to disband the *Tonton Macoutes* and undertook other reforms—all too late. The rioting continued

Jean-Claude ("Baby Doc") Duvalier

and intensified. Amid the chaos, "Baby Doc" and his wife were flown out of Haiti in a U.S. plane for France in February; no other country would receive him. He lived opulently, returning to Haiti in 2010. He is facing charges of human rights violations.

Meanwhile, "Papa Doc's" tomb was raided (his body wasn't there) and others were broken open; skulls were paraded through the streets. The Bennett family was all but wiped out. Shopkeepers closed their shops, frozen with fear, in spite of governmental threats. Among the prime movers behind the revolt were the "liberation theology" priests of the Roman Catholic Church who from the pulpit regularly condemned the government. One of them was a charismatic firebrand named Jean-Bertrand Aristide.

A military regime under General Henri Namphy emerged. The Duvaliers' assets in various parts of the world, including the United States, France and Switzerland, were frozen. However, enough remained untouched to apparently enable "Baby Doc" to live in comfort for life.

The ouster of Duvalier did not end the violence. Mobs sought out the members of the *Tonton Macoutes* and brutally murdered them. There were riots when the head of that organization was allowed to leave for Brazil instead of facing trial.

After a new constitution was adopted in 1987, there followed a procession of presidents averaging eight months in office before being overthrown. They all had initial approval of the military and the elite Haitians, which quickly soured as they tried to expand the bases of their popularity. The last one in early 1990 took the

Haiti

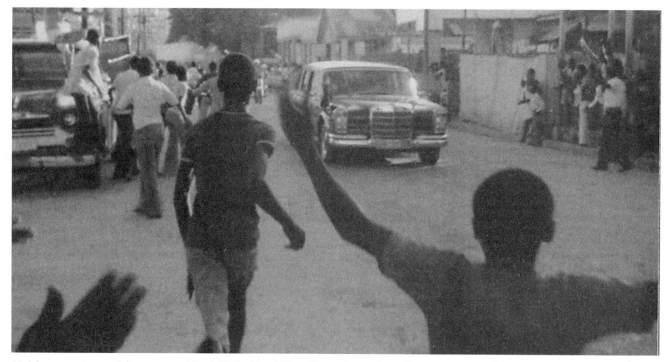

Haitians greet car of former president "Baby Doc" Duvalier, who is throwing money out of the car windows

Photo by Susan L. Thompson

offensive: he had all significant rivals for power seized and beaten, then exiled to Florida. He also went there after the U.S. ambassador persuaded him that there was no choice—either he left or Haiti faced unbridled violence.

Elections were again attempted in late 1990. Jean-Bertrand Aristide, the "liberation theology" priest who had been thundering anti-Duvalier, anti-elite rhetoric from his pulpit (and was defrocked by the Catholic Church for meddling in politics), was elected president by a majority of 70%, despite the opposition of the army, the elite, the Catholic Church and what was left of the *Tonton Macoutes*. But he was revered by the poor. The army commander was able to coerce his men into inaction and silence to ensure free elections.

Lacking military support, President Aristide imported 60 Swiss officers to train a new palace guard loyal to him. Fearing loss of power, the military ousted him on September 30, 1991, and only the intervention of the United States, Canada, France and Venezuela prevented his assassination. He went initially to Venezuela, later entering the United States in 1992, where he spent large sums of money from frozen Haitian assets without accounting for them. General Raoul Cedras became chief of state.

French, EU and U.S. aid to Haiti was immediately suspended and an uneven trade embargo was imposed. The poor of the island became even more desperate,

and began leaving by home-made boats for Florida and Guantanamo Bay, Cuba. The U.S. Coast Guard blocked them, even outside U.S. coastal limits.

Of the Haitians who made it to the United States or Guantanamo, only about 11% were admitted as political refugees. Incredibly poor and uneducated, many of them infected with AIDS and other diseases, they were considered undesirables. Meanwhile, the Black Caucus of the U.S. Congress demanded that Aristide be returned and installed in office by U.S. troops, if necessary.

One of the cruelest hoaxes occurred during the U.S. presidential campaign of 1992. Democratic candidate Bill Clinton promised that, if elected, he would immediately admit refugee Haitians to the United States without limit. When he was elected, countless numbers of Haitians began building boats, using any materials they could find, legally or illegally, awaiting Clinton's inaugural so they could set sail from misery to hope. Literally within hours of taking the oath of office, Clinton decided that it was "wise" to continue the policies of the defeated Bush.

A wedding near Port-au-Prince

234

Haiti

Panoramic view of Port-au-Prince

The question of Haiti appeared to have been solved in mid-1993 when an agreement was signed in New York by Aristide, Cedras and the head of the national police that Aristide would return by October 31. Training officers for the Haitian police appeared at Port-au-Prince aboard U.S. and Canadian vessels, but were prevented from landing by the Haitian military. Cedras did not abide by the agreement.

When President Clinton received black support in Congress on the NAFTA treaty and other measures, he was called upon to respond with more energetic action to remove the military from power in Haiti and to reinstall Aristide. On the refugee problem, the United Nations adopted directives that they be received by all nations (actually meaning the United States).

U.S. Intervention, 1994

Pressures for action mounted and there was increased talk from Clinton threatening invasion. The U.N. Security Council authorized intervention in July 1994. Troops were readied in September, and in a last-ditch effort, Clinton dispatched former President Jimmy Carter, Senator Sam Nunn and retired General Colin Powell to Haiti. They persuaded the military leadership to stand down and leave Haiti, which they did within days.

A force overwhelmingly of U.S. troops entered the island peacefully on September 19 and took up a triple role: janitors, policemen and, later, presidential guard after Aristide returned to the island. Little in their combat training prepared them for such roles.

Both before and after his return on October 15, Aristide modified his former radical positions to become acceptable to the elite. He undertook a disarmament program, but for every weapon obtained, at least 10 were hidden by their owners. Almost 4,000 Haitian refugees were repatriated from Guantanamo Bay. The army, seen as an obstacle to democracy, was disbanded. That move would backfire on Aristide a decade later.

Aristide appointed Smarck Michel as prime minister; together they devised plans for election of a new Parliament in 1995. Plans to withdraw U.S. forces by the fall of 1995 proved impossible. Aristide's supporters started behaving as goons, not as saviors of their nation. A well-known opponent of Aristide was gunned down in 1995, the first of many murders of anti-Aristide Haitians; his personal involvement was suspected.

The Préval Presidency

Aristide floated the idea of canceling presidential elections scheduled for the fall of 1995 so he could remain in office—a proposition that even liberals in the U.S. Congress shrank from in horror. René Préval won in an election with a light turnout; although Aristide hated him, he embraced him at his inauguration in February 1996.

Préval undertook the unenviable task of trying to govern a country still beset by economic, political and social conditions that have made it the basket case of the Western Hemisphere. As if he didn't have problems enough, he inherited a palace guard that was loyal to Aristide and that he did not trust. The United States dispatched a special security team to guard him.

Like so many other recent Latin American leaders, Préval faced economic reality and launched a program aimed at privatizing the inefficient state-owned enterprises. He had the added incentive of meeting requirements of the International Monetary Fund to qualify for additional loans, which accounted for 60 percent of Haiti's budget. Part of the painful austerity program was the elimination of 7,000 of 43,000 public employees. As usually happens, the austerity measures sparked a series of protests in 1997. Préval also undertook an effort to distribute parcels of land to peasants, but the tracts were so tiny—1.2 acres—that they were not commercially viable, and while he won meager appreciation from the recipients of the parcels, he was condemned by those who were left out.

A wave of political violence claimed about 50 lives in early 1997. Préval attributed the killings to remnants of the *Tonton Macoutes*.

The democratic process came close to total breakdown following Senate elections in 1997. Aristide had established an offshoot of his *Lavalas* (Avalanche) Political Organization, or *OPL*, called the *Fanmi* (Family) *Lavalas*, as a vehicle for his re-election in 2000. The Aristide faction was accused of rigging the election, which would have given *Fanmi* a majority in the Senate. Préval indefinitely postponed the runoff elections. Prime Minister Rosny Smarth resigned to protest Aristide's power play. The Chamber of Deputies, in which the *OPL* was the largest bloc with 33, rejected Préval's nominee to succeed him.

Préval then nominated Hervé Denis, an economist committed to privatization of nine state-owned companies. The Chamber voted 34–33 to confirm Denis, but abstentions left him short of a majority. Préval stubbornly re-nominated Denis in 1998, and the *OPL* just as stubbornly vowed not to confirm any nominee until the president dismissed the nine members of the electoral council and had the election results revised. Préval refused, and while this petty contest of wills continued, as much as $300 million in foreign aid packages was tied up because there was no one to negotiate them. It also frightened away foreign investors.

U.S. Secretary of State Madeleine Albright visited Haiti and chided both sides for their failure to resolve the impasse. It seemed the logjam was broken when the Chamber confirmed Denis. But the nomination was blocked in the Senate when it received approval by eight of the 16 senators—not an absolute majority.

While this crisis unfolded, the three-year mandate of the U.N. peacekeeping force, composed of Canadians and Pakistanis, expired on November 30, 1997;

Haiti

the foreign troops withdrew the next day. It was the worst possible timing. Political violence and common street crime engulfed the country, while drug traffickers swarmed into Haiti like cockroaches into a dark, filthy kitchen. Not only was the 5,200-member police force established under U.S. and U.N. auspices incapable of maintaining order, but it killed about 100 people, half of them without apparent justification. Two of Préval's bodyguards and two of his chauffeurs were gunned down (even his dog was stabbed to death), and he asked the United Nations to protect the presidential palace. Two days before the peacekeeping force left, the U.N. Security Council voted to establish a 290-member civilian police force with a one-year mandate.

With the Denis nomination twice rebuffed, Préval nominated his minister of education, Jacques Edouard Alexis. For months, Parliament took no action, and the crisis rumbled on. The Senate, facing the imminent expiration of the terms of eight of its remaining 16 elected members, voted in 1998 to extend those terms until November 1999, apparently expecting new elections before then. It was an act of dubious constitutionality, and the Chamber of Deputies took no similar action to extend its own expiring mandate.

It suddenly seemed the logjam would be broken when, in December 1999, the Senate unexpectedly confirmed Alexis. The Chamber followed suit. The country—as well as the United Nations and the U.S. government—breathed a collective sigh of relief.

Alas, Préval ignored his own deadline and failed to appoint the electoral council. The crisis flared anew on January 11, 1999, the date of the expiration of parliamentary mandates. Declaring that in the absence of new elections there was no longer a parliamentary quorum, Préval announced he would rule by decree. The reaction was immediate and violent, as pro-*OPL* demonstrators, denouncing the move as a ploy by Préval to assume dictatorial powers, took to the streets. So did pro-Préval demonstrators, who blockaded local municipal councils on the pretext that their terms, too, had expired.

Alexis named a cabinet in the absence of Parliament. Once again, Préval set a deadline of February 2, 2000, to name a new electoral council that would call new elections, and once again he let his own deadline pass. Denying he was setting himself up as Haiti's latest dictator, he insisted, "It is democracy we are building."

The Electoral Farces of 2000

If so, the architect and carpenters should have been fired. Three times in 1999 and

2000, the Provisional Electoral Council (*CEP*) set parliamentary election dates only to postpone them. The *CEP* set new dates for the first and second rounds, but Préval disapproved those dates.

The U.S. and the E.U. chided Préval that $500 million in desperately needed aid was contingent upon his calling the long-overdue parliamentary elections. The Haitian people responded with mass demonstrations in March 2000 that left four people dead.

The *CEP* and Préval agreed on a fourth date: May 21, with runoffs on June 25, later moved to July 8. At stake were 19 of the 27 Senate seats and all 83 members of the Chamber of Deputies, plus about 7,500 local offices. During the six-week campaign, at least 15 candidates or campaign workers were murdered, some hacked to death with machetes in traditional fashion.

Another casualty was Jean Dominique, the country's most prominent radio commentator, gunned down in April 2000 as he arrived at work. Dominique had made enemies on both the far right and the far left. Six men believed to be the triggermen were arrested and eventually indicted two years later, but the investigation into who ordered Dominique's death was stymied by intimidation, including the murders of two witnesses. It remains unsolved more than a decade later, though theories abound.

Six opposition groups hastily formed an alliance in a last-ditch effort to prevent a predicted landslide by Aristide's *Lavalas* movement. The election was marred by poor organization and outright manipulation. Many polling places opened late, and at others, the ballots were still being printed! A policeman and a gunman were killed at a polling place, and a local opposition candidate was stoned to death. OAS observers reported cases of fraud and intimidation by pro-Aristide militants, which the U.N.-trained police force seemed uninterested in stopping.

When polls closed, armed goons, presumably from *Lavalas,* stormed several polling places and made off with the ballot boxes. Marked ballots, representing about 10% of those cast, were found lying in the street; workers swept up about 90% of them. It was Haitian "democracy" under construction.

The OAS official in charge of the 200 international observers, with considerable understatement, termed the irregularities "most unfortunate." Former U.S. President Carter, whose Atlanta-based Carter Center also observed the election, said, "It is obvious to me that the election in Haiti was seriously flawed." About the only thing to cheer was the record voter turnout: An estimated 60% of the 4 million eligible voters—a far cry from the 5%

Former President Jean-Bertrand Aristide

who voted in the annulled 1997 elections. Unfortunately, not all their votes were counted.

According to the "results" released by the *CEP* days later, *Lavalas* won 16 of the 19 Senate seats and 23 deputy seats without a runoff. But on June 2, the deputy chief of the OAS observation mission reported that the *CEP* had miscalculated the final percentages for the Senate by counting only the votes for the top four candidates for each seat. Eliminating the votes for lesser candidates gave several *Lavalas* candidates outright majorities they did not actually have. The opposition and the observers claimed that 10 "winning" *Lavalas* Senate candidates should have faced a runoff. When the official results were finally announced, *Lavalas* held all but one of the 27 Senate seats and more than 80% of the seats in the Chamber of Deputies; it also controlled almost all the municipal governments.

This creative tabulating brought international demands, including from U.N. Secretary-General Kofi Annan, that the *CEP* count the votes properly. But the government refused to budge. Two weeks before the runoffs, the president of the *CEP* fled the country, saying government officials had threatened him with death if he did not certify the flawed results. He had refused. Aristide supporters took to the streets to burn tires and to demand that the government release the results. It did—the flawed ones.

This farce continued into the presidential election of November 26, 2000, which the major opposition parties boycotted to protest the parliamentary elections. (In a peripheral farce, two days before the election Parliament finally confirmed Alexis in the office he had held for 20 months.)

Aristide, who almost certainly would have won anyway, was thus opposed only by six unknown candidates, and even they did not campaign because of threats. In the usual pre-election violence, nine bombings killed two people and injured at least 16. The U.S., Canada and the E.U. withdrew their observers rather than participate in a sham. In the balloting, Aristide predictably received 92% of the vote. The government declared the turnout had been 60.5%, but more objective assessments put it at between 15% and 20%, depriving Aristide of a meaningful mandate.

Three weeks later, 15 opposition parties, calling themselves the Democratic Convergence, declared they would form an "alternative government" and even urged *Lavalas* to join them. Aristide brushed aside their call, and he was sworn in on February 7, 2001. The international community largely snubbed the inauguration.

Governing a Cauldron

The opposition rebuffed Aristide's invitation to join his government, saying his election was illegitimate, and demanded new elections. A demonstration at the local OAS headquarters, which had sought to broker a truce, was broken up by Aristide supporters. Three people died.

In April 2001, OAS Assistant Secretary-General Luigi Einaudi arrived in Haiti to jumpstart talks. Aristide supporters staged a tire-burning demonstration and blocked traffic, a signal to the OAS team that while Aristide is open to new talks, they would be on his terms.

The talks broke down in July. Under pressure from the OAS and new U.S. Secretary of State Colin Powell, *Lavalas* and the opposition agreed in principle for a new parliamentary election to be held in November, but the opposition rejected Aristide's "nonnegotiable" demand that the incumbent lawmakers be allowed to serve out their terms, which made new elections pointless.

In December 2001, a band of about 30 armed men stormed the National Palace in an attempted *coup d'etat*, killing two guards and two bystanders. Forces loyal to Aristide recaptured the palace.

Although the attackers appeared to be disgruntled former soldiers from the army Aristide had disbanded in 1994, rather than Convergence activists, Aristide supporters around the country used the attack as a pretext for a rampage. A Convergence headquarters and the homes of three Convergence leaders were burned; four people were burned alive by mobs. Pro-Convergence radio stations received threats. Much of the violence was believed linked to Aristide's personal goon squads, called *chimères*, or ghosts. They hacked to

death another prominent radio journalist, Brignol Lindor, after he allowed opposition representatives on his talk show.

In March 2002, Prime Minister Jean-Marie Cherestal resigned under pressure from Aristide supporters after GDP shrank by 1.2% in 2001. Aristide nominated, and Parliament approved, Senate President Yvon Neptune, who promised new talks with the opposition. Aristide met with Convergence leaders for the first time in two years and promised to satisfy their demands, including reparations for property destroyed by mobs. But stalemate and unrest continued, each side blaming the other for the continued freeze on $500 million in international aid.

In May, Aristide ordered the imprisonment of Amiot Metayer, leader of one of his own *chimères*, the "Cannibal Army." Metayer, who allegedly had burned down houses of a rival gang, was charged with arson. Metayer then turned against Aristide, and his gang used a bulldozer to smash into his jail in Gonaïves and free him and about 150 other inmates. Anti-Aristide demonstrations broke out around the country, while Metayer disappeared— for 13 months.

International pressure increased on Aristide. Haiti joined the Caribbean Community (Caricom) in 2002, and at a summit that December the leaders of the other 14 member nations called for new elections.

In 2003, Einaudi tried again to resolve the impasse and clear the way for aid. He led a delegation from the United States, Canada, the E.U. and OAS and insisted that Aristide disarm the *chimères*, respect human rights and overhaul the police. The delegation set a deadline of March 30 to set up a new electoral council to pave the way for new elections. It was ignored.

Aristide Falls

Two events set things in motion that eventually brought down Aristide. The first was a meeting of representatives of 180 civic groups in Cité Soleil, a teeming slum near the capital that is a stronghold of Aristide supporters, that demanded Aristide's resignation. When the opposition sought to assemble in July 2003, pro-Aristide mobs pelted them with rocks, injuring dozens. The opposition countered with mass anti-Aristide demonstrations in Cap-Haitien, the second-largest city, which turned violent.

In September, Metayer's bullet-riddled body was found. The identity of the assassins was a mystery, but Metayer's supporters accused Aristide of silencing him because of his knowledge of the government's sins. Aristide denied complicity, but it was too late; a large, well-organized, well-armed band of thugs that had been

loyal to Aristide took up arms against him. Over three months, about 50 people died in sporadic violence.

In January 2004, as the country observed the bicentennial of its independence, all hell broke loose. The mandate of the Chamber of Deputies again expired and no elections were forthcoming, so Aristide began ruling by decree as Préval had done. First came a general strike by shopkeepers. Violent demonstrations left two people dead.

Political negotiations came to nothing. A delegation of 14 opposition representatives, calling themselves the Democratic Platform, met with several Caribbean prime ministers during a Caricom summit in the Bahamas. A Caricom delegation came to Haiti and met with Aristide in Kingston, Jamaica. Aristide agreed to disarm his *chimères* and to reform the police. Now it was the opposition that became intransigent, saying Aristide must step down.

Armed groups determined the course of events. Insurrection broke out in at least a dozen towns, and rebels captured Gonaïves, symbolic as the cradle of Haitian independence. The first week, 47 people died. Neptune admitted the 5,000-man police force was incapable of dealing with the uprising—even if it had been so inclined. Policemen often fled as the rebels took town after town. The army, of course, had been disbanded in 1994—by Aristide. It literally became gang warfare, the rebels against the *chimères*.

The rebels, who named their movement the National Resistance Front for the Liberation of Haiti, were far from an army of liberation. They were a rag-tag, unappetizing, improbable collection of disgruntled Aristide loyalists, former soldiers from the former army, even former members of the Duvaliers' *Tonton Macoutes*. The only thing they had in common was a belief in violence as a means for achieving their ends, which they wielded skillfully. At first, the Democratic Platform disavowed the violence and distanced itself from the rebels, many of whose leaders were known killers. But when the rebels began achieving victories, they could not be ignored. Guy Philippe, a more respectable former army officer and the former police chief in Cap-Haitien, emerged as their leader.

Secretary of State Powell admonished Aristide for continuing to unleash gangs of thugs to attack peaceful demonstrations, yet insisted that the U.S. stood by the elected president. Aristide finally yielded to a U.S.-brokered power-sharing plan that would have allowed him to remain in office. The opposition, sensing imminent victory, turned it down.

Then 200 rebels overran Cap-Haitien, and looters went wild. The death toll rose to 80.

Haiti

The rebels moved on Port-au-Prince. A siege mentality gripped the capital as the Aristide gangs erected barricades. Foreign nationals left in droves. U.S. Marines entered Port-au-Prince to safeguard the embassy—just as they had in 1915. Philippe vowed to take the presidential palace and arrest Aristide. Other towns fell to the rebels.

Aristide remained defiant and pleaded for international troops to keep him in power, but by now Powell was questioning whether the man the U.S. had reinstalled in 1994 should continue to misgovern. The United Nations said it would send peacekeeping forces only if Aristide and the opposition reached a power-sharing arrangement, which, of course, the opposition had no incentive to do. Chaos reigned in Port-au-Prince.

On February 29, 2004, Aristide resigned and fled to the Central African Republic. The jubilation in the streets was immediate. Under the constitution, Supreme Court Chief Justice Boniface Alexandre became interim president, but the rebel gangs near the capital were still under arms. Anti-Aristide mobs exacted retribution. A contingent of 100 U.S. Marines and 300 French Foreign Legionnaires arrived as the vanguard of the latest U.N. peacekeeping mission. It was reminiscent of 1915.

The rebels entered Port-au-Prince on March 2, peacefully, as the Marines watched warily. Philippe announced that he was not interested in political power but wanted to be "military chief." Meanwhile, 1,500 more Marines entered Haiti, as did 500 more French and 130 Chilean troops, to maintain order and, unofficially, to prop up the new government.

In March, Haiti moved a step closer to a semblance of a government when a seven-member "Council of Sages" bypassed the Democratic Platform to agree on a prime minister: Gérard Latortue, a former U.N. official and foreign minister during one of the revolving-door presidencies in 1988. Unlike Aristide's figureheads, Latortue had genuine authority. He stated his top priorities were to establish law and order and to arrange new elections.

In a bizarre postscript, Aristide told journalists in his temporary exile that the U.S. had forcibly removed him, in effect, not just abetting but staging a *coup d'etat*. The State Department denied it, but its official declarations made it clear the U.S. was glad to get rid of this embarrassment. Caricom leaders tended to accept Aristide's version and demanded that the U.N. General Assembly and the OAS investigate. Despite objections from the U.S. and the new Haitian government, the OAS General Assembly voted to invoke Section 20 of the charter to determine whether the government of a member country had been unconstitutionally subverted.

Aristide flew to Jamaica, where he announced his final destination: South Africa. He had developed a friendship with President Thabo Mbeke, who had once tried to broker a dialogue with Aristide and the opposition. Aristide arrived in Johannesburg, insisting he was still the legitimate president of Haiti and that the U.S. had forced him out.

The U.S. increased its aid to Haiti for the year to $160 million. In June, the U.N. peacekeeping mission, 8,000 strong, set up its headquarters. The largest contingent was 1,200 Brazilian troops, augmented by 500 Argentines, along with Canadians and Nepalese. The U.S. withdrew in June. The U.N. authorized a force of 5,700, but by August there were only 2,300 U.N. peacekeepers left, far too few to deal with the chaos that was to come.

The new government let the foreigners know it was in no hurry for them to leave, especially after devastating floods in May that killed 1,191 Haitians and left 1,484 unaccounted for. In September, Hurricane Jeanne slammed into Haiti, killing an estimated 3,000 and leaving thousands homeless. It seemed that Haiti was indeed living under a *voodoo* curse. Donor nations pledged $1.3 billion in aid.

Futile Quest for Stability

Aristide's fall was not the panacea for the country's ills his opponents had hoped. The unelected interim government was viewed by many Haitians, and in some international circles, as illegitimate. Meanwhile, Aristide's *chimères* launched a low-grade insurgency roughly analogous to the insurgency in Iraq; indeed, they dubbed their effort "Operation Baghdad." Like the Iraqi insurgents, they hoped for a return to the *ancien régime*. Amnesty International charged that the interim government was little better than the insurgents, accusing it of illegal detentions and summary executions.

Moreover, the former soldiers of the old army who had helped bring down Aristide, still heavily armed, demanded that the interim government reconstitute the army and restore them to their old positions—with back pay. In December 2004, Brazilian troops stormed an estate once owned by Aristide, which some of the former soldiers had converted into a fortress. The ex-soldiers surrendered. Hundreds were allowed to join the new national police force.

The U.N. contingent was boosted to 7,400 to deal with the mounting violence. Brazil again played the leading role.

Latortue announced that elections would be held for president and Parliament, but postponed the date twice until setting a firm date of February 7, 2006. A total of 91 parties participated, including Aristide's

Lavalas. The U.S., Canada, the E.U. and the U.N. funded the elections.

A later wave of violence in 2004 raised the death toll to about 750, including 40 policemen. The U.N. Security Council approved an additional 1,000 troops to safeguard the election.

Violence by rival gangs of pro- and anti-Aristide partisans continued unabated, a lawless scenario reminiscent of the Lincoln County War in New Mexico of the 1870s, only with a much higher death toll. The U.N. peacekeepers and the 3,500 Haitian police found themselves battling both groups; two U.N. peacekeeping troops were killed..

The Return of Préval

The new election began to resemble the electoral farce of 2000, as it was postponed repeatedly. This time it was international advisers who urged the delay, warning that the mechanism for an election was not ready.

Former President Préval declared his candidacy at the head of his new *Lespwa* (Hope) Party, and rejected accusations that he was merely Aristide in sheep's clothing who would allow Aristide to return. Indeed, the two men apparently had had an irrevocable falling-out. Aristide's own *Lavalas* broke into two factions, one that fielded a candidate, and one that called for boycotting an election it believed Préval would win. His only serious opponents were former President Leslie Manigat, overthrown by the military after five months in 1988, and Charles Henri Baker, who represented the business establishment.

Gang-related violence threatened to disrupt the February 7, 2006, election. Two Jordanian U.N. peacekeepers were killed, whereupon the U.N. contingent was increased to 9,000. The turnout was a healthy 63%, about 2.2 million voters, but the vote-counting turned into another sham of democracy. About 85,000 blank ballots—about 4% of the total—were stuffed into ballot boxes, apparently to deprive Préval of an outright majority. Other ballots were stolen and burned. The initial count showed Préval with 63%, but when the tedious count continued and it dropped below 50%, Préval alleged fraud and urged his supporters to protest. They went on a tire-burning rampage that paralyzed Port-au-Prince.

The U.N. oversaw the count, during which the head of the electoral council fled the country because of death threats for disallowing 125,000 blank and suspicious ballots. A compromise was reached, allotting them to the candidates on the basis of the percentages they had obtained without them. That put Préval over the top with 51.5%. Manigat was a distant second with 11.8%.

The new National Assembly had to be in place before Préval could be inaugurated. The elections finally took place in April, and *Lespwa* emerged as the largest bloc in both the Senate and Chamber of Deputies.

Préval was inaugurated for his second term on May 14. 2006. Even before then, he visited Washington, Cuba, Venezuela and Brazil, seeking help for his destitute country. Fidel Castro, also head of a destitute nation, offered the usual medical aid, while Venezuela's Chávez offered the usual discount fuel. Brazil promised to help develop an ethanol program.

Jacques Edouard Alexis, who had been prime minister during Préval's first term, was installed again.

A total of 9,500 peacekeepers—7,500 military and 2,000 police—in the U.N. Stabilization Mission to Haiti, known by its French acronym MINUSTAH, remained in Haiti during Préval's second term. Its mission was to patrol the violence-torn slums. Haitians chafed at the U.N. presence, accusing the troops of firing indiscriminately and wounding civilians. However, when the U.N. Security Council unanimously voted in 2007 to extend the peacekeeping mission, the Haitian government expressed relief and gratitude. The U.N. also named former U.S. President Bill Clinton as its special envoy to Haiti.

Violence in Haiti again made international news in April 2008 when mobs protested the high cost of food, leaving at least five people dead. The protests spread to Port-au-Prince, where rioters stormed the presidential palace to demand Préval's resignation. The mobs looted stores for food. Préval delivered a national address, asking the National Assembly to cut taxes to provide relief and ordering the protesters to stop looting. The riots died out after a few days. The National Assembly forced Alexis to resign to appease the restive population. Haiti became an international *cause célèbre* over escalating food prices.

The Chamber of Deputies rejected two of Préval's nominees to succeed Alexis in 2008 before approving Michèle Pierre-Louis, 60, a U.S.-educated economist who for 13 years had been executive director of liberal American billionaire George Soros' Foundation of Knowledge and Liberty (FOKAL). A leftist and former Aristide supporter who broke with him, she tried to follow a pragmatic economic course and attempted to crack down on drug-based corruption—which won her more enemies than friends.

Haitian economic recovery was the subject of a conference in Bridgetown, Barbados, in April 2009 attended by Pierre-Louis, U.N. Secretary-General Ban Ki-moon, U.S. Secretary of State Hillary Clinton and

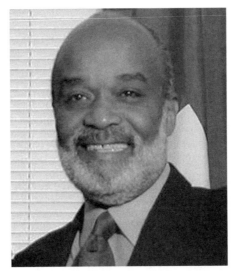

Former President René Préval

the representatives of more than 30 other countries. The new Obama administration implemented a new trade law, called Hope II, which extended preferential tariffs to Haitian products for nine years. Ban urged developed nations to increase investment in Haiti, but also called on Haiti to reform its institutions.

In October 2009, the Senate passed a resolution demanding Prime Minister Pierre-Louis' dismissal because of her perceived failure to come to grips with the country's prodigious problems, especially poverty. Observers speculated the real reason was that some senators were positioning themselves to run for president. She was succeeded by Jean-Max Bellerive, the minister of planning and external cooperation.

The 2010 Earthquake

Bellerive soon found himself facing not only the problems Pierre-Louis bequeathed him, but one that left Haiti devastated and even more desperate. At 5 p.m. on January 12, 2010, a massive 7.0- magnitude earthquake struck, leveling thousands of poorly constructed homes and office buildings—including many government ministries—killing tens of thousands of people and leaving hundreds of thousands homeless. The presidential palace and Parliament were badly damaged, and the executive branch set up an emergency office in a police station. The archbishop of Port-au-Prince was among those killed when the building where he was holding a meeting collapsed. Hillside slums were swept away. About 100 MINUSTAH staffers were killed when the hotel where they were staying collapsed.

International relief efforts were immediate and generous, but the magnitude of the tragedy was more than even disas-

ter- relief experts had bargained for. Haiti simply lacked the institutional or physical infrastructures to cope with such a catastrophe, even with the outpouring of funds, supplies and personnel from around the world.

Because of primitive logistics, food, bottled water and relief supplies sat in airport hangers or in ships offshore as hundreds of thousands went hungry and without shelter. Port-au-Prince's major port was put out of commission. The electrical grid was disrupted, which temporarily halted air traffic control. Landslides blocked roads into the interior. Lack of running water and sewerage sparked outbreaks of disease.

The collapse of several hospitals magnified the suffering. Thousands of unburied corpses rotted in the tropical heat, compounding the nightmare. Mass burials and cremations followed. Looting and gunfights broke out. The parliamentary elections scheduled for February 28 were postponed. About the only good news was that the quake occurred during the dry season, which ended in April.

About 22,000 U.S. military personnel and 2,000 from Canada gradually brought order to the logistical impasse and helped maintain order. A month after the quake, more than 300 tent communities were housing 550,000 people; by October, 1,100 camps housed 1.2 million. It was estimated that 25,000 buildings had been destroyed; the number damaged was even higher. The U.S. joint task force withdrew on June 1, leaving about 850 personnel, mostly engineers. Reconstruction fell to various non-governmental organizations.

The generally accepted death toll from the quake at first was 230,000, although the government later claimed it was 330,000. In 2011, outside estimates put it at 45,000, still a tragedy, but multiple counting and perhaps the government's desire to evoke world sympathy inflated the figure. The actual number may never be known.

The cost of reconstruction was estimated at between $8 billion and $14 billion—twice the country's entire GDP. At a meeting in New York, donor nations pledged $9.9 billion in assistance; by 2011, the amount was up to $12 billion. Former President Clinton supervised the early period of reconstruction.

Just when it seemed things couldn't get worse for Haiti, they did. In October 2010, cholera broke out it one of the camps and quickly spread through others, the result of open sewers. By mid-2011, when the epidemic waned, 6,200 had died.

The U.N. announced in April 2011 that only 37% of the aid money pledged for earthquake recovery had been disbursed, 15 months after the event.

Haiti

Another Electoral Farce

Préval set November 28, 2010, as the date for both the presidential and parliamentary elections. A total of 19 candidates appeared on the presidential ballot, but only four had any chance of making it to the runoff: Jude Célestin, Préval's anointed successor; Mirlande Manigat, wife of the temporary military strongman from the 1980s who lost the 2006 election; and two hip-hop singers, Michel Martelly, better known by the stage name "Sweet Micky," and Wyclef Jean, who were influenced by the *Compas* genre of Nemours Jean Baptiste and Webert Sicot (see Culture). The field narrowed when the electoral council ruled Jean ineligible because he had resided too long in the U.S. and did not meet residency requirements. Jean threw his support to his friend, Martelly. Aristide's *Fanmi Lavalas* Party was barred from the election.

The first round, monitored by the OAS and various international NGOs, was the usual Haitian travesty: stuffed ballot boxes, disappeared ballots, mass confusion in the refugee camps about where to vote. Voter turnout was a pitiful 22.8%. The OAS wearily concluded that despite irregularities, and under the extraordinary circumstances, the election was about as good as could be expected by Haitian standards.

But the OAS and other observers were not quite so acquiescent when it came to the government's official vote count, which put Manigat in first place with 31.4% of the vote while Préval's chosen candidate, Célestin, edged out Martelly for the runoff spot, 22.5% to 21.8%. That was at odds with the exit polls by the OAS and NGOs, which all showed Martelly with a clear second-place finish. In January 2011, a nine-member OAS team concluded that Martelly had received 22.2% to 21.9% for Célestin. Martelly supporters rioted, and the OAS, the U.S., the E.U. and the U.N. all applied pressure on Préval for an honest count. Secretary of State Clinton came to Haiti personally. (The Clintons had honeymooned in Haiti and both claimed a sentimental attachment.) The government agreed to delay the scheduled January 16 runoff to March 20.

During this period of uncertainty, three important events put the country even more on edge.

First, two bad pennies from Haiti's past reappeared from exile. In January 2011, Jean-Claude "Baby Doc" Duvalier, then 59, returned unannounced from his 25-year exile in France. He claimed he was emotionally moved by Haiti's suffering and wished to help—but not to the extent of returning the hundreds of millions of dollars he stole from the treasury as he departed in 1986.

Indeed, he checked into the posh Karibe Hotel. Meanwhile, human rights groups in Haiti and abroad called for his prosecution, both for the massive embezzlement and for the killings and torture that were widespread during his regime. He appeared before a judge for questioning. On February 1, a new Swiss law took effect, actually nicknamed the "Duvalier Law," which makes it easier to confiscate funds plundered from so-called failing states so the funds can be repatriated. At stake was a mere $5.7 million Duvalier had stashed in Switzerland. In 2012, a court ruled he could not be tried for the human rights abuses because the statute of limitations had expired, but that was overturned. He returned to court for more pretrial hearings in 2013.

Next, just days after Duvalier's return, Aristide announced from his exile in South Africa that he was "ready" to return to Haiti as well. His lawyers obtained a passport for him, and Aristide returned to Haiti for the first time in seven years on March 18, two days before the runoff. Like Duvalier, he faced justice for human rights violations, among other misdeeds.

Finally, on February 3, the electoral council announced that a new, revised and more honest vote count put Martelly in the runoff with Manigat. Fortunately, Célestin bowed out gracefully.

Slightly more than 1 million voters participated in the runoff, but the turnout was still just 22.5%. Again, there were some irregularities, but the head of the U.N. peacekeeping mission wearily declared the process an improvement over November 28.

The results were released April 16. This time, there was no cliffhanger:

Martelly	716,986	67.6%
Manigat	336,747	31.7%

Martelly, 50, visited Washington after the election and vowed modernization and transparency for his government. He met with Secretary Clinton and representatives of the IMF, World Bank and the Inter-American Development Bank; and was interviewed at the National Press Club.

One of his major campaign promises was to rebuild the army that Aristide disbanded. He needs one, but a professional one.

He was sworn in on May 14, 2011. His only managerial experience had been as owner of a nightclub in the 1980s and '90s, when he was friendly with the military rulers who replaced Duvalier, and he supported the 1991 coup that toppled Aristide. His highest education was a few classes at a community college in Colorado.

Martelly soon found the same difficulty his predecessors encountered in having a prime minister confirmed. The opposi-

tion controls both houses of the National Assembly, and neither they nor Martelly showed much willingness to govern by consensus. After rejecting two nominees, the Assembly finally approved Garry Conille, a respected academic. He lasted only four months, resigning in February 2012 because of a perceived loss of confidence from the Cabinet. Foreign Minister Laurent Lamothe, a 39-year-old businessman educated in Florida, was sworn in as prime minister on May 16, 2012. Because of this year-long impasse, billions of dollars in earthquake relief remained in limbo, and international donors became impatient with Haiti's bickering rulers.

MINUSTAH Overstays its Welcome

Public opinion turned ugly against MINUSTAH's peacekeeping forces, which Haitians began to regard less and less as benevolent guardians and saviors and more and more as occupiers and abusers. In 2011, experts traced the deadly 2010 cholera epidemic that killed more than 6,000 people to sewage coming from an encampment of U.N. peacekeepers from Nepal. Protesters demanded the withdrawal of MINUSTAH, whose numbers had swelled to 12,000. Protesters clashed with riot police outside the National Palace in July 2011. The protest was broken up with tear gas. Several people were injured, including two foreign journalists. The National Assembly also passed a resolution in 2011 calling for MINUSTAH's eventual withdrawal.

Public opinion was inflamed even more when MINUSTAH soldiers, first from Uruguay and then from Pakistan, were detained in separate incidents in 2011 and 2012 for the alleged homosexual rapes of Haitian boys. Compounding the Haitians' resentment is the fact that MINUSTAH has literally no accountability for such actions. The Uruguayan soldiers were sent home for court-martial; no action was against the Pakistani soldiers.

In response to the protests, U.N. Secretary-General Ban Ki-moon suggested reducing the size of MINUSTAH back to its pre-earthquake level of 7,400. Despite the growing protests, Martelly addressed the U.N. General Assembly in September 2011 and pleaded against a reduction in the size of the force before he is able to resurrect Haiti's army, which Aristide disbanded. He said he envisions an army of 8,000 troops, which raised some eyebrows in human rights circles about how professional such a hastily created army would be. There are fears it would turn into yet another goon squad for the sitting president, as its predecessor had been for the Duvaliers and the military strongmen of the 1980s.

A U.N. Security Council delegation visited Haiti in February 2012 to review the status of the mandate.

By the second anniversary of the earthquake in January, 2012, only $2.38 billion of the massive amount of donations had been spent. Progress had been made toward providing new housing for the 1 million homeless, but by the end of 2012, 350,000 homeless people were still housed in tents. The cholera death toll rose to 7,500, and despite evidence linking the outbreak to sewage from U.N. peacekeeping encampments, the U.N. has washed its hands of culpability or responsibility. The massive aid sent or promised has failed to renovate Haiti, and donors are proving reluctant to throw good money after bad.

In October 2013, the Haitian government actually filed a class-action lawsuit against the U.N. in U.S. federal court in New York, blaming the cholera deaths on "reckless and gross negligence and misconduct." Secretary-General Ban said the U.N. has immunity from lawsuits under an international convention.

Recent Developments

Martelly has spent so much time abroad, like a traveling salesman trying to persuade foreign investors to take a chance on Haiti, that critics wonder whether the huge trip expenses will pay off. Martelly has greased the skids for doing business in Haiti, including a 15-year tax holiday for new investments. As of 2013, his efforts had had mixed results. A U.S.-financed industrial park has not lured tenants. A new terminal for Toussant L'Overture International Airport and some new luxury hotels—for foreign tourists and Haiti's tiny elite—are among the few success stories.

Martelly met with President Obama in the White House on February 6, 2014.

President Michel Martelly

Obama said, "We will continue to stand by the Haitian democracy, the Haitian leadership and the Haitian people."

After ignoring two earlier summonses, Duvalier returned to court in February 2013 for more pretrial hearings for his alleged human rights abuses. He returned to court again on March 4, then was hospitalized for an undisclosed ailment. As of mid-2014, the courts still had made no further progress in the Duvalier prosecution. Amnesty International and Human Rights Watch blamed the three-year delay on "a lack of political will" on the part of the government.

In a potentially significant development, representatives of the executive and

legislative branches and the political parties met at the El Rancho Hotel to hammer out an agreement on holding elections in October 2014 to fill 10 expiring Senate seats. The co-called "El Rancho Accord" was signed on March 14, 2014, and MINUSTAH chief Sandra Honoré hailed it as "an unprecedented step in Haitian political history." The accord failed to gain approved in the Senate; elections are still pending.

CULTURE: Haiti's culture is a singular blend of African and European influences. A minority, the mulattos, relatively better educated in the French-language schools, boast of their European culture and superiority. Educated in medicine and law, they patronize the arts and disdain most manual work. Most are Catholic.

La Citadelle, the famous mountaintop fortress (see photo), is a UNESCO World Heritage Site.

The Haitians are, for the most part, an illiterate peasant society. They practice *voodoo,* a type of animism with African roots with many spirits and deities, and great emphasis on the powers of evil and good spirits. Voodoo, or *voudou* as the Haitians spell it, was sanctioned in the 1987 constitution but was not officially recognized as a religion with legal authority to perform marriages and baptisms until 2003. However, Roman Catholicism is the predominant religion.

Their language reflects their culture. Called *Creole,* or *Kreyòl,* is a blend of French, Spanish, English and Dutch, the foreign influences to which Haiti has been exposed, with roots in African dialects and tongues. Both French and Creole are official languages.

Most artistic expression has *voodoo* overtones. Traditional African designs blend with imaginative contemporary motifs in cloth, wood carving and basketry. Such crafts are valued internationally.

Because of illiteracy, grinding poverty and dictatorship, Haiti never developed a vibrant literature or journalism. A rare exception was the short-lived 19th century poet and playwright Antoine Dupré (1782–1816), who focused on historical themes, such as his play, *Le Mort du General Lamarre* and his poem, *Hymne de la Liberté.* His literary career was truncated in a duel.

Several magazines sprang up in opposition to the U.S. occupation of 1915–34, but press freedom was not one of the American traditions the occupiers were interested in transferring.

Between the end of the U.S. occupation and the beginning of the Duvalier dictatorship in 1957, there was a modest literary movement grounded in social realism. One prominent writer who achieved international recognition during this pe-

Presidents Obama and Martelly discuss Haitian democracy and development in the White House on Februrary 6, 2014.
Credit: whitehouse.gov

Haiti

riod was Jacques Roumain (1907–44), who founded the Communist Party in 1934 and was exiled during the presidency of Stenio Vincent. He worked and wrote at Columbia University and became friends with Langston Hughes, who translated some of his works. Probably his best remembered novel is *Gouveneurs de la Rosée (Masters of the Dew)*. He was allowed to return to Haiti in 1943 and died under mysterious circumstances in 1944, aged 37.

Printed newspapers had tiny circulations because of low literacy. The country's most influential daily is *La Nouvelliste*. Because of Haiti's huge expatriate population in the United States and elsewhere, there are now several daily or weekly Haitian newspapers operating online, some in French, some in Creole, some in both. Freedom House rates the Haitian press as "partly free."

Because of poverty and illiteracy, radio remains the most influential mass medium in the country. There are about 40 stations operating in the capital and 50 in the interior, the overwhelming number of them FM. Because of its mass influence, radio has often played a role in the country's turbulent politics, sometimes with deadly consequences, such as the assassination of anti-Aristide commentator Dominique Jean in 2000, which remains unsolved. The stations also operate websites for the huge émigré population.

There are about 20 television stations, including the government-owned Television Nationale d'Haiti. They also operate websites for émigrés; two are based in New York.

The two most influential figures of Haitian popular music were Nemours Jean Baptiste (1918–85) and Webert Sicot (1930– 85), who competed for the title of founder of a genre of dance music called *Compas*, or *Kompa*, or *Compa Direk*, in the 1950s. Both were saxophonists and composers. The style remains popular and influential today, and has influenced such contemporary artists as hip-hop singers Wyclef Jean and Michel "Sweet Micky" Martelly, who in 2011 was elected president of Haiti (see History). He owns one of the country's television channels.

Despite its destitution, Haiti claims at least 15 universities, most of them small schools established after 1980. The oldest is Episcopal University of Haiti, founded in 1920. The State University of Haiti dates only to 1945.

ECONOMY: Haiti's economy, based on peasant survival at unbelievably low levels, is almost nonexistent. Deforestation, soil erosion, periodic hurricanes and overpopulation all combine to limit agricultural production. The leading cash crops are coffee, cotton, sisal, cacao and sugar.

Low wage scales attract some foreign investment in light industry such as electronic assembly, finished leather goods and tourism. Clothing assembly has been moderately successful. Precut materials are sent from the United States and sewn into garments in Haiti. This substantially lowers import duties when the finished product is shipped to the United States. When former President George H. W. Bush watered down the embargo on Haiti, he did so not out of consideration of Haitians, but because of extreme pressure from the U.S. garment makers and merchants.

During the 1980s the economy suffered from expensive fuel imports, low prices for coffee exports and hurricane damage to crops. Continued U.S. assistance kept the nation economically afloat—barely—before 1987. The already prostrate economy was further stricken by Hurricane Georges in 1998.

Beginning in the 1980s, the desperate economic conditions led to a massive exodus of economic refugees by boat, bound for Florida, the Bahamas, or anywhere they might find a better life; untold numbers died at sea. Those who made it are the source of crucial remittances to their families. Remittances to Haiti grew from $811 million in 2003 to $1.5 billion in 2010. They peaked at $2.1 billion in 2011, falling to just under $2 billion in 2012, 25% of GDP.

Economic growth declined each year from 2001 to 2004. GDP then grew anemically: 1.5% in 2005, 2.5% in 2006, 3.2% in 2007,and 2.3% in 2008, below the Latin American average and only slightly ahead of the birth rate. Yet, in 2009, growth was 2%, higher than the Latin American average, surprising given the global recession and the damage to the economy from the 2008 storms. Because of the massive destruction from the January 12, 2010, earthquake, growth for the year fell –5.4%. Largely because of new construction, the economy grew by 5.6% in 2011 but fell back to 2.8% in 2012, far below international expectations. It was a modest 3.4% in 2013.

Two tropical storms in 2012 caused extensive damage to agriculture.

Unemployment remains about 40%. Haiti's per capita income, roughly at $800 the past three years, is perennially the lowest in the hemisphere, while the infant mortality rate of 70 per 1,000 births is the highest. In 2003, the most recent year with reliable statistics, 80% of the population lived below the poverty line.

Haiti also bears the dubious distinction of being the most corrupt nation of the hemisphere according to Transparency International, which is a drain on economic development.

Reconstruction from the 2010 earthquake, ironically, proved beneficial for

the economy, but only temporarily. The U.N. spent millions in relief funds to hire 220,000 Haitians to clear rubble. In 2011, a Korean firm announced it would build a huge textile industrial park that would create 20,000 jobs and generate $500 million in wages and benefits over 10 years. There are also new efforts by cottage industries to export mangoes. President Michel Martelly, who took office in 2011, has globe-trotted in search of new investors and has made a concerted effort to make it easier to do business in Haiti.

A potential bonanza may lie underground in Haiti's northern mountains. In 2012, foreign mining companies began exploring for gold, silver and copper, and early estimates put the worth of the deposits at $20 billion.

THE FUTURE: The Haitian people have discovered the cruel fact that democracy is not a panacea for two centuries of tenacious poverty and political misrule. Even before the tragic 2010 earthquake, Haiti was the Western Hemisphere's basket case: destitute, illiterate, corrupt, lawless and virtually ungovernable. Its per capita income is the lowest in Latin America, 80% of the population lives below the poverty level and economic growth has averaged 2-3% a year for the past eight years. Haiti desperately needs an enlightened leader, and they have now placed their hope in a rap singer, Michel Martelly, whose qualifications for managing anything, much less coping with Haiti's superhuman woes, are questionable; he even defaulted on several mortgages in Florida.

In a perverse way, the earthquake *could* have represented Haiti's salvation. At least $10 billion in international relief funds was pledged toward a reconstruction that was expected to cost between $8 billion and $14 billion. Haiti could literally have been rebuilt from the ground up, an unprecedented opportunity. It put hundreds of thousands of Haitians to work in reconstruction projects, at least temporarily lowering unemployment and stimulating the overall economy, as it did in Louisiana after Hurricanes Katrina and Rita in 2005. After a calamitous drop of –5.1% in GDP for 2010 because of the earthquake, it grew back by 5.6% in 2011, but the spurt proved temporary. If reconstruction had been planned properly, the new homes, office buildings, hospitals and schools could have been built with affordable techniques that have been used elsewhere, such as Chile, to make them more resistant to earthquakes—and hurricanes. The antiquated telecommunications system could have been replaced with 21st-century fiber-optic technology. Generators burning imported diesel fuel and gas-guzzling buses could have been replaced with those burning locally produced ethanol or biodiesel, and homes and offices could have been fitted with new, low-cost solar panels to harness the tropical sunshine.

But four years on, the opportunity has been lost, the aid money used mainly for temporary relief. Donors now appear reluctant to sink more money into a lost cause.

Martelly, now three years into his five-year term, has proven he was a better entertainer than he is a leader of a destitute nation. He pledged to bring Haiti into the 21st century through "e-governance," to create an independent judiciary and to have transparency to combat corruption. He pragmatically suggested that the billions in aid be in the form of expertise rather than cash, admitting that Haitians do not know how to deal with such large sums. He has globe-trotted in search of new investors, but has lured only a handful, and after 5.6% economic growth in 2011, it fell to a disappointing 2.8% in 2012 and 3.4% in 2013, below the hemispheric average.

He has vowed to rebuild the army that Aristide shortsightedly disbanded in 2001, but will he turn it into his personal goon squad as previous rulers have done?

Martelly's unwillingness to govern by consensus with the opposition-controlled National Assembly has prevented the efficient disbursement of billions of dollars in international relief funds that the country so desperately needs. Even the much-touted "El Rancho Accord" of March 2014, which were designed to hold an election in October for 10 Senate seats, has hit a snag because the opposition alleges that they were excluded from some key meetings.

Haiti still needs an enlightened leader, but apparently it has not found one this time around, either.

The Republic of Honduras

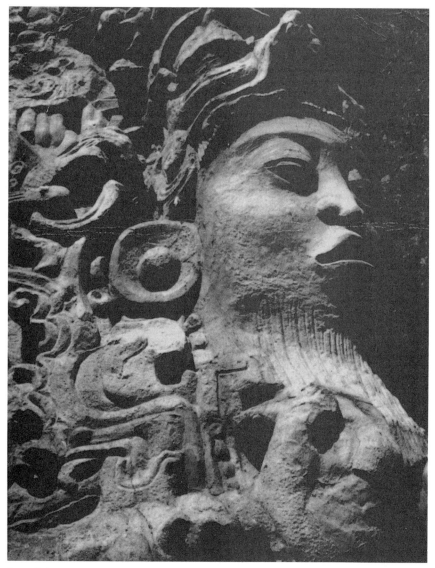

Detail from a carved stone pillar at the Mayan ruins of Copán in western Honduras

Area: 43,266 square miles.

Population: 8,598,561 (2014 est.).

Capital City: Tegucigalpa (Pop. 1 million, 2009 est.).

Climate: Tropical, with clearly marked wet and dry seasons. Heaviest rains occur from May to December.

Neighboring Countries: Nicaragua (Southeast); El Salvador (South); Guatemala (West).

Official Language: Spanish.

Other Principal Tongues: Various Indian dialects.

Ethnic Background: *Mestizo* (Mixed Spanish and Indian, 90%) African (5%), Indian (4%) European (1%).

Principal Religion: Roman Catholic Christianity.

Chief Commercial Products: Coffee, bananas, lumber, meats, petroleum products.

Currency: Lempira.

Gross Domestic Product: U.S. $18.8 billion in 2013 ($2,335 per capita, official exchange rate).

Former Colonial Status: Spanish Colony (1524–1821).

Independence Date: September 14, 1821.

Chief of State: Juan Orlando Hernández Alvarado (b. October 28, 1968), president (since January 27, 2014).

National Flag: Blue, white and blue horizontal stripes, 5 blue stars in a cluster on the center stripe.

Honduras is the second largest of the Central American republics and one of the most thinly populated. Much of the country is mountainous; an irregular plateau in the southwest has peaks approaching 8,000 feet near Tegucigalpa and La Esperanza. The plateau drops to a narrow plain on the Pacific Coast (Gulf of Fonseca). To the north there also is a narrow coastal plain broadening to the east. The valleys of the Ulúa (N.W.) and Aguán (N.E.) rivers extending south from the Atlantic coast (Gulf of Honduras), are important agricultural regions. Running south from the Ulúa to the Gulf of Fonseca is an intermountain valley which is the principal route of communications from the Atlantic to the Pacific oceans. The eastern plains along the Patuca River are covered with jungle and only partially explored.

The central plateau descends into several basins at 2,000 to 4,000 feet, in which are located the principal urban centers. The southern and western highlands contain the majority of the native Indian societies. The black population is found in the banana-raising section along the Atlantic coast. Prevailing winds are from the east, and the Atlantic coastal plain, receiving heavy rainfall, is covered with forests that are also found on the eastern slopes of the plateau and mountains.

HISTORY: Honduras was settled by Spanish treasure seekers from Guatemala in 1524. The mainstream of movement and settlement was along the Guatemala trail, a pattern that today governs the population distribution. The Spaniards ignored the Atlantic coast and the region was untouched until the U.S. fruit companies set up banana plantations in the late 19th century.

Honduras achieved independence from Spain with the other Central American states in 1821, and joined with them in a short-lived federation. Going its own way as a separate state in 1838, Honduras has been subjected to interference from Guatemala, El Salvador and Nicaragua as these countries sought Honduran support in conflicts among and between them. Honduran politics has followed the Central American pattern—two-party conflict between liberal and conservative factions of the elite, little popular participation in the political process and a long list of ever-changing dictatorial regimes.

However, Honduras' dictatorships have been somewhat more benign than those of its neighbors, and several governments have been committed to social and economic reform. Less inclined toward revolution than its neighbors, sparsely populated and with few roads, Honduras has been able to avoid the large-scale bloodshed of its neighbors. Still, during its first 161 years of independence, Honduras witnessed 385 armed rebellions, 126 governments and 16 constitutions. Generally regarded as the most capable presidents were Policarpo Bonilla (1894–99) and Tiburcio Carías Andino (1932–48). Neither made any pretense of democratic rule, governing instead as benevolent despots.

During his 16 years, Carías did more to advance the social and economic well-being of the country than any of his predecessors. Some roads and a few schools were built, and modern agricultural methods were introduced. His regime was maintained by jailing or exiling his critics.

After peacefully surrendering power following 1948 elections, Carías was followed by a series of mediocre presidents. The military seized power in 1963 in a coup led by General Oswaldo López. Honduras joined the Central American Common Market, trade was improved and an industrial development program was initiated in the northern plains region around San Pedro Sula and Puerto Cortés. Presidential balloting held in 1965 resulted in López's election at the head of the National Party to a six-year term.

A long-simmering dispute between Honduras and El Salvador, stemming from the fact that tiny El Salvador is heavily overpopulated, erupted into a brief, but bloody war in 1969 following a contentious soccer match. Since the 1940s, some 300,000 landless peasants have settled illegally on vacant land near the border inside under-populated Honduras. Some Salvadorans fled their homeland to escape the horrors of prolonged civil strife. Others came to Honduras in search of a better life. In time, these highly industrious people were living better than many native Hondurans in the region.

Alarmed by what it viewed as a growing flood of "squatters," Honduras enacted a new land reform law which, among other things, distributed to native Hondurans plots that had been cleared and brought under cultivation by the Salvadorans. All too often, the immigrants would be evicted just before their crops were ready for harvest. The mass deportation of 17,000 Salvadorans created more tension between the two countries.

Although the North American press joked about the 100-hour "soccer war" between the two "banana republics," the conflict claimed more than 2,000 lives and devastated the economies of both countries. Because of the strife, Honduras withdrew from the Central American Common Market.

Capitalizing on his role as a "wartime" leader, President López sought to remain in office by amending the constitution to permit his re-election in 1971. When that effort failed, López persuaded the Liberal and National parties to divide equally most national offices. Under this "Pact of National Unity," Ramón Ernesto Cruz was elected president.

Unable to cope with the nation's growing economic and political problems, the elderly Cruz was ousted in a coup led by López in 1972. To gain popular support, he

promised a major land reform program. The plan was opposed by both the landowners, who rejected any change in the tenure system, and by peasants, who felt the concept was too little, too late. López was himself ousted in a coup in 1975 as a result of a "bananagate" scandal in which high-level government officials were accused of accepting a $1.25 million bribe from the U.S.-owned United Brands Company to lower taxes on banana exports.

The new chief of state, Colonel Juan Alberto Melgar Castro, sought to implement various social and economic development projects. Partly as a result of these efforts, the country enjoyed a healthy GNP growth rate of 6%–8% annually until 1980. Pledging to enact the land reform program promised earlier by López, Melgar also found himself in a deadly crossfire between wealthy farmers and landless peasants.

The heart of the dispute was land. Most of Honduras is mountainous; only 22% is arable. Most has traditionally been controlled by just 667 families (0.3% of the population) and by two U.S. banana firms. In contrast, the peasants (87% of the people) lived as peons on small, difficult-to-till plots. The end result was often widespread malnutrition, particularly among the young. Still, the recent land reform program, while not meeting all expecta-

tions, permitted a larger number of peasants to be resettled on their own property.

Melgar was replaced in 1978 by a three-member *junta* headed by General Policarpo Paz García. Yielding to pressure from the Carter administration, Paz appointed a civilian-dominated cabinet to direct the transition to civilian government. Elections in April 1980 for the 71-seat constituent assembly gave the more reform-minded Liberal Party 35 seats, while the conservative Nationalists took 33.

The Return to Democracy

General elections in 1981 marked the return of democracy and resulted in the presidency of the Liberal Roberto Suazo Córdova, who took office in early 1982. A country doctor, he tried to revive a patient that was suffering from backwardness, a declining economy and growing security problems caused by events in neighboring countries. More than 25,000 Salvadoran refugees flooded into Honduras to escape that nation's war. Many were relocated away from the border and were placed under the U.N. high commissioner for refugees.

After the Marxist *Sandinista* movement came to power in neighboring Nicaragua in 1979, Honduras unwillingly became a sanctuary for the Nicaraguan *Contra* forces opposed to the *Sandinistas*. During the 1980s, there were repeated raids into Honduras from Nicaragua as the *Sandinistas* periodically tried to destroy *Contra* encampments in the remote, inaccessible mountains and jungle along the common border. Losses in coffee production in areas abandoned by farmers because of the conflict were substantial.

The Reagan administration stepped up its military aid commitment to Honduras

Honduras

in response to the *Sandinista* threat. In addition to weaponry, military personnel were sent. Economic aid in large amounts was insufficient to alleviate economic woes, however, because of fluctuations in the prices of bananas and coffee.

Cuba, meanwhile, used Honduras as a transport route to dispatch Soviet-bloc arms and munitions to the *FMLN* rebels in El Salvador. Friction with Nicaragua increased because of the *Contra* presence. In an effort to control the situation, a combined U.S.-Honduran military force established "temporary" U.S. military bases close to the Nicaraguan border. Some thought this was an effort by President Reagan to provoke the *Sandinistas,* justifying direct intervention in Nicaragua.

An incident did occur—*Sandinista* troops entered Honduras in 1988 to wipe out a *Contra* base after a cease-fire had been negotiated between the warring parties. When 3,000 additional U.S. troops were sent into the country, the *Sandinistas* retreated.

With the collapse of the Soviet Union and the end of its support to the *Sandinistas,* a semblance of peace finally came to Central America. But this left a burgeoning, expensive military in Honduras with little purpose. Releasing them would not help in a country where the unemployment- underemployment rate has been close to 50% for more than a generation.

Despite financial and security woes, democracy proceeded reasonably well in Honduras with the elections and peaceful transitions to power of José Azcona (Liberal) in 1985, Rafael Leonardo Callejas (Nationalist), in 1989 and Carlos Roberto Reina (Liberal) in 1993. All was not tranquil, however. Ethnic Indians, largely ignored by the government, became more politically aware and began expressing their dissatisfaction with their status. Vague guerrilla groups periodically appeared and disappeared.

As U.S. aid dwindled to less than $100 million annually, other sources of funding were sought. The International Monetary Fund agreed to loans, but attached a host of conditions that were difficult, including reduction of the size of the legislature and military.

Reina raised eyebrows in 1994 when he launched an anticorruption campaign that saw charges brought against 18 former officials, including former President Callejas, who was immune from prosecution as a member of the Central American Parliament. But it was the paring of the once-omnipotent military that may be regarded as Reina's enduring legacy. He ended the draft, obtained executive control over the armed forces' budget, removed the national police from military control and reduced troop strength; some units were

Former President Carlos Flores Facussé

only 20% of their former size. Moreover, there were Argentine-style efforts to hold the military accountable for human rights abuses during the 1970s and 1980s.

The armed forces complained that the downsizing emasculated their ability to defend Honduras, but to defend against whom? The guerrilla wars in neighboring Nicaragua and El Salvador, which once threatened to embroil Honduras, had ended. Before leaving office in 1998, Reina signed a long-sought border agreement with Salvadoran President Armando Calderón Sol that formally delineated the disputed frontier areas that led the two countries to war in 1969.

Carlos Flores

The presidential and congressional elections in 1997 were the most colorful yet for the fledgling democracy. To succeed the 71-year-old Reina, the Liberal Party made a generational leap to the president of the Congress, 47-year-old Carlos Flores Facussé, who lost an earlier bid to Callejas. The National Party nominated Alba Nora de Melgar, widow of erstwhile military strongman Juan Alberto Melgar Castro and a former mayor of Tegucigalpa. Her link to the days of dictatorship, plus her decision to hire as her campaign adviser Dick Morris, U.S. President Bill Clinton's onetime aide, brought the campaign international attention.

Flores distanced himself from Reina and from the Liberal Party's traditional middle-class base and reached out to the country's impoverished masses, although

he had little in common with them as the scion of two of the country's wealthiest families. He received a degree in industrial engineering from Louisiana State University and held a master's degree in international economics and finance; his wife was American. Ultimately, his populist approach and youthful appeal proved successful, as he defeated Melgar, 53% to 42.4%. Flores was inaugurated on January 27, 1998.

Like his democratic predecessors, Flores found his will tested by the military. The armed forces commander promoted a list of officers without clearing them with the president—who objected to the men chosen and who nullified the promotions.

That was trivial compared with the blow dealt to poverty-plagued and debt-ridden Honduras in October 1998 by Hurricane Mitch, one of the most powerful storms in recorded history. Entire villages on the Caribbean coast were swept away by the winds and floods. In human terms, 5,657 Hondurans were confirmed dead, another 8,058 missing and uncounted thousands more left homeless. The storm also destroyed 170 bridges and damaged 70% of the country's roads; property losses were in the billions of dollars, and 90% of the vital banana crop was destroyed. International relief efforts to alleviate the immediate human misery were quick in coming. The World Bank approved a $200 million loan, and the IMF extended a $215 million credit.

But these were little more than band-aids, and a bewildered President Flores declared to the world that Honduras's debt was "unpayable."

Ricardo Maduro

Hondurans were in the mood for change in 2001. The Liberals nominated a veteran political insider, Rafael Piñeda, 71, president of the Congress. The Nationalists gambled on a 55-year-old businessman, Ricardo Maduro, whose only political office had been head of the Central Bank under the 1990–94 Nationalist administration of Callejas.

As both major parties are center-right, the campaign focused on personalities and the issues of who could better combat crime and promote foreign investment. Maduro, whose own son had been killed in a kidnap attempt in 1997, focused on the crime issue. He visited New York City and promised the "zero-tolerance" approach of then-Mayor Rudolph Giuliani, not only against violent crime but against such petty offenses as littering, vagrancy and defacing public property, all of which, Maduro argued, discouraged tourism and foreign investment. Piñeda, a former elementary schoolteacher, countered that enhanced education was the solution to the crime problem, which had become exacerbated by violent gangs known as *maras*.

In a country plagued by more than 2,000 murders a year, a staggering figure for a nation of only 6.2 million, Maduro's proposal enjoyed widespread support. The violence issue was underscored just two days before the election when a Nationalist candidate for Congress was assassinated; police later arrested three employees of a Liberal deputy.

On November 25, voters gave Maduro a convincing mandate of 53% to Piñeda's 44%. The Nationalists also won the mayoralty of Tegucigalpa, but minor parties kept either of the two major parties from gaining a majority in the 128-seat Congress.

Maduro told his cheering supporters, "We are not just going to administer the country; we are going to effect significant reform." He also vowed "to enforce the laws as never before" and promised to reduce the bloated government payroll, to streamline the bureaucracy and make it more efficient, and to crack down on

Former President Ricardo Maduro

abuses of privileges and frivolous spending by government officials.

The *maras* evidently took Maduro's promises seriously. In January, police foiled a plot by one gang to assassinate the president-elect. He was sworn in on January 27, 2002.

In 2002, the divorced Maduro married a Spanish diplomat, Aguas Ocaña. News reports soon circulated that the couple already had become estranged.

Maduro sought to reform the state-owned water utility in order to facilitate a line of credit from the IMF, which was placed on hold in 2002. As Congress considered the proposal, a demonstration by 10,000 people became uncharacteristically violent. The crowd clashed with police, then stormed inside the Congress.

The president also created controversy in 2003 when he contributed a contingent of 370 troops to the allied coalition in Iraq for a one-year tour. However, after Spain withdrew its contingent following the 2004 terrorist attacks in Madrid, Maduro ordered the troops home.

Gang-related violence remained the country's major problem, other than the endemic poverty that spawns it. But the problem is not Honduras' alone. The *maras*, organized by Central American expatriates in Los Angeles, mostly Salvadorans, have become a serious form of international organized crime, a Mafia

A rack of handmade cigars

Honduras

with tattoos. The most infamous are the *Mara Salvatrucha,* better known as *MS-13,* and *Mara 18.* So serious have they become that the United States, Mexico and most Central American countries launched a joint offensive against them (see El Salvador). In 2003, the Honduran Congress enacted 12-year prison terms for gang membership.

In Honduras, *maras* established control over local areas, posing a greater threat to the central government than did the guerrilla groups of the 1980s. They specialize in spectacular, grisly murders and even massacres to instill terror. In one shocking and senseless attack, the *MS-13* attacked a bus full of Christmas shoppers in 2004 in San Pedro Sula and killed 28 people, six of them children, and wounded 14. The gang's rationale for the attack, left on a note on the windshield: to protest a bill to reinstitute the death penalty! Three *MS-13* leaders were arrested. The government investigated links between the gangs and major drug-trafficking organizations.

In March 2005, Honduras became the second country, after El Salvador, to ratify the Dominican Republic-Central American Free Trade Agreement with the United States. More than 100 left-wing protesters briefly occupied the Congress building to protest the ratification.

Manuel Zelaya

The gang problem again dominated the 2005 presidential campaign. Porfirio "Pepe" Lobo Sosa, 57, the president of the Congress and an advocate of capital punishment, won the National Party nomination. Manuel Zelaya, 53, a wealthy rancher, won the Liberal nomination.

Lobo Sosa pledged to continue Maduro's get-tough approach toward the gangs. Zelaya, who cut a flamboyant cowboy figure with boots, Stetson hat and black mustache, also pledged to get tough with the gangs but advocated life imprisonment rather than the death penalty for criminals deemed "beyond rehabilitation." Zelaya also pledged to create 400,000 new jobs in four years. He campaigned on the populist slogan "citizen power."

The election became the most dramatic cliffhanger of any of the seven since democracy was restored in 1981. Turnout was the usual lethargic 46%, about 1.83 million voters. On election night, the Liberal member of the electoral tribunal declared Zelaya the winner after only 1% of the votes were counted, infuriating the Nationalists. The vote count all but stopped, ostensibly because of computer problems, and 3,000 Nationalists marched on the offices of the tribunal to demand to know why the count was so slow. Zelaya claimed victory, but Maduro and Lobo Sosa refused to

concede. Zelaya said Maduro was "playing with fire," and rumors circulated that Maduro had placed the army on alert, which he denied. Finally, after 10 days, the tribunal released its official tally:

Zelaya	915,075	49.9%
Lobo Sosa	846,493	46.2%
Others	72,142	3.9%

For the first time, members of Congress were elected directly instead of by proportional representation. The Liberals won 62 seats, the Nationalists 55, and three small parties made up the balance of power with 11.

Zelaya was inaugurated on January 27, 2006. He moved quickly to deal with an alarming increase in deaths inside the country's 22 prisons—180 in the previous year—which the president blamed on overcrowding because of Maduro's policy of prosecuting anyone with gang associations. Zelaya also initiated a program to offer job training to gang members who turn in their weapons.

On the negative side, Zelaya demonstrated a decidedly undemocratic attitude toward the country's independent press. In 2007, he introduced legislation that would have outlawed news reports on violent crime, on the theory that such reports "glorify evil." Congress rejected it. He then used his executive authority to require the privately owned television stations to carry two and a half hours of conversation programs a day between government officials and pro-Zelaya journalists. Zelaya said the move was required because the stations were biased against him. It was the most serious attack on freedom of the press under Honduras' 22-year-old democracy.

In 2006, Honduras recorded the fifth-highest murder rate in the entire world, 43 per 100,000 inhabitants; El Salvador was in first place. By March 2008, the wave of gang-related violence became so severe that Zelaya ordered a major crackdown, "Operation Hunter," dispatching 5,000 soldiers and policemen in a nation-wide sweep that rounded up hundreds of suspected gang members. Meanwhile, a U.N. report estimated there are 36,000 gang members in Honduras alone. Not only did it prove ineffective, in 2008 Honduras had the world's *highest* murder rate, 58 per 100,000 people.

Zelaya moved increasingly to the left, bringing Honduras into Venezuelan President Hugo Chávez's *ALBA* organization, a left-wing group that includes Cuba, Bolivia, Ecuador and Nicaragua. Honduras benefited by receiving discounted Venezuelan oil. Zelaya also raised the minimum wage 60% overnight, alienating him further from the business establishment.

Deposed President Manuel Zelaya

Vice President Elvin Ernesto Santos, a 46-year-old engineer and construction company CEO educated at Lamar University in Texas, easily won the Liberal Party primary for the November 29, 2009, presidential election. He then resigned the vice presidency in accordance with the constitution. A month later, the Nationalists renominated "Pepe" Lobo Sosa, then 61, who had narrowly lost to Zelaya. Lobo Sosa is a wealthy businessman and landowner who earned his business degree at the University of Miami. Both candidates discussed the problem of the 1 million undocumented Hondurans living in the United States with Secretary of State Hillary Clinton when she attended the OAS General Assembly session in Tegucigalpa in 2009.

A Constitutional Coup?

Zelaya provoked a constitutional crisis, which led to his overthrow by the Congress and the military, when he called a referendum for June 28, 2009, on whether to place on the November 29 ballot a proposition to elect a constituent assembly to rewrite the 1982 constitution. It was viewed as an attempt to emulate the models of Venezuela's Chávez, Bolivia's Evo Morales and Ecuador's Rafael Correa. Congress rejected the idea; his own Liberal Party was cool to it.

Zelaya defied Congress and proceeded with plans for the referendum, even ordered ballots printed. Critics saw the constituent assembly plan as a ploy to perpetuate himself in power by lifting the ban on re-election, as Chávez, Morales and Correa all had done, and they took him to court. The Supreme Court ruled the referendum unconstitutional. Zelaya defied the Supreme Court and ordered the army to distribute the ballots to polling stations. General Romeo Velásquez, the army commander, refused to comply on the grounds that it was an illegal order. Zelaya fired him. The Supreme Court, on a 5–0 vote, ordered Zelaya to reinstate Velásquez, ruling that he had been dismissed without cause. The same day, the Supreme Electoral Council also ruled the referendum illegal.

At odds with both the legislative and judicial branches as well as the armed forces, Zelaya *still* attempted to proceed with the referendum. On June 25, he and hundreds of supporters forcibly removed boxes of ballots from a military base and took them to the presidential palace. But before daylight on June 28, soldiers raided Zelaya's residence outside Tegucigalpa and arrested him. Within hours, still in pajamas, he was flown to exile in Costa Rica, where he denounced what he called a *coup d'etat.* It was the first forcible removal of an elected president by the military in Latin America since the overthrow of Ecuador's Jamil Mahuad in 2000.

Both major parties, even Zelaya's own Liberal Party, applauded the ouster, and Congress stripped him of his powers through a resolution that said he had "provoked confrontations and divisions," although it was questionable whether that was an impeachable offense. The 1982 constitution does not specifically grant the Congress impeachment power. Congress then elected its Liberal speaker, Roberto Micheletti, as interim president. Micheletti denied what had happened was a *coup d'etat,* saying civilian control and constitutional order were intact and that it was "absolutely a legal transition process," although power had not been passed to the interim vice president. Zelaya supporters protested, but were dispersed by police firing tear gas and water cannons and wielding truncheons. Micheletti declared an indefinite curfew.

International reaction was swift. There were the predictable denunciations from Zelaya's allies, Chávez and Morales, but OAS Secretary-General José Miguel Insulza of Chile also condemned the overthrow, as did U.N. General Assembly President Miguel D'Escoto, of neighboring Nicaragua, and the European Union. President Barack Obama said he was "deeply concerned," declared the overthrow "not legal" and called it "a step backward." He did not recall the U.S. ambassador, but he suspended some aid.

The day after his ouster, Zelaya flew to Nicaragua to meet with Chávez and Nicaraguan President Daniel Ortega. From there, he flew to New York to seek support from the U.N. and to Washington to plead his case to the OAS. The OAS issued a 72-hour deadline for Honduras to reinstate Zelaya. When the deadline expired on July 4, the OAS expelled Honduras.

Presidents Cristina Fernández of Argentina, Rafael Correa of Ecuador and Fernando Lugo of Paraguay joined Zelaya in Washington and at first said they would fly with him to Tegucigalpa to oversee his reinstatement. Citing security concerns, they changed their minds and flew in separate planes. Zelaya attempted to return on July 5—in a Venezuelan plane—but Micheletti denied him permission to land. Thousands of pro-Zelaya protesters had assembled to welcome him at the airport, where security forces opened fire with tear gas and live ammunition, killing one demonstrator and wounding eight. Zelaya and the other presidents, as well as Insulza, diverted to El Salvador.

Costa Rican President Oscar Arias, a Nobel peace laureate, offered to mediate between Zelaya and Micheletti. He met separately with both in San José, but Micheletti returned to Honduras before meeting face-to-face with Zelaya, who insisted that the only solution to the impasse was his reinstatement. Arias' attempts failed.

Micheletti said if Zelaya returned to Honduras he would be arrested to face 18 charges, including treason and dereliction of duty for failing to enforce more that 80 laws passed by Congress. However, he lost the chance to arrest Zelaya when he denied his plane permission to land. No Latin American nation had recognized Micheletti's government, not even the conservative governments of Mexico, Panama, Colombia or Peru, and some had recalled their ambassadors. The U.S., the U.N., the E.U. and the World Bank all applied pressure for Zelaya's reinstatement. In Honduras, pro- and anti-Zelaya demonstrations continued for months, and pro-Zelaya graffiti appeared on buildings all over the capital.

New Elections and the Quest for Legitimacy

Ignoring the international condemnation, Micheletti proceeded with the regularly scheduled presidential and congressional elections on November 29 to choose a constitutional successor to Zelaya and himself.

Zelaya, meanwhile, slipped back into the country and took refuge in the Brazilian Embassy, from where he exhorted his supporters to boycott the election and continued to demand his reinstatement. Micheletti ordered the closure of two pro-Zelaya radio stations; one was allowed to return to the air after it promised to tone down criticism of the government. Zelaya's supporters were hardly champions of free expression, however. They resorted to violence to intimidate would-be voters,

attacking radio and television stations that encouraged people to vote. The country was dangerously polarized.

Philosophically, there was little difference between Lobo and Santos. Both had supported Zelaya's ouster. Graffiti labeled the Liberal Santos *"traidor"* (traitor). Each gave the usual pledges to combat violent crime and to improve the dismal economy, which had grown worse with the global recession (see Economy.)

Despite the boycott campaign, voter turnout actually *increased*, from 46% in 2005 to 50%. The results were a convincing mandate:

Lobo Sosa	1,212,846	56.6%
Santos	816,874	38.1%
Others	114,740	5.4%
Null	92,534	4.0%
Blank	61,086	2.7%

The Nationalists also won a clear majority in Congress with 71 of the 128 seats; the Liberals won 45 and three other parties a total of 12.

In his victory statement, Lobo appealed to the community of nations to respect the will of the Honduran voters and recognize his elected government, saying the United States, France, Germany, Italy, Japan, Indonesia, Switzerland and the United Arab Emirates had assured him they would. In his concession, even Santos called on the world to recognize the new government, saying, "Today Honduras tells the world that we Hondurans . . . know how to solve our problems peacefully and democratically."

At first, only four Latin American countries—Colombia, Costa Rica, Panama and Peru—recognized his electiob. Micheletti, obviously aware he was a pariah, opted not to attend the annual Ibero-American Summit in Portugal, which convened the day after the election.

Lobo was inaugurated on January 27, 2010. That same day, under a safe-conduct agreement Lobo had agreed to, Zelaya left the Brazilian Embassy and went into exile in the Dominican Republic. Honduras re-established diplomatic relations with about 30 countries, including Canada, El Salvador, Guatemala and Mexico. However, 10 of the 12 presidents in the South American Union of Nations (*UNASUR*)—all but Colombia's Álvaro Uribe and Peru's Alan García, both pro-U.S.—threatened to boycott the Sixth EU-Latin American-Caribbean Summit held in Madrid if Lobo attended. Even Chile's new conservative, pro-U.S. President Sebastián Piñera joined in the threat. Lobo took the hint and stayed away. Honduras remained a hemispheric outcast.

The legitimacy of Lobo's government and Honduras' reinstatement into the

Honduras

OAS did not even appear on the agenda of the 40th OAS General Assembly, held in Lima, Peru, in June 2010. Nonetheless, Secretary of State Clinton, in her address to the plenary session, noted that the United States had joined the rest of the OAS in condemning Zelaya's overthrow, saying, "these interruptions of democracy should be completely relegated to the past." However, she added, "Now it is time for the hemisphere as a whole to move forward and welcome Honduras back into the Inter-American community."

But the delegates demurred, passing a resolution saying they needed "more information" and calling on Insulza to appoint a high-level commission to go to Honduras and make a report on the situation by July 30.

An act of historic significance took place in Cartagena, Colombia, on May 22, 2011, when Lobo and Zelaya signed the Cartagena Accord brokered by Presidents Chávez of Venezuela and Santos of Colombia and shook hands. Under the terms, Zelaya was allowed to return to Honduras and his supporters were free to participate in future elections. Lobo called it "a very important day for Honduras," while Ze-

laya told his people, "Do not be afraid of democracy." Most significantly, the accord opened the door for a possible referendum on constitutional changes, the issue that led to Zelaya's ouster. Lobo assured his old antagonist he would be welcomed home and accorded the respect due a former president.

Zelaya returned on May 28. The next day, he declared that his 2009 overthrow was the result of "an international conspiracy" and called for an investigation.

The Cartagena Accord cleared the last obstacle to Honduras' readmission to the hemispheric community. On June 1, 2011, the OAS General Assembly in Washington voted 32–1 to readmit Honduras; Rafael Correa's Ecuador cast the lone dissenting vote, citing concern over supposed human rights violations.

World's Deadliest Country

With the Zelaya crisis resolved, Lobo was preoccupied with the skyrocketing rate of violent crime. After dropping behind neighboring El Salvador in 2009, Honduras has had the ugly distinction since then of having the world's highest

homicide rate: 78 per 100,000 people in 2010, 86 in 2011 and 90.4 in 2012. In a bold move in November 2011, Congress voted to empower the armed forces to perform customary police duties for 18 months. It was designed to circumvent a police force that had become riddled with corruption. Almost 200 police officers were under investigation for a variety of offenses. It even outlawed having more than one male on a motorcycle in an effort to combat drive-by shootings. The violence had grown so frightening that even the U.S. Peace Corps pulled out its 150 volunteers in January 2012.

U.S. Vice President Joe Biden met with Lobo and other Central American presidents in Tegucigalpa in March 2012. He pledged greater U.S. cooperation in combating drug trafficking, including providing police and judicial advising, but he argued against the growing sentiment in the region for legalization.

Lobo turned for help to Chilean President Sebastián Piñera, who dispatched a contingent of Chile's highly respected and professional national police force, the *Carabineros*, to Honduras to conduct a review of the Honduran national police. The Chileans issued a report that led to significant operational changes and high-level dismissals. The revamped national police force was 2,000 strong.

An increasing number of victims of the violence are journalists. Nine journalists were killed in 2010, five in 2011 and four in 2012. One was that of radio talk show host Fausto Valle, who was hacked to death with machetes in March 2012. In May 2012, another prominent radio personality, Alfredo Villatoro, veteran news director of *HRN*, was kidnapped and later found shot in the head. Three men believed tied to a drug gang were being held. The killings were denounced by international journalism organizations, which called upon Lobo Sosa to eliminate the seeming impunity for crimes against journalists. After Valle's murder, a group of 94 U.S. representatives threatened in a letter to Secretary of State Clinton to cut off aid to Honduras unless the government investigate the suspicious rash of killings of journalists. Because of the violence against journalists, Freedom House downgraded the Honduran press in 2012 and 2013 from "partly free" to "not free."

U.S.-Honduran relations became strained even further in May 2012 when a joint operation with Honduran soldiers and U.S. Drug Enforcement Agency agents, flying in U.S.-supplied helicopters, raided a boat in a river near the Miskito Coast, killing four people. Official reports claimed the boat was loaded with cocaine, but it turned out that the four people killed were only diving for lobsters and shellfish. Local residents

**Former President
Porfirio "Pepe" Lobo Sosa**

President Juan Orlando Hernández

burned government offices and demanded the DEA withdraw from the area.

An emerging international gang, *Barrio 18*, now rivals *Mara Salvatrucha* in strength and bloodthirstiness. For the second consecutive year, San Pedro Sula topped a list of the world's 50 most violent cities, with 169 homicides per 100,000 population in 2012. The Associated Press reported that rogue policemen in civilian dress were resorting to death-squad tactics by summarily executing gang members. The U.S. Congress suspended direct aid to Police Chief Juan Carlos Bonilla, nicknamed *"El Tigre,"* because of evidence he was complicit in the death squads.

Honduras also worsened from fifth most corrupt nation in the hemisphere to fourth in Transparency International's Corruption Perceptions Indexes for 2012 and 2013.

In another ranking, the Mitofsky poll showed Lobo Sosa the second most unpopular of 20 Western Hemisphere leaders, with an approval rating of 14%, and international organizations warned that Honduras was on the verge of becoming a "failed state." By October 2013 he had improved somewhat to 32%, the sixth most unpopular.

Suddenly, following the dramatic truce reached between *Mara Salvatrucha* and *Barrio 18* in neighboring El Salvador, the jailed Honduran leaders of the two gangs jointly offered from behind the walls of their prison in San Pedro Sula in May 2013 to lay down their arms if the government would meet certain conditions—which the government found too steep. A year later, the level of violence has not appreciably abated.

The Elections of 2013

In this chaotic environment, Zelaya's wife, Xiomara Castro de Zelaya, 53, declared her candidacy for president in June 2013 under the banner of the newly cre-

ated Liberty and Re-establishment Party, or *LIBRE.* She resurrected her husband's call for a constituent assembly to rewrite the constitution, and she initially led in the polls.

The Nationalists nominated Juan Orlando Hernández, 44, president of the Congress; the Liberals picked Mauricio Villeda, 65, the party leader and son of former President Ramón Villeda (1957-63). Further fragmenting the vote was the candidacy of Salvador Nasralla of the Anti-Corruption Party. Four lesser candidates also were on the ballot.

The goodwill of the Cartagena Accord quickly evaporated, and polls showed the election to be a contest between Castro and Hernández. For Zelaya, of course, his wife's victory would represent vindication and an opportunity to advance his left-wing agenda. Thus, the 2013 election became a referendum over Zelaya's 2009 ouster. The rhetoric was heated, and the stakes were even higher because a simple plurality is all that is needed to win in Honduras, which does not have runoff elections as most Latin American countries do. Fortunately, violence was limited despite the inflamed passions. Hernández, who turned 45 on October 28, erased Castro's lead by pledging to get tougher on the gangs, a *mano dura* approach similar to that of Guatemala's President Otto Pérez Molina. Among other things, he said he would increase the national police from 2,000 to 5,000 but was less clear on how he would finance it. Eight days before the election, he narrowly escaped death in a helicopter crash.

Turnout on November 24 was an unusually high 61.2%. Three hours after polls closed, Castro impetuously declared herself president-elect, citing her party's exit polls. But independent exit polls gave Hernández a three-point lead. He, too, claimed victory. Compounding the drama was the slowness of the vote count. About 500 Castro partisans marched on the headquarters of the Supreme Electoral Tribunal *(TSE)* as a show of force. Yet, Hernández's lead grew. The final count:

Hernández	1,149,302	36.9%
Castro	896,498	28.8%
Villeda	632,320	20.3%
Nasralla	418,443	13.4%

Villeda conceded defeat and congratulated Hernández. But Zelaya denounced the election as a "disgusting monstrosity," claimed it was fraudulent and said his party would refuse to recognize the result. His wife temporarily disappeared from public view. More than 700 international observers who had monitored the election declared it to be transparent and fair. Even Nicaraguan President Ortega, Zelaya's

staunch ally, accepted the outcome and called Hernández to congratulate him.

Besides having a mandate of only 37% of the popular vote, Hernández's National Party won only 48 of 128 seats in the new Congress, a loss of 23. The Liberals won 27, a loss of 18. Taking up the slack were Zelaya and Castro's new *LIBRE*, which won 37 seats, and the Anti-Corruption Party, with 13. The two-party system is no more.

Hernández was inaugurated in the National Stadium on January 27, 2014. *LIBRE* legislators boycotted the ceremony. The presidents of Costa Rica, Colombia, the Dominican Republic, Panama, Kosovo and Taiwan and Spain's Prince Felipe attended; the United States was represented only by Labor Secretary Thomas Pérez.

Honduras found itself in the forefront of a potential humanitarian disaster along the U.S.-Mexican border in June 2014 as tens of thousands of children as young as four years old unaccompanied by adults, most of them from Honduras, Guatemala and El Salvador, suddenly began crossing the U.S. border illegally. They were being housed at various impromptu detention centers, raising international concerns for their welfare. A representative of Honduras met in Guatemala with U.S. Vice President Joe Biden, Guatemalan President Otto Pérez Molina and Salvadoran President Salvador Sánchez Cerén on June 20 to discuss the crisis (see Guatemala).

CULTURE: Honduran culture is almost entirely based on that of its colonial conquerors. The ancient Mayan civilization, the subject of intensive research and archaeological exploration for more than 100 years, had declined many centuries prior to the arrival of the Spaniards. The Mayan ruins of Copan are a UNESCO World Heritage Site.

The Caribbean coast has a significant population of Garifunas, descendants of escaped African slaves. Immigration has further broadened the country's ethnic makeup, including a colony of Palestinian Christians who have thrived in business and banking.

Moorish-Spanish architecture prevails throughout most of the nation, particularly in the beautiful churches built during the centuries since the arrival of Roman Catholicism.

Education is compulsory through the age of 15, but there is a serious shortage of trained teachers, a lack of schools and little effort to enforce the educational law. Honduras has 12 universities, 10 of them established since 1956. The National Autonomous University of Honduras was founded in 1846. Only a tiny percentage of Hondurans attain a higher education.

The folklore and music of Honduras closely resemble those of the other Central

Honduras

American nations. Cultural division exists between the bustling cities and the isolated, mountainous rural areas—the people of the lonely countryside have been almost completely bypassed by the civilization of the more mundane city people.

The high illiteracy rate has hindered the development of newspapers, magazines and book publishing. Among Honduras' best remembered fiction writers were the short-story writer and journalist Froylán Turcios (1874–1943), who compiled many of his stories in *Cuentos del amor y la muerte* (*Stories of Love and Death*) in 1930; and the romantic novelist Lucila Gamero de Medina (1873–1964), whose 1908 novel *Blanca Olmedo* stirred controversy for its criticism of the Catholic Church.

Probably the best-known contemporary Honduran writer is the novelist Roberto Quesada, whose novels have been translated into English. These include *Los barcos* (*The Ships*) in 1992, *The Big Banana* in 2000 and *Nunca entres por Miami* (*Never Through Miami*) in 2002.

The leading newspapers are *El Heraldo* and *La Tribuna* in Tegucigalpa and *Tiempo* and *La Prensa* in San Pedro Sula; all four now circulate nationally. Newspapers remain politically influential, and are owned by families of the ruling elite. *Tiempo*, owned by businessman Jaime Rosenthal, is pro-Liberal, as is *La Tribuna*, owned by former President Carlos Flores. *El Heraldo* and *La Prensa*, both owned by the Canahuati family, are pro-Nationalist. Because of the growing number of journalists murdered in the country's gang-related violence, Freedom House downgraded the Honduran press from "partly free" to "not free" in 2012 and 2013 (see History).

Radio and television are the most popular media and have become well-developed for such an impoverished country. They, too, are owned primarily by wealthy, politically connected families.

ECONOMY: Honduras is a classic example of a "banana republic," with a small aristocracy, a tiny middle class and a large peasant population that lives on a per capita income of $2,000 per year. Most of the nation's farmland was once controlled by U.S.-owned banana firms and by a few huge cattle ranches. Mountainous terrain and periodic droughts limit farm output and methods are primitive. Most industry is foreign-owned. Coffee production replaced bananas as the chief source of foreign exchange, followed by lumber, meat, sugar, cotton and tobacco.

Honduras was devastated by Hurricane Mitch in 1998. Largely because of the devastation to the banana crop, real GDP growth declined –3.0% in 1999. It rebounded to 6.3% in 2000, then dipped before returning to 6.3% in both 2006 and 2007. With the global recession, political unrest and the instability of gang violence, growth declined in 2009 by –3.0%. It increased only 2.8% in 2010, 3.6% in 2011, 3.8% in 2012 and 2.8% in 2013, at or below the regional average.

Remittances from Hondurans working abroad, mostly in the U.S., mushroomed from $484 million in 2000 to $2.56 billion in 2007, more than 25% of GDP. They rose to $2.7 billion in 2008, then shrank to $2.4 billion in 2009 because of the global recession. They have increased gradually each year since, totaling $2.825 billion in 2012. They were projected to total $3.152 billion in 2013, 16.8% of GDP.

Per capita income has grown slowly, from $643 in 1998 to $2,335 in 2013, the third-lowest in the Western Hemisphere, and 60-65% of the population was below the poverty line in 2010. Child prostitution is a growing social problem in Honduras.

Honduras is saddled with a high external debt that was equal to 74.1% of GDP in 2005. It was one of 18 countries—and one of four in the Western Hemisphere—that qualified for a debt-forgiveness program when the so-called Paris Club of creditor nations met in 2005. Since then, it has received about $4 billion in debt relief. At the end of 2008 its debt was $3.6 billion, only about 25% of GDP. It has since risen again, to 35.8% in 2012 and 40.6% in 2013.

About a third of Hondurans are unemployed (4.5% in 2012) or underemployed. Compounding the economic woes is the country's gang-related crime problem, blamed for a devastating 30% decrease in foreign investments in 2001 alone. Kidnapping of business people itself became a lucrative business in the first decade of the 21st century but the situation has improved.

Foreign direct investment in Honduras totaled $687 million in 2010, a one-year jump of 37%, thanks to new government initiatives to lure foreign companies.

A potentially promising experiment in development began in 2011, when Congress approved President Lobo's proposal for a constitutional amendment to set aside a 380-square-mile (1,000 km^2) enclave of undeveloped land on the northern coast near Trujillo for a so-called "special development region," or *RED* in Spanish. It would become a semi-autonomous zone with its own laws that would, in theory, not be handicapped by Honduras' existing corruption and violence. The concept is based on the charter city idea of U.S. economist Paul Romer of New York University, whom Lobo has appointed to a nine-member "transparency commission" of foreign experts to oversee its development. Once developed, it would attract foreign businesses that would create jobs and help stimulate the Honduran economy. It is being compared with post-colonial Hong Kong or Singapore, except that this charter city would be built from scratch.

How democratic its government would be is a still-unanswered question. Moreover, Romer withdrew in 2012, complaining of the government's lack of transparency. A group of investor companies reportedly pledged $15 million to initiate development of the *RED*, but Romer was not consulted and no details were forthcoming.

Then left-wing groups brought suits against the development. The Supreme Court declared it unconstitutional, whereupon the Assembly removed four of the judges! Even pro-government newspapers questioned whether the project would fly; al-Jazeera ridiculed it as "neoliberal Viagra." Lobo left office in January 2014, and the new president, Juan Orlando Hernández, has proposed a similar concept called "exclusive economic development zones," or *ZEDAs*, but details were sketchy when this book went to press.

THE FUTURE: Although passionate about politics, Hondurans seem to be blasé about their democracy. The periodic *Latinobarómetro* survey of 18 Latin American nations published in *The Economist* showed that only 19% of Hondurans in 2013 were satisfied with the way democracy works in their country, the lowest percentage of any country in the survey. The percentage of Hondurans who believe democracy is preferable to any other form of government was 44% in 2013, virtually unchanged from 42% in the first survey in 1996. At the same time, 27% of Hondurans said in 2011 that authoritarianism is preferable to democracy in certain circumstances, the highest of the 18 nations. That fell to 14% in 2013. Yet, for whatever reason, voter turnout on November 24 was a record 61.2%, so apparently they haven't given up entirely.

The overthrow of President Manuel Zelaya in 2009 threw icy water on the democratic process, even though his own party and the Congress insisted his removal was legal and necessary. There was little doubt that the election of the National Party's Porfirio Lobo Sosa was fair and honest and that his 56.6% mandate represented the will of the Honduran people. Zelaya accepted the inevitable and spent a year in exile before being returning home in 2011 under the terms of the historic Cartagena Accords

The defeat of Zelaya's stand-in wife, Xiomara Castro, at the hands of the National Party's Juan Orlando Hernández in the November 24, 2013, election also was fair and square in the eyes of 700 international observers. Zelaya and Castro proved the worst losers of an election since Mexico's

Andrés Manuel López Obrador in 2006 and 2012.

Despite their crybaby antics, however, there is no denying they made history by breaking the rule of the traditional National and Liberal parties. Castro polled almost 29% of the popular vote, and their new *LIBRE* party became the second-largest bloc in the Congress with 37 of the 128 seats. Between them, the National and Liberal parties have a bare majority of 65 seats. Once rivals, the two traditional parties, controlled by the country's oligarchy, will now likely become allies against Zelaya and his left-wing movement. Now that the two-party system appears to be a thing of the past, Congress would do well to amend the constitution to provide for a *segunda vuelta,* or runoff, as most Latin American countries have when no presidential candidate wins an absolute majority.

Armed with a flimsy electoral mandate of only 37% of the vote and a tenuous coalition in Congress, Hernández must now attempt to try to save his destitute, violence-racked country from falling into the category of a failed state—if, in fact, it hasn't already. Honduras has the world's highest homicide rate, it is the third-poorest and the fourth most corrupt nation in Latin America and its public debt is 40% of GDP. Its future looks bleak.

At 45 the youngest president since Callejas, Hernández is a lawyer by training and a successful businessman by profession, but he also holds a master's degree in public administration from New York University. His training there is about to be put to the acid test. Reportedly high on his agenda is a reform of the sales tax, or *IVA,* to eliminate loopholes and help close the chronic budget deficit. He will have to come up with something to pay for the 3,000 extra national policemen he has promised. Balancing his *mano dura* toward the gangs, he also plans to seek foreign assistance for programs aimed at diverting youths away from gangs. He has his work cut out for him, but he has undertaken it with energy, and he has been compared to Franklin D. Roosevelt in his first 100 days. He ordered an investigation of the social security system and all the directors have been charged with corruption. He also extradited the first drug kingpin to the United States. It's an auspicious start.

Jamaica

Dunn's River Falls near Ocho Rios on the north-central coast, a 600-foot stairstep waterfall that is one of the island's favorite attractions.

Area: 4,470 square miles.

Population: 2,930,050 (2014 est.); another 2–3 million live abroad.

Capital City: Kingston (Pop. 937,700 in 2011, estimated).

Climate: The coastal climate is hot and humid; the uplands are moderate, variable and pleasant.

Neighboring Countries: This island state, the third largest of the Greater Antilles, lies about 100 miles south of Cuba and 100 miles west of the southwestern tip of Haiti.

Official Language: English.

Other Principal Tongues: A distinct variety of English spoken with a very rhythmic pattern.

Ethnic Background: African Negro and mulatto, with a very small European minority. There are prominent Chinese and East Indian minorities.

Principal Religion: Protestant Christianity (Anglican); the Roman Catholic Church and other Protestant sects are active, as is Rastafarianism (Rasta).

Chief Commercial Products: Alumina (partially refined bauxite), bauxite, sugar, bananas and other tropical fruits, rum. Tourism and remittances important sources of income.

Currency: Jamaica Dollar.

Gross Domestic Product: U.S. $14.39 billion in 2013 ($4,946 per capita, official exchange rate).

Former Colonial Status: Spanish Colony (1494–1655); British Colony (1655–1962).

Independence Date: August 6, 1962.

Chief of State: Queen Elizabeth II of Great Britain, represented by Sir Patrick Linton Allen, governor-general (since February 26, 2009).

Head of Government: Portia Simpson Miller (b. December 12, 1945), prime minister (since January 5, 2012).

National Flag: A gold diagonal Cross of St. Andrew, with black triangles at each side and green triangles at the top and bottom.

Jamaica is a picturesque, mountainous island about 145 miles long by 50 miles in width. The mountains run east and west, with spurs to the north and south reaching 7,420 feet in the east and descending in the west. The coastal plains are intensively cultivated and are the most densely populated. The Jamaican people are descendants of African slaves imported by Spanish and English planters. Rich soils and adequate rainfall encouraged sugar and cotton production during the colonial period, while the small valleys provided fruits and vegetables for local consumption. Jamaica possesses large deposits of bauxite and gypsum which are commercially exploited.

HISTORY: Jamaica's history is inextricably interwoven with the struggle between Spain and England for domination of Atlantic trade in the 16th and 17th centuries. The island was discovered by Columbus in

Jamaica

1494 during his second voyage to the New World; the Spanish adventurer, Juan de Esquivel, settled the island in 1509, calling it Santiago. Villa de la Vega, (later, Spanish Town) was founded in 1523 and served as the capital until 1872. The native Arawak people were rapidly exterminated and Negro slaves were imported to provide labor.

When Jamaica was taken by the British in 1655, the total population was about 3,000. The Spanish were completely expelled by 1660, at which time their slaves fled to the mountains. These people, known as *Maroons*, resisted all efforts to recapture them, and maintained a state of guerrilla warfare against the British through the 18th century.

British title to Jamaica was confirmed in 1670, and from 1672 on, the island became one of the world's largest slave markets. By the end of the 18th century, Jamaica had a slave population in excess of 3 million, working 70 sugar, 60 indigo and 60 cacao plantations. With a profitable trade with London and an equally great illegal trade with Spanish America, the Jamaican planters were extremely wealthy. The prohibition of slave trade in 1807, freedom of the Spanish colonies by 1821 and the abolition of slavery in 1833–38, ended the plantation economy as the freed slaves took to the hills, occupying small plots of land, where their descendants are found today.

The 19th century was marked by increasing resistance to colonial rule as the economic situation deteriorated. Riots in 1865 brought about changes in the government, while disturbances in 1938 led to the establishment of dominion status in 1944 and an advance preparation for independence, granted in 1962.

Jamaica's history has also been influenced by natural disasters. An earthquake in 1692 destroyed Port Royal and led to the founding of Kingston. It in turn was destroyed by a 1907 earthquake, but was rebuilt. Hurricanes have also exacted their toll and revised the island's agricultural patterns.

The island nation has a parliamentary system of government with a two-chamber legislature consisting of a 21-member Senate and 60-member House of Representatives. The prime minister, selected from the majority party, chooses 13 senators and the remaining 8 are selected by the governor-general with advice from the leader of the opposition party. Technically, Jamaica is still a member of the British Commonwealth and a constitutional monarchy with the queen of Great Britain as the titular head of state. The queen appoints the governor-general (a Jamaican recommended by the prime minister) as her local representative.

By law, elections must be held every five years, but can be called by the party in power sooner. The two major political parties in Jamaica are the Jamaica Labour Party (JLP) and the People's National Party (PNP).

The Manley-Seaga Years

The ensuing two decades after 1972 were dominated by Michael Manley, whose father, Norman Manley, founded the PNP and played a key role in the independence movement, and Edward P.G. Seaga of the JLP. Both were Caucasian. Their policies were energetically directed toward improving Jamaica, and both tried a number of ideas to accomplish this, Manley from the left and Seaga from the right. Both, however, were hamstrung by deep-seated social and economic woes.

Manley, who won the 1972 elections, by 1976 had established a centrally planned economy and forged close ties with the Soviet Union via Castro's Cuba. Government spending increased tremendously and production fell sharply. By 1980, the prime minister's spending habits had all but bankrupted the country, and his popularity, even among the poor, plummeted. Although he counted on subsidies from the Soviet Union like Cuba did, the money and goods never seemed to make it beyond Cuba if, indeed, it had been sent at all by an overextended Soviet Union.

Manley scheduled elections in 1980. Campaign violence claimed an estimated 650 lives. Seaga, despite his party's liberal-sounding name, was right of center. Impoverished Jamaicans listened to his message and gave the JLP 57% of the popular vote and 51 of the 60 House seats.

Seaga established close ties with the new Reagan administration while distancing Jamaica from Cuba. He was instrumental in the creation of Reagan's Caribbean Basin Initiative. Economic growth resumed, although Seaga was criticized over a currency devaluation in 1983. He called elections

Michael Manley

Errol Harvey

abruptly late that year, catching the PNP off balance. The PNP boycotted the election and the JLP won all the seats in the House.

Another devaluation followed, but the economy continued to falter. Export prices for bauxite (aluminum ore) dropped in large part because of widespread recycling of the metal. Discontent over the lack of progress led to a resurgence of Manley's party in 1986, when it captured all but one of the municipal governments. After two more devaluations, the country was plagued by riots in 1987 and 1988, and it sustained widespread damage from Hurricane Gilbert in 1988, which left half a million homeless.

Seaga called new elections in 1989, but he was battling a new edition of Manley, who foresaw the imminent worldwide collapse of communism. Manley had discarded all the old rhetoric and concentrated on attacking Seaga's record and the miserable state of the Jamaican economy. The PNP and Manley returned to power, capturing 44 seats.

Jamaica

Edward P.G. Seaga
Elizabeth Marshall

P.J. Patterson

Faced with continued discontent and in failing health, the 67-year-old Manley retired in 1992. Despite allegations of earlier questionable dealing, his deputy prime minister, Percival James "P.J." Patterson, succeeded him. He was the first post-independence black prime minister.

Patterson called elections in 1993. Patterson and the PNP waged an openly racist campaign against Seaga, appealing to the 75% black population. ("He is one of us"). The PNP won in a landslide, but the PLP alleged fraud. It initially boycotted the Parliament, but returned to claim the eight seats it won.

The JLP fared little better in the general elections of 1997, in which it raised its number of seats only to 10. Overall, the PNP polled 56% of the vote to 39% for the JLP and 5% for the National Democratic Movement, which won no seats. Turnout was low, but so was the traditional political violence. A 60-member team of international observers, headed by former U.S. President Jimmy Carter, declared the elections generally fair, although Carter admitted there had been "serious problems." Chief among these was the peculiar Jamaican tradition of "garrison constituencies" controlled by one party or the other, a practice Carter said he had never seen in monitoring 22 elections in 15 countries.

A political era, and a dynasty, ended when Manley died of prostate cancer on March 6, 1997. Fidel Castro was among those attending his funeral. Manley was buried next to his father.

In July 2001, Patterson mobilized the entire 3,000-man army to quell violence between gangs suspected of ties to the two major parties that left 28 dead in and around Kingston. He and Seaga held a meeting aimed at reducing the violence, but there were new outbreaks in September and October and in January 2002 that left scores dead, including children. There was a total of 1,140 murders in Jamaica in 2001, a 28% increase over 2000, and the violence affected the all-important tourism industry as hotels reported a wave of cancellations.

A special commission investigating the 2001 outbreak concluded its work in 2002, but Amnesty International criticized the report as one-sided because it relied solely on the testimony of the police and military. Not surprisingly, the report concluded that the security forces had acted properly. For his part, Seaga was called to testify before the commission, but he refused.

Patterson also responded to the growing violence by advocating creation of a Caribbean Court of Justice, based in Trinidad, to replace Britain's Privy Council, currently the court of last resort for Jamaica and other British Commonwealth countries in the Caribbean. The new court was seen as a means of expediting hangings of murderers.

Patterson called new elections in 2002. In the three-month campaign, there were 17 politically related deaths—relatively low for Jamaica. Both parties pledged to combat the alarming crime rate. The PNP vowed to seek a 6% growth in GDP, while the JLP stressed education. Patterson won an unprecedented third term, but with a greatly reduced majority: 34 seats to 26. Patterson, then 68, said he would retire before the end of his five-year mandate. Meanwhile, Seaga, 72, said before the election that he would step aside as opposition leader if the JLP lost again and make way for new leadership.

The murder rate for 2004 was 50% higher than in 2003, exceeding 100 per month. In 2005, Jamaica's homicide rate was the highest in the entire world, 58 per 100,000 people. The number of murders hit a record of 1,671, up another 25%. Patterson launched a major crackdown on drug smuggling, which fed much of the gang violence, and brought crime consultants from Britain, the United States, Canada and Australia. In 2006, the homicide rate dropped slightly to 49, still the second-highest in the world after El Salvador.

An old era ended and a new one began in Jamaican politics in 2005 and 2006. Keeping his promise, Seaga stepped down as JLP leader in January 2005, and Orette Bruce Golding, 57, was elected to succeed him in a party convention, becoming the JLP's first black leader. A former member of the House of Representatives who had become a senator, Golding had long been considered Seaga's heir apparent, but he

Former Prime Minister P. J. Patterson

had impatiently bolted the party in 1995 when Seaga declined to retire. However, Golding could not officially become leader of the opposition until he won a House seat, which he did in a by-election in West Kingston. The choice of that constituency would prove fateful. Seaga took a faculty position at the University of the West Indies.

Patterson also retired, and the PNP held a convention in 2006 to elect a new president, who would automatically become prime minister. In the balloting, Portia Simpson-Miller, a veteran member of Parliament and former minister of labor and of tourism, was elected. On March 30, Simpson-Miller, 60, widely known as "Sista P," was sworn in as Jamaica's first woman prime minister. She pledged to combat the endemic violence and corruption, to reform education and to expand the economy.

Golding's Mandate and the Battle of Tivoli Gardens

Simpson-Miller's stewardship was to be short-lived. She called a general election for September 3, 2007. Golding made a surprisingly strong showing in a televised debate with her, emphasizing corruption scandals within the PNP. Unlike past elections, violence was minimal.

The vote was so close the counting went on for two days before Simpson-Miller conceded defeat. The JLP won 50.5% of the popular vote and 32 House seats to 28—a tenuous mandate. Golding was sworn in as prime minister on September 11, ending 18 years of PNP rule. Simpson-Miller remained leader of the opposition.

Later that year, faced like other Third World leaders with escalating oil prices, Golding took a page out of Seaga's book and devalued the currency.

Jamaica recorded another 1,574 murders in 2007, an increase of 17% over 2006; 65 were children.

Golding moved forward with his promise to crack down on corruption, appointing special auditors to investigate the customs service, the National Housing Trust and the Jamaica Urban Transit Company. One auditor, Douggie Chambers, uncovered padded payrolls in the transit company and ordered the dismissal of several managers and almost 500 unneeded employees. On June 27, 2008, Chambers was assassinated in Spanish Town. The prime suspect was a gang called the Klansmen, which has an extortion racket with roots in the transit union. Although Jamaicans had almost become inured to common gang violence, they are unaccustomed to high-level assassinations by contract killers. The murder remains unsolved.

In 2009, Jamaica recorded a record 1,671 murders, moving its homicide rate back up to 60 per 100,000, third highest in the world, behind El Salvador and Honduras.

Golding signed a historic $1.27 billion, 27-month standby agreement with the IMF in 2010 that helped ease the effects of Jamaica's chronic balance of payments deficit (see Economy).

The United States submitted an extradition request in March 2010 for Christopher "Dudus" Coke, 41, the reputed top crime lord in Jamaica, who had been indicted in 2009 by a federal grand jury in New York for trafficking in marijuana and cocaine, especially crack cocaine. The allegorically named Coke was the alleged leader of an international drug- and gun-smuggling organization called the "Shower Posse" that he inherited from his father, Lester Lloyd Coke, who was burned to death in prison under mysterious circumstances in 1992. The organization has tentacles in several major U.S. cities. Like Colombia's late drug kingpin Pablo Escobar, Coke is revered among the poor in the garrison community he controls as a benevolent Robin Hood- or Godfather-like figure. The Shower Posse also has shadowy ties to Golding's JLP; indeed, Coke's garrison community of Tivoli Gardens in West Kingston is in Golding's parliamentary district, and until the extradition request, Coke's attorney was a JLP senator.

That may help explain why Golding, who had routinely agreed to 15 other extradition requests, at first rejected the one for Coke, saying the evidence against him was based on an illegal wiretap. Under U.S. pressure, he relented.

No effort was made to arrest Coke for five days. When that effort did begin, Coke's supporters resisted violently. On May 23, two policemen were killed and six wounded in a gun battle with Coke supporters. The next day, hundreds of po-

Former Prime Minister Bruce Golding

lice and army soldiers stormed into Tivoli Gardens to apprehend Coke. Full-scale combat ensued with well-armed Coke loyalists. Two policemen, one soldier and 26 civilians were killed. By the end of that week, the death toll had climbed to 74, the overwhelming number of them civilians.

Coke partisans alleged to the parliamentary ombudsman that the security forces had engaged in summary executions, which the government denied, while Amnesty International called for an investigation. Dozens more people on both sides were wounded, and about 500 people were arrested; Amnesty International later put the number of arrests at 4,000. The impact on the all-important tourism industry was devastating (see Economy).

Coke remained at large until he was apprehended in Kingston on June 22 and turned over to U.S. authorities two days later. He was taken to New York for trial, where at first he pleaded not guilty. But in August 2011 he suddenly pleaded guilty to various racketeering charges. His sentencing hearing was postponed several times before finally being held on May 22, 2012. Several witnesses gave graphic testimony about killings they said Coke ordered. On June 8 he was sentenced to the maximum—23 years.

On May 23, 2011, the first anniversary of the battle, Amnesty International again called on the Jamaican government to launch a formal investigation into the Tivoli Gardens deaths, saying at least 40 appeared to have been "extrajudicial" killings. AI also alleged that from 2000–2010, there were 2,220 fatal shootings by police in Jamaica, but that only two policemen had ever been convicted of wrongful death.

Golding garnered international attention again in June 2011 when he publicly declared he wanted to sever ties to the

British Crown and make Jamaica a republic in time for the 50th anniversary of independence in 2012. However, a poll by *The Daily Gleaner* showed that 60% of Jamaicans believed the country would be better off if it were a colony again!

The Return of 'Sista P'

Golding stunned the country and even his own party on September 26, 2011, by announcing he was stepping down as prime minister effective as soon as the JLP elected a new leader. In his statement, he did not mention the Coke factor, saying only that "the challenges of the last four years have taken their toll." The party elected Education Minister Andrew Holness, 39, who on October 23 was sworn in as the youngest prime minister in Jamaican history.

Although general elections weren't required before September 2012, Holness perhaps impetuously called a snap election for December 29, 2011, seeking to govern under his own mandate. Theoretically, it was good political timing. After three years of negative economic growth, Jamaica would end 2011 with a tiny, but positive, growth of 1.3%. The murder rate was down dramatically from 52 per 100,000 in 2010, third-highest in the world, to 39 in 2011, tying Belize and Guatemala for fifth place. Polls favored the JLP.

Then the campaign turned ugly, with the JLP belittling Simpson-Miller as uneducated and incompetent compared with Holness, who has a bachelor's degree in management and a master's degree in development from the University of the West Indies. But Simpson-Miller has a degree in public administration from the University

Jamaica

Prime Minister Portia Simpson Miller

of Miami and an advanced management certificate from the University of California at Berkeley, besides participating in the executive program for leaders in development at Harvard's John F. Kennedy School of Government. That tactic boomeranged on the JLP, as most of the electorate has far less education than Simpson-Miller has. Polls then showed the race a tossup.

In a courageous move, Simpson-Miller said she would abandon Golding's ban on gays in the Cabinet. Jamaicans are notoriously homophobic; the anti-gay lyrics of some reggae songs have stirred international condemnation. On one issue she voiced agreement with Golding: Jamaica should become a republic.

It is possible that voters were annoyed over being forced to make an important electoral decision on the Thursday before the festive New Year's weekend. For whatever reason, they gave Simpson-Miller and the PNP a resounding mandate of 42 seats to 21 for the JLP. The PNP also received 463,232 popular votes, or 53.3%, to 405,234 for the JLP. Holness conceded it was a "humbling" defeat.

Simpson-Miller, 61, was sworn in again as prime minister on January 5, 2012. She warned that future austerity measures would be necessary to comply with the $1.27 billion loan agreement Golding concluded with the IMF, and she repeated her intention to proceed with plans to sever ties with the British Crown, saying, "We need to complete the circle of independence."

Queen Elizabeth II issued a brief statement on the issue, saying it is "entirely the matter of the Jamaican government and people." Nonetheless, Prince Harry made a much-publicized visit to Jamaica in March 2012 in honor of the 50th anni-

versary. He was warmly received, even receiving a hug from Simpson Miller, who had hinted that she would "accept" an apology from Britain for the "wicked and brutal" practice of slavery.

Time magazine named Simpson-Miller one of the 100 most influential people in the world for 2012, predicting, "She will have a profound impact as she strives to be a transformational figure in Jamaica."

Recent Developments

Jamaicans had various 50th anniversary celebrations in 2012, culminating in six days of festivities at the newly built Golden Jubilee Village. The National Stadium was packed on August 6, as Jamaicans temporarily put aside their sometimes violent differences to party together.

The independence celebrations came and went, and Jamaica remains part of the British Commonwealth. Both parties seem to have toned down their rhetoric to establish a republic, perhaps because in balance Jamaica has more to lose than gain if it severs its preferential ties to Britain, including economic and military aid. Holness even said during his anniversary speech that showing national maturity and establishing economic independence are more important than a ceremonial name change.

Simpson-Miller's popularity was tested in June 2012 when she extended the sales tax to numerous food items in an effort to come to terms with the crushing budget deficit (see Economy). In order to secure a badly needed $750 million IMF loan, she told bond-holders in February 2013 they would have to accept a lower interest rate and imposed still more tax increases. Higher taxes may exacerbate Jamaica's already serious brain drain (see The Future). In April 2014, she imposed a controversial and highly unpopular tax on bank withdrawals.

Jamaica's homicide rate increased slightly from 39 to 39.3 per 100,000 in 2012. It fell from fifth- to sixth-deadliest country in the world.

CULTURE: The Jamaican people have a vibrant culture. Their musical expression most identifiable with Jamaica is in the hypnotic rhythm of "reggae," grounded in the Rastafarian religion. Rastafarianism, or "Rasta," as its adherents call it, is a Christian cult with African roots. Its central tenet is that Haile Selassie, the late emperor of Ethiopia, was the reincarnation of Jesus Christ. Rasta also permits the ritual smoking of marijuana. The "dreadlock" hairstyle is a distinctive feature of this faith.

Reggae is the basis of a thriving recording industry in Jamaica and has achieved international acclaim. A Best Reggae Album

category was added to the U.S. Grammy Awards in 1985, and Jamaicans have won all but four of them through 2012.

The most iconic figure of reggae was Bob Marley (1945–81), the singer, guitarist and songwriter whose fame spread to the United States and elsewhere with such hits as *One Love, I Shot the Sheriff* and *Buffalo Soldier.* The posthumous 1984 album of his hits, *Legend,* is the largest-selling reggae album of all time, selling 25 million copies. He was awarded the Order of Merit by the Jamaican government shortly before his death.

Marley was only 36 when he died of cancer, but he and his wife, Rita (b. 1946), one of his backup singers, spawned a musical dynasty through their five children. David (aka Ziggy), Stephen, Sharon and Cedella began performing as children with their father. Their group, Ziggy Marley and the Melody Makers, was formed in 1979 and kept performing after the patriarch's death in 1981. It won the Best Reggae Album Grammy in 1989, 1990 and 1998. Stephen Marley won three Grammys on his own, in 2008 and 2010 for two versions of *Mind Control* and in 2012 for *Revelation Part 1: The Root of Life.* Ziggy Marley won a Grammy in 2007 for *Love is my Religion.* The Marleys' youngest child, Damian, who was only 2 when his father died, also grew up to be a reggae singer and has collected two Grammys, for *Halfway Tree* in 2002 and *Welcome to Jamrock* in 2006.

One of the members of Bob Marley's band, The Wailers, who went on to stardom himself was Peter Tosh (1944–87), who won a posthumous Grammy in 1988 for *No Nuclear War.* Another famous contemporary of Bob Marley is Jimmy Cliff (b. 1948), who won a Grammy in 1985 for *Cliff Hanger* and was awarded the Order of Merit in 2003.

Other reggae singers who have won multiple Grammys include Bunny Wailer (1991, 1995 and 1997); and Burning Spear (2000 and 2009).

One who was nominated four times but never won, perhaps because of repeated brushes with the law, was Gregory Isaacs (1951–2010), nicknamed the "Cool Ruler" from the name of a 1978 album. His fame predated Marley's, and he created the reggae style known as "lovers' rock." Both a singer and songwriter, he was regarded as a premier figure of the genre, being called "the Frank Sinatra of Jamaica," but he was arrested 50 times on drug or weapon charges during his career and served six months in a Jamaican prison in 1982–83. Still, there is no denying his prolific body of work of more than 200 albums. His best-remembered songs include *Night Nurse, Lonely Man* and *Don't Let Me Suffer.* He abandoned Jamaica for Britain, where he died of cancer and is buried.

Performing arts have been exemplified by such groups as the National Dance Theatre and the Jamaica Folk Singers, which take the country's dance and song abroad. Kingston and almost all of the larger resort towns have excellent theatrical presentations.

One of Jamaica's most illustrious figures internationally was Louise Simone Bennett-Coverley (1919-2006), a noted folklorist, writer, poet, and radio and television personality. Her poetry was in Creole, and has been collected into several volumes. Perhaps the best-known is *Jamaica Labrish* in 1966. She studied in London, where she had a radio show on the BBC. Returning to Jamaica, she was a popular radio personality, known as "Miss Lou," and also taught poetry and drama at the University of the West Indies. Her trademark phrase was, "Walk good." She became a Jamaican cultural ambassador and in 1960 was named a member of the Order of the British Empire. She was awarded the Jamaican Order of Merit in 1974 for her contributions to the arts and culture. She and her husband emigrated to Canada for him to receive better medical treatment, and she last visited her homeland in 2003. She died in Toronto at 86 but was returned to Kingston for burial. Crowds lined the streets for her funeral.

Jamaica has produced several other writers of distinction, although most chose to spend their careers abroad, typical of Jamaica's brain drain. One notable exception was the white, Canadian-born novelist and journalist John Edgar Colwell Hearne (1926–94), whose Jamaican parents returned to the island when he was 17. He joined the Royal Canadian Air Force during World War II, then studied, taught and wrote in England and Europe for 15 years, publishing his first novel, *Voices Under the Window*, in 1955. For his next four novels he incorporated a technique of Faulkner's of writing about Jamaica under a fictional name, "Cayuna," but the descriptions of the life and issues made it clear that Cayuna was Jamaica. He used this technique in the novels *The Faces of Love, Stranger at the Gate, The Autumn Equinox* and *Land of the Living*, written between 1956 and 1961. He returned to Jamaica in 1962, the year of independence, and spent the rest of his life and career there. He wrote a column for *The Daily Gleaner* under a pseudonym and waited 20 years before publishing his last novel, *The Sure Salvation*, about a slave ship, in 1981.

The Daily Gleaner, established in 1834, is one of the oldest continually published newspapers in the hemisphere and is still Jamaica's newspaper of record.

The National Gallery of Art, established in 1974, houses a collection of priceless works executed by Jamaican artists, but also contains representative works, centuries old and new, from many nations. Local artists, potters, sculptors and weavers produce works that encompass all schools and techniques. They range in price from $10 into the thousands. Many art galleries and craft shops are found throughout the island.

One source of Jamaican pride is its Olympic athletes, especially sprinters. Jamaica has participated in 16 summer games from 1948 through 2012 and won a disproportionately high 67 medals for its size, including 17 gold. Jamaica won 12 medals in London in 2012, including four gold, three of those won by Usain Bolt. Jamaican expatriates often win medals for their adopted countries.

Jamaica has one of the worst brain-drain problems on Earth. Quality higher education is Jamaica is largely lacking, forcing the best and brightest to study abroad, if they can afford it. Too many educated Jamaicans remain abroad where the opportunities are. There are more than a dozen universities, colleges, teacher training schools and community colleges in Jamaica, mostly small, new and expensive. Mico University College in Kingston was founded in 1836. A branch of the University of the West Indies was established in Mona in 1948 and is considered the country's most prestigious school.

Lamentably, Jamaica is characterized by a culture of violence, some political, some common crime. Handguns abound in Jamaica and are the favored means of "settling" disputes. A "Gun Court" was established to hand down stiff sentences for illegal firearm activity. Capital punishment was discontinued in 1988, but reinstituted in 1999. All appeals must be completed within six months; execution is by hanging.

ECONOMY: Rich bauxite (aluminum ore) deposits, sugar and tourism have traditionally dominated Jamaica's economy, and the country's financial condition is tied to these assets. The long-range outlook for the island's economy is linked to diversification and expansion, such as fruits and other agricultural products for the U.S. winter market, which it still has not realized.

An invisible economy revolves around the drug trade, and the gang culture affects politics as well as the economy. Marijuana is plentiful in Jamaica and is exported to the United States informally. Jamaica is also a way station for an estimated 100–120 tons of cocaine per year en route to the United States, Canada and Europe. The gangs also engage in protection rackets, particularly in the construction sector, which increases construction costs by as much as 40%.

Tourism, still the third-largest industry after sugar and mining, is centered around popular resorts like Montego Bay and Ocho Rios on the north coast (far from crime-ridden Kingston) that cater to U.S., Canadian and European vacationers, especially during the Northern Hemisphere winter. It accounts for about $2–$3 billion a year, which represents 20% of GDP, 50% of foreign exchange and 25% of the jobs. It fluctuates according to the global economy and outbreaks of violence. The events of 2009–10 were a "perfect storm" for Jamaican tourism, a global recession and the outbreak of violence surrounding the effort to arrest and extradite reputed drug lord Christopher Coke in May 2010 (see History). The violence caused hundreds of hotel cancellations, and the government estimated losses at $350 million. The Jamaica Tourist Board reported 1,921,678 tourist arrivals in 2010, 1,951,752 in 2011 and 1,986,085 in 2012, an increase of slightly less than 2% a year for three years. Tourism revenue in 2012 was $1.7 billion, or 11.1% of GDP.

Eclipsing tourism as a source of foreign exchange in recent years are the remittances that the estimated 2–3 million Jamaicans living in the United States, Britain, Canada and other developed countries send home to their families. That also means that the country's brightest minds are living and working elsewhere. According to the World Bank, 85.1% of college-educated Jamaicans live abroad, the second-highest brain drain in the world after Guyana. Remittances in 2009 and 2010 were about $1.9 billion. They rose to $2.08 billion in 2011 and $2.37 billion in 2012, or 13.3% of GDP. The Bank of Jamaica reported remittances totaled $2.065 billion in 2013.

Economic growth has been stagnant for two decades. GDP shrank in 1996 and 1997 and was 2% or less from 1998–2004. An increase in the world price of bauxite and an increase in hotel building in 2005–06 increased growth for 2005 to 2.5%. The skyrocketing price of imported fuel and Hurricane Felix slowed growth to 1.5% in 2007. The global recession began in late 2008, with the predictable drop in tourism and remittances. GDP shrank by –.6% in 2008 and –3.0% in 2009. It shrank again in 2010, by –1.2%, probably because the Tivoli Gardens gun battle frightened away tourists (see History). GDP has grown by a minuscule 1.3% in 2011, 0.9% in 2012 and only 0.4% in 2013, the second-slowest in the Western Hemisphere.

An economic dilemma that has no immediate solution is the crushing external debt, which for years has put it among the 10 highest in the world as a percentage of GDP. In 2013 it was 123.6%, the world's eighth-highest. About 70% of government revenues are used just to service the debt.

Jamaica

The per capita GDP of roughly $5,000 is deceptively high, because it is inequitably distributed. An estimated 16.5% lived below the poverty line in 2009. Unemployment has remained stubbornly high for years, and was above 14% in 2011 and 2012. It rose to 16.3% in 2013. This is at least partially responsible for the alarming crime rate.

In 50 years of independence, Jamaica has had only six balanced budgets. The deficit in 2013 was an estimated $263 million, down from $934 million in 2012.

Inflation was a cumbersome 22% in 2008, largely because of the high world price for petroleum. It has fluctuated since, from 8.6% in 2009 to 12.6% in 2010, 7.7% in 2011, 6.8% in 2012 and 9.4% in 2013.

An exciting new venture is Excel Motors, which produced its first 22 "Island Cruiser" automobiles in 2003. It exports them throughout the Caribbean.

In 2008, the money-losing state-owned sugar company became a joint venture with a Brazilian ethanol company, which could lower Jamaica's dependence on expensive foreign oil.

Jamaica signed a 27-month, $1.27 billion standby agreement with the International Monetary Fund in 2010 to ease its chronic balance of payments deficit, after first offering a debt-swap to bondholders that greatly reduced the government's interest payments. In other economic news, the country's first legal marijuana crop has been planted under the auspices of a 16-member licensing board approved by the cabinet.

THE FUTURE: A cynic might well ask, *what* future? Jamaica is plagued by a moribund economy that saw GDP shrink three years in a row and is still stagnant at less than 1% annually, a crushing external debt that in 2013 was the eighth-highest in the world as a percentage of GDP (123.6%), and a culture of political violence and common crime that gave Jamaica the world's sixth-highest homicide rate in 2012 and is threatening the fourth-largest source of foreign exchange: tourism.

In short, Jamaica remains a mess. Then-Prime Minister Golding said he wanted Jamaica to become a republic, free of its attachment to the British Crown, in time for the 50th anniversary of independence in August 2012, and that call was taken up by his successor, Portia Simpson-Miller. That did not happen. Establishing a republic must first pass Parliament with a two-thirds vote and then be approved by voters in a referendum. That may be a hard sell. According to the results of a scientific survey of 1,000 Jamaicans commissioned by the *Daily Gleaner* in 2011, 60% of respondents said they believe Jamaica would have been better off if it had remained a colony; only 17% disagreed. The anniversary was August 5–6, and a year later, Jamaica remains a commonwealth.

Becoming a republic would not prove a panacea for Jamaica's woes. Jamaica has great economic potential, but it must have visionary leadership to make it happen. Simpson-Miller has taken some hard, unpopular economic decisions, such as her recent tax on bank withdrawals, but has not quite lived up to *Time* magazine's glowing predictions for her in 2012 as one of the world's 100 most influential people. Whether she governs a commonwealth or a republic, she has a prodigious task. In fairness to her, it would be a prodigious task for *anyone*.

Sadly, Jamaica's best and brightest continue to gain their educations abroad, and remain there. Tax increases are now forcing others to emigrate. Perhaps that is where a visionary leader for the future can be found—if he or she can be persuaded to return.

Mexico

STATES OF MEXICO

Area: 767,919 square miles.

Population: 120,286,655 (2014 est.; growth, 1.12% per year, est.).

Capital City: Mexico City (Population 8.85 million in the Federal District in 2010, 21.2 million in the metropolitan area).

Climate: Hot, wet on the coast; milder winters, hot summers in the dry north; mild, dry winters in the central highlands.

Neighboring Countries: United States (North); Guatemala and Belize (South).

Official Language: Spanish.

Other Principal Tongues: Various Indian dialects (the census of 1960 identified 52 non-Spanish-speaking groups); English.

Ethnic Background: *Mestizo*, (mixed Spanish and Indian, 60%); Indian and predominantly Indian, (30%); White or predominantly white (9%); other (1%).

Principal Religion: Roman Catholic Christianity.

Chief Commercial Products: Petroleum, petroleum products, border assembly plants, tourism, cotton, coffee, non-ferrous metals, shrimp, sulfur, fresh fruit and vegetables, clothing.

Currency: Peso.

Gross Domestic Product: U.S. $1.845 trillion in 2013 ($11,418 per capita, official exchange rate).

Former Colonial Status: Spanish Colony (1510–1821).

Independence Date: September 16, 1810 (observed); September 27, 1821 (achieved).

Chief of State: Enrique Peña Nieto (b. July 20, 1966).

National Flag: Green, white and red vertical stripes with the national coat of arms (an eagle strangling a snake) in the white stripe.

Mexico is a vast upland plateau lying between the two branches of the Sierra Madre Mountains plus the low lying Yucatán Peninsula. The Sierra Madre range enters Mexico in the south from Guatemala at elevations from 6,000 to 8,000 feet, then dips to low hills in the Isthmus of Tehuantepec and then rises abruptly to a jumble of scenic high peaks and intermountain basins. Mexico City is located in one of the most beautiful of these. From this point northward, the Sierra Madre Occidental (west) runs to Arizona in the U.S. and the Sierra Madre Oriental (east) proceeds northeast to the border of Texas. The eastern mountains are not as high as their counterparts in the west.

Mountains and their plateaus occupy two thirds of the land area of Mexico. The highest elevations are found south of Mexico City, where Citlaltepetl (the highest 18,696 feet) with an almost perfect conical shape, is reminiscent of Fujiyama in Japan. Mountains and plateaus drop gradually toward the north. The western range descends steeply to the Pacific Ocean with few passes, while the eastern range is more gentle, with gaps to the Gulf of Mexico at Tampico and Veracruz.

Mexico

The western mountain slopes, the northern plateau and the peninsula of Lower California (*Baja California*) are arid; the southern inter-mountain valleys receive moderate rainfall; the eastern slopes and the Gulf of Mexico coast receive up to 100 inches of rainfall between the months of June and December.

The whole of Mexico lies in the tropical and subtropical zones; however, climatically, altitude is a more important influence than latitude. Temperatures are hot between sea level and 3,000 feet, temperate between 3,000 feet and 6,000 feet and cold above the latter height. The majority of Mexico's population is found in the southern part of the plateau at elevations between 3,000 and 7,000 feet.

HISTORY: Mexico has a rich, dramatic and colorful history that for the purposes of this chapter can be divided roughly into four periods: pre-Conquest, colonial, post-independence and post-revolutionary. Modern Mexico remains heavily influenced by its past, which must be explored if the current realities and dynamics there are to be understood.

The Pre-Conquest Period

A number of succeeding civilizations thrived in the land area that is now Mexico south of the Tropic of Cancer for more than a millennium before the arrival of the Spanish, among them the Toltecs, Mixtecs, Zapotecs and Olmecs. The Toltecs, who flourished on the central plateau in about the ninth and 10th centuries of the Christian era, are remembered for their development of metallurgy as well as for worshiping a deity known as Quetzalcoatl, or the feathered serpent. When the Toltec civilization collapsed, it was attributed to the departure of Quetzalcoatl to the lands beyond the eastern sea, though he promised to return one day to reclaim his dominions. Six centuries later, it was to become a self-fulfilling prophecy.

Perhaps the greatest of these early peoples, however, were the Mayas, whose empire extended from central Mexico as far south as modern-day Honduras. They were an advanced, if somewhat barbaric, people, paradoxically developing remarkable mathematical, astronomical, engineering, agricultural and medical knowledge even as they practiced rituals that included human sacrifice. The ruins of some of their greatest cities lie in present-day Mexico, such as Chichén Itzá on the Yucatán Peninsula and Palenque in the state of Oaxaca. This great empire suddenly and mysteriously disappeared in about the 15th century.

To the north, even before the decline of the Mayas, another great civilization be-

The ruins of the Maya civilization's temple of Chichén-Itzá near Mérida, Yucatán.

gan to flower: the Aztecs. They, too, developed advanced knowledge in the sciences and medicine, but also practiced a barbaric cruelty to vassal tribes that eventually would lead to their undoing. According to legend, the Aztec god Huitzilopochtli instructed the tribal priests that their capital should be established where they found an eagle perched upon a cactus devouring a serpent. This omen was seen on an island in Lake Texcoco in the great central valley of Mexico in the early 14th century, and consequently the Aztecs began building their great city, Tenochtitlán, upon man-made islands in the lake connected by causeways to the mainland. With its network of canals for streets, the Spanish later dubbed Tenochtitlán, the "Venice of the New World," but the venue also explains why parts of modern-day Mexico City are sinking. The omen, of course, later became the basis for the modern-day symbol of the Mexican Republic, which graces the national flag.

The Aztec empire had reached its zenith by the end of the 15th century, and Tenochtitlán was as resplendent as any city of the Old World. In 1503, Moctezuma II ascended the throne, destined to be the last of the Aztec emperors. In February 1519, a force of 500 Spaniards landed first in Yucatán, then in Tabasco, and finally at Vera Cruz, on the Gulf coast. In command was a young nobleman and soldier-of-fortune determined to make himself rich and famous in this new, unexplored land: Hernán Cortés. Unlike earlier Spanish freebooters who had robbed the coastal Indians, Cortés treated them benevolently and soon found in them willing allies against

their oppressors, the Aztecs. Unknown to Cortés, he also had another ally in the legendary Quetzalcoatl. When this bearded, fair-skinned stranger from across the eastern sea landed in Mexico, the superstitious Indians immediately assumed that he was the reincarnation of the feathered serpent, returning as promised to reclaim his land.

Cortés and his band marched to Tenochtitlán, where Moctezuma, also influenced by the legendary prophecy, greeted him almost as a deity. The wily Cortés, sensing an incredible opportunity, seized the emperor and, through him, issued orders to

Moctezuma II

262

Retreat of the Spanish on *"la noche triste."*

the Aztecs. The plan unraveled, however, when the Aztecs revolted against these uninvited "gods," and in the resulting melee Moctezuma was hit in the head by a rock and killed. On the night of June 30, 1520—remembered in Spanish and Mexican history as *la noche triste*—Cortés and his men had to fight their way across the narrow causeway to the mainland, suffering heavy losses. Reinforced by later arrivals from Cuba, however, he again marched on the Aztec capital with 900 men in early 1521. Meanwhile, Moctezuma had been succeeded by his 20-year-old nephew, Cuauhtémoc, who was to prove less amenable to the invaders than was his uncle. Cortés besieged the capital for three months, but despite starvation and disease, Cuauhtémoc refused to surrender. The Spaniards finally took Tenochtitlán by storm on August 13, 1521, and set it ablaze; Cortés reportedly wept at the destruction of such a beautiful city. Cuauhtémoc was captured trying to escape by canoe and brought before Cortés, who angrily blamed him for the capi-

tal's destruction. Cuauhtémoc requested that Cortés kill him, and the conqueror complied. The remainder of Mexico was subdued quickly, and the Spanish would remain for precisely 300 years.

The Colonial Period

The viceroyalty of New Spain was a vast territory extending from Central America to modern-day California, Colorado and Texas. As was true in Spain's other American colonies, the colonial experience in Mexico differed sharply from that in England's colonies farther north. For example, the wealth of the English colonies lay primarily in their fertile agricultural land, which gave rise to a class of independent small-scale farmers. Mexico, too, had rich farmland in the central plateau, which attracted Spanish fortune-seekers willing to work it. These were not small-scale farmers, however; they were the first of the *hacendados*, who ruled over vast estates like feudal lords.

Moreover, Mexico, like Peru, was blessed—or cursed, depending on one's standing in colonial society—with fabulously wealthy deposits of gold and silver, which filled the coffers of the royal treasury in Madrid and gave rise to a class of idle rich who occupied the top 1% of the social pyramid. Unlike their English counterparts, however, the Spanish did not drive the indigenous peoples from their lands and either exile or exterminate them and import African slaves or indentured servants to perform the heavy labor. Instead, the Spanish drove the Indians from their lands and enslaved them for labor on the *haciendas* and in the mines.

Besides the soldiers and the fortune hunters, the Spanish Crown had another ally in its quest to establish its dominion over this new territory: the Catholic Church. The first priests arrived in tandem with Cortés and set about converting the pagan inhabitants to Christianity. At first, the Indians were loathe to abandon their tribal gods in favor of the one worshiped

Mexico

by their oppressors, and they resented the destruction of their idols. At the same time, the veneration of saints and relics was not terribly unlike their pagan idolatry.

But in 1531, just 10 years after the Conquest, an event occurred that was to accelerate dramatically the conversion of the aborigines and would provide Mexico with an institution that remains part of its national identity. An Indian peasant named Juan Diego reported to the bishop that the Virgin Mary had appeared to him on a hillside outside the City of Mexico and had instructed him to return to gather the roses he would find there. Diego did as he was bidden and found roses lying among the cactus. He gathered them in his cloak and carried them to the bishop, but when the cloak was opened, the roses had disappeared and on the cloak was an image of the Virgin. At first skeptical, the church authorities accepted this version, which the Vatican later recognized as a bona fide miracle. The news that the Mother of God had appeared to a humble Indian peasant electrified the Indians and greatly facilitated the priests' job of bringing them into the bosom of the church. Below the hill where the roses were found was constructed the Shrine of Our Lady of Guadalupe, and over its altar still hangs the cloak of Juan Diego with the mysterious image that modern-day art experts have pronounced unexplainable. In December 2001, the Vatican canonized Juan Diego as a saint, which was a cause for national celebration. Pope John Paul II came to Mexico for the formal canonization in the Shrine of Guadalupe in August 2002.

Apart from the conversion of the Indians, there would be few changes in Mexico during the three centuries of Spanish colonial rule. There was, however, a gradual demographic change that was to have a major impact on the subsequent history of the country. Slowly, the Spanish conquerors began to pass their seed to their Indian subjects, and within a few generations a new, *mestizo* race began to grow and which would constitute a majority by the end of the colonial period. Yet, they were to be a race without any real identity, relegated by the Spanish to second-class citizenship, while resented by the Indians for their mixed ancestry. Although amorous dalliances with Indian women and the spawning of bastard children were commonly accepted, the Spanish men married women of their own race and social position, producing yet another class, the *criollos*, or creoles, people of pure European ancestry born in the New World.

The Spanish colonial experience in Mexico can only be described as exploitative. Her land and peoples were seen to exist only for the enrichment of the Crown. While England experienced the Renaissance, the Protestant Reformation, the Enlightenment and the Glorious Revolution, whose ideals were exported to its American colonies, Spain wallowed in the fear, tyranny and superstition of the Inquisition, which also was exported to America. Unlike the English colonies, there was no large middle class of well educated planters, merchants, craftsmen and intellectuals. Eventually the ideas of Locke, Rousseau and Voltaire did trickle into Mexico via a most unlikely source—the king himself. The sole exception to the succession of reactionary, divine-right monarchs was Carlos III, a reasonably enlightened sovereign who reigned from 1758–1788. Appalled when he learned of the abuses of power that characterized colonial rule in Mexico, Carlos instituted a number of reforms that improved local administration and facilitated trade. He also encouraged science and the arts, expanded education and appointed competent viceroys to carry out his ideas. At the same time, his French-inspired anticlericalism, exemplified by his expulsion of the Jesuits from Mexico, caused alarm within the church, which had heretofore enjoyed great wealth and privileges in the colony. As often happens when reforms are undertaken, there can be no turning back the clock. When Carlos died—on the eve of the French Revolution—he was succeeded by his pathetic son, Carlos IV, who was dominated by his wife who, in turn, was dominated by her unscrupulous paramour, Manuel de Godoy.

The misrule of Carlos IV contrasted so sharply with the enlightened rule of his father that resentment soon set in. Mexico already had enough reason for resentment by the end of the 18th century. The *criollos* resented the social superiority of the Spanish-born elite, whom they referred to disparagingly as *gachupines*, or the ones with spurs. The *mestizos* and the Indians, meanwhile, chafed under the oppression of their Spanish masters. For 20 years after Carlos III's death, these resentments continued to ferment, while news of the American and French revolutions gave rise to talk of independence. Ironically, it was the French themselves, in the form of Napoleon Bonaparte, who were to become the catalysts for Mexican independence.

In 1808, the detested Carlos IV abdicated and was succeeded by his son, Fernando VII. Lured to Paris by Napoleon, both were imprisoned and replaced on the Spanish throne by Napoleon's brother, Joseph, whose "reign" was supported only by French bayonets. The resulting power vacuum in Madrid threw Mexico and all of Spain's American colonies into turmoil. For two years the various factions—the *gachupines* and the *criollos*, the liberals and conservatives—debated whether to maintain their allegiance to an imprisoned king or to rule themselves in his stead. Cells of independence-minded creoles sprang up in the major towns, and the one in the city of Querétaro included a liberal priest from the town of Dolores who had endeared himself to his Indian and *mestizo* parishoners: Miguel de Hidalgo. On September 16, 1810, as a Spanish force moved toward Querétaro to arrest Father Hidalgo and other conspirators, the priest rang the

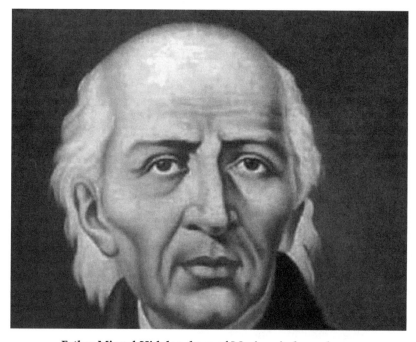

Father Miguel Hidalgo, hero of Mexican independence

bells of the church in Dolores to assemble his parishioners and declared that the moment had come to take up arms against their oppressors. The date of the famous *Grito,* or cry, of Dolores, has been observed ever since as Mexico's independence day.

As with the U.S. War of Independence, the struggle in Mexico was to be long, bloody, tedious and marked by discouraging reverses that would continue for 11 years. Father Hidalgo quickly assembled a rag-tag "army" of peasants who, motivated by a quest for social liberation as much as for independence, eagerly followed their creole leader. The rebels marched inexorably southward, gaining momentum, defeating the better-armed and trained but hopelessly outnumbered Spaniards. Yet, on the very threshold of Mexico City, Hidalgo lost his nerve and retreated. He would never regain the momentum. The Spanish counterattacked and defeated the rebel army at the Battle of Calderón, and Hidalgo fled to the northern mountains. There a trusted comrade betrayed him and other rebel leaders to the Spanish, who captured them. On July 31, 1811, the father of Mexican independence was defrocked and executed by firing squad in Chihuahua, and his head was sent to Guanajuato, where it remained on public display until independence was achieved.

However, the Spanish soon learned that the cause of independence did not die with Hidalgo. Another creole priest, José María Morelos, a man with more military skills than Hidalgo, raised a guerrilla army and took the offensive. Like Hidalgo before him, Morelos enjoyed the initiative for a time, scoring a succession of victories before he, too, was betrayed, captured and shot in 1815. Yet, still more leaders arose to take up the cause.

Meanwhile, the fall of Napoleon and the restoration of Fernando VII to the throne eliminated the issue of who was in charge in Madrid, but by then the movement for independence had taken on a life of its own. Fernando VII dispatched more troops to quell the uprising and, in a Byzantine maneuver, even negotiated with Mexican conservatives a scheme by which Fernando would leave Madrid and become the king of an independent Mexico. This occurred after Spanish liberals had forced him to swear to a constitution he abhorred. A pivotal moment in the war came when Agustín Iturbide, a competent officer in the Spanish army, defected and took up the cause of independence. He issued a decree, called the *Plan de Iguala,* under which an independent Mexico would be governed either by Fernando or another European monarch, the *gachupines* and *criollos* would become social equals, and the church would retain its Privileges. The two principal rebel generals, Vicente

Guerrero and Guadalupe Victoria, embraced the plan, and one by one the major cities fell in behind. Finally, faced with the inevitable, the newly arrived Spanish viceroy also accepted the *Plan de Iguala,* and on September 27, 1821, the Spanish abandoned Mexico City to Iturbide's army—300 years and one month after Cortés had taken it from Cuauhtémoc.

The Post-Independence Period

Just as the colonial period lasted exactly 300 years, the post-independence period would span 99, from 1821, when Iturbide triumphantly entered Mexico City, until 1920, when another military hero, Alvaro Obregón, would assume the presidency and begin to consolidate the gains of the Revolution. Those 99 years would prove to be the bloodiest and most contentious in the country's history, being marked by intrigue, betrayal, dictatorships and civil war. Few of the key players of this period would die quietly in their beds of old age.

The struggle for independence had found the various segments of Mexican society—the Privileged creoles, the *mestizos* and the Indians—fighting together in a peculiar alliance against a common enemy. With the departure of the Spaniards, however, the alliance became unraveled and friction inevitably developed among the classes. Moreover, as they fled, the *gachupines* took with them what little treasure remained, leaving the new country virtually bankrupt. Compounding Mexico's travails, the Spanish did not bequeath a strong governmental infrastructure the Mexicans could build upon for self-rule. As was the case in other emerging Latin American republics, such as Chile and Colombia, Mexico's first century and beyond would be marked by a struggle between the forces of conservatism—the landed gentry and the clergy—and liberalism patterned after the ideals of the French and American revolutions.

The Liberals, understandably in the majority, counted on the support of the *mestizo* and Indian masses, whose cause they ostensibly championed. Fiercely anticlerical, the Liberals nonetheless were pragmatic enough to recognize that the devoutly Catholic masses would never accept such a radical concept as Protestantism. The Liberals' opposition to the properties and Privileges of the church led to the embrace of Freemasonry, a secret society with ancient roots in Europe and the Near East that remains influential among the governing elite to this day.

Unfortunately for the Liberals, the concept of Jeffersonian democracy was to prove unfeasible in a land where the vast majority of the population was illiterate, where there was no democratic tra-

dition to build upon and where the lines of communication were too primitive for effective centralized government. That situation suited the outnumbered Conservatives just fine, many of them being local *caciques,* or strongmen, who wanted no interference from Mexico City. Also unfortunately for the Liberals, the generals who held the genuine power, backed by the cannon, the musket and the bayonet, opted to side with the Conservatives because it was they who possessed what wealth the country still had. The generals, quite simply, were bought off, rewarded for their services with land and treasure. As many a Mexican leader would discover over the next century, the lifespan of the generals' loyalty coincided with that of the payroll.

Iturbide, the conquering hero of the moment but also a man of unbridled ambition and pretentiousness, soon "amended" the *Plan de Iguala.* Instead of a European monarch, he himself would become emperor of Mexico, and he had the military forces to enforce that decision. The country was to witness the tragicomic spectacle of a woefully expensive coronation that the country could ill afford. Iturbide proved a less able administrator than he had a military commander, however. After a little more than a year, his governmental ineptitude, coupled with his profligate spending on the ridiculous trappings of monarchy, left the government bankrupt. That meant, of course, that he couldn't pay the army, which quickly overthrew him and sent the

General Agustín Iturbide

Mexico

Mexico City street scene in the early 19th century

hemisphere's first "emperor" into exile. When he returned uninvited in 1823, he was arrested and shot.

With the fall of Iturbide, Mexico at last became a republic, the Liberals came to power, and in 1824 they promulgated the first of Mexico's three reasonably enlightened constitutions. Guadalupe Victoria (the inspirational *nom de guerre* of Félix Fernández) became the first president, and he was succeeded in 1828 by the third great military hero of independence, Vicente Guerrero. Alas, as was the case with Iturbide before them, their proficiency on the battlefield proved of little value in the halls of government. Both were crude, abrasive men who alienated their own congress as well as the Conservatives. Mexico dissolved into chaos and in 1830 the Conservatives seized power in a *coup d'etat*. When Guerrero fled and took to the field to combat the usurpers, the deposed president was betrayed, captured and shot, like Hidalgo and Morelos before

him. Also like Morelos, a southern state later was named in his honor.

Into this volatile situation was to stride a charismatic figure who was to dominate the country off and on for the next 30 years: Antonio López de Santa Anna. A former Spanish officer who, like Iturbide, had joined the independence movement, Santa Anna was the quintessential Latin American *caudillo*, the charismatic man on horseback who rules with an iron fist to maintain order. At the time of the Conservative coup, he was the commander of the garrison in Vera Cruz (today spelled Veracruz) where the all-important customs house was located. Santa Anna rebelled against the Conservative government in 1832. By the end of the year the grateful Liberals ill-advisedly made him president and Valentín Gómez Farías, a Zacatecan who would be the guiding force of Mexican Liberalism for 30 years, vice president. On the four occasions he would enjoy the supreme power of the republic,

Santa Anna followed a curious practice of retiring to his *hacienda* in Vera Cruz and leaving the day-to-day responsibilities of governing the country to surrogates until such time as the situation demanded his strong hand.

Betraying the Liberals who had mistakenly hailed him as their champion, Santa Anna dissolved the Constitution of 1824, assumed dictatorial powers, and began calling himself the "Napoleon of the West." Liberals in the state of Zacatecas rose in revolt, and Santa Anna mercilessly suppressed them. Then the Anglo-American settlers of the far northern province of Texas, unaccustomed to being ruled by despots, also rebelled. In what is now a legendary epic in Texas history, Santa Anna marched into Texas in 1836 with an army of 6,000 men, killed the 187-man garrison at the mission fortress of the Alamo in San Antonio de Bexar after a desperate and bloody battle, ordered the execution of the 300 Texans who had surrendered the fort at Goliad, then swept eastward almost to the border of Louisiana. There he was defeated and captured by the army of General Sam Houston at the Battle of San Jacinto.

Houston, himself as skilled at politics as he was at war, bartered Santa Anna for Texan independence rather than hanging him, then sent the defeated dictator to Washington to meet with President Andrew Jackson. Santa Anna returned to Mexico in disgrace, retired again to his *hacienda*, and waited patiently for his country's call.

It came in 1838, when the French landed an invasion force to impose collection of debts. In the ensuing battle, Santa Anna's leg was shot off by a French cannon ball, and again he became a national hero. His leg was ceremoniously buried in the ca-

General Antonio López de Santa Anna

thedral in Mexico City and in 1841, at the height of the latest Liberal-Conservative power struggle, he again became dictator. An efficient tax-collector, he was an equally extravagant spender. As had happened to Iturbide, the army deposed him in 1844 when he was unable to meet its payroll and sent him into exile in Cuba.

Meanwhile, a border dispute with the United States erupted into full-scale war in 1846, and Santa Anna was recalled from exile to take the field against the invaders from the north. Cunning as ever, Santa Anna slipped through the U.S. naval blockade by convincing American agents that he would make peace if he returned to Mexico. Instead, he was named acting president and took up arms against the Americans. Defeated by General Zachary Taylor at the Battle of Buena Vista near the city of Saltillo in February 1847, Santa

Anna nonetheless sent back dispatches to Mexico City declaring that he had won a resounding victory.

Returning to the capital a hero, he again assumed dictatorial powers. He next opposed General Winfield Scott's army, which had landed in Vera Cruz and was marching on Mexico City. Again Santa Anna was ignominiously defeated, and the capital fell to the Americans. Under the resulting Treaty of Guadalupe-Hidalgo, Mexico ceded nearly half its territory, from Texas to California. In return, the United States paid Mexico $15 million—a welcome deposit for the bankrupt treasury. Santa Anna again went into exile, this time to Venezuela.

There followed a few years of stable and efficient Liberal civilian governments, but in 1853 Santa Anna, this time the champion of the Conservatives, again was placed in power by *coup d'etat*. To raise money, he sold off another tract of land to the United States—the Gadsden Purchase, in what is today southern Arizona and New Mexico—for $10 million.

Of course, he quickly and frivolously squandered the money. The Liberals, under the leadership of Ignacio Comonfort, rebelled against the dictator and published the *Plan de Ayutla*, which called for the drafting of a new constitution. Santa Anna fell from power for the fourth and final time in 1855 and spent most of the rest of his life in Cuba. Eventually allowed to return, he died in poverty and obscurity in 1876.

Mexico's second Liberal constitution was promulgated in 1857 under the presidency of Comonfort, but it was so anticlerical that the archbishop threatened to excommunicate anyone who took the required oath. By January 1858, the Conservatives had again overthrown the government, but this time the two sides found themselves in full-scale civil war, which was to last for three years and leave the country torn apart. Two Liberal champions emerged during the conflict who would later play decisive roles in Mexican history.

One was a full-blooded Zapotec Indian who was governor of Oaxaca: Benito Juárez. It was he who would become the moral and spiritual guardian of Liberalism and social justice and become revered as the greatest of Mexico's leaders. The other was a *mestizo* guerrilla leader who would betray the cause of reform and become one of Mexico's most reviled villains: Porfirio Díaz.

After Comonfort was deposed, Juárez was named president and removed the constitutionalist government to the north, where it enjoyed the support of the United States. The Liberals won the civil war, and on January 11, 1861, Juárez became the

newest hero to triumphantly enter Mexico City, but in keeping with his humble image he did so in a plain black carriage. He was reelected president, but the Conservatives were not yet ready to admit defeat. They resurrected the old idea of installing a European monarch on a Mexican throne, and they found a willing ally in France's Emperor Napoleon III.

Emboldened by the Americans' distraction with their own civil war, Napoleon landed an army at Vera Cruz and began the traditional march of conquerors to Mexico City. But at Puebla, the stubborn Mexican defenders dealt the French a stinging defeat on May 5, 1862, still commemorated as a national holiday—*el Cinco de Mayo*. The victory was fleeting, however, and the French soon captured the capital. Juárez again fled to the north with his government. In his place the Conservatives invited Archduke Maximilian, brother of the Hapsburg emperor of Austria, to reign as Mexico's second emperor.

Benito Juárez

Maximilian and his wife, Carlotta, a member of the Belgian royal family, are two of history's truly tragic figures. The Conservatives duped Maximilian into believing that he had been elected emperor in a plebiscite, and he and Carlotta arrived in Mexico expecting to be treated as beloved sovereigns. Instead, they found the country at civil war over his intervention. Ironically, Maximilian was himself something of a liberal, and he shocked the Conservatives by implementing some of the very reforms the Liberals had advocated. The Conservatives soon cooled toward their new emperor, and the *Juarista* army began scoring victories over the French

Mexico

and Conservative forces. With the end of the U.S. Civil War, the U.S. government warned Napoleon III to remove its forces from Mexico or the United States would intervene to enforce the Monroe Doctrine. To compound the woes of the beleaguered Maximilian, Carlotta began showing signs of mental instability. She was evacuated to Europe, where she sought unsuccessfully to win an audience with Napoleon III. Faced with the threat of war with the United States and lack of success on the battlefield, Napoleon III abandoned Maximilian to his fate. After a final defeat at Querétaro, the emperor and his army surrendered. Maximilian and two of his generals were executed by firing squad a few days later on June 19, 1867, atop the Hill of Bells, today a national landmark. Carlotta spent the remaining 60 years of her life in insanity.

Once again, Juárez triumphantly entered Mexico City and was soon reelected to a third term. By most accounts, the Juárez presidency was the most honorable and enlightened in Mexico's troubled his-

Emperor Maximilian of Mexico

tory, before or since. There was no shameless self-enrichment such as Santa Anna and others had engaged in. The industrial base began to grow, and railroads were built. Juárez also began to implement the reforms of the Constitution of 1857, and he devoted special attention to secular education, particularly for the hapless Indians who had long been treated as third-class citizens. This, of course, alienated Juárez from even the Liberal creoles. Moreover, in the name of economy and to guard against the praetorianism that had been the bane of Mexico since independence, Juárez had brusquely cashiered most of the officers and soldiers from the army with scant compensation for their services during 10 years of civil war. There were the inevitable military rebellions, which Juárez crushed as ruthlessly as his predecessors had. In the 1867 election, Juárez was opposed by one of his own generals, Porfirio Díaz.

Juárez was elected to a fourth term in 1871, which raised accusations that he hoped to become merely another dictator. In reality, the 1871 election was quite fair by Mexican standards, and Juárez failed to receive a majority, so his election was decided by Congress. Alas, Juárez died suddenly of a heart attack on July 18, 1872, and with him died Mexico's greatest hope for democracy with social reform. Vice President Sebastián Lerdo de Tejada, a respected and honest intellectual, succeeded him and was elected to a full term that fall, but when he chose to run again in 1876 Díaz issued a *pronunciamiento* that cynically purported to uphold the Liberal cause of "effective suffrage, no re-election." After a brief military struggle, the *Porfirista* forces captured the capital and forced Lerdo into exile. Díaz became provisional president, ushering in the longest dictatorship in Mexican history.

The Díaz dictatorship was a veritable yin-yang dichotomy of good and evil, darkness and light. On the one hand, Mexico was to experience unprecedented modernization and economic development during the 35 years he would control the country. On the other, Díaz ruled in the style of the classic Latin American *caudillo*, enjoying absolute power through a principle called *pan o palo* (bread or club). Díaz could be exceedingly generous in return for whole-hearted support, but those who refused his good offices faced imprisonment, economic deprivation, or worse. Turning his back on the Liberal principle of nationalism, he opened the doors to massive foreign investment, chiefly U.S. and British, which capitalized the country and expanded the middle class but left much of Mexico's land and wealth in foreign hands. Himself a *mestizo*, Díaz nonetheless abandoned Juárez's goal of improving the

General Porfirio Díaz

lot of the Indians, who were to continue to languish in the feudalism to which they had been consigned since the Conquest. Díaz surrounded himself with a cadre of creole technocrats, called *científicos*, who managed the economy *so* efficiently that in 1894 Mexico recorded the first budget surplus in its history. The dictator poured much of this revenue into much-needed public works projects and into the beautification of Mexico City, which he wanted to rival the grand capitals of Europe.

Because he had come to power on a platform opposing reelection, Díaz cleverly chose one of his sycophants, Manuel González, to be "elected" in 1880. During his single term, which of course was overshadowed by Díaz, González engaged in corruption on an unprecedented scale, even for Mexico. By 1884, the public was only too happy to forget about Díaz's supposed opposition to reelection and clamored for him to retake the presidency. He maintained himself in power thereafter through six rigged elections, in some of which he awarded himself a unanimous vote! In 1904, he also extended the presidential term to six years. He concentrated all the patronage in his own hands, and enjoyed such power that he literally designated every state governor and member of Congress. Employing a system of divide-and-conquer, he pitted various factions against each other, and if one faction became too strong for his liking, he would undermine it by throwing his support to another. He did much the same thing with the officials in his government, so great was his fear of possible usurpation.

So jealous was he of possible rivals, he made absolutely no preparations for an eventual successor. By the time of his last "election" in 1910, he was 80 years old and showing signs of senility, raising concerns among the ruling elite. But there also was a restiveness among the lower classes who had been bypassed in the economic development of the Díaz years. Mexico was a social powder keg.

The spark that was to set off the inevitable explosion came from an unlikely source, a short, unassuming young man from a wealthy creole ranching family in the state of Coahuila: Francisco I. Madero. Díaz had indicated in an interview with a U.S. correspondent that he would not seek reelection in 1910, a statement that had been intended to mollify the democratic sensibilities of the U.S. government but which soon became reported in Mexico. Díaz then reneged on his promise not to stand again, and the idealistic Madero announced his own candidacy against him. Díaz at first tolerated the opposition of this seemingly insignificant upstart in order to perpetuate the myth of Porfirian democracy, but Madero's campaign appearances began attracting large, enthusiastic audiences. Madero was arrested on a trumped-up charge that he was conspiring to overthrow the regime, and he was kept behind bars until after Díaz had safely "reelected" himself. Symbolically, Díaz's latest power play had coincided with his grandiose centennial celebration of Father Hidalgo's *Grito de Dolores*.

Released from jail, Madero fled to the United States and issued a *pronunciamiento*. Suddenly there were spontaneous demonstrations against the dictatorship. Reentering Mexico, Madero found influential people flocking to his standard, but he also found himself the champion of the lower classes. Among his most important supporters was a legendary bandit from Chihuahua who had become a revolutionary: Francisco "Pancho" Villa. Meanwhile,

in the southern state of Morelos, Emiliano Zapata organized a peasant army that seized the lands of the *hacendados* and engaged in battle with Díaz's federal army. The Mexican Revolution had begun.

Within months, the 35-year-old dictatorship began collapsing like the house of cards it was. When Villa's forces captured the border city of Ciudad Juárez in May 1911, Díaz made the traditional "withdrawal" from the treasury, fled to Vera Cruz and took ship to France. He died in Paris four years later. Madero, meanwhile, became the latest hero to enter the capital to the cheers of the masses.

Unfortunately, for all his noble ideals, Madero was no Benito Juárez. He proved an inept administrator and was easily manipulated by his family and their friends, some of whom had been among Díaz's *científicos*. The masses who had joined his movement expecting genuine social revolution were soon disillusioned. But a graver threat came in the traditional form of military uprisings, this time by counter-revolutionary *Porfiristas*. The Revolution took on the aspect of a free-for-all, with Villa and Zapata battling the counterrevolutionaries in the name of social justice and Madero's creole generals fighting essentially for themselves. The U.S. ambassador, meanwhile, angered by Madero's reversal of Díaz's *carte blanche* to foreign business interests, threw his support behind the counterrevolutionaries. Faced with the possibility of military defeat, Madero entrusted the defense of his government to a general he believed to be loyal: Victoriano Huerta. But in February 1913, with the complicity of the U.S. ambassador, Huerta arrested Madero and Vice President Pino Suárez and ordered them shot, allegedly while trying to escape. Huerta then seized the presidency for himself through a Machiavellian manipulation of the constitution.

Huerta, an alcoholic and drug addict and one of the most treacherous and repugnant figures in Latin American history, immediately found himself faced with formidable opposition. He had arrested Villa shortly before Madero's death, but the wily bandit bribed his way free and fled to the north. After Madero's murder became common knowledge, both Villa and Zapata took to the field against Huerta. In Coahuila, Governor Venustiano Carranza refused to recognize Huerta's regime and in time became the acknowledged leader of the constitutionalist forces. In Sonora, a laborer-turned-businessman-turned-general, Alvaro Obregón, raised yet another army to oppose the usurper.

Meanwhile, Woodrow Wilson became the U.S. president, and Huerta's naked power grab offended Wilson's democratic principles. He replaced the U.S. ambassa-

Francisco "Pancho" Villa

Emiliano Zapata

Francisco I. Madero

Mexico

dor with one who applied pressure on the dictator. When Wilson learned a shipment of German arms was en route to Mexico, he ordered the Marines to seize the port of Vera Cruz in April 1914 to prevent the guns from reaching Huerta. This intervention backfired, however, causing the various warring factions to unite temporarily in their denunciation of this new *gringo* invasion, even as the constitutionalists accepted shipments of U.S. arms.

In one of the most glorious and celebrated periods of Mexican history, the twin northern armies of Villa and Obregón literally raced each other southward, taking city after city from Huerta's forces, while Zapata's revolutionaries fought their way north toward the capital. In August 1914—the very month that Europe exploded into full-scale war—Huerta fled Mexico City and made his way to Texas, where he drank himself to death a year later.

All three revolutionary armies converged on the capital, and for a few days there was near-anarchy. Order was restored as the various leaders met to discuss how Mexico was to be ruled, but peace was not yet at hand. Much to the displeasure of Villa and Zapata, Carranza was elected provisional president, and the two revolutionaries took to the field once again. This time, however, Villa met his match in Obregón, who employed modern concepts from the battlefields of Europe, such as massed machine guns and barbed wire, to decimate Villa's once-invincible cavalry at Celaya. Driven farther north, Villa was outflanked when President Wilson allowed constitutionalist forces to use Texas railroads for troop movements. Enraged, Villa captured some American engineers and had them shot, and in March 1916 he sacked the border town of Columbus, New Mexico, killing 19 Americans. Wilson ordered General John J. Pershing into Chihuahua in pursuit of Villa, a hopeless mission which, once again, served only to unite the warring factions against the invading *gringos*.

Even as the bloodshed droned on, Carranza summoned a constitutional convention that assembled in Querétaro in December 1916 and early the next year finalized the country's third liberal constitution. Unlike the earlier organic laws, this one guaranteed the rights of labor and decreed that property rights were secondary to the public good. The Constitution of 1917, which has decidedly socialist overtones, remains the oldest basic law in effect in Latin America. The constitution should be Carranza's legacy, but he is remembered as much for the rampant corruption that went on during his administration as for his role in the creation of a new Mexico.

The Mexican Revolution, which by most estimates claimed about 1 million lives,

Venustiano Carranza

slowly wound down. A Carranza officer betrayed and assassinated Zapata in 1919. His armed struggle died with him, although the Morelos peasants were permitted to retain the lands they had seized from the *hacendados*. Villa, meanwhile, was bribed into passivity with an amnesty and a huge *hacienda* in Durango. Though he never took up arms again, he remained such a threatening force that he, too, was assassinated in 1923. In 1920, when Carranza sought to circumvent his own constitution's ban on reelection by hand-picking a puppet successor, Obregón and others turned against him. He was forced to abandon the capital and, a few days later, was murdered in his sleep by a trusted

Álvaro Obregón

lieutenant. Obregón's army became the latest to enter Mexico City in triumph, and Obregón was duly elected president and took office in November 1920. After 10 years of Revolution, Mexico was at peace.

The Post-Revolutionary Period

Obregón, unlike earlier conquering generals who became president, proved both an able and enlightened leader, the best since Juárez. There was some of the inevitable corruption, but nothing on the scale of Díaz. Himself a former laborer who became a businessman before the call to arms, Obregón was friendly to labor but chose not to enforce some of the more radical aspects of the new constitution. He did, however, begin a modest land-redistribution program, Primarily to the Indian communal plots, called *ejidos*. He also allowed unprecedented press freedom and adhered to the constitution by stepping aside at the end of his term in 1924—although he essentially dictated who his successor would be.

Largely because of Obregón's guidance during those first critical post-revolutionary years, Mexico embarked on a nominally democratic path with guarantees of civil liberties, rather than embracing the totalitarian experiment of the Bolsheviks who had seized power in Russia the same year the Mexican constitution was drafted. And in 1924, the very year Lenin died and was succeeded by Stalin, Obregón duly relinquished power to another revolutionary general, Plutarco Elías Calles. Although this new president was to succumb to the temptations of near-absolute power, he was certainly no Stalin.

Calles served only one term, but he was destined to wield the actual power for 10 years. His administration basically was a continuation of Obregón's, with whom he maintained a close, harmonious personal relationship. It was suggested that the two men essentially were co-presidents. Calles, however, was even less committed to the social goals of the Revolution than was Obregón, and he slowed even the modest land distribution program.

On the subject of the church, however, Calles was deeply committed to the anticlerical principles that had been embodied in all three liberal constitutions. Both he and Obregón were practicing Freemasons, who are decidedly anti-Catholic and whose influence was believed to be even stronger after the Revolution. When the church opposed Calles' programs, he began enforcing all the radical anticlerical provisions of the constitution. The church's property, even the actual church buildings, were expropriated; priests were forbidden from engaging in political activity or even from wearing clerical garb on the street; foreign priests were expelled, and members of the clergy were required to register with the government. The clergy literally went on strike in 1926, refusing to say Mass for three years. Some fanatical Catholic laymen, called *cristeros*, engaged in acts of terrorism. Church-state relations remained hostile for decades. Not until 1993 did Mexico establish diplomatic relations with the Vatican.

As the election of 1928 approached, Calles and Obregón found themselves unwilling to turn over power to a third man, so the constitution was amended to allow Obregón to run for a second term. Another amendment lengthened the presidential term, as Díaz had done, from four to six years. Obregón was elected over token opposition, but just three weeks later, on July 17, he was shot to death while dining in a restaurant by a young artist who apparently was a *cristero* acting on his own initiative. An eminent intellectual, Emilio Portes Gil, was named interim president until another election could be held in 1929, although it was Calles who actually held the power. During this brief interregnum, however, an institution was established that was to be the dominant force in Mexican political life for the next 71 years. Calles and Portes Gil organized a new political party, the National Revolutionary Party, or *PNR,* that incorporated the revolutionary sectors of *campesinos,* or peasants, and organized labor under its umbrella. Its name would be changed in 1938 to the Party of the Mexican Revolution and yet again in 1946 to its current name, the Institutional Revolutionary Party, or *PRI.* Its candidate in 1929, Pascual Ortiz Rubio, won a suspiciously lopsided victory, a phenomenon that would be repeated over and over again.

Ortiz Rubio's three-year presidency is remembered as little more than a footnote because it was Calles who was really in charge. His control was so complete that when, in 1932, the president fired some officials who enjoyed Calles' support, Calles merely summoned a news conference to announce that Ortiz Rubio had resigned. The hapless president had no choice but to comply. Calles hand-picked Abelardo Rodríguez to fill out the last two years of what was to have been Obregón's term, then likewise designated a well-respected, 39-year-old former revolutionary general, Lázaro Cárdenas, as the official party's candidate for the 1934 election.

Cárdenas won by the predictable landslide, but before long the left-leaning president and the quasi-fascist Calles clashed over policy. A bloodless power struggle ensued, but this time it was Cárdenas who prevailed.

The Cárdenas administration is generally regarded as the most honest and so-

cially conscious of the post-revolutionary period. During his six years in power, Cárdenas redistributed 45 million acres of land to the peasants, compared with 19 million that had been distributed from 1920–1934. He also gave unprecedented moral and official support to organized labor. He refused to recognize the government of the victorious Generalisimo Francisco Franco at the end of the Spanish Civil War and gave refuge to thousands of defeated Republicans. But the act for which Cárdenas is best remembered was the nationalization of foreign oil companies in 1937 after the companies refused the government's terms for settling a prolonged strike. Today, despite the privatization trend sweeping Latin America, oil drilling, refining and fuel retailing remain

Lázaro Cárdenas

in the hands of the state monopoly, *Petroleos Mexicanos,* or *Pemex.*

Despite the near-absolute power Mexican presidents enjoy, there was less abuse under Cárdenas than under many of his predecessors or successors. Press freedom continued to grow, and Cárdenas tolerated the establishment of a conservative opposition movement, the National Action Party, or *PAN,* in 1939. It also was Cárdenas who finally and irrevocably established the revolutionary principle of "no reelection" by stepping aside at the end of his *sexenio,* or six-year term. Although he was to remain a respected and influential voice in Mexican politics until his death in

1970, Cárdenas made no effort to remain the power behind the throne as Calles and others had done.

However, Cárdenas chose to continue, and thus perpetuate, the decidedly undemocratic practice of Obregón and Calles of hand-picking his successor. Referred to in Mexico as *el dedazo,* or the tap of the finger, this practice was followed by all of Cárdenas' successors until Ernesto Zedillo disavowed it in 1999. By tradition, the incumbent conferred in secret about a year before the election with former presidents and a handful of top party leaders to discuss a list of possible candidates. At this stage, the heir apparent was referred to as *el tapado,* or the hidden one, whose identity became the focus of intense speculation by the public and the press. When the president announced his decision, the designated candidate was hailed by all sectors of the party and pro-*PRI* newspapers as a near-messiah and acclaimed as the greatest possible choice. The process more closely resembled the selection of a new pope by the College of Cardinals than the nomination of a presidential candidate in a supposedly democratic system; all that was missing was the emission of white smoke from the presidential palace to announce that a choice had been made. Some scholars have suggested the *PRI*'s selection process was based upon Masonic rites.

Cárdenas' choice was yet another revolutionary general, Manuel Ávila Camacho, who had been Cárdenas' defense secretary. This surprised many, because Ávila Camacho was far to the right of Cárdenas. Moreover, he was a devout Catholic, which represented a sharp break with the anti-clericalism of the past. This transition established a precedent that would be seen again in the ensuing decades of alternating between presidents that were leftist and centrist, also between presidents who were dynamic and passive. Under Ávila Camacho, land redistribution slowed to a glacial pace. But World War II was to result in an economic boom for Mexico, which joined the Allies and declared war on Germany and Japan. Mexican industries churned out war supplies that were exported to the United States; relations in general between the United States and Mexico, strained since the beginning of the Revolution, finally began to improve. Ávila Camacho hosted President Franklin D. Roosevelt at a meeting in Monterrey in 1943, the first time a sitting U.S. president had crossed the southern border.

As his successor in 1946 Ávila Camacho picked Miguel Alemán, his *secretario de gobernación,* or interior minister, the most powerful post in the cabinet, roughly the combined equivalent of the secretary of the interior and White House chief of staff

Mexico

The colorful old downtown of the colonial center of Guanajuato

in the U.S. Traditionally, whoever held it was automatically on the "short list" to be nominated for president. Unlike earlier elections, this time there was a serious opposition candidate in the form of Foreign Minister Ezequiel Padilla, who was disgruntled over not being selected himself. Alemán, of course, was declared the winner with 80% of the vote; that count remains questionable, but for Mexico even 20% for an opposition candidate was extraordinary. The transition was a watershed in modern Mexican history because Ávila Camacho was to be the last general to serve as president.

Like Ávila Camacho, Alemán was a centrist who merely give lip service to the socialist principles of the Revolution, but he was more dynamic and more of a visionary than his predecessor. The Mexican economy was growing, and Alemán devoted much of the increased revenues to mammoth public works projects like highways and dams. He also embarked on the greatest building program since the days of Díaz, and one of the chief beneficiaries of this program was the National Autonomous University of Mexico, or *UNAM*. Moreover, Alemán greatly improved the

efficiency of state-owned enterprises like *Pemex*. On the negative side, corruption reappeared on a scale reminiscent of the days of Carranza and Díaz. The president himself escaped scandal, but it was noted that he and many of his appointees left office far wealthier than they had been before.

Apparently in response to the public discontent over the corruption, Alemán chose his interior secretary, Adolfo Ruíz Cortines, as the *PRI* presidential candidate in 1952. Once again, however, a *PRI* defector, a wealthy businessman and former general named Miguel Henríquez Guzmán, launched a serious independent candidacy. Ruíz Cortines supposedly defeated the popular Henríquez and minor candidates with 77% of the vote—still questionable, but it would be the smallest percentage the *PRI* would admit to for 36 years.

Ruíz Cortines restored an atmosphere of integrity to the presidency. Lacking Alemán's flamboyance and charisma, he often was derided as colorless. But he proved an aggressive, if not demonstrative, reformer. While Alemán had constructed grand projects, Ruíz Cortines focused on roads, irrigation, schools and

hospitals. Among his lasting achievements was extending the suffrage to women in 1953, and in his last year in office Mexico became for the first time a net exporter of food.

Ruíz Cortines selected his young labor secretary, Adolfo López Mateos, as the *PRI* candidate in 1958. The *PAN* for the first time mounted a reasonably serious challenge, but López Mateos won by the usual landslide, about 90%. López Mateos swung the pendulum back to the left and toward more dynamic leadership. As labor minister he had earned the respect of the unions, and there were fewer strikes during his *sexenio* than in the previous three. Land distribution, which had tapered off steadily under his three predecessors, picked up dramatically. López Mateos parceled out about 22 million acres, making him second only to Cárdenas.

The pendulum then swung sharply back toward conservatism and drabness. As his successor, López Mateos picked his interior secretary, Gustavo Díaz Ordáz, a homely, most unpresidential-looking choice. For the first time, the *PAN* garnered more than 1 million votes in the 1964 election, and its percentage rose to just above 10%. There

Manuel Avila Camacho

was nothing particularly breathtaking in the achievements of Díaz Ordáz other than the sports complex that was built for the 1968 Olympic Games. On the very eve of the games, however, something occurred that was to haunt the president until his death. The student unrest that had spread across Europe and the United States in 1968 arrived in Mexico that summer. Federal troops occupied the *UNAM* to quell a lengthy student strike. On the night of October 2, when students staged a peaceful demonstration in the Plaza de Tlatelolco in Mexico City, troops opened fire on the pretext that snipers had fired on them. Little or no evidence supports this, but as many as 300 people were killed, hundreds more wounded and more than 1,000 arrested. It was the greatest outbreak of violence since the *cristero* revolt of the 1920s. More than 40 years later, the "Tlatelolco Massacre" remains a national controversy.

The man responsible for crushing the protests, Interior Secretary Luis Echeverría, was the man Díaz Ordáz selected to succeed him in 1970. This time the *PAN*'s percentage of the vote edged up to 13%. As if to atone for his role in the Tlatelolco incident, Echeverría swung the pendulum dramatically back to the left. Early in his term he freed hundreds of students who had been jailed for two years. He angered the United States by establishing diplomatic relations with the People's Republic of China and by speaking out against the war in Vietnam. He made a point of expressing support for Cuba's Fidel Castro and welcomed Castro on a state visit to Mexico. He refused to recognize the government of General Augusto Pinochet after the 1973 coup that overthrew and killed Marxist President Salvador Allende in Chile, and he granted asylum to

thousands of Chilean leftists. He ordered his U.N. delegate to support a resolution condemning Zionism as racism, but when U.S. Jews launched a boycott of Mexican resorts, he abruptly reversed course. He made pretensions about being a leader of the so-called "Nonaligned Movement" and even sought to become U.N. secretary-general upon his retirement.

On the whole, Echeverría can be described as a fountain of hollow rhetoric. He denounced capitalism, and increased the number of state-owned enterprises from 50 to 750, but pragmatically did little to interfere with free enterprise in Mexico. He talked about democratizing the *PRI*, but didn't follow through. He encouraged the creation of left-wing publications, but when the leftist editor of the daily *Excélsior,* Julio Scherer García, became too critical for his taste, Echeverría used his influence to have him fired. Scherer then launched a weekly newsmagazine, *Proceso,* which the president tried to strangle at birth by refusing to sell Scherer government-subsidized newsprint. *Proceso* survived, however, and today is the leading news weekly. Four months before he left office in 1976, Echeverría set a precedent for future presidents by making a dramatic economic move and leaving the consequences to his successor: he devalued the peso, from 12.5 to 20 to the dollar. He also bequeathed a 50% unemployment/underemployment rate and a 22% inflation rate.

That successor would be Echeverría's finance secretary, José López Portillo, who was elected without any meaningful opposition when the *PAN* refused to field a candidate in 1976 to protest what it called, not incorrectly, *PRI* electoral manipulations. In keeping with tradition, López Portillo swung the pendulum back to the right. The major departure from his predecessor's policy was to stop baiting big business, international lending institutions and the United States. He met with

President Jimmy Carter, sworn in seven weeks after himself, in Washington early in their terms and agreed to an emergency sale of Mexican natural gas to help the U.S. cope with the brutally cold winter of 1977. He also became the first Mexican president to address the U.S. Congress, to which he delivered a fatherly lecture about being good neighbors. Carter would later reciprocate the visit and become the first U.S. president to address the Mexican Congress—in Spanish. López Portillo later would exchange visits with Carter's successor, Ronald Reagan. López Portillo did not, however, distance himself from Castro. He also lent moral and financial support to the *Sandinista* regime in Nicaragua, which came to power in 1979, and opposed Reagan's support for right-wing regimes in El Salvador and Guatemala.

Still, he wisely mended fences with the International Monetary Fund and major foreign banks and succeeded in reassuring them that Mexico was a sound credit risk again. In this he was aided by the discovery in the early 1970s of vast deposits of petroleum, by some estimates rivaling the reserves of Saudi Arabia, in the southern states of Tabasco and Chiapas. *Pemex* brought the fields on line just in time to take full advantage of OPEC's quadrupling of the world market price for oil.

Mexico opted not to join OPEC, but the revenue from petroleum sales began to fill government coffers. López Portillo, like a poor man who has suddenly won the lottery, went on a wild spending spree. When the money ran out, he merely borrowed more from abroad on the assumption that the petroleum gravy train would rumble on indefinitely. He would leave office before the full weight of his folly came crashing down upon his successor.

So, too, would the massive corruption committed by López Portillo and his top officials on a scale unseen since the time of Alemán. He became the embodiment of

Former President López Portillo and family

Mexico

an old Mexican quip about the president: "The first two years he talks about corruption, the next two years he does nothing and the last two years he takes all he can." In López Portillo's case, he acquired a palatial estate called Dog Hill, with five mansions, swimming pools, stables, tennis courts and a gymnasium. On the positive side, he finally moved to give opposition parties a somewhat greater voice, while, of course, not actually jeopardizing the *PRI*'s grip on power. In the 1960s, the opposition had been reserved a maximum of 20 seats in the 197-seat Chamber of Deputies, the lower house of Congress, distributed by proportional representation. López Portillo enlarged the chamber to 400 seats, of which up to 100 could go to the opposition.

In 1982, López Portillo's final year in office, the world price of oil plummeted and Mexico found itself in deep financial trouble. López Portillo was forced to implement a drastic—and exceedingly unpopular—austerity program that threw about 1 million bureaucrats out of work. He also was forced to devalue the peso again. In the midst of this crisis, he broke with convention by selecting as his successor his secretary of planning and budget, Miguel de la Madrid. This also shattered the long-accepted tradition of never picking a *PRI* candidate who speaks English. Not only that, de la Madrid had earned a master's degree in public administration from Harvard. It was, moreover, to establish a new trend of selecting presidents who are technocrats who have never held elective office, reminiscent of Díaz's *científicos*, except that these new ones received their training in the United States.

In the July 1982 election, de la Madrid reportedly received 74.4% to 14% for the *PAN* candidate and 5.8% for the candidate of a coalition of left-wing parties. Just two weeks before he left office, López Portillo did something that not even the leftist Echeverría had dared to do—he nationalized the banks. On December 1, 1982, he turned over the mess he had created to de la Madrid and retired to Dog Hill. He was held in low esteem in public opinion right up until his death on February 17, 2004—and beyond.

De la Madrid was left to cope with the country's gravest economic crisis since the Depression of the 1930s. In 1983, inflation was 60%, and the foreign debt continued to mushroom, from $65 billion in 1983 to $105 billion in 1988—among the greatest per capita debts in the world. Even as the president struggled to cope with this daunting challenge, the country was hammered by a dual blow in 1985. OPEC slashed the price of petroleum by about two thirds, from roughly $30 to $10 per barrel, which completely pulled the rug out from under the debt-ridden economy.

Former President de la Madrid and family

Even nature seemed to be against Mexico; a disastrous earthquake struck Mexico City that year, killing an estimated 10,000 people and causing $3.5 billion in property damage—much of which was attributed to shoddy construction of government-sponsored projects. The peso began to plummet against the dollar, and the country faced the kind of hyperinflation that had once plagued Argentina, Brazil and Peru. Inflation soared to more than 100% on de la Madrid's watch, and the peso dropped from 24.5 to the dollar to 2,800 by 1990.

Compounding the dilemma was Mexico's burgeoning birthrate of 3.2% annually. Even in the boom times the economy had barely been able to absorb the young new workers flooding the labor market, but in these lean times the situation became especially desperate. The cardboard shantytowns on the outskirts of Mexico City grew larger and larger, and more Mexicans than ever were seeking the traditional escape route from their misery—illegal entry into the United States. This, of course, served to strain bilateral relations.

Desperate times do indeed call for desperate measures, and de la Madrid employed them. He allowed the price of Mexican crude oil to "float" instead of pegging it at an artificial price. He also began to sell off some of the government-owned enterprises whose payrolls had become bloated from *PRI* patronage. Attempts to renegotiate the foreign debt satisfied neither Mexico nor its creditors. Finally, de la Madrid succeeded in obtaining a $3.5 billion "bridging" loan from the Reagan administration in 1988.

As if de la Madrid did not have enough problems, early in his administration he was faced with still another—a scandal that erupted over the corruption committed under his predecessor. Among the high-level López Portillo officials accused of financial wrongdoing were the head of *Pemex*, who could not account for a missing 300,000 barrels of oil. Perhaps the most

egregious case, one that especially outraged the public, was that of the Mexico City police chief, who had built himself an unbelievably ostentatious estate complete with air-conditioned doghouses! The chief was prosecuted and his property was expropriated and opened to the public as a "museum of corruption." López Portillo himself managed to escape prosecution (no such action had ever been taken against a former head of state since the Revolution), but the damage to his reputation wrought by his shameless nest-feathering was irreparable and today, even in death, he remains pariah.

The lean economic times and the publicizing of outrageous cases of corruption took a serious toll on the *PRI*. Up to that point, the *PRI* not only had won every presidential election since 1929, but it had never lost an election for a state governorship or a federal Senate seat and rarely lost at any level. Now, for the first time, the *PAN* began winning municipal elections and even won some directly elected seats in the Chamber of Deputies, not merely the scraps the *PRI* reserved for the opposition under proportional representation.

In the 1988 presidential election, the *PRI* was to face the greatest threat to its power in its 60-year history, not from the right, but from the left. Cuauhtémoc Cárdenas, son of the revered former president and himself a member of the *PRI*, abandoned the party to organize a new left-wing movement, the Party of the Democratic Revolution, or *PRD*. As his successor, de la Madrid selected another technocrat who, like himself, spoke fluent English, was schooled at Harvard and had never held an elective office: Carlos Salinas de Gortari. The *PAN*, meanwhile, launched its most determined effort to date with the candidacy of Manuel Clouthier, a wealthy landowner from Sinaloa.

Polls showed that Salinas not only might fail to win an absolute majority, but even more unthinkable, might actually

Mexico

lose to Cárdenas. The campaign was the most contentious until that time, and the actual election on July 6 remains controversial. As the polls had indicated, on election night early returns showed Cárdenas closing on Salinas. Then, suddenly, it was reported the vote count had been delayed by a computer breakdown. Federal troops seized the ballot boxes. The results weren't announced until September 10, and it was reported that Salinas had neatly received a bare majority of 50.36% to 31.06% for Cárdenas and 16.81% for Clouthier. Both opposition parties cried foul, but Salinas was duly sworn in on December 1 under a cloud of suspicion and illegitimacy that haunts him to this day.

Just as Echeverría had sought to atone for the Tlatelolco Massacre by tilting heavily to the left, so Salinas attempted to neutralize the outrage over his suspicious election victory by portraying himself as a political reformer. The timing of the Salinas reforms, beginning in 1989, was especially symbolic. *Perestroika* and *glasnost* were in full flower in the Soviet Union; the democracy movement was underway in China, although it was to be crushed that June; the Berlin Wall came tumbling down in November, and the autocratic regime of Romania's Nicolae Ceaucescu came to a bloody end in December. Moreover, one Latin American dictatorship after another had given way to multi-party democracy. With the temper of these times, Mexico's monopolistic political system suddenly looked as out of place as a man with his fly open at an elegant dinner party. Salinas put out the word that at least some elections must be fair and clean, if only to keep up appearances. As a result, the *PAN* began winning state governorships: Guanajuato, Baja California Norte, Jalisco and Chihuahua. Both the *PAN* and the *PRD* won more directly elected seats in the Chamber of Deputies, and even the *PRI*'s monopoly in the 64-member Senate was finally broken.

Perhaps just as important as the electoral reforms, however, was the relaxation of controls on the media. Salinas abolished *Pipsa*, the government newsprint monopoly that offered paper at subsidized prices but which often had withheld it from overly critical publications. The virtual monopoly enjoyed by the giant pro-*PRI* television network *Televisa* also came to an end as rival network *TV Azteca* went on the air, although it, too, had pro-*PRI* owners. As a consequence, reporting became both more aggressive and more critical. Salinas, and the so-called "dinosaurs," or traditionalists within the *PRI,* soon discovered what Mikhail Gorbachev was to learn: that reforms after decades of repression gain momentum and take on a life of their own; once the forces of openness are

placed in motion, they cannot be reversed without a violent reaction.

Meanwhile, Salinas sought to cope with the economic crisis he had inherited from his predecessor. He negotiated another "bailout" loan in 1990 from President George H. W. Bush, with whom he met several times and enjoyed a satisfactory working relationship. In addition, Salinas embraced the Latin American trend toward privatization of state-owned enterprises. The Mexican Revolution was essentially dead. In its place was a stampede toward free-market capitalism. No longer were foreign, particularly U.S., businessmen viewed as bogeymen. Assembly plants, called *maquiladoras,* sprang up along the northern border. Hundreds of thousands of Mexicans found jobs in them, at wages well below U.S. levels but far above what they had before—nothing.

Slowly the economy improved, and Bush and Salinas discussed a grand scheme designed to benefit both economies—a North American Free Trade Agreement (NAFTA) that would encompass Canada, the United States and Mexico. NAFTA became a hot political issue in the U.S. presidential election of 1992, with organized labor vehemently opposed to it. But after some vacillation, Democratic candidate Bill Clinton also endorsed the concept. The independent candidate that year, tycoon H. Ross Perot, warned that NAFTA would create "a giant sucking sound" as U.S. jobs disappeared south of the border. Clinton won, and the U.S. Senate ratified the treaty in late 1993—after the Canadian Parliament and Mexican Congress already had done so—and it took effect on January 1, 1994.

Modeled loosely after the European Common Market, in theory NAFTA benefits all three countries by eliminating tariffs, thereby stimulating trade and, indirectly, production. Indeed, there has been an explosion of trade. Tractor trailers flow in an endless stream across the Rio Grande in both directions, although in those heading north illegal drugs frequently ride piggy-back with legitimate cargo. In recent years, illegal arms flow south, purchased by powerful drug cartels. The boom in northern Mexico was cut short, however, by yet another disastrous peso devaluation.

By the 1994 elections, Salinas' reforms had ricocheted on him, and the *PRI* was split more than ever between the reformers and the "dinosaurs." The traditionalists contemptuously regarded the reformers, most of whom had held only appointed offices by virtue of their advanced degrees, many of them from the United States, as upstarts who had not paid the necessary dues by coming up through party ranks. Despite his reforms, Salinas was not about to abandon the practice of the *dedazo*. He met privately in 1993 with a handful of influential party leaders before announcing he had selected yet another technocrat with a U.S. doctorate, Luis Donaldo Colosio, as the *PRI* candidate. The party elders regarded him as harmless and pledged to support him.

But Colosio soon demonstrated that he was his own man, not Salinas'. He campaigned as a populist and drew large, enthusiastic crowds, which led to a falling out with Salinas. The rift may have been Colosio's doom. On March 23, 1994, while pressing the flesh with a crowd of cheering supporters in Tijuana, Colosio was shot in the head by a man wielding a pistol and died on the spot. The killing sent shock waves through Mexico, because although violence is relatively common-place in local politics, this was the highest-level assassination since the murder of President-elect Obregón in 1928. The lone gunman was apprehended, convicted and sentenced to 45 years in prison (Mexico does not have the death penalty), and although he never implicated anyone else in the as-

Former President Salinas de Gortari and family

Mexico

sassination, there remains a widespread public belief that the killing was the result of a conspiracy.

Stunned, *PRI* officials met again with Salinas, who chose yet another technocrat, the Yale-educated Ernesto Zedillo Ponce de León. While Colosio had been perceived as shy, Zedillo was seen as colorless and reclusive. He had a flat, uninspiring speaking voice and initially showed no talent for leadership. He had spent his 21 years with the party hidden from the public in various bureaucratic assignments. He received coaching to improve his style, but with dire results. In the spirit of Salinas' reforms, he agreed to meet the *PRD*'s Cárdenas and the *PAN* candidate, Diego Fernández de Cevallos, in a televised debate; his performance was disastrous. Polls after the event showed Fernández leading by 20%.

The well-oiled *PRI* machinery rushed to Zedillo's rescue. Although the "dinosaurs" were lukewarm about having a fourth Ivy League-trained bureaucrat as the nominee, they rallied behind him to ensure victory through the *PRI*'s time-honored methods. Zedillo likely would have won the August 21 vote even without creative vote counting, but like Salinas, he reportedly—and suspiciously—received the magic 50% majority. Fernández supposedly received 26%, while Cárdenas dropped to 17%. The *PAN* and the *PRD* made significant gains in the Congress. The *PRI* won an even 300 of the 500 seats in the Chamber of Deputies, while the *PAN* total rose to 119, the Workers Party (*PT*) had 10 and the *PRD* 7. In the expanded Senate, the *PRI* had 95 of the 128 seats, the *PAN* 25 and the *PRD* 8.

Like his predecessors, Salinas decided in the waning days of his administration to devalue the peso and let Zedillo deal with the consequences. The consequences were terrible; the economic recovery collapsed virtually overnight and the country plunged once again into recession. The trauma of this latest downturn on the newly emerging middle class was to have long-lasting political fallout for the *PRI*. Even today, young urban professionals from different states vote for the *PAN* because of Carlos Salinas.

Even before Zedillo took office on December 1, 1994, the country was shocked by yet another assassination, one that shook the government and the *PRI* to their very foundations. On September 28, *PRI* Secretary General José Francisco Ruíz Massieu, the No. 2 man in the party and a leader in the reform faction, was gunned down. Salinas, whose sister was once married to the slain politician, appointed Ruíz Massieu's brother Mario to investigate the murder. A few months later, after Zedillo had taken office, Mario Ruíz Massieu resigned, alleging that the *PRI* was obstruct-

**Former President
Ernesto Zedillo Ponce de León**

ing the investigation. Ostensibly to ensure a non-partisan investigation, Zedillo appointed as attorney general a *PAN* loyalist, Antonio Lozano. In February 1995, Lozano stunned the nation again by ordering the arrest of former President Salinas' brother, Raúl, on charges of masterminding the Ruíz Massieu murder.

A month later, Carlos Salinas—disgraced as much by his brother's arrest as by the recession already being blamed on him—absconded from the country, first to the United States, then to Canada, and finally to Ireland, which has no extradition treaty with Mexico. He remains a pariah in Mexico to this day, while the Ruíz Massieu assassination and the Salinas brothers' alleged links to it, as well as revelations they may have been linked to drug traffickers, remain grist for the Mexican media. In 1999, Raúl Salinas was convicted of the murder and sentenced to 50 years' imprisonment. In 2005, a three-judge appeal panel shocked the country by overturning the conviction. He walked out of prison a few days later.

The Political Earthquake of 1997

Mexico embarked on an uncharted political course with the midterm elections of July 6, 1997. At stake were all 500 deputies in the lower house of Congress, 300 of them elected directly by district and 200 by proportional representation, and 32 of the 128 senators, allocated by proportional representation. The *PRI* would have had to poll at least 42.2% to retain its absolute

majority in the Chamber of Deputies, but it received only 39%.

Of the 300 deputies elected directly, the *PRI* won 164, the *PRD* won 70, the *PAN* took 65, and the *PT* had one. Proportionally, the *PRI* received 39% of the vote, *PAN* 27% and the *PRD* 25.5%. When the complicated formula was put into effect, the *PRI* fell about 10 seats short of a majority. Its majority in the Senate remained secure.

Buffeted from right and left, the *PRI* also took an unprecedented drubbing in local races. In Mexico City, where the mayor was elected directly for the first time rather than appointed by the president, Cuauhtémoc Cárdenas, the *PRD* presidential candidate in 1988 and 1994, received a landslide victory, polling 47.1% of the vote.

Of the six governorships at stake in the election, the *PAN* won decisive victories in both Nuevo León (Monterrey) and Querétaro. Those triumphs brought to six the number of states the *PAN* had wrested from the *PRI* since 1989, after President Salinas' electoral reforms. The *PRI* retained San Luis Potosí and Colima states, but the *PAN* claimed fraud cost it the governorship of Sonora, which borders Arizona, and of Campeche, in the southeast.

Yet the election apparently was fair. Elections are now conducted under the auspices of the Federal Electoral Institute (*IFE*), an independent, non-partisan entity, not a creature of *PRI* patronage as was the case in the past; each state has a similar body. Since 1994, each voter has a plastic ID card with photo and thumbprint, which is matched against a master list in each polling station. Each party is entitled to five accredited poll watchers at each station. Voters mark their ballots in secret, free from intimidation by *PRI* operatives. After a voter casts his ballot, his thumb is marked with indelible ink to thwart Chicago-style multiple voting. Alcohol sales are banned not only on election day but on election eve.

The business newspaper *El Financiero* had perhaps the most succinct headline the morning after the election: "END TO 70 YEARS OF HEGEMONY." Julio Castrillón, one of the victorious *PAN* candidates for national deputy from Nuevo León, had a prophetic assessment. "This is the death of the one-party system," he proclaimed during an interview with me.

The election went beyond leaving Mexico with an opposition-controlled Congress. Mexico's electoral map showed a troubling polarization between north and south, rich and poor, right and left, which continues today. The *PAN* was clearly on the ascendancy in the prosperous northern half of the country, where jobs were generated by ubiquitous *maquiladora* assembly plants. I was stunned by the increased affluence I found in Monterrey since my

Headlines in the Monterrey newspaper *El Norte* the morning of July 7, 1997, declare the opposition *PAN* candidate, Fernando Canales, the winner of the Nuevo León governor's race, as well as announcing that the opposition parties have broken the *PRI*'s domination of Congress and that the *PRD*'s Cuauhtémoc Cárdenas has won the mayor's race in Mexico City.

Mexico

last visit 14 years earlier. With prosperity, it seems, had come political conservatism. The farther south one goes, however, the worse the poverty and the greater the voting strength of the *PRD*.

For the first year after the historic 1997 elections, the *PAN* and the *PRD* put aside their obvious ideological differences to join forces to wrest control of key committees in the Chamber of Deputies from the *PRI*.

Cárdenas took office as mayor of Mexico City in December 1997, but the euphoria of victory abruptly gave way to the grim realities of governing the world's most populous city. The extent of *PRI* patronage and corruption proved to be even more mind-boggling than had been imagined. The outgoing *PRI* officials had erased the hard drives of all the computers—except for the computers that had mysteriously vanished. The erasures apparently were less an act of sour-grapes sabotage by the losers than a matter of destroying evidence of malfeasance. Meanwhile, scandal after scandal dominated newscasts and the front pages of newspapers in 1998, most of them involving *PRI* officials or wealthy patrons.

But the worst was yet to come. In March 1998, President Zedillo startled the Chamber of Deputies with a cavalier proposal for the government to assume $65 billion in bad debts from the 1994–95 economic crisis. The debts were held by the Bank Savings Protection Fund, the equivalent of the U.S. Federal Deposit Insurance Corporation, known by the acronym *Fobaproa*. Zedillo's plan amounted to a massive bailout of banks that went under during the crisis, with the taxpayers footing the bill. Soon, however, investigative journalists and opposition congressmen began disclosing that many of the bad debts resulted from incredibly stupid loans to multi-millionaires for high-risk ventures. Many of those businessmen, it turned out, had contributed millions to the *PRI*'s 1994 campaign chest.

The public outrage was immediate and intense. For months, the opposition *PAN* and *PRD* deputies joined forces to keep Zedillo's bailout bill hostage in the lower house, while the government made lame efforts to assuage public opinion by arresting more than 180 businessmen for fraudulent loans. The logjam broke when the *PAN* struck a compromise with the *PRI* on the 1999 budget, by which $55 billion of the *Fobaproa* debt would be converted into public debt. The *PRD* denounced the bailout as a travesty, ending the cooperation between the two opposition parties.

Prelude to 2000

With the *Fobaproa* scandal reverberating in the background, Mexicans elected 17 of their 31 governors in 1998 and 1999. With the electoral reforms firmly in place, the outcomes were no longer a foregone conclusion. In Zacatecas, a former *PRI* whip in the Chamber of Deputies, Ricardo Monreal, had bolted the party and was the candidate for the *PRD*, while the *PRI* nominated a longtime party hack. The race was symbolic because Zacatecas had long been a faithful *PRI* stronghold. Monreal won a decisive victory, 43% to 36%, despite evidence of *PRI* vote-buying. That same day, the *PRI* easily held onto the governorship of Durango, and made history in Chihuahua with the first *recapturing* of a governorship from the *PAN*, which had won there in 1992.

A month later, the *PAN* captured the governorship of Aguascalientes for the first time. The same day, the *PRI*'s Miguel Alemán, son and namesake of the former president, won by a large margin in Veracruz, while the *PRI* held onto the governorship of Oaxaca against a determined *PRD* challenge. The *PRD* claimed fraud.

The *PRI* retained the governorships of Tamaulipas in October 1998 and of Puebla and Sinaloa in November. But in tiny Tlaxcala, a former *PRI* loyalist, Alfonso Sánchez Anaya, ran as the *PRD* candidate and pulled off a narrow upset victory, 45% to 43%.

Guerrero and Baja California Sur voted in February 1999; both were battles between the *PRI* and *PRD*. In Guerrero, the *PRI* candidate was declared the winner by 49% to 47%. The *PRD* cried foul, alleging the *PRI* had swapped votes for groceries. But in Baja California Sur, the *PRD*'s Leonel Cota Montana won by a landslide 55% to 36%.

Two weeks later, the *PRI* won in Hidalgo and even in Quintana Roo, where the incumbent *PRI* governor, Mario Villanueva Madrid, was under federal investigation for drug trafficking. In both states, the two opposition parties had failed to present a united front, thus dividing the opposition vote and assuring the *PRI* easy wins. As a bizarre anticlimax to the Quintana Roo election, Governor Villanueva absconded the day before the inauguration of his successor and disappeared. For two years he was an international fugitive before being arrested in Cancún in his home state in May 2001. (In 2010, he was extradited to the United States.)

In July 1999, the *PRI* benefited from a divided opposition to retain the governorship of the populous state of Mexico behind the candidacy of Arturo Montiel, while in Nayarit the *PAN*, *PRD*, and *PT* put aside their ideological differences to field a single candidate, who won, 50% to 44%. The *PRI* defeated an opposition coalition in Coahuila that September.

Thus, voters sent mixed signals in the governorship races of 1998–99. The major psychological winner was the *PRD*, which went into the races with no state governorships and emerged with three, Zacatecas, Tlaxcala and Baja California Sur. The *PAN* didn't quite break even, losing a large, powerful state (Chihuahua) while picking up a smaller, but still influential one (Aguascalientes). An opposition alliance won the governorship of Nayarit but lost in Coahuila. The *PRI* could console itself that it won 13 of the 17 governorships, including the recapturing of Chihuahua, and that it still controlled 21 of the 31, but there was no escaping the mathematics that it suffered a net loss of four states and saw its electoral strength eroded in several more. Of the three parties, it clearly was the major loser.

The Elections of 2000

One of the most pivotal events in 20th century Mexico occurred in 1998 when President Zedillo publicly disavowed the *dedazo*, or "tap," by which for 65 years the incumbent president had personally designated the next *PRI* candidate.

Seven candidates expressed interest in the *PRI* nomination, but the list soon winnowed to four: Manuel Bartlett, former governor of Puebla and interior secretary under de la Madrid, closely identified with the party's "dinosaur" faction; Humberto Roque Villanueva, a former *PRI* chief; Interior Secretary Francisco Labastida, a former governor of Sinaloa, considered a reformist and unquestionably Zedillo's preferred choice; and Tabasco Governor Roberto Madrazo, a dinosaur.

Meanwhile, the *PRD*'s presumed candidate, Mexico City Mayor Cárdenas, who had been the frontrunner for president in most opinion polls throughout 1998, began to suffer a decline in public esteem for his perceived lack of progress. In 1999, a new book alleged Cárdenas had met secretly with Carlos Salinas shortly after the highly suspect 1988 election and agreed not to challenge Salinas' stolen victory.

The *PRI*'s National Political Council (*CNP*) approved the primary election process over a party convention and set November 7 as the date for the primary. The nominee would not be elected directly; the nomination would go to the candidate who polled a plurality of the vote in the largest number of the country's 300 districts for the Chamber of Deputies. The primary was opened to all voters regardless of party affiliation, apparently because the *PRI* did not have party membership cards. The *CNP* required public officials to resign their posts first.

Labastida, Zedillo's favorite, scored a landslide victory, attracting worldwide media attention. He received 5.3 million votes, or 55% of the 9.7 million votes cast, and in the vote that really mattered, carried 274 of the 300 districts for the Chamber of Deputies. Madrazo finished second and Bartlett third. The *dedazo*, it appeared, was not quite dead after all.

Mexico had never seen the likes of the campaign for the July 2, 2000, presidential election. Guanajuato Governor Vicente Fox of the *PAN* had replaced Cárdenas as the frontrunner in all major polls. But once Labastida's landslide primary victory was a fact, he emerged as the front-runner. Attempts to forge an alliance between Fox and Cárdenas failed. Neither man, each known for an oversized ego, would yield to the other.

Fox chiseled away at Labastida's lead, and the race became essentially a contest between them. The Green Party (*PVEM*) forged a coalition with the *PAN* called the Alliance for Change. Later, the candidate of the small but venerable Authentic Party

of the Mexican Revolution (*PARM*) also withdrew and endorsed Fox. The *PRD*, meanwhile, formed a coalition with the *PT* and two smaller left-wing parties.

Fox closed the gap with an April 25 debate, in which the flamboyant Fox was widely seen as the victor over Labastida and Cárdenas. His unorthodox campaign style, heretofore unknown to Mexicans, struck a responsive chord. The six-foot, six-inch Fox enhanced his image by wearing cowboy boots.

In June, Labastida (and Cárdenas) accused Fox of illegally accepting foreign campaign contributions, which Fox adamantly denied. (The *IFE* later confirmed it was true and levied a heavy fine on the *PAN*). Labastida even suggested that the devoutly Catholic Fox would impose his religious beliefs on the country.

As a new feature there were plastic curtains on the voting booths to ensure se-

crecy. On the booths were the words, "The vote is free and secret."

Exit polls showed Fox with 44%, Labastida with 38%, Cárdenas with 16%. Two hours later, Fox's stunning and historic victory became assured. Along Saltillo's Boulevard Venustiano Carranza, thousands of jubilant *Panistas* honked horns, waved banners and posters and flashed the two-fingered symbol for Fox's campaign slogan, *"Ya!"* ("Right now!") There was a far larger explosion of jubilation around the Angel of Independence monument along the Paseo de la Reforma in Mexico City. Mexico's opposition, the wait had been 71 years.

At midnight, a dour President Zedillo addressed his countrymen on television and acknowledged that "it appears unquestionable that the next president will be Licenciado Vicente Fox Quesada." He graciously congratulated Fox on his victory and pledged his cooperation for a smooth transition, but not as graciously spent considerably more time praising Labastida, reminding his viewers what a positive force the *PRI* had been and pledging that the party would remain a vital force in the life of the nation. Soon thereafter, Fox appeared, and graciously praised Zedillo and Labastida. Ironically, July 2 also had been the victor's 58th birthday.

Mexico awoke not to a hangover but what seemed like another impossible dream. Not only had Fox carried 21 of the 31 states, but the *PAN* had near parity with the *PRI* in Congress. Cárdenas carried only two states—Baja California Sur and his home state of Michoacán. To make the *PAN*'s night complete, it picked up the governorship of the southern state of Morelos (the state of Emiliano Zapata) with 58% of the vote. It was the first time the *PAN* had won a governorship outside of its power base in the north.

Meanwhile, the *PRD* candidate for mayor of Mexico City, Andrés Manuel López Obrador, narrowly won with 38% of the vote.

Overnight, Mexico had been turned upside down, and a shell-shocked *PRI* began taking stock of the situation. One of my final images before leaving Mexico was a car with a sign painted on its back window that largely summed up the feelings of a decisive plurality of Mexicans: *"GANO PAN, GANO MEXICO"* ("PAN WON, MEXICO WON").

Final official tabulations by the non-partisan *IFE* were:

Fox	15,988,740	42.52%
Labastida	13,576,385	36.0%
Cárdenas	6,259,048	16.64%

A total of 37,603,924 Mexicans had voted, a respectable turnout of 63.97%. The

The pre-election issue of the weekly newsmagazine *Proceso* carries irreverent caricatures of the three major candidates. At left is Vicente Fox, a Coca-Cola in one hand and an obscene gesture in place of his trademark *"Ya"* sign in the other; around his neck is a cross, symbolizing his devout Catholicism. In the middle is Francisco Labastida, carrying an enormous forefinger representing *"el dedazo,"* meaning he was the favored candidate of President Ernesto Zedillo. On his lapel button is the unpopular former president, Carlos Salinas de Gortari. At right is Cuauhtémoc Cárdenas, portrayed as a moralistic reformer.

Mexico

breakdown in the lower house after the allocation of the 200 seats by proportional representation was: The *PAN*, 208, and its partner, the *PVEM*, 15, for a total of 223 for the Alliance for Change, 27 seats short of a majority; the *PRI*, 209; the *PRD*, 52; the *PT*, 8; the Convergence for Democracy, 3; the Nationalist Society, 3; and the Social Alliance, 2. The breakdown of the 128 Senate seats was 58 for the *PRI*, 53 for the *PAN* and the *PVEM* and 17 for the *PRD*.

The new president was born on a ranch in Guanajuato; his father was of U.S. descent. He received a Jesuit higher education, then went into the family's business. He ran a boot manufacturing company and a frozen fruit and vegetable firm as well as becoming chief of Coca-Cola's Latin American division. He was elected to the Chamber of Deputies in 1988, and was instrumental in passing a constitutional amendment to allow citizens with one foreign-born parent to be elected president; previously, both parents had to be born in Mexico. Fox was elected governor in 1995. and had a solid record of achievement as governor of Guanajuato. Despite his devout Catholicism, he was Mexico's first divorced president.

A New Era Begins

Vicente Fox was inaugurated on December 1, 2000. The inaugural ceremony was attended by such ideologically diverse personalities as Cuban President Fidel Castro, Colombian Nobel Laureate Gabriel García Márquez, U.S. Secretary of State Madeleine Albright and Microsoft chairman Bill Gates.

After receiving the presidential sash from Zedillo, Fox, still wearing cowboy boots, kept a campaign promise by ordering an army withdrawal from Chiapas as his first official act. (see Armed Rebellions). He then did something no *PRI* president could have done: He went to the Basilica of Our Lady of Guadalupe to offer thanks to Mexico's patron saint.

He proposed a breathtaking list of reforms: amending the constitution to permit referenda; a crackdown on corruption; greater environmental protection; streamlining, but not privatizing, *Pemex*; strengthening U.S.-style judicial review over laws passed by Congress; a code of ethics for cabinet secretaries; increased availability to university scholarships; increased incentives for savings and investments; greater government support for small businesses; universal health care; greater autonomy for the states; and the Indian rights bill demanded by the *Zapatistas*.

As foreign secretary, Fox appointed Jorge Castañeda, the noted political scientist; as attorney general, General Rafael

Macedo, the army's prosecutor, who had a reputation for incorruptibility; as interior secretary, the *PAN*'s leader in Congress, Santiago Creel.

Mexican-U.S. relations improved dramatically. Fox met with the new U.S. president, George W. Bush, on Fox's ranch. It was historic symbolism that for the first time ever, a U.S. president opted to make his first foreign visit to Mexico. The two businesslike conservatives with ranching backgrounds got along well and discussed trade, drugs, immigration and energy. Even before he became president, Fox made regular appearances on U.S. interview programs.

Fox made a symbolic gesture by opening the presidential palace of Los Pinos for the first time to the public. That gesture was to boomerang on him, however, when the media reported that the towels in the presidential bathrooms cost $400 and that the remote-controlled curtains cost $17,000. The media immediately labeled the first Fox mini-scandal "Towelgate."

Mexicans learned that their new president was serious about cracking down on corruption. He fired 12 high-ranking government officials after they were caught taking bribes in a sting operation.

Fox obtained congressional support for his Indian rights bill, but he found less enthusiasm when he introduced an ambitious tax reform plan. The Green Party broke with Fox over the tax reform scheme. Congress finally passed a watered-down version that focused on luxury taxes.

Fox averted a possible scandal by marrying his press spokeswoman, Martha Sahagún, on July 2, 2001, his 59th birthday and the first anniversary of his election victory. The nature of their relationship had been the subject of gossip for years, and she was known to be living in Los Pinos. It was reportedly she who had ordered the controversial towels and curtains. The press was not kind to the first lady, criticizing her actions and her taste.

In politics, the *PRI* continued to be plagued with problems after its defeat. An internecine battle for control ensued between the reformers and the dinosaurs, and the party's separation from the reins of power has stripped it of its most powerful tool—patronage. It also continued to lose governorships, beginning with Chiapas to the *PRD*.

In Tabasco, Governor Roberto Madrazo, in true dinosaur fashion, hand-picked the *PRI* candidate to succeed him, Manuel Andrade. In the October 2000 election, Andrade was declared the winner, 44% to 43%, over the *PRD*'s Raúl Ojeda. The *PRD* appealed the decision to the *IFE*, citing the usual evidence of *PRI* vote-buying. Just three days before Andrade's inauguration, the *IFE* made the unprecedented decision

to nullify the election results. The decision threw Tabasco into turmoil. A new election was held in August 2001. Andrade won narrowly, 50.5% to 46%, apparently fairly.

The *PAN* won the Yucatán governorship for the first time in May 2001, bringing to eight the number of states it controlled. That July, the *PAN* easily retained control of the governorship of Baja California Norte for a third straight term. In November 2001, the *PRI* lost the governorship of Michoacán. Lázaro Cárdenas Batel of the *PRD*, son of Cuauhtémoc and grandson and namesake of the illustrious former president, defeated the *PRI* candidate 41.8% to 36.7%. The victory brought to five the number of states, plus the Federal District, that the *PRD* controlled. President Fox himself attended Cárdenas' inauguration.

Fox had promised a fact-finding commission to investigate disappearances during the 1960s and 1970s, but took no action until the high-profile murder in October 2001 of Digna Ortíz, a prominent human rights lawyer. He then commissioned the human rights ombudsman to prepare a report on past abuses, which could only prove an embarrassment to the *PRI*. The 3,000-page report concluded that 532 people who disappeared during that period had been illegally detained by security forces, including the military, and that 275 were murdered and their bodies disposed of. Fox appointed an independent truth commission to investigate the abuses, ostensibly to bring those responsible to justice. In June 2002, he ordered the declassification and release of 80 million intelligence files from the *PRI* period.

Oddly, Fox opposed resuming an inquiry into the 1968 Tlatelolco Massacre, saying it was time to focus on the future, not the past. The Supreme Court disagreed in 2002.

That July, former President Luis Echeverría (1970–76), then 80, was summoned before the commission and interrogated about Tlatelolco, which occurred while he was interior secretary, and about atrocities committed during his term as president, especially the so-called "Corpus Christi Day Massacre" on June 10, 1971, in which an undetermined number of leftists was slain. He refused to answer, saying he would give responses in writing. The prosecutor gave Echeverría 186 written questions; Echeverría refused to comply. Never before had a president or former president been held accountable for his actions.

A year later, on October 2, 2003, the 35th anniversary of the Tlateloleo massacre, declassified documents confirmed that the government had placed 360 snipers around the plaza and had opened fire on the demonstrators. A lower court dismissed the charges against Echeverría in the Corpus Christi Massacre in 2004, ruling that the statute of limitations had expired, but federal prosecutors appealed. In 2005, the Supreme Court ruled 3–2 that Echeverría could be tried. He was eventually arrested on June 30, 2006, and placed under house arrest. But a week later, a federal judge dismissed the charges, saying the 30-year statute of limitations had expired.

The commission released its long-awaited report to the public in 2006, days before Fox left office. It concluded that officials at the highest level in the administrations of Díaz Ordaz, Echeverría and López Portillo had engaged in a systemized plan to exterminate "ideological opponents" and bluntly accused them of "crimes against humanity" and "genocide." It was the first time the Mexican government had ever assigned responsibility to itself for wrongdoing. Echeverría was later recharged, but a judge dismissed the genocide charges in 2009 and ordered his release.

Fox visited Cuba in 2002, seemingly continuing Mexico's tradition of friendship with the Castro regime. Foreign Minister Castañeda stated in Havana that Mexico, as before, would not support a perennial resolution brought before the U.N. Human Rights Commission in Geneva urging Cuba to allow greater freedom of expression. But Fox outraged Castro—and the Mexican left—by meeting with Cuban dissidents. Relations were strained further when more than 20 dissidents invaded the Mexican Embassy in Havana (see Cuba).

Relations with Cuba worsened that April. Fox hosted a U.N. conference on poverty in Monterrey, which Castro decided to attend at the last minute. Castro left in a huff on the first day after making his speech, accusing Fox of pressuring him into leaving before President Bush arrived, which Fox denied. A few days later, in Geneva, Mexico not only voted for the resolution critical of Cuba's human rights record, it co-sponsored it! Castro broke with diplomatic courtesy and released a secretly recorded tape of his conversation with Fox concerning the Monterrey poverty summit that corroborated Castro's contention that Fox had pressured him into leaving; basically, Castro called Fox a liar. Fox replaced the ambassador to Cuba, apparently because he was considered too friendly to the dictatorial regime for his taste. His removal represented a major shift in foreign policy.

In politics, the power struggle between the dinosaurs and the reformers within the *PRI* erupted with a fury during the election for the new party president in 2002. Madrazo, as expected, was the candidate of the dinosaurs (who, not surprisingly, prefer the term *"tradicionalistas,"*) while Beatríz Paredes, speaker of the Chamber

The front page of the Saltillo, Coahuila, daily newspaper *Vanguardia* proclaiming the stunning and decisive victory of Vicente Fox in the July 2, 2000, presidential election.

of Deputies, was the reformists' choice. During and after the campaign, the two rivals came close to disemboweling their party. About 3 million *Pristas* voted, and the count was so close the final results weren't announced until March. Madrazo was declared the winner by a slim 52,000-vote margin, or 1.7 percentage points.

The *PRD* also elected a new leader in a campaign that also was rambunctious but

Mexico

less acrimonious. Former interim Mexico City Mayor Rosario Robles was declared the winner with 60.8%.

An event that had been intended to be spiritual turned out to be political. On July 31, 2002, Pope John Paul II arrived in Mexico for his fifth visit to canonize the Indian peasant Juan Diego, to whom the Virgin of Guadalupe reportedly appeared in 1521 (see The Colonial Period). In the ceremony at the Shrine of Guadalupe, Fox broke with Mexico's long-standing anticlerical tradition and knelt and kissed the pope's ring. Perhaps more significantly, so did Mexico state Governor Arturo Montiel—a *Prista*. Fox made history again when John Paul II died in 2005, becoming the first Mexican president to attend a papal funeral.

The U.S. invasion of Iraq in 2003 strained the warm relations between Fox and Bush. Mexico held one of Latin America's two rotating seats on the U.N. Security Council, and Mexico sided with France, a permanent member of the Security Council, in denying U.N. authorization for an attack if Saddam Hussein did not account for weapons of mass destruction. Fox stated he favored the disarmament of Iraq but preferred to exhaust diplomatic means to accomplish it. The U.S. was forced to withdraw the resolution and invade Iraq without a U.N. blessing.

The gridlock between Fox's *PAN* and the opposition majority in Congress led the president to make a plaintive plea for multipartisan cooperation for the good of the nation in his annual congressional address on September 1, 2002. There were three positive developments: First, the three parties agreed to rotate the speakership of the Chamber of Deputies among them. Second, both houses passed Mexico's first genuine civil service law, creating a five-tiered system of government employees free from the political patronage that the *PRI* had used and abused for so long. Third, Congress enacted a U.S.-style freedom-of-information act that gives citizens—and especially journalists—unprecedented access to government records.

2003 Midterm Elections

All the parties knew they faced high stakes in the midterm elections on July 6, 2003. The *PAN* came under investigation for allegedly receiving $14,000 in illegal funds from the United States for Fox's 2000 presidential campaign. The Federal Electoral Institute *(IFE)* verified a number of irregularities, and fined the *PAN* $32 million.

In the *PRI*, the dinosaurs' Madrazo pulled off a skillful, but politically unwise, power play when he packed the party's list of candidates for the 200 federal deputies chosen through proportional repre-

sentation with his own supporters. The outraged reformists cried foul.

At stake were all 500 members of the Chamber of Deputies, 300 of them directly elected from districts, and six governorships: Campeche, Colima, Nuevo León, Querétaro, San Luis Potosí and Sonora.

Fox hoped to win an outright majority in both houses of Congress or at least increase the *PAN*'s number of seats. The *PAN* scented blood in Sonora, where polls showed a dead heat between the *PRI*'s Eduardo Bours and the *PAN*'s Ramón Corral.

The results of the nationwide voting were a cruel blow to Fox's quixotic dreams of a majority in the lower house. Not only did the *PAN* fail to win a majority and increase its number of seats, but it *lost* 51 of the 206 seats it had. The *PRI* rebounded by slightly increasing its representation. The major winner was the *PRD*, which doubled the size of its delegation.

A dejected Fox acknowledged, "Once again, it is apparent that no single political force will have a majority in the Chamber of Deputies." "The work now begins to build a consensus among us," he added. He also focused on another significant outcome of the elections: the disturbingly low turnout of only 41%. "We hear the voices of those who did not express themselves at the polls," he said. "We all understand your silence."

In terms of raw votes, the *PRI* had received 34.4%, the *PAN* 30.5%, the *PRD* 17.1%. Of the 300 directly elected seats, 163 went to the *PRI*, 67 to the *PAN*, 56 to the *PRD*. After the complex formula was applied for the allocation of the 200 seats by proportional representation, the *PRI* increased its delegation from 211 to 224, 26 short of a majority. The *PAN* wound up with 155 seats, while the *PRD* jumped from 50 seats to 96. The Green Party *(PVEM)* won 15 seats through proportional representation, about the same as before. The *PT* won only eight seats.

The *PAN* suffered another blow with the loss of Nuevo León, 56.4%–33.9%. About the only cause the *PAN* had for cheer on election night was that it captured the governorship of San Luis Potosí for the first time, 44%–37%, and it retained the governorship of Querétaro. In Campeche, the *PRI* pulled off a narrow victory. The *PRI* also retained Colima.

On July 12, the *CEE* declared Bours the winner, 372,467 to 364,544.

Wrangling over Immigration

U.S.-Mexican relations remained problematical in 2005 and 2006 over immigration and over the alarming increase in drug-related violence on the Mexican side of the border (see Other Current Issues: Drugs).

Bush and Fox had once been in accord on immigration, but Fox's proposal for free immigration across the border went nowhere in the U.S. Congress. Bush then advocated a compromise that would allow Mexicans who are offered jobs to work in the United States for up to three years, but they would not be eligible for U.S. citizenship and would be required to return to Mexico.

Fox grudgingly endorsed the watered-down plan and lobbied the U.S. Congress for its passage, but Congress demurred. Then Bush announced the extension of a wall along the California-Baja California border and pushed for legislation requiring states to require proof of citizenship to obtain drivers licenses. The two measures were ostensibly aimed at thwarting terrorists from crossing the border, but they offended Fox and Mexicans in general. Fox's government sent a formal letter of protest.

Next, Fox generated international media attention in 2005with an injudicious remark. Voicing frustration over the lack of progress on immigration, he said Mexican immigrants traditionally have taken jobs that "not even blacks want to do." That sparked a firestorm of criticism from U.S. black organizations, and provided grist for satirists and cartoonists on both sides of the border. Fox said he regretted his remarks had been "misinterpreted," but did not apologize. The Mexicans rallied behind their president; to them, he had merely spoken the truth.

In 2006, a bill was introduced in the U.S. House of Representatives that would make it a felony to hire illegal immigrants. Bush, meanwhile, proposed a controversial plan that would permit up to 400,000 "guest workers" a year and eventually make 11 million illegals eligible for citizenship, which members of his own party rejected as tantamount to an amnesty. On May 1, 2006, illegal immigrants—Mexicans and others—staged a one-day walkout in the United States, refusing to work to dramatize the role they play in the U.S. economy. It coincided with a one-day *"no gringo"* sympathy boycott of U.S. goods and companies in Mexico.

Drugs also strained Mexican-U.S. relations. In 2006, the Mexican Congress passed a bill that would have legalized possession of five grams of marijuana, 500 milligrams of cocaine, 25 milligrams of heroin and small amounts of some hallucinogens such as peyote. The rationale was to have the Mexican authorities divert more of their limited resources toward the traffickers instead of wasting their time busting penny-ante users. Fox declared he would sign it, generating headlines on both sides of the border. The U.S. government leaned heavily on Fox to veto it, arguing that such legalization would lead

A sign of the times: a portion of the fence on the U.S.-Mexico border

to "drug tourism" across the border. Fox sent the measure back to Congress, where it died.

Jockeying for 2006

López Obrador remained high in the polls, but he stood accused of contempt of court in 2001 for refusing to halt work on a road across expropriated private land that he insisted was needed for access to a public hospital. Fox's attorney general's office said López Obrador faced prosecution also for refusing to obey a court order to reinstate 39 city employees who were terminated when he became mayor in 2000.

The mayor responded that the charges were politically motivated. Faced with a possible congressional vote stripping him of his immunity, he defiantly called a mass demonstration in 2004 to declare his presidential candidacy. As trivial as the charges were, they could have forced him from office and disqualified him from running for any public office if convicted.

The *PAN* had its own problems. Energy Secretary Calderón angrily resigned a day after Fox had publicly chastised him for attending a political rally in Guadalajara

at which the governor of Jalisco endorsed Calderón for the *PAN* presidential nomination, even though Calderón had not yet declared his candidacy. Fox declared that he expected his cabinet secretaries to occupy themselves with their duties.

As always, governor's races in the two years prior to a presidential election were closely watched as gauges of the parties' strength. Chihuahua was especially crucial, as the only state that the *PRI* had recaptured from the *PAN*. The *PRD* was defending Zacatecas for the first time. The *PAN* was defending Aguascalientes for the first time, while the *PRI* faced a strong challenge from a peculiar *PRD-PAN* coalition in Oaxaca.

In the balloting on July 4, 2004, the *PRI* retained Chihuahua and Durango and the *PRD* held Zacatecas. The *PAN* won easily in Aguascalientes a month later. But the Oaxaca campaign turned violent the week before the election. The *PRI's* Ulises Ruíz claimed victory, 47% to 45% for Gabino Cué of the *PRD-PAN* alliance. Cué claimed vote fraud had cost him the election. Ruíz belongs to the dinosaur faction.

The *PRI* relished the victory of Jorge Hank Rhon, a controversial racetrack

owner with alleged indirect ties to the Tijuana drug cartel, in the Tijuana mayor's race. The city, and the state of Baja California Norte, are *PAN* strongholds.

The *PRI* retained the Veracruz governorship in September by just 1 percentage point, with just 34.5% of the vote. The *PRI* easily retained the governorships of its strongholds of Tamaulipas and Puebla that November and even recaptured Tlaxcala from the *PRD*.

In February 2005, the *PRD* held onto Baja California Sur and the *PRI* to Quintana Roo. But in poverty-stricken Guerrero, the *PRI* lost for the first time. Like Oaxaca, there was some pre-election violence, but the *PRD* candidate, Zeferino Torrreblanca, a popular former mayor of Acapulco and a successful businessman with a centrist platform, received 55%. The *PRI* retained the governorship of Hidalgo.

When the *PRI* governor of Colima was killed in a plane crash, a special election was called. The *PRI's* Silverio Cavazos defeated the *PAN* candidate.

In July 2005, the *PRI* recaptured the governorship of Nayarit it had lost in 1999 to an opposition coalition, winning with a 46% plurality. That same day, the *PRI* re-

Mexico

tained the crucial state of Mexico, where Enrique Peña Nieto received 47.6%.

In September, the *PRI* won by 55.5% in Coahuila.

The *"Desafuero"* Controversy

The lingering controversy over López Obrador's supposed contempt of court and its effect on his presidential ambitions dominated Mexicans' attention in 2005. What amounted to an impeachment effort in Congress led to an unholy alliance between the *PRI* and the *PAN*, both of which feared López Obrador would win. But to disqualify him for such a picayunish charge appeared opportunistic, even antidemocratic. López Obrador called for "civil resistance" if he were arrested. Polls showed upwards of 80% of Mexicans opposed his prosecution. He declared he would campaign from a jail cell if necessary.

Unintimidated, the Chamber of Deputies voted 360–127, along party lines, for *el desafuero*, paving the way for López Obrador's removal pending trial. Pro-López Obrador demonstrators, 150,000 strong, filled the streets, while *"no al desafuero"* posters filled the capital.

Legal authorities disagreed over whether or not López Obrador could continue serving as mayor. Fox ruled out a presidential pardon. A "silent march" in support of the mayor drew 1 million people. Finally, Fox capitulated by firing Attorney General Rafael Macedo de la Concha, the leading advocate for prosecuting López Obrador, replacing him with Daniel Cabeza de Vaca, who dropped the case. López Obrador and Fox issued conciliatory statements, and the country breathed a sigh of relief. The two men even had an amicable meeting.

López Obrador resigned as mayor on July 31 to devote himself to his presidential campaign.

The Deadlock of 2006

By mid-2006, it seemed López Obrador would coast into Los Pinos. It helped that both the *PRI* and the *PAN* were beset by intra-party rivalries.

In the *PAN*, Fox made no secret that Creel was his anointed heir apparent—a *PAN* version of the *dedazo*. But neither counted on the groundswell of support for the renegade Calderón, who was as charismatic as Creel was lackluster. A member of the party's so-called traditionalist wing, Calderón, who holds a graduate degree in public administration from Harvard, had proven himself an able problem-solver as energy minister. Moreover, polls showed Creel running a poor third behind López Obrador and the *PRI*'s Madrazo. Calde-

Former President Vicente Fox Quesada

rón swept the three party primaries and won the nomination. Fox and Creel closed ranks behind him.

The battle for the *PRI* nomination was uglier. The reformist wing backed outgoing Mexico state Governor Arturo Montiel. Madrazo received the nomination, but the bitterness of the mudslinging left scars.

This time, the small Green Party allied itself with the *PRI* instead of the *PAN*.

As often happens with frontrunners with huge leads, López Obrador had nowhere to go but down once he had actual challengers questioning his record and his proposals and advancing their own. Calderón edged past Madrazo in the polls, and by April he was tied with López Obrador. Calderón challenged López Obrador's vague populist rhetoric and launched a media blitz warning that López Obrador would ruin Mexico the way Hugo Chávez had ruined Venezuela. Calderón probably was aided by the rapidly expanding economy, which benefits the party in power.

López Obrador's most dangerous opponent was himself. His populist rhetoric excited his core constituency of the poor, but to Mexico's growing middle class it lacked specifics and seemed harsh, demagogic—even scary. His constant ridiculing of Fox also backfired; the president still enjoyed an approval rating of about 60%. Finally, the overconfident López Obrador, the political equivalent of Aesop's hare, refused to participate in a televised debate with Calderón, Madrazo and three others. He apparently hoped Calderón and Madrazo would disembowel each other, but voters saw his refusal to debate as cowardly, ar-

rogant or both. He participated in a second debate, but the damage was irrevocable.

The major candidates sounded the same major themes: maintaining good relations with the United States but demanding a better U.S. immigration policy; combating corruption; improving education; investing the windfall from high petroleum prices wisely. Probably the major source of disagreement was Calderón's and Madrazo's call for joint ventures between *Pemex* and foreign firms to exploit deep offshore oil deposits in the Gulf, an idea that was anathema to López Obrador. They also had different approaches to the drug war. López Obrador advocated a greater role for the military; Calderón said he would extradite more kingpins to the United States; Madrazo called for stiffer sentences.

Voter turnout was 58.61%. The vote count was so close between Calderón and López Obrador that both men claimed victory, but the *IFE* said it would have to recount the votes from each precinct beginning July 5. The following day, it released its breathtakingly close official final tally:

Calderón	15,000,284	35.89%
López Obrador	14,756,350	35.31%
Madrazo	9,301,441	22.26%
Others:	1,828,643	4.37%
Null:	904,604	2.16%

López Obrador refused to concede, alleging vote fraud despite a lack of concrete evidence, and said he would challenge the results before the Supreme Electoral Tribunal, which had until September 6 to issue a final ruling.

In the Congress, there was a dramatic new party lineup. The once-omnipotent *PRI* dropped from first place to third in both houses. In the Senate, it decreased from 58 to 27 seats and from 203 to only 49 in the Chamber of Deputies. The *PAN* thus emerged as the largest bloc in both houses, even though it, too, lost seats. It dropped from 48 to 43 seats in the Senate and from 148 to 141 in the lower house. The *PRD* and its allied parties were the major winners, increasing from 15 to 26 seats in the Senate and from 97 to 110 in the Chamber.

The *PAN* held on to the governorships of all three states. In the Federal District, the *PRD*'s Marcelo Ebrard was elected mayor, considered by many the second most powerful post in the country, with 47%.

A map of Mexico's states published in *El Universal* showed graphically just how polarized Mexico had become. While the U.S. has so-called red states and blue states, Mexico's states are literally red *(PRI)*, blue *(PAN)* or yellow *(PRD)*, the parties' official colors. The electoral map in the presidential race showed Mexico painted almost exclusively blue north of Mexico City, and almost solidly yellow to the south and east. In the north, López Obrador carried only Zacatecas, Nayarit and Baja California Sur; in the south, Calderón carried only Puebla and Yucatán. The *PRI*'s Madrazo did not carry a single state, not even his home state of Tabasco! Calderón carried 16 states, López Obrador carried 15 and the Federal District.

López Obrador continued to cry fraud and to use inflammatory rhetoric against Calderón, Fox and even the *IFE*, which in the past had backed the *PRD*'s claims of *PRI* fraud in state elections. Such "proof" that the *PRD* finally produced turned out to be bogus.

López Obrador then incited his followers to take to the streets for what he called "civil resistance" to intimidate the *Trife* into calling a new election. If the Federal Electoral Tribunal, or *Trife*, could not reach a decision by September 6, it would have to do just that, and the badly fragmented Congress would have to name an interim president. He twice filled the Zócalo in Mexico City with hundreds of thousands of *peeredistas*. They also staged demonstrations throughout the country and on September 1, *PRD* congressmen, in an antidemocratic power play, prevented Fox from delivering his annual state of the union address to Congress.

The *Trife* scrutinized returns from tens of thousands of disputed polling places, eerily reminiscent of the disputed 2000 U.S. presidential election. On September 5, the seven *Trife* members announced their *unanimous* conclusion. They disallowed about 220,000 contested ballots, which shrank Calderón's winning margin only by a few thousand votes. Calderón, they ruled, had won the election by 233,831 votes, or .56 percentage points, of the 41.8 million votes cast.

Still, López Obrador refused to concede. He threatened to continue the "civil resistance" and to establish a "shadow government." His supporters remained in the Zócalo, where on September 16, Independence Day, he declared himself "president-elect" and appointed a 12-member "cabinet." Once again, Fox was prevented from following tradition of speaking in the Zócalo on Independence Day.

Gradually, López Obrador's defiance of Mexico's painfully constructed new democratic institutions lost steam. The small Convergence Party, the *PRD*'s coalition partner, announced it accepted the *Trife*'s decision. *PRD* leaders like Cárdenas, who actually *had* been robbed of an election in 1988, told López Obrador to concede. The crowds of protesters began to dwindle.

But López Obrador defiantly claimed he was the legitimate president-elect. His poor sportsmanship and antidemocratic

demeanor began to grate on the Mexicans' nerves; a poll by the newspaper *Reforma* showed that if there were a new election, he would receive only 30%, down five points from his showing on July 2. In an actual bellwether, the *PRD* candidate for governor of López Obrador's home state of Tabasco, who had been favored to win, lost badly to the *PRI*'s Andrés Granier on October 15. López Obrador had campaigned energetically on Ojeda's behalf, and his defeat was widely viewed as a backlash against López Obrador's behavior.

Die-hard *PRD* congressmen then threatened to prevent Calderón from taking the oath in Congress on December 1, camping out in the Chamber of Deputies and attempting to block the doors, *PAN* congressmen seized the chamber in a show of force. Fistfights broke out and *PRD* congressmen threw chairs and cans at the *panistas*, an unparliamentary melee that was shown on television around the world.

Once again, Fox sought to avoid confrontation. In an unprecedented midnight ceremony at Los Pinos, he surrendered the presidential sash. Constitutionally, the president must be sworn in before Congress, so for nine hours Mexico was without a president. Calderón and Fox arrived through a back door to the Chamber of Deputies and went to the podium amid catcalls from the *peeredistas*. Calderón quickly took the oath, then hurried off to deliver his inaugural address at a heavily guarded auditorium across town. The foreign representatives in the gallery, including former President George H. W. Bush and California Governor Arnold Schwarzenegger, President Álvaro Uribe of Colombia and the prince of Asturias from Spain, were there only minutes as the spectacle of bedlam unfolded below. It was not Mexico's finest hour.

A year later, López Obrador was still claiming to be the legitimate president, and he authored a bitter book, *El mafia nos robó la elección (The Mafia Stole the Election from Us)*. He was still able to muster a few thousand demonstrators to the Zócalo on the first anniversary of the election, but a poll by *Reforma* indicated that only 61% of the people who voted for him would do so again. He became such an embarrassment that *PRD* gubernatorial candidates eschewed his support.

Calderón Seeks Consensus and Reform

A serious domestic crisis Calderón inherited from Fox was a near-insurrection in the state of Oaxaca that had left several people dead. It began as a strike by teachers demanding higher pay. The teachers occupied the Zócalo in the state capital until they were forcibly removed by the

unpopular *PRI* governor, Ulises Ruíz, who had narrowly defeated his *PRD* rival in 2004 in an election still considered fraudulent. Other sectors joined the teachers to form the Popular Assembly of the Peoples of Oaxaca *(APPO)*, headed by Flavio Sosa. The protests became so violent that Fox dispatched 4,000 federal police.

The Oaxaca crisis led to a curious alliance between the *PAN* and the *PRI* in the name of expediency. In one of his first acts as president, Calderón ordered Sosa's arrest.

Calderón's unspoken alliance with the *PRI* led to the election of *PRI* members as speaker of the Chamber of Deputies and president of the Senate, and he named a few *pristas* to cabinet posts. Calderón showed himself more skillful than Fox in reaching a consensus. In 2007, Congress passed the pension reform plan Fox had tried but failed to enact. Even the *PRD*, which opposed the pension reform, supported Calderón's electoral and judicial reforms. However, when it came to reorganizing *Pemex* or privatizing electricity, the *PRI* and *PRD* remained united against Calderón.

An important moment in the history of the *PRI* came in 2007 with the election of Beatríz Paredes, a reformer, to succeed Madrazo as party president.

The immigration issue continued to strain relations with the U.S. The long-awaited immigration "reform" compromise reached in the U.S. Congress in 2007, heralded by such polar opposites as President Bush and Senator Ted Kennedy, came under attack from Republicans, Democrats and Mexicans alike. Republicans saw it as tantamount to an amnesty for illegal immigrants. Democrats feared it would threaten organized labor and divide families. Mexicans saw it as demeaning. The issue was so volatile that the Miss USA contestant was booed by the audience at the pageant held in Mexico City.

In state politics, the *PRI* finally savored a triumph in May 2007 when it recaptured the governorship of Yucatán from the *PAN* under the candidacy of Ivonne Ortega, 34, the state's first woman governor. Tijuana Mayor Jorge Hank Rhon hoped to reclaim the Baja California Norte governorship for the *PRI* after 18 years of *PAN* control, but the *PAN*'s José Guadalupe Osuna bested him in August, 50.4% to 44%. The *PRD* retained the governorship of Michoacán in November behind the candidacy of Leonel Godoy Rangel. The term for governor was reduced from six to four years.

In 2007 and 2008, Calderón was preoccupied with three more transcendental reforms Fox tried and failed to enact: taxes, the judiciary and energy, "energy" meaning oil and gas. With horse-trading skills, Calderón forged another congressional

Mexico

consensus with the *PRI* and even some *PRD* legislators, who were still torn between López Obrador's sour-grapes faction that opposed Calderón at every turn, and moderates willing to work toward the good of the country.

Congress overwhelmingly approved the historic tax reform package, badly needed because petroleum production, which had provided 40% of federal government revenue, was expected to begin declining sharply over the next decade. It had already dropped 10% in three years, to 3.3 million barrels per day. The tax package included a corporate income tax of 16.5%, going up to 17.5% in three years, which pleased the left. It also raised gasoline taxes. The overhaul increased the nonpetroleum revenue from 10% of GDP to 12% by the end of Calderón's term in 2012, and it was expected bring in $10.3 billion in 2019. It also provided *Pemex* with funds for new exploration.

To ensure *PRD* support, Calderón agreed to a campaign reform measure that included an institutional overhaul of the Federal Electoral Institute *(IFE)*, which the *PRD* blamed for López Obrador's defeat, a merciful reduction of the year-long presidential campaign period by half and strict limits on campaign advertising.

Congress approved an historic constitutional amendment in 2008 overhauling the judicial and legal systems from top to bottom, including open instead of closed trials, in which judges hear oral testimony instead of documented evidence. Criminal suspects were given the presumption of innocence. Calderón again compromised with the left and human rights advocates by abandoning a provision that would have allowed police to enter a home without a warrant. Retained was a provision that will allow prosecutors to hold "organized crime" suspects for 80 days without charges.

Calderón finally had success with energy reform. Because Mexico must export crude oil and then must reimport 40% of its refined fuel, Calderón proposed allowing *Pemex* to sign contracts with private firms—interpreted as foreign firms—to build refineries and storage facilities. He also proposed contracting with private firms to exploit deep offshore deposits to extend Mexico's dwindling reserves.

It seemed pragmatic, but there is no more sacred cow in Mexico than *Pemex*. López Obrador and the sour-grapes faction of the *PRD* denounced the move. As usual, he threatened to mobilize mass demonstrations. Showing its antidemocratic proclivities once again, the sourgrapes faction seized both houses of Congress to block discussion of the bill. But in October 2008, it passed with the support of *PRI* lawmakers.

Mexico's interior, or government, secretary is traditionally regarded as the second most powerful person in the country. In 2008, Interior Secretary Juan Carrillo Mourino and two former officials died when their government jet crashed in Mexico City. Calderón appointed Fernando Francisco Gómez to succeed him.

The new U.S. president, Barack Obama, made his first state visit to Mexico in April 2009, en route to the Summit of the Americas. He and Calderón discussed the alarming drug violence, which had claimed 5,400 lives in Mexico in 2008, and Calderón urged Obama to crack down on the legal sale of sophisticated firearms to drug traffickers on the U.S. side of the border. Obama agreed that reinstituting a ban on the sale of assault weapons could help stem the flow of arms to the cartels, who are better armed than the authorities. Obama pledged to continue Bush's partnership against the cartels, telling Calderón, "You can't fight this war with just one hand."

The thorny issue of immigration came up, but Obama stated adamantly that nothing would be done before the end of the year.

Calderón's Midterm Setback

Mexico's political landscape was shaken up once again in the midterm elections on July 5, 2009. The *PRI* staged a stunning comeback from near-oblivion to emerge once again as the largest bloc in the Chamber of Deputies. The *PAN* fell from first to second place in the lower house, and the *PRD* dropped to a distant third.

A jubilant Beatríz Paredes said the *PRI*'s alliance with the Green Party *(PVEM)* would give their alliance a working majority. She said the election results show "Mexico is a country in search of proposals, in search of solutions, in search of methods." *PAN* President Germán Martínez resigned the day after the election.

In terms of raw votes, the *PRI* received 36.5% of the 21.6 million votes cast, the *PAN* received 27.8%, the *PRD* 12.2% and the *PVEM*, 6.7%. In "fifth place" were null or blank ballots, totaling 1.3 million or 6 percent, double the percentage in previous elections. Turnout was an anemic 44 percent, but still up from 42 percent in the last midterm elections in 2003.

In the new Chamber of Deputies, the *PRI* won 233 seats, up from 106, and the *PVEM* won 22, up from 17, a potential working majority of 255. The *PAN* fell from 206 seats to 146, and the *PRD* from 127 seats to 72.

The *PAN* also was dealt serious psychological blows in the governor's races, losing Querétaro, which it had held for 12 years, and San Luis Potosí, which it won

for the first time in 2003. It failed a second time to recapture Nuevo León, and lost control of the state legislature. The only bright spot for the *PAN* was winning Sonora for the first time after two near misses, and retaining the mayoralty of Monterrey. The *PRI* easily retained the governorships of Campeche and Colima.

Addressing the nation, Calderón congratulated voters for participating and said, "Today, our political process is more open than ever. Democracy always has the last word." Without mentioning the *PRI,* he called for "collaboration and coresponsibility to confront the great challenges facing the country."

Contrary to expectations, the elections were not marred by the drug-related violence that had become the major political issue, along with the slowdown in economic growth. The army had dispatched 8,500 troops to safeguard the election, 3,500 for ballot security and 5,000 to prevent violence. The election was marred only by the usual charges that the *PRI* was bribing voters with groceries in states it controlled.

Battling Violence and Recession

Recession and violence continued to preoccupy Calderón and his countrymen. In his state of the nation message in 2009, Calderón outlined 10 more reforms, including expansion of the energy and tax reforms already passed. His proposed labor reforms, designed to curb the power of the unions, met a frosty reception, as labor is a sacred cow for both the *PRI* and *PRD*.

He had better luck with tax reform. In an apparent effort to appease the *PRI,* Calderón proposed an increase in the income tax on the wealthy from 28% to 30%. The opposition parties still balked at the idea of allowing contracts between *Pemex* and foreign firms that allow incentives based on production. But with oil production declining by another 10% in 2009, deep offshore wells are the only way to prolong oil production, which continues to account for 40% of federal revenue. If the current production decline continues, Mexico could become an oil importer by 2017.

The number of drug-related murders doubled in 2009 to almost 10,000, while Ciudad Juárez, Chihuahua, officially became the world's most dangerous city and was patrolled by 10,000 army troops (see Other Current Issues—Drugs). The victims include operatives of rival drug cartels, policemen, soldiers, journalists and, increasingly, politicians.

The highest-profile incident was the disappearance of Diego Fernández de Cevallos, a former senator and the 1994 *PAN* presidential candidate, who was

EL NORTE

LUNES

6 de Julio
del 2009
Monterrey, N.L.
México

www.elnorte.com

$ 12.(

124 págin
8 seccior
Año LX
Número 25,7

Gana Rodrigo la Gubernatura de NL; llegan tres Alcaldes menores de 35

Toca a los jóvenes

The Monterrey daily *El Norte* reports the election victory of the *PRI*'s Rodrigo Molina for governor of Nuevo León and the *PRI*'s stunning comeback in the midterm congressional elections of July 5, 2009.

apparently abducted from his ranch in Querétaro in May 2010. Drug traffickers were suspected, and his family asked the government to suspend its investigation, which it did. Fernández was released after his family paid a $20 million ransom.

Eleven journalists were murdered in Mexico in 2010, some of them gruesomely. Other journalists disappeared.

Mexico's booming economy ground to a halt with the U.S. recession, which reduced both Mexican exports to the north and the vital remittances from Mexicans working there who were laid off. The vital tourism industry, also affected, suffered two other blows in 2009: The almost daily reporting on spectacular drug-related killings and massacres, and an outbreak of swine flu in Mexico. The U.S. State Department issued travel advisories. The GDP shrank by 6.5% and tourism by 15% in 2009, to 5.2 million visitors.

The Federal District's legislature made news around the world in 2009 by legalizing same-sex unions, something unheard of even in anti-clerical Mexico. It took effect in March 2010. Several state legislatures quickly amended their constitutions to ban the practice.

Border violence and immigration continued to dominate Mexican-U.S. relations. Very little of the U.S. aid pledged under the Merida Initiative had been disbursed. Secretary of State Hillary Clinton visited Mexico in 2010 and pledged an additional $331 million, but to be spent on social programs and to help upgrade the judicial system. The Mexican government pressed for more stringent control of southbound traffic to curtail the flow of illegal weapons, and the Obama administration complied with stepped-up inspections.

The immigration issue splashed back into headlines in both countries in 2010 when Arizona Governor Jan Brewer signed a controversial new law requiring aliens to carry proof of their immigration status at all times and allowing police to detain people suspected of being in the United States illegally. Mexicans on both sides of the border denounced the law, saying it encourages racial profiling, and there were demonstrations against it in several U.S. states. Obama called it "misguided." Polls, however, showed a majority of Americans, and even a sizable minority of Hispanics, agreed with the law.

The Arizona law overshadowed Calderón's state visit to Washington in May 2010. Obama repeated his opposition to the law. The next day, Calderón addressed a poorly attended joint session of Congress in Spanish and repeated his fear that the law would be used to discriminate against law-abiding Mexicans. On the drug issue, Democrats applauded when he urged Congress to reinstate a ban on automatic assault weapons that had expired; most Republicans remained silent. Thousands of these weapons have been smuggled across the border to drug traffickers.

Bilateral relations remained strained in 2010 and 2011, for a number of reasons. In August 2010, Calderón shocked everyone on both sides of the border by calling for a "public discussion" on the feasibility of legalizing drugs, even as he pressed with his war against the cartels.

Then, in February 2011, two special agents for the U.S. Immigration and Customs Enforcement (ICE) were ambushed while driving in San Luis Potosí State. One, Jaime Zapata, was killed and the other wounded. President Obama publicly pledged to bring the killers to justice, although the killing occurred on Mexican

Mexico

**Former President
Felipe de Jesús Calderón**

soil. Mexican authorities arrested six men connected with *Los Zetas* (see Other Current Problems: Drugs). The suspects claimed they were unaware the victims were U.S. agents. Obama asked for their extradition.

Even more volatile was the release the same week by WikiLeaks of U.S. State Department cables, in which U.S. Ambassador Carlos Pascual reportedly complained about high-level corruption in the Mexican government and about a "dysfunctionally low level of collaboration" in the drug war. An angry Calderón lashed out publicly and undiplomatically, chiding Pascual for his "ignorance" of what was happening in Mexico.

It was against this backdrop that Calderón again flew to Washington for his fifth face-to-face talks with Obama in March 2011. The talks were amicable and ended with a new trucking agreement by which the U.S. would finally live up to its promise to tighten inspections of south-bound cargo to search for weapons. Pascual resigned as ambassador 17 days later. He was replaced by Anthony Wayne, deputy ambassador in Afghanistan and a former ambassador to Argentina,

In politics, 2010 was the important bellwether year in which 12 of the 31 states elected governors. In the past, the elections were spread out through the latter half of the year, but for the first time they were all held the same day, July 4. The states were Aguascalientes, Chihuahua, Durango, Hidalgo, Oaxaca, Puebla, Quintana Roo, Sinaloa, Tamaulipas, Tlaxcala, Veracruz and Zacatecas. Drug-related violence dominated the races in Chihuahua and Sinaloa, where the *PRI* was facing stiff challenges from the *PAN*. But the race that drew the most interest was in Oaxaca. Once again, the *PRD* and *PAN* put aside

their ideological differences to field a unified candidacy behind Gabino Cué, who narrowly lost the disputed 2004 election, against the *PRI*'s Eviel Pérez Magaña.

The results validated the *PRI*'s dramatic comeback the year before. It won nine of the governorships, retaining six—Chihuahua, Durango, Hidalgo, Quintana Roo, Tamaulipas and Veracruz—and recapturing Aguascalientes and Tlaxcala from the *PAN* and Zacatecas from the *PRD*. But the three gains were offset by first-ever losses in Oaxaca, Puebla and Sinaloa; in all three, the *PAN* and *PRD* had forged cross-ideological alliances to offset the *PRI*'s numerical superiority. In Oaxaca, Cué won by a convincing majority of 56%. It could be argued that the three states the *PRI* lost were for local rather than national issues and personalities. The *PRD* and *PAN* began learning to try to govern jointly.

Also of interest was the campaigning on behalf of *PRI* candidates by Mexico State Governor Enrique Peña Nieto, who emerged as leader of the dinosaur faction and was collecting IOUs for his run for president in 2012.

Two governor's races in early 2011 spelled bad news for the *PRI*. In Guerrero, which the *PRD* was defending for the first time, the *PRI* mounted a determined challenge to reclaim its long-time stronghold, which would be an important psychological confirmation of the party's national resurgence. Guerrero was a battleground literally as well as figuratively, with 1,137 drug-related killings in 2010. The campaign for the January 31 election narrowed to the *PRI*'s Manuel Añorve, former mayor of Acapulco, and his cousin, the *PRD*'s Ángel Aguirre, who had defected from the *PRI*. Evidence surfaced that the *PRI* was up to its old trick of buying off voters with groceries when a cache of *dispensas* from the state of Mexico was discovered in Guerrero. The *PAN* candidate, who was running third, withdrew and endorsed Aguirre. The *PRI*'s hopes of a psychological victory were dashed when Aguirre trounced Añorve, 56% to 43%.

Just one week later, on February 6, it was the *PAN* that was to savor a psychological victory in Baja California Sur, which the *PRD* had governed for 12 years, the last six not very well. The *PRI* sensed a pickup because of voter disenchantment with growing drug violence and divisions within the *PRD*. It fielded a strong candidate in Ricardo Barroso, but once again, a defector was to prove decisive. In a peculiar twist, the *PAN* fielded Marcos Covarrubias, a popular federal deputy for the *PRD* who defected when the outgoing governor chose Luis Armando Diaz as the party's nominee. Covarrubias won with 40% of the vote, to 33% for Barrios and 21% for Diaz.

López Obrador announced on February 20 he was taking a "temporary leave" from the *PRD* because of his displeasure over its electoral alliances with the *PAN* in governor's races. Never mind that the alliances had been successful in defeating the *PRI*; López Obrador was still harboring his pique against the *PAN* for his 2006 presidential defeat.

Ultimately, a deal between the *PAN* and *PRD* to form an alliance in the Mexico governor's race fell apart. Because of Governor Peña Nieto's aspirations for the *PRI* presidential nomination, the other two parties had a vested interest in defeating the governor's chosen successor, Eruviel Ávila, two-time mayor of Ecatepec de Morelos, which would have been a humiliation for Peña Nieto and the *PRI* as a whole. In the end, Ávila won with a landslide 62.6% majority.

Two other states, Coahuila and Nayarit, also chose governors on July 3. In Coahuila, the *PRI*'s Rubén Moreira Valdéz polled 59.4% to succeed his brother, Humberto, as governor. In Nayarit, the *PRI*'s Roberto Sandoval Castañeda won with a plurality of 45.9%.

On November 13, the *PRI* not only regained control of Michoacán from the *PRD*, the *PRD* candidate ran third. The *PRI*'s Fausto Vallejo narrowly defeated the *PAN*'s María Luisa Calderón, the president's sister, 35% to 33%. Michoacán is the only state with a four-year term for governor.

In his annual state of the nation address in September 2011, Calderón pledged to purge the prosecutor general's office (*PGR*) of corrupt elements following the dismissal of 400 officers from the agency. He declared he would also forge ahead with his war on the cartels, even as polls showed public support for his hard-line approach waning. A Pew Research Center survey showed only 45% of Mexicans believed the government was making progress in the war and 29% thought it was losing ground. Meanwhile, the death toll for 2011 was a record 16,466, an increase of 8% over 2010, bringing the toll since 2006 to 47,554 (see Other Current Problems: Drugs).

The festering issue of arms smuggled from the U.S. to Mexico exploded into headlines in both countries in 2011. The U.S. Bureau of Alcohol, Tobacco and Firearms, a subsidiary of the Justice Department, reportedly launched a sting operation called Fast and Furious to snare arms traffickers. However, an estimated 1,300 of the 2,000 weapons used as "bait" found their way into the hands of drug cartels. To compound what turned into a political scandal in the U.S. in 2012 and strained U.S.-Mexican relations even more, some of the weapons from the botched sting operation were later found at the scenes of shootouts in which both U.S. and Mexican law enforcement personnel were killed. Attorney General Eric Holder resisted calls from the Republican-controlled House Oversight Committee to produce documents related to Fast and Furious, and Obama invoked executive privilege to prevent their release. The House voted to find Holder in contempt of Congress.

Pope Benedict XVI made his first visit to Mexico in March 2012, and former President de la Madrid died in April at the age of 77.

In April, Calderón made his first official visit to Cuba, which was largely symbolic.

The squabbling political parties put aside their differences to pass an historic carbon-emissions law in 2012, the second in the world and the first for a developing country. It passed the Chamber of Deputies overwhelmingly and the Senate unanimously. (see Other Current Problems: The Environment).

Calderón also was in the international spotlight when Mexico for the first time hosted the G-20 Summit, in Los Cabos, Baja California Sur, June 18–19.

The Elections of 2012

The country's attention became focused on the July 1, 2012, presidential contest. The reformist and dinosaur factions of the *PRI*, realizing their rift caused Madrazo to run a poor third in 2006, buried their hatchet to coalesce behind Peña Nieto, a young, telegenic, articulate and seemingly capable figure. A lawyer and a widower whose first wife died of an apparent epileptic seizure in 2007, he married a popular *telenovela* actress, Angélica Rivera, in 2010. He turned 46 in July 2012. His only opponent for the nomination, Senator Manilo Fabio Beltrones, dropped out, letting Peña Nieto win an unopposed primary in 2011.

López Obrador, or "AMLO," despite his display of pique in "temporarily" abandoning the *PRD*, again won the party's nomination over Mexico City Mayor Marcelo Ebrard. The nomination was decided in a peculiar and unprecedented manner, in a scientific poll of 6,000 voters by two polling firms selected by the two candidates. Ebrard did not contest the results. The *PRD* formed an alliance with the *PT* and the tiny Citizens Convergence.

The *PAN* was more badly divided. Ernesto Cordero, 43, Calderón's finance secretary, declared his intention to run. Santiago Creel, now a senator, who was Fox's chosen successor in 2006 but lost the nomination to Calderón, also entered, as did the *PAN* leader in the Chamber of Deputies, Josefina Vázquez Mota. Calderón made a subtle *dedazo* in favor of Cordero,

but in the *PAN* primary in February 2012, Vázquez Mota won by a decisive 55% to 38% for Cordero and 6% for Creel, becoming the first female presidential candidate of one of the major parties. Her campaign slogan was *"Diferente,"* which was seen as much a reference to the increasingly unpopular Calderón as to her opponents—or her gender.

The tiny New Alliance Party *(PENAL)* fielded Gabriel Quadri.

Early polls showed Peña Nieto with a 30-point lead over his two challengers, with Vázquez Mota in second place and López Obrador a distant third. But as always in Mexican politics, that changed after the candidates came under scrutiny from the press, after they began making gaffes in campaign speeches and after two debates.

Peña Nieto was hurt by a pair of gaffes. In an interview with Spain's *El País,* he was unable to give the price of tortillas, which he attempted to shrug off with the *macho* comment, "I'm not the woman of the household." In an incident reminiscent of Katie Couric's interview with U.S. Republican vice presidential candidate Sarah Palin in 2008, Peña Nieto was unable to tell reporters at a book fair the names of three books that had influenced him.

Yet, a week before the first televised debate on May 6, a major poll still showed Peña Nieto with 37.5%, Vázquez Mota with 21.2% and López Obrador with 17.9%; other polls consistently showed the same rankings.

In the first debate, each of the four accused the others of ties to corruption, and all pledged to continue the war on the drug cartels but without specifically stating what they would do differently. Vázquez Mota and López Obrador both concentrated their main attacks on the frontrunner, who came across as unruffledAfter the first debate, López Obrador overtook Vázquez Mota for second place.

Then something unforeseen happened that *did* rattle Peña Nieto. In May, he went to the private Ibero-American University in Mexico City for a campaign appearance but was prevented from speaking by a group of 131 student hecklers, ostensibly from the reformist wing of the *PRI*, who accused him of benefiting from slanted news coverage. Peña Nieto left angrily, and he accused the group of being paid hecklers for the *PRD*. The video went viral on YouTube, and almost overnight there was a groundswell of anti-Peña Nieto students calling themselves *YoSoy132* (I Am 132). They ridiculed what they called "soap opera democracy," a reference to Peña Nieto's *telenovela* star wife. On May 23, 20,000 of them demonstrated outside the offices of *Televisa.* Then they organized rallies in Mexico City and Guadalajara the

day of the second debate that drew 90,000 participants. The date was also symbolicl; June 10 was the 41st anniversary of the infamous Corpus Christi Massacre in 1971, in which about 120 student protesters were gunned down by security forces. The message was that Peña Nieto represents the *PRI* of the bad old days.

Much was at stake in the second debate. The third-place Vázquez Mota came across as the most aggressive, attacking the records of both Peña Nieto and López Obrador, both of whom went on the defensive but committed no serious gaffes.

Then the British newspaper *The Guardian* reported it had documented evidence that Peña Nieto had, indeed, been paying for positive television news coverage, while López Obrador's campaign was accused of financial improprieties.

On the eve of the election, the *PAN* and *PRD* accused the *PRI* of a 21st-century version of its old trick of swapping *dispensas,* or welfare packages of groceries, for votes or voter cards of opposition voters. *PRI* activists were allegedly distributing thousands of debit cards worth 1,000 pesos, about $77, that could be used at grocery stores. The account was traced to the *PRI* in Peña Nieto's home state of Mexico. The *IFE* concluded there was insufficient evidence the cards were being used to buy votes.

This raised anew the specter of the "old *PRI*," but the polls proved right on target. Turnout nationwide was an unprecedented 63.1%. On election night, incomplete returns from the *IFE* gave Peña Nieto 38.08%, López Obrador 31.68%, Vázquez Mota 25.43% and Quadri 2.3%. Peña Nieto carried 19 of the 31 states.

Vázquez Mota conceded defeat election night, and President Calderón congratulated the winner. But once again, López Obrador refused to concede, said "the last word hasn't been said," claimed he had his "own figures" and vowed to contest the results. It was 2006 all over again, only this time he was more than six percentage points behind, not just one.

The *IFE* yielded to AMLO's demand and recounted the ballots from just over half the 143,000 boxes. On July 5, the *IFE* released the final, official count:

Peña Nieto	19.2 million	38.21%
López Obrador	15.9 million	31.59%
Vásquez Mota	12.8 million	25.40%

AMLO *still* wouldn't concede, charging that the *PRI*'s scheme of swapping groceries for votes and the slanted television coverage Peña Nieto enjoyed were responsible for his 3.3 million-vote loss and arguing that they warranted nullifying the election. Vásquez Mota joined in denouncing the vote-buying, but stopped short of contesting the outcome.

Mexico

Results for the Chamber of Deputies gave the *PRI* and its Green Party partner 175 of the 300 directly elected seats. But after the complex calculations for the 200 seats assigned by proportional representation were completed, the *PRI-PVEM* alliance wound up with 240 seats overall, 11 short of an absolute majority, meaning the fledgling New Alliance Party with 10 seats may prove the kingmaker. The *PRD* and *PT* will have 134 deputies and the *PAN*, just 116.

One fourth of the Senate seats were up in 2012. In the new Senate, the *PRI-PVEM* won 62 seats, the *PAN* 38 and the *PRD* and *PT*, 27.

It was an ignominious defeat for the *PAN*. Not only did it finish third in the presidential race and carry only three states—Guanajuato, Nuevo León and Tamaulipas—but it lost the governorships of Jalisco (Guadalajara) after 18 years to the *PRI*'s Aristóteles Sandoval and Morelos after 12 years to the *PRD*'s Graco Ramírez. It did retain the governorship of Guanajuato, but the number of states it controls has dwindled to five, plus the *PAN*-led coalition in Sinaloa.

The *PRD* carried nine states and the Federal District and retained control of the Federal District; Miguel Ángel Mancera buried the *PRI*'s one-time star, Beatríz Paredes, for chief of government of Mexico City with 63.7% of the vote to her 19.4%. The *PRD* also narrowly won for the first time in Tabasco with the candidacy of Arturo Nuñez Jiménez.

For the first time, the Green Party will have a governor. Manuel Velasco, head of a *PVEM-PRI* coalition, won in Chiapas with 64.6% of the vote.

The *PRI* retained control of Yucatán. Rolando Zapata won 52% of the vote against *PAN* and *PRD* candidates.

At the end of August, AMLO was still claiming fraud, refusing to concede and demanding a recount—even though local *PRD* candidates had won in areas where he lost. The IFE wearily agreed to begin a recount in September but stopped halfway through when it became apparent that there were no irregularities. It verified Peña Nieto's victory.

Old or New *PRI*?

Now that the *PRI* was regaining power, it decided it could stop being an obstructionist to the badly needed reforms Calderón had proposed and embrace them itself—and take the credit, of course. Even before Peña Nieto's inauguration, the *PRI* removed the roadblocks to Calderón's proposed reform of the labor code, the first since 1970. The revisions are reminiscent of the U.S. Taft-Hartley Act of 1947, requiring private-sector unions and the union

of the state-owned *Pemex* to elect leaders by secret ballot and to open their books for auditing. It also eased the restrictions against part-time employment and made severance pay more in line with other countries.

It was a daring move by the *PRI*, as trade unions are one of its core constituencies. The Senate and Chamber tossed the amended bill back and forth for two months before they agreed on a single version, and Calderón signed it into law on November 30—his last day in office.

Four days before his inauguration, Peña Nieto met with President Obama at the White House, unprecedented for a Mexican president-elect.

As they had done with Calderón in 2006, pro-AMLO deputies tried to disrupt the inauguration on December 1 by heckling the new president as he took his oath. Protesters near the National Palace went on a rampage, shattering windows and vandalizing a newly reopened park with pro-AMLO graffiti. But the new Peña Nieto presidency was a reality, and the 46-year-old leader demonstrated at the outset he planned some dynamic changes.

On his first day, "EPN" announced that the *PRI*, *PAN* and *PRD* had agreed on a "Pact for Mexico." Like Martin Luther's Theses, it consisted of 95 proposals affecting labor, energy, taxes, health, education, human rights, telecommunications and security. Miffed at his party's cooperation, López Obrador again bolted from the *PRD* and made plans to establish a new party, which will fragment Mexico's left even further.

As a sign of his intention to govern by multi-party consensus, Peña Nieto appointed Calderón's finance secretary, José Antonio Meade, as foreign secretary. He appointed the *PRD*'s Manuel Mondragón, the police chief of Mexico City and an AMLO backer, to head his security apparatus. Rosario Robles, the former *PRD* president, is social development secretary. Less encouraging, he also appointed some associates of the reviled former President Salinas, and named Zedillo's interior secretary, Emilio Chuayffet, as education secretary. As the powerful interior secretary he appointed the *PRI* governor of Hidalgo, Miguel Ángel Osorio Chong—whom the newsmagazine *Proceso* has accused of ties with *Los Zetas* drug cartel.

In the first few months of 2013, Peña Nieto began making good on his promises. After collaborating with Calderón on the labor code, he next took on another powerful, entrenched force that is one of the *PRI*'s traditional pillars: the teachers' union. He pushed through a constitutional amendment with the *PAN*'s help that imposed certification and evaluations for teachers and provided for removal of

unqualified teachers. It also stripped the union of the power to hire and, more importantly, to pay teachers. As a show of Peña Nieto's determination and muscle, Elba Esther Gordillo, the powerful head of the teachers' union for 23 years, was arrested in February and charged with embezzling $159 million from the union. She had lived and dressed far beyond her means for years.

Peña Nieto next bit another hand that had traditionally fed the *PRI* and had facilitated his election: *Televisa*, the near-monopoly television network, run by Emilio Azcárraga Jean, the 45-year-old grandson of the station's founder. In his proposed reform of the telecommunications industry, another idea inherited from Calderón, the president also took aim at Carlos Slim, the world's richest man (see The Economy). Slim heads the monolithic telephone empire América Móvil, which controls 80% of landlines and 70% of cell phones. The new telecommunications law would open both sectors to more competitors. In television, two new over-the-air channels are to be auctioned off, but *Televisa* and its only real competitor, *TV Azteca*, will not be allowed to bid. Slim, who owns no television assets but aspires to, is allowed to bid.

The gorilla in the room is still drug-related violence, about which Peña Nieto was vague during the campaign. Since his inauguration, he has abandoned Calderón's tough rhetoric, but he unveiled a plan that moved drug enforcement into the Interior Ministry and would create a new, 40,000-member rural gendarmerie to augment the army in violence-prone areas. Existing national police institutions were to concentrate on investigation. In 2013, the first full year of Peña Nieto's presidency, drug-related deaths totaled 16,736, down 16% from 2012 (see Other Current Issues: Drugs).

President Obama made a state visit to Mexico in May 2013 and the two leaders discussed the usual thorny issues of immigration and drugs. The month before, Peña Nieto ended the long-standing open access between parallel U.S. and Mexican agencies and decreed that U.S. agencies must go through the Interior Ministry.

In politics, local elections were held in 14 states on July 7, 2013, including the country's most closely watched election, the governor's race in Baja California Norte, which the *PAN* had held for 24 years. It was the *PAN*'s historic victory there in 1989 that broke the *PRI*'s monopoly of governorships. The *PRI* fielded a formidable candidate, Fernando Castro Trenti, against the *PAN*'s Francisco "Kiki" Vega, a former Tijuana mayor. A loss in this longtime *PAN* stronghold would be embarrassing and symbolic of the party's declining fortunes. Vega sought to boost his chances with an unlikely electoral alliance with the *PRD*.

On election night, the company contracted to tabulate the votes projected Vega the winner, 47% to 44%, but the state electoral commission complained that a problem with the company's "algorithm" invalidated that projection and began the tedious chore of hand-counting the ballots in the boxes that were in doubt. That threw the outcome into confusion—and suspicion. Castro refused to concede until the hand-counting was completed, while the company insisted that the computer problem was fixed quickly and its count was accurate. President Peña Nieto called for calm and for both sides to respect the outcome. (His three-party pact could have come undone if the *PRI* were seen as blatantly stealing the election, like the 1988 presidential race.) The commission declared Vega the winner on July 13.

The *PRI* won the mayoralties of Tijuana and nine of the 14 state capitals contested. The elections were marred by assassinations of candidates and the usual charges of the *PRI* swapping groceries for votes.

Mexico, 2013–14. . .

During the second half of 2013, Peña Nieto forged forward with his promises to implement the promised tax and energy reforms.

Mexico has the lowest tax revenue as a percentage of GDP in Latin America, and the reform measure was designed to bring it up to 4%. He was expected to propose extending the national sales tax, or *IVA*, to groceries and medicines, a most unpopular idea, but needed to reduce the national budget's dependence on oil and gas revenues, which are dwindling. The *PRD* refused to go along with heavier taxes on the poor, while the *PAN* protested raising the income tax cap. For Peña Nieto to keep his Pact for Mexico intact, he had to do a lot of compromising—perhaps too much.

As always, the two chambers played ping-pong before settling on a watered-down version that won the votes of the *PRD* deputies, while the *PAN* voted against it. Peña Nieto backed down on extending the *IVA* to groceries and drugs, but he did end the discounted *IVA* in states that border the United States, Guatemala and Belize, raising it from 11% to the 16% residents pay in the other states. The top income tax rate for people making 3 million pesos ($233,000) or more was raised from 30% to 35%, but lawmakers decided to retain the 30% rate for people making up to 750,000 pesos, while those making more than 750,000 will pay 32%. A plan to reduce the corporate income tax from 30% to 28% was scrapped, prompting *PAN* deputies to stage a walkout. The most con-

President Enrique Peña Nieto

troversial new measure was an 8% excise tax on soda and junk food. The Chamber passed the final version 299-160 on October 31; the Senate followed the next day, 73-50. Peña Nieto signed it into law on December 6. After all the compromises, it is estimated taxes will still only amount to 2.8% of GDP.

Before Peña Nieto could proceed with the even more controversial and contentious energy amendment, he had to soothe the ruffled feathers of the *PAN*, whose votes he would need because this time, it was the *PRD* that was refusing to budge on such issues as allowing foreign companies to drill for Mexican oil in competition with *Pemex*. The *PAN* issued a *sine qua non* to the president: Implement a constitutional amendment on electoral reform first, or forget about the *PAN*'s cooperation on the energy bill.

Peña Nieto acceded. On this issue, the *PRD* was also on board, because the bill was aimed at curbing the kinds of abuses for which the *PRI* was notorious. Among the major provisions, a newly created National Electoral Institute, or *INE*, would take the place of the old *IFE* and would have jurisdiction over both federal and state elections. It would have the power to nullify an election if a candidate exceeded the campaign spending limit by 5% if he or she won by less than 5%. The prosecutor general will now be confirmed by the Senate and operate independently of the executive branch. Beginning in 2018, presidents will be inaugurated on October 1 instead of December 1.

The most earth-shaking change, however, was the chiseling-away at the century-old prohibition against re-election

that was a cornerstone of the 1917 constitution. Federal deputies had already been allowed to seek one additional term. Under the new set of rules, deputies could serve up to four three-year terms and senators could serve two six-year terms. Mayors may now seek immediate re-election, but the one-term rule remains for the president and the chief of government of the Federal District.

It coasted through both houses in early December, a majority of state legislatures quickly ratified it, and Peña Nieto signed it on January 31. Political analysts and columnists complained that the amendment was passed *too* quickly and was not well written.

With electoral reform out of the way, Congress turned to energy reform, which is urgently needed if Mexico is to tap offshore deposits and remain energy independent and an exporter. Peña Nieto dropped the *PRI*'s long-standing resistance to foreign participation in *Pemex*, which is needed for deep offshore exploration and extraction. Although the amendment would break *Pemex*'s 75-year-old monopoly, something almost as sacred to Mexicans as no re-election, and open oil exploration to foreign companies, hydrocarbons below ground would remain the property of the state. The foreign companies would receive a share of profits, but would not have title to the oil itself.

After intense debate, it passed the Senate on December 11, 95-28. The next day, the Chamber engaged in the rowdiest spectacle seen in the lower house since the inauguration of Calderón in 2006. *PRD* deputies yelled epithets like "Traitor!" at *PRI* and *PAN* legislators. Two female legislators engaged in a brawl. A male *PRD* deputy stripped down to his underwear to symbolize the "stripping" of Mexico's natural resources. But it passed, 354-134. A majority of state legislatures ratified it with even more lightning speed than the electoral reform, in four days! The president signed it on December 20.

Mexico finished 2013 with a GDP growth of a mere 1.2%, its slowest in four years and the worst in Latin America. Yet, Peña Nieto ranked as the seventh-most popular leader of the Western Hemisphere in the Mitofsky survey in October, with a respectable approval rating of 56%.

The historic votes on telecommunications, fiscal, electoral and energy reforms were only Round One. Congress next had to enact the enabling legislation, the so-called secondary laws, which occupied the attention of Congress for the first half of 2014.

Not surprisingly, *Televisa* and *TV Azteca* argued against implementation of the telecommunications legislation and even threatened legal action to protect their

Mexico

"biopoly," but Peña Nieto personally intervened to squelch them. The measure bounced back and forth between the two houses for much of March and April before the Senate passed it 108-3 on May 1. The state legislatures followed suit by May 14 and the president signed it on June 10. The process then got underway of accepting bids for the two new over-the-air channels. The winning bids were expected to be announced in September.

The electoral reform legislation passed the Senate on May 14 and the Chamber on May 16, 311-91. But suddenly, the *PRI* began asking for "modifications" to the provisions regarding how parties are governed, and the *PAN* threatened to withhold its support for the secondary energy legislation unless the *PRI* desisted.

Peña Nieto submitted the energy reform secondary legislation at the end of April, and the Senate was taking it up in June when this book went to press.

Mexicans were reminded of *el PRI viejo* in April when a scandal unfolded implicating the party's president in Mexico City, Cuauhtémoc Gutiérrez de la Torre. Acting on a tip, a female undercover radio reporter pretending to be a job applicant recorded a party official explaining that her duties would include providing Gutiérrez with sex. Gutiérrez denounced the station and denied what listeners clearly heard on the recording. He resigned in June.

Gustavo Madero was re-elected *PAN* president in May.

Relations with the United States have continued their usually bumpy course. Peña Nieto was one of the world leaders allied with the United States whose phone conversations were tapped by the U.S. National Security Agency, according to reports leaked to the media in September 2013. The U.S. ambassador was summoned for an explanation. The Obama administration has tacitly acknowledged the eavesdropping and insisted it has been stopped, but Obama has not apologized to Peña Nieto, which has rankled the Mexicans' sensibilities.

Then, in May 2014, U.S. Marine Sgt. Andrew Tahmooressi was jailed in Tijuana when he crossed the border with several weapons in his vehicle. Tahmooressi insists that he took a wrong turn and crossed into Mexico unintentionally. He complained in media interviews that he has been treated harshly. The U.S. government has sought his release, but when this book went to press he was still behind bars.

Meanwhile, a potential humanitarian disaster began unfolding along the U.S.-Mexican border in June as tens of thousands of Central American children as young as four years old, unaccompanied by adults, suddenly began crossing the U.S. border illegally and have been placed in makeshift detention facilities. The reason for the sudden surge in child migration may be a memo Obama signed in 2012 called the Deferred Action for Childhood Arrivals, which defers deportation for illegal immigrants who were brought to the United States as children. The erroneous rumor spread in Central America that if children crossed the border alone and surrendered, they would be allowed to stay.

The surge apparently has been orchestrated by the so-called *"coyotes,"* mostly Mexican, who profit from human smuggling. When this book went to press, 47,000 children had entered the country illegally in 2014 in the so-called "Dream Surge," and it was estimated the figure would reach 70,000 to 90,000 by the end of the year. The children have been placed under the care of the Department of Health and Human Services and were being housed at various military bases and in impromptu detention centers, such as a Border Patrol warehouse in Nogales, Arizona, where 1,100 children were housed in cramped conditions, raising international concerns for their welfare.

The crisis prompted a phone call from Obama to Peña Nieto on June 19. Obama urged his counterpart to tighten immigration from Central America and to crack down on the *"coyotes."* Vice President Biden met in Guatemala on June 20 with Guatemalan President Otto Pérez Molina, Salvadoran President Salvador Sánchez Cerén, Mexican Interior Secretary Osorio and a high-ranking representative of the Honduran government to discuss the surge (see Guatemala).

OTHER CURRENT ISSUES

Drugs

Given the geographic reality of Mexico's 2,000-mile border with the United States, it was inevitable that Mexico would become a conduit in the traffic of illegal drugs from Colombia to the United States. An estimated 70%–80% of the cocaine and heroin entering the United States crosses that border. In addition, vast quantities of Mexican-grown marijuana also stream across the border, as do methamphetamines. It was also inevitable that domestic drug cartels would arise in Mexico, further corrupting already corrupt governmental and law enforcement institutions.

Until 1997 there were three major drug cartels operating in northern Mexico: **the Gulf Cartel** on the eastern flank, based in Matamoros, Tamaulipas, and headed by **Juan García Abregu; the Juárez Cartel,** based in Ciudad Juárez, Chihuahua, and headed by **Amado Carrillo Fuentes;** and **the Tijuana Cartel** in Baja California Norte, run by the **Arellano Félix brothers, Ramón, Benjamín, Eduardo, Francisco Javier and Francisco Rafael.** Of these five brothers—there were a total of 10 siblings—Benjamín was considered the brains behind the business, while Ramón was a bloodthirsty enforcer who himself died in a hail of bullets in 2002. Francisco Rafael would die in a hit in 2013 after he had paid his debt to society.

These three groups had unofficially "divided" the 1,200-mile U.S. border into operational zones. Friction between them erupted into gangland-style violence, which has reached epic proportions. In one legendary case, a lieutenant of the Arellano Félixes infiltrated the Juárez Cartel in 1989, seduced the wife of a Carrillo Fuentes lieutenant, persuaded her to withdraw $7 million from her husband's account, then killed her and sent her head to her husband in a box. He also reportedly threw the couple's two children to their deaths from a bridge in Caracas, Venezuela.

Another still-infamous incident was a 1993 shootout in the Guadalajara airport in which **Cardinal Juan Jesús Posadas Ocampo** was killed, supposedly in the crossfire. Some theories still contend that he was in fact a target because he knew too much of official complicity in the drug trade, and his death remains controversial to this day. Francisco Rafael Arellano Félix was convicted of his role in the archbishop's death, as was **Joaquín Guzmán** of the rival gang. Guzmán escaped in 2001 and was in hiding for 13 years (see Peña Nieto Changes Course below); Francisco Rafael Arellano Félix remains in prison.

In 1996, the Gulf Cartel was beheaded when García Abregu was extradited to the United States and sentenced to 11 life terms by a federal court in Houston. He was known for his high-level influence, among others, it is reported, with Raúl Salinas, brother of the former president, and former federal prosecutor Mario Ruíz Massieu.

In July 1997, Carrillo Fuentes, nicknamed "Lord of the Skies" because of his use of aging jetliners to ferry massive amounts of cocaine from Colombia and believed to head the largest of the three cartels, died while undergoing clandestine plastic surgery to alter his appearance. Reports surfaced in some Mexican media that his death was a "hit" by a rival drug gang, probably the Tijuana Cartel. Although the report never was confirmed, two of his surgeons later were found tortured and killed; a third was granted protection in the United States, where he insisted to investigators that Carrillo Fuentes' death was, indeed, due to nothing more than a botched procedure.

Carrillo Fuentes' brother, Vicente, for a time assumed leadership of the cartel, but he lacked his brother's genius for organization, logistics and control. The dead kingpin was not even in his grave before a monumental turf war erupted between his cartel and that of the Arellano Félix brothers. Both Juárez and Tijuana became war zones, and still are. Most killings are in imaginatively gruesome gangland fashion by strangulation, suffocation with plastic bags or multiple gunshot wounds. Bodies frequently are burned, dismembered or beheaded and stuffed into suitcases, oil drums or automobile trunks. The violence continues to be beyond the capability of federal, state or local police to contend with.

For a time, the Tijuana Cartel gained the upper hand. It was the richest, most powerful, most feared and most bloodthirsty of the cartels. The Arellano Félix brothers maintained their power over public officials with a Godfather-like carrot-or-stick tactic called *"plata o plomo"* ("silver or lead"). They were Mexico's most wanted criminals, and Ramón was on the FBI's 10 Most Wanted List.

The heat on the cartel intensified when it committed a serious tactical error: it began shooting crusading journalists, like Benjamín Flores, the young publisher of a small daily newspaper in Sonora, who was gunned down outside his office in 1997. The same year, **Jesús Blancornelas,** publisher of *Zeta,* a weekly magazine in Tijuana that has been a nemesis of the Arellano Félixes, was critically wounded in an ambush that killed his bodyguard; one of the gunmen also was slain, and was identified as a hit man for the Tijuana Cartel. Other journalists vowed to create unbearable pressure on the Tijuana cartel.

Because of the endemic corruption that riddles government at all levels and the parallel law enforcement agencies, efforts to combat drug trafficking have sometimes taken on the semblance of a comic opera. Frequent changes of top law enforcement officials hamstrung any serious attempt to combat the drug cartels prior to 2000. Mexico had seven attorneys general in eight years during the 1990s.

In 1994, then-President Salinas established the Institute to Combat Drugs (*INCD*), the equivalent of the U.S. Drug Enforcement Administration, but it, too, has had a revolving door. One of its directors, Army General **Jesús Gutiérrez Rebollo,** was arrested in 1997, accused of taking bribes from Carrillo Fuentes. He was sentenced to 13 years and nine months in prison. President Ernesto Zedillo abolished the *INCD* and returned its functions to the attorney general's office.

President Bill Clinton made his first state visit to Mexico in 1997 and ameliorated anti-U.S. feeling somewhat by acknowledging that the root of the drug

trade was not Mexican greed but the insatiable U.S. demand. That good will evaporated in 1998 after a secret, three-year-long sting operation by U.S. agents to nab Mexican bankers involved in money laundering. "Operation Casablanca" involved U.S. agents acting clandestinely in Mexico without the knowledge or approval of Mexican authorities. The operation yielded 150 arrests and $110 million in laundered money, and three Mexican banks were indicted. Mexicans were outraged by what they regarded as a violation of their sovereignty. Clinton offered lukewarm apologies, but there was an implicit message: We don't trust you enough to tell you about undercover drug operations.

Clinton met with Zedillo again in 1999 for a one-day summit in Yucatán that focused on drugs and trade. They worked out a new agreement establishing performance measures of effectiveness (PMEs) for 16 areas of drug control—including reduction of demand in the United States. The United States also agreed to provide increased police training assistance. After the summit, Clinton recertified Mexico as an ally in the drug war.

The Fox Administration

In 2000, the newly inaugurated president, Vicente Fox, pledged a crackdown on corruption, which in Mexico is almost synonymous with drugs. In a meeting with his new U.S. counterpart, George W. Bush, in early 2001, Fox pledged heightened cooperation in the war on drugs, although like his predecessors he voiced disapproval of the U.S. drug certification policy.

The Fox administration scored some significant victories. One was the capture of the fugitive former governor of Quintana Roo, Mario Villanueva, who allegedly aided the Juárez Cartel in smuggling 200 tons of cocaine into the United States. He had been on the run for two years. In 2010, he was extradited to the United States.

Mexican authorities also arrested 21 alleged members of the Gulf Cartel, by then headed by **Osiel Cárdenas,** among them one of the suspected kingpins, **Gilberto García,** known as *"El June."* In 2003, García was sentenced to eight years. Two months after García's arrest, **Juan Manuel Garza,** another of the alleged leaders of the Gulf Cartel, crossed the border from Reynosa into McAllen, Texas, and surrendered to the FBI.

Cárdenas himself, nicknamed *"El Loco"* because he is so brazen he once ordered DEA agents out of "his" territory, and 22 accomplices were apprehended in 2003 after a gun battle in Matamoros, across from Brownsville, Texas.

Drug-related violence then erupted in Nuevo Laredo, and since then a new

turf battle has raged there to fill the latest vacuum at the apex of the Gulf Cartel. By 2003, a band of deserters from the Mexican army, calling themselves *"Los Zetas,"* had become established in Nuevo Laredo and was fighting for a piece of the turf.

The Arellano Félix organization suffered two major blows in 2002. First, Ramón was killed in a shootout, supposedly with police, in Mazatlán. He killed the policeman who killed him in the exchange of gunfire. Because the body was quickly cremated, there was speculation as to whether the corpse was that of an imposter; it was reminiscent of the death of the Juárez Cartel's Carrillo Fuentes in 1997.

A month later, Benjamín was arrested in a raid in Puebla. Benjamín confirmed it was Ramón who had been killed in Mazatlán. DNA samples from Benjamín matched samples taken from blood of the man killed in Mazatlán.

There was a bizarre postscript to Ramón's death. The Associated Press, citing an anonymous "senior U.S. law enforcement official," reported that the police who killed Ramón were in fact part of a hit paid for by **Ismael Zambada García,** head of the new, rival **Sinaloa Cartel.** Officials declined to comment on the report—but did not deny it.

A judge ruled there was insufficient evidence to implicate Benjamín and his imprisoned brother, Rafael, in Archbishop Posadas Ocampo's death in 1993. Another judge dismissed a charge that Benjamín headed a drug-trafficking organization. Another brother, Eduardo, a surgeon, was thought to hold a leadership role. He remained at large until 2008.

With the seeming downfall of the Arellano Félix brothers and the decapitation of the Gulf Cartel, the center of gravity in the drug trade shifted to Sinaloa—the original home of the Arellano Félixes. Sinaloa has a long history in the raising and trafficking of drugs dating to the 19th century, when Chinese immigrants raised poppies for the production of opium, much of it smuggled to the U.S..

At least two major, rival cartels then operated in Sinaloa. One was headed by the **Guzmán brothers, Arturo, known as "the Chicken," and Joaquín, "El Chapo" ("Shorty")** who was serving a 20-year sentence for the accidental shooting death of Archbishop Posadas Ocampo before he escaped in 2001. Arturo was arrested in 2001, but Joaquín remained at large for 13 years until his capture in February 2014 (see Peña Nieto Changes Course below). Arturo is believed to be responsible for an elaborate 1,400-foot tunnel under the U.S. border. Joaquín is believed to be among the drug lords who was trying to fill the vacuum in Nuevo Laredo. Joaquín, who was under a U.S. indictment, was on

Mexico

Forbes magazine's list of billionaires from 2009–13.

The other cartel is headed by **Ismael "El Mayo" Zambada García.** He reportedly attempted to muscle in on the Arellano Félixes' Tijuana operations for at least a decade, fueling speculation he was responsible for Ramón's "execution." His organization became the target of a U.S.-Mexican investigation, Operation Trifecta, after the seizure of a 10-ton cocaine shipment at sea in 2001.

An exceptionally violent turf battle erupted between the Tijuana and Zambada García cartels. Within days of Ramón's death, a suspected Arellano Félix ally was gunned down, sparking a wave of gangland killings.

In 2003, Attorneys General John Ashcroft and Maceda de la Concha announced simultaneously a "significant victory" when Zambada García was named in an unsealed U.S. indictment, along with two of his lieutenants; all three remained at large. Ashcroft and Macedo also announced that Operation Trifecta had yielded 240 arrests and indictments.

Zambada García's brother, **Jesús "El Rey" Zambada García,** also was a major figure in the cartel until his arrest in Mexico City in 2008. He was extradited to the U.S. in April 2012.

President Bush announced in 2004 that the Arellano Félix and Carrillo Fuentes organizations, and Mexicans Eduardo Arellano Félix, Francisco Javier Arellano Félix, and Armando Valencia Cornelio had been placed on a sanctions list, denying them access to U.S. financial institutions or from dealing with U.S. companies or individuals. U.S. authorities arrested Francisco Javier Arellano Félix, the youngest of the brothers, on a yacht off the California coast in 2006.

Juan José Esparragoza, who had been operations chief of the Juárez Cartel, reportedly took over the leadership from **Vicente Carrillo Fuentes** and began building alliances. Carrillo Fuentes went into hiding after his other brother, Rodolfo, was gunned down in 2004 in a hit reportedly ordered by the Guzmán gang. Nonetheless, Esparragoza persuaded the rival Guzmán and Zambada cartels in Sinaloa to put aside their differences and to join the Juárez Cartel. With Benjamín Arellano Félix of the Tijuana Cartel and Cárdenas of the Gulf Cartel both behind bars, this new alliance made the Juárez Cartel the largest in Mexico, and it began a two-front offensive against its rivals. *"El Mayo"* Zambada was the "general" in charge of battling the Tijuana Cartel for control of the drug routes into California and Arizona, while *"El Chapo"* Guzmán fought the Gulf Cartel in Tamaulipas along the Texas border.

In an equally stunning development, Benjamín Arellano Félix and Cárdenas, jailed in the maximum-security La Palma federal prison near Mexico City, formed an unholy alliance of their own to defend their respective turfs against the Juárez-Sinaloa alliance. When the federal government got wind of their collusion, it dispatched troops to surround La Palma. Cárdenas and Arellano Félix were separated, but not before their alliance was created.

The Border Explodes

This clash of titans became spectacularly bloody, generating headlines on both sides of the border and around the world. Gangland-style killings remain a daily occurrence, but the victims are not always members of the two gangs; law enforcement officers, journalists and innocent bystanders die as well. The number of drug-related killings increased from 1,300 in 2005 to 2,100 in 2006. It would go much higher.

The main battlegrounds were once Matamoros, Nuevo Laredo and Ciudad Alemán, border cities in Tamaulipas, where *Los Zetas* were believed to have become enforcers for the Gulf Cartel. In a bold act that shocked both countries in 2005, six guards at the prison in Matamoros were seized by hit men, handcuffed, riddled with bullets execution-style and left in a car. The killings were reportedly retribution for the crackdown on the federal prisons, and were interpreted as a challenge by the drug lords to the national government itself. *Los Zetas* were suspected. Fox sent army troops to cordon off the prison.

The border area remains a veritable war zone. The death toll in 2008 was about 4,500, half the figure of 9,226 civilians killed in Iraq that year. By 2009, the Mexican death toll was 9,635 compared with 4,497 civilian deaths in Iraq. In 2010, it soared to 15,273, a 55% increase. In 2011 there were 16,466 deaths, an 8% increase, bringing the total since 2006 to 47,554.

In Nuevo Laredo, the lawless atmosphere is reminiscent of the Capone-Moran rivalry in Chicago in the 1920s—only bloodier. In 2005, Fox dispatched 600 heavily armed federal policemen there, then added army troops to a force of 700 to help patrol the city, one step short of declaring martial law. When the city finally filled the vacancy for police chief, the new chief was killed his first day on the job. His replacement soon resigned. Another police chief was slain in 2011. The city still averages at least one drug-related murder a day.

But Ciudad Juárez has become the premier slaughterhouse. In 2009, it officially became the world's most dangerous city, with about 2,750 drug-related murders, an average of 12 a day. It was being patrolled by 10,000 federal police and troops, who themselves have been accused of various abuses. In 2010, the death toll in Juárez rose to 3,117, compared with 2,421 civilian deaths in Afghanistan that year. In 2010, 16 teenagers at a New Year's party were slain in what appeared to be a case of mistaken identity. In March, a pregnant U.S. consulate official, her husband and another consular employee became victims, making headlines in both countries. In February 2011, 53 people were killed in just 72 hours, and 41 more died during a four-day period in April. After a policeman was slain when he arrived home in February 2012, the city began housing policemen in hotels to protect them.

The death toll in Juárez declined dramatically in 2011, to "only" 1,933, a 38% decrease. But horrors continue to unfold there. On December 8, 2011, 14 people were killed in a series of incidents, including an ambush of an ambulance that killed four people.

Horrors also continued in Tamaulipas, where *Los Zetas* were believed responsible for the massacre in 2010 of 72 Central American immigrants, mostly Hondurans, near San Fernando. Four members of *Los Zetas* were arrested. In the same area in 2011, eight mass graves yielded 183 bodies. Fourteen dismembered bodies were found in a truck outside the city hall in the town of El Mante.

In Durango state, a mass grave, believed a dumping ground for the Sinaloa Cartel's victims, yielded 219 bodies in 2011. The killings are thought to be the result of internecine warfare within the cartel. A battle between Sinaloa Cartel members and *Los Zetas* erupted in Nayarit state on the Pacific coast in May 2011.

In March 2012, 49 mutilated bodies were found in the desert near Monterrey, Nuevo León. They were believed to be casualties of the turf war between *Los Zetas* and the Gulf-Sinaloa Cartel alliance. A leader of *Los Zetas,* **Daniel de Jesús Elizondo, aka "El Loco,"** was arrested in connection with the massacre, after throwing a grenade and firing on soldiers. He provided details of the massacre.

Meanwhile, *Los Zetas* and *La Familia* are waging a turf war in Guerrero state. In January 2011, 30 people were killed in a four-day period, and 15 decapitated bodies were dumped on a shopping center parking lot in Acapulco.

Jaime Zapata, a U.S. agent for Immigration and Customs Enforcement (ICE) was killed in February 2011 at a roadblock between Monterrey and Mexico City and another agent, Victor Ávila, was wounded, allegedly by members of *Los Zetas.* Calderón ordered four more army battalions to the border area.

On the U.S. side of the border, federal, state and local authorities launched a crackdown on suspected Mexican drug traffickers in reprisal for Zapata's death. The sweep yielded 500 arrests, 16 tons of marijuana, $10 million in cash and 300 weapons. ICE doubled the number of its agents in Mexico and overhauled its security procedures. It was reminiscent of the reaction to the torture-murder of DEA Enrique Camarena in Mexico in 1985. As one ICE agent told the press, "This is personal."

The Targeting of Journalists

Drug traffickers loathe—and fear—crusading journalists only slightly less than they do law enforcement officials who can't be bought. In 2004, for the first time, more journalists were slain in Mexico than in Colombia. According to the Paris-based Reporters Without Borders, Mexico became the second-most dangerous country for journalists in the world after Iraq in 2007. Most of the killings are close to the border.

In Tijuana, **Francisco Ortíz Franco,** assistant editor of Jesús Blancornelas' crusading weekly *Zeta,* was gunned down in 2004. Two months later, **Francisco Arratia Saldierna,** a syndicated newspaper columnist in Matamoros who regularly attacked organized crime, was sadistically tortured and beaten to death. **Gregorio Rodríguez,** a photographer with a newspaper in Sinaloa, was murdered after he took a picture of a drug dealer.

In Nuevo Laredo, two well-known journalists, both of whom reported on the cartels, were murdered in 2004 and 2005. **Roberto Mora,** news editor of *El Mañana,* was stabbed to death, and **Guadalupe García Escamilla,** who hosted a radio crime program, was riddled with bullets outside the station and died 10 days later.

Mexican journalists and international journalism organizations demanded that Fox do more to protect journalists and to apprehend their killers. Yet, in 2006, the offices of *El Mañana* in Nuevo Laredo were attacked with automatic weapons and grenades, and a reporter was critically wounded. The publisher announced that the paper would refrain from any further investigative reporting on the cartels. Self-censorship had begun, and it has grown.

After two grenade attacks on the office of *Cambio,* the evening daily in Hermosillo, Sonora, Mario Vásquez Raña, owner of the Editora Mexicana chain that owns *Cambio,* announced he was "temporarily" closing the newspaper to assure the safety of its employees. It was the first time drug traffickers had succeeding in actually putting a newspaper out of operation.

In 2009, the office of *Televisa* in Monterrey was attacked with grenades and a high-powered weapon, but there were no casualties. Much the same happened in 2009 with the powerful Mexico City newspaper *Reforma* and its sister paper in Monterrey, *El Norte.* Their publisher, **Alejandro Junco de la Vega,** went into self-imposed exile in Austin, Texas, in 2008 because of death threats. He earned his journalism degree there in 1969 at The University of Texas.

The cartels have even targeted musicians who have popularized the so-called drug ballads, or *narcocorridos;* 13 were killed in 2007 alone (see Culture).

Eight more journalists were murdered or disappeared in 2009, 11 in 2010, seven in 2011 and nine in 2012 and early 2013, according to the Inter American Press Association, bringing the total of slain journalists since 2006 to 53. Mexico is the most dangerous country for journalism in Latin America and fourth in the world after Iraq, Afghanistan and the Philippines. Still more are kidnapped. In 2010, four journalists were kidnapped while reporting a story on a prison warden in Durango who allegedly let prisoners free at night to conduct drug-related murders. All four escaped or were rescued, and they reported that their abductors told them they had kidnapped them in order to force the media to report that rival drug gangs had corrupted certain public officials—hardly startling news in Mexico. One of them, a cameraman for *Televisa,* sought asylum in the United States.

A magazine reporter was killed in Veracruz state in 2012, and days later two photojournalists for a local news photo agency in Veracruz were kidnapped. Their dismembered bodies were found stuffed into bags. Two journalists were among 15 people gunned down in a bar in Juárez in April.

Because many news organizations have been cowed into silence, news about the cartels' nefarious activities has been spreading unofficially through the new social media, like Facebook and Twitter. But even using pseudonyms has not protected some of the people relaying information. In 2011, two mutilated bodies were found hanging from a bridge in Nuevo Laredo with a yellow sign laced with misspellings and profanity that warned: "This is going to happen to anyone who posts FUNNY THINGS *(relajes)* on the Internet." It was signed with a "Z," apparently for *Los Zetas.* Meanwhile, the cartels have brazenly been exploiting the social media themselves.

Calderón's War

President Felipe Calderón, who took office on December 1, 2006, was even tougher on the drug gangs than Fox had been. He dispatched 7,000 federal troops to his home state of Michoacán, where a turf battle between the Gulf and Sinaloa cartels killed 600 people in 2006; decapitations are a favorite method there of sending "messages."

In 2007, Calderón dispatched another 3,300 troops to Tijuana, where they supplanted the local police. They even confiscated the weapons of the police to conduct ballistic tests to determine if they had been used in drug-related murders. In 2008, Calderón sent another 2,000 troops to Ciudad Juárez and 2,700 into Sinaloa, bringing to 24,000 the number of troops deployed against the cartels. Mexico began to resemble Colombia.

In two stunning developments, Calderón extradited Osiel Cárdenas and three other kingpins to the U.S. in 2007. He also beefed up and reorganized the new Federal Investigative Agency, or *AFI,* the Mexican equivalent of the FBI, and transferred it from the Justice Ministry to the new Public Security Ministry. The ministry has 30,000 troops under its control.

Benjamín Arellano Félix was sentenced to five years in 2007 on weapons charges. That November, his brother Francisco Javier was sentenced to life without parole in San Diego after entering a guilty plea in exchange for his life. He admitted to numerous murders and issued a surprisingly remorseful letter asking for forgiveness. Benjamín was extradited to the U.S. in 2011.

Calderón and Bush met in Mérida, Yucatán, in 2007 to discuss increased U.S. drug aid. Bush asked Congress to approve a $500-million-a-year aid package for three years to provide Mexico with sophisticated technology. Congress finally approved an initial $194 million of a $1.4 billion aid plan in late 2008, just before Bush left office.

By 2007, there were indications that the bilateral crackdown against the cartels was having an effect. According to the U.S. DEA, the street price of cocaine had jumped 44% in the first three quarters, that of methamphetamines 73%.

Mexican authorities scored another major victory in 2008 with the arrest of **Alfredo Beltrán Leyva,** believed to be Guzmán's enforcer and to be behind shipments of tons of cocaine to the U.S.. The cartels' response was a counteroffensive at the highest levels of law enforcement. Edgar Millán Gómez, acting national police chief, was assassinated, shot nine times as he arrived at his home. Although wounded himself, his bodyguard apprehended the gunman. The killing was believed to have been ordered by Beltrán Leyva's brother, Arturo. The next day, the head of Mexico City's investigative police was murdered. Other victims were the director of organized crime investigation in

Mexico

Mexico City and the deputy police chief in Ciudad Juárez.

Coincidentally, Guzmán's son was slain the same day as Millán Gómez, supposedly by elements of the Juárez Cartel.

That October, Ismael Zambada's brother, Jesús, and 15 other members of the Sinaloa Cartel were arrested after a gun battle with police in Mexico City. Jesús is also suspected of involvement in the Millán Gómez assassination.

Four days after Zambada's arrest, authorities arrested the elusive Eduardo Arrellano Félix after a gun battle in Tijuana. The DEA had tipped off Mexican authorities. He was the last of the brothers active in the cartel to be captured or killed, but it is believed the brothers' role in the cartel has been carved up between their nephew, Luis Fernando Sánchez Arrellano, and Eduardo García Simental. García Simental's brother, Teodoro, split off from the Tijuana Cartel and went off on his own, forging an alliance with the Sinaloa Cartel.

In another example of cartel fragmentation, Arturo Beltrán Leyva split off from the Sinaloa Cartel in 2008 and established his own, entering into an alliance with *Los Zetas* in Tamaulipas and setting up operations in the state of Morelos. He quickly became one of the three most-wanted men in Mexico—but not for long. On December 16, 2009, he and six of his bodyguards died in a 90-minute gun battle with army troops in a house in Cuernavaca, Morelos. The government scored another major success in January 2010 with the arrest of **Teodoro García Simental**. So much for branching off on your own.

Since Beltrán Leyva's death, his brother, Héctor, took up the slack and is operating out of the state of Mexico, but he faced opposition from Texas-born **Edgar Valdéz Villarreal, nicknamed *"La Barbie"*** in high school because of his fair, Ken-like features. Valdéz was indicted for cocaine distribution in Atlanta and arrested August 2010. Héctor Beltrán Leyva remains at large with a $5 million U.S. price tag and a $2.1 million Mexican price tag.

The government's spectacular successes against cartels at war with the Sinaloa Cartel led Calderón's critics to suggest darkly that his administration is in league with the cartel. Indeed, raids and arrests against Sinaloa kingpins seemed suspiciously under-represented compared with those against other cartels. What is possible is that the government has struck a Faustian deal by which the Sinaloa Cartel provides investigators with vital intelligence against its rivals, benefiting both parties. If so, it will be interesting to see what will happen when Sinaloa is the last cartel standing.

A frightening new variable in this already crowded field is a group calling itself *La Familia,* which initially operated exclusively in Michoacán—Calderón's home state. It specializes in methamphetamines but has diversified into extortion. It splashed into the news in 2006 when its members hurled five decapitated heads of rival gang members onto a dance floor. In 2008, eight people were killed and at least 100 wounded when suspected *La Familia* members tossed grenades into a crowd of Independence Day revelers in Morelia, the state capital, apparently just to instill terror. They succeeded, but they also sparked outrage. *La Familia* cloaked itself in a messianic mantle, handing out Bibles and claiming to do God's work. Some members broke off to form the "Knights Templar." It is believed led by **José de Jesús Méndez Vargas.** In 2009, the cartel reportedly tried to reach an accommodation with the government; Calderón responded to the feelers by dispatching 5,000 troops to the state.

The violence nationwide had become so alarming by 2008 that Mexico resembled the sectarian warfare in Iraq, only the killings were even more grisly. Calderón submitted a new security plan to Congress to streamline coordination among the various civilian and military agencies and zero in on corruption. He also summoned a hemispheric drug summit attended by representatives of 34 countries, among them OAS Secretary General José Miguel Insulza and U.S. Attorney General Mukasey. Calderón urged a "continental front" to combat the drug trade from cultivation to demand on the streets of the U.S.. Among the bad news the participants heard: the Colombian deputy defense minister reported that the Revolutionary Armed Forces of Colombia (FARC) was selling cocaine and meth directly to the Mexican cartels.

In August 2010, Calderón did an abrupt about-face and called for a "public discussion" on whether drugs should be legalized.

There were victories, too. *La Familia* suffered a major blow with the arrest of its presumed leader, **José de Jesús Méndez Varga,** in June 2011, the result of collaboration between the U.S. DEA and Mexico's Federal Police. In December 2010, **Nazario Moreno González, known as *"El Más Loco"* (The Craziest One),** the self-proclaimed "spiritual leader" of *La Familia,* was reported killed along with two comrades in a two-day shootout with security forces. Three others were captured. Five federal officers and three civilians also died. *La Familia* had declared a one-month "truce" for December, which it extended inexplicably in January 2011 despite Moreno's reported death. But Moreno's body was never produced, and he was "killed again" in 2014 (see Peña Nieto Changes Course below).

Flavio Méndez Santiago, a founder of *Los Zetas* and one of the 37 most wanted fugitives in Mexico, was captured in Oaxaca in January 2011. He had a $12.2 million price on his head. A month later, **Gilberto Barragán Balderas, alias *"El Tocayo,"*** believed in charge of the Gulf Cartel's defense against *Los Zetas*, was arrested in Reynosa—at his own birthday party. In March, **Victor Manuel Félix, alias *"El Señor,"*** the head of the Sinaloa Cartel's money-laundering operations and father-in-law of *"El Chapo"* Guzmán's son, was arrested along with seven others as part of Operation Beehive in Jalisco and Quintana Roo states. In September 2011, the Mexican navy dismantled a communication system serving *Los Zetas* in Veracruz state and arrested 80 suspects, including six police officers. Another fugitive on Mexico's "Top 37" list, **Raúl Lucio Hernández Lechuga,** a *Zetas* operative nicknamed "El Lucky," was arrested by the navy in December 2011. His arrest brought to 22 the number of those on the Top 37 list who had been killed or captured.

A new development in 2011 was the announcement that U.S. drone aircraft were being deployed over Mexico, with the government's concurrence, for surveillance of drug trafficking. The disclosure created a political controversy in Mexico.

In the U.S., federal agents arrested **José Treviño Morales,** brother of presumed *Zetas* leader **Miguel Ángel Treviño Morales** (see below), and five others in 2012 for allegedly laundering millions of dollars in drug money by raising quarterhorses in New Mexico and Oklahoma. Two of the horses actually had "cartel" as part of their names!

A botched 2011 sting operation by U.S. Alcohol, Tobacco and Firearms agents called Fast and Furious, designed to stem the flow of arms to Mexican drug cartels and capture arms traffickers, led to about 1,300 weapons finding their way to the cartels and were recovered after shootouts in which both Mexican and U.S. law enforcement personnel were killed. The resulting scandal strained bilateral relations.

In his final year as president, Calderón allocated $1.8 billion for the various drug enforcement agencies in his 2012 budget. Reliable figures on the death toll had become elusive by 2012, with the government offering no figures or suspicious ones; news organizations offered their own varying statistics. A generally accepted figure for 2012 was 20,010. News organizations at the end of 2012, when Calderón left office, put the six-year death toll at between 55,000 and 60,000, more than in the war in Afghanistan. An accurate count may never be known.

Two of the cartels suffered high-level losses in 2012. In September, the Gulf Car-

Mexico

tel's **Mario Cárdenas Guillén,** brother of cartel founder **Osiel Cárdenas Guillén,** was arrested in Tamaulipas.

On October 8, **Heriberto Lazcano,** the reputed head of *Los Zetas,* was killed in a gun battle with Mexican marines in Coahuila state. Someone stole his body from a funeral home, apparently to cast doubt on the identity of the slain man, but authorities exhumed the body of Lazcano's mother and confirmed through DNA testing that it was he.

Another high-level figure in *Los Zetas,* **Iván Velásquez Caballero, alias "El Taliban,"** was arrested by marines in San Luis Potosí in September 2012. He was extradited to the United States in November 2013, and his loss is believed to have created a serious void in the cartel leadership. He made his first court appearance in McAllen, Texas. He pleaded guilty in April 2014 to two counts of conspiracy that carry life sentences in what is believed to be a plea bargain for his cooperation in exchange for a reduced sentence. Sentencing was scheduled for July after this book went to press.

Peña Nieto Changes Course

Calderón's successor, the *PRI's* Enrique Peña Nieto, disavowed Calderón's iron-fisted approach to the cartels but was vague about what he would do differently, calling only for a "new dialogue." Soon after taking office on December 1, 2012, he placed drug enforcement under the secretary of the interior and declared he was creating a 40,000-member rural gendarmerie to complement the army in confronting the cartels. The other federal law enforcement agencies would concentrate on investigation. U.S. officials were less than pleased when Peña Nieto announced he was ending the open arrangement Mexico had had with U.S. agencies, which now must go through the Interior Ministry. He appointed Monte Alejandro Rubido as national security commissioner.

The government stopped providing statistics for drug-related deaths in 2012. It claimed the number of "intentional homicides" for 2013 was 16,736, a 16% decrease from the 20,010 in 2012. It further claimed that the number of deaths between gangs had dropped 85%, a figure open to skepticism. It did not itemize the deaths from confrontations between law enforcement and gangs, or how many bystanders were killed. News organizations, the U.S. DEA and international NGOs keep their own tallies, and they vary widely from one another. Human Rights Watch put the total from 2006 through 2012 at 63,000, a generally accepted figure.

There are indications that the traffickers may simply have shifted their focus from murder to extortion and kidnapping for ransom. Also, there has been an increase in disappearances, which are not counted in the death toll unless the bodies are recovered.

Although somewhat diminished, the bloodletting has by no means stopped. Turf battles are being waged between some new and old groups, such as between *Los Zetas* and the so-called Velásquez faction of the Gulf Cartel in the northeast. The faction is named for its captured leader, Iván *"El Talibán"* Velásquez Caballero, a former regional boss for the *Zetas* who returned to the Gulf Cartel until his capture and extradition to the U.S. (see above). Two relatively new gangs, the Knights Templar, an offshoot from *La Familia* in Michoacán and now the dominant group there, and the *Cartel de Jalisco Nueva Generación,* are in a battle to extend their territories in Jalisco, Michoacán, Guerrero and Guanajuato.

Casualties continue to mount as well in battles between the cartels and authorities. Some of the worst violence is now in Michoacán, where in July 2013 protesters took to the streets to denounce the drug violence. Members of the Knights Templar gunned down five of them. The next day, federal authorities arrived in force and were ambushed by the Knights Templar. In the ensuing firefight, two policemen and 20 criminals were killed and 16 people were wounded, the bloodiest incident in months. Peña Nieto has threatened to supplant local government in Michoacán and place it under federal control to maintain institutional order.

Vigilante groups, so-called *"auto-defensas,"* have taken up arms against the Knights Templar in Michoacán and Guerrero. After initially denouncing vigilante violence and calling for the groups to lay down their arms, the authorities are now calling on them to become "institutionalized" and to collaborate with them.

Peña Nieto's plan for a 40,000-member rural gendarmerie went nowhere. A year later, it appeared the government had pared the number back to a mere 5,000—and some of those may be the *auto-defensas.*

There were some high-profile arrests and deaths of cartel kingpins in 2013 and 2014 that made headlines around the world—if not always in Mexico. On July 15, 2013, the *Zetas'* top boss, **Miguel Ángel Treviño Morales,** alias "Z-40," was intercepted in a pickup truck about 40 miles south of Nuevo Laredo. Authorities swooped down on the pickup in helicopters. In the truck were $2 million in cash, eight weapons and hundreds of rounds of ammunition. The Nuevo Laredo newspaper *El Mañana,* cowed into self-censorship, did not even report the arrest, but international wire services and television networks did.

In August, authorities nabbed **Mario Armando Ramírez Treviño, aka "El Melón,"** a suspected leader of the old Gulf Cartel. In September, in the Pacific coast state of Nayarit, they arrested **Alberto Carrillo Fuentes, nicknamed "Ugly Betty,"** who is the brother of the late founder of the old Juárez Cartel Amado Carrillo Fuentes and is believed to be one of the leaders of the "new" Juárez Cartel.

Francisco Rafael Arrellano Félix, one of the five infamous brothers who founded the Tijuana Cartel, who was released from a U.S. prison in 2008 and was no longer a wanted man, was gunned down at his 64th birthday party in a resort in Cabo San Lucas, Baja California Sur, on October 18 by a man dressed as a clown.

Nazario *"El Más Loco"* Moreno González, the spiritual leader of *La Familia* whom authorities claimed to have killed in a shootout in December 2010, actually was not killed but had become a leader of the newer Knights Templar. He was "killed again" in a police raid in the town of Tumbiscatío, Michoacán, on March 9, 2014. This time the police had a body, and fingerprints confirmed it was he.

Arnoldo Villa Sánchez, believed to be the second in command of the diminished Beltrán Leyva Cartel, was quietly arrested during a meeting in Mexico City on April 17. He had been put on the U.S. kingpin list in November 2013.

But no capture or killing made a bigger splash than the news on February 23 that the long-fugitive **Joaquín *"El Chapo"* Guzmán,** the co-founder of the Sinaloa Cartel who escaped from prison in 2001 and had been in hiding for 13 years, was arrested without a shot being fired in a meticulously planned raid by Mexican marines and U.S. DEA agents on a resort in Mazatlán, Sinaloa. At the time of his arrest, the cartel was believed to be a $3 billion-a-year enterprise, and he was one of the world's most-wanted men. Like the late Pablo Escobar of Colombia's Medellín Cartel, Guzmán was revered as a Robin Hood in some circles; in most circles, he was just regarded as a hood.

Peña Nieto, who unlike Calderón has not made media events of the capture or killings of major cartel figures for fear it would glorify them, nonetheless trumpeted Guzmán's capture as evidence of "the effectiveness of the Mexican state, but in no way should it be a motive to fall into triumphalism." Authorities on both sides of the border are watching to see whether his arrest has in anyway disrupted the cartel's operations. When this book went to press, it was not clear which country would prosecute him first.

THE ENVIRONMENT

Mexico City's air pollution has long one of the worst of any of the world's major

Mexico

cities. Because the capital is located in a "bowl" surrounded by high mountains, with a population of 20 million and 3 million cars and trucks, there is literally no air circulation for about eight months a year.

Pemex, the state-controlled petroleum monopoly, was notorious for producing poorly refined, pollutant-laden (particularly sulfur) gasoline, but unleaded fuel has become commonplace, which has led to a dramatic improvement in air quality. An oil refinery that was believed to account for 7% of the city's pollution was closed in 1991.

The No. 1 diseases among the young are respiratory (chronic and debilitating). The response under a succession of presidential administrations was inadequate. But in recent years, factories have been closed or moved, and autos are allotted certain days of the week on which they may be operated.

The Environment Ministry issued new guidelines in 2005 aimed at providing even cleaner-burning gasoline and diesel fuel by 2008. Older cars are inspected twice a year. The result: By 2009, the national ozone limit of .11 parts per million was exceeded in Mexico City on fewer than half the days; in the 1990s, it was exceeded on nine days out of 10.

Mexico City's pollution is exacerbated by hundreds of tons of human and animal waste that is dumped untreated outside the city. It dries, and when the wind blows, it is picked up as a fine dust, further choking the air. Because of this and other pollution problems, educated and wealthy people have left the city for places such as San Luís Potosí, Querétaro and Cuernavaca.

Another environmental concern that has only recently attracted governmental attention is the alarming rate of deforestation through illegal logging. The Environment Ministry estimates that 1.3 million acres of forest are lost to illegal logging each year, even in the 133,000-acre preserve of El Rosario in the state of Michoacán, where the monarch butterflies spend the winter.

Beginning in 1994, experts began measuring how many hectares (2.2 acres) the butterflies occupied. The peak was 18 hectares in 1997, then they began tapering off alarmingly. In 2005 alone, the winter population of the butterflies was only about a fourth what it was the year before. In the winter of 2008–09, it dropped to less than two hectares, but rebounded to four in 2009–10. More than 100,000 tourists visit the monarch preserve each year.

In 2004, the ministry announced that 103 people had been arrested that year for illegal logging, triple the number of the year before, and that sophisticated surveillance had been undertaken to detect the poaching.

Until the government crackdown, the only effort to stem the logging had come from environmental activists, who often were met with violence and questionable charges brought by powerful local *caciques,* or political bosses. Perhaps the best-known group is the Peasant Ecologists of the Sierra Petatlán, in the state of Guerrero. Under national and international pressure, President Vicente Fox intervened to free two of the group's activists in 2001 after they were arrested on what were apparently trumped-up drug and weapons possession charges.

Another member of the group, Felipe Arreaga, was arrested in 2004 on questionable charges stemming from the 1998 murder of the son of a logging company owner. Domestic and international human rights and environmental groups, including Amnesty International, protested he was being framed and demanded his release. Ten months later, after a witness admitted he gave false testimony against Arreaga, he was released. He died in 2009 at age 60. In 2005, yet another of the group's leaders, Albertano Peñalosa, narrowly escaped death in an ambush that killed two of his four sons, aged 19 and 9.

The international environmental group Greenpeace estimates that 40% of the forest in the Sierra Petatlán was logged out between 1992 and 2000.

Also endangered is the Lacandón rainforest in the south, considered by ecologists to be the most biologically diverse jungle in the hemisphere after the Amazon, which also is threatened by illegal logging (see Brazil).

In a positive development, a private campaign by the U.S. group Nature Conservancy and Pronatura of Mexico raised $3 million in 2004 to purchase 370,000 acres of rain forest in Yucatán, which was added to the existing 1.8-million-acre Calakmul Biosphere Reserve. It was the largest private conservation project in Mexican history.

Mexico is believed to be home to 10 percent of all wildlife species on Earth. Four biosphere reserves in Mexico are on UNESCO's list of World Heritage Sites: Sian Ka'an in Yucatán, the whale sanctuary of El Vizcaino on the Sea of Cortéz off Baja California, 244 islands and coastal areas along the Sea of Cortéz and the monarch butterfly sanctuary in Michoacán.

Mexico made history in April 2012 by becoming the first developing nation, and only the second in the world, to pass legislation setting strict deadlines for the reduction of carbon emissions believed to affect climate change. Mexico has become the world's 11th largest emitter of greenhouse gases, about 444 million metric tons a year of CO_2 alone, but under existing U.N. guidelines was not yet required to

take this action. It passed the Chamber of Deputies overwhelmingly and the Senate unanimously, which was phenomenal given the gridlock that had characterized the fragmented Congress since the 2009 midterm elections. President Calderón signed it into law on June 7. "This law adds to the efforts that have positioned Mexico as an international leader in environmental protection," Calderon wrote in a Twitter post. Under the terms of the law, Mexico is supposed to reduce carbon emissions by 30% from existing levels by 2020 and by 50% by 2050. It also is to generate 35% of its energy with non-fossil fuels by 2024. It also creates a National Institute of Ecology and Climate Change.

ARMED REBELLIONS

For all its corruption and political violence, Mexico had not experienced actual armed insurrection since the Revolution. Thus, the country was shocked on New Year's Day 1994 when an organized band of rebels calling itself the *Zapatista* National Liberation Army (*EZLN*) launched a bloody offensive against federal institutions in Chiapas state. The group proclaimed itself the champion of the poor southern peasants, most of them full-blooded Indians, much like the revolutionary hero Emiliano Zapata after whom it is named.

Disputes between the wealthy ranchers and the impoverished masses had been festering in Chiapas for 175 years. The *EZLN*, whose strength was variously estimated at 200 to 2,000, denounced alleged electoral fraud by which the *PRI* had won the governorship of Chiapas. The army was sent in and for 10 days there was some skirmishing in which about 145 people were killed on both sides. Then the government and the rebels agreed to negotiate.

What followed was a media circus. The *EZLN* leader who emerged as its negotiator went by the *nom de guerre* "Subcomandante Marcos," who always appeared in ski mask and with bandoliers containing ammunition incompatible with the shotgun he brandished. This "guerrilla" subsequently was identified as Rafael Sebastián Guillén, son of a wealthy Caucasian family in Tampico in far-off northern Mexico and a former *Sandinista* activist. The unmasking of Subcomandante Marcos largely undermined the credibility of the *EZLN*.

Nonetheless, the *Zapatistas* made up in media savvy what they lacked in military expertise and proved to be skilled in public relations. At first, they aroused sympathy, but support waned in 1995 after the government engaged in a public relations counteroffensive that blamed the rebels for frightening off foreign investments, thus contributing to the crippling recession. For the most part, the *EZLN* has engaged in what one political scientist wryly labeled "guerrilla theater."

Not so with a second group that burst on the scene—also in the south—in 1996. On June 28, peasants in Guerrero state held a memorial service to commemorate the first anniversary of the massacre of 17 peasants by Guerrero police. Dozens of hooded men and women showed up at the service, calling themselves the Popular Revolutionary Army (*ERP*). Unlike the *EZLN*, this group appeared to be well armed with AK-47s and clad more like serious guerrillas, with boots instead of sandals, for example.

Alarmed, President Zedillo dispatched thousands of troops to Guerrero, angering local officials who said the president was "militarizing" the state. Like Chiapas, Guerrero is sharply divided between extreme wealth (Acapulco and other posh Pacific resorts are in Guerrero) and abject poverty. It was the site of a minor insurgency in the 1960s and 1970s, led by the legendary, Robin Hood-like outlaw, Lucio Cabañas, who eventually was slain by security forces in 1974. The Organization of American States sent a team of human rights workers to investigate charges of rights abuses in the state.

That August, the *ERP* stunned the country with a series of well-coordinated attacks against military garrisons and police stations, not only in Guerrero but in Chiapas and Oaxaca as well. They killed at least 18 people, including two civilians.

Since its first spectacular strikes, the *ERP* seemed to fade into the background. Unlike the *EZLN*, the *ERP* has called for the violent overthrow of the government and showed no appetite for negotiation. Also unlike the *EZLN*, it has failed to win public support, judging from opinion polls. Subcomandante Marcos himself distanced the *EZLN* from the new group, saying, "You fight for power. We fight for democracy, liberty and justice."

In February 1996, the government and the *EZLN* reached a tentative agreement in the town of San Andrés de Larráinzar, called the San Andrés accords, that would grant the Indians in the south greater autonomy from the institutionalized state and local governments, almost all of them controlled by the *PRI*. The *Zapatistas* broke off from talks the following September, alleging the government was dragging its feet in implementing the accords. For 15 months the talks were in limbo; it took a shocking tragedy to get things moving again.

The Acteal Massacre

On December 22, 1997, about 70 armed members of a *PRI*-affiliated paramilitary group in Chiapas entered the village of Acteal, about 12 miles north of San Cristóbal de las Casas. Without provocation, they shot anyone who presented a target—men, women, children, even infants in their mothers' arms. People were gunned down as they desperately attempted to flee, others as they huddled in a church, an atrocity reminiscent of My Lai during the Vietnam War or the "ethnic cleansing" in the Balkans. When the firing stopped, 45 Indian peasants had been slain, all but nine of them women or children; four of the women were pregnant. At least 25 others were wounded.

The massacre made international headlines and presented Zedillo with a public relations nightmare. With considerable understatement, the president denounced the massacre as a "cruel, absurd criminal act." In a clumsy effort at damage control, "investigators" from Mexico City hurried to Acteal and initially offered the lame explanation that the massacre had been motivated by a local family feud.

There was a time, before the emergence of viable opposition parties and press reforms, that the *PRI*'s version would have been accepted. Mexico's independent media and foreign journalists, however, interviewed survivors and reported that the gunmen, armed with AK-47s and dressed in blue uniforms, were members of a *PRI* paramilitary group from a neighboring village. One survivor said the gunmen fired in the direction of crying children. Eventually, more than 30 men either were arrested, including a *PRI* mayor, or surrendered. Like the victims, the killers were Indians. The motive for the killings, they explained, was that the villagers were *Zapatista* sympathizers—including, presumably, the slain infants and fetuses.

The opposition *PRD* demanded the resignations of Interior Minister Emilio Chuayffet and the *PRI* governor of Chiapas, Julio César Ruíz Ferro. Zedillo soon sacrificed his No. 2 man on the altar of public opinion and replaced him with Francisco Labastida. Ruíz Ferro yielded to public pressure and resigned.

According to subsequent press reports, such killings of peasants by *PRI*-linked paramilitaries had occurred regularly on a smaller scale in Chiapas, but the Acteal massacre shocked the nation and the world and forced Zedillo to take action. Among other things, he pledged to reduce the army presence in Chiapas (the army was suspected of providing sophisticated weapons to the paramilitaries) and to crack down on paramilitary groups. Most importantly, he introduced sweeping constitutional reforms to Congress in an effort to jump-start the San Andrés accords. His proposal would have recognized the rights of Mexico's 9 million indigenous people and permit them greater autonomy.

As a bizarre postscript, the Acteal massacre returned after 15 years to haunt Zedillo, who in 2012 was teaching at Yale University. A group of anonymous Indians sued him in Connecticut state court for civil damages, but the U.S. government granted him immunity.

The rebels denounced the initiative as providing "the peace of tombs." Moreover, some lawmakers in the *PRI* and the *PAN* opposed the proposal as giving in too much to the rebels, while the *PRD* faulted it for not going far enough. To be enacted, the proposal would have to receive a two-thirds vote of Congress and ratification of 16 of the 31 state legislatures, a goal that seemed all but unattainable. If it failed, of course, Zedillo at least could say, "Well, I tried."

Apparently, he didn't try hard enough. A clash between army troops and a resurgent *EPR* in Guerrero in May 1998 left 11 civilians dead. Three days later, in Chiapas, there occurred the worst violence since the so-called peace process began. The *EZLN* ambushed a combined army-police patrol and in the ensuing clash eight rebels and one policeman were killed.

Negotiations and the 'Zapatour'

Soon thereafter, Mary Robinson, the U.N. commissioner for human rights, rebuked the Mexican government for its alleged rights abuses in Chiapas. U.N. Secretary-General Kofi Annan touched off a diplomatic furor when he suggested the United Nations should play a role in the peace process. Mexico swiftly and vigorously denounced any outside interference. Annan quickly backed off, but visited Mexico to meet with Zedillo and Mexican human rights groups. Although Chiapas was not on the formal agenda, the two leaders discussed it at length. In the end, Annan said the government should exert more effort, but he also urged the rebels to return to the negotiating table, invoking the chiché, "It takes two to tango."

It appeared the "tango" might resume in November 1998 when 29 *Zapatista* delegates showed up in their trademark ski masks for a government-initiated meeting in San Cristóbal de las Casas; Marcos was not among them. The government delegation included six congressmen from all three major parties. The rebels soon dashed any hopes the talks might resume in earnest. They accused the congressmen of being "racists" and refused to return to the bargaining table until the government met the five demands that led to the collapse of the talks two years earlier, including release of *EZLN* prisoners, demo-

Mexico

The Cathedral of Real de Catorce in San Luis Potosí state; once one of the world's greatest producers of silver, now a monument

cratic reforms, disbanding of paramilitary groups and demilitarization of much of southern Mexico.

In April 1999, a potentially explosive incident ended peacefully. About 1,000 unarmed *Zapatistas* came down from the hills and "reoccupied" the city hall in San Andrés de Larrainzar, site of the first talks. The 150 outnumbered state policemen wisely fell back without opening fire. A few days later, 300 state policemen ex-

pelled the few remaining *Zapatistas* without violence or arrests.

For his part, Marcos finally came out of hiding in May 1999 for the first time in 18 months, attending a meeting in the Chiapas village of La Realidad.

The peace process remained moribund until after the 2000 presidential election, and it took the election of the conservative *PAN* candidate, Vicente Fox, followed a month later by the election of *PRD* can-

didate Pedro Salazar for governor of Chiapas, to get it moving again. Fox's first official act after being inaugurated was to fulfill a campaign pledge to order the withdrawal of army troops from Chiapas as a sign of good faith. Fox also introduced a constitutional amendment to Congress in December that would accede to one of the *Zapatistas'* demands, to grant greater autonomy to Mexico's indigenous citizens. With the detested *PRI* out of power both in Mexico City and in Chiapas, and a president in power who seemed serious about peace, the ball was then in Marcos' court. He was now dealing with a president who was at least as astute a public relations practitioner as himself.

What occurred next was typical of Marcos' theatrics, and it garnered worldwide media attention. The *Zapatistas* staged a "caravan" to the capital in March 2001, which the media quickly labeled the "*Zapatour.*" Their stated goal was to lobby Congress directly for the indigenous rights bill. Traveling in trucks and buses, and leaving their weapons at home, Marcos and 23 other *EZLN* members and their entourage traveled through 12 states, receiving tumultuous welcomes from the impoverished Indians along the way, before arriving in the capital. They asked permission to lobby the Chamber of Deputies. Fox agreed, although legislators of his own party adamantly opposed the idea.

The *Zapatistas* remained in the capital for 18 days before they received the invitation to address the lower house. The *EZLN* leaders delivered not strident demands, but respectful requests to the country's lawmakers during a meeting of several hours that was broadcast on national television; the always unpredictable Marcos did not appear. The army, meanwhile, dismantled its last bases in Chiapas.

Congress then debated the indigenous rights bill in earnest. The original bill was based on the accords reached by the *EZLN* and the government in 1996 in San Andrés de Larrainzar. But *PRI* legislators grumbled that the bill infringed on the traditional authority of state governors, while *Panistas* complained it conceded too much to the *Zapatistas.* The Senate unanimously approved an amended version, and the Chamber of Deputies passed it, 386–60. This time the opposition came from the *PRD* and the *PT* on the left, because of language that stressed the preeminence of national sovereignty over indigenous rights. The *EZLN* also opposed the watered-down version because it eliminated the guarantee of rights over land, water and mineral resources.

In July 2001, Michoacán became the 16th state to ratify the amendment. It took effect on August 15, with the *EZLN* still

Famous Zócolo Square, the heart of Mexico City

complaining about "betrayal." The law was challenged, but the Supreme Court ruled 8–3 that it lacked jurisdiction over constitutional amendments.

The world heard little more from the *Zapatistas* until 2005, when Marcos declared a "red alert" and ordered *Zapatista* fighters to assemble in their bases. They announced they would create a new political movement, composed of peasant Indians, laborers and students, and they would begin participating in the mainstream political system.

In 2006, Marcos resurfaced and announced his latest public relations-gimmick: a six-month motorbike tour of Mexico all the way to the U.S. border to coincide with the Mexican presidential campaign. (He quickly abandoned his bike for a car). He addressed a rally of thousands in San Cristóbal de las Casas, where he said the *Zapatista* movement was part of a ground-swell of indigenous political muscle in Latin America. However, the *Zapatistas* declined to participate in the election. Instead, Marcos condemned all the major candidates, and called the *PRD*'s Andrés Manuel López Obrador a "traitor." But there has been no new violence under

the new president, Felipe Calderón of the *PAN*.

Marcos disappeared again for two years, resurfacing again in 2008 to complain that the *Zapatista* movement had "gone out of style" and said he would stop making appearances. Yet, he turned up again in San Cristobal de las Casas on January 15, 2009, to commemorate the 15th anniversary of the 1994 uprising with a four-day conference at which he criticized Calderón's war on drugs and predicted supporters of President Barack Obama would be disappointed with his foreign policy. Still media savvy, he periodically appears in interviews on YouTube.

President Calderón next found himself faced with a resurgent *ERP*. In September 2007, the group took responsibility for six bombings of oil and gas pipelines in the state of Veracrúz, which caused massive disruptions in supply and temporarily closed 1,500 factories. Calderón dispatched 5,000 troops. In 2008, the *ERP* offered to call a cease-fire in return for establishing a commission to investigate its supposed grievances against the government. Calderón refused, and the *ERP* quietly faded away—supposedly.

CULTURE: Appropriately symbolizing Mexico's ethnic composition is a park in Mexico City called *La Plaza de las Tres Culturas*. In Mexico as much as anywhere in the New World, the blending of the Spanish and Indian produced a third, separate race, the *mestizo*, which predominates today. There are 26 historical UNESCO World Heritage Sites in Mexico, representing both the Hispanic and pre-Hispanic cultures. Among the most famous are the Aztec city of Teotihuacán, with its huge pyramids to the sun and moon; the Mayan cities of Chichén Itzá, Uxmal and Palenque; and the colonial centers of Mexico City, Guadalajara, Guanajuato and Zacatecas.

The giant of Spanish America in more ways than population size, Mexico had a rich cultural heritage centuries before the Spanish Conquest. The Aztec, Mayan, Toltec, Mixtec and other indigenous civilizations all have contributed much to Mexican folklore. Just as the mixing of bloods created a new race, so did the infusion of Spanish art, music, literature, food, and architecture, give rise to a new, discrete culture.

Mexico boasts no fewer than 27 precolonial and colonial sites, many of them

Mexico

National University of Mexico Library

still inhabited while others are ruins, on UNESCO's list of 725 World Heritage Sites.

Secular education was virtually nonexistent during the colonial era; what little education was offered was provided by the church. The opposite has been true under the anti-clerical 1917 constitution, which secularized education. Today Mexico boasts about 370 colleges and universities. The oldest, largest and most prestigious is the National Autonomous University of Mexico (UNAM), founded in 1551 as the Royal and Pontifical University of Mexico.

Literature

After independence, cultural development was slow owing to political instability, the crippling civil war between Liberals and Conservatives from 1857–61, the subsequent French intervention and general inattention to public education. Despite the Porfirio Díaz dictatorship rather than because of it, the late 19th and early 20th centuries were marked by the emergence of a distinctly Mexican literature. The most prominent writers of this period were **Amado Nervo, Ramón López Velarde and Manuel Gutiérrez Nájera.**

The demarcation line of Mexican culture, however, was the Revolution of 1910–20. Besides forever changing the political fabric of the country, the Revolution gave birth to a movement in realist art, appropriately called "revolutionary art," music and literature. Two classic revolutionary novels are **Mariano Azuela's** Los de abajo (1916), and **Martín Luís** Guzmán's El aguila y la serpiente ("The Eagle and the Serpent," 1928), both of which focus on social issues. The poetry of **Alfonso Reyes, José Gorostiza and Jaime Torres Bodet** and the novels of **Agustín Yáñez** also are identified with the post-revolutionary period.

Mexico's best-known novelists of the second half of the 20th century were **Juan Rulfo** (1917–86) and **Carlos Fuentes** (1928–2012). Rulfo is best remembered for El llano en llamas (1953), a collection of short stories, and the novel Pedro Páramo (1955). He is considered one of the most influential Latin American writers of the 20th century, inspiring, among others, Colombia's Nobel Laureate Gabriel García Márquez. Rulfo also was an accomplished photographer and screenwriter.

Fuentes, the son of diplomats who became a diplomat himself, also became renowned throughout Latin America and the world. His best-known works that received acclaim abroad include La region más transparente (Where the Air is Clear) in 1957, La muerte de Artemio Cruz (The Death of Artemio Cruz) in 1962 and Terra nostra in 1975. His best-known novel outside Mexico was Gringo Viejo (Old Gringo) in 1985, inspired by American writer Ambrose Bierce's disappearance in Mexico in 1914. The translation became the first best-seller

José Clemente Orozco's portrayal of Mexican hero Benito Juarez

by a Mexican author in the United States and was adapted into a movie in 1989 with Gregory Peck and Jane Fonda. Fuentes received Spain's prestigious Miguel de Cervantes Prize for Spanish-language literature in 1989 and was a perennial candidate for the Nobel, but never received it.

The acknowledged master of the short story was **Juan José Arreola** (1921–2001), a friend of Rulfo's, who developed a half-prose, half-poetry genre called *varia invención*, after the title of one of his stories. He published 16 books of stories, including *Constabulario* (1952), *Punta de Plata* (1958) and *Bestiario* (1972) as well as the highly acclaimed 1963 novel, *La feria.*

But the titan of modern Mexican literature was the poet and essayist **Octavio Paz** (1914–98), who received the Nobel Prize in 1990, the fifth Latin American to receive the garland, and the Cervantes Prize in 1981. His best known works include *El laberinto de la soledad (The Labyrinth of Solitude)* in 1945 and *Piedra de sol (Sunstone)* in 1957. The Nobel Committee cited him "for impassioned writing with wide horizons, characterized by sensuous intelligence and humanistic integrity." His verse was a critical, brutally honest examination of Mexico's hybrid Spanish-Indian culture, which alienated him from many of his leftist intellectual contemporaries. Yet, when he died at age 84 in 1998, his former detractors heaped praise on him, and the government accorded him a state funeral.

Three other Mexican writers have received the Cervantes Prize. The novelist **Sergio Pitol** (b. 1933), author *of Vals de Mefisto (The Dance of Mephisto)* in 1984,

the semi-autobiographical *El arte de la fuga (The Art of Flight)* in 1996 and *El mago de Viena (The Magician of Vienna)* in 2005, received it in 2005. In 2009, it went to novelist, poet and short story writer **José Emilio Pacheco** (b. 1939). The prolific Pacheco also received Spain's Federico García Lorca Prize, among other national and international awards. The French-born nonfiction writer **Elena Poniatowska** (b. 1932) best known for *La noche de Tlatelolco* (tr. *Massacre in Mexico*) in 1971, about the infamous 1968 massacre of anti-government protesters, received the prize in 2013. She is also known for her journalistic work focusing on the plight of women and the poor, and is considered the *"grande dame"* of Mexican letters.

Mexico also lays partial claim to the Colombian-born Nobel Laureate **Gabriel García Márquez** (1927-2014), who spent many of his productive years in Mexico, as well as in Colombia, France and Cuba. Besides novels, he wrote screenplays and non-fiction for newspapers and magazines. He spent the last years of his life in Mexico City, dying there on April 27, 2014. His ashes were to be divided between Mexico and Colombia.

Art and Music

The premier figures of post-revolutionary art were **Diego Rivera** (1886–1957), **José Clemente Orozco** (1883–1949) and **David Alfaro Siquieros** (1896–1974), whose heroic murals epitomize the social struggle of the Revolution. Rivera and Orozco also were at home in the *avant-garde* art crowd of 1920s Paris, and were

friends of Pablo Picasso, the influence of whose abstractionism can be detected in their paintings. Siquieros, a combat veteran of the Revolution, lived and painted for a time in Los Angeles, and fought on the Republican side during the Spanish Civil War.

One of Rivera's four wives, **Frida Kahlo** (1907–54), carved out an international reputation as an artist in her own right and has posthumously become a feminist cultural icon in Europe and the United States. She was the subject of a 2002 U.S. motion picture, *Frida,* starring Mexican actress Salma Hayek (see next page).

Probably Mexico's best-known artist today is the painter and sculptor **Francisco Toledo,** famed for his erotic shaman-based figures.

In photography, the premier figure was the internationally renowned **Manuel Álvarez Bravo** (1902–2002), whose photos ranged from street scenes to nude women.

Mexican music of the post-revolutionary period was dominated by **Carlos Chávez** (1899–1978), who founded the national symphony orchestra in 1928 and whose classical compositions were drawn from Mexico's Indian heritage.

Popular music is characterized both by the *ranchera* style, a guitar-based sound that celebrates Mexico's *vaqueros,* (cowboys), through *corridos,* or ballads, and the quintessentially Mexican *mariachis.* Mexico has long had a thriving popular music industry, one that blends the sounds of traditional Mexican music with the internationalized Latino sounds of the Caribbean and U.S. rock and rap. Mexican singers have achieved renown throughout Latin

Mexico

Frida Kahlo in 1932, sitting beneath her self-portrait

One of Mexico's leading pop icons is **Gloria Trevi** (b. 1968), the so-called "Madonna of Mexico," who has sold more than 20 million records. However, she has been more like the Michael Jackson of Mexico. For five years, she and her lover-manager were the focus of a tawdry international investigation of alleged kidnapping and raping of underage girls. She was jailed in Brazil (where she mysteriously became pregnant and gave birth) and extradited to Mexico, where she was finally acquitted by a judge in 2004 in a court proceeding broadcast on national television. It generated much the same excitement as Michael Jackson's molestation trial and acquittal in the United States. She was 36 at the time of the acquittal and resumed her singing career. Her most recent album was *Me Río de Tí* (I laugh at you) in 2011.

A relatively new Mexican band, called **RBD,** has an enthusiastic following throughout Latin America and the Mexican community in the United States.

An interesting trend since the 1990s has been the singers specializing in the so-called *"narco-corridos,"* inspired by the drug-related violence along the border. In 2007, 13 such singers were murdered, apparently by the drug cartels, including Sergio Gómez and Valentín Elizalde.

Theater and Cinema

Mexico City has a robust theatrical community, though the works of its playwrights to date have been primarily for domestic consumption.

Mexican cinema, on the other hand, developed parallel with that of the United States, and Mexican films have been exported for several decades. Many Mexican film stars went on to successful careers in Hollywood, such as Dolores del Río, Ramón Navarro, Anthony Quinn and Ricardo Montalbán.

Arguably, Mexico's most revered film legend was **María Félix** (1914–2002), perhaps because she eschewed moving to Hollywood and devoted her career to her native country. Known as the "Marilyn Monroe of Mexico," she made 47 films between 1942 and 1970 and was a national icon. Her death in April 2002 brought thousands of mourners to the Palacio de Bellas Artes in Mexico City; President Vicente Fox extolled her as "a great shrine to our country."

The first Mexican film to be nominated for the U.S. Academy Award for Best Foreign Film was *Macario*, in 1960. Since then, seven others have been nominated, although none has won: *Ánimas trujanos (The Important Man)*, 1961; *Tlayucan*, 1962; *Actas de Marusia (Letters from Marusia)*, 1975; *Amores perros*, 2000; *El crimen del Padre Amarro (The Crime of Father Amarro),*

Diego Rivera

2002; *El laberinto del fauno (Pan's Labyrinth),* 2006; and *Biutiful,* 2010.

Amores perros, loosely meaning love is a bitch, directed by **Alejandro González Iñárritu,** is a dark tale linking the lives of three separate people involved in a car accident. *El crimen de Padre Amaro (The Crime of Father Amaro)*, directed by **Carlos Carrera,** is a highly controversial film about sexual abuse in the Catholic Church. Adapted from a Portuguese novel, it is the story of a priest who seduces a 16-year-old girl.

Another box office hit in Mexico and abroad was *Y tu mamá también (And Your Mama, Too.)* directed by **Alfonso Cuarón.**

González Iñárritu (b. 1963), who specializes in Gothic themes, has attained particular international acclaim in the United States and Europe. After *Amores perros,* he directed two more films, both in the United States, in his so-called "Death Trilogy:" *21 Grams* (2003), starring Sean Penn and Benicio del Toro; and *Babel* (2006), starring Brad Pitt and Cate Blanchett. *Babel* won González Iñárritu the Best Director award at the Cannes Film Festival and a nomination for the U.S. Academy Award for Best Director. His 2010 film, *Biutiful,* set in Barcelona and starring Spanish actor Javier Bardém, was nominated for both the Oscar for Best Foreign Film and for the *Palme d'Or* in Cannes.

Cuarón (b. 1961) won the Oscar for Best Director in 2014 for the U.S. movie *Gravity,* starring Sandra Bullock and George Clooney.

Cinema also has been boosted by a new generation of actors, some of whom have also made their marks in Hollywood and

America and in the United States. Hailed as *"El Rey de Ranchera"* is **Vicente Fernández** (b. 1940), who has recorded more than 50 albums and won one Grammy Award and seven Latin Grammys.

Mexicans had won 131 Latin Grammy Awards through 2012, more than any other country. A current sensation is the soft-rock band **Camila,** which in 2010 won Latin Grammys for Song of the Year and Record of the Year for *Mientes* (you lie), and for Best Pop Vocal Album for *Dejarte de Amar* (leaving you to love), which included *Mientes.*

The brother-sister duo **Jesse & Joy,** formed in 2005 by Jesse and Tirza Joy Huerta, won the Latin Grammy as Best New Artist in 2007. In 2012, they received four Latin Grammy nominations and won three. Their album *Con Quién Se Queda El Perro?* was nominated for Best Album and won for Best Contemporary Pop Album. Their song, *Corre!,* won Song of the Year and Record of the Year.

The trio **3Ball MTY,** formed in 2009, won the Latin Grammy for Best New Artist in 2012.

The rock-rap band **Molotov,** which includes the internationally acclaimed guitarist **Tito Fuentes,** has won four Latin Grammys and four MTV Awards. It has stirred controversy because its lyrics are often political and profane.

Europe. One is **Salma Hayek,** nominated for an Academy Award in 2003 for her title role in the U.S. movie *Frida,* based on the life of artist Frida Kahlo; she received Germany's Golden Camera Award as Best International Actress for *Frida.* Another is **Gael García Bernal,** who starred in *Amores perros, Y tu mamá tambien* and *Padre Amaro.* Both have become international sex symbols; in fact, the media have nicknamed García "Sex-Mex." García's co-star in *Y tu mamá también,* **Diego Luna,** later appeared in *Frida* and co-starred with Robert Duval and Kevin Costner in *Open Range.*

Thanks to generous government grants and tax incentives, the number of Mexican film titles tripled from 2000 to 2010, and the country now produces about 70 titles a year, about 40% of the total distributed. Mexico has the world's fifth highest cinema attendance, and it has 4,500 screens, twice as many as Brazil, but U.S. films still account for 95% of box office receipts.

Mass Communication

Mexico's television industry has been characterized by a mix of public-private cooperation. The privately owned *Televisa* network is today one of the world's largest, and Mexican programs, chiefly *telenovelas,* are the most popular in Latin America. By the mid-1990s, a new privately owned channel, *TV Azteca,* made inroads with daring new *telenovelas* that dealt frankly with formerly taboo subjects, such as women's sexuality and official corruption. Some programs began eclipsing *Televisa*'s in the ratings. A new law promulgated by President Enrique Peña Nieto in 2013 broke up this "biopoly" to diversify the number of channels.

The Mexican press is nominally independent, but for more than 60 years the Mexican government controlled the supply of newsprint through a subsidized public entity called *Pipsa.* This allowed the *PRI* to wield a powerful cudgel against overly critical newspapers, which often would find their supply of paper cut off. Meaningful reform came with the Salinas administration of 1988–94, but intimidation of the press continues.

About 30 dailies are published in the capital. The paper once regarded as the most prestigious was *Excélsior,* a cooperative owned by its employees, but in recent years its ties to the *PRI* have hurt the paper's credibility and its bottom line. The workers voted in June 2002 to sell the paper because of declining revenues—and lost wages. Newspapers with greater circulation and with better reputations of independence and aggressive reporting today are *El Universal* and *Reforma.*

Mexico has a more vigorous provincial press than do most Latin American countries; in fact, it is these smaller papers in the interior that frequently are the targets of violence by drug traffickers or corrupt local politicians or police officials who themselves have been targeted by aggressive reporters. Probably the most prestigious of these provincial papers is *El Norte* of Monterrey, owned by *Reforma.*

Mexico also has a sizable magazine industry, producing slick, high-quality, full-color magazines comparable with those in the United States or Europe. Probably the magazine most read abroad is the left-of-center *Proceso,* launched by Julio Scherer García in 1976 after the thin-skinned President Echeverría forced him from the editorship of *Excélsior* for his critical reporting and editorials.

The new role of the Mexican media in exposing corruption cannot be understated. Many, if not most, of the allegations of wrongdoing stem from journalistic rather than official investigations. In the 1980s, this would have been unheard of. The government used the newsprint monopoly as a carrot and stick to keep the print media in line.

The founder of the television giant *Televisa* in 1973, **Emilio Azcárraga Vidaurreta** (1895-1973), was a loyal *PRI* partisan, as was his son and successor, **Emilio Azcárraga Milmo** (1930-97) and his son and successor, **Emilio Azcárraga Jean** (b. 1968). The termination of the newsprint monopoly and the diversification of television with the new network, *TV Azteca,* with the resulting increase in aggressive, investigative journalism, was as significant a factor in curtailing the power of the once omnipotent *PRI* as was the rising electoral strength of the opposition parties. In fact, some have viewed the two parallel developments as a chicken-and-egg analogy—which led to what?

Unfortunately, investigative journalism in Mexico remains a notoriously high-risk endeavor. Journalists investigating links between drug traffickers and public officials have been murdered or intimidated at an alarming rate since 1997, and by 2004 the number of journalists killed in Mexico was the fourth-highest in the world, exceeding the number in Colombia for the first time. By 2007, it had become the second-deadliest country for journalists in the world after Iraq (see Other Current Issues—Drugs). It was still the fourth deadliest in 2010, after Iraq, Afghanistan and the Philippines, and in 2012, after Syria, Somalia and Pakistan. Eleven journalists were murdered in 2011 and 2012, some in gruesome fashion, and more and more news organs were cowed into practicing self-censorship. The situation is now so dangerous for journalists that Freedom House downgraded the Mexican press in 2011 from "partly free" to "not free;" it remained so in 2012 and 2013. Cuba, Venezuela, Honduras and Ecuador are the only other Latin American countries in that category.

This is not to say that all Mexican journalists are martyrs and saints. For decades, government officials and *PRI* leaders routinely paid bribes to low-paid reporters to ensure favorable news coverage, or—even better—no news coverage. This tawdry practice was greatly reduced with the election of opposition governors and an opposition president in 2000, but they resurfaced in the 2012 presidential campaign when the *PRI* candidate, Enrique Peña Nieto, received obviously biased coverage from *Televisa,* which sparked student protests.

In addition, it must be conceded that too many Mexican journalists are overly subjective in their reporting and are not above slanting or even distorting the facts to make a story fit into that medium's particular agenda. Still, the fearless reporting of such Mexico City newspapers as *Reforma* and *El Universal,* as well as that of numerous feisty newspapers and magazines along the U.S. border, is a refreshing change from the old days when almost all the press was either cowed or bought, and it has sent many a corrupt official scurrying for cover like cockroaches from a bright light.

ECONOMY: The Mexican economy is divided into three major sectors: agriculture (20%), industry (30%) and services (50%), a pattern generally associated with advanced nations.

The industrial sector, formerly centered around Mexico City and Monterrey, now is more clustered generally throughout the north, based on factories, called *maquiladoras,* that assemble finished products for export; most are owned by U.S. companies, though joint ventures have become more common. Consequently, the standard of living is significantly higher in the north than in the still-impoverished south.

The quasi-socialist nature of the economy during the seven decades of domination of the *PRI,* and especially after the expropriation of foreign-owned oil companies in 1938, hung a "not welcome" sign for foreign investors. For decades, foreign nationals or businesses could own only a 49% share of real estate or a business. After the 1960s, government participation in industry increased under the *PRI,* which viewed this as a means of extending party power, but was accompanied by inefficiency and corruption.

In the 1990s, this was reversed under former President Salinas. By 1993, more than 363 state-owned companies had been sold or shut down, bringing the government (and *PRI*) more than $22 billion.

Mexico

The *maquiladora* movement greatly stimulated national development, at least in the north. Mexico's hourly wage was less than half that of the United States, and the workforce was literate. The lure of assembling finished goods just across the border at bargain-basement prices was irresistible to U.S. corporations. Of course, it was anathema to organized labor in the United States. The *maquiladoras* led to a veritable boom along the border, and stimulated growth of a middle class. (By 2000, *maquiladoras* accounted for about 48% of Mexico's exports, compared with 10% for oil exports).

The North American Free Trade Agreement (NAFTA) of 1994 accelerated the boom and unquestionably helped the country emerge from the disastrous peso devaluation that year. By 2003, however, Mexico had lost more than 300 companies to China. The NAFTA-generated boom in the north shrank the unemployment rate, from 5.5% in 1996, to 2.3% in 2000, the lowest (officially) in Latin America.

In 1994, in the wake of democratic reforms and the opening up of the economy, Mexico became the first Latin American country to be admitted to the Organization for Economic Cooperation and Development (OECD), a group of the world's richest democracies.

Petroleum remains the only major government monopoly, but it was a hotbed of *PRI* labor and management corruption. For a time there was talk of privatizing *Pemex,* which controls production from the wellhead to distribution at the gasoline station, but public opinion was so vehemently opposed to it that not even the conservative, pro-business governments of Vicente Fox or Felipe Calderón pursued it. *Pemex* still accounts for about 40% of the federal government's revenue.

In the 1980s, *Pemex* departed from production of sulphur-laden, sub-quality gasoline to include unleaded gasoline, called *Magna,* which meets U.S. standards in order to accommodate a burgeoning tourist trade.

Pemex currently is faced with the need to invest in discovery and deep-sea drilling as its existing fields become depleted. Production in 2004 was 3.59 million barrels per day, but as expected, this dropped to 3.42 million in 2007. In 2009, it was only 2.6 million. Mexico remains the world's sixth-largest exporter of crude oil, although it lacks sufficient refining capacity to meet more than 60% of its fuel needs. Current reserves were estimated at only 10.4 billion barrels in 2011, compared with 28 billion in 1999. *Pemex* lacks deep-sea recovery technology, but contracting with foreign oil firms, even if it means keeping Mexico an exporter rather than an importer, is a political taboo in Mexico. If production continues to decline at the current rate, Mexico will become an oil importer by 2017.

Mexico is the world's 16th leading producer of natural gas, at 57 billion cubic meters (2 trillion cubic feet) in 2010. It has proven reserves of 338.8 billion cubic meters (12 trillion cubic feet). It exported 200 million cubic meters (706.2 bcf) in 2010.

President Calderón introduced an energy-reform package in April 2008 that would open up *Pemex* to private investors for deep-sea exploration and refining. Despite fierce opposition from the left, Congress approved it a few months later (see History).

Tourism has long been a major economic pillar, and currently the fifth-largest source of revenue. Various resorts offer complete package vacations to winter-weary neighbors to the north seeking the warm sun. The popularity of these soared in the late 1980s and 1990s as the peso plummeted in value against the dollar. Tourism suffered briefly from the September 11, 2001, terrorist attacks; it has also suffered from drug-related violence along the border and by a new requirement begun in 2005 that Americans have passports to travel to and from Canada, Mexico, and several Caribbean countries.

According to the World Tourism Organization, Mexico was the world's seventh most popular destination in 2007, with 21.4 million visitors from abroad. It increased to 22.6 million in 2008, although dropping to ninth place. With the recession of 2008–09, drug violence and an outbreak of swine flu in 2009, it suffered a 5% drop in 2009, to 21.45 million visitors, 10th place in the world. Foreign exchange from tourism plunged correspondingly by 15% from 2008 to 2009, from $13.3 billion to 12.3 billion. Despite the worsening violence and U.S. State Department travel advisories, tourism jumped back up to 22.4 million visitors in 2010, a 4.2% increase, representing $15 billion.

President Calderón went personally to Las Vegas, Nevada, in May 2011 to address the Global Travel and Tourism Summit, where he assured travel company executives that "almost zero" tourists had been victims of the violence and said $4 billion had been invested in 2011 by foreign travel firms. His pitch must have worked, because the government reported a record 22.7 million foreign tourists for 2011, a 2% increase; the U.N. World Tourism Organization put it at 23.4 million, still 10th place in the world. Domestic tourism also increased.

But foreign tourist arrivals declined by 1.2% in 2012, to 23.1 million, according to the WTO, dropping Mexico to 13th place. The decrease was blamed on reduced border tourism owing to the violence and a reduction in the number of cruise ship dockings. Tourist revenue also fell in 2012 to $12.7 billion, still 7.2% of GDP and 24th largest in the world. Then tourist arrivals jumped in 2013 to 23.7 million.

Agriculture is limited by a lack of arable land and division of what there is into small parcels. The official policy of the government after the Revolution favored redistribution of land, much of it into communal plots called *ejidos,* but the program moved forward at a glacial pace. In 2006, agriculture accounted for only 4% of GDP, and Mexico remains a net food importer.

In 1993, Mexico's economy appeared to be blooming, but it was an illusion caused by increased U.S investment in anticipation of the results of the NAFTA treaty. Mexico printed more pesos, and foreign investors in Mexican bonds demanded more and more interest, as high as 33% per annum to compensate for what they decided was greater risk.

The break came in December 1994, when the peso was devalued by 20% and then allowed to "float" four days later, which led to its decline of 50% by early 1995. The stock and bond markets panicked, contributing to the decline of the peso. The IMF revealed that before the devaluation, individuals and institutions quietly moved $6.7 billion out of Mexico.

President Clinton proposed massive bailout loans to Mexico totaling $13.5 billion, which he got despite widespread opposition in Congress. More than 16,000 businesses ceased operation and more than 2 million Mexicans lost their jobs in 1995. Banks foreclosed on mortgages and repossessed autos at a record rate; more than 12% of bank loans were in default (the rate was about 1.2% in the U.S.).

The loans were guaranteed by the Mexican equivalent of the Federal Deposit Insurance Corporation, known as *Fobaproa.* An organization of creditors, *El Barzón,* correctly charged that the aid being received by Mexico was being used to help depositors, not debtors. *Fobaproa* became the focus of a major political scandal in 1998 when it was learned that many of the failed banks had made risky loans to *PRI* political cronies (see History).

In 1997, amid much media hype, Mexico repaid the last installment of the $13.5 billion loan Clinton had authorized, two years ahead of schedule. What Mexico downplayed was the fact that the loan was repaid by borrowing the necessary amount from European sources.

After the 1994–95 crisis, the economy rebounded into one of the healthiest in Latin America, weathering both the drop in oil prices in 1998 and the Brazilian market panic of January 1999.

The drop in oil prices was probably responsible for a decline in GDP growth from 7% in 1997 to 4.8% in 1998 to 3.4%

in 1999. Growth shot back up to 7.2% for 2000, thanks largely to the continued high price of oil. But the U.S. recession in 2001 and the September 11 terrorist attacks that year proved a double whammy for the Mexican economy. The recession caused trade to plummet, and the terrorist attacks caused a general decrease in tourism, compounded in Mexico's case by the inconveniences caused by tightened security along the border.

Consequently, GDP for 2001 declined by –0.3% and grew by only 0.9% in 2002, not enough to keep up with the growth in the labor market. In 2003, the economy grew by 1.3%, still sluggish. In his state of the nation address to Congress in 2004, a contrite President Fox admitted that the economy had not performed as he had hoped. Growth in 2004 was a more encouraging 4.4% and was about the same in 2005, the result of the spike in world oil prices.

The Fox administration privatized the telecommunications system and in 2005 sold off Mexicana, a state-owned airline.

Growth steadily tapered off under Calderón: 4.9% in 2006, 3.2% in 2007 and 1.4% in 2008. The drop in oil prices from $140 a barrel in mid-2008 to only $70 in mid-2009, coupled with the global recession, sent the economy into a tailspin. The GDP shrank by –6.5% in 2009, but rebounded to a positive 5.6% in 2010. It increased 3.9% in 2011 and 4% in 2012, then fell to a pitiful 1.2% in 2013, an inauspicious beginning for President Enrique Peña Nieto. Taking the heat for the sluggish growth is his MIT-trained finance minister, Luis Videgaray.

Unemployment remained a steady 5.2%-5.6% from 2008 to 2012, dropping to 4.9% in 2013.

Inflation declined gradually from 18.6% in 1998 to 13.7% in 2001 to only 3.2% in 2005 and 3.4% in 2006. However, higher prices for corn pushed consumer prices higher in 2007. With the recession, inflation fell from 6.5% in 2008 to 3.6% in 2009. It was 3.6% in 2012 and 4% in 2013.

One of the mainstays of the Mexican economy for years has been the remittances that Mexican workers abroad, whether legal or illegal, mostly in the United States, send home to their families. Remittances in 2003 totaled $6.3 billion, for the first time surpassing direct foreign investment, which was $5.2 billion, or tourism, which was $4.9 billion. Remittances were second only to oil sales, which were $8 billion. By 2006, remittances were estimated at $23 billion and peaked at $26.07 billion in 2007. They fell 3.6% in 2008, to $25.14 billion, indicative of the beginning of the recession in the United States. Remittances plummeted to $21.2 billion in 2009, a 15% one-year drop. In 2010 they increased just .12%, to $21.27 billion, but in 2011 they jumped a record 7%, to $22.73 billion. In 2012 they were $22.446 billion, down 1.57%, and in 2013 they dropped another 3.8%, to $21.6 billion.

Mexico's growing importance in world financial circles became more apparent when Agustín Carstens, head of the Central Bank, lobbied hard to become the new managing director of the International Monetary Fund. The IMF's French head, Dominique Strauss-Kahn, resigned in disgrace in 2011 after being arrested in New York for attempted rape of a hotel employee. Carstens' leading competitor for the post was French Finance Minister Christine Lagarde. The post has traditionally been held by a European, and Carstens acknowledged his candidacy was a "long shot." Lagarde was elected.

Mexico now claims the distinction of having the world's richest man as a citizen: Carlos Slim (b. 1940), who amassed a fortune mostly in telecommunications in the wake of privatization. His América Móvil controls 80% of the telephone landlines and 70% of the cell phone market. He was worth an estimated $69 billion in 2012. His Grupo Carlo also is involved in technology, finance and retailing.

THE FUTURE: Mexico's democracy has now come full circle with the election of the *PRI*'s Enrique Peña Nieto after 12 years of *PAN* presidents. Many analysts and pundits, including this author, were fearful that the party's "dinosaur" faction would turn back the clock and return to the bad old days of monolithic power and rampant corruption. An editorial cartoon in a Guadalajara newspaper the day after the *PRI*'s July 1, 2012, comeback victory exemplified this expectation. It showed a tyrannosaurus Rex towering menacingly over a humble, working-class home. The caption was a parody of the famous one-sentence Guatemalan short story, *The Dinosaur,* by Augusto Monterroso: "When he awoke, the dinosaur was still there."

It would be hard for Peña Nieto to return to the days of yore even if he wanted

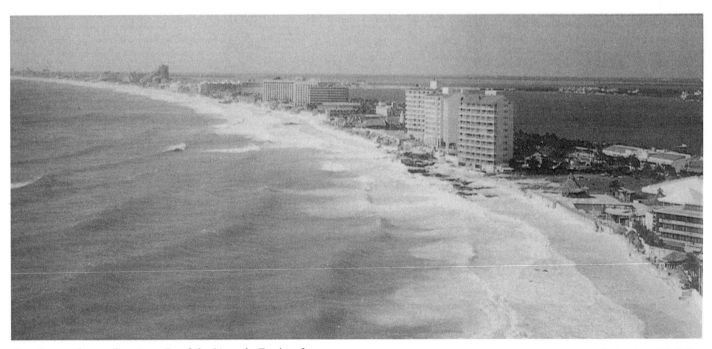

Cancún, on the northeastern tip of the Yucatán Peninsula

Courtesy: Ann and Martin Shuey

Mexico

to, and from what he has demonstrated in his first year and a half, he doesn't intend to.

Anyway, the Mexican press is no longer muzzled by the government as it was before 1989. The TV behemoth *Televisa* might have been expected to turn a blind eye to any wrongdoing by the administration of Peña Nieto, to whom it bestowed shamelessly preferential coverage during the campaign, but Peña Nieto stunned everyone by pushing a new telecommunications law that will break up *Televisa*'s near-monopoly and make way for two new privately owned channels. Those winning bids are expected to be announced in September. Newspapers like *Reforma* and *El Universal* and magazines like *Proceso* now constitute an effective Fourth Estate that should serve as an effective watchdog on corruption and which will howl in protest at any hint of a return to the past. An example of this was the exposé by the radio news station MVS that the head of the *PRI* in Mexico City, Cuauhtémoc Gutierrez de la Torre, had prostitutes on the party payroll to entertain him, forcing him to resign.

Peña Nieto has proven himself to be as skillful a consensus builder as Calderón. But now that the fiscal, electoral, energy and telecommunications reforms are a *fait accompli,* he must devote his own energy to reviving Mexico's sluggish economy. GDP growth in his first year was a pitiful 1.2%, the lowest in Latin America. And although the government claims overall murders declined 16% in his first year, the drug-related violence has by no means stopped.

Mexicans have rightly become jaded by their political system. In *The Economist*'s first *Latinobarómetro* poll in 1996, 53% of Mexicans agreed that democracy is preferable to any other form of government. Alas, two opposition presidential victories do not seem to have strengthened their belief in democracy. By 2009, Mexico ranked at the *bottom* of the 18-nation survey; only 42% said they thought democracy was the best form of government, tying with Guatemala. In 2013, it was still in last place with 37%. Only 22% said in 2013 that they were satisfied with the way democracy works in their country; only Honduras scored lower.

In the legislative elections in June 2015, the PRI polled slightly over 29% of the vote compared to the PAN at 21% and the PDR at 11% (of almost 40 million voters). Whether this will be enough to constitute a mandate for Peña Nieo is yet to be seen.

Nicaragua

A Saturday afternoon native dance in the countryside

Area: 49,163 square miles.
Population: 5,848,641 (2014 est.).
Capital City: Managua (population 1.7 million).
Climate: Tropical, with distinct wet and dry seasons. Rainfall is heavier on the Atlantic coast, with the heaviest downpours from May to December.
Neighboring Countries: Honduras (North); Costa Rica (South).
Official Language: Spanish.
Other Principal Tongues: English, Indian dialects.
Ethnic Background: *Mestizo* (A mixture of Spanish and Indian, 69%), Caucasian (17%), Negro (9%), Amerindian (5%).
Principal Religion: Roman Catholic Christianity.
Chief Commercial Products: Cotton, coffee, bananas, sugar.
Currency: Córdoba
Gross Domestic Product: US $11.28 billion in 2013 ($1,949 per capita, official exchange rate).
Former Colonial Status: Spanish Colony (1519–1821).

Independence Date: September 15, 1821.
Chief of State: Daniel Ortega Saavedra (b. November 11, 1945), president (since January 10, 2007).
National Flag: Blue, white and blue horizontal stripes with a coat of arms on the white stripe.

Nicaragua is the largest and most sparsely settled of the Central American republics. It has three distinct geographic regions: a triangular mountain extension of the Honduran highlands, with its apex reaching to the San Juan River valley on the Costa Rican frontier; a narrow Pacific coastal plain containing two large lakes (Managua, 32 miles long and Nicaragua, 92 miles long); there is a wider Atlantic coastal plain.

The Pacific plain is part of a trough that runs from the Gulf of Fonseca in the northwest through the two scenic lakes and the San Juan River valley to the Atlantic. This is one of the most promising sites for a new interoceanic canal. There is considerable volcanic activity in the northwestern part of this region. Three volcanoes reach-

ing to some 5,000 feet have emerged from Lake Nicaragua, another stands majestically on the north shore of Lake Managua and some 20 more lie formidably between the lakes and the Gulf of Fonseca. The moist easterly winds from the Caribbean Sea drench the San Juan River valley and the Atlantic coastal plains, which are heavily forested.

The Pacific coastal plains receive less rainfall and in some parts require flood control and irrigation for agriculture. The majority of Nicaragua's population is found between the western slope of the highlands and the Pacific Ocean. The few settlements on the Atlantic coast were founded by the British and the population in this region is predominantly of African-West Indian origin, with a few pockets of native Miskito Indians.

HISTORY: The Spanish conquerors reached Nicaragua from Panama in 1519. They found a fairly dense population of agricultural Maya Indians on the shores of Lake Nicaragua, from whom gold ornaments were acquired. The Spaniards re-

Nicaragua

turned in 1524 and founded settlements at Granada and León. By 1570 the flow of gold had ceased, most of the settlers left and the two towns were put under the administration of the captaincy-general of Guatemala.

León, more accessible to the sea, was chosen as the administrative center rather than the larger and more wealthy Granada. The eastern coast was entirely neglected by the Spanish—the towns of Bluefields and Greytown (San Juan del Norte) were established by British loggers cutting mahogany and other valuable timber. By the time of independence, the Lake Nicaragua basin was the site of productive sugar and indigo plantations and the town of Granada was the center of political Conservatism. León, the center of less valuable grain and food production and capital of the province, was the seat of anti-clerical political Liberalism.

Independence came to Nicaragua as a by-product of the movements in Mexico and in the South American states. Through the actions of Guatemala, Nicaragua joined Mexico under Iturbide and became a member of the Central American Confederation, but withdrew from it in 1838. The Liberal-Conservative conflict that marked the period was manifested in Nicaragua by an as-yet unsettled feud between Granada and León.

British interests established a protectorate over the Atlantic region, known as the Autonomous Kingdom of Miskitia, which was not incorporated into the national territory until 1860. During the 1850s and 1860s, Commodore Cornelius Vanderbilt's transit company became involved in ferrying California-bound gold prospectors across Nicaragua, and the Liberals of León invited William Walker, a U.S. soldier of fortune, to head up their army to crush the Granada Conservatives. At the same time, there were conflicts of British and North American interests who backed the various factions.

Walker's successes in León were such that Vanderbilt was induced to aid the Conservatives of Granada. Walker finally was captured and executed in 1860 and the Conservatives established their dominance, which endured for 30 years. They quelled numerous uprisings, installed their presidents and gave the country a semblance of stable government. The cultivation of coffee and bananas was started, gold production was resumed and a few immigrants arrived from Europe.

Factional quarrels among the Conservatives made possible a Liberal coup in 1893 and the seizure of power by youthful José Santos Zelaya. Sixteen years of tyrannical misrule by Santos Zelaya became notorious both at home and abroad. He persecuted his Conservative enemies, betrayed his Liberal supporters and systematically looted both public and private funds. He maintained his position with a ruthless system of spies and police, suppressing all critics. Despite his misrule, the economy prospered, railroads were built and public schools were increased.

His execution of two U.S. adventurers aroused the U.S. government and the dictator fled into exile in 1909. This left the country in a state of near anarchy—the government was bankrupt and foreign creditors threatened intervention. The Conservatives appealed to Washington to intervene while New York financiers bought up foreign bonds and installed economic supervisors to manage the Nicaraguan economy and ensure repayment of their investments.

Liberals revolted in 1912 against a situation in which their country was the ward of foreign banks in. U.S. Marines landed, suppressed the revolt and became involved in a 20-year war for the elimina-

tion of banditry and the establishment of a stable government. While Washington supported the Conservatives, Mexico supported Liberals in a see-saw contest. Larger forces of Marines were introduced in 1927 to control the country; the United States tried to resolve the internal Liberal-Conservative conflict through supposedly free and democratic elections. A guerrilla leader fighting against the Marines became a legendary figure in Nicaragua and most of Central America: Augusto César Sandino, a colorful character sporting a 10-gallon hat and six-shooter.

The Somoza Dynasty

U.S. forces left Nicaragua in 1933, with the government in the hands of a Liberal president, Juan Sacasa, and a peace guaranteed by a Marine-trained police force, the *Guardia Nacional*, under the command of Anastasio "Tacho" Somoza. By 1934 it was obvious that true power lay with the *Guardia* and its commander. Sandino still maintained his guerrilla forces, but had agreed to a cease-fire once the Marines had gone. The government accepted a sweeping amnesty for Sandino's men, additionally offering them land and jobs.

Then the Nicaraguan Congress voted to raise the salary of Sandino's 100-man personal guard while reducing the pay of the military. But not all of Sandino's followers had turned in their arms. The *Guardia* de-

Augusto César Sandino

cided that Sandino had to be eliminated. A supposedly innocent President Sacasa invited Sandino to the presidential palace to discuss outstanding issues, where there were several meetings. But after a farewell supper, the *Guardia* met Sandino at the gate and took him and his men to the airfield, where they were executed and secretly buried.

Anastasio Somoza ruled until his assassination in 1955 and Congress named his son, Luis, to the presidency, which he occupied until 1963. The elections that year were relatively quiet and honest.

In 1967, Luis Somoza's younger brother, Anastasio "Tachito" Somoza Debayle, a West Point graduate, became the third member of the family to occupy the presidency. Barred by law from succeeding himself, Somoza created a caretaker three-man *junta* in 1971 to rule until 1974, when he was "elected" to a second term with 91.7% of the vote. Somoza was a "Liberal" in name only. Nine small opposition parties were barred from the election.

Somoza's second term would be his last. Resentment against the regime grew as increasing numbers of Nicaraguans objected to his heavy-handed tactics and greed. His brutal treatment of political opponents convinced many that the regime would never tolerate democratic elections in the country. The business community was bitter and angry with Somoza's levying of kickbacks on the major commercial transactions conducted in the country. Residents of Managua were outraged by the *junta*'s blatant misuse of international aid earmarked for the city's reconstruction following a disastrous 1972 earthquake. Most Liberals and leftists were offended by the strongman's ostentatious display of wealth: his family owned a half billion dollars worth of investments and 8,260 square miles of Nicaragua, while 200,000 peasants were landless.

Revolution

For the first time, opponents of the regime united, joined by one thing: anti-Somoza feelings (but little else). A broad-based coalition—ranging from Marxist guerrillas to conservative business leaders—was formed. While the business sector continued its strikes to dry up the economy, the guerrillas battled the *Guardia*.

Many moderate opposition groups, wittingly or unwittingly, joined together with the Sandinista National Liberation Front (*FSLN*), named after the legendary nationalist guerrilla leader of the 1930s. The *FSLN*, founded in the 1960s under the auspices of Fidel Castro, grew rapidly when Anastasio Somoza became president. His brutal and corrupt rule pumped new life into the guerrilla movement. As the *Sandinistas* gained strength from association with non-communist elements, Somoza retaliated with sweeping attacks against rural peasants suspected of aiding the guerrillas, which backfired against the regime. Mass support for the *FSLN* developed further following the 1972 earthquake that leveled Managua when it became known that Somoza was pocketing some of the international relief funds and buying up Managua real estate at fire-sale prices.

While the *Guardia* enjoyed a 4–1 manpower edge, the *Sandinistas* and associates nonetheless boasted a force of 3,000 members by 1978. It was actually divided into three groups: two openly Marxist and a third—by far the largest—consisting of

Anastasio Somoza Debayle

socialists and non-Marxist leftist trade unionists, Catholic Church members and a sprinkling of businessmen. Known as the *Terceristas* (Third Force), this last group is best remembered for its daring 1978-occupation of the National Palace in Managua.

Collapse of the Regime

The crucial jolt in the long train of events leading to the overthrow of the Somoza regime came in January 1978, when assassins gunned down Pedro Joaquín Chamorro, longtime Conservative Party critic and publisher of the nation's leading newspaper, *La Prensa*. Although the identity of the killers remains unknown, most Nicaraguans attributed the murder to Somoza. Chamorro was widely respected—10,000 attended his funeral—and his death quickly touched off three days of bloody demonstrations throughout the nation. The *Guardia* responded in a heavy-handed manner; its ruthless mop-up operations in five major cities left 3,000 dead.

The Chamorro murder, combined with the *Guardia*'s indiscriminate killings, cost the regime the vital support of business leaders who then called for a general strike to demand Somoza's resignation. The strike brought more reprisals. As the death toll mounted, the United States proposed a referendum to test national support for the Somoza regime. Somoza quickly rejected the idea, saying, "If they want me to leave Nicaragua, they'll only get me out by force."

The *Sandinistas* were only too willing to oblige him. During its final two years, the Somoza regime was under attack throughout the country. The only significant Nicaraguan sector that continued to support the dictatorship was, as always, the *Guardia*. Meanwhile, the guerrillas continued to score important victories in rural areas, while major power groups in the cities were becoming more militant in their opposition to Somoza. One by one, rural areas fell under rebel control and by the spring of 1979 it was clear that Somoza could not endure.

Still, he refused to budge. Secluded in his Managua bunker—a grim reminder of the last days of World War II in Berlin—Somoza continued to direct the military activities of his *Guardia*. Curiously, Somoza made the same tactical error committed by Hitler during the battle for Stalingrad: He ordered heavy bombing of civilian areas in order to deny the enemy food and shelter. In both cases, the bombed-out buildings provided ideal concealment from which the defenders could fight back. In Nicaragua, the *Guardia*'s bombing of populated areas killed virtually no guerrillas—it merely solidified public opinion against Somoza.

Nicaragua

Sandinistas **celebrate Somoza's overthrow, 1979**

Along with the heavy shelling of civilian areas, Somoza also ordered the summary execution of suspected opponents of his regime. Many of these were youths, whose blindfolded and bound bodies were often found strewn along the shores of Lake Managua. During the final two years of fighting, thousands were killed and left homeless.

By late May 1979, ranking members of the regime began to flee the country. Somoza himself finally abandoned his bunker and flew to the United States, where he boarded a luxury yacht for a leisurely trip to Paraguay, to be given refuge by the Stroessner regime of that country. He left hapless caretakers in charge. Thus ended one of the most durable dictatorships—46 years—in Latin American history.

He lasted only 14 months in Paraguay, however, before he was gunned down by three persons reported to be Argentine guerrillas. He had become depressed, drank to excess and grew fat. Before his death, he was involved in a much-publicized love affair with a former Miss Paraguay—who also happened to be the mistress of Stroessner's son-in-law.

The Sandinista Era

On July 19, 1979, the *Sandinistas* took control of Managua—and a *new* revolution was about to start. Their non-communist allies in the revolution found themselves with little power within the new government.

After Somoza's ouster, the country was administered by a three-member *junta* called the Revolutionary Junta Government (*JRG*). One of the three was Violeta Barrios de Chamorro, widow of the assassinated journalist. This group, in turn, followed policy directives established by a nine-member *Sandinista* National Directorate, controlled by the *FSLN*. Power was shared with a Council of State, a *Sandinista*-dominated legislative body of 47 members representing various political and economic groups as well as the armed forces and the *FSLN*.

Although the Marxist influence was clearly in evidence—especially in the schools, the armed forces and the media—the government was initially primarily nationalistic. But in international relations, Nicaragua quickly joined the non-aligned bloc of Third World nations and established close ties with communist-bloc nations. The regime refused to condemn the Soviet invasion of Afghanistan and in 1982 supported Argentina's invasion of the British Falkland Islands. Trade pacts were signed with various communist nations, including Bulgaria, East Germany, the Soviet Union and Cuba.

Relations became particularly close with the Castro's Cuba. Almost all communist *Sandinista* leaders visited Havana and in mid-1980 Fidel Castro was guest of honor in Managua for the revolution's first anniversary celebration. As many as 6,000 Cuban "advisers" were stationed in Nicaragua; hundreds of Nicaraguan youths were sent to Cuba for educational programs that stressed Marxism.

Although the Carter administration applauded the fall of Somoza and pledged to work with the new regime, the *Sandinistas'* increased ties with communist nations soon led to strained relations with the United States. Some powerful members of the U.S. Congress regarded the *Sandinista* regime as a threat to Central America. Although the Carter administration provided some financial aid to Nicaragua in the hope of strengthening the pro-democratic forces, the new Reagan administration responded with a tough stance against what it concluded was a Soviet-sponsored client state within Central America.

Thus, Washington suspended all aid to Nicaragua in the spring of 1981 after the State Department accused the *Sandinistas* of aiding leftist guerrillas in El Salvador. In late 1981, the Reagan administration again denounced Nicaragua for "arms trafficking to El Salvador," and for building the largest military force "in the history of Central America." In early 1982, Reagan lectured Nicaragua's new ambassador to the United States against "adopting alien influence and philosophies in the hemisphere."

The Pentagon unveiled CIA aerial photos in 1982 to prove that Cuba and the Soviet Union were providing sophisticated military equipment to Nicaragua. Newly enlarged Nicaraguan airfields could be used for bombing raids against the Panama Canal, according to some U.S. officials. Several days later, a badly informed U.S. State Department staged a highly publicized press conference to display a Nicaraguan guerrilla who had been captured in El Salvador. But when the cameras started rolling, the Nicaraguan coolly accused his captors of torture. Highly embarrassed State Department officials promptly deported the man to Nicaragua (where he received a hero's welcome). Nicaraguan strongman Daniel Ortega Saavedra called an urgent meeting of the U.N. Security Council to protest "aggressive and destabilizing acts" by the United States against his country. In 1982, Washington accused Nicaragua of firing on a U.S. helicopter over international waters near the Nicaraguan coast (the United States then recognized a 12-mile territorial limit; Nicaragua claimed 200 miles).

The "Stolen" Revolution

What had been envisioned by in some U.S. circles as a pluralistic revolution in Nicaragua was an illusion. Many elements joined together in the anti-Somoza struggle, but only one had cohesiveness: the *FSLN*. At first, other groups were allowed to participate, but in 1982–83 the true nature of the *FSLN* became apparent. Although U.S. conservatives charged that the *Sandinistas* "stole" the revolution, in fact the *Sandinistas* simply filled a political vacuum and then refused to share it.

In 1984, Ortega was elected president by a predictably wide margin. The opposition was divided and denied access to the media.

During more than 10 years in power, the *Sandinista* regime generated widespread disillusionment and disappointment. Anti-*Sandinista* rallies and meetings were broken up and were later totally prohibited. A prominent leftist within the regime resigned, accusing the *Sandinistas* of planting "a reign of terror . . . a Soviet style Stalinist regime in Nicaragua."

The press that was not directly seized by the government was regularly harassed; *La Prensa* soon became the only non-government newspaper that quickly came to face daily government inspection and approval. Mrs. Chamorro, the publisher, resigned from the *junta* as a result. International credit evaporated as the United States withdrew loan promises and private foreign banks balked at extensions of credit. Somoza had emptied he treasury, compounding the problems of the fledgling government.

Human rights violations sharply increased. Ultimately, an estimated 10,000 people, including former Somoza supporters and former members of the *Guardia*, were jailed and other opponents were sent into exile. A dispute between the government and the Miskito Indians (who had been given a large measure of independence under Somoza) was provoked when the Miskitos were accused of aiding counter-revolutionary Somoza exiles living in Honduras. When the government attempted to resettle about 10,000 tribe members away from border areas, an estimated 20,000 fled to Honduras, from where they started to harass the *Sandinistas*. The government responded by raiding Miskito settlements along the border, leaving an estimated 105 dead. This would lead in the future to an alliance between the Indians and the "*Contras*."

Relations were strained with the Catholic Church durung a visit by Pope John Paul II in 1982. The pope was heckled by Sandinista hardliners while delivering Mass, and he publicly scolded priests who were serving in the *Sandinista* government in violation of his order against priests serving in secular political posts.

In 1985, Reagan requested military aid for the *Contras* ("antis"), a loosely organized but relatively effective opposition to the regime. It had been armed by the CIA. The Democratic-controlled House refused, but did allow $14 million for "humanitarian" aid. Ortega, meanwhile, received pledges of $200 million from Moscow. Reagan imposed a total economic embargo on Nicaragua, and his advisers worked out a secret deal that almost proved the undoing of the Reagan presidency. Arms were illegally sold to Iran, then at war with Iraq, in exchange for Iran's influence in freeing American citizens held hostage by the Iranian-backed Hezbollah guerrillas in Lebanon. The profits from the arms sales were secretly channeled to the *Contras* in defiance of the congressional ban. When the "Iran-Contra affair" became public, Congress held investigatory hearings. Reagan denied knowledge of the deal, but contritely assumed responsibility.

The state-controlled economy ultimately shrank to about one-third of the level it had been before *Sandinista* control. Crops were not harvested because of military pressures and the unwillingness of farmers to accept artificially low prices. Foreign aid dried up by 1987, when the final stages of a precipitous decline was underway in the former Soviet Union and its client, Cuba. Shortages were rampant and housing was shabby and crumbling.

A last-ditch effort was made to overcome the *Contras* located in neighboring Honduras in 1988; the *Sandinista* effort was repulsed when two battalions of U.S. troops were sent to that country.

The Arias Plan

Costa Rican President Oscar Arias offered to broker a Central America-wide peace agreement, for which he would receive the Nobel Peace Prize. Signed by the leaders of Costa Rica, El Salvador, Guatemala, Honduras and Nicaragua meeting in Guatemala City on August 7, 1987, the Arias Plan obligated the *Sandinistas* to negotiate a cease-fire with the *Contras*, allow freedom of the press and other media, cease political repression and allow free, open and democratic elections. Support of rebel forces in adjoining nations would be banned. It further provided for monitoring of all requirements by national conciliation commissions that would include opposition figures, Catholic Church officials and Inter-American Human Rights Commission representatives.

Ortega signed the agreement. Negotiations with the *Contras* and internal opposition groups began in October 1987. They broke down immediately when the *Sandinistas* abruptly announced that "there will never, at any time or any place, be any direct *political* dialogue with the *Contras*." The impasse continued until Cardinal Obando y Bravo volunteered to mediate talks between the parties. His efforts were short-lived: the *Sandinistas* were firm in their ultimatum that they would only accept a military surrender from the *Contras*, not discuss politics. The cardinal walked out in disgust in January 1988, accusing the *Sandinistas* of negotiating in bad faith.

La Prensa and *Radio Católico* were allowed to resume their activities in October 1987, but were again shut down for 15 days in the spring of 1988.

The *Sandinistas* declared a unilateral cease-fire in 1988, *not* because of the Arias peace plan, but because of dire economic conditions within Nicaragua. The cease-fire was extended into 1990.

Daniel Ortega exhorts a group of students about the spirit of the *Sandinista* revolution

Nicaragua

Signing of the Summit Agreement

In 1989, the new Bush administration didn't even bother to ask for military assistance for the *Contras*, settling for more humanitarian aid. Faced with economic and political bankruptcy, the *Sandinistas* engaged in a transparent effort to rig elections set for February 25, 1990.

Chamorro Upsets Ortega

It was clear that the *Sandinistas* were uneasy about the outcome. A cease-fire with the *Contras* was canceled, but the half-hearted military effort that followed was ineffective. Ortega took to the campaign trail. He discarded his khakis and appeared in a variety of costumes and said anything to please everybody, swinging his hips to rock music. Television and newspapers were full of propaganda extolling the party. The *FSLN* outspent the opposition, the National Opposition Union (*UNO*), by at least 10–1.

The *UNO* candidate was Violeta Chamorro, widow of the publisher slain in 1978 under the Somoza regime. *Sandinista* efforts were stepped up, including crude efforts such as bludgeoning those attending opposition rallies.

A Washington Post-ABC poll published predicted a *Sandinista* triumph by a margin of 48% to 32%, although the pollsters issued strong disclaimers as to its accuracy. Chamorro and the *UNO* won by 55.2% to 40.8%! Even the White House was startled. Also surprisingly, Ortega meekly conceded defeat and congratulated Chamorro. She was sworn in on April 25, making history as the first elected woman president in Latin America.

After Chamorro's inaugural, Nicaragua's slim hope for improved conditions evaporated. Much to the dismay of the *UNO*, she appointed Humberto Ortega, Daniel's brother, to continue as defense minister. However, she reduced the army from about 80,000 to zero on the grounds that it was no longer needed. There remained shadowy, informal armed forces, used to protect property seized by the *Sandinistas* by "law" between the time of Chamorro's election and the time she assumed office. The *UNO* coalition in the National Assembly soon turned on Chamorro, claiming she had betrayed her mandate.

The disbanding of the army and of the *Contras* added tremendously (almost 100,000) to unemployment, which rose to more than 50%. Few exiles returned; the wealthy ones in particular, who took much of their money with them, remained outside the country. Conditions on farms, prosperous in the 1970s, were dreadful. Many that were split up and given to peasants and *Sandinista* fighters were idle.

Lower-level *Sandinistas* deserted the *FSLN*, as did former low-income supporters of the movement. The more affluent *Sandinistas* clung tenaciously to the property they had acquired during their years in power.

With the *Sandinistas* in charge of the army, the police and the judiciary, Nicaragua was far from democratic. The president ignored the Assembly and formed an "inner cabinet" to rule the nation. She particularly relied on her son-in-law, Antonio Lacayo, in making crucial decisions that favored the top-drawer *Sandinistas*. The *Sandinista*-controlled Supreme Court nullified all actions of the National Assembly after September 2, 1992, on the dubious grounds that on that date it lacked a quorum! Its ruling was ignored.

The U.S. Congress appropriated $104 million in aid for Nicaragua, to be released in 1992, contingent upon the firing of army commander Ortega, discharge of the police chief, judicial reform, and compensation for seized U.S. property. Chamorro did fire the police chief and said she would "discuss" compensation of U.S. owners. President Bush reluctantly released $50 million after his 1992 re-election defeat.

Following President Bill Clinton's inauguration, Nicaraguan officials intensely lobbied the U.S. Congress for release of the remainder. The Clinton administration sent the funds, citing "important strides that have been made by the Nicaraguan government." An offended senator charged that the money was sent to a "government of thugs."

The Chamorro government promised that Humberto Ortega would leave as army commander—in late 1995, by retirement. Continued U.S. pressure resulted in Ortega's removal in 1994; he was put under house arrest because of alleged involvement in a 1990 crime.

Six years after being elected by hopeful Nicaraguans who had "voted with their stomachs," Chamorro had done little to raise Nicaragua out of its abject poverty.

The Alemán Presidency

Sensing an opportunity for a comeback, Ortega announced his candidacy for the October 1996 presidential election. He entered the race an underdog behind the popular and conservative former mayor of Managua, Arnoldo Alemán, the candidate of the Liberal Alliance. Gone were Ortega's *Sandinista* uniform and his Marxist rhetoric, which he realized had helped defeat him in 1990. Six weeks before the election, the *Sandinistas* even softened the lyrics of their truculent anthem, removing the reference to "the Yankees, enemies of mankind."

Opinion polls indicated that the rehabilitated Ortega, preaching a more social democratic gospel, was running even with Alemán. With 23 candidates, there appeared little likelihood that anyone could garner the necessary 45% to avoid a runoff. But once again, the Nicaraguan voters startled prognosticators by giving Alemán a decisive first-round victory of 48.4% to Ortega's 38.6%—even less than Ortega had obtained in 1990.

Ortega immediately—and unconvincingly—cried fraud. A delegation of OAS observers—including longtime *Sandinista* apologist Jimmy Carter and former Secretary of State James Baker—concluded there was no evidence of major irregularities. Carter persuaded his friend Ortega to accept the results rather than resorting to mass protests as he had threatened to do.

Where Chamorro had pragmatically and almost with flattery sought to placate the *Sandinistas* whom she knew could easily overthrow her, Alemán was confrontational. But then, he had a personal score to settle. A onetime Somoza supporter, Alemán had five farms confiscated by the *Sandinistas* in the 1980s. In 1989, while he was under house arrest, the *Sandinistas* refused even to allow him to accompany his wife, who was dying of cancer, to a hospital.

A lawyer, Alemán was elected mayor of Managua in the same 1990 election that brought Chamorro to power. He compiled an impressive record of achievement in the capital, which still felt the effects of the 1972 earthquake. He improved the traffic engineering system, beautified the city and removed the *Sandinistas*' revolutionary art from walls and billboards.

Alemán was inaugurated on January 10, 1997 for a term that had been reduced to five years, marking the first time in Nicaraguan history that one duly elected civilian president had succeeded another. Alemán delivered a conciliatory inaugural address, offering dialogue with the archrival *Sandinistas*. At first, the *Sandinistas* resisted his overtures and continued their bombastic threats to take to the streets. Yet, perhaps faced with the reality that they could no longer marshal that kind of public support, the Ortega brothers met privately with Alemán.

Alemán promised to reverse the *Sandinistas*' opposition to free-market capitalism and to make Nicaragua more attractive to foreign investors in order to bring in desperately needed capital. He also proposed expanding the free-trade zone Chamorro established in 1992, which attracted Mexican-style *maquiladora* assembly plants, mostly for apparel. His most controversial and divisive proposal was the plan to return land expropriated by the *Sandinistas* to its former owners, compensating the new owners with government bonds.

After months of bickering between the Liberals and the *FSLN*, the two parties came to realize the delay in resolving the title issue was hurting Nicaragua economically by discouraging foreign investment. Moreover, the United States was leaning on Alemán to resolve the issue because of the thousands of Nicaraguans displaced by the Revolution who were residing in the United States. The National Assembly approved, 70–4, a compromise measure that essentially verified the current ownership of most of the 1 million hectares the *Sandinistas* had seized. The new law granted title to those who received rural plots of less than 35 hectares or urban plots of less than 100 square meters. About 5,000 pre-revolutionary landowners thus were frustrated in their hopes of getting their property back.

In 1998, the *Sandinistas* continued to suffer reversals of fortune. The official *FSLN* newspaper *Barricada*, which had been the pro-Somoza daily *Noticias* before it was expropriated in 1979, succumbed to the loss of government subsidies and ceased publication. Its editors accused the Alemán government of retribution through the withholding of government advertising, a time-honored practice of Latin American strongmen, but their protests carried a hollow ring given the *Sandinistas*' own intimidation and censorship of the independent media when they were in power. *Barricada* subsequently reopened in 2000 as a weekly. Later its name was changed to the less combative *Visión Sandinista*.

Another blow, which threatened the very unity of the *FSLN*, came as a bombshell. Ortega's 30-year-old stepdaughter, Zoilamérica Narváez, accused him in an interview in a daily newsletter of having sexually abused her for years, beginning when she was 11 and continuing into the years that he was president. Narvaez's estranged husband, Alejandro Bendaña, like her a committed *Sandinista* and Ortega's former deputy foreign minister, denounced his former boss' "abuse of power."

Ortega adamantly denied the accusation, as did his common-law wife, Rosario Murillo, Narváez's mother. Ortega supporters denounced the charges as "politically motivated" and even accused Narváez of participating in a CIA plot to undermine Ortega. The leader of the Liberals in the Assembly accused Ortega of hiding behind his legislative immunity and called on him to resign. With the storm of controversy swirling around him, Ortega called for party unity. It worked; he was re-elected as *Sandinista* leader. Almost simultaneously, Narváez filed a civil suit against him and also accused high-level *Sandinistas* of aiding and abetting in the sex abuse. Ortega claimed parliamentary immunity, and for weeks the Nicaraguan media reported almost daily "no-I-didn't-yes-you-did" exchanges between Ortega and Narváez.

Ortega attempted to divert attention from the sex scandal. In a mass demonstration, he called Alemán a "dictator" because of his move to re-establish a state security agency similar to that of the Somoza period. Ortega hinted darkly that if the president threatened human rights—as though he himself hadn't—the *Sandinistas* would be called upon "to take up arms." Alemán responded by calling on Ortega to "bury forever the hatchet of war and the rifle of death and let Nicaragua emerge from the poverty in which he left it."

In 1998, Alemán faced a greater adversary even than Ortega: Hurricane Mitch. The storm killed 2,863 Nicaraguans, 948 were missing and more than 867,000 were affected. Seventy-one bridges were destroyed, 70% of the roads were damaged and 30% of the banana crop was wiped out; Mitch also wiped out any hopes of immediate economic recovery. International relief aid poured in to alleviate the appalling human suffering.

Although there was no evidence that this president profited from the disaster as Somoza had in 1972, Alemán was accused of enriching himself while on the public payroll. In 1999, Comptroller General Agustín Jarquín, a member of the Social Christian Party and a longtime political rival of Alemán's, issued a report alleging the president had increased his personal wealth by 900% between 1990, when he was elected mayor of Managua, and 1997, his first full year as president. Alemán maintained the increase had come from property in Nicaragua and Miami that he had inherited from his parents and from his wife's family. He countered that Jarquín was merely out to get him.

Alemán counterattacked when the national police chief, before a crowd of journalists, arrested Jarquín and a well-known television journalist on supposed fraud charges. An appeals court subsequently dismissed the charges.

In 2001, Nicaragua "sued" Colombia before the International Court of Justice in the Hague, Netherlands, over control of some tiny, uninhabited islets in the Caribbean near Colombian-owned San Andrés Island. The court took 11 years to reach a decision (see Recent Developments).

The Power-Sharing Accord

A major political development occurred in 1999 whose long-term implications are still being felt. The long-antagonistic Liberals and *Sandinistas* suddenly concluded an agreement by which they would cooperate in governing the country and would apportion seats on the Supreme Court and the electoral council between them. The

Former President Arnoldo Alemán

Nicaragua

Street scene in Bluefields on the Caribbean Sea

agreement also would reduce the number of frivolous individual presidential candidacies. On the surface, it seemed a welcome respite from the partisan bickering that had plagued the country. However, the minor parties charged—with some justification—that the pact was designed merely to divide the country's political spoils between the two major parties and exclude all others from the public trough. Similar bipartisan pacts had existed in Colombia and Venezuela.

As Alemán neared the end of his term, he could point to a dramatically improving economy as foreign investment poured into the country and shopping malls began to spring up, a sign of a growing consumer economy. But the charges of corruption took a toll on his popularity and even his control over his party. A poll showed that 88% of Nicaraguans believed Alemán was corrupt.

Moreover, members of Alemán's party, now called the Constitutionalist Liberal Party (*PLC*), criticized his autocratic method of hand-picking party candidates for the 2000 municipal elections. They also alleged that his call for a constitutional convention was aimed at allowing him to run for re-election. Defense Minister Antonio Alvarado resigned over these issues. In the end, there was no constitutional convention, so Alemán was barred from seeking re-election.

The effect of the unholy political pact between the *PLC* and the *FSLN*, two parties with decidedly undemocratic ancestries, was seen clearly in the 2000 municipal elections. The two major parties, through questionable challenging of the signatures of voters on party registration petitions, disqualified all parties but them-

selves from participating. In the voting, the *FSLN* won 11 of the 17 departments, and captured the mayoralty of Managua under the candidacy of Herty Lewites, one of the party's moderates.

The Elections of 2001

The *PLC* and the *FSLN* continued their heavy-handed treatment of other parties in the 2001 presidential race. Through their control of the Electoral Council, they denied registration to Jarquín's Social Christian Party, the National Unity Movement of former army commander Joaquín Cuadra and the fledgling party organized by former Defense Minister Alvarado,

among others. Only the venerable Conservative Party was allowed to compete with the two major parties.

Denied registration for his own party, Jarquín challenged Ortega for the *FSLN* nomination. But the *Sandinistas* stuck with Ortega. The *PLC*, meanwhile, nominated former Vice President Enrique Bolaños, 73, who had resigned to make the run. The Conservatives' standard-bearer was Noel Vidaurre.

When Ortega began his fourth campaign for the presidency, polls again showed he had a better than even chance to stage a comeback. Bolaños, who himself enjoyed a reputation for personal honesty, was tarnished by his association with the unpopular Alemán.

Ortega broadened his political base by enticing prominent former *Sandinista* opponents to join his new coalition, called the Convergence. Chief among them was Jarquín, whom Ortega persuaded to become his running mate. Ortega also sought to sanitize his former guerrilla image even more than he had in 1996, abandoning the familiar black and red *Sandinista* colors in favor of the less threatening pink, and as a campaign slogan he adopted, "The Path to Love." He embraced the Liberals' free-market policies, and he even pledged to continue the Liberals' close ties with the United States. His victory appeared all but certain.

But as the November 4 election drew ever nearer, Ortega's lead in the polls shrank. Meanwhile, Vidaurre, reportedly under U.S. pressure not to divide the anti-*Sandinista* vote, withdrew. After the September 11 terrorist attacks on the United States, Ortega vowed to cooperate in the war against terrorism. Bolaños aired em-

Nicaraguan cowboy

barrassing television ads that showed then-President Ortega embracing Libyan leader Muammar Qadhafi and Iraqi dictator Saddam Hussein, both suspected of supporting Islamic terrorism. Ortega was stung further when two of his erstwhile protégés, Sergio Ramirez, who had been his vice president, and Father Ernesto Cardenal, his foreign minister, announced they would boycott the election, saying neither Ortega nor Bolaños was "worthy."

The U.S. ambassador, in a startling breach of protocol, appeared openly at Bolaños rallies and said in interviews that an Ortega victory could jeopardize the future of U.S. aid. Even Florida Gov. Jeb Bush, brother of the U.S. president, got into the act by urging the thousands of resident Nicaraguans in Florida to vote for Bolaños.

Nicaraguan voters once again confounded the pollsters and handed Ortega his third successive humiliating defeat, 56% to 43.5%, prompting jubilant Liberals to take to the streets chanting, "Three strikes, you're out!" Ortega once again graciously conceded defeat, and an equally magnanimous Bolaños praised the *Sandinistas* as "worthy opponents."

The Liberals retained their majority in the 90-seat Assembly with 49 seats to 40 for the *Sandinistas* and one for the Conservatives. In addition, under the Liberal-*Sandinista* pact, the retiring president (Alemán) and the losing presidential candidate (Ortega) both received seats in the Assembly—thus assuring Ortega continued immunity from his stepdaughter's molestation charges and Alemán from charges of illegal enrichment. Ortega later renounced his immunity—once the statute of limitations for prosecuting rape had expired.

The Bolaños Presidency

Bolaños was inaugurated on January 10, 2002. He launched an anti-corruption campaign that soon had him at odds with his predecessor. Alemán was charged with involvement in a $1.5 million embezzlement scheme at the state-owned television station. Bolaños sought to have Alemán, who had been elected president of the National Assembly, stripped of his legislative immunity. Alemán called Bolaños "inept" and called the investigation a "witch hunt" that was "politically motivated."

But prosecutors unveiled additional evidence against Alemán and his associates of mind-boggling proportions. They allegedly had channeled nearly $100 million in public funds to a phantom foundation in Panama. At a time when Nicaragua was desperately trying to emerge from its economic straits, the revelations that its president and his cronies may have enriched themselves on such a scale stirred outrage. It also deepened the schism between the

Bolaños faction of the *PLC* and the so-called *Arnoldistas*.

Bolaños stepped up pressure on the Assembly to strip Alemán's immunity, and the *Sandinistas*—among them, ironically, Ortega—joined that chorus. But the *Arnoldistas* enjoyed a one-seat majority, and they stonewalled the attempts. As the damning evidence and public outrage mounted, Alemán's support eroded. The Bolaños faction and the *FSLN* mustered 47 votes to remove Alemán as Assembly president; 44 *Arnoldistas* boycotted the session.

Several members of Alemán's family and former associates were charged on various counts of embezzlement and money-laundering, including his daughter, María Dolores, who also enjoyed immunity as a member of the Assembly. In December 2002, the Assembly finally stripped Alemán of his immunity. He appeared in court the next day, claiming he still enjoyed immunity as a member of the largely ceremonial Central American Parliament.

In 2003, some of the accused were tried, although Alemán remained under house arrest on his ranch, refusing to answer prosecutors' questions. Prosecutors raised new charges that he stole another $113 million from the treasury, theft on a Somoza-sized scale. The *PLC* was hopelessly rent, with 38 Assembly members abandoning Bolaños, leaving him with only 10 loyal members.

Alemán was eventually convicted and sentenced to 20 years. He went to prison in 2004, but continued to direct the *Arnoldistas*, who remained fanatically loyal. The

U.S. and Panama both sought his extradition for money laundering, but a Nicaraguan court rejected their petitions.

In a Machiavellian maneuver similar to the power-sharing accord of 1999, the *Sandinistas* and *Arnoldistas* joined in an improbable joint effort in 2004 to form a special legislative committee to decide whether to impeach Bolaños on an old, unproven charge of receiving foreign campaign contributions. Between them, they had far more than the 60% needed for removal. Bolaños accused Alemán and Ortega of "a plot to carry out a *coup d'etat.*" The move was motivated, apparently, by revenge from *Arnoldistas* and by fear from *Sandinistas,* who no doubt wondered whether the president would look next at their own sins.

Under pressure from both the U.S. and the OAS, which warned against removing a constitutional president for politically motivated, trumped-up charges, the *FSLN* and the *PLC* backed off, but in 2005 they enacted a new law that curtailed Bolaños' appointment powers, especially the appointment of judges. The crisis eased when Ortega agreed to support Bolaños remaining in office until the end of his term.

The *FSLN* was once again the major winner in the 2004 municipal elections, retaining the mayoralty of Managua and winning in all the major cities.

The skyrocketing cost of petroleum in 2005 sparked violent protests when Bolaños announced an increase in bus fares from 15 to 18 cents. When he tried to address the thousands of student and peasant protesters, they threw rocks at him. The high fuel prices also led the Spanish-

The Metropolitan Cathedral of León, considered the finest examples of colonial architecture in Central America

Nicaragua

owned power company to seek, and receive, an 11.3% increase in electric rates, which Bolaños restricted to major users. The outcry prompted Bolaños to decree a state of economic emergency, which restricted the right of protest. He rescinded the decree three days later.

In October 2005, after bitter debate, the Assembly approved, 49–37, Nicaragua's participation in the Central American Free Trade Agreement (CAFTA) with the U.S. The *Sandinistas* opposed it, and Ortega took part in demonstrations against it. Nicaragua's participation took effect on April 1, 2006.

A feasibility study was begun in 2006 to resurrect a dream dating to colonial times—a canal across Nicaragua. The proposed sea-level canal would cost $18 billion (at that time) and would connect the San Juan River with Lake Nicaragua and the lake with the Pacific, a total of about 173 miles. It would be wider and deeper than the existing Panama Canal, to accommodate large modern cargo ships that are too large for the Panama Canal. Construction would take 12 years.

Ortega Returns to Power

Ahead of the November 5, 2006, presidential and legislative elections, both major parties has serious internal divisions. Herty Lewites, the popular former mayor of Managua, challenged Ortega for the *FSLN* nomination and criticized the power-sharing accord. Ortega demonstrated his latent Marxist-Leninist tendencies by expelling Lewites from the party; so much for pink. Lewites launched the Herty 2006 Alliance. The *Sandinistas* became further fragmented when Ortega's former vice president, Edén Pastora, declared his own candidacy.

The *PLC* also remained split, between the pro- and anti-Alemán factions. When Bolaños' presidency secretary, Eduardo Montealegre, announced his intention to run, the *arnoldistas* expelled him from the *PLC* just as the *Sandinistas* had expelled Lewites. He, too, formed a new movement called the Nicaraguan Liberal Alliance, or *ALN*, and formed a coalition with the old Conservative Party. The *arnoldistas* nominated José Rizo, a former vice president, as the *PLC* candidate.

Under a new election law that Ortega and Alemán had hatched between them, a candidate now needed only 40% instead of 45% to avoid a runoff, or only 35% if a candidate had a five-point lead.

Suddenly, Lewites died of a heart attack in July, throwing the election into turmoil. His party chose his running mate, Edmundo Jarquín, a former official of the Inter-American Development Bank, to replace him. Unlike Lewites, Jarquín was not an experienced campaigner, nor a popular elected official. The question was whether Lewites' followers would stay with Jarquín, drift into the camp of Montealegre, like Lewites a renegade reformer, or go with ideology and return to the *Sandinista* fold and Ortega.

Ortega again scented victory, and he was more determined than ever to come across as a pussycat instead of a jaguar. He adopted the tune of John Lennon's "Give Peace a Chance" as his campaign anthem, which seemed peculiar as Nicaragua had been at peace for 16 years. He mended fences with the Catholic Church, promising to oppose abortion even to protect the life of the mother, and he frequently invoked the name of God in his speeches. He even chose a former *Contra,* Jaime Morales, as his running mate.

The U.S. Embassy made little secret of its support for Montealegre, although its efforts were far less overt than they had been for Bolaños in 2001. Still, there were thinly veiled threats that an Ortega victory could mean an end to U.S. aid.

Nonetheless, Ortega renounced his earlier opposition to Nicaragua's participation in CAFTA, insisted he welcomed foreign investment and downplayed the obvious enthusiasm of Venezuelan President Hugo Chávez for his candidacy.

On November 5, the voters ended the suspense:

Ortega	854,316	38.07%
Montealegre	650,879	29.0%
Rizo	588,304	26.51%
Jarquín	144,596	6.44%
Pastora	6,120	.27%

Montealegre and Ortega met and pledged to work together to create jobs and to reduce Nicaragua's grinding poverty, still endemic after 11 years of *Sandinista* rule and 16 years under three non-*Sandinista* presidents.

The new Assembly was even more fragmented than before, with the *FSLN* win-

LA TRIBUNA

Miedo al año 2000

tribuna@latribuna.com.ni — Sábado 14 de junio de 1997 • Managua, Nicaragua — Año IV nº 1413 • C$ 3.00

EE.UU. deporta a dos nicas

No hubo pérdida de tiempo. Estados Unidos deportó ayer a dos nicaragüenses indocumentados, sólo horas después de que un juez decidió no extender la suspensión de las deportaciones que había aprobado ya en dos ocasiones. El mismo juez que ha pedido más tiempo para tomar una decisión firme. El mismo que solicitó prudencia a las autoridades migratorias hace dos días.

Los dos deportados, originarios de Matagalpa, tenían varios meses de estar detenidos en Estados Unidos tras haber sido detectados trabajando sin autorización en Tucson, Arizona. Las autoridades dijeron que los dos deportados no tienen antecedentes delictivos en Estados Unidos, y fueron expulsados del país por indocumentados.

El juez federal en Miami, Lawrence King, dijo ayer que necesita más tiempo para decidir si suspende de definitivamente las deportaciones de los nicaragüenses. King es el juez a cargo de una demanda entablada por abogados defensores de los nicaragüenses indocumentados. Estos alegan que los Estados Unidos fueron corresponsables de la guerra civil que vivió Nicaragua en la década pasada, y, por lo tanto, deben ahora dar refugio a los nicas que huyeron del país.

Mientras tanto, dos congresistas cubanoamericanos anunciaron que presentarán un proyecto de ley que concedería la residencia legal a los nicaragüenses indocumentados. Los representantes Ileana Ros-Lehtinen y Lincoln Díaz-Balart, ambos de Miami, reconocen sin embargo que lograr la aprobación de dicho proyecto será sumamente difícil.

Información en PAGINA 3A

◇ 6 mil personas con hambruna

Todo un pueblo desnutrido

Nicaragua tiene hambre. **La Tribuna** tituló así hace cuatro días, y hoy presenta una prueba escalofriante. Los 6,000 habitantes de la comunidad de Ranchería, a 15 kilómetros de Chinandega, sufren de desnutrición. El porcentaje no deja lugar a dudas: el 100 por ciento.

Ahora se sabe gracias a la organización Misión Internacional Bautista, que ha hecho el diagnóstico clínico persona a persona y ha dado la voz de alarma: "Es necesaria la ayuda inmediata antes de que los hechos se agra-

ven y la gente comience a morir", afirmó Sennett Lee, jefe del equipo médico.

El alcalde de Chinandega, Rodolfo Gríes, reconoce su frustración, y achaca el problema al desempleo. Se acabaron las plantaciones de banano y algodón y se acabó el único ingreso de centenares de familias. Los vecinos de Ranchería confiesan que no tienen ni para granos básicos, y que el mango es, durante muchos días, lo único que prueban.

Información en PAGINA 4A

Freno al despale

El Ministerio de Recursos Naturales y Ambiente (Marena) comenzó hace unos días a suspender temporalmente ciertos permisos de explotación de recursos forestales, eso que se conoce por despale.

Ayer dio el paso definitivo y dejó en suspenso todos los permisos de las madereras hasta que no esté claro si los mismos se concedieron conforme a la Ley General del Medio Ambiente y al Reglamento Forestal.

La orden se le dio a los delegados departamentales el pasado jueves y, por supuesto, también cierra las puertas por el momento a la autorización de nuevas licencias y a los planes de manejo en vigor.

El Marena advierte que los madereros que estén operando correctamente no tienen nada que temer e insiste: "No se está en contra del progreso, pero se tiene que cumplir la ley".

Información en PAGINA 5A

Pena de muerte para McVeigh

Al jurado le tomó once horas de deliberaciones. Su veredicto: pena de muerte por inyección letal para Timothy McVeigh, declarado culpable hace dos semanas del atentado dinamitero de Oklahoma y a quien la fiscalía llamó "un terrorista cobarde y traidor que merece morir".

El veredicto del jurado, integrado por siete hombres y cinco mujeres, fue recibido emotivamente con lágrimas y abrazos entre los familiares y amigos de las víctimas del más sangriento ataque terrorista registrado en Estados Unidos.

McVeigh, veterano de la Guerra del Golfo Pérsico, fue declarado culpable de haber hecho "volar" un camión cargado de explosivos frente a un edificio federal en Oklahoma, ocasionando la muerte a 168 personas y heridas a más de 500.

Los jurados condenaron a muerte a McVeigh a pesar de las súplicas de grupos opositores a la pena de muerte y de un prelado de la Iglesia Católica, que abogaron por una sentencia de cadena perpetua.

El presidente Bill Clinton agradeció al jurado la "importante decisión" tomada en el juicio. Sin embargo, Clinton evitó comentar sobre la pena de muerte. "Esta investigación y juicio han confirmado la fe de nuestro país en el sistema judicial", indicó Clinton.

La fecha exacta de la ejecución se fijará durante los próximos dos años.

Información en PAGINA 5B

BOB DAEMMERICH / AFP

Timothy McVeigh trasladado por agentes de la Policía, en una imagen de archivo, cuando formalmente fue acusado de terrorismo en 1995.

LOS TOROS SE LLEVAN EL TITULO | ENEL despediría a sindicalistas | SUMARIO

Former President Enrique Bolaños

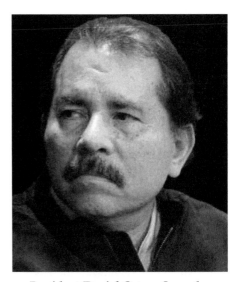

President Daniel Ortega Saavedra

ning a plurality of 38 of the 90 elected seats. The *PLC* won 25, Montealegre's *ALN* won 22 and Jarquín's Sandinista Reform Movement *(MRS)* took 5. The fact that outgoing President Bolaños and Montealegre, the presidential runner-up, also were entitled to seats further complicated matters for Ortega.

Ortega was sworn in on January 10, 2007. Both Chávez and Bolivian President Evo Morales attended the inauguration. The U.S., as usual, sent a mere Cabinet member, Health and Human Services Secretary Michael Leavitt, who met with Ortega and assured him, "Our desire is to work with you." He pledged aid to establish a regional health training facility in Nicaragua, while Chávez promised cut-rate petroleum and fertilizer and said he would pay for 32 badly needed electricity generating plants.

For a time, Ortega maintained a delicate balancing act between his old friends in Cuba and his new ones in Caracas on the one hand, and his old nemesis in Washington on the other. He landed a pledge of $350 million from Iran for port construction, while receiving disaster aid from the U.S. He interjected himself into the Colombian-Ecuadorian border incident in March 2008 on the side of Ecuador (see Colombia and Ecuador), apparently because of ideological kinship with Ecuador's President Rafaél Correa and Nicaragua's long-standing territorial dispute with Colombia over San Andrés Island.

Any further doubts about the unholy alliance Ortega and Alemán had reached in 1999 were dispelled when Ortega succeeded in circumventing the courts by joining with the *arnoldistas* in the Assembly to reduce Alemán's sentence from 20

to five years. He was released from prison but remained under house arrest.

Return of the Cold Warrior

Once back in power, Ortega morphed back into the hardline, Marxist-Leninist Cold Warrior of the 1980s. He brought Nicaragua into *ALBA*, Chávez's anti-U.S. bloc, with Cuba, Venezuela, Ecuador and Bolivia. The old truculent anthems of the 1980s began playing again at *FSLN* rallies. He ordered formation of what became goon squads, funded with Venezuelan money, to intimidate opponents and dissenters.

Dogged by polls that showed his popularity at 20%, Ortega demonstrated his true antidemocratic colors by preventing opposition parties from competing in the November 9, 2008, municipal elections, then by rigging that election so blatantly that it brought world-wide condemnation—except from Ortega's allies in Cuba, Venezuela, Bolivia and Ecuador.

First, Ortega used hurricane damage as a pretext to delay local elections in April 2008 along the Caribbean coast, which sparked riots. Next, he stacked the Supreme Electoral Council, designed to be a neutral, independent body and which certified his 2006 election, with loyal *Sandinistas*. That council then disqualified both Jarquín's *MRS* and Montealegre's *ALN* from participating in the municipal elections; it also disqualified the Conservative Party. Montealegre reconciled with the *PLC* and became its candidate for mayor of Managua.

The municipal elections were the predictable sham. To allay a resounding rebuke predicted by polls, Ortega refused accreditation to the OAS, the European Union and the Carter Center from serving as observers, as they had in 1990 and every election since; Ortega publicly blamed the OAS for his 1990 defeat. He also prevented the Nicaraguan watchdog group, Transparency and Ethics, from monitoring the voting and the count.

On election day, Transparency and Ethics volunteers posted themselves outside polling places and alleged irregularities at one third of them, including the early closing of some polling stations. Polls had showed Montealegre leading the *FSLN*'s Alexis Argüello, a former world boxing champion. But on election night, non-*FSLN* members of the electoral council were expelled from the vote counting, which continued in secret. In the city of León, thousands of ballots marked for Liberal candidates were found in the city dump.

The official results: The *FSLN* won in 94 of the 146 municipalities, and Argüello won in Managua with 51.5% of the vote. Montealegre claimed his independent tally showed him winning handily, and

demanded a recount. His supporters took to the streets, only to be met by *Sandinista* goons wielding clubs and machetes; they also fired home-made mortar rounds at the protesters; police stood by passively. The electoral council agreed to a recount—which took place behind closed doors and independent observers were barred. The results of the "recount" were predictable. The EU expressed its disgust by suspending desperately needed aid, which amounted to a third of the budget. Ortega continued to rely on Chávez's largess.

In 2008, the government investigated two groups that had been critical of Ortega for alleged money laundering: the Center of Media Investigations, headed by Carlos Chamorro Barrios, son of former President Violeta Barrios de Chamorro; and the Autonomous Women's Movement, which had criticized Ortega for opposing abortion even to save the life of the mother, calling it a betrayal of *Sandinista* principles. Their offices were raided. The government also threatened Ernesto Cardenal, the most prominent *FSLN* defector, with legal difficulties after he called Ortega a "thief" and his government a "monarchy."

Ortega also turned the clock back to the Cold War on the international stage. He appointed his former foreign minister, Miguel D'Escoto, an unmellowed Revolutionary Theology defrocked priest, as ambassador to the United Nations, just as Nicaragua's turn came to hold the General Assembly presidency. D'Escoto used the presidency as a pulpit to harangue the U.S. for a litany of real or imagined sins, alienating himself and Nicaragua from Secretary-General Ban Ki-moon.

Nor did Ortega seek amicable relations with the new U.S. president, Barack Obama. At the Fifth Summit of the Americas in Port-of-Spain, Trinidad, in 2009,

Nicaragua

Ortega made a spectacle of himself with a 50-minute, *yanqui*-baiting diatribe, reciting a shopworn list of complaints dating back to the 19th century, as Obama listened indulgently. Ortega even attacked the summit itself because of the exclusion of Cuba. "I don't feel comfortable attending this summit," he said. "I feel ashamed of the fact that I'm participating at this summit with the absence of Cuba."

Obama responded later, "To move forward, we cannot let ourselves be prisoners of past disagreements. I'm grateful that President Ortega did not blame me for things that happened when I was three months old. Too often, an opportunity to build a fresh partnership of the Americas has been undermined by stale debates. We've all heard these arguments before."

Yet, Ortega's contempt for the U.S. has not compelled him to withdraw from CAFTA.

Managua Mayor Argüello was found dead on July 1, 2009 of what was described as a self-inflicted gunshot wound to the heart, but there were allegations of foul play.

In another anti-democratic power play, Ortega pulled a legal sleight-of-hand in October 2009 to get the Supreme Court to nullify the restriction on immediate re-election, allowing him to run again in 2011 without first obtaining a constitutional amendment. He did this by slipping his petition through a subcommittee of *Sandinista* justices; non-*Sandinista* justices were not even informed of Ortega's petition. Tens of thousands of anti-Ortega protesters filled the streets of Managua; tens of thousands of Ortega's supporters counter-demonstrated. That December, the Assembly passed a resolution renouncing what it called the court's "pseudo-ruling" and declaring that Ortega was not eligible to run again. In 2010, two *Sandinista* judges refused to step down at the end of their

term, and anti-*Sandinista* justices boycotted sessions to protest the illegitimate justices. The *Sandinista* president of the court then replaced the boycotting justices with *Sandinista* loyalists, a move of questionable legality. But it provided Ortega with a 13–2 majority, whereupon the full court ruled that barring Ortega from running would violate his human rights!

A year-end poll in 2009 by CID-Gallup put Ortega's approval rating at 22%, and another in May 2010 showed that 56% believe his candidacy would have a negative impact on the country (see The Future).

Undaunted, Ortega set out to boost his faltering popular support two ways. First, in October 2010, he fueled nationalist sentiment by provoking a border dispute with Costa Rica, which has no army. A Nicaraguan dredging operation, backed up by 50 soldiers, established a camp on Calero Island at the mouth of the San Juan River. The river forms the border, but the two countries have long quarreled over navigation rights. Costa Rica moved policemen into the area and lodged a protest, saying the dredgers also were dumping their spill on Costa Rican soil. The Nicaraguans defended their actions by claiming that Google Map showed the location of the camp to be in Nicaraguan territory. Google then publicly declared there was an "inaccuracy" in its map, and said it should not be used to demarcate boundaries.

Costa Rican President Laura Chinchilla appealed to the OAS and brought suit against Nicaragua in the International Court of Justice in The Hague, Netherlands. In March 2011, the court issued a temporary order barring either country from moving civilians or security into the disputed area until it reaches a decision. (On November 21, 2013, the ICJ ruled in favor of Costa Rica and mandated the removal of Nicaraguan forces from Calero Island.)

Next, Ortega used the annual $400 million in Venezuelan aid to ingratiate himself with poor voters by keeping bus fares artificially low despite high fuel prices and by building cinder-block houses to replace slums. He also replaced civil servants with *Sandinista* loyalists and bought off retired generals with high-level jobs. He named one retired general, Omar Halleslevens, a former army commander, as his running mate in 2011.

An Electoral Farce

Jockeying within the opposition to come up with a unified candidate with a chance to unseat Ortega proved futile. Former President Alemán announced his intention to seek a second term, trying to turn his prison term into an asset by nauseatingly comparing himself with Nelson Mandela. Montealegre briefly considered another run, but "sacrificed" his ambition in favor of a candidate who would be more unifying. He threw his support behind a popular, but elderly, conservative radio commentator, Fabio Gadea Mantilla, 79.

Alemán met with Gadea and offered him the vice presidency on the *PLC* ticket if he would abandon his run. Gadea refused, and subsequently named the perennial Jarquín as his running mate under the Independent Liberal Party banner. Another anti-*Sandinista*, Enrique Quiñones of the Nicaraguan Liberal Alliance, also entered the race, further fragmenting the opposition vote and boosting Ortega's chances.

Ortega again began sounding like a moderate, even courting foreign investors with attractive tax incentives, and he ingratiated the Nicaraguan business community by channeling some of the $600 million a year in Venezuelan aid for loans to small businessmen. It worked; campaign contributions to Gadea largely dried up. Ortega made no secret that the largess that Venezuela was bestowing on Nicaragua, such as the business loans and the new housing projects, also would dry up if Gadea were elected.

Ortega also used the state machinery to his advantage, coercing government employees into attending his rallies and commandeering public buses to transport people to rallies. Ortega's image was ubiquitous, while Gadea had only 16 billboards in the entire country.

In the balloting on November 6, EU and OAS observers complained about numerous voting irregularities. There were suspicious delays in delivery of voter identification cards; there was a disproportionate *Sandinista* presence in polling stations; and there was a lack of transparency in the vote tabulations. There were outbreaks of election-related violence that left several

Traditional Dance

people dead. But in the end, the obvious was confirmed by the "official" results:

Ortega	1,569,287	62.5%
Gadea	778,889	31%
Alemán	148,507	5.9%

Thus elected to an unconstitutional third term and an unconstitutional second consecutive term, an exuberant Ortega promised "peace, stability and tranquility." Gadea refused to recognize Ortega's victory. The *Sandinistas* also won 63 of the 92 National Assembly seats, precisely the two-thirds necessary for them to change their own constitution as they see fit, such as allowing Ortega to run for re-election indefinitely.

Ortega's inauguration on January 10, 2012, attracted international headlines. Not only did Chávez attend, as expected, but so did Iranian President Mahmoud Amadinejad, who included Nicaragua on a three-country tour of Latin America along with Venezuela and Cuba. Ortega's "moderation" went out the window during his inaugural address. He voiced his support for Iran's nuclear ambitions, and he lamented the death of the "assassinated" Libyan misruler Moammar Gadhafi. And he must have sent a chill through the domestic and foreign businessmen he had so recently cajoled when he declared, "There is no place on this Earth for savage capitalism."

Yet, Ortega evidently had struck a responsive chord with his countrymen. The Mexican polling firm Consulta Mitofsky reported in April 2012 that Ortega was the fourth most popular leader in the Western Hemisphere, behind Ecuador's Rafael, Colombia's Juan Manuel Santos and El Salvador's Mauricio Funes. By September, he had dropped to seventh place, with an approval rating of 59%. In October 2013, he was back in fourth place with 66%.

Recent Developments

Nicaragua lost to Costa Rica before the ICJ, but it had more luck against Colombia. After deliberating for 11 years, the ICJ issued a stunning decision on November 19, 2012, granting Nicaragua sovereignty over some uninhabited islands in the Caribbean and their surrounding waters, in effect cutting off Colombia's access to San Andrés Island. Also at stake were lucrative fishing rights in those waters, traditionally used by Colombian fisherman. There is also the potential for offshore oil drilling. Colombia reacted angrily to the ruling, but Ortega assured Colombian President Juan Manuel Santos that he would respect Colombia's traditional right of access. The two presidents disavowed military action.

In a controversial and still-mysterious development, Ortega submitted a bill to the Assembly in June 2013 that would grant a 50-year exclusive concession to an obscure Chinese firm, run by an equally obscure tycoon, to build the long-delayed canal across Nicaragua. The *Sandinistas* ramrodded the bill through in just a week, leaving no time for opposing committee testimony from environmental groups or from indigenous communities that may be affected. Opposition legislators cried foul, warning that Ortega was selling out the country's sovereignty and saying it should be decided by referendum. Opponents demonstrated outside the legislative building. On June 19, after white-hot debate, the Assembly approved the concession 61-25, along strict party lines. One Liberal legislator railed, "We can't say you are selling out the country because you are just giving it away!"

Unanswered questions include the exact route of the proposed canal or how long construction will take; about all that has been disclosed is that it will cross Lake Nicaragua, which supplies much of the country with drinking water and irrigation. Another nagging question is, who will finance the $40 billion project?

The concession was granted to a hastily organized company called HKND, based in Hong Kong but registered in the Cayman Islands suspiciously soon before the concession vote. It is owned by 41-year-old Wang Jing, owner of a telecommunications firm called Xinwei, which specializes in wireless telephones. Perhaps not coincidentally, Xinwei recently landed a cell phone contract with Nicaragua. He has visited Nicaragua only once, in September 2012. Wang's only claimed experience in infrastructure construction is a gold mine in Cambodia. He also supposedly owns a hotel management firm, although Reuters reported it could not confirm his connection. Grilled by journalists at a news conference in Beijing after the concession was granted, Wang insisted he is a "normal Chinese citizen" with no ties to the Chinese government. Although he promised transparency for the canal project, he would not reveal at which school he claimed to have studied medicine. He said the $40 billion would come from various international banks, which he would not name.

Ironically, Nicaragua still maintains diplomatic relations with Taiwan.

Digging was tentatively scheduled to begin by the end of 2014, but the head of the canal authority, Manuel Coronel, announced in January that a route had not yet been picked and that construction would "probably" begin sometime in 2015. There still is no transparency.

Nicaragua was one of four Latin American nations, along with *ALBA* partners Bolivia, Ecuador and Venezuela, that offered to grant political asylum to fugitive National Security Agency leaker Edward Snowden in July 2013. Ortega said he would be willing to grant asylum "if circumstances allow it," adding, "We have the sovereign right to help a person who felt remorse after finding out how the United States was using technology to spy on the whole world, and especially its European allies." Snowden requested asylum in Russia, apparently because there was no way to fly from Moscow to any of the Latin American countries without crossing the airspace of a U.S. ally that could order the plane grounded.

In October 2013, Ortega moved to legitimize his illegitimate actions by introducing 39 constitutional amendments, essentially undoing the 1995 constitutional reforms that were aimed at eliminating *Sandinista* abuses. Ortega's "reforms" restores them—and adds some more. The most obvious is the removal of term limits altogether, allowing Ortega to run for president indefinitely. It also removes the 35% requirement to win the presidency, greatly trims the power of the legislative branch, allows Ortega to rule largely by decree, provides constitutional status to the near-sovereignty of HKND to build a canal, and for active military officers to serve in the cabinet. The opposition vainly denounced the measures, warning that Ortega was bent on becoming another Somoza. Along strict party lines, the Assembly approved them on January 28, 2014, by a vote of 64–25.

CULTURE: Though a substantial number of Nicaraguans lead a modern, urban life comparable to that of the large cities of Latin America, the majority, mostly mestizos, live in rural simplicity and poverty. There are enclaves of Miskito Indians and black Garifunas along the Caribbean coast, who have remained fiercely unassimilated.

The 16th century Spanish ruins of León Viejo joined the list of UNESCO's cultural World Heritage Sites in 2000, and the León Cathedral was added in 2011.

Nicaraguan music, derived from the Spanish-Moorish conquerors, is used to accompany a wide variety of local dances and festivals. It is possible to see dramatic and musical productions professionally performed in Managua, and in the interior to view traditional *mestizo* comedies performed in a combination of Spanish and *Hahuatl* or *Mangue*, which are Indian dialects. The African-based music of the Garifunas, descendants of escaped slaves, also has been influential in Nicaragua's musical profile.

Nicaragua contributed one of the world's foremost poets, Rubén Darío (1867–1916), who established the *modernismo* literary

Nicaragua

Rubén Darío

movement in the Spanish-speaking world. He spent much of his productive life in Spain, including a stint as ambassador, and produced such works as *Prosas profanas (Profane Prose)* and *Cantos de vida y esperanza (Chants of Life and Hope)*. Nicaragua's highest cultural award is named for him.

Nicaraguan cinema is underdeveloped, but it claims at least one internationally renowned film: *Alsino y el condor (Alsino and the Condor)*, directed by the Chilean exile Miguel Littín and starring U.S. actor Dean Stockwell. The story of a Nicaraguan boy who befriends a U.S. helicopter pilot working for the Somoza regime during the *Sandinista* revolution, it was nominated for the U.S. Academy Award for Best Foreign Film in 1982 and won the Golden Medal at the Moscow International Film Festival.

Several Nicaraguans have achieved acclaim in popular music, perhaps most notably the singer-composer Carlos Mejía Godoy (b. 1943) and his brother, Luis Enrique Mejía Godoy (b. 1945). They are credited with beginning the *Nueva Canción* (New Song) movement in Central America in the 1970s. They were active participants in the struggle against dictator Anastasio Somoza and served in the *Sandinista* government of 1979–90. However, Carlos later broke with the *Sandinistas* and was Edmundo Jarquín's running mate in the 2006 presidential election (see History). The brothers were jointly awarded the Order of Rubén Darío.

The son of Luis Enrique and nephew of Carlos is the salsa sensation Luis Enrique Mejía López (b. 1962), who goes by the stage name Luis Enrique. He rose to stardom in the 1990s, being hailed as *El Príncipe de Salsa* (the Prince of Salsa). He won two

Latin Grammy Awards in 2009: Best Salsa Album for *Ciclos* and Best Tropical Song for *Yo no sé mañana. Ciclos* also won a mainstream Grammy in 2010 for Best Tropical Album. In 2012, his album *Soy y seré* won the Latin Grammy for Best Salsa Album.

Education was long underdeveloped in Nicaragua. The *Sandinistas* gave it a priority, reducing literacy dramatically. There are at least 34 colleges and universities in Nicaragua, most established since 1979, a mix of state-run, private and Catholic or Evangelical. The premier institution is the National Autonomous University of Nicaragua, founded in 1812, with campuses in Managua and León.

Illiteracy hampered development of the print media, but for decades the country's most influential newspaper has been *La Prensa,* owned by the Chamorro family. Its opposition to the Somoza dictatorship led to the assassination of its editor, Pedro Joaquín Chamorro, in 1978. After Somoza's fall, *La Prensa* then opposed the increasingly dictatorial *Sandinista* regime. When a free election was permitted in 1990, Chamorro's widow, Violeta Barrios de Chamorro, defeated President Daniel Ortega (see History).

The *Sandinistas* confiscated a pro-Somoza newspaper and turned it into a party organ, *Barricada,* which after the return to democracy became a weekly. Xavier Chamorro, Pedro Joaquín's brother, launched a pro-*Sandinista* daily, *El Nuevo Diario,* in 1980.

Because of poverty and illiteracy, radio remains the most influential medium in the country, but it is highly politicized, employed by both sides in Nicaragua's bitter political battles. The opposition candidate who opposed Ortega for re-election in November 2011 was a popular radio commentator, Fabio Gadea.

Television is underdeveloped but popular, and also highly politicized. The adult children of President Ortega control two of the country's channels and the *Sandinista* party controls another. Private stations have reported government intimidation. In 2011, a joint Nicaraguan-Venezuelan business consortium, Albanisa, acquired control of one station and promptly fired a commentator who had been critical of Ortega.

Freedom House still rated the Nicaraguan press as "partly free" in 2012 and 2013.

ECONOMY: Although Nicaragua is largely based on agriculture, which employed 65% of the work force, the increased development of light industry before the revolution gave Nicaragua's economy a degree of hope for a broader base than was found in most other Latin American countries. Underpopulated and

with many unexploited natural resources, the nation has a substantial potential for tremendous economic growth with proper management.

Nicaragua's most important farm commodities are produced in the western region. Rich in volcanic soils, this section is the source of cotton, coffee and sugar. The cattle industry has also expanded in the west. The eastern region is largely devoted to banana production. Nationalization of large producing farms during the *Sandinista* era did not contribute to their efficiency, and the breakup of some into smaller peasant farms actually seriously lowered production.

The U.S. commercial embargo on Nicaragua in the 1980s had a devastating effect. The closing of U.S. ports and a ban on technological imports all but shut down the economy. As in Cuba, Soviet limitations on its economic aid to socialist countries added a somber note to Nicaragua's possibilities for development. During 1986–90, virtually all that was exported was bananas, sold to the Soviet Union and Eastern Europe at inflated prices.

The Chamorro government, hamstrung by the ever-present threat of the *Sandinista* military, accomplished little at reducing unemployment and underemployment, which totaled more than 65%. President Arnoldo Alemán moved more aggressively to bring Nicaragua in line with International Monetary Fund demands and to make the country more attractive to foreign investors. GDP growth was a respectable 5% in 1997. Meanwhile, the IMF extended Nicaragua a three-year, $136 million loan package and praised Alemán for stabilizing the currency and reducing the bloated, featherbedded bureaucracy. The World Bank also granted a $70 million loan to help transform the financial sector from the old Marxist system.

Hurricane Mitch caused billions of dollars in damage to the economic infrastructure in 1998, a blow the country could ill afford and which added another $300 million to the already oppressive $6.2 billion external debt. Surprisingly, however, Mitch did not derail the expanding economy. GDP growth was still 4% for 1998 and 6.2% for 1999. In 2000 it had tapered off slightly to 5.0%. It was 2.5% in 2001 and only 1% in 2002 and 1.4% in 2003.

President Enrique Bolaños claimed a better economic record, with growth in 2004 and 2005 running at about 4% and 3.9% in 2006. Bolaños signed, and the Assembly ratified, the Dominican Republic-Central American Free Trade Agreement with the United States in 2005. It took effect on April 1, 2006.

Nicaragua's per capita income fell lower than Haiti's in 1997, to $436, making it for the first time the poorest country in

Nicaragua

the Western Hemisphere. By 2002 it had dropped even lower, to $370, compared with $440 for Haiti. It has since moved past Haiti, to about $1,500 in 2011, still the second-poorest in the hemisphere. In 2009, the most recent year available, 42.5% of the population lived below the poverty line. Economic growth dropped under Ortega's second term, to 3.2% in 2007 and 2008. With the global recession, it dropped by –2.9% in 2009, recovering slightly by 2.8% in 2010. Growth was 3.1% in 2010, 5.1% in 2011, 4.0% in 2012 and 4.4% in 2013.

Inflation soared under Ortega, from 9.5% in 2006 to 19.9% in 2008. With the recession, it dropped to 3.7% in 2009. In 2013 it was 7.4%.

The official unemployment rate has been about 7.5% for three years, although another 46.5% are underemployed.

Nicaragua has long been saddled with one of the highest per capita foreign debts in the world, a dubious distinction exacerbated by Hurricane Mitch. In 2004, Nicaragua was on the list of 18 heavily indebted nations provided with debt forgiveness by the so-called Paris Club. But in 2008, public debt was still 74.8% of GDP; in 2009, it rose to 87%, 12th highest in the world. In 2011 it was 52.7%, 36th in the world.

Like Mexico and other Central American countries, Nicaragua depends heavily on remittances from Nicaraguans working abroad, mostly in the United States and Costa Rica. Remittances have increased from $655.5 million in 2006 to $768 million in 2009 to $912 million in 2011. They rose 11.23% in 2012 to a record $1.041 billion, or 10.2% of GDP.

Shortly before his re-election in 2011, and despite his avowed socialism, Ortega launched a concerted campaign to lure foreign investors to Nicaragua with attractive tax exemptions, low labor costs and relative tranquility in compared with violence-torn Guatemala, Honduras and El Salvador. Nicaragua's homicide rate in 2010 was 13 per 100,000, compared with 78 in Honduras. His efforts appeared to be bearing fruit, although Nicaragua is still heavily dependent on Venezuela for cut-rate petroleum and direct economic aid.

THE FUTURE: For the past four decades, Nicaragua has been whipsawed from corrupt right-wing dictatorship to corrupt left-wing dictatorship to inept and corrupt democracy and back to a repressive and corrupt left-wing dictatorship, as if on an amusement park ride—only there is nothing amusing about it.

Daniel Ortega, now 68, balding and with a heart condition, rose Phoenix-like from the ashes of three successive defeats to regain the presidency in 2007, hoodwinking his countrymen into giving him a 38% winning plurality, convincing them that he was a different man from the fire-breathing Stalinist of the 1980s. His actions during his second term showed him to be the unreconstructed *yanqui*-hating Cold Warrior he was then, even as he took advantage of Nicaragua's membership in CAFTA. He alienated the United States and the European Union in favor of dubious alliances with Cuba and Venezuela. Then he jerry-rigged the 2008 municipal elections and circumvented the constitution to get himself re-elected in 2011.

Nicaraguans' commitment to democracy has understandably taken a rollercoaster ride. In 1996, in the first annual *Latinobarómetro* survey of Latin American countries, 59% of Nicaraguans said they agreed that democracy is preferable to any other form of government. By 2004, that figure had dropped to 39%, tying with Paraguay for the lowest in Latin America. Perhaps because of the spectacle of seeing the disgraced former President Alemán going to jail, support for democracy rebounded to 61% in 2007. In 2011 and 2013, perhaps because of the sham of democracy, it dropped to 50%, the fifth lowest in the 18-nation survey.

At the same time, Nicaraguans who believe that authoritarianism is sometimes preferable to democracy also has rollercoasted, from 14% in 1996 to 22% in 2001, to 9% in 2010 and back to 15% in 2011 and 20% in 2013. Alas, authoritarianism is what they now have under Ortega.

There is still more unknown than known about the controversial 50-year concession to shadowy Chinese businessman Wang Jing to build a new canal across Nicaragua. The bill was rammed through in a week, with no time to discuss sovereignty, financing or environmental issues. The route of the canal or the expected time of construction has not been revealed; neither has the source of the $40 billion to build it. The only new information is that construction won't begin until 2015. Nicaraguans, and the world, are still waiting for answers.

Ortega's so-called constitutional reforms, which legalized his illegitimate hold on power, were predictable. He is following precisely in the footsteps of his late ally, Venezuela's Hugo Chávez, by allowing indefinite re-election and by emasculating the legislative branch of any meaningful power, letting him run the country by decree as an autocrat. Judging from opinion polls, an overwhelming majority of Nicaraguans approve of his autocracy. In October 2013 he was the fourth most popular leader of the Western Hemisphere, with an approval rating of 66%. Thus, he will likely keep on running and winning until he expires—just like Chávez did.

The Republic of Panama

The almost completed Panama Canal—final blasting of a channel, October 1913

Area: 28,745 square miles.

Population: 3,608,431(2014 est.).

Capital City: Panama City (Pop. 1,346,000 in 2009).

Climate: Tropical, with clearly marked wet and dry seasons. The heaviest rainfall is from May to December.

Neighboring Countries: Colombia (southeast); Costa Rica (northwest).

Official Language: Spanish.

Other Principal Tongue: English.

Ethnic Background: Mulatto (mixed African and European, 72%); African (14%); European (12%); Indians and other (2%).

Principal Religion: Roman Catholic Christianity.

Chief Commercial Products: Bananas, shrimp and apparel.

Currency: Balboa (in reality, the U.S. dollar is the legal tender).

Gross Domestic Product: U.S. $40.62 billion in 2013 ($11,412 per capita, official exchange rate).

Former Colonial Status: Spanish Colony (1519–1821), Province of Colombia (1821–1903).

Independence Date: November 3, 1903.

Chief of State: Juan Carlos Varela Rodríguez (b. December 12, 1963), president (since July 1, 2014)

National Flag: A rectangle of four quarters; white with a blue star, blue, white with a red star, red.

Panama is a very narrow isthmus, 480 miles long and varying in width from 37 to 110 miles, connecting North and South America. Mountainous throughout, the highest elevation is the volcano Baru (11,397 feet) near the Costa Rican border. The Talamanca range continues southeast at an average elevation of 3,000 feet until it drops into the sea just west of Panama City. The San Blas range, rising east of Colón, runs southeast into Colombia; again the average elevation is 3,000 feet. A third range appears along the Pacific coast east of Panama City and runs southeast into Colombia. Both coasts have narrow plains cut by numerous small rivers running into the sea.

Lying in the tropical rainbelt, Panamá's Atlantic coast receives up to 150 inches of rainfall—the Pacific coast receives about 100 inches. The dry season, or "summer," runs from December to April. Four fifths of Panama's territory is covered with jungle and one half lies outside effective

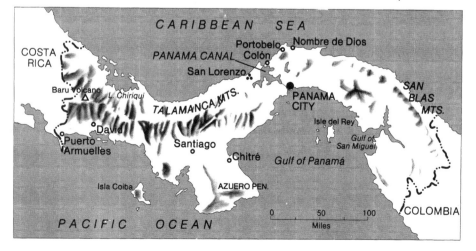

control by the Panamanian government. The principal reason for Panama's existence as a nation and the principal source of its earnings is the geographical accident of the north-south gap between the Talamanca and San Blas ranges, which permitted the construction of a canal between the Atlantic and Pacific oceans. Now the site of the Panama Canal and the nation's major cities, more than half the population is found in a narrow corridor and along the Pacific coast west of the gap.

HISTORY: Columbus discovered Panama in 1498–1500 and called it Veraguas. It assumed importance in 1513 when Vasco Nuñez de Balboa discovered the Pacific. Panama City was established on the Pacific coast in 1518 and connected to three Caribbean ports by trails and rivers.

Nombre de Dios (Name of God) and Portobelo were the principal Atlantic ports maintained by the Spanish. Panama became the base for the outfitting of expeditions into Peru and Central America; it later was a major link in the route over which the wealth of the region was shipped to Spain. This wealth, and Panama's strategic importance, attracted pirates, buccaneers and foreign armies.

The British privateer Sir Francis Drake burned Nombre de Dios in 1573 and 1598; Henry Morgan raided the isthmus, looting and burning Panama City in 1617; British Admiral Edward Vernon captured Portobelo in 1739 and San Lorenzo in 1740. Spain abandoned the Panamanian route in 1746 in favor of the trip around Cape Horn at the tip of Argentina and Chile to reach its colonies in western Latin America.

For nearly 100 years Panama was bypassed by trade and ignored during the wars for independence in Mexico and South America. Panama became a province of Colombia. The discovery of gold in California brought renewed interest in quick transit from the Atlantic to the Pacific coast of the United States. A railroad was constructed between 1850 and 1853, and the De Lesseps Company of France started work on a canal in 1882. The work was abandoned in 1893, in part because of yellow fever epidemics, and in 1904 the United States acquired the assets of the bankrupt company.

There ensued three years of fruitless negotiations between the United States and Colombia. Colombia was gripped by civil war during the period. Philippe Jean Bunau-Varilla, the French agent of the defunct canal company, with the knowledge of the United States, engineered a revolution in Panama with the understanding that the United States would intervene to establish Panama as an independent state and that U.S. financial interests would acquire the right to complete the inter-oceanic canal across the isthmus. President Theodore Roosevelt recognized the independence of Panama three days after its proclamation on November 3, 1903.

Treaty negotiations between the United States and Panama were brief. Bunau-Varilla represented Panama, and the two sides quickly reached an agreement giving the United States virtually sovereign rights "in perpetuity" over the Canal Zone, a 10-mile-wide swath of Panamanian territory from coast to coast. Panamanians were horrified when confronted with Bunau-Varilla's *fait accompli*, but there was little they could do. Construction on the canal started shortly thereafter—as did 70 years of wrangling between the United States and the Republic of Panama over the sovereignty issue. In August 1914, the 400-year-old dream of Spanish, French, British and North American adventurers was accomplished when a vessel sailed through the completed canal from the Atlantic to the Pacific Ocean.

Panama's political history as an independent state was in keeping with the pattern of the Central American and Caribbean nations. Power lay in the hands of a small, elite Caucasian group that exploited the geographic situation for its personal benefit. The population at the time of independence was concentrated in the terminal cities of the trans-isthmian railroad and dependent upon commerce for its income. The influx of labor for the construc-

Panama's Declaration of Independence

Panama

El Casco Viejo, **the old part of Panama City**

tion completely overwhelmed the administrative capabilities of the small nation. A pattern ensued in which actual power was in the hands of the *Guardia Nacional*, whose head was infrequently the actual chief of state; more often he ruled through a figurehead president.

U.S. Patrimony

The United States took what measures it deemed necessary to achieve its purposes while Panama elected or appointed one ineffective government after another. The Panama Railroad, the United Fruit Company, which had established banana plantations during the late 1800s, and the Panama Canal Company, in consort with a small group of Panamanian families, exercised effective political and economic power in Panama. The steady influx of wealth supported a booming economy through the 1940s. Following World War II, the growing population exceeded the service demands of commerce and Panama began to feel the effects of 50 years of lack of direction and failure to invest its earnings in substantial industrial ventures.

Into this volatile political environment there appeared a charismatic and demagogic figure who was to dominate Panamanian politics for the next half-century—and even beyond his death: Arnulfo Arias. The founder of the ultra-nationalist *Panameñista* Party, Arias exploited his people's near-xenophobic dislike of foreigners. He lashed out not only at the United States and the "Zonians" who enjoyed their suburban tropical paradise, but foreign immigrants as well, particularly those from Asia. On those rare occasions when the *Guardia Nacional* allowed Panamanians to vote in fair elections, Arias and his party did well—*too* well, for the *Guardia* and the elite. He was elected president in 1940 and in 1948, only to be deposed by the *Guardia* both times. He won again—and was deposed again—in 1968 and probably won two other elections, in 1964 and 1984, but was denied victory through creative vote-counting.

As the military, in league with the tiny clique of oligarchs, was the actual power in the country, it "elected" one of its own, Police Chief José Antonio Remón, as president in 1952. Oddly enough, Remón was to prove one of Panama's more enlight-

ened rulers, instituting long-overdue social reform, which estranged him from the oligarchy, and cracking down on the more overt corruption. He also was friendlier to the United States than many of his predecessors had been, *too* friendly for some Panamanians. Nonetheless, his more rational policy succeeded in obtaining an increase in the rent for the Canal Zone in 1955 from a paltry $430,000 (it had been only $250,000 until 1939!) to a still-ridiculous $1.9 million. Remón was assassinated that same year, but whether his killers were motivated by social reactionism or anti-Americanism never has been determined.

Remón's antithesis, Ernesto de la Guardia, was elected president in a reasonably fair count in 1956 and began making strident demands on the United States. The war over the Suez Canal that year helped further fan Panamanian passions. Some of the demands were quite legitimate, such as elimination of the inequitable wage scales between Zonian and Panamanian canal employees. President Eisenhower, who had served in Panama as a young Army officer in the early 1920s, acceded to the wage demands, as well as to a demand

326

to allow the Panamanian flag to fly in the Zone. But it seemed the more the Americans conceded, the more antagonistic the de la Guardia government became. On Panamanian Independence Day in 1959, a well-orchestrated mob sought to "invade" the Zone, forcing U.S. troops to deter them with fixed bayonets. Ultra-nationalists and pro-Castro students exploited the incident for propaganda purposes. If nothing else, de la Guardia earned one important distinction for a Panamanian president: he served out his elected four-year term.

A far more moderate figure (and a member of the oligarchy), Roberto Chiari, was elected president in 1960 in what probably was the cleanest election Panama would ever have until 1994. Chiari enjoyed an amicable relationship with President Kennedy, and followed an anti-Castro line pleasing to Washington.

Nonetheless, toward the end of Chiari's term there occurred the worst incident violence yet between Americans and Panamanians. In January 1964, foolhardy Zonian students at Balboa High School tore down the Panamanian flag flying next to the U.S. flag in front of the school and desecrated it. As word got out, Panamanians exploded in fury, and rioters flooded into the Zone, separated from Panama City only by the broad Fourth of July Avenue. In the resulting violence, 23 Panamanians and six Americans, most of them soldiers, were killed. Chiari broke diplomatic relations with the United States, and President Lyndon B. Johnson was faced with his first foreign policy crisis since succeeding the assassinated Kennedy two months earlier. Panama renamed Fourth of July Avenue *Avenida de los Mártires* (Avenue of the Martyrs), and to this day there are ceremonies marking each anniversary of the deadly riots.

In the election of May 1964, Chiari's cousin and fellow oligarch, Marco Aurelio Robles, narrowly defeated the fiery Arias, though the vote counting remains suspect to this day. Robles re-established relations with Washington which, still shaken by the riots, began negotiating seriously about changes to the 1903 canal treaty. Robles withdrew government sanctioning on anti-U.S. demonstrations, and relations gradually improved—for a time.

Torrijos Seizes Power

In the May 1968 elections, the perennial Arias won by a convincing margin that could not be denied. He was duly inaugurated on September 1, but just 11 days into his term, the *Guardia* overthrew him for a third time, ushering in 21 years of despotic military rule as heavy-handed as any in Latin America. For the first 13 of those years, absolute power rested with Colonel

President Jimmy Carter looks on as Panama's Omar Torrijos signs the 1977 Panama Canal Treaty

Omar Torrijos, who later promoted himself to brigadier general, a flamboyant and charismatic figure in the classic style of the Latin American *caudillo*.

Torrijos became a hero to the long-suppressed lower class as he established what amounted to a Panamanian version of a dictatorship of the proletariat. Political activity ceased, and a puppet legislative assembly rubber-stamped Torrijos' dictates. The egomaniacal Torrijos even had his heroic image emblazoned in a new frieze work on the legislative palace. Press freedom vanished as the government expropriated three newspapers owned by Arias' brother, Harmodio, and blackmailed the owner of the venerable and respected *La Estrella de Panama* into becoming a sycophantish parrot of the government line. Critics of the

Brigadier General Omar Torrijos

regime were tortured, and more than a few took a one-way helicopter ride over the Pacific Ocean. Those too prominent to kill were hustled off into exile, often after being beaten as a farewell gesture. Torrijos re-established diplomatic relations with Cuba, and engaged in *gringo*-baiting on a scale not seen since de la Guardia. He attacked traditional corruption long practiced by the elite, but a newer, more sinister version with ties to Colombian drug traffickers soon arose. Torrijos implemented lax banking regulations that attracted branches of major banks from every continent, while the drug traffickers found Panama a veritable paradise for money-laundering.

The New Canal Treaties

National politics was dominated in the 1970s by the lingering dispute with the United States over the canal. Most of this centered around the 1903 treaty that granted the United States virtual sovereignty "in perpetuity" over the 530-square-mile Canal Zone. Widespread resentment against what was regarded as an outdated treaty unified most Panamanian political factions in demanding a new treaty. Key changes sought by Panama included (1) increased rental payments, (2) a large-scale reduction of U.S. military presence in the zone, (3) a greater Panamanian role in operating the canal and (4) recognition of complete Panamanian sovereignty over the zone.

Although there was an effort to place some nationals in management positions within the Canal Company, Panamanians insisted they could, and should, be allowed an even greater role in running their nation's major industry. Panamanians employed in the Canal Zone were

Panama

The Panama Canal at Miraflores locks

usually given menial tasks at low wages. Since its opening in 1914, the canal was operated almost entirely by U.S. staff and supervisors. The zone itself resembled a "company town" as residents were provided with cradle-to-grave programs such as free schooling and medical care.

Because the 1903 treaty granted the United States territorial supremacy over the Zone, Panama said the corridor represented a virtual foreign nation in its midst. It was a valid point. Zonians paid U.S. taxes. The Zone had its own police force. It had a U.S. federal district court, which was part of the 5th Circuit. It had U.S. post offices, although the Zone actually had its own postage stamps. Democrats in the Zone elected delegates to their party's national conventions. Panamanians could even be "deported" from the zone. It contended that U.S. control was a form of colonialism and insisted the 1903 treaty had to be replaced since it was forced on the tiny nation by U.S. "big stick" gunboat diplomacy. Interestingly, however, Americans born in the Zone were entitled to dual nationality. One was now-Senator John McCain.

An eight-point agenda for negotiators was signed early in 1974, during the waning days of the Nixon administration, and talks began shortly thereafter. The negotiations were continued into the Ford administration, and while they were not exactly secret, the administration certainly kept them low-key. In 1976, the canal talks became a campaign issue when Ronald Reagan, running for the Republican nomina-

tion against President Ford, assailed Ford for negotiating to surrender the vital U.S.-controlled waterway to a "tinpot dictator." Ford clumsily denied that he intended to give up the canal, an assertion that immediately drew the ire of the Panamanians. Caught between a domestic political dilemma and an international powder keg, Ford then backtracked and acknowledged that canal negotiations were underway, but he denounced Reagan as "irresponsible" for opposing them. Ford narrowly defeated Reagan for the nomination, but lost the general election to Democrat Jimmy Carter.

Shortly after his inauguration in 1977, Carter gave a high priority to a new canal treaty. Ambassador Sol M. Linowitz was appointed to join Ellsworth Bunker as chief U.S. negotiators, and talks resumed in February 1977.

Completed in August, the new accord consisted of two separate treaties. The first one would permanently guarantee the canal's neutrality and use by all nations. In case of emergency, however, U.S. warships would be given priority over commercial traffic.

The second accord detailed a timetable for gradual transfer of the canal and the Zone from the United States to Panama. At noon on December 31, 1999, Panama would gain control of the whole works. Annual payments to Panama would also be boosted at once from $2.3 million to an estimated $60 million.

Although the two treaties incorporated a number of Panamanian demands, they

left unsettled the question of a larger, deeper sea-level canal. The present facility employs the use of time-consuming locks. The Navy's largest warships and the new generation of super-tankers are too large to pass through the locks. The waterway is also subject to congestion. Both traffic and tonnage had been rising, placing additional burdens on the canal's facilities.

The new treaties were signed with a flourish when leaders from 23 Latin American nations gathered in Washington in September 1977 to witness the historic event. Still, the festive occasion could not hide the fact that the treaties faced a tough fight—both in the U.S. Senate (where critics said Washington gave up too much) and in Panama (where critics said Washington gave up too *little*).

The first test came in Panama, where the treaties were submitted to a national referendum. Despite vocal protests from both leftists and conservatives—who insisted that Torrijos should have held out for more money plus an earlier U.S. withdrawal—the treaties were approved by a comfortable 2–1 margin.

Attention next turned to Washington; for ratification, the agreements needed support from two thirds of the Senate—a tall order for an accord that public opinion polls said was still opposed by a majority of Americans. A campaign by retired and active high government figures was mounted in favor of the treaties. Ten weeks of debate ensued. Seventy-nine amendments were offered. The first treaty was approved in March by 68–32—just one vote more than the necessary two thirds. To gain approval, however, the president had to agree to an amendment permitting U.S. military intervention in Panama should the canal be closed for any reason, including a strike or even technical problems. This amendment caused an immediate uproar in Panama. Nationalists protested that it was not only an affront to Panamanian dignity, but would violate previous U.S.-Latin American agreements that specifically prohibited the concept of unilateral intervention. As the Senate prepared to vote on the second treaty, Torrijos—subjected to a blast of pressure from critics at home—sent a message to 115 world leaders saying Panama could not accept the amendment.

In an 11th-hour attempt to save 14 years of painful negotiations, the White House and Senate leaders agreed to a new provision that promised that the United States would not interfere with Panama's "internal affairs" or "political independence." The lawmakers, obviously tired of the whole matter, voted in April by the same 68–32 margin in favor of the second treaty.

Behind the scenes, Carter had persuaded Torrijos that U.S. Senate ratification of the treaties would be impossible unless he sanitized his odious dictatorship. Torrijos pragmatically agreed to permit competitive elections and to ease restrictions on freedom of expression and of the press, which Carter trumpeted as proof of Torrijos' commitment to democracy. The seemingly close relationship between the U.S. president, who assailed right-wing Latin American military strongmen for their human rights abuses, and the Panamanian dictator who ordered the murders of political dissidents and confiscated newspapers, was most peculiar.

In June 1978, Carter visited Panama to sign the instruments of ratification. At the public ceremony, Carter thrilled the Panamanian crowd by delivering a conciliatory address in his broken Spanish, in which he promised *"no intervención."* Torrijos, by contrast, was a disgrace. On this highly significant occasion in the life of his country, the representative of Panama was so drunk that his speech was badly slurred and he had to brace himself against the podium to keep from falling.

On October 1, 1979, an enormous Panamanian flag was raised atop Ancon Hill, which looms above Panama City and was the site of the U.S. Southern Command headquarters, and titular Panamanian sovereignty over the Canal Zone became a reality. Meanwhile, as window dressing, exiles were allowed to return. A new, more liberal press law was enacted, though the confiscated newspapers remained in government hands and *La Estrella* remained a faithful mouthpiece underneath its Sword

Arístedes Royo

of Damocles. The military established the Revolutionary Democratic Party (*PRD*) as its civilian political façade. In 1980, an ostensible "election" was held in which numerous parties participated, but the winner was predictable: Arístedes Royo, candidate of the *PRD*.

That same year, a group of anti-Torrijos businessmen and intellectuals, headed by Roberto Eisenmann, who had been in exile for four years, put the new press law to the test by establishing a new daily newspaper, *La Prensa*, which soon became a constant irritant to the regime with its investigative reporting of government corruption, biting editorials and iconoclastically satirical cartoons.

Numerous problems faced strongman Torrijos and his protégé, President Royo. Many of the financial benefits expected to flow into Panama as a result of the new treaties were slow to materialize. In 1980 unemployment grew to 20% and growing inflation touched off two days of general strikes that crippled 80% of the country's industries.

The election of Ronald Reagan in 1980 caused shock waves in Panama, where Torrijos feared that the new president might try to sabotage the canal treaties. Given Reagan's long-standing opposition to the pacts, Panama felt it necessary to safeguard its position by obtaining (with the help of Cuba) a seat on the U.N. Security Council in 1980.

Manuel Noriega

The Panamanian political landscape was altered abruptly and dramatically on July 31, 1981, when Torrijos was killed in a plane crash while on an inspection of *Guardia* units in western Panama. Bad weather was cited as the official cause of the crash, though persistent rumors began circulating almost immediately that it was

no accident. Fidel Castro, of course, immediately accused the CIA, then headed by Reagan protégé William Casey, of rubbing out his friend. Torrijos, or what little remained of him, was buried in an elaborate mausoleum on the parade ground of the former U.S. Army installation of Fort Amador. There was a frenzied outpouring of grief for the man who, whatever his shortcomings, had succeeded in reasserting Panamanian sovereignty over the Canal Zone.

Command of the *Guardia* passed initially to Brigadier General Rubén Paredes, and democratic forces held their breath to see what course post-Torrijos Panama would take. Almost a year to the day after Torrijos' death, they found out. On July 30, 1982, Panama experienced a veritable night of the long knives as the military launched a widespread crackdown on dissent. President Royo was summoned to military headquarters and informed that he was resigning for "health reasons"; he readily complied. At the same time, a goon squad invaded the offices of *La Prensa*, vandalized it and beat several of its employees, including women. The paper was padlocked for several days; other independent publications and radio stations also were silenced.

After two years of a behind-the-scenes power struggle, command of the *Guardia*, which had been renamed the Panama Defense Forces (*FDP*), passed to one of the most sinister figures in recent Latin American history: Colonel Manuel Noriega. The longtime chief of the *Guardia*'s G-2, or intelligence section, Noriega was no charismatic *caudillo* like Torrijos. He was squat and ugly, with a face heavily scarred by acne, which led his many detractors to give him the uncharitable sobriquet *"Cara de Piña,"* or "Pineapple Face." Where Torrijos had enjoyed the popularity of the masses, Noriega would rule by raw fear.

Noriega was an alumnus of the U.S. Army's School of the Americas, then located at Fort Gulick, Panama, and had become a paid CIA operative. But he also acted as a double agent, providing intelligence to the Soviets and Cubans. Even more sinister, he enriched himself by providing protection to the Medellín Cartel of Colombia, which used Panama as a safe haven for its cocaine trafficking and money laundering. Noriega's activities were well known, and his ascension to power was seen as the worst possible scenario. As *La Prensa*'s Eisenmann later told me, the difference between Torrijos and Noriega was that Torrijos merely ordered people tortured and murdered; Noriega participated in the torturing and killing and enjoyed it.

Noriega soon demonstrated the extent of his commitment to Torrijos' promise to

Panama

Carter to ease human rights restrictions. In 1984, he dutifully held open presidential elections for an expanded five-year term. As its candidate, the military-backed *PRD* selected Nicolás Ardito Barletta, a respected economist and graduate of the University of Chicago. The *Panameñistas* again nominated the resilient Arias, by then 83. When early tabulations, which were monitored by international observers, showed an unmistakable trend in favor of Arias, the *FDP* abruptly impounded the ballot boxes and continued the vote counting in secret. By independent estimates, Arias would have received a plurality of between 25,000 and 50,000 votes out of 900,000 cast, but through the *FDP*'s creative vote counting, Barletta was declared the winner by 1,700 votes.

Public opposition to Noriega's heavy-handed rule intensified. A curious coalition of the wealthy elite, leftist intellectuals and housewives took to the streets waving white handkerchiefs. Some of the demonstrations were broken up by truncheon-wielding goon squads from *FDP*-backed groups euphemistically named "Dignity Battalions." Not all opponents of the regime fared that well, however.

One of the most prominent Noriega critics was Dr. Hugo Spadafora, a physician who once had served as Torrijos' vice minister of health. He had served both the Nicaraguan *Sandinistas* in their struggle against Somoza and then, when he became disillusioned with their human rights abuses once in power, he lent his support to the *Contras*. He contributed a regular column to *La Prensa*, in which he vilified the Noriega dictatorship, and he announced he would return to Panama from Costa Rica to lead an opposition movement. He never made it. In September 1985, his bus was stopped when it crossed the border and, according to witnesses, he was forcibly removed. Days later, his decapitated body was found stuffed in a mailbag in Costa Rica; the body bore unmistakable evidence of hideous torture.

The Spadafora murder backfired on Noriega the same way the murder of journalist Pedro Joaquín Chamorro had served as the catalyst for the downfall of Nicaragua's Somoza. News of this atrocious crime made headlines around the world, and domestic and international pressure mounted on the regime. A half-hearted investigation concluded that the murder had occurred in Costa Rica and that Panamanian authorities had no jurisdiction. The Costa Ricans disputed that claim, which only served to fuel the mounting public indignation in Panama. Trying to appease public opinion, President Barletta publicly vowed to bring the killers to justice, a declaration he had foolishly made without consulting with Noriega. Like so many of his predecessors, the president was summoned to military headquarters and was informed he would not leave the building unless he resigned; he did. He was succeeded by the vice president, Eric Arturo Delvalle.

That June, Pulitzer Prize-winning reporter Seymour Hersh of the *New York Times* reported what insiders in Panama had known for years, that Noriega was involved in drug trafficking and that he was a double agent. Eventually, the U.S. government acknowledged that Noriega had

General Manuel Antonio Noriega

once been a paid informant and was heavily involved in drug trafficking.

Noriega, of course, played the nationalist card, accusing the *gringos* of trying to undermine him. But in June 1987, one of his own former minions, Colonel Roberto Díaz Herrera, told the press not only that Noriega was a drug trafficker but that he had ordered Torrijos' fatal plane crash. The opposition press gleefully published the charges. On July 26, 1987, Noriega cracked down hard. Díaz was arrested, and *La Prensa* and several other opposition papers and radio stations were shut down. The Reagan administration ostracized the Noriega regime economically. In February 1988, President Delvalle attempted to salvage the country's devastated economy and to restore some degree of respect in the eyes of the world by firing Noriega as *FDP* commander. Noriega, of course, immediately fired Delvalle; Education Minister Manuel Solis Palma was installed to keep the president's chair warm until Barletta's

term expired in 1989. That same year, a U.S. grand jury indicted Noriega on drug trafficking charges.

Incredibly, in May 1989, Noriega went ahead with another showcase election, as though anyone still believed Panama was a democracy. Arias had died in exile in Miami the previous August, and the *Panameñistas*, now renamed *Arnulfistas*, nominated a portly and uninspiring doctor, Guillermo Endara, as the sacrificial lamb to head a coalition opposition ticket. The *PRD* nominated Carlos Duque, a member of the family that published the regime's faithful mascot newspaper, *La Estrella*. Perhaps the most enduring image of this sham campaign was an attack on an opposition rally by Dignity Battalion goons. Guillermo Ford, one of the opposition's two vice presidential candidates, was badly beaten, and international news photographers and cameramen recorded him fleeing for his life, his white *guayabera* shirt drenched bright red with his own blood; these images were carried around the world.

International observers were present for election day. In a replay of the 1984 electoral farce, early returns showed Endara winning by a landslide, and once again the *FDP* halted the vote counting. This time, however, the observers knew Endara had won, so instead of merely proclaiming Duque the winner, the government nullified the election results. The justification: "Foreign interference"! When Barletta's term expired on September 1, the Council of State, composed entirely of *FDP* officers and their *PRD* lapdogs, designated a close associate of Noriega's, Francisco Rodríguez, as the newest figurehead president.

Operation Just Cause

Relations between the United States and Panama deteriorated after the 1989 "election." Noriega suppressed a coup attempt by a group of *FDP* officers in October; they were summarily executed. The CIA made an abortive attempt to abduct Noriega, while President George H. W. Bush (who as CIA director in 1976 had been Noriega's "boss") issued an executive order banning Panamanian registered ships from entering U.S. ports. As Panama was second only to Liberia in the number of registries in world shipping, the order had potentially disastrous implications.

The bombastic Noriega soon proved his own worst enemy. Wielding a machete before a howling crowd of his adherents, he publicly "declared war" on the United States. In December, there were two separate incidents of off-duty U.S. service personnel—and one of their wives—being beaten by goons, and one U.S. serviceman was shot to death at a roadblock.

Faced with these provocations, Bush ordered the bombing of Noriega's headquarters on December 20, 1989, which was followed by an invasion by 9,500 U.S.-based paratroopers and Army Rangers in what was labeled Operation "Just Cause." Army forces stationed in Panama also moved to seize key installations. There were casualties on both sides as the *FDP* and the Dignity Battalions offered some futile resistance. Within days, order was restored, and for once, U.S. troops were actually cheered by the Panamanians, a stark contrast to the riots of 1964. The day after the invasion, Endara was inaugurated as president. Panamanians suddenly found themselves with more individual freedom than they ever had experienced. *La Prensa* and other closed media reopened, the confiscated newspapers were returned to the widow and children of Harmodio Arias, the *FDP* was disbanded and replaced with a more benign civilian constabulary, and the country began building for the future.

Noriega went into hiding, changing his location every few hours. He obtained refuge in the residence of the papal nuncio. A U.S. psychological warfare unit, in a move considered shrewd by some and crude by others, placed powerful loudspeakers outside the building and broadcast heavy-metal rock at an overwhelming volume at the occupants of the building. The horrified nuncio told Noriega that the residence would be moved across the street and Noriega would not be welcome. Gloomily, the beaten man surrendered, to be taken to the United States with the assurance of no death penalty. He was sentenced to 40 years in 1992 and remains behind bars. After serving 18 years of his U.S. term, he was extradited to France in 2010.

Endara unsuccessfully tried to maintain a low profile to disguise his lack of talent. An opposition newspaper ridiculed him as "a non-musician leading an orchestra that does not play." Endara shrugged off chronic unemployment and rampant corruption as normal occurrences. A sardonic in Panama went: "The United States took Ali Baba and left us with the 40 thieves." By 1993 Endara's government had become a caretaker; influential cabinet members resigned to take part in 1994 presidential elections.

Ernesto Pérez Balladares

The organization that had supported Noriega, the *PRD*, nominated Ernesto Pérez Balladares, a former Citi-bank official with a U.S. education, as its presidential candidate. He carefully distanced himself from Noriega, and won the election against a divided opposition. Running a strong second was Mireya Moscoso, the young widow of Arnulfo Arias, running as the *Arnulfista* candidate.

In 1996, U.S. newspapers reported that Pérez Balladares had received funds from drug traffickers for his presidential campaign. The president threatened not to extend the work permit of a Peruvian investigative journalist, Gustavo Gorriti, working at *La Prensa*, accusing him of "masterminding a conspiracy" to undermine his government. A few days later, the president confessed the charges were true but insisted he had not known.

In 1997, *La Prensa* reported that Pérez Balladares had delayed passage of a new antitrust law to give his cousin time to acquire control of a second television station. This time the president revoked Gorriti's work permit, becoming the center of a storm of international condemnation from journalism organizations and human rights groups. He finally relented and agreed to extend Gorriti's permit.

Panamanian officials resorted to yet another time-honored counterattack against media criticism: libel suits. Unlike the United States, Latin American countries have loosely defined defamation laws that allow public officials to sue for the expression of critical opinions; Panamanian officials under both Endara and Pérez Balladares resorted to it; Endara once sued a political cartoonist!

Other critics accused the president of nepotism and cronyism. International shipping companies expressed concerns that as the day inched closer for Panama to take over canal operations, Pérez Balladares was appointing friends and relatives to the Panama Canal Commission, now fully Panamanian. Even members of the president's own party criticized the appointments.

On the positive side, Pérez Balladares put the economy on a solid footing, nationally and internationally, through privatization and fiscal discipline and through a new bank law to curtail the laundering of drug money, thus improving the country's image abroad.

Panama marked a major milestone in September 1997 when the U.S. Southern Command moved its headquarters from Quarry Heights to Miami, turning over the long-time U.S. nerve center atop Ancon Hill on the edge of Panama City to the Panamanians. Albrook Air Base also reverted to Panamanian control. Another milestone in the transfer of the former Canal Zone to Panama came in 1999 when the U.S. Army departed Fort Clayton for the last time, ending a U.S. military presence of 96 years. The Americans' departure also was a reminder that the payroll of the U.S. bases,

Far from the capital's cosmopolitan life: Cuna Indians of the San Blas Islands

Panama

which once pumped $370 million into the economy, was drying up.

Mireya Moscoso

Pérez Balladares became the fourth Latin American president to seek to amend the constitution to permit him to run for immediate re-election. Constitutional amendments require only a majority vote in the National Assembly, then approval by the electorate. In a referendum in August 1998, a resounding 64% voted "no" to Pérez Balladares' attempt to succeed himself, leaving the field wide open.

The *arnulfistas* again coalesced around Moscoso. The *PRD* decided to play the dynasty card as well by nominating Martín Torrijos, the 35-year-old illegitimate son of the former strongman, a businessman who earned an economics degree from Texas A&M and once managed a McDonald's franchise in Chicago.

The two candidates both pledged to maintain the canal efficiently and fairly, for the benefit of all nations. About the only issue that divided them was Moscoso vowed to attack the rampant corruption that had been evident under Pérez Balladares; what could Torrijos say? Torrijos chided Moscoso for her lack of formal training; she had studied interior design at a junior college in Miami. Of course, she had another, unspoken handicap in a *macho* society: her gender.

But the underdog woman suddenly pulled abreast of Torrijos in the polls. In a pathetic attempt to minimize a possible bandwagon effect, *PRD* loyalists bought up 20,000 copies of *La Prensa*, which carried a poll showing Moscoso ahead, and destroyed them.

On election day, May 2, 1999, Moscoso received a clear plurality of 44% to Torrijos' 38% and 18% for a third candidate. With voter turnout 75%, her mandate was solid despite lacking a majority. The combined anti-*PRD* vote represented a dramatic rebuke to the ruling party. Both Pérez Balladares and Torrijos graciously conceded defeat. Moscoso joined a growing number of Latin American presidents elected on their second try.

Thus, from the grave, Arnulfo Arias finally achieved a sweet triumph, as his widow defeated the son of the man who had overthrown him in 1968. Moscoso, 52, had married Arias in exile in 1969, when he was 67 and she was 22, and was with him until his death in 1988. Very possibly it was his memory and his populist message, which she exploited, coupled with disturbingly high unemployment of 12.8%, that was responsible for her victory.

Moscoso was sworn in as Panama's first woman president on September 1, 1999, the 31st anniversary of her late husband's ill-fated inauguration in 1968. Moscoso was only the second elected female president in Latin America, after Nicaragua's Violeta Chamorro.

It was an ugly transition. Pérez Balladares had packed the Supreme Court with last-minute appointees, denied public funds for the open-air inaugural ceremony Moscoso had requested at a stadium, and even ramrodded legislation through the lame-duck Assembly that restricted presidential powers. Pérez Balladares declined to attend the inauguration to place the presidential sash on his successor's shoulders as is traditional.

Moscoso received a sweet consolation for her predecessor's ungentlemanly actions when two small parties, Solidarity and National Liberal, withdrew from their coalition with the *PRD* and joined the *Panameñista Party* in a new coalition, giving it a one-seat majority in the 71-seat National Assembly. As government and justice minister she named Winston Spadafora, brother of the activist murdered under Noriega.

Because of Y2K fears, the date for the ceremony transferring control of the canal was moved from December 31 to December 14, 1999. Representing the United States, appropriately enough, was former President Jimmy Carter, who had signed the new treaties in 1977. With his and Moscoso's signatures, Panama at last enjoyed full sovereignty over its territory and over the canal.

In 2001, a two-year, $300 million project was completed that widened the Gaillard Cut, the "ditch" section of the canal, by 40 yards, increasing its traffic potential by 20 percent. The following year, canal tolls were raised 8%, the first increase since the Panamanian takeover; they were increased another 4% in 2003—the centennial year of the Bunau-Varilla Treaty. The pricing system also was changed from a per-ton basis to the type of ship and cargo. The increases were deemed necessary to keep the canal competitive.

Moscoso proved as thin-skinned about media criticism as her two predecessors. She signed a new press law in 2000 that critics charged restricts freedom of expression, and her attorney general began bringing charges against a number of journalists for alleged defamation. In 2001, Moscoso and Spadafora sought criminal charges for "calumny and injury" against three journalists with the new satirical weekly *La Cáscara (The Shell)* in 2001 after it ran a spoof suggesting a romantic relationship between Moscoso and Spadafora and another minister; a cartoon showed her in their arms. For good measure, the paper was charged with not following legal procedures to open a newspaper—under Torrijos' press law of 1978!

Former President Mireya Moscoso

The journalists apologized to avoid going to prison.

The country experienced a catharsis of sorts in 2002 when a special "truth commission" on disappearances and mysterious deaths during the 1968–89 military regimes presented its report to Moscoso. The commission investigated 168 cases and reached conclusions on 110. Of those, 70 were found to be assassinations of political dissidents, most of them during the Torrijos period. Another 40 remain unsolved.

The remainder of Moscoso's presidency was marred by various allegations of corruption, which proved an albatross around the *Panameñista* Party's neck in the next election. One was that *panameñista* legislators accepted bribes from a consortium seeking to build the so-called Multimodal Industrial and Service Center (*CEMIS*) at the old U.S. military airfield of France Field, near Colón.

In the waning days of her administration, Moscoso provoked a diplomatic row with Cuba. The Cuban government told Moscoso it understood she was considering pardoning four Cuban exiles imprisoned in Panama for planning an assassination attempt on Fidel Castro there in 2000 and warned that it would sever diplomatic relations if she did. Moscoso denied such plans, condemned Cuba for its language, recalled Panama's ambassador to Cuba and ordered the Cuban ambassador to leave Panama. Six days before leaving office, she abruptly pardoned the four for "humanitarian" reasons, saying she feared her successor would extradite them to Cuba, where they would be executed. Cuba broke diplomatic relations, calling Moscoso an "accomplice and protector of terrorism" and the pardons "repugnant

Panama

and treacherous." The Supreme Court voided the pardons in 2008, but by then the prisoners were long gone.

The most notorious of the four men is Luis Posada Carriles, who in 1985 escaped from prison in Venezuela where he was awaiting retrial for masterminding the bombing of a Cuban airliner in 1976 that killed 73 people. Consequently, Venezuela also severed diplomatic relations with Panama because of the pardons. Posada eventually turned up in Miami, where he was arrested in 2005, not on a fugitive warrant but for entering the country illegally. Cuba and Venezuela demanded he be extradited to Venezuela. Posada Carriles was indicted in 2009 by a U.S. grand jury for fraud and entering the United States illegally. He went on trial in 2011, but was acquitted (see Cuba).

Martín Torrijos

Martín Torrijos, still just 39, announced his second bid for the presidency in the 2004 election. He received the *PRD*'s nomination and that of the Popular Party, the descendant of the Christian Democrats, forming an alliance called *Patria Nueva*. The *Panameñistas* nominated Moscoso's personal choice, Foreign Minister José Miguel Alemán, who formed an alliance with two other parties called *Visión de País*. Former President Endara also entered the race as candidate of a movement called *Solidaridad*. Rounding out the field was Ricardo Martinelli, a multi-millionaire supermarket magnate, of *Cambio Democrático*.

Torrijos promised to clean up the endemic corruption (neglecting to mention that it had been also rife in the Pérez Balladares administration, in which he served as a deputy government and justice minister). Unlike his father, he was not a *gringo-baiter*. Educated at Texas A&M, he was a practical businessman and advocated a free-trade agreement with the United States. He even cleaned up the *PRD*'s image for his generation of voters by purging it of some of the unsavory elements left over from the dictatorship. He was endorsed by the popular singer-actor Rubén Blades (see Culture).

On May 2, 76.9% of Panamanians voted, slightly more than in 1999. The results:

Torrijos	711,447	47.7%
Endara	462,766	30.9%
Alemán	245,845	16.6%
Martinelli	79,595	5.3%

The Cuban pardons overshadowed the September 1, 2004 inauguration of Torrijos, who called them "unacceptable," and he quickly restored diplomatic relations with both Cuba and Venezuela. Yet, Moscoso was far more gracious to Torrijos

Former President Martín Torrijos

at his inauguration than Pérez Balladares had been to her. She also had the satisfaction of serving out her full term, something her late husband was denied three times—the last time by the father of the man who succeeded her.

Two months after Moscoso left office, the electoral tribunal revoked her immunity from prosecution. She was asked to account for the alleged disappearance of $70 million in public funds during her presidency. She called the charges politically motivated, even though she brazenly admitted spending $3 million, which she said was justified—to maintain her image! She remains under a cloud of suspicion; in 2011, *La Prensa* reported information from WikiLeaks that Moscoso as president had demanded and received an unspecified bribe from the government of Taiwan.

Torrijos took a businesslike approach to solving pressing economic problems. Although the economy showed encouraging growth (see Economy), he inherited a huge budget deficit, a crushing public debt and a bloated public pension system that was $100 million in the red. Torrijos raised taxes, and his plan to increase the retirement age for men from 62 to 65 and to raise social security contributions led to violent protests in 2005. The National Assembly approved the changes 43–30. The reforms allowed Panama to borrow money at lower interest rates.

Torrijos then turned to expansion of the canal. He called a referendum, held on October 22, 2006, on whether or not to invest $5.2 billion to build a new set of wider, deeper locks on each coast; instead of creating new reservoirs, the water would be recycled. This would create a third "lane" for traffic. About $2.3 billion would be borrowed, the rest raised by increased canal tolls. The project was expected to take seven years and create up to 9,000 jobs at

its peak. Critics warned of environmental dangers and cost overruns, and a former canal authority director said it would be far less costly to transship cargo by land between superports on each coast for the 300 "post-Panamax" ships that are too large to transit the canal. Voter turnout was a disappointing 43% of the 2.1 million eligible, but the voters approved expansion by 76.3%.

Work formally began with a ceremony on September 3, 2007, when part of a hill alongside the Gaillard Cut was blasted away. Torrijos and former President Carter attended the ceremony.

Another project that stirred controversy is the *Cinta Costera*, or traffic beltway, along the coast that circles the colonial-era Casco Viejo section of Panama City. UNESCO threatened to revoke the Casco Viejo's status as a World Heritage Site if the development proceeded, but it was completed in 2009 at a cost of $189 million.

Torrijos entered into free-trade talks with the U.S., which broke down when Panamanian producers of pork, chicken and rice complained that they could be undermined by cheaper U.S. imports. President Bush visited Panama in 2005, and he and Torrijos agreed to push ahead with their bilateral trade talks. Panama was not included in the Dominican Republic-Central American Free Trade Agreement.

Torrijos and Bush signed the FTA in Washington in June 2007 and the Panamanian National Assembly approved it in July, but a new glitch arose when the National Assembly elected as its president Pedro Miguel González Pinzón, who was wanted in the U.S. for the shooting deaths of two U.S. Army sergeants in 1992 during the visit of the first President Bush. González Pinzón was acquitted of the charges in Panama in 1997. The U.S. Congress balked on approval of the FTA. Torrijos wanted González Pinzón to step down for the good of the country, but the *PRD*'s left wing argued it would be an infringement of national dignity to yield to U.S. pressure. González Pinzón agreed not to seek another term as Assembly president when his term expired. Although he left, the U.S. Congress delayed approval until October 2011.

Meanwhile, Manuel Noriega, completed his prison sentence in 2007. Panama had sought his extradition, but Torrijos thought better of it, because Panamanian law prohibits extradition and Noriega was still wanted in France, to where he was eventually extradited by the United States.

Ricardo Martinelli

With a booming economy and a popular president, the *PRD* should have been favored in the 2009 presidential election.

333

Panama

But the *PRD* nominated Balbina Herrera, the housing minister and a member of the party's left wing and a Noriega protégé. Endara again quixotically entered the race as an independent. But instead of the usual fragmentation, the *Panameñistas* and other opposition parties rallied around the *Cambio Democrático* of Ricardo Martinelli, 57, owner of the Super 99 supermarket chain, who had placed a poor fourth in the 2004 race. In a show of unity, he chose the *Panameñista* party president, Juan Carlos Varela, as his running mate.

Martinelli campaigned as a centrist and as an outsider, pledging to combat the corruption that had plagued the administrations of both the *PRD* and the *Panameñistas*. Like Ross Perot, he said he would use his skills as a successful businessman to run the country more efficiently. This time Blades, who served at Torrijos' tourism minister, endorsed Martinelli, whom polls showed the heavy favorite.

Herrera futilely tried to use Martinelli's reported net worth of $400 million against him, and she argued that his plan to cut the corporate income tax rate was a blatant conflict of interest. But the voters liked the message of the handsome businessman with the take-charge attitude, and on May 3, 74% of them went to the polls to deliver their mandate:

Martinelli	952,333	60.1%
Herrera	597,227	37.5%
Endara	36,867	2.0%

It was the first time since the establishment of democracy that a candidate had won with an absolute majority. Martinelli, son of Italian immigrants, became the third consecutive president to win on his second try, and the latest to have been educated in the United States; he earned a bachelor's of business administration from the Uni-

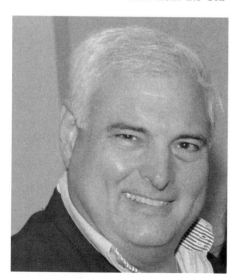

Former President Ricardo Martinelli

versity of Arkansas. His victory was a deviation from the trend of leftist victories in recent years.

Martinelli's *CD* won only 14 of the 71 National Assembly seats, while the *PRD* won 26 and the *Panamañistas*, 22.

Panama's inauguration day was advanced from September 1 to July 1.

In 2009, the Supreme Court agreed to reopen, after four years, the investigation into the *CEMIS* scandal. By 2010, it involved prominent members of both major parties, including former Presidents Moscoso of the *Panameñistas* and Pérez Balladares of the *PRD*, as well as *PRD* presidential candidate Herrera. A U.S. citizen charged under the Foreign Corrupt Practices Act with paying some $200,000 of the bribes was convicted and sentenced to 87 years, the harshest sentence to date under the FCPA. In 2012, Martinelli's new prosecutor asked that former President Torrijos also be tried. The case drags on two years hence.

Former President Endara died of a heart attack from complications of kidney failure on September 28, 2009, at the age of 73. He received a state funeral at the Metropolitan Cathedral.

Noriega's U.S. prison term ended in 2007, but he remained behind bars pending a French extradition request. His U.S. attorneys requested that he be allowed to return to Panama, citing his status as a prisoner of war under the Geneva Convention. Noriega faces two murder charges in Panama, including that of Hugo Spadafora, but because of his age he

legally would be allowed to serve any sentence under house arrest. He turned 76 on February 11, 2010. Federal judges denied his request, and the U.S. Supreme Court to hear his appeal.

Secretary of State Hillary Clinton signed the French extradition request in April 2010. Noriega arrived in France the next day; his attorneys were not even notified the request had been signed. In July, he was convicted of money-laundering charges in France, less serious than murder, and sentenced to seven years. Martinelli's government then filed three extradition requests, including for Spadafora's murder. Panamanian Vice President Varela discussed the extradition with his French counterpart in Paris. Noriega was finally returned to Panama on December 12, 2011, and taken to Renacer Prison—not house arrest—where security had been beefed up to ensure his safety. As of mid-2014, he was still there awaiting trial.

Unlike his predecessors, Martinelli was less eager to use defamation laws to punish journalists, but such punishments have continued. *La Prensa* was ordered to pay $300,000 in damages in 2010 to a former prosecutor for merely *reporting* on her dismissal by the prosecutor general. The same year, two television journalists who exposed a government document, verified for its accuracy, that showed corruption within the Immigration Office were sentenced to 12 months for defamation. Martinelli pardoned the two journalists, saying it "could send mistaken messages,

Carlota—a Panamanian beauty in native costume

nationally and internationally, about the solidity of our democracy." When national policemen arrested and harassed a newspaper photographer in 2010 for photographing policemen at a labor protest, Martinelli apologized.

However, when radio station owner Guillermo Antonio Adames, president of the National Journalism Council, criticized the sentences against the two TV journalists and other attacks against press freedom, his station was subjected to a tax audit. Freedom House for years has rated the Panamanian press as only "partly free."

After five years of delays, the U.S. Congress approved the bilateral FTA on October 12, 2011.

Martinelli unveiled plans for an ambitious nine-mile-long subway line, the first in Central America and ninth in Latin America, under Panama City to alleviate the capital's notoriously congested traffic. Estimated to cost $1.8 billion, the 8.5-mile line was built by a French-Spanish-Brazilian consortium. Work began in 2011 and the Panama Metro opened in April 2014; it is already being expanded to additional stations.

Martinelli found himself faced with a major public relations problem in January 2012 when hundreds of members of the Ngäbe-Buglé Indian tribe blocked the Pan-American Highway in Chiriquí province along the border with Costa Rica to protest the repeal of an amendment that had barred a copper mining operation from tribal lands. The government had agreed to the amendment after the tribe protested the mining operation and planned hydroelectric projects in 2009 and 2010. In 2011, the development-friendly Martinelli persuaded the National Assembly to repeal the amendment, sparking the highway closure. Vital commerce came to a halt. Martinelli offered to fly the chief and other Indian representatives to Panama City in the presidential plane to negotiate, but they refused and said he would have to come there.

Cell phone coverage to the area was cut off, apparently to hamper news coverage, and riot police broke up the roadblock with tear gas, rubber bullets and apparently live ammunition. Despite the blackout, a television network dispatched a helicopter and carried the confrontation live. Casualty reports varied, but apparently at least one protester was killed, 40 people were injured on both sides and 100 protesters were arrested. The crackdown provoked protests by Panama's other indigenous peoples, hundreds of whom descended on the capital to demonstrate in front of the presidential palace. The Inter-American Human Rights Commission expressed its concern, and Amnesty International called for an investigation.

The dispute festered for two months until the two sides signed an accord for legislation that prohibits mining development on tribal lands and stipulates that future hydroelectric projects be approved by local governing bodies near the dams. The Assembly approved the bill in March 2012. The agreement does not provide for a rollback of hydroelectric projects underway, but it provides the tribes with compensation for their inundated lands.

An opinion poll showed that 80% of Panamanians disapproved of the heavy-handed manner in which Martinelli broke up the protest, and his approval rating sank from 80% in 2010 to 33% after the Chiriquí incident, the third lowest in the Western Hemisphere. By September, he had improved to 10th place out of 20 with an approval rating of 52%.

The flamboyant and sometimes erratic president next launched a war of words against his own vice president, Juan Carlos Varela, who had accused Martinelli of accepting a $30 million kickback from an Italian company that received a contract for helicopter and radar services. Martinelli filed a $30 million defamation suit against the *Panameñista* leader in May 2012, attacked his manhood and demanded he resign. Varela has refused. The international media relished the spectacle of a sitting president suing his own vice president.

Another Martinelli scheme that went horribly wrong was a bill he pushed through the Assembly in October 2012 to sell off some of the land in the Colón Free Trade Zone to private companies. Hundreds of workers in the zone protested, complaining that Martinelli was selling assets that benefit Colón; rioting ensued. Martinelli dispatched members of his new border security force to quell the disturbances; a 10-year-old boy was killed. Then protests broke out in the capital against the bill, and shops were looted. After two weeks of unrest, the chastened president had the Assembly repeal the sale.

Panama found itself in the midst of a major international incident in July 2013 when, apparently acting on a tip from U.S. intelligence, it detained a North Korean cargo ship, the Chong Chon Gang, and its 35-man crew as it transited the canal en route from Cuba to North Korea. It was suspected of carrying weapons in defiance of a U.N. embargo against weapons shipments to or from North Korea because it had refused to give up its nuclear weapons development. The crew attempted to resist the Panamanian authorities who boarded the ship, and the captain even attempted suicide. North Korea demanded the ship's release. The tedious search finally revealed two MiG-21 fighter jets, 15 MiG engines, two anti-aircraft missile systems,

nine anti-aircraft missiles and various explosives, hidden under bags of sugar weighing 10,000 pounds. Cuba claimed the weapons were obsolete and were being sent to North Korea to be repaired and returned to Cuba—which, even if true, did not exempt them from the U.N. embargo. In January 2014, North Korea agreed to pay a $666,000 fine for violating the canal's security with the undeclared weapons. Panama then released 32 of the crewmen, keeping three to stand trial for arms smuggling. The ship was allowed to leave in February.

Martinelli also found himself at odds with Venezuelan President Nicolás Maduro after Martinelli called on the OAS to seek a dialogue in the ongoing violent demonstrations against Maduro's government and to help guarantee democracy and human rights. In March, Maduro severed diplomatic relations with Panama, calling Martinelli a "lackey" of the United States and accusing him of working with the United States to destabilize his government. He said Martinelli was "not worthy of his people." Martinelli responded that Maduro's "foul language is inappropriate for the president of a brother country."

By the end of 2013, the canal expansion was behind schedule and cost overruns totaled about $1.6 billion, dashing hopes that the expansion would be complete in time for the centennial of the canal's opening in August 2014. A consortium of two European construction firms, Sacyr of Spain and Salini Impregilo of Italy, halted construction in January 2014 and demanded that Panama pay the additional funds. Martinelli countered by threatening to sue the companies for breach of contract. The consortium resumed work in February, while negotiations continued. The two sides agreed on a compromise settlement on March 14, and the expansion is now scheduled for completion in December 2015. The price tag is now $7 billion.

On a happier note, Panama had Latin America's fastest economic growth in both 2011 and 2012 and the second-fastest in 2013 (see Economy). In the Mitofsky poll in October 2013, Martinelli was the third most popular president of the Western Hemisphere, with an approval rating of 69%.

The Elections of 2014

Constitutionally barred from re-election, the popular Martinelli took a cue from former Dominican Republic President Leonel Fernández and advanced his wife, Marta Linares, for vice president in the May 4, 2014, presidential election. At the top of the *CD* ticket he hand-picked a political novice, José Domingo Arias, 50,

Panama

(no relation to former President Arnulfo Arias), his foreign trade minister. Vice President Varela, also 50, his break with Martinelli definitive, won the *Panameñista* nomination, while the *PRD* nominated former Panama City Mayor Juan Carlos Navarro. Four minor candidates also were on the ballot.

Arias campaigned for continuity, boasting of the new Metro line, the new bypass that eased traffic congestion (in reality begun by Martín Torrijos) and the explosion of new high-rise buildings on Martinelli's watch. Polls at first showed the election to be a two-man race between Arias and Navarro. But then Varela began gaining momentum with a pro-transparency, anti-corruption platform; he, too, tried to claim some credit for the infrastructure improvements and Martinelli's expansion of spending on social programs. He turned Arias' argument around, reminding voters that despite the influx of new wealth, Panama had among the worst income inequality in Latin America. This struck a responsive chord with the one quarter of the population living in poverty.

This time Rubén Blades, who had endorsed Martinelli in 2009, said he would not endorse any of the three but warned that an Arias victory would constitute a re-election of Martinelli and would be a "dangerous risk for Panamanian democracy." Arias also had history running against him: In all four elections since 1989, the ruling party lost.

The campaign was peaceful, but not without dirty tricks, such as fake newspapers reporting that opposing candidates had withdrawn, or a rumor, denied by the U.S. Embassy, that Varela's U.S. visa had been revoked because of ties to drug trafficking.

Voter turnout was even higher than in 2009, 76.8%. One of the voters was Manuel Noriega, voting from his prison cell. The results:

Varela	724,440	39.1%
Arias	582,122	31.4%
Navarro	522,141	28.2%

Martinelli and Arias could take some comfort that *CD* won 29 of the Assembly seats, an increase of 15, to 21 for the *PRD* and only 11 for the *Panameñistas*.

Varela pledged after his victory that he would impose price controls on 22 staples, such as rice, meat and cheese, saying retailers were making huge profits at the expense at the poor. That was an unmistakable dig directed at Martinelli, the supermarket magnate.

Varela was inaugurated on July 1. His vice president is Isabela Saint Malo de Alvarado, 46, a diplomat who earned an international relations degree from St. Joseph's University in Philadelphia, Pennsylvania.

President Juan Carlos Varela

CULTURE: Panama's culture is a reflection of its unique geographical situation as a crossroads of both terrestrial and maritime traffic between two oceans and two continents. There is a polyglot of ethnic groups, not one of which predominates: the indigenous Indians, many of them unassimilated, such as the Cuna tribe of the San Blas Islands on the Caribbean coast that contributed the distinctive *mola* tapestries that have become so identifiable with Panamanian culture; the Caucasians, not merely Spanish descendants but the scions of latter-day European, Arab and Jewish immigrants who today account for a disproportionate share of the country's wealth and political power; the *mestizos*, who outnumber the first two groups; blacks and mulattos, who are about equal in number to the *mestizos*, descended not from slaves as in Brazil, but from workers imported from the British West Indies to help construct the canal; and the sizable community of Orientals, principally Chinese, who have filtered into the country in the decades since the completion of the canal.

Because of this, Panama boasts a distinctive culture, particularly in its folk music, dances and costumes that its tourist industry has helped to preserve.

UNESCO designated the ruins of the Spanish fortress at Portobelo-San Lorenzo on the Caribbean coast as a cultural World Heritage Site in 1980 and the colonial-era Casco Viejo section of Panama City and the nearby Panamá Viejo ruins as a joint World Heritage Site in 1997.

Three Panamanian national parks also have been designated natural World Heritage Sites: Darién, La Amistad and Coiba.

In popular music, Panama's best-known singer and actor, Rubén Blades (b. 1948), won a following in Latin America before appearing in a number of U.S. movies and receiving four U.S. Grammys and one Latin Grammy Award, for Best Singer-Songwriter in 2010 for the album *Cantares del Subdesarrollo*. He ran for president of Panama in 1994 and ran third with 18% of the vote. He served as tourism minister under President Martín Torrijos, and earned a master's degree in international law from Harvard. His many movie credits include *The Milagro Beanfield War*, *All the Pretty Horses* and most recently, *For Greater Glory*.

A newer Panamanian sensation is the raggaeton singer Félix Danilo Gómez (b. 1980), known by the stage name DJ Flex. His biggest hit was *Te Quiero*, from the album *Te Quiero: Romantic Style in Da World*. *Te Quiero* won the Latin Grammy for Best Urban Song in 2008. He also has won eight Latin Billboard Awards.

Panamanians won a total of seven Latin Grammys from 2003 through 2012.

Literacy is relatively high in Panama, but the small population has not been sufficient to support much book or magazine publishing. Panama boasts one of Latin America's oldest daily newspapers, *La Estrella de Panamá*, founded in 1853. Unfortunately, *La Estrella's* owners were blackmailed into editorial support for dictators Torrijos and Noriega, and the paper has never fully recovered from its reputation as a sycophant.

Until the U.S. invasion of 1989 that brought down the Noriega dictatorship, aggressive and critical journalism in Panama was a risky business. *El Panamá América*, expropriated from Harmodio Arias by Torrijos in 1968, was restored to his family and remains the second-leading daily. The country's leading daily, *La Prensa*, was established in 1980 by Roberto Eisenmann and courageously stood up to both the Torrijos and Noriega dictatorships. For this it was repeatedly vandalized and finally closed in 1987. The month after the U.S. invasion in 1989, its repaired presses began rolling again. Even under democratic presidents, the Panamanian press has been the target of defamation suits brought by thin-skinned public officials who dislike criticism or satire. Freedom House rates the Panamanian press as only "partly free."

Despite Panama's relative affluence, few resources have been channeled into public education. The Organization for Economic Cooperation and Development rated Panamanian education 62nd out of 65 emerging economies in 2012. Higher education in Panama was relatively undeveloped until well into the 20th century. The University of Panama was founded in 1935. There are at least 21 colleges and universities, a mix of state, private and campuses of Florida State University and the University of Louisville.

ECONOMY: Panama's economy is based on trade brought to it by an accident of geography. Farm output is unable to feed the population; the major source of income (about 20% of the gross national product) is tied to the Canal. The Torrijos regime sought to diversify the economy, and established incentives to make Panama an international banking center. Passage of the Panama Canal treaties has had the effect of stimulating new industrial investments. An oil pipeline enables the transport of crude by supertankers ocean-to-ocean, compensating for their inability to fit through the narrow canal, providing substantial revenues to Panama.

Much of the impetus for Panama becoming a major international banking center in the 1970s and 1980s stemmed from a Swiss-style banking law that made Panama a favored spot for the laundering of illegal drug money. Not until 1997 did Panama make a concerted effort to change the law and remove this stigma.

The prodigious economic spinoff from the canal, including the thousands of jobs generated by the canal itself and the numerous U.S. military bases, gave Panama among the highest standards of living in Latin America, although income inequality was the second-worst in Latin America in 2008; an estimated 26% of Panamanians still lived below the poverty line in 2012.

Panama received $601 million in remittances from Panamanians living abroad in 2012.

Panama has avoided the hyperinflation that has plagued so many of its neighbors. The reason: The official currency is called the Balboa, but in reality the U.S. dollar is the country's legal tender, which is a boon for international banking and provides monetary stability. (Panama has its own coins, which are identical in size and weight with U.S. denominations and thus are interchangeable in vending machines.) Largely because of the dollar-based economy, inflation has remained manageable. For that reason, Ecuador and El Salvador have emulated Panama by replacing their currency with the dollar.

One of the country's greatest economic success stories is the Colón Free Zone, on the Caribbean side, created in 1948. It imports and re-exports products from all over the world and is now the second-largest free-trade zone in the world after Hong Kong. It accounts for more than $16 billion of imports and re-exports annually as of 2010, $1.3 billion of which is pumped into the Panamanian economy.

On the negative side, Panama has one of the most cumbersome public debts in Latin America. In 2011, the debt was estimated at 44% of GDP, and in 2012 and 2013 it was just under 40%.

The Panamanian takeover of the canal on December 31, 1999, was historic, and while it was no economic panacea, Panama's stewardship has been far more successful than anticipated. When Panama took over, it generated $500 million in revenue; in 2005, it was $1.2 billion, with an operating profit of $183 million. In 2008, revenue hit a record $2.007 billion in the fiscal year that ends on September 30, but it declined to $1.96 billion in 2009 because the global recession reduced traffic. The number of transits has declined slightly in recent years, from 12,987 in 2011 to 12,036 in 2013, but toll revenue rose from $1.728 billion in 2011 to $1.847 billion in 2013, about 4.5% of GDP.

Because 19% of cargo ships are too large to transit the century-old locks, President Martín Torrijos called for reinvesting $5.3 billion in expanding the canal to increase its capacity, which Panamanian approved in a referendum in late 2006. Cost overruns have pushed the price tag up to $7 billion, but its economic spinoffs have had a positive effect. The expansion is scheduled for completion in December 2015.

Panama's GDP growth in 2002 was only 0.9%, but it rebounded to 4.3% in 2003, 6.2% in 2004 and 6.9% in 2005. Its growth was at boom levels for three years, and among the highest in Latin America: 8.7% in 2006, 11.5% in 2007, and 9.2% in 2008. While most Latin American countries saw GDP decline during the 2008–09 global recession, Panama's still grew by 2.4% in 2009. In 2010, in part because of the canal expansion, it grew by 7.5%, tying with Argentina and Brazil as the third-fastest in Latin America. It was 10.6% in 2011 and 10.5% in 2012, the fastest in Latin America both years. In 2013 it was 7.5%, the second-fastest.

Another key to the boom besides the canal expansion has been an enormous influx of foreign direct investment (FDI). In 2010, Panama's FDI of $2.36 billion was 8.8% of GDP, the highest percentage in Latin America. It rose to $2.79 billion in 2011 or 9.1% of GDP. Caterpillar and Procter & Gamble set up their Latin American headquarters in Panama in 2007. Occidental Petroleum and Qatar Petroleum are planning to build a $7 billion oil refinery at Puerto Armuelles on the Pacific coast, while the Chinese are planning a huge new port on the Caribbean side. A British firm is plan-

Washing clothes at an outdoor sluice

Panama

ning to turn the former Howard Air Force Base into an industrial facility, while Donald Trump has plans to build a high-rise hotel and resort.

The boom has reduced chronically high unemployment, which was 8.6% in 2007 and 5.6% in 2008. With the recession, it rose to 6.6% in 2009 and 6.5% in 2010. It went back down to 4.5% in 2011 and 4.4% in 2012.

Inflation rose steadily from 2.4% in 2009 to 5.7% in 2012, but dropped to 4.1% in 2013.

With the boom has come increased international pressure for Panama to tighten regulations of its banks, which are seen as money launderers, much like those in the Cayman Islands. President Ricardo Martinelli responded to the pressure, but slowly, lest he derail the gravy train and appear to be caving in to foreigners.

THE FUTURE: Panama has been a Latin American success story since the fall of the Noriega dictatorship. Its economy is booming, and it has peacefully transferred power five times among three competing parties.

The canal remains Panama's greatest hope for continued economic growth. Plagued by delays and cost overruns, the seven-year, $5.3 billion expansion project, which was supposed to be completed in time for the canal's centennial in August 2014, has now cost $7 billion and is scheduled for completion in December 2015.

President Ricardo Martinelli represented a fresh face and a fresh approach, a successful, multi-millionaire businessman from outside the two major political movements. He inherited an enviable economy, and he used his business skills to run the country efficiently, but he never quite came to grips with Panama's four greatest remaining concerns: institutionalized corruption, a crushing public debt, a substandard public education system and one of the most inequitable income distributions in Latin America.

For whatever reason, the biannual *Latinobarómetro* survey for *The Economist* showed ominously that the percentage of Panamanians who believe that democracy is preferable to any other form of government nosedived from 60% in 2011 to 49% in 2013, the second-largest two-year drop of the 18 Latin American nations in the survey. Curiously, only about 42% of Panamanians said they were satisfied with the way democracy works in their country, a shade above the regional average, while at the same time they gave Martinelli an approval rating of 69%, the third highest in the hemisphere.

In keeping with tradition, Panamanian voters in May 2014 denied a second administration to the party in power, despite Martinelli's high approval rating and his record of success in luring more foreign investment and overseeing the construction of the Panama City Metro. They turned to Vice President Juan Carlos Varela, who had a very public falling out with Martinelli, of the populist *Panameñista* Party, who surged from third place in the polls to win by a convincing 39% plurality.

Varela, who has an industrial engineering degree from Georgia Tech, has promised to tackle that nagging corruption and income inequality. Perhaps he can disarm some of the resentment of the 26% of Panamanians who still live below the poverty line, in the very shadow of the glittering forest of new high-rise office and apartment buildings that have transformed Panama City into a Latin American version of Hong Kong. The question is whether he can accomplish his promises without yielding to the temptation of corruption that has tarnished the reputations of his successors.

The Republic of Paraguay

The Presidential Palace in Asunción

Area: 157,047 square miles.

Population: 6,703,860 (2014 est.).

Capital City: Asunción (Pop. 680,250; 2,164,316 in metropolitan area in 2013, est.).

Climate: The eastern section (*Oriental*) lies in a temperate zone; the western (*Occidental*) section is hot and oppressive. Rainfall is heaviest from February to May; most of Paraguay receives adequate water except for the western plains.

Neighboring Countries: Brazil (East and Northeast); Argentina (South); Bolivia (West and Northwest).

Official Language: Spanish.

Other Principal Tongues: Guaraní, a native Indian dialect, spoken as a first language by half the population.

Ethnic Background: *Mestizo* (mixed Spanish and Guaraní ancestry).

Principal Religion: Roman Catholic Christianity.

Chief Commercial Products: Cotton, soybeans, beef, timber, vegetable oils, coffee, light manufactured goods.

Currency: Guaraní.

Gross Domestic Product: U.S. $30.56 billion in 2013 ($4,614 per capita, official exchange rate).

Former Colonial Status: Spanish Crown Colony (1537–1811).

Independence Date: May 14, 1811.

Chief of State: Horacio Manuel Cartes Jara (b. July 5, 1956), president (since August 15, 2013.

National Flag: Red, white and blue horizontal stripes. The white stripe displays the national seal on one side and the words *Paz y Justicia* (Peace and Justice) on the opposite side. This is the only flag in the world having different sides.

Although Paraguay is landlocked, the Paraná River forms part of the boundary with Argentina and Brazil and links Paraguay with the Atlantic. The north to south Paraguay River, a Paraná tributary, divides the country into two regions with very different characters. Paraguay's third important river, the Pilcomayo, forms the southwest frontier with Argentina and joins the Paraguay opposite Asunción.

The eastern (*Oriental*) region of Paraguay, between the Paraguay and the Paraná rivers, is referred to as Paraguay proper. Containing approximately 40% of the nation's territory, the *Oriental* has fertile rolling plains with scattered hills in the south central portion, rising to the Amam-bay Mountains (2,700 feet) in the northeast along the Brazilian border. This is the most densely populated region of Paraguay.

The western (*Occidental*) region of the nation, commonly called the *Chaco*, is a hot, grassy prairie, interspersed with stands of hardwood known as *quebracho* (axe-breaker). Crossed by numerous unnavigable streams, its underground water is too salty for irrigation or human consumption; until recently this region was largely uninhabited. Today, through the impounding of rainwater, the Chaco is dotted with cattle ranches and the *quebracho* is harvested for tannin.

HISTORY: The history of Paraguay centers on the capital, Asunción, and on the villages within a 60-mile radius around that city on the eastern side of the Paraguay River. To the primitive people who roamed the area prior to the Spanish conquest, the lush plains lying between the Paraguay and the Paraná rivers were their traditional Garden of Eden. Of the many tribes that resided there, most were of the Tupi-Guaraní linguistic group. An amiable people, living by trapping, fishing and simple plantings, they offered little opposition to the Spaniards who explored

Paraguay

the Paraná valley and established a fort at Asunción on August 15, 1537, some 70 years prior to the first English settlement in North America.

Though neglected by the Spanish crown, the colony prospered and at the end of 20 years boasted 1,500 Spanish residents, a cathedral, a textile mill and a growing cattle industry. For two centuries, Asunción and its pleasant valley developed slowly while serving as the seat of Spanish authority in South America east of the Andes Mountains and south of the Portuguese colony in Brazil.

From Asunción, expeditions founded the cities of Santa Fé, Corrientes and Buenos Aires. Beginning in 1588, a company of Jesuit missionaries gathered some 100,000 Indians into mission villages and taught them better methods of farming, stock raising and handicrafts. The Jesuits protected their wards against enslavement by civil governors, settlers and Brazilian slave hunters; in the process, they helped to hold Paraguay and Uruguay for the Spanish. Unfortunately for the colony, the Jesuits were expelled in 1767.

Paraguay's transition from colonial status to independence was swift and unspectacular. In 1810, following the declaration of independence by Buenos Aires, Paraguay was invited to join with the Argentine ex-colony. The invitation was rejected and in 1811 Paraguay defeated a force sent from Buenos Aires to compel acceptance of Argentine leadership. A congress declared Paraguay to be a free and independent state and a five-man ruling council was established.

Dissension erupted; in 1814 a hopelessly deadlocked Congress voted full dictatorial powers to Dr. José Gaspar Rodríguez de Francia, who ruled until 1840. Austere, frugal, honest, dedicated and brutally cruel, he set the dictatorial pattern that persisted until 1989. Francia introduced improved methods in agriculture and in stock raising and was able to force the Paraguayan

soil to produce more than ever before. Although dissent was ruthlessly suppressed, Paraguay was well ordered and well fed.

Francia's death created a power vacuum and a year of turmoil. The man who came to power, Carlos Antonio López, imposed a constitution, but one that let him rule with the same autocratic powers that Francia had. López established trade and diplomatic relations with other countries and groomed his son, Francisco Solano López, to succeed him.

The son enjoyed playing soldier and built up Paraguay's army. After he succeeded his father, he gave himself the rank of *mariscal* (field marshal) and looked around for someone to fight. He foolishly declared war on Brazil, Argentina and Uruguay in 1865, a decision that was to decimate the country's male population. In the bloody, five-year War of the Triple Alliance, Paraguay's three enemies invaded the country and engaged in what today would be called genocide. Of a population of 520,000, at least 300,000 Paraguayans were slaughtered; only 28,746 males survived. It was a demographic cataclysm from which it took the country generations to recover. "Mariscal" López, for whom the main boulevard of Asunción is named today, was himself killed in the Battle of Cerro Corá with the Brazilians in 1870, which ended the pointless struggle, the costliest in the history of post-colonial South America. It says something of the Paraguayan mentality that Solano López

still is revered as a national hero, as is Francia.

Between 1870 and 1932 Paraguay slowly recovered and remained at peace with its neighbors. However, internal turmoil persisted and presidents were put in office by gunplay rather than by elections. From 1870 until 1954, Paraguay had 39 presidents, most of whom were jailed, murdered or exiled before they completed their term. As in many Latin American countries, the Conservative and Liberal parties competed for power, but there was little alternation between them; the Conservatives ruled from 1870–1904, when the Liberals gained power in a modest social revolution and governed until 1936. Economically, there was some progress. Immigrants from Italy, Spain, Germany and Argentina developed the agriculture, stock raising and forestry industries. Of the 800,000 population in 1928, the majority were illiterate and landless; profits from agriculture and industry went to foreign owners, mostly Argentine.

The Paraguay-Bolivia border remained undefined after the war of 1870. A humiliated Paraguay sought to extend its barren Chaco territory. In the 1920s, it granted a concession to Canadian Mennonites to establish a colony in the Chaco, called Filadelfia, which is still there today and accounts for more than half the country's dairy products. Bolivia sought access to the Atlantic via ports on the Paraguay River. War broke out in 1932, ending in a

1935 truce that awarded Paraguay about 20,000 square miles at a cost of 36,000 dead, and a seriously damaged economy. Six of the Chaco War's heroes later became president.

A revolt by Chaco War veterans in 1936 brought Colonel Rafael Franco into the presidency. Like his Spanish namesake who took power that very year, Franco initiated a quasi-fascist economic system that would endure for 50 years. He was deposed in 1937 by Félix Paiva, and a decade of upheaval ensued. Paiva allowed nominally democratic elections in 1939, which the Liberals won behind the candidacy of General Estigarribia, a Chaco War hero. But Estigarribia perished in a plane crash in 1940 and his war minister, Higinio Morínigo, seized power and ruled as dictator for eight years.

In 1947, the old Conservative Party renamed itself the National Republican Association, popularly called the *Colorado* Party, and staged a coup that toppled the dictatorship and began an unbroken period of party dominance that continued until 2008. Five presidents came and went during the next three years, until the election of the *Colorados'* Federico Cháves in 1950.

The Stroessner Era, 1954–89

In July 1954, the army revolted against Cháves and installed General Alfredo Stroessner, son of a Bavarian brewing company accountant and the daughter of a wealthy Paraguayan family. He was "re-elected" to the presidency by a large vote seven times, serving for 35 years. Although he initially allowed opposition elements to contest elections, they were eliminated by 1963. He later allowed the Liberal Party to field candidates in the elections in 1973 and 1978, but the outcomes of all the elections during his rule were preordained.

General Alfredo Stroessner

In 1973, for example, Stroessner received 681,306 votes over his opponent, Gustavo Riart of the Liberal Party, who got 198,096. Abstentions and blank ballots accounted for 35%. Since Stroessner's *Colorado* Party won a majority of the votes, it was by law entitled to two thirds of the seats in Congress. The remaining one third was assigned to the opposition by a prescribed formula.

Two small opposition groups were similar in outlook to the *Colorados*, favoring free enterprise with minimal state intervention in the economy. However, the Liberals favored a more democratic government. Whenever any individual appeared to gain *too much* popularity during Stroessner's years, he was either jailed, exiled or simply disappeared.

With solid military backing, Stroessner ruled Paraguay as his personal fiefdom. He emphasized political stability, road construction and a strong stand against communism. Living standards rose slowly but steadily during his tenure. Political stability also attracted foreign investment.

Relations with the Catholic Church were generally poor, particularly when Stroessner sought to undermine the church's Marandú rural public housing program. Supported with funds obtained in the United States, the effort attempted to provide the nation's 100,000 impoverished Indian population with medical, legal and economic assistance. The conservative elite viewed such attempts to help the Indians as a "communist conspiracy." Five Jesuit priests in the movement were deported and others were jailed. (Even as recently as April 2005, the democratically elected Paraguayan Congress rejected a bill that would have established a 114,000-hectare reserve for the nomadic Ayoreo tribe in the Chaco, the last tribe outside the Amazon to have resisted contact with outsiders.)

Stroessner ruled by "state of siege" legislation that suspended constitutional guarantees. It was renewed every 90 days.

Corruption within the ruling *Colorado* Party was reported by the independent newspaper *ABC Color,* by some radio stations and by the Paraguayan Episcopal Conference in late 1984. The first two were closed down and the latter was ignored.

Stroessner was elected to his eighth term by a majority of 89% in 1988, at the age of 75. There were the usual irregularities and voter apathy. The *Colorado* Party became divided over the issue of a transition. The *tradicionalistas* wanted the aging dictator to step aside, while the *oficialistas* (also called *militantes)* thought Stroessner, barring ill health, should remain in office. The matter was postponed by Stroessner's candidacy for re-election. When *Radio-Ñandutí* became too vocal, it was jammed.

Stroessner Falls

When Stroessner disappeared for 10 days in 1988 there were rumors he had died. He underwent prostate surgery at an undisclosed location; his recovery was slow. Sensing the time was right, the commander-in-chief of the military, General Andrés Rodríguez, staged a coup in February 1989, exiling the now-feeble Stroessner to Brazil without opposition. Low estimates of deaths during the coup were 50, high ones 300. An era had ended.

Taking the opposition by surprise, Rodríguez announced elections for May 1, 1989; Rodríguez became the *Colorado* candidate, assuring his election to a four-year term. He projected the image of a populist in contrast to the aloof, distant Stroessner.

Things didn't really change, however. Rodríguez received more than 74% of the vote, and the *Colorado* Party received the usual two thirds of the seats in Congress. Power struggles erupted within the party between the "democratic" faction and the slightly more conservative "traditionalists." Rodríguez favored the former, even though his daughter was married to Stroessner's son.

Under Stroessner and Rodríguez, Paraguay was a giant fencing operation, the largest in Latin America. If one wanted to buy or sell anything that had been stolen, Paraguay was (and still is, to a large degree) the place to go. Rodríguez was reported to have ties to the drug trade, including to the infamous Auguste Joseph Ricord of *The French Connection* infamy, who sought refuge in Paraguay in the 1960s; the obvious protection he received was a bone of contention between Paraguay and the United States, which sought his extradition. He was extradited in 1972, served 10 years in prison sentence and returned to Paraguay in 1983, dying there in 1985.

The smuggling enterprise was shaken in 1992 when a whistle-blowing colonel disclosed that the army had a virtual monopoly on fencing expensive, stolen cars. Surprisingly, Rodríguez removed four top officers, probably to avoid a charge that he was also involved.

Rodríguez, who was in ill health anyway, was barred by the new 1992 constitution from re-election, so he retired to a palatial estate. When journalists asked him how he could build such an estate on his salary as a general or president, he replied arrogantly that it was from the money he had saved by giving up smoking! He did not quit soon enough; he died of cancer in 1997.

Paraguay

Wasmosy and Oviedo

In late 1992, preparing for primary and general elections, the *Colorados* again became badly divided. The "democratic" faction prevailed and nominated Juan Carlos Wasmosy, a civil engineer and businessman. The conservatives, who had backed a charismatic army general named Lino Oviedo, ultimately supported Wasmosy. There are still suspicions that Wasmosy and Oviedo both stuffed ballot boxes, but Wasmosy's people managed to stuff more than did Oviedo's. Wasmosy was then opposed by two candidates in the May 1993 general election—Domingo Laino, long-time leader of the Authentic Radical Liberal Party *(PLRA)*, and Guillermo Caballero Vargas of the National Encounter Party. Wasmosy won an expanded five-year term with more than 40% of the vote after campaigning on promises to improve the economy and employment. As an encouraging sign of increased pluralization and decentralization, the governors of the 17 departments were elected directly for the first time, and the Liberals captured Central Department, where Asunción is located.

The military promised to continue "co-governing" with the *Colorado* Party. But the main political parties agreed upon a "governance pact" that excluded the police and military from party membership. Its signing was postponed, however, after attacks by *Colorado* supporters on opposition legislators.

A Liberal politician exposed the existence of secret police files in 1992 containing facts behind the disappearance of some 15,000 people during the Stroessner years. It also allegedly contained evidence of the existence of Operation Condor, a cooperative effort against leftists by Paraguay, Chile, Argentina and Uruguay during the 1980s that arranged disappearances of undesired people.

Democratic forces held their breath in April 1996 when Oviedo publicly called for Wasmosy to resign. It amounted to an attempted coup, but the rest of the armed forces failed to move against the civilian president. Wasmosy then summoned Oviedo to his office and ordered him to retire, promising him the cabinet post of defense secretary. For 27 tense hours, Oviedo demurred, provoking fears of a throwback to Paraguay's bad old days of military strongmen. In the end, he relented and retired, but public protests against his accepting the cabinet post led Wasmosy to withdraw the offer.

Paraguay appeared to have established civilian control over the military. Wasmosy went even further, cashiering 207 cavalry officers who he said had supported Oviedo's rebellion. An appeals court upheld the dismissals.

The Oviedo saga continued, however. In the *Colorado* primary in 1997, the 5-foot, 3-inch Oviedo won the nomination for the May 1998 presidential election. This infuriated Wasmosy, and their relations went from poor to deplorable. Oviedo accused the president of incompetence and corruption; Wasmosy, acting on his authority as commander-in-chief, ordered the general arrested for insubordination. Oviedo was a fugitive for 42 days before turning himself in. Wasmosy placed him under house arrest for 30 days.

Legal battles ensued between the two men in both civilian and military courts. In late 1997, the top electoral court rejected Wasmosy's plea to disqualify Oviedo as the *Colorado* candidate. There was another coup scare in January 1998 when, after a judge indicated he might order Oviedo's release because he had never been formally charged, tanks began rumbling in the streets. The military claimed it was merely a practice for a ceremony. A determined Wasmosy assembled a special military tribunal that ordered Oviedo jailed for an "indefinite" term for his abortive 1996 coup. The tribunal then sentenced Oviedo, still a presidential candidate, to 10 years.

When it became apparent Wasmosy might not be able legally to strip Oviedo of the nomination, and faced with polls that showed the Guaraní-speaking Oviedo leading, the president pondered a decidedly undemocratic move: to postpone the election. Paraguay's *Mercosur* partners quickly reminded Wasmosy that democratic government was a condition of membership. The United States also issued a warning against postponement. Wasmosy was rescued from the role of anti-democrat when the Supreme Court voted 5–4 to uphold Oviedo's prison term, effectively disqualifying his candidacy.

Oviedo vowed to campaign from jail, but the party, facing reality, nominated Oviedo's running mate, Raúl Cubas, a businessman. To mollify the Wasmosy faction, they agreed on Luis María Argaña as the new vice-presidential candidate. The 11th-hour termination of Oviedo's candidacy gave a boost to the perennial standard-bearer of the Liberals, Domingo Laino, running this time as candidate of the Democratic Alliance coalition. Now it was the *Colorados* who called for a postponement of the election.

It was just as well for them the vote wasn't delayed. Cubas received 54% to Laino's 42%; the Democratic Alliance claimed fraud, a charge that was largely unsubstantiated. Days before the election, Cubas declared that if the *Colorados* won, "Free, in jail, or wherever he is, Oviedo will have political power." He made good on that promise soon after his inauguration on August 15, 1998.

Assassination, Impeachment, Aftermath

Cubas' seven months in office were marked by Byzantine political intrigues that culminated in a high-level assassination, the president's impeachment and resignation and the ignominious flights into exile of both Cubas and Oviedo. These events sorely tested whether this fledgling democracy would long endure.

Three days after his inauguration, Cubas pardoned Oviedo, which led to jubilant demonstrations by the general's supporters, who chanted, *"Lino presidente!"* Cubas then appointed a new military tribunal, packed with Oviedo sympathizers, which dismissed all charges against the general. This brash action plunged Paraguay into a constitutional crisis, pitting the executive branch against both the legislative and judicial branches; under Stroessner's rule, of course, it would have been a short-lived

The late Lino Oviedo maintained his own Web page

Paraguay

contest. Congress threatened Cubas with impeachment.

In December 1998, the Supreme Court ruled Cubas' pardon and the military tribunal unconstitutional and ordered Oviedo re-incarcerated. Cubas ignored the order, creating a deep schism within *Colorado* ranks. Heading the anti-Oviedo faction was Vice President Argaña, who prevailed in a vote by the *Colorado* leadership days later to expel Oviedo from the party. The president and vice president had not even been on speaking terms since their inauguration.

By February, there were rampant rumors that Cubas was planning a Fujimori-style "self-coup," which he denied.

On February 11, the lower house of Congress voted 71–37 to charge Cubas with abuse of power for his actions the previous August—just two votes shy of the two-thirds-plus-one-vote majority needed for impeachment. Several *Colorado* deputies joined with the opposition Liberals. To further complicate this Byzantine spectacle, the armed forces high command—loyal to Oviedo—dismissed the air force generals

who had refused to participate in Oviedo's barracks revolt in 1996.

As this drama reached a climax, Vice President Argaña was assassinated in broad daylight on March 23, 1999, as he arrived at work. A vehicle containing three or four men in camouflage fatigues curbed Argaña's jeep. One threw a grenade, while others opened fire, hitting Argaña in the heart. He died at the scene. His driver also was killed and his bodyguard wounded. The killing threw the country into even greater turmoil and brought international denunciations. Both Cubas and Oviedo condemned their rival's murder, but not before thousands of Argaña's supporters took to the streets in protest; security forces opened fire, killing seven.

The next day, the Chamber of Deputies overwhelmingly voted to impeach Cubas. The anti-Cubas *Colorado*s and opposition Liberals did not come across as champions of democracy, however; at least one pro-Cubas *Colorado* deputy was roughed up when he arrived at the Congress and prevented from entering. The Senate took

the case up immediately. Conviction and removal were certain.

On March 28, Cubas abruptly resigned and boarded a Brazilian air force plane that flew him into a comfortable exile at a beach house in southern Brazil. Oviedo flew to Buenos Aires, where he was briefly detained for lacking immigration papers. Within a day, Argentina granted him asylum, which precluded extradition. Paraguay requested it anyway.

Senate President Luis Ángel González Macchi, next in the line of succession after the president and vice president, was sworn in as interim president. The army pledged him its crucial support. The new president, a former professional basketball player who had an unspectacular career as a legislator, appointed a new cabinet that included Argaña's brother and even some ministers from the opposition Liberal and National Encounter parties. Such power-sharing was unprecedented in the 52 years the *Colorado* Party had been entrenched in power.

The new government announced it would hold a presidential election in

Itaipu dam on the Paraguay-Brazil border

343

Paraguay

**Former President
Luis Ángel González Macchi**

six months and that a Liberal would be the running mate of the *Colorado* candidate. Later, the Supreme Court ruled that González Macchi could serve the remainder of Cubas' five-year term.

Paraguay recalled its ambassador from Argentina after President Carlos Menem's government refused to extradite Oviedo. In October, the election to succeed Menem in Argentina was won by Fernando de la Rua, who had pledged to extradite Oviedo. Sensing he had overstayed his welcome, the wily general vanished.

Just after New Year's Day, 2000, Oviedo resurfaced, brazenly holding a news conference with a handful of reporters at an undisclosed location in rural Paraguay, which was reported by media throughout Latin America. He maintained his innocence and alleged that his enemies had murdered Argaña to discredit him. Cocky as ever, he boasted to return as the people's champion.

Oviedo supporters in the military, police and Congress gave the country—and the world community—a scare in May 2000 when three armored cars parked in front of the legislative palace and fired two shots at the building. A standoff ensued, as military unit commanders pledged their support for González Macchi, who declared a 30-day state of siege. Denunciations of the revolt poured in from the United States and neighboring democracies. The next morning, about 25 soldiers, a few retired officers, 12 policemen and three pro-Oviedo congressmen surrendered. Oviedo sent a communiqué from his hideout to the newspaper *ABC Color* denying he was involved.

The whereabouts of the elusive general became a national—and international—

obsession. Besides Paraguay and Bolivia, Oviedo sightings were reported in Brazil, which turned out to be correct. In June 2000, acting on information from Paraguayan intelligence authorities who had been tapping and tracing Oviedo's phone calls to supporters back home, Brazilian police arrested him in a posh apartment in Foz do Iguaçu, across the border from Ciudad del Este. Police found a .38 pistol, which allowed them to charge him with illegal weapons possession.

He was in jail until December 2001, when the Brazilian Supreme Court unanimously rejected Paraguay's extradition request as "politically motivated" and ordered Oviedo released. The Paraguayan government was furious. A jubilant and boastful Oviedo vowed to return to Paraguay and run for president again.

In domestic politics, González Macchi's tenuous coalition with the Liberals fell apart in 2000 after the Liberals decided to return to their role as an opposition party to protest corruption. The bone of contention between the two parties was a reform bill that would have streamlined and depoliticized Paraguay's cumbersome bureaucracy, which sucks up more than 80% of the national budget. Hard-line *Colorado*s had resisted because patronage is a traditional tool by which the party ensured support. The president also sought to privatize inefficient state-owned companies, which sparked a protest in front of the legislative palace by workers and by landless peasants demanding free land.

After the *Colorado*-Liberal alliance fell apart, the two parties fielded separate candidates in the special election to fill the vacancy in the vice presidency. The *Colorado*s nominated Argaña's son, Félix, seemingly an unbeatable choice. But the political establishment was stunned when the Liberal candidate, Julio César "Yoyito" Franco, narrowly defeated Argaña. It was the *Colorado*s' first national-level defeat.

With the opposition in the vice presidency, pressure increased on the unpopular—and unelected—González Macchi to step aside. His position was not helped by the continued deterioration of an already sour economy, nor by the embarrassing revelation that his personal BMW, worth about $130,000 but for which he reportedly paid only $80,000, apparently had been stolen in Brazil and smuggled into Paraguay.

For the second year in a row, the U.S. "decertified" Paraguay in 2000 as an ally in the war on drugs, citing inaction at countering smuggling. Paraguay's remote Chaco region is an important way station in smuggling cocaine from neighboring Bolivia. The United States was also displeased when Paraguay re-established diplomatic relations with Cuba in 1999

after a 38-year break, the last South American nation to do so. The United States recertified Paraguay in 2001.

Paraguay, which has a large Arab community, primarily Lebanese and Jordanians, was in the international spotlight following the September 11, 2001, terrorist attacks in the U.S. Paraguayan police raided Arab-owned businesses in Ciudad del Este, notorious as a smuggling center because of the porous borders with Brazil and Argentina, and detained several people. Police seized evidence of links with the Iranian-backed terrorist group Hezbollah, although not with al-Qaeda. Even before 9/11, the U.S. State Department had identified the so-called "Tri-Border" area as a hotbed of Islamic extremists.

González Macchi became even more unpopular in 2002 by declaring a state of emergency after anti-government demonstrations in three cities left two people dead. He blamed Oviedo supporters and implausibly accused Vice President Franco of collaborating with them to bring down his government. Franco called for González Macchi's resignation, and mass protests continued.

Former President Cubas voluntarily returned to Paraguay in 2002 and placed himself at the disposition of the courts. He was placed under house arrest, then released pending trial. In 2007, a judge acquitted him of all charges. He then sought to claim his lifetime non-voting Senate seat as a former president, but the Senate never brought his request to a vote.

González Macchi faced an impeachment trial in 2003 over the stolen BMW and for allegedly mishandling $16 million in state funds; he was acquitted.

Nicanor Duarte Frutos

Nicanor Duarte Frutos, 46, a lawyer and former journalist from the reformist wing of the party, who had served capably as education minister under both Wasmosy and González Macchi, won the *Colorado* primary for the April 2003 presidential election. As his running mate he chose Luis Castiglioni.

After two straight defeats, Laino stepped aside in favor of Vice President Franco for the *PLRA* nomination. Pedro Fadul, a banker, ran as the candidate of a new movement called *Patria Querida* (Beloved Fatherland). Oviedo hand-picked another lackey named Guillermo Sánchez to run as the stand-in candidate of his whimsically named National Union of Ethical Citizens, or *UNACE*.

By 2003, the *Colorado* Party had been in power continuously longer than any party in the world save the North Korean Communist Party, which has ruled since 1945; the Chinese Communist Party came to

Former President Nicanor Duarte Frutos

power two years after the *Colorado*s did. Given the unpopularity of González Macchi and the 2000 election victory of Vice President Franco, it seemed logical that 2003 would be the year the opposition finally broke the *Colorado*s' 56-year grip on power. Logical in any other democracy, perhaps. The fragmented field of candidates divided the opposition vote, and Paraguay, like Mexico and Panama, does not have runoff elections; a simple plurality wins. Moreover, all the candidates vowed to combat corruption.

Turnout was 64.5% of the 2.4 million registered voters, despite the fact that voting is mandatory, possibly a reflection of the widespread disenchantment with the democratic process in Paraguay (see The Future). In the end, voters opted for the status quo:

Duarte Frutos	574,232	37.1%
Franco	370,348	24%
Fadul	328,916	21.3%
Sánchez	208,391	13.5%

The *Colorado*s had little cause for gloating. They won by the smallest percentage yet and lost their Senate majority for the first time. The Liberals also won the governorship of Caaguazú Department for the first time and retained the governorship of Central Department. Oviedo was an even bigger loser, given his stand-in's poor showing. Oviedo congratulated Duarte from his refuge in Brazil, but he ordered the *UNACE* bloc in Congress not to join with the *Colorado*s to form a majority coalition but to remain in opposition. *UNACE,* the *PLRA, Patria Querida* and National Encounter formed an uneasy but majority opposition coalition.

Duarte Frutos, the first president born after the *Colorado* takeover in 1947, soon

stepped on toes, vowing to overhaul the customs and internal revenue services, both notoriously corrupt and riddled with political patronage, which put him on an inevitable collision course with the *oficialista* wing of the party. He publicly vilified the country's Catholic priests as "a bunch of hypocrites" who, he charged, "had manipulated the faith" in favor of Fadul's candidacy.

Duarte Frutos and Castiglioni were inaugurated on August 15, 2003, inheriting a bankrupt government, a stagnant economy, a $2.2 billion public debt and a population that had begun to long for the comparatively prosperous and stable days of dictatorship. The much-reviled outgoing president was not even invited to place the presidential sash on his successor's shoulders. Duarte sounded a populist theme, reiterating his vow to fight the "mafia" that controls smuggling and piracy, but also the "unproductive local oligarchy, who want the government to remain the lackey of its privileges."

Duarte Frutos met with President George W. Bush soon after the inauguration, the first Paraguayan president to visit the White House. Bush was not pleased that Paraguay rejected a U.S. request to send a contingent of troops to Iraq, as the Dominican Republic, El Salvador, Honduras and Nicaragua did. Paraguay also abstained on the vote before the U.N. Human Rights Commission in Geneva in 2004 to condemn Cuba for human rights violations. A large number of Paraguayans study medicine in Cuba, while Cuba has sent many doctors to provide medical care in rural Paraguay.

A stubborn Senate refused to ratify Venezuela's admission into *Mercosur* in 2006. Unanimous approval by the four member countries was required. A majority of senators disapproved of Venezuelan President Hugo Chávez's authoritarian tendencies.

Duarte Frutos seemed eager to back up his populist rhetoric. During González Macchi's tenure, a group of armed peasants invaded a large estate near San Lorenzo and established a colony called Marquetalia, named after the Colombian town where the Revolutionary Armed Forces of Colombia *(FARC)* was formed. Duarte Frutos expropriated 25,000 hectares (62,000 acres) and issued titles to 1,300 peasant families, telegraphing that the way to obtain free land was to arm oneself and become a squatter on someone else's property and the government would back him up. Emboldened peasants invaded another 60 estates in 2004. There are an estimated 300,000 landless peasants, and by some non-governmental estimates, 1% of the population owns 80% of the land.

He also kept his promise to crack down on corruption, especially smuggling, and

at the end of his first year the government reported that customs collections were up by 89%.

Former President González Macchi, still a pariah, was tried but acquitted of illegally diverting $16 million into a New York bank account. He and his wife went on trial over an unexplained $1 million in a Swiss bank account. They were convicted, but an appeals court threw out the convictions.

Meanwhile, the restless ghost of the assassinated Argaña returned to haunt Paraguay. Oviedo embarked on a public relations campaign to clear his name in the murder, and found an ally in the daily newspaper *ABC Color* and the Brazilian newsmagazine *Isto É.* The paper quoted the chauffeur who survived the shooting as saying that Argaña had died of cancer the night before and the assassination was staged by the Argaña faction to discredit Oviedo. *Isto É* contended that Duarte Frutos, then head of the Colorado Party, was a party to this conspiracy. Another conspiracy theory floating about the country was that Argaña's own children rubbed out their ill father in an intra-family estate dispute. Casting doubts on the conspiracy theories is the news videotape shot immediately after the shooting, which shows Argaña's body covered in blood, which would have been impossible if he had died the night before. The news footage also shows the body limp when it was placed on a stretcher. The controversy lingers to this day.

Oviedo announced he would return to Paraguay in June 2004 to face the accusations, but only after several pro-Oviedo lawmakers met with Duarte to extract certain "guarantees." The president shouted that he would not tolerate anyone "destabilizing" the country. Oviedo kept his promise and returned, turning himself in to authorities. He was held in a military jail awaiting trial. In February 2005, he was cleared of charges that he had tried to overthrow González Macchi, but that December, an appeals court denied his release in the case involving the demonstrators killed after Argaña's assassination. Questions about his role in the Argaña assassination also continued to hang over him. In 2006, the Supreme Court, by 7–2, reversed the ruling clearing him of charges in the 1996 coup attempt and ruled he had to serve the remainder of his 10-year prison term. He remained behind bars at the Viña Cué military prison until he was paroled in September 2007 and made plans to run for president.

In 2004 and 2005, Paraguay was plagued by an alarming increase in street crime and kidnappings, something never experienced during Stroessner's iron-fisted regime. The highest-profile kidnapping was

Paraguay

that of former President Cubas' 31-year-old daughter, Cecilia, abducted in broad daylight near her home in September 2004. Raúl Cubas paid a $800,000 ransom, while Paraguayans demonstrated for his daughter's release and put up "Free Cecilia" posters. Her decomposed body was found in February 2005, buried under a house near Asunción. Paraguayans, long inured to non-violent corruption, were horrified, and the national police were criticized for failing to save her after receiving a credible tip as to her whereabouts.

Osmar Martínez, leader of a tiny leftist group, *Patria Libre*, believed to have contacts with Colombia's *FARC*, was arrested in connection with Cubas' death. The *FARC* denied involvement with the kidnapping and murder. So did *Patria Libre*, which claimed it was a scapegoat to justify political repression. Duarte Frutos vowed to use the army if necessary to combat crime, and he promised to recruit 12,000 more policemen, without explaining how he would pay for them. Martínez and other members of *Patria Libre* were convicted and sentenced to long prison terms.

Patria Libre spawned another nettlesome group in 2004, the Paraguayan People's Army *(EPP)*, which remains a significant threat to public order today (see Recent Developments). Its self-proclaimed leader, Alcides Oviedo, was sentenced to 18 years in prison for kidnapping min 2004 and published a manifesto while behind bars.

A peculiar issue arose in 2005. In 2000, the Paraguayan government had endorsed the sale of 1.5 million acres of land around Puerto Casado in the eastern Chaco to the Unification Church of the Rev. Sun Myung Moon, the messianic Korean. The understanding was that the church's practitioners would develop the area, creating jobs. By 2005, however, the Paraguayan residents of Puerto Casado complained that not only had nothing been done but that they were denied entry to the vast tract to collect firewood. They demanded that Congress expropriate part of the tract for the local people. Congress enacted, and Duarte Frutos signed, an expropriation totaling about 115,000 acres.

An era in Paraguayan history ended on August 16, 2006, when Stroessner died in his exile in Brazil. He was 93. He was buried in Brasilia, but the Brazilian government considered it a "transitory" burial until he could reinterred in Paraguay—as though he would contaminate Brazilian soil. Stroessner's family sought unsuccessfully to persuade the Paraguayan government to allow his remains to be buried in his native soil—shabby treatment from his fellow *Colorados*.

Paraguay achieved more international notoriety in 2008 when the United Nations announced that it was the second-largest producer of marijuana in the world in 2006, with 5,900 metric tons out of 41,400 tons worldwide; Mexico was first with 7,400 tons. Paraguayan soil is deemed ideal for growing cannabis. That dubious distinction could help explain the improvement in Paraguay's GDP growth in recent years (see Economy).

Lugo Makes History— and Creates Scandal

The campaign for the April 2008, presidential election turned into an even greater free-for-all than the one in 2003, thanks to a bitter intra-party turf war between two strong *Colorado* candidates, Oviedo's release from jail and the sudden groundswell of popular support for a populist dark horse who vowed to shake up the system.

Vice President Castiglioni resigned to seek the *Colorado* nomination in a primary. Duarte Frutos let it be known his choice was Education Minister Blanca Ovelar de Duarte, whose husband is no relation to the president.

A bitter primary battle between the Castiglioni and the Duarte Frutos-Ovelar factions ensued. The primary was so close that the counting took a month. Ovelar won by a razor-thin 45.04% to 44.5%. A bitter Castiglioni refused to accept defeat and threatened to contest her victory in court, claiming 30,000 of her votes were fraudulent. But her nomination was affirmed.

The expected *PLRA* standard bearer was Federico Franco, governor of Central Department in which the capital is located and brother of former Vice President Julio César Franco, the party's 2003 candidate. But polls suggested a charismatic political newcomer could end the *Colorados'* 60-year reign: Fernando Lugo, 56, a bearded priest and former bishop and revolution theologist who had championed the cause of land reform and expressed admiration for Venezuela's Hugo Chávez.

As bishop of San Pedro, Lugo became popular with landless peasants. Because of his political activities, the church removed him as bishop, a post he had held for 11 years. In 2006, Lugo sought to resign from the priesthood, both because the Vatican prohibits priests from holding civil public office, and because the constitution prohibits priests from serving as president. He established a political movement called *Teko joja*, Guaraní for justice and equality.

In a party convention in 2007, the Liberals *(PLRA)* stunned Franco by narrowly voting to abandon his candidacy in favor of Lugo's on condition that the vice-presidential candidate be a Liberal. The new Lugo-Franco coalition was named the Patriotic Alliance for Change. Lugo suddenly backed away from his earlier pro-Chávez comments.

The enigmatic Oviedo sought and received the *UNACE* nomination. Now, at last, Paraguayans would see whether his popularity could live up to his boasting. Fadul once again stood as the candidate of *Patria Querida*. Three minor candidates rounded out the field.

Voter turnout on April 20 was 65.6%. The historic results:

Lugo	766,502	42.3%
Ovelar	573,995	31.8%
Oviedo	411,034	22.8%
Fadul	41,004	2.5%

Thus, 61 years of *Colorado* Party rule, the longest of any non-Communist party in the world at that time, came to an end with Lugo's inauguration on August 15, 2008.

Although he was entitled to a Senate seat for life as a former president, Duarte Frutos opted to run for a Senate seat, and was elected. He resigned from the presidency on June 23 to qualify for it, but the Senate refused to accept his resignation and told him he was eligible only for the seat-for-life, which is non-voting. He refused to assume it.

The new Congress was as fragmented as the old one. The *Colorados* won 15 of the 45 Senate seats, followed by the *PLRA* with 14; Oviedo's *UNACE*, 9; *Patria Querida*, 4; and Lugo's *Teko joja*, 1 (Lugo did not actively field a slate). In the 80-seat Chamber of Deputies, the *Colorados* had 29, the Liberals 26, *UNACE* 16, *Patria Querida* 3 and *Teko joja*, 1.

Lugo broke with the past by appointing a member of the Aché tribe as minister of indigenous affairs. She was soon forced to resign over allegations she showed favoritism to her own tribe. He also sacked the military high command.

Speaking of indigenous affairs, Paraguayans were unprepared for the scandal that exploded around their new president eight months into his term. In April 2009, Viviana Carrillo, 26, announced she was filing a paternity suit against Lugo, claiming he had fathered her child born in 2007 while he was still a bishop. Evidently the affair began when she was 16. The president acknowledged in passing in a televised Holy Week address that he is the father.

A week later, another woman, Benigna Lequizamón, 27, publicly alleged that Bishop Lugo had fathered her child, born in 2002. One day later, Hortensia Morán, 39, an activist in Lugo's political movement, claimed he had fathered her child born 16 months earlier, but she said she was not filing a paternity suit because the child was "the result of unconditional love." Lugo neither admitted nor denied his paternity of the other two children, but the scandal made news around the world and brought scorn upon the former bishop who could not control his libido. (In 2010, three independent DNA tests showed he was not the father of Moran's child).

Lugo's supporters praised his candor in admitting paternity and said it proved he was a champion of transparency. Not surprisingly, *Colorados* countered that if he were so candid and transparent, why did he wait until he was sued to admit the paternity of Carrillo's child? The bishop of Asunción called on him to assume the necessary responsibilities if he were the father of the other children.

At that point, the president began exhibiting strange, erratic behavior. He canceled a trip to Washington, apparently not wanting to face international media scrutiny over the paternity scandal. Shortly after insisting that he would be making "gradual" cabinet changes, he abruptly fired and replaced four cabinet members—from the same faction of the *PLRA*.

Lugo attended a summit of *ALBA*, the left-wing, anti-U.S. group established by Venezuela's Chávez that also includes Cuba, Bolivia, Nicaragua and Honduras. Lugo denied media reports—and contradicted his own chief of staff—that he had concluded an energy treaty with Venezuela by which Paraguay would purchase cut-rate oil. Lugo called the reports "laughable," even as Chief of Staff Miguel López Perito announced it had been submitted to Congress and *ABC Color* carried the text of the treaty and reported that the Venezuelan Congress had already approved it! The Paraguayan Congress, meanwhile, claimed it had *not* received it, adding to the confusion. Opponents warned that Paraguay was surrendering its sovereignty to Venezuela.

The Paraguayan Senate also continued to refuse to ratify Venezuela's application to join *Mercosur*; it successfully blocked it for six years.

A fourth woman, Teresa Rojas, came forward in 2009 to allege that Padre Fernando had "fathered" her now 20-year-old daughter, Fatima. Lugo did not acknowledge his paternity, but he attended Fatima's wedding and appointed her husband to a government job with the legal department of the Yacyretá Binational Enterprise, raising accusations of nepotism. Lugo's own niece stated publicly that it was common knowledge in their family that Fatima was Lugo's daughter.

The self-styled Paraguayan People's Army *(EPP)*, a radical offshoot of *Patria Libre*, the group blamed for Cecilia Cubas' death in 2005, splashed back into the news in 2008 with a series of kidnappings, including two prominent ranchers, Fidel Zavala and Luis Lindstrom. The specter of a

In this cartoon circulating on the Internet, a journalist asks, "President Lugo, women keep appearing who say they are the mothers of your children. Excuse me for asking, but didn't you take any precautions?" Lugo replies, "Nooo, please, that's against the principles of the church."

guerrilla insurgency created a public outcry, and there were rumors of an imminent military coup. Lugo issued a statement, through the armed forces, denying the rumors. The next day he stunned the country by firing his army, navy and air force commanders, then the armed forces commander. Over three months, he cashiered more than 60 other mid-ranking officers, which led the opposition to charge he was trying to pack the armed forces hierarchy, Chávez-like, with officers sympathetic with his leftist philosophy.

Lindstrom was released two months after his capture after his family paid a $130,000 ransom. Zavala was released underweight but unharmed in January 2010 after his family paid a reported $550,000. Their releases were the cause of national celebration. (Lindstrom was later murdered in May 2013.)

In April 2010, the *EPP* attacked a cattle ranch and killed a policeman and three ranch workers. Lugo declared a 30-day state of exception in five departments, which permitted warrantless arrests and allowed the army to be utilized. Lugo dispatched 1,000 troops to augment a force of 3,000 national police. When the state of ex-

ception expired, the security forces could claim only one arrest. Gabriel Zarate Cardozo, one of the top leaders of the *EPP*, was killed in a shootout with security forces in Canindeyú Department that September.

Lugo claimed a diplomatic triumph in 2009 by extracting an agreement from Brazilian President Da Silva to triple the royalties Paraguay receives from the Itaipu hydroelectric dam, from $120 million to $360 million annually. The Brazilian Congress eventually ratified it in 2011.

Lugo also placed himself in the forefront of international efforts in 2009 to restore deposed Honduran President Manuel Zelaya to power. Lugo initially refused to recognize the government of the newly elected Honduran president, Porfirio Lobo Sosa.

By early 2010, Lugo's approval rating was about 50%, and the opposition in Congress was blocking all his major proposals.

In August 2010, Lugo was diagnosed with non-Hodgkins lymphoma, a common cancer affecting the immune system. He began chemotherapy in September, and by October he was appearing in public bald. He suffered a thrombosis, a common side-effect of chemotherapy, and was

Paraguay

flown to São Paulo, Brazil, for treatment, which was successful. In May 2011, the São Paulo hospital pronounced him cured of the lymphoma as well.

Lugo's illness did not prevent him from effecting yet another military shake-up in September 2010, the second in less than a year and the fourth since 2008. He fired the heads of the three services, then the commander of the armed forces, then worked his way down the echelon to corps, division, regimental and brigade commanders; he even replaced the commander of the band! He explained lamely that it was merely a "routine leadership renewal," while critics renewed their accusations that it was a Chávez-like purge and former generals warned that it was having a negative effect on institutional integrity.

Paraguay enjoyed unprecedentedly good economic news in 2010. After the global recession and a devastating drought that reduced agricultural exports caused the economy to shrink by –3.8% in 2009, the government responded with fiscal and monetary stimulus packages that infused millions of dollars into the economy, particularly construction projects. The private sector also invested heavily in new construction. Fortuitously, the weather also blessed Paraguay in 2010, and soybean and cattle exports reached record highs. By year's end growth was an astonishing 14.5%, the highest in 20 years and the highest in the Western Hemisphere for 2010. "We are economic champions!" Lugo boasted on Christmas Day. In addition, it was learned in 2010 that Paraguay is sitting atop what is now thought to be the world's largest deposit of titanium ore (see Economy).

At the urging of the IMF, Lugo submitted to Congress a bill to resurrect a personal income tax that had been briefly implemented by Duarte Frutos, but the *Colorados* blocked it.

Lugo sacked his interior and public works ministers in June 2011 for no apparent reason other than they publicly opposed a constitutional amendment that would allow him to run for re-election. Two protests were staged in front of the presidential palace to oppose re-election. The first drew only about 50 people. Like the protesters in Tunisia and Egypt, the Paraguayan protesters began communicating via Facebook. The second demonstration drew 350 people. Lugo abandoned his hopes for re-election.

In June 2012, a *fourth* woman, Narcisa de la Cruz, declared that Lugo was the father of her 10-year-old son and that he had been sending her voluntary support payments. Lugo acknowledged he was the father and that he had initiated the legal paperwork to recognize the boy. De la Cruz told the media that she went to Bishop Lugo for "spiritual guidance" because she was having marital difficulties.

Impeachment and International Ostracization

Paraguay's long-simmering dispute between large landowners and peasant squatters finally erupted violently in June 2012, which would end with Lugo's impeachment and removal and his successor's quest for international legitimacy. Lugo had promised in 2008 to redistribute land to 87,000 peasants, but after four years he had failed to make good on that pledge. The peasants, with some legal validity, had long argued that hundreds of square kilometers of land had been seized illegally during the Stroessner regime and parceled out to the dictator's wealthy supporters. A truth commission had concluded as much. Hundreds of peasants had already taken the law into their own lands by invading tracts along the Brazilian border that had been purchased illegally by Brazilians but which now belonged to their Paraguayan-born children, who have Paraguayan citizenship and claim rightful ownership for having worked the land.

In May, 150 peasants invaded and occupied a forested 2,000-hectare (4,400-acre) tract near Curuguaty in Canindeyú department along the Brazilian border owned by influential former *Colorado* Senator Blas Riquelme, a political opponent of Lugo. On June 15, a police special operations unit moved in to evict the squatters, who were suspiciously well-armed. A firefight erupted, leaving six policemen, including the unit's commander, and a reported 11 squatters dead. The unusually bloody incident horrified the country and generated international news. Lugo dispatched troops to restore order, and nine

**Interim President
Federico Franco**

peasants were arrested and charged with murder in the deaths of the policemen. Interior Minister Carlos Filizzola resigned over the incident, as did Police Chief Paulino Rojas.

A few days later, the newspaper *ABC Color* reported it had documentation that suggested the government illegally gave Riquelme the 2,000 hectares in 1967. The government's Rural and Land Development Institute took the case to the Supreme Court to determine whether the government had legal title to the land in the first place when it gave it to Riquelme. Tracing titles in Paraguay can be an onerous legal exercise.

By April 2012, Lugo ranked 13th in popularity out of 19 leaders in the Western Hemisphere, according to the Mexican polling firm Consulta Mitofsky. The media had ridiculed him for his frequent trips abroad, 75 in four years. He had alienated both the *Colorados* and the *PLRA*, which had joined forces in Congress to hamstring him. Then came the fourth paternity incident and the Curuguaty massacre.

In a stunning, unforeseen move, the Chamber of Deputies voted 76–1 on June 21 to impeach Lugo on five somewhat vague counts, including malfeasance in office. His lawyers were given just 24 hours to prepare his "defense" in the Senate the next day, and allotted two hours to present it. Lugo did not attend. The Senate voted 39–4 to remove him from office on June 22. Vice President Franco was quickly sworn in. Within a week, Franco had replaced all but two of Lugo's cabinet ministers, including the most respected, his capable economy minister, Dionisio Borda.

At first, Lugo accepted the decision, although he said Paraguayan democracy was "deeply wounded." Surprisingly few protesters took to the streets to denounce his removal. The media seemed generally supportive of the removal, as did the Catholic Church, which declared its support for Franco. But the reaction from abroad was swift and severe. Technically, the Congress' actions were in accordance with the constitution, but the speed with which they occurred, the lack of opportunity for Lugo to mount a defense and the vagueness of the charges did not sit well in other Latin American capitals. The head of the OAS' Inter-American Commission on Human Rights called it a "parody of justice."

Not surprisingly, Lugo's leftist *ALBA* partners—Venezuela's Chávez, Cuba's Raúl Castro, Bolivia's Morales, Ecuador's Correa and Nicaragua's Ortega—labeled his removal a "coup," recalled their ambassadors and refused to recognize Franco. Chávez cut the exports of discounted oil to Paraguay, even though Paraguay still owed $260 million under that contract. In a touch of irony, Ortega, who is himself serving an unconstitutional third term, called on the OAS not to recognize Franco as the legitimate president.

The leaders of Paraguay's *Mercosur* partners, Argentina, Brazil and Uruguay, who are also left of center, expressed "deep concern" for Paraguayan democracy and recalled their ambassadors; even Chile's conservative president, Sebastián Piñera, denounced Lugo's removal and recalled his ambassador. On June 29, in a hastily called *Mercosur* summit, Paraguay's partners voted to "suspend," but not expel, Paraguay until its next regular presidential election in April 2013. The Union of South American Nations *(UNASUR)* suspended Paraguay the next day.

Argentina, Brazil and Uruguay took advantage of Paraguay's suspension from *Mercosur* to vote to admit Venezuela, which the Paraguayan Senate had refused to ratify for six years. Venezuela joined *Mercosur* on July 31.

Franco was asked to stay away from the annual Ibero-American Summit, held in Cádiz, Spain, in November, because several presidents threatened not to attend if Franco did.

Brazil's government spoke out of both sides of its mouth, decrying the "breakdown of democracy" while at the same time promising to respect Paraguayan sovereignty and disavowing intervention. Brazil had a vested interest in maintaining harmonious relations because of the unresolved issue of land titles for Brazilian settlers and their descendants. A delegation of so-called "Brasiguayos" and Paraguayan legislators met with President Dilma Rousseff to urge her to support the new government.

The U.S. response was cautious and benign by comparison. A spokeswoman for the State Department said only, "We urge all Paraguayans to act peacefully, with calm and responsibility, in the spirit of Paraguay's democratic principles."

Lugo changed his mind and decided to contest his removal, creating a "shadow government." He called for mass demonstrations, and Franco called for counter-demonstrations in support of himself. Lugo succeeded in marshaling a few demonstrations, but they soon fizzled out.

Polls showed that 60% of Paraguayans supported Lugo's ouster. Anti-Lugo graffiti was more prevalent than pro-Lugo graffiti. Many Paraguayans simply didn't like what they saw as bullying from Brazil and Argentina over an internal matter, an insult to their sovereignty.

Franco's own approval rating that September was 36% in the Mitofsky poll, tying with Chile's Piñera as the third most unpopular leader in the Western Hemisphere. One reason was a gaffe he committed by saying that a family could live a "decent life" on the equivalent of $300 a month.

Popular or not, interim president or not, Franco succeeded in taking charge and implementing some breathtaking reforms that his two predecessors had talked about but had failed to enact. First, he finally got Congress to approve a graduated income tax, which treads lightly on the poor and middle class. Second, he outdid Duarte and Lugo by granting titles to unused land and buying up other tracts, which the government sold to independent farmers. Franco also got Congress to approve an allocation for $40 million a year from the revenue from the Itaipú Dam to buy laptop computers for schoolchildren, bringing Paraguayan education into the 21st century. He told his countrymen that in the 14 months he had, he could only "plant the seeds," and urged them to reap the harvest.

Unfortunately, rampant street crime continued unabated, and the *EPP* continued to cause trouble.

The Elections of 2013

Franco let it be known he would not run for a full term in the April 21, 2013, election. His Liberal Party nominated the public works minister, Efraín Alegre. Oviedo, who had supported Lugo's ouster and the interim Liberal government, stood again as the candidate of *UNACE,* confident that the failure of the Lugo experiment would cause voters to turn to him.

Shady millionaire businessman Horacio Cartes, who had been unofficially running for three years, officially declared his candidacy in the *Colorado* primary under the banner *"Honor Colorado."* First he had to cajole the party leadership to suspend the

President Horacio Manuel Cartes Jara

rule that a 10-year party membership is required to run in the primary. He made his fortune in tobacco and soft drink distribution and owned a soccer club, but he had a checkered reputation (see The Future). Moreover, he was a political novice who not only was not a party member, he admitted he had never voted! Yet, Cartes easily won the *Colorado* primary with 59.7% of the vote.

Lugo could not run for a second term, but he organized a movement called *Frente Guasú* (Big Front in Spanish and Guaraní), which nominated Aníbal Carrillo. Lugo chose to run for the Senate. *Patria Querida* nominated Senator Miguel Carrizosa. A new movement called *Avanza País* fielded Mario Ferreira.

Paraguay's political equation was suddenly and dramatically altered on February 4, 2013, when Oviedo, 69, was killed in a helicopter crash en route to Asunción from a campaign rally in Concepción. His pilot and bodyguard also died. Ironically, it was the 24th anniversary of the 1989 coup in which Oviedo was instrumental in toppling Stroessner. Oviedo's party and family immediately charged murder. Franco praised Oviedo as a military hero and vowed to hire international experts to investigate the crash. *UNACE* had no time to field an alternate candidate, so the dead Oviedo appeared on the ballot—and drew almost 1 percent of the vote!

The official investigation into Oviedo's fatal helicopter crash concluded in June 2013 that bad weather was the cause. Oviedo's family and supporters disputed the findings. Like the Argaña assassination in 1999, conspiracy theories may abound for years.

With Oviedo's death, Cartes' victory was even more inevitable. Like Enrique Peña Nieto of Mexico's once-dominant *PRI,* Cartes found himself in the ironic position of being the candidate of change, even reform. But he garnered international notoriety by calling homosexuals "monkeys" and for saying he would cut off his own testicles if one of his sons turned out to be gay. He apologized after the election.

A respectable 68% of voters turned out on April 21. The results:

Cartes	1,095,469	45.8%
Alegre	883,630	36.9%
Ferreira	140,622	5.9%
Carrillo	79,327	3.3%
Carrizosa	27,036	1.1%
Oviedo	19,124	.8%

The *Colorados* fell short of a majority in both houses, requiring government by consensus. Lugo won his Senate seat.

There could be no denying Cartes' mandate or legitimacy in international circles—or Lugo's lack of one from Carrillo's pitiful

Paraguay

showing. During the campaign, Cartes said he expected to bring Paraguay back into *Mercosur*. But on June 24, at a meeting of the U.S.-Paraguayan Chamber of Commerce, he implied coyly that Paraguay may choose not to rejoin an organization that had denied the lawful actions of the Paraguayan Congress. It was a matter of "national dignity," he said.

Cartes was inaugurated on August 15 in a ceremony in Asunción. Juan Eudes Afara, a party regular who had come up through the ranks, was sworn in as vice president. Cartes promised to wage war on poverty and corruption—the same promises Paraguayans hear every five years. Significantly, Presidents Cristina Fernández of Argentina, Dilma Rousseff of Brazil and José Mujica of Uruguay attended, suggesting Paraguay would be welcomed back into *Mercosur*. The presidents of Peru and Chile also were there, conveying more regional legitimacy, as were the president of Taiwan and Spain's Crown Prince (now King) Felipe. But Venezuela's Nicolás Maduro, who had succeeded the dead Chávez in March, did not attend, nor did Ecuador's Correa. The United States, as usual, sent only a third-stringer, Energy Secretary Ernest Moniz.

Recent Developments

As a first step toward Paraguay's reintegration into the hemispheric community, Cartes attended the *UNASUR* summit in Suriname on August 30, where Paraguay was welcomed back into the organization.

However, Cartes stated that he was in no hurry for Paraguay to rejoin *Mercosur,* that he would focus on bilateral relations instead and that he objected to *Mercosur*'s back-door admission of Venezuela while Paraguay was suspended. He declared he would not rejoin while Venezuela was holding the rotating presidency.

Just one month later, Cartes executed a 180-degree change of heart and announced he *did* want Paraguay to rejoin *Mercosur,* saying he expected the conditions would be right early in 2014. He cajoled both houses of Congress into ratifying Venezuela's admission in early December as a sign of goodwill; the fact that Chávez was now dead was undoubtedly a factor in Congress' willingness. Paraguay and Venezuela re-established diplomatic relations on January 14, 2014, and Paraguay was prepared to rejoin at the *Mercosur* summit scheduled in Caracas on January 31. Ironically, after Argentina, Brazil and Uruguay were so eager to admit Venezuela and had bestowed it with the rotating presidency, Maduro had to postpone the summit until March because of the violent street demonstrations against his rule. Then it was postponed again until May, then again be-

cause of the violence. The presidency cannot change until a summit is held.

In domestic affairs, expectations for Cartes were so low because of his shady background that they had nowhere to go but up—which they soon did. He realized immediately that Franco had bequeathed him a massive budget deficit and no remaining presidential operating expenses, so he tackled the problem like a practical businessman. To the dismay of party regulars, he appointed several highly qualified technocrats to cabinet and sub-cabinet posts instead of the traditional party hacks. He pushed through legislation limiting budget increases to 4 percentage points above inflation and limiting the deficit to 1.5% of GDP.

How would he make this happen? He discovered, among other things, that 95% of revenue was earmarked for "fixed" expenses, chiefly government salaries. Then he discovered what veteran *Colorados* already knew, that the government payroll is woefully featherbedded through patronage and nepotism with employees who do little or no work—which keeps the unemployment count deceptively low. When the director of the binational body that operates the Yacyretá Dam disclosed that Paraguay had 3,000 employees on the payroll compared with only 900 for Argentina, Cartes mandated layoffs and ordered that some contracts not be renewed. *Colorado* regulars assumed he was simply paving the way to appoint more party loyalists to those positions, and they were chagrinned when he did not. By the end of the year, 13,000 government jobs or contracts had been eliminated, out of a total of 256,000.

Next, the media reported in October 2013 that one of those Yacyretá contractors was also the nanny for the children of *Colorado* Senator Victor Bogado; she was also on the congressional payroll at a salary almost four times the minimum wage. Allegedly, she was only a figurehead contractor and Bogado was pocketing the money. The media had a field day with the "Golden Nanny" story; the public was indignant.

Simultaneously, the Supreme Court reversed itself in a 2007 ruling in a lawsuit seeking public disclosure of municipal officials' salaries. The suit had been brought by a radio journalist, Daniel Vargas, after local officials had refused to disclose their salaries. The high court had ruled against Vargas, but when the Bogado scandal gained traction through both the mass media and social media, the court ruled that public salaries, including congressional ones, are public record, a long overdue blow in favor of transparency. The newspaper *ABC Color* even created a search engine on its website through which a reader could enter the names of officials and find

out their salaries. Congress stonewalled on disclosing the salaries until Cartes pressured it into doing so.

Bogado's sins thus exposed, a motion was introduced in the Senate in November to strip him of his legislative immunity and pave the way for prosecution. Thirty votes, two-thirds of the 45 members, were needed, but 23 senators voted against stripping Bogado of immunity. The public indignation over Bogado turned to outrage, again widely transmitted by social media and mass media both; the 23 senators became public pariahs. Restaurants actually blacklisted the 23 senators and refused to serve them. About 5,000 protesters braved a rainstorm to demonstrate outside the Congress building. Bogado was stripped of his immunity on December 2. A prosecutorial team has been investigating him, as has a Senate special committee, but as of mid-2014, no charges had been filed.

Paraguay's economy rebounded from the slowest growth in Latin America in 2012 to the fastest in 2013, 12%, thanks to an end to the drought, a bumper crop for soybeans and a favorable market for the commodity (see Economy). Because of Paraguay's new reliance on soybeans, beef and other agricultural products, Cartes announced he would take bids to improve waterway and highway infrastructure. Significantly, a new law allows him to circumvent Congress in the awarding of contracts. Normally, that would be seen as an executive power grab, but in Paraguay, it is a way to keep the *Colorado* hardliners in Congress from enriching themselves (see the Future). Cartes has aggressively courted foreign companies to invest in Paraguay.

Like his three immediate predecessors, Cartes has had to grapple with the growing threat of the *EPP*. Just three days after Cartes' inauguration, the guerrillas launched a raid on a cattle ranch in San Pedro department, killing five security guards. Cartes dispatched 400 troops to the area to complement the outgunned local police. By October, the army had established a semi-permanent outpost in Tacuatí, San Pedro, the *EPP*'s usual area of operations. But later that month, they staged another brazen raid on a cattle ranch in Horqueta, just north of San Pedro, abducted the guards and notified authorities. When police arrived, the *EPP* ambushed the convoy, killing five. In March 2014, it kidnapped 16 people in Concepción.

In April 2014, they kidnapped Arlan Fick, 16, son of a manager of a German-owned ranch, who remains in captivity despite payment of a $500,000 ransom and distribution of $50,000 in foodstuffs to the poor. The country was shocked and alarmed by the group's growing audacity.

In another such attack on a ranch in April 2014, however, responding security forces killed the *EPP*'s third in command, Bernardo Bernal Maíz.

In June, the *EPP*'s acknowledged leader, Alcides Oviedo, attempted to assault the judge when he was brought to a hearing on the kidnapping of the 16-year-old Arlan Fick.

The *EPP* took a page out of the books of Colombian and Peruvian guerrillas and dynamited a high-voltage tower on July 5, which dragged down another tower and left six departments without power for 24 hours. The *EPP* has 60 videos of its attacks it has posted on YouTube. Estimates of the group's current strength vary from 100 to 150.

In April 2014, the Mitofsky poll put Cartes' approval rating at 74%, third-highest in the hemisphere, behind Danilo Medina of the Dominican Republic (90%) and Rafael Correa of Ecuador (75%).

CULTURE: Paraguay's unique culture is a product of geography and politics. Landlocked and cut off from contact with the outside world by a series of 19th century strongmen, Paraguay developed differently from its sister republics. To begin with, the indigenous inhabitants, the Guaraní, were culturally different from tribes on the fringes of the continent. Just as it took a special breed of native to subsist in this hot, dry climate, so it took a special breed of Spaniard to eschew the relative comforts of either coast to pioneer this inhospitable land.

Along with such pioneers came Jesuit priests, who effectively ran the colony in the 16th and 17th centuries, until the Spanish Crown expelled them. The ruins of their mini-civilization can be seen near modern-day Encarnación. In 1993, UNESCO designated two of them, La Santísima Trinidad de Paraná and Jesús de Tavarangue, as a World Heritage Site. Some scholars attribute the Paraguayan trait of obsequiousness to authority to this long-ago Jesuit influence, which inspired the 1986 motion picture, *The Mission*.

Although Roman Catholicism remains the predominant religion, Paraguay's liberal immigration laws and tolerance of other religions has attracted various Protestant sects. In the 1920s, Mennonite pioneers from Canada established the settlement of Filadelfia in the Chaco, and they still account for a disproportionate amount of the country's dairy production. Jews and Jehovah's Witnesses came to Paraguay from less tolerant Argentina. The Assembly of God has grown in size in recent years and has built a huge new complex. The Unification Church of the Rev. Sun Myung Moon purchased a tract of land near Puerto Casado. Lebanese im-migrants, both Christian and Muslim, also constitute a significant minority.

Because Paraguayan leaders placed little value on education, and in no small part because of the genocide committed during the War of the Triple Alliance of 1865–70, Paraguay never developed a European-based literary, artistic or musical tradition as did its neighbors. Paraguayan culture is derived almost wholly from the Guaraní, whose language still thrives and is now in written form; half the population learns Guaraní before Spanish. Several unassimilated Indian tribes still exist in Paraguay, providing tourists with cheap trinkets. But it is from the Guaranís that Paraguay developed the beautiful *ñandutí* lacework that is so identified with the country.

Probably the most identifiable element of Paraguayan culture, however, is its lovely harp-based folk music. During the Stroessner regime, law dictated that 50% of the music played on radio had to be domestic. One Paraguayan folk song in particular, *Recuerdos de Ypacaraí,* is so well known that guitarists or pianists can play it from memory in restaurants or piano bars from Mexico City to Buenos Aires to Madrid.

Paraguay's unofficial musical ambassador in the 1950s, '60s and '70s was Luis Alberto del Paraná (1926–74), a singer and guitarist whose group, Los Paraguayos, performed around the world and appeared together with the Beatles and Rolling Stones, among others. Del Parana recorded about 500 songs, Paraguayan as well as traditional Latin songs from Spain and other Latin American countries, such as Mexico's *La Bamba*. He sold 30 million vinyl records and 650,000 cassette tapes, more than any other Paraguayan. He was especially popular in Europe. His untimely death in London from a stroke at age 48 plunged Paraguay into mourning. His body was returned to Asunción for burial, and President Stroessner was

Augusto Roa Bastos

among the pallbearers at the airport. The streets were filled with mourners for his funeral. His legacy persists. His recordings of *Malagueña* and *Hace Un Año* were part of the sound track of the 1989 U.S. movie *Born on the Fourth of July*. Today there is a Facebook page dedicated to his memory and his music circulates on YouTube and the Internet in general.

Because of dictatorship or lack of economic opportunity, or both, most of Paraguay's truly talented musical, literary and artistic figures have opted to spend their careers abroad.

That was the case with its most internationally renowned literary figure—indeed, the only one—of the 20th century, Augusto Roa Bastos (1917–2005). He served as a medic during the 1932–35 Chaco War with Bolivia. Because of his leftist sympathies and his irreverence toward authority, Roa Bastos voluntarily went into exile in 1947, living and writing abroad for 49 years, first in Argentina, then France and finally Spain. He returned to Paraguay to live in 1996 and died in Asunción.

Unlike many writers who live in exile, however, Roa Bastos did not lose his Paraguayan identity, and he wrote primarily about his homeland. He was known for his use of basing his fiction on historical figures. His best-known work was the novel *Yo, el Supremo (I, the Supreme One)*, published in 1974, which was based on the 19th century Paraguayan dictator José Gaspar Rodríguez de Francia (see History). Two other works, *El Hijo de Hombre (Son of Man)*, a 1960 collection of short stories, and *El Baldio (Vagabond)*, a novel published in 1966, were biting observations on Paraguay's often tragic history. Another, *Vigilia del Almirante (Vigil of the Admiral)*, a novel about Columbus, was published in 1992 to mark the 500th anniversary of the European discovery of the New World. His works were translated into 25 languages. He received Spain's prestigious

Luis Alberto del Paraná

Paraguay

Cervantes Prize in Literature in 1989, and he was often mentioned as a possible Nobel Laureate.

As in many of the Latin American republics, dictatorship and illiteracy stifled the development of viable independent newspapers. A few dailies are published, but only in Asunción. One was the official *Colorado* Party mouthpiece, *Patria*, which has since ceased publication. Beginning in the late 1970s, the others courageously exposed the endemic corruption of the Stroessner regime—although they wisely avoided mentioning the president by name. The country's leading daily is *ABC Color*, founded by businessman Aldo Zucolillo in 1967, which became more and more critical of the dictatorship, until Stroessner ordered it closed in 1984. It didn't reopen until immediately after Stroessner's overthrow five years later. The other dailies are *Diario Popular, La Nación* and *Última Hora*.

Radio has long been an influential medium, so much so that the Stroessner regime closed down stations like Radio Ñandutí, whose reporting became too critical.

Paraguay has seven television stations, two government-owned and five private, and one Argentine-owned cable channel. There is an increasing amount of locally produced programming, mostly reality and comedy programs, but *telenovelas* are still imported.

Despite aggressive newspaper reporting, restrictions on the state-owned TV channel led Freedom House to rate the Paraguayan media as "not free" in 2012. In 2013, it was upgraded to "partly free" again.

Public education has always been substandard in Paraguay, and teachers are barely paid a living wage. There are nine established universities, the oldest being the National University of Asunción, founded in 1889. The Catholic University of Our Lady of Asunción dates to 1960. There has been a proliferation of about 50 "diploma mills" catering to those who could not qualify for the established schools.

ECONOMY: The eastern (*Oriental*) region of Paraguay, with its favorable climate, is the country's primary source of economic wealth. The arid western (*Occidental* or *Chaco*) region was once a wasteland, but in recent years the Mennonite colonies in the Chaco have produced more than half the country's dairy products and a growing percentage of its beef.

Forestry once employed half the workforce, but the forests have been largely logged out, with little attention given to reforestation; the government now prohibits export of raw timber, focusing on finished wood products like furniture.

Approximately 26% of Paraguay's GDP is from agriculture, with beef and soybeans the leading exports. Beef exports now exceed $1 billion, thanks to the virtual eradication of hoof and mouth disease. It made a comeback in 2011. In 2013, it was upgraded to "partly free" again

Paraguay is the world's fourth-largest soybean exporter after Brazil, the United States and Argentina. In 2008, soybean cultivation accounted for 2.4 million hectares (5.3 million acres), 73% of the total area under cultivation. Paraguay's economy has become almost dependent on the vicissitudes of the international market and the weather. Drought devastated the 2011-12 soybean harvest, but in 2012-13, soybean exports totaled $2.4 billion. Other exports include vegetable oils, cotton, leather goods, citrus fruits and tobacco.

About 115,000 hectares are planted in sugar cane for domestic consumption, not export; 30% of the sugar is now used for ethanol production, which has leaped from 53 million liters in 2007 to a projected 190 million liters in 2014, all for domestic consumption. Domestic ethanol consumption was also projected at 180 million liters in 2013. Sugar accounts for 60% of the ethanol; the rest is from grains, mostly corn. Paraguay also is expected to produce and consume 14 million liters of biodiesel fuel in 2014. It is importing thousands of ethanol-burning and flex-fuel vehicles from Brazil and Argentina.

Paraguay's foreign trade is primarily with its *Mercosur* partners, Brazil, Argentina and Uruguay, which account for 49% of exports and 39% of imports. China, with which Paraguay does not have diplomatic relations, has replaced the United States as a major trading partner. China now accounts for 30% of imports, mostly cheap manufactured goods, compared with 5% from the United States.

The economy boomed in the 1970s and 1980s, bolstered by work on two huge hydroelectric dams on the Paraná River: Itaipú, financed by Brazil, and Yacyretá, downstream, financed by Argentina. Yacyretá is the longest river dam in the world, 808 meters, and produced a record 20 trillion watt hours of electricity in 2012. Paraguay exports 90% of its share of the hydroelectric power from the dams to its two energy-hungry neighbors, a leading source of foreign exchange. Itaipú ("big water" in Guaraní) is the largest hydroelectyric dam in the world, with an annual output of about 98 trillion watt hours. Initially, Paraguay agreed to sell the energy to Brazil below market cost, something President Fernando Lugo renegotiated in 2008. Brazilian President Lula da Silva finally agreed in 2009 to triple Paraguay's royalties, from $120 million to $360 mil-

lion, which the Brazilian Congress stalled for two years before ratifying in 2011.

Because of Paraguay's landlocked isolation, and its juxtaposition between two powerful neighbors, smuggling has traditionally been a major but informal pillar of the economy. In recent years, traditional smuggling has been expanded to include drug trafficking, money laundering, gun-running and copyright and trademark infringement. The United States at one point threatened Paraguay with economic sanctions because of the piracy of intellectual properties.

When Raúl Cubas assumed the presidency in 1998, he inherited a dismal economy and a budget deficit that totaled about 4% of the GDP of $10 billion. Paraguay has the lowest tax burden in Latin America. He attempted to crack down on long-accepted tax evasion and black marketeering. He estimated that as much as 55% of taxes were not being paid (the figure today is estimated at 70%). President Nicanor Duarte Frutos briefly imposed a personal income tax, which was repealed because it became an accounting nightmare for both the government and taxpayers. Lugo sought to reimplement it but failed. After Lugo's impeachment in 2012, interim President Federico Franco pushed an income tax through Congress.

Paraguay is one of the few remaining countries with diplomatic relations with Taiwan, but it paid off in 1999 when an appreciative Taiwan lent Paraguay $400 million, which kept the country afloat.

Paraguay's GDP shrank for six out of eight years between 1995 and 2002, when it shrank –2.3%. Four years of modest growth followed, rising to 6.4% in 2007 and 5.5% in 2008, a boom by Paraguayan standards. The improvement was attributed to high world prices for commodities exported by Paraguay, especially soybeans. But the global recession and a severe drought caused GDP to contract by –3.8%, in 2009.

In 2010, Lugo's government responded to the recession with ambitious fiscal and monetary stimulus packages that amounted to 4.7% of GDP. Much of the investment was in construction. There was also significant private investment in construction. Coupled with the construction boom was a fortuitous end to the drought. Soybean production leaped 25%, from 6 million to 7.5 million tons, 5.6 million of which were exported, at a time when world demand and prices were high. The same proved true for beef exports, after a concerted program to eradicate hoof and mouth disease in Paraguay.

Moreover, 465,000 tourists came to Paraguay in 2010, spending about $200 million. It was a perfect, positive, economic storm that gave Paraguay the hemisphere's highest GDP growth in 2010, 14.5%. Tourist arrivals leaped to 539,000 in 2011 and 579,000 in 2012.

Paraguay received more good economic news in 2010 with the announcement of the discovery of major deposits of ilmenite, the ore from which titanium is smelted. A Canadian company, RTA, signed an agreement with the Paraguayan government to invest $3.2 billion in a titanium smelter and estimated Paraguay could produce up to 670,000 tons per year, making it the world's seventh leading producer. The Alto Paraná deposit is now estimated to be the world's largest. The smelter would utilize hydroelectric energy from the Itaipú dam. Work on the smelter was to begin in 2014 and be online by 2016, creating 14,000 jobs.

In 2011, the economy benefited from the additional $240 million in hydroelectric royalties from Brazil, but the construction boom waned. Growth was slower, but a still-respectable 6.4%, above the regional average.

The Economist projected growth for 2012 at 3.5%, but it ended the year with a loss, -0.5%; Paraguay was the only nation in the hemisphere to record negative growth.

An outbreak of hoof and mouth disease in late 2011 devastated the lucrative beef industry, and exports plummeted. Domestic beef prices understandably plummeted, too, because of the glut, much to the delight of carnivorous consumers. A drought in 2012 was also devastated the soybean crop. But with the return of rain in 2013, Paraguay recovered the lost ground with growth of 12%, once again the champion of the hemisphere.

Per capita income declined from a peak of $1,793 in 1996 to only $1,019 in 2003. It increased to $2,920 by 2010, the sixth-poorest in Latin America. It was seventh-poorest in 2011. In 2010, 34.7% of Paraguayans lived below the poverty line, and UNICEF reported that one child in seven suffers from chronic malnutrition.

Official unemployment figures have remained steady for years, from 5.7% in 2008, to 6.9% in 2012 and 6.6% in 2013, but underemployment may be as high as 35%. These factors account for Paraguay's traditional public discontent.

Inflation in the last decade peaked at 11% in 2008, but with the recession it fell back to 1.9% in 2009. It was 3.7% in 2012 and 2.3% in 2013.

An increasingly important economic pillar is the remittances sent by expatriates working abroad, primarily in Brazil, Argentina and Spain, to family members in Paraguay. According to the World Bank, remittances rose steadily each year, from $278 million in 2000 to $587 million in 2008, about 3.5% of GDP. With the global recession, which hit Spain hard, they fell for the first time in 2009, to $579 million. They have increased steadily since: $673 million in 2010, $789 million in 2011 and $804 million in 2012, roughly 3.1% of GDP.

THE FUTURE: The election of Fernando Lugo in 2008, ending 61 years of *Colorado* Party rule, was as historic as Vicente Fox's victory in Mexico in 2000 that ended 71 years of *PRI* domination. Like his predecessors, Lugo pledged to crack down on the endemic corruption that is a leech on the struggling economy.

Paraguayans had heard it all before. They put their hope and faith in Lugo in the belief that not being a *Colorado* or a member of the privileged elite that had long controlled the country, and by having been a priest and bishop, he would be clean, moral, honest and represent genuine change. Not only

Jesuit missions from the 17th century in Trinidad, Paraguay

Paraguay

were they shocked to learn that their president had violated his priestly vows of chastity to father at least three children out of wedlock, one by a 16-year-old girl and another by a married woman, but he proved an erratic decision-maker and an indecisive administrator. He made a Faustian deal with Venezuela's Hugo Chávez for low-price oil that worried his countrymen. He alienated both of the major parties. His behavior became bizarre, even including his attire; he wore a fashion atrocity that appeared to be a cross between a Mao jacket and a priest's cassock.

In 2008, Transparency International rated Paraguay the fourth most corrupt of the 20 Latin American republics. In 2009, Lugo's first full year in office, Paraguay slid back to the *third* most corrupt, ahead of Haiti and Venezuela. In 2010, it was the *second* most corrupt after Venezuela, sliding behind even Haiti. In 2011 and 2012 it was No. 3 again. So much for promises.

Paraguayans also ridiculed Lugo for his 75 trips abroad in four years; when he was home, they joked about him making "a stopover in Paraguay." The infamous Curuguaty Massacre in June 2012, in which 17 peasant farmers and policemen died in an exchange of gunfire, provided the Congress with the pretext it had been looking for to remove Lugo.

In short, Lugo was one more disillusionment. The Congress' lightning-fast impeachment and removal of him was, technically, within its constitutional purview. It impeached President Raúl Cubas in 1999. Still, the impulsive manner in which such an important governmental action was conducted, Lugo's lack of opportunity to present an adequate defense and the vague nature of some of the charges, were not exactly a shining example of democracy at its best.

Interim President Federico Franco, the first member of the Authentic Radical Liberty Party to attain the presidency after 65 years in opposition, faced the same battle for international legitimacy that Roberto Micheletti faced in Honduras when the National Assembly there removed President Manuel Zelaya with the same rapid-

ity in 2009. But in Honduras, the constitutional succession was bypassed; Micheletti was not vice president but president of the National Assembly. Franco, the vice president, was at least the constitutional successor to Lugo. Moreover, Zelaya was sent into exile; Lugo was not.

As happened in Mexico with the return to power of the *PRI* in 2012, Paraguay has now come full circle as voters opted in the April 2013, election to return the *Colorados* to power, this time under the banner of Horacio Cartes, a tobacco empresario and soccer club owner with a checkered reputation. A plane carrying marijuana and cocaine was seized on his rural estate in 2000, Brazil accused him of cigarette smuggling and a U.S. Embassy cable accusing him of money laundering was leaked by Wikileaks. But nothing has stuck.

It is difficult to blame the long-suffering Paraguayans for being cynical about their 24-year-old democracy. The periodic *Latinobarómetro* survey of 17 (now 18) Latin American countries for *The Economist* showed that the percentage of Paraguayans who think democracy is preferable to any other form of government plummeted from 59% in 1996 to just 32% in 2005, lowest of any nation in the survey. As recently as 2007, it was still just 33%; only Guatemala, at 32%, was lower. With the election of Lugo in 2008, the percentage jumped to 53%. But in 2009, in the wake of Lugo's paternity scandals and his lackluster, even bizarre, administrative performance, it slipped back to 46%. In 2010, it rose slightly to 49%, but Paraguay was still one of only three countries in the survey where support for democracy was below 50% (the others were Mexico and Guatemala). It fell from 54% in 2011 to 50% in 2013.

Meanwhile, the percentage of Paraguayans who believe an authoritarian government can be preferable to a democracy "under certain circumstances" increased from 26% in 1996 to 44% in 2005, by far the highest percentage in Latin America. In 2013 it was 32%, highest in Latin America. Only 22% of Paraguayans in 2013 said they were satisfied with the way democracy works in their country, the fourth

lowest in the survey and 18 points below the regional average.

Paraguayans had the opportunity in 2008 to return to strongman rule by voting for Lino Oviedo. But when push came to shove and the voters really had to choose, Oviedo ran a poor third with less than a fourth of the vote. He was hoping to run again in 2013 but died in a helicopter crash.

Now, the Horacio Cartes era has begun. He clearly has a track record as a successful businessman, like Chile's Sebastián Piñera or Panama's Ricardo Martinelli. There are also dark rumors about how much of his fortune he accumulated from smuggling, drug trafficking and money laundering. Still, he was never convicted of anything.

Lugo took office with high expectations, which evaporated. Cartes began with low expectations but he has pleasantly surprised his countrymen so far. Among those he has not pleased are the entrenched regulars of his own party, who had grown accustomed to enriching themselves at the public trough. Cartes' crackdown on nepotism and padded government payrolls, and his surprising expansion of transparency, have been phenomenal for Paraguay. In April 2014, the Mitofsky poll of Mexico put his approval rating at 74%, third-highest in the hemisphere.

The "Golden Nanny" scandal has also demonstrated the growing power of the established media in Paraguay of performing the press' traditional role of society's watchdog, but it also underscored the growing importance of social media like Twitter, Facebook and YouTube in spreading the word of public shenanigans, just as they did in the Arab Spring.

A dark cloud remains, however: the Paraguayan People's Army *(EPP)*. It has grown bolder, the death toll and number of kidnappings continue to mount and it, too, has become savvy in exploiting social media. Numbering probably fewer than 150 effectives, it nonetheless has shown itself a threat to the security of an already struggling state. It is a problem Paraguay doesn't need, and Cartes' top priority now should be to defeat it, perhaps with the aid of foreign counterinsurgency experts.

Peru

Peruvian school girls in Lima

Area: 482,122 square miles.
Population: 30,147,935 (2014 est.).
Capital City: Lima (Pop. 8,473,000, 2007 est.).
Climate: The eastern lowlands are hot and humid; the coast is arid and mild; the highlands are increasingly temperate as the altitude rises.
Neighboring Countries: Ecuador (northwest); Colombia (northeast); Brazil (east); Chile (south).
Official Language: Spanish.
Other Principal Tongues: Quechua and Aymara.
Ethnic Background: *Mestizo* (a mixture of Indian and Spanish ancestry) and pure Indian, 88%; European, mostly Spanish, 12%.
Principal Religion: Roman Catholic Christianity.

Chief Commercial Products: Fish, fishmeal, cotton, sugar, copper, silver, lead, crude petroleum.
Currency: Sol.
Gross Domestic Product: U.S. $210.3 billion in 2013 ($7,046 per capita, official exchange rate).

Former Colonial Status: Spanish Colony (1532–1821).
Independence Date: July 21, 1821.
Chief of State: Ollanta Moisés Humala Tasso (b. June 26, 1962), president (since July 28, 2011).
National Flag: Red, white and red vertical stripes.

Peru sits astride the majestic Andes mountains. The Sierra (upland plateau) is at an average invigorating elevation of 13,000 feet from which ranges of high peaks emerge. The highest, Huascarán, is 22,334 feet; 10 others exceed 20,000 feet and there are many volcanoes in the southern region. The Sierra occupies about one fourth of Peru's surface and is home to more than 60% of the population.

The Sierra is cut and crisscrossed with rivers; those flowing to the west frequently disappear in the desert before reaching the Pacific Ocean; rivers flowing to the east drop into the tropical jungles of the Amazon basin. Some of the eastern rivers have cut scenic gorges into the Sierra 5,000 feet in depth, with tropical climates and vegetation at the lower levels. The Pacific coastal shelf is a narrow ribbon of desert except for a few river valleys where there is sufficient water for irrigation.

The eastern slope of the Andes, known as the *selva* (jungle) contains over 60% of Peru's land and about 14% of the population. There are few roads into this region; travel is along the river valleys.

This area's resources are great, but inaccessibility hampers their exploitation. Peru's climate varies with altitude—tropical in the lowlands, it becomes temperate above the elevation of 3,000 feet and cold above 10,000–12,000 feet, with snow and bitter frost throughout the year on the highest peaks of the Andes. People with respiratory or coronary difficulties dare not venture into these heights—the air is too "thin" to support any but the hardiest of lives.

HISTORY: Peru has been host to civilized people from about the 3rd century A.D. Artistically sophisticated people left pottery and textiles of excellent quality in the southern region that date from the 3rd to the 7th centuries. More primitive people lived in the vicinity of Lima, and a highly skilled culture existed in the north. The southern culture spread to the Sierra and gave rise to the Aymara society at Tiahuanaco, east of Lake Titicaca in the 10th to the 13th centuries. The Inca civilization began to develop in the Cuzco basin about the 11th century and by the end of the 15th century dominated the Andean Sierra and the Pacific shelf from Colombia to the Central Valley of Chile. At the time of the Spanish invasion, a di-

Peru

vision had split the Inca rulers. The legitimate Inca Huáscar ruled the south from Cuzco while his half-brother, Atahualpa, ruled the northern provinces from Quito as a usurper challenging the legitimacy of Huáscar (see Ecuador).

When the explorers Francisco Pizarro and Diego de Almagro landed their small Spanish force in Ecuador in 1531, Atahualpa—apparently seeking allies to assist in his fight against his half-brother—allowed the Spaniards to reach the Sierra. The outnumbered Spanish tricked Atahualpa into an ambush, held him for ransom and killed him after it was paid. As Atahualpa had ordered the assassination of Huáscar, and his person was considered divine by the Incas, no one in the vast empire dared to raise a finger against the Spaniards as long as the emperor was a prisoner. Unopposed, the Spaniards moved into the interior of Peru, occupying the most strategic cities and, after the death of Atahualpa, ruled through puppet Incas until they felt strong enough to proclaim Spain's sovereignty.

Pizarro withdrew from Cuzco, the sacred capital of the Inca empire in 1535 and founded Lima near the coast. Almagro was sent to conquer Chile, but the arid ter-

Atahaulpa is ambushed by Spanish troops

ritory and Indian hostility forced him to return to Lima. A brief struggle for power followed and first Almagro and then Pizarro were killed. Spanish authorities intervened, restored peace and began organizing the new rich colony. Francisco de Toledo, one of the best viceroys Spain ever had, established a firm basis for colonial power. He ruled from 1568 to 1582, adopted many Inca traditions like the "*mita*" (annually every male member of the Inca empires had to work free for the emperor during a few months) for Spain's benefit, and the colony prospered. By the middle of the 17th century, Lima was a splendid city with cathedrals, palaces and a university and the viceroyalty of Peru had become the political and strategic center of the Spanish empire in South America.

Exasperated by the exploitation of the Indians in the mining area, a descendant of the last Inca adopted the name of Tupac Amaru in 1780 and raised the banner of rebellion. Intelligently, he appealed to the creoles (people of Peruvian mixed Spanish-Indian blood), ratified his Catholic faith and proclaimed that he was not fighting against the king, but against his "corrupt officials." The rebellion spread rapidly, but Tupac's Indian followers killed Spaniards and creoles indiscriminately. The alliance of both, plus the condemnation of the Catholic Church, sealed his fate. Thousands of Indians rallied around Spanish authorities (a testimony to Spain's colonial policies) and Tupac was defeated, captured and publicly executed. The rebellion, however, left a lingering fear among the creoles. As in Mexico and Cuba, they remained lukewarm toward an anti-Spanish struggle that could trigger another Indian uprising. The initiative for independence had to come from *outside*.

The arrival of General José de San Martín and his small army of Argentinians and Chileans opened the period of armed insurrection. Unable to defeat the Spaniards, who were supported by many creoles,

Tupac Amaru

San Martín awaited the arrival of General Simón Bolívar, whose victorious army was marching south from Venezuela and Colombia. After meeting with *el Libertador* in Guayaquil and failing to reach an agreement on the impending campaign, a disillusioned San Martín retired to private life. Bolívar and his second-in-command, Antonio José de Sucre, opened the campaign against colonial authorities and in 1824 the battle of Ayacucho put an end to Spanish dominion in South America.

After the battle, Bolívar made an energetic attempt to organize the country. Taxes were cut, convents were turned into schools and the most glaring abuses against the Indians were suppressed. Elected president-for-life, Bolívar could have accomplished much more, but growing resistance on the part of alarmed and conservative Peruvian creoles, and the progressive disintegration of his "Great Colombia" (the union of Venezuela, Colombia, and Ecuador) forced him to leave Peru in 1826. A period of relative stability followed while most of the government and military forces concentrated on solidifying a union with Bolivia in a "Confederation of the North." Unfortunately, Chile considered that union as a threat to its future and invaded Bolivia. Chilean victory at the battle of Yungay forced the confederation to break up. The defeat plunged Peru into political turmoil until

1844, when a capable man, Ramón Castilla, seized power. President Castilla, who served until 1850 and again from 1855–60, united the country, mediated differences between the pro-church Conservatives and the anti-clerical Liberals, established government services, abolished black slavery, ended forced tribute from the Indians and built a few schools.

The national economy, however, was restored by sea birds, whose mountains of dung (guano) on the offshore islands, were highly sought after in European fertilizer markets. The guano trade led to an economic boom and also led to the discovery of nitrate deposits in the southern deserts; the extraction of the mineral was largely in British hands.

The period following Castilla's rule was one of tension and war. Nine presidents occupied the office between 1862 and 1885, of which only two completed their terms. The most competent was Manuel Pardo (1872–76), Peru's first civilian president and founder of the *Civilista* Party. A war with Spain (1862–66) and the War of the Pacific with Chile (1879–83) were brought on by the prosperity that Peru was enjoying. Spain sought to recover its past grandeur and lost; Chile, with British connivance, sought the wealth of the desert nitrate fields and won.

The War of the Pacific was a disaster for Peru—thousands of lives were lost, much property was destroyed, some territory and the port of Arica were ceded to Chile, and the national economy was reduced to a shambles. Huge foreign debts were accumulated, the nitrate beds were lost and the guano deposits were almost exhausted.

British interests funded the foreign debt in exchange for the national railways, the steamers of scenic Lake Titicaca, the exploitation of remaining guano deposits, free use of ports and other trade privileges. Peru's recovery was slow, but a measure of peace and order was established and trade resumed under a succession of *Civilista* presidents.

The major event of the early 20th century was the dictatorship of Augusto B. Leguía (1919–30). Energetic and able, he gave impetus to mining and agriculture and restored Peru's international credit. Leguía called his regime "A New Fatherland," adopted a modern constitution and freed the church from state patronage. Initially an honest administrator, he succumbed to graft and corruption under the temptation of loans proffered by the U.S. banks during the 1920s. When the inevitable protests arose, there was wholesale jailing of critics, restriction of the press and the closing of universities.

By 1930, the Peruvian people were fed up with Leguía's despotism and the economic crisis caused by the worldwide de-

pression. A revolt caused Leguía to flee; he was captured on the high seas and imprisoned on one of the offshore islands, where he died.

APRA is Founded

During the last decade of the 19th century, there developed a movement for liberal reforms in Peru's higher society. Led by Manuel González Prada, a respected intellectual, demands were made to end feudalism, traditionalism and clericalism, which González Prada declared enslaved the people to a handful of powerful men. Among the students attracted to González Prada was Victor Rául Haya de la Torre, a leader in the demand for educational reforms, who founded the American Popular Revolutionary Alliance (*APRA*) in 1924. It remains one of the major political institutions today.

Anti-communist, with ideas borrowed from Russian, Mexican and European models, *APRA* sought to integrate the Indians into Peru's social and economic structure and to terminate the monopoly of political power that had been held by the landowners and the clergy for more than 400 years. During the dictatorship of Leguía, *APRA* grew and became the spokesman for the Indians in the Sierra as well as for urban workers.

APRA won the 1931 elections, but Haya de la Torre was jailed and the party outlawed. The resulting revolts were savagely repressed, and Peru's second dictatorship of the 20th century was launched. Marshal Oscar Benavides ruled somewhat moderately until 1939.

Manuel Prado, a moderate, was president from 1939–45. He made progress in trade, public health, education and sanitation, but simultaneously repressed all popular challengers to the landowner-clergy domination of political power. His successor came to office by a change of *APRA* tactics; reorganizing as the People's Party, *APRA* supported the most liberal of the candidates, hoping to secure congressional seats and cabinet positions.

The *APRA* success in this effort brought on a conservative coup headed by General Manuel Odría, who ruled from 1948–56. No pretense of democracy was maintained; restoring order and suppressing *APRA*, the army ruled with firmness. From a managerial standpoint, the regime gave a good account of itself, restoring confidence in Peruvian industry. Legal elections again returned Prado to leadership, but conditions did not remain stable.

When *APRA* won substantial gains in 1962 elections, the army again intervened by setting aside the results; in more carefully staged elections in 1963, Fernando Belaúnde Terry of the center-right Popular

Peru

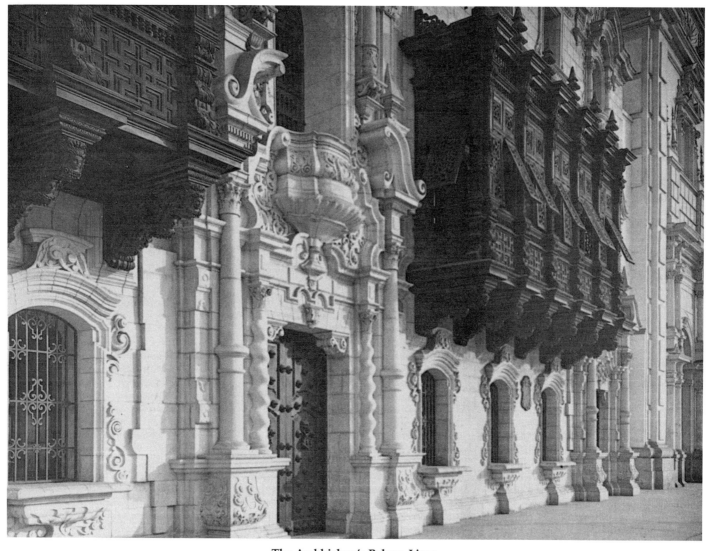

The Archbishop's Palace, Lima

Action Party (*PAP*) won a bare plurality and was named president.

Leftist Military Rule, 1968–80

Charging that the nation's political leaders were insensitive to the needs of the masses, a military *junta* ousted Belaúnde in 1968 and replaced him with General Juan Velasco Alvarado, who served as president for the next seven years. The new regime promised to end the traditional political and economic control of Peru by the "top 40 families" and foreign corporations through a program of "social democracy," patterned loosely on the Yugoslav model, which (they said) would guide the nation on a path between capitalism and communism.

The first phase of the program, largely achieved by 1975, called for state control of strategic sectors of the economy. Thus, the regime nationalized the fishing industry, banks, communications facilities, most

of the news media and U.S.-owned mining operations. A unique feature of the Inca Plan required major industries to grant half-ownership to the workers.

A cornerstone of the economic plan was one of the most extensive land reform programs in Latin America. Before the military seized power, fully 90% of all farmland was owned by just 2% of the population. To break the power of the landed aristocracy, the military seized 25 million acres from large private estates and redistributed them to worker-owned cooperatives and to peasant families.

In foreign affairs, the military government was nationalistic and leftist. Diplomatic ties were extended to many nonaligned and communist nations and Peru became the second nation in the Western Hemisphere to import Soviet weapons and advisers. At international conferences, Peru was a major advocate of Third World causes as well as a frequent critic of U.S. economic power.

These policies naturally strained relations with the United States. Although Peru agreed to pay for some of the seized property, the prices were largely dictated by the *junta*. A low point in U.S.-Peruvian relations came in late 1974 when the *junta* ousted 137 members of the Peace Corps and several U.S. Embassy officials on charges of spying for the CIA.

By combining a nationalistic foreign policy with a state-controlled economy, the *junta* hoped to build what it described as a "new Peruvian man." To speed up the process, the government expanded education programs, increased per capita incomes, promised to spend new oil revenues on social programs and to turn over farms and factories to workers. The expected popular support, however, failed to materialize. Farm workers who received land bitterly opposed sharing their gains with landless peasants. Factory workers continued to strike as often against state-owned industries as they had against the former owners. Part of the problem was rooted in the *junta*'s attempts to run Peru like a military barracks.

Congress was closed, most political parties were banned, and civilians were excluded from key government jobs. Professional organizations and free labor movements were suppressed and the press was censored. Compounding Peru's troubles were collapse of the fishmeal industry (the offshore anchovies disappeared), a plunge in world copper prices and the failure of new oil wells (in which the regime had gambled $1.5 billion) to produce as expected.

The government's economic program scared away badly needed foreign investment and poor management resulted in lowered production in nationalized industries. Benefits of the military revolution failed to filter down to the lower classes; unemployment and inflation cut the living standards of the people.

Velasco Alvarado, partially disabled from circulatory problems and a mild stroke, increasingly ruled by decree, jailing or exiling his critics. When he turned his wrath against fellow military officers, the armed forced finally stepped in and deposed him in a bloodless coup in 1975.

Named as new president was General Francisco Morales Bermúdez, a moderate and former prime minister. Although he pledged to follow the basic goals of the previous regime, he further stated that the

General Francisco Morales Bermúdez

revolution had entered a more conservative "consolidation phase." Faced with a bankrupt treasury, the regime turned away from a policy of rigid state control of industry. A number of major businesses (including the key fishing industry), nationalized by the previous administration, were returned to their former owners. At the same time, the role and power of labor unions were reduced.

Nevertheless, Peru's economy continued to decline during 1977. Hoping to prevent further labor unrest and related political violence, the *junta* announced that plans were being made to surrender power to constitutional government. The first election was set for June 1978, when voters would name delegates to an assembly to rewrite the constitution. Under the plan, an elected president and congress would take control of the country by 1980. However, the military stipulated that the new constitution must embody basic nationalistic principles of the present government which had stressed social reforms and nationalization of major industries.

As an initial step toward the restoration of democracy, voters went to the polls for the first time in 11 years to elect representatives to a 100-seat Constituent Assembly, which drafted he new constitution. The biggest winner, with nearly 40% of the vote, was *APRA*, which campaigned on a slightly left-of-center platform. In second place were the leftists representing six Marxist parties with nearly 28%. The conservatives and moderates, led by the Popular Christian Party, had 27%.

Return to Democracy

When presidential elections were held in May 1980, former President Belaúnde of the *PAP* won easily over 11 other candidates with 43% of the vote. *APRA* was

Panoramic view of Lima with the broad Avenida Alfonso Ugarte in the foreground

Peru

second with 26%, while extremist parties fared poorly.

Belaúnde became Peru's 102nd president, ending 12 years of military rule. The generals refused to attend the inauguration. Because his *PAP* won only 27 of the 60 Senate seats and 95 of the 180 seats in the Chamber of Deputies, Belaúnde had to have the cooperation of *APRA* and the *PCP*. The new administration promised to respect the new constitution, to create an independent judiciary, to promote human rights, to ensure freedom of the press (including return of newspapers and TV stations taken over by the previous military regimes), and to encourage economic development. Programs for construction of roads, housing, increased farm production and water resources and for nurturing foreign investments (especially in oil production) were given high priority.

The Belaúnde administration faced severe political and economic problems, the aftermath of the military regimes' wasteful spending on failed social programs and unnecessary Soviet arms, which brought the nation to the brink of insolvency. Austerity measures were taken to lower inflation and to stimulate financial investments for economic growth.

As usual, the real burden for these reforms fell most heavily on the poor and middle class; the cost of living rose sharply while real wages dropped. Strikes closed down mines, mills, oil installations and schools as workers protested rising prices and clamored for wage increases to catch up with galloping inflation. The volatile atmosphere heated up in 1981 when acts of terrorism became commonplace.

An important diplomatic event occurred for Peru in 1981 when Javier Pérez de Cuellar was named to a five-year term as secretary-general of the United Nations.

Terrorism-Counter-Terrorism

Peru's democracy remained frail, but Belaúnde assured the public that the military would not attempt another coup. This was put to a severe test, however, by the activities of Maoist guerrilla bands calling themselves *Sendero Luminoso* ("Shining Path"). The movement consisted of cells rather than organized larger forces, making it extremely hard to deal with. Founded about 1970 by a philosophy professor, Abimael Guzmán (b. 1935) of the University of Huamanga, in Ayacucho State, it spread quickly to colleges and universities of the highlands, attracting many of Indian ancestry. Its actions, and the government's struggle against it, killed more than 25,000 people.

Guzmán, who went by the *nom de guerre* Presidente Gonzalo, went into hiding in 1975 but remained active. From sketchy accounts of his rigid beliefs and behavior (traditionalist Stalinist, Maoist communism) it was suspected that he was mentally deranged, becoming the leader of a mass cult that he mesmerized. One observer aptly called him "a Charlie Manson with an army to back him up."

Terrorism was committed not only by the *Sendero Luminoso* but also by elite military units sent to the impoverished region inhabited mostly by Indians. A group based in urban areas, the Tupac Amaru Revolutionary Movement, joined in the anti-government effort in 1984; it was named after the 18th century Peruvian Indian who revolted against Spanish rule. It used pipe bombs and heavier explosives to make life in Lima miserable. The city came to be surrounded in the 1980s by "suburbs" of countless shacks and shanties where more than 8 million settled. It was easy in such a setting to bomb strategic locations—banks,

businesses, embassies and the presidential palace—and disappear.

Further complicating life in Peru was the entry of coca production in the Upper Huallaga Valley, which for a time became the source of 75% of coca used to produce cocaine. The hirelings of drug traffickers were merciless and sometimes posed as revolutionaries to divert attention from their actual purposes.

Belaúnde rapidly declined in popularity (from 70% in 1980 to 20% in 1984). By mid-1984 the annual inflation rate reached 120% and Peru looked toward the presidential elections of 1985 with a mixture of hope and despair.

The First García Presidency

APRA candidate Alan García received 46% of the votes in April 1985, and the candidate of the United Left (which included Communist elements), Alfonso Barrantes, popular mayor of Lima, got 21%. In order to discourage voter turnout, both the Shining Path and Tupac Amaru terrorists issued death threats; the Shining Path actually amputated the fingers of peasants to prevent them from voting. Police and military security at the polls was tight.

According to the constitution, if no candidate obtains more than 50% of the votes, a second (runoff) election is obligatory. Before the runoff date was determined, *senderistas* gravely wounded the president of the Electoral Tribunal. Days later, Barrantes, probably trying to avoid a further decline of leftist votes, withdrew from the runoff.

García, just 36, took the oath of office in July 1985. He immediately made dramatic and controversial promises. He stated that no more than an amount corresponding to 10% of Peru's export income would be used to "repay" a foreign debt of almost $16 billion, knowing that such an amount wouldn't even pay the interest on the indebtedness. Peru's international bond rating suffered.

In order to deal with police and army corruption, García fired or retired top figures in both organizations. He declared a state of emergency as lawlessness increased in Lima, ordering armored units from the military to patrol the streets. An American oil company was nationalized (assets: $400 million) without compensation. The United States cut off aid as required by law. A new unit of currency, the *inti*, was introduced, a devaluation of 64 to 1 of the *sol*. It was later devalued several more times.

Conditions deteriorated after 1986. The *senderistas* promoted simultaneous riots at three prisons. The army responded by executing almost 200 prisoners after they had surrendered. The *senderistas* threatened

High school girls in a mountain village

to kill 10 *APRA* leaders for each guerrilla slain. Three universities were raided by 4,000 troops, who seized *senderista* propaganda, violating the traditional security of education institutions. Violence escalated, with the guerrillas resorting to tying bombs to children and burros to carry them to their target. The army's response was equally brutal.

There would have been a military coup, but the military didn't want to inherit an ungovernable country. Much of Peru came under martial law. The *senderistas* then retreated to the upper Huallaga Valley in the northeast, where most of the coca is grown. They imposed a 10% "sales tax" on the farmers "for protection." Because of their hatred for foreigners, the tourist trade all but dried up. The *senderistas* frequently bombed Lima's power grid, reducing power to three hours a day, if any. Polls showed more than half of Peruvians would leave the country if they could.

García nationalized banks and insurance companies in 1987, creating economic havoc. Having defaulted on its external loans, Peru was on a cash-in-advance basis. As many as 50 ships at a time would lie at port, laden with food, but awaiting payment in hard currency before unloading—while Peruvians went hungry. After García left office, evidence surfaced that he had received a kickback for depositing Peru's reserves in BCCI, a shady bank that became the target of an international investigation, and from the construction of an Italian-built electric rail line. The charges were filed in 1992 but García fled into self-imposed exile in Colombia and stayed there for nine years—until the statute of limitations had expired.

The Fujimori Era

When 1990 elections approached, it was generally assumed they would result in another traditional party victory. Polls showed the well-known novelist, Mario Vargas Llosa, the likely winner. But a surprise appeared on the horizon: Alberto Fujimori, an engineer and the soft-spoken son of Japanese immigrants, supported by a substantial number of Protestant evangelicals, entered the contest under the *Cambio '90* ("Change '90") banner. His supporters, going from door to door extolling his virtues, were persuasive. His popularity swelled from 3% to 60% in the runoff a few months later.

A small element within the military, foreseeing Fujimori's victory, attempted a coup just before the elections, replete with a plan to murder him. It failed; his intelligence received word of its time and place.

Following his inauguration on July 28, 1990—his 52nd birthday—Fujimori dismissed the top echelon of the navy and air

force, then the army. He turned inward, trusting no one with basic decisions and policy. He ordered the reorganized military to renew a campaign against the *senderistas* and armed rural peasants.

The *senderistas*, with their strength about 15,000, launched a campaign in 1992 to gain control of Lima. Arms and munitions supplies via Colombia had become unreliable and they needed the support of the vast number of poor people surrounding the city in slums. At the same time, it became evident to Fujimori that the National Assembly, dominated by the traditional political elite, was obstructing him at every turn. He dismissed the body, as well as members of the judiciary, and assumed personal control by decree in April. He had the backing of the military for this so-called "self-coup."

Under pressure from Washington and the OAS, Fujimori called for elections in late 1992. The *senderistas* attempted to disrupt them, but two months before the contest, Guzmán, his girlfriend Elena Iparraguirre and other key members were nabbed by the military and police in a posh Lima apartment. Because he avoided publicity and pictures, little was known of Guzmán; he turned out to be an obese, psoriasis-ridden, ordinary-looking person with remarkable powers of persuasion, not unlike Charles Manson, Jim Jones or David Koresh. Violence had become an end, not a means, for his followers, who engaged in the worst sort of torture, maiming, mutilation and murder of innocent victims. He was sentenced to a 40-year prison term. His and Iparraguirre's capture inspired the novel and movie, *The Dancer Upstairs*.

Fujimori and his supporters drafted a new constitution, which voters approved in 1993 by a narrow margin.

Fujimori's harsh measures began to bear fruit. Violence dwindled to less than 25% of what it had been in 1993. The *senderistas* were reduced to a hard core of fewer than 1,000 who opposed Guzmán's surprising support from his jail cell of the new constitution.

Fujimori's popularity soared. *Cambio '90* changed its name to *Nueva Majoría Cambio '90* ("New Majority for Change 90") for the 1995 elections. Meanwhile, discord surfaced in the presidential mansion. Fujimori and his wife, Susana Higuchi, separated. Forming a new political party, Harmony 21st Century, she announced she would run for president. The National Election Board declared most of the signatures on her application invalid; she accused it of "techno-fraud."

Fifteen candidates filed for president in 1995, including former U.N. Secretary-General Javier Pérez de Cuellar. Higuchi aligned herself with the Police-Military Front. She and her husband divorced soon

Alberto Fujimori

thereafter. Fujimori won 64% of the vote, and his party was assured of a comfortable margin in Congress. He acquired the nickname "Chinochet," a reference to his Asian heritage and the name of Chile's General Pinochet. He declared that Peru needed order, discipline, the principle of authority, sound leadership and administration and honesty. He provided all but the last.

In 1995, Peru fought a brief but bloody war with neighboring Ecuador over a border dispute that had simmered since 1942 (see Ecuador).

The Fujimori government soon faced a new guerrilla threat in 1996 from its other active guerrilla group, the Tupac Amaru Revolutionary Movement (*MRTA*). It differs from the *senderistas* in that it is urban-based and far less bloodthirsty. On December 17, 1996, it raided a Christmas party at the Japanese ambassador's residence in Lima and took more than 400 diplomats and government officials hostage. The *MRTA* demanded release of prisoners, and gradually it released most of the hostages as tense negotiations unfolded.

Peru

The siege attracted worldwide media coverage. After four months, only 73 hostages remained in the compound, but Fujimori steadfastly refused to cave in to the demand to release prisoners. The standoff continued until April 22, 1997, when Peruvian commandos, acting on intelligence that the rebels were engaged in a soccer game, stormed the compound and killed all 14 of the remaining guerrillas, at a loss of only two commandos and one hostage, a Supreme Court justice. There was evidence that at least two women guerrillas attempted to surrender but were gunned down in cold blood, charges the government denied. The operation, and questions about whether guerrillas were summarily executed, later returned to haunt Fujimori.

Fujimori sent up a trial balloon on the possibility of his running for a third consecutive term in 2000, on the pre-text that his first election in 1990 had predated the new constitution. The Constitutional Tribunal rejected the idea. Fujimori merely cajoled Congress, controlled by his allies, to remove three of the tribunal's justices.

By 1997, Fujimori's tendency to play fast and loose with the constitution and with basic civil liberties erupted into a major scandal, which the opposition and its media allies exploited. A female army sergeant assigned to intelligence alleged in a televised interview that she had been tortured and another woman sergeant, Mariela Barreto, murdered for leaking information that military intelligence was wiretapping Fujimori's opponents in Congress and the media and threatening some with physical violence.

When Barreto's dismembered body was found, the public outcry reached a crescendo against the president and the two men who it was widely believed were ruling Peru with him as a triumvirate: intelligence chief Vladimiro Montesinos and General Nicolás Hermoza, chairman of the joint chiefs of staff. Foreign Minister Francisco Tudela, who had been one of the hostages held by the Tupac Amaru guerrillas, resigned to protest the government wiretapping campaign.

The embattled Fujimori responded to the crisis by revoking the Peruvian citizenship of Baruch Ivcher, the Israeli-born owner of *Frecuencia Latina* (Channel 2), the station that televised the interview, a flagrant violation of the constitution. Through a legal maneuver, control of the station passed to two pro-Fujimori shareholders. Spontaneous demonstrations erupted, and volunteers camped out at *Frecuencia Latina* to prevent an armed takeover by security forces. Fujimori's public approval rating nosedived to 19%, the lowest of his seven years in office.

There was more to come. For years, since Fujimori first ran in 1990, there had been rumors that he had been born in Japan and was thus constitutionally ineligible to serve as president. In 1997, *Caretas*, the country's most respected weekly newsmagazine, published documents that disputed Fujimori's claim he had been born in Miraflores in 1938. The media reprinted reproductions of the birth certificate, in which the place of birth obviously had been clumsily erased and the words "Miraflores, Lima" written over the erasure in a different handwriting. Other documents arose, such as Fujimori's mother claiming two children when she immigrated in 1934; Fujimori is her second son. It boiled down to Fujimori's word against the media's. Of course, there was no contest as to who would prevail.

Next came a showdown between Fujimori and the military. Fujimori published a book on the siege of the Japanese ambassador's residence, in which he played up his own role and downplayed that of Hermoza. In an apparent test of his authority, Hermoza summoned all the country's generals to Lima, ostensibly for his birthday party, sparking rumors of an imminent coup. Fujimori quickly ordered the generals back to their posts; just as quickly, they went. Once again, the feisty little president had prevailed in a test of wills.

Fujimori recuperated some of the fading esteem of his people by once again doing battle with a common enemy, not terrorists, but Mother Nature. *El Niño,* the periodic weather phenomenon that affects climate worldwide but which reserves its greatest fury for Peru, returned with a vengeance in December 1997 and continued for months. Flooding destroyed whole villages and killed about 300 people. Fujimori, a professional engineer, went to the affected areas and took personal charge of the efforts to contain the floodwaters. To Fujimori's critics, this was micromanagement at best and shameless grandstanding and exploitation of a tragedy at worst, but it was a take-charge gesture that was typically Fujimori.

In 1998, a popular movement called the Democratic Forum, backed by Fujimori's congressional opposition, collected 1.45 million signatures on a petition demanding a referendum on the issue of whether Fujimori could run again. The petition was presented to the electoral board, which voted 4–1 that only the Congress—controlled, of course, by Fujimori allies—could approve a referendum.

Congress voted down the referendum. Pro-Fujimori and opposition legislators almost came to blows. Police cordoned off the Congress building to repel demonstrators who chanted, "Death to the dictatorship." The vote effectively removed any remaining obstacle to a third-term bid except for one—the Peruvian voters themselves.

In 1999 Fujimoro signed the long-sought peace agreement with Ecuador's President Jamil Mahuad in Brasilia. They dedicated

Machu Picchu

Courtesy: Heather Marion

362

the first border marker in January 2000 and signed bilateral economic development accords in Washington in February (see Ecuador).

On a darker note, Fujimori's government renewed its persecution of exiled television station owner Baruch Ivcher. In December 1998, a Lima court issued arrest warrants for Ivcher, his wife and daughter for allegedly altering the registration forms for his television station. Apparently stung by his growing image as a bully, Fujimori then shifted course and sought to reach an out-of-court settlement, arguing that the case was merely a legal battle between Ivcher and the pro-Fujimori shareholders who controlled the station. When the negotiations broke down, Ivcher took the case before the Inter-American Human Rights Commission, an organ of the OAS. The commission forwarded the case to the Inter-American Court of Human Rights. Fujimori resolved the matter in 1999 in typical fashion: He simply withdrew Peru from the Court of Human Rights. Ivcher remained abroad.

The "Elections" of 2000

The opposition grudgingly accepted Congress' refusal to call a referendum on a third term and set out to defeat the president the only way left: at the ballot box in April 2000. But three strong candidates emerged against him, dividing the opposition.

The early favorite was Lima Mayor Alberto Andrade, of *APRA*, who won a landslide re-election victory of 65% in 1998 against a Fujimori ally. Then a second candidate, Luis Casteñeda, who had earned high marks as head of the social security system, moved up even in the polls to Andrade. Fujimori held a strong first place in the polls, but not the 50% needed to avoid a runoff.

Suddenly, the fourth-ranking candidate, Alejandro Toledo, a 54-year-old economist of pure Indian descent, broke from the rear of the pack and moved up on the outside, emerging as the man for Fujimori to beat. The media made much of Toledo's humble farming background and how he had once shined shoes before going on to earn a doctorate at Stanford and to become an official at the World Bank.

Tension mounted as the opposition, the media and international election monitors uncovered evidence that machinery was in place for vote-rigging. Fujimori insisted the vote would be clean, but he denied the opposition access to the state-owned media, and thugs repeatedly pelted opposition rallies with rocks; no arrests were made. Opposition candidates were also the targets of scurrilous stories in tabloid newspapers.

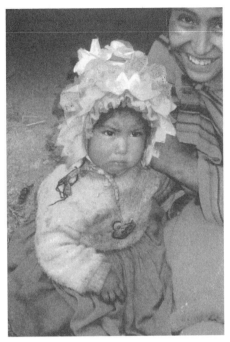

Mother and child in Andean village

The day after the election, it seemed that the worst fears would come to pass. Despite exit polls that showed Fujimori well short of a majority, the first "official" count—suspiciously delayed until April 10—showed Fujimori a hair short of a majority, 49.6%; Toledo was a strong second with 40.6%. It was apparent that as the count progressed, the president would go over the 50% mark. As the tedious count progressed, reports surfaced of such irregularities as soldiers preventing people from voting, ballots with Toledo's name torn off the bottom, pre-filled ballots, and Fujimori campaign officials inserting votes into the electoral commission's computer via an Internet café.

Protests erupted, and the United States and other democracies warned Fujimori they would take a dim view of a fraudulent election. Then, as if by magic, election officials "revised" the final vote count, giving Fujimori 49.89%, just 20,000 short of a majority. Toledo obtained 40.15%.

The opposition took heart from Fujimori's failure to steal the election outright and even more from the results in the congressional election. Fujimori's *Perú 2000* party lost its absolute majority, dropping from 67 seats in the 120-member Congress to 51. Toledo's *Perú Posible* was second with 28 seats. The opposition alleged that Fujimori loyalists were offering $50,000 bribes for legislators to join an alliance with *Perú 2000*.

The eyes of the world were focused on the May 28 runoff, as it seemed obvious Fujimori did not intend to allow a trifle like the will of the people to stand in the way of his retaining power. The domestic watch-

dog *Transparencia* and observers from the OAS and the Atlanta-based Carter Center all concluded it would be impossible to guarantee a fair and honest vote. Toledo proclaimed he would withdraw from the race unless the vote were postponed until June to allow experts time to ensure there would not be the kinds of computer problems and irregularities that marred the first round. The international observers soon joined Toledo's call for a postponement. But Fujimori refused, countering that Toledo merely feared defeat.

Toledo withdrew, saying he refused to lend the appearance of legitimacy to a fraudulent election. Then the OAS and the Carter Center pulled out their observers, saying they could not guarantee the integrity of the vote unless it were delayed. The OAS mission declared that the process "was far from free and fair." "In Venezuela, the election has been postponed, but with integrity," Carter said. "In Peru, the election has been allowed to proceed without postponement, but without integrity."

The Clinton administration warned Fujimori that Peru could face economic sanctions. Street violence broke out as Toledo supporters attacked Fujimori campaign offices. Toledo at first called on his voters to boycott the election, but the $33 fine for failing to vote is too stiff for most Peruvians. He then called on them to deface their ballots by writing, "No to fraud!"

Fabián Salazar, a columnist for the newspaper *La República,* was given videotapes from contacts in the National Intelligence Service that showed Montesinos instructing the head of the electoral commission how to rig the congressional elections to deny seats to certain candidates. As Salazar was viewing the tapes in his office, security agents broke in, confiscated the tapes and sawed Salazar's arm to the bone.

The outcome on May 28 was a foregone conclusion. Fujimori received only a bare majority of 51.1%. Toledo received 17.4%, and 30.3% of the ballots were voided as Toledo had requested.

The U.S. State Department quickly branded Fujimori's victory as "illegitimate," and the presidents of several Latin American countries expressed their concern. Toledo flew to Madrid to ask for support from Spanish President José María Aznar for a new election.

The tarnished election also headed the agenda of a meeting of OAS foreign ministers in Canada. But the Latin American representatives had no stomach for the U.S. position for strong hemispheric action. What emerged was a lukewarm resolution to conduct a fact-finding mission to Peru to study ways to "strengthen democracy" there. There was no mention of sanctions or new elections.

Peru

Fujimori Falls

Fujimori was inaugurated for his third term on July 28, 2000, an event largely snubbed by the international community and vigorously protested in the streets of Lima. Only two presidents, from neighboring Ecuador and Bolivia, attended, compared with nine in 1995. On inauguration eve, Toledo marshaled 80,000 demonstrators for a non-violent protest.

Inauguration day was uglier, as riot police dispersed protesters with tear gas, which wafted toward the presidential palace and into the nostrils of the dignitaries. Uglier still, a bank was torched, and six security guards died in the blaze; each side blamed the other. In his address, Fujimori ignored mention of the democratic reforms he had promised the OAS, focusing instead on economic growth. Meanwhile, as expected, several independent congressmen were "persuaded" to join the pro-Fujimori bloc, giving it a slim 63–57 majority.

For seven weeks, the protesters remained in the streets; usually the protests were non-violent. Among the demonstrators' symbolic protests in front of the presidential palace: Washing the Peruvian flag in a tub of soap and water; using fumigation guns to spray the "rats" in the palace, and surrounding the palace with yellow police tape that bore the legend, "Caution! Mafia at work!" It was clever and effective non-violent protest in the best tradition of Gandhi and Martin Luther King. Still, the entrenched Fujimori hung tough.

In September, evidence became public that Montesinos may have helped transfer arms through Peru to the *FARC* guerrillas in Colombia, which brought increased U.S. pressure on Fujimori. Then a television station broadcast a clandestine videotape of Montesinos attempting to bribe a congressman in the anti-Fujimori faction into switching sides.

The resulting domestic and international pressure finally proved too much. Fujimori stunned the nation in a televised address by announcing he would disband Montesinos' National Intelligence Service (whose Spanish acronym, *SIN*, is amusingly allegorical in English) and that he would call a new election—in which he would *not* be a candidate! He began talks with the opposition, brokered by the OAS, to effect a transition. Fujimori angered the opposition by agreeing to a new election on April 8, 2001, with the new president to succeed him on July 28, but only if the Congress approved an expanded amnesty law to protect members of the armed forces from prosecution in other than human rights cases. The opposition refused, and it prevailed. It demanded Fujimori's immediate resignation, which the president at first rejected, and it made the resignation of Montesinos the *sine qua non* for continued dialogue.

The nation was shocked again by the news that Montesinos had fled to Panama, Latin America's traditional dumping ground for unpopular and venal political figures. Fujimori had just "fired" him under mounting pressure, but his escape smacked of collusion. Others were relieved he was gone. Montesinos sought political asylum in Panama, which demurred, despite pressure from the U.S. and some Latin American countries to allow him to remain, thus removing the possibility of his continuing as a player in Peru's complex power game.

With his tourist visa expiring and no charges awaiting him in Peru, Montesinos returned as suddenly and as unexpectedly as he had left, precipitating a crisis. Rumors flew that the armed forces chiefs, known to owe their first loyalty to Montesinos, were planning a *coup d'etat*. Fujimori went on television to assure the country that he was in "total control" of the armed forces. Montesinos went into hiding, and Fujimori made a publicized effort to "find" him, although most Peruvians believed the president actually was harboring him.

First Vice President Francisco Tudela, long a Fujimori ally, resigned in protest—a decision he may have regretted a month later. Fujimori sought to mollify public opinion by firing the heads of the three armed forces, all Montesinos loyalists. But his new army commander also was a *montesinista*.

For eight months, Montesinos' whereabouts became an international guessing game. Reports circulated in the media that Montesinos and Fujimori had been involved in money laundering, arms dealing and drug trafficking. A federal prosecutor alleged that Montesinos had $48 million in Swiss bank accounts (his monthly salary was just $337). An investigation raised that to $70 million, and further probing suggested Montesinos may have amassed as much as $264 million. Evidence surfaced later that some of the money may have been laundered by two front companies that had been set up in Singapore—by Fujimori.

In November 2000, Fujimori flew to Brunei for a meeting of the Asia-Pacific Economic Cooperation (APEC) conference. By then, defections from Fujimori's bloc in Congress had given the opposition control. Congress deposed his loyal speaker and replaced her with Valentín Paniagua from the now-tiny Popular Action Party. The country was jolted again on November 17, when Fujimori absconded to Japan, his family's homeland. Three days later, he faxed his resignation to Congress—which rejected it. Instead, Congress voted 62–9 to remove him from office as "permanently morally unfit."

At first, Second Vice President Ricardo Márquez, a *fujimorista*, sought to exercise his constitutional right to succeed Fujimori, but Congress appointed Paniagua as interim president. He vowed a "total house-cleaning" and appointed the respected former U.N. Secretary-General Javier Pérez de Cuellar as prime minister. Another positive step: *Frecuencia Latina* was restored to its rightful owner, Baruch Ivcher, and the media were given free rein to report on the upcoming election campaign. Congress also restored the three judges Fujimori had sacked from the Constitutional Tribunal.

Thus, one of the most intriguing eras of *personalismo* in 20th century Latin American history came to an end. In February 2001, Congress formally charged Fujimori with dereliction of duty and other specifications. But Japan granted him citizenship and refused to extradite him. Nonetheless, Fujimori remained as much a fugitive as Montesinos, unable to travel to countries that have extradition treaties with Peru.

He then faced murder charges at home. According to a former Japanese hostage, three of the guerrillas slain in the 1997 commando raid on the Japanese ambassador's residence were seen alive after the raid in commando custody. Fujimori had boasted of his micromanagement of that raid, making it unlikely that the prisoners could have been killed without his approval. It was a shabby end for a man once hailed as the country's savior.

Investigators then seized from Montesinos' home about 2,400 videotapes on which the intelligence chief had unabashedly chronicled his bribes of a dazzling array of officials. Many of the so-called *"Vladivideos"* were released to the media, which kept the public spellbound—and further outraged.

Peruvian authorities received word that Montesinos was in hiding in Venezuela, which President Hugo Chávez denied for months. The Peruvians also learned that Montesinos had a secret bank account in Miami and asked the U.S. FBI to monitor it. Acting on irrefutable evidence from the FBI, the Peruvians confronted the Chávez government with the evidence of Montesinos' whereabouts, and in June 2001, Venezuelan intelligence officials arrested Montesinos in Caracas. Ironically, the Peruvian president-elect, Toledo, was in Caracas for the 13th Andean Summit, where Chávez announced Montesinos' arrest.

Montesinos was hustled back to Lima, not on an extradition request, but as an undocumented alien! His appearance in court, in handcuffs and bulletproof vest, was a hemispheric media event, and the

Peruvian public waited expectantly for new revelations of Montesinos' perfidy like they would an unfolding *telenovela*. Besides the money laundering, drug trafficking and arms smuggling charges, Montesinos also faced a murder charge in the death of the whistle-blowing female army sergeant in 1997. He later was charged with murder in the summary execution of terrorists at the Japanese ambassador's residence in 1997.

New Election, New President

Toledo and nine other candidates presented themselves for the April 2001 election, among them former President García, home after nine years of self-imposed exile in Colombia—just after the statute of limitations on his kickback charges had expired. At first, the García candidacy on the *APRA* ticket was dismissed as a joke, a relic of the dreadful days of guerrilla warfare and hyperinflation. It seemed a foregone conclusion that the two candidates who would face each other in the runoff would be Toledo, candidate of *Perú Posible*, and Lourdes Flores, a veteran congresswoman from the conservative Popular Christian Party.

Suddenly, polls showed García closing in on Flores for the No. 2 spot. That sent a chill through domestic and international financial circles; as president, García had limited debt repayment to 10% of exports, sparking the hyperinflation that Fujimori was elected to combat. Nonetheless, García, an eloquent stump speaker, remained popular with the country's poor majority, who did not feel they had benefited appreciably from 10 years of *fujimorismo*. Still, he pragmatically toned down his fiery populist rhetoric so as not to frighten foreign investors and the ruling elite.

García also was aided by Toledo and Flores, who hurled mud at each other. Toledo was accused of fathering a child out of wedlock and refusing to take a paternity test. Also, *Caretas* magazine reproduced a medical report showing he had tested positive for cocaine in 1998; Toledo countered that the *SIN* had abducted him and framed him.

Peruvians received another jolt on April 8. Toledo led the field with 36.5%, less than he had received the year before in the first round against Fujimori. García won the runoff spot with 26% to Flores' 24%. In the June 3 runoff, Toledo defeated García by a slim 52% to 48%, making history as Peru's first full-blooded Indian president.

Toledo's Troubled Presidency

Toledo was inaugurated on July 28, 2001. He pledged to combat the corrup-

tion left by Fujimori; to restructure the armed forces and police in the wake of Montesinos' departure; to create 400,000 jobs; and to continue cooperating with the United States in the war against drugs. In a symbolic demonstration of pride in his roots, Toledo participated in an Inca "inauguration" ceremony at the ruins of Machu Picchu.

Peru moved toward a catharsis to cleanse itself of the Fujimori legacy, which the disgraced former president continued to defend from his safe haven in Japan. Montesinos admitted Fujimori had ordered him to pay hundreds of thousands of dollars in bribes to key members of Congress to secure his re-election in 2000, and named the members who had accepted them, including several who had just been elected again.

Congress voted unanimously to strip Fujimori of his immunity from prosecution. The attorney general filed formal murder charges against him in connection with two massacres of dissidents: the so-called "barbecue massacre" in the Lima neighborhood of Barrio Alto in 1991 that left 15 people dead, and another in 1992, in which 10 were killed. The massacres allegedly were committed by an infamous paramilitary death squad known as the "Colina Group." Fujimori also was charged with complicity in the 1997 murder and dismemberment of Mariela Barreto, the whistle-blowing intelligence service sergeant.

A judge issued an international arrest warrant for Fujimori. Japan, however, continued to deny his extradition, which strained relations. Congress, meanwhile, questioned the disappearance of $372 million, $260 million of which apparently went into accounts controlled by Montesinos. Another international warrant was issued against Fujimori in 2002 for an alleged $15 million payoff to Montesinos. Fujimori also was charged with ordering the congressional bribes.

Next, prosecutors cited forensic evidence that eight of the 14 guerrillas slain in the recapturing of the Japanese ambassador's residence in 1997 had been shot execution-style, not in combat as had been reported at the time. In 2003, Interpol added Fujimori to its 10 Most Wanted list.

Montesinos faced as many as 70 trials. His was first convicted in 2002, of becoming intelligence chief in an illegal manner, and sentenced to nine years. In 2003 he was convicted of influence peddling and sentenced to five years, then he was convicted of embezzlement and sentenced to eight. In 2006 he was sentenced to 20 years for selling 10,000 assault weapons to Colombia's *FARC* guerrillas.

Meanwhile, former army commander Nicolás Hermoza, the third man in the

Former President Alejandro Toledo

so-called "triumvirate" with Fujimori and Montesinos, was convicted in 2005 of illegally amassing a $22 million fortune and sentenced to eight years.

The Truth and Reconciliation Commission began public hearings in 2002 into human rights abuses committed during the 1980s and '90s. Peruvians were presented with horror stories of past atrocities. A team from the commission flew to Tokyo to interrogate Fujimori himself, who refused to meet with them.

Peruvians were abruptly reminded of another past horror when, in March 2002, a powerful car bomb exploded near the U.S. Embassy in Lima on the eve of a one-day visit by U.S. President George W. Bush, the first visit by a U.S. president. Ten people were killed and 30 injured. Police arrested four members of *Sendero Luminoso* in connection with the bombing.

The prospect of renewed violence by the once-feared group, whose size was estimated variously at 175 to 700, sent a chill through the country. So did the decision by the Supreme Court in 2003 to overturn the conviction of *Sendero Luminoso* leader Guzmán. A second trial ended in mistrial. In 2006 he was finally convicted and sentenced to life in prison. Ironically, his cell is close to Montesinos'.

Toledo's honeymoon with the Congress and the public was brief. Despite the fact that the economy was growing briskly (see Economy), demonstrators took to the streets in 2002 to denounce Toledo for failing to ease unemployment. His job approval rating plummeted to 25%, compared with 59% in August 2001.

Toledo contributed to his own image problem, coming across as inarticulate,

Peru

In this editorial cartoon, President Toledo asks God, "Father, why have You forsaken me?" God replies: "Because of incompetence, frivolousness, insecurity, lying, erratic behavior, irresponsibility, indecisiveness, nepotism, for being dumb, for being a bad father. . ."

unpunctual and indecisive. He changed prime ministers, interior ministers and finance ministers with bewildering regularity, and he replaced technocrats with political hacks. Street protests in the capital and elsewhere became a regular occurrence.

His efforts at privatization also came under attack. In 2002, he dispatched troops and riot police to Arequipa to quell violent protests against plans to privatize two local electric companies. Toledo declared a 30-day state of siege, which prompted his interior minister to resign. Two people died and 200 were injured in the weeklong violence. Toledo called off the sale of the companies.

Former President Fernando Belaúnde, the acknowledged patriarch of Peru's new democracy, died in 2002 at the age of 89. Toledo declared three days of mourning and tearfully praised his predecessor as a "paradigm of democracy."

To enhance decentralization, Congress created 25 new federal-style regional governments. Elections for these new governorships and legislative assemblies were held in November 2002.

In a separate development, Toledo publicly confirmed two days before the election what had alleged and widely believed: that he was the father of a 14-year-old girl born out of wedlock.

Despite the fastest economic growth rate in Latin America, large sectors of the work force grumbled that they were not feeling the benefits of it. In 2003, teachers struck to demand an increase in their $190-a-month salaries. The government offered a $29-a-month raise, which they rejected. Farmers, angered by taxes and low prices, erected barricades on the Pan-American Highway. Civil servants, health-care workers and judicial employees also struck. Toledo responded with another 30-day state of emergency. The government and teachers compromised on a salary increase to $350 a month. Largely as a public relations gesture, Toledo and his top cabinet ministers reduced their salaries by 30%.

Toledo did little to enhance his popularity with his opulent lifestyle. He used the presidential jet to deliver the commencement address at his alma mater, Stanford, in 2003, which cost $100,000, when the university had provided first-class commercial tickets. Toledo's response to his growing unpopularity: another cabinet shuffle! His approval rating dropped to 12%, the lowest of any Latin American president; even Fujimori's was 31%! Toledo's popularity soon dropped even lower.

The Peruvian government stubbornly filed a 700-page extradition request with Japan in 2003, naming Fujimori as the intellectual author of the "barbecue massacre." Japan still took no action, while Fujimori brazenly announced his intention to run for president in 2006—even though he had been barred from holding office until 2010. In 2005, Fujimori's brother and two sisters were arrested on charges that they had embezzled $21 million from a private charity.

The Truth and Reconciliation Commission presented its long-awaited report to Toledo in 2003. It had spent two years and $13 million interviewing 17,000 witnesses and unearthing mass graves. Perhaps its most surprising conclusion was that 69,000 people had been killed during the guerrilla wars of the 1980s and '90s, more than twice as many as the 30,000 that had been generally believed. The commission laid the greatest blame for the deaths at the feet of *Sendero Luminoso,* but also faulted the security services for human rights violations. It criticized the governments of former presidents Belaúnde and García as inept and for not responding forcefully enough, and Fujimori's for responding *too* forcefully.

Faced with an approval rating that had sunk to 6%, the last thing Toledo needed was another scandal. But in 2005, Toledo's sister, Margarita, and 25 others were arrested for allegedly falsifying voters' signatures on the petitions to qualify *Perú Posible* for the ballot in the 2000 election. A

local TV station aired another embarrassing video showing Toledo congratulating followers for collecting the signatures. An investigation revealed that 78% of the party's 520,000 signatures were forged. Toledo neither admitted nor denied the allegations. His only response: another cabinet shuffle.

A congressional committee, on a 3–2 vote, concluded that Toledo was the "co-author" of the forgery scheme. This constituted grounds for impeachment and removal, but Congress voted instead, 57–48, to forward the charges to a prosecutor for Toledo to face criminal charges. Because the president enjoyed immunity, the effect was to allow Toledo to serve out the remaining 14 months of his term.

In the drug war, the United Nations released figures showing that coca production in Peru soared by 55% in 2004. Although the report conceded Peru had eradicated more than 26,000 acres of coca, 42,000 new acres were planted. Experts theorized the crackdown on coca cultivation in Colombia had forced producers to shift operations to Peru, Ecuador and Bolivia. The U.S. government reported that coca production in Peru was up another 38% in 2005.

In 2005, Peru became the 13th nation to sign a bilateral free-trade agreement with the United States; trade between Peru and the U.S. totaled about $6 billion in 2005. Colombia signed one soon thereafter. This technically undermined the purpose of the Andean Pact, from which Venezuela's Chávez angrily withdrew in protest.

On November 7, 2005, the ever-enigmatic Fujimori, then 67, splashed back into the world headlines when he abandoned his safe haven in Japan and arrived unexpectedly in Santiago, Chile, hoping to negotiate his return to Peru. He evidently believed the Chilean government would tolerate his presence, as it had fugitive former Argentine President Carlos Menem (see Argentina). He seriously miscalculated; Chilean authorities arrested him, and a judge denied him bail pending Peru's request to extradite him on 12 counts of corruption and human rights violations. He was freed in May 2006, but was prohibited from leaving Chile until the extradition process was completed, which took more than a year.

García's Dramatic Comeback

The campaign for the April 9, 2006, presidential election was in many ways a replay of 2001: Three major candidates, two of whom also ran in 2001; a surprise finish in the first round; and a close, dramatic runoff. The two holdovers were former President García of the *APRA,* and Lourdes Flores, the conservative whom

García had narrowly nudged out of the runoff.

The long-shot outsider this time was retired army Lieutenant Colonel Ollanta Humala, 43, a leftist nationalist who modeled himself after Venezuela's Chávez and professed admiration for the policies of former military strongman Juan Velasco Alvarado, who ruled from 1968–75. Like Chávez, Humala had participated in a coup attempt while in uniform, a failed attempt to oust Fujimori in 2000; he received an amnesty in 2001, then retired. In August 2005, a poll gave him only 5%, but by December, he had 23%, just behind front-runner Flores. Chávez openly endorsed Humala and compared him to Bolivia's new leftist president, Evo Morales. Toledo recalled Peru's ambassador from Caracas and accused Chávez of "meddling" in Peruvian politics. Humala called the action "desperation" by the ruling elite.

Fujimori, still under house arrest in Chile, bombastically declared his intention to run, even though he was still barred from holding office. His daughter, Keiko, and supporters filed the papers to have him on the ballot, and incredibly, a poll showed him with 15% support. But the electoral commission rejected his candidacy. Fujimori appealed, to no avail. In the end, his hastily created movement, Alliance for the Future, fielded Martha Chávez, a former president of the Congress, as his stand-in. Her running mate was Fujimori's younger brother, Santiago.

Polls hinted that it would be a two-person race between Flores and Humala. Suddenly, just as he had in 2001, the populist García moved up on the outside. Turnout was 88.7%. Once again, García surprised everyone and Flores was again left on the outside looking in. The results:

Humala	3,758,258	30.6%
García	2,985,858	24.3%
Flores	2,925,280	23.8%
Chávez	912,420	7.4%

In the elections for the new Congress, Humala's Union for Peru obtained the most seats, 45 out of 120. *APRA* was second with 36, and Flores' National Unity won 17. Fujimori's Alliance for the Future won 13; one of them went to Keiko Fujimori.

If the prospect of a García presidency frightened the business elite, the U.S. government, international lenders and foreign investors, the idea of a Humala presidency gave them cardiac arrest. Flores' voters, and those of the other losing candidates who comprised more than 20% of the April 9 votes, agonized over whether to vote for a disgraced former president who had wrecked the economy or a left-wing ideologue who wanted to implement a Chávez-like regime Chávez.

García downplayed his past, and while Humala frightened moderate voters by likening himself to Chávez or Morales, García now portrayed himself as a pragmatic populist like Brazil's Lula da Silva or Chile's Socialist president, Michelle Bachelet. While Humala promised greater state control of the economy, García said he would continue Toledo's free-market policies that had given Peru among the highest growth rates in Latin America. García said he would move forward with the free-trade agreement (FTA) with the United States; Humala vowed to scuttle it.

If García's closet was full of skeletons, Humala had some of his own. Charges surfaced that Humala was responsible for human rights abuses during the dirty war against the *senderistas,* and that his abortive coup in 2000 was a diversion designed to help Montesinos flee the country; from his jail cell, Montesinos confirmed the allegations. Humala's brother, leader of a bizarre quasi-fascist paramilitary group, was in jail for leading an attack in 2005 that left four policemen dead. Their father also was notorious for his weird racial philosophy.

Even though millions of voters must have held their noses when they voted in the June 4 runoff, turnout was an impressive 87.7%. The percentages were almost identical to the 2001 runoff, only the loser in 2001 emerged the winner in 2006:

| García | 6,965,017 | 52.6% |
| Humala | 6,270,080 | 47.4% |

The sigh of relief could be heard all the way from Washington.

García pledged an austerity program, including a reduction in the salaries of all elected officials from the president on down, which he kept. He also fired several new government consultants Toledo had appointed in the 11th hour of his term.

García was sworn in on July 28, 2006. At the time, his approval rating was 50%, but with the popular austerity measures—which critics dismissed as populist window dressing—at the end of his first 100 days it was 60%. Besides the salary reductions, he grounded the presidential jet and traveled coach class.

Ironically, he left in place many of the policies of the detested Toledo, and even appointed Toledo's former finance minister, Pedro Pablo Kuczynski, as prime minister for a time. He further assuaged the fears of the business elite and foreign investors by appointing Luis Carranza, a banker and mainstream economist, as finance minister. García met with President Bush in Washington, and he lobbied the new Democratic-controlled Congress to ratify the FTA. It was a far cry from the bogeyman of the 1990s.

Some of his measures proved controversial, such as imposing the death penalty for terrorists and for pedophiles who murder children. He courageously faced the wrath of the powerful teachers' union, part of his constituency, by implementing teacher evaluations as part of badly needed education reform. In their first exams in 2007, the teachers scored abysmally.

As had happened with Toledo, García presided over one of the fastest-growing economies in Latin America: 7.6% in 2006, 8.9% in 2007 and 9.8% in 2008, coupled with 2% inflation in 2007 and a five-point drop in the poverty rate. Yet, just like Toledo, his countrymen did not appreciate him for it. On the first anniversary of his inauguration, his approval rating had plunged to 32%, and by August 2009 it was 27%.

The U.S. Congress ratified the U.S.-Peruvian FTA in December 2007, and Bush signed it. Congress and Bush also extended the Andean Trade Preferences Act, by which Peru and neighboring countries enjoy preferential access to the U.S. market.

Peruvian-U.S. relations grew increasingly warm, surprising given García's past rhetoric. García became one of the few remaining U.S. allies in Latin America under both Bush and Obama. He was one of only four Latin American presidents to join Obama in recognizing the legitimacy of the Honduran election in 2009 to replace the deposed President Manuel Zelaya. Obama hosted García at the White House 2010, where García voiced support for Obama's nuclear non-proliferation initiative aimed at Iran. Secretary of State Hillary Clinton met with García a few days later in Lima, which was hosting the 40th OAS General Assembly.

In 2007, García renounced a 50-year-old agreement with Chile delineating their maritime boundary. He published a map claiming a triangular tract, rich in fish, totaling 14,630 square miles (see Chile). Chile withdrew its ambassador, and García promised to take the case before the International Court of Justice in The Hague, Netherlands. In 2013, the IJC largely upheld Peru's claim (see Recent Developments).

Relations with Chile became strained again in 2009 when a Peruvian air force officer who had been assigned to the Peruvian Embassy in Santiago was arrested and confessed to selling secrets to Chile. Two other officers were arrested as accomplices. Coincidentally, the news broke while García and Chilean President Michele Bachelet were attending an Asia-Pacific Economic Cooperation summit in Singapore. García canceled a workshop with Bachelet and flew home, calling Chile a "pseudo-republic" that has "an in-

Peru

feriority complex" if it buys state secrets. Bachelet retorted that García's remarks were "offensive and haughty." The Chilean Foreign Ministry denied the charges, saying tersely, "Chile does not spy." The controversy eventually died down, with García saying he did not want it to disrupt relations.

For 16 months, the extradition request for Fujimori wound through the Chilean courts. In September 2007, the Supreme Court ordered Fujimori handed over to Peru to face seven specific charges, including the two Colina Group massacres of 1991 and 1992. The ruling thus established an important new precedent for Latin America, where several countries have unsuccessfully sought extradition of venal or bloodthirsty former leaders.

The head of the national police flew to Santiago, and one day later the still-pugnacious former president was back in Lima. In the first of many pending cases, Fujimori pleaded guilty to ordering an illegal search of Montesinos' house and was sentenced to six years; the Supreme Court upheld the sentence in 2008, thus ending the possibility of his running for president in 2011.

Fujimori then went on trial for his involvement in 25 Colina Group murders, including the infamous "barbecue massacre." Ninety witnesses testified during the 16-month trial. In April 2009, a three-judge panel of the Supreme Court found him guilty and sentenced him to another 25 years—one year for each victim? Fujimori showed no emotion when the verdict and sentence were read, but human rights advocates in Peru and abroad reacted with glee, while *fujimoristas* expressed outrage. His daughter Keiko, declared, "We're going into the streets to demonstrate our open support for the best president this country has ever had, for the president who saved Peru from terrorism."

Fujimori faced his final two trials in 2009. He was convicted and sentenced to seven and a half years for paying Montesinos a $15 million bonus from the treasury. As his fourth and final trial was beginning, Fujimori pleaded guilty to authorizing illegal wiretaps and bribing journalists during his 2000 re-election campaign. He was sentenced to six years and ordered to pay $8.4 million in fines.

Fujimori remains in prison, but he was released briefly in 2011 for treatment on a pre-cancerous growth on his tongue.

The *senderistas* resurfaced in 2008, ambushing an army convoy in Tayacaia province and killing 12 soldiers and two civilians. In 2009, another *senderista* ambush left 14 soldiers dead. Two soldiers and at least four *senderistas* died in a firefight in August 2009. *Senderistas* shot down an air force helicopter that was trying to rescue

Former President Alan García

three wounded soldiers a month later, killing two crewmen. Like the *FARC* in Colombia, the *senderistas* were known to have struck a partnership with Peruvian drug dealers, which provides the dealers with protection and the guerrillas with ample funds.

The latest corruption scandal broke in 2008 when an investigative television program aired a video showing prominent *APRA* officials apparently accepting bribes from a small Norwegian oil exploration company. García's cabinet, including Prime Minister Jorge del Castillo, resigned en masse. García's approval rating nosedived to 20%.

García hosted the Asia-Pacific Economic Cooperation (APEC) forum in Lima in 2008. He used the occasion to sign a FTA with Chinese President Hu Jintao.

By March 2011, despite Peru's booming economy, despite the fact that the percentage of Peruvians living below the poverty line had fallen from 49% in 2005 to 35% in 2009, García's approval rating was 26%.

Peruvians and Latin Americans across the political spectrum cheered in 2010 when novelist and former presidential candidate Mario Vargas Llosa was awarded the Nobel Prize in Literature, only the sixth Latin American to receive it and the first in 20 years, since Mexico's Octavio Paz (see Culture).

The Elections of 2011

Polls in 2010 showed the leading contenders for the April 10, 2011, presidential

election were Lima Mayor Luis Castañeda, Fujimori's 35-year-old daughter Keiko, leftist Ollanta Humala and former President Toledo, in that order. But as always happens in Peruvian politics, things changed.

Two-time loser Lourdes Flores, who was running fifth, dropped out ran instead for mayor of Lima in October. Once again, she lost, to moderate leftist Susana Villarán, by less than one percentage point. Then Toledo's former prime minister and finance minister, Pedro Pablo Kuczynski, entered the race under the banner of the Alliance for the Great Change. The venerable *APRA*, handicapped by García's low popularity, did not even field a candidate.

By March 2011, the poll results were almost the reverse, with Toledo of *Perú Posible* leading the pack, followed by Fujimori of Force 2011 and Humala of *Gana Perú* (Peru Wins). One of the major issues was whether mining companies, which were spearheading the country's boom, should pay a windfall profits tax that could be channeled into social programs and education. Toledo, who had had five years to implement a windfall profits tax but didn't, said he favored it, as did Humala; Fujimori, Castañeda and Kuczynski did not.

Having the centrist vote divided three ways ultimately benefited Fujimori on the right and Humala on the left. Five minor candidates also cluttered up the ballot. The results of the first round:

Humala	4,643,064	31.7%
Fujimori	3,449,595	23.6%
Kuczynski	2,711,450	18.5%
Toledo	2,289,561	15.6%
Castañeda	1,440,143	9.8%
Others	103,992	.7%

There were another 1,406,998 blank votes, 8.8% of the total votes, or one voter in 12.

In Congress, Humala's *Gana Perú* party garnered 47 seats to 37 for Fujimori's Force 2011, 21 for Toledo's *Perú Posible*, 12 for Kuczynski's Alliance for the Great Change, nine for Castañeda's National Solidarity and just four for the once-powerful *APRA*.

Humala and Fujimori, faced with the mathematical reality that neither could win the *segunda vuelta* without appealing to the 44% of the voters who chose the three centrist candidates, began reinventing themselves, backtracking on earlier positions. Humala changed his models in midstream, from Chávez to Brazil's pragmatic leftist former President Lula da Silva. He even imported some of da Silva's advisers to help with his campaign. Among their advice: Start wearing business suits instead of a scary revolutionary red shirt, and promise to honor existing contracts with foreign firms. He did both. He also eschewed his nationalistic anti-U.S rhetoric, calling the United States a "strategic partner" against drug trafficking; he even stopped baiting Chile. He changed his position on barring export of natural gas, and brought former Toledo advisers into his inner circle.

Fujimori, just 36, no longer vowed to pardon her father, and even admitted that "mistakes" were made during his regime. Educated in part at Stony Brook University in New York and married to an American, she brought former New York Mayor Rudolph Giuliani to Peru as an adviser on combating crime.

Both pragmatically pledged to continue the successful free-market economic policies that had given Peru one of Latin America's highest growth rates for years.

Toledo threw his support behind Humala, as did the popular and influential Nobel Laureate Vargas Llosa, who assailed Fujimori's father's regime as "one of the most atrocious dictatorships Peruvians have ever had."

On June 5, 15.3 million Peruvians returned to the polls, 7 million of whom were faced with the unenviable choice of deciding which of two unpalatable candidates had really changed his or her spots more. The outcome:

Humala	7,882,968	51.5%
Fujimori	7,427,005	48.5%

Three days after the election, Humala flew to Brazil to meet with Lula's successor, Dilma Rousseff, as if to show he was serious about following the Brazilian rather than the Venezuelan model.

Populism and Pragmatism

Humala, 49, was sworn in on July 28. He stirred controversy by swearing to uphold the pre-Fujimori constitution of 1979 instead of Fujimori's 1993 constitution. Opposition congressmen jeered.

As prime minister, Humala appointed Salomón Lerner, a prominent businessman and banker and former *APRA* activist. His *Gana Perú* party forged a shaky alliance in Congress with Toledo's *Perú Posible,* constituting a three-seat majority.

The president wasted little time making good on his populist campaign promises. Two months after his inauguration, he signed a new law that requires mining companies to consult with indigenous tribes in advance about planned projects on their lands. Lerner also negotiated the windfall profits tax with the mining companies, which would bring in $1 billion in new revenue over five years.

But in October 2011, Humala found himself faced with local protests, just as

President Ollanta Humala

his two predecessors had. At issue was the huge new Conga gold and copper mine in Cajamarca province, which was to be undertaken by the U.S. firm Newmont Mining Corporation, in conjunction with the Peruvian company Minera Yanacocha, which operates the world's second-largest gold mine. The $4.8 billion Conga mine would be the largest in the country's history, and would bring in $3 billion in revenue over 19 years once it was operational in 2015; half that revenue would go to Cajamarca. But local residents blocked roads to protest the project, which they said would lead to environmental destruction and block access of cattle to water.

Humala found himself on the horns of a dilemma: alienate his core constituency by siding with the mining companies, or risk derailing Peru's brisk economic growth by blocking the project. He had already blocked one $800 million mining project, telling the company it needed more environmental safeguards. The protests continued for two months, finally erupting into violence that left 18 people injured. On December 1, Newmont announced it was suspending the Conga project for the foreseeable future. It also ceased operations at the nearby Yanacocha mine because of the protests.

Still the protests continued. Humala, like his predecessors, declared a state of emergency in December, announcing it in one of his rare, brief, television appearances. A week later, Lerner resigned as prime minister, without giving a reason. He was replaced by Interior minister Oscar Valdéz.

More violence erupted in May 2012 at the Swiss-owned Tintaya copper mine, far to the south in Espinar province. Workers had called for an indefinite strike, and a riot erupted that left two people dead

and about 80 police officers injured. Once again, Humala called a 30-day state of emergency, and the local mayor was arrested for inciting the violence.

Indigenous residents near the open-pit Ananina mine complain they havde experienced health problems, that the liocal environment is being destroyed and that the promised benefits from the state's share of the taxes have not materialized.

Dramatic developments unfolded in the war against the *Sendero Luminoso.* In December 2011, the commander of one of two known branches of the *senderistas,* José (or Florindo) Flores, who goes by the *nom de guerre* "Comrade Artemio," declared in an interview with a non-governmental organization that was picked up by CNN that his group was abandoning armed struggle as a means of achieving its goals. Its political aims remained unchanged, he said, but he declared his willingness to negotiate peace with the government. Evidently the government wasn't interested. On February 9, 2012, Flores was gravely wounded in a firefight in the north-central province of Tocache and arrested. Humala boasted that this *Sendero* arm had been defeated, and his approval rating climbed to 59%.

Apparently in reprisal for Flores' capture, the other branch, about 400 guerrillas commanded by Victor Quispe ("Comrade José") in the southern region of the Valley of the Apurimac and Ene rivers *(VRAE)*, kidnapped 36 gas workers in April 2012 and held them hostage. They demanded Flores' release, $10 million and explosives. Police launched a rescue mission with 1,500 men, which freed the workers but resulted in the deaths of eight policemen. The *senderistas* fled, abandoning their captives. Humala, clad in his army uniform, met with the freed hostages and congratulated the police. But Defense Minister Alberto Otarola and Interior Minister Daniel Lozada resigned because of the mounting public criticism of the operation.

Humala's own boost in popularity after Flores' capture was short-lived. In September 2012, the Mitofsky poll of Mexico put it at 40%, ranking Humala 14th in popularity out of 20 Western Hemisphere leaders.

The *senderistas* killed five more soldiers in an ambush in August 2012, but in September they lost one of their commanders in a battle with security forces.

The organization is apparently split between hardliners and relative "moderates." In a jail-cell interview with *The Economist* in September 2012, Guzmán's girlfriend, Elena Iparraguirre, who is serving a life sentence and was the real-life inspiration for the novel and movie *The Dancer Upstairs,* said she is still devoted to the cause but disavowed knowledge of the renegades who she said were defying Guzmán's orders to shun violence

Peru

and participate in the political system. The *senderistas* have formed a political organization called the Movement for Amnesty and Fundamental Rights *(MOVADEF)*, whose only platform is to free imprisoned *senderistas*. The Humala government has not seemed convinced the *SL* has changed its spots, and the political movement has not been recognized. An indication of *SL's* sincerity may come after several *senderistas* sentenced to 20-year terms went free in 2013.

Recent Developments

Fujimori had more mouth surgery in August 2012. Although he had refused to request a pardon because he said it would be an admission of guilt, in October he relented and his family formally asked Humala for a pardon on health grounds. Humala vacillated for eight months between angering Fujimori's enemies and the families of his victims, or being seen as heartless to a sick, old man. On June 7, 2013, he announced, "Having analyzed the interviews of doctors, having spoken to the minister of justice, I have decided to accept the unanimous recommendation given by the Presidential Pardons Commission, and they have not recommended a pardon. Fujimori is the best-kept prisoner in all of Peru." Humala said he would consider a new request if Fujimori's health worsens.

Fujimori finally got some good news in January 2014 when a judge ruled he could not be tried for crimes against humanity in the case of 2,000 rural women who alleged they had been sterilized without their knowledge or consent during Fujimori's campaign to provide tubal ligations in order to reduce poverty. Even human rights groups acknowledged that 300,000 women had willingly participated.

In October 2012, a court acquitted Montesinos of murder in connection with the summary executions of the terrorists who had seized the Japanese ambassador's residence in 1997. Although the judge acknowledged the suspects had obviously been killed execution-style after they surrendered, there was insufficient evidence linking Montesinos directly to their deaths.

First-term Lima Mayor Susana Villarán won some friends and some powerful enemies by cracking down on corruption and lavish spending by the municipal government. Chief among her critics was former Mayor Luis Castañeda. Her enemies collected enough signatures on a petition to force a recall election in March 2013. She survived it with 53% of the vote.

In January 2014, the International Court of Justice in The Hague finally reached a decision on the maritime claim García had filed against Chile in 2007. By a 10-6 vote,

the ICJ reached what can best be called an arbitrary compromise, granting Peru most of the area it had sought but allowing Chile to retain sovereignty over its fish-rich coastal waters. The Peruvians were happier than the Chileans, but the two countries appear agreeable to work out the arrangements.

In a major blow to *Sendero Luminoso*, a two-year investigation by the police and armed forces led to the arrests of 28 *MOVADEF* operatives on April 10, 2014. Among them were the imprisoned Guzmán's lawyer and Humala's own cousin, guitarist and singer Walter Humala.

A drop in the market prices for some of the metals Peru exports caused a modest slowdown in the economy in 2013, but its GDP growth of 5.1%, down from 6.3% in 2012, was still the second-best in Latin America.

The Mitofsky poll in October 2013 gave Humala an approval rating of just 32%, ranking him 15th among 19 hemispheric leaders. He did little to help himself by withdrawing from the public spotlight. His erstwhile supporters on the left have denounced him as a traitor for following a conservative, pro-U.S. policy, unlike Rafael Correa in neighboring Ecuador.

Meanwhile, protests also erupted against Congress in August 2013 after the different factions attempted to appoint party loyalists to the Supreme Court and other supposedly independent bodies. This time, as has happened in the past year in Brazil, Chile and Paraguay, the middle class participated in the spontaneous demonstrations to express their contempt for what they see as a corrupt system.

In April 2014, Humala cracked down on 40,000 illegal gold miners, who are reportedly contaminating rivers. They were given a deadline to legalize their status, which they ignored.

In a larger case of development versus the environment, in 2013 Peru's Vice Ministry of Intercurality *(VMI)* recognized several indigenous tribes in the Napo-Tigre region of the Amazon rainforest as peoples living in "voluntary isolation" and issued a memo endorsing a plan to create an indigenous reserve to protect them and their cultures. Unfortunately, the tract the *VMI* wants to set aside as a reserve overlaps the concessions granted to foreign oil companies for drilling and extraction, including Spain's Repsol, a British-French consortium and the Vietnamese state oil firm. PetroPeru, the state-owned oil firm that is also involved in exploration, asked the Culture Ministry to quash the *VMI's* memo. The ministry suggested that the *VMI* "rescind" it because of lack of scientific evidence to support it. A newly appointed vice minister, deemed friendlier to the oil companies, rescinded

it in December 2013. The NGO Interethnic Association for the Development of the Rainforest *(AIDESEP)* has appealed that decision to the state ombudsman, but PetroPeru has continued to operate in the proposed reserve in the meantime.

CULTURE: The legacy of the Incas is evident in Peruvian folklore, art, music and architecture. Most of the population is full-blooded Indian today, and Quechua is the first language of millions of Peruvians. Still, the inevitable hybridization with Spanish culture produced something that is uniquely Peruvian. UNESCO has named eight Inca or Spanish colonial attractions as cultural World Heritage Sites, including the city of Cuzco, the colonial section of Lima and the famous ruins of Machu Picchu.

Because Peru, like Mexico (New Spain), was a full-fledged viceroyalty that yielded dazzling amounts of gold and silver, the Spanish crown placed a higher value on this colony than on most. Consequently, a strong creole culture developed and along with it a literary tradition. Peruvian literary activity, however, never matched that of, say, Argentina or Chile. One of the most influential writers of the late 19th and early 20th centuries was Manuel González Prada (1844–1918), a journalist, poet and essayist who labored for reform and influenced later generations of idealistic Peruvian writers.

Many of Peru's best-known writers of the first half of the 20th century found their inspiration in politics, including the poet César Vallejo (1892–1938) and the Marxist essayist José Carlos Mariátegui (1894–1930), who, like González Prada, was an major force in the *aprista* movement. The most acclaimed novelists of that period and later years have all stressed indigenous themes, such as Ciro Alegría (1909–67), Julio Ramón Ribeyro (1929–94) and José María Arguedas (1911–69).

Without question Peru's most prominent contemporary writer is Mario Vargas Llosa (b. 1936). He earned a doctorate in Madrid, and consequently his works are more cosmopolitan. His best-known novel, translated into several languages and the recipient of numerous international garlands, remains *La guerra del fin del mundo* (*The War of the End of the World*) (1981). One of his plays, *La señorita de Tacna* (1981), also has been translated into English and other languages and received favorable reviews when performed on Broadway.

Vargas Llosa was Fujimori's opponent in the 1990 presidential election, and his electoral loss was seen as a victory for Peruvian—and Latin American—literature. His 2000 novel *La fiesta del chivo (The Feast of the Goat)*, which was about the assassination of Dominican dictator Rafael

Leonidas Trujillo in 1961, was made into an English-language film by his cousin, director Luis Llosa (see below). In 2003, he published *El paraíso en la otra esquina (The Way to Paradise)* and in 2006 he published *Las travesuras de una niña mala (The Mischief of a Bad Girl),* his first-ever love story.

Vargas Llosa received both of Spain's most prestigious literary honors, the Prince of Asturias Award for Literature in 1986 and the Miguel de Cervantes Prize in 1994. President Alejandro Toledo garlanded him with the Order of the Sun, Peru's highest honor, in 2001. In 2010, after years of anticipation, Vargas Llosa received the Nobel Prize in Literature, the sixth Latin American writer to be so honored and the first in 20 years. The Nobel committee in Stockholm recognized Varas Llosa for "his cartography of the structures of power and his trenchant images of the individual's resistance, revolt and defeat." He received $1.5 million.

Peruvians are as fanatically devoted to their two native musical styles, *música criolla* and Peruvian waltzes, as Argentines are to the tango. The same is true of the national folk dance, the *marinera,* subject of an annual festival in Ayacucho.

The singer-composer Chabuca Granda (1920–83) conveyed these distinctly Peruvian sounds to audiences throughout Latin America. Her song *La Flor de la Canela* (the cinnamon blossom) is considered an unofficial anthem for the capital city of Lima and her performance of it circulates on the Internet.

A contemporary Peruvian singer who has gained international renown is Susana Baca (b. 1944), who is credited with reviving Afro-Peruvian music. She first achieved recognition abroad with her rendition of Chabuca Granda's song *María Lando.* She has won two of Peru's five Latin Grammys: one in 2002 for Best Folk Album for *Lamento Negro,* which also was nominated for a mainstream Grammy for Best World Music Album; and in 2011 for her collaboration with the Puerto Rican band Calle 13 in the song *Latinoamérica.* In July 2011, newly inaugurated President Ollanta Humala appointed her minister of culture, but she resigned in a Cabinet shakeup after just five months.

Peru's other three Latin Grammys went to singer-songwriter Gian Marco (b. 1970), all for Best Singer-Songwriter Album: *Resucitar* in 2005, *Días Nuevos* in 2011 and *20 Años* in 2012. He was named a UNICEF goodwill ambassador for Peru. His father was Javier Zignago, a well-known singer and composer known by the stage name Joe Danova, and his mother is the singer and actress Regina Alcover.

Peruvian theater, cinema and television still lag behind those of such countries as Mexico and Argentina, though some works and artists have achieved recognition abroad. Peru is producing more of its own *telenovelas,* and in 2005 it released the animated 3-D motion picture, *Piratas de Callao (Pirates of Callao),* produced by Hernán Garrido-Lecca, which was distributed throughout Latin America as well as to the United States and China.

Peruvian cinema also is achieving international acclaim through the talents of director Claudia Llosa (b. 1976), Vargas Llosa's niece. Her 2005 film, *Madeinusa,* was named Best Latin American Movie at both the Málaga (Spain) and Mar del Plata (Argentina) film festivals and was selected for showing at the Sundance Film Festival in the United States, among other international awards. Her second film, *La teta asustada (Milk of Sorrows),* an examination of the psychological impact on Peruvian women of the guerrilla wars of the 1970s and '80s, became the first Peruvian film nominated for the U.S. Academy Award for Best Foreign Film in 2010. It won a total of nine international awards, including the Golden Bear at the 2009 Berlin International Film Festival, the Grand Coral Prize in the Havana Film Festival and Spain's Goya Award for Best Spanish-Language Foreign Film.

Another Peruvian director, Luis Llosa, cousin of both Mario Vargas Llosa and Claudia Llosa, achieved fame in the United States with his English-language films in the 1990s. Among others, he directed Sandra Bullock in *Fire on the Amazon* (1993), Tom Berenger in *Sniper* (1993), Sylvester Stallone and Sharon Stone in *The Specialist* (1994) and Jennifer López in *Anaconda* (1997). In 2005, he brought his cousin's novel *The Feast of the Goat* to the screen; he directed it and co-authored the screenplay with Vargas Llosa. In recent years he has devoted himself primarily to producing or directing *telenovelas,* most recently the popular *Condesa por amor,* produced in Venezuela and filmed in the Dominican Republic.

Peru can claim to be one of the birthplaces of Latin American journalism. Even before independence, the literary journal *Mercurio Peruano* appeared in 1791. The leading contemporary daily, *El Comercio,* (see below) was founded in 1839, losing to Chile's *El Mercurio* by two years the distinction of being Latin America's oldest continuously published newspaper. For most of Peru's troubled history, press freedom either was nonexistent or severely limited. During the peculiar social experimentation of the 1968–80 military regime, the major dailies were expropriated and turned over to various "social organizations," such as teachers and labor unions. The result was a journalistic disaster, and the first act of President Belaúnde when he returned to power in 1980 was to restore the newspapers to their rightful owners. Numerous dailies of stature, plus the usual sleazy tabloids, are published in the capital. A newspaper that has come to rival *El Comercio* in journalistic prestige since the restoration of democracy is the pro-*Aprista La República.* Some dailies also are published in the major provincial capitals. There also is a thriving magazine industry, the highest quality probably being *Caretas* and *Oiga.*

Like the press in most Latin American countries, New York-based freedom House rates the Peruvian press as only "partly free," even since the fall of Fujimori.

Education was neglected in Peru for centuries, which has hampered development. There are now about 60 colleges, universities and technical schools of higher learning. The Greater National University of San Marcos, founded in 1551, is one of the two oldest in the Western Hemisphere. Also prestigious is the Pontifical Catholic University of Peru, established in 1917.

Peruvian cuisine is unique, owing to the great variety of seafood provided by the Humboldt Current and the cornucopia of foodstuffs from tropical and Andean ecospheres. Peruvian restaurants have begun cropping up in major cities in Europe and North America. The best-known Peruvian dish abroad is *ceviche* (also spelled *cebiche*), raw fish marinated in lime juice. Pisco, a potent liquor distilled from grapes, is mixed with lime juice, sugar and egg whites to create the Pisco sour, one of South America's favorite cocktails.

ECONOMY: Extraction and marketing of natural resources from mountain areas and the adjacent sea have long been the cornerstone of the Peruvian economy. Because the arid Pacific shelf and the high Andes restrict agricultural output, recent efforts have been made to open the eastern Andean slopes for farming. Water from the eastern slopes is also being used to irrigate former arid regions.

The ambitious land reform program implemented by the military government of 1968–80 provided for the seizure of virtually all of the nation's large farms and their conversion into huge cooperatives rather than small, unproductive peasant plots. Relying on material incentives (profits were to go to the workers), the program was designed to increase farm output and bring—for the first time—larger numbers of peasants into the national money economy. However, because of poor management and a breakdown in the food distribution system, the land reform program fell far short of expectations.

In 1981, Occidental Petroleum reported that new oil fields had been discovered in Peru's Amazon basin. Peru then reported in 1982 that its proven oil reserves increased to 900 million barrels.

Peru

The inflation rate in 1989 was about 2,800%, creating labor unrest and an economically ruinous strike by the miners. President Alan García began privatizing the nation's industry—the military had taken over more than 150 industries while in power. Peru's foreign debt was about $20 billion. To aid in its slow economic recovery, and under strict austerity requirements, the IMF in 1984 extended loans to the government; however, this was half as much as Peru hoped to receive.

When García demurred on payment of Peru's debts in the late 1980s, the IMF declared Peru ineligible to receive further loans, and all other lenders followed suit. This left the nation on a cash-in-advance status—an economic impossibility in a day and age when spare parts, machinery and manufacturing facilities are so vital to growth. It further meant that no government would honor Peruvian currency; the only substitute was foreign currency deposited in a foreign bank in advance to pay for imports.

This was reversed under President Alberto Fujimori. Peru again became creditworthy and received aid and investment from a number of sources. Approval of the constitution in 1993 boosted available lending sources considerably.

Peru is the world's leading producer of raw coca leaf, from which refined cocaine is made, and second after Colombia in production of cocaine. Chewed by the Indians for millennia as a mild anesthetic to allay hunger, coca thrives in the remote Andean valleys. Illegal coca exports once accounted for an estimate d $1 billion a year. But in 1996, Fujimori ordered his air force to begin shooting down planes crossing the border that refused to identify themselves. Total coca acreage that year dropped 18% as peasants accepted a government plan, backed by $45 million in U.S. aid, that provided them with incentives to switch to such alternative crops as coffee, cocoa, yucca and peanuts.

Yucay Sacred Valley

Photo by Susan L. Thompson

Fujimori's much-touted privatization plan, his conquest of hyperinflation and his successful campaign to lure more foreign investors to Peru, received high marks in international financial circles, but they did little to alleviate Peru's grinding poverty. With the modernization that inevitably comes with privatization, industrial jobs were cut by the thousands. The streamlining of the bloated bureaucracy threw middle-class Peruvians out of work as well. The construction boom was concentrated in affluent sections of Lima, with little or no trickle-down effect. Meanwhile, the elimination of government subsidies drove up utility prices, which hit the poor the hardest.

Figures for real GDP were discouraging for several years. From a peak of $65.2 billion in 1997, which was a robust 7% growth from 1996, real GDP dropped to $51.6 billion in 1999. Per capita income also declined, from $2,675 in 1997 to $2,074 in 2001.

Despite the political uncertainty in 2000, real GDP grew by 3.1%, but it slowed to 0.6% in 2001, apparently because foreign investors held back to see what would happen when the dust from Fujimori's fall had settled.

Fujimori's successor, Alejandro Toledo, had a doctorate in economics from Stanford and was once a World Bank official. He was elected on a moderately leftist platform, but he surrounded himself with a retinue of U.S.-trained economists like himself, not unlike the "Chicago Boys" in Chile during the Pinochet years.

The new team had cause for boasting. Peru's GDP growth for 2002 was 5.2%, the highest in Latin America, while inflation was only about 1.2%. Growth was 3.8% in 2003 and 5.07% in 2004; only Chile and Argentina recorded faster growth. For 2005 it was even higher, 6.7%, ahead of Chile and behind only Argentina and the Dominican Republic.

García made a comeback in the 2006 election, but disavowed his fiery populism and pragmatically continued Toledo's policies. As a result, Peru's economy continued to boom, growing 7.6% in 2006, 8.9% in 2007 and 9.8% in 2008. Despite the global recession, it still showed growth of 0.9% in 2009, compared to losses recorded by most Latin American countries. It bounced back to 8.8% in 2010, second-fastest in Latin America. It slowed to 6.9% in 2011, still above the regional average, and was still a respectable 6% in 2012, President Ollanta Humala's first full year in office, the second-fastest in Latin America. It slowed to 5.1% in 2013, still the fourth-fastest.

Peru was awash with good economic news in 2005. Argentina, Brazil, Chile and Uruguay announced plans to begin buying $2.5 billion worth of gas from its new *Mercosur* partner, via a new pipeline

to be built to Chile. Peru has estimated gas reserves of 13 trillion cubic feet in its Camisea field in the Amazon jungle in the south.

Also, the U.S. oil company Petro-Tech announced it had discovered an offshore oil field containing 10–50 million barrels of light crude, the largest discovery in Peru in 30 years. It announced another, larger discovery in 2008. The Spanish oil and gas company Repsol YPF announced discovery of a smaller but onshore field in the Amazon jungle in the north that contains 70 million barrels of heavy crude, which is more difficult to refine than light crude.

Yet, Peru's estimated oil reserves have dwindled to 532.7 million barrels. It produced 152,700 barrels per day in 2011 and only 60,000 in 2012, becoming a net importer.

It has proven natural gas reserves of 345.5 billion cubic meters and it was expected to become self-sufficient and even begin exporting.

Much of the credit for the recent boom goes to the mining sector, which remains Peru's greatest export earner, accounting for 62% in 2006 and remains about the same today. Peru ranked third in the world in zinc production in 2013 with 1.29 million tons; third in copper production in 2013 with 1.3 million tons; third in silver production in 2013, behind Mexico and China, with 3,500 tons; fourth in lead in 2013 with 250,000 tons; and fifth in gold in 2013, with 150 metric tons. Output for some of these metals and Peru's world rankings have begun declining, but high world market prices for these metals remain a godsend for the economy. Peru's copper production was projected to double by 2015.

Another economic activity that shows enormous potential is increased cultivation of sugar cane to produce ethanol for export. In 2006, it was estimated that private investors would be adding 25,000 acres of new sugar cultivation per year. Each acre could produce 650 gallons (2,470 liters) per planting cycle. The only ethanol operation already on line is the $210 million Caña Brava plant in Piura, which opened in 2009. The company owns 6,000 hectares (13,200 acres) and produces 350,000 liters per day. A Spanish company was building a $90 million ethanol plant. A Texas firm, Maple Energy, invested $254 million in 26,200 acres of sugar cane and a distillery to produce 130 million liters of ethanol annually, all for export. It was expected to begin production in the second half of 2011, but delays pushed it back to March 2012. In 2011, the company announced its ethanol would cost $1.42 per gallon. Ethanol production for 2013 was expected to be 240 million liters, a 9% increase over 2012, of which 135 million were for export, a 7% increase. The Netherlands accounts for 54% of the exports.

In 2011, the Peruvian Congress mandated that gasoline must contain 7% ethanol, later raised to 7.8%, while diesel fuel must contain 5% biodiesel.

Unemployment fell from 3.9% in 2012 to 3.6% in 2013. Inflation has see-sawed, from 1.2% in 2004 to 6.7% in 2008, to 1.5% in 2010, to 2.9% in 2013.

Exports increased by about a third in 2004, one of the highest increases in the world, and by 2006 Peru had an $8.8 billion balance of payments surplus. But in 2013, exports plummeted 9.1%, from $45.64 billion to $41.48 billion, which slowed the boom considerably.

Critics on the left complained that the impressive economic growth has not trickled down to the poor. However, the poverty rate under Toledo declined from 54% to 44.5% of the population by 2006. Under García, it reportedly dropped to 35% in 2009 and 31.3% in 2010, which failed to boost his popularity any more than it had Toledo's. By 2012, under Humala, it was down to 25.8%.

In 1998, Peru became a member of the Asia-Pacific Economic Cooperation (APEC), composed of countries around the Pacific Rim, which is designed to foster trade among its members. Peru hosted the 2008 APEC summit.

Peru signed a free-trade agreement (FTA) in 2003 with the *Mercosur* trade bloc (Argentina, Brazil, Paraguay and Uruguay), with tariff barriers to be gradually eliminated over a period of 13 years. In 2005, it signed a FTA with the United States, one with Chile in 2006 and one with China in 2008 (see History). China eclipsed the United States in 2011 as the largest buyer of Peruvian exports, 15.2%, compared with 12.7% for the United States. The United States still accounted for 19.5% of imports, China close behind with 16.6%. The United States is still the largest source of imports, with 24.6% in 2012, compared with 14% for China.

FTAs entered into force with Canada in 2009; South Korea in 2011; Mexico, Japan, and Panama in 2012; and Costa Rica and the European Union in 2013.

With the reduction in terrorism, Peru's tourism industry also is booming, rising from 1.8 million visitors in 2006 to 2.3 million in 2010, 2,598,000 in 2011, 2,846,000 in 2012 and 3,160,000 in 2013. Tourism brought in $3.84 billion in foreign exchange in 2013, accounting for 1.8% of GDP. The tourism industry employed 824,000 people in 2011, 10.8% of the workforce. Much of Peru's popularity as a tourist destination is because of ancient Inca sites like Cuzco and Machu Picchu, but ecotourism to the Amazon rainforest is also growing in popularity. Huascarán and Manú national parks are among UNESCO's natural World Heritage Sites. President Humala created a new tourism ministry.

THE FUTURE: Peru has had one of Latin America's fastest GDP growth rates for more than a decade. Even with the 2008-09 recession, the economy still grew somewhat, while those of most other Latin American nations shrank. Yet, Peruvians reviled both Presidents Alejandro Toledo and his successor, Alan García, who presided over this robust growth. Toledo's approval rating bottomed out at 9%; García's was 26% before leaving office. This robust economic growth has continued under Humala. In 2011, 2012 and 2013, GDP growth was the second-fastest in Latin America.

Yet, Humala saw his approval rating plummet from 80% in 2011 to 32% in October 2013; only three Latin American presidents and Canadian Prime Minister Stephen Harper were less popular. In March 2014, an *El Comercio* poll put it at 25%.

If this seems incongruous, it is. Why, then, does it happen? In large part because the expanding economy has still not trickled down to benefit the impoverished masses; 25.8% of the population still lived below the poverty line in 2012, which is admittedly a dramatic drop from 49% in 2005. But also, Peruvians are notoriously impatient for results. In *The Economist's* annual *Latinobarómetro* survey, the percentage of Peruvians who believe democracy is preferable to any other form of government dropped from 63% in 1996 to just 40% in 2005, in the midst of the boom. By 2010, it was back up to 61%. It was 59% in 2011, one point above the regional average, and 56% in 2013.

In 1996, 13% agreed with the statement that authoritarianism is acceptable under certain circumstances; by 2008, it had risen to 20%. Could they have been nostalgic about Alberto Fujimori? It was 16% in 2013. Only about 22% of Peruvians said in 2013 they were satisfied with the way democracy works in their country. The middle-class revolt against corruption in August 2013 was a symptom of this disgust.

It must be remembered that it was García's wretched performance that led desperate Peruvians to elect Fujimori in the first place in 1990. But in 1990 the economy under García was a shambles, while it was booming when he left office in 2011.

Voters, by a narrow margin in the 2011 runoff, chose the left-leaning Humala over Fujimori's daughter, Keiko. He has walked a tightrope for the past three years, trying to spread some of Peru's newfound wealth to those among his core constituency on the left without killing—or at least alienating—the geese that have been laying these golden eggs, most notably foreign mining and oil companies. Gone is his fire-breathing anti-U.S., pro-Chávez rhetoric. In its place is a leopard with new spots, akin to Brazil's pragmatic leftist Lula da Silva, who effected badly needed social reform and income redistribution without derailing the booming economy.

Humala, now three fifths of the way through his term, has already concluded free-trade agreements on his watch with South Korea, China, Mexico and Panama. That is encouraging, but his country is badly in need of education reform and greater social equality.

If he proves Peru's latest disillusionment, a new face to watch is the politically independent, center-left mayor of Lima, Susana Villagrán, who in March 2013 survived a recall election forced by her enemies with 53% of the vote. Her no-nonsense approach to curbing corruption and government waste in the huge capital city may put her in the national spotlight when the 2016 presidential election rolls around.

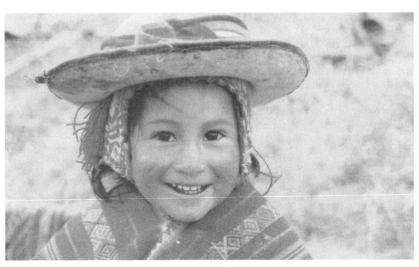

An Andean girl in traditional garb

Suriname

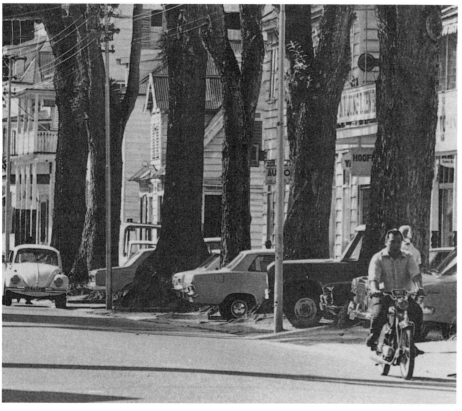

Street scene in the old section of Paramaribo

Area: 63,251square miles (162,820 km²).
Population: 573,311 (2014 est.)
Capital City: Paramaribo (Pop. 224,000, est.).
Climate: Rainy, hot and humid.
Neighboring Countries: Guyana (West); French Guiana (Southeast); Brazil (South).
Official Language: Dutch.
Other Principal Tongues: English, Spanish, Hindi, Javanese, Chinese and a local pidgin dialect called alternately *Sranan Tongo, Taki-Taki* or *Surinamese.*
Ethnic Background: Hindustani, 37%; creole (a person of mixed African and other ancestry) 31%; Asian, 15.3%; Bush Negro, 10.3%; Amerindian 2.6%; European and other, 3.8%. Figures are approximate.
Principal Religions: Hinduism, Roman Catholic Christianity, Islam, Protestant, Christianity.
Chief Commercial Products: Refined aluminum ore, bauxite, aluminum, timber, rice, sugar, shrimp and citrus fruits.
Currency: Suriname Guilder.
Gross Domestic Product: U.S. $5.094 billion in 2013, est. ($8,837 per capita, official exchange rate)
Former Colonial Status: English Colony (1652–67); Dutch Colony (1667–1799); English-controlled (1799–1815); colony of the Netherlands (1815–1948); self-governing component of the Dutch Realm (1948–75).

Independence Date: November 25, 1975.
Chief of State: Desiré Delano "Dési" Bouterse (b. October 13, 1945), president (since August 12, 2010).
National Flag: Two green horizontal stripes, top and bottom, red horizontal stripe in the center, divided from the green by narrow white stripes; a gold five-pointed star is centered in the red stripe.

Separated from neighboring Guyana and French Guiana by large rivers, Suriname lies on the northeast coast of South America. Its 230-mile coastline is rather flat, a strip of marshy land lying mostly below sea level, which needs a series of dikes and canals to hold off the encroaching waters of the Atlantic Ocean. Along this fertile coast and stretching back about 50 of its 300 miles an inland extension is found where about 90% of the country's population lives.

Back from the coastal area, the land turns gradually into a grassland, becoming hilly and then densely forested with some 2,000 varieties of trees, 90% of the land area. This is a broad plateau land that reaches its highest point in the Wilhelmina Mountains. The land then dips down into the dense growth of the tropical rain forest where there are found hundreds of varieties of jungle birds, howler monkeys and all manner of wildlife typical to Brazil. In

the interior is the 600-square-mile W.J. van Blommestein Meer (lake), which provides hydroelectric power for the bauxite industry located downriver.

HISTORY: Although in 1499 the Spanish touched along the coast of what is now Suriname, no attempt at colonization was made. European explorers generally ignored the entire region—the land was not inviting and there were not wealthy native empires to subjugate or loot for the motherlands. Toward the close of the 16th century, the Dutch appeared on the coast, but the first large-scale colonization efforts were made in the early 1650s by the English governor of Barbados, who became the region's first governor. These English colonists established successful sugarcane plantations.

In 1667 the Dutch received Suriname from the English in exchange for the colony of New Netherlands (now New York). Early in the 1680s, workers were brought from Africa to work in the fields since there were few local natives.

The territory again fell to the British during the Napoleonic Wars (1799–1815); a series of agreements between the three powers established the whole of Guiana, as it was then called, into British Guiana (now Guyana), Dutch Guiana (now Suriname) and French Guiana. The latter of these later became infamous for its offshore penal colony, Devil's Island.

The Netherlands emancipated the slaves in 1863 and many of them settled on small farms to cultivate their own produce. This created an immediate and critical labor shortage, which caused the Dutch to import cheap labor from India in the 1870s and from Java in the 1880s.

The territory was slow to develop any political awareness, but since World War II, Far Eastern groups have become increasingly insistent on playing a greater role in the destiny of the land in which they live. This has created a bitter rivalry between the largely agricultural creoles and the prosperous, business-oriented East Indians. The colony became a self-governing component of the Netherlands in 1948 and adopted the name Suriname. After 1950 it controlled its affairs with the exception of defense and foreign relations.

Border clashes between Suriname and the soon-to-be independent British Guiana (Guyana) occurred in 1970. Early in 1973, serious unrest erupted when the government refused to pay increased wages to trade union members. A bloody strike lasted for more than a month before order was restored.

Elections in 1973 for the Legislative Assembly resulted in a victory for an alliance of parties favoring independence. Known as the National Party Coalition (of which the strongest force is the National Party), it gained 13 seats. The Progressive Reform Party won three; this victory by the black-dominated National Party ended a long period of political control by a coalition of East Indians and Chinese.

With the National Party Coalition victory, the colony moved a step closer to independence. Although the Dutch appeared anxious to leave, the large East Indian (Hindustani) population feared that independence would bring serious racial problems similar to those that erupted in neighboring Guyana. The specter of violence soon sparked a mass migration to the Netherlands as independence approached. Nearly a quarter of the population (140,000) fled Suriname.

Despite the damaging exodus, Suriname gained full independence after 308 years of colonial rule on November 25, 1975; the Netherlands agreed to help the new nation adjust to its status by giving it $100 million a year for the next decade—one of the most generous foreign aid programs on a per capita basis in history.

The new minister-president, Henck Arron, urged the nation's former residents to return. The appeal was sincere, as most of those who left were educated and skilled workers; their departure created a severe "brain-drain" for the new nation.

The principal political-economic controversy was whether the aluminum industry should be nationalized or remain in private hands, thus encouraging additional foreign investment? Although Arron's regime was initially leftist, it refrained from nationalization. Further complicating the political scene were ethnic differences and fears. The East Indian and Asiatic communities feared a black-dominated, oppressive regime.

The Bouterse Regime

Arron's policies gradually moderated and relative tranquility prevailed. But economic stability was in reality based on the $100 million annual Dutch subsidy; vital aluminum production was steadily declining. On February 25, 1980, non-commissioned officers ousted the government when it refused to allow them to form a Dutch-style military union. A nine-member National Revolutionary Council (RNC) was formed and backed the election of a government headed by Chin-A-Sen. The military, however, retained actual power; Lieutenant Colonel Desiré "Dési" Bouterse emerged as its leader.

On December 8, 1982, there was an attempted right-wing coup that led to assassinations of two military and 13 civilian opponents of Bouterse. This "December Massacre" remains controversial to this day and is one of Bouterse's lingering political liabilities.

The Dutch suspended aid and conditions rapidly worsened. Bouterse enlarged the military and conditions became extremely tense. He established close relations with Cuba, to the extent that Cuba was viewed as a threat. The government was largely incompetent and inefficient. The "Cuban connection" was brief, ending after the United States invaded Grenada in 1983 (see Grenada).

Economically smarting because of the withdrawal of Dutch aid and lower world prices for aluminum products, Suriname announced a plan for "a return to democracy" in 1984. A 31-member National Assembly consisting of 14 military officers, 11 trade unionists and six from the private sector were to draft a new constitution. The move did not satisfy the Dutch. Bouterse launched a mass political movement, *Stanvaaste*, in a move apparently intended to dominate any future democratically elected administration.

A U.N. report released in 1985 accused the military of involvement in political murders and "suicides."

In 1986, Ronnie Brunswijk (*Bruns*-veek) a Maroon (a descendant of escaped slaves) and former army sergeant, capitalized on the discontent of his people, about 50,000 strong, over the idea of being resettled in towns. They were used to living deep in the interior jungle, speaking their own language. The government had controlled little outside the capital. A group called the Jungle Commando began an armed resistance. The United Nations condemned the tactics of both sides.

Beset with this internal revolt in the interior and pressures from Washington, Bouterse called for elections to an Assem-

Suriname

Lt. Col. Dési Bouterse

bly to be held in November 1987. Balloting was enthusiastic and the National Front for Democracy and Development, a coalition of three ethnic groups, won 41 of the 51 seats. It elected Ramsewak Shankar president for a five-year term in early 1988. Actual power, however, remained with Bouterse and the 7,000-man military until moves got underway to pass control to the civilian government. It was unable, however, to militarily defeat Brunswijk and his followers.

The Dutch, denying aid under the 1975 treaty, continued to exert pressure on Suriname to settle its internal rivalries. Finally, the two factions reached a vague but written agreement for a truce in 1988. Bouterse alleged that the negotiations failed to end the rebellion. Many Maroons had fled to French Guiana to escape the conflict. The Dutch restored aid in generous amounts, but not enough to suit some Surinamese, particularly the military.

The Maroons began returning after assurances that the army would not occupy their traditional territories in the interior. Brunswijk entered Paramaribo in March 1990 under a flag of truce. Bouterse had the army arrest him. This was when the extent of Brunswijk's power (or lack thereof) was felt first-hand.

The following evening, all electrical power in Paramaribo was out; this included vitally needed sources to process aluminum. The Jungle Commando force announced that power would stay off until its leader was freed. President Ramsewak Shankar *ordered* Bouterse to release Brunswijk. After a few hours, Bouterse grudgingly did so. Power was quickly restored.

In 1990, an investigation revealed Suriname was an important link in the Colombia-to-Europe cocaine traffic; both Bouterse and Brunswijk were accused of being heavily involved. When the drugs started

reaching the Netherlands, the Dutch brought pressure, but Bouterse simply threw out President Shankar in a bloodless coup on Christmas Eve 1990 that was labeled the "Telephone Coup" because the president was told over the telephone to resign. The Dutch *again* suspended their aid.

Venetiaan and Wijdenbosch

Elections in 1991 resulted in the coalition selection of Runaldo Venetiaan, former education minister, as president, after five months of wheeling and dealing. Continued Dutch pressure brought about Bouterse's resignation as commander-in-chief in 1992. As the government gained control over the military, it was able in 1992 to negotiate with the Surinamese Liberation Army (Maroon) and *Tucayana Amazonica* (native Indian) rebel movements, leading to a cease-fire in 1992.

Even though Venetiaan's coalition was successful in elections held in May 1996, Bou-terse's National Democratic Party *(NDP)* was the single most popular party.

Not unexpectedly, in elections held in September 1996, Jules Wijdenbosch of the *NDP* was elected president. Venetiaan's New Front had won 24 of the 51 seats in the National Assembly in May general elections, falling short of the two-thirds majority needed to form a government. Thus, the choice for president fell to the United People's Conference (comprising members of the National Assembly and regional and district councils). By a vote of 438–407, Wijdenbosch won.

Wijdenbosch's *NDP* and its coalition partner, the Movement of Freedom and Democracy (*BVD*), initially held a majority of 29 seats in the National Assembly, but the coalition began showing signs of

Former President Jules Wijdenbosch

Former President Runaldo Venetiaan

strain in 1997 when the president fired Finance Minister Motilal Mungra of the *BVD* for criticizing government policy. The schism became more pronounced when Bouterse was charged in absentia in the Netherlands with drug smuggling and the Wijdenbosch government adopted an aggressive response toward the mother country, which still provided Suriname with $65 million a year in aid.

In 1998, four of the five members of the *BVD* abandoned the coalition to protest what they deemed the government's inclination toward dictatorship and for failing to consult with the *BVD* members on policy matters.

Bouterse, meanwhile, now a lumber executive, denied the Dutch charges that he had smuggled 1.3 tons of cocaine into Europe and had ties to Colombian cartels. He announced in 1997 that he was considering running for president in 2001 and that he wanted to wean Suriname away from Dutch aid.

Bouterse was placed on the Interpol wanted list, and he was arrested in Trinidad in July 1998. But that country rejected a Dutch extradition request, and Bouterse returned to Suriname, where he continued to serve in Wijdenbosch's government with the euphemistic title of "presidential aide." In 1999, a court in The Hague issued a summons for Bouterse to appear for trial in March, but he ignored the order; not even his attorney appeared to offer a defense. Apparently to appease the Dutch, whose aid was still welcome, Wijdenbosch fired Bouterse. The Dutch court then began trying Bouterse in absentia. He was convicted, sentenced to 16 years in prison and fined the equivalent of $2.17 million.

To compound Bouterse's legal problems, in 1999 the families of the 15 dissidents slain in the 1982 "December Massacre" coup attempt filed a complaint with an Amsterdam court because Dutch prosecutors had not investigated the deaths. In 2000, a Dutch appeals court ruled that prosecutors did have jurisdiction to investigate on the grounds that the 1982 killings constituted crimes against humanity.

Bouterse then faced an international arrest warrant, much as did Chile's former strongman Augusto Pinochet, but in 2001 the Netherlands High Court dismissed the suit on the grounds that Dutch courts have no jurisdiction over Suriname and because Bouterse is neither a Dutch citizen nor a resident of the Netherlands. The court also ruled that Bouterse could not be tried under a U.N. convention against torture that went into effect six years after the 1982 incident. However, in 2004 a Surinamese prosecutor announced that he would try Bouterse and 25 others for murder in the 15 deaths.

In May 1999, violent street protests erupted against Wijdenbosch's handling of the economy, especially drastic price increases and a precipitous drop in the exchange rate of the guilder. The opposition mustered 27 votes in the 51-seat National Assembly for a no-confidence motion against the president. Wijdenbosch refused to resign, and the constitution is ambiguous as to whether he could be removed. The consensus was that the National Assembly could call new elections by a two-thirds vote, or 34 members; Wijdenbosch's *NDP* had been reduced by defections to 16 seats, not quite enough to block the effort. In an attempt to defuse the move to unseat him, Wijdenbosch announced he would call for new elections no later than May 2000, a year ahead of schedule.

Efforts by the opposition to replace Wijdenbosch with an interim president failed, so Wijdenbosch limped along as a lame-duck president for a full year.

The May 25, 2000, election, in which 23 parties competed and 72% of the 265,000 registered voters participated, was a stinging rebuke both to him and to Bouterse. The New Front of former President Venetiaan won 33 of the 51 Assembly seats, one short of the two thirds needed to name a new president outright. Bouterse's Millennium Combination was second with 10 seats, while Wijdenbosch's Democratic National Platform 2000 won only three.

Venetiaan was inaugurated for a five-year term on August 12, 2000. He immediately inherited an international crisis from Wijdenbosch. The outgoing government had ordered a Canadian offshore oil rig towed from the disputed zone with Guyana at the mouth of the Corantijn River. Both countries moved troops to the area, as diplomats negotiated a peaceful solution. The dispute lingered for seven years, until a U.N. commission awarded most of the disputed area to Guyana (see Guyana).

Boats tied up on the banks of the river at Paramaribo

Paramaribo's *De West*, March 28, 1990: "Military authority criticizes Government's position." Insert shows Ronnie Brunswijk.

Suriname

Internally, the issue of land rights for the black Maroons and indigenous Indian tribes (see Culture) resurfaced in 2004. A legal representative of the Association of Village Leaders of Suriname appeared at a meeting of the Permanent U.N. Forum on Indigenous Issues in New York to complain that mining operations had encroached upon the traditional lands of the Maroons and Indians. She said the government had done little to implement the guarantees of the 1992 peace agreement that ended the rebellion.

Despite the murder charges pending against him for the 1982 massacre and his Dutch conviction for cocaine smuggling, Bouterse announced that he was standing for president again in the general elections of May 25, 2005, as the standard bearer of the *NDP*. Venetiaan coyly avoided saying whether he would seek re-election. In the voting, Venetiaan's New Front again emerged with the most seats, 24, nine fewer than before and two short of a simple majority, much less the two-thirds majority needed to elect the president. Bouterse's *NDP* jumped from seven to 15 seats, while Wijdenbosch's latest vehicle, the People's Alliance for Development, won only six. A new political organization representing the ethnic Maroons, the A-Combination, led by Bouterse's old nemesis Ronnie Brunswijk, won five seats and quickly agreed to join the New Front in a coalition. That still left the New Front five seats short of what it needed to elect a president, whether Venetiaan or someone else. Venetiaan had little choice but to swallow his pride and ask Bouterse to join his coalition; Bouterse refused.

Before the Assembly met to vote, Bouterse withdrew his name and the *NDP* named his running mate, Rabin Parmessar, as its candidate. As expected, no candidate received the needed 34 votes, so the choice fell once again to the 895-member United People's Conference as it did in 1996. Venetiaan was re-elected with a majority of 62.9% on August 3 and was inaugurated on August 12, 2005.

The long-delayed prosecution of Bouterse and others in the "December Massacre" began more or less in earnest in November 2007, when a court-martial subpoenaed him and 25 others. After months of pretrial wrangling, before a court that met only once a month, the actual trial began in April 2008. Several military witnesses have implicated Bouterse, then 64, in the massacre, but he continued to deny it. The trial was stopped for a time, then resumed in November 2009 after six witnesses were brought from the Netherlands.

Bouterse's Stunning Comeback

As the May 25, 2010, National Assembly elections approached, Venetiaan announced he would not stand for a fourth term. Bouterse's *NDP* entered into an alliance with smaller parties called the Mega Combination, and this time he stood himself for president. Venetiaan's New Front for Democracy and Development backed Justice Minister Chandrikapersad Santokhi. Bouterse campaigned vigorously for president, sometimes in a Ché Guevara T-shirt, later in a business suit, even as his trial continued slowly, and which he refused to attend. Astonishingly, polls showed Bouterse's coaltion with a strong plurality, but not a majority. Voter turnout was 73.2%. The results:

Mega			
Combination	95,543	40.2%	23 seats
New Front	75,190	31.65%	14 seats
People's			
Alliance	30,844	13.0%	6 seats
PDDU	12,085	5.1%	1 seat
A-Combination	11,176	4.7%	7 seats

Frantic jockeying began by both the pro- and anti-Bouterse forces to secure the necessary two-thirds majority of 34 of the 51 seats. Venetiaan refused to cut a deal with Bourtese, who then struck an unlikely deal with his old enemy in the civil war, Ronnie Brunswijk of the Maroon A-Combination, which quickly fell apart over how many cabinet seats it would receive. They eventually reached an accord. Ironically, Bouterse and Brunswijk have a common bond: Like Bouterse, Brunswijk is an international fugitive, wanted on drug trafficking charges.

That left former President Wijdenbosch as the kingmaker. His dislike for Venetiaan proved greater than his dislike for Bouterse. His People's Alliance formed a bloc with the A-Combination to negotiate jointly for their 13 seats. On July 19, the world was stunned by the news that the former dictator, fugitive drug trafficker and alleged human rights violator had returned to power in a democratic election, 36–15. Bouterse, then 64, was sworn in on August 12.

The Netherlands quickly suspended its security assistance to Suriname, and although it did not break diplomatic relations, the Dutch foreign minister said Bouterse would not be welcome in the Netherlands "unless it is to serve his prison sentence."

Unlike some rehabilitated former strongmen who regain political power, Bouterse has shown no contrition for his past actions, real or alleged. Quite the contrary, he has seemed proud of his checkered past. His present is just as checkered. He has given his wife a salary of $4,000 a month as first lady, and he appointed his 38-year-old son, Dino, who served a three-year prison term for heading a cocaine

President Dési Bouterse

and weapons ring, as commander of a new counter-terrorism unit. He declared February 25, 2011, the 31st anniversary of his 1980 coup, as a national holiday, calling it a day of "liberation and renewal." In December 2011, he pardoned his foster son, Romano Meriba, who had been sentenced to 15 years in 2005 for the robbery and murder of a store clerk. (Meriba was arrested again in March 2012 for assaulting a police officer.)

The president has warily traveled abroad under his diplomatic immunity, including to Brazil and to address the U.N. General Assembly in New York. But his election has given Suriname the reputation, once again, as an outlaw nation. *Time* magazine labeled him "the dictator who came in from the cold." In early 2011, the Netherlands and the U.S. State Department both alleged that Bouterse is still complicit in drug trafficking, while Wikileaks divulged evidence that he had been at least through 2006. Interpol suspended its warrant while Bouterse is in office.

In 2011, a Wikileaks cable stated that Bouterse had enjoyed a business relationship before 2006 with notorious Guyanese drug trafficker Roger Khan.

Bouterse's trial for the December Massacre dragged on for two more years. Then, on April 5, 2012, the National Assembly voted 28–12 to grant Bouterse immunity for any crimes he may have committed during his earlier regime, effectively halting the trial. Netherlands Prime Minister Mark Rutte recalled his ambassador and said it was "totally unacceptable" to stop the trial.

Recent Developments

Boutersi assumed the rotating presidency of the Union of South American Nations (*UNASUR*) and hosted the *UNASUR*

Suriname

summit in Paramaribo August 30-31, 2013. Whatever international respectability Bouterse might have won from the event was shattered when the news broke during the summit that his prodigal son Dino had been arrested in Panama on a U.S. warrant for cocaine and weapons trafficking—again. Dino Bouterse was taken to New York, where he pleaded not guilty in federal court. In November, the U.S. district attorney in Manhattan announced that he was also being charged with aiding a terrorist organization, alleging that he conspired to provide what he called "toys," meaning weapons, to the Lebanese-based Shi'a terrorist group Hezbollah, to be used to attack the United States. He was sentenced to a 16-year prison term in March 2015.

The alleged sins of the son were visited on his father, who came under increasing pressure to resign. He narrowly survived a no-confidence vote in November. The Netherlands, which still wants Dési Bouterse, asked South Africa if it would detain him when he attended the funeral of Nelson Mandela in December, but withdrew the request because of Bouterse's immunity as a visiting head of state.

CULTURE: The majority of the people are found along the coastal, agricultural zone. Of this group, about a third live in the capital and chief port of Paramaribo, a picturesque city with palm-lined streets and colorful market areas. The Historic Inner Center of Paramaribo is one of UNESCO's cultural World Heritage Sites.

The creole population is well represented in the civil service and mining industries; the East Indians tend to concentrate in commerce and farming activities. There are also about 12,000 native Indians in the Arawak, Carib, Trio and Wayana tribes. There are about 50,000 Surinamese descended from African slaves, called Maroons, who prefer to live in the interior.

Dutch is the official language, and there is a literacy rate of about 80%. Although most students of higher education go to the Netherlands, there are law and medical faculties at Anton de Kom University in Paramaribo. Suriname boasts a cultural center, museums, active theatrical groups, a well-known philharmonic orchestra and a modern sports stadium.

The only institution of higher learning is the Anton de Kom University of Suriname, founded in 1968.

Two newspapers circulate nationally: *Die West* and *De Ware Tijd*.

ECONOMY: Alumina, aluminum and bauxite, the ore of aluminum, account for as much as 85% of the country's exports and some 25% of its tax revenues. The leading bauxite firm is U.S.-owned

Suralco, a subsidiary of Alcoa. Although some bauxite is processed locally, aluminum is now shipped in a finished or semi-finished state to the United States. Panaram, the center of the vital industry, receives its hydroelectric power from Lake van Blommestein.

A Canadian company, Iamgold Corp., obtained rights in 2006 to operate the Gros Rosabel gold mine, which produced 385,000 ounces of gold in 2011, worth about $578 million that year, or almost 15% of GDP. In 2013, the National Assembly increased the state's percentage in the enterprise from 10% to 30%.

Offshore and onshore petroleum deposits have tremendous economic potential; onshore deposits in the Guyana Plateau are estimated at 79 billion barrels. In 2004, the state-owned oil firm, Staatsolie, was pumping 12,000 barrels a day from the Tambaredjo Field, and its refinery capacity is 7,000 bpd, but it was investing $350 million to expand production to 18,000 bpd by 2012 and to expand refinery capacity. Current production of about 14,500 bpd falls slightly short of domestic demands. In 2004, it signed contracts with Spanish and Danish firms to explore for oil in a 7,200-square-mile tract bordering the Tambaredjo Field, which could allow Suriname to become a net exporter. The resolution of the maritime dispute with Guyana (see History) could benefit both nations.

There are few roads; rivers and aircraft provide most of the transportation. The majority of the people are employed in agriculture. The major cash crops are timber, citrus fruits, sugarcane, bananas and corn. Rice is the chief crop and food staple, accounting for half of all land under cultivation and is the source of valuable export income. Major problems facing the economy are high inflation and unemployment. The government is increasing its economic ties with Colombia, Venezuela and Brazil; with the aid of Venezuela it is hoped that new bauxite mines can be developed in the southern part of the country.

In 2001, the economy grew by a sluggish 1.9%. In 2003, growth was a robust 13.2%, which tapered off to 6.2% in 2004 and 4.8% in 2006. It rose slightly to 5.3% in 2007 and 6% in 2008. Much of the growth was attributed to the high world market price for gold, bauxite and alumina, but the global recession caused GDP to shrink by –2.3% in 2009. It has since grown steadily by about the hemispheric average: 4.7% in 2011 and 2013, and 4.8% in 2012.

Unemployment has been steady at about 9% for the past several years. In 2002, the most recent year available, 70% lived below the poverty line despite a relatively high per capita income.

Suriname's leading trading partners are the U.S., which buys 24% of its exports;

Canada, which buys 19.5%; and Belgium, which accounts for 19%. The U.S. is the source of 26% of imports and the Netherlands, 16%.

Tourism remains minuscule, with 266,000 tourist arrivals recorded in 2007, dropping to 205,000 in 2010. It has since grown, to 220,000 in 2011 and 240,000 in 2012, an increasing number of them for ecotourism. The Central Suriname Nature Reserve is one of UNESCO's natural World Heritage Sites.

In 2011, President Dési Bouterse drastically devalued the guilder by 20% and raised taxes.

THE FUTURE: The shocking return to power of Dési Bouterse in 2010 bodes ill for Suriname, giving it a reputation as an outlaw nation as it was in the 1980s when Bouterse ruled as dictator. The intriguing thing about his party winning a plurality of 40% of the popular vote is that much of his support seemed to come from younger voters, who cannot remember his years of misrule.

Thanks to the pardon granted him by the National Assembly in April 2012, he is off the hook for the "December Massacre" of 15 political opponents. The date December 8, 1982, is the Surinamese equivalent of September 11, 2001, despite the relatively small death toll. Suriname needs a catharsis, but that is unlikely unless Bouterse is eventually arrested abroad after he leaves the presidency and extradited to the Netherlands. He is probably too clever for that.

The embarrassing arrest of his son, Dino, who has been indicted in the United States on weapons, cocaine and terrorism charges, has brought further international disgrace on Suriname and has increased pressure on Desi Bouterse to step aside for the good of the country. He has refused. The next election is scheduled for mid- 2015. The voters have a chance to rid themselves of this embarrassment.

Fishing off the coast of Suriname

379

The Republic of Trinidad and Tobago

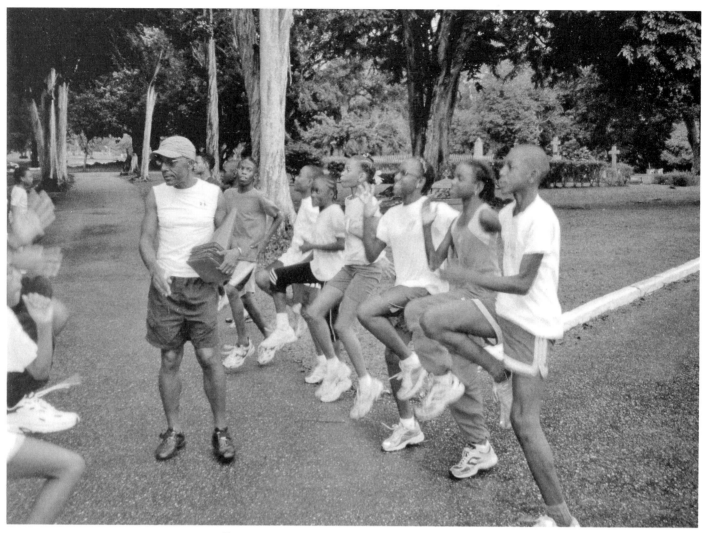

Cross-country runners warm up in Port of Spain

Area: 1,864 square miles (4,268 km²).
Population: 1,223,916 (2014 est.).
Capital City: Port of Spain (Pop. 37,074, 2011 estimate).
Climate: Tropically hot and humid. The heaviest rainfall occurs from May to December.
Neighboring Countries: Trinidad forms the eastern edge of a shelf surrounding the Gulf of Paria on Venezuela's northeast coast, separated from the mainland by narrow channels. Tobago lies 18 miles north of Trinidad.
Official Language: English.
Other Principal Tongues: Hindi, French and Spanish.
Ethnic Background: African Negroid (43%), Asiatic (40%), European and other (17%).
Principal Religion: Protestant Christianity.
Chief Commercial Products: Petroleum, natural gas (including liquefied), chemicals, tourism.
Currency: Trinidad Dollar.

Gross Domestic Product: U.S. $27.13 billion in 2013, est. ($22,143 per capita, official exchange rate).
Former Colonial Status: Spanish Colony (1498–1797); British Colony (1797–1962).
Independence Date: August 31, 1962.
Chief of State: Anthony Thomas Aquinas Carmona, president (since March 18, 2013).
Head of Government: Kamla Persad-Bissessar (b. April 22, 1952), prime minister (since May 26, 2010).
National Flag: A diagonal black stripe bordered with white on a red field.

Trinidad and Tobago both have mountainous spines representing rounded extensions of the Venezuelan coastal ranges. Trinidad's mountains lie along the north coast. Plains extend to the south, rimmed with low, rolling hills. Petroleum and the famed asphalt lake are found in the south of the island. Tobago's mountains on the north are skirted with coral-dotted shelves. Trinidad's soils are rich and well suited to

sugar and other crops. Sea breezes moderate the tropical climate and the annual rainfall of 65 inches is evenly distributed. Trinidad's asphalt has been of commercial significance since the colonial period. The more recent discovery of oil and gas has fostered industrial development. Trinidad and Tobago's population is primarily African and Asian, with smaller groups of cosmopolitan people of Spanish, French and English ancestry.

HISTORY: Columbus discovered Trinidad in 1498 and the Spanish colonized it in the early 1500s. During the French Revolution, a large number of French families were settled on the land that in 1797 was captured from Spain by British forces. Ceded to Britain in 1802, Trinidad was joined by Tobago as a colonial unit in 1889.

The history of the dual-island nation has been rather uneventful. Administered as a British Crown Colony until 1962, its early value was in asphalt and sugar. Slaves had been introduced by the Spanish to work

380

sugar and indigo plantations, and the British continued to add slaves until 1834. With the abolition of slavery, indentured East Indians and Chinese laborers were imported to perform the manual labor. The black and East Indian communities remain the country's two principal ethnic and political groups. The decline of sugar markets hurt the island's economy, but the existence of asphalt and (later) petroleum cushioned the shock and led to a transformation of the economy.

The leasing of bases to the United States during World War II bolstered the economy. The transformation of Trinidad and Tobago from colonial dependency was relatively untroubled. Initially incorporated into the West Indian Federation, its reluctance to tie its healthy economy to the poorer island dependencies was a major factor in the demise of the Federation.

The United States was drawn into the final phases of the negotiations for independence when Prime Minister Eric Williams sought the U.S. base at Chaguaramas as the site for a new capital city. The United States released part of the site in 1960, with the remainder reverting to Trinidad in 1977.

The Eric Williams Era

Independence was attained in 1962, and Williams became prime minister. Parliament consists of an elected House of Representatives, which chooses the prime minister, and an elected Senate. Initially, Queen Elizabeth II was chief of state.

When opposition parties boycotted the May 1971 elections to protest voting procedures, Williams' People's National Movement won all 36 seats in the House of Representatives. Although generally a capable leader, Williams' popularity fell because of his heavy-handed methods. A major crisis developed in 1970 when labor unrest and rioting led to a mutiny by sections of the small army. Williams used government forces in 1975 to quell violent strikes by petroleum and sugar workers.

The dispute soon erupted into a more general strike, joined by transport and electrical workers. Williams jailed key opposition leaders. Despite growing hostility by labor members and some sectors of the business community, Williams' political control remained firm, bolstered by the "mini-boom" caused by the enormous increases in oil prices.

The nation became a republic on August 1, 1976. Although the new constitution severed all ties to Great Britain, the country retains its membership in the British Commonwealth. Named as first president was Governor General Sir Ellis Clarke.

In the general elections held in September 1976, Williams won another five-year term when his People's National Movement (PNM) won 24 of the 36 seats in the House of Representatives. The Democratic Action Congress, traditionally the main opposition party, won only two seats, while a new Marxist-Leninist labor-oriented United Labor Front (UPF) won 10.

George Chambers

Despite the steady flow of oil revenues, stubbornly high unemployment fueled social unrest and persistent criticism of Williams. He died in 1981 at the age of 69. George Chambers, the minister of agriculture, was designated Williams' successor.

In November 1981 elections, six parties vied for the 36 parliamentary seats. Due to the splintered opposition, the PNM scored a major victory, winning 26 seats by the largest margin of votes in the nation's history (219,000).

Relations with Jamaica and Barbados, which had deteriorated in 1982 because of a trade war within the Caribbean Community, became further strained in late 1983 when Trinidad and Tobago opposed the multinational invasion of Grenada. A multi-nation Caribbean organization to promote free trade had been created in 1979, which Trinidad and Tobago joined. At its meeting in 1986, Chambers joined with the other chiefs of state in criticizing President Ronald Reagan's Caribbean Basin Initiative because of its import restrictions on Caribbean products, principally textiles, footwear and oil products.

The collapse of international petroleum prices presented severe economic problems during 1984–87. The sugar industry also became non-existent except for production to meet local needs. The government started importing crude oil for refining because of decreased local production. Despite this, in the 1980s Trinidad and Tobago had one of the higher per capita annual incomes in the area.

A Power Pendulum

The National Alliance for Reconstruction (NAR) led by Arthur Robinson won 33 of 36 seats in 1986 elections, ending the PNM's grip on power.

On July 27, 1990, 114 members of a black Muslim group called Jamaat al-Muslimeen attempted a *coup d'etat*. One group stormed the Parliament building and held the prime minister and several Cabinet ministers hostage. Robinson was shot in the leg and beaten. Another group seized the state-run television station. The siege lasted six days and left 24 people dead, including a member of Parliament. The courts gave amnesty to the rebels, much to the government's displeasure, and the coup leader, Yasin Abu Bakr, continues to run a mosque in Port-of-Spain. The revolt remains controversial to this day.

Trinidad and Tobago

Carnival in Port of Spain

In late 1991, the PNM returned to power with 21 seats. Patrick Manning, the new prime minister, stressed economic improvement and lowered black-Indian tensions.

The pendulum swung again in 1995, this time in favor of the Indian community, when the United National Congress (UNC) won a two-seat majority and elected Basdeo Panday as prime minister. He pledged to be "the leader of all the people," but blacks still feared Indian domination. Panday also was faced with a burgeoning crime rate, a divided judiciary and police corruption related to drug trafficking. Trinidad made international headlines in 1999, and brought condemnation from human rights groups, when it hanged 10 convicted murderers, justified as a deterrent to rising crime. The public seemed to approve of the hard-line policy.

Trinidadian courts have continued to hand down death sentences, although the crime wave has continued, as have international protests. In 2002, the Inter-American Court of Human Rights, an arm of the Organization of American States to which Trinidad and Tobago belongs, ordered the country not to carry out the executions of 31 men and one women on the grounds that their rights had been violated.

Panday's UNC was narrowly returned to power in general elections in December 2000, winning 19 of the 36 seats to 16 for the PNM, still led by Manning. The NAR won the remaining seat.

In his second term, Panday created a business-friendly environment that attracted new foreign investment. But critics, including three of his own cabinet ministers, complained he was becoming *too* friendly with business. Rumors circulated of kickbacks from an airport construction project. In 2001, Attorney General Ramesh Maharaj and two other cabinet ministers publicly alleged corruption within the government. Panday fired Maharaj, precipitating a crisis that Panday unwisely sought to resolve by dissolving Parliament and calling a new election for December, only a year after being returned to power. The election results led to a constitutional crisis when the UNC and the PNM each won 18 seats.

Panday and Manning struck a deal by which they would let President Robinson of the PAR, usually only a figurehead, decide who would be prime minister, who would then head a unity government. Robinson, who like Manning is black, chose Manning to head the government, giving only a vague explanation for his reasons. A miffed Panday reneged on his promise to cooperate in a unity government.

Parliament did not meet until April 2002, barely beating a six-month deadline that would have forced a new election. For two days, Parliament deadlocked on the election of a speaker, and the tension between the two parties—and hence the two ethnic groups—threatened to turn ugly.

In August 2002, Panday dissolved Parliament and called elections for October,

the third in three years. The campaign was predictably bitter, with the PNM pointing to the criminal charges that Panday had a secret London bank account in which he had allegedly stashed hundreds of thousands of dollars and the UNC running advertisements linking Manning to the black Muslim terrorist group that had attempted the 1990 coup. A woman also alleged that Manning had fathered her 2-year-old daughter. Voters gave the PNM 51% of the popular vote and a majority of 20 of the 36 seats. Turnout was 69.8%.

Panday, then almost 70, announced he would step down as leader of the opposition. However, he reneged.

In 2003, Parliament elected George Maxwell Richards, 71, a former dean of the University of the West Indies who is of African descent, to succeed Robinson as president. Richards, who is not a member of either party, pledged he would govern without regard to race.

In 2005, Panday, his wife, his former works minister and a businessmen were arrested and charged with offering or accepting a $45,600 bribe for the airport construction contract. Thousands of UNC supporters demonstrated in support of Panday and paid the equivalent of $104,000 for his bail. He later was charged in connection with the secret London bank account.

In September 2005, Panday anointed Winston Dookeran to succeed him as political leader of the party, although Panday remained chairman and resisted calls to step down as leader of the opposition. A power struggle developed between the Panday and Dookeran factions.

Ex-Prime Minister Patrick Manning

Prime Minister Kamla Persad-Bissessar

**President
Anthony Thomas Aquinas Carmona**

**Former President
George Maxwell Richards**

In April 2006, Panday, then 73, was convicted of fraud in connection with the secret bank account and sentenced to two years at hard labor, although four days later he was released from jail because of ill health. President Richards revoked Panday's title as leader of the opposition and named the UNC's deputy political leader, Kamla Persad-Bissessar, 54, a former attorney general, as the new opposition leader. This caused a serious rift within the UNC, with Panday seeking to reclaim the title of opposition leader.

Manning called elections for an expanded 41-seat House of Representatives in November 2007. Manning and the PNM received a decisive mandate this time, 26 seats to 15 for the UNC. Voter turnout was 66%, about the same as 2002.

In 2008, the already high murder rate soared by 38% to 550 homicides, or about 42 per 100,000, the third-highest in the world after Honduras and Venezuela that year.

Against this backdrop, Trinidad and Tobago hosted the Fifth Summit of the Americas in April 2009.

First Woman Prime Minister

In January 2010, the simmering rivalry between Panday and Persad-Bissessar for the UNC leadership came to a showdown when Panday challenged her leadership in a vote of the party's legislators, which Persad-Bissessar won overwhelmingly.

Apparently believing the divided and scandal-plagued UNC was mortally wounded, Manning called an early snap election on May 24, 2010. Voter turnout was 80% of the 1.3 million registered voters. In a stunning upset, the UNC-led coalition called People's Partnership won 29 of the 41 seats. Manning conceded on television, saying, "I take full responsibility for the defeat." He resigned as PNM leader but kept his seat in the House.

Two days later, Persad-Bissessar, 58, was sworn in as Trinidad and Tobago's first female prime minister. Keith Rowley became leader of the opposition, and she named her former rival Dookeran foreign secretary.

Trinidad and Tobago recorded another 472 murders in 2010, a rate of 37 per 100,000, still the fourth-highest in the world and seven times greater than the U.S.. Public sentiment swelled to resume hangings; there were already 42 prisoners on death row.

There had been no hangings since the 10 in 1999, because a 1993 ruling by the Privy Council in London, Trinidad and Tobago's court of last resort, had put a limit of five years between sentencing and execution of sentence. Most appeals take longer than five years. A Privy Council decision can be overturned only by a constitutional amendment, which requires a three-fourths majority in Parliament. Persad-Bissessar endorsed the amendment, despite opposition from human rights groups, calling hangings "a weapon in our arsenal." Opponents questioned the deterrent value, noting that the number of murders had quintupled since the 1999 hangings. To pass it required the support of the PNM, but the vote in March 2011 was 29–11, a strict party-line vote.

With that "weapon" denied her, Persad-Bissessar resorted to one her predecessor had been reluctant to use lest it frighten foreign investors. On August 21, 2011, she declared a state of emergency in Port-of-Spain and three other towns, which included a 9 p.m. curfew. Days later, two armed robbers were shot to death.

Whether or not the state of emergency was responsible, murders declined by a fourth in 2011 to 354, or 28 per 100,000, which still made the country among the 11 deadliest in the world. It began 2012 with four killings on New Years Day, and ended the year with 379, a 6.5% increase. The rate per 100,000 was 28.3, among the word's 13 deadliest.

Meanwhile, the government appointed a commission in 2010 to investigate the causes of the infamous 1990 Muslim revolt, which remains a sore subject for Trinidadians because the rebels were given amnesty and no one was held accountable for the 24 deaths. Four years later, the commission was still interviewing witnesses willing to testify voluntarily, because the commission was not granted subpoena power.

Recent Developments

President Richards retired in 2013 and Persad-Bissessar nominated Anthony T.A. Carmona, a judge on the International Court of Justice respected by both races, to succeed him. The PNM backed the nomination, and he was sworn in as the fifth president on March 18.

U.S. Vice President Joe Biden included Trinidad and Tobago as part of a three-nation goodwill tour in May 2013. Besides meeting with Carmona and Persad-Bissessar, Biden met with several other leaders from the Caribbean as a mini-summit to discuss trade, assistance, security and energy. Other participants were the presidents or prime ministers of the Dominican Republic, the Bahamas, Grenada, St. Vin-

Trinidad and Tobago

cent and St. Kitts and Nevis. The closed-door meetings were reportedly heated at times.

Even as Biden was leaving, the new president of China, Xi Jinping, arrived in Port-of-Spain to meet with the same leaders, underscoring the emerging rivalry between China and the U.S. in the region.

The PNM won eight of 14 municipalities in local elections on October 21, 2013, to five for the People's Partnership coalition. A deadlock in the 14th municipality was broken when a minor party councilor crossed over to the PNM. A video of an apparently drunk Persad-Bissessar claiming victory when in fact her party had lost went viral on YouTube (http://www.youtube.com/watch?v=Rhf1eP_7zkg).

In March 2014, Venezuela arrested 19 Trinidadian Muslims on suspicion of terrorist activities. One of those detained had been questioned during the 2011 state of emergency on suspicion of conspiring to assassinate Persad-Bissessar.

CULTURE: The people of Trinidad and Tobago, about 40% of East Indian (Gujerat) ancestry and 37.5% of African descent, have remained in distinct ethnic groups, but managed social and political integration during the period of British rule.

The African element has acquired renown for its calypso music. The people learned that through hours of heating, tempering and pounding that the steel oil drums from World War II could be tuned into unique musical instruments that are world-familiar today. Although most speak English, it is with a unique lilt.

Religious expression is unhampered, with popular participation in the *Carnival* of the Christians as well as the Islamic festival of Hosein.

Probably Trinidad's most noted calypso musician was Rupert Grant (1914–61), better known by the stage name Lord Invader. He is best remembered for the songs *Don't Stop the Carnival,* which he recorded in 1939 and was later recorded by Harry Belafonte, and *Rum and Coca-Cola,* which became a hit by the Andrews Sisters in the 1940s and was the object of a successful copyright suit by Grant.

Another famous Trinidadian calypso performer was Frederick Wilmoth Hendricks, better known as Wilmoth Houdini (1895–1977), whose 1939 hit *He Had it Coming,* changed to *Stone Cold Dead in the Markets* in the United States, was performed by Ella Fitzgerald and Louis Jordan and was on the top of the rhythm and blues chart for five weeks. He moved to New York and spent the rest of his life there.

The Indian population has contributed the genre of so-called chutney music.

Trinidadians felt a sense of pride in 2001 when Vidiadhar Surajprasad (V.S.) Naipaul (b. 1932), a Trinidad-born novelist, was named recipient of the Nobel Prize for Literature, only the second West Indian to be so honored. Their pride was muted somewhat by the fact that Naipaul had spent 50 of his 69 years in Britain and has ridiculed his homeland as "primitive." Scion of a literary family, Naipaul attended Oxford and opted to stay in Britain, vowing to "beat them (the British) at their own language." Yet, he used Trinidad as the setting for some of his novels, which include *A House for Mr. Biswas, The Suffrage of Elvira, The Mimic Men, Guerrillas,* and *In a Free State;* his first published

novel, *The Mystic Masseur,* was made into a movie in 2001 and was filmed in Trinidad. The Nobel committee praised the iconoclastic Naipaul for his "incorruptible scrutiny" of the post-colonial West Indies, but he also had attracted notoriety for his attacks on Islam and for ridiculing such literary greats as C.S. Forrester and James Joyce.

Besides the University of Trinidad and Tobago, established in 2004 in Wallerfield, there are four campuses of the University of the West Indies, established in 1948 and supported by 18 Caribbean countries, and the private University of the Southern Caribbean, founded by the Seventh-day Adventist Church in 1927.

Three daily newspapers circulate nationally and on line. *The Guardian,* founded in 1917, is the country's newspaper of record. Its competitors are the *Daily Express,* established in 1967, and its sister paper, *Newsday,* which dates to 1993. Freedom House rates the Trinidad and Tobago press as "free."

ECONOMY: Although the nation contains rich soils and agriculture is important, the economy is based on oil and natural gas production. The only Caribbean country with oil deposits, Trinidad and Tobago was at one time the hemisphere's third-largest oil exporting nation. This has been declining since 1982. The government has offered tax advantages to oil firms to encourage exploration.

As oil production has declined, Trinidad and Tobago has cashed in on its vast natural gas reserves, although they, too, have been declining for a decade. At the end of 2010, estimated gas reserves were 13.46 trillion cubic feet, down from 19.67 tcf in 2000. Liquefied natural gas (LNG) is increasingly exploited and exported; the United States obtains 75% of its imported LNG from Trinidad and Tobago.

In 2002, Prime Minister Patrick Manning announced plans for a gas pipeline under the Caribbean with branches to Cuba, Puerto Rico, Barbados, Guadaloupe, Martinique, Antigua and St. Kitts. The project cost $500 million.

Trinidad and Tobago is also the world's leading exporter of methanol and ammonia. In 2006, a Trinidad-German consortium announced plans for a new $1.2 billion methanol plant.

During the days of the oil boom of the 1970s, per capita income was among the highest in the hemisphere, more than $7,000, but that plummeted to $3,800 at the depth of the recession of the late 1980s and early 1990s. By 2007, with the oil and chemical industries booming, it was $14,000 although as is the case in many oil-rich countries, it was not equitably distributed and it led to a high cost of living for housing and basic goods. In 2007, 17%

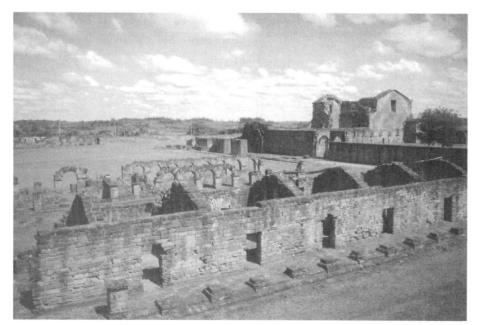

Jesuit Ruin of Trinidad

of the population lived below the poverty line, much less than in Latin America.

A serious problem had been the external debt, which in 1999 stood at $1.42 billion, nearly 25% of GDP. In 2012 it was up to 46.6% of GDP.

Trinidad and Tobago has gone from boom to bust to boom to bust. Real GDP declined for eight consecutive years, from 1988–95. Growth averaged only 3%–4% from 1996–98, but was a robust 7.1% in 1999 and 6.9% in 2000. It peaked at 12.2% in 2006, largely because of the price of crude oil, dropping back to a still-healthy 5.5% in 2007. It fell to 3.5% in 2008 because of the fall in oil prices and the beginning of the global recession late in the year. GDP shrank by –3.5% in 2009, had zero growth in 2010 and shrank by –2.6% in 2011. It grew by an insignificant .2% in 2012 and 1.6% in 2013, among the worst in the hemisphere.

Unemployment fell from 8.4% in 2004 to 5.3% in 2008. It was 5.6% in 2012 and 5.9% in 2013.

Inflation reached 12% in 2008. With the recession, it dropped to 7.6% in 2009, then rose to 11.3% in 2010. It was down to 9.2% in 2012 and 5.4% in 2013.

Tourism, now principally on Tobago, would provide more profits than drug trafficking and would help diversify the oil-and-gas-dependent economy, but as in Jamaica, tourists are shunning this would-be tropical paradise because of an alarmingly high crime rate. In 2008, Trinidad and Tobago recorded 550 homicides or 55 per 100,000, the third-highest in the world that year, higher even than Jamaica. In 2010, it was still fourth-highest, with 37 homicides per 100,000. Both the United States and Great Britain issued travel advisories for the country. The homicide rate dropped to 28 in 2011, still among the 11 highest in the world, but the number of murders increased again in 2012 by 6.5%, to 377.

Tourism peaked at 463,000 arrivals in 2005. Arrivals declined –2.5% in 2007, –2.5% in 2008 and –4.2% in 2009, a double whammy of violent crime and the 2008-09 global recession. Tourist arrivals in 2010 were 388,000, down anoter 4.4%, but still accounting for 3.8% of GDP. Arrivals finally increased slightly in 2011 to 402,000, according to the World Bank. Interestingly, the EU's Council on Tourism and Trade named Trinidad and Tobago its top tourist destination for 2012. The government predicted a 4.4% increase in 2012, but the figures are still unavailable.

THE FUTURE: The UNC's upset in the snap elections of 2010 and the ascension of Kamla Persad-Bissessar as the country's first woman prime minister opened a new and uncertain chapter in the country's history. Over four years, she has shown herself to be a capable and determined prime minister. She is a former teacher with degrees from Trinidad and Britain who became an attorney and rose through her party's ranks.

She faced her first major challenge, the country's alarming murder rate, by calling for a constitutional amendment that would expedite hangings. She failed, on a strict party vote in 2011, to obtain the necessary three-fourths in Parliament. More hangings would be little more than a feel-good approach to the problem. Polls show the public overwhelmingly favors capital punishment, which is legal but hasn't been used since 1999.

Her imposition of a state of emergency in 2011 was definitely a step in the right direction. If she can get a handle on the crime crisis, tourists may start returning to this island paradise that gangs have turned into a hell.

General elections have been scheduled for September 7, 2015.

Rural scene

The Oriental (Eastern) Republic of Uruguay

Gauchos **enjoy folk music in the countryside**

Area: 72,150 square miles (186,861 km²).

Population: 3,332,972 (2014 est.)

Capital City: Montevideo (Pop. 1,395,000 in 2012, est.)

Climate: Temperate throughout the year. There is a warm season from November to April and a milder season from May through October. Rainfall is moderate and evenly distributed.

Neighboring Countries: Brazil (north); Argentina (west)

Official Language: Spanish.

Other Principal Tongues: Portuguese and English.

Ethnic Background: European (90%), *mestizo* (a mixture of European and Indian ancestry, 10%).

Principal Religion: Roman Catholic Christianity.

Chief Commercial Products: Hides, leather products, beef and other meat, wool, fish, rice.

Currency: New Peso.

Gross Domestic Product: U.S. $57.11 billion in 2013, est. ($17,179 per capita, official exchange rate).

Former Colonial Status: Spanish Colony (1624–80); contested between Spain and Portugal (1680–1806); captured by Great Britain (1806–07); War for Independence (1807–20); Portuguese Brazilian Colony (1820–25); contested between Brazil and Argentina (1825–28).

Independence Date: Independence was proclaimed on August 25, 1825, but Uruguay did not actually become independent until August 27, 1828, when a treaty was signed with Brazil and Argentina as a result of British intervention in the dispute between Uruguay's two neighboring countries.

Chief of State: Tabaré Ramón Vázquez Rosas (b. January 17, 1940), president (since March 1, 2015), (previously president 2005–2010).

National Flag: Four blue and five white horizontal stripes; a rising sun of 16 alternating straight and wavy rays on a white square is in the upper left hand part of the flag.

Uruguay, the second smallest of the South American countries, is a land of rolling hills covered with lush grasses and a few scattered forests. The highest elevation is about 2,000 feet; the country is crossed by numerous small streams and is bounded by the Atlantic and several large rivers. The estuary of the Río de la Plata and the Uruguay River, separating Uruguay from Argentina, are navigable and provide an important means of transportation. The River Negro, which arises in Brazil and crosses Uruguay from northeast to southwest is also navigable for some distance.

The rich, black soils produce a high quality of grasses, which have encouraged cattle and sheep raising. Equally suited to agriculture, less than 10% of the land is used for farming. The climate is mild, though damp. Winter (June–August) temperatures average 57° to 60° F., with occasional frosts; summer (December-February) temperatures average 75° to 79° F. Rainfall is evenly distributed during the year, averaging 40 inches annually. Nature and history have caused Uruguay to become a pastoral country.

HISTORY: The Spanish explorers of the Río de la Plata in the 16th century passed up the hills of Uruguay as unlikely to have treasure in gold and precious stones. The warlike Charrúa Indians also discouraged invasion. Military expeditions against the Indians were uniformly unsuccessful, but Jesuit and Franciscan missionaries were able to establish missions in 1624. Cattle are supposed to have been introduced by Hernando Arias in 1580 during one of the unsuccessful military expeditions. A counter-invasion by the Portuguese from Brazil came in 1680, following slave raids on the missions and cattle roundups of the wild herds that roamed the grasslands.

The Portuguese founded Colonia de Sacramento on the Río Plata as a rival to Spanish Buenos Aires. In 1995, the old quarter of Colonia was named a UNESCO World Heritage Site. The remainder of Uruguay's colonial history is one of war between the Spanish and Portuguese contenders for control of the river.

Montevideo was planned by the Portuguese, built by the Spanish and taken by the British in 1806, but abandoned in 1807 when an attack on Buenos Aires failed. A Brazilian attack in 1811 was resisted by the Uruguayan cattleman and patriot José Artigas, who declared Uruguay's independence.

Uruguay

The struggle continued until 1820 when Montevideo fell to the Brazilians and Artigas fled to Paraguay, where he died in a comfortable self-imposed exile. A group of 33 exiles returned from Buenos Aires to take up the cause in 1825, and with Argentine assistance, they defeated the Brazilians at Ituzaingo in 1827 (the city of Treinte y Tres is named in honor of that band of exiles). At this point, Great Britain intervened. Both Brazil and Argentina renounced their claims and Uruguay became independent in fact on August 27, 1828.

The settlement of Uruguay proceeded slowly from the first missionary stations. The *gauchos* (cowboys) who hunted the cattle in the 17th and 18th centuries were nomads and not interested in the land. Slaughtering the cattle for hides, they sold their wares to merchants from Argentina. By the time of independence, the nomads had disappeared and large ranches had taken up the land. Farming was practiced only around Montevideo, where a market for produce was assured. Following independence, Italian and Spanish immigrants settled in the farming belt where their descendants still live today.

The early history of the republic was a chaotic period of civil war as the factions fought for power. Two parties emerged—the *Blanco* (White), representing conservative ranchers, and the *Colorado* (Red), favoring liberal reforms. The parties and politics established in the 1830s have been hardened in more than 150 years of combat and still persist today. A 10-year civil war was fought between the factions with support from other powers that intervened, including French, English and Italian. The foreign intervention terminated with the unseating of Argentine dictator Rosas in 1852; however, the Uruguayans continued the civil war for another 10 years.

Further strife in 1863 led to Brazilian support for a *Colorado* despot who unseated his *Blanco* opponent in 1865. The Paraguayan dictator Francisco Solano-Lopez came to the aid of the *Blancos*, precipitating the Triple Alliance (Argentina, Brazil and Uruguay) war against Paraguay. The defeat of Paraguay left the *Colorados* in power, which they retained for nearly a century except for the military period.

The year 1870 marked a turning point in Uruguayan history. The rancher with his *gaucho* army was out of place. The demand for better quality meat, hides and wool required more modern methods and business-like management of the huge estates. Railroads were built, European immigrants settled in the cities and a middle class mercantile society developed. Clashes continued between the two parties through the remainder of the 19th cen-

tury, but a growing group of responsible citizens emerged. Three *Colorado* dictators ruled from 1875 to 1890 with some degree of moderation. Two more ruled from 1890 to 1896 with such disregard for the law that civil war again broke out, resulting in the division of the country into *Colorado* and *Blanco* provinces. This uneasy arrangement lasted until 1903 and the election of Uruguay's foremost statesman and leader, José Batlle y Ordóñez.

The Batlle Era

Uruguay's 20th century history was dominated by Batlle—who assumed the leadership of a bankrupt, battle-torn and divided nation—even after his death. His first term, 1903–07, was spent in crushing civil war, uniting the country and securing popular support for sane, democratic government. From 1911–15 he campaigned for his plan, which included replacing the powerful presidency with a council, an idea based loosely on the Swiss model but unheard of in Latin America. He encountered considerable opposition, but by 1917 a new constitution was adopted, and full franchise and progressive social legislation was enacted. Using the editorial pages of *El Día*, Montevideo's leading newspaper, Batlle pleaded his case and educated the people.

By the time of Batlle's death in 1929, Uruguay was the most literate, democratic, well-fed state in Latin America. His unique plural executive system was in use until 1933 and again from 1951–67. His nephew, Luis, served twice as president, though far less effectively than the uncle.

Batlle's reforms did not, however, create the economic base needed to support the welfare state he had created. The next two presidents tried to carry out his programs,

Uruguay

José Batlle y Ordóñez

but they were restricted by the nine-member national council that wielded considerable power. Social and economic reforms were completely stopped when Uruguay went into an economic depression with the rest of the world in 1931.

Confusion, near-anarchy and no progress marked the years 1931–51, replete with military dictators and corruption. Batlle's plural executive form of government was readopted as a result of a plebiscite in 1951 and its nine members functioned as the executive arm of government until 1967. The long-dominant *Colorados* again were returned to power, but high inflation and other economic woes led to disenchantment.

In the 1958 elections, the *Blancos* won for the first time since 1865. They were re-elected in 1962. However, they proved no more capable of dealing with the economic crisis than had the *Colorados*, largely because neither party had the courage to deal with the bloated bureaucracy and overly generous retirement system that the welfare state had wrought.

In desperate need of dynamic leadership, Uruguayans voted overwhelmingly to return to a presidential executive in elections and a plebiscite in 1966. The *Colorados*, in the minority for eight years, elected a former air force general, Oscar D. Gestido, to the presidency, bypassing Jorge Batlle, grand-nephew of the reformer. When Gestido died in 1967, he was succeeded by the vice president, Jorge Pacheco Areco, a civilian. Encumbered by an inefficient bureaucracy and runaway inflation, and lacking forceful leadership abilities, Pacheco also proved incapable of solving economic

stagnation, corruption and rising urban terrorism by the *Tupamaros*—Latin America's most infamous urban guerrilla force in the 1960s.

Promising law and order and economic reform, the *Colorados* received another mandate in 1971 with the presidential candidacy of Juan María Bordaberry. Most of the president's program was soon blocked in the National Assembly, however, where he lacked a majority.

The *Tupamaros* achieved international notoriety by kidnapping and murdering an agricultural official with the U.S. Embassy, Dan Mitrione, whom the *Tupamaros* alleged was a CIA agent who was training the Uruguayan security forces in torture techniques. As the *Tupamaros* increased their terrorism, and under U.S. pressure because of the Mitrione incident, Bordaberry turned to a new power source: the armed forces. With stunning efficiency, the military systematically routed some 2,000 guerrillas by early 1973. Then, instead of returning to the barracks, the military demanded major reforms in the nation's welfare programs, which it believed had been the basis for rampant political corruption and economic decay.

Military Rule, 1973–85

On February 8, 1973, the armed forces staged a *coup d'etat*. The generals agreed to allow Bordaberry to remain in office, provided he agreed to governmental reform and a crackdown on the *Tupamaros*. He did. Backed by the armed forces, Bordaberry dissolved the National Assembly, banned eight political parties, closed the nation's only university, broke up labor unions, instituted strict press censorship and jailed 6,000 political opponents. Under the new order, all power was vested in the military-controlled Council of the Nation, which ruled by decree. The Mitrione incident and the subsequent *coup* inspired the 1973 Costa-Gavras film, "State of Siege."

Bordaberry decided he wanted to become president-for-life with the military backing him in 1977, but the military, favoring a gradual return to democracy, ousted him in a bloodless coup in 1976. An interim president was named, who was chief of a 27-member Council of State formed to replace the dissolved National Assembly.

Under the military's master plan, the new president was to serve for three years, at which time a duly elected president would serve another five years. Full democracy would then be restored at the end of this eight-year period. Further, the military was prepared to purge top leaders from the *Colorado* and *Blanco* parties before they would be permitted to participate

in elections set for 1984. All other parties would be banned.

The master plan went awry when the new president unexpectedly refused to issue a decree abolishing the nation's top political leadership. The military ousted *him* and, after consultation with top conservatives, the generals recruited a new civilian president, Dr. Aparicio Méndez, who dutifully nullified the political rights of 1,000 leaders from all existing parties for a 15-year period.

In foreign affairs, the military government received increased criticism for its violation of human rights. Yet, the *junta*, ruling through a civilian "front" administration, felt secure enough to submit a new constitution for popular approval in 1980. Although it provided for free congressional elections, it also established a National Security Council, empowered with final approval of almost all governmental activity and limited the presidential election to a *single* candidate approved by the military. On November 30, 1980, the voters rejected the constitution by a margin of 58% to 42%—to the utter amazement of the *junta*.

Rival factions divided the military: hardliners urged an end to the liberalization policy; others focused on the power struggle to name the presidential candidate. Meanwhile, *Blanco* and *Colorado* leaders demanded removal of a ban on political activity and restoration of a free press. Despite these appeals and the plebiscite, the military did not intend to surrender control, as more than 1,200 political prisoners languished in jail.

Transition to Democracy

General Gregorio Álvarez, former army commander, was appointed president and began preliminary discussions with the political leaders of the two traditional parties for free general elections prior to March 1985 when his "term" expired. Negotiations stalled on the issue of membership of the commission to set rules for political activity and for framing a constitution to be submitted to a national referendum. The armed forces wanted guarantees that they would enjoy sufficient power under the democratic regime, but the opposition insisted that the army's place is in the barracks. The armed forces hinted at the necessity of a "transitional period" between the military regime and return to democracy. Most political parties had either opposed the idea or stressed the brevity of such a "transitional period."

Sanguinetti and Lacalle

Held on November 25, 1984, the elections resulted in the victory of Julio María

Uruguay

Sanguinetti, a *Colorado*, who received 39% of the vote; the *Colorados* also won a plurality in both houses of the National Assembly. Democracy was restored officially when the Assembly convened on February 15, 1985, and Sanguinetti was inaugurated on March 1 for a five-year term.

As in most of Latin America, the new president, considered a centrist, had to face the rising expectations of a population free of military rule, the political inexperience of many of his advisers and a serious economic situation. Strikes were rampant. The government suspended two banks, and reassured the public that the "restlessness" of the armed forces, provoked by a cut in the military budget and investigations into the actions of the past military regime, would be peacefully solved.

An avowed agnostic in a nominally Catholic but traditionally secular country, Sanguinetti once stirred controversy by not kneeling to kiss the ring of Pope John Paul II during a papal visit.

A delicate matter was resolved in 1986: what to do with the military, which, as in other Latin American countries, had committed numerous human rights violations. To try them would be an invitation to a military takeover. An oral agreement was reached prior to the return to civilian rule that there would be no trials of either *Tupamaros* or the military. A reluctant but practical Assembly passed the Law of General Expiration at Sanguinetti's request. The military then acknowledged that some officers had committed "transgressions of human rights."

The amnesty enraged human rights advocates and relatives of dissidents who were slain or "disappeared." The matter was seemingly settled in 1989 when in a referendum the amnesty was upheld by a margin of 57% to 43%. But the issue did not go away.

A moderate *Colorado* candidate was expected to win 1989 elections, but Luis Lacalle of the *Blanco* Party captured a plurality of 37%. He had entered into a pre-election coalition with the leftist *Frente Amplio* (Broad Front), the candidate of which received 21%. Thus a loose combination of leftists, including Communists, became a force to be reckoned with in Uruguayan politics, and it remains so today.

Although nominally leftist, Lacalle followed a program of privatization of government enterprises, arousing opposition from surplus employees of these industries. Privatization of the telephone system was halted by a 1992 referendum, in which 72% opposed the measure.

Lacalle made Uruguay a charter member of *Mercosur*, the free-trade bloc with Argentina, Brazil and Paraguay. High inflation plagued Uruguay in 1993–94, which led to voter discontent.

The 1994 election was virtually a three-way tie and left no party with a mandate. Former President Sanguinetti was returned to the presidency with a bare plurality of 34.3%. The *Blanco* Party's Alberto Volonte was second with 33%. The Broad Front, an alliance of the left-wing Progressive Encounter with the Socialists and Communists, fielded Montevideo Mayor Tabaré Vázquez, an oncologist, who received 32.8%, the left's strongest showing yet. The traditional two-party dominance of Uruguayan politics effectively ended.

Largely because the vote was so fragmented, the Assembly introduced a *segunda vuelta*, or runoff, for future presidential elections. Sanguinetti's second term continued to emphasize trade, especially within *Mercosur*. The economy experienced modest growth until late in his term, when the economic woes of neighboring Argentina and Brazil proved contagious.

Jorge Batlle

About half the country's 2.4 million voters participated in the party primaries in 1999 and a clear plurality, just over 37%, voted in the *Colorado* primary. The winner was Senator Jorge Batlle, grand-nephew of the party's illustrious founder and son of Luis Batlle, who served twice as president, in 1947–51 and 1954–58. A former journalist, Batlle had failed in four earlier presidential bids.

Making his second bid, Vázquez received about 80% of the vote in the Progressive Encounter primary, while former President Lacalle easily won the *Blanco* primary.

Once again, the old Communist and Socialist parties coalesced around the Progressive Encounter to form the Broad Front. In the first round on October 31, Vázquez scored a convincing first-place finish with 39.8%, to 32.7% for Batlle and 22.2% for Lacalle. Moreover, the Broad Front stunned the two traditional parties by emerging as the largest force in the new Assembly, winning 40 of 99 seats in the Chamber of Deputies and 12 of the 30 Senate seats. Voter turnout was 91.8%.

Clearly, the left wing had come a long way since the 1973 coup, but the prospect of a Vázquez presidency alarmed the political establishment. The defeated Lacalle swallowed his pride and endorsed Batlle, who pledged to continue Sanguinetti's moderate free-market reforms and derided the "crazy ideas" of his leftist opponent. In the November runoff, the results were:

Batlle	1,138,067	53.9%
Vázquez	972,197	46.1%

Batlle was inaugurated on March 1, 2000, at the age of 72. With 40% of the seats in both houses, the Broad Front forced the

Former President Jorge Batlle

traditionally rival *Colorados* and *Blancos* to form a legislative marriage of convenience. This coalition ended in 2002 when the *Blanco* cabinet ministers resigned, but the two parties continued to present a united front in the Assembly.

The Batlle government at first resisted the hemispheric trend toward wholesale privatization, then reluctantly began making moves to reform the bloated public sector in order to appease the International Monetary Fund (see Economy).

Batlle found himself in the maelstrom an international controversy in 2002. Uruguay co-sponsored a resolution before the U.N. Human Rights Commission that called upon Cuba to democratize and to respect human rights. When Cuban President Fidel Castro called Batlle a "lackey" of the United States, Batlle broke diplomatic relations, which had been restored in 1986 after a 25-year break (see Cuba).

Uruguay faced the same type of socioeconomic crisis that led to the chaos in Argentina in 2001. In 2002, the government issued a surprise decision to let the peso float, and it plummeted from 17 to the dollar to 28. When Uruguayans began withdrawing their savings in a panic, and bank deposits dropped from $13 billion at the end of 2001 to just $8.8 billion, Batlle declared a "temporary" bank holiday. Violence and looting broke out in Montevideo. The Bush administration authorized a $1.5 billion emergency loan, the first time Bush had approved a direct loan to a Latin American country. Within days, the loan was repaid when the IMF approved a $3.8 billion loan.

The crisis continued into 2003, and despite international predictions of a default,

Uruguay

Uruguay serviced its debt through painful austerity measures that led to more street protests, but even the opposition Broad Front proclaimed them necessary.

Faced with grim economic choices, the *Blancos* and *Colorados* boldly voted to slaughter the sacred cow of state-owned monopolies in 2003 by approving a bill that dismantled the inefficient state oil monopoly, *ANCAP*, and opened it up to badly needed foreign investors. But the Broad Front had enough votes to force a referendum on the law. In a replay of the 1992 referendum on telephone privatization, 62% of the electorate voted to repeal the privatization.

As had been done in other Latin American countries, a peace commission was created in 2003 to come to terms with the abuses committed during the dictatorship. It found that 29 dissidents had been killed in Uruguay, while another 150 were killed across the river in Argentina.

Vázquez Prevails

In 2004, the Broad Front renominated Vázquez, the *Colorados* nominated former Interior Minister Guillermo Stirling, and the *Blancos* rejected former President Lacalle in favor of Jorge Larrañaga, a former governor and senator. By then the economy was rebounding, but it was too late for either of the now-discredited major parties, especially the *Colorados*.

Like Presidents Ricardo Lagos of Chile and Luiz Inácio da Silva of Brazil, Vázquez suddenly moderated his long-standing socialist rhetoric and emerged as a pragmatic, statesmanlike figure. He rejected a radical approach, pledging to couple an emphasis on social programs with moderate economic policies. It was a message the recession-weary Uruguayans, who were still reluctant to scrap their overly generous social welfare system, wanted to hear. The result was a stunning first-round victory for Vázquez:

Vázquez	1,121,622	50.5%
Larrañaga	762,715	34.3%
Stirling	230,434	10.4%

Vázquez was inaugurated on March 1, 2005, Uruguay's first leftist president; the 170-year grip on power by the *Colorados* and the *Blancos* was finally broken. The Broad Front also emerged with a working majority in the Assembly. The inauguration proved a fiesta for the South American left. Cuba's Castro was uncharacteristically absent, but Vázquez's first act as president was to restore diplomatic relations with Cuba, three years after Batlle's spat with Castro.

In keeping with his campaign promises, Vázquez, himself a physician, announced a $100 million social program to provide medical care and nutrition. At the same time, he continued the grudging efforts toward, if not outright privatization, a mixed economy that created partnerships between the state and private industry. It was much the approach he followed as mayor of Montevideo. He also succeeded in satisfying the IMF and the World Bank (see Economy).

A Quest for Justice

Following the lead of Argentina and Chile, Vázquez made an effort for Uruguay to atone for the human rights abuses of the 1973–85 dictatorship. He struck a deal with the military by which he agreed to abide by the amnesty law, while the military would cooperate in recovering bodies of those who disappeared during the dictatorship to give their families closure.

In 2009, the Supreme Court ruled the 1986 amnesty law unconstitutional, but it remained in force pending repeal by the Assembly or the voters.

But the amnesty deal did not exempt civilians. In 2006, former President Bordaberry, then 78, who abetted the military seizure of 1973 and ruled as dictator, and his foreign minister, Juan Blanco, were arrested for the 1976 murders in Buenos Aires of two exiled leftist legislators, Senator Zelmar Micheneli and Deputy Héctor Gutiérrez, and two *Tupamaro* rebels. The charges were later expanded to include 14 other murders. Commented President Vázquez, *"Habló la justicia"* (justice has spoken).

Justice spoke slowly. They were jailed for weeks, then placed under house arrest to await trial. Like the Pinochet case in Chile, the case involved two and a half years of legal wrangling. Bordaberry returned to jail in 2009, after which he was hospitalized for a respiratory condition. The trial resumed, and on February 9, 2010, the judge found Bordaberry, then 81, guilty of the two homicides, of nine disappearances and of "crimes against the constitution." He was sentenced to 30 years. Because of his deteriorating health, he was given house arrest. He died at his home on July 17, 2011, at age 83.

Another president from the dictatorship, General Gregorio Álvarez, who ruled from 1980-85, was arrested and indicted in 2007 for kidnapping Uruguayan activists in Argentina, who were returned to Uruguay and killed; the amnesty did not cover kidnapping. In October 2009, when the amnesty law's validity was uncertain, Álvarez, then 82, was convicted of 37 counts of murder and human rights violations and sentenced to 25 years. Now 88, he remains behind bars. A former navy captain was sentenced at the same time to 20 years for 29 cases of murder.

The Pragmatic Populist

In economics, Vázquez did prove to be a pragmatist like da Silva, rather than a firebreathing Marxist like Chávez, which irked some hardliners in his own movement while delighting the middle class and the IMF. He followed Batlle's prudent policies that had begun to extract Uruguay from its devastating recession; in 2005 the country recorded GDP growth of 6.6%, and in 2008, it was 8.5%, among the highest in Latin America.

Uruguay allowed firms from Spain and Finland to invest $1.5 billion in two huge paper mills on the Río Plata, the largest

President Tabaré Vázquez

Source: BBC

single foreign investment in Uruguayan history. But the projects elicited concerns about pollution from greens in Vázquez's coalition as well as from the Argentines across the river, who feared dioxin contamination. Argentine protesters blocked a border bridge for two months in 2006. The Spanish firm abandoned the project. The Finnish firm "finished" its mill in 2007, as 20,000 Argentines protested the opening on their side of the river. The plant was expected to add 1.6% to GDP and increase export revenue by 15%.

In 2006, Uruguay paid a $630 million installment to the IMF nine months ahead of schedule, saving $8.4 million in interest payments. Finance Minister Danilo Astori also hinted at leaving *Mercosur* to enter a more lucrative free-trade agreement (FTA) with the U.S., heresy for Latin American leftists. Ironically, Vázquez had joined Venezuela's Chávez in hamstringing the U.S.-sponsored Free Trade Area of the Americas (FTAA) at the Summit of the Americas in Argentina two months earlier, and Chávez had just agreed to bring Venezuela into *Mercosur*.

Vázquez upped the ante again in 2007 when Uruguay signed a trade and investment framework agreement with the United States, the first step toward a FTA. Uruguay was one of five countries on President Bush's goodwill tour of Latin America that March. The two presidents had an amicable meeting, at which free trade was tops on the agenda. Chávez timed an anti-Bush rally in Buenos Aires the same day. Uruguay and the U.S. signed two more protocols in advance of a FTA in October 2008, but it has not yet been finalized. (In 2011, WikiLeaks reported on a 2006 diplomatic cable that then-Argentine President Néstor Kirchner had worked behind the scenes to block it.)

Vázquez visited Washington in 2009 and met with Secretary of State Hillary Clinton. He echoed her criticism of Venezuela's arms buildup, saying, "We believe

that it is quite inconvenient to the region to devote such significant economic resources toward purchasing arms."

Vázquez angered women's rights advocates, part of his core constituency, in 2008 when he vetoed a bill to permit abortion in the first trimester. The Assembly had narrowly passed the measure, although the Roman Catholic bishop threatened legislators who supported it with excommunication. The physician-president said he opposed abortion "philosophically and biologically." The Assembly made global news again in 2009 by passing Latin America's first same-sex adoption law.

José Mujica

As his chosen successor, Vázquez endorsed Finance Minister Astori, who was challenged by Senator José Mujica, a former *Tupamaro* guerrilla who spent 14 years in prison before and during the military regime. In party primaries in June 2009, Mujica, 74, narrowly defeated Astori. In the *Blanco* primary, former President Lacalle, 68, defeated Senator Jorge Larrañaga, the party's 2005 standard bearer. The *Colorados* nominated the jailed former President Bordaberry's son, Pedro, 49, who was proclaiming his father's innocence. Two minor candidates were also on the ballot.

In the first round on October 25, turnout was 89.9% of the 2,563,250 registered voters. The results:

Mujica	1,105,262	47.96%
Lacalle	669,942	29.07%
Bordaberry	392,307	17.02%

Also on the ballot was the latest referendum initiative to annul the amnesty law for human rights abuses committed by the military. It failed again, 48%–52%, showing just how polarized Uruguayans remain on the volatile issue.

Bordaberry endorsed Lacalle for the runoff. But Mujica's huge lead proved insurmountable. In the runoff, the turnout was 89.2%. The results:

Mujica	1,197,638	52.4%
Lacalle	994,510	43.5%
Blank	53,100	2.3%
Null	40,103	1.75%

In the General Assembly, the Broad Front holds a one-seat majority in both houses. In the Senate, the Broad Front has 16 seats to 9 for the *Blancos* and 5 for the *Colorados*. In the Chamber of Deputies, the Broad Front has 50 seats, the *Blancos* 30, the *Colorados* 17 and the Independent Party, 2.

Mujica, who made news when he announced that he owns no property other than a 1987 Volkswagen Beetle and that his bank accounts and other property are

Former President José Mujica

in his wife's name, may be officially the world's poorest chief of state. He was inaugurated on March 1, 2010. The oldest elected president in Latin America, he turned 76 on May 20, 2011. He and his wife declined to use the presidential residence, living instead on a small farm outside the capital. Mujica has become something of an international celebrity by his refusal to wear a tie on even the most formal occasions.

Again to the surprise of leftist hardliners who thought Mujica was one of them, Mujica continued Vázquez's prudent, center-left course. GDP growth in 2010 was 8.5%, second-highest in Latin America. In 2011, it was still 6.5%, although it slowed to 3.9% in 2012 and 3.5% in 2013.

The issue that won't go away, annulment of the 1986 amnesty for human rights abuses committed by the military during the dictatorship, resurfaced in 2011. The Inter-American Human Rights Court, an organ of the OAS, ruled that Uruguay should remove the obstacles to prosecuting human rights abuses. The Assembly took up the latest initiative. Critics on the right complained that the amnesty for the guerrillas would remain in effect. The Senate approved the annulment by a single vote, but it died in the Chamber of Deputies in May on a 49–49 tie when a deputy in the ruling coalition abstained. Mujica called the defeat "a shame." Protesters took to the streets. The Assembly eventually annulled the amnesty that October, and a judge was appointed to investigate 55 cases of murder and disappearance.

But the Supreme Court stunned the country, and international human rights groups, on February 22, 2013, by ruling the 2011 law annulling the military amnesty unconstitutional on grounds it was retroactive. The court also transferred the investigating judge, Mariana Mota, to a

Uruguay

civil court for "procedural reasons." Outraged Assembly members summoned the justices to appear before the Assembly to explain their ruling, which they refused to do. Mujica threatened to impeach the justices, which would have subverted the principle of separation of powers.

Yet, Mujica acted on a ruling by the Inter-American Court of Justice in 2012 by paying $513,000 to an Argentine woman, Macarena Gelman, as compensation for Uruguay's role in the kidnapping and murder of her mother during Operation Condor in the 1970s. Gelman was one of the babies of slain dissidents who were illegally adopted by military families. Gelman learned as an adult who her real parents were and that she is the granddaughter of the famous Argentine poet, Juan Gelman (see Argentina-Culture).

And in May 2013, for the first time, an active duty officer was convicted of a murder of a dissident during the dictatorship. General Miguel Dalmao was sentenced to 28 years for the murder of a 24-year-old Communist activist, Nibia Sabalsagaray, in 1974. He claimed the woman committed suicide in custody. He has appealed.

Mujica splashed into international headlines in July 2012 by submitting a bill that not only would legalize marijuana production, sale, possession and use, making Uruguay the first country in the world to do so, but would make the state the sole supplier—in effect, socialized head shops. But in December, faced with polls that showed two thirds of Uruguayans opposed to the idea, he told his party to back off because "the time is not ripe." One year later, he decided it was (see Recent Developments).

Uruguay was in the world headlines again in September 2012 when the Assembly resurrected the bill Vázquez had vetoed to legalize abortion in the first trimester. The bill stipulated a five-day waiting period. It squeaked through the Chamber of Deputies 50–49, and the Senate approved it, 17–14, on October 17. Mujica signed it into law a few days later, making Uruguay the first democratic Latin American country to legalize abortion on demand. It is also legal in Cuba, Guyana and Mexico's Federal District. Its opponents, backed by the Catholic Church, continued to fight. They succeeded in calling for a "consultative ballot" to force the issue to a referendum. They needed 655,000 people to vote in the consultative ballot to force the referendum, but in the balloting on June 23, 2013, only 226,653 participated.

Uruguay again made history, and broke with Latin American convention, by becoming the second Latin American country after neighboring Argentina to legalize same-sex marriage. The Chamber of Deputies approved it 71-21 in December 2012.

The Senate followed suit in April 2013, 23-8, and Mujica signed it into law.

In September 2012, the Mexico-based Mitofsky poll ranked Mujica as one of the seven least popular of 20 Western Hemisphere leaders, with an approval rating of 40%; he tied with Peru's Ollanta Humala. By October 2013 he had moved up to 45%, ranking 10th out of 19 leaders.

Recent Developments

Perhaps motivated both by a recommendation by 34 OAS foreign ministers in June 2013 to consider "new approaches" to the drug issue, as well as by the legalization of recreational marijuana use by the U.S. state of Colorado, Mujica decided the "time was ripe" to reintroduce the measure to legalize the drug, even though polls showed 63% of Uruguayans still opposed. Mujica said he was willing for Uruguay to become a test case for legalized cannabis, calling it a "contribution to humanity."

On July 31, the Chamber of Deputies approved it after 12 hours of debate, 50-46, along strict party lines. The Senate followed through on December 10, 16-13, generating news around the world. Despite the historic nature of the bill, Mujica signed it into law on December 23 behind closed doors and without fanfare. Uruguayans over 18 years of age who join a club of from 15 to 45 members will be allowed to purchase up to 40 grams (1.4 ounces) of marijuana a month at authorized pharmacies, rather than government-owned shops, and grow 99 plants a year. This requirement will likely prevent Uruguay from becoming a pilgrimage site for pot-smoking tourists. The law went into effect in April, but the bureaucratic mechanism for enforcing it was still not in place when this book went to press.

Mujica, the former guerrilla, met with President Obama in the Oval Office on May 12—without a tie, as usual. The two leaders chatted amiably and Obama praised Uruguay for its contributions to the U.N. force in Haiti and Mujica for his commitment to democracy and human rights. But Obama pointedly did not mention Uruguay's marijuana legalization. Mujica lectured Obama about officially making the United States a bilingual nation.

The country is now focused on the upcoming October 26 presidential and legislative elections. The still-popular Vázquez announced his candidacy for a second term in November 2013 and on June 1, 2014, won 84% of the vote in the Broad Front primary. He is facing two sons of ex-presidents. Pedro Bordaberry again won the *Colorado* primary, with 69% of the vote. Luis Lacalle Pou defeated perennial candidate Jorge Larrañada, who favored repealing marijuana legalization, with 53% of the

vote in the National Party primary. A Cifra poll of party, not candidate, preferences in March 2014 gave the Broad Front 45%, the National Party 28% and the *Colorados* just 15% (see The Future).

CULTURE: Almost entirely Caucasian, the result of Spanish colonization and Italian immigration, Uruguay in many ways resembles an extension of Europe, and this certainly is true in its culture. Like Chile, highly literate and prosperous Uruguay has made cultural contributions far out of proportion to its small size. Also as in Chile, this cultural development was made possible by a climate of political stability and virtually unlimited freedom of expression.

Uruguay's contributions to art and music are not insignificant, but it is in the field of literature that the country has attained its greatest recognition beyond its borders. One of the most distinguished writers was José Enrique Rodó (1872–1917), whose 1900 essay, *Ariel*, extolled Latin American culture and denounced the United States as lacking in appreciation for cultural values. Needless to say, this essay was revered by latter-day Marxists and *dependentistas* throughout Latin America.

Regarded as leading representatives of the romantic period in Uruguay were the novelists Eduardo Acevedo Díaz (1851–1921) and Carlos Reyes; the poet Juan Zorilla de San Martín bridged the gap between romanticism and modernism. Two women of the post-modernist period, Delmira Agustini and Juana de Ibarbourou, also achieved international recognition.

Some of Uruguay's leading 20th century writers abandoned the country during the military regime of 1973–85, the two best known being the novelists Juan Carlos Onetti (1909–94) and Mario Benedetti (1920–2009).

Onetti's first novel, *El pozo (The Pit)*, was considered a trendsetter in Latin American literature. Taking a technique from William Faulkner, whom he admired, Onetti created the fictional town of Santa María in his 1950 novel *La vida breve (The Short Life)* and used it in several of his 25 novels. He was jailed by the military regime, and when he was released, he spent the rest of his life in Spain, refusing even to visit Uruguay after the return to democracy. He received Spain's prestigious Cervantes Prize in 1980, the only Uruguayan ever to be so honored.

Benedetti was a poet, novelist, playwright and journalist. He wrote two plays and 11 novels, perhaps the best known being *La tregua (The Truce)* in 1960, later made into a movie, and *El cumpleaños de Juan Ángel (Juan Ángel's Birthday)* in 1971. He, too, was jailed by the military and went into exile in Argentina, Peru, Cuba and Spain, but he returned to Uruguay after the restoration of democracy and died in Montevideo on May 17, 2009.

Uruguay's cinema has always been overshadowed by neighboring Argentina, which has traditionally lured Uruguay's best talent away. Two exceptions were the collaborative directors and screenwriters Pablo Stoll (b. 1974) and Juan Pablo Rebella (1974–2006). Their 2001 independent film, *25 Watts,* an urban comedy set in Montevideo, won Best First Feature Film Award at the Havana Film Festival and Best Feature Film Award at the Rotterdam International Film Festival. Their 2004 dark comedy, *Whisky,* a joint Uruguayan-Argentine-Spanish-German production, won the Regard Original Award at the Cannes Film Festival and International Filmmakers Award for Latin America at the Sundance Film Festival. Rebella committed suicide in 2006 at the age of 32.

Traditional Uruguayan music includes several distinct styles: *milonga, candombe* and *murga. Candombe* has been recognized by UNESCO as an Intangible Cultural Heritage of Humanity. Argentine tango also has influenced Uruguayan music and musicians.

Raúl Jaurena, age uncertain, is an internationally renowned Uruguay-born tango composer and *bandoneón* (accordion) master. He won the Latin Grammy for Best Tango Album in 2007 for *Te Amo Tango.* He has lived in New York for more than 20 years but has a tango school in Montevideo.

An Uruguayan singer-songwriter who has achieved international acclaim but hasn't abandoned the country is Jorge Drexler (b. 1964). Son of a Jewish father who fled to Uruguay from Germany, Drexler became an ear, nose and throat specialist while achieving fame in music. He combines traditional Uruguayan sounds, like *milonga,* with tango. His song, *Al Otro Lado del Río,* which he sang, appeared in the sound track of the movie *The Motorcycle Diaries,* a biopic about the young Ché Guevara, and won the U.S. Academy Award for Best Song. His album *Cara B* was nominated for the Grammy Award for Best Latin Pop Album in 2009. In 2010, he, his album *Amar la Trama (Loving the Plot)* and one of its songs, *Una Canción Me Trajo Aquí (A Song Brought Me Here)* received four Latin Grammy nominations, for Record of the Year, Song of the Year, Best Singer-Songwriter Album and Best Long Form Music Video.

Uruguay's oldest band, formed in 1980, is *El Cuarteto de Nos,* which despite its name now has five members. Its album *Porfiado* won the Latin Grammy in 2012 for Best Pop/Rock Album, and Roberto Musso, a founding member of the group

who left it in 2009, won the Latin Grammy for Best Rock Song, *Cuando Sea Grande.* They brought to four the number of Latin Grammys Uruguay has won.

Uruguayan journalism is highly developed but also highly politicized. The leading daily remains *El Día,* founded in 1886 by the future President of the Republic José Ordóñez y Batlle as a mouthpiece for his *Colorado* Party, which it still is today. Ordóñez's picture remains on the editorial page like the image of a patron saint. The *Blanco* Party has its own organ, *El País,* founded in 1918. The third major daily is *El Diario,* also pro-*Blanco.*

Uruguay has always placed an emphasis on education, giving it one of the highest literacy rates in the Western Hemisphere. There are seven major colleges and universities, four of which have been established since the return to democracy in 1985. The University of the Republic was founded in 1833.

ECONOMY: Uruguay's economy is almost totally dependent on its cattle and sheep-raising industry, which accounts for more than 40% of all exports. Because of heavy taxation on farm products, as well as inefficient state management of the economy, the gross national product actually declined between 1955 and 1975. Inflation has also been a serious problem. Prices rose by an incredible 1,200% in the decade following 1968. To help control inflation, the government imposed new tax and credit policies. Steps were also taken to increase farm output, stimulate exports and begin offshore oil exploration.

Economic growth declined for several years during the country's economic crisis of 1999–2002 (see History). Real GDP shrank by –3.2% in 1999, –1.3% in 2000, –3.4% in 2001 and –10.8% in 2002. It finally grew by 2.5% in 2003 and 12.3% in 2004, but that did not even recover the ground lost during the recession.

It then grew steadily for four years: 6.6% in 2005, 7% in 2006, 7.2% in 2007 and 8.5% in 2008. With the global recession, it grew by only 2.6% in 2009. In 2010, it rebounded to 8.5%, the second-highest in Latin America after Paraguay. It was 6.5% in 2011, but slowed to 3.9% in 2012 and 3.5% in 2013, about the hemispheric average.

Unemployment remained stubbornly in the double-digits for several years and peaked at 20% in 2002 during the economic crisis. It was still 10.8% in 2006. It was down to 6% in 2011 and in 2012, rising to 6.5% in 2013.

Inflation reached 26% in 2002 during the crisis. It was 8.1% in both 2011 and 2012 and 8.3% in 2013.

Much of the blame for the 1999–2002 crisis could be placed on the dire economic situation in neighboring Argentina. Ar-

gentines who once crowded the beautiful beaches at Punta del Este stayed home in droves in the summer of 2002. Even worse, they began withdrawing millions they had deposited in Uruguayan banks for safekeeping. The crucial beef industry was simultaneously affected by an outbreak of mad cow disease, which caused exports to nosedive.

Uruguay's seemingly enviable cradle-to-the-grave social welfare system and generous retirement benefits helped give Uruguay one of the hemisphere's best standards of living for decades, and the per capita income for years was second only to Argentina's among the Latin American republics. It was $6,300 in 1998, but it dropped steadily during the devastating recession of 1999–2002. The per capita income of $3,300 in 2004 ranked seventh in the region. The situation has improved dramatically. Uruguay's per capita income of $11,860 in 2011 was third-highest in Latin America behind Argentina and Chile, and in 2012, Uruguay was second-highest behind Chile, at $13,580, according to the World Bank's Atlas method. Only 18.6% of the population was below the poverty line in 2010, far below the Latin American average.

The long-cherished social welfare system has come at a high price; external debt in 1999 was $6.3 billion, about 30% of GDP, even then a heavy burden for such a small country, and by the end of 2004 it was about 90% of GDP, the ninth highest in the world. Severe austerity measures brought it down to 57% in 2008. In 2012 it was still 57.2% in 2012, 49th in the world, but in 2013 it was 30.8%, in 84th place.

In 2002, the international rating for Uruguayan bonds was reduced, thus making it more costly to borrow money. The Batlle administration responded with an economic austerity plan, which included privatization of state-owned utilities, telecommunications, airports and even highways, and a cut in the bloated civil service pensions. Batlle also promised to reduce the budget deficit, which was 4.2% of GDP in 2001, to 2.5% in 2002 and to balance the budget by 2004. The move was popular with the International Monetary Fund, which approved $743 million in loans in March 2002, another for $1.5 billion in May and $3.8 billion in August. Uruguay and the IMF agreed to restructure its bond indebtedness, thus extending the term of its bonds. But a law privatizing the state-owned oil company, *ANCAP,* proved unpopular with the voters; 62% of them voted to repeal it in a referendum in December 2003.

Despite his leftist tilt, President Tabaré Vázquez, elected in 2004, bent over backward to reassure foreign investors and creditors that he would honor Uruguay's

Uruguay

debt commitment (about $11 billion when he took office in March 2005), and he moderated his long-standing opposition to free trade. Thus, he more closely resembled Brazilian President Luiz Inácio da Silva and former Chilean President Roberto Lagos, two socialists who pragmatically moved to the center, than the confrontationist Presidents Néstor Kirchner of Argentina and Hugo Chávez of Venezuela.

His pragmatism paid off, literally; in 2005, the IMF approved a $1.13 billion loan and the World Bank approved an $800 million, five-year loan to help the country recover from the recession. In 2006, Uruguay paid $630 million to the IMF ahead of schedule and paid another $1.1 billion in 2007.

Vázquez's successor in 2010, José Mujica, is a former *Tupamaro* guerrilla who, like Vázquez, has mellowed in recent years. He has not radically changed his predecessor's prudent and pragmatic policies.

THE FUTURE: Uruguay was once the embodiment of Churchill's comment that democracy is the worst possible form of government—except for all the others. Uruguayans have been reluctant to abandon their cherished welfare state and state-owned monopolies, which had be-

come luxuries the economy could not afford. They punished any party at the polls that sought to do so, but gradually they succumbed to reality and accepted badly needed austerity measures.

They do cherish their democracy. In the annual *Latinobarómetro* survey of 18 Latin American nations published by *The Economist*, 71% of Uruguayans said in 2013 they believed democracy is preferable to any other form of government, the third-highest percentage in the survey. That was down, however, from 78% in 2003, when it tied with Costa Rica for the highest. In 2013, 81% said they were satisfied with the way democracy works in their country, the highest in the survey.

They have reason to be satisfied. Dr. Tabaré Vázquez and now José Mujica finally accomplished at the ballot box what the *Tupamaros* failed to do with terror—bring the left to power and break the grip of the two traditional parties. But like so many other erstwhile Latin American left-wing firebrands, they moderated their Marxist rhetoric and eschewed a radical approach. Vázquez embraced the pragmatic socialism of Brazil's Lula da Silva, rather than the meat-ax Marxism of Venezuela's Hugo Chávez. His performance as president was impressive. He reassured

foreign investors and attracted new industry—despite environmental risks. He repaid IMF loan installments ahead of schedule. The economy showed encouraging growth on his watch. At the same time, he sought justice for the human rights abuses of the military regime. Mujica has essentially followed Vázquez's lead, deciding not to try to fix something that isn't broken.

Whether or not to grant amnesty for human rights abuses of the 1970s and '80s remains an emotional issue for Uruguayans, who remain almost evenly divided: justice or reconciliation? Ironically, most Uruguayans now are too young to have any memory of the military dictatorship. Mujica, a former guerrilla who remembers it only too well, has not been in a forgiving mood.

Uruguayans are also emotional over their country making history by becoming the first country in the world to legalize marijuana cultivation, sales, possession and use in 2013. A poll at the time showed 63% opposed to the bill. Could this backfire on the ruling front?

Probably not. Vázquez became the Broad Front's nominee for a second term in October 26, and was returned to office in March 2015.

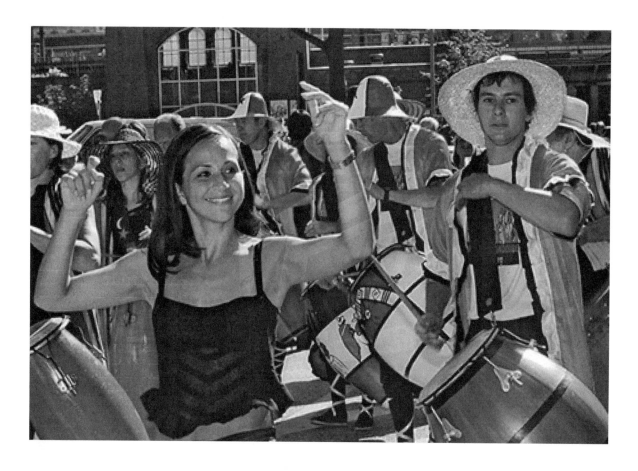

The Bolivarian Republic of Venezuela

Caracas and the mountains

Venezuela

Area: 352,150 square miles.

Population: 28,868,486 (2014 est.).

Capital City: Caracas (Pop. 5 million, estimated).

Climate: Tropical in the coastal lowlands, increasingly temperate at higher elevations in the interior. Heaviest rainfall is from June to December.

Neighboring Countries: Guyana (East); Brazil (Southeast and South); Colombia (Southwest and West); Trinidad and Tobago are islands lying a short distance from the northeast coast.

Official Language: Spanish

Other Principal Tongue: English.

Ethnic Background: Mulatto-*mestizo* (mixed European, African and Indian ancestry, 83%); European (10%); African (5%); Indian (2%).

Principal Religion: Roman Catholic Christianity.

Chief Commercial Products: Petroleum and petroleum products, aluminum, alumina and bauxite, agricultural products, small manufactured products.

Currency: Bolívar.

Gross Domestic Product: U.S. $367.5 billion in 2013 ($12,913 per capita, official exchange rate).

Former Colonial Status: Spanish Colony (1498–1811).

Independence Date: July 5, 1811. Venezuela seceded from *Gran Colombia*, also known as New Granada, on September 22, 1811.

Chief of State: Nicolás Maduro Moros (b. November 23, 1962), president (since March 5, 2013).

National Flag: Yellow, blue and red horizontal stripes with seven yellow stars in a semi-circle on the red stripe.

Venezuela has four distinct geographic regions: the Venezuelan Highlands to the west and along the coast, the Maracaibo Lowlands around freshwater Lake Maracaibo, the *Llanos* or plains of the Orinoco River and the Guiana Highlands. The Venezuelan Highlands are an extension of the eastern mountains of Colombia and are Venezuela's most densely populated region, with Caracas, Maracay and Valencia located in the fertile inter-mountain basins. The northern slope of the Highlands is relatively arid, but the basins receive adequate rainfall and because of elevation, are temperate and suited to agriculture.

The Maracaibo Lowlands, encircled by mountains, are windless and one of the hottest regions in South America, famous for the great lake (129 miles long and 60 miles wide) under whose water are some of the most extensive oil deposits in the world. Rainfall in this region is heavy along the slopes of the highlands, gradually diminishing toward the coast.

The *Llanos* of the Orinoco are the great treeless plains of the Orinoco River valley, which run east and west between the Venezuelan Highlands and the Guiana Highlands. Extending some 600 miles in length and 200 miles across, these plains are low and wet; intersected with slow moving streams, this region has been plagued with periodic floods and drought, but the poor soil has supported cattle raising. Presently, the government is undertaking flood control and irrigation projects to make this land available for agriculture and to support the development of new breeds of cattle.

The Guiana Highlands, south of the Orinoco, comprise more than half of Venezuela's territory. Rising in steep cliffs from the *Llanos*, this area is a flat tableland that extends to the Brazilian border. Heavily forested in part, it contains vast deposits of iron ore and bauxite. Gold and diamonds also exist in this region, which has been explored only superficially.

HISTORY: At the time of the Spanish conquest, Venezuela was inhabited by warlike tribes of Carib and Arawak Indians who offered brave but ineffective resistance to the invaders. The first landing was in the Gulf of Paria, where pearls were discovered. Under Spanish direction, Indian divers soon stripped the beds of the Gulf. The first settlement was established at Cumaná in 1520, with additional settlements at Coro (1520), Barquismeto (1551), Valencia (1555) and Caracas (1567).

Indians were utilized to pan the rivers for gold, but the results were disappointing and the settlers turned to agriculture. The wealth found in Peru and Mexico caused the Spanish government to lose interest in Venezuela, and options to explore its potential were leased to Dutch and German adventurers. The Spanish settlers gradually consolidated their small holdings, but it was nearly a century later before a serious attempt was made to explore the interior. The enslaved Indian laborers perished on the coastal plantations, and black slaves were imported from Africa to work the sugar and indigo crops. The neglected planters, with little merchandise to ship to the Spanish markets and forbidden to trade with the growing American markets, revolted against Spanish authority in 1796.

Two additional abortive attempts to set up an independent government were made in 1806 and 1811 under the leadership of Francisco de Miranda. At his urging, a republican congress declared independence on July 5, 1811, but the so-called First Republic lasted only a year. Venezuela's national hero, Simón Bolívar, took up the struggle and fought a limited, but de-

ceptive, guerrilla war against local armies in the pay of Spain until his capture of Angostura in 1817. Here he was joined by British veterans of the Peninsular War in Spain and by cattlemen from the *Llanos* with whom he made a dramatic march on Bogotá. The Spanish were finally expelled from northern Latin America in 1819 and the country achieved full independence, becoming a part of the Republic of Gran Colombia, led by President Simón Bolívar and Vice President Francisco de Paula Santander, and including present-day Colombia and Ecuador. Dissension and the subsequent illness of Bolívar led to the dissolution of Gran Colombia; Venezuela withdrew in 1830.

General José Antonio Páez, the country's first president and a hero of independence, dominated Venezuelan politics from 1830 to 1848. He later returned as a dictator from 1861 to 1863. A capable and popular leader, he was effective in restoring order to war-torn Venezuela and in the establishment of governmental services and control. He was followed in 1848 by 13 years of repressive dictatorship by the Monagas brothers, who forced him into exile.

In 1861, Páez raised another force of cattlemen to regain power in Venezuela. He ruled for two years, but was less tolerant of opposition than he had been during his first tenure; he was ousted in 1863 and intermittent civil war wracked the country until 1870 as young liberals fought conservatives.

Antonio Guzmán Blanco emerged from the chaos of civil strife; as strongman, he served as president or ruled through puppets for 18 years. Well educated, arrogant and completely unscrupulous, he enforced honesty among his ministers while converting a substantial part of the national treasury to his personal use. A careless despot who enjoyed living in Paris, he left his office in the hands of a puppet once too often and was overthrown in 1888.

Eleven years of confusion ensued, punctuated by violence and short-term presidents. An illiterate soldier of fortune who had been exiled to Colombia, Cipriano Castro, captured the presidency with the help of a private army in 1899. His nine-year rule was the most repressive in Venezuela's troubled history. His high-handed dealing with European powers resulted in a blockade of the Venezuelan coastline by British, German and Italian naval units. After intervention by President Theodore Roosevelt, the matter was settled by arbitration. Castro turned the government over in 1909 to Juan Vincente Gómez, who ruled until 1935.

Gómez gave Venezuela its most able and its most savage administration. Oil had been discovered and he arranged lucrative contracts with U.S., British and

Dutch interests for extraction and processing. Simultaneously, he fostered agriculture and public works, established sound foreign relations and paid off the national debt. He also mechanized the army to support his regime and built a personal fortune. By comparison with his predecessors, Gómez left Venezuela in a prosperous condition when he died, but totally bereft of qualified leaders to administer the wealth he had accumulated or to control the army, which he had enlarged and modernized.

From 1935 to 1948 a series of moderate, but ineffective presidents occupied the office; during this period, political parties were allowed to organize, the largest being *Acción Democrática* (Democratic Action), a center-left party that had attempted to consolidate rural labor into a mass organization. Fearful of a rigged election in 1945, the party revolted and named Rómulo Betancourt as provisional president.

Venezuelans were delighted with democratic government, and action was taken to recover some of the wealth from Gómez's estate and from others who had privately benefited during his rule. In the first free and honest elections in Venezuela's history, Rómulo Gallegos, a well-known novelist, was chosen as president in 1947. Moving too fast to accomplish his goals, he frightened the army, which feared loss of its power and position in the government; he was ousted by a coup within three months of his inauguration. The army declared that it would save the country from communism, and exiled Gallegos and Betancourt, establishing another dictatorship under General Marcos Pérez Jiménez. He loosed a reign of terror and with reckless abandon spent the income from oil on public works in the city of Caracas and on poorly planned industrial ventures, with a handsome cut to friends and to the army. By late 1957 Venezuelans had had enough—resistance increased to the point that even the pampered army refused to oppose the popular will. Pérez Jiménez fled in January 1958, and a combined military and civilian committee took over.

Democracy Takes Root

Three moderate parties competed for the presidency in elections that December: Democratic Action, or *AD*; the Democratic Republican Union (*URD*), and a social Christian movement with a cumbersome name that is better known by the acronym *COPEI*. The *AD*'s Betancourt was returned to the presidency with a 47% plurality and was sworn in for a five-year term on February 13, 1959, beginning an unbroken line of nine presidential

administrations that has continued to the present, an enviable record of stability for Latin America.

An enlightened leader, Betancourt oversaw the adoption of a liberal constitution in 1961, but he also had to deal with a leftist insurgency incited by Cuba's Fidel Castro. Nonetheless, left-wing political parties such as the Movement to Socialism (*MAS*) were allowed to compete under Betancourt's tolerant constitution. One of the fundamental tenets of that document, designed to guard against another Gómez or Pérez Jiménez, was that no president could be re-elected for 10 years after leaving office. The popular Betancourt was succeeded in 1964 by Raúl Leoni, also of *AD*, who received a 33% plurality.

In the December 1968 election, *COPEI*'s Rafael Caldera was elected with only a 29% plurality. Caldera was instrumental in establishing the Organization of Petroleum Exporting Countries (OPEC).

AD was returned to power in 1973 elections in which Carlos Andrés Pérez won a landslide (by Venezuelan standards) 48% of the vote over his principal opponent. Both candidates had run on almost identical center-left platforms. Voters firmly rejected both the radical left and right—the Marxist-Socialist candidate received only 4.2% of the vote and the right-wing candidate, a former associate of Pérez Jiménez, got less than 1%. In congressional races, *AD* won 24 of 49 seats in the Senate and 102 out of 200 seats in the Chamber of Deputies. Pérez launched new, ambitious programs in agriculture and education, which amazed even his own supporters.

Venezuela took charge of the U.S.-operated iron mines near Ciudad Guyana in 1975. The nationalization of the oil industry occurred in 1976. The 40 private firms, most of them U.S.-based, were granted compensation of $1.2 billion, which Venezuela asserted was equal to the book value of their assets. The companies claimed the true value to be between $3.5 and $5 billion.

Although Pérez maintained that nationalization of the oil industry would make Venezuelans "masters of their destiny," the nation continued to depend heavily on foreign oil companies to refine, transport and market the oil. In addition, the oil firms provided technical assistance to the state-owned oil organization, *Petroven*. Ironically, the fees charged by the private firms for these services were almost as high as the profits they made before nationalization. Such a lucrative arrangement led to criticism of the Pérez administration by those who claimed that "oil nationalization needs more nationalization."

In 1973, when it joined OPEC in raising prices by more than 400%, Venezuela experienced windfall profits. With its oil income rising from $2 billion in 1972 to $10.4 billion in 1974 and $14.5 billion in 1983, Venezuela earned more from oil during the two years following the price hike than in the previous 56 years it had been exporting oil.

The gush of petrodollars swamped the nation with more money than it could realistically absorb. To control the resulting inflation, which rose from the usual rate of 2–3% to 20% in 1974, the government

Birthplace of the Great Liberator, Simón Bolívar in Caracas

Venezuela

The sprawl of modern Caracas

channeled half the money out of the country. Some was invested in international lending agencies while some was lent to developing nations, particularly in the Caribbean. To further reduce the cash inflow, and to conserve the nation's dwindling oil reserves (then estimated at 12–15 billion barrels), Venezuela cut production from an average of 3.3 million barrels a day in 1973 to 2.2 million in 1976.

Oil income vastly increased Venezuelan influence in Latin America. By raising contributions (and therefore voting power) in international lending organizations, Pérez hoped to make these agencies less subject to "humiliating vetoes" of loans to nations out of favor with the United States. Venezuela also helped to finance the establishment of cartels—such as in banana and coffee production and marketing—so that developing nations could charge more for raw materials sold to industrialized countries.

In foreign relations, Venezuela became an advocate for Third World causes and for Latin American economic independence. Pérez also played a major role in advocating greater respect for human rights in the region, and condemned the use of torture by the military regime in Chile.

Relations with the United States remained cordial. In 1977, Pérez visited the United States, where he praised the Carter administration's campaign for human rights. Carter gave Venezuela high

marks for its refusal to join a 1973 OPEC oil embargo against the United States arising out of the Arab-Israeli conflict, and for shipping extra quantities of oil to North America during the unusually cold winter of 1976–77.

Venezuela had one of the highest per capita incomes in Latin America, but most of that was concentrated in the upper class (5%) and the middle class (15%), both of which literally went on a spending spree. Signs of the "good life" abounded—swimming pools, comfortable homes and beach villas. A 350% tax on luxury cars didn't slow demand. Although domestic car production reached record levels, there was a waiting list for buyers.

In this jewel of opulence, fully 80% of the people lived in poverty (and still do), with malnutrition afflicting half the nation's people. Almost none of the oil money filtered down to the poor. Pérez warned, "Our country is rich, but our people are poor." Ironically, he was one of the "fat cat" class engaged in open thievery.

The search for jobs and a better life lured 80% of the population to urban areas, where they settled in filthy slums surrounding major cities. This caused not only a costly drop in farm output and a jump in food prices, but created immense problems of how to provide basic services to this population encircling the cities. More than 70% of the population of Caracas, then and now, lives in sordid *ranchos*,

where even the police hesitate to go, in sharp contrast to the gleaming skyscrapers of the city. Incentives encouraging slum dwellers to move back to the country failed.

Investment during the first Pérez administration centered on the oil, steel and electrical industries, traditional sources of income for the super-rich of Venezuela.

In 1978, Venezuela suffered its largest balance of payments deficit in its history ($1.7 billion). Exports (mostly oil) were down 7.5% from the previous year. During the five years Pérez was in office, imports rose by more than 230%.

As is often common during periods of rapid economic expansion, there was also widespread government fraud, inefficiency, administrative waste and a decrease in social services. Living standards actually declined for the lower-income masses. Although Pérez boasted that unemployment had been largely eliminated, the inflation rate ranged between 10% (officially) and 20% (more accurate). Urban residents also complained of overcrowded schools, shortages of water and electric power and declining quality of health facilities.

Increased economic problems set the stage for the 1978 presidential elections, when voters turned to the *COPEI*'s Luis Herrera Campíns, who won with 46.6% of the 5.5 million votes cast. The *AD*'s candidate trailed with 43%. During the campaign, Herrera Campíns repeatedly charged that the nation's oil income had been squandered through government corruption, waste and deficit spending.

The new president, a former journalist, was widely regarded as an intellectual. He promised to emphasize state development of major industries while also encouraging greater private investments. He also pledged to pay more attention to the problems of the poor as well as to expand the nation's school system. Herrera Campíns also made an effort to diversify the economy from its over-dependence on oil.

He criticized the Reagan administration for its "treatment" of Nicaragua, its support of the right-wing government in El Salvador and for its backing of Britain in the Falkland Islands invasion by Argentina in 1982.

A burning issue was Venezuela's long-simmering border dispute with neighboring Guyana. Venezuela claimed a full five eighths of Guyana's territory! There was strong anti-British feeling in Venezuela—exacerbated by the Falklands dispute. British warships shelled Venezuela's ports early in the 20th century when Venezuela failed to repay loans to British banks. Herrera Campíns wanted to settle the border dispute through negotiation. However, the amount of territory claimed made a solution almost impossible to reach. The area claimed is rich in timber—and potentially rich in oil, minerals and precious gems.

Venezuela's oil wealth attracted a flood of immigrants from its poorer neighbors. Efforts to register the newcomers were inadequate. The ethnic makeup of the country was also altered by the presence of more than 1 million European and Arab immigrants, who worked in the technological aspects of petroleum production.

By 1981, it was clear Venezuela's governments had not been able to follow the wise advice of Rómulo Betancourt "to sow the oil," meaning diversify the economy and avoid the country's increasing dependence on oil exports. Limited industrialization, declining agricultural production and a lack of serious planning made the economy highly vulnerable to any change in the price of oil.

Consequently, the oil gluts of 1979–80 and 1986–90 hit Venezuela hard. In 1982, the country suffered from a severe cash crisis produced by falling oil revenues, a sharp decline in international reserves and a lack of confidence of potential investors. The government re-evaluated its gold holdings and placed the state oil company under central bank jurisdiction. Unaccustomed to austerity, the Venezuelans reacted with mounting criticism to the government's erratic policies.

Presidential and congressional elections in 1983 demonstrated the general dis-

content with *COPEI*. Jaime Lusinchi, the presidential candidate of *AD*, won easily, receiving more than 50% of the vote over the respected former President Rafael Caldera of *COPEI*. *AD* also received a majority in Congress.

Lusinchi not only did not ease the austerity measures, he devalued the currency by almost half, increased fuel prices by more than 100% to eliminate what amounted to an annual subsidy of $85 million, and instituted temporary wage-price freezes in large sectors of the economy.

Venezuela placed a moratorium on the repayment of its foreign debt in 1983, but under pressure from international banks, it renegotiated the obligation and agreed in 1986 to resume payment. Although large reserves indicated the ability to maintain payments, at the same time the debt payment resumption was finally negotiated, Venezuelan oil was in the process of dropping from $28 per barrel to less than $10 in the face of increased Saudi Arabian and world production.

The 1988 presidential campaign was lively, but as usual there was little difference between the two powerful political parties. *COPEI* was still dogged by its association with the sharp economic drop in the early 1980s. Within *AD*, Lusinchi opposed the nomination of former President Pérez, but Pérez accurately accused the president of maintaining the illusion of prosperity by emptying the treasury. Pérez himself had been convicted of theft during his first term, but departed for Spain to avoid going to prison. The voters' memory didn't reach back that far, and he received a majority of 53%.

Lusinchi announced yet another moratorium on debt repayment shortly before leaving office. Pérez negotiated additional aid from the International Monetary Fund in return for imposing reforms, including a 90% increase in the price of gasoline (from 15 cents to 25 cents a gallon), a doubling of bus fares, unfreezing prices on almost everything and ending numerous subsidies.

Crisis and Corruption

Suddenly, the poor were faced with the brutal realization that the free lunch they had been enjoying was over. Riots broke out in Caracas in 1989 and quickly spread to other cities. Common criminals took advantage of the unrest to loot stores. Pérez declared martial law and ordered the army to crush the rioters. At least 300 people were killed and more than 2,000 injured in what came to be called the "*Caracazo*." It remains controversial to this day, just as the 1968 Tlatelolco Massacre is in Mexico.

Conditions deteriorated swiftly in 1988–89 in spite of nominally improved

Former President Carlos Andrés Pérez

economic conditions. Caracas' homicide rate was more than 1,500 per year. Drug trafficking became rampant. Wages for all but the elite remained incredibly low. The mass of people enveloped by abject poverty began to fully realize who had benefited from more than a half century of oil exportation.

In 1992, Venezuela's once-admired democracy was shaken to its very foundations. There were two abortive military *coups*, one of which was nearly successful but collapsed when commanders of key units failed to join the effort to oust Pérez. The instigator, a charismatic paratrooper named Lieutenant Colonel Hugo Chávez, was sentenced to two years in prison. The same year, Pérez was accused of pilfering $17 million in public funds. He issued a clumsy, unconvincing, almost arrogant denial, and public opinion turned harshly against him.

Pérez's party, his majority in the Congress and his hand-picked Supreme Court turned on him in 1993. Congress voted for impeachment, and he was forced to step down. The Senate appointed José Ramón Velásquez to head an interim government for the rest of his term. For good measure, Pérez was convicted in a criminal court and served 28 months in prison. In 1998, then 74, Pérez was again placed under house arrest when he and his mistress were charged with "illegal enrichment" for depositing large sums of undisclosed origin in U.S. banks. Pérez went into self-imposed exile in Miami, where he died on Christmas Day 2010.

In the 1993 elections, the voters rejected the two principal political parties, voting for Caldera, now 80, who had ended his association with *COPEI*. He was the candidate of a 17-party coalition, the *Convergencia Nacional* (*CN*—"National Convergence"). He won with a plurality of only 30.5% in a four-man race.

Venezuela

Caldera's first term had been uncontroversial and somewhat uneventful during a period of relative Venezuelan wealth. This time, he inherited an absolute nightmare when he took office in February 1994. Despite decades of oil money, Venezuela was in dire financial straits. A controversial value added tax (VAT) was initially extended, then canceled because of popular opposition in 1994. The second-largest bank collapsed, with fallout in the form of a run on all banks. The cause: massive thievery; 83 were arrested.

Venezuela's years of drunken-sailor spending had given it a foreign debt in excess of $27 billion, more than half of GDP, which threatened the country with insolvency. The crisis was so severe that in 1996 Caldera was forced to sign a reform package with the IMF, something he once vowed he would never do. Among other things, the package eliminated the gasoline subsidy and abolished price controls. The measures were annoying to Venezuela's small, crybaby middle class but were especially painful to the poor, who still accounted for 80% of the population.

The crisis lumbered on into 1997. The state-owned airline, *Viasa*, went bankrupt. At the end of the year, Caldera, the one-time populist, privatized the money-losing state-owned steel company, *Sidor*, and announced plans to sell off the state's aluminum company. In 1998, the government was hit with a new fiscal blow when the price of oil, on which the government pegs its budget estimates, suddenly dropped. The government had drawn up a $23 billion budget based on an estimate of $15.50 a barrel, but the price fell to $12.80. Moreover, despite efforts to reduce the size of the cumbersome bureaucracy (see Economy), the public payroll in 1997 actually *increased* by 4%! Inflation was reduced to a still-high 38% in 1997, the highest in Latin America, due mostly to a 75% pay increase for public employees.

The Elections of 1998

Like a retreaded tire, the second Caldera administration blew out and the country lumbered along for the last year of his term, as Venezuelans desperately searched for a mechanic. So eager were they for a fresh face offering dynamic new leadership that for a time it seemed they would entrust their future to Irene Sáez, the 1981 Miss Universe, who had compiled a respectable record as mayor of the Caracas suburb of Chacao. Polls showed the 35-year-old Sáez with a commanding lead, but her poll figures dropped when she failed to offer any substantive solutions for the country's ills; she was, it seemed, little more than a still pretty-face with name recognition.

Not so Hugo Chávez, leader of the abortive 1992 coup, who declared his own independent candidacy in early 1998 under the banner of the Fifth Republic Movement. His candidacy sent chills through the heavily entrenched political and economic establishments, but he soon gained a following among the downtrodden masses.

Chávez was a dynamic speaker, whose *macho*, charismatic mien and populist rhetoric were reminiscent of Latin American *caudillos* of old. Instead of a white horse and fringed epaulets, however, this late 20th-century savior had his red paratrooper's beret. Born into the middle class in 1954, he is the son of two schoolteachers. As a boy, he sold fruit on a street corner, and the army recruited him because of his skill as a baseball pitcher. Besides the appeal of his humble beginnings, his vow to clean up the country's cumbersome, corrupt political system, to wrest power away from the elite and to effect genuine socioeconomic reforms electrified Venezuela's destitute, long-suffering and resentful masses. As his bandwagon gained inertia, more alienated political groupings jumped aboard, forming an alliance called Patriotic Pole. At the same time, Chávez's open admiration for Fidel Castro alarmed the elite, as well as foreign investors.

The campaigns for the November 1998 congressional and regional elections and the December presidential election were the most bizarre of Venezuela's 40-year-old democracy. As Chávez's lead in the polls widened, the two traditional parties panicked and grasped for ways to stop this juggernaut. *COPEI* offered its nomination to Sáez, who foolishly accepted. Now identified with one of the establishment parties blamed for the country's woes, she fell even further behind Chávez. *AD*, meanwhile, initially nominated a 76-year-old party hack. Filling out the race was another independent, Henrique Salas, a respected 62-year-old businessman and Yale graduate, who formed a movement called Project Venezuela.

In the November 8 elections, Patriotic Pole became the largest force in the new Congress, winning 34% of the seats in the 48-member Senate and 189-member Chamber of Deputies. *AD* was a distant second with 22%; Salas' Project Venezuela won 12% of the seats, and *COPEI* won a pitiful 11%. Patriotic Pole also won seven of the 23 governorships; Chávez's father, also named Hugo, was elected governor of Barinas. *AD* fell from 11 governorships to eight.

Chávez then suddenly softened his fiery populist, anti-establishment rhetoric. Evidently aware that he was on the brink of full power, he seemed to be reassuring foreign investors and domestic financial kingpins on whose support he would depend to resuscitate the moribund economy.

In an unprecedented Machiavellian maneuver, *AD* and *COPEI* jettisoned their own candidates on November 20 and

The Caracas daily *El Universal* reports the landslide reelection victory of President Chávez on July 30, 2000.

400

rallied behind Salas, who was second in the polls. Chávez sneered that this only proved that *AD* and *COPEI* had conspired all along to share power.

But this last-ditch ploy failed. On December 6, an uncharacteristically high 65% of the electorate turned out to vote. Chávez polled a landslide 56.5%, to 39.5% for Salas; Sáez was a microscopic third. The flamboyant Chávez suddenly appeared humble and conciliatory, and reached out to *AD* and *COPEI* for a consensus on how to solve the country's problems. He also reassured the business establishment that he did not seek to dismantle the capitalist system.

Even before the new Congress was installed, the president-elect declared his intention to call for a referendum dissolving Congress and the judiciary and calling for the installation of a constituent assembly to rewrite the 1961 constitution. The traditional parties vowed to block Chávez's initiative, prompting Chávez to denounce what he called a "conspiracy" and to threaten to dissolve Congress and rule by decree. It was to be the first of many bombastic threats to circumvent democratic institutions.

New President, New Constitution

Chávez was inaugurated on February 2, 1999. He reiterated his plans to scrap the constitution he had just sworn to uphold, deriding it as "moribund," and proclaimed what he called the "Bolívarian revolution." He set the date for the first of three referenda on constitutional reform. Among his proposals for the new basic law: removal of the ban against immediate re-election, saying he needed at least 10 years to put Venezuela's house in order.

Like a weary parent trying to placate a willful child, Congress acceded to Chávez's demands and gave him the

Former President Hugo Chávez Frías

power to make sweeping economic decisions without congressional approval for six months.

In the April referendum, which had a 60% turnout, a stunning 90% voted *"sí"* for a constituent assembly. The election for the 131 members of the constituent assembly was held in July 1999. Predictably, 121 of the 131 members elected were members of Patriotic Pole, including Chávez's wife, Marisabel, and his brother.

In August, the assembly formally voted to strip Congress of its powers and sealed off the gold-domed capitol building, which sparked protests by Chávez opponents. Several opposition members of Congress scaled the fence around the *Capitolio* in defiance of the assembly's decision, while pro- and anti-Chávez factions clashed in the street outside. Violence appeared imminent.

The Catholic Church mediated a peaceful solution, preventing another bloody *Caracazo* that would have benefited neither side. The agreement stipulated that Congress would continue to serve as the law-making body, including the power to approve the budget, until after the referendum on the new constitution. (Chávez later broke that promise.)

The assembly soon renewed its attack on the judiciary. It appointed a special judicial investigative committee, which summarily removed 130 judges who had been under investigation for bribery and other sins. Few had any sympathy for the sacked judges, as the judiciary had become notoriously corrupt, but the lack of due process was troubling. The Supreme Court meekly upheld the judges' dismissal.

The assembly moved like a steamroller on the new constitution. The final document had Chávez's fingerprints all over it. It renamed the country the Bolívarian Republic of Venezuela. It established a new 165-member unicameral National Assembly, abolishing the Senate. The presidential term was increased from five to six years, and immediate re-election was permitted. The president was to enjoy far greater authority than under the old constitution. The state and local governments were replaced by regional and municipal councils. Active-duty members of the military were given the right to vote for the first time. There was no prohibition against abortion, which drew fire from the Catholic Church. It reduced the work week from 48 to 40 hours, which upset businessmen. It declared that Venezuelans have a right to "free, truthful, uncensored information," but left unsaid who would determine what is "truthful," a clause seen as an attempt to silence Chávez's critics in the media. The cries of naysayers that the new organic

law was drafted too hastily and concentrated too much power in the president's hands were drowned out in an avalanche of public approval. On December 15, 1999, voters overwhelmingly ratified it by 71.8%.

Renewed Mandate

The constituent assembly abolished the old Congress and the Supreme Court, then created a 23-member standing committee, nicknamed the "*Congresillo*," to act as the legislative authority pending the election of the new National Assembly. Elected president of the *Congresillo* was Luis Miquilena, a close Chávez ally who was y regarded as the second most powerful man in the country.

Chávez announced he would subject himself to the electorate under the new constitution to seek a renewed mandate. All other officials established under the new constitution would be selected in the same "*Megaelecciones*," scheduled for May 28, 2000.

In February 2000, the first schism appeared in Chávez's Bolívarian revolution. To mark the eighth anniversary of the 1992 coup attempt, three of Chávez's former comrades-in-arms broke with the president, accusing him of corruption and of betraying the goals of their revolutionary movement. Among them was Francisco Arias Cárdenas, governor of Zulia State, widely regarded as the intellectual author of the 1992 coup attempt. Though not as charismatic or brash as Chávez, Arias was generally respected as more reasoned moderate. To use a Steinbeckian metaphor, Arias played the role of George to Chávez's Lenny. An even unkinder metaphorical cut for Chávez came, symbolically, on March 15—the Ides of March—when Arias declared that he would run for president against his former friend and chief. A former mayor of Caracas, Claudio Fermín, also declared his candidacy.

Chávez wisely eschewed the intellectually superior Arias' invitation to a debate. Arias aired a television commercial in which he "debated" a hen, which represented his "chicken" opponent.

There was an ominous cloud over the campaign. The five-member National Electoral Council, or *CNE*, all of them Chávez appointees, warned that it was unsure it could resolve computer problems in time for the election. The *CNE* blamed the problems on a U.S. firm that had the contract to tabulate the votes, while the company complained that the *CNE* had made 11,000 last-minute changes to the database. This prevented the company from having the flashcards needed to program the computers that would be

Venezuela

The Cienpies Exchange, Caracas

used in more than half the 8,400 polling stations ready in time. Days before the election, Chávez dispatched an air force jet to Omaha, Nebraska, to receive the flashcards.

In Caracas, Arias had held his closing rally in the Avenida Bolívar the previous day, and Chávez's closing rally was in full sway that night, also in the Avenida Bolívar. The president's electrically charged voice sounded more like that of a soccer announcer than a politician. The atmosphere at his rally resembled Mardi Gras more than a political event. A majority of those in the almost entirely working-class multitude—many of them wearing Chávez's trademark red beret—appeared inebriated.

The following day, the *CNE* postponed the election because of technical difficulties. Chávez and Arias both expressed support for the delay, although Arias demanded dismissal of the *CNE* for incompetence. Reaction ran the gamut from outrage to nonchalant acceptance.

Former U.S. President Jimmy Carter, who had become a sort of self-appointed guardian of Latin American democracy, held a news conference in Caracas to endorse the postponement which, he said, "was for a good reason." In response to my question, he drew a contrast with the obviously rigged election in Peru that

would be held the following day (see Peru) and predicted that the Venezuelan election ultimately would be held and would "accurately reflect the will of the Venezuelan people."

On one point, there was almost universal agreement: the *CNE* had botched its job. Chávez sacked the five members and replaced them, at Carter's suggestion, with a group less partisan and more representative. It contracted with a Spanish firm to conduct the election, and the new election was set for July 30, 2000, which I also covered.

Chávez was resoundingly re-elected with 59.2% of the vote, a mandate even greater than in 1998. His Fifth Republic Movement (*MVR*) received 57.6% of the votes for the new National Assembly, which translated into 92 of the 165 seats. That fell short of the two-thirds majority needed for constitutional amendments and confirmation of judicial appointments, but it gave Chávez the three-fifths majority needed to pass emergency legislation that would allow him to rule by decree. *AD* was second with 19.7%, giving it 35 seats. Arias' *Proyecto Venezuela* was a distant third with 4.9%, or eight seats, while *COPEI* was a poor fifth with a mere 2.4%, or four seats. The *MVR* and its ally, the Movement to Socialism (*MAS*), won 15 of the 23 governorships.

Dissent and Repression Grow

Chávez had to contend with such pressing domestic issues as declining living standards. One solution: Create a new labor organization, predictably named the Bolívarian Workers' Force, to replace the Confederation of Venezuelan Workers (*CTV*), long affiliated with the discredited *AD*. As usual, he called a referendum, in December 2000. Critics warned this was merely another attempt to concentrate more power in Chávez's hands. Chávez received the expected lop-sided majority for his plan, but he was stunned by the anemic 25% voter turnout. In municipal elections, the *MVR* won 40% of the seats.

Strikes protesting the state of the economy became common, as Chávez grew increasingly impatient with dissent, something he no doubt picked up from his friend in Havana. He long had assailed the Venezuelan press as controlled by the oligarchy. In one case of legalized suppression, Pablo López, editor of the gadfly Caracas weekly *La Razón*, went into exile in 2000 rather than face house arrest for charges he had defamed a wealthy friend and financial benefactor of Chávez's and Miquilena's. The judge had refused to allow López to introduce evidence that the articles published in *La Razón* about influence peddling were true.

In many countries with a Hispanic legal tradition, truth is not a defense in libel or defamation cases; all that must be proven is that the plaintiff was offended. López's lawyer took his case to the Inter-American Commission on Human Rights (ICHR) in Washington, an organ of the Organization of American States. In 2001, the ICHR ruled in López's favor and ordered the Venezuelan government to stop persecuting him. Chávez responded that the matter is a judicial one, and López remains in self-imposed exile in Costa Rica.

Chávez also lashed out at the independent television station *Globovisión*, known for hard-hitting reporting that often embarrasses the government. The station was notified that it was being investigated under a broad provision of the new constitution that prohibits "false or misleading" information. This harassment continued has for a decade.

Rangel announced the establishment of pro-Chávez neighborhood groups called "Bolívarian Circles." Rangel denied they were patterned after Cuba's Committees for the Defense of the Revolution. Another parallel with Cuba was the application of a clause in the new constitution to teach "Bolívarian principles" in the public schools.

In a move reminiscent of Salvador Allende's land reform program in Chile, Chávez presented the deeds to 105,000 acres of idle land to small farmers in 2001, and he warned large landowners that they should "donate" unused land to the state for redistribution or face confiscation. Chávez touted his agrarian reform plan as a means of relieving the crowded, squalid conditions in the slums around Caracas, something chillingly reminiscent of the Khmer Rouge in Cambodia.

Chávez stunned the nation in 2001 with a list of 49 decrees affecting virtually all economic sectors, especially the all-important oil industry. One decree doubled royalties on foreign oil companies from 16.5% to 30%, a move that would drive away badly needed capital investment. This action had the unintended effect of forging an unlikely alliance between *Fedecamaras*, the country's main business lobby, led by Pedro Carmona, and the *CTV*, whose president, Carlos Ortega, had defeated Chávez's hand-picked candidate. *Fedecamaras* and the *CTV* called for a 12-hour general strike. Chávez ridiculed the strike and its organizers, but millions participated in the stoppage.

By 2002, Venezuela became irrevocably polarized between passionate pro-Chávez and anti-Chávez camps. The president's approval ratings slipped below 50% for the first time, and few Venezuelans remained ambivalent about Chávez and his revolution. There was growing dissent

as well within the ranks of the military, which had become riddled with corruption as the administrator of Chávez's $100 million social program, *Plan Bolívar 2000*. The president was embarrassed by revelations that his hand-picked army commander had pocketed millions from the fund; Chávez fired him. Yet, when the auditor-general uncovered still more examples of embezzlement of funds destined for the poor, Chávez responded by firing the auditor-general.

Chávez's popularity dropped to 30%, and anti-Chávez demonstrations and pro-Chávez counter-demonstrations became commonplace. Suddenly, Chávez began to sound conciliatory. He agreed to moderate some of his more radical economic decrees. He called for understanding from the opposition, and said he hoped he could "sheath my sword." He attempted to mend fences with the church. He even condemned Colombia's *FARC* guerrillas. But this era of good feeling proved fleeting.

Events unfolded quickly and dramatically in 2002 after Chávez fired the president of the state-owned oil company, *Petroleos de Venezuela* (*PDVSA*) and replaced him with a leftist economist. *PDVSA* white-collar workers protested with marches, but held off on calling a strike that would halt oil exports.

Then two high-ranking officers, Vice Admiral Carlos Molina Tamayo and Air Force General Roman Gómez Ruíz, publicly declared their opposition to their commander-in-chief for what they regarded as corruption and mismanagement of the armed forces; Gómez Ruíz called on Chávez to resign.

Rumors of an imminent coup began to fly, and the media reported that dissident officers had approached U.S. diplomats for support. The State Department expressed its support for democratic institutions. The crisis escalated in March when *Fedecamaras* and the *CTV* issued a plan for a post-Chávez Venezuela. The protests at *PDVSA* continued, threatening to upset the world oil market; production dropped by 450,000 barrels a day—about 20%. Venezuelans and the world watched anxiously to see what would happen next.

Coup and Counter-Coup

In April, *Fedecamaras* and the *CTV* declared a one-day general strike, which was so successful it was extended indefinitely—meaning, until Chávez resigned. When 150,000 people poured into the streets, pro-Chávez goons opened fire on them, killing 17 and wounding at least 100. The armed forces high command declared later that Chávez had ordered them to implement *"Plan Ávila,"* the code

name for the use of deadly force to protect the Miraflores Palace, but that they had refused to fire on unarmed civilians; a leaked audiotape corroborated their account.

After midnight on April 12, 2002, the generals acted, using the violence against the peaceful demonstrators as justification to restore order. The president was taken into "protective custody" on the island of La Orchila; accounts leaked later revealed that Chávez broke into tears when he surrendered. By Chávez's own account later, he was told to sign a resignation statement, but he refused. Nonetheless, General Efraín Vásquez, the army commander, announced that Chávez had stepped down. As interim president, the military named *Fedecamaras'* Pedro Carmona. Meanwhile, the U.S. State Department issued a statement, which later backfired, suggesting that Chávez's forcible removal was the will of the Venezuelan people. The United States also sought to allay an OAS resolution denouncing "the alteration of the constitutional order," but in the end it supported it.

Carmona unwisely said he was abrogating Chávez's 1999 constitution and dissolving the Assembly and the Supreme Court; he called for new congressional elections in eight months. This was too much even for those delighted by Chávez's ouster, and it brought international rebuke—even from the Bush administration, which directed its ambassador to try to dissuade Carmona. Mexican President Vicente Fox refused to recognize the interim government. To make matters worse, Carmona did not name any representatives of the *CTV* in his interim cabinet. Within hours, the new "government" unraveled.

On April 13, hundreds of thousands of furious *chavistas* poured into the streets around the country and rioted to demand Chávez's reinstatement. Fighting broke out, and at least 50 people were killed and hundreds injured. Some of the *chavistas'* rage was directed against the opposition media. Suddenly, a schism appeared within the ranks of the armed forces, which had been thought to be almost solidly opposed to Chávez. Loyalist midranking unit commanders rebelled against the rebellion and stormed the Miraflores Palace; among them were the paratroopers, whence Chávez had sprung. That night, Carmona resigned; to fill the power vacuum, the high command agreed to allow Chávez's vice president, Diosdado Cabello, to take charge until Chávez returned. Carmona was placed under house arrest. An estimated 80 officers also were detained.

On April 14, Chávez was back in power. Although brief, his forcible removal marked only the third military *coup* in

Venezuela

more than 20 years of democratic reforms in Latin America, following that in Haiti in 1991 and Ecuador in 2000. In the days following the coup and counter-coup, Chávez appeared chastened and, again, conciliatory. "Let's put our house in order," he said, and he promised not to seek revenge. He lamented having "sown hatred." He accepted the resignations of the entire *PDVSA* board and said that he was willing to compromise to settle the dispute with the *PDVSA* management.

Oil production returned to normal. Chávez appointed Ali Rodríguez, the OPEC secretary-general and a former Venezuelan oil minister, as president of *PDVSA*. He also replaced Vice President Cabello with Defense Minister Rangel, and relieved Vásquez from command of the army.

The U.S. government denied abetting the *coup* attempt. Then-security adviser Condoleezza Rice did little to quell international suspicions when she stated in a televised interview that she hoped Chávez had received the "message" of the Venezuelan people and that he "takes advantage of this opportunity to right his own ship, which has been moving, frankly, in the wrong direction for quite a long time."

Political Stalemate

OAS Secretary-General Cesar Gaviría, a former Colombian president, met with Chávez and leaders of the umbrella opposition body, Democratic Coordinator, urging them to effect a reconciliation. But the opposition remained intransigent. Chávez invited former President Carter to Caracas to broker an agreement, but those talks ended in failure.

Chávez's dropped the conciliatory tone and vilified those who instigated the *coup* as "Nazis." Carmona escaped from house arrest and sought asylum at the Colombian Embassy. Colombian President Pastrana, no doubt delighted to repay Chávez for his support of the *FARC*, granted it. Carlos Fernández succeeded him as *Fedecamaras* president.

Then Chávez, who was himself once jailed for leading a *coup* attempt, sought to prosecute four officers involved in the coup against *him*. The officers—two navy admirals and an army and an air force general—appealed to the Supreme Court to block their trial, arguing that Chávez's own constitution makes it lawful to disobey orders from an authoritarian government, in this case, an order to fire on unarmed civilians. They also argued that they had acted to prevent anarchy when they believed Chávez had resigned. The court, packed with Chávez appointees, nonetheless voted 11–8 to dismiss the charges, citing insufficient evidence. Furious Chávez supporters tried to storm the

court building but were repulsed by security forces. Surprisingly, Chávez accepted the decision and appealed to his supporters to "swallow the decision like a fish with bones."

Animated by the court decision, the opposition filed criminal charges against Chávez, including abuse of power and accepting illegal campaign contributions. Chávez also was criticized by international journalism organizations for his harsh rhetoric against the opposition media and for the alarming number of physical attacks on journalists.

Chávez next found himself in a test of wills with Alfredo Peña, the opposition mayor of Caracas. Chávez accused the Caracas police of treating pro-Chávez demonstrators more harshly than anti-Chávez demonstrators; Peña alleged that his police were ambushed by *chavistas* when they responded to a disturbance call. In retaliation, Chávez grounded Peña's helicopter. Fighting broke out between the police and *chavistas*. Pro-Chávez policemen began a strike, dividing the police force.

Representatives of the United Nations, the OAS and the Carter Center attempted to jump-start the dialogue between Chávez and the Democratic Coordinator. Chávez reiterated that he was agreeable to a recall referendum, but not before August 2003, the mid-point of his term, as specified in the constitution. The talks failed.

Events turned uglier in November 2002 when the opposition staged a march to the *CNE* to present petitions containing 2 million signatures calling for a referendum on December 4. *Chavistas* attacked the marchers, and Caracas police intervened. In the resulting melee, dozens of people were injured, more than 20 by gunfire.

Chávez refused to call the referendum. Tensions between the two factions of the police force erupted into violence that left two people dead and dozens wounded. Chávez ordered a federal takeover of the Caracas police, sending in national guardsmen to augment them. Demonstrators banging pots and pans, Latin America's traditional *cacerolazo* form of non-violent protest, filled the streets almost daily, and violence erupted. Venezuela appeared on the brink of anarchy.

General Strike

Fedecamaras and the *CTV* called for an indefinite general strike, to begin December 2, 2002. At first it was not universally observed and the vital oil industry continued functioning. The government proclaimed the strike a failure. But it continued day after day, and the economy soon felt the pinch. On December 6, *chavista* gunmen fired into an opposition rally, killing three and wounding 28. *Chavistas*

also stepped up their vandalism against *Globovisión* and other anti-Chávez media, egged on by the president. Yet, Chávez disavowed the violence.

Rebels seized a government oil tanker; Chávez ordered the navy to retake it. By the fourth day, striking port workers had brought oil exports from the world's fifth-largest producer almost to a halt. Production dropped from 3 million barrels a day to 400,000, then to 200,000; the world oil market shivered. The price of crude jumped accordingly, to more than $30 a barrel. Chávez assailed the opposition as "fascists," "traitors," "terrorists," "saboteurs," "coup-plotters" and "hijackers." He broke off the OAS-sponsored negotiations until the strike ended, and used foreign reserves to import food, medicine and, ironically, fuel.

The nation remained paralyzed for weeks. Neither side budged, and the economy languished. The opposition now set February 2, 2003, as a date for the referendum. Gaviría, Carter, the Bush administration and the European Union all advocated early elections to defuse the crisis. Chávez offered a *binding* referendum after August 2003, but refused to resign under duress. The divided army backed Chávez, saying the strike was threatening the national well-being.

In January 2003, with street violence continuing, Chávez met with U.N. Secretary-General Kofi Annan in New York to discuss a diplomatic solution. Meanwhile, newly inaugurated Brazilian President Luiz Inácio da Silva offered his intercession and invited the United States, Spain, Portugal, Chile and Mexico to form a "Friends of Venezuela" group to mediate an end to the crisis. Annan agreed to send an emissary. Carter returned and met with both sides and with Gaviría against the backdrop of violent demonstrations.

Suddenly, the general strike lost its steam as small businesses, faced with bankruptcy, began reopening. By the end of January, oil production was back up to about 1 million bpd. Private banks reopened on February 3. The non-oil sector began operating normally. Chávez claimed victory and threatened to prosecute the strike's organizers. In reality, there were no winners, as the strike had cost $6 billion and left the economy in a shambles (see Economy), not to mention the lives lost. Finance Minister Tobías Nobrega justifiably called the 61-day general strike a "kamikaze attack."

The Recall Movement

The opposition returned to petition-gathering, this time claiming 4 million signatures. Chávez hung tough, saying there could be no vote before August 19, 2003.

Gaviría and the "Friends of Venezuela" finally persuaded the two sides to agree to an eight-point resolution that renounced violence. It also called for the government to respect freedom of expression and for the media to show restraint in their rhetoric. But the deal quickly unraveled.

The opposition threatened to resume the general strike, and international condemnation poured in on Chávez. The president accused the United States and Spain of siding with the opposition and even reprimanded Gaviría, who had spent three months patiently trying to effect an agreement, for meddling in Venezuela's internal affairs!

In April, the two sides finally agreed on the terms for a referendum. The opposition agreed to wait until after August 19, 2003, and Chávez pledged not to try to delay the vote and to resign if he lost. However, he said the signatures collected earlier were invalid and that the opposition would have to go through the petition process again after August 19. Chávez soon reneged on the agreement, raising a new condition that the opposition's elected officials also face a recall referendum.

In May, the two sides finally signed an agreement on a referendum, for both Chávez and some opposition legislators. Moreover, the National Assembly, in which the *chavistas* enjoyed a small majority, would have to appoint a new CNE. Chávez reneged again, arguing that the terms did not specify that he *must* call a referendum.

Still, the Democratic Coordinator pressed on with plans for a binding referendum, which would require 20%, not just 10%, of the more than 12 million registered voters, or 2,436,083 valid signatures. The turnout would have to be at least 25% and the votes to remove Chávez would need to match or exceed the 3.76 million votes Chávez received in his 2000 re-election. Also key would be the date. If held before August 19, 2004, the fourth anniversary of Chávez's re-election, the CNE would be required to call a new election within 30 days. If after that date, Vice President Rangel would serve out the remainder of his term.

On August 20, 2003, one day after the mid-point of Chávez's term, the Democratic Coordinator presented the CNE with petitions containing 3.4 million signatures. Chávez declared the signatures invalid, not explaining how he could know that, and ridiculed his opponents as "crazy."

The Supreme Tribunal appointed a new five-member CNE, approved by Chávez, the Democratic Coordinator, Gaviría and the United States. The CNE ruled that the petitions were invalid because the signatures were collected *before* the August 19 mid-point. It said the Democratic Coordinator would have to collect the needed signatures again during a four-day window, a hurdle the CNE perhaps believed to be insurmountable, but in November the opposition succeeded in collecting 3.4 million signatures.

The CNE stalled until March 2004, when it ruled that only 1.83 million signatures were valid, 140,000 were invalid and 1.1 million more were in doubt. Changing the rules in the middle of the game, the CNE announced that the Democratic Coordinator had the burden of confirming the signatures of enough of the questioned signatures to reach the necessary number, or about 600,000, and gave it four days to do so. Riots erupted throughout the country, in which six died.

After more legal wrangling, the two sides agreed on the four-day verification window, during which signers were required to come forward and verify their signatures. Again the Democratic Coordinator presented its petitions to the CNE, and again the country and the world held their breaths. This time, although it disallowed about 110,000 signatures, the CNE could not escape reality. On June 3, it announced that the Democratic Coordinator had collected 2,451,821 valid signatures—15,738 more than required.

Instead of his usual defiance, Chávez accepted the CNE's conclusion and insisted that he "welcomes the challenge" of the recall election, but his followers went on a violent rampage in Caracas, attacking Mayor Peña's office and the offices of opposition media.

The CNE postponed the agreed date to August 15 so the new computer system could be in place. After a tempestuous but relatively non-violent campaign, hundreds of international observers and foreign journalists observed the climax of the two-year-long recall effort. A total of 70% of Venezuela's 14 million registered voters participated, voting "*Sí*" to remove Chávez, or "*No.*" The results stunned both sides:

Sí	3,989,008	40.74%
No	5,800,629	59.25%

Chávez claimed victory before jubilant supporters at the Miraflores Palace. Becoming a bit messianic, he declared that "the will of the people is the will of God."

The opposition suffered another stinging defeat in state and municipal elections in October 2004, losing control of Caracas and losing 20 of the 23 state governorships.

The Screws Tighten

For the first time in more than two years it seemed peace would return. Those hopes were jarred on November 19, 2004, when a car bomb killed Danilo Anderson, the prosecutor in charge of the cases against about 400 opposition figures implicated in the 2002 coup attempt.

Two brothers who are former policemen and their cousin were convicted in 2005 and sentenced to terms of from 27 to 30 years. In November 2005, four other people were arrested as the "intellectual authors" of the murder. These included Nelson Mezerhane, a respected banker and co-owner of *Globovisión,* and Patricia Poleo, editor of the opposition newspaper *El Nuevo País.* All proclaimed their innocence, and international journalism organizations questioned whether the charges against Poleo and Mezerhane were trumped up to intimidate the opposition media.

Oil derricks, Lake Maracaibo

Venezuela

Chávez consolidated more and more power in his hands. A new law placed municipal and state police forces under unified national—meaning his—control. The addition of 12 new justices to the Supreme Court took effect in 2004. He appointed another loyalist to the *CNE*, giving it a lop-sided 4–1 majority. He stepped up seizures of privately owned rural land under the 2001 land reform act. He ingratiated himself to the armed forces with a 50–60% pay increase.

Chávez also tightened the screws on privately owned broadcast stations with the Radio and Television Social Responsibility Law, which has such vague language that domestic and international media organizations and the OAS's Inter-American Human Rights Commission denounced it as an attempt to censor content. The law, ostensibly designed to protect children, states that images of sex or violence, including news coverage of violent demonstrations, cannot be aired between 7 a.m. and 11 p.m. It also provides for 70 minutes of government programming per week. Violators can be fined or have their licenses revoked for carrying programming that is deemed slanderous, that "incites disruption of public order" or that is "contrary to national security," all defined by the government on a case-by-case basis.

Several journalists were charged with violations. The government's taxing agency levied fines against several anti-Chávez television stations, not under the terms of the new law but for allegedly airing opposition propaganda for free during the general strike of 2002–03 and for back taxes. The stations appealed, and eventually the amount of back taxes was reduced.

Equally onerous were Chávez's revisions to the penal code, which in effect outlawed peaceful dissent. It subjects journalists to up to 12 months in jail for criminal defamation, which is loosely defined, and five years for "causing panic" by disseminating "false information," not just by the mass media but by e-mail or other means; presumption of innocence in such cases was eliminated. Demonstrators engaging in banging pots and pans, the traditional Latin American *cacerolazo*, could be arrested for "intimidating" public officials!

Next, Chávez got his government into the mass media business itself in 2005 with the creation of a regional all-news television channel, *Telesur,* in conjunction with the friendly governments of Argentina and Uruguay; Brazil and Cuba provide technical support. While Chávez extolled the channel as a counterweight to the domination of U.S. and European all-news channels, critics complained it carried little more than left-wing, anti-U.S. propaganda.

Chávez also tightened the screws on domestic and foreign businesses. He greatly increased the government's role in the private sector through the creation of more than 65,000 cooperatives, euphemistically named "social production companies," and new laws mandated that private companies be "co-managed," meaning that workers have a greater share in decision-making. Companies that do not embrace "co-management" have been denied government contracts, and the mandate has continued to widen to include more companies.

Chávez stunned foreign oil companies in 2005 by announcing they would be required to sign new contracts with the government or leave the country by January 1, 2006. This raised serious legal questions about breach of contract. Chávez said under the new contracts, taxes would be raised from 34% to 50% and royalties to the government from 1% to 30%. With oil selling then for $50 a barrel, the companies still stood to benefit, so they grudgingly agreed.

The last remaining political check on Chávez's growing power—the opposition in the National Assembly—was eliminated in the congressional elections of December 2005. It wasn't a power grab by Chávez, but a rather a surrender of it by the major opposition parties, which boycotted the election. The *AD, COPEI* and Project Venezuela complained that the fingerprint-reading machines used to confirm voters' identification were synchronized with the vote-counting machines so that it would be possible to match a person with how he or she voted. (There already were suspicions that businessmen who voted to recall Chávez in 2004 were being denied government services.) The *CNE* agreed to turn off the fingerprint machines, but the opposition then called for a delay in the election, which the government refused. The result: Chávez's Fifth Republic Movement and its allies won all 167 seats in the expanded Assembly. Chávez could then amend his constitution at will.

Venezuelan-U.S. relations continued to deteriorate. In May 2005, the United States arrested Luis Posada Carriles, an anti-Castro Cuban exile who bribed his way out of a Venezuelan prison in 1985. Posada was awaiting retrial for the bombing of a Cuban airliner off Barbados in 1976 that killed 73 people. Venezuela requested his extradition, after assuring the United States that Posada would not be sent to Cuba, where he almost certainly would be shot. The United States refused extradition on the grounds that the request did not contain the required evidence against Posada, who already had been acquitted in Venezuela of the bombing. Posada was tried in the United States in early 2011 and acquitted (see Cuba).

Chávez announced in 2005 that he planned to begin talks with Iran for a Venezuelan nuclear program. That was too much even for friendly Brazil, which said it would not cooperate in helping Venezuela establish a nuclear program if Iran were involved.

Chávez then complained that the United States was not keeping its agreement to supply spare parts for Venezuela's fleet of 21 F-16 fighter aircraft, purchased in 1983, and threatened to contribute some of the jets to Cuba and China. The U.S. Embassy provided documentary proof that spare parts were in fact being delivered, and reminded Venezuela that such transfer of technology to third countries would violate the terms of the sale.

The United States escalated the conflict in 2006 when it invoked its legal rights to refuse a license for Spain to sell to Venezuela 12 Spanish transport and surveillance aircraft that contained U.S. parts. The deal was worth $2 billion for Spain, a U.S. ally.

Chávez responded with a thinly veiled threat—which he was later to repeat often—to stop oil exports to the United States. It was not an idle threat; Venezuela is the United States' fourth-largest supplier of oil, amounting to 1.5 million barrels a day, about 13% of the total. Venezuela also has 70% ownership in Citgo, which owns three refineries and 14,000 stations in the United States. However, Venezuela cannot afford to reduce its exports by 13% overnight, and the United States could retaliate with a food embargo; one fourth of Venezuela's food imports are from the United States.

In 2006, Chávez said he would begin buying fighter aircraft from Russia. In addition to the 100,000 AK-47 and AK-103 assault rifles that arrived from Russia, Chávez announced that the first factory in South America to manufacture the popular Kalashnikov rifles would be built in Venezuela.

The Election of 2006

Two years after the recall referendum, the opposition to Chávez was still in disarray. The various groups were at odds over whether they should contest the December 3, 2006, presidential election or boycott it, and if they opted to contest it, who their candidate should be. They agreed that more than one candidate was a recipe for defeat. Their last boycott only produced a Cuban-style one-party Congress. Opinion polls confirmed that their chances of unseating Chávez were as quixotic as they had been in 2004.

Three political veterans expressed interest in taking on the increasingly dictatorial president: Manuel Rosales, the popular governor of Zulia State of the *Un Tiempo Nuevo* party; Teodoro Petkoff, a moderate leftist former planning minister and the publisher of the nettlesome opposition newspaper *Tal Cual*; and Julio Borges, head of a center-right movement called Justice First. Ultimately, the opposition coalesced around Rosales.

Rosales attacked Chávez where he was most vulnerable: corruption, which had worsened in the eight years since Chávez was first elected on a promise to clean up the corruption of the past, and violent crime, which had become epidemic. He chided Chávez for squandering billions of dollars in aid to try to secure a seat on the U.N. Security Council (see Hugo Chávez: An International Loose Cannon) instead of using it to reduce unemployment and build housing. He promised to channel 20% of oil revenue directly to the poor through the use of a debit card.

Chávez reminded voters of the billions of dollars in oil profits he *had* channeled into such social programs as subsidized groceries for the poor and free universities. He vowed to consolidate his revolution and implement what he called "21st century socialism." The Chávez campaign was embarrassed by the release of a clandestine video that showed Rafael Ramírez, head of *PDVSA*, threatening to fire employees who did not support Chávez.

About 75% of the 15.9 million eligible voters turned out. The results:

Chávez	7,309,080	63.1%
Rosales	4,292,466	36.9%

Rosales conceded defeat (he lost every state, even Zulia) but promised to try to keep the opposition intact and to defend Venezuelan democracy, or what was left of it. Chávez hailed his victory as one for his socialist revolution, saying "socialism is love" and "a new era has begun."

Third Term

Chávez soon unveiled some chilling details of his "new era," things he hadn't outlined *before* the election. Although he insisted he would respect private property, he said democracy is incompatible with capitalism. He proposed merging his Fifth Republic Movement and the other groups of his Patriotic Pole into one homogenous political party—under his control. The Communist Party and other groups balked, but Chávez forged the United Socialist Party of Venezuela *(PSUV)*.

Chávez also announced that the license for privately owned Radio Caracas Television, or *RCTV*, the oldest and most popular station in the country, would not be renewed when it expired in May 2007. He made no secret that this was retribution for the station's opposition to him and for what Chávez alleged was its complicity in the 2002 coup. His announcement met swift criticism from international journalism organizations and from OAS Secretary-General José Miguel Insulza of Chile. Chávez called Insulza, himself a leftist of long standing whom Venezuela had supported for the post, an "idiot." The heretofore friendly governments of Brazil and Chile concurred with Insulza.

At midnight on May 27, 2007, *RCTV*'s signal went black, and a few seconds later the new station was on the air on that channel, opening with a pro-Chávez anthem. Unexpectedly, thousands of demonstrators, mostly students, took to the streets in Caracas and other cities to protest the closure. Police opened fire with tear gas and plastic bullets, injuring several. Two days of rioting ensued. Chávez ordered a counter-demonstration in support of the closure.

RCTV's closure left *Globovisión* as the only openly anti-Chávez station, and the station's management vowed it would not be intimidated. *RCTV* soon returned as a cable and satellite channel, but could claim only 40% of its previous audience. Two other privately owned channels, *Televen* and *Venevisión*, began practicing self-censorship to avoid the same fate.

Next, Chávez said he planned to renationalize the electric and telecommunications utilities, something he had not advocated during the campaign. Without explanation, he abruptly removed Vice President Rangel, perhaps because his prominence in the socialist movement rivaled his own. He replaced him with Jorge Rodríguez, head of the *CNE*, seen as more devoted to Chávez.

Chávez was sworn in on January 10, 2007, declaring "fatherland, socialism, or death!" He announced more features of his "new era:" nationalizing foreign-owned refineries and natural gas operations, and constitutional amendments that would curb the powers of state and local officials and, more ominously, permit his indefinite re-election. Finally, he asked his rubber-stamp National Assembly for the power to rule by decree. For the first time, he declared himself a "communist" and said he had been one since 2002, something else he neglected to mention before the election. (Polls showed a majority of Venezuelans oppose a Cuban-style totalitarian regime.) Jesus Christ, Chávez argued, was "an authentic communist."

The National Assembly dutifully gave Chávez the power to rule by decree for 18 months, officially putting Venezuela under one-man rule. He purchased the 28.5% stake of the U.S. firm Verizon in Venezuela's largest telephone company, *CANTV*, for $572 million. Chávez had accused *CANTV* of tapping his telephone conversations.

The government also applied more pressure on its print media critics. In 2007, Laureano Márquez, one of the country's most popular humorists, wrote a satirical editorial in Petkoff's newspaper *Tal Cual* that lampooned the suggestion attributed to Chávez's nine-year-old daughter, Rosines, to change the national coat of arms to show a horse galloping to the left instead of to the right. In the editorial, Márquez asked Rosines to suggest changing the horse to a faithful golden retriever or to a tortoise "to symbolize our sluggishness in everything." A judge, citing child-protection laws, imposed an $18,600 fine on *Tal Cual's* publishing company for "violating the honor, reputation and privacy" of the girl. The judge fined Márquez separately. Márquez ridiculed the government for its sensitivity to traditional satire.

Chávez announced Venezuela's withdrawal from both the World Bank and the IMF in 2007. Venezuela had already paid its debts to the two institutions.

Then he announced the government was assuming operational control from ExxonMobil, ConocoPhillips, Chevron, British Petroleum, Norway's Statoil and France's Total over the exploitation of the tar deposits of the Orinoco Belt. The companies were converting 600,000 barrels of heavy crude a day into synthetic oil. They were told they would have to agree to harsh new contractual terms if they wanted to remain in the country. Exxon Mobil and ConocoPhillips refused, although the others agreed. In 2008, Exxon Mobil fought back, obtaining an injunction freezing $12 billion in *PDVSA* assets in the United States, Great Britain and the Netherlands to recover what it said it had lost from Venezuela's breach of contract. Chávez, as usual, threatened to cut off the flow of oil to the United States. In 2008, the National Assembly passed a new law that also expropriated the foreign companies' filling stations and a fleet of 1,200 trucks.

Meanwhile, a 500-page blueprint for a new education system was leaked to the press. It is unmistakably patterned on the Cuban model, with the purpose of indoctrinating children in Marxist ideology.

The National Assembly next approved 69 constitutional amendments, among them extending the presidential term from six to seven years and allowing indefinite re-election. Elected state and municipal governments would have to share power with so-called regional councils, appointed by the president. The Central Bank would lose its autonomy to him. He would be able to expropriate private property by decree and to declare an

Venezuela

Hugo Chávez's Legacy: An International Loose Cannon

Hugo Chávez sought to make Venezuela—in reality, himself—a player on the world stage. He made it a point to make high-profile visits to rogue states and leaders like Iraq's Saddam Hussein, Libya's Muammar Qadhafi, Iran's Mahmoud Ahmadinejad and Syria's Bashar al-Assad. His main purpose, of course, was to bait the United States.

Chávez idolized Fidel Castro. When Castro fell gravely ill in 2006, Chávez regularly came to his bedside. When Chávez fell gravely ill with cancer, he came to Cuba for treatment.

While cultivating ties with sinister dictators and promoting his Marxist agenda, he managed to alienate Venezuela, at one time or another, from Colombia, Peru, Chile, France, Spain, Mexico, Israel, even friendly Brazil with his brash, undiplomatic behavior.

At an OPEC summit Chávez hosted in Caracas in 2000, his was the loudest voice in favor of curtailing production to drive up oil prices—then $30 a barrel, the highest since Gulf War I. Every $1 increase in the price of a barrel added $1 billion a year to his government's revenue, which he used to fund his "social revolution" at home and to buy influence abroad. He sold oil at discount prices to Cuba and other allies.

Chávez strained relations with Colombia and Peru in 2001. Venezuela arrested, then released, a guerrilla from the National Liberation Army (ELN) of Colombia wanted in an airplane hijacking. Chávez was known to be sympathetic to the ELN and to the Revolutionary Armed Forces of Colombia (FARC).

Chávez denied reports in 2001 that the fugitive former Peruvian intelligence chief, Vladimiro Montesinos, was hiding in Venezuela (see Peru). Only when Peruvian authorities presented him with conclusive evidence from the U.S. FBI that Montesinos was in the country did Chávez order Montesinos arrested and flown back to Peru.

Chávez relished being in the spotlight at the Third Summit of the Americas in Quebec in 2001, where he was the only one of the 34 heads of state who opposed the idea of a Free Trade Area of the Americas (FTAA). He argued that subregional integration should come first, and warned of U.S. domination of the FTAA. He also irked his fellow presidents by balking at the requirement that signatories to the FTAA be "representative democracies;" he said he preferred "participatory democ-

racy," which could be more loosely construed. U.S. President George W. Bush snubbed Chávez by avoiding a one-on-one meeting.

Then came September 11, 2001. Chávez dutifully denounced the terrorist attacks on the U.S. as "abominable," but Chávez defended his close ties with Iraq, Iran and Libya, calling them "our brothers and partners." He also criticized the post-9/11 U.S. bombing campaign in Afghanistan as "using terror to fight terror." The U.S. recalled its ambassador. Relations were strained again in 2003 when Chávez condemned the U.S. invasion of Iraq. Media reports also circulated that the large Arab community on the Venezuelan island of Margarita had become a haven for Hamas and Hezbollah terrorists.

Chávez next irritated the French by expressing his concern over the welfare of the notorious Venezuelan-born terrorist Ilyich Ramírez, known by the sobriquet Carlos the Jackal, who was incarcerated in a French prison after two decades as an international fugitive.

In 2003, it was Chile's turn to become annoyed with Chávez's loose tongue. He commented that he dreamed of one day visiting a Bolivian beach, a reference to Bolivia's ongoing quest to regain the seacoast it lost to Chile in the 1979–84 War of the Pacific (see Bolivia, Chile). Chile protested the comment and recalled its ambassador.

In 2004, Colombia announced it had arrested Rodrigo Granda, FARC's "foreign minister." Chávez charged that Granda was abducted in Caracas and whisked across the border by Venezuelan national guardsmen who, Chávez said, had been "bribed" by the Colombians. President Álvaro Uribe called the payment for Granda's abduction a "reward." Chávez denounced Colombia's violation of Venezuelan sovereignty and demanded an apology from Uribe, who not only refused but accused Chávez of having harbored a representative of a known terrorist organization. Chávez recalled his ambassador and canceled a bilateral agreement to build a $200 million gas pipeline. Eight national guardsmen were arrested and charged with treason. The two presidents met in Caracas and announced that the crisis had been resolved, that the pipeline deal was back on, and that Venezuela was mindful of Colombia's security concerns. There still was no apology from Uribe.

Relations with Spain improved with the election victory of José Luis Rodríguez Zapatero's Socialist Party in 2004. Zapatero turned foreign policy 180 degrees from that of his conservative predecessor, José María Aznar, whom Chávez had loudly accused of complicity in the 2002 coup attempt. Zapatero signed a $1.7 billion arms deal by which Venezuela purchased eight ships and 12 planes planes. Spain also sold Venezuela an oil tanker and agreed that Repsol, Spain's oil company, would increase its investments in Venezuela. The U.S. later blocked the sale of the planes by a NATO ally.

The announcement that Venezuela was buying 100,000 AK-47 and AK-103 assault rifles and 40 Mi-35 assault helicopters from Russia drew a quick protest to Russia from U.S. Secretary of State Condoleezza Rice, who called Chávez a "negative force" in the region. Defense Secretary Donald Rumsfeld questioned during a visit to Brazil why Venezuela needed 100,000 assault rifles and suggested they would wind up in the hands of the Colombian rebels. Russia later sold Venezuela three submarines.

At the Fourth Summit of the Americas in Mar del Plata, Argentina in 2005, Chávez gloated that he had dealt the FTAA a "knockout." He was joined by the four members of Mercosur—Argentina, Brazil, Paraguay and Uruguay. Chávez sought to bring Venezuela into Mercosur, seen as a challenge to Brazil's da Silva for regional leadership. Paraguay's Senate, however, refused to ratify Venezuela's entry. Mexico's Vicente Fox, one of the leaders at the summit who supported the FTAA, suggested that the 29 pro-FTAA countries could proceed without the other five. Chávez later accused Fox of selling out to the U.S. Fox demanded an apology; Chávez withdrew his ambassador.

Between 2005 and 2009, Chávez's regional influence was boosted by the election victories in Bolivia of Evo Morales, who had promised to join with Cuba and Venezuela as part of a "Bolívarian alternative;" and of Manuel Zelaya in Honduras, Daniel Ortega in Nicaragua, Rafael Correa in Ecuador, Fernando Lugo in Paraguay, Mauricio Funes in El Salvador and José Mujica in Uruguay. Chávez had openly endorsed all of them.

But when he tried the same thing in Peru, it blew up in his face. Chávez enthusiastically supported left-wing candidate Ollanta Humala in Peru's 2006 presidential election. Chávez even ridiculed Humala's two major opponents, calling former President Alan García a "thief" and a "crook" and conservative Lourdes Flores "the candidate of the oligarchy." He even suggested he would break diplomatic relations if García won. García, Flores and President Toledo denounced what they called Chávez's interference in domestic Peruvian politics, and Toledo recalled his. Humala narrowly lost to García in the runoff; Chávez's interference was widely viewed as the deciding factor that cost Humala the election. Five years later, Humala won the 2011 runoff, but only after he dropped his pro-Chávez rhetoric.

Chávez's scuttling of the FTAA also backfired on him. In 2005 and 2006, Colombia and Peru, two of Venezuela's Andean Pact partners, signed lucrative bilateral free-trade agreements with the U.S. A furious Chávez withdrew Venezuela from the Andean Pact.

In 2006, Chávez addressed the U.N. General Assembly in New York, something he once denigrated as a "dialogue of the deaf." He sparked global controversy by referring to President Bush as "the devil." Angry Americans boycotted Venezuelan-owned Citgo. Chávez also announced he wanted Venezuela to receive one of Latin America's two rotating seats on the U.N. Security Council, making no secret that he intended to use it to oppose the U.S. Guatemala was already in line for the seat, and the contest caused serious intra-regional tension; Chávez called in his IOUs from countries on which he had lavished foreign aid. After more than 20 inconclusive ballots in the General Assembly, the Latin American ambassadors settled on Panama as a compromise.

Chávez visited Argentina and Bolivia in 2007 in an obvious attempt to steal the limelight during President Bush's visits to Brazil, Uruguay and Colombia. He addressed large, anti-American rallies; Bush ignored him.

Chávez further alienated himself from his old friend da Silva during an energy conference Chávez hosted in Caracas in 2007. Da Silva supported Bush's proposal to use arable land in Latin America for sugar cane to produce biofuels such as ethanol for export and to reduce dependence on imported petroleum. Chávez, who depends on oil exports to fund his socialist revolution and to bribe other countries, ridiculed the idea, saying it would remove land from cultiva-

tion to feed the poor. Da Silva countered that Latin America has sufficient arable land for both food and ethanol.

Chávez's defense of North Korea's and Iran's nuclear programs caused even his Latin American sympathizers to cringe.

Chávez next alienated himself from the heretofore friendly Spanish government of Zapatero. During the Ibero-American Summit in Santiago, Chile, in 2007, Chávez railed in undiplomatic language against former Spanish President Aznar, whom he was still accusing of complicity in the 2002 coup attempt, calling him among other things a "fascist." That proved too much even for Zapatero, who came to the defense of his predecessor and arch-rival and admonished Chávez for using such language against a chief of government who had been duly elected by the Spanish people. Chávez repeatedly tried to interrupt Zapatero, until Spain's King Juan Carlos finally told Chávez, *Por qué no te callas?* ("Why don't you shut up?") Chávez threatened to break diplomatic relations with the best friend he had in the European Union. Of course, he did not.

Chávez's brashness almost led to war with Colombia in 2008, when Colombia launched a raid on a *FARC* camp just across the border in Ecuador. President Correa moved 3,200 troops to the border, whereupon Chávez ordered 10 battalions moved to the Colombian border. Chávez, Correa and Uribe met in the Dominican Republic to resolve the matter without bloodshed.

However, Colombia turned over to Interpol several laptop computers confiscated from the *FARC* camp which, among other things, reportedly prove that Chávez has channeled $300 million to the *FARC*, despite Chávez's many denials. Interpol's experts verified that the files on the laptops had not been tampered with. Chávez called the Interpol report a "clown show." Even before the border incident, Chávez had shocked the EU by asking it to remove the *FARC* from its list of terrorist organizations.

When Bolivia expelled the U.S. ambassador in 2008, Chávez impetuously expelled the U.S. ambassador from Caracas in "solidarity" with Bolivia, prompting the U.S. to expel the Venezuelan ambassador. Relations remained frozen for the remainder of Bush's term and beyond. In January 2009, he just as impetuously expelled the Israeli ambassador and broke diplomatic relations with Israel over the Israeli invasion of Gaza. Israel returned the favor.

Venezuela and Russia held joint naval exercises for the first time in 2008, much to Bush's annoyance. In 2009, Venezuela acquired Russian surface-to-air missiles.

As usual, Chávez grandstanded at the Fifth Summit of the Americas in Port-of-Spain, Trinidad, in 2009. There was speculation on whether he would meet with the new U.S. president, Democrat Barack Obama, whom he already had called "ignorant" and said has "the same stench as Bush." Chávez interrupted a plenary session by approaching Obama and, as the cameras rolled, presented him a copy of a leftist book, *Latin America's Open Veins—Five Hundred Years of the Pillage of a Continent* by Uruguayan author Eduardo Galeano. An awkward-looking Obama shook his hand and thanked him. Twice Chávez told Obama in English at the summit, "I want to be your friend." Chávez also approached Secretary of State Hillary Clinton to voice his willingness to restore ambassadorial-level relations. Clinton responded coolly. Later, the State Department announced it "welcomes" the restoration. Ambassadors were exchanged in June.

At a post-summit news conference, Obama insisted he wanted to be an equal partner with Latin America, but he chided Chávez for his tendency to play to the TV cameras and for years of "inflammatory" rhetoric toward the U.S. Ultimately, he said, "The test for all of us is not simply words but also deeds."

Chávez took the lead international role in demanding the reinstatement of his ally, Honduran President Zelaya, who was deposed in 2009 for allegedly attempting to impose a new, Chávez-style constitution. Chávez failed, but he succeeded in preventing his allies from recognizing the elected government of Zelaya's successor, Porfirio Lobo Sosa. Eventually, Chávez and the new Colombian president, Juan Manuel Santos, put aside their differences to broker an agreement between Zelaya and Lobo by which Zelaya returned to Honduras and Lobo is recognized as president.

Chávez visited Russia, Iran, Syria and six other countries in 2009. In Syria, he accused Israel of "genocide." In Iran, President Ahmadinejad agreed to provide Venezuela with nuclear technology while Chávez agreed to provide Iran with gasoline if the rest of the world applied sanctions against Iran for refusing to abandon its nuclear program. Ahmadinejad reciprocated by visiting Caracas in 2012. In Russia, Chávez obtained a

Venezuela

$2.2 billion credit to buy tanks, short-range missiles and air-defense radar, which led Secretary Clinton to accuse Chávez of starting what could be a regional "arms race."

In 2010, a Spanish judge alleged that Venezuela had long served as an intermediary between the *FARC* and the Basque separatist group, *ETA*, which was linked to 800 deaths in terrorist attacks over nearly half a century. Then the Spanish media reported that two arrested *ETA* terrorists had stated that they had received weapons training in Venezuela. The Spanish government nervously downplayed the reports, which Chávez dismissed as a "broken record."

In the first half of 2011, even as the rest of the world was condemning Libya's Gadhafi and Syria's al-Assad for suppressing mass demonstrations by brute force, Chávez voiced his continued support for his fellow autocrats. He called al-Assad, whose security forces had slaughtered thousands of unarmed demonstrators, a "brother."

For the first time, he missed the Summit of the Americas, held in April 2012 in Cartagena, Colombia, weakened by the cancer that would claim his life less than a year later. He exuberantly remained an international loose cannon to the end.

---

open-ended state of emergency and suspend civil liberties, including presumption of innocence and the right to fair trial. Domestic and international human rights groups labeled the power grab for what it was, a move toward absolute dictatorship.

The 69 amendments were lumped together in two separate "blocks." The campaign turned violent when *chavistas* opened fire on an opposition rally of 80,000 students in November; eight were wounded. Chávez, accustomed to lopsided election victories, was confident this one, on December 2, 2007, would be no different. But only 45% of the electorate turned out to vote, handing him—and an anxious world—a stunning surprise:

	"Block A"	
Sí	4,379,392	49.29%
No	4,504,354	50.71%
	"Block B"	
Sí	4,335,136	48.94%
No	4,522,332	50.06%

Chávez said he accepted the will of the voters, claiming that it proved that Venezuela is a genuine democracy. He even admitted he had tried to push the country too far too fast, and said his revolution would focus on "three Rs: revision, rectification and relaunching." He reshuffled his cabinet and once again ejected his vice president, Jorge Rodríguez, replacing him with Ramón Alonso Carrizales, a retired colonel and a member of the Socialist Party.

Several factors contributed to Chávez's first electoral defeat. One was resentment over his suspension of the highly popular *RCTV*. Another was the frightening crime wave that still continues; in 2006, Venezuela's murder rate of 49 per 100,000 inhabitants was second-highest in the world after El Salvador. Another was the perception that Venezuela's vast oil riches had done little to alleviate the grinding poverty despite Chávez's new social programs. The individual components of his coalition, such as Communists and Socialists, balked at his plan for an umbrella organization under his control. Finally, most Venezuelans simply don't want a dictatorship.

Chávez's self-professed mellowing did not stop him from renationalizing Sidor, the steel complex that had been run by an Argentine-Italian consortium. The nationalization, ironically, strained relations with Argentina; he ignored his friend, former President Néstor Kirchner, who had lobbied him not to do it.

In 2008, Human Rights Watch, the hemispheric ombudsman group, released a 267-page report critical of Venezuela's growing repression. Speaking in Caracas, José Miguel Vivanco, the Chilean executive director of the group, said, "During this decade, democracy and its key institutions have become seriously weakened, judicial power has lost independence, civil society has less space, the news media, too, and the unions—the big, strong ones—cannot exercise their rights." As though to verify Vivanco's point, Chávez expelled him.

Chávez also came under criticism from Poland's Nobel Peace Laureate, Lech Walesa. Speaking in Warsaw, Walesa said, "I am the best proof that communism failed because it is a bad system, and introducing it there (Venezuela) is the biggest mistake of the region." Walesa then canceled a speech at a pro-democracy forum in Venezuela sponsored by Chávez critics when the Venezuelan government said it could not guarantee his security.

Venezuelans voted again in November 2008 to elect 22 state governors and 330 mayors and municipal councils. Turnout was 55%. Chávez's electoral machinery "disqualified" some of the opposition's strongest candidates on flimsy pretexts, and during the campaign Chávez made naked threats against the opposition. In one state, he even threatened to call out his tanks if the "oligarchy" won.

But voters chafed at such intimidation. *Chavistas* won 17 of the governorships, but the opposition took cheer from winning the two largest states, Zulia and Miranda, and the Caracas mayoralty. It also won the governorships of Carabobo, Táchira and Nueva Esparta, meaning a majority of Venezuela's population would be governed by the opposition. Two of Chávez's past presidential opponents won office, Henrique Salas as governor of Carabobo and Manuel Rosales as mayor of Maracaibo. Antonio Ledezma won the Caracas mayoralty with 52.4% over a hand-picked Chávez protégé. Especially embarrassing was the victory of Enrique Capriles over Governor Diosdado Cabello in Miranda; Cabello had been Chávez's vice president and was a member of his inner circle. But perhaps the most humiliating—and ominous—loss for the *chavistas* was the mayoralty of Sucre, which contains some of Caracas' sprawling suburban slums and which had been a bastion of regime support.

The *chavistas* won a majority of the 10.22 million votes cast, 53.1% to 43.2% for the opposition and 3.4% for independents, but that was a dramatic drop from the 59% he received in 2000 or the 2004 recall referendum or the 63% he received in 2006.

Chávez soon announced he was "open" to the idea of *another* referendum to lift the ban on term limits; the Assembly quickly acted. Chávez also replaced several of the functions of the Caracas municipal government under federal—meaning his—control. The police were nationalized, as well as a sports stadium and a parking lot that were important revenue sources for the city.

When Ledezma took office, he was appalled at the degree of featherbedding he found in the municipal government, with thousands of employees on the government payroll—including a suspicious number of beautiful young women—who apparently did no work. When he announced their contracts would not be renewed, hundreds staged an occupation of city hall. Chávez blamed Ledezma for creating the problem.

The new referendum on term limits was held February 15, 2009. This time, Chávez took no chances. The media blitz in favor of a "*Sí*" vote was of Orwellian proportions. He mobilized the workers of *PD-VSA* and the state-owned telephone company, making it clear their jobs depended on a favorable outcome. This time the turnout was 70.3% and the outcome was more to his liking:

Sí	6,316,482	54.85%
No	5,193,839	45.15%

His winning percentage, despite the heavy turnout, was far less than what he was accustomed to, and the results showed that Venezuelans were as polarized as ever.

Chávez was forced to slow down, but not stop, his nationalizations in 2009 because the price of oil had dropped below $70 a barrel from a high of $140 in 2008. He expropriated a Cargill rice mill, but abandoned a $1.2 billion takeover of Spain's Banco de Santander branch. Incredibly, Chávez invited foreign oil companies to make bids for exploration!

In the next move to suppress opposition, the government ordered Manuel Rosales, his 2006 election opponent and the newly elected mayor of Maracaibo, to appear in court in March 2009 on charges that he had illegally enriched himself while serving as governor of Zulia. Rosales denied the charges, went into hiding, and in April sought political asylum in Peru, which granted it.

Chávez made several grandstanding appearances on the world stage in 2009. When Honduran President Manuel Zelaya, a Chávez ally, was deposed, Chávez was instrumental in denying Latin American recognition to the interim government and to the new president, Porfirio Lobo Sosa, duly elected that November. Ultimately, Chávez and the new Colombian President, Juan Manuel Santos, brokered an accord between Zelaya and Lobo in 2011 (see Honduras).

When the U.S. and Colombia announced that Colombia would allow U.S. forces use of seven Colombian military bases, Chávez denounced the deal as a "declaration of war" and threatened to sever diplomatic relations with Colombia. He didn't, but he restricted trade and reduced Colombian imports by 70%. Hostilities appeared imminent. Venezuela closed two bridges on the border, disrupting commerce. Relations normalized after the Colombian Supreme Court ruled the base deal unconstitutional.

Carrizalez resigned as vice president and defense minister in 2010 and was replaced by Elías José Jaua, a leftist academic.

In September 2010, Chávez made a nine-country tour of Iran, Syria, Russia, Libya, Algeria, Turkmenistan, Belarus,

Italy and Spain. Returning home, he announced a $2.2 billion arms-purchasing credit from Russia that included, among other items, 92 T-72 tanks and short-range missiles with a 55-mile range, as well as an anti-aircraft system with a 185-mile range. U.S. Secretary of State Hillary Clinton used a meeting with visiting Uruguayan President Vázquez, heretofore a Chávez ally, to denounce what she called a regional "arms race." Vázquez agreed, saying Latin America would be better served channeling its resources to social problems rather than weapons.

Domestically, Chávez continued moving Venezuela inexorably toward a Cuban-style dictatorship. In 2009, Diosdado Cabello, now the minister of public works and housing, who oversaw broadcasting and was then regarded as the second most powerful man in the country, announced he was not renewing the broadcast licenses of 34 privately owned radio stations, ostensibly because their owners had had a case of mass amnesia and all neglected to complete the proper paperwork. The owners protested they had tried for two years to seek guidance on what kind of paperwork was required but that the government ignored them.

The closures led to mass anti-Chávez demonstrations, not only in Venezuela but in Colombia, Honduras, the U.S. and Europe. Cabello responded by announcing that an additional 29 stations would be closed! He also filed another legal complaint against the beleaguered *Globovisión*, saying that during its coverage of the demonstrations it had carried tickers at the bottom of the screen calling for a *coup*. Pro-Chávez goons vandalized the station; Chávez unconvincingly condemned the attack.

The radio station closures were followed by a new media law that tightened the provisions of the existing law. The surviving private radio stations could not share national news but could report only local news. In 2010, *RCTV* was also barred from cable TV after it refused to adhere to a new regulation that cable channels also must carry Chávez speeches live. Its second closure also drew protest rallies.

The government went after *Globovisión* again in 2010. First, it arrested Oswaldo Álvarez Paz, former governor of Zulia and a presidential candidate in 1993. Álvarez Paz said in an interview on *Globovisión* that Venezuela had become a haven for narcotraffickers and that it was secretly supporting the Marxist rebels in Colombia. He was charged with conspiracy against the government, public incitement to commit a crime and spreading false information. The government dropped the conspiracy charge—the most serious—against Álvarez Paz and released him

on bail. In 2011, he was convicted of the remaining charges and sentenced to two years of house arrest.

Two weeks after Álvarez Paz's arrest, Guillermo Zuloaga, president of *Globovisión*, was arrested for allegedly disseminating false information that created panic. How? By criticizing Chávez during a meeting of the Inter American Press Association in Aruba, saying he was seeking to divide Venezuelans and suppress freedom of expression. Zuloaga's house also was raided twice for evidence that he had hunted endangered species; no evidence was found. He was also charged with stockpiling 24 cars to sell them for a profit. The IAPA condemned Zuloaga's arrest.

Globovisión faced 40 civil complaints. Zuloaga went to Washington to plead his case to the OAS' Inter-American Commission on Human Rights (ICHR), challenging the Venezuelan government to prove the charges against him. The ICHR had already denounced both arrests and issued a 319-page report accusing Venezuela of "routinely" committing human rights violations and of persecuting people for their political beliefs. In late 2010, Chávez alleged that Zuloaga and other opponents were trying to raise $100 million to have him assassinated. In 2011 a judge fined the station $2 million, and the Supreme Court upheld the fine five months later.

It was not just Chávez's opponents who were at risk. One of Chávez's own judges, Lourdes Afiuni, released a dissident banker, Eligio Cedeño, on bail in 2009 because he had been held three years without trial. Under Chávez's constitution, a suspect may be help up to two years without trial. Chávez promptly had Afiuni herself arrested on corruption charges, calling her a "pirate" and demanding she be sentenced to 30 years. She was finally released in 2013, but remained under house arrest, and became an international *cause célèbre*. Her arrest ended any lingering doubt about whether Venezuela has an independent judiciary.

The government announced the takeover in 2010 of two glass manufacturing plants owned by the U.S. firm Owens-Illinois, then expropriated another privately owned steel manufacturing plant, Sidetur, owned by the Venezuelan firm Vivencia. The government's justification for the Sidetur takeover: It wasn't providing enough steel to meet the nation's needs—as though it would be more efficient under state control. The year before, Sidor produced 4.3 million tons; under state control, it produced about 2 million in 2010. More than 200 companies were nationalized in 2010, about half the total nationalized since Chávez came to power. By the end of the year, the government also had seized a total of 3 million hect-

Venezuela

ares of farmland and expected to confiscate another 450,000 in 2011.

The 2010 Assembly Elections

The National Assembly passed a new electoral law in 2009 that replaced proportional representation with a district system that gives the party with the highest percentage of the votes a disproportionately large share of Assembly seats. It delegates to the *CNE,* not the Assembly, the task of reapportioning the districts. The *CNE* conducted the redistricting in 2010, which was an obvious gerrymander to favor Chávez's *PSUV.* The rural areas loyal to Chávez were grossly over-represented.

These moves toward increased authoritarianism, as well as the 2.9% decline in GDP caused by stagnant world oil prices and the global recession, took a toll on Chávez's popularity. By the beginning of 2010, his approval rating had slipped to 46%, and 66% of poll respondents said they did not want him to be elected again in 2012. He decreed a 10% devaluation, which was designed to give the economy a short-term boost by making Venezuelan goods cheaper abroad.

Realizing the folly of their 2005 boycott of the National Assembly elections, and faced with the mathematical necessity of having a united front to face Chávez's *PSUV* in the 2010 Assembly elections, 16 national and 34 regional opposition groups hammered themselves together in an umbrella organizationcalled Coalition for Democratic Unity *(MUD).* It even included the old *MAS,* once a member of Chávez's coalition. They chose Ramón Guillermo Avelado as their leader. This hodge-podge of groups had only one common bond: the goal of defeating Chávez and thus salvaging Venezuelan democracy.

At stake in the September 26, 2010, elections were the 165 Assembly seats. Chávez needed to retain 110 to keep his two-thirds "supermajority" that allowed him to amend the constitution and to rule by decree. Besides the two main coalitions on the ballot was a small opposition left-wing group, Fatherland for All *(PPT).*

The opposition had ample ammunition: violent crime that had claimed 20,000 lives, or 48 per 100,000, the world's third-highest homicide rate in 2010; chronic power shortages and other lapses in public services; continued corruption, that had made Venezuela the most corrupt nation in Latin America in 2010, according to Transparency International; and a scandal involving 130 tons of badly needed imported foodstuffs that were left to rot in a government warehouse because of bureaucratic ineptness. Chávez's approval rating was a record low of 40% in mid-2010.

This already highly charged electoral atmosphere was overshadowed by the death in August of a hunger striker, 49-year-old Franklin José Brito, a farmer who had fought a six-year legal battle against the government after his neighbors occupied part of his land. He alleged that his accusations of corruption against a local *chavista* mayor sparked the invasion, which he said was instigated by the government's land reform agency. The government denied it. He and his wife also lost their jobs as schoolteachers. Brito held a total of eight hunger strikes and once amputated his own finger in protest, which brought him national and international media attention. Toward the end, the government rushed Brito to a military hospital in a frantic attempt to keep him alive, but he died of cardiac arrest. The opposition made him a martyr for private property rights. The government labeled the opposition "vultures" and claimed Brito never had clear title to his land.

Voter turnout was 66%. The results proved historic, if confusing:

PSUV	5,451.419	48.3%	96 seats
MUD	5,334.309	47.2%	64 seats
PPT	354,677	3.1%	2 seats
Others	155,429	1.4%	3 seats

Both sides claimed victory, but the government's claim was hollow. It had lost its supermajority and had failed to poll a majority of the vote. It was only because of the *CNE*'s creative gerrymandering of district lines that the government won a disproportionate majority of seats, which Avelado called a "perversion" of democracy. If proportional representation had still been in effect, the non-*PSUV* parties would have won outright control.

Chávez's response to this impending limiting of his powers was predictable. Two weeks before the new Assembly was to convene, the lame-duck Assembly voted to give him the power to rule by decree for the next 18 months, using a flood as a pretext. The Assembly then adopted new laws and internal procedures that effectively emasculated the legislative branch as a governmental power; it was required to meet only four days a month. New legislation stripped state and local governments of more power, transferring functions to socialist communes. For good measure, two of the newly elected *MUD* legislators were arrested on corruption charges.

Chávez accelerated his nationalizations and his suppression of opposition media. The lame-duck Assembly passed an Internet regulation amendment that allowed the government to control the content of websites and the information coming into Venezuela from abroad or being

sent from Venezuela. The vaguely worded law permits the government to squelch information that "promotes, defends, or incites breaches of public order," that is "contrary to the security of the nation" or that causes "anxiety or unrest." The Committee to Protect Journalists, the Inter American Press Association and the U.S. State Department all condemned the new restrictions on freedom of expression.

The Assembly next passed an amendment to the telecommunications act requiring broadcast station owners to appear in person to reapply for their licenses, a measure obviously aimed at *Globovisión's* exiled Zuloaga. It also moved so-called "adult content" programming from prime time to after midnight. Chávez denied the new laws were attempts at censorship, and one of his Assembly members rationalized that the new measures "reaffirmed" freedom of expression!

Chávez's latest provocation against the U.S. came in December 2010, when he refused to accept the credentials of the newly nominated U.S. ambassador, Larry Palmer. Palmer had said at his Senate confirmation hearing that there were "clear ties" between Venezuela and the *FARC.* The Venezuelan government termed these and other remarks "unacceptable." The U.S. retaliated by revoking the U.S. visa of the Venezuelan ambassador. It was against this backdrop that Chávez had a brief and uneasy encounter with Secretary Clinton in January 2011 in Brasilia, where they attended the inauguration of Brazilian President Dilma Rousseff. Neither side released details of what they discussed, but news agencies disseminated photos of a smiling Chávez and a wary-looking Clinton shaking hands.

A total of 82 students staged a three-week hunger strike across the country in February 2011 to demand the release of political prisoners. The government, not wanting another martyr like Brito, had doctors monitor them. The students ended the strike when four of the strikers passed out. The government insisted the prisoners in question were guilty of corruption or murder, but the day after the strike ended Biagio Pileri, a newly elected Assembly member who had been under house arrest on corruption charges, was released.

Disgraced former President Carlos Andrés Pérez died in self-imposed exile in Miami on Christmas Day 2010 at the age of 88. A court fight immediately erupted between his wife, who said Pérez had asked to be buried on his native soil, and his long-time mistress, who insisted Pérez had told her he did not want to be buried in Venezuela while Chávez was in power. He was eventually buried in Venezuela in October 2011.

Venezuela's relations with Colombia improved steadily after Juan Manuel Santos replaced Uribe as president in August 2010. Chávez declined Santos' personal invitation to attend his inauguration, but sent Foreign Minister Nicolás Maduro to carry a "message of love and solidarity." Chávez and Santos met three days after the inauguration and met many times since in meetings that were far less strained than the meetings with Uribe had been. They met most recently in December 2011, signing bilateral agreements on agriculture, trade and security. There were indications that the greatest remaining source of antagonism, that of *FARC* guerrillas taking refuge in Venezuela, had also dissipated as the guerrillas have increasingly abandoned Venezuela.

Uncertainty, Re-Election and Death

Chávez underwent surgery in Cuba in June 2011 for removal of an abscess in his pelvis and remained to convalesce. He addressed the nation on TV from Cuba and revealed that a malignant tumor had been removed. His illness and prolonged absence raised questions about the lack of any established transition. Chávez flew regularly to Havana for chemotherapy or surgery for the next year and a half.

His head bald from chemo, he declined to offer details of the cancer, insisted he was cured and said his illness would not prevent him from running again in 2012. Nonetheless, he advanced the date for the election from December to October 7. He made far fewer TV appearances, and when he did his speeches were much shorter. Yet, he came across as strong and in high spirits. The self-proclaimed Communist also admitted he had sought divine intervention. "I say to Christ, 'Give me more life,' because it's not for me, it's for your plan, so that your plan for Venezuela can advance," he said.

In January 2012, Chávez effected the latest shakeup in his cabinet and ruling circle. He named former Vice President Diosdado Cabello first vice president of the *PSUV* and president of the National Assembly, raising speculation that he was being groomed as his possible successor if the cancer interfered with his vision of rule-without-end. He replaced Defense Minister Carlos Mata Figueroa with General Henry Rangel Silva, whom the U.S. put on its drug kingpin list in 2008 for allegedly facilitating the *FARC*'s drug trafficking through Venezuela. He appointed a 10-member Council of State headed by Vice President Jaua and including the resurrected José Vicente Rangel, the former vice president. Its very creation fueled even further speculation that the president was mindful of his impending mortality.

Chávez again hosted Iranian President Mahmoud Ahmadinejad during his three-country Latin American tour in January 2012, and Chávez reiterated his support for Iran's ambition to develop nuclear energy. The two men also joked—supposedly—about directing "a big atomic bomb" at Washington.

Even as Ahmadinejad was in Caracas, the U.S. declared Livia Acosta, the Venezuelan consul in Miami, *persona non grata* and expelled her from the country. The State Department did not explain, but the media reported that she and some Iranian diplomats were allegedly linked to a scheme by a leftist Mexican professor to hack into the computers of the White House, Pentagon, FBI and U.S. nuclear plants. Chávez closed the Miami consulate, a move that may have been designed to make life more difficult for anti-Chávez dissidents living there.

Two *MUD* governors, Henrique Capriles in Miranda and Pedro Pérez in Zulia, competed in the opposition primary in February 2012. So did former Caracas Mayor Leopoldo López after the Inter-American Human Rights Commission ruled in 2011 that the government's 2008 order preventing him for running for office was illegal. He later withdrew and became Capriles' campaign manager. Capriles, 39, whom polls showed as the only opposition candidate with a chance of defeating Chávez, won the primary with 62% of the vote. Violence erupted in one municipality after the primary between opposition supporters and local police, who attempted to seize the voter list.

Capriles' primary opponents coalesced around his candidacy. Chávez refused to debate his opponent, dismissing Capriles as a "fly." He later called Capriles a "pig" and, his favorite epithet for those who opposed him, a "fascist."

Passions during the campaign became unruly, and in one instance, deadly. Two opposition leaders were stopped at a roadblock in Barinas state and gunned down in cold blood. Chávez condemned the killings, and suspects reportedly were arrested.

Chávez used the full force of incumbency to boost his chances, lavishing public works projects on a scale that was to boost GDP growth that year to 5%, third-highest in Latin America. He also saturated the airwaves of state-owned radio and television with ostensibly "non-political" messages boasting of his government's accomplishments, while Capriles was legally limited to three minutes a day of advertising. Chávez downplayed questions about whether a deadly refinery fire in August that killed 50 people was the result of milking *PDVSA* for cash to pay for public works at the expense of proper maintenance.

A more nagging question on everyone's mind was the president's health and whether he could live through another six-year term. Chávez assured his countrymen he was "completely cured" of cancer. Indeed, he seemed healthy and ebullient at his rallies.

Turnout on October 7 was 80.5%. In the end, Chávez's assurances and the advantages of incumbency prevailed:

Chávez	8,191,132	55.1%
Capriles	6,591,304	44.3%

It was far less than the winning percentages Chávez had received in the past. Capriles made a gracious concession, and the two men reportedly exchanged pleasantries by telephone. But two days after the election, Chávez referred to the 44% who voted against him as the "bourgeoisie."

On December 8, the president who assured his countrymen two months earlier that he had been completely cured of cancer, announced to them that he had to return to Cuba immediately for more surgery because the cancer had "returned." In an equally stunning announcement, he anointed former Foreign Minister Nicolás Maduro, a Marxist-Leninist hardliner whom he had appointed the latest vice president in October, as his successor. It was the closest he had come to admitting he was dying. It had long been believed that National Assembly President Diosdado Cabello was his preferred heir-apparent.

The opposition was dealt a second bitter disappointment in the regional elections on December 16, when it won only three of the 23 state governorships. Capriles regained the governorship of Miranda in a close race with one of Chávez's disposable vice presidents, Elías Jaua, whom Chávez had replaced with Maduro. The opposition also won in Amazonas and Lara.

Chávez remained in Cuba and disappeared from public view for 10 weeks, provoking an international deathwatch. When he missed his own inauguration on January 10, confusion reigned as to who was constitutionally in charge. Although there were constitutional provisions for declaring the president temporarily incapacitated, which would have made Cabello acting president, they were not taken. In accordance with Chávez's direction, Maduro took charge, insisting unconvincingly that he was not acting president. Former Vice President Jaua became foreign minister. Chávez's mascot Supreme Court justices upheld this deviation from Chávez's own constitution. As in other autocracies, Chávez *was* the constitution.

The only proof he was still alive were two photographs released in Cuba show-

Venezuela

ing Chávez with his two daughters. Finally, Chávez returned to Caracas on February 18. There was no media coverage of the nighttime arrival, and he was whisked immediately to a military hospital. It was apparent he had come home to die on his native soil.

On March 5, he did. Hours later, Maduro, 50, a former bus driver, was sworn in as interim president, pending an election that the constitution said had to be held within 30 days.

Raúl Castro and Iran's Ahmadinejad attended the funeral on March 8, as did several *USASUR* presidents. The official U.S. delegation was composed of U.S. Representative Gregory Meeks, D-N.Y., senior Democrat on the House Foreign Affairs Committee, and former Representative William Delahunt, D-Mass. Attending unofficially were the Reverend Jesse Jackson and the actor Sean Penn, both Chávez admirers. At first, the government announced that Chávez's body would be embalmed and put on permanent display, as the Soviets had done with Lenin and Stalin, but a month later it announced that the technology was unavailable and that Chávez would be buried like an ordinary mortal.

Maduro's Dubious Mandate

Deviating again from the constitution, Maduro called the election for April 14, 10 days past the 30-day deadline; skeptics had wondered whether he would even bother with the formality of an election.

Maduro found himself faced with handicaps that would have been fatal to an incumbent in any true democracy. Chávez's spending spree before the October election had finally taken the inevitable economic toll. The *Bolívar* had been kept deliberately overvalued against the dollar to make vital imported goods affordable, but by early 2013 it was no longer sustainable. Consumers were faced with shortages of basic foodstuffs like wheat and corn flour, rice, sugar and cooking oil. The dying president, or someone acting in his stead, effected two currency devaluations in early 2013. Inflation was 20.9% for 2012, the highest in Latin America, and by April it was running at an estimated 30% for the year. Then there was the alarming crime rate, which Chávez had chosen to ignore. In 2012, Venezuela was the second-deadliest country in the world with a homicide rate of 53.7 per 100,000 population.

The opposition again fielded Capriles, who now had name recognition, voter disenchantment with the government and, most importantly, an opponent who was not Hugo Chávez.

Maduro was a relatively lackluster campaigner, and although he emulated

President Nicolás Maduro
Courtesy Agência Brasil

Chávez's style by playing a guitar and singing at campaign rallies, he simply did not have his mentor's charisma. But like Chávez, he took full advantage of the government's machinery to dominate the airwaves and plaster the country with propaganda that proclaimed, "A vote for Maduro is a vote for Chávez." The dead president was elevated to the plane of political sainthood; indeed, Maduro even called him "the Christ of Latin America," which brought a quick rebuke from the Roman Catholic bishop in Caracas.

The rhetoric between the two candidates grew increasingly ugly and personal, with Maduro implying Capriles is gay because he is not married and calling him a "prince of the bourgeoisie." Capriles called Maduro a "bird brain" and said he'd rather be a bachelor than have a wife as ugly as Maduro's. It was not democracy at its best. Polls showed the race too close to call, or had diametrically opposite findings.

The actual results did nothing to resolve Venezuela's political crisis:

Maduro	7,587,532	50.6%
Capriles	7,363,264	49.1%

Maduro carried 15 states, Capriles eight. Capriles immediately called for a recount, and alleged widespread irregularities. Meeting with domestic and foreign journalists, he claimed opposition pollwatchers had been forced out of 282 voting stations, sometimes at gunpoint. At more than 1,200 stations, he alleged, Maduro had suspiciously received more votes than Chávez had in October. The National Electoral Council (*CNE*) reported it had audited 54% of the votes and verified their accuracy. Capriles demanded the *CNE* audit all 100%, which it agreed to do in May. The results were so questionable that even Chávez's old *UNASUR* allies told Maduro

that a proper recount would have to be made for them to attend his inauguration.

When Capriles demanded that the signatures and fingerprints also be audited, the *CNE* refused and abruptly certified Maduro as the winner, well before the legal appeal process had expired. He was hastily sworn in on April 19 with the cloud of illegitimacy hanging over his head. The inevitable protests erupted, some non-violent, like the traditional *cacerolazo*, others not. When the 67 opposition *MUD* members of the National Assembly refused to recognize Maduro's victory, their salaries were frozen and a free-for-all broke out in the chamber, captured on smartphones.

The opposition filed suit challenging the election results, citing a list of irregularities that totaled 180 pages. Like the "birther" campaign against Obama in the United States, the lawsuit also alleged that Maduro was born in Colombia and thus ineligible to be president under Chávez's constitution. On August 7, to no one's surprise, the Supreme Court upheld Maduro's election.

Recent Developments

Two weeks after the election, *Globovisión*, the last remaining opposition TV channel, was sold to Juan Domingo Cordero, an insurance company owner seen as sympathetic to the government. The station's exiled owner, Guillermo Zuloaga, told employees in a letter that the station had become economically unviable because of all the government fines and that he could not raise salaries enough to keep up with skyrocketing inflation. International journalism and human rights groups lamented the sale as a major blow to freedom of expression.

Maduro was one of four Latin American presidents, all of *ALBA* countries, who offered to grant political asylum to fugitive U.S. National Security Agency leaker Edward Snowden in July 2013. Snowden had been stranded in a transit lounge of the Moscow airport, and there were conflicting reports as to whether he had formally requested asylum in Venezuela. If Snowden had gone to Venezuela, Maduro could have regarded it as payback for the United States' refusal to extradite Luis Posada Carriles, the anti-Castro Cuban terrorist wanted for the bombing of a Cuban airliner off Venezuela in 1976 (see Cuba/The Posada Carriles Case). But Snowden requested asylum in Russia, apparently because there was no way to fly from Moscow to any of the Latin American countries without crossing the airspace of a U.S. ally that could order the plane grounded.

Venezuela's economic crisis worsened in late 2013 as the *Bolívar's* black-market value continued to slide against the dollar. Inflation was running at more than 50% for the year. The scarcity of basic food items and necessities, even toothpaste and toilet paper, led to long queues outside stores that still had the items to sell; other stores were closed. Power blackouts became commonplace. The deprivation was now affecting the *PSUV*'s core constituency, the poor, as the country approached the December 8 municipal elections. Maduro blamed everyone else for the situation: the United States, the opposition, the few remaining privately owned media outlets, the business elite.

In September 2013 he expelled three U.S. diplomats, accusing them of conspiring with the opposition to foment violence and to sabotage the electrical grid. But he offered no evidence. He called the managers of the newspaper *Diario 2001* "bandits" for publishing an investigative piece about gasoline shortages in this oil-producing country. Self-censorship became more common.

Armed with autocratic powers, he pulled off an astute but economically preposterous maneuver. In November, he simply decreed that the prices of major appliances, such as refrigerators and plasma TVs, would be rolled back to what they were in September. Retailers had no choice but to comply, and shops were flooded with customers taking advantage of the bargains; some shops were looted. Dozens of businessmen were arrested for "usury" and for what Maduro called "waging economic war."

It gave him the desired bump in the polls. Once again he exploited the airwaves for political purposes, while the non-government media were afraid to provide coverage of *MUD* candidates or rallies.

In the December elections, turnout was 59%. Both sides found cause to claim victory. In the popular vote, the *PSUV* obtained a plurality of 49% to 43% for the *MUD*; the remainder went to independents. Scores of races were too close to call on election night, but on December 10 the *CNE* declared that the *PSUV* had won 255 mayoralties to only 75 for the *MUD* and five for independents. The opposition took comfort that the non-*PSUV* vote was a clear majority, and that *MUD* candidates had won the mayoralties of Caracas and the other three largest cities, as well as nine of the 23 state capitals.

The chronic shortages continued, and prices continued to soar. Maduro's response was, once again, to order price controls, which put even more pressure on the *Bolívar*, which in turn made imports more expensive. In January, Maduro ordered a partial devaluation, through a complicated "secondary exchange rate" designed to stop the hemorrhaging of dol-

lar reserves, which had hit a 10-year low. Foreign airlines and other businesses were clamoring for billions of dollars that were owed to them.

Venezuelans' concern over the alarming wave of violent crime that had made Venezuela the second-deadliest country in the world after Honduras was magnified in January 2014 when Monica Spear, 28, who had been Miss Venezuela in 2004, and her ex-husband were shot to death by armed robbers when their car broke down in Carabobo state. Their 5-year-old daughter was shot in the leg. The killings shocked an already jaded country, and street protesters demanded something be done about crime. Venezuela was once again a powder keg.

On February 12, it exploded when national guard troops opened fire on a loud but peaceful march in Caracas, killing three protesters. The march had been called by the Popular Will faction of the *MUD*, led by Leopoldo López, which advocates a non-violent but more confrontational policy against the government. The day after the fatal protest, the government issued an arrest warrant for López, 42, for conspiracy, murder, terrorism and arson; López pointed his finger at the government for the deaths. Maduro, as always, labeled the opposition "fascists" who were plotting a coup.

On February 15, opposition demonstrators, overwhelmingly young, took to the streets again across the country to protest the three deaths and to generally express their rage against the shortages, inflation, oppression and high crime. As has happened with mass protests in other countries around the world, the new social media became a vital medium for disseminating information about the protests because the government had threatened the remaining privately owned mass media with reprisals if they reported on them. López, in hiding, used Twitter and YouTube to exhort his followers.

National guardsmen seized a CNN camera at gunpoint at one demonstration. Maduro threatened to expel CNN if it did not "rectify" its coverage of the protests, but relented the next day. He accused U.S. journalists of falsely conveying the idea that Venezuela is in a civil war.

Maduro next blamed his usual whipping boy, the United States, and again expelled three diplomats on February 17 for allegedly conspiring against his government— again without presenting any proof. The U.S. called the allegations "baseless and false." The day after the expulsions, the erratic president said he wanted a "dialogue" with President Obama.

When Panamanian President Ricardo Martinelli called on the OAS to initiate negotiations between the government and

opposition to quell the violence, Maduro called him a "lackey" of the United States and severed diplomatic relations.

The growing unrest forced Maduro to cancel a scheduled summit of *Mercosur*, to which Venezuela had just been admitted. Maduro was serving as its rotating president. He has been forced to postpone the summit twice more as the violent disturbances continued.

Coincidentally, the nation took a little time amid the growing unrest to mourn the passing on February 19 of Simón Díaz, 85, the country's most beloved singer, known internationally for his folk ballads called *tonadas*. Maduro tweeted a presidential tribute to him (see Culture).

López tweeted to his followers, and told CNN, that he would present himself in front of the Justice Ministry on February 20, but urged his supporters to remain non-violent. López appeared, and images of his shouting defiantly as he was manhandled into a waiting national guard vehicle were transmitted around the world. López's first court hearing was held behind the walls of his military prison, a violation of the constitutional guarantee that court proceedings be public. The murder charges against him were dropped. In April he was formally charged with conspiracy, arson, property damage and public incitement.

All Maduro accomplished was to create an opposition martyr. Street protests intensified, and the death toll on both sides mounted, including another beauty queen. The escalation of violence put López in a confrontation with the more moderate Capriles as well. Although Capriles condemned López's arrest, he warned that the demonstrations would get out of hand and play into the government's hands. Popular Will supporters denounced Capriles as a "traitor." Yet, in March, Capriles called via Twitter for the opposition to organize "popular defense committees" to maintain the pressure on the government. He demanded the release of López and student protesters. Significantly, he acknowledged that the opposition would have to begin to appeal to the poor if it were going to cut into the *PSUV*'s power base.

As a possible sign of cracks within the regime, Maduro ordered the arrests of three air force generals in March for allegedly plotting a coup. Whether they really were, or whether it was another example of presidential paranoia, remains unclear.

The protests continued, and by April more than 30 people had been killed. A chastened Maduro asked the Vatican secretary of state, Cardinal Pietro Parolin, to mediate talks with the opposition. Capriles agreed, but the talks were denounced by the López faction. The two sides agreed to form a truth commission, but as weeks

Venezuela

went by and the government refused to release López or even one political prisoner, the opposition broke off the talks. The López faction had the satisfaction of saying, "We told you so." By May, the death toll had passed 40. Maduro issued an edict requiring government permission to stage protests—which, of course, generated more student protests.

López continues to languish behind bars. Besides the dead, hundreds more have been injured or arrested. The opposition accused the government of torturing several prisoners. International human rights organizations called for a renewed dialogue and faulted Maduro for his heavy-handed response. In May, the Republican-controlled U.S. House of Representatives passed a bill that would ban visas and freeze assets of Venezuelan officials who commit human rights violations. Its passage by the Senate was doubtful, because President Obama opposes it on the grounds that it could prolong the stalemate in Venezuela.

Meanwhile, Venezuela's economic crisis continues unabated, largely because of the government's bizarre economic lever-pulling. In April, Maduro promised to cough up almost $4 billion in hard currency toward the $13 billion Venezuela owes to importers and airlines. The airlines alone account for $4 billion. Air Canada and Alitalia of Italy have suspended all service to Venezuela, while other airlines have reduced service. In June, the already financially troubled American Airlines announced it was suspending 38 of its 48 weekly flights to Venezuela and would fly to Caracas only from Miami until Venezuela pays it the $750 million it owes.

When this book went to press in June, the violent protests had largely dried up, but the atmosphere remained tense.

CULTURE: Venezuela's ethnic make up is an intriguing blend of European, Indian, *mestizo*, black and mulatto. The crippling succession of dictatorships took a heavy toll on cultural development, however. The Spanish colonial heritage is still visible in the port of Coro, which became a UNESCO World Heritage Site in 1993.

Its two most distinguished men of letters both spent many of their most productive years abroad. The 19th century intellectual and writer Andrés Bello (1781–1865), left Venezuela at the age of 19 in 1810, then spent 19 years in London and the remainder of his life in Chile.

In the 20th century, Rómulo Gallegos (1884–1969) spent two decades in Spain during the Gómez dictatorship. His best known novel, *Doña Bárbara*, was published in 1929—in Madrid, not in Caracas. Two more of Gallegos' best-known works were written in Barcelona: *Cantaclaro* (1934) and *Canaima* (1935). Returning to Venezuela after Gómez's death in 1935, Gallegos wrote *Pobre negro* (1937) *and El forestero* (1942), but they never achieved the critical acclaim of his novels written in Spain. Perhaps that was because he was more absorbed by his political activities; he was elected president of the republic in 1948 (see History). He went into exile again during the Pérez Jiménez dictatorship of the 1950s, this time to Mexico. The Romulo Gallegos International Novel Prize, now one of the most prestigious in Latin America, was created in his honor in 1965.

Another outstanding literary figure was Arturo Uslar Pietri (1906–2001), a playwright, novelist, poet, journalist, television producer and short story writer, but primarily renowned as an essayist. He received Spain's prestigious Prince of Asturias Award for Literature in 1990 and the Romulo Gallegos Prize for his novel, *La visita en el tiempo*, in 1991. He twice won the National Prize for Literature, in 1954 and 1982.

In art, Venezuela has produced a few figures with a regional reputation, but in classical music and theater it still largely borrows from abroad.

In popular music, however, Venezuela has produced several singers who have achieved acclaim throughout Latin America and beyond.

Simón Díaz (1928-2014) specialized in the genre of the *tonadas,* or Venezuelan folk ballads. He composed and sang hundreds of *tonadas,* which celebrate the bygone lifestyle of the farmers and cowboys of Venezuela's high plains, called *musica llanera,* much as Woody Guthrie did with his folk ballads about the common man in Oklahoma. His signature song is a love ballad, *"Caballo Viejo,"* which the French group Gypsy Kings co-opted for its international smash hit *"Bamboleo"* in 1989. Díaz later received a copyright infringement settlement.

Long a popular television personality in Venezuela, Díaz, widely known as "Tío Simón," became famous throughout Latin America, and in 2004 he released a CD in the United States, *"Mis Canciones."* In 2008, he received the Latin Grammy Lifetime Achievement Award, and he is the only singer to have been awarded the Order of the Liberator, Venezuela's highest honor. He died on February 19, 2014, at age 85. Flags were flown at half-staff, and President Nicolás Maduro paid tribute, saying, "Tío Simón has gone, embraced by his love *tonada* and leaving us unforgettable memories of his contribution to our culture."

José Luís Rodríguez (b. 1943), also known by the sobriquet *El Puma,* has been a regional megastar of Latin pop-rock, for

Andrés Bello

more than three decades, recording his first hit in Venezuela in 1978. His three-volume *"Inolvidable"* album, released between 1997 and 2001, has been among his most popular. His two most recent albums are *Los Grandes del Amor* and *Mi Amigo El Puma,* both in 2009. He has also acted in *telenovelas*. Despite his regional popularity and his prolific output of songs, a Grammy has eluded him.

Another Venezuelan veteran singer-songwriter who has achieved hemispheric fame is Franco de Vita (b. 1954), who has recorded 14 albums since 1984. His 1990 song *No Basta* was at the top of the Billboard Latin charts in the U.S. for four weeks and won an MTV Award. He received two Latin Grammy Awards in 2011, for Best Male Pop Vocal Album for *En Primera Fila*, which was also nominated for Album of the Year and three other Grammys; and for Best Long Form Music Video.

In all, Venezuelans had won 15 Latin Grammys through 2012.

Venezuelan *telenovelas* are marketed abroad, but the fledgling film industry has suffered from brain drain. Venezuela's two best-known directors and screenwriters are Fina Torres (b. 1951) and Sebastián Gutiérrez (b. 1974). Both have chosen to work primarily abroad, Torres in Mexico and the United States and Gutiérrez in the United States.

One exception was Torres' *Oriana* in 1985, her directorial debut, set in Venezuela with the Venezuelan actress Doris Wells in the title role. It won Torres the *Camera d'Or* for Best First Feature at the Cannes Film Festival. Her 2000 English-language film *Woman on Top* was shot in Brazil and San Francisco, California, and starred Spanish actress Penélope Cruz. Her latest film, *Habana Eva,* is a romantic comedy filmed in Spanish in Cuba; it stars the Mexican actor Juan Carlos García and the Venezuelan actress Prakriti Maduro. It was named Best Picture at the 2010 New York International Latino Film Festival.

Gutiérrez's best-known film is the 1998 U.S.-made crime drama *Judas Kiss,* his directorial debut, with Emma Thompson and Alan Rickman. It premiered at the Toronto International Film Festival and was Critics' Choice at the 1999 Cognac Police Film Festival in France.

Beauty contests are a national passion in Venezuela, where special schools that groom young women for competition, and plastic surgeons who enhance their looks, have become thriving industries. Five Venezuelans have won the Miss World title since its inception in 1951, the most recent in 1995. Four Venezuelans have won the Miss Universe title since it was created in 1953, in 1979, 1981, 1986 and 1996. One, Irene Sáez (1981), later went into politics and ran for president in 1998 (see History).

Venezuela has 43 colleges and universities. The national university is the colonial era Universidad Central de Venezuela, in Caracas, founded in 1721. Its main campus is now the Ciudad Universitaria de Caracas, built between 1945 and 1960 and designed by the Modern Movement architect Carlos Raúl Villanueva (1900–75). It was designated a UNESCO cultural World Heritage Site in 2000.

The absence of free expression before the advent of democracy in 1958 also hamstrung the press. Press freedom caused the number of newspapers and magazines to mushroom. The capital's two prestigious dailies are the venerable *El Universal,* founded in 1909, and *El Nacional,* which dates to 1943. High-quality magazines include *Resúmen, Momento, Bohemia, Elite, Auténtico* and *Zeta.* However, freedom of the press came under increasing attack from President Hugo Chávez (see History), and the New York-based Freedom House has rated the Venezuelan media as "not free" for several years.

ECONOMY: Venezuela's economy is completely dominated by petroleum production. Oil revenues account for about half of all government in come and 90% of the nation's exports; Venezuela is the world's fifth-largest oil producer and the fourth-largest exporter of oil to the United States.

Extracting oil from the tar-like deposits of the Orinoco oil belt led to an $8 billion project to develop those resources. A large field was discovered in the eastern state of Monagas with an estimated 8.6 billion barrels in 1987. Total reserves, including "heavy" oil, are about 300 billion barrels. In 2003, the state oil company announced the discovery of still another new field in

Monagas containing an estimated 350 million barrels of light crude and 870 million cubic feet of natural gas.

There has been renewed oil drilling in the Maracaibo area. Twenty-one years after Venezuela nationalized its oil industry, it began inviting oil companies to come back in 1996 to explore in promising areas. But President Hugo Chávez, elected in 1998, reneged on those contracts in 2007 and demanded tough new terms that Exxon Mobil and ConocoPhillips refused to accept (see History).

Venezuela's bloated, featherbedded, inefficient and corrupt bureaucracy became the horror story of Latin America. The bureaucracy was padded with phantom employees and real employees who were notoriously lazy and inefficient. This discouraged foreign investors and lenders and drove up inflation. Despite President Caldera's effort to reduce the public sector, the workforce actually *increased* by 50,000 in 1997. Why? Because of de-centralization, laid-off federal workers entered the payrolls of state and local governments. Another reason was the traditional dark side of democracy: spoils and patronage. To gain or keep power, politicians swap jobs for votes.

Chávez was elected in 1998 ostensibly to rescue the economy and battle the corruption that was such a drain. Economic statistics confirmed the severity of the crisis he inherited. Real GDP growth in 1997 was an illusionarily rosy 5.1%, but that gain followed negative growth of –0.4% the year before. In 1998, the year of the free-fall in world oil prices, growth declined by –0.3%, and in 1999, Chávez's first full year in office, it plummeted by

a devastating –6.1% despite skyrocketing oil prices. In 2000, Venezuela showed positive growth of only 3.2%, almost entirely the result of the continued high price of oil on the international markets, but it was not enough to overcome the losses of the previous three years.

Growth in 2001 was 3%, but in 2002, largely because of the abortive coup and a crippling general strike (see History), GDP fell again by –8.9%. Growth in 2003 was about 9% and in 2004 was a robust 17.9%, the highest in Latin America. Growth was 9.3% in 2005 and 10.3% in 2006, again the highest in Latin America, the result of the spiraling world price of petroleum. Growth was still 8.4% in 2007, but tapered off to 4.8% in 2008 as the price of oil plummeted late in the year. In 2009, with the global recession and reduced demand for oil, GDP shrank by –3.2%, the worst year since 2002, and it shrank another –1.5% in 2010. Only Haiti had worse economic growth in Latin America.

In 2011, it grew 4.2% because of the sudden jump in the price of oil in the last two quarters. Growth in 2012 was 5.7%, thanks to oil prices and Chávez's lavish spending on public works to boost his electoral chances, the third-fastest growth in Latin America after Panama and Peru. But in 2013, as the country sank into economic crisis, it was only 1.6%, the second worst in Latin America.

Unemployment remained stubbornly in the double digits from 1997 to 2005, peaking at 20% in 2003. It fell to 8.9% in 2006 and 8.5% in 2008. Despite the global recession, it fell slightly to 7.9% in 2009, then leaped to 12.1% in 2010. It dropped back to 8.2% in 2011, and 7.9% in 2013.

Wall of the Thousand Columns (top of the Auyán-Tepui)

Venezuela

Inflation declined from a paycheck-stealing 103.2% in 1996 to 12% in 2001. In 2003 it was back up to 27.1%, the highest in Latin America. It has remained high: 17% in 2006, 22.5% in 2007, 31% in 2008, 27.1% in 2009 and 29.8% in 2010—again the highest in Latin America.

It was 26.1% in 2011 and 21.1% in 2012 still, then soared to 56.2% in 2013, helping to fuel public protests (see History). Both Chávez and his successor, Nicolás Maduro, exacerbated the crisis by attempting to manipulate the exchange rate of the *Bolívar* by fiat.

Oil wealth once gave Venezuela among the highest standards of living in the region, but inflation and negative economic growth have steadily eroded it. In 2008 its per capita income of $9,230 was the third-highest of the 20 Latin American republics after Mexico and Chile, and in 2009 it was the highest at $10,090, but it is inequitably distributed. It was fourth-highest in 2012.

The government claimed it has reduced the percentage of the population living below the poverty line from 37.9% in 2005 to 31.6% in 2011.

The public debt has fluctuated from 29% of GDP when Chávez became president to 18% in 2009 back to 34.2% in 2013.

Three decades after oil production was nationalized, the state oil company, *PDVSA*, has become increasingly dependent on foreign companies once again to maintain production, which in 2008 was 2.643 million barrels per day, the fifth-highest in the world. Part of the reason for this is that Chávez largely politicized *PVDSA* after the crippling general strike of 2002–03; he fired more than 40% of *PDVSA* managers and workers and replaced them with political loyalists with no regard to expertise.

The change did not improve efficiency. *PDVSA* entered into joint ventures with U.S., British, Dutch, Spanish and Brazilian oil firms to try to bring production up to 5 million bpd by 2009, but in 2010, the government had to settle for 2.375 million. It was still just 2.3 million bpd in both 2011 and 2012. Estimates varied for 2013, but the U.S. Energy Department put it at 2.49 million bpd.

Venezuela's proven oil reserves are still the largest in the world, 298 billion barrels.

Chávez's government abruptly canceled existing contracts in 2005 and 2007 and forced foreign companies to sign new ones on even more favorable terms for the government, which led ExxonMobil to obtain an injunction freezing $12 billion in *PDVSA* assets (see History).

With the price of oil at $70 per barrel in mid-2006, it became economically feasible to exploit the heavy crude in the Orinoco tar belt. Natural gas production was expected to increase as well. The government offered new leases in the Orinoco in 2009, but not on attractive terms. Still, it had some takers.

In mid-2008, oil skyrocketed to $140 a barrel, which prompted more drunken-sailor spending by Chávez for his foreign adventures. But the boom quickly turned to bust as the price of oil plummeted to as low as $37 a barrel by the end of 2008, not enough to finance Chávez's grandiose foreign and domestic agendas. It stabilized at about $70 in 2010, then spiked again at about $100 in early 2011 because of the political turmoil in Libya, Bahrain and elsewhere in the Middle East. The price of oil climbed back to about $110 a barrel in early 2012, but declining world demand pushed it back to $80 a mid-year. In mid-2014, it was back up to $106.

By 2010, Chávez's government had expropriated 400 domestic- and foreign-owned firms.

After five years of artificially pegging the *Bolívar* at 2.15 to the dollar despite double-digit inflation each year, Venezuela was faced with a severe dollar shortage in 2010. Chávez devalued the *Bolívar* in January 2010 to 4.3 to the dollar in a desperate attempt to shore up the economy and bring in hard currency, but GDP still shrank by –2.9% in 2010. Chávez also cracked down on black-market currency trading and replaced legal currency brokerage houses with a government entity to control the currency and bond markets, as though he could command monetary stability the way he commanded everything else. The black market value for *Bolívares* rose to nine to the dollar, although penalties are now severe. There were two more devaluations in early 2013 as Chávez lay on his deathbed, and another partial devaluation by Maduro in January 2014. In March, the *Bolívar* was allowed to float freely, whereupon it plunged 88% against the dollar. Maduro imposed severe penalties for black market exchanges.

THE FUTURE: What is Hugo Chávez's legacy to his country? In 1998, the year Chávez was elected on a platform to clean up the country's endemic corruption, Transparency International rated Venezuela tied with Ecuador as the 12th most corrupt of the 15 Latin American republics it rated that year, and 77th most corrupt in the world. In 2012, after 13 years of *chavismo*, TI rated Venezuela as tied with Haiti as the two most corrupt nations in the Western Hemisphere and 165th out of 174 rated countries in the world.

In addition, Chávez promised to battle Venezuela's alarming crime rate. But by 2011, Venezuela was up to 67 homicides per 100,000, about 20,000 murders, fourth place in the world behind Honduras, El Salvador and Saint Kitts and Nevis. In 2012, it was in second place behind Honduras. There were also a reported 3,000 kidnappings.

Finally, although he was duly elected four times, he persecuted political opponents and opposition media, to the point that Venezuelans now live in fear, not only of common crime but of the midnight knock on the door for criticizing the regime.

Some legacy.

Chávez's long overdue, if involuntary, departure from power created a gigantic sucking sound as politicians across the political spectrum tried to fill the void his oversized presence created. The 2013 election between Nicolás Maduro, Chávez's designated successor, and Miranda Governor Henrique Capriles demonstrated just how sharply polarized the electorate is. The *chavista*-dominated National Electoral Council quickly declared Maduro the winner with a 1.5 percentage point edge, despite credible evidence of widespread fraud. The Supreme Court, of course, rejected the opposition's lawsuit challenging the results.

But there is also a schism developing within Chávez's ruling party, the *PSUV*. Until October 2012, it was widely believed that Diosdado Cabello, now 51, a former army officer, vice president, interior minister, governor of Miranda and one of Chávez's henchmen in the failed 1992 coup, was Chávez' choice to succeed him. But Chávez did not appoint him to the new, Politburo-like, 10-member Council of State. Then Chávez replaced Vice President Elías Jaua with Maduro, the long-time foreign minister, also now 51, who unlike Cabello was a former bus driver and a more dogmatic Marxist-Leninist, but who like Cabello had been a loyal Chávez sycophant for two decades. Cabello became president of the National Assembly and enjoys a following within the officer corps of the armed forces. He is known to be ambitious. A power struggle between the two *chavistas* seems virtually unavoidable.

Ironically, support for democracy remains high in Venezuela. In the perennial *Latinobarómetro* survey of Latin American countries for *The Economist*, 62% of Venezuelans in 1996 said they believed that democracy was preferable to any other form of government. In 2011, it was 77%, and in 2013, it was 87%, the highest in Latin America both years. By the same token, the percentage of those who believe that an authoritarian form of government is sometimes preferable to democracy declined, from 19% in 1996 to 14% in 2011 to just 8% in 2013, the lowest percentage in Latin America.

Does this overwhelming support for democracy mean Venezuelans are satisfied with the system they have—or wistful over the one they would *like* to have?

The 2013 *Latinobarómetro* poll also showed that only about 42% of Venezuelans are satisfied with the way democracy works in their country, about the regional average. The results of the 2013 presidential election in April and the municipal elections in December underscored just how sharply polarized Venezuelans are.

Venezuela has become a classic "tyranny of the majority." Like Perón, or Louisiana's Huey P. Long, Chávez did not understand that in a democracy, the losers are still entitled to civil liberties, the right of dissent and a free press. His response to losing his supermajority in the National Assembly in 2010 was simply to have the lame-duck Assembly give him the power to rule by decree for 18 months and to render the legislative branch impotent.

Venezuela is facing an uncertain future. Maduro thinks like Chávez, but Maduro is *not* Chávez, and all the posters proclaiming Chávez the "eternal commander" cannot fill his void. The violent protests that erupted in February 2014 were inevitable, with inflation running at an annual rate of 60% or more, shortages for everything from rice and cooking oil to toothpaste and toilet paper, violent crime running unchecked, the mass media either controlled by the government or cowed into self-censorship, the value of the *Bolívar* evaporating and political opponents like Lorenzo López imprisoned for exercising their rights.

Unfortunately, just when the opposition needed to stand united, it has been rent into two factions, the confrontationists who follow López's lead, and the moderates led by Capriles, who correctly has pointed out that the opposition must reach out to the poor if it is ever going to come to power through the democratic process. The only one who benefits from their feud is President Maduro.

Angel Falls

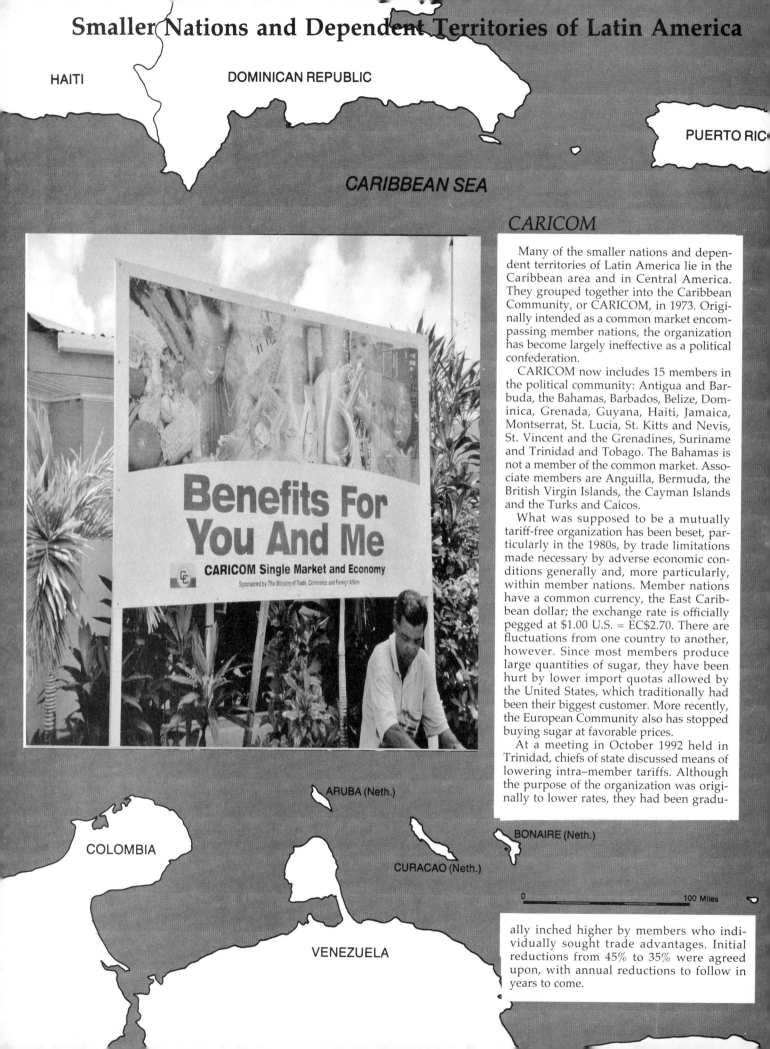

HAITI

DOMINICAN REPUBLIC

PUERTO RICO

CARIBBEAN SEA

ARUBA (Neth.)

BONAIRE (Neth.)

COLOMBIA

CURACAO (Neth.)

0   100 Miles

VENEZUELA

CARICOM

Many of the smaller nations and dependent territories of Latin America lie in the Caribbean area and in Central America. They grouped together into the Caribbean Community, or CARICOM, in 1973. Originally intended as a common market encompassing member nations, the organization has become largely ineffective as a political confederation.

CARICOM now includes 15 members in the political community: Antigua and Barbuda, the Bahamas, Barbados, Belize, Dominica, Grenada, Guyana, Haiti, Jamaica, Montserrat, St. Lucia, St. Kitts and Nevis, St. Vincent and the Grenadines, Suriname and Trinidad and Tobago. The Bahamas is not a member of the common market. Associate members are Anguilla, Bermuda, the British Virgin Islands, the Cayman Islands and the Turks and Caicos.

What was supposed to be a mutually tariff-free organization has been beset, particularly in the 1980s, by trade limitations made necessary by adverse economic conditions generally and, more particularly, within member nations. Member nations have a common currency, the East Caribbean dollar; the exchange rate is officially pegged at $1.00 U.S. = EC$2.70. There are fluctuations from one country to another, however. Since most members produce large quantities of sugar, they have been hurt by lower import quotas allowed by the United States, which traditionally had been their biggest customer. More recently, the European Community also has stopped buying sugar at favorable prices.

At a meeting in October 1992 held in Trinidad, chiefs of state discussed means of lowering intra–member tariffs. Although the purpose of the organization was originally to lower rates, they had been gradually inched higher by members who individually sought trade advantages. Initial reductions from 45% to 35% were agreed upon, with annual reductions to follow in years to come.

ST. THOMAS

ST. JOHN

U. S. VIRGIN ISLANDS

ST. CROIX

BRITISH VIRGIN ISLANDS

ANGUILLA

ST. MARTIN

ST. BARTHELEMY (Fr.)

SABA (Neth.)

ST. EUSTATIUS (Neth.)

ST. KITTS

NEVIS

REDONDA

BARBUDA

ANTIGUA

MONTSERRAT

GUADELOUPE

MARIE GALANTE

DOMINICA

MARTINIQUE

ST. LUCIA

ST. VINCENT

GRENADINES

GRENADA

BARBADOS

ATLANTIC

OCEAN

TO

TRINIDAD

Plans were made in 1993 for a pact between member nations that would provide for taxation of income at the place of its origin rather than the location where it is received; the agreement has not been finalized. Further complicating the economic picture has been the NAFTA treaty (Mexico, U.S., Canada) and the General Agreement on Tariffs and Trade (GATT), both lowering and/or abolishing tariffs.

Because of the relative political stability of most CARICOM countries and the success with offshore banking on many of them, they tended to enjoy favorable credit ratings, which led many of them to overborrow and to become heavily indebted. Of the 10 countries in the world with the highest debt as percentage of GDP in 2004, six are CARICOM members. In order of percentage, they are Guyana, St. Kitts and Nevis, Antigua and Barbuda, Dominica, Grenada and Belize.

Most of the members are heavily dependent on tourism for foreign exchange, and thus suffered from the fall in tourism following the September 11, 2001 terrorist attacks on the United States. That sector has recovered, but violent crime is frightening away tourists from such idyllic destinations as Barbados, St. Kitts and Nevis, and Trinidad and Tobago.

In 2001, 12 of the English-speaking countries and dependencies signed a treaty to establish the Caribbean Court of Justice in Port-of-Spain, Trinidad, which would replace the British Privy Council as the region's court of last resort. The court was formally established on April 16, 2005, although only two of the signatories, Barbados and Guyana, have enacted the necessary legislation to forward cases to the new court.

SOVEREIGN NATIONS
Antigua and Barbuda (Independent November 1, 1981)
The Bahamas (Independent July 10, 1973)
Barbados (Independent November 30, 1966)
Grenada (Independent February 7, 1974)
Dominica (Independent November 3, 1978)
St. Kitts and Nevis (Independent September 19, 1983)
St. Lucia (Independent February 22, 1979)
St. Vincent and the Grenadines (Independent October 27, 1979)

THE DEPENDENT TERRITORIES
British Virgin Islands (colony)
Anguilla (British Crown colony)
Cayman Islands (British colony)

Falkland Islands (British colony)
Turks and Caicos (British colony)
Montserrat (British colony)
French Guiana (French overseas department)
Guadeloupe (French overseas department)
Martinique (French overseas department)
Puerto Rico (U.S. commonwealth)
U.S. Virgin Islands (territory)

The Commonwealth of the Bahamas

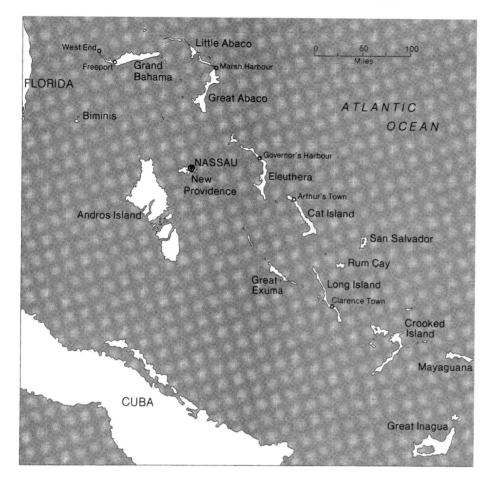

Area: 5,389 square miles, encompassing about 700 islands and islets only 35 of which are inhabited. In addition, there are over 2,000 cays which are low reefs of sand or coral.

Population: 321,834 (2014 est.).

Capital City: Nassau, on New Providence Island (Pop. 244,400 in 2009).

Climate: Sunny and semi-tropical, with prevailing sea breezes; there is a hurricane season from June to October.

Official Language: English.

Ethnic Background: African (80%), White (10%), Mixed (10%).

Chief Commercial Ventures: Tourism, gambling, banking and drug smuggling.

Gross Domestic Product: U.S. $8.373 billion in 2013, est. ($27,364 per capita, official exchange rate).

Former Colonial Status: Crown Colony of Great Britain, 1717–1964; self-governing colony 1964–73.

Independence Date: July 10, 1973.

Chief of State: Queen Elizabeth II of Great Britain, represented by Governor-General Arthur A. Foulkes (since April 14, 2010).

Head of Government: Perry Gladstone Christie (b. August 21, 1943), prime minister (since May 8, 2012).

Like the fragments of a broken piece of pottery, the Bahama Islands spread their natural beauty over about 100,000 square miles of ocean, making a gently curving arc 700 miles long from a point off the Florida coast down to the islands of Cuba, Haiti and the Dominican Republic. Only 35 of the islands are inhabited, with New Providence Island having more than half of the nation's population.

HISTORY: In October 1492 Christopher Columbus first sighted his New World at the island he promptly named San Salvador—"the Savior"—lying on the eastern edge of the island group. The exact landing site has since been disputed. San Salvador is also known as Watlings Island. The Arawak Indians who populated these islands were exterminated over a brief period of years by Spanish slave traders, who shipped them off to the large Spanish-owned islands to work on the sugarcane plantations.

Thinly populated, the islands were virtually ignored for a century and a half until 1647 when a former governor of the English island of Bermuda sailed south and landed on the long, narrow strip of land called Eleuthera. He and his party were seeking greater religious freedom than was found on Bermuda.

The tourist boom started in the late 1930s and early 1940s. Today the islands record more than 5 million tourist arrivals annually.

The Progressive Liberal Party (PLP) was formed in 1953 by Bahamians (pronounced Ba-haim-yans) who resisted rule by a small group of businessmen then in control of political and economic life on the islands ("The Bay Street Boys"). Continually gaining strength, the PLP was voted into office in 1967, and in 1972 it won 29 of 38 seats in the House of Assembly.

In July 1977, Bahamians voted in the island's first elections since independence in 1973. Although Prime Minister Lynden O. Pindling ("Black Moses") had been severely criticized for his economic policies, voters gave his PLP 31 of the 38 House seats. The government's "black power" image hurt the all-important tourist industry.

Pindling followed a trend found throughout the Caribbean: increased state control over the economy. The government forced many businesses to hire local workers to replace foreigners. New taxes were placed on foreign workers and on the sale of property to non-Bahamians. The government claimed that these programs produced a black middle class.

One impact of these measures was an end to the Bahamas' former status as a tax-free haven for the rich. Many of the so-called suitcase companies moved from the Bahamas to the Cayman Islands, where taxes remain low.

General elections in mid-1982 saw Prime Minister Pindling's PLP win with 53% of the vote and a majority in the House of Assembly. A similar victory occurred in 1987, despite repeated accusations that the prime minister was involved in drug trafficking, including eyewitness testimony linking him to Everette Bannister. The latter was known as "Mr. Fixit" of the Bahamas, and widely suspected as a drug smuggler.

**Former Prime Minister
Hubert A. Ingraham**

Prime Minister Perry Gladstone Christie

In August 1992, elections resulted in victory for the opposition Free National Movement (FNM) and selection of Hubert Ingraham as prime minister, ending the 27-year rule of Pindling. An investigation of corruption in state owned enterprises during the Pindling years ensued. Ingraham's government also has stressed economic development through inviting foreign investment. The FNM was returned to power in general elections in March 1997, winning 35 seats to only four for the PLP.

In the general elections of May 2002, the PLP returned to power, winning 29 of 40 seats. Perry Christie became prime minister.

The pendulum swung back in the next elections on May 2, 2007. The FNM accused the PLP of corruption and of making it too easy for foreigners to buy the limited amount of land in the Bahamas. The FNM won 23 seats to 18 for the PLP.

By the time Ingraham called an under-the-deadline election for May 7, 2012, unemployment had risen to 15%, home foreclosures were increasing and the crime rate was threatening the vital tourism trade. The Bahamas recorded a record 127 murders in 2011, or 36 per 100,000, the sixth-highest in the world. The voters returned the PLP to power with 48.6% of the popular vote and 29 seats, to 42.1% and just nine seats for the FNM. Christie was sworn in again as prime minister. Ingraham won his seat, but announced his intention to retire. Hubert Minnis was sworn in as opposition leader on May 10, 2012.

Several new resorts were scheduled to open in 2013, but despite the Bahamas' popularity as a tourist destination, it had the unsavory distinction of having a homicide rate in 2012 of 29.8 per 100,000, the seventh-highest in the Western Hemisphere.

CULTURE: The people of the Bahamas, approximately 90% of whom are of Afri-

can ancestry, are good-humored and generally prosperous. Most derive their living from the tourist trade. Among their many festivals is a special holiday—Junkanoo—a carnival not unlike the New Orleans Mardi Gras, which takes place during Christmas week. A sportsman's paradise, the islands provide excellent fishing, first-rate golf courses, a lively night life, visiting ballet companies, concerts and other theatrical productions. Goombay is a musical sound which is exclusively Bahamian; it blends a combination of goatskin drums, maracas and saws scraped with nails. The rhythm is fast-paced, exciting and non-stop.

The College of the Bahamas, located in Nassau and founded in 1974, is the country's tax-supported institution of higher learning. There is also a satellite program of the University of the West Indies in Nassau for training in tourism and hotel management. The private Galilee College focuses on business and computer science.

The Nassau Guardian, founded in 1844, is the country's newspaper of record and one of the oldest continuously published newspapers in the Western Hemisphere.

ECONOMY: Tourism is the number one industry, accounting for 60% of GDP. Most visitors are from the United States on excursion cruises out of Miami who stay one or two days. Europeans, who stay for an average of two weeks, spend much more, and strong efforts are being made to cultivate this trade. New hotels and vacation facilities have been constructed in the "outer" islands. The Bahamas recorded more than 5 million tourist arrivals in 2010, a 15% increase over 2009, bringing in about $500 million in foreign exchange. There were a record 5,94 million tourist arrivals in 2012, a 6% increase over 2011, the tourism minister reported. He said he was anticipating another 6–7% increase for 2013.

Ranking second to tourism is the international banking industry (15% of GDP), with more than 350 banks located on the islands. Because there is no income tax and great secrecy of financial transactions, the Bahamas has traditionally been a major tax haven and scene of widespread "laundering" of money from illegal drugs. The government has attempted to broaden the base of the economy by lowering import duties and other attractive incentives. Production of bauxite is important. Oil refining and transshipment from large ships to smaller vessels at new terminals is a major source of income, together with cement production.

Another source of income is "dummy" registration of ships, which can be returned to U.S. registry in the event of a war. Better terms are being offered than those of Liberia; Bahamian registry includes huge supertankers. Commercial fishing is also being expanded. Lavish and lively gambling casinos, in operation around the clock, see millions of dollars changing hands each

week, but they have felt the effect of U.S. state lotteries and legalized gambling.

Although new building developments are encroaching on the limited arable farmlands, "double cropping" each year in this warm climate makes most food plentiful, but imports have increased. Citrus fruit groves have replaced dairy farming as the most important sector of agriculture. Huge groves were planted to take advantage of severe frosts in Florida in the 1980s. Oranges, limes and other tropical fruit are plentiful and some are shipped to the United States. Other major exports include rum and salt.

Limitations on the economy include the presence of a large number of unskilled Haitians requiring high levels of social services.

The Bahamas have had meager or negative growth for years. The growth rate was 2.8% in 2007 and 1.5% in 2008. With the global recession, which always impacts tourism heavily, the economy shrank by –4.0% for 2009 and another –.5 in 2010. It grew by just 1.7% in 2011, 1.8% in 2012 and 1.9% in 2013.

Unemployment rose from 8.7% in 2008 to 15% in 2011, which was an issue in the May 7, 2012 election. It was still 14% in 2012 and 2013.

THE FUTURE: Blessed with the highest annual per capita income in the Western Hemisphere after the United States and Canada, the Bahamas is relatively prosperous; this does not include a considerable amount of money generated by illicit drug trafficking. As in most prosperous places of the world that are popular tourist destinations, prices are high. So is unemployment and crime. Perry Gladstone Christie returned to power in 2012 and must now deal with them this time.

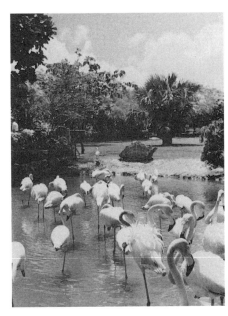

Flamingos at Nassau's Ardastra Gardens

Barbados

Former Prime Minister Owen Arthur

Area: 166 square miles.

Population: 289,680 in 2014 (est.).

Capital City: Bridgetown (Pop. 96,578 in 2006).

Climate: Tropical, but pleasant, with moderate rainfall from June to December.

Ethnic Background: African (77%); mixed races (17%); European (6%).

Chief Commercial Products: Sugar, molasses, rum.

Gross Domestic Product: U.S. $4.262 billion in 2013 ($4,761 per capita, official exchange rate).

Former Colonial Status: Colony of Great Britain, 1627–1966.

Independence Date: November 30, 1966.

Chief of State: Queen Elizabeth II of Great Britain, represented by Governor-General Elliott Belgrave.

Head of Government: Freundel Jerome Stuart (b. April 27, 1951), prime minister (since October 23, 2010).

Barbados is an island 21 miles in length and 14.5 miles at its greatest width, lying in the Atlantic Ocean 100 miles east of the Lesser Antilles. The island is surrounded by colorful coral reefs and has but one natural harbor, Carlisle Bay, on the southwestern coast; the island's high elevation is Mt. Hillaby (1,115 feet) on the northern part. The land slopes to the south in gentle terraces. Temperatures of the tropical climate are moderated by sea breezes. Fertile soils and adequate rainfall have favored sugar production.

HISTORY: Barbados was occupied by the British in 1625 and remained continuously in British control until its independence in 1966. Until the mid-19th century, sugar produced great wealth for the planters. The abolition of slavery in 1838 disturbed, but did not destroy, the island's economy. By comparison with other West Indian islands, Barbados' history has been tranquil. Riots occurred in 1876 and in 1937 because of efforts to federate the island with other British possessions. Ministerial government with partial self-rule was granted in 1954 by Britain. In 1961 Barbados became internally self-governing within the British Commonwealth. Full independence was achieved in 1966. The House of Assembly is the second-oldest legislative body in the Western Hemisphere, having first met in 1639.

Elections in 1971 were won by Prime Minister Errol Walton Barrow's Democratic Labor Party. Disturbed by the decline in the national economy, voters in 1976 turned to the Barbados Labor Party headed by J.M.G. (Tom) Adams. But in 1986 elections, in the presence of a declining economy, the people again turned to Barrow, who won a landslide victory in mid-1986, but died in June 1987. He was succeeded by his deputy, Erskine Sandiford.

Winning half the vote in January 1991, the DLP captured 18 of the 28 seats in the House of Assembly. Sandiford, who continued as prime minister, had promised to carry out the policies of his predecessor.

The BLP had revitalized itself under the leadership of Owen Arthur since 1993 and promised competition based on the flagging economy in the next election.

Tax reforms, including a value-added tax, highlighted 1993, as did the development of tax reductions and incentives intended to boost export of small manufactured goods, including clothing.

In elections held in September 1994, the BLP ended the eight-year rule of the DLP winning 18 of the 28 seats in the House of Assembly, and Arthur became prime minister. Arthur and the BLP won a landslide re-election victory in January 1999, winning 26 seats. Two seats were added to the Assembly before the May 21, 2003 elections, which the BLP won again, taking 23 of the 30 seats.

Crime has become such a serious problem, threatening the vital tourism industry, that the Arthur government followed Trinidad and Tobago's and Jamaica's lead in reinstating death by hanging. The last hanging was in 1984, but the British Privy Council, which has a five-judge panel that hears Caribbean appeals, commuted several sentences. In response, on April 16, 2005, 12 Caribbean members of the British Commonwealth established a new Caribbean appeals court of last resort, which will sit in Port-of-Spain Trinidad that will replace the Privy Council. So far, only Barbados and Guyana have ratified this change.

In February 2005, Prime Minister Arthur went a step further and advocated abolish-

Prime Minister Freundel Stuart

ing Barbados' recognition of the queen as chief of state and establishing a republic. He said the change would be submitted to voters in a referendum.

That referendum was to have been held concurrently with the general election for a new House of Assembly on January 15, 2008, but was postponed. In the parliamentary elections, the DLP was returned to power after 14 years, winning 20 of the 30 seats. David Thompson, 46, who held several cabinet posts under Sandiford, was sworn in as prime minister the next day.

Thompson announced in May 2010 he was stepping aside pending the results of medical treatments abroad for an undisclosed illness, later revealed to be pancreatic cancer. Deputy Prime Minister and Attorney General Freundel Stuart governed in his absence until Thompson died on October 23, 2010. Stuart was sworn in as the seventh prime minister the same day.

CULTURE: The people of Barbados are descendants of British colonists and African slaves. They have a typically West Indian culture with a blend of English tradition. Their rhythmic dances and calypso music, backed by steel drum bands (see Trinidad and Tobago), are in strange contrast to their love of cricket, always the joy of the British upper classes, but in Barbados the game of the people. African influence is as dominant as British, except in political and economic institutions, where the latter is maintained. Barbados is densely populated, with more than 1,500 people per square mile. The historic section of Bridgetown and its garrison, with its 17th, 18th and 19th century Brityish architecture, was designate a cultural World Heritage Site in 2011.

One of the three physical campuses of the University of the West Indies is located at Cave Hill, Barbados.

The Barbados Advocate has been publishing since 1895, but it now trails in circulation behind *The Daily Nation,* founded in 1973. There are also a few online-only publications.

ECONOMY: Sugar production and tourism account for a large percentage of the nation's foreign exchange earnings. Fish, fruit and beef output barely meet domestic needs of the nation, one of the world's most densely populated regions. A lack of mineral wealth hampers economic growth. To help reduce unemployment and racial tensions, the government has been making a concerted effort to involve its large, literate (97% adult literacy rate) black population in tourism to offset a decline in sugar production. Production of sugar has been steadily declining in the face of falling world prices.

The tourism boom of the 1990s has made Barbados a relatively prosperous little country, with an estimated per capita income well above that of most of the 20 "Latin" republics. There were 532,000 tourist arrivals in 2010 and 568,000 in 2011, twice the island's population.

GDP grew by 3.7% in 2000, well above the 0.7% annual population growth rate.

But it declined by .6% in 2001 and another 0.4% in 2002, reflecting the global drop in tourism in the wake of the September 11, 2001 terrorist attacks on the United States. It grew by 3.4% in 2004, 4.1% in 2005 and 3.9% in 2006, 3.3% in 2007 and 1.5% in 2008. With the global recession, it declined by –4.7% in 2009. It showed anemic growth of .2% in 2010, .8% in 2011 and 0% in 2012. It shrank by -0.8% in 2013

Unemployment remains stubbornly high, although the rate of 9.8% in 2004 was a record low. It was 11.4% in 2013. The income tax rate, 25%, is one of the highest in the region.

Barbados' public debt in 2013 was 90.5% of GDP, one of the world's highest.

Tourism, which accounts for three-fourths of GDP, helps offset the serious balance of trade deficit. In 2013, Barbados imported $1.675 billion in goods and exported only $1.05 billion.

THE FUTURE: Persistent unemployment has made crime a perennial problem. Tourism has not grown as rapidly as might be expected because of this. Establishing a republic may give Barbadians a greater sense of identity, but it is not likely to solve their economic problems.

The Village of Bathsheba

Grenada

Area: 133 square miles, including the islets of Carricou and Petit Martinique in the Grenadines.
Population: 110,152 in 2014 (est.).
Capital City: St. George's (Pop. 34,000, est.).
Climate: Tropically rainy and dry, hot, with prevailing ocean breezes.
Official Language: English.
Ethnic Background: African.
Chief Commercial Products: Nutmeg, tropical agricultural products.
Gross Domestic Product: $811 million in 2013 ($7,400 per capita, official exchange rate).
Former Colonial Status: Ruled alternately by French and British, 1650–1783; colony of Great Britain, 1783–1974.
Independence Date: February 7, 1974.
Chief of State: Queen Elizabeth II of Great Britain, represented by Governor-General Cécile LaGrenade (since May 7, 2013).
Head of Government: Keith Claudius Mitchell (b. November 12, 1946), prime minister (since February 20, 2013).

Prime Minister Keith Mitchell

Like a large pearl, Grenada (pronounced Greh-NAY-dah) is the southernmost of the Windward Island chain, lying peacefully at the edge of the Caribbean Sea and the Atlantic Ocean. Blessed with beautiful beaches, clear water and a pleasant (but tropical) climate, the island is 21 miles long from north to south and only 12 miles horizontally at its widest point. Grenada has heavily wooded mountains watered by many streams that feed the quiet, lush valleys. There is the calm of smooth beaches and the rockbound coasts where the surf pounds and churns endlessly.

HISTORY: Discovered in 1498 by Columbus, Grenada was originally inhabited by the Carib Indians. In the 1650s the island was colonized by the French, who established large tobacco plantations. England acquired Grenada in 1763 by the Treaty of Paris, under which (among other exchanges of territory) France ceded Canada to the English. The new rulers of the island imported slaves from Africa to work the sugarcane plantations.

For over 200 years, Grenada basked peacefully in obscurity, harvesting its crops and almost oblivious to the rest of the world. During this period it was administered as a separate British Colony until its membership in the short-lived West Indian Federation (1958–72). The federation collapsed partly because one key member, Trinidad, did not want to tie its own healthy economy to that of its poorer federation neighbors.

Elections held in 1972 brought an overwhelming victory to the Grenada United Labor Party of Premier Eric Gairy (13 out of 15 seats in the House of Representatives), whose major platform during the election was the complete independence of the island nation. As a result of talks in London soon afterward, a constitutional conference was set for May 1973.

Grenada gained its independence in 1974. The most prominent figure in the nation's politics since 1962, Gairy continued to control Grenada through his domination of powerful labor unions. However, his corrupt and brutal rule generated widespread resentment at home, while abroad he generated notoriety over his stated belief in UFOs. Opponents, led by the "new left" black-power New Jewel Movement, ousted him in 1979.

The new regime, headed by London-educated Maurice Bishop, 34, promptly dissolved Parliament and promised a new constitution that would make the island a "socialist democracy." Although it restricted personal liberties (no press free-

dom, no elections), the regime somewhat improved living conditions for the poor. Private enterprise remained largely intact.

In foreign affairs, Bishop embraced the Castro regime. Cuba responded with technical and military assistance for Grenada's new "People's Revolutionary Army."

The Reagan administration viewed the Grenada regime as a tool of Moscow via Cuba and imposed a blackout of the island. When a group of hard-line Marxist army officers deposed and murdered Bishop in October 1983, anarchy ensued. A force of U.S. Marines and Army Rangers and troops from other Caribbean nations and territories invaded. Several hundred Cuban troops were taken prisoner and returned to Cuba; vast amounts of Soviet and Cuban military equipment was found. The occupying force was withdrawn after elections were held in December 1984.

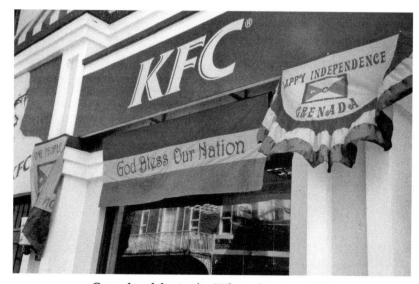

Grenada celebrates its 35th anniversary, 2009

426

Grenada

Former Prime Minister Tillman Thomas

Herbert Blaize, leader of the New National Party, was selected prime minister over a coalition government that split in 1989; Blaize died shortly thereafter. Inconclusive elections in 1990 resulted in Nicholas Braithwaite being selected to lead another coalition government. He stumbled badly in 1993, failing to find economic measures acceptable to the media and people, and he resigned on February 1, 1995. In June elections, the New National Party (NNP) led by former Works and Communications Minister Keith Mitchell, defeated the NDC, taking eight of the 15 seats in the House of Representatives.

As prime minister, Mitchell embarked on a successful campaign to lure foreign investors to the island, but there were signs that his government corrupted itself in the awarding of public works contracts. When two of his ministers defected to the opposition in late 1998 over the allegations of corruption, Mitchell lost his one-seat majority

and was forced to call general elections 18 months early. On January 18, 1999, voters resoundingly indicated they were more concerned about the jobs Mitchell had brought to the island than with the corruption charges: The NNP won all 15 seats in the House. Mitchell himself received 89% in his district. The leader of one opposition party complained that with the snap election and short six-week campaign, "We were caught with our pants down."

In the next election on November 27, 2003, and the NNP was returned to power but with only a one-seat majority of 8–7.

Grenada was hit harder than any other country by Hurricane Ivan in 2004, the most powerful storm in the Caribbean in at least 20 years. An estimated 85% of the homes and other buildings on the island, including Mitchell's home and the prison, were destroyed or damaged.

Mitchell waited the maximum five years before calling the latest election on July 8, 2008, probably because of a sluggish economy that actually shrank in 2006 (see Economy). The NDC's leader, Tillman Thomas, promised to lead Grenada out of the "disaster" he said Mitchell had created. The NDC won 11 of the 15 seats, and Thomas, a 63-year-old attorney who had been jailed by Maurice Bishop, became prime minister the following day. He promised to practice the "politics of inclusion."

But in the next general elections on February 19, 2013, the voters "excluded" the NDC, giving the NNP all 15 seats. Mitchell was sworn in the next day to begin his second premiership.

CULTURE: The people of Grenada, 95% of whom are black or mulatto, are a fun-loving and hard-working group. Grena-

da's capital and main port, St. George's, rises steeply from the bay and the red-roofed houses are painted in pastel shades of pink and green. Nightlife in the city is often punctuated by continuous music from colorful Calypso bands.

St. George's University, which has a medical school, is the only institution of higher learning. One of the rationales for the U.S. invasion in 1983 was to rescue U.S. students studying medicine there.

ECONOMY: Grenada is called the Isle of Spice, and for centuries its economy has been based on its nutmeg. It is presently the world's second-largest exporter of this product. Most exports go to EC countries. Grenada and the Windward Islands were greatly favored by EC import limitations on bananas from other Caribbean sources. Other exports include bananas, sugar, cacao and mace.

GDP grew by only 0.6% in 2002, due in part to the general downturn in tourism following the September 11, 2001, terrorist attacks on the United States. Grenada has a public debt that in 2004 was 112% of GDP, the eighth highest in the world. The devastation of Hurricane Ivan in September 2004 was an economic catastrophe from which Grenada may take several years to recover.

The economy shrank by –1.1% in 2006, then grew by 4.3% in 2007 and 3.7% in 2008. The global recession caused it to decline in 2009 by –7.7%. It shrank another –1.3% in 2010 and showed only tiny growth of 1% in 2011. It shrank by -.8% in 2012 and grew by .8% in 2013.

THE FUTURE: The sluggish economy and corruption remain problems that need to be addressed.

Mixed feelings still exist concerning U.S. invasion in 1983

Photo by Susan L. Thompson

427

THE DEPENDENT TERRITORIES

The dependencies in the Western Hemisphere have a wide variety of relationships with the nations controlling them. Those of Great Britain have various degrees of internal self-government. In the Caribbean area, the British attempt to unite several territories into the West Indian Federation failed, and Barbados, Guyana and Jamaica became sovereign nations shortly thereafter.

The islands of Guadeloupe and Martinique, and mainland French Guiana, are governed as *départments* of France. The Netherlands Antilles are internally self-governing. Puerto Rico is a commonwealth within the United States that possesses internal autonomy, and the U.S. Virgin Islands are federally administered territories of the United States. The Falkland Islands, lying off the coast of Argentina, are governed by the British and claimed by the Argentines.

Fort-de-France, Martinique; Mt. Pelee looms behind the capital. *Photo by Miller B. Spangler*

British Dependencies

CAYMAN, TURKS AND CAICOS ISLANDS

Area: 269 square miles.
Population: 51,384 in Cayman Islands; 44,819 in Turks and Caicos (2011 est.).
Administrative Capital: Georgetown (Pop. 4,700, estimated).
Heads of Government: Helen Kilpatrick (Caymans); Gordon Wetherell (Turks and Caicos), governors.

These two groups of islands were administered by the Governor of Jamaica until 1962 when they were placed under the British Colonial Office. With the closing of the Colonial Office, administration passed to the Commonwealth Relations Office. The Cayman Islands lie midway between Jamaica and the western tip of Cuba. Turks and Caicos Islands are geographically a portion of the Bahamas. There are some 35 small islands in these groups, of which only eight are populated. The predominantly black and mulatto people eke a meager existence from fishing and the production of salt. Because of their limited resources, these islands cannot sustain themselves as independent nations. The Cayman Islands have become increasingly popular as a tax haven since the Bahamian government ended tax exempt status there for foreign corporations. There are numerous banks catering to "commerce," which means "laundering" money, the source of which is desired to be secret—usually narcotics. Crime associated with drug trade is increasing sharply. There are 532 banks, 80 of which actually have offices in the islands—one for every 53 people; more than 25,000 companies are registered to do business.

A five-member executive council is elected in the Caymans; political activity is minimal. Turks and Caicos Islands have a 20-member Legislative Council and an eight-member executive council.

FALKLAND ISLANDS

Area: 4,618 square miles.
Population: 3,140 (2008 estimate).
Administrative Capital: Port Stanley
Head of Government: Colin Roberts, governpr (since 2014); Keith Padgett, chief executive (since 2012).

The Falkland Islands are made up of two large and 200 small islands, treeless, desolate and windswept, which lie off the southern tip of Argentina in the Atlantic Ocean.

The British discovered and named the islands in 1690; the French established a small colony on one of the larger islands in 1764 and the British started a settlement on the other large island in the following year. France gave up its possession to Spain in 1767 and the Spanish drove the British from the island they occupied. The territory was abandoned by the Spanish in 1811, and Argentina, after gaining independence, established a small colony on the islands in 1824. This settlement was destroyed by the U.S. Navy in 1831 in retaliation for Argentine harassment of whaling ships from Boston.

The British again gained possession of the islands in 1833 and have held them since that time. Argentina claims the islands based on its effort of 1824. Originally of strategic importance because of their closeness to the Atlantic-Pacific sea route around the Cape, with the opening of the Panama Canal their value greatly decreased. However, the British Navy successfully struck from the islands against the German Navy in both world wars.

The islands are an economic liability to Britain, but are still a symbol of its sovereignty, not to be relinquished. When Argentina suddenly invaded the Falklands in April 1982, Britain met the challenge head on . . . successfully. A later dispute was resolved when Britain and Argentina agreed upon a joint, 200-mile fishing boundary around the islands calculated to exclude Japan, Russia and Taiwan.

Development of oil deposits within the 200-mile radius, and a new Argentine constitution reaffirming sovereignty over what it calls the *Islas Malvinas*, have created problems that will be difficult to solve.

A new constitution went into effect on January 1, 2009.

FRENCH GUIANA

Area: 34,740 square miles.
Population: 221,500 (2010 estimate).
Administrative Capital: Cayenne (Pop. 61,550, 2006 estimate).
Head of Government: Rodolphe Alexandre, regional president (since 2010).

French Guiana lies on the north coast of South America, north of Brazil and east of Suriname. The land consists of fertile, low plains along the coast, rising to the Tumuc-Humac Mountains on the Brazilian frontier. The Isles of Salut (Enfant Perdu, Remire and Ile du Diable—Devil's Island), lying off the coast, form part of the territory administered as a French *département*. The climate is tropical, with an average temperature of 80°F. The rainy season is from November to July, with the heaviest downfall in May.

Guiana was awarded to France in 1667, attacked by the British in the same year, taken by the Dutch in 1676 and retaken by France in the same year. In 1809 it was seized by a joint British-Portuguese effort based in Brazil, and remained under Brazilian occupation until 1817, when the French regained control. Gold was discovered in 1853, inspiring disputes with Brazil and Suriname which were not settled until 1915. The colony is best known for its infamous prison colony, which was closed in 1945.

Guiana has fertile soils, 750,000 acres of land suitable for stock raising, vast resources of timber and coastal waters abounding in shrimp and fish. However, only some 12,000 acres are cultivated and most foodstuffs are imported. The population consists of creoles (descended from African black ancestors), Europeans, Chinese and a few native Indians. The principal products are shrimp, gold, hardwood and rum. French Guiana has adequate resources to support itself as an independent state, but little or no effort has been made to exploit these resources.

For a brief interval, French Guiana loomed in France as a 20th century *El Dorado*. During a three-day visit to Guiana in 1975, Olivier Stirn, minister of territories, announced a resettlement plan for the French colony, one part of which would initially require 10,000 settlers to develop a pulp and lumber industry. The plan was adversely received by Guiana local leadership and was condemned by 11 Caribbean chiefs of state. Nevertheless, French immigration to the territory proceeded. A satellite-launching base was constructed at Kourou, and continental French now constitute about a third of the population of Guiana. They have gathered in an ultraconservative political movement, the *Front National*, and, of course, oppose independence; the local movement for this faded quickly.

Political expression is mainly through the Guianese Socialist Party affiliated with the Socialist Party in France and the opposition Rally for the Republic, a Gaullist party affiliated with that of France. Guiana is one of 26 regions of France, called an overseas department, governed by a regional president with the advice and consent of a General Council and a Regional Council.

Vast unused resources remain under the dense rain forest that covers more than 70% of the land area. Intense farming is done by the industrious Hmong people of Laos who were transplanted here more than three decades ago. Timber and fish are the most important exports. Hydroelectric installations completed in 1993 provide all electricity needed, albeit at a substantial cost in local animal and bird life. As in so many other tropical settings of the region, social and economic unrest is at a high level and probably has no "cure."

GUADELOUPE

Area: 657 square miles.
Population: 405,500 (2008).
Administrative Capital: Basse-Terre (Pop. 44,864).
Head of Government: Victorin Lurel, president of the Regional Council (since May 2, 2014).

Guadeloupe consists of two islands separated by a narrow channel. Five small French islands in the Lesser Antilles are administered as a part of the Department of Guadeloupe (Marie Galante, Les Saintes, Desirade, St. Barthelemy and one-half of St. Martin).

Guadeloupe dependencies are occupied by the white descendants of Norman and Breton fishermen (and pirates) who settled there 300 years ago—the population is predominantly of mixed European and African derivation. The climate is tropical, with the rainy season extending from July to December.

Guadeloupe's principal products are bananas, sugar, rum, coffee, cocoa and tourism. Although this is an island of call for Caribbean cruises, it has excellent accommodations for extended vacations. The balance of trade is unfavorable and the *département* has little hope for independence.

The people are apparently content with a Regional Council and a General Council, the latter of which exercises executive power. Elections are on a party basis and are spirited; the one in 1992 had to be voided because of "irregularities." The right wing prevailed in a re-run.

A new World Trade Center opened on Guadeloupe in 1994 and is the seat of numerous efforts to boost Euro-Caribbean trade.

Guadeloupe

MARTINIQUE

Area: 420 square miles.
Population: 412,305 (2012 estimate).
Administrative Capital: Fort-de-France (Pop. 120,000, estimated).
Head of Government: Serge Letchimy, regional president (since March 21, 2010).

Martinique has been in French possession since 1635 except for two short periods of British occupation. Mountainous, with Mt. Pelee reaching 4,800 feet, its climate is tropical; the rainy season extends from July to December; violent hurricanes are frequent during this period. An eruption of Mt. Pelee in 1906 killed 10,000 people. The population is predominantly of mixed European and African origin.

Martinique's principal products are sugar, rum, bananas and other tropical fruits. This island also is an attractive tourist haven, with modern facilities available widely. Cattle raising is a steady industry, but presently produces enough for local consumption only.

Netherlands Dependencies

NETHERLANDS ANTILLES

Area: 395 square miles.
Population: 183,000 (2005 estimate).
Administrative Capital: Willemstad (Pop. 75,000, estimated).

The Netherlands Antilles consist of two groups of three islands each—one group lies off the north coast of Venezuela; the other lies just east of the Virgin Islands. Fully autonomous in internal affairs since 1954, the islands are organized into four self-governing communities—Aruba, Bonaire, Curaçao, and the Leeward Islands (southern portion of St. Martin, St. Eustatius and Saba). The population consists of about one third European ancestry and two thirds of mixed blood. Dutch is the official language. Spanish, English and a local *lingua franca* called Papamiento are

also spoken. All of the islands are popular calls for cruise ships, and have, with the exception of St. Eustatius and Saba, have good facilities for extended vacations.

The economy of the Netherlands Antilles is based on the large oil refineries on Curaçao and Aruba. Almost all articles for consumption must be imported because fishing does not fill local needs and an arid climate coupled with poor soil do not support agriculture. The islands of Bonaire, St. Martin, St. Eustatius and Saba are of little economic importance. Despite some discontent among the non-European population, it is not likely that the islands will seek independence. Aruba was granted separate status from the other islands in 1986, with full independence set for 1996.

The lingering question of independence was probably laid to rest by balloting in 1993 on Curaçao and in 1994 on the remaining islands. Voters chose to remain a Dutch territory by a large majority, rejecting even the semi-independence that had been granted to Aruba. They undoubtedly wished a continuation of benefits derived from an annual Dutch subsidy of U.S. $160 million. Aruba, originally scheduled to become completely independent in 1996, instead continues in "special status."

The island of Curaçao has evidently been chosen as a drug outlet by Colombian, Surinamese and Dutch traffickers—rivals and their hired thugs fought pitched battles in late 1993.

Willemstad, Curaçao

430

El Morro fortress for centuries guarded the entrance to the harbor at San Juan.

PUERTO RICO

Area: 3,423 square miles.

Population: 3,620,897 (2013 est.).

Capital: San Juan (Pop. 395,326 in 2010 census, greater metropolitan area).

Gross domestic product: $101.5 billion in 2012, est. ($25,382 per capita, official exchange rate).

Head of Government: Alejandro Javier García Padilla (b. August 3, 1971) governor (since January 2, 2013).

The easternmost and smallest island of the Greater Antilles, Puerto Rico is somewhat rectangular in shape, measuring 111 miles from east to west and about 36 miles north to south at its widest point; it includes four offshore islands, two of which are populated. Centrally located at almost the middle of approximately 7,000 tropical islands, most of them very tiny, hardly more than atolls, much of the island is mountainous or hilly—three quarters of the terrain is too steep for large-scale, mechanized cultivation. Puerto Rico is a *commonwealth* of the United States—while not a state, it is legally within the territorial jurisdiction of the U.S. The people are by language and culture part of the Caribbean and Latin America. Since it is not

a state, Puerto Rico has no voting representation in Congress, but does have an elected resident commissioner with a four-year term who holds a seat, can speak out on issues, but does not have a vote. Otherwise, he enjoys the same privileges and immunities of other congressmen.

HISTORY: Columbus discovered Puerto Rico in 1493. There were at least three native cultures on the island, mostly of Arawak origin from the South American mainland. They were a peaceful group,

quickly enslaved by the Spaniards and eventually died out as a race. Columbus claimed the island for Spain and named it San Juan Bautista (St. John the Baptist). After many years of colonization, the island was given the name Puerto Rico (Rich Port) and its capital city became San Juan.

Its first governor was Juan Ponce de León, who was later to discover Florida in his fabled search for the Fountain of Youth. Almost from the time of early colonization, Puerto Rico was a military target due to its strategic location. The French, British and

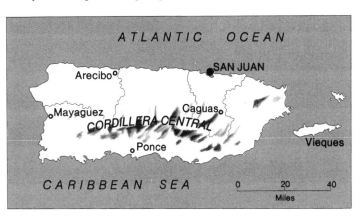

Puerto Rico

Dutch were repelled over the centuries and massive fortifications were erected by Spain to guard the harbor at San Juan.

The 18th century was rather uneventful, and during Latin American wars for independence, Puerto Rico remained faithful to Spain. Sugar, tobacco and coffee produced on the island found a ready market in the United States, as did its flourishing rum industry. Toward the middle of the 19th century, Puerto Rican social consciousness came slowly to life. In 1868 there was a revolution against Spain, which was quickly snuffed out.

Slavery was abolished in 1873. As the 19th century came to a close, Spain granted Puerto Rico broad powers of self-rule, but only days after the new government assumed its duties the Spanish-American war broke out. The U.S. public had been appalled by the stories of harsh treatment of Cuban revolutionaries, which caused a growing anti-Spanish sentiment in the United States, carefully fed by the press, which printed sensational stories of supposed atrocities. After the battleship *U.S.S. Maine* was mysteriously blown up in Havana harbor on February 15, 1898, the United States declared war on Spain. One of the operations was the invasion of Puerto Rico by American forces under General Nelson A. Miles the following July.

The treaty of peace signed in Paris in December after the brief conflict forced Spain to withdraw from Cuba, and ceded to the United States were Puerto Rico, Guam and the Philippines. The Spanish-American War established the United States as a world power. A military government was set up in Puerto Rico, and in 1900 the first civil government was established. It gave the U.S. government full control over island affairs, with the president appointing the governor, the members of the Executive Council (legislature) and the island's Supreme Court. Members of the House of Delegates, which functioned as a second legislative branch, were popularly elected. All trade barriers with the United States were removed as Puerto Rico was placed within existing U.S. tariff walls. The island, the Philippines and Guam, were collectively designated an "unincorporated territory."

With the advent of civil government, men were again allowed the right to vote as they had under Spain. Also, the island was exempted from paying federal taxes; duties and excise taxes collected in Puerto Rico on foreign products and on Puerto Rican products sold in the United States were handed over to the island treasury. Between 1900 and 1925, foreign trade increased from $16 million to $178 million annually; it now more than $14 billion. A corresponding population increase occurred: from some 950,000 in 1905 to 1.3 million in 1921.

The school system expanded rapidly, reducing illiteracy from about 90% to less than 50%. A more worrisome condition was the gradual concentration of wealth in fewer hands. Two half-mile tunnels were opened in 1909 through the mountains that provided irrigation for the south side of the island, very dry due to the constant trade winds. On the eve of World War I, Congress granted U.S. citizenship to Puerto Ricans and replaced the appointed Executive Council with a popularly elected Senate. However, the island remained exempt from federal taxes and was allowed to design its own tax system and raise its own revenues. Trade with the United States grew by leaps and bounds so that the island became one of the top consumers of U.S. goods in Latin America.

When the United States declared war on Germany in 1917, the Selective Service Act was extended to Puerto Rico by request of the island's government and some 18,000 men were inducted into service.

During the first decades of the 20th century, Puerto Rico developed its sugar production, but most of the profits went to absentee landlords in the United States. By the time of the Great Depression of 1929, there was mass unemployment, malnutrition and deteriorating health conditions. By 1930, unemployment stood at a frightening 60%. When the Roosevelt administration came into office in 1933, it extended a large measure of relief to the stricken island. Because of the dire conditions, a strong nationalist movement emerged seeking complete independence. The movement reached its peak in 1937, when police fired on a nationalist demonstration in the southern city of Ponce, killing 20 people.

Commonwealth Status

Puerto Rico played an important defense role in the Caribbean region during World War II. President Truman appointed a Puerto Rican governor for the island in 1946 and one year later signed a law permitting it to elect its own governor. In 1948, voters elected Luis Muñoz-Marín of the Popular Democratic Party (PDP). In 1950, U.S. Congress allowed the island to draft its own constitution, which was approved with amendments by the Congress and then ratified in a plebiscite in 1952. Governor Muñoz-Marín claimed the constitutional process and plebiscite were an act of self-determination, thus marking an end to American colonial rule. The Commonwealth was officially established on July 25, 1952, the 54th anniversary of the day the U.S. forces landed in 1898.

Despite the move toward self-determination, a small but aggressive minority of "nationalists" still clamored for full independence, eventually resorting to terrorism. A band of nationalists attempted to assassinate President Truman in a bloody shootout in Washington in 1951. Three years later, nationalist terrorists opened fire from the gallery of the U.S. House of Representatives, wounding five congressmen. Militant nationalism resurfaced in the 1970s with the creation of the so-called Armed Forces of National Liberation, or *FALN*. Between 1974 and 1983, the *FALN* was believed responsible for 130 terrorist bombings in the continental United States that killed six people and wounded dozens of others. The worst bombing, on a tavern in New York's Greenwich Village in 1975, killed four.

Muñoz-Marín laid the foundations for the industrial development of the island, aided by important incentives at home and aggressive promotion abroad. The program, called "Operation Bootstrap," was one of the 20th century's great success stories—Puerto Rico's economy was transformed from one based on a single crop (sugar) to a broadly based manufacturing one, creating a strong middle class and one of the highest standards of living in all of Latin America. Per capita income has increased geometrically since 1940. Further, university and college enrollment soared from about 5,000 students in 1945 to about 150,000 by the mid-1980s.

In a 1967 plebiscite, 60% of the voters favored continuation and improvement of the commonwealth status with the United States while 38% voted for statehood. The major independence groups boycotted the plebiscite. The pro-statehood New Progressive Party (PNP) won the governorship in 1968, winning again in 1976 and 1980. The pro-commonwealth PDP won in 1972, 1984 and 1988. These frequent

Former Governor Pedro J. Rosselló

432

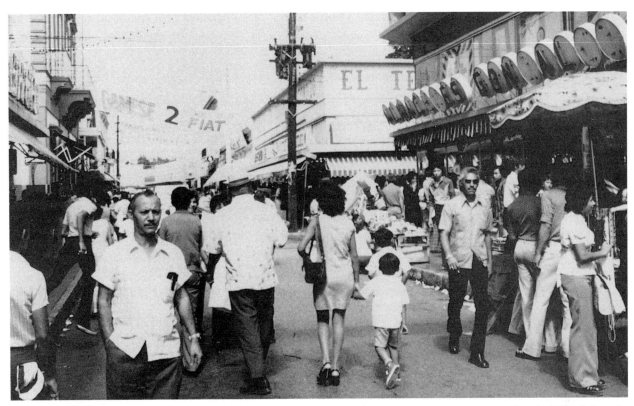

Street scene in Ponce, Puerto Rico's second largest city

Photo by Miller B. Spangler

changes in power produced a virtual stale-mate on the political status of the island. This still goes on; the effect is to discourage investment in job producing facilities in Puerto Rico.

In spite of then-President George H. W. Bush's support for Puerto Rican statehood, the matter was bottled up in Congress in 1989–91; the Republicans did not wish to give Democrats an opportunity to tighten their hold on both houses of Congress. In a gesture of defiance, Puerto Rico enacted a measure providing that Spanish was the only official language. It was later repealed by a measure in 1993 recognizing both Spanish and English. Only the wealthy and middle-class are genuinely bilingual.

Roselló and Referenda

In the 1992 elections, the *PNP* and its candidate for governor, Pedro J. Rosselló, a physician, again ran on a platform advocating statehood. The *PDP* favored continuing commonwealth status, and was soundly trounced in its worst defeat in its 44-year history. The victors held another referendum (non-binding) on statehood in November 1993. Fully 73% of the electorate participated and the result was 48.4% for commonwealth status and 46.2% for an application for statehood. Less than 5% favored independence. Rosselló, ignoring the result, insisted the struggle for statehood would go on.

Rosselló was re-elected in 1996, which he interpreted as a mandate to continue his quest for statehood. Responding to his persistent efforts, the U.S. House of Representatives voted in 1998 for a *binding* referendum that ostensibly would decide the issue once and for all; the measure passed by only one vote, however, and the Senate failed to follow up.

Marking the 100th anniversary of U.S. occupation in July 1998, Rosselló then called for yet another non-binding referendum for December. Five options were listed on the complicated ballot: statehood, independence, an ambiguous "free association," continued commonwealth and "none of the above." The opposition *PDP*, however, advocated instead what it called an "enhanced commonwealth" by which Puerto Rico could enter into treaties with other nations and would have the power to annul federal laws, definitely the best of both worlds but which likely would never win congressional approval. As its "enhanced commonwealth" was not on the ballot, the *PDP* campaigned vigorously for "none of the above." The 1998 referendum was a near-duplicate of the 1993 plebiscite, only this time "none of the above" won a slim but absolute majority of 50.2%, while the vote for statehood was virtually unchanged at 46.5%. Independence received 2.5%, "free association" 0.3% and commonwealth only 0.1%. This sent the ambiguous message

that Puerto Ricans were ready to change their status, but didn't yet know what that status should be.

Meanwhile, a corruption scandal exploded in 1999 that tarnished Rosselló's reputation and credibility and proved a major political liability for the *PNP* in the 2000 elections. The former comptroller of the San Juan AIDS Institute—an entity Rosselló had approved in 1987 when he was health director of San Juan—pleaded guilty to conspiracy and testified that $2.2 million in federal funds intended for AIDS victims had been diverted to the political campaigns of both the *PNP* and *PDP*, including Rosselló, who allegedly received $250,000 for his 1992 campaign. Rosselló dismissed the allegations as a "character assassination." Although the governor himself was never indicted, he underwent the ignominy of appearing on the witness stand in the trials that ended in 2000 with the convictions of two high-ranking officials.

Then, in August 2000, 18 *PNP* officials, including two mayors, were indicted on federal charges that they received $800,000 in campaign donations in exchange for $56 million in government contracts. Several of them also were convicted in 2001.

Rosselló also stood accused by pro-*PDP* newspapers of employing the time-honored cudgel of Latin American dictators of withholding government advertising from them. *El Nuevo Día*, which lost its

Puerto Rico

government advertising after several investigative articles on corruption, sued the government in 1997. In 1999, the paper and the government reached a settlement by which the government restored the advertising, established a policy for distributing advertising fairly and expressed its respect for press freedom, but while the paper granted the government discounted rates.

In 1999, President Clinton sparked controversy by granting clemency to 12 convicted members of the *FALN* and another militant group, the *Macheteros*, or machete wielders, in exchange for their promise to renounce terrorism. None had been convicted of any of the bombings of the 1970s and '80s, but on charges of seditious conspiracy and weapons possession. Nine of the prisoners accepted the clemency offer, and returned to heroes' welcomes in Puerto Rico. Even Governor Rosselló supported Clinton's offer. Not so the Republican-controlled Congress, which passed a stinging censure resolution against the president for his perceived softness on terrorists. Other critics alleged the clemency bid was designed to help Hillary Clinton win Puerto Rican votes in her successful campaign for the U.S. Senate from New York in 2000.

Independence activists seized the national spotlight again in 1999 and 2000 with their support for the 9,100 residents of the island of Vieques, who were protesting the island's use by the U.S. Navy as a bombing and gunnery range. The Navy had bombarded Vieques since 1941, but residents complained that they were endangered by the exercises and by unexploded ordnance. Protests began when an island resident was killed by a stray bomb in 1999. President Clinton announced a five-year withdrawal plan to placate the islanders. But they were not placated. In 2000, 200 residents staged a nonviolent occupation of the range, forcing federal agents to take them into custody for trespassing on federal property. The occupation and arrests became the focus of national and international media attention.

More protesters were arrested in 2001, while others sought redress in federal court to enjoin the Navy from using the range. A federal court ruled in favor of the Navy, which resumed target practice. Even pro-commonwealth Puerto Ricans were offended by the Navy's arrogance. The Rev. Al Sharpton believed to be currying favor among Puerto Rican voters there for his presidential run, was among several protesters arrested on Vieques for trespassing on the range.

In a 2001 referendum, the island's residents voted 68% for the Navy to leave immediately. President George W. Bush

Former Governor Sila María Calderón

announced that the Navy would abandon Vieques in 2003—not soon enough for many critics.

First Woman Governor

The corruption scandals of the Rosselló administration forced him to decide, wisely, not to seek a third term in 2000. Instead, the wounded *PNP* nominated Carlos Pesquera, while the *PDP* nominated Sila María Calderón; the Puerto Rican Independence Party (*PIP*) nominated Rubén Berrios.

The Vieques issue overshadowed the campaign, with Pesquera largely avoiding it, Berrios trumpeting it and Calderón making only vague statements in support of the island's residents. An extraneous issue was interjected into the campaign when a pro-statehood federal judge in San Juan ruled in favor of 11 residents who demanded the right to vote in the U.S. presidential election between Al Gore and George W. Bush. The *PDP* and the *PIP* challenged the ruling, and the 1st U.S. Circuit Court of Appeals in Boston ruled that Puerto Ricans did not have that constitutional right.

The gubernatorial election was another reminder of how divided Puerto Ricans are on the statehood issue, and the results were a virtual replay of the 1998 referendum: Calderón narrowly won with 48.5% of the vote to 46.1% for Pesquera and 4.9% for Berrios. The *PDP* also won clear majorities in the House and Senate.

After her inauguration on January 2, 2001, as Puerto Rico's first woman governor, Calderón became more strident in demanding that the Navy leave Vieques. She discussed the issue with President Bush in Washington soon after his own inauguration.

The Vieques controversy simmered for two years. In 2002, the Navy notified Calderón that it would resume bombing exercises on the island, which brought a tart rebuke from the governor. But in October, the Navy did an about-face and announced that it would abandon Vieques. On May 1, 2003, the bombing range—along with six decades' worth of unexploded ordnance—reverted to Puerto Rican control. Jubilant celebrations, some of which turned ugly, marked the transition. Calderón sought federal help in cleaning up the ordnance.

The commonwealth-statehood-independence debate continued to raise controversy between elections and referenda. The Calderón administration issued new license plates that contained the legend, "Free Associated State." Both the *PNP* and the *PIP* denounced the plates as a *PDP* political statement.

Deadlock and Gridlock

Calderón opted not to seek re-election in 2004, and the *PDP* nominated Aníbal Acevedo Vila, Puerto Rico's resident commissioner to the U.S. Congress. Despite the past scandals, the *PNP* nominated former Governor Roselló instead of Pesquera. The *PIP* again ran Berrios. Acevedo raised the corruption issue and promised to come to terms with the alarming increase in crime that was frightening and angering Puerto Ricans. Calderón had been compelled to put the National Guard on the streets of San Juan in 2004 to complement the police force. By year's end, Puerto Rico experienced a record 790 murders, up from 780 the year before.

Puerto Ricans had become accustomed to closely divided elections, but the November 2, 2004, contest was closer than ever. In the preliminary vote count, Acevedo led Roselló by a mere 3,880 votes out of 1,990,372 cast. Acevedo received 48.38% to Rosello's 48.18%. By law, when the difference is less than 0.5 percentage points, a recount is mandatory. The results of the recount by the elections commission reconfirmed Acevedo's razor-thin margin:

Acevedo	963,303	48.40%
Roselló	959,737	48.22%
Berrios	54,551	2.74%

In an eerie replay of the contested 2000 presidential vote count in Florida, the *PNP* disputed about 7,000 ballots that had been ambiguously marked for both the *PIP* as a party and for Acevedo for governor. Roselló went to U.S. district court in San Juan to have the votes disallowed. The *PDP* argued in the commonwealth court system that the ballots were valid votes for Acevedo. The Puerto Rico Supreme Court ruled that the ballots should be counted,

Former Governor Aníbal Acevedo Vila
Source: BBC

while the federal judge said they should be counted pending his review of them. The *PDP* appealed to the 1st Circuit Court of Appeals in Boston, arguing that the election was a commonwealth, not federal, matter. A three-judge panel agreed that the Puerto Rico Supreme Court has jurisdiction over elections. On December 28, just five days before the inauguration, the elections commission certified Acevedo's 3,566-vote margin.

Roselló conceded, but added he still considered the results "irregular and unjust." He could console himself that Acevedo had a legislature with a *PNP* majority of 18 of the 27 Senate seats and 34 of 51 House seats. A Roselló protégé, Luis Fortuño, was narrowly elected the new resident commissioner to Washington. It was the first time the governor and commissioner had been from different parties.

At his January 2, 2005, inauguration, Acevedo called for an end to the partisan bitterness that has so sharply divided Puerto Ricans. He also declared that he favored a U.S. withdrawal from Iraq within six months. At the time, 23 Puerto Ricans had been killed in the war.

In March, Acevedo laid off more than 23,000 public employees in an effort to reduce a $740 million budget deficit. The crisis surrounding the deficit continued, as the *PDP* governor and *PNP*-controlled legislature deadlocked on a solution and each blamed the other for the gridlock. On May 1, 2006, the commonwealth officially ran out of money, and about 100,000 public employees, including 40,000 teachers, were furloughed indefinitely. The impasse was temporarily resolved when the legislature approved, and Acevedo signed, an emergency loan measure designed to keep the government running until the end of the fiscal year on June 30.

Acevedo failed to come to grips with the alarming crime rate. The U.S. Justice Department sent a special task force in 2007 to combat gangs. In 2008, Puerto

Rico recorded 800 murders, a 12-year high, which was a rate of 19.6 per 100,000, higher than any U.S. state.

The 2008 Election

Acevedo ran for re-election in 2008, and he endorsed Democratic presidential candidate Barack Obama. But in March 2008, Acevedo and 12 others were charged in federal court with 19 counts of conspiracy to violate U.S. campaign finance laws and of giving false statements to the FBI. He was not jailed, although five of the suspects were arrested and appeared in court in handcuffs. They were accused of illegally raising money to pay off Acevedo's campaign debts. Acevedo maintained his innocence and claimed he was being persecuted by federal authorities because he criticized an FBI raid in 2005 in which a Puerto Rican nationalist activist was killed. He refused to resign or abandon his re-election bid.

Besides the pending charges, Acevedo was haunted during the campaign by a miserable economic record that actually saw a decline in the island's GDP in 2007 and 2008 (see Economy).

Fortuño, the resident commissioner to Washington, defeated former Governor Roselló in a *PNP* primary in March with almost 60% of the vote. The *PIP* nominated Edwin Irizarry Mora, while the "Puerto Ricans for Puerto Rico Party" fielded Rogelio Figueroa. The outcome of the voting on November 4, 2008:

Fortuño	1,014,852	52.8%
Acevedo	793,753	41.3%
Figueroa	53,033	2.8%
Irizarry	39,170	2.0%

Fortuño's winning margin of 220,000 votes was the largest in the commonwealth's history. His handpicked choice for resident commissioner, Attorney General Pedro Pierluisi, also was elected. Incredibly, the *PNP* swept all the Senate seats with 81.5% of the vote and almost all the House seats with 72.5%, but by law the opposition is guaranteed representation. The *PNP* thus held 22 of the 27 Senate seats and 37 of the 51 House seats.

Fortuño, who holds a bachelor's degree from Georgetown University and a law degree from the University of Virginia, was inaugurated on January 2, 2009.

Puerto Ricans of all parties were understandably electrified in 2009 when President Obama nominated Sonia Sotomayor, an appeals court judge of Puerto Rican parentage, to the U.S. Supreme Court. Sotomayor herself was born in the Bronx, New York, and educated at Princeton and Yale.

Inheriting a $3.2 billion budget deficit, Fortuño ordered a 10% cut in non-essen-

**Former Governor
Luis Guillermo Fortuño**

tial government spending, mostly perks like vehicles and cell phones. But when he announced plans to lay off almost 17,000 government employees, much as Acevedo had done, thousands of civil servants, students and clergymen staged a one-day general strike in October 2009. Fortuño's office argued that 70% of the budget goes for employee salaries and that Puerto Rico has a higher proportion of government workers per capita than any of the 50 states. The layoffs compounded an unemployment rate estimated at 15%, a result of the global and U.S. recessions.

In mid-2011, Fortuño boasted in an interview with the Public Broadcasting Service that when he took office the budget deficit was the worst of any U.S. state or territory but had improved to 20th. However, unemployment then was still 15.7%, compared with about 9% for the United States as a whole.

In 2010, the U.S. House of Representatives passed, 223–169, the Puerto Rico Democracy Act, sponsored by Pierluisi, the first time Congress had initiated a referendum on Puerto Rican self-determination. But the Senate failed to take action, and the measure died when the 111th Congress adjourned. The Republicans, who have been cool to the idea of statehood for Puerto Rico because they believe it will elect Democratic senators and representatives, won control of the House in the 2010 midterm elections.

As a further reminder of Puerto Rico's role in U.S. politics, President Obama made a five-hour visit to Puerto Rico in June 2011, the first president to visit the island in exactly 50 years, since John F. Kennedy went there in 1961. Although the 3.7 million Puerto Ricans on the island cannot vote in presidential elections, there are now 4.6 million Puerto Ricans living

Puerto Rico

on the mainland, concentrated in key states like New York, Florida and Connecticut. The city of Orlando, Florida, has the second-largest concentration of Puerto Ricans after New York City. Obama raised $1 million on the visit for his re-election campaign, sparking criticism from the Republican-allied *PNP* that Obama had not discussed Puerto Rico's future status or the pressing issues of unemployment or crime during his visit.

Fortuño generated controversy in 2012 when he proposed a plan requiring all school curriculums to be taught in English rather than Spanish. He insisted his motive was not to facilitate Puerto Rican statehood but to enhance job opportunities for younger Puerto Ricans. Critics argued that it would undermine Puerto Rico's cultural heritage. Fortuño had been hinted as a possible Republican vice presidential candidate for Mitt Romney.

Fortuño proved no more able to deal with crime than was Acevedo or Calderón. The murder rate soared to 890 in 2009, a 12-year high, giving Puerto Rico a homicide ratio per capita of 22.4 per 100,000, higher than any U.S. state except Louisiana. Like Calderón before him, Fortuño called out the National Guard. In 2011, the murder rate soared even higher to a record 1,136, an estimated 80% of it related to drug trafficking; Puerto Rico had turned into a "mini-Mexico." The rate per 100,000 was 30.5, ranking Puerto Rico as 11th deadliest in the world if it were a sovereign nation. The rate for the U.S. as a whole in 2010 was 4.8 and the worst rates on the mainland were 21.9 in the District of Columbia and 11.2 in Louisiana. Fortuño allocated an additional $20 million for police equipment and training.

It apparently had some effect; there were "only" 1,004 murders in 2012, a 14% decrease. The island's violence garnered attention from the news media on the mainland when the retired boxer, Hector "Macho" Camacho, 50, who once defeated Sugar Ray Leonard, was shot while he sat in a parked car in San Juan in November and died four days later.

Two Electoral Surprises

The congressionally authorized referendum was placed, for the first time, on the same ballot as that for governor, resident commissioner and the legislature in 2012. It was in two parts. The first asked whether voters agreed that Puerto Rico should continue with its present territorial status. The second asked which nonterritorial options they preferred, statehood, independence or "sovereign free associated state," essentially the same as the existing commonwealth but with supposedly enhanced autonomy.

Governor Alejandro García Padilla

Fortuño ran for re-election, while a young senator, Alejandro García Padilla, 41, received the *PDP* nomination. Juan Dalmau Ramírez stood for the *PIP*.

The voters sent some decidedly mixed signals on November 6. For the first time, a clear majority of 54% voted "no" to continued territorial status. Again for the first time, statehood not only finished first, but with a 61.1% majority of the valid votes. But in "second place" were 480,000 blank votes, 26% of the total votes cast, which were not valid votes. A "free associated state" was next with 33.3% of the valid votes, and independence, once again, was a distant third with 5.6%. Out of the total number of votes cast, however, those percentages are much lower (see The Future).

With this clear shift toward statehood, Fortuño of the pro-statehood *PNP* should have coasted to victory. But the voters surprised everyone:

García	896,060	47.7%
Fortuño	884,775	47.1%
Ramirez	47,3312	2.5%

Just as surprising, the *PNP*'s Pierluisi was narrowly re-elected resident commissioner over the *PDP*'s Rafael Cox, 48.4% to 47.3%. The *PDP* regained control of both the Senate and the House, winning 18 of the Senate seats to 8 for the *PNP* and 1 for the *PIP*, and 28 of the 51 House seats.

Fortuño initially conceded defeat, then a few days later changed his mind and asked for a recount, even though the difference was greater than .5 percentage points. The elections commission upheld García's victory, and he was inaugurated on January 2, 2013.

Although García had opposed public-private partnerships during the cam-

paign, after the election he promised not to scuttle the new $2.57 billion deal to privatize San Juan's Luis Muñoz Marín International Airport.

García stirred controversy in April 2013 when he mandated a shakeup of the University of Puerto Rico's board of governors and reduced the terms of the members. The move led to the mass resignations of the presidents of the university's 11 branches. García backed down from imposing an $800 fee on students after it sparked protests and caused a drop in enrollment.

Puerto Rico's alarming homicide has now dropped two years in a row, from 1,136 in 2011 to 1,004 in 2012 to 883 in 2013. But it started off 2014 with 13 murders in the first five days.

CULTURE: For centuries the Spanish presence in Puerto Rico left an indelible imprint on the island, but it also has been a true melting pot, a blend of the Spanish with Indians and Africans. Color lines are thus blurred and racial tensions hardly exist. The colonial-era fortress, La Fortaleza, is a UNESCO's World Heritage Site, along with the San Juan National Historic Site.

The abundant literature of Puerto Rico emphasizes its colonial past and the island's fight to retain its Hispanic identity. Leading authors include Luis Rafael Sánchez, Pedro Juan Soto, José Luis González and Enrique Laguerre.

In art, José Campeche (1752–1809) produced some magnificent portraits and points of historical and religious themes. Francisco Oller (1833–1917) was influenced by the great figures of French impressionism—two of his paintings hang in the Louvre Museum in Paris. Today the island is particularly strong in silk screening and plastic arts, with recognized masters such as Lorenzo Homar, Rafael Tufiño, Julio Rosado del Valle, Manuel Hernández Acevedo, Carlos Raquel Rivera and later, Antonio Martorell, Myrna Baez and Luis Hernández Cruz.

Francisco Rodón (b. 1934) is one of Latin America's leading portrait artists. He has painted such leading Latin American cultural figures as Peruvian Nobel Laureate Mario Vargas Llosa and Cuban prima ballerina Alicia Alonzo. At the 1992 World's Fair in Seville, Spain, he was proclaimed Puerto Rico's greatest artist of the 20th century.

Augusto Marín (1921–2011) was regarded as Puerto Rico's finest muralist, whose works combined religious and Caribbean themes. Governor Luis Fortuño ordered flags flown at half-staff for three days in his honor when he died in 2011.

In the mainland United States, Puerto Rican performers in the movies, popular music, television and legitimate theater have included José Ferrer, Rita Moreno, Chita Rivera, Raúl Julia, Erik Estrada, Justino Díaz, Pablo Elvira and Benicio del Toro. Many others are born in the mainland U.S. and achieve stardom, such as Jennifer López.

Puerto Ricans had collected a total of 55 Latin Grammy Awards through 2012, in fifth place behind Mexico, Brazil, Spain and Colombia. In 2011, Puerto Rico accounted for 11 of the 58 Grammys, eight of them going to the duo Calle 13, composed of René Pérez Joglar and Eduardo José Cabra Martínez. Their Grammys included Record of the Year for *Latinoamérica* and Album of the Year for *Entren Los Que Quieren*. They have won a total of 19 Latin Grammys and two mainstream Grammys. To the chagrin of many of their fans, they are active in the pro-independence movement.

In 2012, the Puerto Rican reggaeton singer Don Omar, whose real name is William Omar Landrón Rivera, won two Latin Grammys: Best Urban Music Album for *Don Omar Presents MTO²: New Generation*, and Best Urban Song for *Hasta Que Salga el Sol*.

Puerto Rico's favorite sport is baseball, and it has contributed more than 240 players to the Major Leagues since the 1940s. In 1984, Willie Hernández of the Detroit Tigers was the American League's Most Valuable Player. The unforgettable Pittsburgh Pirate Roberto Clemente is in Baseball's Hall of Fame. There were 50 Puerto Ricans on Major League rosters in 2011.

There are 26 institutions of higher learning in Puerto Rico that offer baccalaureate or graduate programs or both, many of which have multiple branches. The University of Puerto Rico, founded in 1903, now has 11 campuses, including a medical school. There are at least two other medical schools and several law schools. University of the Sacred Heart (*Universidad del Corazón Sagrado*) was founded in 1880.

The dean of the Puerto Rican press is the century-old *El Nuevo Día*, which is published in the San Juan municipality of Guaynabo and circulates island-wide. It traces its roots to the Ponce newspaper *El Diario de Puerto Rico*, which was changed to *El Día* in 1911. It is owned by the family of former Governor Luis A. Ferré, who bought it in 1948. His son moved it to San Juan in 1970 and renamed it *El Nuevo Día*. Three other dailies circulate island-wide, *El Vocero* of San Juan, *Primera Hora* of Guaynabo and the English-language *Puerto Rico Daily Sun*, an offshoot of *The San Juan Star*, which was published from 1959–2008. As in the United States, the newspapers are struggling financially.

ECONOMY: Although the Puerto Rican economy is reasonably strong, it has its problems. The main pillar of the economy is manufacturing. The island has nearly 2,000 plants, the majority of which are subsidiaries of U.S. companies attracted to Puerto Rico mainly because of tax advantages. The 1987 tax reforms, however, altered these incentives. These industries are geared to producing export items—the famous Bacardi Rum, for example, is produced on the island. Puerto Rico is a favorite location for U.S. pharmaceutical manufacturers because of particular tax advantages derived from locating on the island.

With industrialization, agricultural production, the dominant sector of the economy, commenced a decline starting in the 1950s. Agricultural workers first went to San Juan and then immigrated to the United States in search of jobs. As a result, about 3 million people of Puerto Rican heritage are now living in the United States.

Tourism, after manufacturing and agriculture, has been one of the mainstays of the economy. It now stands seriously threatened by crime directly connected to a burgeoning drug traffic from Colombia to the United States. It is relatively easy to get cocaine to the island and difficult to prevent it from entering the mainland United States because Puerto Ricans are citizens and need pass no more than the security check for weapons on flights to the United States.

If Puerto Rico were independent, its per capita income of about $25,000 would be the highest in Latin America. state. In relative terms, that is only half the per capita income of the U.S. mainland, and less than the poorest state, Mississippi, but it is five times as much as Puerto Rico's closest sovereign neighbor, the Dominican Republic. Because wages are so much higher than in other Caribbean countries, Puerto Rico is at a disadvantage in the competition for tourism.

Economic growth has dismal or nonexistent for years. In 2006, growth was only 0.5%; it declined by –1.8% in 2007, –2.0% in 2008, –3.2% in 2009, –5.8% in 2010 and –1.5% in 2011. Various sources projected growth at about 1% for 2012.

Public debt in 2013 was about $70 billion.

Although Puerto Ricans pay no federal income tax, they qualify for welfare and unemployment benefits. Unemployment was 16% in 2012 and 15.4% in 2013, compared with 7.5% on the U.S. mainland. Moreover, the island receives about $10 billion in aid from the mainland.

THE FUTURE: President Obama's visit to Puerto Rico in 2011 was the first by a sitting president in 50 years, a shameless record of neglect of an island and a people who have contributed sons, and now daughters, in all U.S. wars since World War I; more than 1,200 have given their lives. By June 2013, 50 Puerto Ricans had lost their lives in Iraq and 15 in Afghanistan, and about 300 had been wounded.

The confusing results of the November 6, 2012, elections have raised more questions than they answered about what Puerto Ricans want to do. The pro-statehood Governor Luis Fortuño was narrowly ousted from office. In the status referendum, a clear majority indicated they do not agree that Puerto Rico's current status should continue. But what do they want to replace it with? Statehood finished in first place for the first time. But why did 26% cast blank ballots on that question? In reality, statehood received the support of only 44.6% of the 1,848,000 people who voted, an enhanced commonwealth received 24.3% and independence just 4.1%.

Obama said he would respect whatever decision the Puerto Ricans make. The trick now is trying to determine what the decision was. Meanwhile, the island's population declined by more than a quarter of a million in just the last three years as Puerto Ricans, plagued by chronic unemployment and a murder rate six times that of the mainland, seek their futures elsewhere.

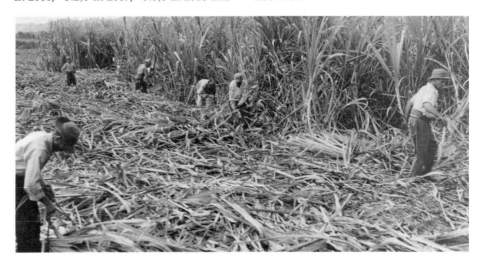

U.S. VIRGIN ISLANDS

Area: 132 square miles
Population: 109,666 (2011 est.).
Administrative Capital: Charlotte Amalie (Pop. 19,000, 2004 estimate).
Head of Government: Kenneth Mapp, governor (since January 5, 2015).

The U.S Virgin Islands lie about 40 miles east of Puerto Rico and consist of three major islands (St. Croix, St. Johns and St. Thomas) and some 50 small islands and cays, mostly uninhabited. The islands were acquired by purchase from Denmark in 1917 and are administered as a Federal Territory by the U.S. Department of the Interior. Although voters turned down a proposed new constitution in 1978, attempts are being made to write a new charter. Most residents seem to prefer commonwealth status—rather than independence or statehood—with the United States.

The islands are hilly, with arable land given to small farms. The climate is tropical, with a May to November rainy season.

The population is about 20% North American and European descent; the remainder is of African and mixed heritage. The principal products for export are rum and bay rum, the fragrant distilled oil of the bayberry leaf. Cattle raising and truck farming are important for local consumption. The islands do not possess resources adequate for support as an independent entity.

Prosperity in the 1970s brought a tremendous influx of immigrants—now only about 40% of the islanders are natives. The ethnic derivation of these "newcomers" was about 75% black from neighboring Caribbean nations, including Haitians, and 25% white U.S. mainlanders. Because the Virgin Islands in the past relied principally on rum taxes for government expenses, tax changes have seriously undermined this scheme. The response was increased taxes on just about everything in the last several years—very unpopular to say the least. Tourism has been a mainstay of the economy and is being promoted. Unemployment remains very low by Caribbean standards—about 5%.

A referendum of the islands' future relationship with the United States was held in late 1993 after being postponed because of a hurricane. Ninety percent voted for continued or enhanced status—the status quo. But only 27% of the electorate bothered to participate in the balloting; it thus did not meet validation requirements.

After an unsuccessful run in 2002, John de Jongh was elected governor in 2006. In 2012 he came under suspicion of bribery and was threatened with a possible recall election.

Selected Bibliography of Key English Language Sources

WEB SITES
Useful General Web Sites:
www.un.org (Web site for United Nations. Many links.)

www.unsystem.or (Official UN website)

http://europa.eu.int (EU server site)

www.oecd.org/daf/cmis/fdi/statist.htm (OECD site)

www.wto.org (World Trade Organization site)

www.worldbank.org/html/Welcome. html (World Bank news, publications with links to other financial institutions)

www.ceip.org (Carnegie Endowment for International Peace, using a fully integrated Web-database system)

www.cia.gov/index.html (Central Intelligence Agency)

www.odci.gov/cia (Includes useful CIA publications, such as *The World Factbook* and maps)

www.state.gov/www/ind.html (U.S. Department of State, including country reports)

http://usinfo.state.gov (U.S. Department of State)

lcweb2.loc.gov/frd/cs/cshome.html (Library of Congress with coverage of over 100 countries)

www.embassy.org/embassies (A site with links to all embassy web sites in Washington D.C.)

www.psr.keele.ac.uk\official.htm (Collective site for governments and international organizations)

www.desdecuba.com/generationy/

Newspapers, Journals and Television with good coverage on Latin American affairs:
www.chicagotribune.com (Named best overall U.S. newspaper online service for newspapers with circulation over 100,000.)

www.csmonitor.com (*Christian Science Monitor.* Named best overall U.S. newspaper online service for newspapers with circulation under 100,000.)

www.dallasnews.com (*The Dallas Morning News)*

www.diariolasamericas.com (*Diario las Américas*, Miami*)*

www.economist.com (British weekly news magazine)

www.miami.com/mld/miamiherald/ news/world/americas/ (*The Miami Herald*)

www.nytimes.com

www.washingtonpost.com

www.washingtontimes.com

www.foreignaffairs.org (One of best-known international affairs journal)

www.cnn.com (Latest news with external links)

www.news.BBC.co.uk (British Broadcasting Corporation site)

www.c-span.org (Includes C-SPAN International)

www.sun-sentinel.com (South Florida Sun-Sentinel, Fort Lauderdale)

General
Adelman, Jeremy, ed. *Colonial Legacies: the Problem of Persistence in Latin American History.* New York: Routledge, 1999.

Alcántara Sáez, Manuel, ed. *Politicians and Politics in Latin America.* Boulder, CO: Lynne Rienner, 2008.

Álvarez, Sonia E. *Cultures of Politics, Politics of Cultures: Revisioning Latin American Social Movements.* Boulder, CO: Westview Press, 1998.

Appelbaum, Nancy P., Anne S. Macpherson, and Karin Alejandra Rosemblatt, eds. *Race and Nation in Modern Latin America.* Chapel Hill: University of North Carolina Press, 2003.

Arnson, Cynthia. *Comparative Peace Processes in Latin America.* Stanford, CA: Stanford University Press, 1999.

Atkins, G. Pope. *Latin America and the Caribbean in the International System.* Boulder, CO: Westview Press, 1998.

Atkins, G. Pope. *Latin America in the International Political System.* Boulder, CO: Westview Press, 3rd. ed. 1995.

Barham, Bradford L. and Oliver T. Coomes. *Prosperity's Promise: the Amazon Rubber Boom and Distorted Economic Development.* Boulder, CO: Westview Press, 1996.

Barton, Jonathan R. *A Political Geography of Latin America.* London: Rutledge, 1997.

Beezley, William H. and Linda Curcio-Nagy, eds. *Latin American Popular Culture: an Introduction.* Wilmington, DE: Scholarly Resources, 2000.

Berg, Janine, Christoph Ernst and Peter Auer. *Meeting the Employment Challenge: Argentina, Brazil and Mexico in the Global Economy.* Boulder, CO: Lynne Rienner, 2006.

Bethell, Leslie, ed. *A Cultural History of Latin America: Literature, Music and the Visual Arts in the 19th and 20th Century.* New York: Cambridge University Press, 1998.

Bethell, Leslie, ed. *Latin America since 1930.* New York: Cambridge University Press, 1994.

Black, Jan Knippers, ed. *Latin America: Its Problems and Its Promise.* (3rd Edition) Boulder, CO: Westview Press, 1998.

Blake, Charles H. *Politics in Latin America.* St. Charles, Il: Houghton Mifflin, 2004.

Bonilla, Frank, et al., eds. *Borderless Borders: U.S. Latinos, Latin Americans, and the Paradox of Interdependence.* Philadelphia, PA: Temple University Press, 1998.

Britton, John A. *The United States and Latin America: a Select Bibliography.* Langham, MD: Scarecrow Press, 1997.

Brysk, Alison. *From Tribal Village to Global Village: Indian Rights and International Relations in Latin America.* Stanford, CA: Stanford University Press, 2000.

Bulmer-Thomas, Victor. *The Economic History of Latin America since Independence.* New York: Cambridge University Press, 1994.

Burkholder, Mark A. and Lyman L. Johnson. *Colonial Latin America.* New York: Oxford University Press, 3rd ed. 1998.

Cameron, Maxwell A., & Eric Hershberg, eds. *Latin America's Left Turns: Politics, Policies, and Trajectories of Change.* Boulder: Lynne Reinner Publishers, 2010.

Castañeda, Jorge G. *Utopia Unarmed: the Latin American Left after the Cold War.* New York: Random House, 1993.

Centeno, Miguel Angel, *Blood and Debt: War and the Nation-State in Latin America.* University Park: The Pennsylvania State University Press, 2002.

Chasteen, John Charles. *Born in Blood and Fire: a Concise History of Latin America.* New York: W.W. Norton & Company, 2000.

Chomsky, Noam. *Latin America: from Colonization to Globalization.* Hoboken, NJ: Ocean Press, 1999.

Chong, Nilda and Francia Baez. *Latino Culture: A Dynamic Force in the Changing American Workplace.* Yarmouth, ME: Intercultural Press, 2005.

Cleary, Edward L. and Timothy J. Steigenga, eds. *Resurgent Voices in Latin America: Indigenous Peoples, Political Mobilization and Religious Change.* New Brunswick: Rutgers University Press, 2004.

Cockcroft, James D. *Latin America: History, Politics, and U.S. Policy.* Chicago, IL: Nelson-Hall, 2nd ed. 1996.

Cooper, Andrew F. and Jorge Heine, eds., *Which Way Latin America? Hemispheric Politics Meets Globalization.* Washington: The Brookings Institution Press, 2009.

Craske, Nikki. *Women and Politics in Latin America.* Piscataway, NJ: Rutgers University Press, 1999.

Davis, Darien J. *Slavery and Beyond: the African Impact on Latin America and the Caribbean.* Wilmington, DE: SR Books, 1995.

Dealy, Glen Caudill, *The Latin Americans: Spirit & Ethos.* Boulder, CO: Westview Press, 1992.

De la Campa, Romban. *Latin Americanism.* Minneapolis, MN: University of Minnesota Press, 1999.

Dent, David W. *Monroe's Ghosts.* Westport, CT: Greenwood Publishing Group, 1999.

Diamond, Larry et al. *Democracy in Developing Countries: Latin America.* Boulder, CO: Lynne Rienner, 1999.

Dominguez, Jorge I. and Michael Shifter, eds., *Constructing Democratic Governance in Latin America,* 2nd Ed. Baltimore: The Johns Hopkins University Press, 2003.

Dominguez, Jorge I. *Democratic Politics in Latin America and the Caribbean.* Baltimore, MD: Johns Hopkins University Press, 1998.

Bibliography

Dominguez, Jorge I., ed. *Latin America's International Relations and Their Domestic Consequences: War and Peace, Dependency and Autonomy, Integration and Disintegration.* New York: Garland Publishing, 1994.

Dominguez, Jorge I., ed. *Race and Ethnicity in Latin America.* New York: Garland Publishing, 1994.

Early, Edwin. *A History Atlas of South America.* Old Tappan, NJ: Macmillan Publishing Company, 1998.

Ellis, R. Evan, *China in Latin America: the Whats and Wherefores.* Boulder, CO: Lynne Rienner, 2009.

Fagg, John E. *Latin America: a General History.* New York: Macmillan Publishing Company, 3rd ed 1977.

Fauriol, Georges A. *Fast Forward: Latin America on the Edge of the Twenty-First Century.* New Brunswick, NJ: 1997.

Ferman, Claudia, ed. The Postmodern in Latin America Cultural Narratives: Collected Essays and Interviews. New York: Garland Publishing, 1996.

Ferreira, Francisco H.G., et al, *Economic Mobility and the Rise of the Latin American Middle Class.* Washington: The World bank, 2012.

Ferreira, Leonardo. *Centuries of Silence: The Story of Latin American Journalism.* Westport, CT: Praeger, 2006.

Fitch, John S. *The Armed Forces and Democracy in Latin America.* Baltimore, MD: Johns Hopkins University Press, 1998.

Foders, Frederico and Manfred Feldsieper, eds. *The Transformation of Latin America.* Northampton, MA: Edward Elgar Publishing, 1999.

Foster, Dean. *The Global Etiquette Guide To Mexico and Latin America.* New York: John Wiley & Sons, Inc, 2002.

Fowler, Will, ed. *Ideologues and Ideologies in Latin America.* Westport, CT: Greenwood Publishing Group, 1997.

Franco, Jean, et al. *Profane Passions: Politics and Culture in the Americas.* Durham, NC: Duke University Press, 1999.

Galagher, Kevin P., and Roberto Porzecanski. *The Dragon in the Room: China and the Future of Latin American Industrialization.* San Jose: Stanford University Press, 2010.

Galeano, Eduardo, *Open Veins of Latin America—Five Hundred Years of the Pillage of a Continent.* New York: Monthly review Press, 1997.

Garreton, Manual Antonia et al. *Latin America in the Twenty-First Century: Toward a New Sociopolitical Matrix.* Boulder, CO: Lynne Rienner, 2003.

Garreton, Manuel Antonia and Edward Newman, eds. *Democracy in Latin America.* Washington D.C.: Brookings, 2002.

Gilderhus, Mark T., et al., eds. *The Second Century: U.S.-Latin American Relations since 1889.* Wilmington, DE: Scholarly Resources, 1999.

Gill, Anthony. *Rendering Unto Caesar: The Catholic Church and the State in Latin America.* Chicago: University of Chicago Press, 1998.

Goodwin, Paul Jr. *Latin America (10th Ed).* Guilford, CT: The Dushkin Publishing Group, Inc., 2003.

Graham, Carol and Eduardo Lora, eds., *Paradox and Perception: Measuring Quality of Life in Latin America.* Washington: The Brookings Institution Press, 2009.

Green, Roy E., ed. *The Enterprise for the Americas Initiative: Issues and Prospects for a Free Trade Agreement in the Western Hemisphere.* New York: Praeger, 1993.

Gutteridge, William F. *Latin America and the Caribbean: Prospects for Democracy.* Brookfield, VT: Ashgate Publishing Company, 1997.

Gwynne, Robert N. *Latin America Transformed: Globalization and Modernity.* New York: Oxford University Press, 1999.

Halebsky, Sandor and Richard L. Harris, eds. *Capital, Power, and Inequality in Latin America.* Boulder, CO: Westview Press, 1995.

Hamill, Hugh M., ed. Caudillos: *Dictators in Spanish America.* Norman, University of Oklahoma Press, 1992.

Harris, Richard L. and Jorge Nef, eds. *Capital, Power and Inequality in Latin America and the Caribbean, New Edition.* Lanham, MD: Lexington Books, 2008.

Hartlyn, Jonathan et al. Eds. *The United States and Latin America in the 1990s: Beyond the Cold War.* Chapel Hill: The University of North Carolina Press, 1992.

Harvey, Robert. *Liberators: Latin America's Struggle for Independence.* New York: The Overlook Press, 2000.

Henderson, James D., et al. *A Reference Guide to Latin American History.* Armonk, NY: M.E. Sharpe, 2000.

Hillman, Richard S., ed. *Understanding Contemporary Latin America,* 3rd ed. Boulder, CO: Lynne Rienner Publishers, 2005.

Hofman, André A. *The Economic Development of Latin America in the Twentieth Century.* Northampton, MA: Edward Elgar Publishing, 2000.

Howe, Brendan, Vesselin Popovski and Mark Notaras, eds., *Democracy in the South: Participation, the State and the People.* Washington: The Brookings Institution Press, 2010.

Jackiewicz, Edward L., and Fernando J. Bosco, eds. *Placing Latin America: Contemporary Themes in Human Geography.* Boulder, CO: Lynne Rienner Publishers, 2008.

Jorge, Antonio, et al., eds. *Capital Markets, Growth and Economic Policy in Latin America.* Westport, CT: Greenwood Publishing Group, 2000.

Kanellos, Nicolas and Cristelia Perez. *Chronology of Hispanic-American History.* Detroit, MI: Gale Research, 1995.

Keen, Benjamin and Mark Wasserman. *A History of Latin America (6th Edition).* Boston: Houghton Mifflin Company, 2000.

Kelly, Philip. *Checkerboards & Scatterbelts: The Geopolitics of South America.* Austin: The University of Texas Press, 1997.

Landau, Saul. *The Guerrilla Wars of Central America: Nicaragua, El Salvador, and Guatemala.* New York: Saint Martin's Press, 1993.

Langley, Lester D. *The Americas in the Age of Revolution: 1750–1850.* New Haven, CT: Yale University Press, 1996.

Logan, Samuel, *This is for the Mara Salvatrucha—Inside the MS-13, America's Most Violent Gang.* New York: Hyperion Books, 2009.

Lombardi, Cathryn L. and John V. *Latin-American History. A Teaching Atlas.* Madison, WI: The University of Wisconsin Press, 1983.

Loveman, Brian. *For la Patria: Politics and the Armed Forces in Latin America.* Scholarly Resources, 1999.

Loveman, Brian and Thomas M. Davies, Jr., eds. *Politics of Anti-Politics: The Military in Latin America.* Boulder: SR Books, 1997.

Lowenthal, Abraham F., Theodore J. Piccone and Lawrence Whitehead, eds. *The Obama Administration and the Americas: Agenda for Change.* Washington: Brookings Institution Press, 2009.

Lowenthal, Abraham F., et al, eds. *Shifting the Balance: Obama and the Americas.* Washington: Brookings Institution, 2011.

Lynch, John, ed. *Latin American Revolutions, 1808–1826: Old and New World Origins.* Norman, OK: University of Oklahoma Press, 1994.

MacDonald, Scott B. and Georges A. Fauriol. *Fast Forward: Latin America on the Edge of the Twenty-First Century.* Piscataway, NJ: Transaction Publishers, 1998.

Mace, Gordon, Jean-Philippe Thérien and Paul A. Haslam, eds. *Governing the Americas: Assessing Multilateral Institutions.* Boulder, CO: Lynne Rienner, 2007.

Mainwaring, Scott, ed. *Presidentialism and Democracy in Latin America.* New York: Cambridge University Press, 1997.

Maldifassi, José and Pier A. Abetti. *Defense Industries in Latin American Countries: Argentina, Brazil, and Chile.* New York: Praeger, 1994.

Manzetti, Luigi. *Privatization South American Style.* New York: Oxford University Press, 2000.

Margheritis, Ana, ed. *Latin American Democracies in the New Global Economy.*

North South Center Press, Miami: University of Miami, 2003.

Márquez, Ivan, ed. *Contemporary Latin American Social and Political Thought: An Anthology*. Lanham, MD: Rowman Littlefield Publishers, 2008.

Martz, John D., ed. *United States Policy in Latin America: a Decade of Crisis and Challenge*. Lincoln, NE: University of Nebraska Press, 1995.

Mendez, Juan E., et al., eds. *The (Un)Rule of Law and the Underprivileged in Latin America*. Notre Dame, IN: Notre Dame Press, 1999.

Millett, Richard L. and Michael Gold-Biss, eds. *Beyond Praetorianism: The Latin American Military in Transition*. North South Center Press, University of Miami, 1996.

Mills, Kenneth and William B. Taylor, eds. *Colonial Spanish America: a Documentary History*. Wilmington, DE: Scholarly Resources, 1998.

Morales, Juan Antonio and Gary McMahon, eds. *Economic Policy and the Transition to Democracy: the Latin American Experience*. New York: Saint Martin's Press, 1996.

Morley, Samuel A. *Poverty and Inequality in Latin America: the Impact of Adjustment and Recovery in the 1980s*. Baltimore, MD: Johns Hopkins University Press, 1995.

O'Brien, Thomas F. *Century of U.S. Capitalism in Latin America*. Albuquerque, NM: University of New Mexico Press, 1999.

Oppenheimer, Andres. *Saving the Americas: The Dangerous Decline of Latin America and What the U.S. Must Do*. Mexico City: Random House Mondadori, 2007.

Orr, Bernadette M, and Cruz. *Americas: Study Guide*. New York: Oxford University Press, 1993.

Park, James William. *Latin American Underdevelopment: a History of Perspectives in the United States, 1870–1965*. Baton Rouge, LA: Louisiana State University Press, 1995.

Payne, Leigh A. *Uncivil Movements: the Armed Right Wing and Democracy in Latin America*. Baltimore, MD: Johns Hopkins University Press, 2000.

Peeler, John. *Building Democracy in Latin America*. Boulder, CO: Lynne Rienner Publishers, 1998.

Peeler, John. *Building Democracy in Latin America*. Third Edition. Boulder, CO: Lynne Rienner, 2008.

Peruzzotti, Enrique and Catalina Smulovitz, eds. *Enforcing the Rule of Law: Social Accountability in the New Latin American Democracies*. Pittsburgh: University of Pittsburgh Press, 2006.

Pion-Berlin, David, ed. *Civil-Military Relations in Latin America: New Analytical Perspectives*. Chapel Hill: University of North Carolina Press, 2001.

Ramsey, Russell, *Guardians of the Other Americas: Essays on the Military Forces of Latin America*. Lanham, MD: University Press of America, Inc., 1997.

Rist, Peter H., *Historical Dictionary of South American Cinema*. Lanham, MD: Rowman and Littlefield, 2014.

Roberts, Paul. *The Capitalist Revolution in Latin America*. New York: Oxford University Press, 1997.

Rochlin, James F. *Vanguard Revolutionaries in Latin America: Peru, Colombia, Mexico*. Boulder, CO: Lynne Rienner, 2003.

Roseberry, William, ed. *Coffee, Society, and Power in Latin America*. Baltimore, MD: Johns Hopkins University Press, 1995.

Rosenberg, Kincaid and Logan, eds. *Americas, an Anthology*. New York: Oxford University Press, 1992.

Rosenberg, Tina. *Children of Cain*. New York: Penguin Books, 1991.

Scheina, Robert L., *Latin America's Wars (Vol. 1)—The Age of the Caudillo, 1791–1899*. Washington: Brassey's Inc., 2003.

Sáez, Manuel Alcántara. *Politicians and Politics in Latin America*. Boulder, CO: Lynne Rienner, 2007.

Schoultz, Lars. *Beneath The United States: A History of US Policy Toward Latin America*. Cambridge: Harvard University Press, 1998.

Schoultz, Lars, et al., eds. *Security, Democracy, and Development in U.S.-Latin American Relations*. North South Center Press, University of Miami, 1996.

Schwaller, John F., et al., eds. *The Church in Colonial Latin America*. Wilmington, DE: Scholarly Resources, 2000.

Silva, Patricio, ed. *The Soldier and the State in South America*. Great Britain: Palgrave, 2001.

Skidmore, Thomas and Smith, Peter. *Modern Latin America*. (7th Edition). New York: Oxford University Press, 2009.

Smith, Gaddis. *The Last Years of the Monroe Doctrine: 1945–1993*. New York: Hill & Wang/Farrar, Straus & Giroux, 1994.

Smith, Peter H. *Democracy In Latin America*. Oxford: Oxford University Press. 2005.

Smith, Peter H. *Talons of the Eagle: Dynamics of U.S.-Latin America Relations*. New York: Oxford University Press, 1996.

Smith, William C., ed. *Politics, Social Change, and Economic Restructuring in Latin America*. Coral Gables, FL: University of Miami, North/South Center Press, 1997.

Stahler-Sholk, Richard, Harry E. Vanden and Glen David Kuecker, eds. *Latin American Social Movements in the Twenty-first Century: Resistance, Power and Democracy*. Lanham, MD: Rowman Littlefield Publishers, 2008.

Stallings, Barbara and Wilson Peres. *Growth, Equity and Employment: the Impact of the Economic Reforms in Latin America and the Caribbean*. Washington, DC: Brookings Institution Press, 2000.

Stephenson, Skye. *Understanding Spanish-Speaking South Americans: Bridging Hemispheres*. Yarmouth, ME: Intercultural Press, 2003.

Swenson, Russell G. and Susana C. Lemozy, eds. *Democratización de la función de inteligencia: El nexo de la cultura nacional y la inteligencia estratégica*. Washington: National Defense Intelligence College, 2009.

Taylor, Lance, ed. *After Neoliberalism: What Next for Latin America?* Ann Arbor, MI: University of Michigan Press, 1998.

Tenenbaum, Barbara A. *Encyclopedia of Latin American History and Culture*. New York: Scribner, 1996.

Thorp, Rosemary. *Progress, Poverty and Exclusion: an Economic History of Latin America in the 20th Century*. Washington, DC: Inter-American Development Bank, 1998.

Tulchin, Joseph S., and Ralph H. Espach, eds. *Combating Corruption in Latin America*. Baltimore: Woodrow Wilson Center Press, 2000.

Tulchin, Joseph S. and Ralph H. Espach, eds. *Latin America in the New International System*. Boulder, CO: Lynne Rienner, 2001.

Tulchin, Joseph. S. and Meg Ruthenberg. *Citizenship in Latin America*. Boulder, CO: Lynne Rienner, 2007.

Turner, Barry. *Latin America Profiled: Essential Facts on Society, Business and Politics in Latin America*. New York: Saint Martin's Press, 2000.

Ungar, Mark. *Elusive Reform: Democracy and the Rule of Law in Latin America*. Boulder, CO: Lynne Rienner, 2002.

Valtmeyer, Henry and James F. Petras. *Dynamics of Social Change in Latin America*. New York: Saint Martin's Press, 2000.

Vanden, Harry E. And Gary Prevost, *Politics of Latin America*. New York: Oxford University Press, 2008.

Vargas Llosa, Alvaro. *Liberty For Latin America*. New York: Farrar, Strauss and Giroux, 2005.

Vera, Leonardo. *Stabilization and Growth in Latin America: a Critique and Reconciliation*. New York: Saint Martin's Press, 2000.

Von Mettenheim, Kurt and James M. Malloy. *Deepening Democracy in Latin America*. Pittsburgh, PA: University of Pittsburgh Press, 1998.

Wiarda, Howard J., *The Soul of Latin America: The Cultural and Political Tradition*. New Haven: Yale University Press, 2001.

Youngers, Coletta A. and Rosin, Eileen, eds. *Drugs and Democracy in Latin America. The Impact of U.S. Policy*. Boulder, CO: Lynne Rienner, 2004.

Andes Region

Crandall, Russell, et al, eds. *The Andes in Focus: Security, Democracy, and Economic*

Bibliography

Reform. Boulder, CO: Lynne Rienner, 2005.

Caribbean

Allahar, Anton, ed. *Caribbean Charisma: Reflections on Leadership, Legitimacy, and Populist Politics*. Boulder, CO: Lynne Rienner, 2001.

Beckles, Hilary M. and Verene Shepherd, eds. *Caribbean Freedom: Economy and Society from Emancipation to the Present*. Princeton, NJ: Markus Wiener Publishers, 1998.

Braveboy-Wagner, Jacqueline and Dennis J. Gayle, eds. *Caribbean Public Policy Issues of the 1990s*. Boulder, CO: Westview Press, 1997.

Braveboy-Wagner, Jacqueline, et al. *The Caribbean in the Pacific Century: Prospects for Caribbean-Pacific Cooperation*. Boulder, CO: Lynne Rienner Publishers, 1993.

Braveboy-Wagner, Jacqueline A. *The Caribbean in World Affairs: the Foreign Policies of the English-Speaking States*. Boulder, CO: Westview Press, 2000.

Carvajal, Manuel J. *The Caribbean, 1975–1980: a Bibliography of Economic and Rural Development*. Lanham, MD: Scarecrow Press, 1993.

Craton, Michael. *Empire, Enslavement and Freedom in the Caribbean*. Princeton, NJ: Markus Wiener Publishers, 1997.

Desch, Michael C., et al., eds. *From Pirates to Drug Lords: the Post-Cold War Caribbean Security Environment*. Albany, NY: State University of New York Press, 1998.

Dominguez, Jorge I., ed. *Democracy in the Caribbean: Political, Economic, and Social Perspectives*. Baltimore, MD: Johns Hopkins University Press, 1993.

Dominguez, Jorge I. *Democratic Politics in Latin America and the Caribbean*. Baltimore, MD: Johns Hopkins University Press, 1998.

Granberry, Julian, ed. *An Encyclopaedia Caribbeana: a Research Guide*. Detroit, MI: Omnigraphics, 2000.

Griffith, Ivelaw L. *The Political Economy of Drugs in the Caribbean*. New York: Saint Martin's Press, 2000.

Griffith, Ivelaw L. *The Quest for Security in the Caribbean: Problems and Promises in Subordinate States*. Armonk, NY: M.E. Sharpe, 1993.

Grugel, Jean. *Politics and Development in the Caribbean Basin: Central America and the Caribbean in the New World Order*. Bloomington, IN: Indiana University Press, 1995.

Hillman, Richard S. and Thomas D'Agostino, eds. *Understanding the Contemporary Caribbean*. Boulder, CO: Lynne Rienner, 2003.

Maingot, Anthony P. *The United States and the Caribbean: Challenges of an Asymmetrical Relationship*. Boulder, CO: Westview Press, 1994.

Marshall, Don D. *Caribbean Political Economy at the Crossroads: NAFTA and Regional Developmentalism*. New York: Saint Martin's Press, 1998.

Meditz, Sandra W. and Dennis M. Hanratty. *Islands of the Commonwealth of the Caribbean: a Regional Study*. Washington, DC: U.S. GPO, 1989.

Palmer, Ransford W., ed. *U.S.-Caribbean Relations: Their Impact on Peoples and Cultures*. Westport, CT: Greenwood Publishing Group, 1998.

Payne, Anthony and Paul Sutton, eds. *Modern Caribbean Politics*. Baltimore, MD: Johns Hopkins University Press, 1993.

Portes, Alejandro, ed. *The Urban Caribbean: Transition to the New Global Economy*. Baltimore, MD: Johns Hopkins University Press, 1997.

Sheperd, Verene, ed. *Women in Caribbean History*. Princeton, NJ: Markus Wiener Publishers, 1999.

Smith, Robert Freeman. *The Caribbean World and the United States: Mixing Rum and Coca-Cola*. Boston, MA: Twayne Publishers, 1994.

Stallings, Barbara and Wilson Peres. *Growth, Equity and Employment: the Impact of the Economic Reforms in Latin America and the Caribbean*. Washington, DC: Brookings Institution Press, 2000.

Taylor, Patrick. *Nation Dance: Religion, Identity and Cultural Difference in the Caribbean*. Bloomington, IN: Indiana University Press, 2000.

Tulchin, Joseph S. and Ralph H. Espach, eds. *Security in the Caribbean Basin: the Challenge of Regional Cooperation*. Boulder, CO: Lynne Rienner Publishers, 2000.

Central America

Alexander, Robert J. *Presidents of Central America, Mexico, Cuba and Hispaniola: Conversations and Correspondence*. New York: Praeger, 1995.

Booth, John A., Christine J. Wade and Thomas W. Walker. *Understanding Central America*, 5th Ed. Boulder: Westview Press. 2010.

Brockett, Charles D. *Land, Power and Poverty: Agrarian Transformation and Political Conflict in Central America*. Boulder, CO: Westview Press, 1998.

Coatsworth, John H. *Central America and the United States: the Clients and the Colossus*. Boston, MA: Twayne Publishers, 1994.

Dominguez, Jorge I., ed. *Democratic Transitions in Central America*. Gainesville, FL: University Press of Florida, 1997.

Foster, Lynn V. *A Brief History of Central America*. New York: Facts on File, 2000.

Krenn, Michael L. *The Chains of Interdependence: U.S. Policy toward Central America, 1945–1954*. Armonk, NY: M.E. Sharpe, 1996.

Langley, Lester D. and Thomas Schoonover. *The Banana Men: American Mercenaries and Entrepreneurs in Central America, 1880–1930*. Lexington, KY: University Press of Kentucky, 1995.

Lentner, Howard H. *State Formation in Central America: the Struggle for Autonomy, Development, and Democracy*. Westport, CT: Greenwood Publishing Publishing, 1993.

LeoGrande, William M. *Our Own Backyard: the United States in Central America, 1977–1992*. Chapel Hill, NC: University of North Carolina Press, 1998.

Logan, Samuel, *This is for the Mara Salvatrucha—Inside the MS-13, America's Most Violent Gang*. New York: Hyperion Books, 2009.

Meara, William R. *Contra Cross: Insurgency and Tyranny in Central America, 1979–1989*. Annapolis: Naval Institute Press, 2006.

Moreno, Dario. *The Struggle for Peace in Central America*. Gainesville, FL: University Press of Florida, 1994.

Paige, Jeffery M. *Coffee and Power: Revolution and the Rise of Democracy in Central America*. Cambridge, MA: Harvard University Press, 1997.

Scott, Peter D. *Cocaine Politics: Drugs, Armies and the CIA in Central America*. Berkeley, CA: University of California Press, 1998.

Torres-Rivas, Edelberto. *History and Society in Central America*. Austin, TX: University of Texas Press, 1993.

Walker, Thomas W. and Ariel C. Armony, eds. *Repression, Resistance and Democratic Transition in Central America*. Wilmington, DE: Scholarly Resources, 2000.

Weaver, Frederick Stirton. *Inside the Volcano: the History and Political Economy of Central America*. Boulder, CO: Westview Press, 1994.

Woodward, Ralph L. Jr. *Central America: a Nation Divided*. New York: Oxford University Press, 1999.

Argentina

Adelman, Jeremy. *Republic of Capital: Buenos Aires and the Legal Transformation of the Atlantic World*. Stanford, CA: Stanford University Press, 1999.

Alonso, Paula. *Between Revolution and the Ballot Box: the Origins of the Argentine Radical Party*. New York: Cambridge University Press, 2000.

Armory, Ariel C. *Argentina, the United States, and the Anti-Communist Crusade in Central America*. Athens, OH: Ohio University Press, 1997.

Balze, Felipe A.M. de la. *Remaking the Argentine Economy*. New York: Council on Foreign Relations, 1995.

Berg, Janine, Christoph Ernst and Peter Auer. *Meeting the Employment Challenge:*

Argentina, Brazil and Mexico in the Global Economy. Boulder, CO: Lynne Rienner, 2006.

Biggins, Alan. *Argentina.* Santa Barbara, CA: ABC-CLIO, 1991.

Cavarozzi, Marcelo. *Argentina.* Boulder, CO: Westview Press, 1999.

Deutsch, Sandra McGee and Ronald H. Dolkart, eds. *The Argentine Right: Its History and Intellectual Origins, 1910 to the Present.* Wilmington, DE: Scholarly Resources, 1993.

Epstein, Edward and David Pion-Berlin. *Broken Promises? The Argentine Crisis and Argentine Democracy.* Boulder, CO: Lynne Rienner Publishers, 2008.

Erro, Davide G. *Resolving the Argentine Paradox: Politics and Development, 1966–1992.* Boulder, CO: Lynne Rienner Publishers, 1993.

Escude, Carlos. *Foreign Policy Theory in Menem's Argentina.* Gainesville, FL: University Press of Florida, 1997.

Feitlowitz, Marguerite. *A Lexicon of Terror: Argentina and the Legacies of Torture.* New York: Oxford University Press, 1998.

Foster, David W. and Melissa F. Lockhart. *Culture and Customs of Argentina.* Westport, CT: Greenwood Publishing Group, 1998.

Hinton, Mercedes S. *The State on the Streets: Police and Politics in Argentina and Brazil.* Boulder, CO: Lynne Rienner, 2006.

Horvath, Laszlo. *A Half Century of Peronism, 1943–1993: an International Bibliography.* Stanford, CA: Hoover Institution Press, 1993.

Ivereigh, Austen. *Catholicism and Politics in Argentina, 1810–1960.* New York: Saint Martin's Press, 1995.

Keeling, David J. *Contemporary Argentina: a Geographical Perspective.* Boulder, CO: Westview Press, 1997.

Manzetti, Luigi. Institutions, Parties, and Coalitions in Argentine Politics. Pittsburgh, PA: University of Pittsburgh Press, 1993.

Munck, Gerardo L. *Authoritarianism and Democratization: Soldiers and Workers in Argentina, 1976–1983.* University Park, PA: Pennsylvania State University Press, 1998.

Rein, Monica. Translated by Martha Grenzeback. *Politics and Education in Argentina, 1946–1962.* Armonk, NY: M.E. Sharpe, 1998.

Rock, David. *Authoritarian Argentina: the Nationalist Movement, Its History and Its Impact.* Berkeley, CA: University of California Press, 1993.

Sawers, Larry. *The Other Argentina: the Interior and National Development.* Boulder, CO: Westview Press, 1996.

Shumway, Nicolas. *The Invention of Argentina.* Berkeley, CA: University of California Press, 1996.

Tulchin, Joseph S., ed. *Argentina: the Challenge of Modernization.* Wilmington, DE: Scholarly Resources, 1998.

Barbados

Beckles, Hilary McD. *A History of Barbados: from Amerindian Settlement to Nation-State.* New York: Cambridge University Press, 1990.

Belize

Merrill, Tim L., ed. *Guyana and Belize: Country Studies.* Washington, DC: U.S. GPO, 2nd ed. 1993.

Sutherland, Anne. *The Making of Belize: Globalization in the Margins.* Westport, CT: Greenwood Publishing Group, 1998.

Wright, Peggy and Brian E. Coutts. *Belize.* Santa Barbara, CA: ABC-CLIO, 2nd ed. 1993.

Bolivia

Gallo, Carmenza. *Taxes and State Power: Political Instability in Bolivia, 1900–1950.* Philadelphia, PA: Temple University Press, 1991.

Gill, Lesley. *Teetering on the Rim: Global Restructuring, Daily Life and the Armed Retreat of the Bolivian State.* New York: Columbia University Press, 2000.

Hudson, Rex A. and Dennis M. Hanratty, eds. *Bolivia: a Country Study.* Washington, DC: U.S. GPO, 3rd ed. 1991.

Lehman, Kenneth D. *Bolivia and the United States: a Limited Partnership.* Athens, GA: University of Georgia Press, 1999.

Leons, Madeline B. and Harry Sanabria, eds. *Coca, Cocaine, and the Bolivian Reality.* Albany, NY: State University of New York Press, 1997.

Morales, Waltraud. *Bolivia: Land of Struggle.* Boulder, CO: Westview Press, 1992.

Morales, Waltraud Q. *A Brief History of Bolivia.* New York: Checkmark Books, 2004.

Brazil

Baronov, David. *The Abolition of Slavery in Brazil: the "Liberation" of Africans through the Emancipation of Capital.* Westport, CT: Greenwood Publishing Group, 2000.

Berg, Janine, Christoph Ernst and Peter Auer. *Meeting the Employment Challenge: Argentina, Brazil and Mexico in the Global Economy.* Boulder, CO: Lynne Rienner, 2006.

Boer, Werner. *The Brazilian Economy: Growth and Development.* Boulder, CO: Lynne Rienner, 2007.

Boxer, C.R. *The Golden Age of Brazil: Growing Pains of a Colonial Society.* New York: Saint Martin's Press, 1995.

Brainard, Lael and Leonardo Martínez-Díaz, eds., *Brazil as an Economic Superpower?* Washington: The Brookings Institution Press, 2009.

Bresser-Pereira, Luiz Carlos. *Economic Crisis and State Reform in Brazil: Toward a New Interpretation of Latin America.* Boulder, CO: Lynne Rienner Publishers, 1996.

Bresser-Pereira, Luiz Carlos. *Developing Brazil: Overcoming the Failure of the Washington Consensus.* Boulder, CO: Lynne Rienner Publishers, 2005.

Burns, E. Bradford. *A History of Brazil.* New York: Columbia University Press, 3rd ed. 1993.

Capistrano de Abreu, João. *Chapters in Brazil's Colonial History, 1500–1800.* New York: Oxford University Press, 1997.

Cavalcanti, Clovis de Vasconcelos, ed. *The Environment, Sustainable Development and Public Policies: Building Sustainability in Brazil.* Northampton, MA: Edward Elgar Publishing, 2000.

Cavaliero, Roderick. *The Independence of Brazil.* New York: Saint Martin's Press, 1993.

Chaffee, Wilber A. *Desenvolvimento: Politics and Economy in Brazil.* Boulder, CO: Lynne Rienner Publishers, 1997.

De la Barra, Ximena and Richard A. Dello Buono. *Latin America after the Neoliberal Debacle: Another Region is Possible.* Lanham, MD: Rowman Littlefield Publishers, 2008.

Eakin, Marshall C. *Brazil: Once and Future Country.* New York: Saint Martin's Press, 1997.

Fausto, Boris. *A Concise History of Brazil.* New York: Cambridge University Press, 1999.

Goertzel, Ted G. *Fernando Henrique Cardoso: Reinventing Democracy in Brazil.* Boulder, CO: Lynne Rienner Publishers, 1999.

Gordon, Lincoln. *Brazil's Second Chance. En Route toward the First World.* Washington, D.C.: Brookings, 2003.

Hanchard, Michael. *Racial Politics in Contemporary Brazil.* Durham, NC: Duke University Press, 1999.

Hecht, Tobias. *At Home in the Street: Street Children in Northeast Brazil.* New York: Cambridge University Press, 1998.

Hinton, Mercedes S. *The State on the Streets: Police and Politics in Argentina and Brazil.* Boulder, CO: Lynne Rienner, 2006.

Hudson, Rex A., ed. *Brazil: a Country Study.* Washington, DC: U.S. GPO, 5th ed. 1998.

Hunter, Wendy. *Eroding Military Influence in Brazil: Politicians against Soldiers.* Chapel Hill, NC: University of North Carolina Press, 1997.

Kingstone, Peter R. and Timothy J. Powers, eds. *Democratic Brazil: Actors, Institutions and Processes.* Pittsburgh, PA: University of Pittsburgh Press, 2000.

Kinzo, Maria, ed. *Brazil under Democracy. Economy, Polity, and Society since 1985.* Washington, D.C.: Brookings, 2003.

Lesser, Jeff. *Negotiating National Identity: Immigrants, Minorities, and the Struggle*

Bibliography

for Ethnicity in Brazil. Durham, NC: Duke University Press, 1999.

Levine, Robert M. Brazilian Legacies. Armonk, NY: M.E. Sharpe, 1997.

Levine, Robert M. and John J. Crocitti, eds. The Brazil Reader: History, Culture, Politics. Durham, NC: Duke University Press, 1999.

Levine, Robert M. Father of the Poor? Vargas and His Era. New York: Cambridge University Press, 1998.

Mainwaring, Scott. Rethinking Party Systems in the Third Wave of Democratization: the Case of Brazil. Stanford, CA: Stanford University Press, 1999.

Matos, Carolina. Journalism and Political Democracy in Brazil. Lanham, MD: Lexington Books, 2008.

Page, Joseph A. The Brazilians. Reading, MA: Addison-Wesley, 1995.

Power, Timothy J. The Political Right in Postauthoritarian Brazil: Elites, Institutions and Democratization. University Park, PA: Pennsylvania State University Press, 2000.

Purcell, Susan K. Brazil under Cardoso. Boulder, CO: Lynne Rienner Publishers, 1997.

Reiter, Bernd. Negotiating Democracy in Brazil: The Politics of Exclusion. Boulder, CO: Lynne Rienner Publishers, 2009.

Ribeiro, Darcy and Gregory Rabassa. The Brazilian People: the Formation and Meaning of Brazil. Gainesville, FL: University Press of Florida, 2000.

Robinson, Roger. Brazil. Des Plaines, IL: Heinemann Library, 1999.

Roett, Riordan, The New Brazil. Washington: The Brookings Institution Press, 2010.

Skidmore, Thomas E. Brazil: Five Centuries of Change. New York: Oxford University Press, 1999.

Topik, Steven C. Trade and Gunboats: the United States and Brazil in the Age of Empire. Stanford, CA: Stanford University Press, 2000.

Von Mettenheim, Kurt. The Brazilian Voter: Mass Politics in Democratic Transition. Pittsburgh, PA: University of Pittsburgh Press, 1995.

Weyland, Kurt Gerhard. Democracy without Equity: Failures of Reform in Brazil. Pittsburgh, PA: University of Pittsburgh Press, 1996.

Willumsen, Maria J., ed. The Brazilian Economy: Structure and Performance. Coral Gables, FL: University of Miami, North/South Center Press, 1997.

Webber, Jeffrey R. From Rebellion to Reform in Bolivia: Class Struggle, Indigenous Liberation, and the Politics of Evo Morales. Chicago: Haymarket Books, 2011.

Chile

Bosworth, Barry P., ed. The Chilean Economy: Policy and Challenges. Washington, DC: Brookings Institution Press, 1994.

Collier, Simon and William F. Sater. A History of Chile, 1808–1994. New York: Cambridge University Press, 1996.

Constable, Pamela and Arturo Valenzuela. A Nation of Enemies: Chile under Pinochet. New York: W.W. Norton, 1993.

Davis, Madeleine, ed. The Pinochet Case. Washington, D.C.: Brookings, 2003.

Franceschet, Susan. Women and Politics in Chile. Boulder, CO: Lynne Rienner, 2005.

Hachette, Dominique and Rolf Luders. Privatization in Chile: an Economic Appraisal. San Francisco, CA: ICS Press, 1993.

Franceschet, Susan. Women and Politics in Chile. Boulder, CO: Lynne Rienner, 2005.

Hojman, David E. Chile: the Political Economy of Development and Democracy in the 1990s. Pittsburgh, PA: University of Pittsburgh Press, 1993.

Hudson, Rex A., ed. Chile: a Country Study. Washington, DC: U.S. GPO, 3rd ed. 1994.

Huneeus, Carlos. The Pinochet Regime. Boulder, CO: Lynne Rienner, 2007.

Lomnitz, Larissa Adler and Ana Melnick. Chile's Political Culture and Parties: an Anthropological Explanation. Notre Dame, IN: University of Notre Dame Press, 2000.

Lonregan, John B. Legislative Institutions and Ideology in Chile. New York: Cambridge University Press, 2000.

Monteon, Michael. Chile and the Great Depression: the Politics of Underdevelopment, 1927–1948. Tempe, AZ: Arizona State University, Center for Latin American Studies, 1998.

Oppenheim, Lois Hecht. Politics in Chile: Democracy, Authoritarianism, and the Search for Development. Boulder, CO: Westview Press, 2nd ed. 1998.

Oxhorn, Philip. Organizing Civil Society: the Popular Sectors and the Struggle for Democracy in Chile. University Park, PA: Pennsylvania State University Press, 1995.

Petras, James, et. al. Democracy and Poverty in Chile: the Limits to Electoral Politics. Boulder, CO: Westview Press, 1994.

Pietrobelli, Carlo. Industry, Competitiveness and Technological Capabilities in Chile: a New Tiger from Latin America. New York: Saint Martin's Press, 1998.

Puryear, Jeffrey. Thinking Politics: Intellectuals and Democracy in Chile, 1973–1988. Baltimore, MD: Johns Hopkins University Press, 1994.

Quereshi, Lubna Z. Nixon, Kissinger and Allende: U.S. Involvement in the 1973 Coup in Chile. Lanham, MD: Lexington Books, 2008.

Roberts, Kenneth M. Deepening Democracy? The Modern Left and Social Movements in Chile and Peru. Stanford, CA: Stanford University Press, 1999.

Siavelis, Peter. The President and Congress in Post-Authoritarian Chile: Institutional Constraints to Democratic Consolidation. University Park, PA: Pennsylvania State University Press, 1999.

Sigmund, Paul E. The United States and Democracy in Chile. Baltimore, MD: Johns Hopkins University Press, 1993.

Silva, Eduardo. The State and Capital in Chile: Business Elites, Technocrats, and Market Economics. Boulder, CO: Westview Press, 1996.

Solimano, Andres. Distributive Justice and Economic Development: the Case of Chile and Developing Countries. Ann Arbor, MI: University of Michigan Press, 2000.

Spooner, Mary Helen. Soldiers in a Narrow Land: the Pinochet Regime in Chile. Berkeley, CA: University of California Press, 1994.

Valdes, Juan Gabriel. Pinochet's Economists: the Chicago School in Chile. New York: Cambridge University Press, 1995.

Verdugo, Patricia. Chile, Pinochet, and the Caravan of Death. Boulder, CO: Lynne Rienner, 2001.

Wheelan, James R., Out of the Ashes: Life, Death and Transfiguration of Democracy in Chile, 1833–1988. Washington: Regnery Gateway, 1989.

Colombia

Ardila Galvia, Constanza. The Heart of the War in Colombia. London: Latin American Bureau, 2002.

Brittain, James J. Revolutionary Social Change in Colombia: The Origin and Direction of the FARC-EP. London: Pluto Press, 2010.

Bouvier, Virginia M., ed. Building Peace in a Time of War. United States Institute for Peace Press, 2009.

Cathey, Kate. Culture Smart: Colombia. Kuperard. 2011.

Crandall, Russell. Driven By Drugs: U.S. Policy Toward Colombia. Boulder, CO: Lynne Reinner, 2002.

Davis, Robert H. Historical Dictionary of Colombia. Lanham, MD: Scarecrow Press, 2nd ed. 1993.

Drexler, Robert W. Colombia and the United States: Narcotics Traffic and a Failed Foreign Policy. Jefferson, NC: McFarland & Company, 1997.

Duzan, Maria Jimena. Translated and edited by Peter Eisner. Death Beat: a Colombian Journalist's Life inside the Cocaine Wars. New York: HarperCollins, 1994.

Gonsalves, Marc, Tom Howes, Keith Stansell and Gary Brozek, Out of Captivity: Surviving 1,967 Days in the Colombian Jungle. New York: Harper Collins, 2009.

Hanratty, Dennis M. and Sandra W. Meditz, eds. Colombia: a Country Study. Washington, DC: U.S. GPO, 4th ed. 1990.

Hristov, Jasmin. Blood and Capital: The Paramilitarization of Colombia. Athens: Ohio University Press, 2009.

Kirk, Robin. *More Terrible Than Death: Massacres, Drugs, and America's War in Colombia.* New York: Public Affairs, 2003.

Kline, Harvey F. *Colombia: Democracy under Assault.* Boulder, CO: Westview Press, 2nd ed. 1995.

Kline, Harvey F. *State Building and Conflict Resolution in Colombia, 1986–1994.* Tuscaloosa, AL: University of Alabama Press, 1999.

LaRosa, Michael J., and Germán R. Mejía. *Colombia: A Concide Congtemporary History.* Lanham, MD: Rowman and Littlefield, 2013.

McFarlane, Anthony. *Colombia before Independence: Economy, Society, and Politics under Bourbon Rule.* New York: Cambridge University Press, 1993.

Menzel, Sewall H. *Cocaine Quagmire: Implementing the U.S. Anti-Drug Policy in the North Andes-Colombia.* Lanham, MD: University Press of America, 1997.

Mohan, Rakesh. *Understanding the Developing Metropolis: Lessons from the Study of Bogota and Cali, Colombia.* New York: Oxford University Press, 1994.

Posada-Carbo, Eduardo. *Colombia.* New York: Saint Martin's Press, 1997.

Rabasa, Angel and Peter Chalk. *Colombian Labyrinth: The Synergy of Drugs and Insurgency and Its Implications for Regional Stability.* Santa Monica: Rand Corp, 2001.

Rausch, Jane M. *The Llanos Frontier in Colombian History, 1830–1930.* Albuquerque, NM: University of New Mexico Press, 1993.

Safford, Frank and Marco Palacios. *Colombia: Fragmented Land, Divided Society.* New York: Oxford University Press, 2002.

Thorpe, Rosemary. *Economic Management and Economic Development in Peru and Colombia.* Pittsburgh, PA: University of Press, 1991.

Thoumi, Francisco E. *Political Economy and Illegal Drugs in Colombia.* Boulder, CO: Lynne Rienner Publishers, 1995.

Wade, Peter. *Blackness and Race Mixture: the Dynamics of Racial Identity in Colombia.* Baltimore, MD: Johns Hopkins University Press, 1993.

Costa Rica

Basok, Tanya. *Keeping Heads above Water: Salvadorean Refuges in Costa Rica.* Toronto: University of Toronto Press, 1993.

Biesanz, Mavis H., Richard Biesanz and Karen Z. Biesanz. *The Ticos: Culture and Social Change in Costa Rica.* Boulder, CO: Lynne Rienner, 1999.

Booth, John A. *Costa Rica: Quest for Democracy.* Boulder, CO: Westview Press, 1998.

Colesberry, Adrian and Brass McLean. *Costa Rica: the Last Country the Gods Made.* Helena, MT: Falcon Press, 1993.

Creedman, Theodore S. *Historical Dictionary of Costa Rica.* Lanham, MD: Scarecrow Press, 2nd ed. 1991.

Edelman, Marc. *Peasants against Globalization: Rural Social Movements in Costa Rica.* Stanford, CA: Stanford University Press, 2000.

Helmuth, Chalene. *Culture and Customs of Costa Rica.* Westport, CT: Greenwood Publishing Group, 2000.

Honey, Martha. *Hostile Acts: U.S. Policy in Costa Rica in the 1980s.* Gainesville, FL: University of Florida Press, 1994.

Miller, Eugene D. *A Holy Alliance? The Church and the Left in Costa Rica, 1932–1948.* Armonk, NY: M.E. Sharpe, 1996.

Rottenberg, Simon, ed. *Costa Rica and Uruguay.* New York: Oxford University Press, 1993.

Stansifer, Charles L. *Costa Rica.* Santa Barbara, CA: ABC-CLIO, 1991.

Wilson, Bruce M. *Costa Rica: Politics, Economics, and Democracy.* Boulder, CO: Lynne Rienner Publishers, 1998.

Yashar, Deborah J. *Demanding Democracy: Reform and Reaction in Costa Rica and Guatemala, 1870s–1950s.* Stanford, CA: Stanford University Press, 1997.

Cuba

Arbdeya, Jesus. Translated by Rafael Betancourt. *The Cuban Counterrevolution.* Athens, OH: Ohio University Press, 2000.

Baloyara, Enrique and James A. Morris. *Conflict and Change in Cuba.* Albuquerque, NM: University of New Mexico Press, 1993.

Benjamin-Alvarado, Jonathan. *Power to the People: Energy and the Cuban Nuclear Program.* New York: Routledge, 2000.

Blight, James G, et al. *Cuba on the Brink: Castro, the Missile Crisis, and the Soviet Collapse.* New York: Pantheon Books, 1993.

Bunck, Julie Marie. *Fidel Castro and the Quest for a Revolutionary Culture in Cuba.* University Park, PA: Pennsylvania State University, 1994.

Corbett, Ben. *This is Cuba.* Boulder, CO: Westview, 2002.

Diaz-Briquets, Sergio and Jorge Perez-Lopez. *Conquering Nature: the Environmental Legacy of Socialism in Cuba.* Pittsburgh, PA: University of Pittsburgh Press, 2000.

Fernandez, Damian J. *Cuba and the Politics of Passion.* Austin, TX: University of Texas Press, 2000.

Fursenko, Alexandr and Timothy J. Naftali. *"One Hell of a Gamble": Khrushchev, Castro and Kennedy, 1958–1964.* New York: W.W. Norton & Company, 1997.

Gonzalez, Edward and McCarthy, Kevin F. *Cuba After Castro. Legacies, Challenges, and Impediments.* Santa Monica, CA: Rand, 2004.

Gott, Richard. *Cuba: A New History.* New Haven: Yale University, 2004.

Halperin, Maurice. *Return to Havana: the Decline of Cuban Society under Castro.* Nashville, TN: Vanderbilt University Press, 1994.

Hernandez, José M. *Cuba and the United States: Intervention and Militarism, 1868–1933.* Austin, TX: University of Texas Press, 1993.

Huddleston, Vicki and Carlos Pascual, *Learning to Salsa: New Steps in U.S.-Cuba Relations.* Washington: The Brookings Institution Press, 2010.

Ibarra, Jorge. *Prologue to Revolution: Cuba, 1898–1958.* Boulder, CO: Lynne Rienner Publishers, 1998.

James, Ian Michael. *Ninety Miles: Cuban Journeys in the Age of Castro.* Lanham, MD: Lexington Books, 2008.

Jordan, David C. *Revolutionary Cuba and the End of the Cold War.* Lanham, MD: University Press of America, 1993.

Kirk, John M. *Canada-Cuba Relations: the Other Good Neighbor Policy.* Gainesville, FL: University Press of Florida, 1997.

Klepak, Hal. *Cuba's Military 1990–2005: Revolutionary Soldiers During Counter-Revolutionary Times.* New York: Palgrave MacMillan, 2005.

Kornbluh, Peter, ed. *Bay of Pigs Declassified: the Secret CIA Report.* New York: New Press, 1998.

Leonard, Thomas M. *Castro and the Cuban Revolution.* Westport, CT: Greenwood Publishing Group, 1999.

Luis, Julio Garcia. *Cuban Revolution Reader: a Documented History of 40 Years of the Cuban Revolution.* Hoboken, NJ: Ocean Press, 2000.

Luis, William. *Culture and Customs of Cuba.* Washington: Brookings Institution Press, 2001.

Mesa-Largo, Carmelo, ed. *Cuba after the Cold War.* Pittsburgh, PA: University of Pittsburgh Press, 1993.

Moses, Catherine. *Real Life in Castro's Cuba.* Wilmington, DE: Scholarly Resources, 2000.

Oppenheimer, Andres, *Castro's Final Hour: The Secret Story Behind the Coming Downfall of Communist Cuba.* New York: Simon & Schuster, 1992.

Paterson, Thomas G. *Contesting Castro: the United States and the Triumph of the Cuban Revolution.* New York: Oxford University Press, 1994.

Perez, Louis A., Jr. *On Becoming Cuban: Identity, Nationality and Culture.* Chapel Hill, NC: University of North Carolina Press, 1999.

Perez, Louis A., Jr., *Cuba: Between Reform and Revolution.* New York: Oxford University Press, 2005.

Perez-Lopez, Jorge F. *Cuba at a Crossroads: Politics and Economics after the Fourth*

Bibliography

Party Congress. Gainesville, FL: University of Florida Press, 1994.

Perez-Lopez, Jorge F. *Cuba's Second Economy: from behind the Scenes to Center State.* New Brunswick, NJ: Transaction Publishers, 1995.

Perez-Stable, Marifeli. *The Cuban Revolution: Origins, Course, and Legacy.* New York: Oxford University Press, 2nd ed. 1999.

Purcell, Susan Kaufman and David Rothkopf, eds. *Cuba: the Contours of Change.* Boulder, CO: Lynne Rienner Publishers, 2000.

Quirk, Robert E. *Fidel Castro.* New York: W.W. Norton, 1993.

Ritter, Archibald R.M. and John M. Kirk, eds. *Cuba in the International System: Normalization and Integration.* New York: Saint Martin's Press, 1995.

Roy, Joaquín. *Cuba, the United States, and the Helms-Burton Doctrine: International Reactions.* Gainesville, FL: University Press of Florida, 2000.

Santi, Enrico Mario, ed. *Cuban Studies XXIV.* Pittsburgh, PA: University of Pittsburgh Press, 1994.

Schwab, Peter. *Cuba: Confronting the U.S. Embargo.* New York: Saint Martin's Press, 2000.

Schulz, Donald E. *Cuba and the Future.* Westport, CT: Greenwood Press, 1994.

Skoug, Kenneth N. *The United States and Cuba under Reagan and Shultz: a Foreign Service Officer Reports.* New York: Praeger, 1996.

Stubbs, Jean, et al. *Cuba.* Santa Barbara, CA: ABC-CLIO, 1996.

Suchlicki, Jaime. *Cuba: from Columbus to Castro and Beyond.* McLean, VA: Brassey's, Inc.: 4th ed. 1997.

Szulc, Tad. *Fidel. A Critical Portrait.* NY: Avon Books, 1986.

Tulchin, Joseph S., et al., eds. *Cuba and the Caribbean: Regional Issues and Trends in the Post-Cold War Era.* Wilmington, DE: Scholarly Resources, 1997.

Dominican Republic

Atkins, G. Pope. *The Dominican Republic and the United States: from Imperialism to Transnationalism.* Athens, GA: University of Georgia Press, 1998.

Baud, Michiel. *Peasants and Tobacco in the Dominican Republic, 1870–1930.* Knoxville, TN: University of Tennessee Press, 1995.

Bedggood, Ginnie & Ilana Benady. *Culture Smart: Dominican Republic.* Kuperard. 2010.

Haggerty, Richard A., ed. *Dominican Republic and Haiti: Country Studies.* Washington, DC: U.S. GPO, 2nd ed. 1991.

Hall, Michael R. *Sugar and Power in the Dominican Republic: Eisenhower, Kennedy and the Trujillos.* Westport, CT: Greenwood Publishing Group, 2000.

Hartlyn, Jonathan. *The Struggle for Democratic Politics in the Dominican Republic, 1961–1996.* Chapel Hill, NC: University of North Carolina Press, 1998.

Howard, David. *Dominican Republic: a Guide to the People, Politics and Culture.* Northampton, MA: Interlink Publishing Group, 1999.

Roorda, Eric. *The Dictator Next Door: the Good Neighbor Policy and the Trujillo Regime in the Dominican Republic, 1930–1945.* Durham, NC: Duke University Press, 1998.

Sagás, Ernesto. *Race and Politics in the Dominican Republic.* Gainesville, FL: University Press of Florida, 2000.

Ecuador

Alchon, Suzanne Austin. *Native Society and Disease in Colonial Ecuador.* New York: Cambridge University Press, 1991.

De la Torre, Carlos. *Populist Seduction in Latin America: the Ecuadorian Experience.* Athens, OH: Ohio University Press, 2000.

Gerlach, Allen. *Indians, Oil, and Politics: A Recent History of Ecuador.* Wilmington: Scholarly Resources, Inc, 2003.

Goffin, Alvin M. *The Rise of Protestant Evangelism in Ecuador, 1895–1990.* Gainesville, FL: University Press of Florida, 1994.

Hanratty, Dennis M., ed. *Ecuador: a Country Study.* Washington, DC: U.S. GPO, 3rd ed. 1991.

Herz, Monica and J.P. Nogueira. *Ecuador vs. Peru: Peacemaking Amid Rivalry.* Boulder, CO: Lynne Rienner, 2002.

Hey, Jeanne A.K. *Theories of Dependent Foreign Policy and the Case of Ecuador in the 1980s.* Athens, OH: Ohio University Press, 1995.

Isaacs, Anita. *The Politics of Military Rule and Transition in Ecuador, 1972–92.* Pittsburgh, PA: University of Pittsburgh Press, 1993.

Muratorio, Blanca. *The Life and Times of Grandfather Alonso: Culture and History in the Upper Amazon.* New Brunswick, NJ: Rutgers University Press, 1991.

Roitman, Karem. *Race, Power and Ethnicity in Ecuador: The Manipulation of the Mestizaje.* Boulder, CO: First Forum Press, 2009.

Selverston-Scher, Melina. *Ethnopolitics in Ecuador: Indigenous Rights and the Strengthening of Democracy.* North South Center Press, Miami: University of Miami, 2001.

El Salvador

Angel, José, et al. Strategy and Tactics of the Salvadoran FMLN Guerrillas: Last Battle of the Cold War, Blueprint for Future Conflicts. New York: Praeger, 1995.

Beirne, Charles Joseph. *Jesuit Education and Social Change in El Salvador.* New York: Garland Publishing, 1996.

Didion, Joan. *Salvador.* New York: Vintage, 1994.

Doggett, Martha. *Death Foretold: the Jesuit Murders in El Salvador.* Washington, DC: Georgetown University Press, 1993.

Grenier, Yvon. *The Emergence of Insurgency in El Salvador: Ideology and Political Will.* Pittsburgh, PA: University of Pittsburgh Press, 1999.

Haggerty, Richard A., ed. *El Salvador: a Country Study.* Washington, DC: U.S. GPO, 2nd ed. 1990.

Hammond, John L. *Fighting to Learn: Popular Education and Guerrilla War in El Salvador.* New Brunswick, NJ: Rutgers University Press, 1998.

Hassett, John and Hugh Lacey, eds. *Toward a Society that Serves Its People: the Intellectual Contribution of El Salvador's Murdered Jesuits.* Washington, DC: Georgetown University Press, 1991.

Marenn, M.J. *Salvador's Children: a Song for Survival.* Columbus, OH: Ohio State University, 1993.

Pelupessy, Wim. *The Limits of Economic Reform in El Salvador.* New York: Saint Martin's Press, 1997.

Popkin, Margaret L. *Peace without Justice: Obstacles to Building the Rule of Law in El Salvador.* University Park, PA: Pennsylvania State University, 2000.

Quizar, Robin O. *My Turn to Weep: Salvadoran Women in Costa Rica.* Westport, CT: Greenwood Publishing Group, 1998.

Ucles, Mario L. Translated by Amelia F. Shogun. *El Salvador in the 1980's: Counterinsurgency and Revolution.* Philadelphia, PA: Temple University Press, 1996.

Williams, Philip J. *Militarization and Demilitarization in El Salvador's Transition to Democracy.* Pittsburgh, PA: University of Pittsburgh Press, 1998.

Wood, Elisabeth Jean. *Insurgent Collective Action and Civil War in El Salvador.* Cambridge: Cambridge University Press, 2003.

Grenada

Heine, Jorge, ed. *A Revolution Aborted: the Lessons of Grenada.* Pittsburgh, PA: University of Pittsburgh Press, 1990.

Guatemala

Benz, Stephen Connely. *Guatemalan Journey.* Austin: University of Texas Press, 1996.

Dosal, Paul J. *Doing Business with the Dictators: a Political History of the United Fruit in Guatemala, 1899–1944.* Wilmington, DE: Scholarly Resources, 1993.

Dosal, Paul J. *Power in Transition: The Rise of Guatemala's Industrial Oligarchy, 1871–1994.* New York: Praeger, 1995.

Bibliography

Goldman, Francisco, *The Art of Political Murder: Who Killed the Bishop?* New York: Grove Press, 2007.

Grandin, Greg. *The Blood of Guatemala: a History of Race and Nation.* Durham, NC: Duke University Press, 2000.

Handy, Jim. *Revolution in the Countryside: Rural Conflict and Agrarian Reform in Guatemala, 1944–1954.* Chapel Hill, NC: University of North Carolina Press, 1994.

Hendrickson, Carol. *Weaving Identities: Construction of Dress and Self in a Highland Guatemalan Town.* Austin: University of Texas Press, 1995.

Jonas, Susanne. *Of Centaurs and Doves: Guatemala's Peace Process.* Boulder, CO: Westview Press, 2000

Jones, Oakah L. *Guatemala in the Spanish Colonial Period.* Norman, OK: University of Oklahoma Press, 1994.

Levenson-Estrada, Deborah. *Trade Unionists against Terror: Guatemala City, 1954–1985.* Chapel Hill, NC: University of North Carolina Press, 1994.

Lovell, George W. *A Beauty That Hurts: Life and Death in Guatemala.* Austin, TX: University of Texas Press, rev. ed 2000.

McCleary, Rachel M. *Dictating Democracy: Guatemala and the End of Violent Revolution.* Gainesville, FL: University Press of Florida, 1999.

McCreery, David. *Rural Guatemala, 1760–1940.* Stanford, CA: Stanford University Press, 1994.

Nelson, Diane M. *A Finger in the Wound: Body Politics in Quincentennial Guatemala.* Berkeley, CA: University of California Press, 1999.

Perera, Victor. *Unfinished Conquest: the Guatemalan Tragedy.* Berkeley, CA: University of California Press, 1993.

Schirmer, Jennifer. *The Guatemalan Military Project: a Violence Called Democracy.* Philadelphia, PA: University of Pennsylvania Press, 1998.

Shea, Maureen E. *Culture and Customs of Guatemala.* Westport, CT: Greenwood Publishing Group, 2000.

Stanley, William. *Enabling Peace in Guatemala: The Story of MINGUA.* Boulder, CO: Lynne Rienner, 2009.

Stoll, David. *Between Two Armies: in the Ixil Towns of Guatemala.* New York: Columbia University Press, 1993.

Stoll, David. *Rigoberta Menchu and the Story of All Poor Guatemalans.* Boulder, CO: Westview Press, 1998.

Trudeau, Robert H. *Guatemalan Politics: the Popular Struggle for Democracy.* Boulder, CO: Lynne Rienner Publishers, 1993.

Wilkinson, Daniel. *Silence On The Mountain: Stories of Terror, Betrayal, and Forgetting in Guatemala.* Boston: Houghton Mifflin Company, 2002.

Woodward, Ralph Lee. *Guatemala.* Santa Barbara, CA: ABC-CLIO, rev. ed. 1992.

Woodward, Ralph Lee. *Rafael Carrera and the Emergence of the Republic of Guatemala.* Athens, GA: University of Georgia Press, 1993.

Yashar, Deborah J. *Demanding Democracy: Reform and Reaction in Costa Rica and Guatemala., 1850s–1950s.* Stanford, CA: Stanford University Press, 1997.

Zimmerman, Marc. *Literature and Resistance in Guatemala: Textual Modes and Cultural Politics from El Señor Presidente to Rigoberta Menchu.* Athens, OH: Ohio University Press, 1995.

Guyana

Da Costa, Emilia Viotti. *Crowns of Glory, Tears of Blood: the Demerara Slave Rebellion of 1823.* New York: Oxford University Press, 1994.

Gibson, Kean. *The Cycle of Racial Oppression in Guyana.* Lanham, MD: University Press of America, 2003.

Merrill, Tim L., ed. *Guyana and Belize: Country Studies.* Washington, DC: U.S. GPO, 2nd ed. 1993.

Williams, Brackette F. *Stains on My Name, War in My Veins: Guyana and the Politics of Struggle.* Durham, NC: Duke University Press, 1991.

Williams, David P., et al., eds. *Privatization vs. Community: the Rise and Fall of Industrial Welfare in Guyana.* Lanham, MD: Rowman & Littlefield, 1998.

Haiti

Chambers, Frances, ed. *Haiti.* Santa Barbara, CA: ABC-CLIO, 2nd ed. 1994.

Fatton, Robert Jr. *Haiti's Predatory Republic: The Unending Transition to Democracy.* Boulder, CO: Lynne Rienner, 2002.

Fatton, Robert Jr. *The Roots of Haitian Despotism.* Boulder, CO: Lynne Rienner Publishers, 2007.

Gibbons, Elizabeth D. *Sanctions in Haiti: Human Rights and Democracy under Assault.* Westport, CT: Greenwood Publishing Group, 1999.

Fatton, Robert Jr. *Haiti's Predatory Republic: The Unending Transition to Democracy.* Boulder: Lynne Reinner Publishing, 2002.

Fatton, Robert Jr. *The Roots of Haitian Despotism.* Boulder, CO: Lynne Rienner, 2007.

Haggerty, Richard A., ed. *Dominican Republic and Haiti: Country Studies.* Washington, DC: U.S. GPO, 2nd ed, 1991.

Hein, Robert Debs and Hein, Nancy Gordon. Revised and Expanded by Hein, Michael. *Written in Blood. The Story of the Haitian People 1492–1995.* Lanham, MD: University Press of America, 1996.

Kumar, Chetan. *Building Peace in Haiti.* Boulder, CO: Lynne Rienner Publishers, 1998.

Laguerre, Michel S. *The Military Society in Haiti.* Knoxville, TN: University of Tennessee Press, 1993.

Langley, Lester D. *The Americas in the Age of Revolution, 1750–1850.* New Haven, CT: Yale University Press, 1996.

Perusse, Roland I. *Haitian Democracy Restored, 1991–1995.* Lanham, MD: University Press of America, 1995.

Rotberg, Robert I., ed. *Haiti Renewed: Political and Economic Prospects.* Washington, DC: Brookings Institution Press, 1997.

Stotzky, Irwin P. *Silencing Guns in Haiti: the Promise of Deliberative Democracy.* Chicago: University of Chicago Press, 1997.

Weinstein, Brian and Aaron Segal. *Haiti: the Failure of Politics.* New York: Praeger, 1992.

Zephir, Flore. *Haitian Immigrants in Black America: a Sociological and Sociolinguistic Portrait.* Westport, CT: Bergin & Garvey, 1996.

Honduras

Euraque, Dario A. *Region and State in Honduras, 1870–1972: Reinterpreting the "Banana Republic."* Chapel Hill, NC: University of North Carolina Press, 1996.

Merrill, Tim L. *Honduras: a Country Study.* Washington, DC: U.S. GPO, 3rd ed. 1995.

Meyer, Harvey Kessler and Jessie H. Meyer. *Historical Dictionary of Honduras.* Lanham, MD: Scarecrow Press, 2nd ed. 1994.

Jamaica

Butler, Kathleen Mary. *The Economics of Emancipation: Jamaica and Barbados, 1823–1843.* Chapel Hill, NC: University of North Carolina Press, 1995.

Davis. Nick. *Culture Smart: Jamaica.* Kuperard. 2011.

Gray, Obika. *Radicalism and Social Change in Jamaica, 1960–1972.* Knoxville, TN: University of Tennessee Press, 1991.

Heuman, Gad. *The Killing Time: the Morant Bay Rebellion in Jamaica.* Knoxville, TN: University of Tennessee Press, 1994.

Hewan, Clinton G. *Jamaica and the United States Caribbean Basin Initiative: Showpiece or Failure?* New York: Peter Lang Publishing, 1994.

Ingram, K.E. *Jamaica.* Santa Barbara, CA: ABC-CLIO, Inc., revised ed. 1997.

Keith, Nelson W. and Novella Z. Keith. *The Social Origins of Democratic Socialism in Jamaica.* Philadelphia, PA: Temple University Press, 1992.

Lundy, Patricia. *Debt and Adjustment: Social and Environmental Consequences in Jamaica.* Brookfield, VT: Ashgate, 1999.

Mordecai, Martin and Pamela Mordecai. *Culture and Customs of Jamaica.* Westport, CT: Greenwood Publishing Group, 2000.

Bibliography

Moser, Caroline and Jeremy Holland. *Urban Poverty and Violence in Jamaica.* Washington, DC: The World Bank, 1997.

Payne, Anthony J. *Politics in Jamaica.* New York: Saint Martin's Press, rev. ed. 1994.

Zips, Werner. Translated by Shelley L. Frisch. B*lack Rebels: African-Caribbean Freedom Fighters in Jamaica.* Princeton, NJ: Markus Wiener Publishers, 1999.

Mexico

Alonso, Ana Maria. *Thread of Blood: Colonialism, Revolution, and Gender on Mexico's Northern Frontier.* Tucson, AZ: University of Arizona Press, 1995.

Aspe, Pedro. *Economic Transformation in the Mexican Way.* Cambridge, MA: MIT Press, 1993.

Berg, Janine, Christoph Ernst and Peter Auer. *Meeting the Employment Challenge: Argentina, Brazil and Mexico in the Global Economy.* Boulder, CO: Lynne Rienner, 2006.

Bondi, Loretta. *Beyond the Border and Across the Atlantic. Mexico's Foreign and Security Policy Post-September 11.* Washington: Brookings, 2004.

Bosworth, Barry P., et al., eds. *Coming Together? Mexico-U.S. Relations.* Washington, DC: Brookings Institution Press, 1997.

Britton, John A. *Revolution and Ideology: Images of the Mexican Revolution and the United States.* Lexington, KY: University Press of Kentucky, 1995.

Brunk, Samuel. *Emiliano Zapata: Revolution and Betrayal in Mexico.* Albuquerque, NW: University of New Mexico Press, 1995.

Bulmer-Thomas, Victor, et al., eds. *Mexico and the North American Free Trade Agreement: Who Will Benefit?* New York: Saint Martin's Press, 1994.

Butler, Edgar. *Mexico and Mexico City in the World Economy.* Boulder, CO: Westview Press, 2000.

Camp, Roderic A., *Politics in Mexico: The Democratic Consolidation.* New York: Oxford University Press, 2006.

Castañeda, Jorge G. *The Mexican Shock: Its Meaning for the U.S.* New York: New Press, 1995.

Chand, Vikram K. *Mexico's Political Awakening.* Notre Dame, IN: University of Notre Dame Press, 2000.

Clough-Riquelme, Jane. *Equity and Sustainable Development: Reflections from the U.S.-Mexico Border.* Boulder, CO: Lynne Rienner, 2006.

Cope, R. Douglas. *The Limits of Racial Domination: Plebeian Society in Colonial Mexico City, 1660–1720.* Madison, WI: University of Wisconsin Press, 1994.

Corchado, Alfredo, *Midnight in Mexico: A Reporter's Journey Through a Country's Descent into Darkness.* New York: Penguin Press, 2013.

Cornelius, Wayne A., and Jessica M. Lewis, eds. *Impacts of Border Enforcement on Mexican Migration: The View from Sending Communities.* Boulder, CO: Lynne Rienner, 2007.

Crandall, Russell, et al, eds. *Mexico's Democracy at Work: Political and Economic Dynamics.* Boulder, CO: Lynne Rienner, 2004.

Davidow, Jeffrey. *The U.S. and Mexico: The Bear and the Porcupine.* Markus Weiner, 2004.

Davis, Diane E. *Urban Leviathan: Mexico City in the Twentieth Century.* Philadelphia, PA: Temple University Press, 1994.

Dominguez, Jorge I. and James A. McCann. *Democratizating Mexico: Public Opinion and Electoral Choices.* Baltimore, MD: Johns Hopkins University Press, 1996.

Dominguez, Jorge I. and Alejandro Poire, eds. *Toward Mexico's Democratization: Parties, Campaigns, Elections and Public Opinion.* New York: Routledge, 1999.

Edmonds-Poli, Emily and David A. Shirk. *Contemporary Mexican Politics.* Lanham, MD: Rowman Littlefield Publishers, 2011.

Eisenhower, John S.D. *Intervention! The United States and the Mexican Revolution, 1913–1917.* New York: W.W. Norton, 1993.

Erfani, Julie A. *The Paradox of the Mexican State: Rereading Sovereignty from Independence to NAFTA.* Boulder, CO: Lynne Rienner Publishers, 1995.

Fehrenbach, T.R. *Fire and Blood: a History of Mexico.* New York: Da Capo Press, 1995.

Foster, Lynn V. *A Brief History of Mexico.* New York: Facts on File, 1997.

Garber, Peter M., ed. *The Mexico-U.S. Free Trade Agreement.* Cambridge, MA: MIT Press, 1994.

Gledhill, John. *Neoliberalism, Transnationalism and Rural Poverty: a Case Study of Michoacan, Mexico.* Boulder, CO: Westview Press, 1995.

Grayson, George W. Oil and Mexican Foreign Policy. Pittsburgh: University of Pittsburgh Press, 1988.

Hamnett, Brian. *Juarez.* White Plains, NY: Longman Publishing, 1994.

Harvey, Neil, ed. *Mexico: Dilemmas of Transition.* London: British Academic Press, 1993.

Homedes, Núria, and Antonio Ugalde, eds. *Decentralizing Health Services in Mexico.* Boulder, CO: Lynne Rienner, 2006.

Johns, Christina Jacqueline. *The Origins of Violence in Mexican Society.* New York: Praeger, 1995.

Johnson, Stephen, *Mexico's 2012 Elections: From Uncertainty to a Pact for Progress.* Lanham, MD: Rowman and Littlefield, 2013.

Jones, Richard C. *Ambivalent Journey: U.S. Migration and Economic Mobility in North-Central Mexico.* Tucson, AZ: University of Arizona Press, 1995.

Katz, Friedrich. *The Life and Times of Pancho Villa.* Stanford, CA: Stanford University Press, 1998.

Krauze, Enrique. *Mexico-Biography of Power: a History of Modern Mexico, 1810–1996.* New York: HarperCollins Publishers, 1997.

Krooth, Richard. *Mexico, NAFTA and the Hardships of Progress: Historical Patterns and Shifting Methods of Oppression.* Jefferson, NC: McFarland & Company, 1995.

Markiewicz, Dana. *The Mexican Revolution and the Limits of Agrarian Reform, 1915–1946.* Boulder, CO: Lynne Rienner Publishers, 1993.

Merrell, Floyd. *The Mexicans. A Sense of Culture.* Boulder, Co: Westview, 2003.

Merrill, Tim L. and Ramon Miro, eds. *Mexico: a Country Study.* Washington, DC: U.S. GPO, 4th ed. 1997.

Meyer, Michael C., et al. *The Course of Mexican History.* New York: Oxford University Press, 1998.

Middlebrook, Keven J., ed. *Dilemmas of Political Change in Mexico.* Washington: Brookings, 2004.

Morris, Stephen D. *Political Corruption in Mexico: The Impact of Democratization.* Boulder, CO: Lynne Rienner Publishers, 2009.

Morton, Adam David, *Revolution and State in Modern Mexico: The Political Economy of Uneven Development.* Lanham, MD: Rowman and Littlefield, 2013.

Oppenheimer, Andres. *Bordering on Chaos: Guerrillas, Stockbrokers, Politicians and Mexico's Violent Struggle.* New York: Little, Brown, 1996.

Peters, Enrique Dussel. *Polarizing Mexico: the Impact of Liberalization Strategy.* Boulder, CO: Lynne Rienner Publishers, 2000.

Preson, Julia and Dillon, Samuel. *Opening Mexico: The Making of a Democracy.* New York: Farrar, Straus and Giroux, 2004.

Purcell, Susan K. and Luis Rubio, eds. *Mexico under Zedillo.* Boulder, CO: Lynne Rienner Publishers, 1998.

Rodriguez, Victoria E. and Peter M. Ward. *Opposition Government in Mexico.* Albuquerque, NM: University of New Mexico Press, 1995.

Roett, Riordan, ed. *Political and Economic Liberalization in Mexico: at a Critical Juncture?* Boulder, CO: Lynne Rienner Publishers, 1993.

Rubio, Luis and Purcell, Susan Kaufman, eds. *Mexico Under Fox.* Boulder, CO: Lynne Rienner, 2004.

Ruíz, Ramon E. *On the Rim of Mexico: Encounters of the Rich and Poor.* Boulder, CO: Westview Press, 1998.

Schulz, Donald E. and Edward J. Williams, eds. *Mexico Faces the 21st Century.* Westport, CT: Greenwood Publishing Group, 1995.

Sernau, Scott. *Economies of Exclusion: Underclass Poverty and Labor Market Change in Mexico.* New York: Praeger, 1994.

Shirk, David A. *Mexico's New Politics: The PAN and Democratic Change.* Boulder, CO: Lynne Rienner, 2004.

Staudt, Kathleen A. *Free Trade? Informal Economies at the U.S.-Mexican Border.* Philadelphia, PA: Temple University Press, 1998.

Thomas, Hugh. *Conquest: Montezuma, Cortes, and the Fall of Old Mexico.* New York: Simon & Schuster, 1994.

Tulchin, Joseph S. and Andrew D. Selee, eds. *Mexico's Politics and Society in Transition.* Boulder, CO: Lynne Rienner, 2002.

Wise, Carol. *The Post-NAFTA Political Economy: Mexico and the Western Hemisphere.* University Park, PA: Pennsylvania State University Press, 1998.

Womack, John Jr. *Rebellion in Chiapas: an Historical Reader.* New York: New Press, 1999.

Netherlands Antilles

Brown, Enid. *Suriname and the Netherlands Antilles: an Annotated English-Language Bibliography.* Lanham, MD: Scarecrow Press, 1992.

Sedoc-Dahlberg, Betty, ed. *The Dutch Caribbean: Prospects for Democracy.* New York: Gordon and Breach, 1990.

Nicaragua

BiondiMorra, Brizio N. *Hungry Dream: the Failure of Food Policy in Revolutionary Nicaragua, 1979–1990.* Ithaca, NY: Cornell University Press, 1993.

Gambone, Michael D. *Eisenhower, Somoza and the Cold War in Nicaragua, 1953–1961.* Westport, CT: Greenwood Publishing Group, 1997.

Hale, Charles R. *Resistance and Contradiction: Miskitu Indians and the Nicaraguan State, 1894–1987.* Stanford, CA: Stanford University Press, 1994.

Kagan, Robert. *A Twilight Struggle: American Power and Nicaragua, 1977–1990.* New York: Free Press, 1996.

Luciak, Ilja A. *The Sandinista Legacy: Lessons from a Political Economy in Transition.* Gainesville, FL: University Press of Florida, 1995.

Merrill, Tim L., ed. *Nicaragua: a Country Study.* Washington, DC: U.S. GPO, 3rd ed. 1994.

Miranda, Roger and William Ratliff. *The Civil War in Nicaragua: Inside the Sandinistas.* New Brunswick, NJ: Transaction, 1993.

Prevost, Gary. *The Undermining of the Sandinista Revolution.* New York: Saint Martin's Press, 1997.

Randall, Margaret. *Sandino's Daughters: Feminism in Nicaragua.* New Brunswick, NJ: Rutgers University Press, 1994.

Ryan, David. *US-Sandinista Diplomatic Relations: Voice of Intolerance.* New York: Saint Martin's Press, 1995.

Sabia, Debra. *Contradiction and Conflict: the Popular Church in Nicaragua.* Tuscaloosa, AL: University of Alabama Press, 1997.

Spalding, Rose J. *Capitalists and Revolution in Nicaragua: Opposition and Accommodation, 1979–1993.* Chapel Hill, NC: University of North Carolina Press, 1994.

Vanden, Harry E. and Garry Prevost. *Democracy and Socialism in Sandinista Nicaragua.* Boulder, CO: Lynne Rienner Publishers, 1993.

Walker, Thomas W. *Nicaragua. Living in the Shadow of the Eagle.* Boulder, Co: Westview, 2003.

Walker, Thomas W., ed. *Nicaragua without Illusions: Regime Transition and Structural Adjustment in the 1990s.* Wilmington, DE: Scholarly Resources, 1997.

Walter, Knut. *The Regime of Anastasio Somoza, 1936–1956.* Chapel Hill, NC: University of North Carolina Press, 1993.

Whisnant, David E. *Rascally Signs in Sacred Places: the Politics of Culture in Nicaragua.* Chapel Hill, NC: University of North Carolina Press, 1995.

Panama

Conniff, Michael L. *Panama and the United States: the Forced Alliance.* Athens, GA: University of Georgia Press, 1992.

Donnelly, Thomas, et al. *Operation Just Cause: the Storming of Panama.* New York: Lexington Books, 1991.

Guevara Mann, Carlos. *Panamanian Militarism: a Historical Perspective.* Athens, OH: Ohio University Press, 1996.

Johns, Christina Jacqueline and P. Ward Johnson. *State Crime, the Media, and the Invasion of Panama.* New York: Praeger, 1994.

Leonard, Thomas M. *Panama, the Canal and the United States: a Guide to Issues and References.* Claremont, CA: Regina Books, 1993.

Major, John. *Prize Possession: the United States and the Panama Canal, 1903–1979.* New York: Cambridge University Press, 1993.

Meditz, Sandra W. and Dennis M. Hanratty, eds. *Panama: a Country Study.* Washington, DC: U.S. GPO, 4th ed. 1989.

Noriega, Manuel and Peter Eisner. *America's Prisoner: the Memoirs of Manuel Noriega.* New York: Random House, 1997.

Pearcy, Thomas L. *We Answer Only to God: Politics and the Military in Panama, 1903–1947.* Albuquerque, NM: University of New Mexico Press, 1998.

Perez, Orlando J., ed. *Post-Invasion Panama: the Challenges of Democratization in the New World Order.* Lanham, MD: Lexington Books, 2000.

Ward, Christopher. *Imperial Panama: Commerce and Conflict in Isthmian America, 1550–1800.* Albuquerque, NM: University of New Mexico, 1993.

Paraguay

Gimlette, John, *At the Tomb of the Inflatable Pig: Travels Through Paraguay.* New York: Alfred A. Knopf, 2003.

Hanratty, Dennis and Sandra W. Meditz, eds. *Paraguay: a Country Study.* Washington, DC: U.S. GPO, 2nd ed. 1990.

Kracy, Hendrick, and Thomas Whigham, eds., *I Die With My Country: Perspectives on the Paraguayan War, 1864–70.* Lincoln: University of Nebraska Press, 2004.

Lambert, Peter and Andrew Nickson, eds. *Transition to Democracy in Paraguay.* New York: Saint Martin's Press, 1997.

Leis, Paul H. *Political Parties and Generations in Paraguay's Liberal Era, 1869–1940.* Chapel Hill, NC: University of North Carolina Press, 1993.

Miranda, Carlos R. *The Stroessner Era: Authoritarian Rule in Paraguay.* Boulder, CO: Westview Press, 1990.

Mora, Frank O. and Jerry W. Cooney. *Paraguay and the United States: Distant Allies.* Athens: The University of Georgia Press, 2007.

Nickson, R. Andrew. *Historical Dictionary of Paraguay.* Lanham, MD: Scarecrow Press, 2nd ed. 1993.

O'Shaughnessy, Hugh, and Edgar Venerando Ruíz Díaz, *The Priest of Paraguay: Fernando Lugo and the Making of a Nation.* London: Zed Books, 2009.

Whigham, Thomas, *The Paraguayan War (Vol. 1)—Causes and Early Conduct.* Lincoln: University of Nebraska Press, 2002.

Peru

Cameron, Maxwell, A. *Democracy and Authoritarianism in Peru: Political Coalitions and Social Change.* New York: Saint Martin's Press, 1994.

Clayton, Lawrence A. *Peru and the United States: the Condor and the Eagle.* Athens, GA: University of Georgia Press, 1999.

Gootenberg, Paul. *Imagining Development: Economic Ideas in Peru's "Fictitious Prosperity" of Guano, 1840–1880.* Berkeley, CA: University of California Press, 1993.

Gorriti, Gustavo. *The Shining Path: a History of the Millenarian War in Peru.* Chapel Hill, NC: University of North Carolina Press, 1999.

Bibliography

Hudson, Rex A., ed. *Peru: a Country Study*. Washington, DC: U.S. GPO, 1993.

Jacobsen, Nils. *Mirages of Transition: the Peruvian Altiplano, 1780–1930*. Berkeley, CA: University of California Press, 1993.

Kirk, Robin. *The Monkey's Paw, New Chronicles From Peru*. Amherst: University of Massachusetts Press, 1997.

Klaren, Peter Flindell. *Peru: Society and Nationhood in the Andes*. New York: Oxford University Press, 2000.

Lockhart, James. *Spanish Peru, 1532–1560: a Social History*. Madison, WI: University of Wisconsin Press, 1994.

Masterson, Daniel M. *Militarism and Politics in Latin America: Peru from Sanchez Cerro to Sendero Luminoso*. Westport, CT: Greenwood Publishing Publishing, 1991.

Palmer, David Scott, ed. *The Shining Path of Peru*. New York: Saint Martin's Press, 1992.

Peña, Milagros. *Theologies and Liberation in Peru: the Role of Ideas in Social Movement*. Philadelphia, PA: Temple University Press, 1995.

Quiroz, Alfonso W. *Domestic and Foreign Finance in Modern Peru, 1850–1950: Financing Visions of Development*. Pittsburgh, PA: University of Pittsburgh Press, 1993.

Roberts, Kenneth M. *Deepening Democracy? The Modern Left and Social Movements in Chile and Peru*. Stanford, CA: Stanford University Press, 1999.

Seligmann, Linda J. *Between Reform and Revolution: Political Struggles in the Peruvian Andes, 1969–1991*. Stanford, CA: Stanford University Press, 1995.

Sheahan, John. *Searching for a Better Society: the Peruvian Economy from 1950*. University Park, PA: Pennsylvania State University Press, 1999.

Starn, Orin, Carlos Ivan Degregori, and Robin Kirk, eds. *The Peru Reader: History, Culture, Politics*. Durham: Duke University Press, 1995.

Stern, Steve J. *Peru's Indian Peoples and the Challenge of Spanish Conquest: Huamanga to 1640*. Madison, WI: University of Wisconsin Press, 2nd ed. 1993.

Stern, Steve J., ed., *Shining And Other Paths*. Durham: Duke University Press, 1998.

Tarazona-Sevillano, Gabriela. *Sendero Luminoso and the Threat of Narcoterrorism*. New York: Praeger, 1990.

Tulchin, Joseph S. and Gary Bland, eds. *Peru in Crisis: Dictatorship or Democracy?* Boulder, CO: Lynne Rienner Publishers, 1994.

Watters, R.F. *Poverty and Peasantry in Peru's Southern Andes, 1963–90*. Pittsburgh, PA: University of Pittsburgh Press, 1994.

Puerto Rico

Acosta-Belén, Edna, and Carlos E. Santiago. *Puerto Ricans in the United States: A Contemporary Portrait*. Boulder, CO: Lynne Rienner, 2006.

Dietz, James L. *Puerto Rico: Negotiating Development and Change*. Boulder, CO: Lynne Rienner, 2003.

Suriname

Brown, Enid. *Suriname and the Netherlands Antilles: an Annotated English-Language Bibliography*. Lanham, MD: Scarecrow Press, 1992.

Dew, Edward M. *The Trouble in Suriname, 1975–1993*. New York: Praeger, 1994.

Hoefte, Rosemarijn. *In Place of Slavery: a Social History of British Indian and Javanese Laborers in Suriname*. Gainesville, FL: University Press of Florida, 1998.

Hoefte, Rosemarijn. *Suriname*. Santa Barbara, CA: ABC-CLIO, 1991.

Trinidad and Tobago

Anthony, Michael. *Historical Dictionary of Trinidad and Tobago*. Lanham, MD: Scarecrow Press, 1997.

Ewbank, Tim. *Culture Smart: Trinidad and Tobago*. Kuperard. 2011.

Regis, Louis. *The Political Calypso: True Opposition in Trinidad and Tobago, 1962–1987*. Gainesville, FL: University Press of Florida, 1998.

Yelvington, Kelvin A. *Trinidad Ethnicity*. Knoxville, TN: University of Tennessee Press, 1993.

Uruguay

Gillespie, Charles Guy. *Negotiating Democracy: Politicians and Generals in Uruguay*. New York: Cambridge University Press, 1991.

Gonzalez, Luis E. *Political Structures and Democracy in Uruguay*. Notre Dame, IN: University of Notre Dame Press, 1991.

Hudson, Rex A. and Sandra W. Meditz, eds. *Uruguay: a Country Study*. Washington, DC: U.S. GPO, 2nd ed. 1992.

Preeg, Ernest H. *From Here to Free Trade: Essays in Post-Uruguay Round Trade Strategy*. Chicago: University of Chicago Press, 1998.

Rottenberg, Simon, ed. *Costa Rica and Uruguay*. New York: Oxford University Press, 1993.

Sosnowski, Saul. *Repression, Exile, and Democracy: Uruguayan Culture*. Durham, NC: Duke University Press, 1992.

Venezuela

Canache, Damarys J. and Michael R. Kulisheck, eds. *Reinventing Legitimacy: Democracy and Political Change in Venezuela*. Westport, CT: Greenwood Publishing Group, 1998.

Coppedge, Michael. *Strong Parties and Lame Ducks: Presidential Partyarchy and Factionalism in Venezuela*. Stanford, CA: Stanford University Press, 1994.

Coronil, Fernando. *Magical State: Nature, Money and Modernity in Venezuela*. Chicago: University of Chicago Press, 1997.

Corrales, Javier and Michael Penfold. *Dragon In The Tropics: Hugo Chavez and the Political Economy of Revolution in Venezuela*. Washington: Brookings Institution Press, 2011.

Ellner, Steve and Hellinger, Daniel, eds. *Venezuelan Politics in the Chávez Era: Class, Polarization, and Conflict*. Boulder, CO: Lynne Rienner, 2004.

Ellner, Steve and Miguel Tinker Salas, eds. *Venezuela: Hugo Chávez and the Decline of an "Exceptional Democracy."* Rowman & Littlefield Publishers, Inc: Lanham. 2007.

Ellner, Steve. *Rethinking Venezuelan Politics: Class, Conflict and the Chavez Phenomenon*. Boulder, CO: Lynne Reinner Publishers, 2008.

Enright, Michael J., et al. *Venezuela: the Challenge of Competitiveness*. New York: Saint Martin's Press, 1996.

Golinger, Eva. *The Chavez Code: Cracking U.S. Intervention in Venezuela*. Northampton, MA: Olive Branch Press, 2006.

Goodman, Louis W., et al., eds. *Lessons of the Venezuelan Experience*. Baltimore, MD: Johns Hopkins University Press, 1995.

Gott, Richard. *In The Shadow of the Liberator: Hugo Chávez and the Transformation of Venezuela*. Verso Press: London, 2000.

Gott, Richard. *Hugo Chavez and the Bolivarian Revolution*. London/New York: Verso, 2005

Haggerty, Richard A. *Venezuela: a Country Study*. Washington, DC: U.S. GPO, 4th ed. 1993.

Hillman, Richard S. *Democracy for the Privileged: Crisis and Transition in Venezuela*. Boulder, CO: Lynne Rienner, 1994.

Jones, Bart. *Hugo: The Hugo Chavez Story, From Mud Hut to Perpetual Revolution*. Hanovger, NH: Steerforth Press, 2007.

Kozloff, Nikolas. *Hugo Chavez: Oil, Politics, and the Challenge to the U.S.* New York: Palgrave MacMillan, 2006.

Nelson, Brian A. *The Silence and the Scorpion: The Coup Against Chavez and the Making of Modern Venezuela*. New York: Nation Books, 2009.

Rudolph, Donna K. and G.A. Rudolph. *Historical Dictionary of Venezuela*. Lanham, MD: Scarecrow Press, 1996.

Schoen, Douglas, and Michael Rowan. *The Threat Closer to Home: Hugo Chávez and the War Against America*. Free Press, 2009.

Wilpert, Gregory. *Changing Venezuela By Taking Power: The History and Policies of the Chavez Government*. London/New York: Verso, 2007.

THE Basics OF
Communication
2
EDITION

THE Basics OF
Communication
A Relational Perspective

2
EDITION

Steve Duck
David T. McMahan

Los Angeles | London | New Delhi
Singapore | Washington DC

For information:

 SAGE Publications, Inc.
2455 Teller Road
Thousand Oaks, California 91320
E-mail: order@sagepub.com

SAGE Publications Ltd.
1 Oliver's Yard
55 City Road
London EC1Y 1SP
United Kingdom

SAGE Publications India Pvt. Ltd.
B 1/I 1 Mohan Cooperative Industrial Area
Mathura Road, New Delhi 110 044
India

SAGE Publications Asia-Pacific Pte. Ltd.
33 Pekin Street #02–01
Far East Square
Singapore 048763

Printed in Canada

Library of Congress Cataloging-in-Publication Data

Duck, Steve.
The basics of communication : a relational perspective/Steve Duck, David T. McMahan. — 2nd ed.
    p. cm.
Includes bibliographical references and index.
ISBN 978-1-4129-8109-5 (pbk. : acid-free paper)
    1. Communication. I. McMahan, David T. II. Title.

P90.D833 2012
302.2—dc22   2010048516

This book is printed on acid-free paper.

10   11   12   13   14   10   9   8   7   6   5   4   3   2   1

Executive Editor:	Diane McDaniel
Acquisitions Editor:	Todd Armstrong
Associate Editor:	Aja Baker
Editorial Assistant:	Nathan Davidson
Production Editor:	Eric Garner
Copy Editor:	Melinda Masson
Typesetter:	C&M Digitals (P) Ltd.
Proofreader:	Wendy Jo Dymond
Indexer:	Sheila Bodell
Cover Designer:	Bryan Fishman
Marketing Manager:	Helen Salmon
Permissions Editor:	Karen Ehrmann

Brief Contents

Detailed Contents

CHAPTER 3 ■ Nonverbal Communication

CHAPTER 4 ■ Listening   77

CHAPTER 5 ■ Identities and Perceptions   101

CHAPTER 6 ■ Talk and Interpersonal Relationships   **133**

CHAPTER 7 ■ Groups and Leaders 161

CHAPTER 8 ▪ Culture and Communication   189

CHAPTER 9 ■ Technology in Everyday Life   213

CHAPTER 10 ■ Relational Uses and Understanding of Media   239

CHAPTER 11 ■ Preparing for a Public Presentation   265

CHAPTER 12 ■ Developing a Public Presentation   **293**

Chapter 15 ■ Interviewing   367

Preface

*T*he Basics of Communication: A Relational Perspective was developed with the belief that basic communication courses play a central role in the discipline by attracting new majors, providing a foundation for upper-level courses, and supporting the entire academic community as important general education requirements and preparations for future life. The basic course is not just about training students in a discipline; it is about educating them more broadly for life beyond college and instilling within them an inquisitive curiosity that will serve them throughout their lives. It is one of the most important courses a student of any discipline will take.

Accordingly, we did not want to present students and the discipline with a cookie-cutter book that looked much like every other basic course textbook published in the past few decades—even though many publishers with whom we spoke encouraged us to do just that! Rather, if we were to develop a new textbook, it had to bring something fresh and meaningful to the study of communication. We believed that our relational perspective would provide students with a coherent structure to their study of communication and an opportunity to apply the material to their everyday personal and professional lives. We also believed that while some traditional material such as verbal communication, nonverbal communication, and listening should be included in any basic course, other material such as relational technology, social media, and culture was conspicuously absent from other books in spite of being an integral part of students' lives. We believed that pedagogical tools such as boxes and photos should be focused on learning. Finally, we believed that ancillary materials should be developed that would benefit students, new instructors, and experienced instructors alike.

In order to substantiate, challenge, and build upon these beliefs, we engaged in extensive discussions with our fellow basic course instructors and directors as well as students throughout the United States and other countries. We wanted to know what they needed in a basic course textbook, what worked and did not work with previous textbooks, and what innovations must be included. Primarily due to their input and encouragement during all facets of its development and production, the first edition of *The Basics of Communication* was met with an overwhelmingly positive response. These discussions continued once the first edition was published, and remained fundamental in the development and production of this edition.

New to This Edition

This second edition enabled us to advance the components that worked well in the first edition and to include additional features and modifications to enhance its use in communication classrooms. In general, we have streamlined much of the text in order to increase its readability for students. Forty-two tables have also been included to help students synthesize the material. Margin notes proved very popular with both instructors and students. Consequently, their numbers have been increased in this edition. The same holds true for the photographs included throughout the book, which also serve as learning tools for students. Most of the original photographs have been replaced, and many additional photographs have been included. Three new pedagogical boxes (Contrarian Challenge, Case in Point, and College Experience) have been included in each chapter. In response to reviewer and student comments, the coverage of some material has been rearranged, removed, increased, or added. Specific examples include an increased focus on perception when dealing with the development of identities and an entirely new chapter on interviewing. The latest research and findings have been incorporated throughout each of the chapters, as have updated discussions and examples.

We are thankful for the success of the first edition and are excited about the potential impact of the second edition. In what follows, we discuss the relational perspective, outline the pedagogical features of the book, and provide a final note about instructor support.

A Relational Perspective

This book allows all of these topics to cohere and coalesce by pointing out the *relational* basis of all communication as a major feature of students' everyday lives. By "relational basis" we mean the influences created by and upon relationships during the course of activities *other than* relational development, management, and intimacy creation—for example, the effects of a personal relationship on one's ability to persuade a person with health advice. In short, we deal not only with the creation of relationships but also with the way relationships flow into many other daily experiences. We then apply this perspective to basic issues in communication.

The Intersection of Communication and Relationships

The key feature of this text, then, is the idea that relationships make, are present in, modify, and create all communication. Our coverage of relationships is not as containers created by emotions; instead, we stress the importance and implications of the fact that they are perpetually *managed and enacted* daily experiences. In short, we emphasize the vital intersection of communication with relational contexts. We believe that this point provides both insight and coherence with reference to the topics normally covered in a basic text and simultaneously integrates such material with the increasingly popular and important, but previously independent, research on relationship communication, which is gradually refining or even replacing the traditional concept of "interpersonal communication." All of our coverage of traditional topics is extended and developed from this point of view.

The Social Context of Everyday Experience

The relational approach makes the importance and operation of communication more understandable through direct connections to student experience and therefore will facilitate classroom discussion while channeling and capitalizing on students' natural interests. We use this idea to illuminate the daily lives of students, and we offer the pedagogical purpose of showing how the students' experiences can be clarified through the principles of communication theory. Our goal is to help students understand their own daily lives by increasing the analytic awareness of their experiences and to show how communication theory and research can illuminate them. We further emphasize the social context of everyday experience, not only at the level of dyadic relationships and membership in networks but also by noting that people's interactions with one another create the location of society's influence on the individual: Social partners are the human face of such abstract notions as "society" and "culture." Our relational approach helps pedagogically by showing how much of life's experience (even of "society at large") is in fact perceived through direct social connections with other people. Only through our direct experience with others who represent "culture" and "society" do we feel these abstractions' influence at all.

A Way of Understanding the World

Given the variety of their educational backgrounds, demographic characteristics, and experiences, all students share the fact that their understanding of the world has been formed and influenced by relationships. Therefore, we focus not on the traditional approaches based on intimacy development but instead on the ways relationships create epistemics and rhetorical visions—that is, ways of understanding and (re)presenting the world—and we interweave this claim into traditional topics in interpersonal communication and media to show how much of life's apparently personal experience is in fact processed through social connections. By adopting an overall coherence of approach, it is possible to prevent segmentation of topics by use of the guiding overarching theme and hence to tie together several previously—but to us always artificially—separate aspects of communication, which will help communication majors develop further as their courses proceed and allow them to see connections between presently disparate areas of communication study. This basic hybrid text will therefore lay the groundwork for a lifetime of learning, as well as present a strong overview of communication for those whose only exposure to the work of communication scholars will be this book. In this way, we hope to make the book relevant to business majors, to those in training for the health professions, and to many other students with an interest in communication studies.

Pedagogical Features

We view the pedagogical features within textbooks as fundamental elements in the comprehension and incorporation of the material being presented. Unfortunately, chapter boxes and other pedagogical elements, often sidebar features, are frankly overlooked by students and instructors alike. Accordingly, we have included pedagogical features with a fundamentally integrative and summational force, which will give students an immediate and visible structure for what they study in the text. These pedagogical tools are located throughout, as well as at the end of, each chapter.

Overview

To help guide the students, each chapter begins with a pedagogical overview: "These are the key things you need to know about this topic. Now let's look at them in more detail and go on to extrapolate and develop the complexities." Focus Questions are then posed to further direct students through the chapter. These questions are positioned *after* an opening narrative rather than at the very beginning to increase the likelihood that students will use them.

Chapter Boxes

The main body of the chapters includes the following pedagogical boxes: (1) Make Your Case, (2) Strategic Communication, (3) Listen In On Your Life, (4) Contrarian Challenge, (5) Case in Point, and (6) College Experience. Make Your Case boxes provide students with opportunities to develop their own positions or to perform an exercise about the material, which then can be used as a basis for class discussion. Within the nonverbal communication chapter, for example, students are asked to consider a situation where they felt uncomfortable in the presence of another person. Strategic Communication boxes present students with guides to integrate the material into their lives when influencing others. For instance, the technology chapter asks students to consider how the purpose of their messages and the technological preferences of the person they are contacting will determine the appropriateness of face-to-face, telephone, or computer-mediated interaction. Listen in on Your Life boxes ask students to consider the material in relation to their lives and lived experiences. Specifically, this feature will sensitize students to issues and encourage them to become careful observers of the activities and events going on in their lives, compelling them to examine and apply the material. For example, the listening chapter asks students to consider friends, family, classmates, or coworkers they would label as *good* and *bad* listeners. Students are then asked to consider what behaviors led them to these evaluations and then to determine measures to enhance others' listening skills. Contrarian Challenge boxes encourage critical thinking by asking students to consider positions that counter or contest those presented in the text or commonly held in society. For instance, in the "delivering a public presentation" chapter, we encourage students to use manuscript delivery only when careful wording is required and maintain that novice speakers, especially, should avoid this delivery style. However, we ask students to develop an argument for why novice speakers would benefit from manuscript delivery. Though students may agree with what is presented in many instances, we want to encourage the critical examination of all material discussed in the book. Case in Point boxes encourage students to apply what they have learned in the analysis of everyday life situations. For instance, the culture chapter asks them to find a public space where members of a unique cultural group are gathered and observe the ways they communicate. Finally, College Experience boxes encourage students to apply the material discussed to better understand and perhaps manage situations encountered in academic contexts. A major factor in the retention of students is their development of relationships with classmates, instructors, advisors, and others on campus. These boxes have been developed to help students evaluate and handle academic life and relationships. Chapter 1, for example, asks students to consider how academic-based relationships such as those between instructors and students frame interactions, influencing what is said and how communication is interpreted.

Margin Notes

Margin notes are also included in each chapter to provide students with additional information or open-ended questions to ponder as they study the material. Accordingly, some margin notes serve to enhance student interest in the material by providing unique information, such as who invented the Internet. Other margin notes urge students to reflect upon the material by posing such questions as whether families would be considered groups.

Photographs

Photographs included in each chapter also serve as pedagogical tools. Each photo caption is stated in the form of a question that corresponds with material being discussed. Students will be asked to examine the photograph and answer the accompanying question based on their understanding of the material. Rather than being open-ended, these questions have specific answers that appear at the end of each chapter.

End-of-Chapter Pedagogical Materials

Each chapter also ends with pedagogical materials that bring the overview and focus questions full-circle. Focus Questions Revisited is implemented as a way of summarizing chapter material via pedagogical structure rather than as a simple (and usually ignored) chapter summary. Also, instead of including review questions, which often serve only to establish lower levels of comprehension, each chapter includes (a) Ethical Issues, (b) Media Links, and (c) Questions to Ask Your Friends. These features enable students to further examine how the chapter material fits within their communicative lives as a whole. Ethical Issues urge students to contemplate and develop a position regarding ethical quandaries that arise in communication. For example, the technology chapter asks students to consider whether employers should use material on social networking sites, such as Facebook or Twitter, when making hiring decisions. Media Links lead students to draw from media in order to further explore the issues discussed in each chapter. For example, the relationships chapter instructs students to examine the Sunday newspaper section of marriages, engagements, and commitment ceremonies for similarities in attractiveness. Finally, Questions to Ask Your Friends provide students with questions to ask their friends in order to further increase their awareness of the material and integrate it into their lives. In the culture chapter, for example, students are urged to ask their friends about themes in their favorite children's stories and to connect those themes to cultural ideals and norms.

Conversational Tone

To further assist student learning, we have adopted an informal tone in our writing. This is intended primarily to invite students into the conversation about the issues that we present as basics of communication. We also want to engage their capacities to reflect about a problem and work through it with us, leaving them with a greater sense of having mastered the material. We continually refer to everyday issues that students may have encountered or heard about from others, and we challenge them from time to time to reflect on and apply to their own lives what they have been reading about here.

Instructor Support

Although a fundamental feature of the book is, of course, to update discussion of topics by integrating the latest research while providing a new relationally based perspective on the material normally included in traditional texts, this is a two-edged sword. A challenge associated with developing a new textbook—especially one offering an original approach and addressing more up-to-date issues of communication—is that many instructors already have their courses in good shape and do not need the extra burden of rewriting those courses to fit a completely new text. We have therefore sought to add material in a way that supplements and develops rather than replaces traditional material. By this means, we seek to support those teachers who have developed courses on the basis of older material and who want to add some spice from the newer research without having to completely revise their existing lectures and notes. Thus, although the present text updates much of the theory and research included in older-style texts, we have constructed this book to reflect the traditional, basic text design. A host of ancillary materials are also available that would benefit both new and experienced instructors of the basic course.

In sum, we see the advantages of this book as fourfold:

1. It presents a coherent reformulation of communication around the theme of relational and everyday experience.

2. It recognizes transformations within the discipline of communication and covers material increasingly relevant to students' lives.

3. It has strong self-reflective pedagogical features applied to students' own personal experiences and is thus different from many older texts.

4. It can be readily adopted without major restructuring of existing courses because it adds, we think, a more interesting approach to existing topics rather than entirely redrawing the map.

See if you agree.

***

The Basics of Communication: A Relational Perspective (Second Edition) is accompanied by the following supplements, tailored to match the content of the book.

Ancillaries

Student Study Site

www.sagepub.com/boc2e

An open-access student study site provides a variety of additional resources to build on students' understanding of the book content and extend their learning beyond the classroom. The following resources are featured for each chapter:

- **Self quizzes** with multiple-choice and true/false questions for every chapter allow students to independently assess their progress in learning course material.
- **E-Flashcards** reinforce student understanding and learning of key terms and concepts that are outlined in the book.
- **Web resources** to various sites on the web for further research related to the chapter topic.
- A "**Learning From SAGE Journal Articles**" feature provides access to recent, relevant full-text articles from SAGE's leading research journals. Each article supports and expands on the concepts presented in the chapter. Discussion questions are also provided to focus and guide student interpretation.
- Carefully selected, web-based **video** and **audio link** resources feature relevant content for use in independent and classroom-based exploration of key topics.
- **Web exercises** direct students to various sites on the web and ask them to apply their knowledge to a particular topic.

Instructor Teaching Site

www.sagepub.com/boc2e

A password-protected instructor teaching site provides one integrated source for all instructor materials, including the following key components for each chapter:

- An updated **electronic test bank**, available to PCs and Macs through Diploma software, offers a diverse set of test questions and answers to aid instructors in assessing students' progress and understanding. The software allows for test creation and customization and each chapter includes multiple choice, true/false, and essay questions. The test bank is also available in Microsoft Word.
- **PowerPoint presentations** designed to assist with lecture and review, highlighting essential content, features, and artwork from the book.
- **Chapter outlines** and **key terms** have been provided for each chapter that can be used to structure daily lesson plans.
- **Classroom activities**, **discussion questions** and **course projects** are provided to reinforce active learning.
- **Web resources** to various sites on the web for further research related to the chapter topic.
- Carefully selected, web-based **video** and **audio link** resources feature relevant content for use in independent and classroom-based exploration of key topics.
- **Sample syllabi** provide suggested models for creating the syllabus for your course.
- **Speech evaluation** and **format guidelines** assist in grading student speeches and provide the "how to" of putting a speech together.

Acknowledgments

A book such as this is a far larger undertaking than we realized when proposing the first edition. Although our two names appear on the front cover of both editions, many other people have contributed to their development. Chief among these and to whom we owe the largest debt is our editor, the inestimable Todd Armstrong. Working with Todd has been a genuine pleasure, and this project benefited enormously from his experience and wise guidance. Like many authors, we signed with SAGE specifically because of Todd's professionalism, enthusiasm, keen intellect, and appreciation for both the discipline and the written word. His pioneering vision and commitment to knowledge further position him without equal among those in the publishing industry. Plus, he has great taste in ties.

We are grateful to those colleagues and friends who took the time to read drafts and redrafts of manuscripts at all stages of development—from initial outlines to re-revised "final" versions—for their wisdom and suggestions. We would also like to thank our students, both graduate and undergraduate, who knowingly or unknowingly provided observations, examples, and thoughtful discussion of the ideas presented here.

We are also thankful to the instructors and students who used the first edition of the book for allowing us into their classrooms. Many of them enabled us to live out the relational perspective through personal contact by phone and e-mail and through visits on campuses and at conferences. Their feedback and encouragement are greatly appreciated and have enhanced this second edition in immeasurable ways.

Involvement in books such as this takes an enormous toll on family life. We are grateful to our respective spouses and families that we have managed to complete another project and still remain married. Their forbearance provides a supportive atmosphere for us to manage the long hours and extended absences required to bring such projects to completion.

Finally, we would like to thank all of our parents, siblings, nieces and nephews, extended families, friends outside academics, acquaintances, strangers we have encountered, people we like, people we do not like, detested colleagues, and despised enemies, all of whom have provided us with ideas for a relational perspective on communication and an awareness of the importance of everyday life relating.

We are also indebted to the following for their unstinting generosity in commenting on the textbook in spite of their incredibly busy schedules and for making many brilliant suggestions that we were all too happy to borrow or appropriate without acknowledgement other than here. They generously contributed to whatever this book in its turn contributes to the growth and development of the field. We could not have developed the relational perspective without their professionalism and thoughtfulness.

Matt Abrahams
De Anza College

Brent E. Adrian
Central Community College–Grand Island

Allison Ainsworth
Gainesville State College

Elizabeth R. Alcock
Bristol Community College

Carlos Alemán
James Madison University

Melissa W. Alemán
James Madison University

Alicia Alexander
Southern Illinois University–Edwardsville

Karen Anderson
University of North Texas

Alice Araujo
Mary Baldwin College

Christine Armstrong
Northampton Community College

Kevin Backstrom
University of Wisconsin–Oshkosh

Bryan H. Barrows III
Lone Star College–North Harris

Douglas Battema
Western New England College

Sally Bennett Bell
University of Montevallo

Keith Berry
University of Wisconsin–Superior

Robert Betts
Rock Valley College

Robert Bodle
College of Mount St. Joseph

David M. Bollinger
University of North Carolina–Wilmington

Deborah Borisoff
New York University

Jay Bower
Southern Illinois University–Carbondale

Kathy Brady
University of Wisconsin–Whitewater

Michele Bresso
Bakersfield College

Paulette Brinka
Suffolk County Community College

Pamela Brooks
Arizona State University Polytechnic

Stefne Lenzmeier Broz
Wittenberg University

Nancy J. Brule
Bethel University

Dale Burke
Hawai'i Pacific University

Linda Cardillo
College of Mount St. Joseph

Sheena M. Carey
Marquette University

Anna Carmon
North Dakota State University

Laura Cashmer
Joliet Junior College

Mindy Chang
Western New England College

Yvonne Yanrong Chang
University of Texas–Pan American

April Chatham-Carpenter
University of Northern Iowa

Denise M. Chaytor
East Stroudsburg University

John Chetro-Szivos
Fitchburg State College

Daniel Chornet-Roses
Saint Louis University–Madrid

Carolyn Clark
Salt Lake Community College

Brian Cogan
Molloy College

Sarah Cole
Framingham State College

Janet W. Colvin
Utah Valley University

Anna Conway
Des Moines Area Community College

Erica Cooper
Roanoke College

Gil Cooper
Pittsburg State University

Lisa Coutu
University of Washington

Miki Crawford
Ohio University Southern Campus

Alice L. Crume
Kent State University–Tuscarawas

Kevin Cummings
Mercer University

Kimberly M. Cuny
University of North Carolina–Greensboro

David D'Angelo
Kent State University–Tuscarawas

Roberta A. Davilla
Western Illinois University

Quinton D. Davis
University of Texas–San Antonio

Jean Dewitt
University of Houston–Downtown

Linda B. Dickmeyer
University of Wisconsin–LaCrosse

Aaron Dimock
University of Nebraska–Kearney

Marcia D. Dixson
Indiana-Purdue University–Fort Wayne

Shirley K. Drew
Pittsburg State University

Michele Rees Edwards
Robert Morris University

Michael Elkins
Indiana State University

Larry A. Erbert
University of Colorado–Denver

Suzanne Stangl-Erkens
St. Cloud State University

Billie Evans
Graceland University

Lisa Falvey
Emmanuel College

Jeanine Fassl
University of Wisconsin–Whitewater

Sarah Bonewits Feldner
Marquette University

Diane Ferrero-Paluzzi
Iona College

Jerry E. Fliger
Toccoa Falls College

Sherry Ford
University of Montevallo

Jil M. Freeman
Portland State University

John French
Cape Cod Community College

Tammy French
University of Wisconsin–Whitewater

Todd S. Frobish
Fayetteville State University

Jodi Gaete
Suffolk County Community College

Beverly Graham
Georgia Southern University

Darlene Graves
Liberty University

Dawn Gully
University of South Dakota

Suzanne Hagen
University of Wisconsin–River Falls

Donna L. Halper
University of Massachusetts–Amherst

Thomas Edwards Harkins
New York University

Martin L. Hatton
Mississippi University for Women

Patrick J. Hebert
University of Louisiana–Monroe

Susan Hellweg
San Diego State University

Valerie Hennen
Gateway Technical College

Deborah Hermach
Lane Community College

Annette Holba
Plymouth State University

Lucy Holsonbake
Northern Virginia Community College

Sallyanne Holtz
University of Texas–San Antonio

David Hopcroft
Quinebaug Valley Community College

Alec R. Hosterman
Indiana University–South Bend

Gayle E. Houser
Ball State University

Bill Husson
University at Albany—SUNY

Rebecca Imes
Carroll University

Ann Marie Jablonowski
Owens Community College

Amir H. Jafri
Davis and Elkins College

Lori Johnson
University of Northern Iowa

Michelle Johnson
The College of Wooster

Bernadette Kapocias
Southwestern Oregon Community College

Jim Katt
University of Central Florida

William M. Keith
University of Wisconsin–Milwaukee

Doug Kelley
Arizona State University

Elizabeth Kindermann
Mid Michigan Community College

Branislav Kovacic
University of Hartford

Shelley D. Lane
University of Texas–Dallas

Rachel Lapp
Goshen College

B. J. Lawrence
Bradley University

Kathe Lehman-Meyer
St. Mary's University

Amy Lenoce
Naugatuck Valley Community College

Nancy R. Levin
Palm Beach Community College

Kurt Lindemann
San Diego State University

Judith Litterst
St. Cloud State University

Deborah K. London
Merrimack College

Karen Lovaas
San Francisco State University

Louis A. Lucca
F. H. LaGuardia Community College (CUNY)

Julie Lynch
St. Cloud State University

Valerie Manusov
University of Washington

Lawrence M. Massey
Spokane Falls Community College

Masahiro Masuda
Kochi University

Marie A. Mater
Houston Baptist University

Nelya McKenzie
Auburn University–Montgomery

Bruce McKinney
University of North Carolina–Wilmington

Donald S. McPherson
Indiana University of Pennsylvania

Shawn Miklaucic
DeSales University

Jean Costanza Miller
George Washington

Yolanda F. Mitchell
Pulaski Tech

Thomas Morra
Northern Virginia Community College

Kay E. Neal
University of Wisconsin–Oshkosh

Vicki Nelson
Curry College

John Nicholson
Mississippi State University

Michael E. Nitz
Augustana College

Carey Noland
Northeastern University

Kristen Norwood
Trinity University–Texas

Laura Oliver
University of Texas–San Antonio

Rick Olsen
University of North Carolina–Wilmington

Susan Opt
Salem College

Miri Pardo
St. John Fisher College

Nan Peck
Northern Virginia Community College–Annandale

Lynette Sharp Penya
Abilene Christian University

Frank G. Perez
University of Texas–El Paso

Jeffrey Pierson
Bridgewater College

Jon Radwan
Seton Hall University

Rita L. Rahoi-Gilchrest
Winona State University

Pravin Rodrigues
Ashland University

Tracy Routsong
Washburn University

M. Sallyanne Ryan
Fairfield University

Erin Sahlstein
University of Nevada–Las Vegas

Jim Schnell
Ohio Dominican University

David P. Schultz
Trinity Lutheran College

Pamela Schultz
Alfred University

Pam L. Secklin
St. Cloud State University

Marilyn Shaw
University of Northern Iowa

Tami Spry
St. Cloud State University

Gina Stahl-Ricco
College of Marin

Suzanne Stangl-Erkens
St. Cloud State University

John Stone
James Madison University

John Tapia
Missouri Western State University

Jason J. Teven
California State University–Fullerton

Avinash Thombre
University of Arkansas–Little Rock

Amy Torkelson Miller
North Dakota State University

April R. Trees
Saint Louis University

David Tschida
St. Cloud State University

Stephen Thompson
College of DuPage

Jennifer Tudor
St. Cloud State University

Jill Tyler
University of South Dakota

Ben Tyson
Central Connecticut State University

Michelle T. Violanti
University of Tennessee–Knoxville

Catherine E. Waggoner
Wittenberg University

John T. Warren
Southern Illinois University–Carbondale

Sara C. Weintraub
Regis College

Scott Wells
St. Cloud State University

Richard West
Emerson College

Joel Whittemore
McMurry University

Bruce Wickelgren
Suffolk University

Sarah M. Wilde
University of North Carolina–Greensboro

Daniel Wildeson
St. Cloud State University

Richard Wilkins
Baruch College

Bobette Wolensenky
Palm Beach Community College South

Denise Woolsey
Yavapai College

Sarah Wolter
Gustavus Adolphus University

Yinjiao Ye
University of Rhode Island

Lance Brendan Young
Iowa City VA Medical Center

Mei Zhang
Missouri Western State University

We would also like to extend our deep appreciation to the following student reviewers of the published first edition for their keen insight as those for whom this book is truly intended.

Fayetteville State University: Katrina Faison, Kristy Mitchell, Jourdan Scruggs, Elvia Stangle, and Desiree Thomas; *University of Iowa:* Daniel Usera; *Lone Star College–North Harris:* Lyndi Bryson and Beverley Church; *Molloy College:* Karenlyn Barone; *University of Nevada, Las Vegas:* Jenny Farrell; *McNeese State University:* Scott Backstrom, Dontae Cannon, Halie Cooper, Hunter Duhon, Jordan Gandy, Ilias Khidhr, Jeremie Mitchell, Brandon Regis, Chad Robertson, Rae Williams; *Owens Community College:* Stephen Traxel; *University of Tennessee, Knoxville:* Kathleen Adgent, Holly Albright, Sarah Arnold, Mary Ashritz, Noel Austin, Joseph Barnes, Alyson Bauer, Flora Katherine Bell, Amanda Betts, Jessica Bishop, Tanya Bishop, Erica Boozer, David Bottoms, Ciarra Bragg, Mary Brandon, Krysta Elise Brown, Sayers B. Burgess, Kyle Cantrell, Preston Chandler, Elizabeth Darnell, John Daunais, Andrea Davis, Jasmine Davis, Krista Davis, Timothy Dembek, Tyrone Dowell, David Drew, Weston Duke, Katherine Duncan, Ashley Dupree, Jay Faris, Matthew Farris, Darren Flanery, Joseph Franklin, Russell Garner, Allison Goo, Richard Graves, Andrew Hamilton, Shani Hammonds, Myosha Hardnett, Ashley Harris, Carrie Hatcher, Robert Hayes, Max Healy, Brad Hernandez, Jonathan Hill, Charles Hodges, Cara Holloway, Brian Hopson, Cathleen Hosfield, Jessica Howell, Sara Horne, Morgan Hutcheson, Lacie Hyder, Lauren Kedrow, Caroline Johnston, Allison Kelly, Traci Kerr, Alyssa Knight, Jennifer Lea, Patrick Lees, Kijeka Lewis, William Lewis, Senwhaa Lim, Rachel Mathis, Ashley McClusky, Elizabeth McPherson, Brooke Mooney, Manika Moore, Rachel Moore, Lara Ann Muldowny, Cori Mullaney, Emmanuel Negedu, Jessica Newsom, Joseph Ohman, Kelly Paley, Kensey Parker, Jessica Pensinger, Rebecca Perkins, Devin Phillips, Jessica Pinkston, Chasen Plunkett, Sarah Polston, Andrew Puryear, Cary Queen, Cara Rains, Rachel Robinson, Adriana Rodriguez, Christian Ross, Carrie Rowland, Brent Russell, Ian Salter, Gina Sarli, Courtney Schiller, Hannah Schwartz, Richard Sharp, Sharina Sheehan, Jessica Shipp, Lindsey Sowders, Ben Sproul, Robyn Steffen, Hannah Strickland, Charles Treadway, Victoria Treece, Ellis Turner, Brittany Vaughn, Mark Vick, Marie Waller, Phil Walters, Samantha Weinschreider, Madi Weller, Eric White, Chris Williams, Krisgianna Woods, Michael Young; *Washburn University:* Lisa Bellanga, Garrett Bendure, Adam Forbes, Andrew Foxhoven, Blaine Grooms, Kari Hadl, Janelle Hill, Kaitlin Marsh, Tessa Okruhlik, Elise Richardson, Carmen Romero-Galvan, Lindsey Scott, Talia Van Anne, Cassandra Wall Gaddis, and Shannon Ware; *Winona State University:* Jana Heydon, Chris Johnsen, Jennifer Lamont, McKenzie Larson, Kate Perardi, Amanda Peters, Brad Reiter, Erin Rieckenberg, Paul Rohde, Emily A. Schultz, Katrina Theis, Danielle Topka, and Brent Vyvyan; *University of Wisconsin–Milwaukee:* Angela McGowan.

About the Authors

Steve Duck taught at two universities in the United Kingdom before taking up the Daniel and Amy Starch Distinguished Research Chair in the Department of Communication Studies at the University of Iowa in 1986, where he is also an adjunct professor of psychology. He was recently promoted to Collegiate Administrative Fellow and works with the deans' caucus in the College of Liberal Arts and Sciences, and as an extension of this position for 2010–2011 he has been appointed interim chair of the Rhetoric Department. He has taught several interpersonal communication courses, mostly on interpersonal communication and relationships but also on nonverbal communication, communication in everyday life, construction of identity, communication theory, organizational leadership, and procedures and practices for leaders. Always, by training, an interdisciplinary thinker, Steve has focused on the development and decline of relationships from many different perspectives, although he has also done research on the dynamics of television production techniques and persuasive messages in health contexts. Steve has written or edited 50 books on relationships and other matters and was the founder and, for the first 15 years, the editor of the *Journal of Social and Personal Relationships.* His 1994 book *Meaningful Relationships: Talking, Sense, and Relating* won the G. R. Miller Book Award from the Interpersonal Communication Division of the National Communication Association. Steve cofounded a series of international conferences on personal relationships that began in 1982. He won the University of Iowa's first Outstanding Faculty Mentor Award in 2001 and the National Communication Association's Robert J. Kibler Memorial Award in 2004 for "dedication to excellence, commitment to the profession, concern for others, vision of what could be, acceptance of diversity, and forthrightness." He was the 2010 recipient of the UI College of Liberal Arts and Sciences Helen Kechriotis Nelson Teaching Award for a lifetime of excellence in teaching. He was elected in 2010 as one of the National Communication Association's elite Distinguished Scholars. He hopes to someday appear on *The X Factor* and be famous.

David T. McMahan has taught courses that span the discipline of communication, including numerous courses in interpersonal communication, media, communication education, theory, and criticism. David's research interests also engage multiple areas of the discipline with much of his research devoted to bridging the study of relationships and media. This work includes examining the discussion of media and the incorporation of catchphrases and media references in everyday communication. A great deal of research has been derived from his experiences in the classroom and his commitment to education. His early work in this area focused on communication competence, self-conception, and assessment. His focus has since shifted toward topics that include both media and relationships, such as contradictions within advisor–advisee relationships and discussions of media in the classroom. His diverse research experiences include studies on symbolic displays of masculinity and violence in rural America, media-based political transformations of the world's nation-states, *The New York Times*' reporting of mass-murder suicide, and primetime animated series. His work has appeared in such journals as *Review of Communication, Communication Education,* and *Communication Quarterly,* as well as edited volumes. A member of the Central States Communication Association, Eastern Communication Association, Iowa Communication Association, National Communication Association, Southern States Communication Association, Speech Communication Association of Puerto Rico, and Western States Communication Association, David has served numerous roles within these organizations. He has received multiple awards for his work in the classroom and has been the recipient of a number of public service and academic distinctions, most recently being named a Centennial Scholar by the Eastern Communication Association. He hopes to someday appear on an updated version of *Tic Tac Dough* and beat the dragon.

1

An Overview of Communication

If you think there is anything important in your life that does not involve communication, leaf idly through this book and see if it makes you challenge your first thought. It will take only a couple of minutes, and then you can put the book back on the shelf. In reality we do not think you will be able to come up with any aspect of life that does not involve communication and that would not be made better by your ability to understand communication more thoroughly. We are passionate about the study of communication, and we believe very strongly that you can benefit from knowing more about how communication works. We wrote this book partly because we believe that everyone needs to know something about communication. *The Basics of Communication: A Relational Perspective* will help you better understand—and even improve—your life through better understanding communication.

The Relational Perspective and Everyday Communication

What makes this book different from other communication textbooks is the *relational perspective* taken when considering communication. The constant guide in understanding communication will be the relationships that you have with other people. The relational perspective is based on the belief that communication and relationships are intertwined processes. Any type of communication you ever participate in has a relationship assumed underneath it.

The relationship shared by people will influence what is communicated, how it is shared, and the meanings that develop. People generally talk with friends in a different way than with their parents. Coworkers generally talk with one another in a different way than with their supervisor. The meanings of communication also change depending on the relationships. For instance, saying "I love you" will take on different meaning if said to a romantic partner, a friend, a family member, a supervisor, or someone you just met. In turn, communication creates, reinforces, and modifies all relationships.

Saying "I love you" can do many things. It can lead to the creation of a new relationship, strengthen a relationship, maintain a relationship, or result in the realization that people do not view a relationship in the same way. Ultimately, the link between relationships and communication is undeniable, and it can be used to study all communicative activity.

Something else that sets this book apart from other basic course textbooks is its focus on *everyday communication*. The discipline of communication has traditionally focused on the "big" moments or seemingly extraordinary events of human interaction. These instances include initial encounters, betrayals, disclosure of secret information, family upheavals, and other dramatic experiences you may occasionally encounter during your lifetime. These events may be memorable, but they do not make up much of a person's lived experiences. For instance, romantic relationships only rarely feature moments in which partners hold hands, gaze into one another's eyes, and share their deepest darkest secrets and declarations of unending love.

Most interactions of romantic partners include brief conversations as they get ready for work or school, a quick phone call or text between classes or during a break, talking in the car while in traffic, or chatting while watching television. The content of these conversations is seemingly mundane and may include topics such as schedules, weather, what to eat, what to watch on television, what bills need paying, or the source of a foul odor.

Everyday communication may not always be memorable, but it does *constitute* (i.e., compose) a person's life, and it happens to be incredibly important. It is through routine, seemingly mundane everyday communication (more than through extraordinary events) that major portions of a person's life take shape.

Everyday communication creates, maintains, challenges, and alters relationships and identities as well as culture, gender, sexuality, ethnicity, meaning, and even reality. When discussing all types of communication, we will continuously interconnect them with your everyday life and experiences.

We sincerely believe that your life as a student, friend, romantic partner, colleague, and family member can be improved through the study of communication from a relational perspective.

Whatever your purpose in reading this book, and whatever your ultimate goal in life, we hope that it will

- enrich your experience,
- sharpen your abilities to observe and analyze communication activity,
- make your life a little bit more interesting, and
- help you understand the processes going on around you.

Before fully jumping into our exploration of communication, let's take a look at some of the features of this book.

Features to Guide Your Learning

Because we are convinced of the importance of the topic and because we are passionate about helping people learn about it, we have used some special features designed to make it particularly interesting and relevant to you.

First of all, the tone of this book is somewhat different from that of other textbooks you may have come across. We have deliberately adopted an informal and conversational tone in our writing, and we even throw in a few jokes. We are not attempting to be hip or cool: Trust us; we are far from either, so much so that we are not even sure if the words *hip* and *cool* are used anymore. Instead, we use a conversational voice because we believe that it makes this book more engaging to read. Plus, we genuinely enjoy talking about this material. We want to share our enthusiasm in a way that we hope is infectious. We have become used to seeing the significance of communication as if it speaks for itself, but we realize that not everybody sees communication that way. Because we are also deeply committed to the importance of studying communication, we want to discuss it all in such a way that is clear, understandable, and applicable to your life. We hope that this will make it as exciting to you as it is to us.

Everything that appears in this book—even every picture—does so for a reason. That reason centers on increasing your understanding, your application, and even your enjoyment of the material. For example, the pictures do not have standard captions, but each asks a question that you can answer for yourself (although we provide a possible answer at the end of each chapter). The pictures are here not just to make the book look pretty, but they serve the purpose of teaching you something and *making you think for yourself.*

Instead of beginning each chapter with questions to focus on before you know what the chapter is about, our **Focus Questions** follow an opening narrative for each chapter. They are so positioned because we want to ensure that you read them *after* you have seen the basic issues with which the chapter deals. We personally skipped Focus Questions when we were in school because they were not any help to our learning: They appeared at the very beginning of the chapter, and we did not yet know what they were about.

For this book, we strongly encourage you to read them. Because they come after the narrative that sets up the questions in each chapter, they will guide you through the chapter and provide you with insight as to what you should focus on as you read. Because they are important, we will also revisit and answer them at the end of each chapter so that you can see if your answers match ours. In fact, we do this instead of summarizing the chapter in the conventional way. The end of every chapter is therefore directly connected to the beginning.

We did not want to include boxes in support of material just to break up the text or just because they are generally included in other textbooks. We thought very carefully about what types of boxes would be most beneficial to your understanding of the material and to applying the material in your life. Ultimately, each chapter includes the following six types of boxes: (1) Make Your Case, (2) Strategic Communication, (3) Listen in on Your Life, (4) Contrarian Challenge, (5) Case in Point, and (6) College Experience.

Make Your Case boxes provide you with opportunities to develop your own positions or to perform an exercise about the material that might be used during class discussion. In the verbal chapter, for example, you are asked to find out the secret languages that you and your friends speak without realizing it.

Strategic Communication boxes help you integrate the material into your life when influencing others. For instance, the technology chapter asks you to consider how the purpose of a message and the technological preferences of the person you are contacting will determine the appropriateness of face-to-face, telephone, or computer-mediated interaction.

Listen in on Your Life boxes ask you to consider the material in relation to your own life and lived experiences. We want you to start recognizing communication in your life and how the material addressed within this book applies. For example, the listening chapter asks you to consider friends, family members, classmates, or coworkers you would label as *good* and *bad* listeners. You are then asked to analyze what behaviors led to these evaluations and to determine measures to enhance the listening skills of others. These exercises, therefore, will also serve to further your understanding and comprehension of the material.

Contrarian Challenge boxes invite you to think more carefully about what you have read and see if we have persuaded you or if you can see another side to what we have written. For example, in the chapter on delivering a public presentation, we encourage you to use manuscript delivery only when careful wording is required and maintain that novice speakers, especially, should avoid this delivery style. However, through the Contrarian Challenge box, we ask if you can make an argument for why a novice speaker would benefit from manuscript delivery. In many instances, such as that one, we think you will come to agree with us. However, we want to encourage you to critically examine all that is discussed in the book and not just take what we say without evaluation.

Case in Point boxes encourage you to apply what you have learned in the analysis of everyday life situations. For instance, the culture chapter asks you to find a public space where members of a unique cultural group are gathered and observe the ways they communicate. Doing so and answering questions posed within the box will help you better understand the ways in which culture and communication are connected.

College Experience boxes encourage you to apply the material discussed to better understand and perhaps manage situations encountered in academic contexts. The majority of people reading this book are students (or our relatives). Whether you are navigating your first-year experiences or still figuring things out after a few semesters or terms, these boxes will help you evaluate and handle academic life and relationships. For example, this chapter will ask you to consider the ways in which academic-based relationships such as those between instructors and students frame interactions, influencing what is said and how communication is interpreted.

Also included in each chapter are **margin notes,** which provide additional information about the material or open-ended questions to ponder as you study it. Accordingly, some margin notes provide unique information, such as when the first "smiley face" emoticon was sent, who invented the Internet, or what percentage of people believe that they are shy enough to need treatment. Other margin notes urge you to reflect on the material by posing questions, such as whether or not families would be considered "groups."

The very end of each chapter includes features to further enhance your mastery and comprehension of the material. Once again, we thought very carefully about what to include here. We did not want questions that ask you to merely memorize and repeat what you read in this book. Parrots can do that; rather we wanted you to *think* about the material outside of class as you carry out the rest of your life. We wanted to include features that ask you to go beyond each chapter's content and engage in higher levels of thinking.

Accordingly, each chapter also includes the following features: (a) Ethical Issues, (b) Media Links, and (c) Questions to Ask Your Friends.

Ethical Issues urge you to contemplate and develop a position regarding ethical quandaries that arise in communication. For example, the technology chapter asks you to consider whether employers should use material on social networking sites, such as Facebook, when making hiring decisions, and the relationships chapter asks if it is ever ethical to have two romantic relationships going on at the same time and why (or why not).

Media Links ask you to draw from media in order to further explore the issues discussed in each chapter. You are asked to watch a TV newscast and discover ways in which the newscasters establish a relationship with the audience, for example, and to read a newspaper article looking for examples of logical fallacies. The relationships chapter invites you to examine the Sunday newspaper section of marriages, engagements, and commitment ceremonies for similarities in attractiveness. Believe it or not, romantic partners often look alike!

Questions to Ask Your Friends provide you with questions to ask your friends in order to further increase your awareness of the material and integrate it into your life. In the chapter on preparing for a public presentation, for example, you are urged to ask your friends about two people whom they consider to be very different. If they wanted to try to convince each person of the same idea, how would they have to adjust their strategy with each one? Examining this issue will help you—and your friends—better understand the need to adapt presentations to particular audiences. Plus, these activities will help underscore the significance of relationships in your life. As with the boxes, we are serious about having you try out these instructional tools to improve your study of the material.

A **Student Study Site** is also available to improve your study of the material. It includes electronic flash cards to check your knowledge of key terms and concepts, study quizzes, Internet activities and resources, links to video and audio clips, and a link to the Facebook group created for the book. You can access the site for free at **www.sagepub.com/boc2e.**

Ultimately, we want to invite you into the conversation about the issues we present as basics of communication. As part of that, we are trying to stretch your capacity to think about a problem and work through it with us, leaving you with a greater sense of having mastered the material by thinking through it for yourself, under guidance.

Within this initial chapter, we invite you to start thinking more carefully about communication and how it works. In doing so, we will examine what makes communication more complex than many people may believe. We will also explore what communication entails by discussing a few of its key characteristics. So, with that in mind, let's get started with those focus questions we mentioned above.

Focus Questions

1. What are symbols?
2. How is meaning established?
3. Why should communication be considered cultural?
4. Why should communication be considered relational?
5. What are communication frames?
6. What does it mean to view communication as both representational and presentational?
7. What does it mean to view communication as a transaction?

What Is Communication Anyway?

In introductory chapters such as this one, you might expect the primary subject to be defined. In this case, you might be looking for an authoritative definition of *communication* that may very well show up on an examination you will take in the near future. Well, here is one you might like: *Communication* is the transactional use of symbols, influenced, guided, and understood in the context of relationships. Actually, that definition is not half bad, but it does not really do justice to what communication really entails. Your instructor may provide you with a better one.

There are a number of definitions of communication out there, and many of those definitions are very acceptable. Communication scholars Frank Dance and Carl Larson (1976) once compiled a list of 126 definitions of communication appearing in communication scholarship. Imagine the number of definitions that must have emerged in the four decades since then! Of course, education should go beyond memorizing a definition and rather should explore deeper issues or characteristics of an issue or a topic, so that is exactly what will be done in this chapter.

One fact that makes the study of communication unique, as opposed to, say, chemistry, is that you have been communicating your entire life. Previous experience with this topic can be very beneficial, since you will be able to draw from relationships and events in your own life when studying the material. You will even be able to apply the material, hopefully improving your communication abilities and life in general along the way.

You will notice that when we refer to someone else's work or ideas, we will list the surname of the author(s), a date, and a page number when quoting the author(s) directly. The date gives the year in which the original paper or book was published, and the page number is where the original quote can be located. This format is used in most social science textbooks and professional writing, with the full reference at the end of each chapter or at the end of the book. You may also be asked to use this format when you write your own papers or speeches.

The drawback to previous experience is that people may not see the value in studying something that is such a common part of life. You may even be asking the "big deal" questions: What is so problematic about everyday communication? Why bother to explain it? Don't people know what it is about and how it works? Communication is just about sending messages, right?

True: Most of the time, people communicate without thinking, and it is not usually awkward. But if communicating is so easy, why do people have misunderstandings, conflicts, arguments, disputes, and disagreements? Why do people get embarrassed because they have said something thoughtless? Why are people misunderstood, and why do people misunderstand others?

If communication is simple, how do people know when others are lying (if all that matters is listening to their words as a straightforward representation of a situation)? Why would anyone be agitated or anxious about giving a public talk if talk is just saying what you think? Why is communication via e-mail or text message so easy to misinterpret?

Make Your Case

If you are not already convinced, the importance of communication will hopefully become increasingly clear as you continue reading this chapter and finish the entire book. You may be using this book for a required course in your major, a required general studies course, or an elective course. Make the case for a basic communication course being required for all graduates at your school. To get you started, people in the professional world consistently rank effective communication a vital trait for new hires and necessary for advancement. What are some other reasons a communication course should be required?

People would never disagree about what happened in a conversation if the students who asked the above "big deal" questions were right. Why, then, are allegations of sexual harassment sometimes denied vigorously, and how can there ever be doubt whether one person intentionally touched another person inappropriately? Why are coworkers so often a problem for many people, and what is it about their communication that makes them difficult?

When first coming to the study of communication, many students assume that communication simply involves the sending of messages from one person to another through e-mails, phone calls, gestures, instant messages, text messages, or spoken word. That basic view has some truth to it, but communication involves a lot more than merely transmitting information from Person A to Person B.

As you read this chapter, you will likely start to recognize that communication is more complex than it initially appears. Let's begin by examining a common situation, a restaurant server speaking to customers:

> "Hi! My name is Alice, and I'll be your server today. Our special is witchety grub stewed in yak fat with broccoli sautéed in mushroom sauce for $24.95. If you have any questions about the menu, let me know."

6. What does it mean to view communication as both representational and presentational?

Communication describes facts or conveys information (representation) while conveying the perspective or worldview or slant of the person sending a message (presentation). Communication gives other people and audiences a way of looking at the world that is based on how the source of a message prefers them to see it.

7. What does it mean to view communication as a transaction?

Viewing communication as a transaction means understanding that communication is more than just the simple exchange of messages. Rather, communication involves the construction of shared meanings or understandings between two (or more) individuals. Moreover, communication constitutes, or creates, aspects of life such as relationships, culture, gender, and even reality.

KEY CONCEPTS

communication as action   17
communication as interaction   18
communication as transaction   18
constitutive approach to
    communication   18
frames   15
meaning   11

medium   12
presentation   16
representation   16
signs   9
social construction   11
symbols   9

QUESTIONS TO ASK YOUR FRIENDS

1. Ask your friends to define communication. In what ways do their definitions align with the characteristics of communication discussed in this chapter? In what ways do their definitions counter these characteristics?

2. Ask your friends to consider the difference between signs and symbols. Do they find it difficult to view some symbols as being completely arbitrary?

3. Ask your friends whether a message must be received in order for communication to occur. What do their answers tell you about viewing communication as an action?

MEDIA LINKS

1. In what ways do song lyrics not merely entertain but also *present* particular ways of living, particular attitudes, and particular styles? Find examples that present relationships differently (e.g., from The Killers, Lady Gaga, Otis Redding, Toby Keith, Mel Tormé, The Beatles).

2. Watch a political discussion on C-SPAN, on a television news channel, or online. How are opposing positions being *presented?* Is the distinction between representation and presentation obvious or hidden?

3. Watch the audio and visual coverage of a live event on television or online. Then read about the same event in a newspaper the next day. How does the medium impact your understanding of the event and the meanings you assign to the event?

ETHICAL ISSUES

1. What assumptions appear to be built into people's speech concerning race, gender, sexuality, and age? Are such assumptions justified, or should no assumptions be made concerning these aspects of a person?

2. Is communicating in a manner consistent with someone's cultural expectations but inconsistent with your normal communication style unethical?

3. Your communication with someone may appeal to certain relational obligations. For instance, friends may be expected to do certain things (give someone a ride) if they are truly friends. Is it ethical to appeal to such obligations, or is it simply part of being a friend? Are there any limits to what a person may ask someone else to do based on their relationship?

ANSWERS TO PHOTO CAPTIONS

Photo 1.1 ■ No. Communication is actually quite complex.

Photo 1.2 ■ Traffic signs are really symbols rather than signs.

Photo 1.3 ■ Physical context entails the actual location in which a symbol is used.

Photo 1.4 ■ The women are probably close friends as demonstrated by obvious enjoyment of the conversation as well as their physical closeness and touch, which are signs of intimacy.

Photo 1.5 ■ Though it could result in an interaction or in the occurrence of a transaction, simply sending a text message would be considered an act.

STUDENT STUDY SITE

Visit the study site at **www.sagepub.com/boc2e** for e-flashcards, practice quizzes, journal articles and additional study resources.

REFERENCES

Dance, F. E. X., & Larson, C. E. (1976). *The functions of human communication: A theoretical approach*. New York: Holt, Rinehart & Winston.

Hauser, G. (1986). *Introduction to rhetorical theory*. New York: Harper & Row.

Hopper, R., Knapp, M. L., & Scott, L. (1981). Couples' personal idioms: Exploring intimate talk. *Journal of Communication, 31*, 23–33.

Watzlawick, P., Beavin, J., & Jackson, D. (1967). *Pragmatics of human communication: A study of interactional patterns, pathologies and paradoxes*. New York: Norton.

Wood, J. T., & Duck, S. W. (Eds.). (2006). *Composing relationships: Communication in everyday life*. Belmont, CA: Thomson Wadsworth.

2

Verbal Communication

A man walked into a bar. A second man walked into a bar. A third one didn't, because he ducked. You know the word *bar*, and you know that in our culture jokes and stories often start with the phrase "A man walked into a bar." Such cultural knowledge frames your expectations about the story you are being told. A *frame*, you recall, is a context that influences the interpretation of communication. However, the word *bar* has different meanings. If you were faintly amused by the opening sentences here, it is partly because the word is used in the first sentence differently than you expected on the basis of the frame of the story. The punch line works only because you are misled—twice—into thinking of a different kind of "bar." Familiarity with the story's cultural form frames your expectations in a way that pulls the last sentence right out from under you.

As we mentioned in Chapter 1, *verbal communication* involves the use of language. Whenever you speak, you *use* language in ways that take much for granted, and the study of *language use in talk* is the subject of this chapter. Language has a grammatical structure, but when used conversationally, it uses cultural and relational assumptions. These are represented by symbols, frames, and meanings. In this chapter you will learn more about the workings of these aspects of the spoken language of everyday life and how they serve to build and sustain relationships.

In everyday talk, words weave together seamlessly within a context that includes nonverbal communication. Examples of nonverbal communication include facial expressions, hand gestures, movements, changes in posture, and pacing or timing of speech. In practice, nonverbal aspects of communication help frame your expectations and interpretation of what someone means. For convenience, though, we have to separate verbal and nonverbal communication into two parts: verbal, or language, in Chapter 2 and nonverbal in Chapter 3. Keep in mind, however, that this split is artificial when it comes to understanding everyday life.

Focus Questions

1. What are the differences between grammatical language (*langue*) and talk in everyday use (*parole*)?
2. What frames your understanding of talk and gives it meaning?
3. What values are hidden in the speech you use?
4. How does everyday talk make use of relationships to frame meanings?
5. How do different types of talk work, and how do they connect to relationships?
6. What is talk style, and how does it frame meaning?
7. What are the key elements of stories?

How Do You Know What Talk Means?

When you use the word *cat,* everyone assumes you are referring to an animal. You know what animals are and, specifically, what a cat looks like. When you started to learn to read, "The cat sat on the mat" may have been one of the first sentences you ever came across. In everyday life talk, however, if you say to a person, "You really are catty" (Norwood, 2007), you are speaking not literally but relationally or metaphorically. A listener would understand what you mean, even though the words are literally not true: He or she is not a cat. This example emphasizes an important point: The formal grammar of a language is different from use of that language in everyday talk.

Linguists like Ferdinand de Saussure (Komatsu, 1993) therefore draw a distinction between *langue* (pronounced "longg") and *parole* (pronounced "pa-rull"). **Langue** is the formal grammatical structure of language that you will read about in books on grammar. **Parole** is how people actually use language, with informal and ungrammatical phrases that carry meaning to us all the same. "Git 'er done!" is an example of parole but would earn you bad grades in an English grammar course (langue). When people feel relaxed in a close relationship, they are much more likely to use parole. People in a formal setting are more likely to use langue. Communication is used loosely in close personal relationships because they are quite informal, but formal relationships are more uptight. Relationships frame both what gets said and how it gets understood.

Language and your use of talk are also based on other frames. One is familiarity with the other person: The friendlier you are with the other person, the more you use relaxed, informal language. Other influences on your speech affect the words you choose or the relational messages sent by the words you pick out ("Hey, you!" is different from "Excuse me, sir").

Other frames for talk depend on the times that you live in and the items that are familiar to you. Your great-grandparents may have called their father "sir" whereas you probably call yours "Dad" or something less formal.

A final frame requires that you know how the strict rules of grammar may be bent when you speak language out loud. We are sure that our readers normally speak in perfectly polished grammatical sentences; after all, you are educated people. However, quite probably you also know that in everyday talk you can speak in ungrammatical ways that everyone else understands. For example, "Ain't no way I'm gonna do that!" does not make a lot of sense from a strictly grammatical point of view. All the same it sends messages of defiant resistance to anyone who speaks a current modern form of English. "A pox on you, knave" means something when you are reading Shakespeare, but you would be unlikely to say it in everyday life today.

Multiple Meanings: Polysemy

Words, gestures, and symbols can have different meanings on different occasions/circumstances according to the particular frame for talk. Communication scholars and philosophers call this **polysemy**, multiple meanings for the same word (Ogden & Richards, 1946). Even though you already knew that the same word could carry multiple meanings, knowing the academic term for it becomes important for deepening your insights into the way that everyday conversation actually works. You need to know how, in a particular sentence, you work out which meaning a person is using. If every communication—whether words, facial expressions, or gestures—can have several different meanings, then each time you speak or hear a word, you must determine which meaning applies.

Ambiguity

Polysemy exists as a feature of all communication, and you must always deal with the ambiguities that it creates. Ability to deal with this ambiguity is very important in everyday communication because that talk consists of many types of utterance (both formal and informal). Some examples of everyday talk are technical jargon, ordinary slang, put-downs, boasting, euphemisms, and even occasional cursing.

In the course of a single conversation, the partners can switch between styles and vocabularies. So they need to be sure that the context/frame clarifies what is going on when these switches occur. If a friend moves from informal to formal talk, suddenly curses, or switches from slang to technical talk, is he or she angry with you, or is there another explanation? Look at it the other way, too. If an acquaintance switches from formal to informal talk, this might mean that he or she wants to develop a friendly relationship in place of a previously more formal one. The most important point in this chapter, then, is that *relationships frame the meaning of talk*. So a strong and close connection exists among language, talk, and relationships.

Uncertainty

Uncertainty about meaning decreases as your understanding of frames that relationships and other contexts give you increases. The best and most helpful guide to a person's meaning is the personal knowledge you have from a close relationship with him or her. People tend

Did you know that a "cat" is not only an animal but a kind of whip (cat-o'-nine-tails), a movable penthouse to protect soldiers besieging a medieval castle, a jazz fan (a "cool cat"), and a brand of tractor (Cat, short for Caterpillar)?

special and closer. Uninformed listeners, however, can always request that the hypertext be unpacked, expanded, or addressed directly.

How Friends Understand One Another

You and your friends talk in coded, hypertextual language all the time. Only when you encounter someone who does not understand the code do you need to further explain. In the previous example, "De'Janee" is hypertext until you have been introduced to her, and the "hot date" is hypertext until you learn that De'Janee has a new love interest. After that initial explanation, the term *hot date* might become a shared reference. Even the friend from out of town now knows what it means. If, later in the conversation, someone starts to talk about "De'Janee's hottie," the out-of-town friend will be included in the shared knowledge. At that point, the group of friends will have created a new hypertext to the conversation and the relationship that even the out-of-town friend understands.

Research shows how you can tell, just from their talk, whether people know one another because of the way they treat conversational hypertext as needing no further explanation. Planalp and Garvin-Doxas (1994) reported studies where they played tapes of talk to an audience and asked the listeners to say whether the people on the tape were friends. Listeners were very skilled at making this identification. They could easily tell whether two conversational partners were acquainted or merely strangers. What made the difference was whether the talkers took information for granted or whether they explained the terms used. Said without explanation, "Jim was worried about his foot again" identified the two conversers as friends. On the other hand, the following showed them to be unacquainted: "Jim—that's my friend from high school—was worried about his foot again. He has gout and has to be careful about setting it off. It is a problem that keeps coming back. It worries him a lot, so he usually calls me when it flares up, and I help him deal with it."

Essential Functions

People very easily underestimate the extent to which talk and its nonverbal wrapping *are* a relationship. Of course, even when you are in a relationship, you and your partner do not spend every moment with each other. You experience absences, breaks, and separations: They may be relatively short (one person goes shopping), longer (a child goes to school for the day), or extended (two lovers get jobs in different parts of the country, go on vacation separately, or are involved in a commuter relationship).

Because these breaks occur, there are ways to indicate that, although the interaction may be over, the relationship itself continues. For example, you might say, "See you next week," "Talk to you later," or "Next week we will be discussing the chapter on informative and persuasive speeches." All of these phrases are examples of the **essential function**

Think about a situation where you overheard two people talking and you could tell—you just *knew*—that they were not close but that one of them was trying to impress the other and get into a relationship with him or her. What did you notice that made you sure you were right about the person doing the "impressing"? How did you know whether or not the other person was impressed?

of talk. Talk makes the relationship real and talks it into being by simply assuming that it exists. The above examples, talking about the continuance of the relationship beyond an upcoming absence, demonstrate that the relationship will outlast the separation.

Most of the time, however, talk creates and embodies relationships in other ways, both implicitly ("I've got you, babe") and explicitly ("You're my friend"). There can be direct talk that embodies the relationship ("I love you") or indirect talk ("What shall we do this Friday night?") that recognizes the relationship's existence but does not mention it explicitly. The essential function of talk operates in

Case in Point

Spend some time listening for different types of talk that occur in everyday life. Listen for the ways in which relationships are essentialized and transacted. Up to this point, we have not said a lot about how "talk" can be divided into different categories. We have treated "talk" as a unitary and consistent "thing." But it is not. How many different types of "talk" can you identify?

hidden ways as simple as more frequent references to "we" and "us" or inclusion in talk where joint planning is carried out or nicknames are used. Linguistic inclusion (*let's, we, us*), also known as **immediacy**, is a seemingly small but powerful way to essentialize the relationship in talk. Nicknames, even as obvious as *honey* or *Jimbo* rather than *James,* clearly show familiarity. Inclusion in planning ("Let's do something really special tonight") signals the essentializing of the relationship as a taken-for-granted part of the speaker's life.

Politeness and Facework

Different kinds of talk essentialize relationships in different ways. For example, a polite conversation is different in style from an impolite one and essentializes a different type of relationship. Of course, other frames may indicate whether the impoliteness results from dislike or the informality that characterizes close friendship.

Politeness

Let's start with politeness, since in one way or another, most of our everyday talk is polite even with strangers. Communication scholars Bill Cupach and Sandra Metts (Cupach & Metts, 1994; Metts, 2000) speak of **facework**, a term that refers to the management of people's "face," meaning dignity or self-respect. When people are ashamed or humiliated, you might talk of them "losing face." Although that is a metaphor, it is worth noticing how often people who are embarrassed or who feel foolish cover their faces with their hands. An almost automatic reaction to shame or to the recognition that we have done something foolish, it makes our point that "face" is connected to moral appearance in the social world as a composed and centered social being. You might also see that the term *boldfaced lie,* used for a particularly daring falsehood, refers to the same idea. Doing facework or presenting a strongly favorable image of yourself, a particularly important aspect of giving talks, speeches, or interviews, is even more basic to daily conversation.

Accommodation: Convergence and Divergence

Just as you can set the frame, you can change it. You can choose a particular way to say something. You may change or adapt it either to suit an audience or to see changes in feelings or in the relationship that occurs during the course of the interaction.

Giles and his colleagues (1973) have shown that people will change their accent, their rate of speech, and even the words they use to indicate a relational connection with the person to whom they are talking. They called this process **accommodation** and identified two types: convergence and divergence. In **convergence**, a person moves toward the style of talk used by the other speaker. For example, an adult converges when he or she uses baby talk to communicate with a child, or a brownnosing employee converges when he or she uses the boss's company lingo style of talk. In **divergence**, exactly the opposite happens: One talker moves away from another's style of speech to make a relational point, such as establishing dislike or superiority. A good example is how computer geeks and car mechanics insist on using a lot of technical language with customers, instead of giving simple explanations that the nonexpert could understand. This form of divergence keeps the customer in a lower relational place.

The different ways of sending the same content in a message are another instance of how meaning and relationships are inextricably tied together. Talking conveys content and something about your identity. It conveys even more about your sense of the ongoing changes in your relationship with others and how it may be altered by the course of an interaction.

Photo 2.4 People tell stories every day, whether about the crazy commute that made them late to work or a funny interaction with a bank teller. How do you know that one of the people in this photo is telling a story, and what role does storytelling seem to play in their relationship? (See page 46.)

Narration: Telling Stories

The multilayered framing aspect of talk is quite noticeable when people tell stories. Communication scholars use the term *narrative* to cover what is involved when you say *what* people are doing and *why* they are doing it. This applies whether talk includes funny events, tragic events, significant emotional experiences, or relational stories (meeting new people, falling in love, breaking up). You may not always notice that talk has the features of a story. You have heard many examples—"How We Met," "How My Day Was," and even "I Couldn't Do the Assignment," which may not at first strike you as a story. A **narrative** is any organized story, report, or prepared talk that has a plot, an argument, or a theme, or can be interpreted as having one. In a narrative, speakers do not just relate facts but also arrange the story in a way that provides an account, an explanation, or a conclusion. Often stories make the speakers look good or are told from their own particular point of view (i.e., their talk appears representational when it is really presentational). Some remarks do not appear story-like but follow the same pattern all the same: for example, "I couldn't do the assignment; it was way too hard." This relates a fact and presents a conclusion. You said you couldn't do it because it was too hard. Your instructor may have thought you did not do enough work. Different stories!

Strategic Communication

Kenneth Burke's (1969) pentad can help you analyze the stories of others. However, it can also be used as you develop your own stories. Consider when it might be more appropriate to emphasize scene, agent, act, agency, and purpose when sharing particular stories with others.

Everyday Stories: Part of Human Nature

Much of everyday life is spent telling stories about yourself and other people, whether or not they walk into bars. For example, you may tell a story about when you went into a shop and something funny or unexpected happened. Or you may tell your friends how when you were, like, working in the pizza parlor, some guy came in and couldn't, like, make his mind up about whether he wanted, like, double cheese or pepperoni, and you, like, stood there for, like, 5 minutes while he made up his mind.

Communication scholar Walter Fisher (1985) pointed out that much more of human life than we suspect is spent telling stories. He even coined the term *homo narrans* (Latin for "the person as a storyteller or narrator") to describe this human tendency. Indeed, he suggested that storytelling is one of the most important human activities. Stories are also a large part of relating, so we need to spend some time exploring how people narrate and justify their action in stories.

Everyday talk can be "a story." Narratives often appear to be special kinds of talk, but they are hidden in straightforward talk. They are elaborate frames, too, that provide excuses for your actions. For example, in the cheese and pepperoni case, the end of your story might be "I was so mad." The details about the person failing to make up his mind are used to justify (frame) the fact that you felt irritated.

People often give excuses and tell stories that help explain their actions within a set of existing frames. This section looks at how stories use, and provide, frames for your talk to present you incidentally as a relationally responsible and attractive person (facework).

Burke's Pentad

All stories have particular common elements that were identified by Kenneth Burke (1969) as a **pentad**; *pentad* is a word derived from the Greek for "five" (see Table 2.2 for a listing of the elements).

Table 2.2 Common Elements of Stories That Make Up Burke's Pentad

1. Scene (setting)	*Where* it happened
2. Agent (character)	*Who* was involved
3. Act (single event or sequences of events)	*What* (facts) unfolded in time
4. Agency (plotline)	*How* (the way in which) acts happened
5. Purpose (outcome)	*Why* (What was the result or goal?)

The outcome usually offers a moral result (the moral of the story). The next time you hear people telling stories in everyday life communication, you can check how far their reports fit this framework for justifying and explaining their actions.

Elements of the Pentad

Stories start out with a *scene* in which something happened (*act*) ("I was working in a pizza parlor last night, and this guy came in . . ."; "My professor told me yesterday during office hours that . . ."; "My mom was driving home from work last night and realized . . ."; "I was talking with my boyfriend yesterday, and we decided to break up because . . ."). These elements of talk introduce the main characters (*agents*), often yourself and someone you know ("I was working . . . this guy came in"). Stories involve the interaction and intersection of characters (*agency*)—"He couldn't make up his mind"; "I stood there for 5 minutes waiting"—and their plotlines are based on a sequence of events that result in an *outcome* ("I was so mad").

The simple pizza story now looks quite different. For one thing it is organized and structured in the way Burke (1969) proposed. Although you may not previously have been able to name the terms this story encompasses, you now know more about stories than you did before.

Burke's Pentad as Frame

The important point is how the story is used to frame its outcome as reasonable and inevitable. Table 2.3 shows how the punch lines of stories—even news stories and scientific reports or tales of

Table 2.3 How a Story Is Used to Frame Its Outcome as Reasonable or Inevitable

Agent:act ratio	• Uses a person's character to explain actions • For example, "He's the kind of guy who does that"; "Friends don't let friends drive drunk."
Scene:act ratio	• Uses a situation or circumstances to justify action • For example, "Desperate times call for desperate measures"; "This is war and we need to use harsh methods to obtain the truth from prisoners."
Scene:agent ratio	• Uses a situation to explain the kinds of characters who are found there • For example, "Politics makes strange bedfellows"; "Miami is a sunny place for shady people."
Scene:agent:act ratio	• Uses a situation or circumstances (e.g., a disintegrating parental marriage) to explain a person's actions • For example, "Children of divorced parents are more likely to be insecure in relationships and get divorced themselves later in life."

people walking into bars—are seen as reasonable and acceptable. It all depends on how they are set up in such ratios of justification and presentation.

Stories and People's Frames

The elements of the pentad that show up in a person's typical accounts of everyday life experience give insight into how the person thinks. The terms of the pentad used by a narrator present selected aspects of the world. When a person highlights an element

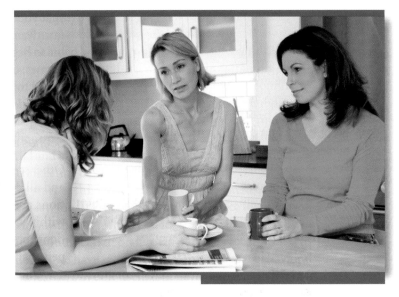

Photo 2.5 The woman on the left is telling her friends about the series of events that she encountered that day. Which pentadic element is most likely being highlighted? (See page 46.)

of the pentad, that gives insight into the way he or she thinks about the world. From this point of view, stories are not simply narrations of events but personalized ways of telling: The narration indicates presentation of a perspective or personal frame.

One significant frame that sets the scene for all narratives comes from

1. the character of the agent telling the story, making the speech, giving a toast, reporting the gossip, or talking the talk, and

2. the relationship between the speaker and the audience (a latent agent-to-agent ratio).

In formal settings a toastmaster may wear a uniform, a priest who is speaking may wear the clothes of office, or speakers may wear business clothes to clarify their importance, professionalism, and seriousness. However, even in informal settings all speakers invite you to accept the important frame that they *matter* whether or not they are giving a formal presentation.

The bottom line of many stories really comes down to "I'm a decent person, and what I'm telling you is essentially a good idea/I did the right thing, didn't I?" Outside of therapy, you rarely meet anyone who does not, at root, like to think he or she is a good person, essentially decent and OK. Now you may recognize that these story "bottom lines" are offering justifications and accounts for acts. Also the features in this chapter relate the speaker and the audience. Speaking to any audience is always an act set in a relational scene.

Character as Frame

A speaker's character frames what he or she says and justifies his or her attempts to persuade an audience. It is the same whether the speaker addresses a formally seated audience at a political rally or gives a business speech or is just talking with a friend.

All speakers want to make relational partners, potential friends, and other audiences appreciate or even like them. In most everyday life conversations, the chances are often also contains codes that indicate the depth of relationship you have with the person to whom you are speaking.

4. How does everyday talk make use of relationships to frame meanings?

Everyday talk draws on the relationship that exists between two people in a conversation to indicate what is appropriate or inappropriate for them to do and say to one another. Friends who know one another well may talk in ways that are inappropriate between strangers.

5. How do different types of talk work, and how do they connect to relationships?

We already pointed out politeness, conflict, and rudeness, but other types of talk could include information, questions, argument/persuasion, jargon, euphemism, instructions, assignments, profanity, rituals, catch-up talk, hostility, harassment, bullying, comforting, social support, advice, small talk, planning, speechmaking, confession, and forgiveness. Many of these forms of talk represent ways to keep a relationship together; others are ways of keeping people away.

6. What is talk style, and how does it frame meaning?

The style of talk can be carried out in high code or low code. High code is appropriate for formal settings, and low code is appropriate for informal settings. The choice to use one or the other frames the meaning of the interaction, and switching between the two types of code is a way of creating greater closeness or distance, depending on which direction the switching takes place in. Convergence is when two people speak in the same style and indicates closeness or liking, but divergence is when they speak in different styles and indicates distance or disliking.

7. What are the key elements of stories?

According to Burke's pentad, the key elements of stories are scene, agent, act, agency, and purpose/outcome. The act is what is done, the scene is where it takes place, the agent is the person performing the act, the agency is how the act is done, and the purpose or outcome is basically the result or endpoint of the story, often tinged with moral judgment.

KEY CONCEPTS

QUESTIONS TO ASK YOUR FRIENDS

1. Try conducting a conversation with one of your friends where you use only high code. Afterward, ask your friend how long it took to notice something wrong or inappropriate in the situation.

2. Ask your friends if they ever find it hard to know when you are kidding and what makes it hard.

3. Have your friends report an occasion when they caught someone in a boldfaced lie and how they knew. How did they handle it (thinking of facework)?

MEDIA LINKS

1. Find news stories that are structured in ways that illustrate the pentad.

2. How do news anchors introduce stories intended to be seen as "not serious" as compared to those regarded as serious and important?

3. What techniques do news anchors use on television in order to relate with their audience and seem friendly, likeable, and credible?

ETHICAL ISSUES

1. Note how sexist, racist, and heterosexual (marking) language is relational and always places one group of people in an inferior position relative to another group of people. Is it ever ethical to use this kind of language?

2. Should the stories you tell always be true? Why or why not?

3. Should you always be polite and save people's face when they do something embarrassing?

ANSWERS TO PHOTO CAPTIONS

Photo 2.1 ▪ The U.S. Constitution stipulates the separation of church and state, but this pair of street signs indicates that this is the point where Church and State intersect. Someone who finds it amusing would have to know about the U.S. Constitution and the fact that Americans do not say the word *street* when talking about the intersection of two roads.

Photo 2.2 ▪ Clearly these two women are close friends (context cues about their personal familiarity are their physical closeness and the whispering). The subject matter of their conversation is both secretive and funny. One has her hand up "to stop other people from hearing," so we know that the conversation is private and personal. This and their shared laughter indicate that they both share some of the same common knowledge about people and events and have a similar sense of humor.

Photo 2.3 ▪ Indexical or essential function. They seem very at ease and familiar in speaking with each other; the talk is occurring in a kitchen at night, which suggests that they are friends and must be relaxed by the atmosphere because the chairs certainly wouldn't help.

Photo 2.4 ▪ The individuals are relaxed, indicating a friendship and shared bond. Everyone is looking at the person who is gesturing and telling the story (actually it is Sir Lancelot). The story presumably confirms him as a hero and those around him as sharing the same heroic values and seeking the same results, affirming their bonds of loyalty to one another.

Photo 2.5 ▪ Scene is most likely being featured in this person's story.

STUDENT STUDY SITE

Visit the study site at **www.sagepub.com/boc2e** for e-flashcards, practice quizzes, journal articles and additional study resources.

REFERENCES

Burke, K. (1966). *Language as symbolic action: Essays on life, literature and method.* Berkeley: University of California Press.

Burke, K. (1969). *A grammar of motives.* Berkeley: University of California Press.

Cupach, W. R., & Metts, S. (1994). *Facework*. Thousand Oaks, CA: Sage.

Duck, S. W. (2002). Hypertext in the key of G: Three types of "history" as influences on conversational structure and flow. *Communication Theory, 12*(1), 41–62.

Duck, S. W. (2007). *Human relationships* (4th ed.). London: Sage.

Duck, S. W., & Pond, K. (1989). Friends, Romans, Countrymen; lend me your retrospective data: Rhetoric and reality in personal relationships. In C. Hendrick (Ed.), *Review of social psychology and personality: Close relationships* (Vol. 10, pp. 17–38). Newbury Park, CA: Sage.

Fisher, W. R. (1985). The narrative paradigm: An elaboration. *Communication Monographs, 52*, 347–367.

Giles, H., Taylor, D. M., & Bourhis, R. Y. (1973). Towards a theory of interpersonal accommodation through language use. *Language in Society, 2*, 177–192.

Goffman, E. (1971). *Relations in public: Microstudies of the public order*. New York: Harper & Row.

Kelly, G. A. (1969). Ontological acceleration. In B. Mather (Ed.), *Clinical psychology and personality: The collected papers of George Kelly* (pp. 7–45). New York: Wiley.

Kirkpatrick, C. D., Duck, S. W., & Foley, M. K. (Eds.). (2006). *Relating difficulty: The processes of constructing and managing difficult interaction*. LEA Series on Personal Relationships. Mahwah, NJ: Lawrence Erlbaum.

Komatsu, E. (Ed.). (1993). *Saussure's third course of lectures on general linguistics (1910–1911)* (R. Harris, Trans.). London: Pergamon.

Metts, S. (2000). Face and facework: Implications for the study of personal relationships. In K. Dindia & S. W. Duck (Eds.), *Communication and personal relationships* (pp. 72–94). Chichester, UK: Wiley.

Norwood, K. M. (2007). *Gendered conflict? The "cattiness" of women on "Flavor of Love."* Paper presented at the Organization for the Study of Communication, Language, and Gender, Omaha, NE.

Ogden, C. K., & Richards, I. A. (1946). *The meaning of meaning* (8th ed.). New York: Harcourt Brace Jovanovich.

Planalp, S., & Garvin-Doxas, K. (1994). Using mutual knowledge in conversation: Friends as experts in each other. In S. W. Duck (Ed.), *Dynamics of relationships* (Understanding relationship processes 4, pp. 1–26). Newbury Park, CA: Sage.

Sapir, E. (1949). *Selected writings in language, culture and personality* (D. Mandelbaum, Ed.). Berkeley: University of California Press.

Scott, M. B., & Lyman, S. M. (1968). Accounts. *American Sociological Review, 33*, 46–62.

Whorf, B. (1956). *Language, thought, and reality: Selected writings of Benjamin Lee Whorf* (J. Carroll, Ed.). Boston: MIT Press.

3

Nonverbal Communication

Nonverbal communication is always present in talk in normal interaction and carries messages over and above the words you speak. For example, a smile makes your words seem friendly, but a sneer makes the same words seem sarcastic. Nonverbal communication most often goes along with and supports talk, although not always. You might say, "I'm *not* angry" but look as if you are really angry. Or you might say, "I love you" and only have to exchange a glance with your partner for him or her to see that you really mean it. Nonverbal communication frames talk, but it can also frame other people's assessments and judgments of you before you even speak. It also indicates how you feel about other people. The way you move, look, and sound (the speed and pitch of your voice) conveys relational messages to others. These others can be friends chatting in a lounge or an interviewer considering you for a job or patients as you tell them bad news. All nonverbal communication conveys something about your sense of relaxation and comfort with the person(s) with whom you're speaking. Nonverbal communication also indicates your *evaluation or assessment* of that person. In short, nonverbal communication is an essential *relational* element of all interaction, and you cannot have interactions without nonverbal communication; nor can you have interactions without the *relational messages* that nonverbal communication sends.

Classic research claims that about 80% of the meaning of a message is conveyed nonverbally.

Nonverbal communication, or NVC, has been tied up with your communication all of your life. That can make it difficult for you to appreciate its importance because it is so "obvious." But is NVC something worth understanding and learning about? You bet!

How Nonverbal Communication Works

Having discussed the two sides and modes of NVC, we can now discuss the operation of nonverbal symbols in your everyday experiences. Both verbal and nonverbal communication are symbolic and share many of the same characteristics, such as being personal, ambiguous, guided by rules, and linked to culture. As we discuss the nature of NVC, we address the characteristics it shares with verbal communication as well as how they materialize. We also discuss characteristics unique to NVC, such as its continuous nature and that it is often beyond your full control. This comparison will help you understand the workings of NVC and should also add to your understanding of verbal communication, with which it often occurs (Knapp & Hall, 2002; Remland, 2004).

Symbolic

Both nonverbal and verbal communication are symbolic. The key difference between them is that verbal communication involves the use of language and NVC involves the use of all other symbolic activity.

Like verbal symbols, nonverbal symbols can be described as polysemic; that is, a single nonverbal symbol can have multiple meanings. The ambiguity of nonverbal symbols often makes it difficult to decide their intended meanings. For example, what does a stare mean: affection, anger, hostility, interest, longing, or "Be quiet!"?

Guided by Rules

Nonverbal communication is guided by rules. Rules guide the choice of nonverbal symbols that should be used in specific situations and with certain people. You would probably shake his or her hand rather than give your instructor a high five. The appropriateness of greeting someone with a kiss depends on whether he or she is your romantic partner, an attendant behind the counter at a gas station, or someone from a culture where a kiss on the cheek is an accepted greeting even between persons of the same sex (Russia or Italy, for example).

Rules also guide evaluation of nonverbal behavior. For instance, you know that nonverbal expressions of gratitude include shaking a person's hand, smiling, and talking in an appreciative tone of voice as opposed to avoiding eye contact, pouting, and talking in a surly tone of voice. A brisk handshake is evaluated differently than a hearty handshake; a slight smile is evaluated differently than a broad smile. You can even gauge the extent of a person's degree of appreciation through slight alterations in his or her tone of voice.

As opposed to those guiding verbal communication, the rules guiding NVC are learned indirectly and primarily through your interactions with others (Remland, 2004). This course may be the first time you have ever formally studied NVC, but you have been studying verbal language in school for years. In your English classes, for example, you learned the difference between nouns, verbs, adjectives, and adverbs and about proper sentence structure. In grade school, you learned vocabulary skills and the meanings of certain words. With NVC, you have learned nearly everything, from the meaning of particular nonverbal symbols to the structure of their use, informally throughout your lifetime as you have interacted with other people, though when you were a kid, your parents may have said directly, "Don't stare. It's rude," or "Look at me when I'm talking to you."

Cultural

Nonverbal communication is linked to cultural appropriateness (Knapp & Hall, 2002). In the United States, eye contact is often viewed as a display of courtesy, honesty, and respect. In other countries, making eye contact, especially with a superior, is considered improper and highly disrespectful. Meanings of nonverbal messages also depend on culture, including use of space, touch, and time. Dialect and accent can also indicate that a person comes from a particular country or region, and particular cues may be associated with stereotypes—for example, sexiness (French accent), slowness (Southern drawl), or cheeky friendliness (Irish accent). Also, many gestures are acceptable in some cultures but impolite or offensive in others (although in our culture the forefinger-to-thumb "O" means "perfect," in other cultures it is an offensive sexual suggestion). Many nonverbal behaviors and symbols are perhaps universally recognized (the smile, for example), but they do not necessarily have universal meaning in the same contexts (Remland, 2004).

A disability called NLD (nonverbal learning disorder) exists (http://www.nldline.com/) where people fail to understand NVC. They may stand too close to you, get in your way when you try to get past them, fail to read your tone of voice correctly, or be unable to distinguish anger from nonanger. Several otherwise high-functioning intelligent people (including Albert Einstein, some believe) suffered from this particular disorder, showing that it is possible to be both extremely intelligent and nonverbally disabled.

Personal

Nonverbal communication can be very personal (Guerrero & Floyd, 2006). Similar to verbal communication, you develop your own personal meanings and use of nonverbal symbols. A person's use of some nonverbal symbols may even become idiosyncratic over time. Some people may not like to hug or be hugged, for example. One person may view the peace sign (shown in Figure 3.1) as cliché and may look at celebrities flashing the peace sign at cameras with disdain. Another person may view this sign as still having great meaning and value and may regard its use with admiration. Others still may cover themselves with tattoos.

Photo 3.2 How does static NVC work, and what work does it do in communication? (See page 74.)

always obvious, but you are generally skilled at detecting it—especially when you share a close, personal relationship with the speaker. Faced with contradiction, you will be more likely to believe the person's nonverbal over verbal communication. Why? (Hint: Spontaneous NVC is less subject to your control than is verbal communication.)

Regulates Interactions

NVC also helps regulate your interactions. Nonverbal communication aids in starting or ending interactions. Used to determine whether you should actually engage in interactions with another person, NVC helps you know when to send and when to receive verbal messages.

Regulators are nonverbal actions that indicate to others how you want them to behave or what you want them to do. One familiar regulator occurs at the end of most college classes: Students begin closing their books and gathering their belongings to signal to the instructor that it is time to end class. Other regulators include shivering when you want someone to close the window or turn up the heat, a look of frustration or confusion when you need help with a problem, and a closed-off posture (arms folded, legs crossed) when you want to be left alone.

Nonverbal communication can indicate whether you will actually engage in conversation. If one of your friends walks past you at a rapid pace with an intense look on his or her face, it shows that he or she is in a hurry or not in the mood to talk. In this case, you might avoid interacting with your friend at this time. If someone looks frustrated or confused, however, you may decide to interact with him or her because the nonverbal behavior signals a need for help.

Photo 3.3 How does NVC regulate (begin, maintain, and end) interactions? (See page 74.)

Nonverbal communication also serves to *punctuate* how you talk to other people; it starts and ends interactions and keeps them flowing. Specifically, NVC creates a framework within which interaction happens in proper sequence. Most of the time it is perfectly effortless and unconscious, but you must *act* to get in and out of conversations: For example, you must "catch the server's eye" to start ordering in a restaurant.

You follow elaborate nonverbal rules to begin and to break off interactions. Consider what happens when you see someone walking toward you in the distance and wish to engage in conversation. Kendon and Ferber (1973) identified five basic stages in such a greeting ritual, as shown in Table 3.1.

Nonverbal communication also signals the end to an interaction. You may, for example, stop talking, start to edge away, or show other signs of departure, such as looking away from the other person more often or checking your watch. You might also step a little farther back or turn to the side. When the interaction is coming to an end, speakers join in rituals of ending, such as stepping back, offering a handshake, or stating directly that it's time to go.

Table 3.1 Kendon and Ferber's (1973) Five Basic Stages of a Greeting Ritual	
1. Sighting and recognition	Occurs when you and another person first see each other
2. Distant salutation	Used to say hello with a wave, a flash of recognition, a smile, or a nod of acknowledgement
3. Lowering your head and averting your gaze (to avoid staring)	As you approach the other person you break off your visual connection till you get close enough to talk and be heard
4. Close salutation	Most likely involves some type of physical contact: a handshake, a kiss, or a hug, which brings you too close for a comfortable conversation
5. Backing off	Taking a step back or turning to the side to create a slightly larger space, the actual size of which is dictated by the type of relationship you share with the other person

Identifies Others

Nonverbal communication also functions to identify specific individuals. Just as dogs know each other individually by smell, humans recognize one another specifically from facial appearance. You also use physical cues like muscles, beards, skin color, breasts, and the whiteness of a person's hair to identify him or her as a particular sex, age, race, or athletic ability.

Clothing is an identifying signal for someone's sex (men rarely wear dresses), personality (whether a person wears loud colors, sedate business attire, or punk clothing), favorite sports team, and job (police, military, security). Clothing can also identify changes in people, such as whether they have a special role today (prom outfits, wedding wear, gardening clothes), or indicate specific differences about their lives (casual Friday).

People can also distinguish others' scents: What perfume or cologne do they wear? Do they smoke? Are they drinkers? People often do not comment on these kinds of clues, but if your physician smells of alcohol, you may well identify him or her as professionally incompetent to deal with your health concerns.

Make Your Case

Note the date (1973) of Kendon and Ferber's greeting ritual research. When discussing touch later in this chapter, we reference works by Heslin and Jourard, which were conducted at around the same time (1974 and 1971, respectively). In a later chapter, we encourage you to be cautious when using references that are dated. However, some material may stand the test of time. There are two cases for you to make here. First, has Kendon and Ferber's greeting ritual research stood the test of time, or have changes in greetings occurred since it was conducted? Second, will the meanings of some nonverbal behaviors never change, or is all communication and meaning open to change?

of interests you may have. Even in dorm rooms, though they are generally less than spacious, roommates find a decorative way to assert ownership of "their" areas.

You establish *secondary territory as your own through repeated use,* even if it is space that is not central to your life or exclusive to you. A good example of secondary territory is the room where your class is held. Chances are pretty good that you and your fellow students sit in the exact same seats that you sat in on the first day of class. Even though this space does not belong to you, others associate it with you because of repeated use. Accordingly, if you came to class one day and someone was sitting in "your" seat, you would probably get irritated or uncomfortable during class if you were forced to sit elsewhere.

Public territory is space open to everyone but available for your sole temporary occupancy, such as park benches or seats in a movie theater. Secondary and public territory can involve the same type of physical space, such as a table at a restaurant, so consider this: If you go to the same restaurant every day for lunch and always sit at the same table, eventually it will become your secondary territory. Although it is open to everyone, once you claim that space for your temporary use, you assume exclusive control over it for the time being and would not expect anyone to violate that.

There are cultural variations in the use of public territory. In the United States, for example, if you and your date went to a restaurant and were seated at a table for four, the two additional seats would remain empty regardless of whether other people were waiting to be seated. In many European countries, however, it would not be surprising if another couple you do not know were eventually seated at your table.

Markers, used to establish and announce your territory, are surprisingly effective. People mark space by putting their "stuff" on it. Markers are common when using public territory that is open and unrestricted. For example, when you lay a jacket over the back of a chair, you have claimed that chair. Should someone want to move the chair, he or she would probably ask your permission rather than simply removing the jacket and taking the chair. Markers are often used to indicate privacy and control; you feel uncomfortable if someone else enters the space without permission. People meet this "invasion" with varying degrees of disapproval, but blood pressure frequently goes up (Guerrero & Floyd, 2006).

A friend of ours was traveling home on a plane. The woman in front of him kept grabbing the top of her seat and draping her fingers down his movie screen. In those tight seats, her wiggly fingers were just 14 to 16 inches from his face and distracting him from the movie. At one point, he coughed. She must have felt the air on her hand because she quickly jerked it back and never placed it on his movie screen again. This is a great example of "spoiling the space" for her and reclaiming it as his.

Personal Space and Distance

You carry around with you an idea of how much actual space you should have during an interaction. This idea will be affected by your status, your sex, and your liking for the person with whom you are talking. It also will be affected by the situations in which you find yourself.

Personal space refers to that space legitimately claimed or occupied by a person for the time being. Close friends are literally closer to you—people generally stand closer to people they like. In fact, if you look around, you can tell whether people are friends or strangers according to the amount of space between them.

All of us have a **body buffer zone**, a kind of imaginary aura around people that they regard as part of themselves. People differ in the size of their body buffer zone. If you step into the body buffer zone that someone feels is "his space," even if it is beyond what you would normally expect, you may be in for trouble. Your friends and family can enter your body buffer zone more freely than other people. You react to space and its use depending on the kind of situation in which you find yourself. An early pioneer of personal space research, E. T. Hall (1966) distinguished among intimate distance (contact to 18 inches), personal distance (18–48 inches), social distance (48–144 inches), and public distance (12–25 feet) (see Figure 3.2). Although valuable, this early research does not explain cultural differences. It has become accepted that people from Latino and Arab cultures require less space for each type of encounter than do Northern Europeans and North Americans.

Intimate Distance: 18 inches

Personal Distance: 18–48 inches

Social Distance: 48–144 inches

Public Distance: 12–25 feet

Figure 3.2 Hall's (1966) four types of personal space

Proxemics and Everyday Life

The meaning of space or distance is framed by your relationships with others. What it means for someone to stand mere inches away from you will differ depending on whether he or she is a friend, an adversary, or a complete stranger. A friend moving the backpack you placed on a table in order to sit near you would mean something entirely different than a complete stranger doing the same thing.

Your use of space and distance enacts these relationships. Subordinate individuals tend to give more space to individuals in leadership positions. An employee, for example, would stand at a greater distance when talking with an employer than with a coworker, indicating the superior–subordinate nature of that relationship and enabling both interactants to perform their respective roles.

Physical space is often laid out to indicate and perform leadership or power roles. A formal chair of a meeting sits at one end of the table, usually in a special seat, and everyone else lines up along the length of the table at right angles to the chair. In contrast, a more secure or less formal leader might sit anywhere at the table. From seemingly minor physical facts about the distribution and use of space, then, you can determine relational information about the people in a setting—who is in charge and who is not—as well as the leader's preferred style of interaction, formal or informal.

Space and distance also allow relational negotiation to take place. For instance, a friend who desires a more intimate relationship with you may begin standing a bit closer to gauge your reaction. Similarly, a subordinate decreasing the amount of space granted to a superior may be indicating a desire for a more equal relationship. Either attempt could be accepted or rejected depending on the other person's view of the relationship. Such relational negotiation frequently takes place in families once adolescent sons or daughters start to claim bedrooms as their own space that is now private from invasive parents.

Space and distance also guide interactions with others. If your friend has books, papers, and other material spread out over a large space, it could indicate that he or she prefers to be alone. In this case, you might ask your friend before you move these items to the side, or you might avoid going over altogether. Your instructor working in his or her office with the door wide open could be indicating that he or she is available to see students. Still, you would probably attempt to knock or at least announce yourself before entering the office, because you are essentially invading the instructor's primary space. The reactions of your friend sitting at a table or your instructor working in the office—looking up and smiling or expressing annoyance—will probably dictate what you do next, which brings us to the next element of NVC.

Photo 3.4A and B Notice the difference between these two photos. The first photo is a scene from a Western city in which people are noticeably uncomfortable by their lack of personal space. The second photo captures Japanese train pushers, whose job is to cram as many people onto a subway car as possible. Little consideration is given to lack of personal space in this Eastern city. What imaginary aura around people that they regard as part of themselves is obviously more restricted in the latter photo? (See page 74.)

Kinesics: Movement

Kinesics refers to the movement that takes place during the course of an interaction. While interacting, you may move around quite a bit, shift position, walk around as you talk, cross and uncross your legs, lean forward on a table, or sit back in a chair. Kinesics can be broken down into posture, gesture, and eye contact/gaze. In every case, whether separately or in combination, these cues convey messages about your relationship to the speaker or your audience, about the subject you are discussing (discomfort or relative ease), or about the situation as a whole. Movement can be either very intimate or very aggressive, especially if you move into somebody's space.

Posture

The position of your body during an interaction may be relaxed and welcoming or tense and off-putting. For example, someone draping him- or herself over a chair will look very relaxed, and someone sitting up straight or standing to attention will not. You can probably look around the room now and see people with different postures. Even during class, you likely draw conclusions about whether people are interested just from the posture they adopt.

In an open posture, the front of the body is observable, and in a closed posture, the front of the body is essentially shut off, usually because the arms are folded across the chest or the person is hunched over. Both types of posture convey the three attitudes noted before: (1) attitude about self (confidence, anxiety, shyness, a feeling of authority), (2) attitude about others (liking, respect, attention), and (3) attitude about the situation (comfort, ease). An open posture conveys positive messages, and a closed posture conveys negative messages. When someone feels "down," he or she tends to look "down," slumping over, slouching, and generally being depressed ("depressed" means pressed down). These postures send messages about a person's relaxation, attention, confidence, comfort, and willingness to communicate.

Gesture

Gesture can be defined as a movement of the body or any of its parts in a way that conveys an idea or intention or displays a feeling or an assessment of the situation. Suppose you were in a foreign country, one of your friends suffered heatstroke, and no one knew the word for *dehydrated* in that country's language. You would likely indicate your need for water by making a "drinking" gesture.

When people think of gestures, hand or arm movements most often come to mind, but facial expressions also count as gestures for our purposes. Quite frequently, your face and the rest of your body work together to express meaning. For instance, when a person is expressing an emotion, the face will provide information about the exact emotion being expressed, and the body will provide information about its extent. You could, for example, be angry and scowling while your body is fairly loose and fluid, indicating low-intensity anger. However, you could be scowling, holding your body tight and rigid, and almost shaking, which would indicate great anger and tell others to use their knowledge of proxemics to give you plenty of space!

Gestures can be split broadly into two sorts: those that signal a feeling not expressed in words (emblems) and those

Richard Nixon and Winston Churchill each used a version of the emblematic "V is for victory" to denote a different political message. Nixon's use indicated his personal victories, and Churchill's use related to the British people's fight against Germany in World War II. Can you think of a female historical figure who used an emblematic gesture?

[Handwritten note: Posture indicates 3 things. (1) attitude about self. (2) attitude about others (3) attitude about the situation. gestures: (1) emblems - signal a feeling if not expressed in words. illustrations - signal something said in words]

palm of your hand off your forehead n[...] it before?"

Illustrators

Illustrators are directly related to speech [...] or emphasize its content. For example, turning your palm down and then rotating it as you describe how to unscrew a bottle cap is an illustrator, and scrunching up your face while saying "This tastes disgusting" is an illustrator using facial expression. Like other NVC, gestures can also regulate interaction. While making a speech, you might raise a finger to draw attention to the fact that you wish to make a key point.

Eye Contact Versus Gaze

Eye contact refers to the extent to which you look directly into the eyes of another person. Someone who "looks you in the eye" while talking is generally seen as reliable and honest; someone with shifty eyes is treated as suspicious and untrustworthy.

Gaze—distinguished from eye contact, where both interactants look at each other—describes one person looking at another and, most of the time, is seen as rewarding. Most people generally like to be looked at when they are talking to someone else. In fact, if you gaze at a speaker and smile or nod approvingly, you will probably find that the speaker pays more attention to you, looks toward you more often, and engages in eye contact with you. Try this with your instructor the next time you are in class, and see if he or she responds to you personally in this way.

Starting with the broad generalization that gaze and eye contact convey mostly positive messages, note that eye contact indicates engagement in interactions, and eye contact and orientation can start conversations or establish the likelihood of interaction. A continued positive pattern of eye contact shows that you are paying attention to someone and are interested in what he or she is saying.

Although most eye contact is positive, it can also convey negative messages. A wide-eyed stare can mean a disbelieving "Excuse me?!" or be a threat. Years ago, Ellsworth and her colleagues (Ellsworth, Carlsmith, & Henson, 1972) stood at the intersections of roads and stared at some drivers and not others. Those who were stared at tended to drive away more speedily, suggesting that a stare is a threatening stimulus for flight. Gaze can therefore be threatening and negative as much as it can be enticing and positive. Something for you to think about, then, is how this particular element of NVC helps you determine whether a positive or negative message is being sent (hint: NVC is a system of different parts that interrelate).

A recent television show, *Lie to Me,* is based on the idea that expert observers of nonverbal communication can tell whether people are lying and help solve crimes.

Eye contact or gaze is often used to gather information or acquire feedback from the speaker as you are listening and from the listener when you are talking. If you are looking at someone, you can see how he or she is doing and get a better idea of what is going on. If you are talking, this allows you to assess whether another person is paying attention, how he or she responds to what you are saying, and how he or she evaluates you.

Some people (shy people, for example), afraid that others will evaluate them negatively, tend to decrease eye contact (Bradshaw, 2006), which cuts out negative inputs from other people. For shy people, this is a distinct advantage, but it also reduces the amount of information they can gather about a listener's reaction to what they say. Many outsiders assume that decreased eye contact is evidence of other social flaws, such as deception, so a shy person who avoids eye contact through fear of feedback may eventually create an impression of being shifty and unreliable. Burgoon and colleagues (Burgoon, Coker, & Coker, 1986) found that gaze aversion produces consistently negative evaluations of interviewees. Typically, unconfident behavior (as in shy people) involves not only low eye contact but also nervous speech, poor posture, tendency for long silences in conversation, and lack of initiative in discussion.

Eye contact is also used to regulate interactions. Some characteristic patterns of eye movements go along with talk in conversations to regulate its flow. The speaker tends to look at the listener at the start and end of sentences (or paragraphs, if the speaker is telling a longer tale) but may look away during the middle parts. A listener who wishes to speak will tend to look hard at the present speaker, and a person asking a question will look right at the person to whom it is directed, maintaining his or her gaze while awaiting a reply. Listeners look at speakers more consistently than speakers look at listeners. When giving a speech to a group or large audience, it is important that you not only look at your audience (rather than at your notes) most of the time but also distribute your gaze around the room, looking both left and right.

Interaction is further regulated through use of eye contact to manage the turn taking noted earlier, a kind of eye-based "over and out." In cultures where simultaneous speech is taken as a sign of impoliteness, rather than of active and desirable involvement in the interaction, eye contact is used to end or yield a turn (a speaker looks longer toward the audience at the end of sentences), as well as to request a turn (a listener establishes longer eye contact with a speaker in order to signal willingness to enter conversation). You leave conversation by breaking off eye contact (typically 45 seconds before departure) and then, when the talking stops, turning toward an exit.

Vocàlics: Voice

Vocalics, sometimes called paralanguage, refers to vocal characteristics that provide information about *how verbal communication should be interpreted* and how you are feeling. For example, the tone of your voice can be strained when you are angry or high-pitched when you are anxious, and your talking speed may be fast when you are excited. Vocalics indicate your degree of comfort and whether you like the person to whom you are talking or feel upset by him or her. You can also signal how you feel about what you are saying. You must manage your paralanguage when giving a speech, for example, to let people know you're interested in your topic.

A main element of vocalics involves the sound of your voice (voice quality) and how it can change during the course of an interaction or a speech, referring not to what you say but to how you say it. Sometimes you can tell who is calling on the phone just by the way a call begins; some people do not need to identify themselves directly to you since you just know how their voices sound. Even people who do not know you can tell something about you from your accent and tone of voice. For example, your accent can give people information about where you come from (the Deep South as opposed to Minnesota). The sound of your voice alone can indicate your age and sex. Also, some people make decisions about your attractiveness on the basis of the sound of your voice, with some accents preferred over others.

You often use the tone or pitch of your voice to emphasize the parts of a sentence that you think are the most important. A loud scream or a shout of "Fire!" or of "Help!" conveys the situation as urgent in a way that a simple conversational tone would not. These aspects of vocalics are used to emphasize elements of an interaction to which an audience must pay more attention. You can make a speech more interesting, for example, by varying vocalic pitch and tone in a way that keeps the audience attentive and helps the audience identify the most important parts of the speech. Tone of voice also enables you to determine what someone really means and is especially important when trying to determine whether or not a person is being sarcastic.

What do you think when you hear a person with a Southern accent, a New York accent, or a British accent? How do you think people perceive you based on your accent?

Another aspect of vocalics is speech rate, or the speed at which someone talks. When a teacher wants you to pay special attention to what is being said, he or she will sometimes slow down so you realize the importance of the point. Someone who speaks too fast is likely to be treated as nervous or possibly shy. In everyday life, where people are relaxed among friends, their speech rate tends to be lively and fluent rather than stilted or halting. In stressful circumstances, however, their speech rate may be hesitant or uneven.

One surprising part of vocalics is silence. You have likely heard the seemingly contradictory phrases "Silence is golden" and "Silence is deadly." Tending to differ on the extent to which they view silence as one or the other, people evaluate silence depending on contextual and relational factors surrounding its use. Most people in the United States—especially on a date or in an interview—meet silence or a prolonged break in conversation with discomfort. Silence could indicate embarrassment, anxiety, or lack of preparation as well as shyness, confusion, or disrespect. Silence can also be used to show anger or frustration, such as when you are mad at someone and give him or her the "silent treatment," or relational comfort, in that people do not feel pressured to keep the conversation going. "Shared inactivity" can be an indication of the absolute comfort in one another's presences as when you and a partner just veg out in front of the TV.

Giles (2008) shows that people can indicate their membership in a particular group by the way they use vocalic nonverbal behavior. For instance, if you are from the South, you might use a heavier accent in your conversation with others from your state or region, but you might tone down your accent when talking to people from the Northeast. Where people wish to maintain a distance from the person they are talking to, they will diverge, or hang on to differences in accent. When they want to become closer to the other person, they will tend to converge, or match their way of talking to the other person's. You may notice yourself copying the speech styles of people you like.

Vocalics and Regulation

In addition to sending relational messages, people use vocalics to regulate their interactions. A sharp intake of breath indicates shock, pain, or surprise; *uh-huh* or *um*, known as **backchannel communication** (vocalizations by a listener that give feedback to the speaker to show interest, attention, and/ or a willingness to keep listening), may be used either to encourage someone else to keep talking or to indicate that a speaker does not want to yield the floor because he still has something to say but has not yet decided what.

The most common use of vocalics in regulating your interaction is with **turn taking**, which is when you hand over speaking to another person. This handover happens much less obviously than does a radio form of communication, where an airline pilot or a trucker, for example, says "over" or "comeback" to indicate that he or she has finished speaking and wants another person to respond.

Case in Point

People often find that they unconsciously adopt a similar posture to another person in an interaction (for example, they fold their arms when the other person does). Go to a public space on campus and observe whether people's nonverbal behavior mirrors that of people they are with.

In your normal interactions, you don't need to say "over" because you can tell from the speaker's tone of voice or eye movements (referring back to kinesics) that he or she wants you to begin speaking, but you still need to signal a handover. For example, when someone asks a question, raising the pitch of his or her voice afterward serves to prompt you that the questioner now expects an answer. You also know when people are coming to the end of what they want to say because they will generally slow down somewhat and drop the pitch of their voice. That is how students know when a lecture is coming to an end and that they should start closing their books!

Chronemics: Time

Chronemics encompasses use and evaluation of time in your interactions, including the location of events in time. For example, the significance of a romantic encounter can often be determined by when it occurs. You might see a lunch date as less meaningful than a late-night candlelit dinner. Whether you are meeting for lunch or dinner, however, your meal will have a time structure and pattern. You probably have the salad before the ice cream.

Chronemics also involves the duration of events. Boring lectures seem to last forever. You may also have had the experience that people often end their college romances after about 18 months or during the spring semester, when one partner might be graduating or going away for the summer. You are quite likely to comment if you run into someone whom you have not seen for "a-a-a-ges." Also, you would probably feel the need to apologize if you left an e-mail unanswered for too long, did not answer a text message, or were late for an appointment. Cultural differences in attitudes toward time also exist; some cultures especially value timely completion of tasks over attention to relationships, respect, or status, while others place the priorities exactly in reverse, feeling that it is discourteous to get down to the task before taking plenty of time to create a good relational atmosphere first.

The meaning of nonverbal behavior depends on the *context* of the interaction and the relationship of the interactants. Is your arriving 20 minutes late to class acceptable? What if your instructor does it?

Chronemics and Regulation of Interaction

Chronemics can affect the structure of interactions. You all have an expectation about the number of milliseconds that are supposed to elapse between one person finishing speaking and the other joining in. When this timing gets disrupted, interaction becomes uncomfortable for everybody—one reason why people who stammer or who are shy create difficulty for others in interaction by not picking up the conversational baton when they are expected to (Bradshaw, 2006). You also recognize that when someone is really paying attention to you and is interested in what you are saying, he or she will tend to be engaged and maintain "synchrony." He or she will not allow too much time to elapse between utterances and try to synchronize his or her interaction and behavior with yours. In addition, you can indicate interest in somebody else by answering his or her questions promptly, a chronemic activity. You also convey information about your knowledge and expertise by keeping your talk flowing freely and by not allowing yourself too many hesitations. Both fluency and the absence of hesitation count as chronemic elements of nonverbal communication since they are about the timing of speech.

Haptics: Touch

Haptics is the study of the specific nonverbal behaviors involving touch. When people get into your personal space, they will likely make actual physical contact with your most personal possession, your body. Touch is used not only as a greeting to start an interaction (a handshake or a kiss) but also in ceremonies, whether baptism, the confirming laying on of hands, holding a partner's hands while making wedding vows, or as a means of congratulation from a simple handshake to a pat on the back to those piles of players who form on top of the goal scorer in sports.

Psychologist Sidney Jourard (1971) observed and recorded how many times couples in cafés casually touched each other in an hour. The highest rates were in Puerto Rico (180 times per hour) and Paris (110 times per hour). Guess how many times per hour couples touched each other in the mainland United States? Twice! (In London, it was zero. They never touched.) Jourard also found that French parents and children touched each other three times more frequently than did American parents and children.

Heslin (1974) noted that touch, of which there are many different types, has many different functions, as shown in Table 3.2. These forms of touch show positive feelings, but each could also produce negative feelings: Someone you feel close to shakes your hand instead of hugging you, or someone you are not close to tries to hug you. Touch can also indicate influence. Have you ever seen a politician who places one arm on the back of a visiting foreign dignitary to indicate a place to which the person should move? The two actions together serve to indicate politely to the other person where the next stage of a discussion or proceedings will take place. Touch can also serve as a physiological stimulus, for example, in sexual touch or from a reassuring back rub.

Table 3.2 Heslin's (1974) Functions of Touch	
Functional/ professional	Touch is permitted by the context—for example, during a medical exam, someone you hardly know may touch parts of your body that even your best friend has never seen.
Social/polite	Touch is formal—for example, a handshake.
Friendship/ warmth	Touch is an expression of regard.
Love/intimacy	Touch is special, permitted only with those with whom you are close.

As with all other NVC, touch can play a role in interaction management. For example, you can touch someone on the arm to interrupt the flow of conversation. Also you both begin and end encounters with handshakes on many occasions, indicating that the beginning and ending of the interaction have essentially relational consequences because you imply, through touch, continuance of the relationship beyond the specific interaction.

The Interacting System of Nonverbal Communication

In the last few pages, we have split NVC into separate parts to give a better understanding of the complicated system that makes it work, but we promised to reassemble them at the end. It has probably struck you that elements of NVC carry double messages or, at least, that they can be "read" in more than one way. A stare can be a threat or a sign of longing; a touch can be an intimate caress or a sexual harassment violation; a move toward someone can be loving or aggressive. Same behavior, different meaning! How do you know what to make of the behavior and how it should be understood?

Essentially, you can interpret the meaning of NVC in four ways that recognize that it occurs as part of a system and is related to other parts of an interaction:

Photo 3.5 From how many types of NVC can you tell that these two people like each other? (See page 74.)

1. Nonverbal communication has a relationship to the words used with it. It can affect how words are understood, and words can affect how NVC is understood. Someone caressing your thigh and saying "I love you" is doing something different from someone touching your thigh and saying "Is this where it hurts?"

2. Any NVC has a relationship to other NVC that happens simultaneously. If someone is staring at you with a scowl and clenched fists, you can assume that the stare is intended as a threat; if the stare is accompanied by a smile and a soft expression, it is intended as friendly. Likewise, a smile accompanied by agitated gestures, sweating, or blushing probably means the person is nervous, but someone smiling and looking relaxed with an open posture is probably feeling friendly and confident.

3. The interpretation of NVC depends on its context. If someone stares at you in class, it feels different from a stare across a crowded singles bar; a scream at a sports match probably means your team just scored, but a scream in your apartment could indicate the discovery of a spider.

4. How NVC is interpreted is also affected by your relationship to another person. If the person caressing your thigh is a nurse, you're probably right to assume that the touch is part of a treatment or medical exam, so stay there and get well. If the person is your instructor, it's time to leave—and leave quickly.

We have referenced a few of the errors and violations that can occur in NVC (such as sitting in someone else's special chair or touching someone when he or she does not want to be touched), but we have not given you direct guidance for how it can be improved. The preceding four guidelines should generally help you avoid serious errors, but we can go further and address specific ways to improve NVC overall.

Improving Your Use of Nonverbal Communication

Let's start with what you already know. People can be poor at encoding their intentions or at decoding others' meanings. The goal of improving NVC suggests immediately that you can identify errors that need to be improved or avoided.

A violation is a serious breach of NVC rules, such as invading someone's territory or personal space in ways discussed earlier. In general, a violation openly breaks a rule that ignores the four guidelines in the previous section that help interpret the interacting system of NVC. All the negative interpretations that follow violations of NVC rules derive from the fact that the violations are taken to *indicate a negative attitude or relationship* toward the other person, usually of dislike or disrespect. Although any NVC rule can be violated, the most fateful are violations of touch since the body is the most personal and primary area of space. Invasion of someone's body or personal space is a deeply disrespectful or extremely intimate act.

Successful conversation and use of NVC depend in large part on how people tune in to one another and respond appropriately. Recall the earlier distinctions between encoding and decoding. Someone who is socially skilled is a good encoder *and* a good decoder. You tend to notice, though, when someone is bad at encoding and continually producing inappropriate NVC. For example, some very young children do not yet understand the rules and often need to be told directly, "Don't stare; it's rude," or "Look at me when I am talking to you." It is harder to notice when someone is a poor decoder and just "doesn't get it."

One way to become a better decoder is to make sure that you *attend* to whether other people pay attention to NVC and seem to understand it. A good decoder also *bonds* with the speaker and watches out for the signals that the speaker sends about comfort in the situation. A good decoder will notice when the speaker is anxious and will smile more often or reward the speaker with head nods and encouraging NVC to put him or her at ease. A good listener also *coordinates* with the speaker and responds to his or her cues so the interaction runs smoothly with no awkward silences. Skilled listeners should also *detect/decode* the undercurrents of a speaker's talk by attending carefully to eye movements and gestures that "leak" what the speaker truly feels. Finally, a good listener is *encouraging* and invites the speaker to continue, shows interest, looks at the speaker directly, is focused, and makes the speaker the center of attention in the conversation.

Listen in on Your Life

Think about a situation where you felt uncomfortable in the presence of another person. Inside, you may have been filled with anxiety. How do you think the other person could have known that you were anxious? Were you sweating, blushing, agitated, speaking too fast, or jumpy? What did you do to try to conceal your nerves? Have you ever seen other people trying to appear calm, but you weren't fooled? What were they doing? What were their bodies saying to you in these languages of NVC? What behaviors gave away their anxiety?

Table 3.3 Encoding and Decoding Skills	
Speaker/encoder	**Listener/decoder**
Affirming	Attending
Blending	Bonding
Consistency	Coordinating
Directness	Detecting/decoding
Emotional clarity	Encouraging

What about skilled encoding? A good speaker will *affirm* the listener by encoding approval and liking while talking—that is, by smiling or good eye contact. Good speakers also *blend* their NVC with the talk to allow for *consistency* between what is said and what is delivered in the NVC channels. *Directness* is achieved by making sure that NVC is done clearly and unambiguously, and *emotional* clarity is presented by good signaling of what is felt. Good speakers and good actors are able to convey the emotions of their words by matching their nonverbal expression of emotion to the meaning of the words.

The skills listed in Table 3.3 can be broadly summarized by saying that two people in an interaction should not disrupt the usual patterns of normative interaction. They show the importance of NVC in regulating interaction while also sending positive messages about the other person and yourself—in short, about the relationship between the two people.

FOCUS QUESTIONS REVISITED

1. What is nonverbal communication?

Nonverbal communication (NVC) is everything that communicates a message but does not include words. Among other things space and distance, movement, vocal tone and pitch, time, gestures, touch, eye movements, and posture are NVC.

2. How does nonverbal communication work, and what work does it do in communication?

NVC conveys attitudes about self, others, and interaction and regulates interaction.

3. How does nonverbal communication regulate (e.g., begin and end) interactions?

Nonverbal communication regulates interaction by initiating conversation, regulating the turns with which people speak, and defining when interactions have reached their end. It does this through eye movements, vocalics, and gestures, among other things.

4. What are the elements of nonverbal communication, and how do they interconnect?

Elements of NVC are proxemics, kinesics, vocalics, chronemics, and haptics. They work as an interacting system so a particular cue (e.g., a stare) can be interpreted in the context of other cues (e.g., a grim or friendly expression). The overall meaning is determined by the combination within the system and by the frame of the relationship in which it happens.

5. How can you improve your use of nonverbal communication?

There are two sides of NVC that can be improved: encoding and decoding. Improvement of encoding involves better projection of your emotions and feelings; improvement of decoding involves paying more attention to the other person in an interaction and fully understanding what he or she means.

KEY CONCEPTS

backchannel communication   67
body buffer zone   61
chronemics   68
decoding   50
dynamic   50
encoding   50
haptics   68
kinesics   62

leakage   54
personal space   61
proxemics   59
regulators   56
static   50
turn taking   67
vocalics   66

QUESTIONS TO ASK YOUR FRIENDS

1. Ask your friends how good they believe themselves to be at determining when other people are not telling the truth.

2. Ask your friends whether they can tell when you are embarrassed or uncomfortable even though you might not tell them. What nonverbal behaviors inform them of your embarrassment or discomfort?

3. Ask your friends whether they think they could get away with telling you a lie.

MEDIA LINKS

1. Look for television news stories involving police putting people into cars. What percentage of police touch the person's head? In what other circumstances, if any, do people open the car door for someone else and then touch the head of the person getting in? What do you think is being conveyed?

2. How many news stories can you find where a fight got started because someone felt another person was "looking at him in a funny way" or infringing upon his personal space?

3. How do television shows use the placement of furniture to add something to the story?

ETHICAL ISSUES

1. Now that you know more thoroughly some of the behaviors involved in nonverbal communication, would it be ethical for you to use this information to deceive other people?

2. Would it be unethical for you to use your knowledge to reveal when other people are being deceptive?

3. If a member of another culture is breaking a rule of nonverbal communication in your culture, should you tell him or her? Why or why not?

ANSWERS TO PHOTO CAPTIONS

Photo 3.1 ▪ There are static cues and dynamic cues: Static cues include the hairstyle, wristband, chain, and necklace, all identifying him as a "punk." Although this is a still photo, he has taken a posture that in everyday conversation would be part of a dynamic system of movement. His posture is aggressive, threatening, or hinting at menace.

Photo 3.2 ▪ Bodily adornment can create images of power and intimidation in enemies. People sometimes adopt body modifications in order to raise their status or inspire fear.

Photo 3.3 ▪ First, nonverbal communication regulates interaction through recognition (we recognize someone as the individual he or she is by sight, by touch, or in the case of animals and human beings by smell/fragrance), and then there are various rituals of behavior that begin interactions (catching someone's eye, shaking hands, bowing, or sniffing) and behaviors that are used to end interactions, such as a handshake, a bow, a wave, or a wag of the tail.

Photo 3.4 ▪ The body buffer zone is more restricted.

Photo 3.5 ▪ You can tell they like each other from at least the following: physical closeness, touching together parts of the body not normally touched with strangers (thighs and calves), and smiling at an intimate distance. Their similar dress codes and open postures indicate comfort with each other; the woman's body (her left shoulder) and head lean toward the man. There are also static cues: Where they are sitting is an intimate place.

STUDENT STUDY SITE

Visit the study site at **www.sagepub.com/boc2e** for e-flashcards, practice quizzes, journal articles and additional study resources.

REFERENCES

Bradshaw, S. (2006). Shyness and difficult relationships: Formation is just the beginning. In C. D. Kirkpatrick, S. W. Duck, & M. K. Foley (Eds.), *Relating difficulty: The processes of constructing and managing difficult interaction* (pp. 15–41). Mahwah, NJ: Lawrence Erlbaum.

Burgoon, J. K., Coker, D. A., & Coker, R. A. (1986). Communicative effects of gaze behavior: A test of two contrasting explanations. *Human Communication Research, 12,* 495–524.

Duck, S. W. (2007). *Human relationships* (4th ed.). London: Sage.

Ellsworth, P. C., Carlsmith, J. M., & Henson, A. (1972). The stare as a stimulus to flight in human subjects: A series of field experiments. *Journal* of *Personality and Social Psychology, 21,* 302–311.

Giles, H. (2008). Communication accommodation theory. In L. A. Baxter & D. O. Braithwaite (Eds.), *Engaging theories in interpersonal communication* (pp. 161–173). Thousand Oaks, CA: Sage.

Guerrero, L. K., & Floyd, K. (2006). *Nonverbal communication in relationships.* Mahwah, NJ: Lawrence Erlbaum.

Hall, E. T. (1966). *The hidden dimension.* New York: Doubleday/Anchor.

Heslin, R. (1974). *Steps toward a taxonomy of touching.* Paper presented at the meeting of the Midwestern Psychological Association, Chicago.

Jourard, S. M. (1971). *Self-disclosure.* New York: Wiley.

Kendon, A., & Ferber, A. (1973). A description of some human greetings. In R. P. Michael & J. H. Crook (Eds.), *Comparative ecology and behavior of primates* (pp. 591–668). New York: Academic Press.

Knapp, M. L., & Hall, J. A. (2002). *Nonverbal communication in human interaction* (5th ed.). New York: Holt, Rinehart & Winston.

Manusov, V., & Patterson, M. L. (2006). *Handbook of nonverbal communication.* Thousand Oaks, CA: Sage.

Remland, M. S. (2004). *Nonverbal communication in everyday life* (2nd ed.). New York: Houghton Mifflin.

Seiter, J. S., & Sandry, A. (2003). Pierced for success? The effects of ear and nose piercing on perceptions of job candidates' credibility, attractiveness, and hirability. *Communication Research Reports, 20*(4), 287–298.

4

Listening

What if we told you that we could provide you with the secret to academic success, career advancement, and improved relationships? It does not involve giving copies of this book to your instructors, employers, friends, and family—although that is a tremendous idea! Imagine the look of joy on their faces when they open the package and see their very own copy of Duck and McMahan, the perfect gift for the young and young at heart! OK . . . sorry for the shameless self-promotion. The truth is, though, that we can tell you the secret to these things, and it is something many people rarely consider: listening.

Effective listening entails more than merely going through the motions of the listening process. Effective listening means being an active, engaged, critical, and relationally aware listener who recognizes and overcomes the many obstacles to listening encountered in everyday communication.

In this chapter, we discuss the objectives for listening, such as relational development, gaining and comprehending information, critical evaluation, enjoyment, and therapeutic goals. We also address the process of active listening and discuss how listening and hearing are not the same thing, even though the terms *listening* and *hearing* are often used interchangeably. Discussions of listening frequently do not go beyond the active listening process, but communication involves more than simply listening carefully and intently. We specifically examine engaged listening and relational listening as we discuss how people may go beyond active listening in the communication process.

You do not have to read this book to realize that people listen more effectively on some occasions than on others; however, you may not be fully aware of the many obstacles that people actually face when listening. Accordingly, we address these obstacles and discuss how you might overcome them. You may very well be a listening champion once you finish studying this chapter! Even if you do not receive an award for listening, your listening skills will significantly improve, assisting you in school, your career, and your relationships.

Focus Questions

1. Why is listening important enough to have an entire chapter devoted to it?
2. What are the objectives of listening?
3. What does it mean to listen actively?
4. What are engaged and relational listening?
5. Why do people sometimes struggle when listening?
6. What is critical listening, and why is it so important?
7. What are fallacious arguments?

The final part of this chapter is dedicated to critical listening. Being critical does not necessarily entail finding fault or disagreeing with messages, but it does involve determining their accuracy, legitimacy, and value. This process may lead just as often to a positive evaluation of a message as to a negative evaluation of a message. We discuss the prevalence of critical evaluation in everyday life and examine the four elements of critical evaluation. We also explore the use of fallacious arguments, those that seem legitimate but are in reality based on faulty reasoning or insufficient evidence. Fallacious arguments, actually quite evident in everyday communication, appear in many of the commercials and advertisements you come across each day. After reading this chapter, you will be better equipped to recognize—and not be fooled by—these arguments.

Why Is Listening Important?

Listening is the communication activity in which people engage most frequently. In fact, studies conducted over the past 80 years have consistently ranked listening as the most frequent communication activity (Barker, Edwards, Gaines, Gladney, & Holley, 1980; Janusik & Wolvin, 2009; Rankin, 1928; Weinrauch & Swanda, 1975). One of the most recent studies examining the amount of time spent listening found that people dedicate nearly 12 hours daily to listening-related activities, such as talking with friends, attending class, participating in a business meeting, or listening to music on an iPod (Janusik & Wolvin, 2009). In other words, you probably spend half of each day listening!

As frequently as people engage in listening, its significance in daily life is not always given a lot of consideration. Since listening is so pervasive, people may tend to take this essential communication activity for granted. Perhaps the most mundane activity of everyday life (Halone & Pechioni, 2001), listening is nevertheless crucial to everyday interactions in a number of important contexts.

Listening and Education

Listening—often the primary channel of instruction at all levels of education—is a fundamental element in instruction and key to academic success. Listening is also a critical component in the relationships that develop between students and their instructors and between students and their academic advisors. Both instructor–student and advisor–advisee relationships demand effective listening by everyone involved. Ironically, while listening is the primary method of instruction and is so fundamental to academic achievement, it remains the least-taught type of communication skill (see Beall, Gill-Rosier, Tate, & Matten, 2008).

Listening and Career

Effective listening skills are also crucial to career success and advancement. Employers frequently rank listening as one of the most sought-after skills. Furthermore, most success and achievement from both organizational and personal career standpoints can be connected in large measure to effective listening (see Flynn, Valikoski, & Grau,

Strategic Communication

We will remind you to do so when examining obstacles to effective listening, but as you read this chapter, consider the ways in which your listening in the classroom can be enhanced. Also, consider how interactions with your instructors, your classmates, your advisors, and others with whom you share an academic-based relationship can be improved through engaged and relational listening.

2008). Surveying the importance of listening in all professions and its significance in developing occupational areas, one listening scholar concluded "job success and development of all employees, regardless of title, position, or task will continue to be directly related to the employees' attitudes toward, skills in, and knowledge about listening" (Steil, 1997, p. 214).

Listening and Religion and Spirituality

Although in this context it has received less attention from researchers, listening is also an important component in religion and spirituality. Surveying this context, it was noted that listening in this area includes intrapersonal listening when engaged in meditation and prayer. Interpersonal listening occurs in such instances as listening to sermons or music and studying sacred and holy texts. Finally, interfaith listening occurs when one is attempting to understand the beliefs and perspectives of other religions (Schnapp, 2008).

Listening and Health Care

Listening is also a fundamental element of health care. The extent to which both patients and providers listen effectively has a tremendous impact on whether correct diagnoses are established and on whether patients accurately follow provider instructions. Listening is also vital to suc-

Photo 4.1 Enabling someone to talk about a problem or concern is known as what type of listening? (See page 80.)

cessful communication among health care workers such as when nurses receive instructions from doctors or when nurses update doctors on patient information (Davis, Thompson, Foley, Bond, & DeWitt, 2008).

Listening and Relationships

Listening also plays a fundamental role in relationship development and maintenance. Those relationships in which both partners engage in effective listening tend to be successful, long lasting, and positive, while relationships in which one or both partners fail to engage in effective listening tend to struggle and provide less satisfaction and enjoyment. Effective listening is an essential component of every action that takes place within relationships at all stages of development.

Listening Objectives

People generally have reasons for listening in most situations and contexts. While they may have a primary objective for listening, a single communicative exchange can have multiple listening goals. Table 4.1 presents these listening goals in isolation, but keep in mind that all listening situations may entail more than one objective.

Table 4.1 Listening Objectives	
Relational development and enhancement	People may engage in listening for the development and enhancement of relationships. Through listening, you can gain a greater understanding of yourself, your partner, and the relationship—even when these are not being discussed directly.
Gaining and comprehending information	People also listen to gain and comprehend information. As a student, you are likely well aware of this listening objective as you listen to lectures during class or to a classmate during a class discussion.
Critical listening	The goals of critical listening include evaluating the accuracy of a message as well as its value in a given situation. For example, you may listen critically during a class lecture or when listening to a salesperson discussing a product. Critical listening may lead to negative or positive evaluations of the message.
Enjoyment and appreciation	People also listen for enjoyment or appreciation: listening to a friend tell a story about a recent trip, listening to music on an iPod, or listening to crickets chirp and birds sing while you walk through a wooded area. The objective of these listening experiences is to gain pleasure.
Therapeutic listening	Therapeutic listening enables someone to talk through a problem or concern. Examples of therapeutic listening include listening to a coworker complain about a customer or client or listening to a neighbor talk about financial difficulties. In these situations, the person might simply be needing to express certain anxieties or frustrations, might be seeking approval or justification for feelings, or might be seeking advice and counsel about appropriate actions.

The Process of Active Listening

Many people use the terms *hearing* and *listening* interchangeably. Although connected, they are not the same. **Hearing** is the passive physiological act of receiving sound that takes place when sound waves hit your eardrums. If someone starts beating on a desk, the resulting sound waves will travel through the air and hit your eardrum, the act of which is an example of hearing. As a passive act, hearing does not require much work or energy to occur; you can hear without really having to think about it. **Listening** is the active process of receiving, attending to, interpreting, and responding to symbolic activity. As opposed to hearing, listening is active because it requires a great deal of work and energy to accomplish. It is also referred to as a process rather than an act, since multiple steps or stages are involved.

Receiving

The first step in the listening process is the act of **receiving** sensory stimuli as sound waves travel from the source of the sound to your eardrums. As mentioned above, listening and hearing are connected, and receiving is the point at which that connection is established. As you continue reading, keep in mind that the entire listening process is not limited to aural stimuli. Multiple sensory channels, including taste, touch, smell, and sight, can be used to make sense of a message you have received.

Attending

Attending to stimuli, the second step in the listening process, occurs when you perceive and focus on stimuli. You are constantly being inundated with competing stimuli, only some of which you pick up. The stimuli that receive your attention are generally those you deem most necessary to accomplish the task at hand. In a conversation with your boss about an important project that must be completed by the end of the day, for example, you will probably attempt to concentrate on what he or she is saying rather than on competing stimuli, such as other conversations taking place nearby or music playing in the background. Although you may attempt to focus primarily on those stimuli that enable you to complete your task, it is sometimes challenging to maintain your focus. There is a reason it is referred to as an active process!

Interpreting

The third step in the listening process, known as **interpreting**, is when you assign meaning to sounds and symbolic activity. You use multiple sensory channels and accompanying stimuli when listening, especially sight and visual stimuli. Returning to the earlier example of a person beating on a desk, if you see his or her hand hitting the desk each time that sound is received, this cue will assist you in making sense of what you hear. Likewise, visually perceiving a smile or a scowl when a person is speaking to you will help determine whether he or she intended a caustic remark as a sarcastic joke or as a serious retort.

Responding

An additional step in the listening process, **responding** is essentially your reaction to the message or communication of another person. Your response, or feedback, to messages occurs throughout the entire communication process. Even though you may not express yourself verbally while another person is speaking, you may express yourself nonverbally as you react to a message being received. Responding to a message while it is being received shows another person you are indeed listening to what he or she is saying. In addition to letting someone know you are listening, responding

Traditional positive feedback or response to a message includes leaning forward, smiling, and nodding your head in agreement, while negative feedback or response includes leaning away from the source, frowning, and shaking your head in disagreement. Feedback can also include looks of shock, excitement, boredom, and confusion.

while a message is being received enables the sender to know how you feel about the message.

After receiving a message, you may respond with verbal feedback in which you explain your interpretation of the message. **Reflecting**, sometimes referred to as paraphrasing, involves summarizing what another person has said in your own words to convey your understanding of the message ("I understand you to mean that our team has until the end of the week to finish the project"). Sometimes these reflections or paraphrases are accompanied by requests for clarification or approval ("Do you mean it will be impossible to receive my order by the first of the month?"). Reflecting primarily assists in ensuring accurate understanding of the message, but it serves the secondary function of exhibiting attentiveness to the message and concern about its accurate interpretation.

Engaged and Relational Listening

For quite some time, the process of active listening described above has been viewed as the ideal method of listening. It has been included in many communication textbooks and corporate training sessions throughout the years. Acknowledging the responsibilities of both the source and the listener in the communication process, active listening demands that the listener fully take part in the communication process by attempting to accurately interpret a message as it was intended and by responding to the message source. This description is correct for the most part; however, participating in the communication process involves more than listening carefully to what is said, even if you listen intently and can repeat it. A tape recorder can accomplish both of these things! We are not saying that active listening is wrong; we are saying that it is not enough. Two other types of listening are necessary for truly effective communication to take place: engaged listening and relational listening.

Engaged Listening

Engaged listening entails making a personal relational connection with the source of a message that results from the source and the receiver actively working together to create shared meaning and understanding. Not just listening actively, engaged listening involves caring, trusting, wanting to know more, and feeling excited, enlightened, attached, and concerned.

Disengaged Listening

Perhaps the best way to explain what we mean by engaged listening is by first demonstrating what it is *not*. Examples of disengaged listening include standard attempts to be friendly and positive in boilerplate responses to technical support questions and apologies from the bank/airline/hotel after receiving a complaint. Most of these responses start off saying how important you are while the rest of the message in both form and content conveys a contrasting meaning.

Perhaps the most obvious example of being actively involved but not engaged emerges in the nonverbal attentiveness that managers and other customer service providers learn during training courses. Taught many of the active listening response behaviors, such as eye contact and displays of warmth and understanding, the really bad managers and customer service providers learn to do this without ever learning engagement. They simply go through the motions, with no real meaning underlying their behaviors.

Photo 4.2 Customer service representatives often appear to be listening actively, but they do not really understand the point of view of the customer. If they attempted to make a personal connection with the customer and actively worked to create shared understanding, what type of listening would they be doing? (See page 80.)

Engaged Listening for a Transactional World

Engaged listening accompanies the view of communication as a transaction rather than a mere action or interaction. If communication were merely an action or interaction, active listening would be more than sufficient. However, communication involves more than the sending or exchanging of symbols. It involves the construction and negotiation of shared meaning between people and the personal connections that they subsequently develop. Communication is a transactional process that demands engaged listening to be effective.

Engaged listening enables you to grasp a deeper understanding of the message that goes beyond what can be achieved through mere active listening. Take reflection, the routine approach to active listening described earlier. While you may be able to paraphrase or repeat what you hear, this ability does not guarantee you will actually understand the overtones of what is said. For example, active listeners may be able to understand and "reflect" that when someone says, "As a father, I am against the occupation of Iraq," he is stating opposition to the situation in a foreign country. Active yet disengaged listeners,

Make Your Case

Recall an experience with a customer service representative in which you felt that you were not listened to. What about the customer service representative's responses made you feel this way? If you were training customer service providers, how would you prepare them to be good listeners?

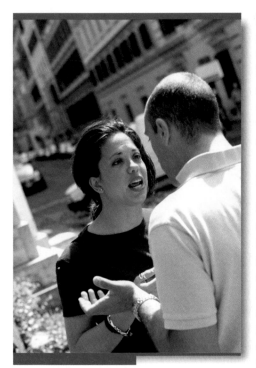

Photo 4.3 What must be considered when engaging in relational listening? (See page 80.)

however, may miss the deeper significance of the first three words. Apparently irrelevant to the rest of the sentiment expressed, they were probably uttered because they are central to *the speaker's view of self* and to *the speaker's view of his relationship with others* and therefore constitute a major part of what he wants to tell the world. Engaged listeners would be able to pick up on this additional meaning.

Relational Listening

Relational listening involves recognizing, understanding, and addressing the interconnection of relationships and communication. Vital to understanding how your personal and social relationships are intrinsically connected with communication, listening relationally will also enhance your understanding of your personal relationships and the meaning of communication taking place. When engaging in relational listening, you must address two features of communication and relationships: how communication impacts the relationship and how the relationship impacts communication.

All communication between people in a relationship will impact that relationship somehow. Some exchanges may have a greater impact than others, but all communication will exert influence on the relationship. Relational listening entails recognizing this salient feature of communication, considering how a given message impacts the relationship, and addressing this impact in an appropriate manner. The relationship people share will also influence what is (or is not) communicated, how it is communicated, and its meaning. Relational listening when receiving a message would thus entail addressing the questions listed in Table 4.2.

Table 4.2 Questions to Consider When Receiving a Message

1. What impact does this message have on my understanding of this relationship?

2. What impact may this message have on the other person's understanding of this relationship?

3. Does this message correspond with my understanding of this relationship?

4. Is something absent from this message that would correspond with my understanding of this relationship?

5. Is this message being communicated in a manner that corresponds with my understanding of this relationship?

6. What does this message mean based on my understanding of this relationship?

7. What does this message tell me about the other person's understanding of this relationship?

How you answer these questions will determine the actions that result from the message you receive. First, these questions will guide your actual response to the message, given your relational understanding of its meaning and its impact on your relationship. Second, your answers to these questions will change your perception and understanding of the relationship. Sometimes these changes in perception and understanding will be quite profound, while other times your perception and understanding will be only slightly modified. All communication will change your relationship, once again underscoring the importance of listening.

Recognizing and Overcoming Listening Obstacles

Effective listening is fundamental in the development of shared meaning and understanding, allowing you to comprehend and appreciate the perspectives of others and providing others with insight about you. It accounts for many of the positive attributes derived from our interactions with others. Yet, while effective listening can lead to many positive outcomes, ineffective listening (frequently resulting from obstacles inherent in and associated with listening) can lead to equally negative outcomes and cause problems in your relationships. In this section of the chapter, we discuss listening obstacles along with suggestions for overcoming them. Recognizing these obstacles and the detrimental impact they have on everyday communication is the first step in overcoming them.

Environmental Distractions

Environmental distractions result from the physical location where listening takes place (Wood, 2009). If you have ever tried listening to a friend when loud music is playing at a bar or restaurant, for example, or if people are whispering in class or texting while you are attempting to focus on

College Experience

Listening has a profound impact on classroom performance. As you explore obstacles to effective listening, consider how you can enhance your listening abilities in the classroom by recognizing and overcoming these obstacles. Which of these obstacles do you find most common in the classroom? What can you do to manage them?

your instructor, you already know well that the environment can hinder effective listening. However, a host of environmental distractions can obstruct listening, and these distractions go beyond competing sounds that make it difficult to hear and pay attention. The temperature of a room can distract you from fully listening if it happens to be uncomfortably warm or cool. Activity and movements of people not involved in a conversation can also distract you from focusing on a message being received.

Medium Distractions

Medium distractions result from limitations or problems inherent in certain media and technology, such as mobile phones or Internet connections. You have probably needed to include the phrases "Are you still there?" and "Can you hear me now?" in a conversation with someone when at least one of you was using a cell phone. You also likely have continued talking long after a call has been disconnected only to realize the disconnection when your phone starts ringing in your ear. Such distractions make it very difficult not only to pick up on the words being spoken but also to fully concentrate on the message. Similar to problems encountered with cell phones, problems involving poor connections and delays also occur when using instant and text messaging, making it very difficult to concentrate on the messages being exchanged.

Source Distractions

Source distractions result from auditory and visual characteristics of the message source. Vocal characteristics—for example, an unfamiliar or uncharacteristic tone and quality of voice, extended pauses, and such repeated nonfluencies as *um, uh,* or *you know*—can distract you from listening to someone's message. A person's physical appearance, proxemics, haptics, and artifacts may also serve as distractions. For instance, someone may be standing too close to you or touching you more than you find appropriate or comfortable.

Factual Diversion

Often a problem students experience when taking notes while listening to a lecture in class, **factual diversion** occurs when so much emphasis is placed on attending to every detail of a message that the main point becomes lost. Students become so intent on documenting every single detail that they lose the main point of the discussion. Imagine you are in a history course studying the American Revolution. The instructor is discussing Paul Revere's "midnight ride," which just so happens to be her area of expertise. As a result, throughout the discussion she offers multiple details about this infamous ride, including the type of buttons on Revere's jacket, the color and name of his horse, the temperature, and even what he ate for breakfast that morning. You begin to furiously write them all down in your notes. In fact, you note every single detail but one—the purpose of his ride! You know the color and name of his horse but not what he was doing on top of it. When you focus too much on every detail of a message, you very likely will miss the main idea.

Semantic Diversion

Semantic diversion takes place when people are distracted by words or phrases used in a message through negative response or unfamiliarity. People tend to respond positively or negatively to words they encounter. The intensity of this response will vary, with some words eliciting a strong or weak response in one direction or the other (Osgood, Suci, & Tannenbaum, 1957). Semantic diversion occurs when your response to a certain word used during a message causes you to focus unnecessary attention on that word or prevents you from listening to the rest of the message. For example, you may hear a word that elicits a strong negative response, such as a racial or sexual slur, and focus on your feelings about that word rather than fully attend to the message. Semantic diversion also involves letting unfamiliar words or phrases cause us to stop listening to or shift our attention away from the message. People often encounter unrecognizable words in a message; for instance, during a lecture your instructors may occasionally use a word with which you are unfamiliar.

Content (Representational) Listening

Content (representational) listening occurs when people focus on the content level of meaning, or literal meaning, rather than the social or relational levels of meaning. Content listening occurs when you focus solely on the surface level of meaning and fail to recognize or engage in determining deeper levels of meaning. A classmate may remark, "This project I have been working on is more difficult than I anticipated." If you listen only at the content level, you may see this statement as a mere observation; however, it may very well have a deeper meaning: Listening at a deeper level may uncover that this classmate needs your assistance, is seeking words of motivation, or is determining if your relationship is one that would provide such support. Content listening does not engage in seeking the deeper levels of meaning inherent in most messages and only focuses on surface-level meaning.

Selective Listening

Selective listening occurs when people focus on the points of a message that correspond with their views and interests and pay less attention to those that do not. Essentially, people pick up on the parts of a message that correspond with their views or that they find most interesting and disregard the rest. Imagine meeting a friend for lunch when you are particularly hungry. Upon meeting your friend, she begins telling you about her morning. You drift in and out of the conversation until she asks what restaurant you prefer. At that moment, you become very interested in the conversation and focus on what is being discussed.

Egocentric Listening

Egocentric listening occurs when people focus more on their message and self-presentation than on the message of the other person involved in an interaction. This type of listening is frequently observed during disagreements or arguments when people concentrate so much on what they are going to say next that they fail to listen to others. Perhaps you are in the middle of a heated discussion with a rival coworker and have just come up with a brilliant sarcastic remark. You cannot wait until your coworker's lips stop moving so that you may use this line. The problem is that you have stopped listening to your coworker. You are so absorbed in developing and presenting your own message that you have failed to listen to his or hers.

Listen in on Your Life

Which of your friends, family members, classmates, or coworkers would you consider *good* listeners? What behaviors do these people enact when interacting with others? In what ways could their listening still improve?

Which of your friends, family members, classmates, or coworkers would you consider *poor* listeners? What behaviors do these people enact when interacting with others? In what ways could their listening improve?

Photo 4.4 Why are wandering thoughts so common? (See page 80.)

Wandering Thoughts

Wandering thoughts occur when you daydream or think about things other than the message being presented. This lack of attention happens to everyone from time to time. No matter how intent you are on focusing on a message, your mind wanders, and you start thinking about other things. Consider listening to a lecture in class when your mind starts to wander. You think about a high school classmate, the great parking space you found last week, where you will eat after class, or a YouTube video that you have seen at least 20 times. Wandering thoughts are caused not necessarily by lack of interest in the topic but rather by the connection between the rate of speech and the ability to process information, which can directly impact listening comprehension (Preiss & Gayle, 2006). People speak on average between 100 and 150 words per minute, but listeners process information at a rate of between 400 and 500 words per minute. An effective way to overcome this obstacle is to take advantage of the extra time by mentally summarizing what the speaker is saying. This strategy will enable you to remain focused, as well as increase your understanding of the message.

Experiential Superiority

Experiential superiority takes place when people fail to fully listen to someone else because they believe that they possess more or superior knowledge and experience than the other person (Pearson & Nelson, 2000). If you have worked at the same job for a number of years, you might choose not to listen to a recently hired employee's suggestion about your work. You might feel that because you have more experience in the position, you do not need to listen because you will not hear anything new. Unfortunately, the new hire's suggestion might be good, but you will never know because you did not listen.

Message Complexity

Message complexity becomes an obstacle to listening when a person finds a message so complex or confusing that he or she stops listening (Wood, 2009). At times, you may listen to a person discussing a topic that you feel is beyond your grasp. You may try to listen intently to comprehend what is being discussed, but you just find it too confusing and difficult to understand. In this situation, you feel tempted to stop listening because you believe you cannot glean anything valuable from paying further attention. You might, however, actually gain some understanding from continuing to listen, and the discussion might actually start making sense. Unfortunately, you will lose this understanding if you continue to ignore the remainder of the message.

Past Experience With the Source

Past experience with the source becomes an obstacle to listening when previous encounters with the message source lead people to ignore the message. You may know people who habitually lie or who seem to be wrong about nearly everything they say, and your past experience with these individuals may compel you to not listen to them. Although they may have something worthwhile to say, you will never know because you decided not to listen. Of course, just because you should listen to that person does not mean that you should believe what he or she tells you. We talk more about the need to critically examine messages in the next section.

Critical Listening

Critical listening involves analyzing and evaluating the accuracy, legitimacy, and value of messages and is part of the more general process of critical evaluation of everything in life. Being critical does not necessarily mean being negative or finding fault with a message. Students often see the term *critical* and initially believe that critical listening entails disagreement or disapproval. However, critical listening can just as easily result in a positive evaluation of a message. Much like movie critic Roger Ebert, who rates movies with either a "thumbs down" or a "thumbs up," as a critical listener, you may evaluate messages positively or negatively. In addition, a message will likely have both positive and negative qualities, in which case you must decide whether the positive attributes outweigh the negative ones or vice versa. Few messages can be evaluated as entirely negative or entirely positive, with the actual evaluation ranking somewhere in between. Rather than "thumbs up" and "thumbs down," perhaps "thumbs slightly askew upward" and "thumbs slightly askew downward" are more appropriate.

Critical Evaluation in Everyday Life

Critical evaluation encompasses every aspect of daily life and all symbolic activity. People are constantly being called to make critical evaluations and judgments as they encounter others' messages and general life experiences. Your critical choices can range from major life-altering decisions, such as deciding to attend college, to seemingly less important but still significant decisions, such as which television program to watch or where to meet a friend for lunch. The need for critical listening pervades your daily life.

Elements of Critical Listening

Now that we have introduced critical listening we can examine the four elements that compose it.

Evaluation of Plausibility

Some messages seem legitimate and valid whenever you first listen to them. When encountering other messages, however, you immediately get the feeling that something is just not right. Even if you cannot immediately pinpoint the problem with these messages, you feel as if something is amiss. When you experience these feelings, you are evaluating the **plausibility** of the message, or the extent to which it seems legitimate (Gouran, Wiethoff, & Doelger,

1994). You might not believe that diaper-wearing winged monkeys were spotted flying over campus because this event is implausible. The plausibility of other messages might not be as obvious, but something might still strike you as problematic. For example, an automobile dealership guaranteeing "free maintenance for life on all new cars sold this month" may strike you as plausible but problematic. You may feel that the message does not provide sufficient information or is not entirely genuine. When you are unsure of a message's legitimacy, it is best to follow your instincts. The evaluation of plausibility is your first line of defense as a critical listener, and often your first impression of a message is accurate.

Evaluation of Source

When critically examining a message, you must evaluate its source. As mentioned when discussing listening obstacles, you may know people who never provide you with good advice or who always seem to be wrong about everything. While you should still listen to these people in case they offer a worthwhile message, your past experiences with them may dictate the degree of belief and value that you place on their messages. The **status of the source** will also impact the extent to which you critically engage a message. People tend to be more critical of messages from individuals of equal status than of those from higher-status individuals. For instance, you may not critically evaluate a message from your instructor because you assume he or she will be correct (Pearson & Nelson, 2000).

Photo 4.5 Are there some types of relationships or areas of life that do not require critical evaluation? (See page 80.)

Evaluation of Consistency

Consistency concerns whether the message is free of internal contradiction and in harmony with information you already know is true (Gouran et al., 1994). Earlier in this chapter, we mention the importance of listening. If we contend later in the chapter that listening is not very important in your everyday life, this contradiction should strike you as problematic. One of these two statements is obviously wrong or misrepresented, and this contradiction might lead you to question the information being provided. (Incidentally, you do not need to search for that statement later in the chapter. We have a great editor who would prevent such a situation, and we really do believe in the importance of listening.) Consistency also entails whether the information provided agrees with information you already know as true. If someone is describing the best route to travel through the South and mentions that "once you enter Mississippi, just keep driving south until you reach Tennessee," you might question the message given your previous knowledge that Tennessee is actually located north of Mississippi. The information being offered is not consistent with previous information you know to be true.

Evaluation of Evidence

As a critical listener, you must also evaluate the evidence by considering the following criteria: verifiability, quantity, and quality. **Verifiability** indicates that the material being provided can be confirmed by other sources or means (Gouran et al., 1994). If someone tells you during the day that the sky is blue, you can verify this by going outside and looking for yourself. If someone tells you Alexander Hamilton was shot in a duel with Aaron Burr, you can verify this by confirming the information in a book about these historic figures. Some material may be more difficult to verify, in which case you must evaluate other aspects of the message. When it comes to the quantity of evidence, there is no magic number to indicate a well-supported argument or claim. Such judgment is based on other evaluations of a message as well as the quality of evidence that is included. Evaluations of quality include determining such issues as a lack of bias, sufficient expertise, and recency. The evaluation of evidence and sources will be discussed further in Chapter 11.

Critical Listening and Fallacious Arguments

Engaging in critical listening requires the recognition of **fallacious arguments**, or those that appear legitimate but are actually based on faulty reasoning or insufficient evidence.

Argument Against the Source

Argument against the source occurs when the source of a message, rather than the message itself, is attacked. This fallacy is traditionally known as *argument against the person* or *ad hominem (to the human being) argument,* but we prefer to call it *argument against the source* to recognize the growing trend in attacking not only people but also media sources. Political analysts are often guilty of this fallacy. For instance, you might hear a political analyst say, "The senator's latest proposal is not acceptable because she is nothing but a pathological liar." Rather than critically evaluating the actual proposal, the analyst attacks the source of the proposal. Challenging the source of a message instead of the message itself may indicate the message as sound; otherwise, the flaws of the message would be challenged. Sometimes actual media sources or systems are challenged. For instance, when discussing a television news segment you just watched with a friend, he might say, "That cannot be right because television news is biased against the current administration," challenging not the information within the segment but the media source of the information.

Appeal to Authority

Appeal to authority happens when a person's authority or credibility in one area is used to support another. Sports heroes and actors, for example, have been used to sell

Contrarian Challenge

Arguing against the source rather than the message is considered a fallacious argument. However, are there times when it would be appropriate to question the source of the message?

everything from magazine subscriptions to underwear. However, just because a person has particular knowledge or talent in one area does not mean he or she is knowledgeable or talented in all areas. Ask most college administrators to change the oil in an automobile and see what happens!

Appeal to People (Bandwagon Appeal)

Appeal to people (bandwagon appeal) claims that something is good or beneficial because everyone else agrees with this evaluation. Consider the many products that boast their own popularity in advertisements: "Squeaky Clean is the nation's top-selling brand of dish soap" or "See *British and Redneck Professors Go to Vegas,* the movie that audiences have made the number one comedy for 2 weeks in a row." No mention is made of dexterity in removing grease from pans or of wonderful acting. These products' popularity is offered instead, and you are asked to join the crowd. As a critical listener, you should recognize when the appeal to people fallacy is being used and question why other evidence was not provided.

Sometimes it is not the messages of others that make people susceptible to the appeal-to-people fallacy but rather their own intrapersonal communication, or communication with the self. They convince themselves of the value of an object or a behavior because of the actions of other people. Making a decision based on what you perceive others to be doing is referred to as social proof (Cialdini, 1993).

Appeal to Relationships

Appeal to relationships occurs when relationships are used to justify certain behaviors and to convince others of their appropriateness. Communication scholar Erin Sahlstein (2000) has noted that people often refer to the relationship they share with another person in an interaction when attempting to convince him or her to behave a certain way. When someone says, "Could you be a friend and give me a ride to the library?" the inclusion of the relational term *friend* underscores the existence of the relationship and reminds the other person of behaviors and duties associated with that sort of relationship. You might expect a "friend" to provide transportation when requested, but not an "acquaintance." The use of relational terms also justifies requests being made. A "friend" *could make* and *be asked to make* this sort of request without great loss of face by either interactant. Appealing to a relationship may be somewhat legitimate but also fallacious. Asking a friend for a ride to the library is one thing; asking a friend to drive the getaway car while you rob a convenience store is another. Certain obligations are associated with each type of relationship, but each responsibility also has limitations. As a critical listener, you must determine when the use of relational terms is legitimate and when it is unreasonable.

Post Hoc Ergo Propter Hoc *and* Cum Hoc Ergo Propter Hoc

Latin for "after this; therefore, because of this," **post hoc ergo propter hoc** argues that something is caused by whatever happens before it. According to this logic, the following statement is true: A man kissed a woman, and 2 weeks later she was pregnant; therefore, the kiss was responsible for her pregnancy. You likely see the inherent problem with this statement. Admittedly, the above example may seem a bit obvious. However, the use of this sort of reasoning is actually quite common and frequently evident in advertising.

Cum hoc ergo propter hoc argues that if one thing happens at the same time as another, it was caused by the thing with which it coincides. Once again, we are dealing with a Latin phrase. *Cum hoc ergo propter hoc* translates into "With this; therefore, because of this." As with its *post hoc* companion, this fallacy argues that one event causes another due to their association in time. While *post hoc* argues that something occurring *before* something else is the cause, *cum hoc* argues that something occurring *at the same time* as something else is the cause. Someone might remark, "I wore a new pair of socks on the day of my communication midterm and earned an A on the test. Wearing new socks must have been the reason I scored so high. From now on, I'm going to wear a new pair of socks each time I take a test." If this were all it took to score well on an examination, life would be pretty sweet! Wearing new socks at the same time you ace an examination, however, will not guarantee you a high score on your next exam. If you really want to improve your exam scores, try visiting **www.sagepub.com/boc2e**. Although quite common and often very convincing, these fallacies are difficult to prove when challenged.

Upon recognizing them, as a critical listener, you may question and expect the speaker to prove two things: First, does a direct link actually exist between what is deemed the cause and what is deemed its effect? Second, if a link between the cause and its effect exists, did any additional variables work to produce the effect?

Case in Point

Watch television and analyze the commercials being aired. What fallacious arguments are evident in these commercials? Are some forms of fallacious arguments more prevalent than others?

Hasty Generalization

Hasty generalization arises when a conclusion is based on a single occurrence or insufficient data or sample size. Asked about where to purchase a new car, someone might remark, "My coworker bought a car at that dealership east of town, and it broke down a week later. If you buy a car at that dealership, it will probably be a lemon." Just because the dealership sold a faulty car once does not mean it will sell another defective car. Sometimes, the hasty generalization is based on a small sample size. In other words, the people involved or questioned are not significantly representative of a given population. When defending a new policy on campus, someone might say, "I asked people in my algebra class, and they all agreed that a campus-wide attendance policy is a good idea. So I guess the policy is a good one that the students like." Simply because a few people agreed with this policy in one class does not mean it is good or that the majority of students agree with the policy.

The name "red herring" comes from the phrase "draw a red herring across the trail," derived from the practice of 17th-century dog trainers. They would drag a smoked herring across the trail of a fox to determine how well dogs could remain focused on the original scent (Urdang, Hunsinger, & LaRouche, 1991).

Red Herring

Red herring describes the use of another issue to divert attention away from the real issue. This fallacy is especially common when someone wishes to avoid a particular topic. When talking about the cost of higher education, you might hear "I find it difficult to fathom that you insist on addressing higher-education funding when the spotted pygmy squirrel is on the verge of extinction" or "Sure, the cost of higher education is staggering, but so is the cost of health care, which has become a major burden on millions of people." During an argument between romantic partners, you might hear the following use of a red herring: "Why are we talking about me going out with my friends when we should be talking about your inability to commit to this relationship?" This example contains a strategic attempt to divert attention away from the issue of going out with friends by dragging commitment to the relationship across the conversational trail.

False Alternatives

False alternatives occur when only two options are provided, one of which is generally presented as the poor choice or one that should be avoided (Pearson & Nelson, 2000). One flaw in this reasoning is that there are usually more options than the two provided. Traveling by plane, for example, comes with the likelihood of delays caused by mechanical problems and the always kind and supportive airline personnel who have been known to use false alternatives by explaining, "You can either endure a delay while we find a plane that is functional, or you can leave as scheduled and travel in a plane that is not working correctly." Waiting for a functional plane seems much better than facing possible mechanical problems after takeoff; however, this overlooks the other equally probable option: having a functional plane available to begin with by ensuring proper maintenance is accomplished well before the flight is scheduled to depart. As a note of caution, pointing out this option to airline personnel at the gate will severely decrease your chances of receiving a seat upgrade on that particular flight!

In addition, quite possibly the option deemed less favorable is not as negative as it is portrayed, and the preferred option is not as beneficial. Likewise, an auto mechanic may explain, "You can either replace the serpentine belt in your car now or face being stranded should it end up breaking at one of those cracks." It is possible that the serpentine belt does not need immediate repair, as well as that you would not be stranded somewhere should it actually break. Such claims and options often go unchallenged unless a person recognizes this fallacy is being utilized and critically examines the statements being made.

Composition and Division Fallacies

Composition fallacy argues that the parts are the same as the whole (Pearson & Nelson, 2000, p. 118). According to this fallacy, any student at your school could be picked at random to represent all students at your school. Common sense tells you that one person cannot accurately represent an entire group of people, but this fallacy nevertheless remains quite common. Consider how often entire populations are represented in newspaper articles by one person or perhaps a few people. An article might say, "Students on campus are in favor of the tuition increase to pay for the new sports complex. When asked about the increase in tuition, sophomore Emalyn Taylor noted, 'If it takes an increase in tuition to replace the old sports complex, that's what needs to be done.'" This report essentially says that if one student (part) is in favor of the tuition increase, all students (whole) are in favor of it as well.

Division fallacy argues the whole is the same as its parts (Pearson & Nelson, 2000, p. 118). For instance, when being set up on a date by a friend, you might argue, "Everyone you have ever set me up with has been a loser, so this person is going to be a loser too." This statement essentially reasons that if previous dates have been losers (whole), this date (part) will also be one.

Equivocation

Equivocation relies on the ambiguousness of language to make an argument. The equivocation tactic is frequently used in commercials. You might hear an announcer proclaim, "Squeaky Clean dish soap is *better!*" This sounds good, but you cannot be certain what Squeaky Clean is actually better than. Is it better than using no dish soap at all or washing dishes by dropping rocks into the sink? Is it better than other brands of dish soap? The use of equivocation leaves such questions unanswered, often the point of this fallacy. When ambiguous words and phrases, such as *improved, bargain, good value, delicious,* or *soothing,* are used, listeners must fill in the context on their own, which often results in a product or an idea being received in a much more positive manner than warranted. The makers of Squeaky Clean dish soap could say, "We never said *it was better than all other brands;* we just said it was *better.*" While this tactic is tricky, this statement would be absolutely true. The good news is now that you are able to recognize the use of equivocation, you will be well equipped to find the best dish soap—whatever *best* means!

FOCUS QUESTIONS REVISITED

1. Why is listening important enough to have an entire chapter devoted to it?
Listening is not only the communication activity in which you engage most frequently but is also fundamental to success in education, careers, and relationships. Often the most common activity in classrooms, listening has been directly linked to academic achievement, is one of the most sought-after skills by employers, and is critical to success and advancement in the workplace. Effective listening in relationships leads to greater satisfaction and is essential for successful relational development.

2. What are the objectives of listening?
There are five objectives of listening:

- Relational development and enhancement
- Gaining and comprehending information
- Critical listening
- Enjoyment and appreciation
- Therapeutic listening

Even though these objectives were discussed in isolation, remember that a single communicative exchange can involve multiple listening goals.

3. What does it mean to listen actively?
Active listening is a process of receiving, attending to, interpreting, and responding to symbolic activity. Receiving auditory stimuli is the first step in the listening process. Attending occurs when you perceive and focus on stimuli. Interpreting involves assigning meaning to sounds and symbolic activity. Responding, the final step in the active listening process, entails reacting to this symbolic activity.

4. What are engaged and relational listening?
Engaged listening and relational listening are advanced types of listening that demand more of the listener than active listening. The engaged listening process entails making a personal relational connection with the source of a message that results from the source and the receiver actively working together to create shared meaning and understanding. Relational listening involves recognizing, understanding, and addressing the interconnection of relationships and communication.

5. Why do people sometimes struggle when listening?
You may encounter a number of obstacles to listening. Recognizing and overcoming these obstacles are crucial to effective listening.

6. What is critical listening, and why is it so important?
Critical listening is the process of analyzing and evaluating the accuracy, legitimacy, and value of messages. Involving the evaluation of a message's plausibility, source, argument, and evidence, critical listening has a profound impact on personal relationships, learning, and the evaluation of persuasive messages.

7. What are fallacious arguments?
Fallacious arguments are those that appear legitimate but are actually based on faulty reasoning or insufficient evidence. The ability to recognize fallacious arguments will enable you to become a more critical listener.

KEY CONCEPTS

appeal to authority   91
appeal to people (bandwagon appeal)   92
appeal to relationships   92
argument against the source   91
attending   81
composition fallacy   94
consistency   90
content (representational) listening   87
critical listening   89
cum hoc ergo propter hoc   93
division fallacy   95
egocentric listening   87
engaged listening   82
environmental distractions   85
equivocation   95
experiential superiority   88
factual diversion   86
fallacious arguments   91
false alternatives   94
hasty generalization   93

hearing   80
interpreting   81
listening   80
medium distractions   85
message complexity   88
past experience with the source   88
plausibility   89
post hoc ergo propter hoc   92
receiving   81
red herring   94
reflecting (paraphrasing)   82
relational listening   84
responding   81
selective listening   87
semantic diversion   86
source distractions   86
status of the source   90
verifiability   91
wandering thoughts   88

QUESTIONS TO ASK YOUR FRIENDS

1. Ask a friend to recall a time when he or she misunderstood someone else. Have your friend describe the situation and determine if problems with listening had anything to do with the misunderstanding. If so, how could the misunderstanding have been prevented through effective listening behaviors?

2. Evaluating your listening, in what ways do your friends consider you a good listener? What suggestions do they have for improving your listening?

3. Ask a friend to describe a time when he or she made a purchase based on the recommendation of a salesperson that he or she later regretted. Was a lack of critical listening partially responsible? What suggestions could you offer your friend when making future purchases?

MEDIA LINKS

1. Find videos of two people talking. These videos could include actual interactions or fictionalized interactions such as a television program or movie. Select one video

in which one or both of the interactants are listening effectively, and select another video in which one or both of the interactants are listening ineffectively. What made you characterize them as effective or ineffective respectively?

2. Watch a political talk show, such as *Fox News Sunday, Meet the Press,* or *The O'Reilly Factor.* What obstacles to listening are evident during interviews and panel discussions on these programs?

3. Concurrent media exposure occurs when two or more media systems are used simultaneously. For example, you may be using the Internet while listening to the radio or reading a newspaper at the same time you are watching a movie on television. What impact might concurrent media exposure have on listening to media?

ETHICAL ISSUES

1. When would you consider the appeal-to-relationships fallacy *appropriate?* When would you consider this fallacy *inappropriate?*

2. We mentioned that you should be aware of your limitations when engaged in therapeutic listening. When would you consider it appropriate to suggest that a friend seek professional assistance?

3. Consider a situation in which you were engaged in therapeutic listening and a friend told you in confidence that he or she was doing something harmful or dangerous. Would it be appropriate to tell someone else if you believed it would prevent your friend from being harmed or harming others? If you believe it would be proper to tell someone else, in what circumstances would this behavior be appropriate?

ANSWERS TO PHOTO CAPTIONS

Photo 4.1 ▪ Therapeutic listening enables someone to talk through a problem or concern.

Photo 4.2 ▪ Engaged listening entails making a personal relational connection with the source of a message that results from the source and the receiver actively working together to create shared meaning and understanding.

Photo 4.3 ▪ When listening relationally, a person must consider (a) how communication impacts the relationship and (b) how the relationship impacts communication.

Photo 4.4 ▪ Listeners are able to process information at a faster rate than people generally speak.

Photo 4.5 ▪ No. All relationships and even the most mundane parts of life require critical evaluation.

STUDENT STUDY SITE

Visit the study site at **www.sagepub.com/boc2e** for e-flashcards, practice quizzes, journal articles and additional study resources.

REFERENCES

Barker, L., Edwards, R., Gaines, C., Gladney, K., & Holley, F. (1980). An investigation of proportional time spent in various communication activities by college students. *Journal of Applied Communication Research, 8,* 101–109.

Beall, M. L., Gill-Rosier, J., Tate, J., & Matten, A. (2008). State of the context: Listening in education. *International Journal of Listening, 22,* 123–132.

Cialdini, R. B. (1993). *Influence: The psychology of persuasion.* New York: Morrow.

Davis, J., Thompson, C. R., Foley, A., Bond, C. D., & DeWitt, J. (2008). An examination of listening concepts in the healthcare context: Difference among nurses, physicians, and administrators. *The International Journal of Listening, 22,* 152–167.

Flynn, J., Valikoski, T.-R., & Grau, J. (2008). Listening in the business context: Reviewing the state of research. *The International Journal of Listening, 22,* 141–151.

Gouran, D. S., Wiethoff, W. E., & Doelger, J. A. (1994). *Mastering communication* (2nd ed.). Boston: Allyn & Bacon.

Halone, K. K., & Pechioni, L. L. (2001). Relational listening: A grounded theoretical model. *Communication Reports, 14,* 59–71.

Janusik, L. A., & Wolvin, A. D. (2009). 24 hours in a day: A listening update to the time studies. *The International Journal of Listening, 23,* 104–120.

Osgood, C. E., Suci, G. J., & Tannenbaum, P. H. (1957). *The measurement of meaning.* Urbana: University of Illinois Press.

Pearson, J. C., & Nelson, P. E. (2000). *An introduction to human communication* (8th ed.). New York: McGraw-Hill.

Preiss, R. W., & Gayle, B. M. (2006). Exploring the relationship between listening comprehension and rate of speech. In B. M. Gayle, R. W. Preiss, N. Burell, & M. Allen (Eds.), *Classroom communication and instructional processes* (pp. 315–327). Mahwah, NJ: Lawrence Erlbaum.

Rankin, P. T. (1928). The importance of listening ability. *English Journal, 17,* 623–630.

Sahlstein, E. M. (2000). *Relational rhetorics and RRTs (Relational Rhetorical Terms).* Unpublished manuscript. Iowa City, IA.

Schnapp, D. C. (2008). Listening in context: Religion and spirituality. *The International Journal of Listening, 22,* 133–140.

Steil, L. K. (1997). Listening training: The key to success in today's organizations. In M. Purdy & D. Borisoff (Eds.), *Listening in everyday life: A personal and professional approach* (pp. 213–237). Lanham, MD: University Press of America.

Urdang, L., Hunsinger, W. W., & LaRouche, N. (1991). *A fine kettle of fish and other figurative phrases.* Detroit: Invisible Ink.

Weinrauch, J. D., & Swanda, R., Jr. (1975). Examining the significance of listening: An exploratory study of contemporary management. *Journal of Business Communication, 13,* 25–32.

Wood, J. T. (2009). *Communication in our lives* (5th ed.). Boston: Wadsworth Cengage Learning.

5

Identities and Perceptions

We don't know you, and you don't know us. From reading this book you might have some impressions of us. You know who *you* are, though—not just name and address but the kind of person you are. You have an **identity**, and we don't just mean an ID that you show people to prove your age. You are an individual who is friends with other individuals, each perhaps quirky with a unique personality and identity. You might see these individuals and yourself as persons with a history deep inside, a childhood set of experiences that made them who they are and you who you are. You know things about yourself that no one else knows. You are you, you-nique!

This chapter will teach you that you have multiple identities and that these identities are transacted through communication. Some are created by the situation in which you find yourself or in the company of certain people but not others. (Do you really behave the same way with your mother as you do with your best friend?) Others are the result of cultural symbols attached to "being gay or lesbian" or "being a go-getter or a team player." Some are performed for an audience. In intimate relationships, you can perform and express most of your true self. In a police interview, you may want to conceal some of what you are. In a hospice at the end of your life, you may want to hang onto a little *dignity*. You lose control over the skills, performances, and parts of your body and self that used to compose your identity, and you become physically more dependent on others. Those old folks who look a lot older than you now could be how you will be someday. Think about it.

Identity is partly a *characteristic* (something that you possess), partly a *performance* (something that you do), and partly a *construction of society*. For example, society tells you how to be "masculine" and "feminine" and indicates that "guys can't say that to guys" (Burleson, Holmstrom, & Gilstrap, 2005). This restricts the way in which men can give one another emotional support. Society also provides you with ways to describe a personality;

Focus Questions

1. Some textbooks picture a person's identity like an onion, built layer by layer and communicated slowly as intimacy increases. Does this really make any sense?
2. How do daily interactions with other people form or sustain your identity?
3. How much of your "self" is a performance of social roles where you have to act out "who I am" for other people?
4. What is meant by a symbolic self, and why do we have to account to other people for who we are?
5. What is the role of culture in your identity experiences?

the media focus you on some traits more than others. Categories like *gluttonous, sexy, short, slim, paranoid,* and *kind* are all available to you, but they are not all equally valued.

The ways you express yourself and the ways you respond to other people in your social context *transact* part of your identity. Your identity is partly constructed through your interactions with other people. Have you had the experience of being with someone who makes you nervous when you normally aren't nervous or who helps you relax when you feel tense? In these instances, your identity is molded by the person, situation, or communication. You'll get used to a rather odd phrase in communication studies: "*doing* an identity," used instead of "*having* an identity." Communication scholars now pay close attention to the ways in which people's behavior carries out, enacts, transacts, or *does* an identity in talk with other people.

The transaction of identities is guided in part through perceptions of yourself, others, and various components of an interaction. In other words, your internal views of yourself and others influence the external construction of identities. This notion may be somewhat difficult to comprehend, and we discuss this matter in more detail later in the chapter.

Up front, though, this is a very significant consideration and sets the discipline of communication and this textbook apart from others. Identities, relationships, cultural membership, and the like are not located within people or embedded within their minds waiting to be discovered. These things are instead created symbolically through interactions with others. At the same time, how a person views the world, organizes what is seen, and evaluates this information will influence the symbolic activity that does take place, and ultimately how that symbolic activity is viewed, organized, and evaluated. It is therefore important that these activities are also taken into account when exploring the transaction of identities.

Who Are You?

Bob is a really nice guy. He is a good friend, loyal, trusting, open, honest, comforting, seriously devoted to his kids, caring, charitable, active in his religious community organizing charitable events (especially for mentally challenged kids), giving, respectful, a fabulous cook (he specializes in the cuisines of other cultures), and very caring to his aging parents (he never misses a visit and takes them on a short trip each weekend even though his father does not remember any longer who he is and his mother is seriously arthritic). Bob is the kind of guy who would give you one of his kidneys if he matched and you needed it. Everyone in the neighborhood knows and loves Bob; at some time or another everyone in Baxter Close has experienced his stellar generosity, whether the single-parent family that found groceries on their doorstep the week they ran out of food stamps or the feisty senior lesbian who just lost her lifetime partner and

Dr. Harold "Fred" Shipman was a respected family practitioner in England, working in two practices in the 1980s and 1990s and even appearing on TV in a discussion about the way to treat mentally ill patients. He was a quiet but well-respected pillar of the community. He was also England's most prolific mass murderer and in January 2000 was convicted of murdering 15 patients. Subsequent inquiries revealed that he was directly responsible for the murders of at least 215 people, and that figure is probably a serious underestimate.

needed someone to talk to. He is active in the PTA, does long Saturdays coaching and refereeing the blossoming mixed-sex soccer group that he started, and does a spectacular comedic turn as George W the Orangutan.

At work Bob is the most hated SOB in the Border Security branch of Homeland Security. There is no one who is such a completely ruthless, nasty, dogged, suspicious, awkward cuss. He is an officious, pettifogging a-hole, and there is no one better at interrogation. He nails people who make illegal applications for a green card and has the highest record in the whole border area for catching cheats. People lie to him, and he gets them every time (he read Chapter 3); people fudge, and he owns them; people say things that do not match up with what they wrote on their forms, and he gets it right away without even looking. Nobody gets past Bob. He asks all the right probing questions, uncovers the half truth and the full-out lie, trusts no one, and never accepts at face value anything on an application form (he even caught the fact that one person could not spell his own name the same way in two different places on the same form). He regularly has grown men breaking down in tears in his office. If you get interviewed for immigration by Bob and are not 100% straight up, then he will get you. Believe it.

We all know a version of Bob. We all know a supervisor who is a pain in the buttermilk plant where he rules without mercy, gives no one any breaks, and cuts no slack, but in the rest of his life he is a beacon: a leading member of his church community, a giving and generous community member, and a social delight as long as there is no one there from the workplace.

Other examples surround us everywhere in everyday life. The same person may be unfriendly and distant on one occasion but funny and sociable on another. You may know someone whom you consider to be kind, yet one of your friends sees the person as nasty. In both cases you're talking about the same person, but people can have mood swings as a result of periodic hormonal imbalances, drinking too much, gluten intolerance, or just having had a series of really unfortunate events happen to them on a bad hair day.

College Experience

Consider the situation of nontraditional students and identities, which may apply to you personally or to other students in your classes. Nontraditional students have the same concerns as all students such as getting their work done on time and receiving good grades at the end of the semester or term. However, they view themselves differently. Nontraditional students frequently return to school after working for a number of years, perhaps the result of deciding their line of work was not satisfying or the result of losing their job in a rough economy. Many of these students have been quite successful, and yet they are very apprehensive about entering the classroom. Such students are used to being obeyed, someone to whom people turn for advice, a leader, a mentor, and an example. Which is the *real* person: the successful professional and authoritative leader or the obviously older student in a classroom where previous experience counts for very little?

Now consider the situation of traditional students, which again may apply to you personally or to other students in your classes. These students most likely experienced some success in high school. Many entering students graduated with honors, participated in many activities, received a number of awards and distinctions, were well known in their school, and were looked upon with admiration by others. Now, these students may view themselves as isolated in a sea of people who were equally or even more successful in high school. Which is the *real* person: the standout high school student who excelled at everything or the awkward first-year student seeking some sort of recognition?

Return to these questions once you have read the entire chapter and see if your perspective has changed.

That is perhaps not terribly surprising since many changes in mood are temporary, relatively unimportant, and reversible. Get the hormones back into balance, let them sleep off the hangover, and let the sun shine in, and then they will be back to their same old self.

What is much more complicated for communication scholars is the question of why different people disagree about whether someone is *essentially* good or bad. Why might two professors argue about whether a particular student is (a) intelligent or (b) someone who stands no chance of improving? Why might the bosses in an organization argue about whether someone should be promoted or passed over? If every person had just one identity at the core of his or her multi-layered onion of personality, then these kinds of questions would make no sense.

If people had a stable core inside a set of layers we could peel away to reach "the truth," then we would never be able to change our mind about someone. If someone were a good and loyal friend, he would never turn into an enemy unless he had a personality transplant. Yet you've most likely had the experience of seeing someone in a different light over time. This is a real problem for scholars of communication thinking about the nature of identity and self and why some people do not include "self" in their courses: far too mushy.

When a stranger does something unkind, your first thought may be to blame personality: This is an evil person, perhaps with psychopathic tendencies. Or you could put it down to the identity that had been constructed during childhood when there were some bad experiences. Lawyers often explain their clients' bad behavior in such terms. On the other hand, the "unkind stranger" probably saw identity in personality terms, too, but more favorable ones—as a good decent person who was being irritated by an annoying stranger (you!) and walked away thinking, "What a jerk [or some other non-specific and dehumanizing term]!"

Of course, *you* (and your friends) have never done anything that dehumanizes, stereotypes, or depersonalizes others, have you? You have never called anyone "an illegal" or "a frat boy" or lumped someone together with all other "college kids" or chanted, "Oh, how I hate the team from State."

Framing Identity

Earlier chapters talked about frames for situations and thinking. Shotter (1984) sees identity as a frame for interpreting other people's actions: Your beliefs about other people set the stage for your understanding of how they act. Burke (1969) also saw motives and personality language as helpful frames for interpretation (see Chapter 2). In short, your identity will be revealed in a language that reflects the priorities of a particular culture or relationship and its frames for thinking about how humans should act and describe themselves.

Human beings talk about their identities in ways that are steered by social norms and conventions in their society. In return you expect other people to present such narratives and behaviors. Your culture frames identity as a stable inner self; it therefore feels quite normal for you to think in those terms, so you can easily understand the idea that someone would reveal a private self layer by layer. However, you would be thought crazy if you said, "My identity is blue with an elephant spirit inside." You'd soon be locked up.

You have to use terms and phrases that your audiences recognize as symbolically meaningful in the culture: "I'm a go-getter but quite private, ambitious yet introverted." In other words, you *frame* your talk about yourself and your identity in the language that your culture has taught you to use.

Perceiving Encounters and Transacting Identities

Your framing of an encounter is based, in part, on the perceptions you develop. **Perception** is a process of actively selecting, organizing, and evaluating information, activities, situations, people, and essentially all the things that make up your world. In what follows, we explore this process and its influence on identity construction.

Selecting

In Chapter 4, we discussed how receiving stimuli does not necessarily mean you will recognize their presence or direct your attention to them. Imagine going up to a friend whose concentration is focused on a book (or a newspaper, a television program, a computer screen, a ball game, or any number of objects or activities). You greet her by saying hello or by saying her name, but she does not seem to recognize you are speaking. This person continues to focus solely on the book. You speak again, a little louder this time, and still receive no response. You may have to tap her on the shoulder, hit her over the head, or practically scream to get her attention away from that book. You are not being ignored; this person is simply not attending to, or selecting, the sound of your voice.

You select and focus more on some things going on around you and less on other things. Certain factors influence exactly to what extent you focus. If something stands

In Chapter 10, we discuss how you are more likely to select and attend to particular media that support your beliefs, attitudes, and values using the principle of selective exposure.

out for whatever reason, you are more likely to focus your attention on that. For instance, if you scan a room of people wearing similar clothing, you will likely focus on a person whose clothing is dissimilar to that of the others. Another factor influencing focus is *selective exposure*, which means you are more likely to focus on and expose yourself to that which supports your beliefs, values, and attitudes.

During your interactions with others, you will be more likely to pick up on activities that support your views of the world and pay less attention to those that do not. If you view yourself as a competent person, you will be more likely to pick up on the behaviors of others that uphold this view such as compliments and less likely to focus on behaviors that counter this view such as criticism. The opposite, of course, would happen if you viewed yourself as an incompetent person.

Organizing and Evaluating

Observations of the world are not floating randomly around in your head. Instead, they are organized in ways that allow you to retrieve them when necessary, and new information is connected to previous information that is already organized and stored. **Schemata** are mental structures that are used to organize information in part by clustering or linking associated material. For example, information about relationships can be stored and connected in "relationship" schemata and drawn from when needed. Since this information is stored in a relatively accessible manner, it can be used to make sense of what you are experiencing and to anticipate what might happen in a given situation.

This particular approach is based on the work of George Kelly (1955), who saw people as scientists making hypotheses about everyday life and then testing their effectiveness. When researchers conduct experiments, they make calculated guesses about what will happen and then decide if what they anticipated actually occurred once the experiment has been completed. Kelly maintained that people do the same thing in their everyday lives. For instance, upon meeting you may greet someone in a particular way because—based on past experience and observations—you believe doing so will lead to approval from the other person and a proper relational connection. If your expectations are proved *correct*, your existing way of viewing the world will be strengthened, and you will be more likely to perform the same action in the future. If your expectations are proved *incorrect*, you will likely revise your way of viewing the world, and you will be less likely to perform the same action in the future.

Your organizational system is constantly being updated and modified based on new experiences and as a result of evaluating its accuracy and usefulness. This system seems pretty efficient and beneficial. However, it is not without its disadvantages. Kelly (1955) maintained that a person's processes are "channelized" by the ways in which events are anticipated. As a result, certain ways of acting and viewing the world become more deeply ingrained in your thinking. Imagine running the end of a stick in a straight line over and over in the same spot on the ground. Eventually, an indentation begins to develop and becomes deeper and deeper as you continue to run the end of that stick in the same place. The same thing can be imagined with certain ways of behaving and viewing the world. The more you behave in a certain way and the more often you view the world in the same way, the deeper and more ingrained it becomes in your thinking. After a while, it becomes difficult to imagine behaving in another way or viewing the world in a different way.

Consequently, Kelly (1955) urged people to imagine a table as being soft. When touching a table, you probably anticipate that it will be hard, and most of the time you will be correct. However, you should always consider the possibility that the table will be soft. Always consider the opposite, and always consider other possibilities. When done consistently, a person's behaviors and views frequently become seen as correct and natural rather than things that should be constantly evaluated and reassessed. Alternatives may or may not be better, but they should always be considered.

Kelly's (1955) work has resulted in a better understanding of the ways in which people think and relate to others. It can also be used to better understand how our perceptions influence the transaction of identities through prototypes, personal constructs, and scripts.

Prototypes

A **prototype** is the best-case example of something (Fehr, 1993). You may have a prototype of an ideal romantic partner, for instance. This prototype could be a composite of different people or an actual person. Accordingly, your romantic partner prototype could be compiled from characteristics of past romantic partners, or it could be a single romantic partner. It could be made up of people you actually know, people you have observed, and media representations. All prototypes are influenced culturally.

When identities are transacted they are broadly measured using prototypes as standards. Someone attempting to construct the identity of a romantic partner would use his or her prototype as a model, and other people would use their respective prototypes of a romantic partner in order to evaluate and make sense of this person.

Personal Constructs

Personal constructs are bipolar dimensions used to measure and evaluate things. Whereas prototypes tend to be broad categories, personal constructs are narrow and more specific characteristics. These personal constructs can be used in the development of a prototype and to determine how close someone may come to meeting all the criteria. Using romantic partners again as an example, the following personal constructs could be used:

Attractive–Unattractive

Kind–Mean

Passive–Aggressive

Intelligent–Ignorant

Humorous–Dull

Employed–Unemployed

Like prototypes, personal constructs are used to make sense of the world and to evaluate what is taking place. Personal constructs, though, are more specific and detailed. They can be used to determine just how well a person measures up according to certain categories.

Scripts

Scripts are guides for behavior developed from our system of knowledge. A movie or television script informs actors what they should be doing and saying. Such scripts assist actors in performing a character. Likewise, you use scripts when performing social roles and enacting identities in everyday life. For example, you know what to say and how to act when performing the role or identity of a student. You are following the script of a student. Using the running example of romantic partners, you know what you should do and say as a romantic partner through scripts developed from personal experience and observations of others. You know when the other "actors" are following a script correctly and performing an identity accurately. You also know when they have forgotten their lines and are giving a horrible performance.

While following scripts is important, most actors are required to improvise their performance from time to time. They also explore the creation of a character by saying different things and behaving in different ways. You must do the same thing when you are performing particular identities. You develop your own spin on an identity. Furthermore, you must improvise and edit scripts when scenes or contexts change.

Listen in on Your Life

How would you describe yourself? Would you give your national identity, ethnic identity, gender identity, sexual identity, age identity, social class identity, religious identity, or anything else?

Now check the categories that you can use to personalize your profile on Facebook or another social networking site. People are generally asked to identify themselves by association with particular categories and such items as favorite videos and music, hobbies, and sexual orientation. Are these the categories you would use to describe yourself to a child, an employer, or a new neighbor? How would you feel if your instructor composed a slide show of all the Facebook profiles of the people in your class and showed it to everyone?

Scripts are subject to change and revision through experience and assessment. Sometimes a person discovers the table is soft! Beyond careful evaluation, however, scripts change with the passing of time. This change is especially noticeable with scripts involving identities associated with close personal relationships. For instance, the script of a friend in elementary school is different from the script of a friend in high school. Both scripts are different from the script of a middle-aged friend. Returning yet again to the example of romantic partners, the script of a romantic partner early in the relationship will likely be different from the script of a romantic partner after a number of years in the same relationship.

Ultimately, scripts focus our attention on the mutual influence of perception and the transaction of identities. Identities are performed though interactions with others, and perceptions guide our understanding of what should be done and the evaluation of symbolic performance. In what follows, we examine how people may view themselves as having an established inner core or identities to be revealed, but in actuality identities are performed though communication and personal relationships.

Identity as Inner Core: The Self-Concept

We start with the "commonsense" idea that you have a true inner self. By the end of the chapter, however, we will show that there is more to learn about personal identity built by relationships with other people. The chapter connects identity to language; to other people; to the norms, rules, and categories in society/culture; and to narratives of origin and belonging to other relationships. This identity may be represented by such statements as "I'm an African American" or, on a bumper sticker, "Proud parent of an Honor Roll student at City High." These examples make statements of identity that claim it through relationships with other people or membership in groups, not just as a person with an inner core.

Psychic/Reflective Self

When you think about persons as having some true personal, private, and essential core, covered with layers of secrecy, privacy, and convention, this is known as a **self-concept**. Because everyone is assumed to have this core, you are alarmed by people who have multiple personalities or are bipolar. Someone should have only one consistent personality; people who have more parts are disturbed or irrational. Your identity may be hard for other people to reach, but according to many self-help books and celebrity biographies, it is reachable. Communication serves to help people *talk about* or *express* what is inside, perhaps in greater depth as they get to know one another better. Communication scholars can teach you the skill of expressing yourself well or help you be open and honest and let "the real you" be heard.

The Weirdness of Consistent Expectations

A consistent inner self would be made up of the person's broad habits of thought (e.g., someone is kind, outward-looking, introverted, or self-centered). You might see that self revealed communicatively in styles of behavior (e.g., someone is aggressive, calm, ambitious, reliable, hardworking, or manipulative) or in characteristic styles of perception (e.g., someone is paranoid, trusting, insightful, or obstinate). *Personality* is the label that you would first use to describe someone's *identity* if you were asked about it casually in a conversation by someone who wanted to know what that person was like.

Photo 5.1 How do daily interactions with other people form or sustain your identity? What is being communicated here about gender, identity, and culture? (See page 129.)

But it's a very odd idea indeed. People are too complex. A person can *simultaneously* be many identities. For example, a person can simultaneously be a loving parent, a vegetarian, a conservative, quick-tempered, a good dancer, a bad cook, business savvy, and a team player. You also have a choice in the identity you describe: a relational identity (friend/parent), an interactional identity (worker/customer/server), a sex or gender identity (male/female/masculine/feminine/GLBT), a racial/ethnic identity (the boxes to check on government forms), or a behavioral identity (extrovert/introvert). It's a choice, then, to describe your identity.

Unstable Behaviors

Another key point about identity comes from everyday experience. People are multilayered and can have different moods, being good company on one day and bad on another. People can fluctuate during the course of the day, and events may happen to them that cause them to act "out of character." These fluctuations help demonstrate that it's a peculiar idea that somebody could have a *fixed* inner identity if it can also be so variable and complex over time.

The best you can hope for, then, is that the more you get to know someone through talk, the more you can understand the person's usual self. You can learn about what triggers a tailspin or a rant.

The upshot, though (and we are sorry to spoil it for you), is that all the magazine articles that offer to tell you about "the real [Lady Gaga/Beyoncé/Ashton Kutcher/

	Known to Self	Unknown to Self
Known to Others	Arena	Blind Spot
Unknown to Others	Façade	Unknown

Figure 5.1   The Johari Window

Source: From "The Johari Window: A Graphic Model of Interpersonal Awareness," by J. Luft and H. Ingham, 1955, in *Proceedings of the Western Training Laboratory in Group Development* (Los Angeles: University of California, Los Angeles).

Joseph Stalin/Sarah Palin]" are always going to be nonsense. The notion that someone has a real single inner core is suspect for communication scholars from the get-go. Also, if identities could not be changed or reviewed, there would be no therapists or communication textbooks with advice on how to develop your communication and presentation skills (i.e., how to present your "true self" more effectively).

The Johari window, developed in 1955 by two guys called Joe (Luft) and Harry (Ingham)—and we're not kidding—distinguishes between what a person knows about self and what others know about the person. As you can see in Figure 5.1, people have *blind spots:* Everyone but the person in question can see something obvious (for example, that Bob is "a pain"). In other cases we pretend (*façade*), concealing from people something that we know about ourselves (guilty secrets and so forth). The *arena* is basically where we openly act out a public identity that everyone else knows and recognizes.

Describing a Self

Ask people to tell you who they are. They will tell you their name and start revealing information about themselves, usually with a narrative that places their self in various contexts. *Steve Duck* indicates to someone in your culture that the person is male and has to put up with many very unoriginal jokes about his name. Although he has lived in the United States of America for more than 25 years, he is a Brit, or English as he prefers to think of it. His family comes from Whitby in North Yorkshire, England, where the first recorded Duck (John Duck) lived in 1288. John Duck and Steve Duck share the same skeptical attitude toward authority figures. John is in the historical record because he sued the Abbot of Whitby over ownership of a piece of land. John was descended from the Vikings who sacked and then colonized Whitby in about 800 A.D. *Duck* is a Viking nickname–based surname for a hunchback. (Have you ever ducked out of the way of anything? If so, you have crouched like a hunchback.)

Steve Duck is also relatively short for a man, is bald but bearded, likes watching people but is quite shy, and can read Latin, which is how he found out about John Duck while researching his family tree. Steve likes the music of Ralph Vaughan Williams, enjoys doing cryptic crosswords, knows about half the words that Shakespeare knew, and has occasionally lied. He resents his mother's controlling behavior, was an Oxford college rowing coxswain (cox'n), loves reading Roman history, and is gluten intolerant. He thinks he is a good driver and is proud of his dad, who was a Quaker pacifist (that antiauthority thing again) who won three medals for bravery in World War II for driving an unarmed ambulance into the front line of a war zone in order to rescue two seriously wounded (armed) comrades. Steve has lived in Iowa for 26 years. He has had two marriages and four children, carries a Swiss Army knife (and as many other gadgets as will fit onto one leather belt), and always wears two watches. He is wondering whether to get the new Swiss Army knife that has a data storage capacity, a laser pointer, and a fingerprint password. Sweet.

Self-Description and Stereotypes

Notice that some of this information about Steve's identity is *self-description*. That is, these words describe him in much the same way that anyone else could without knowing him personally (e.g., male, bearded, short, bald, two watches, magnetic sex appeal).

Self-description usually involves information about self that is obvious in *public* (or on your résumé). If you wear your college T-shirt, talk with a French accent, or are short, this evidence about you is available even to strangers who can see your physical appearance or hear how you sound. "Identity" in this sense is communicated publicly and physically. It parks the individual in categories (national, racial, or ethnic groups) or else lumps him or her into stereotypes. It isn't really an individual identity but is more about group membership.

Case in Point

Analyze recent interaction with people you would consider a friend, an acquaintance, and a stranger. What, if any, disclosure took place? What does this tell you about disclosure and relationships?

Self-Disclosure

Some points in Steve's description of himself count as **self-disclosure**: the revelation of information that people could not know unless Steve *made* it known. In the above example, these are the points that describe particular feelings and emotions that other people would not know unless Steve specifically disclosed them. The *resents, is proud of, enjoys, thinks*, and *is wondering* parts give you a view of his identity that you could not directly obtain any other way, though you might work it out from what Steve says or does.

These parts, since they are spoken as insights, are self-disclosure, not self-description. The term *self-disclosure* is limited to revelation of private, sensitive, and confidential information relevant to identity. Values, fears, secrets, assessments, evaluations, and preferences all count as such confidences that you share with only a few people.

The Importance of Being Open

Jourard (1964, 1971) wrote about self-disclosure as making your identity "transparent" to others. People who make the most disclosures are acting in the most psychologically healthy manner. Early research also connected self-disclosure with growth in intimacy. Classic reports (e.g., Derlega, Metts, Petronio, & Margulis, 1993) found that the more people become intimate, the more they disclose to each other information that is both broad and deep. Also, the more you get to know someone's inner knowledge structures, the closer you feel to him or her.

Closeness generally develops only if the information is revealed in a way that indicates it is privileged information that other people do not know. For example, if a man lets you (and only you) know the secret that he has a serious invisible illness (such as diabetes, lupus, or prostate cancer), an unusually strong fear of spiders, or a significantly distressed marriage, you feel valued and trusted, because he let you into his inner life.

Openness and Closeness

There is an important relational process going on here: When someone tells you about inner identity, you feel honored and valued by someone's revelation of the inner self, or you may actually not care for what you are hearing. The important point is that disclosure itself does not make a difference to a relationship; the relationship makes a difference to the value of disclosure. If you feel the relationship is enhanced by self-disclosure, it is. If you don't, no matter how intimate the disclosure, the relationship does not grow in intimacy.

Later research has refined this idea (Dindia, 2000; Petronio, 2002). For example, too much disclosure of identity is not necessarily a good thing at all times. You've probably been bored by somebody telling you more than you wanted to know—TMI! By contrast, people who are closed and don't tell anything about themselves are regarded as psychologically *un*healthy.

Communication scholar Kathryn Dindia (2000) points out that the revelation of identity is rarely a simple progression and is certainly not just the declaration of facts and then—*bam!*—intimacy. Self-disclosure is a dynamic process tied to other social processes that relate to your identity and how you disclose yourself over time. It continues through the life of relationships and is not a single onetime choice about whether to disclose or not. Part of your identity is the skill with which you reveal or conceal information about yourself and your feelings, as any good poker player knows.

Make Your Case

Consider the following example: José learns more about Juanita's identity when she discloses something about herself that makes him feel positive about their relationship. It also makes him nervous because, in the past, he did something that her disclosure shows she would not like. So he tells her what he did and how sorry he is about it. Juanita likes the fact that he confides in her and feels better about the relationship as a result. She wonders if José is still the same person he was when he did the bad thing or if he is genuinely sorry and has changed.

Using this example, make the case that identity, self-disclosure, and relationships are mutually connected *transactions,* not just simply the peeling away of layers.

Dynamics of Revelation

In fact, the revelation of your identity, like identity itself, is an open-ended process that continues indefinitely in relationships even after they have become deeply intimate. It is dynamic, continuous, and circular so that it is hard to say where self-disclosure or identity begins or ends. It is also influenced by the behavior and communication of the other person(s)—the audience. Both self-disclosure and identity occur in the context of a relationship that has ups and downs.

Dialectic Tensions

Everyone places a limit on the amount of information that he or she reveals to others, and some choose to remain private, even in intimate relationships. Baxter and Montgomery (1996) identify a push-pull **dialectic tension** of relationships. These tensions occur whenever you are in two minds about something or feel a simultaneous pull in two directions. Some communication scholars (e.g., Baxter, 2004, 2011; Baxter & Braithwaite, 2008) suggest that there simply is no singular core of identity but a dialogue

Photo 5.2 How do you explain the fact that a person can experience different sides of self and hold different views simultaneously? (See page 129.)

between different "voices" in your head. For example, in relationships, you want to feel connected to someone else, but you do not want to give up all of your independence. You can see how you—and your identity—can grow by being in a relationship, but you can also see that this comes at a simultaneous cost or threat to your identity, independence, and autonomy.

The autonomy–connectedness dialectic is one dialectic tension, but another is openness–closedness, where people feel social pressure to be open yet also want to retain control over private information. This tension leads to people sometimes giving out and sometimes holding back information about themselves. Even in the same relationship, a person can feel willing to reveal information sometimes but crowded and guarded at other times. A personal relationship is not a consistent or a simple experience any more than identity is. Each affects the other over time. Also you may tell different versions of your identity to different audiences on different occasions.

Identity and Its Boundaries

In fact, people in relationships negotiate boundaries of privacy (Petronio, 2002). Part of the difference between friendship and mere acquaintance is that you have stronger boundaries around your identity for acquaintances than you do for friends.

As Jon Hess (2000) notes, you simply don't like some people. You don't want them to know "personal stuff" and may actively limit what they find out. Caughlin and Afifi (2004) have shown that even intimate partners sometimes prefer to completely avoid topics that may annoy or provoke the other person.

Petronio (2002) deals with the inconsistencies in the revelation of information by pointing to the importance of boundary management of the topics within different relational settings. People experience a tension between a desire for privacy and a demand for openness differently in different relationships. Couples make up their own rules for controlling the boundaries of privacy. So, for example, two people may define, between themselves, the nature of topics that they will mention in front of other people and what they will keep to themselves. A married couple may decide what topics it can discuss in front of the children, for instance, and these topics may change as the children grow older. In other words, people show, employ, and work within different parts of their identity with different audiences at different times.

Self-Disclosure and Boundaries: Who Am I, for Whom?

One of Petronio's (2002) key points is that the suitability of something for disclosure is itself affected by relational context and by agreement between the partners. There are no absolutes.

She also draws attention to the ways in which a couple can decide how much to disclose. Amount, type, or subject of self-disclosure can be a topic for discussion (often called *metacommunication* or communication about communication). In contrast to Jourard's (1964, 1971) idea that there are absolute rules about self-disclosure of identity, Petronio (2002) demonstrates that it is a matter of personal preference, worked out explicitly between the partners in a relationship through communication.

The upshot of this discussion of self-disclosure questions identity as a straightforward, layered possession of your own inner being. Your self-disclosure and your identity are jointly owned by you and a partner. There is more to identity than just *having* or *revealing* one,

Self-disclosure reacts to a **norm of reciprocity** (an unspoken rule about fairness and giving back about as much as you receive). If you say something self-disclosing to someone, that person should tell you something about himself or herself in return. If one person keeps telling information but gets nothing back, the person will stop doing it. Oddly enough, the norm of reciprocity can actually be used to interrogate people or find out information about them indirectly. If you say something personal about yourself, that loads an obligation on the other people to respond by saying something equally personal about themselves.

then. The norms of appropriateness for reciprocity, the rules about amount of revealed information (especially negative information) show that there is a social context for communication about identity. Identity is revealed within that set of social rules, cultural norms, and contexts.

Identity and Other People

Saying that there is a social context for identity is basically making two points:

1. Society as a whole broadly influences the way you think about identity in the first place.

2. The other people who meet a person may influence the way that person's identity is expressed.

When you reveal your identity, you often use stories to tell the audience something about yourself and help its members shape their sense of who you are. As with self-disclosure, so too with stories: They are influenced by both society/culture and the specific persons or audience to which you do the telling.

Narrative Self and Altercasting

People tell stories about themselves and other people all the time and pay special care to what they will say, particularly for occasions like job interviews, sales pitches, and strategic communication of all sorts. You may have noticed that you adapt stories of your identity for consumption by other people in a social context (see Chapter 2).

Stories We Tell

A report about your identity characterizes you by means of a memory or history in its narrative or a typical or an amusing instance that involves character (your identity), plot, motives, scenes, and other actors (see Chapter 2). Even when you reveal an internal model of self, this story organizes your identity in ways other people understand in terms of the rules that govern accounts, narratives, and other social reports. As Kellas (2008) has pointed out, narratives can be an *ontology* (how I came to be who I am), an *epistemology* (how I think about the world), an *individual construction,* or a *relational process,* such as when romantic partners tell the story about how they first met.

Origin Stories

Reports about an identity have a narrative structure that builds off both the sense of origin derived from early life and a sense of continuity. The self comes from somewhere and has roots—"I'm Hispanic," "I'm a true Southerner," "I'm a genuine Irish McMahan."

Identity comes in part from narratives of origin. These can be personal, cultural, or species ("What was my great-grandfather like?" "Where did I come from?" "Where did our culture come from?" "How did humans get started?"). A sense of origin leads, for most people, straight back to their family, the first little society that they ever experienced (Huisman, 2008). The specific context of family experience is the first influence on a person's sense of origin and identity. It gives the person a sense of connection to a larger network of others. Indeed, in African American cultures, "the family" can be seen as a whole *community* that goes beyond the direct blood ties that define "family" in other cultures. The earliest memories give you a sense of origin as represented by your experiences in a family-like environment.

Origin, Memory, and the Telling of Your Self

However, early memories are not neutral facts. They are loaded, like dice, by the experiences you think you had in your family. A childhood seen as terrible can make you absorb an identity that gives you low self-esteem, for example (Duck, 2011), and could lead you to treat later relational opportunities with great caution. People treated respectfully by parents end up confident and secure about themselves, whereas those treated by their parents as nuisances come to see themselves that way. They also become anxious in relationships or avoid them altogether.

Table 5.1 Early Experiences and Influences on Your Later Life

Early experiences affect your thought worlds/worlds of meaning.

They influence your sense of identity.

They create identity narratives about you and your history.

They influence feelings about self, the goals that you set for life, the levels of ability you feel you have, the ways you relate to other people, the dark fears that you hoard all your life, your beliefs about the way to behave properly (religious beliefs, rituals about birthdays, who cares for people emotionally, whether sports "matter"), and whether you see life as peacefully cozy or violently conflicted.

A key point, then, is that by both direct and indirect means, your interactions and communication with other people shape your views of yourself. This happens even when you don't realize it or necessarily want it to happen—and this influence is not automatically something you just grow out of. Therapists get paid to put clients' childhood into better perspective! Early experiences in "the family" lay down many of the tracks upon which your later life will run.

Stories about you must fit with what your audience believes to be coherent and acceptable. It is not just that you *have* a self but that you shape the *telling* of your identity in a way that your audience (culture, friends) will accept.

Photo 5.3 How is your sense of identity represented by connections to the past? (See page 129.)

This distinction is like the difference between the words in a joke and the way someone tells it: The telling adds something performative to the words, and a person can spoil a joke by telling it badly. Likewise with identity, it has to be performed or told in appropriate ways. When Bob, the nontraditional student, the Purdue fan, or the frat boy brags about his achievements to friends, he probably tells his identity differently than he would to former workmates, the police, Indiana University fans, or the dean of students.

Labeling

Identity is also made by **labeling** the characteristics that you want to stand out. One of our faculty colleagues refers to himself as "Dr. Dave," which creates a certain kind of image, a mixture of professionalism and accessibility that is also an amusing cross-reference to the cultural icon Dr. Phil. Such nicknames and labels can be used for reinforcement of a type of identity. In the case of *other people,* a technical term used in discussion of communication and identity is **altercasting**. Altercasting refers to how language can give people an identity and then force them to live up to the description, whether positive or negative (Marwell & Schmitt, 1967). For example, you are altercasting when you say, "As a good friend, you will want to help me here" or "Only a fool would . . ." These label the listener as a certain kind of person (or not), by positioning the person to respond appropriately (as a friend or not as a fool). Even such small elements of communication transact your identity and the identities of those people around you.

When you communicate about yourself, therefore, you assume that the audience will understand you, so you assume a shared basis for understanding other people. On top of that, you assume that special people—friends, for example—not only understand your "self" but also do reality checks for you. When people talk about identity, then, they assume their audience will be able to comprehend, interpret, and probably support it.

The earlier description of Steve, for example, mentions a Swiss Army knife because that particular item is well known in the culture. Any description of an identity is therefore steered by beliefs about the criteria, categories, and descriptions that will matter to, or even impress, the audience. For example, people project a professional identity by wearing smart business clothes to a job interview. People also communicate their cultural identity through their accent and behavior. Thus "who you are" is a *relational* point.

Symbolic Identity

Your sense of self is influenced by language frames, culture, origin, membership, and other people's thoughts about you. But don't you actually *do* a lot of your identity for specific people, such as your priest, your neighbor, your best friend, and your coworkers and customers?

The Many Yous

Most people have a range of identities that they can turn on as necessary according to where they are and who is there with them. In that case, identity is not so much something that you *have* as it is something that you *do* in ways that people recognize as suitable.

Do you ever feel like a different person when you are with your friends compared to when you're talking to your mother? Are you the same person all the time, or do you have good and bad days? Do you ever do things you regret or regard as not typical? Ever say things you regret?

Most people have protested that someone has misrepresented them. Until now you would not have called that resistance to an altercasting by refusing to accept it, but that is what it is. A hostile or negative person can make you feel very bad about yourself. Have you ever met anyone who didn't really "get" what you are about?

On the other hand, you may have had a close relationship with a partner that felt good because you were able to be your *true self* around the other person or because the person helped bring out sides of you that other people could not. Did you struggle to assert an identity independent from your parents when you were a teenager?

You must already be wondering how any of that is possible if "you" are one identity. You may also have started to think about how advertising, religion, and social fashions influence the ways you dress and act. Other people can affect your values, the choices you make, and how these feed into your sense of identity. Your culture and your identity at the very least interact with one another. At most, culture and its icons (pop stars, fashion models, celebrities) account for quite a lot of your identity, by showing you how to dress and how to behave and what standards of belief are "OK."

Symbolic Self

The lesson is simple: Your identity is shaped by culture and the people you interact with. This is because you can

Contrarian Challenge

If you do not have a central core that is "you," then how come people who know you well can apparently predict what you will do and know how you should be dealt with?

reflect that your "self" is an object of other people's perceptions and that they can do critical thinking or listening about you as well. In short, your identity is a **symbolic self**, a self that exists for other people and goes beyond what it means to you; it arises from social interaction with other people. As a result, you fit identity descriptions into the form of narratives that your society and your particular acquaintances know about and accept. Hence, any identity that you offer to other people is based on the fact that you all share meanings about what is important in defining a person's identity.

Symbols and Identity: Reflection

Another way of thinking about identity, then, is in terms of how broad social forces affect or even transact an individual's view of who he or she is. This set of ideas is referred to as **symbolic interactionism**. In particular, George Herbert Mead (1934) suggested that people get their sense of self from other people and from being aware that others observe, judge, and evaluate one's behavior. How many times have you done or not done something because of how you would look to your friends if you did it? Has your family ever said, "What will the neighbors think?"

Mead (1934) called this phenomenon the human ability to adopt an **attitude of reflection**. You think about how you look in other people's eyes or reflect on the fact that other people can see you as a social object from their point of view. Guided by these reflections, you do not always do what you want to do but what you think people will accept. You may end up doing something you don't want to do because you cannot think how to say no to another person in a reasonable way. You cannot just stamp your foot and shout "SHAN'T!"

Your identity, then, is not yours alone. Indeed, Mead (1934) also saw self as a transacted result of communicating with other people: You learn how to be an individual by recognizing the way that people treat you. You come to see your identity through the eyes of other people, for whom you are a meaningful object. People recognize you and treat you differently from everyone else, as distinct in their eyes and so in your own.

Self as Others Treat You

Relationships connect through communication to the formation of your identity. If other people treat you with respect, you come to see yourself as respected, and self-respect becomes part of your identity. If your parents treated you like a child even after you had grown older, they drew out from you some sense that you were still a child, which may have caused you to feel resentment. If you are intelligent and people treat you as interesting, you may come to see yourself as having different value to other people than does someone

Physically attractive people often act confidently because they are aware of the fact that other people find them attractive. On the other hand, unattractive people have learned that they cannot rely on their looks to make a good impression. They need other ways of impressing other people (e.g., by developing a great sense of humor; Berscheid & Reis, 1998). In a phrase, you come to see yourself as others see you.

who is not treated as intelligent. You get so used to the idea that it gets inside your "identity" and becomes part of who you are, but it originated from other people, not from you.

If you are tall, tough, and muscular (not short, bald, and carrying a Swiss Army knife), perhaps people habitually treat you with respect and caution. Over time, you get used to the idea, and identity is enacted and transacted in communication as a person who expects respect and a little caution from other people (Duck, 2011). Eventually, you will not have to act in a generally intimidating way in order to make people respectful. Your manner of communicating comes to reflect expected reactions to you. Although your identity began in the way you were treated by other people, it eventually becomes transacted in communication.

Society as Other Individuals: Society's Secret Agents

Another way of thinking about this is to see how "society" gets your friends to do its work for it. You have never met a society or a culture, and you never will. You will only ever meet people who (re)present some of a society's key values to you. This contact with other folks puts them in the role of *Society's Secret Agents*. These people you meet and talk with are doing your society's work by enacting ways that culture represents the values that are desirable within it.

When you communicate with other people in your culture, you get information about what works and what doesn't, what is acceptable and what isn't, and how much you count in that society—what your identity is "worth." For example, the dominant culture in the United States typically values ambition, good looks, hard work, demonstration of material success, and a strong code of individuality. People stress those values in their talk ("The American Dream"/"Winners") or else feel inadequate because they don't stack up against these values ("Losers").

Of course, you are forced to interact with some people whether you like them or not (coworkers, professors, or relatives, for example). The principle is the same even though you most often think of the influence of your friends and relatives or key teachers on your identity. Nonfriends may challenge aspects of your sense of identity and make you reflect on the question, "Who am I?" Sometimes this reflection results in reinforced confidence in your opinions, but

Photo 5.4 What is meant by a symbolic self, and why do we have to account to other people for who we are? (See page 129.)

sometimes it undermines, modifies, or even challenges them. Either way, discussions of everyday communication transact some effect on your view of self, your identity. Your sense of self/identity comes from interactions with other people representing society as a whole.

Individuals acquire their individuality through the social practices in which they carry out their lives. Accordingly, they encounter powerful forces of society that are enacted by Society's Secret Agents in ordinary interactions. That "raised eyebrow" from your neighbor/instructor/team fan was actually society at work! Your "self" is structured and enacted in relation to those people who have power over you in formal ways, like the police, but most often you encounter the institutions within a society through its secret agents: public opinion. The people you know who express opinions about moral issues of the day and give you their judgments—they are Society's Secret Agents, guiding what other people do and thinking just as they do. And for that matter, your talk with other people makes you an agent also. Every time you comment on someone else's behavior, dress, relationships, or speech, you (yes, you) are helping to enforce social norms and practices.

Transacting a Self in Interactions With Others

In keeping with this book's theme, you can't have a self without also having relationships with other people—both the personal relationships you choose and the social relationships you reject. A person cannot have a concept of self without reflection on identity via the views of other people with whom he or she has relationships. Your identity is *transacted* or constituted in part from two things: First, you take into yourself the beliefs and prevailing norms of the society in which you live. Second, you are *held to account* for the identity that you project. As a football fan, you lose face if you don't know the score during a game or cannot name your own team's quarterback. As a student, you are expected to know answers about the book you are reading for your class.

Banality of Life as an Identity Maker

Again, your identity is a complex result not only of your own thinking, history, and experience but also of your interaction with other people and their influence on you, both as individuals and as Society's Secret Agents. Behind all those things that you think of as abstract social structures, like "the law," are real individuals acting in relation to one another (you and the police officer). These social relations get internalized into yourself. You slow down at speed-limit signs not because you want to but because you saw the police car and don't need another ticket.

Strategic Communication

People develop impressions of others through social networking profiles. Consider what your profile says about you. Does your profile convey the identity or identities you desire? If not, what might be changed to help construct the desired identities? If your profile is working, how can it be enhanced?

The routine ordinary banality of everyday life talk with friends who share the same values and talk about them day by day (a) actually does something for society and (b) helps make you who you are. Daily routines like meeting at 11 A.M. for coffee in the coffee room put events in a predictable framework of meaning through trivial and pedestrian communication (Wood & Duck, 2006). But—here's the point of this section, so remember it well—you *do* your identity in front of the audiences, and they might evaluate and comment on whether you're doing it right.

The same kinds of processes occur in interaction when you profess your undying allegiance to one football team and your supposed hatred of the opposing team, or say that murder is wrong or that bankers are gouging customers. The people around you do not resent it but actually encourage you and reinforce your expression of ideas that make up your identity. They share it and support it. Just as Bob and his colleagues dehumanize "illegals" as targets for his most diligent attention and scrutiny—and his colleagues admire him for it—so do you when you categorize the opposing team as some kind of enemy. The underlying idea—that a group of people can be treated as nothing more than depersonalized, dehumanized others with no appreciable individuality—runs through team loyalty and rivalry, town versus college kids, treating older students as aliens, and any other kind of stereotyping.

Performative Self

Other people influence who you are and how you are treated. Other people use labels and judge your behavior. You are not just an inner core but part of a heritage. You are not just you; you are a symbol in a cultural and social structure.

On top of that, add the curious idea that you don't just *have* an identity; you actually *do* one. Identity is not just *having* a symbolic sense of self but *doing* it in the presence of other people and doing it well in their eyes. This is an extremely interesting and provocative fact about communication: Everyone *does* his or her identity for an audience, like an actor in a play. **Performative self** means that selves are creative performances based on the social demands and norms of a given situation. As we will now discuss, you try to present the right face to people you are with and do your identity differently in front and back regions.

Mock put-downs are a common form of intimate banter in English-speaking countries but not in Eastern cultures. This suggests that face is culturally influenced on top of everything else that influences it. For instance, direct challenges to a person's competence ("You are a failure!") are openly offensive. Friends, though, may have a running joke between them that allows them to say it to one another.

Facework Revisited

Facework is part of what happens in everyday life communication (Chapter 2), and people have a sense of their own dignity. This gets transacted in everyday communication by polite protection of the person's "face."

This idea is about the performance of one's identity in public, the presentation of the self to people in a way that is intended to make the self look good.

Erving Goffman (1959) indicated the way in which momentary social forces affect identity portrayal. Goffman was interested in how identity is performed in everyday life so that people manage their image to make everyone "look good" (Cupach & Metts, 1994). The concept of "looking good" of course means "looking good *to other people*." It is therefore essentially a relational concept. (Table 5.2 provides challenges to a person's face.)

Table 5.2 Embarrassments and Predicaments

Embarrassment is when you perform a behavior that is inconsistent with the identity you want to present (Cupach & Metts, 1994; Metts, 2000). Someone who wants to impress an interviewer but instead spills coffee on his or her lap undercuts "face" of professional competence by being clumsy. Someone who wants to present a "face" of calmness and confidence but who suddenly blushes or twitches allows nonverbal behavior to contradict the identity of being cool and composed. The *performance* of an identity (face) is undercut by a specific behavior that does not fit.

Predicaments present a longer challenge to the performative self (think of predicaments as extended embarrassment). If you go to a job interview and your very first answer makes you look stupid, you still have to carry on, with the interviewers all thinking you are a hopeless, worthless, and unemployable idiot. You cannot leave; you have to sit it out watching their polite smiles and feeling terrible.

It takes you one step closer to looking at the interpersonal interaction that occurs on the ground every day. Rather than looking at society in an abstract way, Goffman (1959) focused on what you actually *do* in interactions. In part, your portrayal of yourself is shaped by the social needs at the time, the social situation, the social frame, and the circumstances surrounding your performance. Remember the server from Chapter 1? She does not introduce herself that way to her *friends* ("Hi, I'm Alice, and I'll be your server tonight") except as a joke, so her performance of the server identity is restricted to those times and places where it is appropriate.

Front and Back Regions

Goffman (1959) differentiated a **front region** and **back region** to social performance: The front region/front stage is *not a place* but *an occasion* where your professional, proper self is performed. For example, a server is all smiles and civility in the front stage of the restaurant when talking to customers. This behavior might be different from how he or she performs in the back region/backstage (say, the restaurant kitchen) when talking with the cooks or other servers and making jokes about the customers or about being disrespectful to them. But again, the back region is not just a place: If all servers are standing around in the restaurant before the customers come in and they are just chatting informally among themselves, the instant the first customer comes through the door, their demeanor will change to "professional" and they will switch to a front-region performance.

That means the performance of your identity is not sprung into action by your own free wishes but by social cues that this is the time to perform your "self" in that way. An identity is a performance. It shows how a person makes sense of the world not just alone but within a context provided by others.

Any identity connects to other identities. You can be friendly when you are with your friends, but you are expected to be professional when on the job and to do student identity when in class. So is this what allows Bob to be "two people," one at work and one in the social community? Is he just doing a front-region SOB performance at work?

Individuals inevitably draw on knowledge shared in any community, so any person draws on information that is both personal and communal. If you change from thinking of identity as about "self as character" and instead see it as "self as performer," you also must consider the importance of changes in performance to suit different audiences and transactive situations.

Self Constituted/Transacted in Everyday Practices

We have seen that identity is not just a personal inner core but a communicative performance molded by surrounding cultural influences, the way that you *do* your identity and how you are recognized as having one. Your practical performance of "being yourself" is affected by the social norms that are in place to guide communication in a given society. People judge your identity performance in a practical world and expect you to explain or account for yourself.

Practical Self

Your identity is performed in a material world that affects who you are. For example, the fact that you can communicate with other people more or less instantaneously across huge distances by mobile telephone materially affects your sense of connection to other people. This practical self is born from the ability to do practical things and is illustrated by the importance to many young people of learning to drive a car. When you can drive, not only do you go through the transformation of self as "more of a grown-up," but when you have a car you also can do what you cannot do when you do not have one. The ability to drive and obtain access to a car expands your identity in a practical way.

Part of your *performance* of self is connected to the practical artifacts, accompaniments, and "stuff" that you use in your performance. If you have the right "stuff" (professional suit, bling, or a sports car), the self that you project is different from the self you perform without it.

Accountable Self

An important element of doing an identity in front of an audience is that you become an **accountable self**, which essentially allows your identity to be morally judged by other people. What you do can be assessed by other people as right or wrong according to existing habits of society. Any performance of identity turns identity into a moral action. That is, identity becomes a way of living, based on choices made about actions that a person sees as available or relevant. Others will judge and hold the performance to account. The social construction of identity is influenced by societal value systems. Society as a whole encourages you to take certain actions (do not park next to fire hydrants, protect the elderly and the weak, be a good neighbor, recycle!).

Moral accountability is a fancy way of saying that society as a whole makes judgments about your actions and choices. It holds you to account for the actions and choices that you make, but it also forcefully encourages you to act in particular ways and to see specific types of identity as "good" (patriot is good, traitor is bad; loyalty is good, thief is bad; open self-disclosure is good, passive aggression is bad, for example). As noted before, "society" does this through everyday performances and communications by Society's Secret Agents—including you.

Improvisational Performance

The identity that you thought of as your own personality, then, is not made up of your own desires and impulses but is formed, performed, and expressed within a set of social patterns and judgments. These are reinforced by the practices in a community through the relationships that people have with one another. The Indiana University fan is not asked why she is cheering for Indiana University by other Indiana University fans; Bob is not asked by his colleagues why he is so tough on "illegals."

A person's identity is a complex and compound concept that is partly based on history, memory, experiences, and interpretations by the individual, partly evoked by momentary aspects of talk (its context, the people you are with, your stage in life, your goals at the time), and partly a social creation directed by other people, society and its categories, and your relationship objectives in those contexts. Your performance of the self is guided by your relationships with other people, as well as your social goals. Even your embodiment of this knowledge or your sense of self is shaped by your social practices with other people. Your self-consciousness in their presence influences the presentation of yourself to other people. Although a sense of self/identity is experienced in your practical interactions with other people, you get trapped by language into reporting it abstractly as some sort of disembodied "identity," a *symbolic* representation of the routine practices and communication styles that you experience in your daily interactions with other people. Once again, then, another apparently simple idea (identity, personality, self) runs into the relational influences that make the basics of communication so valuable to study.

Photo 5.5 What can you say about a transgender person who has had reassignment surgery? What problems might a transgender person encounter in relation to identity as discussed in this chapter? (See page 129.)

Table 5.3 summarizes what you've learned in this chapter about identity and relationships.

Table 5.3 Some Ways to See Identity Communication and Relationships	
Psychic/ reflective self	*Habits of thought/of behavior/of perception identify a person's "personality."*
	What you normally think of as identity a priori: Your communicative behavior just expresses the inner self.
Symbolic self	*Broad social forces affect self differentiation/characterization.*
	Self arises out of social interaction and not vice versa; hence, it does not "belong to me." You are who you are because of the people you hang out with, interact with, and communicate with; you can be a different identity in different circumstances.
Performative self	*Present social situation affects self-portrayal.*
	Selves are acted out in a network of social demands and norms; you do your identity differently in front and back regions and try to present the right "face" to the people you are with.
Practical self	*Material world affects self/how you think of self.*
	Practical aspects of materiality transform the concept of self. Your identity is represented by objects that symbolically make claims about the sort of person you are.
Accountable self	*Social context influences broad forms of portrayal.*
	Personality is just an abstract concept. People act within a set of social ideas and habitual styles of thinking, allowing other people to comment and steer how they behave.
Improvisational performance	*There is a rhetorical spin to this and how "self" is presented.*
	Ideology affects the manner of presentation of terms, characteristics, and so on. We try to narrate ourselves in the way that our society expects us to represent identity.

FOCUS QUESTIONS REVISITED

1. **Some textbooks picture a person's identity like an onion, built layer by layer and communicated slowly as intimacy increases. Does this really make any sense?**
For some reasons and purposes, it makes sense for us to see identity this way, but it really is not the only way that "identity" actually works in the everyday encounters of relationship life.

2. **How do daily interactions with other people form or sustain your identity?**
In at least two ways: Their responses to us affect the way we feel about ourselves; also, they act as Society's Secret Agents by innocently enforcing society's norms and beliefs through their comments on our own styles of behavior and identity performance.

3. **How much of your "self" is a performance of social roles where you have to act out "who I am" for other people?**
Much of what you do in everyday life is steered by your awareness of yourself as a social object for other people. Hence, you perform roles and styles of behavior that

are appropriate in the circumstances. Your "inner self" may be constrained by this awareness.

4. What is meant by a symbolic self, and why do we have to account to other people for who we are?

Your "self" is presented to other people as a symbol, and you have to describe yourself in terms and phrases that your audiences recognize as symbolically meaningful in the culture. You are also able to take an attitude of reflection that recognizes that you are an object of other people's perceptions and judgment. You will remember from Chapter 1 that people can observe your behavior and "go beyond" it to its symbolic meaning.

5. What is the role of culture in your identity experiences?

Culture has multiple roles in identity experience. For one, cultures regard "individuality" differently; for another, your origin from a particular culture steers the way you think about people and their styles of behavior; for still another thing, your culture is part of your identity, and people proudly claim their cultural heritage as part of "who they are."

KEY CONCEPTS

accountable self 124	perception 105
altercasting 117	performative self 122
attitude of reflection 119	personal constructs 107
back region 123	prototype 107
dialectic tension 113	schemata 106
front region 123	scripts 108
identity 101	self-concept 109
labeling 117	self-disclosure 112
moral accountability 125	symbolic interactionism 119
norm of reciprocity 115	symbolic self 119

QUESTIONS TO ASK YOUR FRIENDS

- Discuss with your friends or classmates the most embarrassing moment that you feel comfortable talking about, and try to find out what about the experience threatened your identity. What identity were you projecting at the time, and what went wrong with the performance?

- Have your friends look at how advertisers sell the *image* of particular cars in terms of what they will make the owner look like to other people; the advertisers recognize that identity is tied up in material possessions. Discuss with your friends the following topics: How is your identity affected by your preferences in music, the Web, fashion magazines, resources, or wealth?

- Get a group of friends together and ask them each to write down what sort of vegetable, fish, dessert, book, piece of furniture, style of music, meal, car, game, or building best represents their identity. Read the responses out loud and have everyone guess which person is described.

MEDIA LINKS

- Watch the movie *Sideways* (Payne, 2004) and fast-forward to the veranda scene during which Miles talks to Maya about his preference for wine and it becomes apparent that he is using wine as a metaphor about himself. He projects his identity through his knowledge about the subtleties of wines. Basically he uses it to describe himself, and his hope is that Maya will learn to understand him.

  Maya: You know, can I ask you a personal question, Miles?

  Miles: Sure.

  Maya: Why are you so into Pinot?

  Miles: [laughs softly]

  Maya: I mean, it's like a thing with you.

  Miles: [continues laughing softly] Uh, I don't know, I don't know. Um, it's a hard grape to grow, as you know. Right? It's, uh, it's thin-skinned, temperamental, ripens early. It's, you know, it's not a survivor like Cabernet, which can just grow anywhere and, uh, thrive even when it's neglected. No, Pinot needs constant care and attention. You know? And in fact it can only grow in these really specific, little, tucked away corners of the world. And, and only the most patient and nurturing of growers can do it, really. Only somebody who really takes the time to understand Pinot's potential can then coax it into its fullest expression. Then, I mean, oh its flavors, they're just the most haunting and brilliant and thrilling and subtle and . . . ancient on the planet.

- Collect examples that demonstrate how media representations of ideal selves (especially demands on women to be a particular kind of shape, but try to be more imaginative than just these images) are constantly thrown in our path.
- How do television talk shows encourage us to be open, honest, and real? Do these programs teach us anything about the "right" ways to be ourselves?

ETHICAL ISSUES

- If your identity is partly constructed by other people, how does this play out in relation to diversity, cultural sensitivity, and political correctness versus speaking the truth?

- Analyze the difficulties for someone "coming out" in terms of performance, social expectations, norms, and relationships with those around the person.

- If you have a guilty secret and are getting into a deep romantic relationship with someone, should you tell him or her early on or later? Or should you not tell him or her at all?

ANSWERS TO PHOTO CAPTIONS

Photo 5.1 ▪ There are messages about identity both "inside" the picture and "outside" it: The performance of femininity and womanhood is being communicated to the girl, a sense of the importance of looks and the enhancement of natural appearance in private. The picture also communicates to outsiders the role of personal hygiene in personal identity.

Photo 5.2 ▪ Baxter (2011) points out that people have different dialogues available to them at each moment to draw them one way or another. Dialectical tensions are a constant part of daily life, and you may often feel pulled in two directions at once, whether in expressing what you feel or in enacting your identity.

Photo 5.3 ▪ Interactions and experiences with older people give us a sense of our own identity and where we came from. This boy is learning how to connect himself to the past of his family.

Photo 5.4 ▪ Symbolic self means that your identities represent something to other people and not just yourself. Furthermore, identities are transacted symbolically through your interactions with others. Many of the roles that you enact in everyday life are drawn from cultural expectations about the kind of person you "should" be. Part of your identity is therefore always an act. Identity can be "performed," and the performance takes over the identity. We all know who the impersonator is *trying* to be, but . . . he's not that person. We actually just saw the real guy working at a truck stop in Omaha and going by the name *Barry!*

Photo 5.5 ▪ Sometimes physical self needs to be aligned with inner self through sex reassignment surgery. The transgender person still has to perform (dress, behave) in a way that convinces others that the correct sex has now been assigned. Family members need to learn new labels for the person: Who was once a son is now a daughter; an aunt is now an uncle; a sister is now a brother (Norwood, 2010).

STUDENT STUDY SITE

Visit the study site at **www.sagepub.com/boc2e** for e-flashcards, practice quizzes, journal articles and additional study resources.

REFERENCES

Baxter, L. A. (2004). Distinguished scholar article: Relationships as dialogues. *Personal Relationships, 11*(1), 1–22.

Baxter, L. A. (2011). *Voicing relationships: A dialogic perspective*. Thousand Oaks, CA: Sage.

Baxter, L. A., & Braithwaite, D. O. (2008). Relational dialectics theory: Crafting meaning from competing discourses. In L. A. Baxter & D. O. Braithwaite (Eds.), *Engaging theories in interpersonal communication* (pp. 349–361). Thousand Oaks, CA: Sage.

Baxter, L. A., & Montgomery, B. M. (1996). *Relating: Dialogs and dialectics*. New York: Guilford Press.

Berscheid, E., & Reis, H. T. (1998). Attraction and close relationships. In D. T. Gilbert, S. F. Fiske, & G. Lindzey (Eds.), *The handbook of social psychology* (4th ed., pp. 139–281). Boston: McGraw-Hill.

Burke, K. (1969). *A grammar of motives*. Berkeley: University of California Press.

Burleson, B. R., Holmstrom, A. J., & Gilstrap, C. M. (2005). "Guys can't say that to guys": Four experiments assessing the normative motivation account for deficiencies in the emotional support provided by men. *Communication Monographs, 72*(4), 468–501.

Caughlin, J. P., & Afifi, T. D. (2004). When is topic avoidance unsatisfying? Examining the moderators of the association between avoidance and dissatisfaction. *Human Communication Research, 30*(4), 479–513.

Cupach, W. R., & Metts, S. (1994). *Facework*. Thousand Oaks, CA: Sage.

Derlega, V. J., Metts, S., Petronio, S., & Margulis, S. T. (1993). *Self-disclosure*. Newbury Park, CA: Sage.

Dindia, K. (2000). Self-disclosure, identity, and relationship development: A dialectical perspective. In K. Dindia & S. W. Duck (Eds.), *Communication and personal relationships* (pp. 147–162). Chichester, UK: Wiley.

Duck, S. W. (2011). *Rethinking relationships: A new approach to relationship research*. Thousand Oaks, CA: Sage.

Fehr, B. (1993). How do I love thee: Let me consult my prototype. In S. W. Duck (Ed.), *Understanding relationship processes* (Vol. 1, pp. 87–120). Newbury Park, CA: Sage.

Goffman, E. (1959). *Behaviour in public places*. Harmondsworth, UK: Penguin Books.

Hess, J. A. (2000). Maintaining a nonvoluntary relationship with disliked partners: An investigation into the use of distancing behaviors. *Human Communication Research, 26*, 458–488.

Huisman, D. (2008). *Intergenerational family storytelling*. Iowa City: University of Iowa Department of Communication Studies.

Jourard, S. M. (1964). *The transparent self*. New York: Van Nostrand Reinhold.

Jourard, S. M. (1971). *Self-disclosure*. New York: Wiley.

Kellas, J. K. (2008). Narrative theories: Making sense of interpersonal communication. In L. A. Baxter & D. O. Braithwaite (Eds.), *Engaging theories in interpersonal communication* (pp. 241–254). Thousand Oaks, CA: Sage.

Kelly, G. A. (1955). *The psychology of personal constructs*. New York: Norton.

Luft, J., & Ingham, H. (1955). The Johari window: A graphic model of interpersonal awareness. *Proceedings of the Western Training Laboratory in Group Development*. Los Angeles: University of California.

Marwell, G., & Schmitt, D. R. (1967). Dimensions of compliance-gaining behavior: An empirical analysis. *Sociometry, 30*, 350–364.

Mead, G. H. (1934). *Mind, self, and society*. Chicago: University of Chicago Press.

Metts, S. (2000). Face and facework: Implications for the study of personal relationships. In K. Dindia & S. W. Duck (Eds.), *Communication and personal relationships* (pp. 74–92). Chichester, UK: Wiley.

Norwood, K. M. (2010, April 26). *Here and gone: Competing discourses in the communication of families with a transgender member.* Unpublished PhD thesis, Department of Communication Studies, University of Iowa.

Payne, A. (Director). (2004). *Sideways* [Motion picture]. United States: Fox Searchlight Pictures.

Petronio, S. (2002). *Boundaries of privacy.* Albany: State University of New York Press.

Shotter, J. (1984). *Social accountability and selfhood.* Oxford, UK: Basil Blackwell.

Wood, J. T., & Duck, S. W. (Eds.). (2006). *Composing relationships: Communication in everyday life.* Belmont, CA: Thomson Wadsworth.

6

Talk and Interpersonal Relationships

W e want you to rethink relationships: They're not just about emotion. Instead, they are about knowledge, ways of understanding the world (Duck, 2011) and connecting symbolically to people. Communication helps you make connections between people and knowledge, and you really cannot have one process without the other, of course. Communication and relationships, as well as what you know and how you know it, are directly connected.

Everyday talk occurs in an evaluative context involving critical thinking and (moral) judgment. Critical thinking applies not only to big stories told in politics or persuasive appeals but also to small talk. Critical thinking about relationships can be based on the internal coherence of a breakup story, for example—whether it all seems to hang together—or the plausibility of the talk. You have heard friends tell a story about how they acted well in a romance and, while listening politely and smiling pleasantly, privately thought skeptically to yourself, "Yeah, right!"

This chapter covers four topics:

1. how communication in relationships supports your knowledge,

2. how everyday communication increases intimacy levels,

3. how everyday communication decreases intimacy levels, and

4. critical evaluation of the concept of relational stages.

Focus Questions

1. How does your everyday communication with other people transact your relationships?
2. How does your talk compose your relationships during everyday conversation?
3. How do relationships grow or change, and how does this show up in speech?
4. What are the different types of communication that take place when a relationship is coming apart?
5. Do relationships develop and break down in a linear fashion?

What Is the Best Way to Connect Talk, Relationships, and Knowledge?

How many of your present beliefs do you discuss with friends and family? How much of *what* you know depends on *whom* you know? You may discuss your life, current news, the nature of the outside world, and how to interpret the events that happen in it with people at work. Researchers have shown that you typically prefer to hang out with people who share similar attitudes and beliefs (Byrne, 1997; Kerckhoff, 1974; Sunnafrank, 1983; Sunnafrank & Ramirez, 2004). Who knew? You tend to respect their judgments and enjoy talking to them because they often reinforce what you believe (Weiss, 1998)! Of course, you will occasionally disagree, but mostly your friends let you talk about yourself in ways you like. In turn, they talk about themselves in ways you like, adopt the attitudes and beliefs you like, and see the world in broadly the same way you do.

Also very likely to have similar social, religious, racial, economic, and educational backgrounds, your friends live in worlds very like your own. When you communicate with them, you feel broadly supported—as a person who lives in a similar world of meaning (Duck, 2011).

How much of your daily talk involves comparison of ideas with someone else ("What do you think of the way she's dressed?" "I didn't like that lecture, did you?" "I forgot to check Facebook this morning. What's new?")? Even casual chatter serves to compose your experience of life and your relationships (Wood & Duck, 2006). Your interactions with friends may often seem light and unimportant—not, in fact, very productive. On the contrary, even small talk serves to reestablish the relationship, provide you with reality checks, give you information, transmit news, bring you up to date, and, most important of all, make you feel included. That is a relational outcome: *Inclusion* is a relational term; any talk, however small, that acknowledges and includes you serves a relational purpose.

Relationships and What You Know

Everyday communication reinforces both your relationships and what you know. All forms of communication show how you rely on your connections with other people to filter your knowledge and help you critically evaluate events, people, and situations. Because communication involves information, the people you know and with whom you spend your time affect your knowledge. They influence/steer/select the messages you send or attend to, the information you believe, the type of critical thinking you do, and how you evaluate the outcomes. So, not just a *result* of communication, relationships are also significant in the opposite process, the formation and transaction of knowledge—the creation of the world of meaning you inhabit.

Relationships also exert influence on the distribution of information. You tell secrets to your friends that you would not tell to strangers, and news travels through networks of folks who know one another (Bergmann, 1993;

Make Your Case

Pay careful attention to media discussions of whatever happens to be the romance of the month, the breakup of the month, or the cheater of the month. How do such stories set ideals for society about romance and at the same time reinforce moral values about the ways in which relationships should be conducted? Watch out for words like *perfect couple, betrayal, lie, cheat, stand by your (wo)man,* and *ashamed,* all of which are secretly telling you what are the right and wrong ways to do romantic relationships.

Duck, 2007). Relationships also affect what you believe or challenge about the world in general, how you think about other people, and how you evaluate their behavior (whom you gossip about and why, for example). The marketing world knows about the power of the connection among relationships, information flow, critical thinking, and "knowledge." Marketers use WOM (word of mouth) campaigns that exploit the fact that we respect our friends' opinions about the right purchases to make and what is "cool." In the latest marketing fad, "buzz agents" are paid to tell their friends about particular products, thereby creating "buzz" and influencing people to buy them (Carl, 2006).

Building and Supporting Relationships

Robert Weiss (1974) identified six specific areas where relationships provide us with something special, needed, or valued. These six **provisions of relationships** are as follows.

Belonging and a Sense of Reliable Alliance

The major benefit that people desire from relationships is *belonging and a sense of reliable alliance:* You like to feel that someone is "there" for you. Quite often, you state this desire explicitly, but more often you just learn from daily interaction that someone looks after your interests, cares for you, inquires about your state of mind/health, and can usually be relied upon to help when asked—and sometimes even without being asked. That's what Weiss (1974) meant by "reliable alliance." It comes over in talk not only directly ("I'm here for you") but also indirectly as you listen to another person and realize (transact) from the talk that he or she really is reliable and interested in your welfare (Leatham & Duck, 1990).

Emotional Integration and Stability

Other people provide you with emotional support in the form of a shoulder to cry on. In daily communication, friends often offer comfort and support in gender-specific ways (Burleson, Holmstrom, & Gilstrap, 2005). They also, however, support your knowledge base. Carl and Duck (2004) indicated how much people rely on each other to verify, support, or do reality checks on the world in their everyday communication. Drawing on the previous work by Weiss (1974), they indicated the importance of using other people as sounding boards for emotions or responses to situations. For example, people often ask friends, "Did I do the right thing?" "Do you think I should believe what this person says?" or even "Should I take this job?" Friends also give you information about the rules for conducting relationships (Baxter, Dun, & Sahlstein, 2001) and offer you advice about other problems in life (Goldsmith & Fitch, 1997).

Opportunity to Talk About Yourself

Opportunity to talk about yourself not only is enjoyable but subtly gives you extra chances to derive the above provisions from other interactions. People like to put themselves into their talk, offer their opinions and views, be important in stories they tell, and otherwise be part of a narrative of their own lives that makes them appear valuable and good. Indeed, one of the main things that makes a relationship more rewarding to people, according to Robert Weiss (1974), is a sense of being known, so it is hardly surprising that self-disclosure largely comprises what happens in relationship growth and maintenance.

Opportunity to Help Others

Humans also like the feeling of being there for others, which is Weiss's (1974) fourth provision. A request for advice is flattering and implicitly recognizes the value of your world of meaning. It also allows you to talk about yourself and thus simultaneously fulfills another provision noted above. Manusov, Kellas, and Trees (2004) examined how friends told and listened to one another's stories about a failure in their life and explored the facework (making someone "look good") done in the accounts. People who asked about the event and then received a very long and complex explanation felt more burdened, despite the fact that the speakers imagined such accounts were more acceptable from the listeners' points of view. So, those who took the opportunity to help others ended up feeling burdened by an overly lengthy response, but at least the speakers appreciated the chance to talk about themselves!

Provision of Physical Support/Reassurance of Worth and Value

Relationships ratify and gratify your world by providing support when you need it. Weiss (1974) divided this support into two provisions: the *provision of physical support* and the *reassurance of worth and value.*

Physical support is offered by friends and relatives: If you have to move a heavy piano, you need other people; or you might need someone to drive you to the airport or look after your pet rat while you are on vacation. These are the favors that friends do for one another as part of the role of friendship.

You may find a subtle reassurance of your worth when someone gives up time for you in this way, but you certainly find it confirming when someone says, "Good job!" "Sure! Drop that jerk. You deserve better anyway," or "I'd love to help solve that with you." More important, relationships show you how other people see the world, how they represent/present it, what they value in it, what matters to them, and how your own way of thinking fits in with theirs. In such talk and action, they reassure your worth and value as a human being (Duck, 2011).

Everyday communication provides reassurance and other provisions seamlessly. People advise, seek advice, help, seek help, encourage, reveal things about themselves, and talk to one another in ways that offer the above provisions all the time, often without being obvious. In the course of everyday life, you communicate with people who offer you ways to check your knowledge of the world, and you share knowledge about other people in return.

Suppose someone praises you ("Great job!" "I love your outfit!" "You did well on the test—and you are making great comments in class. You are obviously a good learner"). What subtle processes are going on? The speaker not only claims the relational right to make comments about you but also shows a desire to connect positively and make you feel good. Organizing, reaffirming, correcting, or otherwise presenting a view of you that affects your knowledge of self and how you appear to other people, the person emphasizes those parts of the world in which you do things right and perform commendably.

Support for an area of your knowledge about yourself transacts validation for that part of your identity. In contrast, criticism undermines confidence about your performances. Criticism also claims the other person's relational rights to comment on you (or else you resent that the person claims such a right: "Who does s/he think s/he is?"). Validation of your world, as well as what challenges or undermines it, demonstrates the tight connection between relationships and what you know and believe about yourself.

Photo 6.1 How does your end-of-day communication with other people transact your relationships? How are the relationships between the people here conveyed and transacted in talk? (See page 156.)

Composing Relationships Through Talk

Talk transacts knowledge and relationships. Part of what is composed during the tight connections among talk, relationships, and knowledge is a range of different relationships. These relationships are recognized by different styles of talk. Every culture has its own way of thinking about relationships, so the transactions of culture and relationships connect very directly in this chapter. For example, Japanese language differentiates more than 200 ways of indicating a speaker and a listener's relationship, and whenever two Japanese speakers converse, they inevitably and directly signal their status relationship at very complex levels. By contrast, American culture often splits up relationships into a very basic distinction between "formal" and "informal." This broad differentiation includes important subtleties (e.g., hookups, cross-sex nonromantic relationships, speed dates, nonresidential parents, in-laws, buddies, "the 'rents").

Types of Relationships Recognized in Talk

People in Western culture differentiate among strangers, neighbors, friends, family, and romantic partners, sometimes within categories. For example, among romantic partners, you can differentiate between dates, affairs, and spouses. Aware of the overtones, you might decide to think carefully about how you sign off on an e-mail, a job application, or a postinterview thank-you letter, recognizing that *yours, love, see ya*, and *cordially* connote different relational messages. When denoting different relationship types, some types are given more value in a given culture than other types. Table 6.1 reviews the assessment of status in Confucian philosophy and in the United States.

Table 6.1 Status and Types of Relationships

Confucian philosophy in Chinese culture represents six basic types of relationships (all of which center on men and five of which are essentially structured as superior–subordinate relationships): emperor–subject; father–son; husband–wife; elder brother–younger brother; teacher–student; and one of equality, friend–friend.

In the United States, titles used in talk, such as *Professor, sis, pal,* and *Mom,* that directly indicate the status relationship of one speaker to another.

Western scholars make a distinction between social and personal relationships. **Social relationships** involve essentially interchangeable people. For example, your relationships with Alice the witchety grub server, store assistants, bus drivers, and prison guards are not truly personal. Any of them could change shifts with other individuals who continue to perform the same tasks and functions. Only specified and irreplaceable individuals (e.g., your mother, father, brother, sister, or very best friend), on the other hand, may engage in **personal relationships** with you. You can't just pick a random person off the street and make him or her instantly into your best friend—and certainly not into your father or sister. You could in time attempt to turn servers, bus drivers, or checkout clerks into acquaintances, dates, or lovers. You cannot, however, just switch people around in personal relationship roles in the way that you could pick one cashier over another and still be served politely in an interchangeable social relationship.

One of the authors was out to lunch with two deans. At the end of the meal one said to the other, "I see you don't like the way they do potatoes here," and the other replied, "Sure, have them if you want." That struck us as a terrific example of the assumptions and taken-for-granted information that give away the fact that two people know one another very well and that each of them can interpret what is said in that light.

Keeping Relationships Going in Talk

Communication theorist Stuart Sigman (1991) considered how even small talk can keep relationships going by acknowledging that the relationship still continues even when the partners are *not* face-to-face and may be apart from one another. Technically this type of communication is called **relational continuity constructional units (RCCUs)**. In less complex and more memorable terms these are simple conversational symbols that indicate that you expect relationships to exist through time even when the partners are physically distant. You can anticipate an absence, acknowledge that you are apart but the relationship still exists, or recognize that you have just met up again and reaffirm the relationship. Sigman divided these symbols into *prospective, introspective,* and *retrospective* types, and they are not as frightening as the names suggest: In fact they are so obvious that you probably overlook them or take them for granted.

Listen in on Your Life

Listen to how you talk with friends differently than you do with strangers during a chosen day. Note the kinds of differences in the relationships involved. How many relationships are with intimate strangers or, more accurately, with familiar acquaintances (people you talk to and whom you know well enough not to ignore but do not feel close to)? Look at the lists you have created in this exercise, and identify the differences between communication with friends and communication with strangers. What topics do you talk about with friends but not strangers? What range of topics do you talk about in each type of relationship? Does the topic, style, or range of topics make a difference between the relationships, or is it something else?

Prospective Units

Prospective units provide recognition that an interaction is about to end but the relationship continues. In essence, prospective units refer to a coming absence, and they create a conversational leapfrog that gets you over it. Prospective units include "Let's set the agenda for next time" and "When shall we three meet again, in thunder, lightning, or in rain?" Other examples are "See you later" and "Talk soon."

Any other form of communication—even nonverbal communication—that suggests the likelihood of the partner's return is also a prospective unit. For example, if one partner leaves a toothbrush in the other's apartment, the toothbrush indicates the missing partner will likely return. It offers recognition that the absence is temporary but the relationship remains intact. Sigman (1991) referred to such nonverbal evidence as "spoors," like the track marks made by deer in snow, that indicate the partner's previous physical presence (and expected return). Grieving parents often keep a dead child's room just the way it was the day the child died, as if they expect a return. Queen Victoria kept Prince Albert's desk and dressing room spick and span for 40 years with a new shirt laid out each day. As noted in the previous chapter, parents of transgender people often experience "ambiguous loss" (Norwood, 2010) because they are not sure whether, during any gender reassignment surgery, they have lost a daughter or gained a son. It takes time for them to adjust.

College Experience

For those of you who recently graduated high school, we have what may be some surprising news. For those of you who have been out of high school for a while, you are well aware of this news but will still learn something about recent research.

Regardless of how many times "B[est] F[riends] F[orever]" has been written in high school yearbooks, very few relationships last after graduation. In fact, you will never again see many of the people with whom you graduated, and most will become nothing but a faded memory. If you are suddenly worried about losing your friends, do not worry too much. You will soon make new even closer friends in college. Also, some high school friendships do last long after graduation. Those that do survive are those in which regular contact is maintained. Cummings, Lee, and Kraut (2006) discovered that high school relationships maintained through e-mail and instant messaging declined less rapidly than those primarily maintained by phone and even face-to-face contact. The authors speculate that these findings resulted more from increased contact through online communication than from any other factor.

Introspective Units

By contrast, *introspective units* are direct indications of a relationship's existence during the physical absence of one partner. The difference between introspective units and prospective units is that prospective units note that the absence is *about to happen* whereas introspective units acknowledge it already has. Examples include wedding rings worn when away from the spouse, greetings cards, phone calls, mediated contact, and, of course, e-mail messages, as well as photos of family on your desk at work.

Retrospective Units

Retrospective units directly recognize the end of an absence and the reestablishment of the relationship through actual interaction. The most familiar nonverbal example is a hug or handshake or kiss upon greeting. The most common forms of conversation that fit this category are catch-up conversations and talk about the day (Vangelisti & Banski, 1993) but also counted are "Hi!" "What's up?" "How ya doin'?" and "Long time, no see."

By reporting on their experiences during the day, partners emphasize their psychological togetherness, as well as a shared interest in one another's lives and the events that happened in those lives during their physical separation. Hence, in these communicative moments, or "end-of-the-day talks," with your partner or friends, you are relating to each other as well as simply reporting what happened. The talk reestablishes the relationship.

Even little bits of small talk often serve relational purposes, and such phrases as *talk soon* do something to compose relationships in everyday life: They reinforce your relationships and establish you as connected with other people. They demonstrate conversationally that the people are important to you and that you want them to know about your life experiences. This connection is the essential function of talk (Chapter 2). People's favorite complaint when they miss someone is that they cannot talk to that person as often as they wish. If you have ever been in a long-distance relationship, you know what we mean (Sahlstein, 2004, 2006); it's just not the same when you cannot talk to people on the spur of the moment, side by side—though cell phones help out here.

Your normal daily conversations compose and essentialize relationships in a stronger way than do long-distance relationships. The casual conversation you have with the people you know is a steady, if overlooked, reinforcement of your relationships. Frankly, many of your conversations with friends are probably not big slices of intimacy, just a lot of small stuff that makes you feel connected—the "essential function" of talk.

Talk and Relational Change

Any relationship between people is partly indexed and essentialized (see Chapter 2) by the kinds of talk that they do—either the content or the way they talk. But how does your talk with someone change your relationship—turning a casual friend into a best friend, for example—or how do you get acquainted with people in ways that increase intimacy? The hypertext (Chapter 2) in your conversation helps you identify and maintain your intimacy level. Your willingness to tell each other your private thoughts helps you recognize your deeper connection to one another as individuals.

Photo 6.2 The man in this photo just said, "We'll see you this weekend." Which type of relational continuity constructional unit was displayed here? (See page 156.)

Relationships are *indexed* in talk, but friendships are also based on increased personal knowledge about someone else. Your talk reflects such changes as it indicates a growing understanding of another person. Your talk represents a greater ability to move around in the map of his or her psyche and way of being. Once again, knowledge, communication, and relationships interconnect.

Obviously, as relationships change, so degrees of intimacy are altered, whether in growth or in decline (it's almost a matter of definition). As you get more involved, so you see more of another person; as you fall apart, so time together is stressful and you seek more time alone—or at least apart.

Along with this behavioral change, talk itself can alter the form (or comfort level) of the relationship. As a relationship becomes more intimate, partners obviously change the ways they talk with one another (otherwise you would not be able to distinguish close friends from acquaintances). As you grow closer, your talk relaxes and gets informal; as you grow apart, your talk gets sharper and less welcoming. In Chapter 2 we reported that Planalp and Garvin-Doxas (1994) showed that people are skilled at differentiating between friends and acquaintances in speech they overhear. Therefore, it must be true that as a relationship grows in intimacy, at least one partner is driving it forward by opening up intimate topics or changing to more-relaxed styles of talk.

Moving Between Types of Relationships

If you know there are different kinds of relationships, it must also be true that we can transition from "not allowed" to "allowed" or from "inappropriate" to "appropriate" behaviors as a change to suit the new relationship level.

Crossing Boundaries

Any development of relationships must involve *crossing boundaries* between one level and another, between one set of permitted behaviors and another, and between one definition of the relationship and another. When you move from acquaintances to friends, dates to partners, lovers to enemies, or spouses to divorcés, you are moving across the boundaries between different types of relationships in your culture. Accordingly you say and do different things together.

Most of what we say about crossing boundaries, particularly in romance, reflects the idea of a progression from "no emotion" to "intimacy" and then to "greater intimacy." Of course, in today's world, social media such as the Internet, cell phones, and Twitter have altered how people experience romance. Hookups occur without any traditional relationship development (Paul, 2006), and relationships on the Internet between people who have not yet met face-to-face are more common. There are even "virtual churches" (e.g., www.virtualchurch.com/) where the congregations never congregate. This new approach to relational communities, to romance, and to sexuality necessarily separates older-fashioned ideas that intimacy and sexual involvement increase steadily and together. The new relational order invalidates much of the old research that was based on outdated romantic practices inappropriate to the experience of people nowadays, whether younger or older.

It does not, however, invalidate the thesis of this book that relationships of all sorts are reflected in talk, communication, and two people's knowledge about one another (Duck, 2011). Instead of doing so in private, people these days are much more comfortable *relating in public*—by talking on their cell phones (see Chapter 9). They will be conducting and doing relationships in talk. They are not in any traditional sense transacting relationships in emotion alone.

The connection between relationships and communication is inescapably built into talk that occurs. "Respect" for a superior is transacted in communication, and there are acceptable and unacceptable ways in which closeness can be spoken. Think about going up to your instructor and saying, "I love you," or "I hate you." How do you think he or she would respond? Why?

Signaling Changes

So how do you signal change in relationships through communication? Most research on romantic relationships has been carried out on college students, some in the 1980s and 1990s before cell phones, the Internet, Facebook, or other social media. On the basis of that research, relational development from initial contact to romantic involvement is represented as a developmental progression driven by a simple growth of personal/internal emotions, from first impression to long-term affection.

Forget for the moment that this research completely fails to represent the experience of older people, those with lives outside college, or those not involved in a romantic relationship. Note instead that it underestimates how often networks and people introduce partners to one another. Actually this happens approximately 60% of the time (Parks, 2006). It also understandably underestimates the extent to which people connect on the Internet before ever meeting face-to-face.

Yet, the development of romance is reported in most books as something that two people do for themselves. Other books tell you it is based on individual and internal feelings of love and initial attraction that people express and communicate in affectionate ways. Relationship development is all too rarely seen as a change in talk based on the information individuals know (or have inferred) about each other's ways of thinking about the world (Duck, 2011). Because talk essentializes relationships rather than merely indexes them, any change in a relationship involves change in content of talk and the style of communication. Neither talk nor style is a trivial thing—that's why we study communication!

How do talk and communication connect at these different levels to relating and emerging differences in relationships? You can change relationships subtly or directly by talk intended instrumentally to change them.

Direct and Indirect Talk to Change Relationships

People do direct relational talk in special ways, on special occasions, and with very special care. Any direct talk about a relationship forces the partners to focus on its explicit definition. This can force a definition of "the state of our relationship" in a way that they had not foreseen or do not find truly welcome.

"The State of Our Relationship"

In 1985, Baxter and Wilmot pointed out the difficulties people have when they raise certain topics for discussion in a relationship. It is difficult to make the relationship a topic of discussion. Hearing "Let's talk about our relationship" sends chills down the spine of most people, particularly men (Acitelli, 1988). There seems to be no escape once the topic comes up.

You cannot talk about the relationship without ending up somehow defining it and its meaning to the two partners involved. For at least one of them, the result may be unwanted. One may hope that the relationship would be defined as stronger and with a better future than the other person is willing to accept. The best outcome is that the two people agree to see the relationship in a particular way that they both accept. All other outcomes are bad for at least one of the people involved.

Contrarian Challenge

We have noted that talk changes as relationships change, but this is a chicken-and-egg problem. Which comes first? Is it that easy to work out the sequence?

Indirect Talk About Relationships

Talk that changes relationship types tends to be indirect. Asking someone "Will you have sex with me?" is a direct and very high-risk strategy whereas many indirect strategies are more effective without being threatening (e.g., a warm kiss, a bunch of flowers, a deep sigh, a longing look, or even a smart or sexy outfit). For this reason, flirtation is one of the key ways people push the envelope in relationships through *indirect* communication.

Flirtation is a safe way to propose relationship growth: First, it generally serves as an indirect form of relationship question; second, it can be taken as a simple statement of fact, a friendly joke, or something more sexually or relationally loaded. Because it is ambiguous in this way, flirtation is *deniable*. You can always claim you were "just teasing." If the person you flirt with is interested in a relationship, the response will accept the relationally loaded reading of the message. If the person is not interested, the message can be treated as fun or fact and nothing more. For example, a friend of ours was interested in a cashier at a local supermarket, and when he paid by check, the cashier asked, "Is everything current?" He replied, "Yes, especially the phone number." This could be read as a statement of fact or as an invitation to call. Actually, the cashier did call him, and they ended up in a long-term relationship (for 10 years!).

Stages in Relationship Development

Popular cultural beliefs state that relationships go through stages, from initial contact to strong attachment. Honeycutt (1993) questioned whether the stages actually exist or are merely *assumed to exist* in our culture. He found that stages in relationships (dating, engagement, and marriage, for example) are convenient labels for a much more complex process. Many an engagement has had a rocky road or been called off temporarily: It is not a straightforward signpost on the path toward marriage. Sometimes, relationships take a step "backward." Couples sometimes revert from engagement to dating, to just being friends, or even to being enemies.

Development of relationships is really a cultural ideal: We assume that relationships will develop from initially meeting the ultimate romance in a warm, fuzzy, and uncomplicated way. In the stark cold daylight of real life, the development of a relationship is far more complex: One person might not want it to move ahead too fast and may resist his or her partner's attempts to make it grow. Some people might be wary of letting others into their lives and will try hard to keep them at a distance—the intrusive neighbor, the undesirable coworker, or the unwanted romantic who won't take no for an answer.

Despite this readily observable fact of everyday life, relationship development is often treated in research as if it is based on individual feelings or attitudes toward another person. These are assumed, as emotions deepen, to lead to progression in the relationship. As feelings intensify, they are just worked out unproblematically and translated into behavior. The relationship develops more or less straightforwardly from emotions without the involvement of—and certainly not with any particular behavioral effort from—the individuals concerned.

Hess (2000) indicated that people have an extensive range of communicative strategies for keeping disliked people at a distance, from simply ignoring them to treating them as objects to direct and open hostility and antagonism. In normal life people know that unwanted relationships happen and have strategies to deal with them, so the rosy assumption that all relationships develop positively is too simplistic.

How the relationship actually develops in behavioral or communicative terms is often not explained but merely measured as an increase in intimacy assessed by means of scales and self-reports. If people report steadily increasing "intimacy," they must have a steadily deepening relationship. The relationship must have become progressively deeper as their intimacy grew. This theory is often called "the evolutionary course of personal relationships." Think, though: Is it all that realistic? Not at all for those shy, awkward, or inept people who desperately want to relate to others but cannot summon the courage to develop their relationships.

The theory represented in this research is, of course, an invention of researchers (Duck, 2011) and is not really real in other ways, either. As Jesse Delia (1980) pointed out long ago, most of our relationships are shallow and do not really develop at all, even with frequent contact. How much deeper is your "relationship" with your regular supermarket checkout clerk than it was the first time you went to the grocery store?

Also, many relationships are deliberately kept at a careful distance, and there are many people you don't ever want to get to know in great and intimate depth (such as your defense attorney, your boss, your professor, or even, in some cases, your roommate).

Weak Ties

By far, the majority of your relationships in everyday life are weak ties of this loose and distant nature (Granovetter, 1973). Can you generalize about the development of relationships, then? The next section explores a different model for relationship progression.

Photo 6.3 How do relationships grow or change, and how does this show up in speech? (See page 156.)

The Relationship Filtering Model

Duck's (1998, 1999) Relationship Filtering Model suggests that people pay attention to different cues in sequence as they get to know someone. Basically you use whatever evidence is available in order to form an impression of another person's underlying thought structure. The sequence in which you pay attention to characteristics of other people is basically the sequence in which you encounter them: physical appearance, behavior/nonverbal communication, roles, and attitudes/personality. At each point in the sequence, some people are filtered out as people you do not want as partners. Only those who pass all filters become friends or lovers. The model follows the intuitive process through which you get to know people layer by layer. It assumes your basic goal is to understand others on the basis of whatever cues are available at the time. At each deeper level, you get a better understanding of how they tick, and you let them deeper into your world (see Figure 6.1).

Basic Facts About Others

Think about meeting and getting to know strangers. When you meet obvious members of your culture, it is reasonable to assume you share common language and probably a set of beliefs about your culture's workings. Typically careful of strangers, however, newly acquainted people engage in safely noncontroversial small talk. You never know if someone is an ax murderer and just hasn't told you yet. The conversation normally stays on safe topics unless you meet in a singles' bar, on a speed date, or in a context clearly intended to promote relational growth (such as "welcome to the neighborhood" events or orientation weeks).

When you meet strangers, all you have to go on initially is how they look and sound. In everyday life when basic personal information is missing, you seek it out by asking questions. Interactions with strangers focus on information gathering, and providing information about yourself. This small stuff covers where you come from, your general background, and perhaps some of your personal views. Mostly, this information appears inconsequential: Who really cares which high school you attended, where you work, or whether you have grandchildren?

Well, the answer is that this sort of trivial information provides evidence about your background—even your religion, socioeconomic class, or style of thinking—that can be useful to your "audience." If you go on to make evaluative remarks about your school, you could give your audience helpful insights into your general attitudes,

Strategic Communication

An interview is a special situation where the interviewer has more personal information about you than you have about him or her. How do you think this inequality affects your ability to build a relationship with this person? What could you do to gain knowledge about the interviewer? Check out Chapter 15 for more information about interviews!

Figure 6.1 The Relationship Filtering Model

ways of thinking, and values. These pieces of information might be important in building a picture of yourself that will help other people make a decision. Are they interested in allowing you through to the next filter to become their acquaintance or friend? You can even make some deductions about strangers' looks that might help you judge their values and personality so you know how to talk to them. If someone is young, he or she probably won't have much to say about arthritis, and if someone is wearing a suit and carrying a Bible, you might not start a conversation about Darwinism.

Information and Inference

The more you get to know people—whether colleagues at work or people in your classes—the better your map of their world of meaning. Most of your classmates are, at best, little-known acquaintances. Yet you share some experiences and knowledge that would create some common topics to talk about if you happened to get stuck in an elevator or had to sit together on a long bus journey. You'd have some common topics of knowledge and an idea of each other's position on issues—though perhaps not the depth of understanding that talk with a friend has established.

As Duck (2007, p. 80) notes, however, "The development of relationships is not simplistically equivalent to the revelation of information nor to the decrease of uncertainty. The process of relationship development is created by the *interpretation* of such things by the partners, not by the acts themselves."

In other words, the relationship grows not from the information that you learn about the other person but from how you "go beyond" it. Physical appearance, nonverbal communication, roles, and attitudes are *information-loaded nuggets.* You can "go beyond" them to make inferences about a person's worlds of meaning.

Similarity Begins Near Home

You are much more likely to meet people of the same race, educational background, socioeconomic status, and religion as you. This leads to a tendency to assume, when you meet such people, that you share common values at some level. Later interaction may prove that you share fewer values than you first thought, but at least you began the relationship with a good working hypothesis.

When you first meet people, therefore, the Relationship Filtering Model asserts that you will *assume,* unless they demonstrate otherwise, they are similar to you. Your goal is ultimately to understand them, so the assumptions that you make initially may need to be modified with time. The same principle applies to all other "stages" of the Relationship Filtering Model. Your goal is to understand more accurately how the other person thinks—and sees the world.

The Assumption of Similarity and Difference

When you first see people, even from a distance, you may make assumptions about them just on the basis of their appearance. You can observe their age, race, sex, dress, number of tattoos and body piercings, height, and physical attractiveness. You can also see any marked social stigmas, such as extremely unusual hairstyles or disfigurements, visible disabilities, or physical peculiarities.

Although these cues do not necessarily provide accurate information, people make inferences from such things to the inner world of meaning. The Relationship Filtering Model assumes that you filter out people who do not appear to support your ways of seeing the world or confirming self and thus that they are not prospects for the kind of relationship you like or are seeking.

As you begin to interact more, you can adjust your perceptions in order to make more accurate judgments about whether people are likeable or unlikeable and whether they support your worldviews. If they pass the filter, you may begin to make extra efforts to include them in your social circle.

In all of your filtering interactions, you are really trying to find out what people are like at the level of their deeper worlds of meaning, so you aim all the questions you ask and all the communication strategies you adopt toward finding these deeper selves. The more fully you understand somebody, the more you understand how he or she thinks.

The Relationship Filtering Model proposes this ultimate goal of understanding people's thinking as the goal of all communicative activity in relationship development. The more you understand someone and the more he or she appears to support your world of meaning, the more you want to hang out with him or her and, accordingly, the more you use emotional labels like *friendship* and *love* to represent this connection.

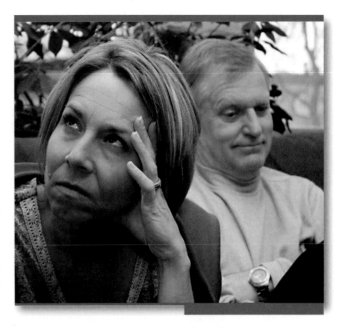

Photo 6.4 As relationships come apart, people, especially couples, find it harder to interact and tend to become more hostile and unsympathetic in their behaviors toward each other. What are the signs that these partners are in distress about their relationship? (See page 156.)

Coming Apart

Unfortunately, not all relationships work, and some come apart at the seams. Duck (1982) and Rollie and Duck (2006) have proposed a basic model to explain the workings of relational breakup—in particular, the conversational changes that take place at different points in the process.

Models of Breakup

The original model (Duck, 1982) proposed five stages, moving from the negative thoughts inside an individual's head to how the broader social network eventually becomes involved with the final story about ending a relationship. This old model focused on the uncertainties surrounding the end of relationships, which involve the partners and others in the network.

In the **intrapsychic process**, an individual simply reflects on the strengths and weaknesses of a relationship. Should it be ended? The person highlights the advantages of leaving over the disadvantages, as well as the disadvantages of staying over the advantages. Next, the **dyadic process** involves confronting the partner and openly discussing a problem with the relationship. This confrontation may be unpleasant or lead to greater understanding and forgiveness. If not, the process goes on to the third phase, the **social process**. Here, the person tells other people in the network about the relationship problem, seeking either their help to keep the relationship together or their support for his or her version of why it has come apart. You would like people to hear your side of things. What's more, you would like them to agree with your presentation! Fourthly, the **grave dressing process** involves creating the story of why a relationship died and erecting a metaphorical tombstone that summarizes its main points from birth to death.

Communication and Breakup

More recently, Rollie and Duck (2006) added a further **resurrection process**, which deals with the ways people prepare themselves for new relationships after ending an old one. The end of a particular relationship is not the end of all relational life, and one of people's major tasks once any single particular relationship has finished is to begin seeking a replacement. The Rollie and Duck model is strongly focused on the types of communication that occur during each process.

Rollie and Duck (2006) discuss the talk *topics* and *patterns* of communication that go with each process. For example, in the intrapsychic process, the person withdraws, reflects alone, and pulls back from the partner. In the dyadic process, the person speaks specifically with the partner and focuses on the relationship itself ("Our Relationship Talks"). Because these discussions take time from other activities, friends may notice they do not see as much of the person as before. In the social process, the person actively seeks greater contact and communication with third parties—not with the partner—to get advice, to cry on someone's shoulder, to get supportive commentary, or even to have his or her evaluation of the partner confirmed ("I always told you he was a jerk!").

The grave dressing process involves storytelling, and you've probably heard a lot of breakup stories yourself. The most usual form of breakup story follows a narrative structure that portrays the speaker as a dedicated but alert relater who went into the relationship realizing it was not perfect and needed work. After all, the speaker wants to look like a good person, not a fool! The speaker then tells of the work that went into the relationship. The partner was unresponsive or unhelpful, or perhaps both partners were mature enough to realize their relationship was not going to work out, so they made the tough but realistic decision to break it off. Such a narrative is advantageous in its presentation of the person. Not as "damaged goods" but as perfectly reasonable, this good relational worker is ripe and ready for a resurrection in a new healthy relationship. So this kind of breakup story projects a person's identity as attractive to other people looking for relationships.

Other sorts of relationship breakup stories normally indicate how a partner betrayed the speaker, but all these accounts follow a basic narrative form (Chapter 2) and make the speaker look OK, if somewhat shocked. Listen for such stories. You can learn a lot about human nature and about particular people by listening to the stories they tell about relationships. Figure 6.2 shows the breakdown process model.

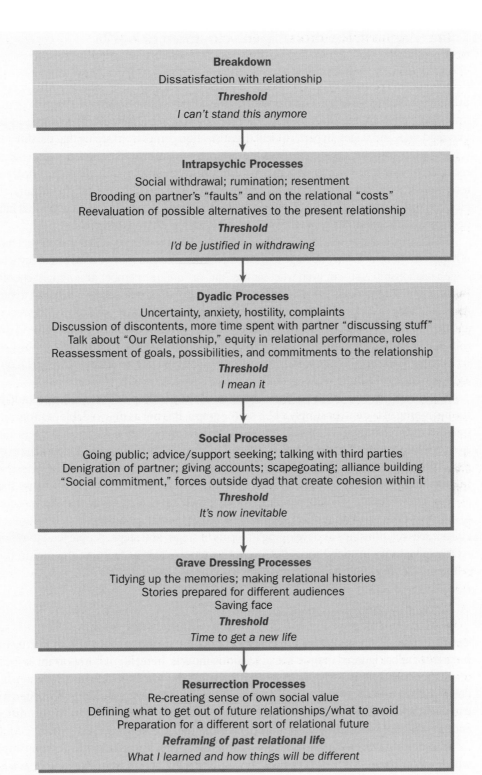

Figure 6.2   Breakdown Process Model

So Are There Stages in Relationship Development or Not?

In our experience, students find the linear progression idea built into "stages" both informative and frustrating. Although familiar with the idea that relationships take steps, grow, or pass from one stage to another, they recognize the messiness of life. Relationships do not easily fall into rigid steps and stages. In part, student dissatisfaction comes from seeing that the different types of relationships are not so similar. One date is not necessarily like another, every engagement has unique features, and all personal relationships are importantly different. Life is just too complex to fit into simple boxes, categories, stages, and progressions, but all the same the idea of stages is appealing. How do we reconcile this? Easy! Stages are not literally what happens, but they help us to see how relationships ebb and flow or grow and decline.

That is why it makes sense that you have probably also experienced relationships that have not moved smoothly from one stage to the next. Sometimes you may be hard put to say what stage a relationship is at—or even whether it is "on" or "off" (remember junior high school?). In particular, stage models tend to underestimate the extent of individuals' resistance to progression. In the case of a declining relationship, people very often try hard to stop the decline and do not want it to happen. It hurts! So they often propose to reconcile or make up and stop things from falling apart. Much of their activity seems to suggest that they do not—as the stage models might suggest—see a breakup as inevitable. However, like a map, a stage model is only a guide to the terrain but does not actually look like what you see out of the car window.

Not always obvious to the partners at the time, the breakup of a relationship could be the beginning of the end or simply a blip on the graph. It is not as unavoidable or programmatic as researchers assume. You may already have seen one reason why: Researchers tend to ask people to report on what has happened to them, which of course focuses them on reports of the past ("retrospective reports"). When people give retrospective reports, they fit everything into a narrative structure in the form discussed in Chapter 2. Because they already know what happened, people can shape their reports in a way that makes sense of events—even those that may have been messy or uncertain at the time. Because our culture sees relationships as developing in terms of stages and steps, people tend to report relational activity in such terms. Retrospective reports also accentuate the notion that relationships are plainly goal oriented even when life is less clear cut.

The Accidental/Confused Breakup

The possibility that relationships are redefined quietly and almost thoughtlessly during the progress of talk is ignored in most social scientific models. In reality, it is important to focus on relational change as a whole—not just big changes but the little ones too. Relationship development is not always strategic or conscious or directed in linear fashion. Most often it is based on the uncertainty that surrounds the future outcome of relationships and the different ways they are essentialized in the talk of everyday life.

These bits of talk can lead to questions about the nature and form of the relationships, which is how change occurs. Is dissolution a special case of human processing or just an extension of these processes? It is one more example of how talk changes relationships in the context of uncertainty about the future.

People talk, things happen, and relationship consequences arise. In short, your talk reflects cultural expectations and can lead to self-fulfilling prophecy. Processes of change may be connected to everyday experiences in complex ways and are not necessarily different just because researchers (and particularly researchers' methods) treat them as such. If you listen critically to how talk makes relationships work, we hope you will agree.

You have probably noticed that every relationship that benefits you also brings you difficulties, what Jackie Wiseman (1986) elegantly referred to as the bond/bind dilemma. To be in a successful relationship with someone, you must give something up or be prepared to make sacrifices. If you want to benefit from a bond with another person, you must also be prepared to put up with the binds, such as driving him or her to the airport, and to supply the other provisions of relationships that we discussed at the beginning of the chapter. We humans do not simply *need* these provisions for ourselves but also *supply* them for others, so the provisions of relationships are a two-way street.

Photo 6.5 Do relationships develop and break down in a linear fashion? (See page 156.)

A more complicated illustration of this idea by Baxter and Montgomery (1996) pays attention to the dialectic tensions present in relationships that people have to manage day-to-day. A dialectic tension is essentially a built-in contradiction between two aspects of the same dimension, such as **autonomy–connectedness** or **openness– privacy**. Everyone wants to be autonomous and independent; everyone simultaneously wants to connect with someone else. For that reason, from time to time you

When searching for a "breakup" photo for this page, the only photos we could find featured women who were brokenhearted rather than men. Even though the picture we finally selected includes a man who appears to be upset, a woman is clearly at the forefront. What does this tell you about cultural views of relationships?

experience the tension between autonomy and connectedness and must make choices about how to handle it. In the same way, you recognize that you must be open and honest with your partners in relationships, but you also need some privacy and do not always wish to tell them everything. The operation of these two dialectics, demonstrated in the talk that individuals have with one another, is often very significant in relationships. The simultaneous push/pull that individuals experience in negotiating their relational activities tends to show through in their talk. Once again, it seems that stages are not clearly laid out in relationships but rather that you experience ups and downs, pushes and pulls, and tensions and countertensions in almost all of your relational experiences. If your talk reflects a degree of ambivalence about what is happening in a relationship, that is because relationships are very complicated to conduct successfully.

Given all these pieces of evidence, then, it is not surprising that relationships are often turbulent and that stage models of relationship growth and decline can be viewed as too simplistic in the real world. Certainly, as we indicated at the beginning of the chapter, relationships are not simply driven by emotions but are the result of complex management of competing forces handled in both direct and indirect talk.

FOCUS QUESTIONS REVISITED

1. How does your everyday communication with other people *transact* your relationships?

Everyday communication with other people transacts your relationships by supporting your knowledge base and providing some of the psychological and other needs for support and understanding. Several forms of communication serve to include people in relationships, thus transacting the intimacy between them. There are several forms of communication that build support and sustain relationships, ranging from direct intimacy talk to indirect discovery of similarity.

2. How does your talk compose your relationships during everyday conversation?

Talk composes your relationships both directly (for example, through requests for friendship and connection or requests to end a relationship) and indirectly by demonstrating social and personal relationships in the kind of talk two persons engage in. Everyday chitchat can show that a relationship still exists between two people, and friends as compared to acquaintances tend to take much more for granted and do less explaining in their conversations. Relationships are also sustained by relational continuity constructional units, or small-talk ways of demonstrating that a relationship persists through absence.

3. How do relationships grow or change, and how does this show up in speech?

Relationships grow and change in several ways, as people become more knowledgeable about one another and more relaxed in each other's company. In the early stages of a relationship's development, conversation tends to be about broad and uncontroversial topics, where people need to fill in details about themselves and their past history so the other person can understand. As the relationship becomes more developed, individuals need to fill in less background information and are able to take much more for granted.

4. What are the different types of communication that take place when a relationship is coming apart?

The breakdown of relationships is marked by changes in both the topic of conversation and the audience to which the person communicates. In the early parts of a breakup when an individual is simply contemplating ending a relationship, he or she tends to withdraw from social contact and become very brooding. The second phase of a breakup is characterized by confrontation with a relational partner and less time spent with other friends. A third phase develops where the person decides to tell friends and associates about the breakup and to enlist their support. In the fourth phase, the person develops and tells a story to the world at large, explaining how the breakup occurred and making himself or herself "look good." The final (resurrection) phase is characterized by communication aimed at developing new relationships and letting go of the past.

5. Do relationships develop and break down in a linear fashion?

No. There are many cultural reasons why people would like to believe that there are stages in relationships, but these cultural beliefs tend to force their narratives of relationship into a pattern that conforms with their beliefs and therefore creates a self-fulfilling prophecy. People can make sense of both the development and the breakup of relationships, often a messy process, only retrospectively, and it is easy to make a relationship look as if it moved in linear fashion even when it did not.

KEY CONCEPTS

autonomy–connectedness   153
dyadic process   150
grave dressing process   150
intrapsychic process   150
openness–privacy   153
personal relationships   138

provisions of relationships   135
relational continuity constructional units
   (RCCUs)   139
resurrection process   150
social process   150
social relationships   138

QUESTIONS TO ASK YOUR FRIENDS

1. Write the story of your most recent breakup. Does it follow a neat progression? Have a friend read it and ask you questions about particular details. Does this questioning make you want to revise your narrative in any way?

2. What turning points are there in relationship growth or decline that you and your friends believe you can identify through talk?

3. The next time your friends ask, "How was your day?" ask what they think they are accomplishing. Enter into a broad and fulfilling discussion on retrospective RCCUs and how even small talk serves to maintain relationships during absence.

MEDIA LINKS

1. Look at several Sunday paper sections on marriages and engagements. Check for similarities in attractiveness level between the people involved. Next take these pictures and cut them down the middle. How easy is it to reconnect the right people?

2. Take any movie where a romance develops between two main characters. Does it either develop or dissolve according to the proposal made in this chapter, and if not, how?

3. What models of "true romance" are presented in different kinds of movies? Is the romance depicted in action films, if any, the same as or different from that presented in romantic comedies? In what ways?

ETHICAL ISSUES

1. Do you think that someone who is ending a relationship with someone else has an ethical duty to explain to the other person why?

2. What is unethical about having two romantic relationships at the same time?

3. Can you think of a time when the autonomy–connectedness dialectic presented you with an ethical dilemma (e.g., made you think about lying in order to maintain your freedom without losing a relationship)? Don't use that example, but try to find others.

ANSWERS TO PHOTO CAPTIONS

Photo 6.1 ▪ A husband and wife talking about the books they are reading at the end of the day might compare notes about their reactions to their reading and share their enjoyment. Reading to one another is also a great pleasure to many couples. The activity reaffirms connection and also highlights the parts of the reading that each person values, thus reaffirming the connection of their worlds of meaning.

Photo 6.2 ▪ It is an example of prospective units, providing recognition that an interaction is about to end but the relationship continues.

Photo 6.3 ▪ People self-disclose their inner thoughts, secrets, worries, and concerns as they become closer. This conversation between friends (look at the distance between them, the place where the talk is happening, and their postures) is obviously very intense and deep, not shallow and uninvolving.

Photo 6.4 ▪ The expressions—hostile resentment and dejected resignation—on the two people's faces are clear, and the woman has literally turned her back on the man and is looking upward, as if for help from the skies, while close to tears. The man's closed posture shows difficulty, but the surroundings are comfortable and the man and woman are sitting close to one another, suggesting that they are either at home or in counseling.

Photo 6.5 ▪ No. Relationships do not break down linearly, though people often report as if they do.

STUDENT STUDY SITE

Visit the study site at **www.sagepub.com/boc2e** for e-flashcards, practice quizzes, journal articles and additional study resources.

REFERENCES

Acitelli, L. K. (1988). When spouses talk to each other about their relationship. *Journal of Social and Personal Relationships, 5,* 185–199.

Baxter, L. A., Dun, T. D., & Sahlstein, E. M. (2001). Rules for relating communicated among social network members. *Journal of Social and Personal Relationships, 18,* 173–200.

Baxter, L. A., & Montgomery, B. M. (1996). *Relating: Dialogs and dialectics.* New York: Guilford Press.

Baxter, L. A., & Wilmot, W. (1985). Taboo topics in close relationships. *Journal of Social and Personal Relationships, 2,* 253–269.

Bergmann, J. R. (1993). *Discreet indiscretions: The social organization of gossip.* New York: Aldine de Gruyter.

Burleson, B. R., Holmstrom, A. J., & Gilstrap, C. M. (2005). "Guys can't say that to guys": Four experiments assessing the normative motivation account for deficiencies in the emotional support provided by men. *Communication Monographs, 72*(4), 468–501.

Byrne, D. (1997). An overview (and underview) of research and theory within the attraction paradigm. *Journal of Social and Personal Relationships, 14*, 417–431.

Carl, W. J. (2006). What's all the buzz about? Everyday communication and the relational basis of word-of-mouth and buzz marketing practices. *Management Communication Quarterly, 19*(4), 601–634.

Carl, W. J., & Duck, S. W. (2004). How to do things with relationships. In P. Kalbfleisch (Ed.), *Communication yearbook* (Vol. 28, pp. 1–35). Thousand Oaks, CA: Sage.

Cummings, J. N., Lee, J. B., & Kraut, R. (2006). Communication technology and friendship during the transition from high school to college. In R. Kraut, M. Brynin, & S. Kiesler (Eds.), *Computers, phones, and the Internet: Domesticating information technology* (pp. 265–278). New York: Oxford University Press.

Delia, J. G. (1980). Some tentative thoughts concerning the study of interpersonal relationships and their development. *Western Journal of Speech Communication, 44*, 97–103.

Duck, S. W. (1982). A topography of relationship disengagement and dissolution. In S. W. Duck (Ed.), *Personal relationships 4: Dissolving personal relationships* (pp. 1–30). London: Academic Press.

Duck, S. W. (1998). *Human relationships* (3rd ed.). London: Sage.

Duck, S. W. (1999). *Relating to others* (2nd ed.). Milton Keynes, UK: Open University Press.

Duck, S. W. (2007). *Human relationships* (4th ed.). London: Sage.

Duck, S. W. (2011). *Rethinking relationships.* Thousand Oaks, CA: Sage.

Goldsmith, D. J., & Fitch, K. (1997). The normative context of advice as social support. *Human Communication Research, 23*, 454.

Granovetter, M. S. (1973). The strength of weak ties. *American Journal of Sociology, 78*, 1360–1380.

Hess, J. A. (2000). Maintaining a nonvoluntary relationship with disliked partners: An investigation into the use of distancing behaviors. *Human Communication Research, 26*, 458–488.

Honeycutt, J. M. (1993). Memory structures for the rise and fall of personal relationships. In S. W. Duck (Ed.), *Individuals in relationships* (Understanding relationship processes 1, pp. 60–86). Newbury Park, CA: Sage.

Kerckhoff, A. C. (1974). The social context of interpersonal attraction. In T. L. Huston (Ed.), *Foundations of interpersonal attraction* (pp. 61–77). New York: Academic Press.

Leatham, G. B., & Duck, S. W. (1990). Conversations with friends and the dynamics of social support. In S. W. Duck with R. C. Silver (Eds.), *Personal relationships and social support* (pp. 1–29). London: Sage.

Manusov, V. K., Kellas, J. K., & Trees, A. R. (2004). Do unto others? Conversational moves and perceptions of attentiveness toward other's face in accounting sequences between friends. *Human Communication Research, 30*(4), 514–539.

Norwood, K. M. (2010, April 26). *Here and gone: Competing discourses in the communication of families with a transgender member.* Unpublished PhD thesis, Department of Communication Studies, University of Iowa.

Parks, M. (2006). *Communication and social networks.* Mahwah, NJ: Lawrence Erlbaum.

Paul, E. L. (2006). Beer goggles, catching feelings and the walk of shame: The myths and realities of the hookup experience. In C. D. Kirkpatrick, S. W. Duck, & M. K. Foley (Eds.), *Relating difficulty: Processes of constructing and managing difficult interaction* (pp. 141–160). Mahwah, NJ: Lawrence Erlbaum.

Planalp, S., & Garvin-Doxas, K. (1994). Using mutual knowledge in conversation: Friends as experts in each other. In S. W. Duck (Ed.), *Dynamics of relationships: Understanding relationship processes* (Vol. 4, pp. 1–26). Newbury Park, CA: Sage.

Rollie, S. S., & Duck, S. W. (2006). Stage theories of marital breakdown. In J. H. Harvey & M. A. Fine (Eds.), *Handbook of divorce and dissolution of romantic relationships* (pp. 176–193). Mahwah, NJ: Lawrence Erlbaum.

Sahlstein, E. M. (2004). Relating at a distance: Negotiating being together and being apart in long-distance relationships. *Journal of Social and Personal Relationships, 21*(5), 689–710.

Sahlstein, E. M. (2006). The trouble with distance. In C. D. Kirkpatrick, S. W. Duck, & M. K. Foley (Eds.), *Relating difficulty: Processes of constructing and managing difficult interaction* (pp. 119–140). Mahwah, NJ: Lawrence Erlbaum.

Sigman, S. J. (1991). Handling the discontinuous aspects of continuous social relationships: Toward research on the persistence of social forms. *Communication Theory, 1,* 106–127.

Sunnafrank, M. (1983). Attitude similarity and interpersonal attraction in communication processes: In pursuit of an ephemeral influence. *Communication Monographs, 50,* 273–284.

Sunnafrank, M., & Ramirez, A. (2004). At first sight: Persistent relational effects of get-acquainted conversations. *Journal of Social and Personal Relationships, 21*(3), 361–379.

Vangelisti, A., & Banski, M. (1993). Couples' debriefing conversations: The impact of gender, occupation and demographic characteristics. *Family Relations, 42,* 149–157.

Weiss, R. S. (1974). The provisions of social relationships. In Z. Rubin (Ed.), *Doing unto others* (pp. 17–26). Englewood Cliffs, NJ: Prentice Hall.

Weiss, R. S. (1998). A taxonomy of relationships. *Journal of Social and Personal Relationships, 15,* 671–683.

Wiseman, J. P. (1986). Friendship: Bonds and binds in a voluntary relationship. *Journal of Social and Personal Relationships, 3,* 191–211.

Wood, J. T., & Duck, S. W. (Eds.). (2006). *Composing relationships: Communication in everyday life.* Belmont, CA: Thomson Wadsworth.

7

Groups and Leaders

Researchers have been writing about small groups for years and years and years. Small groups (say, fewer than 15 people)—from committees in Congress to juries to college admissions committees to job interview panels—can affect our lives in multiple ways. Juries, for example, can deprive us of life, liberty, and the pursuit of happiness.

Obviously you want to be sure that groups make good decisions—or at least do not make bad ones. Many questions arise about how group members communicate with one another when they are making decisions and what communicative mistakes they make. Feminist scholars have recently drawn attention beyond the different communicative styles of men and women in groups to marginalization in groups and the effects of group composition on group communication and behavior.

Communication scholars focus on a number of questions about groups. For example, why do groups sometimes make bad decisions even though they have talked about all the issues very thoroughly? Why is group conflict such a common experience? What makes most group meetings so tedious and boring? Does a group leader communicate, or relate, differently than other members of a group (and, if so, in what ways)? How can a good leader influence a group ethically and directly? What sorts of leadership communication styles help a group reach good decisions or complete tasks on time and well? How much difference do leaders make to whether groups get along?

There are many different theories about these questions (Poole & Hollingshead, 2005), including psychodynamic perspectives seeking to understand the psychological forces that lead group members and leaders to act how they do (McLeod & Kettner-Polley, 2005). Others deal with social identity and how groups (try to) make themselves coherent and at the same time distinctive from other groups (Abrams, Hogg, Hinkle, &

Otten, 2005). Some look at a network perspective on groups and explore the connection of one group to another (especially in a larger organization—say, "sales" in relation to "marketing") and of the relationship of one group member to another, whether familiar with each other or not (Katz, Lazer, Arrow, & Contractor, 2005). Others look at how groups form, develop, and change and how communication among members changes in style and form during these processes (Arrow, Bouas Henry, Poole, Wheelan, & Moreland, 2005).

A growing style now is to stress that both group membership and leadership are kinds of *relationships* that exist behind communication in groups (Northouse, 2009). For one thing, a leader needs good relationships with group members, and groups that are cohesive and get along well are usually more successful. By contrast, conflict that happens in groups should be seen not simply as a battle of *ideas* but as a battle between *people who have ideas.* This again makes group activity relational. If you have ever been involved in group conflict in class or with people in your friendship network, you know how painful and difficult it is to deal with. Not really about ideas, arguments, and abstractions, group conflict is about emotions, feelings, and relationships—and the *people* who *hold* the ideas and *make* the arguments.

Focus Questions

1. What exactly is a group, and what makes it different from an assembly, a collective, or a team?
2. Can you define groups only in terms of the kinds of communication that take place between members, or must you look at the relationships that lie behind the communication? Does communication transact the existence and nature of the group?
3. How do groups form, and what changes in their communication?
4. What communicative and relational skills make a leader into a good leader?
5. In what ways are discussions of team-based organizing and communication different from traditional approaches to small-group communication?
6. How can a group promote its own decision-making capacities in more effective ways?

What Makes a Group?

We first must decide what a group is and is not. Is a group just one more person than a dyad and one person short of a crowd? Or is it less a matter of numbers than the activities that groups carry out? In this section, we give you some pointers about how groups communicate or transact their "groupness." Think of any group you belong to, and you have already answered the question "What is a group?" by referencing your sense of *membership.* The key point is that essentially a collective becomes a group once it recognizes itself as one and its members identify themselves as such.

Defining a Group

Beyond the recognition of membership a simple assembly or collection of people is not really a group unless it has a **common purpose.** That is, people are working toward the same goal, or are collected as a group to achieve a particular result (such as a sales group wanting to find ways to increase sales). Beyond that minimum requirement, however, people in groups are *organized*, have *awareness* of one another as *members* of the same group, and carry out *communication* among themselves.

Different groups communicate differently (some formally, some casually), and everyone in a group does not necessarily have to talk to everyone else for it to count as a group. For example, in a college discussion section, the students may all talk to the discussion leader but not to one another. A discussion section still counts as a group rather than a random collection of students because there are a common purpose, a set time to meet, some rules, and a leader (i.e., an implied organizational structure). Most important, the people see themselves as more than just a bunch of folks and as members of something shared.

There are many types of small groups that might be part of your experience: Bible study groups, board meetings, sorority/fraternity committees, friends deciding what kind of pizza to order on Friday night, chat rooms, focus groups, or sets of roommates working out a cooking schedule. In each of these groups, when decisions are made, someone essentially persuades someone else, in the context of the rules that govern the relationship. Everyday life relating involves informal persuasion of people in a group just as persuasive speeches to large audiences have an underlying set of assumptions about the relationship of speaker to audience (Chapter 14). Here, we look only at the processes by which decisions get made by small interactive groups. By and large the principles—the transactive principles of communication now familiar to you—are broadly similar in all of these cases: They depend on relationships.

A collection of cancer patients visiting a hospital for chemotherapy is not a group. The stay-at-home dads waiting outside to pick up their children from school are not a group, although they arrive at the same place at the same time with the same goal (to pick up their kids). If they get to know one another and start to talk routinely, *then* they become a group transacted by talk (their talk creates an interchange of information and creates a sense of belonging). So now they have a recognized, organized, social, or even personal relationship with each other. They shared a purpose all along, but communication and sense of knowledge makes them more than just a collection of bodies waiting for something else to happen.

Photo 7.1 What exactly is a group, and what makes it different from an assembly, a collective, or a team? How many of each of these can you see in this picture? (See page 185.)

Communication and Transaction of Groups

Scholars have most often looked at group decision making in terms of quality of information and message transmission. Much information transfer and decision making takes place relationally. You listen to complaints, give advice, carry out tasks, and do favors for friends without really giving the prospect much thought. It's what friends do for one another, offering advice, knowledge, information, help, and support. The *kind* of communication and how it is carried out makes the group the sort that it is (see Table 7.1).

Table 7.1 Types of Groups

Type of group	Primary/fundamental purposes	Features	Examples
Formal groups	Task oriented, general management oversight, outcome focused, often legislative or formally structured to run an organization	Membership is restricted or delegated; attendance is expected. There is a clear structure; power is vested in the chair; there is an agenda. There may be formal rules for speaking/turn taking; there may be voting.	Congress, congressional committees, debate clubs, shareholder meetings, annual general meetings of organized bodies, executive committees of unions, student government organizations, legislative assemblies
Advisory	Task specific, usually evidentiary or evaluative, with the intention of producing an outcome that is a focused "best solution" to a specific problem or arrangement of an event	Membership is specific and restricted; there may be a chair, there may be structure, and there may be an agenda. Discussion is usually open, informal, and focused on the weighing of evidence or alternatives. Critical and evaluative argument of different proposals is encouraged.	Sorority and fraternity social affairs committees, homecoming committees, juries, accident investigation boards, review boards for awards and prizes
Creative	Evaluation of concepts or creation of new products or approaches to complex problems	Membership is usually invited. There is a lack of structure; individuals are discouraged from critical comment on the ideas generated by others. The point is to generate as many ideas as possible and evaluate them later.	Brainstorming; consciousness raising; creativity groups; focus groups; test-bed groups for developing specifications and criteria for complex projects, such as the beta versions of new software, advertising logo development teams
Support	Advising, comforting, sharing knowledge, spreading information, and raising consciousness about specific issues	Membership is loosely defined; members come and go as needed; participation is voluntary as and when desired.	Alcoholics Anonymous, breast cancer survivors, grief support groups, study groups, PFLAG (Parents, Families and Friends of Lesbians and Gays)
Networking	Obtaining, building, or sustaining relationships, usually online	Membership is not defined; members join and leave as desired.	Chat rooms, social networking groups, MySpace, Facebook

Many communication courses focus exclusively on deliberate and purposive persuasion, especially in groups that make formal decisions or in public presentations and speeches. There is a relational basis to this kind of communication, too, founded on immediate trust or liking for a speaker with whom the listener is unacquainted.

In contrast, discussion in real-life groups involves interaction with people you know over time. We live in groups, at work, in school, and in the local community, and the effective forms of communication that help such groups reach decisions are focused on set tasks and objectives (such as a team responsible for deciding whether to launch a space shuttle, business associates meeting to decide a sales plan, or a jury deciding on guilt or innocence).

You may not have been in such important decision-making groups or meetings yet, but you may have taken part in a dorm meeting or class discussion about whether or not to do a particular class exercise. You will certainly be familiar with group decision making that does *not* occur in formal groups: for example, family discussion about chores, friends' discussions about pizza toppings to order, and other group decision making that happens between people in longer-term relationships.

College Experience

Students who are unhappy and those who quit school often indicate that they do not feel "connected" to the school or that they feel out of place. What they are actually saying is that they do not feel relationally connected. Relationships with a school are not those between students and a bunch of buildings, sidewalks, and landscaping. Rather, students' relationships with a school are represented in their relationships with faculty, staff, administrators, and one another. If you are feeling disconnected with your school or you just want to enhance your college experience, we encourage you to seek out groups on campus. Doing so will increase your sense of connection as well as bring about a host of other benefits and opportunities.

Formation of Groups

Groups created for experimental purposes and those in real organizational settings develop their own ways to conduct business. Bruce Tuckman (1965), a psychologist, proposed five stages of group development, and another similar phase model was proposed by communication scholar Aubrey Fisher (1970).

Tuckman's Five Stages of Group Development

1. *Forming:* The group comes into existence and seeks direction from a leader about the nature of its task and procedures.

2. *Storming:* The group gets creative. Focusing on its goals, it may become entangled in socioemotional and relationship storms and interpersonal conflict between individuals.

3. *Norming:* The group defines its purposes, roles, and procedures, moving more formally toward a solution.

4. *Performing:* Having established *how* it will perform its task, the group now does so. Members seek solutions to their problems but are careful about one another's feelings.

5. *Adjourning:* The group reflects on its achievements, underlines its performative accomplishments, and closes itself down. A good leader will summarize what has been done, repeat who has been assigned tasks to be done before the next meeting (or by a date certain), and then thank everyone and, if truly appropriate, do some congratulation: "Good job, everyone."

Fisher's Model of Group Progression

- *Orientation:* Group members get to know one another and come to grips with the problems they have convened to deal with.
- *Conflict:* The group argues about possible ways of approaching the problem and begins to seek solutions.
- *Emergence:* This occurs when some daylight of consensus begins to dawn. The group sees the emergence of possible agreement.
- *Reinforcement:* The group explicitly consolidates consensus to complete the task.

Communication and Relationships in Groups

Fisher (1970) supposed that the types of communication in a group would identify, as well as promote, the particular stage. For example, if someone says, "That's a really good idea. I think we're getting somewhere," and others mutter, "Yeah," or just nod, then that would count as emergence as well as moving people to the general sense that they are moving from conflict to consensus. His model helps researchers who watch a decision-making group to see where it is headed or to help it through toward the final conclusive stage. He assumed that the stage of the group produces certain identifying types of communication, whereas we would say it is vice versa.

Listen in on Your Life

Regular "friendship groups" or "social networks" are not included in Table 7.1. Why do you think researchers would see a friendship group as different from the other types of groups, and does it matter? One obvious point is that friendships have very little structure and are based on the notion of equality, whereas many other groups have a formal structure that gives people different rank or powers. What other differences do you notice between the "groups" you belong to and the "friendships" you have?

Speech Style Differences

We have emphasized the importance of everyday communication throughout this book, and you can immediately recognize that groups, whether or not they change their speech styles in the exact stages proposed by Fisher (1970), certainly speak differently than when friends chat.

One feature that makes formal groups feel different is that they affect everyday speech by adopting rules that alter the patterns of speaking from those of everyday speech. "Will the senator yield?" and "If it pleases the court" are not remarks you often hear outside of formal decision-making groups!

What are the effects of the differences between everyday communication and the confining formal speech that happens in group decision making? For one thing, you must know the right language to belong to a group: The Speaker of the House of Representatives does not begin the business of the day by announcing, "Yo, dogs, wassup?"

Is your family a group? If so, is it the same as or different from the other groups you belong to? Which parts of it make up the group, and how far do you extend membership (e.g., do you count cousins, stepsiblings, or neighbors who are "just like family")? Where are your boundaries?

There is a prescribed formula, not widely known to outsiders: After the Pledge of Allegiance, the chair asks, "Shall the Journal stand approved to date?"

One element of group membership, then, is created by *knowledge of the styles and rules governing talk* in the group. They will differ from everyday life conversation.

A Key Point About Groups and Communication

For this reason—the nature of assumptions in communication and its styles—seeing "the composition" of groups as just a counting of heads is a mistake. Groups are not structures but communicatively related membership systems. It only makes sense to identify the composition of a *collective* in terms of names, ranks, sex, age, and other general demographic information. *Groups* interact not because of their "composition" (numbers of females or males, old or young) but because of *communicative relationships* and the kinds of talk shared between specific people involved.

A "group" can be those attending a business meeting or just a set of friends talking to one another to decide where to go for dinner. *All* groups are not simple structures but dynamic, communicative, relationally transacted entities.

Photo 7.2 Three Scotsmen in 1877 judge a prize canary, their equivalent of a beauty pageant. Which of Fisher's stages do they portray? (See page 185.)

Features of Groups

Many different sorts of researchers study groups, ranging from management studies to jury decision making to military mission control. We repeat our emphasis on

Strategic Communication

Recognizing the relational elements of groups will greatly assist you when promoting a particular agenda or decision. Groups are not structured as bodies, numbers, and depersonalized decision makers. Within a general structure sit real human beings who have relationships with one another. Review the following example and consider how it can apply to groups to which you already belong and groups to which you may belong in the future.

The "board of executives'" decision may be influenced by the friendship between Alina and Sangeet. Distrust of six members for the chair makes the group less effective. An agreement made before the meeting by Kristen, Bianca, and Brendan to "stick together on this one" may cause the good arguments against a proposition to fail all the same. A board meeting can be seen as a formal structure in an organization tasked with making top-level decisions, but the specific people put into it will develop personal relationships with one another that can influence their decisions. Within the board, Jim may be friends with Sarah; Sarah trusts Chitra; Juanita resents Jamaal . . . and formal and informal relationships can clash. For example, Sarah trusts Chitra interpersonally, but in a board setting, they both have to act not on their personal feelings but in the service of their own department goals. Success of the group is more important than Sarah's personal trust for Chitra. Anyway, in service of the company Sarah and Chitra may have to carry out tasks that strain their personal trust: For example, they may be asked to decide which of their personal employees to fire so the business can cut costs.

relationships in all cases. Groups are necessarily dynamic interpersonal relationships between members.

Togetherness: Cohesiveness and Relationships in Groups

The members of a group are first defined by their common motives and goals (Thibaut & Kelley, 1959). For example, a city council advisory committee shares the task of coming up with a thoughtful report. A homecoming committee shares the goal of making this the best homecoming ever, with the smartest ideas and themes.

Interdependence

A related feature of groups is that they divide the labor in a way that leads to **interdependence**. That is, everyone relies on everyone else to do his or her part of the job well. The team cannot function properly if its members do not work interdependently. For example, members of a football team are interdependent because the performance of the whole team depends on the coherent yet distinct performance of each of its members.

Interdependence involves the division of labor into particular jobs so the members can achieve their goals. Interdependence works as a transacted outcome of the communication between team players. The coaches and the captain have the job of communicating and coordinating the other members' performances in a way that hangs it all together.

Commitment

Group members usually show *commitment* to each other and to their group's goals when a group is working well (Harden Fritz & Omdahl, 2006). One transactive feature that makes a group "a group" is that individual members share a commitment to the overall group goals. They want to be team players, and communicate that desire in talk and behavior.

The members may also show commitment to one another, watch each other's backs, and look out for one another, particularly in effective groups. The more people share commitment to one another as members of a group, the more they help the whole group move forward toward its goals. The group may show commitment to individual members through caring for their welfare, as well as aiming to achieve the goals of the group.

Cohesiveness

Cohesiveness, essentially another word for *teamwork,* describes people working in unison (Hogg, 1992). You may have seen a motivational poster of a team of rowers all pulling their oars together. They are synchronized and cohesive: They work in time together with one another. If they pulled their oars whenever they felt like it rather than all at the same time, they would show low cohesiveness and keep getting in each other's way. Their oars would clash, and the boat would go nowhere (take it from an Oxford rowing coxswain!).

Another goal of many groups is to maintain high morale and civility by making sure that members do not disrespect each other. Maintaining good relationships between members, another example of cohesiveness, is a goal of any group that seeks to be effective. Cohesiveness, however, or the degree to which members are attracted and committed to one another, is a primary output of groups' social emotional exchanges in talk and thus is a transactional and relational consequence of communication.

Avoiding Out-Groups

In any small group there can develop a power cell of disgruntled folks who feel undervalued, mistreated, disrespected, not included, or overlooked. Often dubbed "out-groups" such people can be either disruptive or constructive, and a

Make Your Case

Consider whether these count as groups: a family; an audience of people watching a football game in a sports bar; an audience at a public lecture on campus; the people watching a movie at the cinema; witnesses to a car accident talking to one another as they watch the police take notes. You might also reflect on whether or not you are in a group when you use the speakerphone feature on a mobile/cell phone in a public place. Who is in the group, and who is out? What communicative features are different in the above cases?

In football, not everyone can be a quarterback; people in the offense have different jobs than those in the defense. The work is divided because the team as a whole shares a purpose: namely, winning the game. The ultimate success of the whole team will depend on whether every member does an assigned job. If everyone tried to do the same task (all tried to throw the ball, all tried to block the other team, all tried to catch passes), it would be ineffective because the other jobs would not get done.

good leader can use them in the better role to challenge and question group assumptions by listening carefully to their concerns.

Disruptive out-groups will tend to prevent the rest of the group from completing its business. Out-groups can, however, serve a useful purpose by making the majority members of the group discuss more options, reflect more carefully on their opinions, answer challenges, and rethink their arguments.

Expectations About Performance

Groups usually expect particular behavior from members. This is a specialized, localized version of the larger society as it makes assumptions and enforces behaviors as a whole on identity (Chapter 5). We saw that others' expectations work as Society's Secret Agents to influence our own behaviors and the performance of our identity. Small groups have more specific expectations about behavior and influence the group itself. Correct behavior elicits a reinforcing response, which then influences further expectations of and for other people. This is another example of the constitutive and transactive way in which communication sustains behavior.

Group Norms

Group norms involve established status relationships, values, and sanctions. They are informal rules and procedures that occur in a group but not outside it. A group norm may be that everyone should speak in turn and that all voices should be heard, as is common in meetings in the Netherlands, for example. Another group norm could be that everyone should speak in order of seniority, follow the leader, or speak creatively without fear of being criticized. Some group norms may require that "nobody rocks the boat and everyone should be a team player." Most groups have a norm that requires mutual respect.

How do various groups to which you belong show their commitment to membership? Don't just list your college "fight song" but report on specific examples of communication that transact commitment.

Negative Norms

Some therapy groups try to break down people's defensiveness about their egos. This is intended to lead to a norm of making honest, even if negative, comments about each other with no attempt to dress them up politely (sensitivity groups and encounter groups; Weigel, 2002).

A stronger version of this norm is found in military training groups. The purpose here, in part, is to break down the recruits' individuality. This can involve insulting them and getting them used to the idea of doing whatever they are told without objecting or answering back. In all of these cases, though, the group sets its own norms and ways of ensuring their enforcement.

Enforcing the Norms

Most groups have their own **group sanctions**, or punishments for "stepping out of line," speaking out of turn, or failing to accept the ruling of the chair or leader. For example, an unruly member—one who persistently violates the norms—may be thrown out of a meeting. This has the effect of silencing his or her participation in, and influence on, the group.

More subtly, everyone else in the group may shun a dissenter and classify him or her as to be avoided outside and ignored inside the meetings. "Shunning," or excluding people from participation in the group, or not even acknowledging their presence, is a very powerful social, relational, and communicative punishment used by such religious communities as the Amish and the Jehovah's Witnesses.

Member Roles

Other expectations about performance concern roles. You know about roles from movies: A role is when someone acts out a part that fits in with parts other people play in "the drama."

Erving Goffman (1959) pointed out that people perform a lot of life as if it were drama, and in Chapter 5, we discussed the *performance* of identity. In many groups the role of leader is key, but groups with a continuous existence tend to mark out other roles as well.

In formal organizations, these roles have titles, like *sales director* or *manager*. If you have ever bought a car, you know that one dealer will often play the role of "the friendly guy" while another one will play the role of "hardnose." That way they can soften you up first and then play hardball in the negotiations over price.

Photo 7.3 Sidelining a player for an offense during a soccer game is a good example of a particular group behavior. What is that? (See page 185.)

Informal Roles

Groups that meet more than once and interact frequently with an expectation of continued future existence also develop roles. In groups of coworkers, "the sales team," or a college discussion section, roles evolve for several people involved. Patterns of interaction that repeat themselves and reinforce these roles evolve as well. People in that group likely will be categorized and informally assigned particular roles ("the joker," "the grinch," "the loose cannon," or "the rising star," for example).

If two friends are in a sales-team group decision-making situation where one is "the leader," which role should the leader adopt if the friend says something funny but irrelevant—the "stay-on-track leader" role or the "have-fun-with-friends" role?

Roles and Traits

The identification of members' roles was based at first on the idea that certain people are better suited to some roles than others or have the personality traits that make them better than other people in certain roles. In particular, leadership in groups was regarded as a role for which some people may show early evidence in traits.

An early hope of research in group processes (e.g., Hollander, 1958) largely grew from research done in World War II. The military wanted to identify future leaders early in their careers and give them fast-track promotion to leadership roles. Even today, the military identifies individuals as "flyers" and places them on the fast track as a result of tests during the first few weeks of their enlistment.

This style of research assumes that leadership is an inborn trait and has run into the objection that it takes too little account of how people adapt to situations and circumstances. Communication in group interaction can generate unexpected skills or adaptations in people, especially since situations are constantly changing and need adaptive techniques. Usually groups have a culture that steers their decisions in particular ways.

Group Culture

A **group culture** is another form of expectation set that affects groups. Group culture is evident in how members talk to one another, the clothes they wear while working as a group, or the special terms and language or jokes they use. For example, an organization may have a formal dress code in the workplace except on "casual Friday," or group members may talk in ways that reflect an organizational hypertext language specific to their particular organization.

Workers on a construction site may have a group culture that particularly values physical strength rather than managerial thinking. Such workers tend to play down any evidence of thoughtfulness. Dennis Mumby (2006) illustrates this kind of group culture when he writes about his experiences as a college student working in a manual labor job. The other workers mocked the fact that, with all his "college boy" intelligence, he could not drive some of the machinery as well as they could. The very use of the term *college boy* to describe him represents, in talk, the group culture that "book learning" is less important than practical skills.

All of these expectations in groups (norms, roles, culture) are important ways of stressing communicatively that a person belongs to a group and must play particular parts in its performances. They all transact the relationships between people, and that communication makes groups what they are (revisit Table 7.1).

In the cult film *Office Space,* one element of group culture in the restaurant where the Jennifer Aniston character ("Joanna") works is the wearing of "flair" (badges and decorations on the servers' uniforms). In one scene, a manager points out that Joanna is wearing only the *minimum* amount of flair and therefore is not demonstrating adequate commitment to the group culture. By the way, the manager in that scene is actually writer and director Mike Judge!

Leadership

In real life, groups usually have an appointed leader. Your first thought is likely that **leadership** is the formal position where a specific person has power over the others in the group: a boss in the workplace, a team leader in a task group, a chair of any committee, or an elder of a religious community. Indeed, such people are required to communicate authoritatively, to run the agenda, and to move the group forward in particular ways that others should follow.

Case in Point

Listen for the norms, roles, and culture of two or three of the groups to which you belong. Identify their differences in terms of each kind of respective group.

Leadership Styles

The classic discussion of leadership, since Bales (1950), has divided leaders into those who are focused on the **task** and those who focus on the **socioemotional** well-being of the members of the group. As discussed below, more recently leaders have been regarded as group stewards or *team* leaders (Northouse, 2009).

Task Leaders

A task leader

- stresses the activity of the group,
- keeps members on topic,
- follows the agenda,
- makes sure decisions get made,
- is responsible for defining the group's intended accomplishment,
- is charged with directing what happens to fulfill the set tasks of the group,
- makes sure the group reaches a conclusion at the end of its allotted meeting time,
- summarizes what got done in a meeting, and
- sets the agenda for the next meeting.

This kind of leader also is responsible for ensuring that proper procedures are followed during the course of discussion. The chair of a committee of Congress, for example, must know the proper rules of parliamentary procedure encoded in Robert's Rules of Order. These procedures may involve such matters as who may propose a motion, the form in which a motion may be proposed, how amendments may be discussed, and the order in which motions must be debated.

Socioemotional Leaders

A socioemotional leader

- pays attention to how everyone feels in the group,
- ensures that members feel comfortable with the decision-making process,

- allows everyone to get a turn in the discussion,
- makes members happy with the outcome,
- keeps the personal relationships between group members on an even keel, and
- manages people's "face" and handles their feelings.

Of course, the task leader and the socioemotional leader can be one and the same. For example, in *Apollo 13*, "Flight" manages to rally his team members by recognizing their anxieties, providing firm authority and so calming them down, inviting their input and inclusion in the discussion, and then forcing them to be realistic.

Different forms of communication are involved in the two tasks (Parsons & Bales, 1955), and a person may be good at one element of the group process (task) but poor at the other (keeping everyone happy). When the two roles are performed by separate people, most often the formal leader focuses on goals at the expense of the feelings of the people involved.

Types of Leadership Power

Talk sometimes creates conflicts between formal power and informal power, making power itself a transactive result of communication. A leader is said to have **formal power** when power has been formally allocated by a system or a group. However, a group may communicate in a way that this power doesn't mean much. For example, the chair may be ineffective, and another member may be better at communicating or more respected than the chair. **Informal power** is based on liking, relationships, and communication competence. This type of leadership power has not been formally granted but rather has been developed through the group's interactions.

Informal Power

John Hepburn and Ann Crepin (1984) studied the relationships between prisoners and guards in a state penitentiary. The formal structure of power seems obvious: The guards are in control, and the prisoners are not. But think again. The system cannot work if only formal power is taken into account. Informal power must also be taken into account within this system.

First, the prisoners outnumber the guards. At any time, if they acted together, they could overpower a single guard, whether or not the guard is carrying weaponry.

There is one obvious example from your own life where a person who appears powerful over you might find things turning around unexpectedly. Your instructors appear to have power over you, but you get to rate them at the end of their courses in a way that may influence their careers or pay status.

Second, the guards' superiors take note of how they handle prisoners. Particular guards get a reputation for being good with prisoners, while other guards are seen as incompetent. The good ones receive bigger pay raises than the others. Once again the prisoners can influence the outcomes for the guards in unexpected ways.

If the prisoners choose to communicate cooperatively with a particular guard, the superiors will see that guard as doing the job well. If the prisoners decide to make a particular guard's life difficult by disobeying orders or showing disrespect in their talk, he or she will be frequently pulled into conflicts. The superiors will eventually see this as evidence of inability to get the job done well.

So the guards need to play along, communicating with prisoners in a constructive and amiable way that helps them develop decent working relationships so they can do their job at all. So who *really* has the power?

An informal system of power also exists among the prisoners: Some prisoners are top dogs while others are not. The guards must pay attention to this informal hierarchy and not treat them all equally. Otherwise, the prisoners will stir up trouble for the guards. Again, power is transacted into being by how two parties relate and communicate.

Power in groups, then, is not always as clear as it seems from group structure. As you can tell, power is always a transactional concept and is always related to relationship dynamics. It depends on acceptance by followers as well as on its execution by a leader.

More Types of Power

French and Raven (1959) went further and distinguished five types of power (see Table 7.2), and indeed the exercise of power is more complicated than it may appear at first.

Table 7.2 French and Raven's Five Types of Power

Type of power	Features of the type	Examples
Legitimate	Conferred by a person's office rank or official status	Police officer, judge, CEO, two-star general, elected political official
Expert	Created through special knowledge of a particular topic	Mechanical engineer, electrician, automotive expert, nurse, lawyer
Referent	Created by the allegiance of one group of people to another person or group	Singers, popular politicians, celebrities, star actors (for as long as they are popular)
Reward	Created by the power to give benefits to other people, or to manage or withhold them	Paymasters; instructors who can give or withhold good grades; lobbyists who can corrupt politicians with bribes, gifts, free lunches, and the usual political trough
Coercive	Having the power to punish (as distinct from withholding of rewards, this means actual applicant of punishment)	Executioners, prison guards, instructors who penalize students for absences from class

Note that a single person can often have more than one of these types of power. For example, a police officer has legitimate power, some expert power (knowledge of traffic law, for instance), and coercive power (the power to write tickets, to deprive you of liberty through arrest, and to restrain you from going where you want to go if it would involve crossing "Police: Do Not Cross" tape). In a group it is more of a problem if the "legitimate power-holder" is not also the expert. If one other member of the team knows more than the boss and so can legitimately contradict some of the boss's ideas, then that can make

Most research on group decision making assumes that the structure and the style of communication are more important than the personal relationships among members. Which do you think is more important?

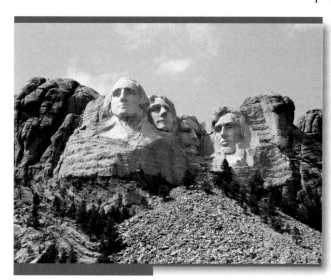

Photo 7.4 Which communicative and relational skills make a leader a good leader? (See page 186.)

relational life difficult in the group. The assumption that "the leader" has all of the power is not always justified.

Leadership Is Transacted

The preceding discussion really means that leadership is not a trait and that there are complicated social influences from other people in a group. These influence how a leader behaves—and relationships between group members are part of that. This really means that leadership is an *interpersonal process*, not a trait.

Leadership is a communicative relationship between one person and others such that when one gives a direction and another gladly carries it out, leadership has been successfully *transacted* in the interchange. Leadership is not *in a person* but *between people*.

It is true that a leader, manager, director, or department head has real control over resources that other team members need. But French and Raven (1959) teach us that these apparent powers can be undermined by the existence and use of other kinds of relational power. Sometimes, particular members of decision-making groups come up with consistently better ideas than the designated leader, and eventually people start to see those members as the true influencers. Or sometimes followers just refuse to obey.

Recent work on leadership (Northouse, 2009, 2010) has emphasized leaders' roles as "stewards" of either people or resources during their tenure at the helm. This emphasizes that the rest of the group should still be coherent and effective as a team once a new steward takes over.

Of course the term *team* has a rhetorical spin that presents interdependence, cooperation, effective division of labor, common goals, coordination, and mutual respect. Relational communicative terms, no? Relational aspects of an effective team are at least as important as the group's task outcomes. Hence, research on teams places emphasis on making people feel valued as well as getting the job done (Clampitt, 2005).

Any nasty despot can force slaves to build pyramids, but very few leaders can make their underlings feel important afterward. Julius Caesar's leadership qualities included making a point of knowing the names of as many of his men as humanly possible—he had a staggering memory—and addressing each one personally as often as he could. By paying attention to their feelings as people, he built his legions into formidable teams that would do for him what they would do for no one else (Dando-Collins, 2004).

Effective teams and their leaders are therefore interdependent. They all attend to personal relationships and carry out the friendly and respectful communication necessary for truly "personal" relationships. Personal communication transacts a collaborative climate, strong personal commitment, high regard for other team members, and a unified commitment to excellence. This enables the group to achieve its goals as clearly articulated by a good leader (Northouse, 2009). Clarity and purposefulness, two extra features of a leader's communication, thus help the team once interpersonal trust and mutual respect have been built.

Group Decision Making

In the movies, decisions are always important, are always made in futuristic glass-paneled executive suites, and usually have the subplot that one of the group decision makers is an inside traitor (*The Negotiator, V for Vendetta, Michael Clayton, Avatar,* and *Rendition,* to name a few).

In research on group decision making, random strangers are pulled together to make up a group and then given weird problems like deciding how to get back from the moon, using only a few pieces of special equipment.

Real life resembles neither of these scenarios, and for that reason much research on group decision making is remote from your experience. You experience the fact daily that groups of different types make decisions all the time in ways that this formal, stilted, and illusory way does not adequately represent. Most everyday life groups are not made up of extremely powerful people, and most decisions are not based on the availability of unlimited resources. Most important, the most familiar groups that make decisions are composed of people who already know one another both inside and outside the group decision-making scenario. When you and a group of friends decide which movie to see, the stakes are a lot lower than in the earlier examples, but you have to live with the result in your future dealings with these friends.

Even formal groups can come to conclusions and make decisions in a

Many people, including leaders, naively assume that groups are immediately inspired and immediately willing to adapt themselves when a leader proposes a new vision. For at least 100 years it has been documented that this is a stupid assumption, and whole volumes have been dedicated to "resistance to change in organizations."

Cornford (1908) noted that *organizations are motivated to oppose change* and presents their resistance to change in arguments that we can still recognize as opposing any suggestions for novelty. Among these were *the principle of unripe time* (this is not the right time to make this move; let's wait . . . until it's too late to do it); *the principle of the wedge* (if we do this now, then we will be facing a larger problem in the future); and *the dangerous precedent:*

The Principle of the Dangerous Precedent is that you should not now do an admittedly right action for fear you, or your equally timid successors, should not have the courage to do right in some future case, which, ex hypothesi, is essentially different, but superficially resembles the present one. Every public action which is not customary, either is wrong, or, if it is right, is a dangerous precedent. *It follows that nothing should ever be done for the first time.* (Cornford, 1908, p. 17) variety of ways, such as voting, consensus, straw polls, or mandates from the boss. They usually do this when formally in session "as a group." When the people meet informally, business can still be conducted, but in different ways. Informal discussions could still influence the outcome of a group deliberation. For example, a formal committee session may be influenced by a private discussion between the chair and a committee member before the meeting. Likewise, faculty members' votes on a particular issue may be influenced by concerns about tenure, promotion, and fear of future retaliation. Informal meetings and the personal concerns about later consequences are significant and meaningful.

Group Goals and Functions

Leaders are supposed to keep a group on track, but the group often strays onto other stuff because groups are boring and the people want to take account of one another's face and emotionality as well as the task. Formal groups work better when they have a number of objectives very clearly worked out beforehand, but the leader may not be able to hold group members to the agenda.

Much research in communication studies has looked at the best way groups can be sure to make "effective decisions," but since the effectiveness of a real-life decision cannot be known until its results play out, most of this research involves 20/20 hindsight analysis to identify where the group went wrong. Given that reservation, a particularly influential approach to this question is the functional theory of group decision making (Gouran & Hirokawa, 1996). This approach suggests that the "most effective sequence" in group decision making is rather obvious: to define the problem, analyze the issues, establish the criteria, generate solutions, evaluate solutions, choose and implement the best solution, and then develop an action plan to monitor the solution.

It is most important for a group to start with problem analysis. The group must first decide what requires improvement or change in a situation, and to do so, the members must analyze the problem carefully and thoughtfully to ensure that they understand it fully before trying to solve it, making sure they have a good grasp of what is at stake.

Having understood the nature of the problem, the group's next task is goal setting, or what it needs to do to solve the problem. The group must establish criteria by which it can work out whether the problem has been solved and then effectively evaluate whether its solution is better than other possibilities. To do this evaluation, the group must identify and discuss alternative ways to solve the problem and then evaluate effectively whether each will work. Assessing and evaluating the positive and negative consequences of each possibility are important in order to see whether the solution is better than the problem. For example, a medical team that decides to cut off a patient's hand because his or her palm constantly itches has probably not thought the problem through properly or evaluated alternative solutions effectively.

Communication That Helps Group Decision Making

There are three forms of communication that can help a decision-making group achieve its goals, divert from its goals, and get back on track, respectively: (1) **promotive communication,** (2) **disruptive communication,** and (3) **counteractive communication,** as described in Table 7.3.

Table 7.3 Three Forms of Communication in Decision-Making Groups	
Promotive communication	• Helps a decision-making group achieve its goals by specifying them • Works toward moving the agenda along and keeping people on track (i.e., serves their objectives in effective ways) • For example, a person may help the group focus by telling a story about how he or she solved a similar problem (Glidewell, Tucker, Todt, & Cox, 1982)
Disruptive communication	• Diverts the group from its goals and takes it down side alleys • Does not push the group forward toward achieving its goals • Does not help the group toward goals but may raise morale or lower tension • Somebody who tells an amusing story from his or her own life that has very little connection to the group's goals would be a disruptive communicator
Counteractive communication	• Gets the group back on track by reminding its members of its purposes • For example, in *Apollo 13*, Flight reminds the team members that they are telling him *what they need* to solve the problem of how to return the space capsule safely to Earth, and he is telling them what they have to work with. In short, he uses counteractive communication to bring them back to reality and to tell them that resources are limited and unalterable—they simply must work within the available means.

Leadership and Group Decision Making Are About Relationships

In discussing the group decision-making process, we have pointed out that group culture, group history, group future, group norms, and cohesiveness or conformity are all in their own way relationship concepts (see Table 7.4).

Bad Group Decisions

An attempt to be cohesive at the expense of anything else, however, can sometimes get in the way of a group's effective functioning. If everyone wants to keep everyone else happy rather than make tough decisions, this leads to a special kind of *conformity*. Sometimes, people would rather preserve good relationships than make good decisions.

Irving Janis (1972) famously referred to this negative kind of consensus-seeking cohesiveness as "groupthink." In groupthink, members place a higher priority on keeping the process running smoothly and agreeably than they do on voicing opinions that contradict the majority opinion. The group prefers the well-being of its members, morale, and teamwork at the expense of proper critical evaluation of ideas. Groupthink can result in faulty decision making because a group prefers to be a *happy* ship rather

THE BASICS OF COMMUNICATION

Table 7.4 Relationship Concepts in Group Decision Making	
Group culture	The relationships that exist between the people in a group
Group history	A sense of collectivity and common origin, which, as you recall from Chapter 5 on identity, is important in how people and groups enact themselves. Groups are often aware that they have to live up to their own history and not let down those who have gone before them
Group future	Indicates that the members of a group feel they will still be connected and committed in the future (many lab research groups lack this sense)
Group norms	Defined ways of behaving that set the standard for that behavior
Cohesiveness	How people treat one another and regard the group as an important relational component of their common life irrespective of the achievement of other goals
Conformity	Going along with the group even if you disagree; adopting a style of dress, behavior, or language that makes you fit in through a strong desire to be accepted or liked
Groupthink	A type of conformity based on the desire to have a happy consensus in the group rather than a real debate about the issues; unwillingness to disagree caused by desire not to upset others in the group

Photo 7.5 What (usually undesirable) characteristic of groups is depicted in this photograph? (See page 186.)

than a ship going in the right direction. Although usually a good thing, cohesiveness can lead to negative consequences.

Group Decision Making and Persuasion

Persuasion is based on relationships, even in groups. Your friends persuade you and you persuade them, but people in groups reach decisions in a more formal way than friends do day-to-day. The question is really whether the formality of groups changes how persuasion works or whether relationships lie at the bottom of it all.

Because power in groups is manifold (see Table 7.2), leaders do not always get their own way. Your relational standing in the group will influence whether people do what you want. Bosses control resources (such as pay), agenda, policy, and other norms to do with dress code and organizational expectations, so they are supposed to have power in an organization. Incompetent, bullying, and authoritarian bosses can rule with a stick, but everyone still hates them and often takes any quiet chance to undermine them in everyday chatter around the water cooler and in privately circulated e-mail exchanges. By contrast, popular and inclusive or supportive bosses and leaders can get people to do more than absolutely required and encourage greater efforts without force. In these cases, people do what their bosses ask because they like them and do not resent the request (referent power).

Group Decisions Are Influenced by Outside Relationships and Interactions

Formal group decision making is normally presented in textbooks as if it were a rational type of interaction, where groups sit around and work through decisions smartly and thoughtfully. This just seems to be wrong, and if you have ever sat in on a group making a decision, you will know that.

The type of decision making that gets overlooked in all the books is the everyday persuasion that is often masked or unnoticed. When you separate decision making into the activities of groups in meetings, you tend to overlook just how much persuasion of group members actually occurs in other settings for other reasons. Sometimes, people vote for a proposal not because it is compelling but because they like the person who proposed it or dislike the person who opposed it, for instance. Groups are made up of *people*. Members (e.g., members of a work team) have relationships with one another *outside* as well as *inside* their meetings. After the formal discussion, when the group splits up, the members go on with the rest of their lives, which can mean chatting to other group members in places outside the group. Real-life groups exist continuously both as groups (e.g., "The work team meets every Friday," "Bible study group is Wednesday night," "The book club meets every Thursday") and as individuals whose lives may be connected outside the group (e.g., two members of the same work team may be friends, Bible study group members may also be neighbors, book club members could be in the same family).

All your lives, you are embedded in various groups: families, workplace groups, friends, servers/diners, salespeople/shoppers. Our point is that these outside-world processes of interpersonal communication can apply even to formal, small-group decision making. Instead of isolating group decision making like a big animal in a zoo that needs its own diet and treatment, it makes more sense to see all human communication as part of the same interdependent ecosphere where creatures (like family communication or persuasive speeches) roam in different spaces but, as it were, essentially share about 99.9% of the common communication DNA.

In real life, people *do* sit down and make actual decisions about what to do, but often the banal routine of everyday life does it for them. If you know it is your job to clean up the dishes after a meal on Wednesday night, the group does not have to keep deciding it. Sometimes you may need reminding about an existing decision still in force ("It's Wednesday, your day for the dishes"). A group can also, of course, sit down and make a decision again and change the roster. Most of the time, however, previous decisions are assumed to still be in force and have power, unless they are explicitly brought up for reconsideration.

It is a mistake to overlook the influence on groups and leaders defined by preexisting decisions. If your group has a ritual way of "doing Friday night," few decisions are needed on any particular Friday. Everything just follows the regular path. People show up at the expected time and place without being reminded, and then the Friday runs the

Contrarian Challenge

The research literature in interpersonal communication concerning group decision making is most often attentive to formal groups that have power and resources. Although the studies that have been done to test theories of group decision making were often based on more limited types of groups with few resources, the intention was always for the results to apply to those groups in the outside world that are more fully endowed with importance and possibility. To what extent does this literature on group decision making actually apply to real life as you know it? Is it legitimate to make broad generalizations using limited types of groups?

same course as always. Everyone is happy and does not sit down to decide to change the ritual.

You are influenced by your groups whether you notice it or not, just as your interaction with specific people (as we saw in Chapter 5 when thinking about symbolic interactionism) brings out your identity in interesting ways.

What we have written about decision making draws on the existing research literature about it with skepticism. A tension exists between treating group decision making as a special case of human behavior and seeing it as a species of behavior that has more in common with the rest of life. In this textbook, we emphasize the relational underpinnings of every aspect of life. We see this underpinning as the core of most behavior that happens during communication episodes—whether or not they happen in groups.

FOCUS QUESTIONS REVISITED

1. **What exactly is a group, and what makes it different from an assembly, a collective, or a team?**

A group may be regarded as an organized structure composed of individuals having a common purpose, interdependence, and division of labor. The key elements that make a group different from a random collection of people, however, are that group members are aware of one another as such and communicate it through their talk. Groups are different from teams in that teams are more concerned with the strength of the relationships among members and involve mutual respect and concern among members. Team members want to avoid anyone in the group feeling bad about a particular outcome or decision.

2. **Can you define groups only in terms of the kinds of communication that take place between members, or must you look at the relationships that lie behind the communication? Does communication transact the existence and nature of the group?**

Group communication is all about everyday talk and relationships, especially the relationships between people who have, hold, and use different sorts of information in the group. Indeed, it is not so much that groups transact communication but that, when communication and relationships are seen as interconnected, the very notion of a group is a transacted and symbolic concept. Through communication, the group members see themselves as belonging to a group, and the group sees itself as an entity with meaning sustained and created by its own symbolic actions. Groups are not structures or composites but dynamic human relationships and processes transacted within and by means of norms and roles.

3. How do groups form, and what changes in their communication?

The formation of groups has most often been studied in experimental settings, and how they form in normal life has been less clearly understood. Where formation of groups has been studied, it appears that changes in the nature of talk occur, with the first stages being general orientation toward one another and the later stages representing discussion or conflict, which resolves itself in the solution of a task and is followed by mutual congratulation. In longer-term groups, not simply focused on the completion of a particular task in a specific time frame, people will more likely move from formal and superficial talk toward deeper and more meaningful personal talk, much in the way that self-disclosure occurs, though they will also focus their talk on any tasks or objectives the group has in front of it.

4. What communicative and relational skills make a leader into a good leader?

Leaders need to focus on the task and have knowledge that allows them to direct and guide other people toward its completion. A good leader is also able to handle the socioemotional activity in a group and make people feel they are valued members of a team. A really good leader has a combination of communicative skills that help solve problems and present judgment clearly, listens carefully to understand other people's perspectives, and is able to reflect the value of members' contribution to the team. Frequent communication with team members and openness of communication that lets people know what is going on help sustain members' sense of value to the group. Clarity and purposefulness are also communicative features of a good leader.

5. In what ways are discussions of team-based organizing and communication different from traditional approaches to small-group communication?

Team-based organization and communication differ from traditional approaches to small-group communication in that they place much more emphasis on the value, personal feelings, mutual respect, and internal cohesiveness of the members of the team. The division of labor, and the interdependence of team members specifically, builds bonding among them that can outlast the tenure of a particular steward of the team. The team, therefore, does not fall apart once the leader is changed, and the emphasis of team-based organization is to sustain the team as a coherent, self-respecting, and mutually respecting unit, irrespective of the specific problems it is dealing with at a particular time and of the leader nominally in charge for the moment.

6. How can a group promote its own decision-making capacities in more effective ways?

A group can promote its own decision-making capacities by setting a definitive agenda, doing a thorough problem analysis, assessing its goals, and thoroughly assessing alternative possibilities. The group should establish its goals explicitly and realistically, setting goals that are attainable within a specified timeline, and have clear criteria by which it can evaluate the outcomes. Promotive communication and counteractive communication are ways to keep groups on task.

KEY CONCEPTS

cohesiveness   169
common purpose   163
counteractive communication   179
disruptive communication   179
formal power   174
group culture   172
group norms   170

group sanctions   171
informal power   174
interdependence   168
leadership   173
promotive communication   179
socioemotional   173
task   173

QUESTIONS TO ASK YOUR FRIENDS

1. How does your group of friends decide what to do on Friday night? Ask your friends this question to determine their perspective. Which processes discussed in this chapter can you see at work there?

2. Who do your friends think is a good leader, and what makes a person so?

3. What group norms and rituals can you identify in the small groups and organizations to which you belong? Ask your friends in these groups this question and then compare answers.

MEDIA LINKS

1. The following three movies offer good instances of groups in action and cover some of the concepts discussed in this chapter: *Office Space, Apollo 13,* and *12 Angry Men* (the original Henry Fonda black-and-white version). Each movie demonstrates something different about groups: The opening sequence of *Office Space,* for example, gives you a good idea of a group culture, and some of the characters represent different leadership styles (analyze Lumbergh's—ugh!—power and leadership style). *12 Angry Men* demonstrates how a task leader can bring emotionally led individuals back on track by using promotive communication but also handle the socioemotional concerns of different members. What aspects of leadership and group norms can you identify in the group communication that takes place in *Apollo 13?*

2. The next time you are in a group, pay attention to any discussions about media. For instance, someone might bring up a television program viewed the previous evening or a newly discovered website. In what ways could such discussions be considered

disruptive communication? In what ways could such discussions actually enhance group relationships?

3. In any reality shows you watch, how do groups form, what are their dynamics and transactions, and what are their weaknesses?

ETHICAL ISSUES

1. Some say that leaders must use authority to mobilize people to face tough decisions when the followers are struggling with change and personal growth. Others stress that leaders should take care of and nurture their followers. What do you think?

2. Should groups and organizations do what is right even if it results in lower dividends to stakeholders to help finance their operations? For example, should oil companies make more real and substantial contributions to environmental protection even if it means that shareholders receive no dividend in a particular year? Should tobacco companies stop selling cigarettes?

3. What conditions would make it wrong, and what conditions would make it right, to blow the whistle on your group irrespective of the consequences to you personally?

ANSWERS TO PHOTO CAPTIONS

Photo 7.1 ■ A group has a common purpose, and members are aware of each other, have organization, and communicate with one another. A collective may have a common purpose but lack organization, so the audience (which has to be imagined in this picture, as is so often the case in English cricket, an exceptionally tedious game to watch) is a collective. Each side in the game is a team as well as a group, since the members (presumably) care for one another's welfare and play together more effectively by creating chances for each other or not trying to do it all on their own. It is hard to tell one from the other in cricket, where both sides wear all white, but the one with the bat is on one side and the others are on the other side. The man in black trousers is the umpire. The people sitting in chairs are most likely players on the batsman's side waiting their turn to bat. Contact the authors on Facebook for an explanation of the rules.

Photo 7.2 ■ Orientation. They are sizing up the problem before they begin to offer their competing views.

Photo 7.3 ■ The use of group sanctions to enforce norms. People who break the rules are not allowed to stay in the group until they have repented, apologized, or served a fixed amount of penalty time. The "silent treatment" is another example of this group sanctioning, where people refuse to speak to a group member who disobeys norms or does not support the group. In England the term *sending someone to Coventry* is used to describe the refusal of trade union members to speak to another member who has not backed a strike. It can last from a few days to several years.

Photo 7.4 ▪ The ability to identify with the audience shows understanding of their concerns, a sharing of their feelings, and having answers that will work. A good leader focuses people on issues, motivates people to address solutions, and helps them to achieve their goals. Leadership is not in a person but is transacted between people, as the leader acts as steward of their interests, for the moment.

Photo 7.5 ▪ Conformity. They all look exactly alike, and in humans this can indicate an undesirable overruling of independence by the desire to be accepted. Look around you and observe that conformity can often be paradoxical: All students look alike in *not* looking the same (sweatshirt, jeans, possibly a baseball cap).

STUDENT STUDY SITE

Visit the study site at **www.sagepub.com/boc2e** for e-flashcards, practice quizzes, journal articles and additional study resources.

REFERENCES

Abrams, D. B., Hogg, M. A., Hinkle, S., & Otten, S. (2005). The social identity perspective on small groups. In M. S. Poole & A. B. Hollingshead (Eds.), *Theories of small groups: Interdisciplinary perspectives* (pp. 99–137). Thousand Oaks, CA: Sage.

Arrow, H., Bouas Henry, K., Poole, M. S., Wheelan, S., & Moreland, R. (2005). Traces, trajectories and timing: The temporal perspective on groups. In M. S. Poole & A. B. Hollingshead (Eds.), *Theories of small groups: Interdisciplinary perspectives* (pp. 313–367). Thousand Oaks, CA: Sage.

Bales, R. F. (1950). *Interaction process analysis.* Cambridge, MA: Addison-Wesley.

Clampitt, P. G. (2005). *Communicating for managerial effectiveness.* Thousand Oaks, CA: Sage.

Cornford, F. M. (1908). *Microcosmographia academica: Being a guide for the young academic politician.* Cambridge, UK: Bowes & Bowes Publishers.

Dando-Collins, S. (2004). *Caesar's legion: The epic saga of Julius Caesar's elite tenth legion and the armies of Rome.* Chichester, UK: Wiley.

Fisher, B. A. (1970). Decision emergence: Phases in group decision making. *Speech Monographs, 37,* 53–66.

French, J. R. P., Jr., & Raven, B. (1959). The bases of social power. In D. Cartwright (Ed.), *Studies in social power* (pp. 48–67). Ann Arbor: University of Michigan Institute for Social Research.

Glidewell, J. C., Tucker, S., Todt, M., & Cox, S. (1982). Professional support systems— The teaching profession. In A. Nadler, J. D. Fisher, & B. M. DePaulo (Eds.), *New directions in helping 3: Applied research in help-seeking and reactions to aid* (pp. 163–184). New York: Academic Press.

Goffman, E. (1959). *Behaviour in public places.* Harmondsworth, UK: Penguin.

Gouran, D. S., & Hirokawa, R. Y. (1996). Functional theory and communication in decision-making and problem-solving groups. In R. Y. Hirokawa & M. S. Poole (Eds.), *Communication and group decision making* (2nd ed., pp. 55–80). Thousand Oaks, CA: Sage.

Harden Fritz, J. M., & Omdahl, B. L. (2006). Reduced job satisfaction, diminished commitment, and workplace cynicism as outcomes of negative work relationships. In J. M. Harden Fritz & B. L. Omdahl (Eds.), *Problematic relationships in the workplace* (pp. 131–151). New York: Peter Lang.

Hepburn, J. R., & Crepin, A. E. (1984). Relationship strategies in a coercive institution: A study of dependence among prison guards. *Journal of Social and Personal Relationships, 1,* 139–158.

Hogg, M. A. (1992). *The social psychology of group cohesiveness: From attraction to social identity.* London: Harvester Wheatsheaf.

Hollander, E. P. (1958). Conformity, status and idiosyncrasy credit. *Psychological Review, 65,* 117–27.

Janis, I. (1972). *Victims of groupthink.* Boston: Houghton Mifflin.

Katz, N., Lazer, D., Arrow, H., & Contractor, N. (2005). The network perspective on small groups: Theory and research. In M. S. Poole & A. B. Hollingshead (Eds.), *Theories of small groups: Interdisciplinary perspectives* (pp. 277–312). Thousand Oaks, CA: Sage.

McLeod, P. L., & Kettner-Polley, R. (2005). Psychodynamic perspectives on small groups. In M. S. Poole & A. B. Hollingshead (Eds.), *Theories of small groups: Interdisciplinary perspectives* (pp. 63–97). Thousand Oaks, CA: Sage.

Mumby, D. K. (2006). Constructing working-class masculinity in the workplace. In J. T. Wood & S. W. Duck (Eds.), *Composing relationships: Communication in everyday life* (pp. 166–174). Belmont, CA: Wadsworth.

Northouse, P. G. (2009). *Introduction to leadership concepts and practices.* Thousand Oaks, CA: Sage.

Northouse, P. G. (2010). *Leadership: Theory and practice* (5th ed.). Thousand Oaks, CA: Sage.

Parsons, T., & Bales, R. F. (1955). *Family, socialization and interaction process.* Glencoe, IL: Free Press.

Poole, M. S., & Hollingshead, A. B. (2005). *Theories of small groups: Interdisciplinary perspectives.* Thousand Oaks, CA: Sage.

Thibaut, J. W., & Kelley, H. H. (1959). *The social psychology of groups.* New York: Wiley.

Tuckman, B. W. (1965). Developmental sequence in small groups. *Psychological Bulletin, 63,* 384–399.

Weigel, R. G. (2002). The marathon encounter group—vision and reality: Exhuming the body for a last look. *Consulting Psychology Journal: Practice and Research, 54,* 186–198.

8

Culture and Communication

As we begin our exploration of culture, we want to address two issues involving the ways in which people often think about culture. First, when most people think of culture, they tend to think of it as something involving *other* people—wearing unusual clothes, eating strange foods, participating in odd customs, living in unique structures (bamboo huts, Roman temples, Chinese pagodas), and doing strange things with coconuts and tulips.

However, what is considered abnormal by one culture is considered perfectly normal by another. In fact, *you* perform cultural practices and communicate in ways that those from another culture might regard as odd, even though these practices and ways of communicating may seem to you to be natural and right. For instance, if you follow a traditional U.S. approach to time, many cultures would view arriving at a very specific time quite strange, utterly obsessive, absurd, and valueless. After all, you should stop to the smell the roses, or the tulips. In short, it seems just as normal and natural and right to the Japanese, the Italians, the Serbo Croatians, and the Tutsi to act the way they do as it does to you to do what you do.

Believing that your culture is the benchmark for all others is called **ethnocentric bias**: Your own cultural way of acting is right and normal, and all other ways of acting are only variants of the only really good way to act (yours!). If

As you study the material in this chapter, it will be important to be as detached as possible and to treat your own culture as objectively as you treat others—as far as that can be achieved. Cultural influences run so deep within your routine talk and relational performance that you do not recognize them at first, but this chapter shows you how.

this manner of thinking seems familiar, you are not alone, and it does not necessarily make you a bad person. However, appreciating and recognizing the value of other cultures will assist you personally and professionally, especially given an ever-expanding multicultural world. Doing so will also increase your appreciation for and understanding of your own cultural behaviors.

The second issue to address is that many people think of culture as something that is possessed or something to which a person belongs. Actually, you do not just have or belong to a culture; you *transact* and *perform* culture. This notion is similar to that discussed in Chapter 5 when examining identities. Identities and cultures are transacted (or constructed) symbolically and performed when interacting (or relating) with other people.

Accordingly, cultures do not create different communication; rather, different communication creates cultures. Thus, cultural groups are distinct not because they live in different places but because they communicate in different ways. Culture is created symbolically, not through positioning in a physical location.

Of course, relationships remain fundamental to the actual creation and maintenance of culture. Using the relational perspective to examine identities in Chapter 5, we noted that the only way you ever meet *society* is through other people you meet. Similarly, your exposure to *culture*, whether your own or another, is not exposure to an abstraction. You meet culture when you encounter people performing that culture; you perform your own culture when you communicate with other people. Society's (and Culture's) Secret Agents are the very friends you meet, other people on the streets, human beings you observe, and everyone who communicates with you.

In what follows, we examine the two primary approaches to identifying and studying culture: structured and transacted. From a structural approach, we discuss cultural differences concerning context, individualism/collectivism, time, and conflict. Examining culture as a transaction, we further explore the connection between culture and communication using a relational perspective. Specifically, we examine how culture is embedded in communication and how cultural membership is enacted or denied through communication.

Focus Questions

1. What does it mean to view culture as structured?
2. What does it mean to view culture as transacted?
3. How is communication organized to reflect cultural beliefs about context, collectivism/individualism, time, and conflict?
4. What does it mean to say culture is coded into communication?
5. What does it mean to say that cultural groups are created through communication?
6. How do people enact cultural membership through communication?

How Can Culture Be Identified and Studied?

We begin our exploration by examining how culture has been identified and studied. As mentioned above, the two primary ways in which culture has been examined are as a structure and as a transaction. The most common approach to studying culture has been to view it as structural. Increasingly, however, the limitations of this perspective have become more obvious. Nevertheless, using this approach has provided a wealth of information about culture and should not be shoved aside without full consideration.

Culture as Structured

Viewing *culture* from a structural standpoint has a long history in the communication discipline. This way of seeing culture focuses on large-scale differences in values, beliefs, goals, and preferred ways of acting among nations, regions, ethnicities, and religions. We could therefore differentiate Australian, Indian, Japanese, Dutch, and Canadian cultures. Clear distinctions could be made between Eastern and Western cultures and the communication styles displayed among people of these areas.

Cross-Cultural Communication and Intercultural Communication

A great deal of valuable research has been conducted from a structural standpoint, examining communication within and among nations or physical regions. This research is usually referred to as cross-cultural communication or intercultural communication.

Cross-cultural communication compares the communication styles and patterns of people from very different cultural/social structures, such as nation-states. For example, Seki, Matsumoto, and Imahori (2002) looked at the differences in intimacy expression in the United States and Japan. They found that the Japanese tended to think of intimacy with same-sex friends in relation to such expressive concepts as "consideration/love" and "expressiveness" *more* than did the Americans. The Japanese placed *more* stress than the Americans on *directly* verbalizing their feelings when considering intimacy with mother, father, and same-sex best friend. On the other hand, Americans placed more value than the Japanese on *indirectly* verbalizing their feelings for others.

Examining the influence of social networks on romantic relationships, Jin and Oh (2010) discovered that Americans tend to involve their friends and family in romantic relationships more often than Koreans. Social networks among Americans also provide more support for romantic relationships.

As Nakayama, Martin, and Flores (2002) point out, White adults and especially "white children do not need to attend to the norms and values of minority groups unless they have direct exposure in their neighborhoods and schools. Minority children, however, are exposed to and compare themselves to [the dominant] white cultural norms through television, books, and other media" (p. 103). Whereas White people can act without knowledge or sensitivity to other cultures' customs in a White society, minority groups are rapidly disciplined for failing to observe White cultural norms.

Listen in on Your Life

Consider the television programs and fairy tales you enjoyed as a child and their accompanying cultural themes. For example, many children's programs in the United States stress the importance of a person's individuality and his or her ability to achieve everything he or she desires through hard work and determination. This belief accompanies the U.S. beliefs in rugged individualism and achievement. What was your favorite program as a child? What themes were reinforced?

Intercultural communication deals with how people from these cultural/social structures speak to one another and what difficulties or differences they encounter, over and above the different languages they speak (Gudykunst & Kim, 1984). Chiang (2009), for instance, examined office-hour interactions involving international teaching assistants and American college students. Potential linguistic and cultural issues were isolated, and strategies for improving communication among these groups were offered.

Examining cultural metaphors related to health care, Le and Chiu (2009) examined Asian views of health care in Australia. The purpose of their research was to assist health care providers and patients in understanding respective views of medicine and the implications of health care.

Limitations and Benefits

While this view of culture has provided a better understanding of different groups and has improved interactions among people, it is not without its limitations. For example, when you start looking at cultures as identifiable national or regional groups, you rapidly notice some important points: First, multiple "cultures" exist in one national or regional group. Second, multiple *social communities* coexist in a single culture and talk amongst themselves as part of their conduct of *membership* (for example, bikers, car mechanics, vegetarians, and ballet dancers).

Nevertheless, from a communication point of view, we can study how all members of a nation partake of the customs or beliefs of the nation and its communication patterns and styles. Although broad, such distinctions nevertheless seep down to a person's way of thinking, and they are structured into meaning systems used in everyday communication. Accordingly, while a social community of construction workers (or any other group) may communicate in unique ways, members' styles of communication are still impacted by those of the larger social structure in which they are embedded.

Culture as Transacted

As we have maintained throughout this book, it is through communication (or symbolically) that relationships, identities, meanings, and realities are created or transacted. Culture is no exception. As we have also maintained, relationships are key to realizing and understanding how it all happens. Culture is an ideal example. You belong to sets of people who share meanings and styles of speaking, systems of beliefs, and customs. In other words, you live your life in the context of communicating sets of individuals who transact universes of thought and behavior, which emerge and are supported through unique cultural styles of communication.

Cultural ways of communicating, beliefs, and values are established and imposed through everyday communication. You are constantly reminded of them by your contacts with other people (Society's/Culture's Secret Agents). Your conformity to culture is constantly and almost invisibly reinforced in the daily talk that happens informally in the interactions with such agents as your friends, your family members, your coworkers, and even strangers. The nature of culture and your connection to society is conducted through the specific relationships you have with other individuals whom you meet fairly frequently and with whom you interact daily.

Cultural groups are recognized and labeled as such when some consistency and distinctiveness is observed in their behavior and communication. For example, the *shared relational* use by goths, punks, and emos of symbols like hairstyles, body piercing, cutting, and self-harm along with a relevant music genre and vocabulary transacts their identity and collectively forms the goth, punk, or emo culture. Similarly, rednecks and redneck culture have been identified and caricatured through particular stories and jokes (for example, by Jeff Foxworthy and Larry the Cable Guy).

Photo 8.1 The Harajuku area of Tokyo is a popular destination for teenagers, many of whom dress in such cultural styles as gothic lolita, visual kei, and decora. Are artifacts such as clothing the primary distinction between cultural groups? (See page 209.)

You may or may not be a goth, a punk, an emo, a redneck, or a goth-redneck. If you are, you may be able to relate to the above examples. If not, we can try another angle. Even if you belong to a strict nudist culture, we are going to go out on a limb and assume you generally wear clothing in public. Aside from the possibility of breaking a handful of laws (which themselves uphold social norms) and aside from protecting yourself from the weather, why do you wear clothes? After all, you probably would be much more comfortable without them. Well, you wear clothes because you have been convinced that it is the culturally proper and right thing to do. It was not some abstract notion of culture that convinced you. Rather, it was developed and maintained from observing the behavior of people around you. It was developed and maintained from being taught to wear clothes by your parents or guardians, who were taught the same thing by their parents or guardians. It was developed and maintained from knowing that negative evaluations or consequences could arise through friends, family, and other people in your life. Once again, Society's/Culture's Secret Agents are on the case!

Coded Systems of Meaning

What makes this approach to studying culture different from a structural approach is that culture is seen as a **coded system of meaning**. Culture is not just a structured bureaucratic machine but a set of beliefs, a heritage, and a way of being that is *transacted* in communication. From this point of view, then, you can think of culture as a meaning system.

If you think of culture as a system of norms, rituals, and beliefs, any group with a system of shared meaning is a culture. Farmers, athletes, gamers, members of business organizations, comic book fans, health professionals, truckers, fast-food employees, and musicians could all be considered members of a unique culture. The list of unique cultural groups is virtually unending.

Case in Point

Go to a public space where members of a unique cultural group are gathered and observe the ways they communicate. (Naturally avoid dangerous places and situations. We do not want you injured and cannot afford to bail you out of jail.) There are many groups from which you may choose, but based on some of those mentioned here, you might observe farmers at a cattle auction barn, comic book fans at a comic book store, or truckers at a truck stop. What is unique about their communication? What does their communication tell you about their cultural beliefs and values?

Viewing societies and cultures as unique meaning systems provides an opportunity to go beyond a traditional structural view of cultures. Although these conventional views can still provide a great deal of valuable information, they tend to overlook numerous, distinct meaning systems within larger structure-based labels such as *nation-state*. You cannot legitimately maintain that everyone in the United States communicates the same way, that everyone in Lithuania communicates the same way, that everyone in India communicates the same way, or that everyone in any other nation-state or region communicates the same way. There are many different cultures within the United States (and other nation-states) communicating in very unique ways.

Studying how culture is symbolically transacted enables us to examine how styles of communication serve to include people in or exclude people from cultural communities and groups. We can focus on how people "speak themselves into culture" and how membership in a particular culture is done through communication.

Structure-Based Cultural Characteristics

Although we have indicated that it is far too simplistic to equate culture *exclusively* with nation-states or regions, some very broad differences between such groups have been observed and should be taken into account. As we mentioned earlier, all members of a nation or citizens of a country are impacted in some way by the most general communication styles and patterns.

Children learn to view the world in culturally appropriate ways as they learn to communicate and interact with others. For example, small children may be rushed from the store by embarrassed parents who have just been asked loudly, "Why is that man so ugly?" and they will certainly be taught a culture's nonverbal rules: "Look at me when I'm talking to you" and "Don't interrupt when someone is talking." "Remember to say thank you" is another way children are taught culture's rules about respect and politeness as they learn to talk.

During your childhood and introduction to culture (socialization), you learned how to behave, interact, and live with other people as you learned to communicate. These styles of behavior readily became more and more automatic—and hence were automatically included in your later communication—as you grew up. If this did not happen, you could not communicate with other people in your society. Thus, learning to communicate includes learning the habits of your particular culture or society.

Strategic Communication

When attempting to persuade someone or to develop a positive relationship with someone, communicating in a manner consistent with his or her culture will increase your chances of success. However, check out the Ethical Issues at the end of this chapter for more on this matter.

It makes sense to look at the rich list of differences uncovered among cultures—even if these sometimes amount to stereotypes that you hold about other nations when representing how people there *typically* act. In what follows, we examine the following cross-cultural characteristics: (a) context, (b) collectivism/individualism, (c) time, and (d) conflict. As these communication styles and meanings are discussed, keep in mind how they are learned and reinforced through interactions with friends, families, and others with whom relationships are shared.

Context

Context involves the emphasis placed on the environment, the situation, or relationships when communicating. Some cultures tend to leave much unsaid, with the assumption that others will understand what is meant based on such influences as circumstances encompassing the interaction and relationships among those communicating. Other cultures tend to be more explicit and straightforward when communicating, rather than relying on contextual factors. Cultures are accordingly categorized as being either high-context or low-context.

High-Context Cultures

Some societies, known as **high-context cultures** (Samovar, Porter, & McDaniel, 2010), place a great deal of emphasis on the total environment or context where speech and interaction take place. In a high-context society, spoken words are much less important than the rest of the context—for example, the relationships between the people communicating. It is much more important for people to indicate respect for one another in various verbal and nonverbal ways than it is for them to pay close attention to the exact words spoken.

In such countries as China and Iraq, for example, a person's status in society is extremely important, and people tend to rely on their history and their relationship to the speaker or the audience. In Iraq and some African countries, additional importance may be attached to a person's religious or tribal group to assign meanings to conversation. Such cultures greatly emphasize and give major priority to relationships among

There often exist contextual-based differences between the marketing or sales force in a business and the technicians or engineers who actually make the product. For marketing team members and salespeople, it is very important to have good relationships with their customers and with a network of other sales personnel. For the technicians who actually make and service products, it is more important that accurate information be conveyed to customers than that the customers be made to feel good interpersonally. This difference of emphasis sometimes leads to conflict between the same organization's marketing and technical personnel.

family members, friends, and associates. Therefore, it is regarded as ethical to favor one's relatives or as fair to give contracts to friends rather than to the highest bidder. Everything is connected to this background context of relationships and other personal contexts of status, influence, and personal knowledge.

Low-Context Cultures

By contrast, when communicating in a **low-context culture**, the message itself means everything, and it is much more important to have a well-structured argument or a well-delivered presentation than it is to be a member of the royal family or a cousin of the person listening (Samovar et al., 2010).

In a low-context society, therefore, people try to separate their relationships from the messages and to focus on the details and the logic. Detailed information must be given to provide the relevant context, and only the information presented that way counts as relevant to the message. In low-context societies, people may remove themselves from decision-making roles if a friend or family member is involved. Nepotism, or favoritism shown to a family member or friend, is evaluated negatively in low-context cultures.

Collectivism/Individualism

An entire chapter of this book is dedicated to identity (Chapter 5), but the very notion of a personal identity is more of a Western than an Eastern idea. Some cultures stress collectivism/togetherness, and some stress individualism/individuality.

Collectivist Cultures

As traditionally noted (Gudykunst, 2000; Morsbach, 2004), Eastern societies, such as Japan, tend to be **collectivist**—that is, to stress group benefit and the overriding value of working harmoniously rather than individual personal advancement. Collectivist cultures place greater importance on the whole group, stressing common concerns and the value of acting not merely for oneself but for the common good. Accordingly, in a collectivist culture, your value is based on your place in a system—portraying you as just a single bee in a beehive—more than your special and unique qualities as an individual.

These characteristics are developed and reinforced through personal relationships and interactions with others. Within a collectivist society, an individual who acts to achieve personal rather than collective goals would be viewed as simply selfish and disrespectful. He or she would be brought back into line and made to understand and accept the value of community and collectivity. Such reprimands, especially made by someone with whom a close relationship is shared, would bolster the prevailing view of society.

Individualist Cultures

Western societies, such as the United States, are generally characterized as **individualist**, or focusing on the individual person and his or her personal dreams, goals and achievements, and right to make choices (Gudykunst, 2000; Morsbach, 2004). Individual desires and freedoms are emphasized, and your value is measured according to your personal accomplishments.

As with collectivist cultures, these characteristics are constructed and strengthened through relationships. Contrary to collectivist cultures, within individualistic cultures, personal achievement is lauded and reinforced through conversations with others. For instance, supervisors may talk with employees about the development of personal goals and post "employee of the month" placards to single out individual achievements. Next time you see such a placard, think of it as an example of American cultural ideals being transacted before your very eyes!

Time

Cultures are also categorized and differentiated according to their views of time. Consider how time is perceived in the United States, where the phrase *time is money* is quite common. Time is valuable, and so it is important to not waste it. Therefore, showing up on time helps create a positive impression. Many employees are required to punch in on a time clock or log into a computer system when arriving and leaving work, so precise time can be measured. And, if a person consistently arrives late for work, he or she will likely lose the job.

Contrarian Challenge

Some research presents a sharp distinction between individualist and collectivist cultures. Can you think of contrary examples in U.S. culture where the individual is required to subordinate personal goals to the collective good? If you can, does this undercut the whole idea of the great distinction between collectivism and individualism?

Because cultures differ in how they view time, the importance of brisk punctuality, as opposed to that of leisurely relationship building, is also given different weight. This broad difference of emphasis on activity or relationships in time is labeled as a distinction between monochronic and polychronic cultures.

Monochronic Culture

If you think of time as a straight line from beginning to end, you are thinking in terms of *monochronic time*, where people do one thing at a time or multitask only because it helps them work toward particular goals with tasks in sequence and communication fitting into a particular order.

Photo 8.2 This man seems very concerned about time. Would his perception of time be considered monochronic or polychronic? (See page 209.)

Monochronic cultures, such as the United States, the United Kingdom, and Germany, view time as a valuable commodity and punctuality as very important. People with a monochronic view of time will usually arrive at an appointment a few minutes early as a symbol of respect for the person they are meeting. In the United States, after first establishing a pleasant atmosphere with a few brief courtesies, people will more likely bring up the matter of business fairly early in the conversation.

Polychronic Culture

If you think of time as the ever-rolling cycle of the seasons or something more open-ended, you are thinking in terms of *polychronic time,* where independent and unconnected tasks can be done simultaneously and also where people may carry out multiple conversations with different people at the same time.

Polychronic cultures have a relaxed attitude toward time. Indeed, as Calero (2005) noted, the predominant U.S. notion of time translates as "childishly impatient" to polychronic cultures. This notion of time is true even in relation to food, specifically in, say, Italy or France where two-course meals can take 3 hours. In polychronic societies, "promptness" is not particularly important, and as long as the person shows up sometime during the right day, that will count as doing what was required. Some Mediterranean and Arab countries do not regard as impolite being late to an appointment or taking a very long time to get down to business. Indeed, placing so much emphasis on time that people's relationships are ignored is regarded as rude and pushy; instead, time should be taken to build the relationships. In the same way, it is important in some countries not to get to the point too quickly, and a lot of time is spent talking about relational issues or other matters before it is polite to bring up a business question.

Future and Past Orientations

Cultures also differ in the way they pay attention to the past, the present, and the

Make Your Case

The United States is generally regarded as monochronic. However, the increased use of cell phones has tended to alter our perception of time. For instance, schedules are frequently loosened as a result of being able to contact someone immediately and alter plans. Make your case for one of the following:

The United States will remain a monochronic culture.

The United States will become a polychronic culture.

future. Different cultures tend to assume that the present is influenced either by one's goals and the future or by past events, and fatalism and preordained destiny tend to control to a greater extent what happens in the present. In the United States, many groups place much greater emphasis on future orientation, particularly in the short term, than on their control over present and distant

> Polychronic views of time are more likely to be connected with high-context cultures, while monochronic views of time are more likely to be connected with low-context cultures.

future events. Some Asian societies, on the other hand, pay more attention to the distant future and, like South American and Mediterranean cultures, tend to assume a greater influence of the past on the present and that destiny or karma affects what happens to us in the present moment (Martin & Nakayama, 2007).

Conflict

Cultures can also be compared according to their understanding of and approach to **conflict**, which involves real or perceived incompatibilities of processes, understandings, and viewpoints between people. Communication scholars Judith Martin and Thomas Nakayama (2007)—drawing from the work of Augsburger (1992)—differentiate two cultural approaches to conflict: conflict as opportunity and conflict as destructive (pp. 404–413).

Conflict-as-Opportunity Cultures

Conflict-as-opportunity cultures tend to be individualist, such as the United States. This approach to conflict is based on the four assumptions listed in Table 8.1 (Martin & Nakayama, 2007, p. 404).

Table 8.1 The Four Assumptions of Conflict-as-Opportunity Cultures

1. Conflict is a normal, useful process.
2. All issues are subject to change through negotiation.
3. Direct confrontation and conciliation are valued.
4. Conflict is a necessary renegotiation of an implied contract—a redistribution of opportunity, a release of tensions, and a renewal of relationships.

Source: Martin & Nakayama, 2007, p. 404.

Members of these cultures view conflict as a normal and useful process, an inherent part of everyday life. Naturally experienced when interacting with people, conflict will lead, if handled constructively, to the enhancement of personal and relational life. This cultural view of conflict also understands all issues as subject to change, meaning that all personal or relational processes, goals, or outcomes can be altered. When a person wants to make changes in his or her relationships or personal life, he or she is expected to fully express and work with others to achieve these desires. Finally, members of these cultures view conflict as not only normal and useful but also a necessary requirement for renewing relationships and for achieving personal goals and overall well-being.

Individualist cultures tend to view conflict as opportunity, while collectivist cultures tend to view conflict as destructive.

Conflict-as-Destructive Cultures

Stressing group and relational harmony above individual needs and desires, **conflict-as-destructive cultures** tend to be collectivist or community-oriented such as many Asian cultures. Religious groups, such as the Amish and Quakers, also view conflict as destructive. David's dad attended Quaker meetings as a child and adhered to pacifist ideals even on the playground. He has told stories of other children hitting him, knowing he would not fight back. As instructed in the Bible, he would literally turn the other cheek, and the other children would promptly hit that cheek as well. Nevertheless, David's dad remained steadfast in his culturally based belief in the destructive nature of conflict. As with conflict-as-opportunity cultures, four assumptions guide this approach to conflict, as listed in Table 8.2 (Martin & Nakayama, 2007, p. 406).

Table 8.2 The Four Assumptions of Conflict-as-Destructive Cultures
1. Conflict is a destructive disturbance of the peace.
2. The social system should not be adjusted to meet the needs of members; rather, members should adapt to established values.
3. Confrontations are destructive and ineffective.
4. Disputants should be disciplined.

Source: Martin & Nakayama, 2007, p. 406.

Contrary to conflict-as-opportunity cultures, this cultural approach views conflict not as a natural part of everyday experience but rather as unnecessary, detrimental, and to be avoided. Also contrary to conflict-as-opportunity cultures and reflective of collectivist cultures in general, members of conflict-as-destructive cultures do not view individual needs and desires as more important than group needs and established norms. Furthermore, rather than valuing direct confrontation, members consider confrontations futile and harmful to relationships and the group as a whole. Accordingly, those who engage in confrontation should be disciplined to discourage such destructive behaviors since they undo relationships and solidarity.

Managing Conflict

Of course, conflict occurs in all relationships and among all groups, even those viewing conflict as destructive. However, the management of conflict will also differ among cultural groups. When conflict occurs, people generally engage in one of five styles of conflict management: (1) dominating, (2) integrating, (3) compromising, (4) obliging, and (5) avoiding (Rahim, 1983; Ting-Toomey, 2004).

Photo 8.3 The person on the left did not want to engage in conflict, so he did not say anything when his friend wanted to order a pizza topping he did not like. What cultural orientation to conflict do his actions represent, and what style did he use to manage the conflict? (See page 209.)

Dominating. Dominating styles involve forcing one's will on another to satisfy individual desires regardless of negative relational consequences. For example, you and a friend decide to order a pizza, and as you call in the order, your friend mentions a desire for pepperoni. You would rather have sausage and reply, "Too bad. I'm making the call, and we are having sausage."

Integrating. Integrating styles necessitate a great deal of open discussion about the conflict at hand to reach a solution that completely satisfies everyone involved. You and your friend differ on what pizza topping you would like, so you openly discuss your positions and the options available until you reach a solution that fulfils both of your desires—perhaps getting both toppings or half sausage and half pepperoni.

Compromising. Compromising styles are often confused with integrating styles because a solution is reached following discussion of the conflict. However, making a compromise demands that everyone must give something up to reach the solution, and, as a result, people never feel fully satisfied. Returning to the pizza quagmire, you and your friend discuss the conflict and decide to get mushrooms instead of sausage or pepperoni.

Obliging. Obliging styles of conflict management involve giving up one's position to satisfy another's. This style generally emphasizes areas of agreement and deemphasizes areas of disagreement. Using this style of conflict management, as you and your friend discuss what topping to include on your pizza, you probably mention that the important thing is you both want pizza and then agree to order pepperoni instead of sausage.

Avoiding. Finally, avoiding styles of conflict are just that: People avoid the

Cultural beliefs and values are first learned in childhood and then reinforced by relationships throughout your entire life. In this way, you do your culture by using the filters you learned in your early years without even realizing it, rather like wearing glasses. The lenses, for example, affect what you see to make perception more effective. Most of the time, people are not aware of wearing glasses because of their lenses' "transparency," but nevertheless, they affect what the wearer sees and how he sees it. So too with culture: Though it shapes and to some extent distorts perceptions and focus, people are largely unaware of culture and how it affects them.

conflict entirely either by failing to acknowledge its existence or by withdrawing from a situation when it arises. So, your friend expresses a desire for pepperoni on that pizza, and even though you really want sausage, you indicate that pepperoni is fine and place the order.

Transacting Culture

The preceding section emphasized a set of broad and general differences resulting from seeing culture in structural or geographical terms. Structural discussions of cultural characteristics treat culture very broadly and categorically: If you are a Westerner, you will behave and communicate in the Western way. Although such broad-brush ideas are very helpful in many circumstances, especially when traveling to other countries, dealing with international relationships, or discussing the clash of cultures and/or diversity, it is important to go beyond the broad ideas and add some finer detail.

Indeed, a lot of *who you are* depends on *where you are*, or at least on *where you come from,* as well as on the groups you belong to and how they expect people to behave. You are not alone: You *belong* and do not always have a choice. You belong to many groups, some small (groups of friends or neighbors), some large (your citizenship or your ethnic group), some central to your life (family, friends), and some probably peripheral (your tax group, your shoe size). Somewhere in there, somewhere in your sense of yourself, however, is the culture (are the cultures) that you see as yours.

Studying culture as a transaction requires you to consider how your membership in cultural groups goes beyond such structural categories as nation-state, ethnicity, or religion. Instead, you must focus on how culture is created symbolically through communication and is reinforced through your relationships with others and your everyday experiences. Cultural codes are embedded within your communication, and you "speak" culture each time you communicate. Accordingly, it is through communication that cultural groups are established and cultural membership is achieved.

In a sense, people create culture symbolically and then are bound by that which they create. For example, standing a certain distance from a particular person might be considered the norm among members of a cultural group, because proper distances have been socially constructed over time. Yet, members of this group are constrained and must adhere to what they have created, because there may be repercussions if cultural norms involving distance are violated.

Culture Is Embedded Within Your Communication

Your culture is coded in your communication not only in the language you speak but also in the thoughts you express and the assumptions you make. Obviously, talk accomplishes this in the straightforward sense: French men and women speak French. But they also speak "*being* French." Accordingly, every time a person communicates, other people know something about his or her culture. When someone is seen wearing "cultural clothes," difference is assumed, but that person actually *wears* his or her culture in talk and behavior, too.

Your two authors, Steve and David, are different. Steve is English; David is American. When we travel in the United States, people say to Steve, "I love your accent," but when we travel in the United Kingdom, they say it to David. So which of us has an accent? No one in either place ever says with marvel to us, "You speak good English," though when we go to France, people might say, "You speak good French" (if we did). In the United Kingdom, people can tell that Steve is from "the West country," and in the United States, they know David is *not* from "the South." All of them can tell, even on the phone, that we are not ethnic Dutch or Indonesian. They also know we are not women or 5 years old. This is not only a result of vocalic differences but also a result of what we say and how we say it.

Photo 8.4 Would someone studying biker culture within the United States be more likely to take a structural approach to culture or a transacted approach to culture? (See page 209.)

When Steve first met a new colleague (an Eastern European), the conversation lasted only briefly before the colleague said, "You're not American." Steve said, "Oh, the old accent gives me away yet again!" but the colleague said, "No, actually. I'm not a native English speaker, and I can't tell the difference between English and American accents. It was something in your *style* that announced you as 'other.'"

David grew up on a farm in rural Indiana, and like everyone, his communication styles and assumptions about the world were influenced and informed by people around him. He views the world differently and communicates differently than someone who was raised in the city, someone who grew up wealthy, or someone who has never worked the land. His rural Indiana cultural beliefs and values are displayed by what he says and how he says it. Rural Indiana communication styles and patterns are embedded in his talk.

Culture Goes Beyond Physical Location

Notwithstanding the importance of a person's place of origin, Steve is not just "West country," and David is not just "rural Indiana." Steve is a coxswain. David is a radio announcer. Steve is a father. David is a bartender/bouncer. Steve is a genealogist. David is a singer. Both of us are academics. These cultural activities and roles—past and present—have influenced our views of the world and our communication styles. Furthermore, each is cultural in its own right. Steve communicates coxswain culture, father culture, genealogy culture, and academic culture. David communicates radio announcer culture, bartender/bouncer culture, singer culture, and academic culture. At times one may be more pronounced than others. Also at times it may be more important to enact membership into one culture than another. For instance, at academic conferences, we tend to communicate academic culture rather than coxswain or bartender/bouncer culture—although doing the latter may be a way to liven up future conferences!

What ultimately becomes clear—other than we have just spent too much time talking about ourselves—is that people belong to multiple cultures and that cultural membership is enacted through communication.

Cultural Groups Are Created Through Communication

As we have discussed in great detail, a structural understanding of culture as being encompassed by a nation-state, a region, an ethnicity, or a religion is restrictive. It does not give an entirely accurate depiction of culture in everyday life. For instance, several cultures may exist within one country (Houston & Wood, 1996). These cultural groups are recognized and differentiated through their unique communication and meaning systems.

Co-cultures

Co-cultures are smaller groups of culture within a larger cultural mass. For instance, most countries have regions regarded as different and distinctive (the South, the Midwest, Yorkshire, the Valley). The belief systems in these small and diverse groups are often recognized as somewhat different and distinct from those within the larger society or nation. A large group like "Americans" can be broken down into smaller groups ("Northern Americans" and "Southern Americans") containing smaller sets of both nations and societies, such as Irish Americans, Southerners, Sioux, African Americans, Iowans, or Republicans.

Sociologically and demographically, discussions of co-cultures are significant because they underscore the vast number of cultures that can be explored and that encompass a person's life. However, there is still the tendency to take on a structural approach to their study. Accordingly, someone might say, "Republicans communicate this way, while Democrats communicate that way."

Speech Communities

A more communication-based view labels these cultures as speech communities (Hymes, 1972; Philipsen, 1975, 1997). **Speech communities** are cultures defining membership in terms of speaking patterns and styles that reinforce beliefs and values of the group. Essentially, cultural groups are set apart based on their unique communication styles. In this way, various **speech (communication) codes**, or a culture's verbalizations of meaning and symbols, tend to have built into them certain ways of understanding the world that guide the particular talk patterns people use in conversation with one another.

One characteristic of any culture is what it takes for granted. For example, in a particular culture, certain topics can be talked about and certain ideas are taken for granted, even during persuasion. Kristine Muñoz (Fitch, 2003) has written about these taken-for-granted

In a male offenders' prison, Julia Wood (2004) uncovered a special kind of talk, based on physical strength and the assumed right to control other people, in spouse abusers.

assumptions as **cultural persuadables**, certain topics that people in a society never bother to persuade anyone else about because their arguments are always raised against a background of common understanding and shared beliefs. For instance, some speech communities adhere to very traditional notions of gender roles. Accordingly, it is unnecessary to say anything directly about these gender roles because they are implicit in everything that is communicated.

Teamsterville and Nacirema

So, multiple cultures exist based on the unique ways in which they communicate and what is taken for granted in communication. As mentioned earlier, we can therefore pinpoint and study an essentially limitless number of cultures throughout the world. Two classic studies examining the cultures of "Teamsterville" and "Nacirema" exemplify this approach and laid the groundwork for subsequent research.

Communication scholar Gerry Philipsen (1975) explored the talk in Teamsterville, a pseudonym for a working-class community in Chicago showing a "man's communication style." For members of this community, the style of speech occasionally prefers action to words and is based on talking only when power is equal or symmetrical. In this community, a man demonstrates power by punching someone rather than arguing about a problem. Speech is regarded as an inappropriate and ineffective way of communicating in situations when demonstrating power. For example, if a man were insulted by a stranger, the culturally appropriate way to deal with the insult would be to inflict physical damage rather than discuss the issue. In Teamsterville, speech in such a situation would be characterized as weak. On the other hand, when a man in Teamsterville is among friends, his speech is permitted to establish his manliness. If a man's friend made a derogatory remark about the man's girlfriend, the man would either take the remark as a tease or simply tell the friend not to say such things, and violence would not result as it would in the case of strangers saying the same thing.

Photo 8.5 How might break time at a factory be an opportunity to learn about and enact cultural membership within this culture? (See page 210.)

In addition to his identification of the cultural Code of Honor carried out by the men of Teamsterville as they "do manliness," Philipsen (1997) identified a cultural Code of Dignity, which he identified as characteristic of the "Nacirema" (*American* spelled backward). This communication code emphasizes relationships, work, communication, and individual/self and is quite easily discovered on TV talk shows and in the broader context of speech in large parts of America. The work by Philipsen and others (e.g., Fitch, 1998) helps us see that speech (communication) codes create membership within a given culture.

College Experience

Contemplate how members of an academic community can be considered a unique cultural group. This approach to academic communities can be applied to people in academics in general, and it can also be applied to your very own school.

1. What unique communication styles and accompanying meaning systems are performed at your school? In other words, how is membership into that particular academic community enacted and displayed?

2. Do you consider yourself a member of this cultural group? If so, how does your communication when on campus reflect that of others in the group? If you consider yourself a member of this group, you probably feel more connected than when you first arrived on campus. How did this sense of connectedness develop? (Warning: If you do not include interactions and relationships in your answer, your authors may shed many tears!)

3. If you do not consider yourself a member of your school community, why do you think that might be? Do you choose not to perform membership into this group? Is it possible that you display cultural membership more than you realize?

4. Finally, how many different cultural groups do you observe while on campus? What is unique about the communication of these groups? Are some groups more exclusive or separate than others?

Cultural Membership Is Enacted Through Communication

Enacting membership in a cultural group means communicating and assigning meaning in ways similar to other members of that group. For instance, musicians enact membership into a musician culture by communicating like members of that culture. It can be broken down further, and we can distinguish musician cultures related to jazz, blues, death metal, hip-hop, rhythm and blues, country, bluegrass, rockabilly, and barbershop just to name a few. Once again, each cultural group communicates in unique ways, and enacting membership requires communicating as such.

However, enacting membership into a cultural group is more complicated and restrictive than it may initially appear. If you want to be a rapper, you cannot just talk like a rapper and suddenly become one. It is not just the act of communicating that establishes membership into a cultural group; it is also, and more important, knowing the meaning of that communication that does so. A cultural understanding is required. If you do not know how to perform membership in a particular community, you are excluded from it. Membership in a culture can be represented in and restricted by one's knowledge of speech (communication) codes.

The unique ways of communication and the underlying meaning of that communication create a sense of otherness or separateness. Some cultural groups may rejoice in their exclusivity. For instance, certain clubs or organizations may have secret ways of communicating concealed from everyone but their members. When "outsiders" attempt to enact membership into certain cultural groups, they may be referred to as "fakes" or "wannabes." Members of rural communities often view people who move into the area with suspicion. These new people may be living in the same area, but they do not automatically become members of the culture.

Cultural speech (communication) codes must be learned and understood before a person can fully enact membership into a group. Doing so requires interacting and forming relationships with members of that cultural group. It is through relating that cultural understanding is transferred and maintained. Cultural understanding is fundamental to enacting cultural membership, and it is through relationships that this understanding is learned.

FOCUS QUESTIONS REVISITED

1. What does it mean to view culture as structured?

Viewing *culture* from a structural standpoint has a long history in the communication discipline. This way of seeing culture focuses on large-scale differences in values, beliefs, goals, and preferred ways of acting among nations, regions, ethnicities, and religions. Research using this perspective is often referred to as either cross-cultural communication or intercultural communication.

2. What does it mean to view culture as transacted?

When viewing culture from a transactional standpoint, culture is seen as a coded system of meaning. Culture is a set of beliefs, a heritage, and a way of being that is *transacted* in communication. When viewing culture as a system of norms, rituals, and beliefs, any group with a system of shared meaning can be considered a culture.

3. How is communication organized to reflect cultural beliefs about context, collectivism/individualism, time, and conflict?

Cultures can be categorized as either high context or low context. High-context cultures place a great deal of emphasis on the total environment or context where speech and interaction take place. In a low-context culture, people try to separate their relationships from the messages and to focus on the details and the logic.

Cultures can be categorized as either individualist or collectivist. Collectivist cultures place greater importance on the whole group, stressing common concerns and the value of acting not merely for oneself but for the common good. Individualist cultures focus on the individual person and his or her personal dreams, goals and achievements, and right to make choices.

Cultures can be categorized as either monochronic or polychronic. Monochronic cultures view time as valuable and adhere to schedules. Polychronic cultures view time more holistically and have a much more relaxed attitude toward schedules. Cultures also differ in their orientation to past, present, and future events.

Cultures can be categorized as viewing conflict as either opportunity or destructive. Cultures viewing conflict as opportunity perceive conflict as a normal and useful process, an inherent part of everyday life. Cultures viewing conflict as destructive perceive conflict as unnecessary, detrimental, and something to be avoided.

4. What does it mean to say culture is coded into communication?

Culture is coded in communication not only in the language spoken but also in thoughts expressed and assumptions made. Every time a person communicates, other people know something about his or her culture. Cultural beliefs and values are displayed by a person's communication.

5. What does it mean to say that cultural groups are created through communication?

Multiple cultural groups are recognized and differentiated through their unique communication and meaning systems. Speech communities are cultures defining membership in terms of speaking patterns and styles that reinforce beliefs and values of the group. Essentially, cultural groups are set apart based on their unique communication styles.

6. How do people enact cultural membership through communication?

Enacting membership in a cultural group means communicating and assigning meaning in ways similar to other members of that group. However, it is not just the act of communicating that establishes membership into a cultural group; it is also, and more important, knowing the meaning of that communication that does so. Membership in a culture can be represented in and restricted by one's knowledge of speech (communication) codes.

KEY CONCEPTS

co-culture   204
coded system of meaning   193
collectivist   196
conflict   199
conflict-as-destructive culture   200
conflict-as-opportunity culture   199
cross-cultural communication   191
cultural persuadables   205
ethnocentric bias   189

high-context culture   195
individualist   197
intercultural communication   192
low-context culture   196
monochronic culture   198
polychronic culture   198
speech (communication) codes   204
speech communities   204

QUESTIONS TO ASK YOUR FRIENDS

1. Have your friends tell you about their favorite children's stories, and then discuss the themes demonstrated by those stories and connect them to the cultural ideals.

2. Ask your friends in how many cultures they view themselves as having established membership. In what ways do they establish these memberships?

3. Ask your friends to describe a recent intercultural experience. What did they find most challenging? What did they find most rewarding?

MEDIA LINKS

1. Select and analyze a movie with intercultural themes (i.e., *The Namesake*) to show how individuals from different cultures build relationships and develop understanding. Describe how culturally relevant concepts and ideas from this chapter are shown in the movie's characters, plot, setting, script, and acting styles.

2. How are different cultures represented on television and in movies? Compare current with 30- or 40-year-old shows and movies. What differences do you see?

3. How are other cultures represented by newspapers, television news, or online news sources? Can you identify any ethnocentric bias in these reports?

ETHICAL ISSUES

1. As mentioned in the Strategic Communication box, communicating in a manner consistent with another person's culture will generally make you more persuasive. If this counters your own cultural perspectives, are you being deceitful? Is there a difference between adapting a message and being disingenuous?

2. Evaluate a problem currently being discussed in this society that grows out of cultural dynamics. Explore at least two possible solutions to, for example, immigration or racial/ethnic/religious profiling.

3. Should people of the world be accepting of all cultural behaviors? For instance, in some cultures, women are forced into subservient roles. Children of some cultures must endure rites of passage that might be viewed as disgraceful or dangerous in other cultures. Some cultural groups disfigure their bodies in certain ways. Should other cultures intervene in some circumstances?

ANSWERS TO PHOTO CAPTIONS

Photo 8.1 ■ No. While clothing is part of a person's cultural identity and perhaps one of the first things people of other cultures notice, it is just one of many symbolic behaviors through which culture is transacted.

Photo 8.2 ■ He seems to view time as a valuable commodity and punctuality as very important, which means he has a monochronic view of time.

Photo 8.3 ■ He likely views conflict as destructive rather than as opportunity. He used the avoiding strategy to manage the conflict.

Photo 8.4 ■ Someone studying biker culture or other speech communities would likely be taking a transacted approach to culture rather than a structural approach.

Photo 8.5 ▪ Break time at a factory would provide an opportunity to interact with coworkers and establish relationships with them. It is through interaction and relationships that cultural meaning is truly recognized and understood.

STUDENT STUDY SITE

Visit the study site at **www.sagepub.com/boc2e** for e-flashcards, practice quizzes, journal articles and additional study resources.

REFERENCES

Augsburger, D. W. (1992). *Conflict mediation across cultures: Pathways and patterns.* Louisville, KY: Westminster/John Knox.

Calero, H. (2005). *The power of nonverbal communication: What you do is more important than what you say.* Los Angeles: Silver Lake.

Chiang, S.-U. (2009). Dealing with communication problems in the instructional interactions between international teaching assistants and American college students. *Language and Education, 23,* 461–478.

Fitch, K. L. (1998). *Speaking relationally: Culture, communication, and interpersonal connection.* New York: Guilford Press.

Fitch, K. L. (2003). Cultural persuadables. *Communication Theory, 13*(1), 100–123.

Gudykunst, W. (2000). *Asian American ethnicity and communication.* Thousand Oaks, CA: Sage.

Gudykunst, W. B., & Kim, Y. Y. (1984). *Communicating with strangers: An approach to intercultural communication.* New York: Random House.

Houston, M., & Wood, J. T. (1996). *Gendered relationships.* Mountain View, CA: Mayfield.

Hymes, D. (1972). Models of the interaction of language and social life. In J. Gumperz & D. Hymes (Eds.), *Directions in sociolinguistics: The ethnography of communication* (pp. 35–71). New York: Holt, Rinehart & Winston.

Jin, B., & Oh, S. (2010). Cultural differences of social network influence on romantic relationships: A comparison of the United States and South Korea. *Communication Studies, 61,* 156–171.

Le, Q., & Chiu, C. (2009). Culturally-informed health metaphors on health service delivery. *International Journal of Social Health Information Management, 2,* 48–59.

Martin, J. N., & Nakayama, T. K. (2007). *Intercultural communication in context* (4th ed.). New York: McGraw-Hill.

Morsbach, H. (2004). *Customs and etiquette of Japan.* London: Global Books.

Nakayama, T. K., Martin, J. N., & Flores, L. A. (Eds.). (2002). *Readings in intercultural communication* (2nd ed.). New York: McGraw-Hill.

Philipsen, G. (1975). Speaking "like a man" in Teamsterville: Culture patterns of role enactment in an urban neighborhood. *Quarterly Journal of Speech, 61*(1), 13–22.

Philipsen, G. (1997). A theory of speech codes. In G. Philipsen & T. Albrecht (Eds.), *Developing theories in communication* (pp. 119–156). Albany: State University of New York Press.

Rahim, M. A. (1983). A measure of styles of handling interpersonal conflict. *Academy of Management Journal, 26,* 368–376.

Samovar, L. A., Porter, R. E., & McDaniel, E. R. (2010). *Communication between cultures* (7th ed.). Belmont, CA: Wadsworth.

Seki, K., Matsumoto, D., & Imahori, T. T. (2002). The conceptualization and expression of intimacy in Japan and the United States. *Journal of Cross-Cultural Psychology, 33*(3), 303–319.

Ting-Toomey, S. (2004). The matrix of face: An updated face-negotiation theory. In W. Gudykunst (Ed.), *Theorizing about intercultural communication* (pp. 71–92). Thousand Oaks, CA: Sage.

Wood, J. T. (2004). Monsters and victims: Male felons' accounts of intimate partner violence. *Journal of Social and Personal Relationships, 21*(5), 555–576.

9

Technology in Everyday Life

Communication and relationships increasingly center on the use of technology and media. For the sake of organization only, this chapter is primarily concerned with such technologies as cell phones and iPods. Chapter 10 is dedicated to what has been traditionally termed "mass" media, such as television, radio, movies, books, video games, and newspapers. As both a mass media system and an interactive technology, the Internet will be discussed in both chapters, with this one discussing more of its social and interactive nature and the next one discussing it from a mass media perspective.

Even though we are separating these concepts into two chapters, we recognize that they are rapidly becoming integrated and will no doubt continue to merge into relational life. Television, no longer confined to a large-screened unit in such social spaces as your home, waiting rooms, and restaurants, can now be watched in a variety of locations through cell phones, iPods, and similar technologies. Movies, books, newspapers, video games, and millions of songs are available for download onto these devices, just waiting to help you accomplish a variety of personal and relational needs.

This separation is still legitimate at the present time but may not be suitable in the future. The continuously changing nature of human communication in general and the use of technology in particular to fulfill relational connections are among the features that make the discipline of communication so intriguing but also challenging. Accordingly, you may notice throughout the chapter a recurring theme of technological change and evolution but a constant awareness of their embeddedness in relationships. In fact, we use the term *relational technologies* quite a bit more than just *technology*.

This chapter first explores the use of relational technologies and their influence on the construction of personal and relational identities. We examine how the use of these technologies conveys particular meanings to others. We then look at the construction of identity through the Internet, specifically focusing on screen names, e-mail addresses, content creation, social networking sites, and features of Internet activity that impact everyday life. The second half of the chapter is dedicated to the use of technology when interacting with others and how technology influences personal relationships. We first examine the distinct relational features of cell phone interactions and then explore the characteristics of online communication and its influence on relationships and social networks.

Focus Questions

1. How have emerging technologies generally been viewed?
2. What factors influence identity construction through the use of relational technologies?
3. What do your screen name and e-mail address tell others about you?
4. How are content creation and social networking sites impacting the construction of identity and self-disclosure?
5. How do cell phones impact interactions with others?
6. What makes online communication different from other forms of communication?
7. How is online communication impacting personal relationships and social networks?
8. Do people interact with technology like they interact with other people?

How Do People (and Scholars) View Technology?

A person's perspective will influence how something is understood and how it is studied. Accordingly, your view of technology will influence how you comprehend and evaluate the information provided in this chapter. Within this initial section, we discuss how the perspectives of communication scholars have impacted how technology is studied. We also discuss how emerging technologies are traditionally viewed by people in general along with how relationships (surprise!) play a fundamental position in the ways in which technologies are used and understood.

Academic Views of Technology

Most people currently conducting research and writing textbooks about technology—including both of your authors—remember a time without cell phones, iPods, and the Internet. You may have heard these technologies referred to as *new* media because, for those writing the textbooks and conducting the research, they are new. However, even with growing numbers of nontraditional students, the majority of students studying this research and reading these textbooks do not view this technology as new but view it as something that has always been around and that has always been a very significant part of their lives. Accordingly, the term *new media* will not be used when discussing the Internet, cell phones, iPods, and similar devices. Instead, these technologies will be referred to as *relational technologies* in recognition of their truly relational nature.

Beyond the designation of these technologies, the media experience of researchers also influences how technology gets discussed in most current research. Much of what is written about the Internet, cell phones, and other relational technologies frames them as intrusive and threatening, and they are evaluated according to standards and criteria associated with what are thus viewed as traditional or "normal" media and technology. Actually an increasingly vital, essential, and beneficial part of everyday life, these technologies should be studied and evaluated according to their own unique standards and norms.

The term *new media* is nothing new. In 1954, a classic study on parasocial relationships—a topic that will be addressed in the next chapter—noted that the impact of new media would be explored. The new medium studied was television!

Cave Drawings and Other Concerns

Fears and apprehensions surrounding the latest technology are nothing new and concern people other than scholars from previous media generations. The emergence of any new communication technology has historically elicited choruses of concern and anxiety, surprisingly similar in nature.

People tend to worry about the effects of emerging technologies on family, community, and, of course, children. While no evidence exists, we imagine focus groups were developed by well-meaning cave people to examine the potentially negative impact of cave drawings on innocent and susceptible cave children. Documented criticism of more recent technologies shows people expressed similar fears when radio began appearing in homes in the 1920s, and these fears were nearly identical to those expressed about television when it began appearing in homes during the 1950s. Actually, many of these criticisms are still being expressed! The even more recent introduction of the Internet led to concerns about diminished physical activity and social interaction among its users. Such criticisms are strikingly similar to questions raised in 1926 by the Knights of Columbus Adult Education Committee about telephones in homes, including "Does the telephone make [people] more active or more lazy?" and "Does the telephone break up home life and the old practice of visiting friends?" (as quoted in Fischer, 1992, p. 1).

Of course, the introduction of a new technology is not without its supporters, although voices of praise are usually overwhelmed by those of criticism. As with similarities among the concerns, the praise offered for each emerging technology is often quite similar. A public relations announcement by the American Telephone & Telegraph Company (AT&T) had this to say about telephones: "The telephone is essentially democratic; it carries the voice of the child and the grown-up

The Luddites (named from their leader Ned Ludd) were an early 19th-century British social movement that protested innovations of the Industrial Revolution and were involved in armed conflicts with the British army. Today, *Luddite* refers to a person who opposes any innovation, especially technology.

Case in Point

Find news reports about advances in technology. How are these technological advances being characterized? Does the source of these reports impact these characterizations? For instance, do print newspapers report them differently than podcasts or online sources?

with equal speed and directness. . . . It is not only the implement of the individual, but it fulfills the needs of all the people" (as quoted in Fischer, 1992, p. 2). These sentiments sound strikingly similar to those surrounding the democratic and equalizing nature of the Internet.

Every Technology Is Relational

Technologies do impact society and the world in which you live. Regardless of whether its influences are positive or negative, each technology changes how people communicate and interact. The one constant among all technologies, from cave drawings to the Internet to whatever technologies arise next, is that they are inherently relational in their understanding and use. At the center of all criticism and praise of technologies rest their influence and effect on social interaction and connections among people. This influence is probably why criticism and praise surrounding each emerging technology have sounded so similar; relationships among people have been the one constant throughout all human technological development. Adapted to accomplish and meet relational needs, all technologies have influenced how you interact and relate with others.

Relational Technology and the Construction of Identities

Technological devices do not merely connect you with other people or provide you with information, music, and video. Personal and relational identities are created and maintained through your use of these technologies. We refer to cell phones and iPods as **relational technologies** to emphasize the relational functions and implications of their use in society and within specific groups. Throughout this section of the chapter, we examine how the use of technology creates and conveys information about the self, groups, and relationships.

The Meaning of Relational Technology

The use of relational technologies develops unique meanings for particular social groups. Perceiving and using technology in a manner consistent with these groups assists in establishing membership into these groups and developing particular identities. For instance, some groups view the cell phone less as a device to contact others and more as a means of displaying social status and membership (J. Katz, 2006). The social meanings accompanying technologies, along with their significance, vary according to the social system in which they are used. Members of some organizations, for example, may view text messages as a more appropriate means of communication, while members of other organizations may prefer contact through calling or face-to-face interactions. The views governing the use of these technologies are developed in large part by how other members of these organizations use and discuss each technology.

Technology and Media Generations

A major influence on people's perceptions and use of technology is the generation in which they were born. In fact, media scholars Gary Gumpert and Robert Cathcart (1985) have maintained that the traditional notion of separating generations according to time can be replaced by separating generations according to media experience. What separates generations is not just the chronological era in which they were born but also the media and technology that encompass their world. **Media generations** are differentiated by unique media grammar and media consciousness based on the technological environment in which they are born. Before the introduction of radio, past generations understood the world according to the printed word and standards associated with literacy. Radio generations eventually gave way to television generations, which gave way to digital and Internet generations, which will eventually give way to whatever technology and media generations are on the horizon.

The meaning and use of technology often vary among people of different countries. When cell phones first appeared in the United States, for example, they were marketed as business tools to be used primarily by businesspeople. In the United Kingdom, they were marketed as social relationship tools to be used by everyone. Consequently, cell phones became popular much sooner in the United Kingdom than in the United States.

Each technology influences people's thinking, sense of experience, and perceptions of reality in very unique and specific ways. Media generations and societies as a whole consequently develop different standards and methods for evaluating knowledge, experience, and reality (Chesebro, 1984). If you were born into the Internet generation, you think differently and perceive the world differently than someone born before the introduction of the Internet, and vice versa. Furthermore, those born during a particular media era privilege the perspectives or orientations brought about by their dominant technology. Someone from the Internet generation may accept and enjoy an abbreviated podcast or webcast of a full-length television episode, but someone from a television generation may find it difficult to follow. Likewise, media generations born into a digital world undervalue books and traditional television in favor of the Internet and digital products.

Technology and Social Networks

Your social network is an equally powerful force in guiding perceptions and use of technology. While generational influence is largely determined by the *availability* of technology, the influence of social networks on your use and perceptions of technology is determined by the actual *use and incorporation* of technology and the social meanings that subsequently develop. Friends, family,

Photo 9.1 What social influence may be impacting the use of technology in this picture? (See page 236.)

Strategic Communication

The medium through which you contact someone can make a difference in his or her reception of your message. The purpose of your message and the technological preferences of the person you are contacting will determine the appropriateness of face-to-face, telephone, or computer-mediated interaction.

classmates, coworkers, and others with whom you share a particular relationship direct and shape your assumptions about the value of technology and what its use represents both relationally and personally. For instance, cell phone adoption, along with attitudes toward products and services, is often shared among members of a social network (Campbell & Russo, 2003). Whether or not you own particular relational technology is based in large part on whether or not your friends own that particular relational technology. Likewise, your use of relational technologies and your attitude toward them are likely to mirror those of your friends and other members of your social network.

Your use of technology will, of course, vary according to the person with whom you are in contact and what you want to achieve through the interaction. You belong to multiple social groups, each of which likely views technology and its use differently. For example, you may be more likely to contact members of one group via e-mail and members of another group through text messages. The technological tendencies of a group may also impact its ability to achieve social status and acceptance. For instance, the use of iPods may be less common in some groups, and owning one may earn you a higher social status. On the other hand, among groups in which these devices are quite common, owning an iPod may not indicate higher social status but establish group membership and acceptance through the common use of this technology. Each social group to which you belong will help shape and mold your view and use of technology, with the group you view as most important for what you wish to achieve personally and relationally likely providing the greatest influence of all.

Technological Products and Service Providers

In addition to adoption and incorporation of relational technologies, identities are also created though the use of specific products and services. Scholars have long studied the diffusion of innovations, or how new ideas and technologies are spread throughout communities (e.g., E. Katz, Levin, & Hamilton, 1963). Some individuals desire to own the latest relational technology and related accessories as a means of demonstrating technological savvy or social status. Aside from issues associated with cost, those whose technological devices appear dated may care little about possessing the latest products and even purposefully delay adopting new technological devices as a means

"Friends and family" cell phone plans in the United States were developed when the relational turn in their use was recognized. Though developed based on consumer use, these plans now have a normative influence—essentially telling people whom they should be calling.

of conveying technological indifference or mistrust. The majority of people adopt technological devices at relatively the same time. In all three cases of technological adoption, the technological device being used communicates specific attitudes about that technology.

Beyond the speed at which technological devices and services are adopted, specific meanings are associated with the use of particular products and service providers within a social system. The use of these devices allows people to associate themselves with accompanying perspectives and attitudes related to these technological products. One study (Lobet-Maris, 2003) found that, when purchasing a cell phone, young people are influenced less by quality or available features and more by the image associated with that particular phone. Each style of cell phone is symbolically connected to certain lifestyles, activities, or media personalities, and the use of these phones enables the construction of associated identities. Not limited to the phone model, these connections also include the actual service provider. Individuals in the study linked cell phone networks with specific social features, such as humanitarianism, professionalism, and family. Thus, the use of specific networks may enable people to feel associated with groups sharing certain values or orientations.

College Experience

Consider how relational technologies are viewed by people on campus compared to other groups with which you may interact. For instance, if you have recently graduated from high school, how do meanings of technology use there differ from those on campus? If it has been a while since you were in high school, how does technology use on campus compare with that in places where you have worked?

Ringtones

Ringtones do not simply inform someone of an incoming call or message; they can be viewed as a method of identity construction. People frequently select favorite music or dialogue from television programs or movies. Using these media products as ringtones announces your media preferences to others and underscores their importance in your life. As we discuss in the next chapter, identities constructed through media preferences are equally as meaningful as other sorts of identities. The selection of ringtones—media-based or otherwise—is meaningful and is based largely on how a person wants to be perceived by others.

If you are reading this book in public or the next time you are around other people, look around at the cell phones and other relational technologies that people are using. Chances are the majority of people will be using cell phones and other relational technologies that look very similar, a few people will be using devices that appear more modern and advanced, and the remaining few will be using relational technologies that look a bit outdated.

Photo 9.2 This photo was taken just before the student's instructor took the phone and threw it against the wall. Is it ever a good idea to use cell phones while in class? (See page 236.)

Of course, some people tend to keep their cell phone set on silent or vibrate rather than an audible ring tone. This decision could be an indication that the person does not desire to draw attention to his or her use of the technology. It could also indicate that the person does not wish to be socially compelled to answer, which provides greater choice in social contexts. Once again, this selection is not just personal but also relational and is influenced by how a person wishes to be understood.

Performance of Relational Technology

Finally, the use of relational technologies can be considered a performance through which identities are constructed. The proper use or performance of technology has been established socially and will likely change over time. However, behaviors are judged according to present norms and prevailing expectations. Violating social standards associated with the use of technology often leads to negative responses and evaluations by others.

The appropriate use of technology is often determined by location and occasion. For instance, there are numerous locations and occasions where the use of technology may be deemed socially unacceptable. You might not expect the use of cell phones, MP3 players, and other technological devices during religious services, weddings, or other special events. The use of cell phones while watching a movie at a theater can really irritate other members of the audience. Likewise, the use of relational technology is usually discouraged in the classroom. Your instructors may ban the use of cell phones in the classroom, but they are not the only ones who disapprove. Other students consider mobile phones ringing or vibrating during class to be just as distracting and annoying as faculty do (Campbell, 2006).

The appropriate use of technology also encompasses content. There are certain subjects people would normally avoid discussing with someone else when they are physically together in public, but often these topics are discussed freely while engaged in a conversation on a cell phone. Perhaps there is a heightened sense of privacy considering the other person cannot be seen or heard, but it is still very much a public performance. Whether they have been personal discussions of intimacy or graphic descriptions of a rash that just will not go away, you have probably overheard cell phone conversations that you would have rather avoided.

Online Activity and the Construction of Identities

Having discussed the influence of relational technologies on the construction of personal and relational identities, we now turn our attention to the Internet. Research concerning the development of online identities has focused on identity construction through chat room discussions. While this line of research has provided valuable insight into Internet activity and personal identity, we would like to focus instead on matters of Internet activity that have received less attention but are continuing to grow in importance in everyday life.

Screen Names

Identity development is accomplished in part through the selection of screen names. Of course, screen names are frequently selected when participating in chat rooms but are also evident when playing MMORPGs (massively multiplayer online role-playing games), uploading videos on YouTube, leaving online comments and evaluations, and even selling items on eBay. A person is sometimes known to others only by his or her screen name, which may or may not provide an accurate representation of the person behind the screen. What is known about that individual is often limited to his or her Internet activity, with his or her life away from the Internet frequently unknown. A person may also establish a number of screen names and create multiple online identities.

Users may select screen names based on genuine perceived characteristics of the self or uncharacteristic traits they wish to establish online. Such screen names as *shyguy24* or *toughgrl17* may be used by those who view themselves as outgoing or aggressive, as well as by those who see themselves as introverted or passive off-line but who wish to create a unique online persona. In other words, people may select a screen name based on characteristics they usually attempt to develop through off-line interactions with others. They may also select a screen name based on characteristics usually not developed through off-line interaction as a way to test these characteristics in what may be an anonymous and nonthreatening environment.

Although former Vice President Al Gore once infamously took credit, no single person can be considered the inventor of the Internet. However, chief among the early major contributors are Leonard Kleinrock and J. C. R. Licklider. Leonard Kleinrock was the first person to publish a paper on packet switching, an essential component of the Internet. J. C. R. Licklider is considered the first person to conceive of a worldwide network of computers, which he labeled a "galactic network."

Screen names may represent other aspects of individuals beyond personality traits. Selecting such names as *HoopsFan90* or *Bears85* may symbolize an interest in a particular sport or team. Choosing such names as *SimpsonsGeek3564* or *GreysAnatoAmy53* may represent an interest in specific movies, television programs, or other popular-culture products. The screen names that people select may also embody personal relationships (*ProudPapa35, EmalynMom64, OlderSister124, ILuvDarvin95*) or represent people's professions, hobbies, and majors (*CrookedCop10_4, OilPainter23, CommStudiesRules73*). Selecting screen names based on these aspects of the self symbolizes their significance in a person's life and how that person wishes to be perceived by others.

Somewhat related to screen names are e-mail addresses, which may also influence and assist in constructing identities. The key components of e-mail addresses and their potential impact on identity construction are presented in Table 9.1.

Table 9.1 E-mail Addresses and Identities

User name: located before the @ symbol

webmaster@sagepub.com

As with screen names, multiple aspects of the self can be constructed when a person is allowed to select a user name. Be aware that screen names or user names may create undesired impressions; *2Sexy4U* or *KegLuvver,* for example, may be fine when corresponding and interacting with friends online but not in professional situations.

Domain name: located immediately after the @ symbol

webmaster@**sagepub**.com

The domain name can reveal service provider, profession, or affiliation. Domain names may display the Internet service provider, which—as with cell phone providers—could be selected based on how people wish to portray themselves to others. Companies and schools usually have their own domain name, enabling employees and students to signify their affiliation.

Top-level domain: located at the end of the address

webmaster@sagepub**.com**

The top-level material may also reveal information to others. Such codes as *.edu, .gov, .mil,* and *.org* indicate a connection with education, government, military, or an organization, respectively. Addresses originating in countries other than the United States come with a two-digit country code, such as *.uk,* which provides further information about the user.

Content Creation

The Internet has become both an instrument and a site for self-expression and, accordingly, the construction and performance of identities. This identity work is partially accomplished through online **content creation**. Social networking pages, blogs, and the posting of original pictures, videos, reviews, comments, and other personal online creations enable people to share and display their thoughts, interests, talents, and experiences and convey themselves to others in ways they wish to be viewed and understood.

Just as they do in face-to-face interactions, people make strategic choices when presenting themselves (via their creations) online. Choice of content, along with the presentation of the material included, represents a symbolic display of a person's worldview, providing specific insight into how he or she wishes to be viewed by others. For instance, the

Identity work online also takes place through the creation of avatars and the exploration of such virtual worlds as Second Life, Gaia, and Habbo. Presently only around 8% of online teens and 4% of online adults visit virtual worlds (Lenhart, Purcell, Smith, & Zickhur, 2010). These numbers have remained relatively steady in the past few years but will likely increase as the relational nature of the Internet continues to develop.

creation of a picture display on Snapfish or a similar picture site does not merely serve to archive or document experiences. Relational and identity-based decisions are made concerning what pictures are shared and what messages these pictures convey to others. Similarly, it has been discovered that people use self-presentation strategies frequently in blogs to achieve acceptance and approval and to appear socially competent (Bortree, 2005).

> It can be argued that social networking sites began in the form of online communities. If this is the case, Well.com, launched in 1985, would be among the first. In their current form—in which people create a profile, compile a list of connections, and visit the profiles of other members—Classmates.com, launched in 1995, and SixDegrees.org, launched in 1997, were among the first social networking sites.

Social Networking Sites

The development of profiles on such social networking sites as Facebook, MySpace, and LinkedIn, along with activity on these sites, remains the most widespread form of content creation. Findings from the Pew Internet & American Life Project indicate that 73% of online teens (12–17 years old), 72% of online young adults (18–29 years old), and 40% of online adults (30 years old and above) have at least one profile on a social networking site (Lenhart et al., 2010). These sites have become important tools in the display and creation of personal and relational identities.

Perhaps the most obvious identity work on these sites takes place through the creation of unique member profiles. Some sites allow people to establish unique backgrounds; to include images from television, movies, video games, and other media; and to incorporate music, all of which convey to visitors how a person wishes to be digitally perceived. Personal information including demographic information, self-descriptions, favorite quotes, interests, and media preferences are frequently offered through these profiles and serve to develop a particular view of the profile's creator. Once again, as with face-to-face interactions, people make strategic choices about how they hope to be perceived through their profiles. The information provided in or excluded from these profiles is cast to portray a person in the ways in which he or she hopes to be seen by others.

In addition to the creation of profiles, such social networking site activities as updating your status, uploading photos, sharing websites, commenting on the profiles, and even playing games like Farm Town, Mafia Wars, and Bejeweled are used in the development of identities. Status updates, for example, do not simply let others in a network know what a person is doing or what a person is thinking.

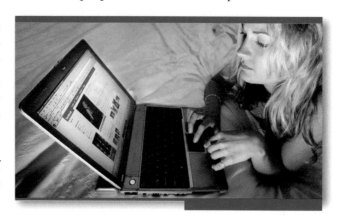

Photo 9.3 What activities are related to identity construction on social networking sites like Facebook? (See page 236.)

Listen in on Your Life

If you have your own page on a social networking site, what do you believe it conveys to other people about you? How do these perceptions compare with how you view yourself? Do your friends agree about the messages being conveyed?

These updates present a person's worldview to others and how he or she wishes to be seen.

A person's activities and disclosures on social networking sites are often very strategic, but sometimes people include information without fully considering how it will impact the way others see them. Likewise, in face-to-face interactions, people do not always consider the impact of what they say and do on how they are perceived by others. Regardless of similarities with other forms of communication, however, the disclosure and corresponding identity development involved make social networking sites very unique.

Self-disclosure taking place on social networking sites has led communication scholars to question many classic studies and observations related to disclosure. Communication scholars previously believed that self-disclosure occurs gradually as trust is established in a relationship, but these sites instead provide a tremendous amount of personal information all at once. Peripheral, or relatively minor, information, such as favorite music, appears on these sites at the same time as more personal information, such as relationship history and sexual preferences. Scholars also believed that peripheral information about the self would be shared initially; that deeper personal information would be shared later; and, further, that information shared with one person would be different from that shared with another person, depending on the relationships between these individuals. More information, in general, and more personal information, specifically, would be shared with close friends than acquaintances. Unless access is blocked and sometimes in spite of access being blocked, anyone—regardless of his or her relationship with a creator—can view the information included on most social networking site pages. You may have heard stories about people being kicked out of school or losing a job because of the content shared on their social networking webpage. Someone had access to information that he or she would not have gained otherwise.

Relational Technology and Personal Relationships

Having examined the influence of technology on identities, we can now fully explore how technology and relationships are connected and mutually influential. Examining the influence of technology on relationships, Kraut, Brynin, and Kiesler (2006) have observed that on one level changes in technology simply allow people to achieve relatively stable relational goals in new ways. People exchange birthday greetings, for example, through e-cards rather than a traditional card sent through the postal service. Correspondence takes place through phone calls rather than letters. These authors also maintain, however, that more than simply altering how traditional goals are met, technological transformation also changes what can be accomplished, creating new relational goals and norms.

Cell phones, online communication, and other technological advancements are changing how people communicate and form relationships with others, as well as altering established relational goals and norms. This section of the chapter examines the impact of cell phones and other relational technologies on interactions among people. We then examine the characteristics of online communication and its influence on relationships and social networks. Finally, we consider how people interact not only with one another but also with technology itself.

Cell Phones and Personal Relationships

Cell phones have come to represent constant connection to those who possess your number, and how freely people give out their cell phone numbers varies. Giving or denying someone access to your cell phone number establishes both the *boundaries* and the *degree of closeness* desired and expected within the relationship. Limiting the availability of contact with a person establishes specific relational boundaries. How that person views and evaluates such limits depends on your relationship. Refusing to provide a cell phone number to a friend may be viewed negatively; therapists not providing clients with their numbers may be viewed as legitimate.

Providing another person with your cell phone number suggests a desire for connection with that individual and perhaps an indication of the type of relationship you wish to establish. For instance, making your number available to an acquaintance could imply a desire to develop a closer type of relationship. As above, the evaluation and meaning of this action generally depend on your relationship with that person. Although it serves to maintain the existence and importance of your relationship, providing a close friend with your cell phone number may be expected. Patients receiving the cell phone number of their doctor along with instructions to call at any time may see this action as more meaningful or consequential because it runs counter to the expectations associated with that relationship.

David rarely gives out his cell phone number, and his wife is the only person who ever calls him on that phone, which for him has become an exclusive symbol of their relationship. Although many colleagues and friends know Steve's U.S. cell phone number, very few people know the number of the cell phone he uses while in Europe—including his coauthor! When returning home to England, Steve becomes symbolically and literally separated from all but a few individuals in his social network. As is the case for many other people, our cell phones have brought about personal and social connotations that dictate their use, including who is able to contact us.

Constant Connection and Availability

Connection and availability are fully established when calls are actually made and text messages are sent. There are times when the content of these messages is less important than the actual contact itself. Such instances are similar to how seemingly mundane everyday talk keeps relationships going without necessarily adding much

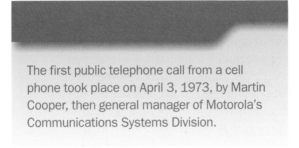

The first public telephone call from a cell phone took place on April 3, 1973, by Martin Cooper, then general manager of Motorola's Communications Systems Division.

in terms of substance. Connecting with another person reestablishes the existence and importance of the relationship, confirming for both parties its existence and value in their lives. At other times the content of these messages is vitally important, especially during the enactment of relational information and other relational maintenance strategies. Of course, letters sent via the Pony Express in 1860 accomplished the same things, so what makes cell phones so different? We are glad you asked!

Cell phones allow people to be in "perpetual contact" with others (J. Katz & Aakhus, 2002). If you have your cell phone with you, you have your social network with you as well. The ability to make instant contact with another person regardless of geographic location creates a symbolic connection unlike that created by any previous communication technology. Research indicates that 70% of couples with cell phones contact each other at least once a day just to say hello or to chat briefly, whereas only 54% of couples who do not own cell phones do this (Kennedy, Smith, Wells, & Wellman, 2008).

This constant connection with others can provide comfort and security in a relationship or can lead to challenges. Relationships require connections between people, as well as autonomy and independence (Baxter & Montgomery, 1996). While the feeling of constant connection made possible through cell phones can be beneficial, it may decrease feelings of autonomy, equally important and necessary in relationships.

New relational expectations have also developed as a result of constant availability through cell phones. When calling someone's cell phone, you expect he or she will be readily available. If he or she does not answer the phone, you generally expect him or her to return the call in a timely manner and provide a plausible excuse for not answering in the first place. The same expectations apply when sending someone a text message. Failure to respond to a text message in a timely manner—or failure to respond, period—can constitute a violation in the relationship (Ling, 2004).

Photo 9.4 In what ways could the use of a cell phone create shared experiences? (See page 236.)

Shared Experience

We can discuss shared experience derived from the use of cell phones in two ways. First, the actual use of cell phones constitutes shared technological experience. Especially when people correspond through text messages, they engage in the use of the same technology. As discussed earlier in the chapter, particular groups assign great significance and meaning to the use of particular technology. More than simply transmitting information, the act of sending and receiving text messages both announces and establishes shared membership and acceptance into a group.

Cell phones also enable people to engage in shared experience even when physically separated. The immediate transmission of voice, picture, sound, and video provides people with the sense of experiencing an event or occasion together. A person in a disagreement with a romantic partner can be in simultaneous contact with a friend offering guidance and support and subsequently sharing in the experience. Joyous occasions and celebrations can likewise be shared with others who are physically absent.

Social Coordination

One of the greatest relational consequences of the cell phone encompasses its use in coordinating physical encounters with others. Face-to-face interactions are created and synchronized through the use of cell phones. The ability to establish the physical location of others while in public creates opportunities for spontaneous physical interaction. If you call a friend while studying in the library only to discover that he or she is studying in the adjacent building, this discovery could lead to a decision to meet and take a break together. The revelation of proximity made possible through cell phones makes such encounters possible.

Cell phones enable people to synchronize their activities to the point of microcoordination. Making plans to meet someone previously involved establishing a fixed time and physical location for the interaction to occur, but the massive adoption of cell phones has resulted in time and physical location for contact becoming increasingly fluid. **Microcoordination** refers to the unique management of social interaction made possible through cell phones. Rich Ling (2004) has observed three varieties of microcoordination: (1) midcourse adjustment, (2) iterative coordination, and (3) softening of schedules (see Table 9.2).

Table 9.2 Ling's (2004) Three Varieties of Microcoordination	
Midcourse adjustment	Involves changing plans once a person has already set out for the encounter—for example, contacting the other person to change locations or to request that he or she pick up someone else on the way
Iterative coordination	Involves the progressive refining of an encounter. Cell phones have made actually establishing location and time unnecessary. Instead, people increasingly plan to meet without specifying an exact time or location. For instance, friends may agree to meet sometime tomorrow. As a result of progressive calls or messages, they eventually "zoom in on each other" (p. 72).
Softening of schedules	Involves adjusting a previously scheduled time. If you planned to meet a friend for coffee at 3:30 P.M. but a meeting with your advisor took longer than expected and you are running late, cell phones make it much easier to reach your friend and inform him or her of the delay.

Source: Ling, 2004.

Online Communication and Personal Relationships

Characteristics of Online Communication

Before discussing the influence of online communication on personal relationships, we want to first consider the unique characteristics of online communication. Recognizing that there are a number of unique forms of online communication, such as e-mail, chat rooms, message boards, and instant messaging, we examine the similarities among them.

Richness

One characteristic of online communication—and, for that matter, all text-based inter-actions—is the lack of nonverbal cues available to help determine meaning. Nonverbal communication, such as vocalics and kinesics, is incredibly valuable when crafting and interpreting messages. The number of verbal and nonverbal cues available through a medium or technology determines its **richness**. Face-to-face interactions are consid-ered richer than other types of interaction since verbal communication and a range of nonverbal cues are available to convey and interpret meaning. Phone conversations are less rich since they are limited to verbal communication and vocalics. Online commu-nication is limited to verbal communication, with no nonverbal cues available to assist in conveying and interpreting messages.

Accordingly, misunderstandings will more likely occur during online interac-tions than during telephone conversations or face-to-face interactions. This possi-bility does not automatically mean that all online interactions will result in misunderstandings, but it does mean that individuals engaging in online communication must carefully con-sider the messages they craft and care-fully interpret the messages they receive. **Emoticons**, text-based symbols used to express emotions online, often help alleviate problems associated with a lack of nonverbal cues. The general absence of nonverbal cues, however, poses a distinct challenge when interacting online.

The very first "smiley face" emoticon :-) was used at 11:44 A.M. on September 19, 1982, by professor Scott E. Fahlman while contributing to an online bulletin board.

Asynchronous

A second characteristic of online communication is its asynchronous nature. In **syn-chronous communication**—for example, face-to-face interaction—people interact in real time and can send and receive messages at once. In **asynchronous communication**, containing a slight or prolonged delay, the interactants must alternate between sending and receiving. E-mail and even instant messaging represent asynchronous communi-cation. Although some online interactions are close to real time, they still contain a delay, and people must take turns being sender and receiver. The asynchronous nature of online communication provides more time to consider the messages of others and to formulate messages.

While sometimes beneficial, the asynchronous nature of online communication also poses a challenge, especially when it comes to instant messaging. Boneva, Quinn, Kraut, Kiesler, and Shklovski (2006) have shown that instant messaging provides as much social support as face-to-face interactions and phone conversations, but people using instant messaging report feeling more disconnected from those with whom they use it to interact. While this finding may be the result of

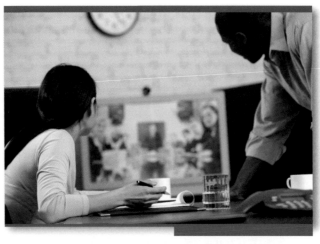

diminished nonverbal cues mentioned above, these authors maintain it may actually be the result of multitasking. Specifically, a person may have multiple instant messaging windows open at the same time, while also browsing the Internet, listening to the radio, watching television, and engaging in other activities.

Photo 9.5 In what ways does a webcam affect the richness and asynchronous nature of online communication? (See page 236.)

Quality

Due in large part to fears associated with new technologies mentioned earlier, many researchers have wrongly positioned face-to-face communication as superior to online communication in quality and influence. Conversely, online communication has been positioned as fraught with challenges and potential harm. Baym, Zhang, and Lin (2004), however, have noted that "face-to-face [interaction] may not always be the rich, deep, and inherently superior means of communication that it is often presumed to be" (p. 316). Comparing face-to-face, telephone, and online interactions, these authors found the quality of telephone and face-to-face interactions only slightly higher than that of online interactions. Quite often when online communication is evaluated harshly, the norms and practices of other forms of interaction have been used. This type of evaluation is no more legitimate or fair than using norms and practices of online communication to evaluate face-to-face or telephone interactions.

Two observations about the quality of online communication and other forms of interaction become clear. First, all forms of interaction have unique benefits and challenges. In this regard, online communication is no different from face-to-face communication, telephone conversations, or any other interaction. Second, how online communication is

Make Your Case

Some people have denounced online communication as inferior to face-to-face communication. Do you believe this evaluation? What are the advantages and disadvantages of both forms of communication? In what ways are online communication and face-to-face communication similar? In what ways are they different?

used has as much to do with its quality as its actual nature. Again, this use makes it no different from other forms of human communication. What does differentiate online communication is that it is still a relatively new form of interaction for many generations. People's perceptions of quality surrounding online communication are likely associated with their comfort and familiarity with interacting online, and as they continue to integrate online communication into their lives, it will become just as normal and commonplace as face-to-face communication.

Personal Relationships and Social Networks

Online communication enables people to maintain and enhance existing relationships, reinvigorate previous relationships, and create new relationships. Fears that the Internet will decrease social interaction and diminish the quality of relationships appear unfounded. In fact, increased use of the Internet allows for increased interaction with friends and family, not only online but also face-to-face and over the telephone. Furthermore, the majority of Internet users indicate that it has improved the quality of their relationships (Howard, Rainie, & Jones, 2002).

Contrarian Challenge

We have emphasized the positive aspects of online communication. What negative aspects of online communication can you come up with?

Accessibility of contact is perhaps what makes online communication so useful in maintaining existing relationships. Relationships take a great deal of effort to maintain, the basis of which involves enacting them through regular contact. The ease with which contact can be made online may very well increase the likelihood that it will take place at all.

Online communication appears to supplement rather than replace traditional forms of interaction. As people use the Internet to connect with friends, family, and acquaintances, it appears as if face-to-face interactions and telephone calls actually increase. While it seems everyone spends a great deal of time online, face-to-face communication remains the most frequent type of interaction among college students (Baym et al., 2004).

The type of online communication used appears to be associated with distance. People use both e-mail and instant messaging when interacting with others regardless of distance. However, they are less likely to use e-mail to contact people who live nearby and more likely to use it to contact long-distance friends and family (Quan-Haase & Wellman, 2002). On the other hand, people are much more likely to use instant messaging to interact with others living nearby (Boneva et al., 2006).

Social Networks

Online communication is dramatically changing the construction and nature of social networks. For instance, Internet users are more likely to maintain larger and more diverse social networks. Studying the impact of the Internet on social networks, Boase, Horrigan, Wellman, and Rainie (2006, p. 5) distinguished two types of connections in social networks: core ties and significant ties (see Table 9.3). Core ties tend to remain the same

---

Table 9.3 Core Ties and Significant Ties

Core ties include people with whom you have a very close relationship and are in frequent contact. You often discuss important matters in life with core ties, and you often seek their assistance in times of need.

Significant ties, though more than mere acquaintances, represent a somewhat weaker connection. You make less contact with significant ties and are less likely to talk with them about important issues in your life or to seek help from them, but they are still there for you when needed.

---

regardless of Internet activity, while Internet users report a greater number of significant ties. While the size of core ties may remain, Internet use has been shown to increase the diversity of core ties. For instance, Internet users are more likely to have nonrelatives as members of their core network (Hampton, Sessions, Her, & Rainie, 2009).

Another consequence of online communication is the geographic diversity of social networks. Traditionally, social networks have developed around geography-based communities. In other words, people in social networks tend to live in the same town or at least nearby. While physical proximity still plays a large role in the development of social networks, online communication has resulted in more geographically dispersed networks (Boase et al., 2006). Some people decry the fact that fewer and fewer people socialize with or even know their neighbors, but this does not necessarily mean people are antisocial or lack strong social support in times of need. Socialization and social support increasingly come from the Internet rather than next door. At the same time, Internet users are still just as likely as nonusers to visit with their neighbors (Hampton et al., 2009).

The Media Equation

While a great deal of research has focused on technology's impact on relationships between people, one research program has instead looked at relationships between people and technology. Before you start making dinner reservations at a fancy restaurant for you and your computer, this research program has not revealed the co-construction of shared meaning, reality, and other features of human-to-human relationships. It has, however, uncovered something incredibly fascinating.

Introduced by Byron Reeves and Clifford Nass (2002), the **media equation** maintains that interactions with technology are the same as interactions with other people, and people use the same social rules and expectations when interacting with both. You interact with your computer as if it is an actual person.

When they first hear about the media equation, many people deny that they treat technology similarly to people. Yet, have you ever pleaded with your computer to go faster when experiencing a slow connection or yelled at your computer when it crashed? You may even have talked to or humanized other inanimate objects and technology. Accordingly, it may not be so inconceivable that your interactions with technology mirror your interactions with other people, especially given the interactive nature of more recent technological innovations.

To test the media equation, Reeves and Nass (2002) found research involving people-people interaction; erased one of the references to *people* and replaced it with *computer, television,* or another technology; and conducted the study using the same techniques that established the people–people findings. If the study found "people like people who compliment them," they would change this finding to "people like *computers* who compliment them," and then they would test it using the same methods that established the original findings. The results of the people–technology experiments consistently mirrored the results of the original people–people experiment.

I Am Me; I Am My Computer (Personality)

People generally prefer to be around and interact with people who are similar to them rather than people who are different. If you have a dominant personality, you will prefer interacting with other people with dominant personalities. Likewise, if you are submissive, you will prefer interacting with other submissive people. People, it turns out, not only perceive computers as having dominant or submissive personalities but also prefer computers whose personality is similar to their own. Furthermore, people are able to recognize that these computers have such similar personalities.

People's relationships with technology may become especially close in the relatively near future. David Levy (2007) convincingly argues in the book *Love and Sex with Robots* that by the year 2050, "robots will be hugely attractive to humans as companions because of their many talents, senses, and capabilities. They will have the capacity to fall in love with humans and to make themselves romantically attractive and sexually desirable to humans" (p. 22).

Computers Say the Kindest Things (Flattery)

Remember that "brownnoser" or "suck-up" from your high school, the one who always complimented the teachers on their clothing or that "wonderfully crafted and inspirational" examination or assignment? That person knew what he or she was doing. The official term for this behavior is *ingratiation*, and it turns out to be quite effective, whether or not it is genuine or deserved (Gordon, 1996). People like other people who compliment them, and the same evaluative response holds true for computers: People, it was discovered, like computers who offer them praise more than computers that offer no evaluation.

Be Nice to Your Computer (Politeness)

When someone asks for your feedback on a project he or she has completed or asks about his or her performance on a task, you generally provide him or her with a positive response. If someone else asked you about that person's performance, your response would be more negative than if that person asked you directly. Not necessarily deceitful, you are just not being as negative as you could be because you do not want to hurt his or her feelings. The same patterns of interaction were found to take place with computers. When asked to evaluate a computer while using the same computer to type their responses, people responded much more positively than when typing their responses on a different computer. They did not want to hurt the computer's feelings. On a personal note, we would like to acknowledge the extraordinary contribution of the computer we are using to type this section of the book—and we hope it does not crash!

FOCUS QUESTIONS REVISITED

1. How have emerging technologies generally been viewed?

The emergence of any new communication technology has historically elicited choruses of concern and anxiety, surprisingly similar in nature. Of course, the introduction of a new technology is not without its supporters, although voices of praise are usually overwhelmed by those of criticism. As with similarities among the concerns, the praise offered for each emerging technology is often quite similar. At the center of all criticism and praise of technologies rest their influence and effect on social interaction and connections among people. This influence is probably why criticism and praise surrounding each emerging technology have sounded so similar; relationships among people have been the one constant throughout all human technological development.

2. What factors influence identity construction through the use of relational technologies?

There are a number of factors influencing the meaning of relational technologies. For instance, media generations develop unique standards and methods for evaluating technology and consequently respond to relational technologies in different ways. The actual use and incorporation of relational technology by a social network will determine the social meanings that subsequently develop. The speed at which new technologies are adopted will influence the meaning associated with the use of particular products and services. Further, specific meanings are associated with the use of particular products and service providers within a social system. Ringtones do not simply inform someone of an incoming call or message; they also can be viewed as a method of identity construction. Finally, the use of relational technologies can be considered a performance through which identities are constructed. The proper use or performance of technology has been established socially and includes such issues as where relational technologies should be used and content.

3. What do your screen name and e-mail address tell others about you?

The selection of a screen name or user name may inform others of genuine perceived characteristics or characteristics you wish to establish online. E-mail addresses can reveal service providers, professions, affiliations, and other personal information.

4. How are content creation and social networking sites impacting the construction of identity and self-disclosure?

Social networking pages, blogs, and the posting of original pictures, videos, reviews, comments, and other personal online creations enable people to share and display their thoughts, interests, talents, and experiences and convey themselves to others in ways they wish to be viewed and understood. Social networking sites, especially, have led communication scholars to question classic studies and observations related to disclosure. Self-disclosure on these sites does not take place gradually; rather, people provide a tremendous amount of personal information all at once. Furthermore, they reveal relatively minor information at the same time as deeper personal information. Finally, they give the same personal information to everyone instead of disclosing certain information to or hiding certain information from individuals with whom they share a particular relationship.

5. How do cell phones impact interactions with others?

Cell phones have come to represent constant connection to those who possess your number. Giving someone your cell phone number or denying someone access to your number establishes both the boundaries and the degree of closeness desired and expected within your relationship with that person. A new relational expectation of constant availability has developed as a result of the constant availability made possible through cell phones. Also, shared experience develops from the actual use of cell phones and from the immediate transmission of voice, picture, sound, and video. Finally, the use of cell phones makes possible the microcoordination of physical social interaction.

6. What makes online communication different from other forms of communication?

The richness of a medium or technology, determined by the number of verbal and nonverbal cues available, differs among forms of communication. Online communication is considered less rich than face-to-face and telephone interactions. Further, online communication is considered asynchronous, meaning there is either a slight or a prolonged delay of the sending and receiving of messages. Face-to-face and telephone interactions are considered synchronous, meaning the people involved interact in real time and can be at once senders and receivers.

7. How is online communication impacting personal relationships and social networks?

Online communication enables people to maintain and enhance existing relationships, reinvigorate previous relationships, and create new relationships. Online communication also appears to supplement rather than replace traditional forms of interaction. Further, online communication enables people to maintain larger and more diverse social networks.

8. Do people interact with technology like they interact with other people?

According to the media equation theory, people's interactions with technology are the same as their interactions with other people, using the same social rules and expectations. While the media equation corresponds with basic views of human interaction, it has not yet been applied to the more advanced conceptions of human interaction and relationships examined in communication studies.

KEY CONCEPTS

asynchronous communication   228
content creation   222
emoticons   228
media equation   231
media generations   217

microcoordination   227
relational technologies   216
richness   228
synchronous communication   228

QUESTIONS TO ASK YOUR FRIENDS

1. Ask your friends at school how they feel when someone's cell phone rings during class. Do they find it irritating or believe it is acceptable behavior? If you have friends attending another school, ask them how they feel when someone's cell phone rings during class. How do their answers compare with those of friends at your school?

2. If you have your own page on a social networking site, ask your friends to compare how you present yourself on this page to how you present yourself off-line. In what ways are they different and similar?

3. Ask your friends about their most recent technology purchase and why they purchased that particular product. Are there any similarities in the products purchased by your friends? Are there any similarities in their reasons for making the purchase?

MEDIA LINKS

1. Examine how characters on television programs use and perform relational technology. Do their use and performance of technology parallel that of your friends, family, coworkers, or classmates?

2. Describe how relationships are featured in the television, print, and Internet advertisements of cell phone companies.

3. Visit the official websites of various television series and movies. How many of these sites have chat rooms or discussion boards available to connect fans and viewers? How might establishing these relational connections influence the number of people watching these series and films? How might the establishment of these connections influence the interpretation and use of this material?

ETHICAL ISSUES

1. In many ways, it is easier to fool people in chat rooms or when instant messaging than when talking with them face-to-face. Do you think deceitfulness online is more pardonable than being deceitful when talking with someone face-to-face?

2. Students have been suspended from some schools for content on social networking sites. Should schools be allowed to suspend students for this content? Would your assessment change depending on whether the content *did* or *did not* pertain to school-related issues, activities, or people?

3. Employers have based hiring decisions on social networking site content. Do you believe these actions are justified? In what ways do employers using social networking sites for the evaluation of job candidates compare and contrast with school officials using these sites for student discipline?

ANSWERS TO PHOTO CAPTIONS

Photo 9.1 ▪ The generations in which these gentlemen were born will likely influence their perceptions and use of technology.

Photo 9.2 ▪ It is never a good idea to use a cell phone in the classroom. The use of cell phones annoys classmates just as much as it annoys instructors—and it *really* annoys most instructors!

Photo 9.3 ▪ Identity construction on social networking sites includes the creation of profiles along with status updates, uploading photos, sharing websites, commenting on the profiles, playing games, and other activities.

Photo 9.4 ▪ Shared experience derived from the use of cell phones can come from a shared technological experience and from enabling people to engage in shared experiences when physically separated.

Photo 9.5 ▪ Webcams increase the richness of online interaction by increasing the number of nonverbal cues available. They also enable online communication to become more synchronous.

STUDENT STUDY SITE

Visit the study site at **www.sagepub.com/boc2e** for e-flashcards, practice quizzes, journal articles and additional study resources.

REFERENCES

Baxter, L. A., & Montgomery, B. M. (1996). *Relating: Dialogues and dialectics.* New York: Guilford.

Baym, N. K., Zhang, Y. B., & Lin, M.-C. (2004). Social interactions across media: Interpersonal communication on the Internet, telephone, and face-to-face. *New Media & Society, 6,* 299–318.

Boase, J., Horrigan, J. B., Wellman, B., & Rainie, L. (2006, January 25). *The strength of Internet ties: The Internet and email aid users in maintaining their social networks and provide pathways to help when people face big decisions.* Washington, DC: Pew Internet & American Life Project.

Boneva, B. S., Quinn, A., Kraut, R., Kiesler, S., & Shklovski, I. (2006). Teenage communication in the instant messaging era. In R. Kraut, M. Brynin, & S. Kiesler (Eds.), *Computers, phones, and the Internet: Domesticating information technology* (pp. 201–218). New York: Oxford University Press.

Bortree, D. S. (2005). Presentation of self on the Web: An ethnographic study of teenage girls' weblogs. *Education, Communication & Information, 5,* 25–39.

Campbell, S. W. (2006). Perceptions of mobile phones in college classrooms:

Ringing, cheating, and classroom policies. *Communication Education, 55,* 280–294.

Campbell, S. W., & Russo, T. C. (2003). The social construction of cell telephony: An application of the social influence model of perceptions and uses of cell phones within personal communication networks. *Communication Monographs, 70,* 317–334.

Chesebro, J. W. (1984). The media reality: Epistemological functions of media in cultural systems. *Critical Studies in Mass Communication, 2,* 111–130.

Fischer, C. (1992). *America calling: A social history of the telephone to 1940.* Berkeley: University of California Press.

Gordon, R. A. (1996). Impact of ingratiation on judgments and evaluations: A meta- analytic investigation. *Journal of Personality and Social Psychology, 17,* 45–70.

Gumpert, G., & Cathcart, R. (1985). Media grammars, generations, and media gaps. *Critical Studies in Mass Communication, 2,* 23–35.

Hampton, K. N., Sessions, L. F., Her, E. J., & Rainie, L. (2009). *Social isolation and new technology.* Washington, DC: Pew Internet & American Life Project.

Howard, P. E. N., Rainie, L., & Jones, S. (2002). Days and nights on the Internet. In B. Wellman & C. Haythornwaite (Eds.), *The Internet in everyday life* (pp. 45–73). Malden, MA: Blackwell.

Katz, E., Levin, M. L., & Hamilton, H. (1963). Traditions of research on the diffusion of innovations. *American Sociological Review, 28,* 237–252.

Katz, J. E. (2006). *Magic in the air: Cell communication and the transformation of social life.* New Brunswick, NJ: Transaction.

Katz, J. E., & Aakhus, M. A. (Eds.). (2002). *Perpetual contact: Cell communication,* *private talk, public performance.* Cambridge, UK: Cambridge University Press.

Kennedy, T. L. M., Smith, A., Wells, A. T., & Wellman, B. (2008). *Networked families.* Washington, DC: Pew Internet & American Life Project.

Kraut, R., Brynin, M., & Kiesler, S. (Eds.). (2006). *Computers, phones, and the Internet: Domesticating information technology.* New York: Oxford University Press.

Lenhart, A., Purcell, K., Smith, A., & Zickhur, K. (2010). *Social media & mobile Internet use among teens and young adults.* Washington, DC: Pew Internet & American Life Project.

Levy, D. (2007). *Love and sex with robots: The evolution of human-robot relationships.* New York: HarperCollins.

Ling, R. (2004). *The cell connection: The cell phone's impact on society.* San Francisco: Morgan Kaufmann.

Lobet-Maris, C. (2003). Cell phone tribes: Youth and social identity. In L. Fortunati, J. E. Katz, & R. Riccini (Eds.), *Mediating the human body: Technology, communication, and fashion* (pp. 87–92). Mahwah, NJ: Lawrence Erlbaum.

Quan-Haase, A., & Wellman, B. (with Witte, J. C., & Hampton, K.). (2002). Capitalizing on the Internet: Social contact, civic engagement, and sense of community. In B. Wellman & C. Haythornwaite (Eds.), *Internet and everyday life* (pp. 291–324). Malden, MA: Blackwell.

Reeves, B., & Nass, C. (2002). *The media equation: How people treat computers, television, and new media like real people and places.* Stanford, CA: Center for the Study of Language and Information.

10

Relational Uses and Understanding of Media

Think about the amount of time people actually spend using media each day. How much time do you think the average person spends watching television, listening to music, reading, playing video games, watching movies, and using the Internet?

To determine the most accurate measure of media use, the Middletown Media Studies compared the results of telephone surveys, diary records in which people documented their own activities, and direct observation in which people were followed and observed during every waking moment of the day (Papper, Holmes, & Popovich, 2004). It was discovered that people actually spend double the amount of time using media than they believe. These studies also established that people do not use media in isolation but often use two or more media systems simultaneously, an activity referred to as **concurrent media use**. For example, you may be reading this book while listening to the radio or watching television. Including concurrent media use, the most media-active person observed in these studies spent more than 17 hours using media each day, and the least media-active person observed spent a bit more than 5 hours using media each day. The average amount of time spent using media daily was nearly 11 hours.

While the sheer amount of time spent using media is reason enough for the importance of media use as an area of study, perhaps more significant is the

The Middletown Media Studies also uncovered that while the majority of media use occurs in the home, 34% of media use occurs outside the home in such locations as businesses, automobiles, schools, and workplaces. This percentage will likely increase in the coming years as video, music, and the Internet become more accessible through cell phones and other relational technologies.

A study on the media use of children uncovered numbers similar to those established through the Middletown Media Studies. Including concurrent media use, the average child uses media for 10 hours and 45 minutes daily (Rideout, Foehr, & Roberts, 2010).

impact of media on relationships and the impact of relationships on the use of media. Media use at home frequently occurs in the presence of family members, close friends, and romantic partners, while media use outside the home often occurs with those with whom you share more social relationships, such as classmates, coworkers, acquaintances, and even strangers. In fact, the influence of relationships on your use of media is even evident when you are physically alone. The most common medium used concurrently with television was found to be the telephone (Papper et al., 2004). Unless the people in the study were listening to recorded messages and not talking with someone else, their use of television occurred in the context of their relationships.

This chapter first explores early views of media and the media audience. We then position the media audience as active consumers of media products who assign unique meaning to media texts and use media for specific reasons. Next, we discuss the relational uses and functions of media, including how media provide a context for relationships, inform people about relationships, and function as an alternative to relationships. We then examine the use of media in everyday communication, looking specifically at the prevalence of media as a topic of conversation, the impact of media in the understanding and dissemination of media messages, and the role of media in the development of relationships and identities.

Focus Questions

1. Why is the term *mass media* inappropriate?
2. Why might audience members be considered active consumers of media?
3. What are the relational uses and functions of media?
4. What functions does talk about media serve in everyday communication?

Is *Mass Media* an Appropriate Term?

Media were originally thought to exert absolute and uniform influence on the lives of "the masses." This view assumed that all media messages were being received and interpreted by members of the audience in the same manner and that they all resulted in the same impact or effect on each audience member. If everyone in your class watched the same episode of a television program, this view would hold that it would be received by every member of your class in the exact same way; the episode would mean the exact same thing to everyone in your class and have the exact same effects on each of you. This belief in the inescapable and standardized nature of media messages has been characterized as the *hypodermic needle* or *magic bullet* capability of media.

Media scholars have now debunked as incorrect the notion of all-powerful media exerting unrestricted influence on a susceptible audience. Media do not exist independently from the cultural, political, and economic systems in which they are embedded (Chesebro & Bertelsen, 1996). Further, media audiences are not passive receptors but rather actively engaged users of media. The classic view of media also overlooked the profound influence of relationships, which play a huge role in the reception of media messages, how they are interpreted, how they are used, and their potential impact on opinion and behaviors. We discuss these issues in more detail later in the chapter.

Before addressing these issues, however, there is another problem with labeling media audiences as *mass* that must be discussed. Although people occasionally use terms like *mass media* and *mass audience,* the use of these terms is based more on tradition than on actual conditions. The term *mass* is indicative of media's ability to reach large numbers of people, an essentially massive audience. However, these numbers are not as large as one might be led to believe. In what follows, we discuss (a) the increased availability of media, (b) narrowcasting, and (c) the creation of unique media experiences.

Increased Availability

As the number and availability of media products have increased throughout the years, a less massive audience is receiving the same media product. Think about the changes in the amount and accessibility of media products that have taken place in the past century. For quite some time, people could choose among three broadcast television stations, which meant that on a given evening, television viewers watched one of three different programs. The hundreds of programs now available on demand with the use of DVRs, webcasts, and podcasts increase the number of available options even more. Radio was once limited to the few stations that could be received with a good antenna. Satellite radio has radically increased the number of channels available, and many traditional radio stations worldwide are now available through live Internet feeds. People were once limited to local newspapers. Now hundreds of newspapers—even international ones—are available online, and many newspapers are digitally reproduced and distributed in multiple cities throughout the country.

While the audience of some media still numbers in the millions, comparing present numbers with past illustrates the dramatic drop that has taken place. The highest-rated half-hour television program of all time is "The Giant Jackrabbit" episode of *The Beverly Hillbillies*, which aired on January 8, 1964, with a 65 share.

Case in Point

Keep a record of how much media you use in a given day. How do you think it will compare to the averages discovered through the Middletown Media Studies? Make sure you record media use as it happens. Do not forget to count concurrent media use as well as exposure to media while in public spaces.

Remnants of this view of media are still evident when people blame television, video games, music, movies, or other media for increases in crime, school shootings, or other tragedies that befall society.

Table 10.1 Nielsen TV Ratings for Network Prime-Time Series: Top 10

Rank	Program Name	Network	Day	Time	Household Rating/Share	Household Audience	Viewers
1	AMERICAN IDOL	FOX	Wed	9:00 PM	13.7/21.0	15,685,000	23,574,000
2	AMERICAN IDOL	FOX	Tue	8:00 PM	13.4/21.0	15,319,000	23,414,000
3	DANCING WITH THE STARS	ABC	Mon	8:00 PM	12.6/19.0	14,430,000	20,278,000
4	MENTALIST, THE	CBS	Tue	9:00 PM	10.4/16.0	11,854,000	16,678,000
5	NCIS	CBS	Tue	8:00 PM	10.4/17.0	11,917,000	16,723,000
6	GREY'S ANATOMY	ABC	Thu	9:00 PM	10.3/16.0	11,800,000	15,546,000
7	DANCING W/STARS RESULTS	ABC	Tue	9:00 PM	9.4/14.0	10,763,000	14,556,000
8	CSI	CBS	Thu	9:00 PM	9.2/15.0	10,589,000	14,912,000
9	CRIMINAL MINDS	CBS	Wed	9:00 PM	8.9/14.0	10,176,000	14,128,000
10	CSI: MIAMI	CBS	Mon	10:00 PM	8.7/14.0	9,979,000	13,718,000

Source: http://tvlistings.zap2it.com/ratings/weekly.html.

This means that 65% of all television sets in use at that moment were tuned to that episode! Current top-rated programs (see Table 10.1) usually average a third of that number.

Narrowcasting

Coupled with and at least partially responsible for the rise in the number of media options available has been an increased tendency to focus a particular media product on specific audiences. **Narrowcasting** is the tendency to focus media products on specific audience members connected by a common bond. These common bonds can be based on demographics, hobbies, political affiliations, occupations, and other characteristics. For instance, a mass audience may not be interested in scrapbooking or model trains, but a small, narrow audience interested in these topics will seek out and use media devoted to them.

To comprehend this media trend, consider the number of magazines being

Four decades ago, Gary Gumpert (1970) introduced the term *mini-com* to describe media becoming increasingly directed and adapted to multiple "small mass audiences" connected through interest in particular content (p. 286).

published. National magazines, such as *Life*—which once boasted huge numbers of subscribers—no longer exist. The thousands of magazine titles now available target specific populations, such as budget travelers, fishing enthusiasts, and Angus cattle farmers. Someday, a publisher may even aim a magazine called *British and Redneck Professors Monthly* exclusively at us!

Creating Individual Media Experiences

Beyond increased media options and a focus on specific audiences, members of an audience have always possessed the ability to create original and distinct media products through their individual and unique use of each media system. As you flip through the channels while trying to find something to watch on television or go back and forth between two or more channels, you create a distinct television product unavailable to people not watching with you. The selection and arrangement of songs on your iPod or MP3 player are distinctive and organized in ways unimaginable by the producers of those songs. Your scanning of headlines and pictures in the newspaper, along with your selection of stories, comics, sports reports, horoscopes, advice columns, letters to the editor, classifieds, and other material, will be unique compared to the experience of any other reader.

The Active Use of Media

As we mentioned earlier, classic views of the media audience positioned its members as passively receiving media messages without any thought, critical evaluation, or resistance. In reality, audience members actively select and attend to media, assign unique meanings to media messages, and use media for specific and often very relational reasons.

Contrarian Challenge

We characterize the audience as active consumers of media. However, can you think of examples where the audience is more passive than active? Are audiences always as active as we maintain?

Selecting and Attending to Media

Characterizing audience members as selective users highlights the discriminating nature of the media audience. People do not consume everything available during mediated experiences; nor do they provide their full attention to the media products they use. When you last visited a news site on the Internet, you probably used some areas of the site and not others. This manner of consuming media is the result of needing only some parts of a media product and receiving greater satisfaction from some parts of a media product than from others.

Selective Exposure

People generally attend to media that support—and avoid media that counter—existing beliefs, values, and attitudes (Zillmann & Bryant, 1985). You are more likely to

Photo 10.1 According to the Middletown Media Studies, what type of media use seems to be taking place? (See page 259.)

listen to radio talk show hosts who support your political views and avoid those hosts who counter your views. A favorite song coming on the radio will likely result in an increase in volume, and a disliked song will lead to changing the station or turning off the radio. As you might imagine, selective exposure research has undergone profound changes through the years resulting from massive increases in the amount of media products available, along with changes in technology, such as recording devices and even the remote control (Bellamy & Walker, 1996).

Attention to Media

In addition to the actual selection of media, the amount of attention audience members provide to media will fluctuate. One reason attention fluctuates is that people often *engage in multiple activities* when using media. Someone on a bus may glance at passing cars or watch other passengers while reading a book. People often talk to one another while watching a television program at home, which decreases their focus on the program being viewed. As we discussed earlier, people often engage in concurrent media use. Consequently, you may listen to music while using the Internet and vary your degree of concentration on one or the other at any given moment.

A second reason the amount of attention provided to media fluctuates has to do with *involvement* with the media. Involvement entails getting into or becoming engrossed in the media product or experience (Biocca, 1988). An example of high involvement is really enjoying and becoming engrossed in a movie and feeling a part of the action. An example of low involvement is watching a boring movie at the request of a friend and mentally formulating tomorrow's to-do list instead of paying attention to the action on-screen.

Commercial breaks may impact your involvement in a television program, but one study suggests that lower involvement is not the only thing that may happen during commercial breaks. People who are really engrossed in a television program will actually respond negatively to products advertised during commercial interruptions (Wang & Calder, 2006).

A final reason for fluctuation in the amount of attention paid to media takes us back to their actual selection. If you *need* the information provided by a particular media product, you will be more likely to focus your attention on it than if you do not. If you are in the market for a new automobile and an automobile commercial comes on the screen, you will likely pay more attention to it than to an advertisement for a product you have little interest in purchasing.

The Polysemic Nature of Media Texts

The polysemic nature of media texts is a fundamental assumption of the active audience approach to media. Words—and all symbols, for that matter—do not have a single meaning but instead are capable of having multiple meanings depending on occasions, circumstances, and how they are used. Media texts, which can include words, visuals, and sounds among other symbolic events, are no different. Rather than having a single meaning, media texts are open to a variety of meanings and are given these multiple meanings by members of the media audience.

A number of factors influence the meaning given to media texts. For instance, one study found that people's understanding and interpretation of television fiction differed significantly according to their cultural backgrounds (Liebes, 1988). An individual's ethnicity, gender, economic status, and other demographic and relational variables will influence how he or she interprets a given media text.

The variety of circumstances in which that person finds himself or herself and why that particular media text is being consumed will also influence his or her interpretation. For instance, a person listening to a political advertisement of a candidate he or she opposes will naturally interpret the information provided in a different manner than if he or she supported that candidate.

Consuming media with others will also impact the interpretation of media text. For instance, laughter from others in a movie theater may lead you to view events on the screen as funnier than you may have otherwise experienced. Talking about media both during the consumption of media texts and after they have been consumed will also influence the meanings people assign to media texts.

The Uses and Gratifications of Media

Research into the selection of media and the attention provided to it, the primary focus of **uses and gratifications** research, has attempted to determine why media systems are used and what audience members gain from their use. Uses and gratifications research originated from the study of radio soap opera audiences conducted in the early 1940s (Herzog, 1944) and grew in prominence during the 1950s and 1960s when researchers sought to determine the effectiveness of media campaigns (Blumler, 1980). Communication scholars James Chesebro and Dale Bertelsen (1996) have summarized the primary findings of this research, as shown in Table 10.2.

Table 10.2 Why People Use Media According to Uses and Gratifications Research	
1. Escapism	To avoid ongoing reality systems
2. Reality exploration	To secure basic information and to understand the world in which one exists
3. Character reference	To find suitable models for one's own life
4. Incidental reasons	A kind of miscellaneous category in which it is recognized that each individual may use or be gratified by media for very different, personal, and unique reasons

Source: Chesebro & Bertelsen, 1996, p. 35.

Exhibiting the importance of taking a relational perspective when studying media, it has been discovered that people have unique motives for watching news videos on YouTube and unique models for sharing them with others (Haridakis & Hanson, 2009).

While uses and gratifications research has provided us with a more accurate and realistic view of media use by an actively engaged audience, it is not without its limitations. Chesebro and Bertelsen's (1996) characterization of incidental reasons for media underscores the major limitation of uses and gratifications research. Essentially, this research focuses on *individual* uses of media rather than *relational* uses of media. Although some studies recognize the use of media for relational reasons, media research in general de-emphasizes these uses of media. However, a relational view of media is becoming increasingly vital as more and more of the world becomes mediated and interconnected in everyday life with relationships.

Relational Uses and Functions of Media

Photo 10.2 Do you think using the Internet as a family will become a shared media experience like watching television as a family? (See page 259.)

While often overlooked in the past, media are increasingly viewed as playing an influential role in people's relational lives. We next examine three key areas in which media enable relationships and fulfill social and relational needs.

The Use of Media Is a Shared Relational Activity

The use of media such as television often takes place in the company of others and for specific relational reasons. Most media—especially electronic media—enable interaction to take place and quite frequently are the actual basis for interaction. Print media, such as books, newspapers, and magazines, are more isolating, but, as Bausinger (1984) reminds us, people are still not alone when reading because "it takes place in the context of the family, friends, and colleagues" (p. 350).

A sense of connection also exists through shared experience with others through all types of media. In the case of television, regardless of decreases in the amount of people watching the same program and the uniqueness of each viewer's experience, still potentially millions of people watch the same material as you at the exact same time. This phenomenon has led Saenz (1994) to describe television as providing viewers with "the feeling of being present at a 'busy' live cultural site" (pp. 578–579). Using the Internet while watching television increases this feeling, with increasing numbers of people making comments and chatting with others while watching a program.

The use of media as a shared relational activity enables people to accomplish certain relational needs. Table 10.3 addresses four relational needs satisfied through the shared use of media.

Table 10.3 Relational Needs and the Shared Use of Media

Promoting interaction
Media enable interactions to take place. Even in media-rich households with multiple television sets, computers, and other media systems, families often use media together, which provides an opportunity for interactions to occur.

Withdrawing from interactions
Media also allow people to withdraw from social interaction (Lull, 1980). Watching a movie is a common first-date activity since it enables people to be together without being forced to talk.

Differentiating relationships
The shared use of media has even been shown to distinguish particular relationships from others. It was discovered that watching television was the most frequent activity shared by spouses (Argyle & Furnham, 1982). Friends and siblings may play video games together more than those involved in other forms of relationships.

Enacting and evaluating roles
The shared use of media also enables people to establish and enact specific relational roles, expectations, and boundaries (Lull, 1980). Participation in massively multiplayer online role-playing games (MMORPGs) has been found to enable romantic couples to learn more about one another's personality and worldview. Furthermore, parents who take part in these games with their children find they are able to develop a better understanding of their child's identity and social behavior (Yee, 2006).

Media Inform People About Relationships

People base their understanding of relationships and their actions within relationships in part on portrayals in media. In fact, scholars have noted that knowledge of the world and of society is increasingly based on media rather than on socialization by social networks (Cohen & Metzger, 1998). Books, magazines, newspapers, the Internet, movies, songs, and television programs feature both fictional and real social and personal relationships, the depictions of which fluctuate culturally and with the passing of time (LaRossa, 2004). Of course, a variety of sources inform your understanding of relationships, and you can compare the information you gain from one source with the information gained from other sources as you develop your own unique understanding of relationships.

Stereotypical gender roles in relationships are also reinforced in media. In prime-time television programs, women tend to fulfill relational roles involving family, friends, and romance. Men, on the other hand, tend to fulfill roles involving the workplace (Lauzen, Dozier, & Horan, 2008).

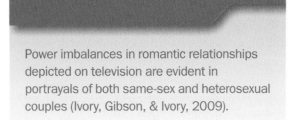

Power imbalances in romantic relationships depicted on television are evident in portrayals of both same-sex and heterosexual couples (Ivory, Gibson, & Ivory, 2009).

Media Inform Us How Relationships Should Look

Media representations of relationships provide information about relational roles and demographic characteristics. Essentially, people can learn about what relationships look like and what to expect from them based on their depiction in the media. The relationships depicted on television are not always realistic, however. People have the ability to compare relationships depicted in media with relationships observed or enacted in their physical lives, but media representations of relationships may nevertheless create unrealistic expectations and beliefs about how relationships should be enacted and what they should offer (Bachen & Illouz, 1996).

Relationships depicted in media do not always look like those that audiences personally experience. Multiple races, religions, sexual orientations, socioeconomic categories, and relationship configurations are underrepresented in television and in all media (Dates & Stroman, 2001; Heintz-Knowles, 2001; Robinson & Skill, 2001). Relationships portrayed in media do not look like most relationships. However, there is a tendency for people to believe that those relationships are normal and that their relationships should be compared to those in media.

Inaccurate portrayals of relationships in media may create unrealistic expectations. For instance, research has shown that viewing romantic genres, such as romantic comedies and soap operas, is associated with unrealistic and overly idealistic expectations about marriage (Segrin & Nabi, 2002). Watching romantically themed television has also been found to influence adolescents' expectations of romantic partners (Eggermont, 2004). In spite of what people may learn from watching sitcoms, problems that families experience are generally not resolved and forgotten in half an hour.

Photo 10.3 The sitcom *Modern Family* is a fantastic comedy that features three families. While diversity exists among these families, one traditional expectation of what a family should look like remains. Can you name it based on this picture? (See page 259.)

Even though media representations may lead to inaccurate expectations of relationships, they may be necessary when people are faced with a lack of models in their physical world. This use of media has proved critical in the formation of sexual identity among gay teens and adolescents, who frequently encounter a lack of physical life models to inform their sexuality (McKee, 2000; Meyer, 2003). Unfortunately, unrealistic expectations about relationships depicted in media may be especially influential in the absence of physical life comparisons (G. Jones & Nelson, 1996).

Media Inform Us How to Behave in Relationships

The second area in which media inform people about relationships is through the depiction of behaviors and interactions within relationships. Depictions of relationships in media provide models of behavior that inform people about how to engage in relationships. This use of media encompasses the **socialization impact of media**. Through media representations of relationships, people are informed how to enact the behaviors consistent with various relational roles and how to properly engage in interactions within these relationships.

Numerous studies have examined the depiction of family interactions on television and generally observed positive behavior and relational maintenance strategies. B. Greenberg (1980) examined television family interactions as either going toward, going against, or going away, as described in Table 10.4. Going toward actions were found to occur with much greater frequency among television families than the other two actions combined. Subsequent studies have found that television family behavior has changed throughout the decades but generally remains positive (Bryant, Aust, Bryant, & Venugopalan, 2001; Larson, 1993, 2001).

While the behaviors exhibited on *The Jerry Springer Show* are frequently based on conflict and violence, even this program has been shown to promote positive family behaviors. Through negative audience reaction to the transgressions and misbehavior of guests, Grabe (2002) has argued that the show actually imparts "frequent moral lessons about the virtues of family life in opposition to promiscuous behavior" (p. 314) and "might contribute to the promotion of traditional family values" (p. 326).

Table 10.4 B. Greenberg's (1980) Types of Television Family Interactions	
Going toward actions	Positive acts of relationship maintenance, such as sharing or seeking information, showing concern, and overall acceptance
Going against actions	Negative acts such as ignoring, opposing, or attacking others
Going away actions	Acts through which a person distances him- or herself from others either physically or psychologically

Source: B. Greenberg, 1980.

Naturally, this use of media is not limited to families or television. All media systems depict a host of personal and social relationships used to inform us about behavior in relationships along with interaction techniques we might employ. Examples include what might happen on a first date, interactions with friends (Baxter, De Riemer, Landini, Leslie, & Singletary, 1985), interactions with annoying coworkers, and even communication between teachers and students (Freedman, 2003). Incidentally, we are still waiting to hear from Dwayne "The Rock" Johnson and Patrick Dempsey about portraying us in case this book is ever turned into a movie!

College Experience

Before coming to college, most of what you knew about the experience probably came from media portrayals. Naturally some depictions of college life are more accurate than others. Describe the differences between what you now know about college and what you thought you knew based on media portrayals. Have you had any difficulty managing expectations and realities?

Photo 10.4 Based on research findings about family interactions on television, what types of interactions would you expect to find on *Family Guy*? (See page 259.)

In any case, people use media depictions to inform them of their own relationships. Like relational roles and demographic characterizations, media portrayals of relationship interactions and behaviors may not always mirror those in people's physical lives (Brinson, 1992), but they provide a vital source of information that people use in formulating and interacting in their actual relationships.

Media Function as Alternatives to Personal Relationships

Media serve many of the same uses and provide many of the same benefits as personal relationships. Needs and desires gained from personal relationships, such as companionship, information, support, control, intimacy, and entertainment, can be gained from media with the same level of satisfaction and fulfillment. In this sense, media and relationships have been described as "coequal alternatives" (Rubin & Rubin, 1985, p. 39).

Notice that the header for this section of the chapter and the description just mentioned label media as *alternatives* to rather than a *substitution* or *compensation* for personal relationships. Researchers have previously speculated that people might turn to media to compensate for a lack of companionship or substitute media when social and relational interaction is unavailable (Rosengren & Windahl, 1972). While this might be the case in some circumstances, media use has actually been found to enrich already satisfied social and personal lives (Perse & Butler, 2005). Furthermore, words like *substitution* imply an inferior entity is filling in or taking the place of a superior reality. As we will discuss, both personal relationships and media are more effective at fulfilling some needs and desires than others, but neither can be legitimately labeled as superior. Media and personal relationships are equally functional and interchangeable alternatives.

Companionship and Relational Satisfaction From the Actual Use of Media

The relational and social satisfaction derived from media comes in part from their actual use and position within the home. Research has indicated that some people think of media, such as television or the computer, as a friend or member of the family (Gauntlett & Hill, 1999). Watching a movie, reading a book, browsing the Internet, playing a video game, or using any other type of media can provide the same amount of relational satisfaction and experience as going out with a group of friends. In Yee's (2006) study of MMORPGs, 27% of respondents named something that occurred during the game as their most satisfying experience of the past week. The same study found 33% of respondents indicated that their most negative experience of the past week had also occurred while playing the game, which indicates people's emotional investment in media.

Cohen and Metzger (1998) have observed that many motives for using media correspond with motives for engaging in personal relationships. These authors have specifically compared social and relational needs surrounding feelings of security, such as intimacy, accessibility, control, and relaxation. In all instances but intimacy, media seem to have the advantage.

Some people may actually prefer the companionship provided by media to that provided by those in their social network. Certainly, on some occasions people would rather use media than be with other people. Think back to a time when you wanted to spend time by yourself reading, watching television, listening to music, or using other media. Whether this use of media served to achieve a sense of companionship or to satisfy another need, you quite possibly enjoyed being away from other people and felt quite satisfied with your mediated experience.

Companionship and Relational Satisfaction From Parasocial Relationships

While media systems themselves can satisfy social and relational needs, many of these needs are met through relationships established with media characters and personalities, known as **parasocial relationships** (Horton & Wohl, 1956). Relationships people form with media characters and personalities have proved just as real and meaningful as those within their physical social networks. People consider and treat media characters and personalities just like they do family and friends who live next door.

When first learning about parasocial relationships, students often consider the concept a bit outrageous and often claim they do not form such relationships. They often associate these relationships with stalkers or those who are obsessed with particular characters or media personalities. However, these relationships are actually quite normal and extremely common. In fact, we are fairly confident that you have formed parasocial relationships with media characters and, at a minimum, thought of and talked about fictional characters as if they were actual people.

Make Your Case

Research indicates that parasocial relationships are just as meaningful and fulfilling as relationships in our physical world. Nevertheless, some people view these relationships as inferior to those in our physical social networks. Make a case for whichever assessment of parasocial relationships you believe is more accurate.

Parasocial relationships have consistently been found to parallel relationships in physical social networks. Some of these research findings are listed in Table 10.5.

Table 10.5 Parasocial Relationships Research Findings

- Similar to other relationships, people are often attracted to media characters and personalities with whom they perceive a certain degree of similarity (Turner, 1993).

- People use similar cognitive processes when developing parasocial relationships and other relationships (Perse & Rubin, 1989).

- People follow the same attachment styles used in physical relationships in their other relationships (Cole & Leets, 1999).

- Parasocial and other relationships provide similar levels of satisfaction (Kanazawa, 2002).

- As with face-to-face contact, parasocial contact has been shown to lower levels of prejudice (Schiappa, Gregg, & Hewes, 2005).

- Parasocial relationships are measured using similar criteria to those used to evaluate other relationships (Koenig & Lessan, 1985).

- Parasocial relationships and relationships with people in physical social networks have been found to follow similar patterns of development, maintenance, and dissolution. When parasocial relationships end (e.g., when a television character "dies"), people experience this loss in much the same manner as they do losing a close friend (Cohen, 2003).

The Use of Media in Everyday Communication

Media frequently provide the basis for conversation in social and personal relationships. While a definitive number of any topic of conversation is unattainable, reports have indicated that anywhere from 10.5% to half of all conversations involve media to some extent (Alberts, Yoshimura, Rabby, & Loschiavo, 2005; Allen, 1975, 1982; S. Greenberg, 1975). Even using a conservative estimation, these numbers position media as among the most frequent topics—if not the most frequent topic—of conversation among people. Discussions about media occur both while people are using the media system and while people are away from the media system and engaged in a number of other activities. Conversations about media serve six important functions in social and personal relationships.

Photo 10.5 What are some things that can happen when a couple talks about media? (See page 260.)

Media Provide a General Topic of Conversation

Media have long been recognized as providing people with a general topic of conversation (Berelson, 1949; Boskoff, 1970; Compesi, 1983; Katz, Hass, & Gurevitch, 1973; Lazarsfeld, 1940; Mendelsohn, 1964; Scannell, 1989; Smith, 1975). Much like discussing the weather, the pervasiveness of media enables people to establish a shared topic of discussion that in many cases will not lead to a heated disagreement. As a general topic of conversation, media play a vital social and relational role. Yet, even when media simply appear to provide a topic of conversation, important social and relational work takes place, and other functions of media talk discussed here are ultimately accomplished.

Talk About Media Impacts Their Interpretation and Understanding

Talking about media significantly affects such things as the meanings derived from them as well as emotional responses and attitudes. You may have previously discussed with others the impact or value of certain types of media, such as video games, television, movies, music, and books. Discussions of media value also involve actual media products and genres. People might tell you they absolutely love a new book just published or tell you about a great website they just found. Although not always immediately recognized as such, these discussions of media have influenced your use and understanding of media in some manner.

A more noticeable influence of discussions of media is their impact on the understanding and interpretation of particular media products. Some discussions of media products serve *directional* purposes, such as explaining the plot of a television program to someone who started watching it a few minutes late or describing what happened in a movie to someone who just returned from the restroom. Other examples of this type of media discussion involve repeating dialogue for someone who missed what was said or walking someone through a video game when playing it for the first time. While these examples usually result from requests for clarification or guidance, other directional media talk is offered without prompting.

Discussions of media often bring about new understanding and meaning of media texts and also of relationships (Babrow, 1990; Fiske, 1989; Hodge & Tripp, 1986). Discussions of plot, characters, or actors playing certain roles can change people's interpretation of a movie or a relationship. A prime example is discussing what you watched on television the previous evening with friends at work or school the next day. Such discussions of media products can clarify the meanings attached, alter convictions about their significance, and adjust levels of appreciation.

Talk About Media Impacts Their Dissemination and Influence

Media do not have an all-powerful role in people's understanding of the world, knowledge, decisions of value and importance, or behavior, but they do play a significant role in the development of people's thoughts and actions. Discussions of media not only aid in the dissemination of media messages but also enhance their impact and are a relational phenomenon.

Even when someone has not watched a program on television, read the latest newspaper, or visited particular websites, discussing these media with others can still spread the information contained within them. You may not have caught a recent video online,

A study found that media attempts to promote breast cancer screening influenced middle-aged women more than younger women, who were more influenced by interpersonal discussions with friends, family, and health care providers who often received the information from media sources (K. Jones, Denham, & Springston, 2006).

but when friends who have watched the video tell you about it, the content of that video has nevertheless been spread to you. Especially with online content and podcasts, these conversations may lead to personal viewing or coviewing (Haridakis & Hanson, 2009). Media information is being spread, and relational connections are being enhanced at the same time.

The influence of media may be enhanced through their discussion with others. Because of the issues of trust and concern inherent in close relationships, information gained from media but conveyed through a friend, a family member, or another close relationship may quite possibly be considered more significant and valid than information received directly from a media source. A magazine article about the dangers of texting while driving, for instance, may not convince you to stop this dangerous behavior. However, a friend may read this article and pass along the information to you. Since this information comes from someone with whom you share a close personal relationship, you may view it as more meaningful than if personally reading it in the magazine.

Talk About Media Promotes the Development of Media Literacy

David's mom likes to tell the story of when David and his younger brother, Kevin, were watching a Bugs Bunny cartoon when they were 6 and 3 years old, respectively. When something outlandish happened in the cartoon, Kevin turned to David and asked, "How did they do that?" David confidently replied, "It's just the magic of television." Perhaps deep inside the recesses of his mind, striving to provide his brother with a better answer may be one of the reasons David started studying communication in the first place—and perhaps the reason he still enjoys watching Bugs Bunny cartoons. Regardless of the accuracy of the original answer, this tale of the McMahan family highlights another consequence of talk about media, specifically the promotion and development of media literacy.

Media literacy entails the learned ability to access, interpret, and evaluate media products. Discussion of media content impacts people's understanding and evaluation of this material, as well as their comprehension of its production and influence. Talking about media with those with whom you share close relationships significantly influences your actual use of media and your development of media literacy.

Discussions regarding the use and interpretation of media, especially television, often occur among family members. Parents and older siblings frequently demonstrate the use of media to young children and guide their understanding of the material both directly and indirectly. Research has indicated that parents greatly influence both what a child learns from television and a child's attitude toward television. There exist both indirect and direct forms of parental influence on children's interpretations of television (Austin, 1993). *Indirect influences* include children's modeling of viewing behaviors exhibited by their parents. *Direct influences* include rulemaking and actively mediating children's interpretations of television content through communication about observations on television.

Of course, the promotion of media literacy through discussions of media is not limited to those occurring among family members (Geiger, Bruning, & Harwood, 2001). Much of what people know about media literacy and their ability to critically evaluate media products has developed from interactions with friends, classmates, professors, coworkers, romantic partners, and others with whom they share a relationship.

Talk About Media Influences Identification and Relationship Development

Talking about media enables people to recognize and promote shared interests, understanding, and beliefs, while also serving to highlight differences among people. A connection or disconnection with others can be based solely on the recognition of shared media experience. Discussions with a coworker about movies both of you have seen may promote feelings of similarity. These discussions are influential not only because they allow people to recognize shared media experiences but also because they allow people to recognize shared understanding of those experiences. Conversations about media experience can also develop feelings of separation, such as when a classmate talks about a band you have never heard before.

While the actual consumption of media can promote perceptions of similarity and dissimilarity, evaluation of media plays an important role in the development of these views. For instance, if someone (like one of our relatives) mentions that his or her favorite book of all time is *The Basics of Communication: A Relational Perspective* and this happens to be your all-time favorite book, you may feel a sense of connection with that person. Someone else may discuss a new website that he or she finds deplorable, but if you enjoy that website, you may feel division or separation from that person. Perceptions of similarity and difference derived from conversations about media can be fundamental in the evaluation of others and can play a strong role in the development of relationships.

Of course, discussions of media content can uncover areas of similarity and difference beyond actual media use and evaluation. For example, discussing a blog entry can lead to the realization that you share certain political views with someone else. Talking about a podcast can bring about recognition of shared interests. Talking with a romantic partner about a romantic relationship portrayed in a movie can provide a sense of how that person views relationships and whether or not you share such views. The topics included in media are essentially limitless, and thus, so too are the areas of similarity and difference that can be explored through their discussion.

Strategic Communication

Consider how discussions of media can engender feelings of connection or disconnection with others. When would such discussions be most helpful?

Talk About Media Enables Identity Construction

Media that you use and enjoy are a significant part of who you are as an individual and play a major role in informing people of your identity. Your **media profile**, a compilation

Listen in on Your Life

Create your own media profile, using the questions listed in Table 10.6 as a guide. What do you think your media profile would tell people about you? Consider how your own media identity is created through talk with others. Do you discuss aspects of your media use and preferences with some people and not others? If so, why do you think this is the case? If you have one, how is this reflected in your Facebook or MySpace profile?

of your media preferences and general use of media, informs others about who you are as a person or at least the persona you are trying to project.

David, for instance, loves watching television, and his favorite shows include, among many others, *The Andy Griffith Show, Family Guy, The Dukes of Hazzard, The A-Team, Married . . . With Children, Night Court,* and *The Golden Girls.* He enjoys most music and especially likes blues, classic soul, Southern rock, alternative music from the '80s, and anything by Eric Clapton and Prince. Thanks to Steve's introduction, David also enjoys listening to the music of Ralph Vaughan Williams but does not care much for Symphony No. 7. His favorite movie of all time, *The Blues Brothers,* is probably responsible for his initial interest in and enjoyment of blues and soul music. He rarely plays video games but tends to be fairly good when he does play them. He never reads fiction (except for the Jack Reacher series by Lee Child) but is a voracious reader of newspapers and academic literature. His Internet use is primarily dedicated to reading these newspapers along with watching television programs and listening to music.

What does David's media profile inform you about him? What does it tell you about who he is as a person, where and when he grew up, his past experiences, and his additional interests and preferences, along with the beliefs, attitudes, and values he might hold?

Identities constructed through media consumption and subsequent discussions are just as meaningful as other identities (McMahan, 2004). In some cases, this identity construction surrounds the actual use or disuse of particular media systems. Some people wish to portray themselves as never watching television, while others may pride themselves on being dedicated gamers. Media identity construction also involves particular media products. These identities, though especially evident among fan cultures (Amesley, 1989; Jenkins, 1992), can occur among all consumers of media. A person may enjoy listening to country music, watching game shows, reading romance novels, or watching action movies, and these preferences and activities become part of this person's identity. Some people may enjoy a particular television program and pride themselves on knowing multiple details about the series. Some people you know may gain pleasure from listening to music acts that few other people have heard of.

Media preferences emerge through everyday communication with others, either through purposeful self-disclosure ("Hello. Nice to meet you. My name is David, and I love watching *The Golden Girls*") or unintentionally through the course of a conversation ("That story reminds me of something that once happened on *The Golden Girls*"). The first example contains a specific reason that David wants to disclose this information, perhaps to create a sense of identification with another fan of the show or someone who enjoys that type of program. Or perhaps the show is such a significant part of David's life that he is disclosing this information to provide a meaningful view of

Table 10.6 Some Questions to Consider When Creating Your Own Media Profile

1. Do you like watching television? If so, what are some of your favorite programs?

2. Do you like listening to music? If so, what are some of your favorite artists and songs?

3. Do you like watching movies? If so, what are some of your favorite movies?

4. Do you like to read? If so, what are some of your favorite books, newspapers, magazines, and so forth?

5. Do you like playing video games? If so, what are some of your favorite games?

6. Do you like using the Internet? If so, what are some of the sites you visit most often?

7. What television programs, music, movies, print material, video games, and Internet sites do you dislike?

8. Do you access television programs, music, movies, and newspapers through the Internet or your cell phone?

himself for another person. David may not have intentionally mentioned *The Golden Girls* in the second example, but it nevertheless indicates to the other person that David is a fan of the show, watches it occasionally, or has seen at least one episode that was meaningful enough for him to remember.

Discussions of media not only enable us to fully enact those identities related to media but also provide an opportunity to construct other parts of the self. Discussions of media have been shown to perform important roles in the construction of age and gender (Aasebo, 2005). Further, discussions of media can provide a sense of voice and empowerment (Brown, 1994; Jewkes, 2002) and allow media-based identities to be constructed, enacted, and displayed while serving a vital role in the enactment of multiple types of identities.

FOCUS QUESTIONS REVISITED

1. Why is the term *mass media* inappropriate?

The term *mass media* implies that large numbers of people receive the same media product, interpret it in the same way, and are influenced by it in the same way. This characterization ignores personal, social, and relational influences on the interpretation, evaluation, and use of media messages. "Mass" in particular implies that massive numbers of people receive the same media product. However, while millions of people may have access to media products, the ever-increasing number of media options has resulted in fewer people experiencing the same media product. Finally, individual audience members have the ability to create original and distinct media products through their use of each media system.

2. Why might audience members be considered active consumers of media?

Not just passive consumers receiving media messages without any thought, critical evaluation, or resistance, members of the audience actively select and attend to media, interpret and assign meaning to media messages in unique ways, and use media for a variety of relational reasons.

3. What are the relational uses and functions of media?
The use of media is a shared relational activity that enables people to come together, withdraw from relationships, and enact specific relational roles. Media also inform people about how relationships should look and how people should behave in relationships. Media function as coequal alternatives to personal relationships through the actual use of media and the formation and maintenance of parasocial relationships.

4. What functions does talk about media serve in everyday communication?
Beyond providing a general topic of conversation, talk about media impacts the interpretation and understanding of media. Talk about media also impacts the dissemination and influence of media, promotes the development of media literacy, influences identification and relationship development, and enables identity construction.

KEY CONCEPTS

concurrent media use   239
media literacy   254
media profile   255
narrowcasting   242

parasocial relationships   251
socialization impact of media   249
uses and gratifications   245

QUESTIONS TO ASK YOUR FRIENDS

1. Ask your friends to estimate the amount of time they spend using media every day. How do their responses compare with the average daily media use revealed by the Middletown Media Studies? If there is a significant difference between your friends' estimations and the numbers discovered in the Middletown Media Studies, why do you think this discrepancy exists?

2. Ask a few of your friends separately to describe their media profile, and then compare their responses once you have compiled a list of these preferences. Do you notice any similarity among their responses? If so, why do you think this similarity exists? What impact would this similarity of media preferences have on the relationships among your friends?

3. Ask your friends how often they find themselves talking about media with other people. What media do they discuss most frequently? With whom do they talk about media most often? How have discussions about media influenced their use of media? How have discussions about media influenced their understanding of media?

MEDIA LINKS

1. Examine how relationships are portrayed in the media. What types of relationships are most common? Do media systems (i.e., Internet, books, television, movies) differ on the types of relationships represented? How are these relationships depicted?

2. Compare how relationships are portrayed in recent media with their portrayal in media from past decades. What changes do you recognize?

3. Visit a newsstand or store that sells magazines and examine the titles available. What does the concept of mini-com tell you about the available collection of magazines? Is the new issue of *British and Redneck Professors Monthly* out yet?

ETHICAL ISSUES

1. Many concerns about media entail the impact of media on children, which has the potential to be both positive and negative. Who should be most responsible for regulating media used by children: producers of media content or parents?

2. Should people base their perceptions of others on discussions of media? What are the limitations or advantages of using these discussions to evaluate other people?

3. Media content is often shared through digital files, used in mash-ups to create new products, and used in fan-produced webpages dedicated to media. Many producers of this content discourage these uses of media and frequently take legal action to prevent this behavior. Do you believe the three uses of media content mentioned above should be considered violations of the law? Do you believe any of these uses of media are less of an infraction than the others? If so, why?

ANSWERS TO PHOTO CAPTIONS

Photo 10.1 ■ It is an example of concurrent media use.

Photo 10.2 ■ Using the Internet as a family appears to be an increasingly common relational experience. Research indicates that over half of Internet users living with a spouse and children go online with others at least a few times each week and an additional 34% do so occasionally (Kennedy, Smith, Wells, & Wellman, 2008).

Photo 10.3 ■ Each family includes at least one child, with children remaining a traditional component of the way many people expect a "family" to look. Each family also has two parents, which further reinforces traditional expectations of a "family."

Photo 10.4 ■ Although Stewie may wish Lois was dead and Meg is not always treated well, many episodes of *Family Guy* feature positive feelings among family members. Television family behavior is usually quite positive.

Photo 10.5 ▪ Talk about media can provide a couple with a topic of conversation, promote the development of media literacy, increase identification, enable identity construction, and impact the dissemination and understanding of the media product.

STUDENT STUDY SITE

Visit the study site at **www.sagepub.com/boc2e** for e-flashcards, practice quizzes, journal articles and additional study resources.

REFERENCES

Aasebo, T. S. (2005). Television as a marker of boys' construction of growing up. *Young: Nordic Journal of Youth Research, 13,* 185–203.

Alberts, J. K., Yoshimura, C. G., Rabby, M., & Loschiavo, R. (2005). Mapping the topography of couples' daily conversation. *Journal of Social and Personal Relationships, 22,* 299–322.

Allen, I. L. (1975). Research report—Everyday conversations about media content. *Journal of Applied Communications Research, 3,* 27–32.

Allen, I. L. (1982). Talking about media experiences: Everyday life as popular culture. *Journal of Popular Culture, 16,* 106–115.

Amesley, C. (1989). How to watch *Star Trek. Cultural Studies, 3,* 323–339.

Argyle, M., & Furnham, A. (1982). The ecology of relationships. *British Journal of Social Psychology, 21,* 259–262.

Austin, E. W. (1993). Exploring effects of active parental mediation of television content. *Journal of Broadcasting & Electronic Media, 37,* 147–158.

Babrow, A. S. (1990). Audience motivation, viewing context, media content, and form: The interactional emergence of soap opera entertainment. *Communication Studies, 41,* 343–361.

Bachen, C. M., & Illouz, E. (1996). Imagining romance: Young people's cultural models of romance and love. *Critical Studies in Mass Communication, 13,* 279–308.

Bausinger, H. (1984). Media, technology and daily life (L. Jaddou & J. Williams, Trans.). *Media, Culture, and Society, 6,* 343–351.

Baxter, R. L., De Riemer, C., Landini, A., Leslie, L., & Singletary, M. W. (1985). A content analysis of music videos. *Journal of Broadcasting & Electronic Media, 29,* 333–240.

Bellamy, R. V., Jr., & Walker, J. R. (1996). *Television and the remote control: Grazing on a vast wasteland.* New York: Guilford Press.

Berelson, B. (1949). What "missing the newspaper" means. In P. F. Lazarsfeld & F. N. Stanton (Eds.), *Communications research 1948–1949* (pp. 111–129). New York: Harper & Brothers.

Biocca, F. A. (1988). Opposing conceptions of the audience. In J. Anderson (Ed.), *Communication yearbook* (Vol. 11, pp. 51–80). Newbury Park, CA: Sage.

Blumler, J. G. (1980). The role of theory in uses and gratifications research. In G. C. Wilhoit & H. DeBock (Eds.), *Mass communication: Review yearbook* (Vol. 1, pp. 201–228). Beverly Hills, CA: Sage.

Boskoff, A. (1970). *The sociology of urban regions* (2nd ed.). Englewood Cliffs, NJ: Prentice Hall.

Brinson, S. L. (1992). TV fights: Women and men in interpersonal arguments on prime-time television dramas. *Argumentation and Advocacy, 29,* 89–104.

Brown, M. E. (1994). *Soap opera and women's talk*. Thousand Oaks, CA: Sage.

Bryant, J., Aust, C. F., Bryant, J. A., & Venugopalan, G. (2001). How psychologically healthy are America's prime-time television families? In J. Bryant & J. A. Bryant (Eds.), *Television and the American family* (2nd ed., pp. 247–270). Mahwah, NJ: Lawrence Erlbaum.

Chesebro, J. W., & Bertelsen, D. A. (1996). *Analyzing media: Communication technologies as symbolic and cognitive systems*. New York: Guilford Press.

Cohen, J. (2003). Parasocial breakups: Measuring individual differences in responses to the dissolution of parasocial relationships. *Mass Communication & Society, 6,* 191–202.

Cohen, J., & Metzger, M. (1998). Social affiliation and the achievement of ontological security through interpersonal and mass communication. *Critical Studies in Mass Communication, 15,* 41–60.

Cole, T., & Leets, L. (1999). Attachment styles and intimate television viewing: Insecurely forming relationships in a parasocial way. *Journal of Social and Personal Relationships, 16,* 495–511.

Compesi, R. J. (1983). Gratifications of daytime TV serial viewers. *Journalism Quarterly, 57,* 155–158.

Dates, J. L., & Stroman, C. A. (2001). Portrayals of families of color on television. In J. Bryant & J. A. Bryant (Eds.), *Television and the American family* (2nd ed., pp. 207–228). Mahwah, NJ: Lawrence Erlbaum.

Eggermont, S. (2004). Television viewing, perceived similarity, and adolescents' expectations of a romantic partner. *Journal of Broadcasting & Electronic Media, 48,* 244–265.

Fiske, J. (1989). Moments in television: Neither the text nor the audience. In E. Seiter, H. Borchers, G. Kreutzner, & E. Warth (Eds.), *Remote control: Television, audiences, and cultural power* (pp. 56–78). London: Routledge.

Freedman, D. (2003). Acceptance and alignment, misconception and inexperience: Preservice teacher, representations of students, and media culture. *Critical Studies—Critical Methodologies, 3,* 79–95.

Gauntlett, D., & Hill, A. (1999). *TV living: Television, culture, and everyday life*. London: Routledge.

Geiger, W., Bruning, J., & Harwood, J. (2001). Talk about TV: Television viewers' interpersonal communication about programming. *Communication Reports, 14,* 49–57.

Grabe, M. E. (2002). Maintaining the moral order: A functional analysis of *The Jerry Springer Show*. *Critical Studies in Media Communication, 19,* 311–328.

Greenberg, B. S. (1980). *Life on television: Content analysis of US TV drama*. Norwood, NJ: Ablex.

Greenberg, S. R. (1975). Conversations as units of analysis in the study of personal influence. *Journalism Quarterly, 52,* 128–130.

Gumpert, G. (1970). The rise of mini-com. *Journal of Communication, 20,* 280–290.

Haridakis, P., & Hanson, G. (2009). Social interaction and co-viewing with YouTube: Blending mass communication reception and social connection. *Journal of Broadcasting & Electronic Media, 53,* 317–335.

Heintz-Knowles, K. E. (2001). Balancing acts: Work-family issues on prime-time television. In J. Bryant & J. A. Bryant (Eds.), *Television and the American family* (2nd ed., pp. 177–206). Mahwah, NJ: Lawrence Erlbaum.

Herzog, H. (1944). What do we really know about daytime serial listeners? In P. Lazarsfeld (Ed.), *Radio research 1942–1943* (pp. 2–23). New York: Duell, Sloan, and Pearce.

Hodge, R., & Tripp, D. (1986). *Children and television: A semiotic approach*. Palo Alto, CA: Stanford University Press.

Horton, D., & Wohl, R. R. (1956). Mass communication and para-social interaction: Observations on intimacy at a distance. *Psychiatry, 19,* 215–229.

Ivory, A. H., Gibson, R., & Ivory, J. D. (2009). Gendered relationships on television: Portrayals of same-sex and heterosexual couples. *Mass Communication and Society, 12,* 170–192.

Jenkins, H. (1992). *Textual poachers: Television fans and participatory culture.* New York: Routledge.

Jewkes, Y. (2002). The use of media in constructing identities in the masculine environment of men's prisons. *European Journal of Communication, 17,* 205–225.

Jones, G. D., & Nelson, E. S. (1996). Expectations of marriage among college students from intact and non-intact homes. *Journal of Divorce and Remarriage, 26,* 171–189.

Jones, K. O., Denham, B. E., & Springston, J. K. (2006). Effects of mass and interpersonal communication on breast cancer screening: Advancing agenda setting theory in health contexts. *Journal of Applied Communication Research, 34,* 94–113.

Kanazawa, S. (2002). Bowling with our imaginary friends. *Evolution and Human Behavior, 23,* 167–171.

Katz, E., Hass, H., & Gurevitch, M. (1973). On the use of the mass media for important things. *American Sociological Review, 38,* 164–181.

Kennedy, T. L. M., Smith, A., Wells, A. T., & Wellman, B. (2008, October 19). *Networked families.* Washington, DC: Pew Internet & American Life Project.

Koenig, F., & Lessan, G. (1985). Viewers' relations to television personalities. *Psychological Reports, 57,* 263–266.

LaRossa, R. (2004). The culture of fatherhood in the fifties. *Journal of Family History, 29,* 47–70.

Larson, M. S. (1993). Family communication on prime-time television. *Journal of Broadcasting & Electronic Media, 37,* 349–357.

Larson, M. S. (2001). Sibling interaction in situation comedies over the years. In J. Bryant & J. A. Bryant (Eds.), *Television*

and the American family (2nd ed., pp. 163–176). Mahwah, NJ: Lawrence Erlbaum.

Lauzen, M. M., Dozier, D. M., & Horan, N. (2008). Constructing gender stereotypes through social roles in prime-time television. *Journal of Broadcasting & Electronic Media, 52,* 200–214.

Lazarsfeld, P. F. (1940). *Radio and the printed page: An introduction to the study of radio and its role in the communication of ideas.* New York: Duell, Sloan, and Pearce.

Liebes, T. (1988). Cultural differences in the retelling of television fiction. *Critical Studies in Mass Communication, 5,* 277–292.

Lull, J. (1980). The social uses of television. *Human Communication Research, 6,* 197–209.

McKee, A. (2000). Images of gay men in the media and the development of self esteem. *Australian Journal of Communication, 27,* 81–98.

McMahan, D. T. (2004). What we have here is a failure to communicate: Linking interpersonal and mass communication. *Review of Communication, 4,* 33–56.

Mendelsohn, H. (1964). Listening to the radio. In L. A. Dexter & D. M. White (Eds.), *People, society, and mass communications* (pp. 239–249). New York: Free Press.

Meyer, M. D. E. (2003). "It's me. I'm it.": Defining adolescent sexual identity through relational dialectics in *Dawson's Creek. Communication Quarterly, 51,* 262–276.

Papper, R. A., Holmes, M. E., & Popovich, M. N. (2004). Middletown media studies: Media multitasking . . . and how much people really use the media. *International Digital Media & Arts Association Journal, 1,* 4–56.

Perse, E. M., & Butler, J. S. (2005). Call-in talk radio: Compensation or enrichment? *Journal of Radio Studies, 12,* 204–222.

Perse, E. M., & Rubin, R. B. (1989). Attribution in social and parasocial relationships. *Communication Research, 16,* 59–77.

Rideout, V. J., Foehr, U. G., & Roberts, D. F. (2010). *Generation M²: Media in the lives of 8- to 18-year-olds*. Menlo Park, CA: Henry J. Kaiser Family Foundation.

Robinson, J. D., & Skill, T. (2001). Five decades of families on television. In J. Bryant & J. A. Bryant (Eds.), *Television and the American family* (2nd ed., pp. 139–162). Mahwah, NJ: Lawrence Erlbaum.

Rosengren, K. E., & Windahl, S. (1972). Mass media consumptions as a functional alternative. In D. McQuail (Ed.), *Sociology of mass communications* (pp. 166–194). Middlesex, UK: Penguin.

Rubin, A. M., & Rubin, R. B. (1985). Interface of personal and mediated communication: A research agenda. *Critical Studies in Mass Communication, 2,* 36–53.

Saenz, M. K. (1994). Television viewing as a cultural practice. In H. Newcomb (Ed.), *Television: The critical view* (pp. 573–586). New York: Oxford University Press.

Scannell, P. (1989). Public service broadcasting and modern public life. *Media, Culture, and Society, 11,* 135–166.

Schiappa, E., Gregg, P. B., & Hewes, D. E. (2005). The parasocial contact hypothesis. *Communication Monographs, 72,* 92–115.

Segrin, C., & Nabi, R. L. (2002). Does television viewing cultivate unrealistic expectations about marriage? *Journal of Communication, 52,* 247–263.

Smith, D. M. (1975). Mass media as a basis for interaction: An empirical study. *Journalism Quarterly, 52,* 44–49, 105.

Turner, J. R. (1993). Interpersonal and psychological predictors of parasocial interaction with different television performers. *Communication Quarterly, 41,* 443–453.

Wang, A., & Calder, B. (2006). Media transportation and advertising. *Journal of Consumer Research, 33,* 163–172.

Yee, N. (2006). The psychology of MMORPGs: Emotional investment, motivations, relationship formation, and problematic usage. In R. Schroeder & A. Axelsson (Eds.), *Avatars at work and play: Collaboration and interaction in shared virtual environments* (pp. 187–207). London: Springer-Verlag.

Zillmann, D., & Bryant, J. (Eds.). (1985). *Selective exposure to communication*. Hillsdale, NJ: Lawrence Erlbaum.

11

Preparing for a Public Presentation

A relational basis exists in all communication, and public speaking is no exception. A relational connection between speakers and audiences is essential to effective public speaking and must be established in the preparation, development, and delivery of presentations.

At first glance, public speaking—in which both the speaker and the audience play active roles based on and guided through socially established norms and expectations—may appear as merely the enactment of social roles. If public speaking were simply the enactment of social roles, a speaker and an audience would be interchangeable—much like a given customer at a fast-food restaurant and a given cashier. However, public speaking more closely resembles the unique personal relationships that you share with your friends, family, and romantic partners in which the people are irreplaceable; that is, if a speaker or an audience were replaced, the interaction would be totally different. Audience members' characteristics, perceptions, and needs will govern what they expect from a speaker, and public speakers must adapt to each audience accordingly.

Recognition of the relationship between speakers and an audience begins with acknowledging the similarities between public speaking and personal relationships. In personal relationships, people seek to inform, understand, persuade, respect, trust, support, connect, satisfy, and evoke particular responses from one another, and such objectives exist in public speaking situations. In personal relationships, people must adjust to one another just as speakers must adjust to each unique audience to satisfy the goals of a public presentation. People transact their personal relationships though communication and create meaning and understanding that go beyond the simple exchange of symbols, and the same transactions occur during public presentations. In this way, what you already know about personal relationships and everyday communication can guide your understanding of public presentations.

It is quite possible that you are feeling very nervous and apprehensive about delivering a public presentation. Even talking about its preparation may be somewhat upsetting. You are not alone! These feelings are perfectly normal and are extremely common. We talk about communication apprehension—the technical term for the fear or anxiety you may experience when speaking in public—in Chapter 14 and encourage you to skip ahead and read that part of the book first if you are particularly worried.

This chapter is dedicated to the *preparation* of public presentations. We examine the groundwork that must be conducted before the development and delivery of presentations. The success of public presentations depends largely on what takes place during this phase of the process. We spend a great deal of time discussing how you can analyze your audience, which will help you determine how to construct a presentation and is what speech texts normally cover, but we go further and teach you how to establish a relational connection with the audience. Also in this chapter, we discuss the selection of topics and the development of a purpose and a thesis for your presentation. We also examine evidence and support material that you can use to develop your thesis, to support the claims made in your presentation, and to connect relationally with your audience. Finally, we explore the process of collecting and using quality sources, often vital to the success of presentations and your ability to connect with the audience. Of course, the one constant throughout our entire exploration of public presentations is the audience members and their relationship with the speaker, and here we begin.

Focus Questions

1. What factors should you consider when analyzing and relating to an audience?
2. What factors should you consider when determining the topic of a presentation?
3. What strategies can you use when searching for the topic of a presentation?
4. What are the general purpose, specific purpose statement, and thesis of a presentation?
5. What types of evidence and support material can you use to develop a presentation?
6. What factors should you consider when selecting sources for a presentation?
7. What factors should you consider when conducting research and gathering material?

How Do You Analyze and Relate to Audiences?

Analyzing audiences and adapting a presentation and its delivery accordingly are fundamental to effective public speaking. As a speaker, you must determine the best way to develop and maintain a positive relationship between yourself and audiences and between audiences and the material.

Ultimately, you must adapt to an audience all elements and components of a presentation—including introductions, sources, types of evidence and support material, organizational patterns, and conclusions—except one very important thing: what you believe and wish to argue, maintain, or claim. For instance, suppose you are presenting a speech about hunting ordinances before members of your community and want to maintain that hunting is necessary to control certain wildlife populations. Although a large part of your audience opposes the hunting of animals for any reason and will likely disagree with your speech, you should not adjust your beliefs to match the audience's and thus present a speech urging a hunting ban. If you suspect your audience will oppose your speech, however, you will likely provide different evidence, organize and deliver your speech differently, and establish different relational connections with the audience than you would if you were giving a speech to a prohunting audience.

You must adjust the speech—that is, how you state your beliefs—to your audience, but do not adjust what you personally believe. In what follows, we discuss various factors that will impact approaches to the audience and provide suggestions and guidelines for developing effective presentations.

Relationship With the Speaker

As mentioned above, you must establish and maintain an appropriate relationship with an audience and base all decisions about a speech in part on that relationship. A relationship with an audience may already exist outside the public speaking context. An audience, for example, may consist of colleagues, supervisors, employees, classmates, group members, or community members, and their preexisting relationships with you will impact how they view you personally and what they expect from your presentation. Identities created in other contexts will influence the public speaking identity created through a presentation, and vice versa. Additionally, the relationships that exist outside the public speaking context will impact the relationship created with the audience through a presentation, and vice versa.

Listen in on Your Life

Think back on times when friends or strangers tried to convince you of something. How much influence did the relationship shared with each person have on your decisions? Did the primary dimensions of credibility influence your decisions?

How an audience views you personally has a profound impact on presentations. A speaker's credibility is crucial to the success of a presentation. The most successful individuals tend to be those who are (a) considered knowledgeable about the topic, (b) trusted, and (c) concerned about the audience.

These characteristics touch on the three primary dimensions of credibility: knowledge, trustworthiness, and goodwill (Gass & Seiter, 2011). Speakers must convey to an audience that they are knowledgeable about the topic, that they can be trusted, and that they have the audience's best interest at heart. Notice that these components are often

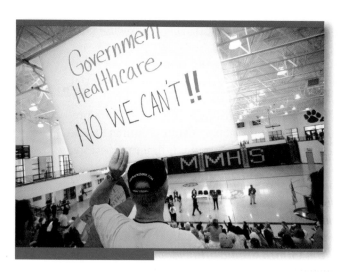

Photo 11.1 If you know an audience will disagree with your position, should you change your position to match that of the audience? (See page 291.)

attributed to those with whom you share a personal relationship. In fact, perceptions of credibility are often based largely on the actual relationship shared with someone (i.e., you trust a person because he or she is your *friend,* or you distrust someone because he or she is your *enemy*).

If the audience has no previous knowledge of your credentials or experience with an issue or perceives you negatively, you may need to spend more time explaining your credibility and developing a positive relationship with audience members. Also especially important, you must provide strong evidence for assertions made throughout the speech along with a clear focus and development of the topic to maintain a strong relational connection.

If the audience members already perceive you as credible and view you in a positive manner, you will be more easily able to establish a strong relational connection with them. However, you still must engage in behaviors that will enable full development and maintenance of such a relationship.

Relationship With the Issue and Position

You must also determine an audience's relationship with the issue being addressed or the position being advanced. An audience may have a positive, a negative, or an impartial view of an issue before a speaker even begins to speak. You must take this existing evaluation into consideration when preparing a speech because it will likely impact how the audience receives the presentation and the audience's relationship with you. If the audience opposes your position, you may have to spend additional time establishing your credibility and developing a positive relational connection with audience members.

If you anticipate the audience will receive the issue in a positive manner, you might spend less time defending and more time clarifying and outlining a position. Also, while establishing credibility and a positive relationship with the audience is always necessary, it will be easier if the audience agrees with the position being advanced. People view individuals whose positions mirror their own as *more* credible than those with opposing beliefs.

You must also adjust your speech if you believe the audience is impartial to the issue, in which case you will probably need to spend more time stressing its importance and its impact on audience members' lives. The audience may not fully understand the issue, so you may need to spend more time describing what it entails.

Previous knowledge of the issue by an audience will also impact a presentation. The audience may be very knowledgeable or have little knowledge about the issue. The level of audience knowledge and understanding of an issue will dictate the depth and intricacy of a speech and what evidence and support material are used, the language used and whether terminology must be defined or explained, and how much time must be spent orienting the audience to the topic.

Audience View of the Occasion

How the audience views the occasion will also impact your speech, including the extent to which the audience desires to listen to your presentation. A **captive audience** is forced to listen to your presentation. Classmates may be listening to your speech because of an attendance policy, or colleagues may be listening to your presentation because your employer has required their attendance. A captive audience does not mean a hostile audience, but you must work that much harder to make such an audience appreciate the value of your presentation and ensure that the audience members will actually enjoy your presentation. It is especially important that you grab their attention at the beginning of the speech and establish how they will benefit personally from listening to the presentation. Though not a definite characterization, a captive audience is more likely than a voluntary audience to have limited knowledge of your topic, which will also increase the importance of making audience members see the relevance of the presentation, bringing them up to speed on the topic in the introduction, and engaging their attention rapidly. The limited previous knowledge may also require you to moderate the depth at which you discuss material.

A **voluntary audience** listens to your speech because its members have personally chosen to be there. This may be because they have particular interest in your topic or a particular need, such as wanting to learn how to accomplish a task, to learn more about your topic, or to learn your particular "take" on it. It is still imperative that you orient audience members to the topic and establish why they should listen to your presentation specifically. While they may already recognize their connection with the topic, you must reinforce their relationship with the material provided. A voluntary audience may possess more knowledge and experience with the topic, allowing you to go into greater depth or use more technical terms. However, you must determine whether members of your audience are there to increase their understanding of the topic or to learn about it for the first time.

Photo 11.2 If an audience listening to these speakers were required to be in attendance, what type of audience would it be? (See page 291.)

Attitudes, Beliefs, and Values

Determining audience attitudes, beliefs, and values also provides a speaker with insight into how an audience may evaluate and respond to an issue and how audience members may view their relationship with him or her.

Attitudes

Attitudes are learned predispositions to evaluate something in a positive or negative way that guide thinking and behavior (Fishbein & Ajzen, 1975). For example, you may dislike the taste of a particular type of food, which will guide your response to decline eating it should a plateful be passed your way at dinner. Or you may like a particular type of music, which may guide your decision to listen to that genre online. Attitudes usually do not change readily but instead remain relatively constant. Generally, the longer you hold an attitude and the more support you discover in its favor, the less likely you will be to change it.

Audiences' attitudes will impact their view of you as a speaker, the topic, the occasion, and even the evidence provided to develop and support an argument. Some audience members will respond more favorably to statistics while others will respond more favorably to examples or illustrations. Similarly, members of an audience will also possess attitudes regarding the sources of evidence. Some may view the Internet as providing unreliable information while others may view it as providing the most current and accurate information.

College Experience

It is possible that in college you may experience greater change in your attitudes and beliefs than at any other time in your life. What changes in attitudes and beliefs have you experienced since starting college? What led to these changes? How might these experiences inform you when attempting to change the attitudes and beliefs of other people?

Beliefs

Beliefs, or what people hold to be true or false, are formed like attitudes through your direct experience, as well as through media, public and personal relationships, and cultural views of the world. Whereas attitudes are evaluations of something favorable or unfavorable, beliefs are evaluations of something true or false. Like attitudes, your beliefs can change, but they are generally even more stable than attitudes.

Knowing the beliefs of audience members will help determine their attitudes, but the value of this knowledge does not stop there. Knowing the beliefs of an audience can also assist in focusing a presentation. For instance, if you are discussing the problem of illegal immigration, the audience may or may not believe that an illegal immigration problem even exists. If the audience *does not* believe this problem exists, you might focus your speech on establishing its existence. If the audience *does* believe that a problem exists with illegal immigration, you may then explore other issues involving this topic.

Knowing the beliefs of an audience will also impact how completely you must support the facts or opinions included in your presentation. Depending on an audience's beliefs, some statements or claims of belief may need more or less support. If claiming that "the Earth is round," you might feel fairly confident that an audience will not look for proof, and unless that statement is critical to your argument, you would not need to include a great deal of support and development. Statements such as that one would be considered a **given belief**—that is, the majority of people in the audience will hold the same perspective of either true or false. However, saying something like "The issue of illegal immigration has been a problem for decades" might require additional support and development since not all members of an audience may agree with or be aware of this statement of belief. In the majority of cases, it is generally best to support all statements. However, knowing the beliefs of an audience will determine how much development should be included and whether or not the audience will agree with a given statement.

Values

Values are deeply held and enduring judgments of significance or importance that often provide the basis for both beliefs and attitudes. The values you hold are what you consider most important in this world. When listing values, people often include such things as life, family, truth, knowledge, education, personal growth, health, freedom, and wealth. Although all the items on this list might sound good to you, people do not agree on their importance. For instance, a person may not view wealth as all that important in life, and not all people believe in the importance of family.

When considering the influence of audience values on a presentation, three points emerge. First, you can use values to form an understanding of audience beliefs and attitudes, and vice versa. However, it is not always possible to establish supportive links between these variables. A person may profess to value health but have a positive attitude toward drinking alcohol in excess. Second, you can use audience values to determine and successfully convince audience members of their relationship with a topic and why they should listen to a presentation. If audience members value family, you can use the impact the issue has on family life to show them the importance of the issue and why they should listen to the presentation. Finally, changing a person's values is very difficult and will take more than a single presentation to accomplish. You might be able to change audience beliefs and attitudes through a single presentation, but values are another story.

Demographics

Demographics are characteristics of a person or an audience that can provide insight into one's knowledge, experiences, interests, needs, attitudes, beliefs, and values. Demographic characteristics of an audience include such things as age, gender, ethnicity, education, occupation, political membership, religion, and place of residence. Demographic characteristics provide generalized information but do not necessarily provide an entirely accurate reflection of any particular person or audience. Just because someone is the same age as you, for instance, does not mean that person possesses the same knowledge, experiences, interests, needs, attitudes, beliefs, and values that you do. However, it may be more likely that people of the same age share some similarities that set them apart from people of a different age. Table 11.1 presents common demographic characteristics that may be used when analyzing audiences.

Table 11.1 Demographic Characteristics

Age

Age may provide insight into the life experiences of audience members and what issues are most important to them. An audience whose members average 55 years in age may be more concerned about retirement issues than an audience whose members average 20 years in age. Age may also impact the degree of change that is possible. As people age, it becomes more difficult to change existing attitudes, beliefs, and values.

Sex and gender

Sex is based on biological makeup, being born with female or male reproductive organs, usually with either an XX or XY chromosomal pair. Gender is a socially created and maintained symbolic concept of femininity or masculinity. Be careful to avoid stereotypical views of women and men, such as being feminine or masculine or as having conventionally gendered interests. Men and women have likely encountered different experiences and different expectations of behavior because of social constructs and demands and not because of personal characteristics.

Education

Education should not be equated with level of intelligence. Still, the level of education of your audience and especially audience members' major course of study may provide information about knowledge of a topic and areas of interest. Accordingly, the education of your audience can indicate the extent to which you must define terms that you will be using, how in-depth you may go in your presentation, and how likely your audience will be to find the information interesting and valuable.

Occupation

The occupations of your audience also may provide information about knowledge of a topic and areas of interest. An audience of carpenters may have a greater interest in a speech about the latest construction techniques than would an audience of accountants. The occupations of your audience can often tell you the education and training members may have had, which will allow you to use information about their education discussed above.

Income

Income may indicate what topics an audience deems most worthwhile. An audience struggling with bills would probably not be interested in a speech about traveling the French Riviera; a wealthy audience would probably not be interested in a speech about cutting grocery expenses. Always adapt a speech to the audience. If presenting a speech about travel to an audience struggling with money, you might discuss ways to save money when traveling. Or you could discuss affordable trips to nearby locations.

Political memberships

The political memberships of your audience may indicate attitudes, beliefs, and values. However, political membership does not mean a person adheres to the entire platform of a particular party. There may be some issues for which there exists strong agreement and other areas for which there exists considerable disagreement.

Religion

The religious affiliations of your audience may also provide information about attitudes, beliefs, and values, but they may also provide inaccurate information. Just as there may be some planks of a political platform not accepted by all members of a political party, there may be some aspects of a religious doctrine not embraced by all members of a religion. Also, be certain to recognize that members of the audience may belong to various religions and that your language and perspective are inclusive.

Place of Residence

Places of residence may provide information about what topics an audience finds useful. Someone living in the Midwest would likely find a speech about what to do in the event of a tornado more valuable than a speech about what to do in the event of a hurricane. Places of residence may also provide insight into experiences and knowledge. Audience members living in the Midwest would be more likely to recognize the destructive qualities and nature of a tornado than audience members living in areas where tornados are less common.

Selecting Your Topic

Now that we have discussed the audience, we can begin to explore your preparation for the development and delivery of your presentation. First, you must determine the topic of your presentation. For some public speaking occasions, a topic or an area will already be established for you. Other occasions may require you to select the topic yourself. Even when a topic has already been established, you often have some degree of flexibility with what you will share with the audience. Coming up with a topic is sometimes challenging, so in what follows, we discuss how to select your topic and factors you should consider in that selection.

Consider Yourself

When selecting a topic for your presentation, the best place to begin is by considering yourself. In doing so, consider your knowledge, your experiences, and what you find important.

Knowledge

Consider areas about which you are knowledgeable. You do not need an advanced degree to claim knowledge about a subject. You may not be a certified mechanic, but you may know how to repair a car; you may not possess a degree in computer programming, but you may know how to develop a website. Many people possess knowledge of particular areas they do not believe others would consider worthy of acknowledgment. For instance, you may have every episode of *The Boondocks* on Adult Swim practically memorized; you may know the story of how your favorite video game was developed. This sort of knowledge often proves very worthwhile and valued by many people.

Experiences

You may have derived much of your knowledge about a topic from your experiences. Just as people sometimes underappreciate their knowledge base, they also underestimate the value of their experiences. Consider where you grew up. Contemplate your numerous life experiences during your search for a topic. Reflect on the jobs you have had. Ponder the activities and organizations in which you have been involved at your school and in your community. Think about your experiences with family and friends. You may consider many topic areas by simply looking at your own life. Selecting a topic from your experiences will also provide benefits similar to those gained by selecting a topic about which you possess prior knowledge.

Importance

Search for a topic that you consider important. Your topic must impact the audience (and your relationship to audience members) in a meaningful way, but it should also be meaningful to you. You may consider some topics important because they have directly impacted your life. Of course, topics important to you are not limited to those that affect you directly. As with knowledge and experiences, do not underestimate the importance of things that are meaningful to you. Selecting a topic you consider important will enhance the overall quality of your presentation, especially when it comes to connecting relationally with your audience and establishing credibility. If you do not consider your topic important and worthwhile, you will not be able to express genuine enthusiasm, and it will be difficult to convince the audience members that you care about them and that they should care about your presentation.

Consider Your Audience

Just as you should consider yourself when selecting a topic, you must also consider your audience. Since we have already talked a great deal about audiences, we will not spend much time discussing them again in this section of the chapter. However, we want to underscore one factor that is vital to the success of your speech.

You must establish a relationship between the audience and your topic. The topic you select must impact the audience in a meaningful way. During the introduction of your speech, you must tell the audience members how the topic affects them and why they should listen to your presentation. Selecting a topic meaningful to your audience will assist you in maintaining audience attention, connecting relationally with audience members, and enhancing your credibility. You do not have to select a life-altering topic. A presentation about a new video game system may not save the lives of your audience members but could impact them in a profound way. Also do not think that you must select a topic they already know is important or meaningful in their lives. Some of the most powerful speeches introduce audiences to a topic about which they previously knew nothing or enable them to view an issue in an entirely new way.

Searching for a Topic

Selecting a topic for a presentation often takes a great deal of time and contemplation. Even after considering themselves and their audience, people sometimes struggle to find an appropriate topic for a presentation. If you find yourself struggling to find a topic, the following four methods can help in your search.

Brainstorming

Brainstorming is a method of gathering and generating ideas without immediate evaluation. Essentially, you just write down everything that comes to mind for a specific (generally brief) period. You do not evaluate these ideas as they come; you simply gather a list of ideas. You also generate ideas, because one idea may trigger or prompt another, which in turn may trigger another, which may prompt another, and so on. So, sit down at a computer or with a pen and paper; select a brief time limit, such as 5 minutes; and then start writing. Before you know it, you will have a list of topics to consider. Once this list is compiled, you can critically examine these topics, singling out some ideas as possible speech topics and eliminating others entirely.

You can use two types of brainstorming when searching for a topic. When **open brainstorming**, you generate a list of ideas with no topic boundary. When **topic-specific brainstorming**, you generate a list of ideas encompassing a specific topic (i.e., Civil Rights Movement). Sometimes, the topic has been derived from an open brainstorming session. Other times, you may have an existing topic area in mind but not know what to examine or the best way to narrow your focus.

Current Issues and Events

When searching for a speech topic, also consider looking at current issues and events. Examining an Internet news site, reading a newspaper, watching a news channel, or listening to a radio program will provide a ready-made list of topics for you to consider. This method would certainly provide you with a recent topic to explore. Even if you do not select a current event or issue, these topics may trigger one you do want to discuss.

Individual Inventory

We previously discussed selecting a topic based on your knowledge, experience, and evaluation of importance. One way to derive such a topic is by compiling an **individual inventory**, or a listing of a person's preferences, likes, dislikes, and experiences. You are a unique individual with distinct experiences, knowledge, and perspectives, and compiling an individual inventory will help you pinpoint your distinguishing characteristics. Create your inventory by providing items for the categories listed in Table 11.2 or any other categories. Completing an individual inventory may provide you with a topic for your speech or trigger another topic to examine.

Strategic Communication

Develop your individual inventory using the model in this chapter. Once your inventory is complete, examine the list for possible topics for an informative presentation and for a persuasive presentation. You may wish to engage in topic-specific brainstorming to narrow your focus.

Suggestions From Other People

Getting suggestions from other people can also help you establish a topic for your presentation. An especially helpful method when speaking to an organization or at an event, asking the person who provided the invitation about past speakers and topics, as well as what sort of topics the audience might enjoy, often provides invaluable perspective on topic selection and the audience.

Table 11.2 Individual Inventory Categories	
Favorite television programs	Favorite food
Favorite movies	Goals
Favorite music	Fears
Favorite Internet sites	Employment
Favorite magazines	Hometown
Last book read for fun	Things you do for fun
Most valuable possession	Favorite classes in school
Heroes or people you admire	Interesting or memorable experiences
Things that annoy you	Qualities that make you unique

Determining the Purpose and Thesis of Your Presentation

Establishing and maintaining a clear goal is crucial to developing an effective presentation, and the first step in this process is the development of an explicit purpose and thesis for your presentation. In this section, we discuss the general purpose, the specific purpose, and the development of a thesis.

General Purpose

The **general purpose** is the basic objective you want to achieve through your presentation. Most presentations are developed to achieve the following three basic objectives: (a) inform, (b) persuade, and (c) evoke. When your general purpose is to **inform**, you want to develop audience understanding of a topic through definition, clarification, demonstration, or explanation of a process. When your general purpose is to **persuade**, you desire either to influence audience beliefs, values, or attitudes or to influence audience behaviors. The types of presentations you will encounter most often and be asked to develop most likely in class are informative and persuasive presentations. Chapter 13 is dedicated to these types of presentations, so we will not spend a great deal of time discussing them here.

Contrarian Challenge

We believe there are elements of all three types of speeches in any public presentation. Can you think of any speeches in which this would not be the case?

Some presentations seek to generate an emotion from the audience. Communication scholars Jo Sprague and Douglas Stuart (2003) use the term **evoke** to describe presentations designed to "elicit a certain feeling or emotional response" (p. 65) from the audience. Textbooks, such as this one, often use the term *entertain* to describe these presentations, but we agree with Sprague and Stuart that this term detracts from the emotional depth that these presentations can achieve and limits them to "fun" only. Evocative presentations can entertain in a traditional sense by providing laughter or escape, but they can also "inspire, celebrate, commemorate, bond, or help listeners to relive" (p. 65). They can elicit happiness, sadness, joy, fear, excitement, reverence, or a combination of emotions from the audience.

Although one general purpose usually dominates, it is fair to say that most presentations contain elements from all three types of speeches. As you explain how to accomplish something, you can use your relationship with audience members to convince them that they must enact certain steps to achieve the desired outcome. You may also entertain or inspire the audience members as you teach them how to conduct each step. As you convince the audience members that something is true, you also inform them of reasons they should believe you. Emotional responses often provide a way of persuading the audience to do something or enact a particular behavior. The overlap among general purposes can sometimes make staying focused as you develop the speech quite complicated. The specific purpose of your speech, along with your thesis, will allow you to focus its development and your presentation of the material.

Specific Purpose

The **specific purpose** of your presentation, or exactly what you want to achieve through your presentation, differs from the general purpose in that it is not a broad objective. Rather, the specific purpose of your speech encompasses the narrow, explicit goal of your presentation and entails the precise impact you want to have on your audience. Developing a specific purpose statement helps ensure that you personally stay focused on achieving an explicit goal though your presentation.

Photo 11.3 What type of speech is most likely to occur at a wedding or another celebratory event? (See page 291.)

The specific purpose statement should include the goal of your speech, and this goal should correspond with the general purpose of the speech. The goal of a speech might be to inform or explain (*speech to inform*), persuade or convince (*speech to persuade*), or reminisce or excite (*speech to evoke*).

> *The purpose of this presentation is to inform . . .*

> *The purpose of this presentation is to convince . . .*

> *The purpose of this presentation is to reminisce . . .*

The specific purpose statement should also refer to the audience to underscore its importance in the development of the presentation.

> *The purpose of this presentation is to inform the audience . . .*

> *The purpose of this presentation is to convince the audience . . .*

> *The purpose of this presentation is to reminisce with the audience . . .*

Finally, the specific purpose statement should include the explicit focus of the presentation.

> The purpose of this presentation is to inform the audience *about the three primary types of financial aid available to students at the university.*

> The purpose of this presentation is to convince the audience *to volunteer with the city's literacy program.*

> The purpose of this presentation is to reminisce with the audience *about Mason Steven's contributions to the revitalization of the downtown business district.*

Thesis Statement

A **thesis statement**, or what you will argue or develop throughout the entire presentation, encapsulates your entire speech. A statement rather than a question, the thesis of your presentation should focus on a single idea. Being as explicit as possible will help guide the development of your entire presentation and sustain your relationship with the audience.

Student financial aid opportunities include loans, scholarships, and work study.

Volunteering with the city's literacy program provides benefits for volunteers and for the city.

Mason Steven's tireless efforts on behalf of the downtown business district have resulted in its revitalization.

Evidence and Support Material

You will use evidence and support material to develop your thesis and back the claims made throughout your presentation. In the next chapter, we discuss the creation of an argument, which essentially consists of a thesis and support for that thesis. Your thesis will be supported by main points, which will in turn be supported by subpoints. These main points and (especially) subpoints will consist of evidence or support material, such as facts, testimony, definitions, examples, comparisons and contrasts, and statistics. In what follows, we discuss the various sorts of evidence and support material you can use for your presentation and then discuss guidelines for their selection, making them particularly relevant to the relationship that you have with each particular audience.

Definitions

Definitions provide the meaning of a word or phrase. Definitions assist in audience understanding and help clarify your topic of discussion. The abstract and ambiguous nature of language often requires you to define terms for your audience. Contextual factors can enable an audience to determine the meaning of a word, and the different meanings may be obvious. However, not all words or phrases are obvious to the audience.

Operational definitions are concrete explanations of meaning that are more original or personal than what a dictionary might provide. This type of definition is often necessary to clarify what you mean by a word or phrase and to focus audience perspective on a particular aspect of that word or phrase. For example, if you discuss *Internet activity,* do you mean all activities taking place online? Or do you wish to distinguish between exploration and use of Internet sites and person-to-person correspondence through e-mail or instant messaging? This distinction could make a big difference in your point.

Facts and Opinions

As you gather material to develop your presentation, you will discover both facts and opinions concerning your topic. In many instances, you will find both within the same article, Internet site, or television news broadcast. **Facts** are provable or documented truths that you can use as evidence to support your claims. "The first broadcast of *American Idol* occurred on June 11, 2002" and "Richard Nixon was the only American president to resign from office" are facts because they can be verified through credible documentation. "Water freezes at 32 ºF" and "Large-mouth bass spawn each spring when water temperatures average around 65 ºF" are facts because they can be proved or demonstrated and verified through credible documentation.

Facts and opinions are not the same but are often used interchangeably, and people often confuse their meanings. **Opinions** are personal beliefs or speculations that, while perhaps based on facts, have not been proved or verified. "Using top water baits is the most exciting way to catch largemouth bass" and "*American Idol* is the most influential television program ever produced" are opinions because they cannot be proved even though many people may find the use of top water baits exciting and appreciate the influence of *American Idol.*

You can use both facts and opinions in support of your presentation, but you should manage them in different ways. As with all types of evidence and support, the facts and opinions used in your presentation must come from cited, credible sources. Since opinions have not been proved or verified, it is especially important that the audience perceive and recognize the source as credible. Further, facts are more likely than opinions to be able to stand alone without any additional support. Above all, a speaker's perceived credibility and relationship with the audience members will influence their reaction to these types of evidence and support.

Comparisons and Contrasts

Comparisons and contrasts are often used to assist in audience comprehension and understanding. **Comparisons** demonstrate or reveal how things are similar, and **contrasts** demonstrate or reveal how things are different. Sometimes used to show trends among concepts, ideas, or objects, comparisons can also establish connections between two items to associate their favorable or unfavorable characteristics. You may, for example, compare profitable yet unstable investment programs with the dot-com industry of the late 1990s in attempts to warn investors of possible risks. Contrasting is frequently used to distinguish something supported by the speaker from something considered negative by the audience. For example, you could contrast a new recycling program for the city with an existing, less favorable recycling program. In all cases of comparisons and contrasts, the audience must be familiar with at least one of the items being connected.

Testimony

Testimony consists of declarations or statements of a person's findings, opinions, conclusions, or experience. There exist three types of testimony: (1) personal testimony, (2) expert testimony, and (3) lay testimony.

Personal Testimony

Personal testimony comes from oneself and is enhanced by one's connection with the audience. Discussing your own experience with a topic, a powerful method of enhancing audience members' perceptions of credibility and their relationship with you as a speaker, often conveys to the audience that the topic has special significance for you and that you possess exceptional insight that can enhance understanding of the topic. While important, your personal testimony is not enough to support an entire presentation. Additional evidence and support material must be included to develop the presentation.

Expert Testimony

Expert testimony comes from someone with special training, instruction, or knowledge in a particular area. If you give a speech about dental hygiene, for example, you may include testimony from a dentist. You must observe certain ethical considerations when using expert testimony. First, make absolutely clear that this testimony is not your own through accurately referencing the source. This action not only prevents you from plagiarizing the material but also enhances the believability of the statements you make. Second, critically evaluate the testimony because your audience may not. People often readily believe testimony from experts because they evaluate these messages less critically than those they receive from someone without perceived expertise in an area. Therefore, as a speaker, make certain that this testimony is as accurate and truthful as possible.

Make Your Case

Research indicates little difference in the influence of the various types of evidence and support material. Accordingly, statistics may be more influential in some situations, and testimony may be more influential in others. Further, the influence of evidence and support material will vary among different people. Having learned all of this and considering only statistics and testimony, which do you generally find most influential and convincing? Why do you favor that type of evidence and support material? How might your choice change with changes in context? What does this tell you about yourself as an audience member?

Lay Testimony

Lay testimony comes from someone without expertise in a particular area but who possesses experience in that area. It comes from a regular person providing his or her experience with your topic. For instance, in a speech about dental hygiene, you might use the testimony from someone who has not followed a proper dental hygiene regimen and is suffering the consequences. Lay testimony can be just as meaningful and powerful as personal or expert testimony, but make sure this testimony is worthwhile and comes from a legitimate source. If your lay testimony comes from an interview, make sure the person you interview is a legitimate source rather than a convenient source, such as your roommate or Uncle Billy-Bob. Lay testimony from your roommate or uncle may be legitimate, but the personal connection may require you to provide additional justification for its inclusion in your speech.

Examples

Examples, or specific cases used to represent a larger whole to clarify or explain something, can involve the concrete or tangible (a schnauzer is an example of a dog) or the abstract or intangible (the ability to vote is one example of the many freedoms we enjoy in this country).

Examples can serve two very important functions in your presentation. First, they can help an audience better understand your discussion and relate to the material. The audience members may not know what a particular term means, and providing an example will help them comprehend its meaning. When using examples, it is important that you select those most familiar to your audience. Second, examples may also help your audience better appreciate or grasp the importance or significance of an issue. Providing examples of injuries suffered by someone abused by a spouse may help the audience better understand the meaning of *domestic violence* and appreciate its dire nature.

Illustrations, or examples offered in an extended narrative form, can enhance the understanding and appreciation of your audience and also help you maintain audience attention. The most effective illustrations use vivid imagery, engaging audience senses virtually through your description of the example. For example, you might illustrate possible difficulties encountered when visiting the financial aid office on campus. Furthermore, audience members often remember illustrations long after they have forgotten other support material and evidence that you provided during your presentation.

Hypothetical illustrations are fabricated illustrations using typical characteristics to describe particular situations, objects, or people, as well as illustrations describing what could happen in the future. It is very important to disclose to your audience that your illustration is hypothetical; otherwise, you are being dishonest and will lose credibility, which can hinder your relationship should the audience realize this deception.

Statistics

Statistics are numbers that demonstrate or establish size, trends, and associations. Consider the examples in Table 11.3.

Table 11.3 Statistics in Use: Sizes, Trends, and Associations

- According to the Surgeon General, 2 out of 3 Americans experience problems with acid reflux—size (frequency).

- According to the *Mayberry Gazette,* 25% of Camden County residents overpaid an average of $570 in local taxes last year—size (scope).

- According to noted economist Jake N. Elwood, the amount of credit card debt accrued by the average American has tripled in the past 5 years—trend.

- The amount of money a person earns each year is related to his or her level of education. An article from *Money Quarterly* revealed that individuals who have earned a bachelor's degree can expect to earn an average of $15,000 more each year than those with only a high school diploma. Individuals who have earned their master's degree earn an additional $10,000—association.

Recognizing and Overcoming Problems With Statistics

Statistics can accomplish a great deal during your presentation, but you must endeavor to use them appropriately and cautiously. While they can be very effective, using them inappropriately can make them equally ineffective. Further, while many are accurate and valid representations, statistics can be extremely misrepresentative. You can very easily mislead the audience with statistics, so do all you can to ensure the relevance and accuracy of the statistics you use during your presentation. Some cautions and guidelines to assist you in the selection and use of the most accurate and representative statistics follow below.

In fact, 25% of all statistics have been made up. OK, we just made up that last statistic, but see how easy it is? While we are at it, 99.5% of all students using this textbook think its authors are handsome. Pity the tastes of the remaining 0.5%! It has also been discovered that reading this textbook in public will make you appear 5 times more attractive to others and increase your chances of being asked out on a date by 55%. We can do this all day long!

Statistics may be fabricated. Sometimes people are dishonest about data they provide. Although many statistics you come across will be authentic, some may be absolutely bogus. Some fabricated statistics have been used so often, they have almost become given beliefs. For a number of years, news reports claimed higher spousal abuse on Super Bowl Sunday than on any other day of the year. Supposedly, watching football makes a person more violent, and since record numbers of people watch football on that day, this results in more visits to hospital emergency rooms by abused spouses. In reality, none of this is true. Someone simply made up these statistics. Using trustworthy and credible sources will help you avoid using fabricated statistics in your presentation.

Statistics and time. Time is often an issue in the misuse of statistics. Compared to other types of evidence and support material, the shelf life of many statistics is especially short. What is statistically true today is often untrue tomorrow. Using dated statistics to describe current situations misleads your audience. Strive to use the most current statistics available, and if you use somewhat-dated statistics, disclose this to the audience and explain why you included these particular statistics in your presentation. For instance, using the amount of pumpkins sold during the month of October in anticipation of Halloween to represent year-round sales would be misleading.

Statistical averages: mean, median, and mode. Statistical averages may not always provide an accurate description. When you selected a college or a major, you may have looked at the average class size or the average number of students enrolled in each class. An academic department may offer five courses with a maximum enrollment of 12 students, two courses with a maximum enrollment of 14 students, four courses with a maximum enrollment of 15 students, and one course with a maximum enrollment of 600 students. If all of these classes were full, there would be 748 students enrolled in that department's 12 classes. This total would result in an average class size of 62.3 students, which, while statistically correct, does not provide an accurate description of the class size of most of that department's courses.

- **Mean** refers to the average number, which may or may not provide an accurate description or representation. The average of 62.3 students in the above example would be the mean number of students.

- **Median** is the number that rests in the middle of all the other numbers; half of the numbers are less than this number, and the other half are more than this number. In the above example, the median number would be 14 students, with half the numbers below this number and half above this number (12 12 12 12 12 **14 14** 15 15 15 15 600).

- **Mode** is the number that occurs most often. Once again using the number from the above example, the mode would be 12 students, since that number occurs most often (**12 12 12 12 12** 14 14 15 15 15 15 600).

Photo 11.4 Using statistics to support her presentation, this speaker is using the number that occurs most often. What is this number called? (See page 291.)

Population and base. Statistics can also be misleading when the population and base are not disclosed. **Population** refers to whom or what a study includes. Such populations as "registered voters" are often provided with survey results. Changes in the population will generally lead to changes in the results of a study. Asking more Republicans than Democrats about their voting intentions to gauge a candidate's popularity with voters as a whole will provide a misleading characterization of that candidate's approval or disapproval among all voters.

The statistical **base** refers to the number of people, objects, or things included in a study. Problems with the statistical base frequently surround the use of a small sample size rather than not including a representative population. The finding that 75% of students favor a tuition increase may sound like

Sometimes surveys are used to promote a rumor and skew results of questions. Consider the possible results if respondents were asked these two questions in the following order: (a) "If it is true that Duck and McMahan Medicated Cream causes uncontrolled itching, would it impact whether or not you use this product?" and (b) "Which product would you be most likely to use: Duck and McMahan Medicated Cream or Wood Medicated Ointment?" The first question accomplishes two different things. First, it promotes an absolutely false rumor about the high-quality and reasonably priced Duck and McMahan Medicated Cream. Look for it in your local pharmacy! It also plants a seed of doubt in the benefits of that product, and this doubt will likely influence how people answer the second question.

a convincing mandate for raising tuition rates. However, such a finding would not be nearly as convincing if it were based on a poll conducted in a single class with 25 students.

Asking the questions. How a question is posed and how an issue is defined can also influence statistical results. Imagine the outcome of a political survey that asked likely voters, "Would you be more likely to vote for the incumbent, who has lowered taxes each year while in office and visits with the elderly each weekend, or the challenger, who wants to abolish Social Security and is rumored to frequently drown baby kittens in the river?" Regardless of a person's attitude toward felines or the elderly, how the question is phrased would certainly benefit the incumbent. Not all surveys are this blatant, but many are quite biased in the ways they present questions.

Using Statistics Effectively

Having discussed some of the problems related to statistics, you should now be aware of some of the pitfalls and consequences associated with their use. Table 11.4 provides guidelines and suggestions for incorporating statistics in your presentations.

Table 11.4 Increasing the Effectiveness of Statistics
• *Statistics should come from a trustworthy and credible source.* Using statistics from trustworthy and credible sources will enable you to incorporate them into your presentation with a greater confidence in their accuracy and legitimacy.
• *Use statistics sparingly.* Do not overwhelm your audience with statistics. When you use multiple statistics in the development of your speech, the audience will find it increasingly difficult to determine what each statistic means and how it supports your presentation.
• *Use statistics that personally involve and impact the audience.* Statistics that personally involve or impact your audience will have the greatest effects.
• *Simplify the statistics.* Statistics should be memorable and easy to process for your audience, and a good way to achieve these characteristics is by making the statistics as simple as possible: Round them to a whole or major number ("more than 3 million" is more memorable than "3,065,453"); present them as fractions and percentages.
• *Explain the statistics to your audience.* Endeavor to make statistics meaningful for your audience. Explain them to your audience, and translate them into terms that the audience will easily understand ("Last year, wildfires destroyed 8 million acres of land. To put this in perspective, that amount of land is 4,000 times the size of this campus and nearly 90 times the size of this state").

Selecting and Using Evidence and Support Material

We must address three additional questions before moving on to the next section of the chapter:

1. How much evidence should be included in a presentation?

2. How important is the quality of evidence?

3. Is one type of evidence and support material better than others?

The Quantity of Evidence and Support Material

You should strive to develop your presentation with a sufficient amount of quality evidence to take advantage of its positive influence on audience members' perceptions of the message and of your credibility and relationship with the audience. No magic number exists as to the amount of evidence and support material that must be included. The impact of evidence quantity will vary according to audience involvement or relationship with the topic. Those individuals not highly involved with the topic will be more influenced by the quantity than by the actual quality of evidence when compared with highly involved individuals (Petty & Cacioppo, 1986). You should not include large amounts of poor evidence just to convince audience members not highly involved with the topic of your speech. Instead, include large amounts of high-quality evidence to satisfy all members of the audience.

Photo 11.5 As you select sources for your presentation, should you limit the types of sources that you use, such as only gathering evidence and support material from the Internet or from books? (See page 291.)

The Quality of Evidence and Support Material

Using quality evidence and support material will enhance the effectiveness of a presentation. This impact is further enhanced when using **oral citations** (O'Keefe, 1998), or references to the source of the evidence and support material used during your presentation. The use of quality evidence will also enhance audience members' perceptions of your credibility and of their relationship with you. Audiences will view as more credible a speaker who uses highly credible sources and as less credible a speaker who uses sources of lower credibility. Naturally, the use of such evidence will hinder the development of a meaningful relationship with the audience.

Case in Point

Visiting the library on campus may not appeal to everyone, and for others it can be somewhat intimidating. However, the more familiar you are with what it has to offer, the better equipped you will be to find effective sources for your presentations and papers. Go to the library and start exploring. Begin running searches for topics that interest you. Always be sure to ask librarians for assistance when you need it. Your library may also offer tours or seminars to help people unfamiliar with what it offers.

Comparing the Effectiveness of Evidence and Support Material

None of the types of evidence and support material discussed in this chapter have consistently proved more persuasive or effective than other types. An analysis of studies examining this area found that statistical evidence may be "slightly more effective" than other types of evidence (Allen & Preiss, 1997, p. 128). This finding

Types of sources include books; dictionaries and encyclopedias; magazines; newspapers; scholarly journals; pamphlets; television, video, and radio; Internet sites; blogs; and interviews.

especially holds true when the vividness of evidence is held constant (Hoeken, 2001). Ultimately, however, the effectiveness of each type of evidence and support material depends on such factors as audience members' attitudes toward the topic (Slater & Rouner, 1996), their involvement with the issue (Baesler, 1997), cultural differences among audience members (Hornikx & Hoeken, 2005), and ultimately their relationship with you and with the topic and the material. Use multiple types of evidence when supporting and developing your presentation to satisfy all members of your audience.

Selecting and Searching for Sources

The quality of the sources used during your presentation will in part determine audience members' perceptions of your credibility and your relationship with them, as well as the overall effectiveness of your presentation. Indeed, your presentation is only as good as the sources used in its development. As you search for material to support your speech, your goal should be finding the most accurate and credible sources available. Table 11.5 provides guidelines to critically evaluate and determine the quality of potential sources for your speech.

Table 11.5 Selecting Quality Sources

Unbiased

You should select unbiased sources—those that provide a balanced view of an issue—in the development of your speech. Most sources slant one way or another when it comes to issues, but some sources may be very obvious and open about their point of view, such as material from prolife or prochoice organizations, gun control organizations, and environmental groups.

Editorial review

You can usually trust sources that have undergone a review process—in which more than one person has determined their accuracy—more than those that have not. Many of the books, journals, magazines, and newspaper articles you discover when conducting research will have undergone a review process. While you can generally be more confident in the accuracy of a source that has undergone editorial review, you should still evaluate this source critically.

Expertise

The sources you use should have expertise in the area examined. Consider the background or qualifications of an author when evaluating the quality of a book or an article to determine if you should consider the author an expert in the area discussed. For instance, while perhaps an expert in journalism, a newspaper or magazine reporter, would not be considered an expert in fitness even if authoring an article about the topic.

Recency

The sources used in the development of your presentation should be as recent as possible. How recent a source should be depends on the topic. Use your knowledge of the topic to determine whether the source has become outdated. Have significant changes occurred in the area that would alter the information available from the source? Does the topic area undergo rapid change and development? Also, consider the evaluation of your sources by the audience. Would your audience view the source as outdated and question its legitimacy and accuracy?

Credibility of a source's sources

The sources and evidence that a source uses in its development can also determine its quality. Carefully consider whether the source you are evaluating includes recent, unbiased material. Determine if the source's sources have undergone editorial review and can be considered experts in the area. If you determine that the sources supporting the source you are evaluating are not legitimate, you should not use that particular source for your presentation. If a source makes claims without any form of support, you should question the legitimacy of that source.

Credibility for your audience

Keep in mind that your audience will evaluate and use the types of sources you use in a presentation to determine the accuracy of the evidence supplied, the value of your presentation, and your credibility as a speaker. Your audience may judge certain types of sources as more worthwhile and accurate than others.

Searching for material to support and to develop your speech can sometimes be a challenging process, especially when someone is relatively new to the process. Table 11.6 provides some guidelines and suggestions to follow when conducting research and gathering material.

Table 11.6 Guidelines for Conducting Research and Gathering Material

Start early

One of the biggest mistakes you can make when conducting research is waiting until the last minute. Delaying the collection of support material will impede the actual development of the speech and limit the amount of time available to practice the delivery of your presentation.

Use multiple types of sources

It is best to use multiple types of sources when developing your research. Including multiple sources will enable you to satisfy the various preferences of the audience and to ensure the thoroughness of your research.

Go to the library

You will need to actually go to the library to conduct adequate research for your presentation. A great deal of material is available online, but more material is still physically available at the library itself.

Use multiple search engines and databases

When conducting searches, you should use multiple search engines and databases. While there are some very powerful search engines and databases available, none are complete. Many are dedicated to particular topics or areas, which will allow you to conduct a more thorough and efficient search. Using multiple search engines and databases will enable you to conduct the most complete search for materials.

(Continued)

Table 11.6 (Continued)

Do not read everything

As you review potential sources, do not feel as if you have to read all of these pieces in their entirety. A quick but conscientious review of the material will help you determine whether or not you should examine it in more detail. Reviewing a book's index to pinpoint particular information will help establish its potential usefulness, as will reading abstracts or key sections of journal articles, magazines, or other periodicals. However, you will have to read the material in more detail once you determine it will be used.

Take notes as you proceed

You should take notes as you conduct your search for information to find the information later and to ensure the accurate citation of material. When you have examined multiple sources, it is easy to forget where particular evidence and support material originated.

Pay attention to the citations of others

Regardless of how thorough your search may be or how expansive your search engine may be, it is impossible to discover every available source related to your topic. The reference sections of the material you do find provide ready-made lists of potential sources that can be used for your presentation. Just because a source has been previously used by someone else does not mean that it cannot be used by you. However, you must actually locate and read these other sources on your own.

Engage in multiple searches and trips to the library

Conducting research is not something that should be done all at one time. It would be unwise to think that a single trip to the library will enable you to conduct a thorough search for sources and provide all the material you need. Conducting adequate research requires multiple searches and multiple trips to the library.

Eventually you must develop your presentation

While you must conduct a thorough search of the material and there will always be additional sources that you can find, you will eventually have to start developing and then practicing your presentation. Especially keep this in mind if you are particularly nervous about speaking in public. Such speakers often spend more time than necessary conducting research and less time developing the speech for a particular audience and practicing the presentation (Ayres, 1996).

FOCUS QUESTIONS REVISITED

1. What factors should you consider when analyzing and relating to an audience?
When analyzing an audience, you should consider audience members' relationship with you, their relationship with the topic, and their view of the occasion. You may also consider audience attitudes, beliefs, and values as well as demographic characteristics.

2. What factors should you consider when determining the topic of a presentation?
Some occasions may warrant a particular topic, or a topic may already be selected for you. On occasions when you must select your own topic, consider yourself and the audience.

3. What strategies can you use when searching for the topic of a presentation?
When searching for a topic for a presentation, you can brainstorm, examine current issues and events, create an individual inventory, and gather input from others.

4. What are the general purpose, specific purpose statement, and thesis of a presentation?

The general purpose is the basic objective you want to achieve through your presentation. Most presentations are developed to achieve the following three basic objectives: (a) inform, (b) persuade, and (c) evoke. The specific purpose of your presentation is exactly what you want to achieve through your presentation. A thesis statement, or what you will argue or develop throughout the entire presentation, encapsulates your entire speech.

5. What types of evidence and support material can you use to develop a presentation?

You can use definitions, facts and opinions, comparisons and contrasts, testimony, examples, and statistics as evidence and support material to develop a presentation.

6. What factors should you consider when selecting sources for a presentation?

As you critically evaluate and determine the quality of a source, determine whether it is unbiased and whether it has undergone editorial review. You should ensure that sources have the proper expertise and experience, determine the recency of a source and the credibility of its sources, and, above all, determine audience evaluation of the source.

7. What factors should you consider when conducting research and gathering material?

When conducting research and gathering material, you should start early, use multiple types of sources, go to the library, use multiple search engines and databases, not read everything, take notes, pay attention to citations, engage in multiple searches and trips to the library, and eventually start writing.

KEY CONCEPTS

QUESTIONS TO ASK YOUR FRIENDS

1. What types of evidence and support material do your friends find most convincing? Which of this material do they find least convincing? Do their evaluations change depending on circumstances or what is discussed?

2. What types of sources do your friends find most convincing? Which sources do they find least convincing? Once again, do their evaluations change depending on circumstances or what is discussed?

3. Ask your friends to think about two people whom they consider to be very different. If they wanted to try to convince each person of the same idea, how would they have to adjust their strategy with each one? What does this tell you about the need to adapt your presentations to particular audiences?

MEDIA LINKS

1. Scan a newspaper for articles that include examples of evidence and support material. What types of this material are most prevalent? Do you find these articles convincing? To what extent do you believe your evaluation is based on the evidence and support material provided?

2. Gather examples of sources used in media that you consider *credible*. Now gather examples of sources used in media that you do not consider credible. Explain why you evaluated these sources in the manner that you did.

3. Gather examples of sources used in media that you consider *biased*. Now gather examples of sources used in media that you do not consider biased. Explain why you evaluated these sources in the manner that you did.

ETHICAL ISSUES

1. Taking concerns of privacy into account, what limitations would you place on audience analysis? To what lengths do you think a person is justified in going when gathering information about people for use in the development of a presentation?

2. Organizations and administrations sometimes misrepresent statistics, facts, and other types of evidence and support material for what they would consider the "greater good." Do you consider this use of evidence and support material justified? How would you support your response?

3. Graphic images are sometimes used as presentation aids to shock an audience. To what extent should a speaker be held responsible for such images? Do you consider the use of these images justified? How would you support your response?

ANSWERS TO PHOTO CAPTIONS

Photo 11.1 ■ No. You should adapt all elements of a presentation to a specific audience except the position you intend to argue.

Photo 11.2 ■ An audience required to be in attendance is known as a captive audience.

Photo 11.3 ■ Most likely to occur at a wedding or another celebratory event is a speech to evoke.

Photo 11.4 ■ Mode is the number that occurs most often.

Photo 11.5 ■ No. You should use a variety of sources to ensure thorough research has been conducted and to satisfy multiple members of the audience.

STUDENT STUDY SITE

Visit the study site at **www.sagepub.com/boc2e** for e-flashcards, practice quizzes, journal articles and additional study resources.

REFERENCES

Allen, M., & Preiss, R. W. (1997). Comparing the persuasiveness of narrative evidence using meta-analysis. *Communication Research Reports, 14*, 125–131.

Ayres, J. (1996). Speech preparation processes and speech apprehension. *Communication Education, 45*, 228–235.

Baesler, E. J. (1997). Persuasive effects of story and statistical evidence. *Argumentation and Advocacy, 33*, 170–175.

Fishbein, M., & Ajzen, I. (1975). *Belief, attitude, intention, and behavior: An introduction to theory and research.* Reading, MA: Addison-Wesley.

Gass, R. H., & Seiter, J. S. (2011). *Persuasion, social influence, and compliance gaining* (4th ed.). Boston: Allyn & Bacon.

Hoeken, H. (2001). Anecdotal, statistical, and causal evidence: Their perceived and actual persuasiveness. *Argumentation, 15*, 425–237.

Hornikx, J., & Hoeken, H. (2005, May). *The influence of culture on the relative persuasiveness of anecdotal, statistical, causal, and expert evidence.* Paper presented to the International Communication Association Annual Conference, New York.

O'Keefe, D. J. (1998). Justification explicitness and persuasive effect: A meta-analytic review of the effects of varying support articulation in persuasive messages. *Argumentation and Advocacy, 35*, 61–75.

Petty, R. E., & Cacioppo, J. T. (1986). *Communication and persuasion: Central and peripheral routes to attitude change.* New York: Springer-Verlag.

Slater, M. D., & Rouner, D. (1996). Value-affirmative and value-protective processing of alcohol education messages that include statistical evidence or anecdotes. *Communication Research, 23*, 210–235.

Sprague, J., & Stuart, D. (2003). *The speaker's handbook.* Belmont, CA: Wadsworth/ Thomson Learning.

12

Developing a Public Presentation

I n the previous chapter, we discussed how you select a topic, determine the purpose and thesis of your speech, and gather support material, and we showed how you must accomplish all of these activities with your relationship to your audience in mind. At this point in the speech development process, you know its purpose and what you want to argue. You even have support material to back up your claims. However, public speakers cannot just haphazardly throw around a thesis statement, statistics, quotations, illustrations, and other support material. They must combine and organize their material and package it in a manner that will have the greatest impact on a particular audience. They must also develop the material in a way that further connects them relationally to the needs and desires of an audience. Developing and presenting a speech to an audience is not just logical but relational. A speaker must connect with an audience, motivate its members to listen, present a well-argued case, and conclude with a logical and relational uplift.

In this chapter, we talk about developing an argument in that relational context. Argumentation is not just another word for *disagreement* but a careful way of laying out your thoughts. Something you engage in every day, developing an argument is not as unfamiliar as it may seem. This discussion will assist you when developing your speeches and when writing papers for this class and others. Talk about more bang for your academic buck!

Inherent in the development of a public presentation is the continued enactment of a relational connection with an audience. Having previously established the purpose of the presentation to meet audience needs and desires, you must organize your support material for your audience in a clear and understandable way that exhibits your ability to satisfy these needs and desires. You can select from several strategies (or patterns) to organize your material. We discuss ways of selecting the best organizational pattern for your speech based on your topic, the purpose of your speech, and, of course, the audience. Clear organization of an argument results in audience understanding and increased audience liking of the speaker.

The introduction and conclusion of your presentation also enact the relational connection with your audience. These parts of your speech, just as important as its body, must accomplish a great deal. Within the introduction, you must establish credibility and a relationship with your specific audience, stress the importance of the topic (i.e., how it relates to the audience), and prepare your audience for the remainder of the speech, using the same skills, techniques, and ways of relating to your audience discussed in the previous chapter. This relational connection continues when you reach the conclusion, in which you must reinforce your thesis and purpose, summarize your material, stress audience involvement, and provide adequate closure. While both introductions and conclusions include a lot of material, we break them down into manageable components to help you better understand and develop them. In addition, you should not write your introduction or conclusion until you have finished the body of your speech, so we begin by discussing that part of your presentation.

Focus Questions

1. What are the four principles of speech organization and development?
2. What organizational patterns can you use in the development of the speech body?
3. What components must you include in a speech introduction?
4. What components must you include in a speech conclusion?

The Body: How Do You Develop an Argument?

The **body** of your speech is where you develop and present your argument. When we talk about arguments and argumentation, we do not necessarily mean disagreeing with someone or engaging in a heated discussion. Rather, an argument is presented when you provide a thesis or claim and then back it up with evidence and support material discussed in the previous chapter.

Providing claims and then support for those claims is actually something you do quite often. Whenever you try to convince a friend to do something, or whenever you explain or describe something to a colleague, you are essentially engaged in argumentation. For example, you may find yourself with a group of friends trying to decide what to do on a Friday evening. You really want to see a particular movie, so you tell your friends that you should all go to the theater and watch this movie. You might then describe the movie and provide reasons you should all go see it. Whether you realize it or not, you are engaging in a form of argumentation. Your thesis or claim is that you should all go to the movie. Your support comes from the various reasons your friends should do what you suggest—the movie has received favorable reviews, the theater is not very far away, and nothing tastes better than a $50 box of popcorn. So, while developing an argument might sound like an unfamiliar task, the basic ideas behind the process are nothing new. The primary difference between constructing an argument for an academic, civic, or professional setting and presenting an argument to friends, family, or romantic partners is that the former is generally more structured and has undergone more development and planning.

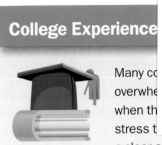

College Experience

Many co overwhe when th stress t a clear argument in their speeches or papers. Developing an argument is not always taught or required in high school, yet suddenly students are expected to know how to do it as soon as they enter college. If you feel stressed out by these demands, rest assured that you are not alone. Even better, once you finish this chapter, you will know how to do it!

Principles of Speech Organization and Development

To better describe how to construct the body of your speech and develop your argument, we discuss the four principles of speech organization and development that can help you maintain a clear focus: points, unity, balance, and guidance. The first three principles underscore the logical development of an argument, and the final principle emphasizes relational development. You must adhere to all four principles to properly develop a presentation and to fully connect with an audience.

Points Principle

The **points principle** highlights the basic building blocks of an argument: the main points and subpoints. The body of your speech will include **main points**, or statements that directly support or develop your thesis statement. As a general rule, include five main points at the absolute most. Ideally, you should include at least two but no more than three main points when supporting or developing your thesis statement. Including too many main points will make it difficult to provide adequate support and development.

Subpoints, or statements that support and explain the main points of your speech, will include much of the support material we discussed in the previous chapter. The actual number of subpoints you include to support each main point will vary. Similar to limiting the number of main points, you do not want to overwhelm your audience with too many subpoints. Including a limited number of strong subpoints to support a main idea is more effective than including numerous weak ones.

Being able to visualize the construction of an argument is sometimes helpful, which is one of the reasons your instructor may have you develop an outline for presentations you deliver in the classroom. While not an actual outline, Figure 12.1 will help you visualize the structure of an argument.

Thesis

Main point 1 supporting thesis
Subpoint supporting main point 1
Subpoint supporting main point 1
Subpoint supporting main point 1
Subpoint supporting main point 1

Main point 2 supporting thesis
Subpoint supporting main point 2
Subpoint supporting main point 2
Subpoint supporting main point 2
Subpoint supporting main point 2

Main point 3 supporting thesis
Subpoint supporting main point 3
Subpoint supporting main point 3
Subpoint supporting main point 3
Subpoint supporting main point 3

Figure 12.1 Visualizing the structure of an argument

Unity Principle

The **unity principle** maintains you should stay focused and provide only information that supports your thesis and main points. This principle sounds reasonable and easy to follow, but speakers often struggle to abide by it. As you conduct research for your speech, you will come across a wealth of information about your topic. You can use some of this material to support your thesis and include some of it in your presentation. Other material, while related to your topic, will not directly support your thesis or main points and should therefore not be included.

The most obvious example of not adhering to the principle of speech unity involves the selection of main points that do not support the thesis. For instance, imagine you are presenting a speech in which you want to inform the audience about the treatments of a particular disease. In your first main point, you address one common type of treatment. In your second main point, you address another common type of treatment. In your third main point, you suddenly shift gears and begin discussing common symptoms of this disease. While the matter of symptoms associated with this disease is naturally associated with your topic, your speech is supposed to be about the treatment of the disease. You have not followed the principle of speech unity.

You might be thinking, "Wait a second. If I were telling my audience about the treatment of a disease, why would I not want to talk about the symptoms?" Depending on your audience, addressing the symptoms might be important; however, your main argument involves the treatments associated with this disease. Including anything else in the body of your speech will prevent you from fully explaining the treatments, what you set out to do in the first place. If you think it is important to let the audience know the symptoms associated with this disease, you can briefly discuss them in the introduction of your speech. We discuss introductions later in the chapter and, during something called *orientation to the topic*, specifically address such instances as the preceding, so stay tuned!

Balance Principle

The **balance principle** maintains that the points of the body must be relatively equal in scope and importance. You must devote to them equal time and an equal amount of development and support. Your main points, as well as the subpoints

Photo 12.1 This speaker is providing members of her audience with a clear transition between sections of her speech in order to help them better understand the presentation. Which principle of speech organization and development emphasizes the relational development of a presentation? (See page 316.)

supporting them, must also be equally important in their support of your thesis.

One common violation of the principle of balance involves the amount of time and support you devote to a particular main point. Suppose you have three main points in your speech. You have discovered a lot of material to support and develop your first main point, so you spend most of your time discussing it. When it comes to your second and third main points, you have not found as much support material or have not found them as interesting, so you devote less attention to them during your speech. While you have done an excellent job explaining and supporting your first main point, your other main points are not developed enough to support your thesis. Regardless of its strength, that first main point will not sufficiently support your thesis. Make sure to spend relatively equal time developing and discussing your main points (O'Hair, Stewart, & Rubenstein, 2001).

Guidance Principle

The **guidance principle** maintains a speaker must guide and direct the audience throughout the entire speech. Fundamental to the effectiveness of a speech are audience members' understanding and establishing a strong relational connection with them. Guiding them through a speech helps ensure that audience members comprehend the support provided and recognize and understand how it supports your thesis. Guiding the audience members throughout the presentation will also enhance your credibility and relational connection with them, because it indicates your true concern for their understanding of your presentation as you construct the identity of a speaker who cares for the audience. Just as you help guide and support your friends through difficult problems when they need your direction and advice, you must guide your audience through the logic of your presentation. We talk about components of the introduction and conclusion that help guide the audience later in the chapter, but here we address the use of transitions.

Transitions, or phrases or statements that serve to connect the major parts or sections of the speech and to guide the audience through the presentation, should be included between the introduction and the body of the speech, between each main point, and between the body of the speech and the conclusion. These transitions should guide the audience members and inform them of where you are, where you have been, and/or where you are going in the speech. Examples of transitions include the following:

To begin, let's examine the issue of . . .

Now that we have talked about X, let's turn our attention to the matter of Y.

The first item we must consider is . . .

This brings us to our second issue . . .

The examples provided here might differ from transitions you have studied in English or writing classes. When taught about transitions in those courses, you were probably instructed that they guide the reader and set up the next paragraph or section of the paper or story. Transitions included in written work and transitions included in oral presentations are very similar. The key difference between them is that transitions included in oral work must be more obvious than those included in written work, and they must fully direct the audience through the speech.

To really grasp the need for such explicit transitions and the importance of the guidance principle in general, consider the difference between reading an article or a book and listening to a speech. When reading, you have the ability to reread a paragraph or section. You can flip back a few pages and remind yourself of what came before. You can scan ahead to see what comes next. When you listen to a speech, you do not have these luxuries. As a speaker, you must be aware of this limitation of the medium and fully guide the audience throughout the entire speech. You must maintain your relationship with the audience members by acting as their page turner or reviewer, constantly helping them recognize and remember the key points.

Having talked about principles of speech organization, we can now discuss the variety of organizational patterns you can use to structure the presentation of your claims and support.

Strategic Communication

Consider how the act of reading is similar to and different from listening to a public presentation. In addition to transitions, what do these similarities and differences tell you about the needs of a listening audience? Compile a list of strategies based on your responses that you could implement as a public speaker to assist your audience.

Organizational Patterns

As we discussed with the principles of speech organization and development, the most effective speeches are focused, ordered, and understood by the audience. Consider how difficult even your friends might find it to follow and understand a story that offers main points at random. So too with an audience: One would have trouble following a speech where evidence, such as statistics, testimony, and examples, is simply scattered about. Members of the audience would find it very difficult to comprehend the material, and therefore, you would have a very difficult time successfully achieving the purpose of your speech and constructing a positive relationship with the audience. You must arrange the speech in a way that will allow the audience to clearly grasp the material and that will most effectively achieve your purpose.

An **organizational pattern** is an arrangement of the main points that best enables audience comprehension. Some organizational patterns are more effective for certain types of speeches and audiences than for others, and the following discussion covers various organizational patterns you may choose and when they might be most appropriate given the circumstances surrounding your speech.

Chronological Pattern

When using the **chronological pattern**, you arrange the main points according to their position in a time sequence. Often selected when explaining a process to the audience, this pattern conveys a sense of development, either forward or backward depending on your topic and purpose. For example, you may explain the process of passing legislation through Congress:

1. First, legislation is introduced and sent to the appropriate committee.

2. Second, legislation is debated and voted on by both the House of Representatives and the Senate.

3. Finally, legislation undergoes additional committee discussion and approval before being submitted to the president.

Spatial Pattern

In the **spatial pattern**, the main points are arranged according to their physical relation, such as from left to right, top to bottom, north to south, or forward to backward. For instance, you may describe the layout of a new building on campus using this pattern:

1. The bottom floor of the new student union building will feature the bookstore and a food court.

2. The second floor of the new student union building will house student organization offices.

3. The third floor of the new student union building will include additional classrooms and a technology lab.

Causal Pattern

When a **causal pattern** is used to organize the body of a speech, the main points are arranged according to cause and effect. The order in which you choose to place these two matters will depend on your purpose, topic, and audience. This pattern works best when you are attempting to explain to members of an audience or convince them that one thing causes another. For example, you could use the causal pattern to discuss the impact of capital gains taxes on investment and development:

1. There has been a steady increase in the amount of capital gains taxes.

2. Small-business investing and development have substantially decreased in recent years.

Fundamental to the causal pattern is convincing the audience that a definite link exists between what you classify as a cause and what you claim are its effects. In the above example, you would have to convince the audience that the decrease in investments and development was the primary result of increased capital gains and not the result of federal guidelines, interest rates, global investments, or a host of other factors. A causal pattern sometimes proves challenging for speakers to use effectively. When using this pattern, make sure you provide a clear connection between your cause and its effects.

Question–Answer Pattern

Using the **question–answer pattern** involves posing questions an audience may have about a subject and then answering them in a manner that favors your position (Gronbeck, German, Ehninger, & Monroe, 1995). When selecting which questions to include, make sure they are important to the audience and not just the easiest to answer in a way that supports your stance. You will likely use this pattern when addressing a voluntary audience with concerns about an issue (Chapter 11). For instance, you may address a community group with questions about the impact of a particular city project. This organizational pattern may also be appropriate when speaking to your fellow students about issues on campus. For example, if you deliver a speech about possible tuition increases, arranging your main points in a question–answer format might be effective:

1. The major question students are asking is, "Why is this tuition increase necessary?"

2. A second common question among students is, "Can we expect similar increases over the next few years?"

3. Students are also wondering, "How will this tuition increase affect grants, scholarships, and other financial assistance?"

Topical Pattern

The **topical pattern** arranges support material according to specific categories, groupings, or grounds. At times, the order of your assertions may follow a natural progression. In the next example, when discussing available scholarships with your audience, you could begin with the scholarship offering the least amount of money and progress to the one offering the largest amount of money:

1. The Caton Scholarship pays for half of tuition for the entire academic year.

2. The McNeece Scholarship pays for full tuition for the entire academic year.

3. The Cutter Scholarship pays for full tuition for the entire academic year plus full room and board for the recipient.

Other times, the order in which each main point in a topical pattern is presented does not really matter. For instance, you may provide your audience with reasons for a spike in medication prices:

1. Additional research and development by pharmaceutical companies have increased the price of medication.

2. Increased demand for different medications has led to an increase in their prices.

3. Federal legislation has resulted in the increased price of medication.

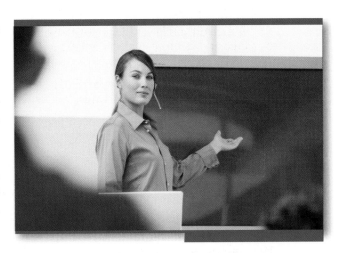

Although in a topical pattern the main points may not always follow a natural progression, do not place your main points at random without any thought or consideration. When using the topical pattern, you might use one main point to prepare the audience for another and should therefore address it first.

Problem–Solution and Elimination Patterns

We discuss the final two organizational patterns somewhat in tandem to emphasize the importance of considering the audience when selecting which pattern to use in the organization of your speech. First, the **problem–solution pattern** divides the body of the speech by first addressing a problem and then offering a solution to that problem. You may want to convince your audience that an increase in domestic oil drilling will help lower gasoline prices:

Photo 12.2 This speaker wants to convince her audience that a particular solution should be enacted to address a problem the audience does not know exists. Which organizational pattern would be most appropriate in this situation? (See page 316.)

1. An overreliance on foreign-based oil has led to a significant increase in gasoline prices in the United States.

2. Increased domestic oil drilling and exploration will reduce U.S. reliance on foreign oil and lower the price of gasoline.

Using the problem–solution pattern, it is naturally imperative that the solution indeed solve the problem. Furthermore, you must convince the audience that your solution is practicable and realistic.

The **elimination pattern** offers a series of solutions to a problem, systematically eliminating each one until the solution remaining is the one you support. When using this particular organizational pattern, make sure that the solutions offered are widely accepted or legitimate and that the reasons for eliminating them are reasonable (Gronbeck et al., 1995). We can illustrate the elimination pattern using the above example. You want to convince your audience that an increase in domestic drilling is the best solution for lowering the price of gasoline. In doing so, you provide other possible solutions, eliminating each of them until only the one that you support remains:

1. While increasing gasoline taxes to curb consumption has been proposed as a way of lowering prices, it will result in more hardships for consumers.

2. Decreasing government regulations oil companies must follow has been suggested as a way of lowering gas prices, but this will only be a short-term fix.

3. Increasing domestic oil drilling and exploration will reduce U.S. reliance on foreign oil and lower the price of gasoline.

Both the problem–solution pattern and the elimination pattern are most often used to convince an audience of a particular action's suitability to eliminate or manage a given problem. However, the problem–solution pattern is most appropriate when an audience does not know that the problem exists or does not recognize the pervasiveness or impact of the problem. Consequently, you will want to dedicate part of your speech to explaining to the audience the extent and impact of the problem in addition to promoting an acceptable solution. In the above example, if your audience were unaware of the problems surrounding high gasoline prices, the problem–solution pattern would be most appropriate. The elimination pattern, on the other hand, best suits an audience that is already aware of the extent and impact of a problem. However, these listeners are either unaware of possible solutions or aware that certain solutions exist but uncertain about which one to support. If your audience were already well aware of issues related to high gasoline prices but unaware or undecided about how they might be lowered, the elimination pattern would be most appropriate.

Listen in on Your Life

Recall an occasion when a friend tried to convince you to do or believe something. Did that person organize his or her ideas according to one of the organizational patterns discussed here? What impact did his or her use/nonuse of organizational patterns have on the outcome? What difference would it have made if the person had been a stranger?

Now recall a time when a stranger informed you about something. Did this person organize his or her ideas according to one of the organizational patterns discussed in this chapter? What impact did his or her use/ nonuse of organizational patterns have on your understanding and comprehension of the material? What difference would it have made if the person had been a friend?

Introductions and Conclusions

In addition to the body of your speech, you need to include an **introduction** that lays the foundation for the speech and establishes a positive relational connection with the audience. You will also need to include a **conclusion** that reinforces and completes the speech while also reinforcing a relationship with the audience. Here, we talk about why these parts are so important to your speech and then offer guidelines for developing effective introductions and conclusions.

Beginning speakers often wonder how much time they should devote to introductions and conclusions. A classic study (Miller, 1946) suggested that introductions make up approximately 10% and conclusions make up around 5% of all speeches. While this study was conducted more than 60 years ago, these numbers are not too far off from what we see today. Generally, communication scholars recommend that you devote somewhere between 10% and 25% of your speech to the introduction and 5% to 15% to the conclusion. Given the particular importance of establishing a relational connection with your audience at the beginning of your presentation, reinforcing this connection through the end of the presentation, and developing a logical foundation and closing, we recommend dedicating around 25% of your speech to the introduction and 10% to 15% to the conclusion. If you give an 8-minute presentation, your introduction should finish at around the 2-minute mark, and your conclusion should occupy approximately the last minute of the presentation. Spending more time than this will not allow you to fully develop the body of your speech. Spending less time will not allow you to adequately connect with the audience, lay the foundation for the speech, or conclude the speech effectively.

While you will spend less time presenting your introduction and conclusion, these parts of your speech are just as important as its body. Sure, you devote more time to the body during the presentation of your speech, and you may spend more time working on the body during its preparation. However, it is impossible to present an effective presentation with a weak introduction or conclusion. You must support the body of your speech with a strong introduction and finish the speech with a thorough conclusion.

When considering how introductions and conclusions are just as important as the body of a speech, you might liken the development of a speech to the development of a house. No matter how strong the walls and frame are, without a solid foundation, the house will collapse and crumble to the ground. Further, regardless of how solid the foundation is or how strong the walls and frame are, without a durable roof on top, the house is not complete and will likely deteriorate. Likewise, you must support the body of your speech with a strong introduction and reinforce the speech with a thorough conclusion.

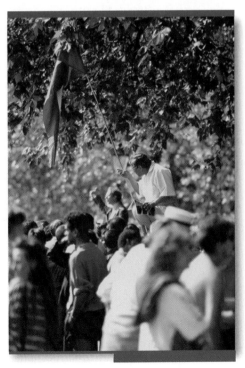

Photo 12.3 What is the first component that must be included in the introduction of a presentation? (See page 316.)

Introductions

When meeting someone for the first time, your initial impressions have a lasting impact on your perceptions of that person and determine if you desire additional contact. Often within the first few moments of a conversation, you determine if you would like to prolong your conversation and develop a relationship, if you would like to see this person in the future, or if you hope never to endure the excruciatingly painful experience of seeing this person again. Whether or not you actually engage in a relationship with someone is regularly determined in the first few moments of contact. The same holds true for the initial moments of a public presentation.

The first impressions an audience forms of you are critical for the reception of your presentation. As the audience members listen to you introduce yourself during the introduction to your speech, it is important that you perform your identity in an appealing manner so that the audience members can determine what type of relationship they will share with you. Whether you are speaking about an issue the audience supports or opposes, it is important that audience members respect and, ideally, like you as a person and a speaker. You must construct the identity of a credible speaker and develop a positive relationship with the audience. During the introduction of your speech, you must begin to establish your credibility and connect with the audience on a relational level; reinforce connections among the topic, your audience, and yourself to increase the audience's desire to listen; and lay the groundwork for the remainder of the speech. Below we discuss six components to include in the introduction of your speech (see Table 12.1). Including each component and following the guidelines offered will help you develop a strong, effective foundation for your speech.

Table 12.1 Brief Guide to Introductions

Attention-getting device

Gain the attention of your audience

Purpose and thesis

Inform your audience of the purpose of your speech and state your thesis

Credibility and relational connection

Explain why your audience should listen to you speak on the topic and discuss your personal connection with the audience

Orientation phase

Familiarize your audience with the topic and define terms if necessary

Impact of the topic and speech

Explain how the topic impacts your audience and why the audience should listen to the speech

Enumerated preview

Outline the main points of your speech for your audience

Attention Getter

The first thing to include in your introduction is an **attention getter**, a device used to draw the audience to you and hence your presentation. The placement of the remaining components of the introduction can vary, but the attention getter, ranging from one sentence to a few lines, always comes first. Some common types of attention getters are offered in Table 12.2.

When selecting the most appropriate attention getter, consider the topic, the audience, and yourself. Your attention getter must relate to the *topic* at hand in terms of both subject matter and tone. Many fascinating stories, colorful quotations, and extraordinary facts exist in the world, but the one you choose to gain your audience's attention must relate to the topic at hand and the occasion.

Table 12.2 Attention-Getting Devices

Illustration

A brief topic-related narrative can be used to grab your audience's attention. These narratives can be real or hypothetical, but if you provide a hypothetical narrative, make sure you tell the audience up front.

Personal reference

Providing a personal narrative or an anecdote can be a very effective way of gaining your audience's attention. Personal references allow you to begin establishing your credibility and a relational connection with your audience, which you can also gain by establishing a level of trust between you and your listeners.

Provocative facts or statistics

Provocative facts or statistics that shock or surprise an audience can also be effective attention getters. When selecting such facts and statistics, it is especially important to make sure they are relevant to the topic and the audience.

Rhetorical question

A rhetorical question—that is, one to which you do not expect the audience to offer a verbal response—gains audience members' attention by actively engaging them and causing them to think about their position or experience with a topic. A good rhetorical question also helps maintain audience attention throughout the speech, since members of the audience often wonder if their answer is accurate or appropriate.

Quotation

A relatively brief introduction can help gain attention and properly introduce the topic of your speech. Never just utter a quote and expect the audience to understand its relevance, why it was included, or who said it. Always explain why you selected a quote or what it may suggest.

Humor

A joke is an effective way to open a speech and gain your audience's attention, as long as it relates to your topic and allows you to effectively prepare the audience for your speech. Of course, a humorous opening does not have to be in the form of a joke. It can apply to all of the preceding attention-gaining strategies.

You must also consider the *audience* when selecting your attention getter. If audience members are very familiar with your topic, startling facts or statistics may not shock them as much as an audience unfamiliar with the topic. If audience members are unfamiliar with your topic, they may not fully understand complex illustrations, which thus may be ineffective at establishing a relational connection with them and capturing their attention.

Finally, when selecting an attention getter, you must consider *yourself*. Select an attention getter that is most comfortable for you. Some people feel awkward citing a quotation or reciting lines of a poem. Others feel ill at ease when attempting humor. Select an attention getter that is most suitable and natural for you. In particular, select one that lets you connect yourself to the audience.

Purpose and Thesis

In the introduction, you must also inform your audience of both the purpose of your speech and your thesis. Be as explicit as possible when stating your thesis or central idea. Tell audience members exactly what you intend to argue; they should not wonder what your speech is about. In the most effective speeches, the audience knows precisely what the speaker will argue. Earlier, we discussed the need to guide the audience throughout the entire speech. When you provide your thesis statement, you are telling the audience the direction you are heading and that everything included in the body of your speech will support this statement.

Supplying the purpose of your speech performs a few different functions. It often reinforces your thesis statement and will increase the listeners' understanding of the information you provide. When you get to the body of your speech, they will better understand why this particular material is included and its overall purpose.

Providing the purpose of your speech also enhances your credibility by establishing a sense of goodwill. By placing audience members at the forefront, you are letting them know that they are the reason you are speaking. You are presenting this information not for personal gain or because you like to hear yourself speak but because you care about the audience members and want to impact their lives in a meaningful and beneficial way.

Informing the audience of your purpose also helps comfort the audience and establishes trust. Especially if the audience is suspicious, it is good to be straightforward about your intentions. Letting the audience know your motives for presenting the speech will help you establish a trusting relationship, enhance your credibility, and ultimately help ensure the effectiveness of your presentation.

Credibility and Relational Connection

As a speaker, you must convey to the audience that you are knowledgeable about the topic, that you can be trusted, and that you have its best interest at heart. As mentioned in Chapter 11, these characteristics touch on the three primary dimensions of credibility: knowledge, trustworthiness, and goodwill (Gass & Seiter, 2011). Notice once again that these components would likely be used to characterize someone with whom you share a positive relationship. Perceptions of credibility are closely connected to and frequently based on relationships.

The three primary dimensions of credibility are established throughout the introduction and throughout the speech, but knowledge is the one dimension that you must explicitly convey to your audience in the introduction. You need to assure the audience that you are knowledgeable and experienced in this area. You must establish a sufficient degree of expertise. Of course, by doing so, you also reinforce trustworthiness and goodwill. As someone knowledgeable and experienced in this area, the information you provide is probably accurate. As someone with personal experience in this area, you care enough about it and the members of your audience that you feel it is important to share it with them. Furthermore, you establish for the audience your personal relationship with the material.

As a speaker, at minimum you must relate your expertise and your personal experience with the topic about which you speak. You can best express this expertise to your audience members by informing them of your experience exploring and learning about this topic. Sometimes this credibility comes already partially established and embedded in a person's credentials. A person's rank, title, or advanced degree carries a certain degree of expertise. Of course, you do not need an advanced degree in an area to claim expertise or experience. Explaining to your audience how you have carefully studied the topic or have extensive experience or background with the material is often sufficient.

As a speaker, you must also establish a relational connection with the audience. You can accomplish this connection by noting your identification with the audience or how you and the audience are alike (Burke, 1969). People tend to trust and like others whom they perceive as similar to them. Additionally, through identification, the meaning framework of a speaker becomes apparent. People feel as if they understand the way a speaker thinks and views the world because of the similarities between them. Consequently, a speaker's words become more understandable and more believable because the audience members are able to match the speaker's ways of thinking to their own. As long as they are legitimate, noting similarities, such as having the same connection with the topic, the same experiences, or the same desires, fears, and joys, can connect you with the audience and create this sense of identification.

Contrarian Challenge

We believe it is important to discuss your credibility in the introduction of speech. However, doing so could possibly be perceived as bragging by the audience, which might prevent you from developing a positive relational connection with audience members. Do you believe a person can overdo the discussion of his or her credibility? How might discussing credibility be accomplished without appearing to boast?

Orientation Phase

In the **orientation phase**, you provide the audience members with any information you believe will allow them to better understand and appreciate the material you will present in the body of your speech. The actual information you include will vary according to your topic and the audience. It could include definitions of unfamiliar terms you will use during your speech. A brief explanation of what the topic entails might benefit the audience, as might an overview of the historical development of an issue.

Describing your approach to a topic or your particular meaning can sometimes dramatically alter your audience's perspective and the speech itself. For instance, when you are giving a speech about abortion, some members of the audience may approach your speech differently depending on whether you define abortion as occurring in the first trimester or the last trimester.

During our discussion of the unity principle, we mentioned that the orientation phase is the place to include information you feel is

Photo 12.4 Why might this speaker include an orientation phase as part of her introduction? (See page 316.)

important for the audience to know but whose inclusion in the body would get you off-track. So, returning to the example from a few pages ago, say you are informing the audience about the treatment of a disease, but you think it is important for audience members to know about the symptoms of the disease. Briefly include this material in the orientation phase.

Essentially, when providing an orientation to the topic during the introduction, you are getting the audience members up to speed on the topic and preparing them for the body of the speech. Include whatever information you consider most relevant to audience understanding and a successful speech.

Impact of the Topic and Speech

As a speaker, it is your job to tell the audience members how the topic impacts their lives and how they might benefit from listening to your speech. In other words, you are establishing their relationship with the material and giving them a reason to listen to your presentation. This approach also enhances your credibility by conveying to the audience a concern about its well-being. The fact that you are aware of and are satisfying members' needs will assist in the establishment of an audience's relationship with you.

When considering how to explain the impact of the topic, you must fully consider the audience members and what they already likely know or believe. Do not take for granted that they already know the importance of the topic or fully understand its impact on their lives. Perhaps your topic does impact their lives and should be important to them, but they just do not realize this, in which case you need to inform them of the connection and importance during the introduction. Reinforce this link even if you feel audience members are already fully aware of the topic's impact on their lives.

When explaining how the topic impacts the audience, ensure that you make it as personal as possible. For example, if you are presenting a speech on preparing for floods, do not just say, "Many people will be affected by flooding this year." Instead, inform the audience members of the chances that they, a friend, or a relative will sustain damage or encounter danger as a result of flooding. Such comments as "Lots of people are affected" or general circular statements like "This is important to know because it is really vital" are not sufficient. Saying something like "If the people in this room represent the entire population of the state, five of us will have our homes devastated in a flood by the end of the year" will be much more effective.

When they are developing this part of their speech, we often encourage our students to imagine cynical audience members saying, "Who cares?" or "Big deal." You need to tell them why they should care and why it is a big deal. Do not worry; most audiences are not cynical and will provide you with encouragement. You can be certain that your classmates will be very encouraging, if you are giving a speech in class. After all, you are all in the same boat or floating on the same educational raft.

Enumerated Preview

Finally, you must provide an enumerated preview of your main points during the introduction of your speech. Essentially, you must list the main points of your speech. "First, I will talk about X. Then, I will talk about Y. Finally, I will talk about Z." You may include this list at any point in the introduction following your attention getter, but generally it is located at the very end.

An enumerated preview helps position your audience for the body of your speech and provides a nice lead into your argument. Plus, remember how important it is to fully guide your audience throughout the speech. In an enumerated preview, you are guiding audience members by providing markers or landmarks for them to follow and recognize along the way.

An enumerated preview also helps the audience remember your main points. We have heard an adage, which has been attributed to many groups. Among others, it has been referred to as an Irish saying, a Native American saying, and an Eskimo saying. No matter its origin, the saying and its meaning remain the same: Tell them what you are going to tell them. Tell them. Then tell them what you told them. In other words, the more often you say something, the more likely your audience will remember it. In the introduction, you tell audience members what you are going to tell them. In the body of your speech, you tell them. Finally, in your conclusion, you tell them what you told them. We have already gone through the *tell them what you are going to tell them* and the *tell them* stages. Now, we can discuss the part in which when you *tell them what you told them.*

Concluding Your Presentation

As we mentioned previously, the introduction, body, and conclusion are equally important. However, many speeches we hear often end with a very weak conclusion and just seem to stop—as if the speaker had run out of ideas and wanted to run out of the room. The introduction and body might be very well done, but the conclusion of the speech needs a great deal of additional development. If the speaker is so relieved to be near the end of the speech that he or she just abruptly quits after finishing the body, or if the speaker is not quite sure how to end the speech, any credibility he or she has developed up to that point will be diminished, and the relational connections established with the audience will be weakened, lessening the overall value and effectiveness of an otherwise good speech.

The conclusion is not just a logical end to your presentation; it entails the maintenance of the relationship between speaker, audience, and the material presented. At the end of a conversation with a friend, you draw a clear line to indicate that the interaction is over but that the relationship continues. Speakers need to make the audience members feel that their relationship to the ideas and commitments expressed by the speaker will continue beyond the interaction they have just experienced.

Photo 12.5 Why should audience members clapping at the very end of a presentation not be the primary focus of a speaker when developing a conclusion? (See page 316.)

During the conclusion, you must reinforce your thesis and purpose, underscore audience involvement, and provide adequate closure. The impression made at the end of your speech will be long lasting and plays a predominant role in whether the audience uses the information you provided or is persuaded by your presentation. You must strive to make a positive lasting impression and end your presentation in a manner that is most effective and maintains your relational connection with the audience and the material presented. Conclusions contain six components that will help get this accomplished (see Table 12.3).

Table 12.3 Brief Guide to Conclusions

Wrap-up signal

Signal the beginning of the conclusion for your audience.

Restatement of thesis

Restate your thesis for your audience.

Summary of main points

Provide your audience with a complete summary of your main points.

Audience motivation

Encourage members of your audience to incorporate the material you have provided into their lives or to behave/think in a certain manner.

Relational reinforcement

Reinforce the relationship between your audience and the material and between your audience and yourself.

Clincher statement

Provide your audience with a memorable line or phrase that will enable you to end strongly and smoothly.

Wrap-Up Signal

The first thing you must provide for the audience when concluding a speech is a **wrap-up signal**. You must indicate to the audience both verbally and nonverbally that you have reached the conclusion and are essentially wrapping things up. We have said it before, and we are saying it again: You must guide your audience through the entire speech.

Verbally, incorporating phrases like "As we draw to a close," "As we look back on what has been discussed during this speech," and "As we near the end of this presentation" will signal the audience that you have reached your conclusion. The old standby "In conclusion" can also be used, but many people consider this cliché and a bit dull. Nonverbally, you can indicate with your tone of voice that you have reached the final part of your presentation. An extended pause will work in some cases, as will a decrease in your rate of speaking. Whatever you include, make sure the audience knows that you have reached your conclusion.

While a wrap-up signal is valuable in guiding your audience through the speech, some audience members may view it as a cue to stop listening or to begin gathering their things in anticipation of leaving. Make sure that the wrap-up signal is clear, but do not dwell on it. Instead, move quickly to the remaining components of the conclusion. Clarify to your audience that you have reached not the end of your speech but the beginning of your conclusion. You will be able to maintain audience members' attention in part through the full development of the conclusion, making it worthwhile for them to listen.

Restatement of the Thesis

You must also restate the thesis during the conclusion of your speech to underscore the main idea and help your audience remember it afterward. When you restate the thesis is up to you. Like the components of the introduction, some components of the conclusion can occur at any point. Aside from providing a wrap-up signal at the very beginning of the conclusion and ending with the clincher statement (we discuss this one shortly), the order in which these components appear will be based on what you believe works best for your speech.

Summary of Main Points

A summary of the main points allows you to stress the main points of your speech and helps the audience retain the information. Remember that in the introduction you provided an enumerated preview of the main points. There, you simply listed the main points of the speech without elaboration. When summarizing your main points during your conclusion, you do not simply list them but instead remind your audience what

they are, briefly review each one, and accentuate their support of your thesis. Summarizing your main points is crucial to audience retention and understanding of the material.

Audience Motivation

You must also strive to motivate the audience to take action as a result of listening to the speech. In the introduction, you explained to the audience the importance of the topic and provided the audience with reasons for listening to your

Make Your Case

We suggest verbally indicating to an audience that you have reached the conclusion of a presentation. However, a few communication professionals discourage the use of wrap-up signals because of the possibility that audience members will cease listening as carefully once they have been informed that the presentation is nearing the end. Make a case for the value of wrap-up signals and what you should do to limit the possible drop in audience attention.

We have found that providing a complete summary of the main points instead of just listing them is the area in which beginning speakers struggle the most when developing conclusions. Keep the importance of the summary in mind when speaking in the community, on the job, or in the classroom.

presentation. During the conclusion, reiterate why you gave the speech in the first place and encourage audience members to act as a result of the speech. A positive relationship with the speaker will increase the likelihood that an audience will go along with whatever is asked of it.

In speeches to persuade, this reaction is relatively easy to accomplish because the audience response is a bit more obvious. For instance, if the purpose of your speech is to get your audience members to wear their seat belts when traveling in a vehicle, urge them to always wear their seat belts when traveling in a vehicle. Do not assume your audience members will understand what course of action you want them to take or remember the purpose of your speech. It is important to be explicit by telling the audience members exactly what you want them to think or do. If the purpose of your speech is to convince the audience members that something is true or a certain policy should be enacted, tell them exactly what you want them to believe or support.

During speeches to inform, your purpose is to increase audience understanding or recognition of the topic. An effective informative speech will generate or enhance interest in your topic and will actually be used by your audience. To ensure members of your audience make full use of the material, encourage them to utilize the information and go beyond what you provide.

The impact of any message is greatest while heard and immediately afterward. As time goes on, this impact grows increasingly weaker. You have the most impact on your audience while presenting the speech, and as soon as you finish, the effects of your speech will increasingly diminish. The best way to ensure a lasting impact is to motivate the audience to use the information.

Relational Reinforcement

You must also reinforce the relationship between the audience and the material and between the audience and yourself. Emphasizing the importance of the material in audience members' lives, like you did in the introduction, will increase their motivation to use the material and to act or think the way you want. By reinforcing their connection with the material, you also ensure that this relationship will not end with your presentation, just as a relationship among friends lasts after a conversation has drawn to a close.

In the conclusion, you must also remind the audience members of your relationship with them. You may want to touch upon the ways the material impacts your life just as it does theirs. You could also note other similarities with the audience members by emphasizing your connections with them. Much like reinforcing their relationship with the material, audience members should recognize that your relationship with them will continue once the presentation concludes.

Case in Point

Analyze a public presentation on television or on the Internet. Which elements of conclusions discussed in this chapter are evident? Are any elements of conclusions absent from that presentation? What could the speechwriter have done to improve the conclusion?

Clincher Statement

You must end your speech with a **clincher statement**, a phrase that allows you to end your speech strongly and smoothly. Your clincher statement needs to encapsulate your entire speech and leave the audience in the proper frame of mind. This technique will help make the speech memorable, and knowing the last line of your speech is often a comfort.

Many of the attention-getting strategies used in speech introductions can be used here. Sometimes humor is most appropriate. A final illustration or anecdote can be used as a clincher statement. Linking the clincher statement to your introduction is often an effective way of ending your speech and completely wrapping up the entire presentation. For instance, if you began with a rhetorical question, providing an answer as your final statement may reinforce your thesis. Audiences often remember the last thing said longer than anything else in the speech, so make sure you carefully choose your conclusion.

Never, however, end your speech by saying, "Thank you." This is incredibly forgettable and ineffective. We are sure you are a considerate person who will be eager to expresses your gratitude to the audience for its attention. However, most presenters who end their speeches this

Comedians always know their last joke or line before they go up to the microphone. Once on stage, they may vary the rest of their act, but that last line will remain the same. They want their audience laughing when they finish, ending in a memorable fashion. Previously establishing the last line of their act and knowing its strength also reassures and helps calm them through the rest of their performance. Your speeches may not end with a huge laugh from the audience, but they will need to end in a memorable way.

way are doing so not out of appreciation for the audience but because they are finished and the audience does not know it. Ending a speech without making the audience aware of it results in the speaker staring at the audience, the audience staring back at the speaker, and nobody knowing quite what to do next. So, the speaker meekly utters, "Thank you." At this point, the audience members realize it is over and start clapping, primarily because they are relieved to know what is happening. The speaker in the above example likely did not guide the audience through the entire speech, include a wrap-up signal, or incorporate any of the other components of an effective conclusion. After reading this book, you will be certain to fully guide your audience through the speech. You know what components to include when developing a successful conclusion, and you will end strongly with a memorable clincher statement.

Of course, you can still express gratitude and appreciation for your audience by saying, "Thank you," but wait until the applause has died down following your clincher statement and the audience has finished showering you with roses and words of praise.

FOCUS QUESTIONS REVISITED

1. What are the four principles of speech organization and development?
The four principles of speech organization and development are (a) points, (b) unity, (c) balance, and (d) guidance. The points principle highlights the basic building blocks of an argument: main points and subpoints. Unity is a principle of speech organization and development that maintains you should stay focused and provide only information that supports your thesis and main points. Balance is a principle of speech organization and development that maintains the points of the body must be relatively equal in scope and importance. The amount of time you devote to the main points and to the amount of development and support you provide for them must be relatively equal. Guidance

is a principle of speech organization and development that maintains a speaker must guide and direct the audience throughout the entire speech.

2. What organizational patterns can you use in the development of the speech body?
An organizational pattern is an arrangement of the main points that best enables audience comprehension. You should base the selection of an organizational pattern for your speech on the topic, your purpose, and the audience. Use the chronological pattern when arranging the main points according to their position in a time sequence. Use the spatial pattern when the main points are arranged according to their physical relation. Use a causal pattern to organize the main points according to cause and effect. The question–answer pattern involves posing questions an audience may have about a subject and then answering those questions in a manner that favors your position. The topical pattern arranges support material according to specific categories, groupings, or grounds. The problem-solution pattern divides the body of the speech by first addressing a problem and then offering a solution to that problem. Finally, the elimination pattern involves offering a series of solutions to a problem and then systematically eliminating each one until the only solution remaining is the one you support.

3. What components must you include in a speech introduction?
During the introduction of a speech, you must begin to establish your credibility and connect with the audience on a relational level, reinforce connections between the topic and your audience to increase its desire to listen, and lay the groundwork for the remainder of the speech. Six components must be included in the introduction to achieve these requirements. The first thing to include in your introduction is an attention getter, a device used to draw the audience into your presentation. The placement of the remaining components of the introduction may vary, but the attention getter will always come first. In the introduction, you must inform your audience of both the purpose of your speech and your thesis. You must tell the audience members why they should perceive you as credible, and you must develop your relationship with them. You must orient the audience members by providing them with any information that will allow them to better understand and appreciate the material you will present in the body of your speech. You must inform the audience members of the importance of the topic and its impact on their lives. Finally, you must provide an enumerated preview of your main points during the introduction of your speech.

4. What components must you include in a speech conclusion?
During the conclusion, you must reinforce your thesis and purpose, underscore audience involvement, and provide adequate closure or sense of finality. Six components of the conclusion will help you accomplish these requirements. You must first provide the audience with a wrap-up signal when concluding a speech. You must indicate to the audience both verbally and nonverbally that you have reached the conclusion and are essentially wrapping things up. You must restate the thesis during the conclusion of your speech. You must summarize the main points to reinforce them and help the audience retain the information. You must strive to motivate the audience to take action as a result of listening to the speech. During the conclusion of your speech, you must also reinforce the audience members' relationship with the material and their relationship with you. Finally, you must end your speech with a clincher statement, a phrase that allows you to end your speech strongly and smoothly.

KEY CONCEPTS

attention getter   304
balance principle   297
body   294
causal pattern   299
chronological pattern   299
clincher statement   312
conclusion   302
elimination pattern   301
guidance principle   297
introduction   302
main points   295

organizational pattern   299
orientation phase   307
points principle   295
problem–solution pattern   301
question–answer pattern   300
spatial pattern   299
subpoints   295
topical pattern   300
transitions   298
unity principle   296
wrap-up signal   310

QUESTIONS TO ASK YOUR FRIENDS

1. What types of attention getters do your friends find most effective? Which types of attention getters do they find least effective? Do their evaluations change depending on circumstances or what is discussed?

2. Ask your friends to describe the characteristics of what they consider an effective public presentation. Limit their responses to those *not* involving delivery. Consider their responses in regard to the guidelines for developing public presentations discussed in this chapter.

3. Ask your friends to recall an occasion during which they listened to a presentation they considered confusing. What do they believe made it difficult to understand? As a speaker, what would you have done differently?

MEDIA LINKS

1. We discussed how written transitions are often less obvious than oral transitions. Find examples of written transitions in magazines, newspapers, and books. Once you have gathered these examples, turn each one into an oral transition that would clearly and effectively guide a listening audience.

2. As you did with Case in Point, watch a public presentation on television or on the Internet. Which elements of introductions discussed in this chapter are evident? Are any elements of introductions absent from that presentation? What could the speechwriter have done to improve the introduction?

3. Locate examples of archived speeches from at least 20 years ago. Many can be found on the Internet. Then find examples of recent speeches. In terms of development, how are these speeches similar, and how are they different? How has the passing of time altered the development of public presentations?

ETHICAL ISSUES

1. What are the necessary qualifications for a speaker to claim expertise and experience with a topic? Are determining these qualifications and evaluating expertise and experience the responsibilities of the speaker, the audience, or both?

2. When describing the importance of the topic to an audience, some speakers may feel compelled to embellish the facts to make the topic seem more vital and to enhance audience attention. They may consider this necessary as part of the greater good. Are there occasions when this deceitfulness would be appropriate? Why or why not?

3. When developing a presentation concerning a topic about which there are multiple opposing positions, is it necessary to provide equal coverage for all sides of the issue? Are there certain topics or occasions when this may or may not be necessary? Be sure to support your answers.

ANSWERS TO PHOTO CAPTIONS

Photo 12.1 ▪ The guidance principle emphasizes the relational development of a presentation.

Photo 12.2 ▪ The problem–solution pattern would be most appropriate in this situation.

Photo 12.3 ▪ The first thing that must be included in an introduction is an attention getter. The order of the remaining components may vary, but the attention getter always comes first.

Photo 12.4 ▪ As a speaker prepares an audience for the body of the presentation, the orientation phase enables the audience to better understand and appreciate the material presented.

Photo 12.5 ▪ A conclusion is not simply the end of a presentation but an important part of a speech that requires careful and complete development.

STUDENT STUDY SITE

Visit the study site at **www.sagepub.com/boc2e** for e-flashcards, practice quizzes, journal articles and additional study resources.

REFERENCES

Burke, K. (1969). *A rhetoric of motives.* Berkeley: University of California Press.

Gass, R. H., & Seiter, J. S. (2011). *Persuasion, social influence, and compliance gaining* (4th ed.). Boston: Allyn & Bacon.

Gronbeck, B., German, K., Ehninger, D., & Monroe, A. H. (1995). *Principles of speech communication* (12th ed.). New York: HarperCollins.

Miller, E. (1946). Speech introductions and conclusions. *Quarterly Journal of Speech, 32,* 181–183.

O'Hair, D., Stewart, R., & Rubenstein, H. (2001). *A speaker's guidebook: Text and reference.* Boston: Bedford/St. Martin's.

13

Relating Through Informative Speeches and Persuasive Speeches

At first glance, it may appear as if little difference exists between informative speeches and persuasive speeches. Speakers generally inform their audiences of various facts or ideas when persuading them to believe something or to perform a particular action. Certain aspects of persuasion are evident when speakers inform an audience about something. Informative and persuasive speeches are alike in many ways, not the least of which is the need to develop a relationship with the audience. However, a clear and concrete distinction exists between these two types of speeches: the purpose of the presentation, or the primary impact you wish to have on the audience as a result of the presentation. The purpose of an informative speech is to increase audience knowledge or understanding of something, while the purpose of a persuasive speech is to impact either the thinking (attitudes and beliefs) or the behavior of the audience.

That observation is actually a pretty big distinction. Yet, except for that very meaningful difference, these types of speeches share many similarities. Both, of course, show similarity of relationship to the audience. You will neither inform nor persuade people who do not trust or believe what you say. Therefore, performance of an identity as a "truth speaker" is essential in all cases, whether among friends or strangers. Many components of both the introduction and the conclusion are the same and necessary for both speeches. The principles of speech development and organization are the same for each type of speech, along with the requirements and guidelines for using credible evidence and support. The need to develop and maintain credibility, as well as a relationship with the audience, is the same for both speeches, as are the elements of effective delivery. Some organizational patterns are more commonly associated with either informative or persuasive speeches, but you can use all of the patterns discussed earlier for either persuasive or informative presentations. Many of the other concepts and guidelines included in this chapter that are primarily discussed with one type of speech can actually be used in the development and enhancement of both types of speeches. For all of these similarities, though, the distinction of purpose is significant enough to make these two very different types of speeches.

In what follows, we bring together much of the material discussed in the previous two chapters as we explore informative and persuasive speeches. We examine various types of informative speeches and discuss guidelines for increasing the success of informative presentations. We then examine persuasive presentations, discussing various types of persuasive speeches along with artistic proofs and the theory of social judgment.

Focus Questions

1. What are the types of informative speeches?
2. What strategies exist for achieving successful informative presentations?
3. What are the types of persuasive speeches?
4. How might preexisting beliefs and attitudes of the audience influence speeches to convince?
5. How might speeches to actuate affect audience behavior?
6. What are the artistic proofs?
7. What is the social judgment theory, and how can it impact persuasive attempts?

What Are Informative Speeches?

We begin our discussion of informative speeches by examining the various types of informative speeches you may present in your community, your workplace, your school, and other areas of your life. We then discuss ways to increase the success of your informative presentations.

Speeches of Definition and Description

Speeches of definition and description provide the audience with an extended explanation or depiction of an object, a creation, a place, a person, a concept, or an event. After listening to a speech of definition or description, your audience should have a greater understanding and recognition of the topic. For example, you may develop a speech informing the audience about Kobe beef, BlackBerry cell phones, the television series *It's Always Sunny in Philadelphia*, or the role of quarterback in football.

All of the components of introductions and conclusions discussed in Chapter 12 should be included in speeches of definition and description. As with all presentations, you must establish a relationship with the audience throughout the presentation. You are more likely to deliver these types of speeches to audiences with little prior knowledge and

Concrete words represent tangible objects that can be experienced through sensory channels (touch, taste, smell, hearing, seeing) and include real people, objects, actions, and locations. Abstract words, in contrast, represent intangible objects that cannot be experienced through your senses and include ideas, beliefs, and feelings. *Patriotism* is an abstract word that could be conveyed more concretely by describing a flag and acts of patriotism that provide the audience with a clearer mental picture and greater understanding of what you mean by that term.

Descriptive language provides the audience with a clearer picture of what you are discussing by *describing* it in more detail. Consider the difference between merely saying "There is a meadow" and using descriptive language to provide a clearer picture of a meadow by invoking multiple senses of your audience. For example, you could describe the meadow as having grasses swaying majestically in a gentle breeze caressing your skin and carrying the fragrance of thousands of wildflowers and a bubbling brook flowing underneath a cobalt sky filled with singing birds. This passage might sound like something from a bad romance novel, but used correctly, descriptive language will provide members of your audience with a clearer understanding of what you are discussing, help maintain their attention, and connect them to the material.

Relate Unknown Material to Known Material

Relating new or unknown material to familiar or known material will enable your audience members to better understand what you are discussing and help them retain the material. For example, your audience members may not have prior experience with nuclear reactors or prior understanding of how these reactors actually work. However, they may have a basic understanding of how a toaster works. Comparing the process involved with nuclear reactors (unknown) to the process involved with a toaster (known) will help the audience understand what you are discussing. Members of your audience may also be more likely to recall your presentation the next time they fix a piece of toast. Naturally, it is important to select something with which your audience is actually familiar. This criterion highlights once again the need for careful audience analysis, especially when using something other than a common household item.

Motivate Your Audience

"Use it or lose it" refers to more than just muscle mass. If the audience members do not incorporate into their lives the information that you provide, they will likely forget the material provided during your presentation. Recall that, during the conclusion of a presentation, you must reinforce relational connections and motivate your audience to act on the information provided. Encouraging your audience members to use the information provided will help them retain the information and fully recognize the importance of the

College Experience

The focus of this chapter is what a speaker should do rather than what audience members should do. However, you might consider yourself an audience member when listening to a lecture in class. Even if your instructor does not do so, try relating the material you are learning to things you already know. It will likely increase your understanding and retention of what is being discussed.

topic in their lives. Effective informative speeches prompt or increase interest in the topic and compel the audience to utilize the information. Motivating your audience to utilize the information provided will help ensure that these actions occur following your presentation.

What Are Persuasive Speeches?

Now that we have discussed informative speeches, we can turn our attention to persuasive speeches, of which two basic types exist: speeches to convince and speeches to actuate. These types of persuasive speeches are distinguished by their specific purpose. In both cases, as with informative speeches, establishing a positive relationship with the audience is vital to the success of your presentation. You must also determine how the audience members will view their relationship with you as a speaker given a preexisting relationship or a desired relational connection. This consideration is especially relevant when you want to significantly alter the thinking or behavior of an audience.

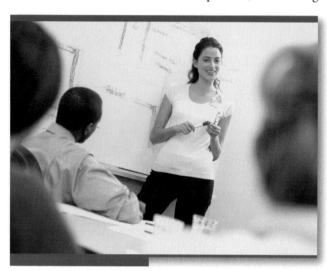

Photo 13.3 Why would a positive relational connection with an audience be important when attempting to persuade? (See page 340.)

Speeches to Convince

Speeches to convince are delivered in an attempt to impact audience thinking. They encompass a primary claim—essentially, what you are trying to convince your audience to believe. For example, you might want to convince your audience that Puerto Rico should remain a territory of the United States rather than becoming a state, that tuition increases at your school are detrimental, that a need exists for after-school programs in your community, or that recycling needs will change within the next decade. The four primary types of persuasive claims that can be developed through a speech to convince include (a) policy, (b) value, (c) fact, and (d) conjecture.

Claims of Policy

A **claim of policy** maintains that a course of action should or should not be taken. For example, you may wish to convince the audience that an attendance policy should be instituted at your school, same-sex marriage should be legalized in your state, or stricter automobile emissions standards should be enacted. When supporting a particular policy, a speaker must demonstrate the need for such a policy, how the policy will satisfy that need, and that the policy can be successfully enacted. A speaker may also be required to prove that the policy advocated is superior to an existing policy or another policy being proposed.

A claim of policy does not have to support a policy. You could also oppose the institution of an attendance policy, the legalization of same-sex marriage, or stricter automobile emissions standards. When opposing a policy, a speaker could argue that the need for such a policy does not exist. If a need for such a policy does exist, a speaker might demonstrate that a proposed policy does not satisfy the need, that the policy could not be successfully enacted, or that other policies are superior to the one being presented for consideration.

Note that a claim of policy does not necessarily involve individual action but rather involves action of a more collective nature, such as a community, corporation, school, or nation-state. We talk about persuasive speeches involving individual action (speeches to actuate) later in the chapter.

Claims of Value

A **claim of value** maintains that something is good or bad, beneficial or detrimental, or another evaluative criterion. Claims of value deal largely with attitudes, which were discussed earlier. You may want to convince your audience that Andrew Jackson was the worst American president or that playing video games is beneficial to child development.

When developing a claim of value, you must let the audience know what criteria you used to determine and judge the value you support. Then, you need to exhibit how the object, person, or idea meets those criteria. You would need to explain to the audience how to determine "the worst president in U.S. history" and how Andrew Jackson would then be ranked the worst. You would need to explain to your audience what you mean by "beneficial to child development" and why playing video games meets those criteria. Claims of value go beyond simply offering your opinion about something. You must establish criteria and provide evidence to support your claim.

Claims of Fact and Claims of Conjecture

Claims of fact and claims of conjecture are related but have one key distinction. A **claim of fact** maintains that something is true or false at the *present time* or was true or false in the *past*. A **claim of conjecture**, though similar to a claim of fact in that something is determined to be true or false, contends what will be true or false in the *future* (Gouran, Wiethoff, & Doelger, 1994). Examples of claims of fact and conjecture include

Photo 13.4 The speaker in this photo is attempting to convince her audience that her university should provide each incoming student with a laptop computer. What type of claim is she making? (See page 340.)

ncing your audience that decreases in taxes result in increases in consumer spend-
hat slow drivers cause the majority of traffic fatalities, that banning handguns would
to an increase in crime, and that education costs will triple within the next 10 years.
Both claims of fact and claims of conjecture require solid evidence and support. Claims
conjecture are somewhat unique, however, since a speaker is arguing that something will
the case or will exist in the future. Accordingly, you are speculating about what might
happen and do not have established facts or statistics to support your claim. However, existing facts and statistics can be used to support the presentation. Such evidence is used all the
time when economic predictions are made. Economists examine current trends, statistics,
and even past events to speculate about the future economic picture. It is particularly important that the evidence offered as support pertain to the claim being developed, and you as
the speaker must establish a clear connection between these elements for the audience.

Audience Approaches to Speeches to Convince

Regardless of the type of claim being advanced, an audience's existing beliefs and attitudes will influence what you attempt to achieve with your presentation and the methods you employ. They will also influence how the audience members perceive you and
your relationship with them. You can impact the thinking of your audience in the three
different ways discussed in Table 13.1.

Table 13.1 Impacting Audience Thinking	
Reinforcing an existing way of thinking	In this case, you desire to strengthen your audience members' convictions and ensure them of their accuracy and legitimacy. Speeches that reinforce an existing way of thinking usually offer additional reasons in support of a particular way of thinking along with new or recent evidence. In these situations, audiences generally view their relationship with the speaker in a very positive manner.
Altering an existing way of thinking	Here, you essentially tell the audience members that their current way of thinking is wrong or should be modified. This approach does not automatically mean that the audience will be hostile toward you or your position. However, when attempting to bring about this change, it is especially important to develop a very positive relationship with the audience. It is also especially important to enhance audience perceptions of your credibility, particularly of your goodwill.
Creating a new way of thinking	In this situation, members of your audience will probably be more willing to accept your claim than they would if you attempted to change their position. However, you may need to spend additional time developing the audience members' relationship with the material and stressing the importance of the issue in their lives. As always, establishing a positive relational connection with your audience will increase your likelihood of success.

Speeches to Actuate

Speeches to actuate are delivered in an attempt to impact audience behavior. You
may want members of your audience to join your cause, volunteer with a charitable
organization, limit their consumption of natural resources, or vote Quimby for mayor
of Springfield. You may end up influencing audience thinking as a consequence of a
speech to actuate, but that is not the ultimate goal of such a speech. The ultimate goal
of a speech to actuate is to impact the behavior of your audience. You can impact your
audience in the five different ways discussed in Table 13.2.

Table 13.2 Impacting Audience Behavior

Reinforcing an existing behavior	In this case, you desire to strengthen audience members' conviction about performing a behavior and ensure that they continue performing it. Reinforcing existing behavior often entails providing new reasons or evidence for enacting this behavior, along with increasing audience confidence and excitement about performing the behavior.
Altering an existing behavior	Here, you are asking the audience not to stop performing a certain behavior or to enact a totally new behavior but to modify an existing behavior. It is important that you stress the value of continuing to perform this action and its positive influence in audience members' lives, but you must urge them to perform this action in the more effective or beneficial manner you suggest.
Ceasing an existing behavior	An audience will probably be less supportive of this type of presentation, since you are essentially telling audience members that they are doing something wrong. Be careful not to offend them but be resolute in your support of ceasing that behavior. It is especially important to develop a positive relationship with the audience. Stress that you are doing this for members' well-being.
Enacting a new behavior	The key to successfully persuading your audience members to enact a new behavior is determining why they are not behaving this way in the first place. Are they opposed to the behavior? Do they not know the behavior can be done? Do they not recognize the value of the behavior? Do they believe that performing the behavior is more trouble than it is worth? Do they view the behavior as unaccomplishable? Answering these questions will enable you to develop the presentation in a relational manner that best fits your audience and that will most likely persuade audience members to enact the desired behavior.
Avoiding a future behavior	When attempting to impact an audience in this manner, you are not necessarily reinforcing an existing behavior but encouraging your audience to avoid a specific new behavior. Such behaviors may be a concern now or in the future. These speeches often require that you provide the audience members with reasons and strategies for avoiding this behavior.

Persuasive Speaking and Artistic Proofs

Each type of persuasive speech can be enhanced through the recognition of the artistic proofs *ethos*, *pathos*, and *logos*. Aristotle laid out these artistic proofs more than 2,000 years ago, but the ideas behind them remain significant.

Ethos

Ethos involves the use of speaker credibility to impact an audience. We have already talked about the importance of establishing and maintaining your credibility as well as a positive relational connection with an audience. For members of an audience to judge the information provided by a speaker as accurate, valuable, and worthy of their

Listen in on Your Life

Listen for attempts to change someone's behavior during your interactions with friends, family, and other people with whom you share a personal relationship. Which of the five ways of impacting behavior discussed in this chapter is most evident? How are the persuasive appeals supported when interacting one-on-one with someone? How can these attempts at persuasion inform the development and delivery of speeches to actuate?

Photo 13.5 Evoking feelings of sadness from an audience when attempting to persuade would entail which artistic proof? (See page 340.)

attention and consideration, they must view that speaker as knowledgeable, trustworthy, and concerned about their well-being. Audiences must also perceive a relational connection with the speaker. Audiences' perceptions of speaker credibility and their relationship with the speaker are critical to the success of persuasive attempts. We urge you to consider the great impact that audience perceptions of your credibility will have on the success of your presentations.

Pathos

Pathos involves the use of emotional appeals to impact an audience. The use of such emotions as excitement, sadness, happiness, guilt, and anger can be quite effective when persuading an audience. You may have also witnessed the use of emotional appeals when attending or watching political rallies during which speakers elicit feelings of excitement about a particular candidate and perhaps anger toward political rivals. These emotional appeals are usually quite effective in achieving the desired response. Furthermore, the relational connections necessary for effective presentations often entail certain emotional qualities that will assist speakers persuading an audience.

Discussing emotion in a communication textbook may initially strike some people as peculiar. Emotions are often considered things that people *feel internally,* which seems far removed from the discussion of symbolic activity. It is true that emotions involve internal activities and feelings. Neuroscientists can even pinpoint changes in the brain when people experience specific emotions. Changes in heart rate, blood pressure, and temperature and a host of other physical changes occur when you experience any emotion.

Yet, emotion is also very much a *symbolic activity* and a *relational activity.* Symbolically, emotions and the feelings that accompany them are given meaning within a culture or society. Emotions bring about physical change, but this physical change is understood and evaluated according to established meaning. Happiness, sadness, fear, and all other emotions have meaning beyond physical experience or a given instance. These symbolic characteristics of emotions are learned *relationally.* Relationships are about knowledge, connecting symbolically to others, and understanding the world. Accordingly, it is through relationships that people come to understand emotion. Your understanding of emotions and of their appropriate display has

In a classic study, Schachter and Singer (1962) demonstrated that physiological arousal itself is not sufficient for people to define their emotions. People need some socially developed label to determine what they are experiencing.

developed through everyday communication and interactions with your friends, family, classmates, neighbors, romantic partners, acquaintances, and others with whom you share a relationship. Incorporating this knowledge of emotions from your everyday life can assist you when attempting to persuade others in a public speaking situation.

Logos

Logos involves the use of logic or reasoning to impact an audience. The two primary types of reasoning are inductive reasoning and deductive reasoning.

Make Your Case

Public discourse has been traditionally focused on reasoning and evidence (logos), but the use of emotion (pathos) is becoming increasingly evident in persuasive attempts. Do you think/ feel that pathos will overtake logos as the central focus of public discourse? How would you support your view?

Inductive Reasoning. **Inductive reasoning** involves deriving a general conclusion based on specific evidence, examples, or instances. If you go to a restaurant and receive bad service, your friend goes to the same restaurant on another night and receives bad service, and a classmate goes to the restaurant and also reports having received bad service, you may conclude based on these specific instances that this restaurant has bad service. When using inductive reasoning, a sufficient number of examples or instances must exist from which to draw a legitimate conclusion, and these examples or instances must be relevant to the conclusion being established.

Deductive Reasoning. **Deductive reasoning** involves using general conclusions, premises, or principles to reach a conclusion about a specific example or instance. Thus, you may decide that since Duck and McMahan products are generally high in quality, a Duck and McMahan television set would be a high-quality product. Such reasoning frequently takes the form of syllogisms. A **syllogism** is a form of argumentation consisting of a major premise, a minor premise, and a conclusion. The *major premise* of a syllogism is a statement or conclusion of a general nature, while the *minor premise* entails a more specific statement about a particular instance or example. The *conclusion* is then derived from the logical connection between the major and minor premises. This may sound a bit confusing, but examining the following syllogism based on the example above might clear things up for you:

Major Premise: Duck and McMahan products are high in quality.
(This statement involves a general conclusion about Duck and McMahan products.)

Minor Premise: This television is a Duck and McMahan product.
(This statement involves a specific example connected to the major premise about Duck and McMahan products.)

Conclusion: This television is high in quality.
(The conclusion is based on the major and minor premises. If Duck and McMahan products are high in quality and this television is a Duck and McMahan product, this television must be high in quality.)

This method of reasoning is sometimes presented in a slightly modified form known as an enthymeme. An **enthymeme** is a syllogism that excludes one or two of the three components of a syllogism. An enthymeme may be used when one of the premises is readily understood, accepted as true, or so obvious that it does not even need to be stated. People often use enthymemes when talking with others. If a salesclerk at an electronics store was attempting to sell you the Duck and McMahan television, he or she might exclude both the minor premise and the conclusion in the example syllogism above and simply establish the major premise by saying, "Duck and McMahan products are very high in quality." The fact that this television set is a Duck and McMahan product might be obvious, perhaps as would the natural conclusion. Beyond dealing with the obvious, however, incorporating enthymemes into one's message often seems more natural than speaking in syllogisms. If the salesclerk includes all the parts of a syllogism and says, "Duck and McMahan products are high in quality; this television is a Duck and McMahan product; this television is high in quality," you might determine the salesclerk either is a robot or really needs a coffee break.

Sir Arthur Conan Doyle, creator of Sherlock Holmes, modeled his character's skills of deduction on Professor Joseph Bell. By the way, never in the 56 short stories and four novels featuring the famous detective did he ever say, "Elementary, my dear Watson." Now that you know how deductive reasoning works, though, it may become just that.

As a speaker, you must determine whether it is most appropriate to present the material in the form of a syllogism or an enthymeme. As with other choices involving the development and delivery of a public presentation, this decision will be determined by your analysis of the audience. If your audience is adequately familiar with the material, you could probably use an enthymeme successfully. However, if the audience is unfamiliar with the material or will not readily accept the major or minor premise as true or accurate, you should present the material in the form of a syllogism.

Persuasive Speaking and the Social Judgment Theory

A more recent offering than artistic proofs and also valuable in increasing the effectiveness of persuasive presentations is the theory of social judgment. The **social judgment theory** (C. Sherif, Sherif, & Nebergall, 1965; M. Sherif & Hovland, 1961) explains how people may respond to a range of positions surrounding a particular topic or issue. This theory can be understood as dealing with an audience's relationship with the topic or issue. Using this theory, imagine an audience responding or relating to the various positions connected to a topic or an issue in one of three ways: acceptance, rejection, and noncommitment. These positions can in turn be placed in three types of ranges, referred to as latitudes (see Figure 13.1). The **latitude of acceptance** includes the range

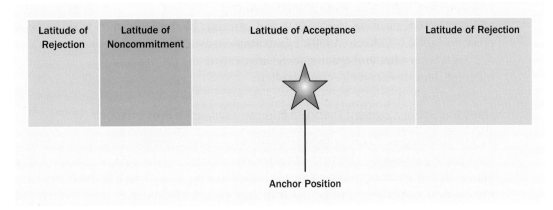

Latitude of Rejection	Latitude of Noncommitment	Latitude of Acceptance	Latitude of Rejection

Anchor Position

Figure 13.1 Components of the Social Judgment Theory

of position that the audience deems acceptable. At some point within this latitude of acceptance is the **anchor position**, which represents the preferred or most acceptable position. The **latitude of rejection** includes those positions that the audience deems unacceptable. Finally, the **latitude of noncommitment** includes positions that the audience neither wholly accepts nor wholly rejects.

Variables Impacting Social Judgment

The size of the latitudes is affected by the audience's level of involvement or relationship with the issue. **Audience involvement** is based on audience members' recognition of the issue's significance and importance in their lives. The greater the significance and importance audience members perceive the issue as having in their lives, the more involved they will be with the issue, and vice versa. As audience members' involvement with an issue increases, so does the size of their latitude of rejection. Audiences highly involved with an issue will have relatively small latitudes of acceptance and noncommitment because people will spend more time thinking about and evaluating the concerns surrounding an issue if they view it as important and meaningful. People will spend less time engaged in those behaviors if they do not view the issue as such. Thus, people highly involved with an issue will have developed a more focused view of what is acceptable.

Audience members will often perceive messages as either closer to or farther away from their position than they actually are. These perceptions are based on the **assimilation effect**, which maintains that if someone advocates a position within your latitude of acceptance, you will view it as closer to your anchor position than it really is, and the **contrast effect**, which maintains that if someone advocates a position within your latitude of rejection, you will view it as farther from your anchor

The assimilation effect and contrast effect are similar to what happens in interpersonal relationships. Depending on their view of someone, people generally believe they are either more similar to or more different from that person than they actually are.

position than it really is. Assimilation and contrast effects are more likely to occur when an actual position is not clear and can thus be minimized by making your position explicit (O'Keefe, 1990). For example, advocating *harsh penalties* for drug dealers is somewhat ambiguous, while advocating the *death penalty* as the punishment for drug dealers is clear and explicit.

Using the Social Judgment Theory to Improve Persuasive Presentations

As you can imagine, determining the social judgment of a group of listeners takes thorough audience analysis. Also true is that various members of the audience will probably hold different anchor positions when it comes to your issue. You will not likely have specific data supporting a precise illustration of audience latitudes. However, you could use audience analysis to provide a rough idea of how the general audience latitudes might appear, which could prove very useful when developing your presentation. Furthermore, elements of the social judgment theory also provide key insight into improving the effectiveness of persuasive presentations in general.

Be Explicit. First, the assimilation and contrast effects underscore the need to be very explicit in conveying your goals to the audience. The audience members must know exactly what position you support and want them to accept. When dealing with the contrast effect, if the position you desire is within audience members' latitude of rejection, it may not be as far away from their anchor position as they would assume if you did not explicitly state your position. Audience members may view your position as not even remotely considerable, when in reality it is closer to their anchor position than they realize.

Explicitly stating your position is also necessary when dealing with assimilation effects. Having your audience members believe your position is closer to their anchor position than it actually is might appear to be beneficial. However, this can actually reduce the effectiveness of your presentation. According to O'Keefe (1990), the audience will view you as seeking less change than you actually seek. In fact, "in the extreme case of complete assimilation, receivers may think that the message is simply saying what they already believe—and hence receivers don't change their attitudes at all" (p. 38). Both the assimilation effect and the contrast effect emphasize the need to state your position explicitly.

Consider Audience Involvement. Second, considering audience perceptions of positions related to your topic will also assist you in determining how to develop your presentation. Audiences with a considerably large latitude of noncommitment may not be particularly involved with the topic or fully aware of its importance in their lives. The size of either the latitude of acceptance or the latitude of rejection may dictate which organizational pattern you use to develop your presentation. People new to public speaking often wonder whether they should include both sides of the issue when presenting a persuasive speech. As with most questions involving presentations, the answer depends on the audience. If you believe the audience will strongly oppose your stance, it might be a good idea to present both sides of the issue to address the limitations of the opposite side. When an audience is neutral or somewhat unopposed to your position, presenting only your side of the issue will usually suffice.

Degree of Change. Finally, considering the social judgment of your audience will help you ascertain the degree of change you should seek with your audience. If the anchor position of the audience is far away from the position being advocated, a speaker will be hard-pressed to convince many members of the audience to accept that new position. This reality should not discourage you as a speaker. Rather, you should simply be aware that persuasion is often a continual and gradual process.

FOCUS QUESTIONS REVISITED

1. What are the types of informative speeches?

The following are the four primary types of informative speeches: (a) speeches of definition and description, (b) expository speeches, (c) process speeches, and (d) how-to speeches. Speeches of definition and description provide the audience with an extended explanation or depiction of an object, a person, a concept, or an event. Expository speeches provide the audience with a detailed or in-depth review or analysis of an object, a person, a concept, or an event. These speeches seek higher levels of understanding on the part of the audience than speeches of definition or description. Process speeches describe the procedure or method through which something is accomplished without the expectation that the audience will actually perform the process. The audience will be able to explain and understand the process once you finish speaking. How-to speeches describe the procedure or methods through which something is accomplished with the expectation that the audience will be able to perform the process at the speech's conclusion.

2. What strategies exist for achieving successful informative presentations?

To achieve successful informative presentations, speakers should maintain a narrow focus, adapt the complexity of the presentation, be clear and simple, use clear organization and guide the audience, stress significance and utility, provide a clear mental picture, relate unknown material to known material, and motivate the audience.

3. What are the types of persuasive speeches?

The two primary types of persuasive speeches are speeches to convince and speeches to actuate. Speeches to convince are delivered in an attempt to impact audience thinking, and they encompass a primary claim—essentially, what you are trying to convince your audience to believe. The following are the four primary types of persuasive claims that can be developed through a speech to convince: (a) policy, (b) value, (c) fact, and (d) conjecture. Speeches to actuate are delivered in an attempt to impact audience behavior.

4. How might preexisting beliefs and attitudes of the audience influence speeches to convince?

Depending on preexisting beliefs and attitudes of the audience, a speaker may attempt to reinforce an existing way of thinking, change an existing way of thinking, or create a new way of thinking.

5. How might speeches to actuate affect audience behavior?

As a result of a speech to actuate, audience members may reinforce, alter, or cease an existing behavior; enact a new behavior; or avoid a future behavior.

6. What are the artistic proofs?

The artistic proofs are ethos, pathos, and logos. Ethos involves the use of speaker credibility to impact an audience. Pathos involves the use of emotional appeals to impact an audience. Logos involves the use of logic or reasoning to impact an audience.

7. What is the social judgment theory, and how can it impact persuasive attempts?

The social judgment theory explains how people may respond to a range of positions surrounding a particular topic or issue. Underscoring the need to be very explicit when conveying your goals to the audience, this theory will assist you when determining how to develop the presentation and the degree of change you should seek with your audience.

KEY CONCEPTS

anchor position   335
assimilation effect   335
audience involvement 335
claim of conjecture   329
claim of fact   329
claim of policy   328
claim of value   329
concrete words   327
contrast effect   335
deductive reasoning   333
descriptive language   327
enthymeme   334
ethos   331
expository speech   321

how-to speech   321
inductive reasoning   333
latitude of acceptance   334
latitude of noncommitment   335
latitude of rejection   335
logos   333
pathos   332
process speech   321
social judgment theory   334
speech of definition and description   320
speech to actuate   330
speech to convince   328
syllogism   333

QUESTIONS TO ASK YOUR FRIENDS

1. Ask a friend at school to recall the most recent lecture in one of his or her classes. Would your friend consider that lecture more of an informative presentation or more of a persuasive presentation? What characteristics of that lecture led to your friend's judgment? Do you agree with his or her assessment?

2. Ask a friend to describe a time when someone tried to explain something to him or her, but your friend had difficulty understanding what that person was attempting to explain. Why does your friend think that he or she had difficulty understanding? Based on what you now know about informing others, what could that person have done differently to assist in your friend's understanding and comprehension of the material discussed?

3. Ask a friend to describe a time when someone tried to convince him or her of something but was not successful. Why does your friend think that he or she was not convinced? Based on what you now know about persuasion, could that person have done anything differently to increase the likelihood of convincing your friend?

MEDIA LINKS

1. Read letters submitted to the editor of your local newspaper. Which of the following claims are addressed or presented most often: policy, value, fact, or conjecture? What type of support—if any—is provided in these letters?

2. Watch a presentation before Congress on C-SPAN or online, and look for evidence of ethos, pathos, and logos. Which artistic proof is most prominent?

3. Watch advertisements on television or online and look for evidence of ethos, pathos, and logos. Which artistic proof is most prominent? Does the prominent artistic proof change depending on the product or service advertised? If so, why do you think this change exists?

ETHICAL ISSUES

1. Emotions can be very powerful tools of persuasion. To what extent do you think people should elicit fear, guilt, sadness, anger, and other "negative" emotions when persuading an audience? Are there limits to which speakers should adhere when inducing these emotions? Does your perspective change depending on the purpose of the speech?

2. Review the discussion of fallacious arguments in the chapter on listening. These flawed arguments are often quite effective when used to persuade someone. Are there any occasions that would justify the use of fallacious arguments? If you believe such occasions exist, how would you support your answer?

3. Freedom of expression is a major tenet in the United States. Do you believe people should have unlimited freedom of expression? If so, how would you support this response? Do you believe in limits to an individual's freedom of expression? If so, provide examples where freedom of expression should be limited and support this assessment. Think about these questions for a while—the Supreme Court has!

ANSWERS TO PHOTO CAPTIONS

Photo 13.1 ■ The chef is delivering a how-to speech since he is describing a procedure or method with the expectation that the audience will be able to perform the process once he has concluded his presentation.

Photo 13.2 ■ Audience members will be more likely to pay attention to a message and incorporate the information into their lives if they view it as important and meaningful.

Photo 13.3 ▪ A positive relational connection with members of an audience increases their perceptions of a speaker's credibility and enhances their willingness to accept what the speaker wants them to think or do.

Photo 13.4 ▪ The speaker would be making a claim of policy.

Photo 13.5 ▪ The artistic proof pathos involves the use of such emotions as sadness.

STUDENT STUDY SITE

Visit the study site at **www.sagepub.com/boc2e** for e-flashcards, practice quizzes, journal articles and additional study resources.

REFERENCES

Gouran, D. S., Wiethoff, W. E., & Doelger, J. A. (1994). *Mastering communication* (2nd ed.). Boston: Allyn & Bacon.

Gregory, H. (2002). *Public speaking for college and career.* New York: McGraw-Hill.

O'Keefe, D. J. (1990). *Persuasion: Theory and research.* Newbury Park, CA: Sage.

Schachter, S., & Singer, J. E. (1962). Cognitive, social, and physiological determinants of emotional state. *Psychological Review, 69,* 379–399.

Sherif, C. W., Sherif, M., & Nebergall, R. (1965). *Attitude and attitude change: The social judgment-involvement approach.* Philadelphia: W. B. Saunders.

Sherif, M., & Hovland, C. I. (1961). *Social judgment: Assimilation and contrast effects in communication and attitude change.* New Haven, CT: Yale University Press.

14

Delivering a Public Presentation

In the previous chapters, we talked about the preparation that goes into a presentation and about developing a presentation that actually connects relationally with an audience. We discussed how to develop the purpose and thesis of your presentation and gathering material to support your claims both logically and relationally. We examined what it means to develop an argument and how to determine the best way to organize your speech to connect you, the audience, and the material. We addressed the importance of introductions and conclusions and the logical and relational components that must be included in each of these areas to ensure an effective presentation. We also examined the specific development of various informative and persuasive presentations. A constant presence throughout our discussion of this material has been audiences and the need to connect relationally with them. It is now time to actually present the speech to them and develop this relational connection.

Before going any further, though, we must address **communication apprehension**, the technical term for the fear or anxiety you may experience when speaking in public. This fear is actually quite common, and in fact, the *Book of Lists* (Wallechinsky & Wallace, 1995) indicates that more people are afraid of speaking in public than are afraid of death!

Because of its pervasiveness and its impact on people's lives, communication apprehension has been a sustained area of study in the discipline of communication for the past four decades (McCroskey, 1970). We realize this fact does not make it any easier to get up in front of an audience of friends, acquaintances, colleagues, classmates, or strangers to speak, but knowing that the majority of people in the world experience the same concerns may provide a bit of comfort. At least they know how you feel.

A number of politicians, actors, singers, and even communication professors report that they get nervous when speaking or performing in public.

Near the end of this chapter, we discuss communication apprehension in greater detail and give you some suggestions for dealing with your concerns. We do not attempt to fool you into believing that presenting a speech to an audience is simple and carefree, because it takes a good deal of preparation and effort. However, we do tell you with great certainty that you will be able to do it.

Communication apprehension can be linked to relationships shared with the audience. In some cases, speakers might know members of the audience (e.g., coworkers, group members, classmates) on a personal level and not want to look foolish to them, since it might damage their relationship outside of the presentation. On other occasions, speakers might not know the audience personally but might feel anxious about how to best perform an appropriate identity that satisfies audience members' expectations.

Some of your anxiety probably comes from not knowing what to expect or how to actually present a speech. If you are like most of your classmates, you probably have had little experience speaking to public audiences and delivering formal public presentations. While you may not have much experience delivering speeches in public, through studying material from the previous chapters, you now better understand what developing a public presentation entails and what you must do to develop an effective speech. This chapter provides guidelines and suggestions for presenting speeches that will assist you in delivering an effective presentation and give you a better understanding of speech delivery, which will likely help alleviate some of your anxiety.

As always, the relationship between a speaker and an audience is of paramount importance. Within this chapter, we discuss styles of delivery, providing benefits and drawbacks to each one along with strategies for selecting and enacting each delivery style. We discuss the choices you will face as a speaker when determining the most appropriate style. We also address the goals of effective delivery, which include developing and enhancing your credibility, connecting with the audience relationally, and ensuring audience understanding of the material.

Focus Questions

1. What are three guidelines for effective delivery?
2. What are the styles of delivery?
3. What are the goals of effective delivery?
4. What are the components of effective delivery?
5. What are presentation aids?
6. What is communication apprehension, and how can it be managed?

Guidelines for Effective Delivery:
What Are the Answers to Common Questions?

In the course of this chapter, we talk about effective delivery styles and techniques. Before fully addressing specifics, we first want to introduce three guidelines to follow when delivering a presentation. Based on years of experience working with student and novice speakers, these guidelines have been derived from answers to questions these speakers frequently have. They wonder, for instance, how they should act, what they should sound like, and what happens if they mess up or are nervous. Here are the answers: (a) Always be yourself, (b) strive to make your speech conversational, and (c) avoid drawing undue attention to mistakes and to nerves.

Always Be Yourself

Even before reading this book, you could probably recognize and distinguish particular qualities that really good public speakers possess. You can no doubt imagine an incredible speaker who is capable of relating with audience members and working them into a dramatic frenzy of emotion and awareness and who, upon ending a speech, is showered with praise and cheers from the crowd. You may have such fabulous speakers as Ronald Reagan, Winston Churchill, and Oprah Winfrey in mind as you study public presentations and gain a better understanding of why they are or were so effective at speaking and relating with an audience. You may even wish to emulate their speaking styles in hope of improving your own speaking ability. However, imitating Ronald Reagan, Winston Churchill, Oprah Winfrey, or any other speaker you admire will not make you a good speaker.

The most effective way of delivering a presentation is by being you, not by pretending to be someone else. You must deliver your presentations in the most natural way. Doing otherwise will make you appear artificial, uncomfortable, and less credible to your audience. Consequently, you will not be able to connect relationally with your audience. If you admire particular characteristics of another speaker, you can attempt to integrate these qualities into your own delivery style. Ultimately, however, you must adapt these qualities to your personal style.

Ronald Reagan was often called The Great Communicator. When he first began in radio, he noted his ability to connect with listeners was achieved by imagining he was talking with a group of friends at a barbershop.

Of course, all speakers have particularly strong areas of delivery and other, weaker areas in need of development. When we advise you to be yourself, we are not implying that you should just get up in front of the audience and whatever happens will be just fine. Instead, we want to encourage you to feel relaxed and to bring out the best aspects of yourself and your personal delivery while working to modify or eliminate aspects of your delivery that may hinder your presentation. This chapter will help you recognize your own personal strengths, provide guidelines for their promotion, and allow you to recognize possible areas in need of development. As you are learning how to become an effective speaker, strive to incorporate the strategies offered here into your own personal style.

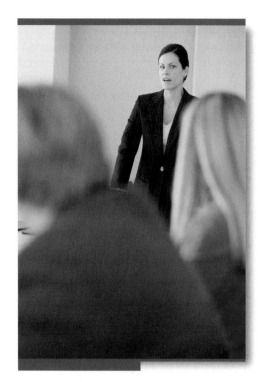

Photo 14.1 This speaker admires the speaking style of her supervisor, who happens to be a very effective public speaker. Should she imitate her supervisor's style? (See page 364.)

Strive to Make Your Presentation Conversational

You may wonder what your natural speaking style is like. If so, think back to the last conversation you had with a close friend. That is it! In the most effective speeches, the speaker connects with the audience in a relational way. Rather than delivering your speech as if you were speaking down to the audience from on high, you can accomplish this connection through a natural conversational tone, the kind you have with friends, family members, colleagues, and others with whom you share a personal or social relationship. In fact, you should consider the delivery of a speech as nothing more than a conversation in which you just happen to be doing all the talking for an extended period. You can adapt and understand many aspects of delivery discussed in this chapter in terms of your everyday relational experiences.

Avoid Calling Attention to Mistakes and to Nerves

When delivering a speech, people commonly worry about the possibility of making a mistake. They fear, for example, that they may forget to include a phrase they had wanted to incorporate or that they may stumble over a word. You may make mistakes, but it probably will not matter. Think back to the last time you spoke with an acquaintance who stumbled over a word. Were you traumatized by the experience, and did you hope to never again be forced to speak with this person? Unless your acquaintance drew unnecessary attention to it, you probably did not think much about it.

The only way that such mistakes will distract from your speech and significantly damage your credibility and your relationship with the audience is if you draw attention to them. Worse yet is dramatically apologizing for them or questioning your ability by saying something like, "Oh, I am so terribly sorry for ruining this speech." By drawing attention to your mistake, you direct more attention toward it than toward your message and your relationship with the audience.

Sometimes you must acknowledge a mistake for the sake of honesty or accuracy, but do it without great elaboration or excessive apology. For instance, if you provide the wrong oral citation, provide an erroneous statistic, or misquote testimony, you should quickly clarify the mistake and move on.

In addition to not calling attention to mistakes, do not point out to your audience that you are nervous about speaking. Nerves themselves do not necessarily decrease a person's credibility, but calling attention to and obsessing over them might. If nothing else, you will draw your audience members' attention away from your message and on to something they may not have even noticed. In fact, most of the time, an audience will have no idea you are nervous unless you point it out.

Styles of Delivery

With these three guidelines in mind, we can now discuss the three delivery styles to choose between when delivering public presentations. Each delivery style comes with inherent advantages and disadvantages, with some styles more suitable for particular circumstances than others. This section will help you understand the characteristics of each delivery style. You will also discover how to successfully utilize each style when delivering a public presentation and relating with an audience.

Manuscript Delivery

Manuscript delivery involves having the entire speech written out in front of you when you speak. Speakers using this method of delivery generally utter every word and phrase on the page exactly as written. This style of delivery applies when accurate wording is required. Members of Congress often use a manuscript style of delivery when speaking in the House of Representatives or Senate. The president uses a manuscript delivery when presenting the State of the Union address, and so do many political candidates making major speeches. Your professors may use the manuscript method of delivery when presenting their research at academic conferences when they desire careful wording of specific findings.

When using a teleprompter for manuscript delivery, the words of the speech are projected onto slanting clear screens to the left and right of the speaker. The screens appear clear to the audience, but because of their angle (using a technique called Pepper's ghost), text can be read off the screens by the speaker. This allows for eye contact with the audience—and explains why speakers address the left and right of the audience so much more often than the center where there is no such screen to help them.

While the advantage to this style of delivery is an increased accuracy of the material presented, the glaring disadvantage to using a manuscript is that the delivery often suffers dramatically. Frankly, the delivery often stinks! Using a manuscript to deliver a presentation will often lead to decreased eye contact with audience members, since you will focus your eyes on the page in front of you instead of on them. Further, the speech often sounds like it is being read since, essentially, it is. Also, if a speaker holds on to the manuscript, the number and quality of gestures and other movements will diminish, and the manuscript may distract the audience. With these disadvantages often outweighing the advantage, we encourage you to use a manuscript style of delivery only when absolutely necessary.

Memorized Delivery

Memorized delivery is exactly what it sounds like: delivering a speech without the use of a manuscript or any notes whatsoever. This delivery style comes with some obvious advantages. Without any notes, absolutely no chance exists of reading the speech. Speakers using memorized delivery will probably maintain eye contact, and the speech will not sound like it is being read. They need not worry about notes distracting the audience or hindering the use of gestures and movement. While these points might sound good, some disadvantages of memorized delivery make it less beneficial than you might imagine.

One disadvantage of a memorized style of delivery is that committing an entire speech to memory is very difficult. When delivering a speech from memory, speakers will likely remember certain parts or phrases but forget many of their ideas or present them in a random and confusing manner.

Another disadvantage to delivering a speech completely from memory is that it often sounds memorized rather than natural and conversational, which hinders the development of a relational connection with the audience. People memorize and remember information in bits.

If you do not believe us, recite your telephone number with area code or your Social Security number to yourself. We will wait. . . . Seriously, we mean it. . . . Did you do it yet? . . . OK, glad you are back. More than likely, when reciting your phone number, you gave the three numbers of the area code, briefly paused, gave the next three numbers, paused again, and then gave the final four numbers. When presenting your Social Security number, you probably gave the first three numbers, paused, gave the next two numbers, paused, and then gave the final four numbers. If you still do not believe us and argue that this results from both series of numbers being separated that way, recite the alphabet. . . . You probably recited *A* through *G*, *H* through *P*, *Q* through *S*, *T* through *V*, *W* and *X*, and *Y* and *Z* almost musically. You may even have sung the jingle at the end.

See: You have been doing this for years. Notwithstanding years of success, what works fine for telephone numbers, Social Security numbers, and the alphabet is not appropriate when presenting a speech. When someone delivers a completely memorized speech, it often sounds unnatural and uneven and seems emotionless and mechanical rather than natural and conversational. A relational connection with the audience becomes incredibly difficult to establish.

Contrarian Challenge

We encourage you to use manuscript delivery only when careful wording is required. In addition, perhaps more so than even memorized delivery, it should not be attempted by novice speakers. It requires a great deal of speaking experience to successfully accomplish. This aspect might seem counterintuitive. It might seem to you that novice speakers would be better off having the entire speech written out in front of them. Can you make an argument for why novice speakers would benefit from manuscript delivery? If you take everything into consideration, we believe you will agree with us on this one!

Extemporaneous Delivery

Generally recommended as the way to achieve a natural and conversational delivery while ensuring the accuracy of ideas and connecting relationally with an audience, **extemporaneous delivery** involves the use of minimal notes. Speakers using this method prepare an entire speech but do not use a manuscript when presenting the speech. Rather, they include key words, phrases, or, at most, brief sections of the speech in their notes.

This style of delivery provides many of the advantages of manuscript and memorized delivery without the disadvantages. With minimal notes, you will not be tempted to concentrate on them rather than engaging in eye contact with your audience. You will not read to your audience, so you will probably speak in a conversational tone of voice. You will not have multiple sheets of paper or cards in front of you, so your notes will less likely distract your audience. At the same time, using notes will help you stay focused and ensure that your presentation includes key points and vital ideas. The extemporaneous style of delivery requires a great deal of practice and preparation to perform effectively, but it will enable you to deliver an effective, relationally developed presentation.

College Experience

We are stretching the connection between this box and what you have been studying in this chapter quite a bit. However, what we are about to tell you will assist your college experience. It has been established that people remember things in bits. Getting even more specific, people tend to remember those bits appearing at the beginning and those bits appearing at the end. So, if you were shown a list of numbers, and these numbers were then taken away, you would likely recall the numbers at the beginning of the list and the numbers at the end of the list. You would likely forget the numbers in the middle. The same thing happens when people study! Accordingly, you are more likely to remember things at the beginning of a study session and at the end of a study session. It is much more effective to have multiple study sessions lasting shorter periods than to study for 10 hours straight the night before an examination. Trust us—we tried both ways when we were in school.

Goals of Effective Delivery

Regardless of which style of delivery you use, the objectives of effective delivery remain the same. Essentially, effective delivery entails developing and enhancing audience perceptions of your credibility, increasing audience understanding, and establishing a relational connection with the audience. In this section we discuss these elements in more detail and then talk about aspects of delivery that allow you to establish and maintain them.

Developing and Enhancing Credibility

Drawing from decades of research, communication scholars Robert Gass and John Seiter (2011) maintain the existence of three primary dimensions of credibility

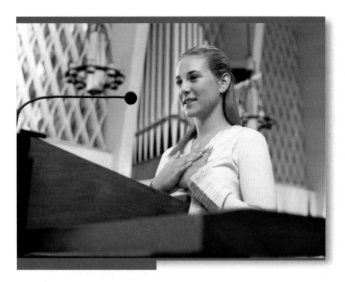

Photo 14.2 What will this speaker's minimal use of notes and careful preparation enable her to achieve? (See page 365.)

and four secondary dimensions of credibility. The three primary dimensions—expertise, trustworthiness, and goodwill—no doubt sound familiar since we talked about their importance in the development of the speech itself. Yet these primary dimensions are fully transacted through the delivery of your speech. Later in this chapter, we discuss various components of delivery and how you can properly convey these dimensions. Presented in Table 14.1, the four secondary dimensions of credibility include dynamism, composure, sociability, and inspiring. You may notice how these dimensions connect especially to relational qualities and can be established through the delivery of your speech.

Table 14.1 Secondary Dimensions of Credibility

Dynamism involves being energetic and enthusiastic. Certainly, you want your audience members to perceive you as interested and concerned about your topic, your speech, and them personally. Make sure your enthusiasm is sincere and appropriate; otherwise, other dimensions of credibility, such as trustworthiness, will be called into question, as will a genuinely meaningful relationship with the audience.

Composure entails the ability to appear calm under pressure. Audience members will view someone who cracks under pressure as less credible than someone who is able to overcome potential obstacles and unforeseen circumstances, and they will not desire a relationship with such a person. Again, nervousness does not necessarily mean a lack of composure. Actually, delivering the speech proves your ability to manage feelings of stress and discomfort. Your audience will only question your composure if you draw unnecessary attention to your nerves.

Sociability involves being personable and likeable. As with personal relationships, people want to be around individuals they perceive as good-natured and pleasant. On the other hand, people avoid individuals they perceive as gruff and unfriendly. Speakers who convey an open and congenial demeanor through their delivery are often most effective, in part because they appear to meet the primary dimensions of goodwill and trustworthiness. They are the type of people with whom others would want to develop a relationship.

Inspiring entails the ability to instill enthusiasm in others. Again supporting the primary dimensions, people often view individuals who inspire them as knowledgeable, honest, and concerned. It is not precisely clear whether people view them in this manner because they inspire people or whether they inspire people because people view them as knowledgeable, honest, and concerned. Most likely it is a combination of both, with one reinforcing the other. As with other dimensions of credibility, people are more likely to desire a relationship with inspiring individuals.

Increasing Audience Understanding

The delivery of your speech must also work to increase and guide audience understanding. Gestures and movement can help explain and reinforce the material you present to the audience. Pauses can help guide the audience when you are moving from one section or part of your speech to another.

An especially significant role of delivery is the expression of emotion. If you are discussing a serious or solemn topic, your voice, facial expression, and body should correspond and convey the appropriate emotion or tone. Likewise, if your speech deals with a topic that makes you angry, you should reflect and express this feeling in your delivery. The same applies to such other emotions as fear, excitement, happiness, and pleasure. This coordination both reinforces what you say and underscores your approach to the issue.

Your expression of an emotional tone lets the audience members know how they should feel about and approach the topic. This experience arises in part from a general transference of emotion. When someone is sad or upset, for example, other people around him or her act in a manner that supports this emotion. They might also begin feeling upset themselves. Setting the emotional tone also acts as a cue for the audience.

Think about it in terms of the effects of background music when you are watching a movie. The music sets the mood and lets you know how you should feel or what to expect. This association especially holds true in horror movies. Eerie or creepy music plays as someone approaches a closet door. You feel uneasy, your heart may begin racing, and you know something is going to jump out. It may be just a cat, but you know something is definitely going to happen. The same holds true when delivering a presentation. Your delivery and expression of emotion will let the audience members know how they should feel and what to expect, whether it is an issue that should make them concerned or angry, a solution to a problem that should comfort and delight them, or a psychotic killer jumping out from behind a closed door.

Strategic Communication

We discuss nonverbal components of effective delivery later in the chapter, but here is something for you to keep in mind when delivering presentations. Facial expressions and body positioning work together to convey emotions. Your facial expressions inform people what emotion you are experiencing, while your body informs them of the intensity of that emotion. For instance, your face may be conveying anger, but your body may be loose and fluid—indicating a low level of anger. On the other hand, your face may be conveying anger, but your body may be tense and rigid—indicating a high level of anger. Remembering how these nonverbal elements work together can assist you when conveying emotion to an audience.

Connecting Relationally With the Audience

Through the delivery of a public presentation, you must also strive to develop a positive relational connection with the audience. In all personal and social relationships, people

Although accommodation may increase perceptions of similarity, be careful that you do not overdo it. Both Hillary Clinton and Barack Obama have been chastised for speaking with disingenuous Southern dialects when speaking to voters in the South.

convey nonverbally how they feel about others. Public audiences should feel that the speaker likes and cares about them. You can transact this alliance by smiling when appropriate and using a concerned and compassionate tone of voice when discussing the importance of your topic in their lives. You can also develop a connection with the audience members through an openness of gestures and bodily movements toward them.

Further, you can develop a relational connection through identification with the audience members by communicating similarity with them. Studies in accommodation have shown that people adjust their rates of speech, accents, facial expressions, and bodily movements to match those with whom they interact to indicate and develop a relational connection (Giles, 2008). When speaking in public, you may also accomplish this association through appearance and style of dress or through dialect and the similar pronunciation of words or other vocal characteristics. As with all forms of communication, when delivering a public presentation, speakers communicate more than just content; they transact a relationship with the audience.

Components of Effective Delivery

Now that we have examined the goals of effective delivery, we can discuss how to achieve them through the components of effective delivery. This book proposes that the same nonverbal relational techniques work in dyadic and public speaking situations. We now apply elements of Chapter 3 accordingly.

Make Your Case

Select a person you know or a public figure you consider an effective public speaker. What characteristics of his or her delivery do you find most impressive? What could this individual do to improve his or her delivery of public presentations?

Now select someone you consider a poor public speaker. What characteristics of his or her delivery do you find most in need of improvement? What suggestions would you provide this person to improve his or her

Personal Appearance

Personal appearance—including clothing, hairstyle, jewelry, tattoos, makeup, and other artifacts—reflects who you are and how you want other people to perceive you and your relationship with them. Personal appearance is so powerful that people often make judgments based more on another person's appearance than on his or her words or actions. Through your appearance, you must seek to connect relationally with the audience and convey credibility. This strategy means dressing in a manner that is consistent with audience expectations and conveys professionalism or a specific relationship. Audiences view those dressed professionally—again determined by audience expectations—as more knowledgeable and trustworthy. Dressing in a professional manner also conveys to your audience members that you care enough about them and the occasion to dress appropriately.

Vocalics

Just as in dyadic interaction, a speaker's voice is a key component in the development of a conversational and relational style of delivery, which is accomplished in part though variation of pitch, rate, pauses, and volume.

Pitch

Pitch involves the highness or lowness of your voice. You have a range at which you normally speak, and you should use this same range when speaking in front of an audience. Whether you speak with a high or a low tone of voice, you must speak using a variety of pitches within your natural range. Speaking without variations in pitch means speaking in monotone, which will cause audiences to lose interest in your presentation and prevent you from connecting with them relationally.

Rate

Rate is how fast or slow you speak, generally determined by how many words you speak per minute. On average, people speak at around 150 words per minute. You may speak at a faster or slower rate in a normal conversation, and speaking at approximately the same rate when delivering a speech should work out just fine. Times will occur when your rate of speech is either faster or slower than others, depending on your emotional state, intensity of language, and emphasis on certain words.

Volume

The **volume** of your presentation is determined by how loudly or quietly you speak. When presenting your speech, strive to speak as naturally as possible. Just like other elements of the voice, volume should rise and fall during the delivery of your speech to make the presentation appear more natural and conversational, which will help you maintain audience attention and connect with the audience in meaningful ways. You can also use changes in volume (e.g., speaking more quietly as you reach the end of a major section) to provide emphasis, to underscore emotion, and even to direct the audience.

Speak as naturally as possible, but obviously the audience should be able to hear you. Demosthenes, an ancient Greek orator, trained himself to speak by trying to project his voice over the roaring ocean waves. If you cannot make it to a beach in Greece, though, here is another option. The volume of your voice increases naturally as the amount of air being released increases. Therefore, when attempting to speak in a louder voice, remember to take deep breaths and expel more air.

Pauses

Pauses, or breaks in the vocal flow, serve to direct the audience, add emphasis to areas of your presentation, and allow you to, um, avoid, like, nonfluencies and stuff. You may wish to include a brief pause when shifting from one main point to another or from one section of the speech to another. This action allows the audience members to recognize that something is going on and fully prepares them for movement within the speech.

Pauses also allow you to add emphasis to what you say or are about to say. If you have said something particularly profound, a pause will allow the audience to reflect on it. If you are getting ready to say something especially important, a pause will signal the audience members that they need to pay particular attention to what comes next.

Finally, pauses will help you avoid **nonfluencies**, meaningless vocal fillers that often distract from a presentation. Common nonfluencies include *um, uh, like, OK, you know,* and *you know what I'm saying.* A brief moment of silence will not distract the audience or seem out of place and, certainly, will not be more distracting or inappropriate than a nonfluency.

Eye Contact

Maintaining eye contact with the audience members will allow you to maintain their attention, as well as enhance your credibility and relational connection. There are a few issues to keep in mind when considering eye contact.

First, many cultures view eye contact as a sign of trustworthiness and as a means of relating with another person. However, some cultures consider eye contact, especially between a subordinate and a superior, a sign of disrespect. Be aware of and prepared for any cultural differences that might arise during a speaking situation.

A second consideration involves where you focus your eye contact. Make sure that you scan the entire room when speaking rather than focusing on one area of the audience. Of course, you should not look side to side like when watching a tennis match. You want to make your scanning appear as natural as possible.

A third consideration when incorporating eye contact is to look pleasant and engaging. A fine line exists between a friendly glance in someone's direction and the piercing stare of a psychopath. You do not want to get into a staring contest with the audience, and blinking from time to time is more than appropriate. Once again, strive to make your eye contact with the audience as natural as possible.

As with shy people communicating in one-on-one situations (Bradshaw, 2006), people who feel apprehensive about speaking in public may decrease eye contact to reduce what they believe will be negative reactions from the audience. This reduces the amount of audience feedback they can gather—much of which may very well be positive—and may actually lead to negative audience reactions. Apprehensive people who avoid eye contact may be misunderstood as deceptive or uncaring about the audience—just another reason to maintain eye contact with audiences and to address anxieties you may experience about speaking in public.

Facial Expression and Body Position

Your facial expression is key to establishing a relational connection with the audience members and directing them emotionally. A smile and a pleasant look on your face go a long way in establishing a positive connection with the audience. Sociability—a secondary dimension of credibility—deals with a person's likeability. People generally enjoy being around people who seem pleasant and congenial. Plus, an amiable nature may serve to underscore and establish the primary dimensions of trustworthiness and goodwill.

Facial expression, along with body position, will allow you to guide the audience emotionally. As mentioned above, your delivery serves to direct the audience members by letting them know how you feel and what they should feel. Your facial expression will let them know the emotion, and your body position will tell them the intensity of that emotion. It is important to remember that your displays of emotion must match your language.

Photo 14.3 How might this speaker's use of gestures benefit his presentation? (See page 365.)

Gestures

Including gestures in the delivery of your speech will assist you in increasing audience understanding and allowing you to channel nervous energy. Gestures can help guide the audience through the presentation. For example, you may emphasize a transition by holding out one hand and saying, "Now that we have addressed X," and then holding out the other hand and continuing, "let's turn our attention to Y."

Gestures are also an effective and productive way to expend the nervous energy you may experience when speaking in front of an audience. Most people feel apprehensive when speaking in front of an audience, which results in a buildup of nervous energy. Releasing this nervous energy allows people to feel more at ease; however, this relief unfortunately results in mannerisms that can distract the audience. **Distracting mannerisms**, or bodily movements that allow a person to discharge nervous energy, serve no actual purpose in the presentation and often divert attention from the message. Such mannerisms include rubbing your hands together, pecking on the sides of the lectern with your fingertips, playing with your watch or jewelry, rubbing the back of your neck, playing with your hair, and rocking from side to side. Here, the importance of gestures comes into play. Gestures allow you to expend this nervous energy while also increasing audience understanding and giving life to your presentation.

Presentation Aids

Presentation aids—objects, images, graphs, video clips, sound, and PowerPoint presentations—are tools used by a speaker to enhance audience understanding,

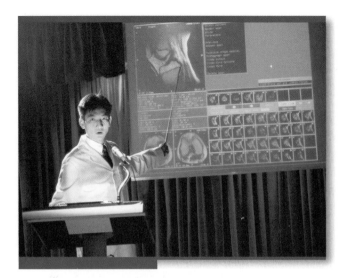

Photo 14.4 What is the speaker doing to remain the primary focus of the audience while addressing a presentation aid? (See page 365.)

appreciation, retention, and attention, as well as a speaker's credibility. Usually auditory and visual in nature, presentation aids can also invoke such senses as taste, touch, and smell. We begin by discussing the ways in which they enhance presentations.

Enhance Audience Understanding

Understanding increases when multiple senses are involved. Someone can explain what it means when something tastes bitter, but actually tasting a sour lemon will provide a better understanding. A person can explain a crescendo, but hearing an example of one can provide a clearer understanding of that musical device. Presentation aids compel audience members to use multiple senses, which increases their understanding of the material presented.

Enhance Audience Appreciation

Often used to allow an audience to appreciate the extent or magnitude of something, presentation aids help your audience fully comprehend what you say or fully recognize its importance or impact. During a speech urging audience members to avoid eating fast food, a speaker might display a pile of cooking lard equivalent to the amount of fat consumed during a typical meal at a fast-food restaurant. When using statistics, incorporating pie charts or line graphs will allow audience members to visually realize and appreciate the magnitude of an issue or fully grasp trends or changes. Images can be powerful tools that enable audience members to fully recognize the importance of your topic. For instance, during a speech about poverty or world hunger, the image of a hungry child will enable the audience to put a human face to the discussion.

Enhance Audience Retention

Along with the use of vivid and memorable support material, presentation aids can help the audience remember the material and retain key information. Quite often, audience members remember presentation aids long after other parts of the speech.

Enhance Audience Attention

If audience members are able to understand, appreciate, and retain the material presented, they will be more likely to pay attention to the speaker and the presentation. Because presentation aids entail change (additional movement by the speaker, something new to look at, an alteration in thought processes, the use of additional senses), they can regain and reinforce audience attention.

Enhance Speaker Credibility

When a speaker conveys information in a manner that allows the audience to understand, appreciate, and retain the material, audience members' perceptions of that person's credibility will improve, as will their perceptions of their relationship with the speaker. A well-developed presentation aid can positively enhance audience members' perceptions of a speaker's overall credibility and their relationship with that speaker. Of course, the opposite holds true as well, and a poorly executed and shoddy presentation aid will most certainly negatively affect a speaker's credibility and his or her relationship with the audience. Table 14.2 provides guidelines for the development and incorporation of presentation aids.

Table 14.2 Presentations Aids Should Be . . .

Fully prepared

Poorly created presentation aids diminish audience perceptions of a speaker's credibility and relationship with the audience, because the speaker appears not fully prepared for the presentation.

Limited in number

Presentation aids can greatly enhance your presentation, but using too many may become a distraction, and the value of each will subsequently diminish. A general guideline to follow for brief presentations: Include no more than two presentation aids for each main point of your speech.

Relatively simple

Presentation aids should convey a single idea.

Inoffensive

Graphic or explicit images can gain the attention of members of your audience and make them appreciate what you are discussing, but these images can also offend and hinder your relationship with them.

Easily seen

It is important that all members of the audience, not just those closest to you, be able to clearly see your presentation aid.

Fully discussed

Fully incorporate presentation aids into your discussion. Do not assume that the audience will recognize the significance of pictures, objects, or any other presentation aid you use.

Incorporated seamlessly

Continue talking as you incorporate and remove your presentation aid rather than stopping your presentation. Use the period immediately before incorporating the presentation aid to prepare the audience members for what they are about to see or hear, and use the period after exhibiting the presentation aid to discuss what they just experienced.

The secondary focus

As a speaker, you should remain the primary focus of the audience, and the presentation aid should be the secondary focus. Accordingly, keep presentation aids out of view when not addressing them, avoid looking directly at them, and do not pass them around.

Managing Communication Apprehension

Feeling nervous or apprehensive about speaking in public is a common occurrence and perfectly natural. While this fact might not alleviate your anxiety about the thought of speaking in front of others, it might reassure you to know you are not alone. Nearly everyone feels nervous when speaking in public. Of course, some people are more apprehensive than others, but it is a common experience, and many people really dread the thought of it.

You might be surprised to learn that a bit of nervousness can actually benefit your presentation. Nervous energy gives your presentation spark and vibrancy that enliven your speech and help maintain audience attention. Without it, your voice will lack enthusiasm, your body will appear listless, and it will be difficult to connect with the audience relationally. Your overall presentation will seem dull, flat, and lifeless. We recognize that this sounds a bit like a shampoo and conditioner commercial. So, we will not go so far as to say that nervous energy will make your presentation easier to style and will prevent frizz and split ends. However, we will continue to maintain that nervous energy will give life to your speech, and without it your presentation will not be as effective.

All joking aside, knowing that nervousness is a normal experience and can benefit your presentation if it is not overwhelming does not diminish the fact that many people consider it a major cause for concern. Communication apprehension can result in a great deal of uncomfortable stress and overall lousy feelings. The good news is that ways exist to deal with nervousness and stress associated with speaking in public.

Recognizing and Knowing What You Fear

The first way to deal with stress and anxiety related to public speaking is to recognize exactly what worries you. Especially when people have little or no actual experience speaking in front of others, they are less afraid of actually speaking in front of an audience and more afraid of the unknown. As a result, people generally imagine things as a whole lot worse than they actually turn out to be.

Fear of the unknown as a major cause of communication apprehension may be supported in part by the finding that the second greatest point of anxiety related to public speaking in the classroom comes at the moment the speech is assigned, with the moment of greatest anxiety occurring right before speaking (Behnke & Sawyer, 1999). In most cases, the assignment is provided before public speaking has fully been discussed in class. The requirements of giving an effective presentation are largely unknown—a frightening proposition. Reading this book and discussing speeches in class will help minimize many of those unknowns, but you can do more.

Listen in on Your Life

Research indicates that most people have at least some apprehension about speaking in public. What would you consider your greatest concerns about speaking in front of an audience? What could you do to minimize these concerns?

Alleviating the Unknown

Often, fear of the unknown emerges from a sense of not having control over a situation. The best way to handle this anxiety is to do as much as possible to eliminate those unknown variables and address your specific fears. This control will require a great deal of preparation and practice but essentially entails meeting the requirements of an effective presentation, something you have to do anyway. Table 14.3 provides guidance when limiting the unknown factors of a presentation.

Table 14.3 Knowing the Unknown

Knowing the audience relationally

Audience analysis can alleviate much of the fear of not knowing what to expect from an audience. Conducting a thorough audience analysis enables you to gain a better understanding of your audience's experience, knowledge, and general view of the world and you personally. Audience analysis also enables you to mold the speech to fit your audience members specifically, which means you will be able to share the material in the most effective way and to connect with them on a relational level.

Knowing the topic

If you feel particularly nervous about speaking in public, we strongly suggest that, when possible, you select a topic about which you are already knowledgeable. Familiarity with a topic will increase your confidence and alleviate fear that comes from speaking to others. Of course, familiarization with your topic also comes from the rigorous exploration of the topic through careful research and the thorough development of your argument.

Knowing the speech will be worthwhile

As you thoroughly examine a topic, you will likely develop a greater appreciation for its significance and its relational importance in the lives of your audience members. Knowing that your speech is worthwhile and recognizing that it will positively affect your audience members' lives will provide you with greater confidence and alleviate anxiety related to your presentation.

Knowing the speech's beginning

Constructing a solid introduction and conclusion will also help diminish any fears. Confidence in your attention getter and overall introduction is especially vital since presenters generally experience the most anxiety at the very beginning of a presentation, just before they start speaking (Behnke & Sawyer, 1999). Belief in your introduction will allow you to face the moment of greatest anxiety straight on with confidence.

Knowing the presentation aids

Some research indicates that using presentation aids may help reduce anxiety related to speaking in public (Ayres, 1991). At the same time, they can be an issue of concern. Recognize the value of presentation aids, and ensure that you devote enough time and consideration to their preparation. Avoid overly complicated and unpredictable presentation aids, such as children and animals. Allow plenty of time to organize or ready each presentation aid before beginning your speech. Finally, include the demonstration of presentation aids in practice sessions. Doing so will make you aware of and adequately prepare you for possible problems that may arise and ensure the seamless integration of each presentation aid into your speech.

Practicing Your Presentation

Practicing your presentation will help you manage your nerves by increasing your familiarity with the material and the speech, as well as your confidence as a speaker. Practicing a speech, especially in front of others, has been shown to reduce apprehension related to public speaking and increase one's willingness to speak in public (Ayres, Schliesman, & Sonandre, 1998). In what follows, we discuss some guidelines to consider when practicing the delivery of a presentation.

In addition to physically practicing your presentation, some scholars (e.g., Ayres & Hopf, 1990) have suggested visualizing the successful delivery of your presentation as a way to manage communication apprehension.

Practice Actual Delivery. Practice presenting your speech in the manner in which you will actually deliver it. This means presenting the material out loud, incorporating full gestures and movement, and including presentation aids. When initially preparing for a presentation, many people read the speech silently to themselves. This practice may allow you to familiarize yourself more with the speech, which is fine, but we recommend presenting the material out loud as soon as possible. A big difference exists between reading something to yourself and presenting material orally. The sooner you begin focusing on the latter, the better prepared you will be to effectively deliver the material to others. Also, although it might be more comfortable, do not practice your speech while lying across your bed or sprawling across a chair. You will not be able to fully incorporate and practice gestures, movement, or even eye contact; nor will you be able to get an accurate sense of delivering your presentation in front of an audience. Make your practice sessions as close to the real thing as possible.

Watch and Listen to Yourself. People can imagine what they look and sound like, but a difference often exists between what they imagine and what they actually do. At minimum, we recommend practicing your speech in front of a mirror to observe and assess your facial expressions, eye contact, and gestures. You can also tape-record yourself and play it back to evaluate your tone of voice, rate of speech, and possible use of nonfluencies. Preferably, you will be able to videotape yourself speaking and review the entire package at once. Doing so will allow you to consider the integration of vocal variety and bodily movement and which elements of delivery you accomplished most effectively.

Photo 14.5 Which practicing guideline is the speaker in this photo following? (See page 365.)

Practice in Front of an Audience. We also recommend that you practice delivering your speech in front of actual people, such as family members, friends, roommates, or strangers you drag off the street. The people listening to you practice will be able to provide constructive criticism to help you improve the actual speech and your delivery. Practicing in front of people will also provide a more accurate sense of what delivering your speech will actually be like, which will help improve your presentation. In fact, practicing your presentation in front of other people has been shown to increase the quality of your speech (Menzel & Carrell, 1994). If you are still not convinced, how about this? Practicing your speech in front of other people has also been shown to improve the grade you earn on the speech (Smith & Frymier, 2006). We thought you might like that one! In fact, one study concluded that increased preparation time overall will bring about higher grades on classroom speeches, and activities related specifically to delivery appear the most important (Pearson, Child, & Kahl, 2006). Finally, practicing a speech in front of others has been shown to reduce communication apprehension and increase a speaker's willingness to give a presentation (Ayres, 1996). We urge you to practice in front of others as part of your preparation, especially if you are apprehensive about speaking in public. This type of preparation may not appeal to you, but you will greatly benefit from it.

A bit of unfortunate irony exists. Highly communication-apprehensive people generally spend more time preparing for their speeches than less-apprehensive people (Ayres & Robideaux-Maxwell, 1989). However, this preparation is less likely to include communication-oriented activities (Ayres, 1996). While people who feel highly apprehensive about speaking in front of others may spend a great deal of time conducting research and constructing their speech, they will probably avoid practicing the delivery of their presentation, an unfortunate situation given the tremendous benefits that come from such practice. If you are particularly apprehensive about speaking in public, be sure to avoid succumbing to this trend.

Experience and Skill Building

Experience and skill building will also help you manage anxiety related to public speaking. Experience in public speaking helps eliminate some of the unknowns associated with it, while learning skills and how to develop them through experience provides added confidence. As with most things, the more you engage in public speaking, the better you will become at presenting a speech.

If you are about to present your very first speech or have spoken before a public audience only a few times in the past, you may think a discussion of experience and skill building does not do you any good. However, the impact of skill building largely comes from the self-recognition that you know how to develop an effective speech and know the elements of effective delivery. Having read and studied these chapters and discussed this material in class, believe it or not, you now possess this knowledge. By the time you actually deliver your speech, you will have come a long way from the beginning of class when you were unfamiliar with what public speaking entails. You know

Case in Point

 Videotape your delivery of a presentation, and then analyze your performance using the guidelines and criteria offered in this chapter. Play the tape at least three times— once with the sound off, once with the sound on but without looking at the screen, and once focusing on the integration of your voice, body movement, and facial expression. What did you do well? What areas of your delivery do you need to develop? What can you do to improve these areas and your overall delivery?

the fundamental components of effective presentations and are in the process of implementing this knowledge and fully developing skills of effective delivery. We know that you possess this knowledge and ability, but it is more important that you recognize it.

Although you have increased your understanding of speech development and presentation, you still may not possess a great deal of actual experience as a public speaker. Realize, however, that the more you speak, the better you will become. We would like to make one more appeal for practicing your speech in front of others: This practice will provide you with experience from which you may draw when actually presenting the speech.

Of course, even the most experienced speakers are often apprehensive about speaking in public. Experience and skill building will not lead to the complete elimination of anxiety related to public speaking, and you would not even desire this result, since some nervous energy is necessary to give life to your presentation. Experience will often lower your level of anxiety, however. Plus, you will increasingly improve the management of nerves related to speaking in public as you gain additional experience.

A Final Thought About Communication Apprehension

If you feel extremely apprehensive about speaking in public, we encourage you to talk with the instructor of your course. Communication apprehension is a legitimate concern and should be taken seriously. Sometimes breaking down the unknown, practicing your speech, and gaining skills and experience do not suffice. While we are certain these strategies will help you, we also realize that they cannot do enough in some cases. Realize that you are not alone in your concern about public speaking. This uneasiness is quite common, and your instructor can help prepare you for the experience and assist you in dealing with any anxieties. We are confident that you will be able to do it.

FOCUS QUESTIONS REVISITED

1. What are three guidelines for effective delivery?

As a speaker, you should (a) always be yourself, (b) strive to make your presentation conversational, and (c) avoid calling attention to mistakes and nerves.

2. What are the styles of delivery?

The styles of delivery are manuscript, memorized, and extemporaneous. Manuscript delivery involves having the entire speech written out in front of you when speaking. This style is usually used when accurate wording of the speech is required but often results in poor delivery. Memorized delivery is done without any notes whatsoever. While reading the speech and distracting notes become nonissues, it is difficult to memorize an entire speech, and the delivery often sounds unnatural and uneven. Extemporaneous delivery involves the use of minimal notes and is generally recommended as the way to achieve a natural and conversational delivery while ensuring the accuracy of ideas.

3. **What are the goals of effective delivery?**

The goals of effective delivery are developing and enhancing audience perceptions of your credibility, increasing audience understanding, and establishing a relational connection with the audience.

4. **What are the components of effective delivery?**

The components of effective delivery include personal appearance, vocalics, eye contact, facial expression and body position, and gestures and physical movement. These components must work together to achieve the effective delivery of a presentation.

5. **What are presentation aids?**

Presentation aids are audio and visual tools used by a speaker to enhance audience understanding, appreciation, retention, attention, and a speaker's credibility.

6. **What is communication apprehension, and how can it be managed?**

Communication apprehension is the fear or anxiety people experience about speaking in public. Feeling nervous about speaking in public is quite common and perfectly normal. Nervous energy can actually help enhance a presentation as long as it is managed effectively. One way of dealing with communication apprehension is recognizing and knowing what you fear. Practicing the presentation, as well as gaining public speaking skills and experience, will also help you manage communication apprehension and increase your overall confidence as a speaker.

KEY CONCEPTS

communication apprehension   343
composure   350
distracting mannerisms   355
dynamism   350
extemporaneous delivery   349
inspiring   350
manuscript delivery   347
memorized delivery   348

nonfluencies   354
pauses   354
pitch   353
presentation aids   355
rate   353
sociability   350
volume   353

QUESTIONS TO ASK YOUR FRIENDS

1. Ask your friends to describe the characteristics of an *effective* public speaker. Limit their responses to those involving the delivery of a presentation. Consider their responses in regard to the guidelines and criteria for delivering public presentations discussed in this chapter.

2. Ask your friends to describe the characteristics of an *ineffective* public speaker. Limit their responses to those involving the delivery of a presentation. Consider their

responses in regard to the guidelines and criteria for delivering public presentations discussed in this chapter.

3. Ask your friends if they will listen to you practice your presentation. You should have known we would bring this up yet again! Seriously, practicing a presentation in front of an actual audience will improve your overall performance and help you manage communication apprehension.

MEDIA LINKS

1. Watch a public presentation on television or the Internet. Which components of effective delivery discussed in this chapter are evident? What does the speaker do well? How could the speaker improve his or her delivery?

2. Watch a public presentation on television or the Internet. Then find the transcript of that presentation. The transcripts of major presentations, such as those delivered by a president or a prime minister, are often included in newspapers the following day and almost immediately available online. In what ways would you have responded differently had you read the speech rather than watched and listened to it being delivered? What about the speaker's delivery led to these differences?

3. Think about the issues with which a speaker must contend when delivering a presentation to both a physically present audience and an audience watching the presentation on television or the Internet. How can a speaker nonverbally connect with both audiences? Assuming a smaller viewing screen, would a podcast change what a speaker must do to connect with the audience?

ETHICAL ISSUES

1. Audience members perceive a speaker's credibility in part through his or her personal appearance. In what ways would you consider such judgment either justified or unfair?

2. With the above considerations about personal appearance in mind, is it ethical for a person to alter his or her usual appearance for a public presentation situation?

3. We discussed how you should always be yourself when speaking in public but that you may integrate certain qualities of speakers you admire into your own speaking style. Where would you position the boundary between integrating qualities of that person's delivery into your own personal style and becoming a caricature or mimic of that person? Addressed another way, is it possible to plagiarize a delivery style?

ANSWERS TO PHOTO CAPTIONS

Photo 14.1 ▪ No. Speakers should always be themselves when speaking in public and not try to pretend to be someone else.

Photo 14.2 ■ Extemporaneous delivery enables this speaker to convey her ideas accurately while maintaining a conversational tone of voice and connecting relationally with the audience.

Photo 14.3 ■ His use of gestures helps reinforce verbal communication, gives life to the presentation, and channels nervous energy to avoid distracting mannerisms.

Photo 14.4 ■ The speaker is not looking directly at the presentation aid, ensuring that his primary focus is relating with the audience.

Photo 14.5 ■ He is practicing his speech in front of a mirror to observe and assess his facial expressions, eye contact, and gestures.

STUDENT STUDY SITE

Visit the study site at **www.sagepub.com/boc2e** for e-flashcards, practice quizzes, journal articles and additional study resources.

REFERENCES

Ayres, J. (1991). Using visual aids to reduce speech anxiety. *Communication Research Reports, 8,* 73–79.

Ayres, J. (1996). Speech preparation processes and speech apprehension. *Communication Education, 45,* 228–235.

Ayres, J., & Hopf, T. S. (1990). The long-term effect of visualization in the classroom: A brief research report. *Communication Education, 39,* 75–78.

Ayres, J., & Robideaux-Maxwell, R. (1989). Communication apprehension and speech preparation time. *Communication Research Reports, 6,* 90–93.

Ayres, J., Schliesman, T., & Sonandre, D. A. (1998). Practice makes perfect but does it help reduce communication apprehension? *Communication Research Reports, 15,* 170–179.

Behnke, R. R., & Sawyer, C. R. (1999). Milestones of anticipatory public speaking anxiety. *Communication Education, 48,* 165–172.

Bradshaw, S. (2006). Shyness and difficult relationships: Formation is just the beginning. In C. D. Kirkpatrick, S. W. Duck, & M. K. Foley (Eds.), *Relating difficulty: The processes of constructing and managing difficult interaction* (pp. 15–41). Mahwah, NJ: Lawrence Erlbaum.

Gass, R. H., & Seiter, J. S. (2011). *Persuasion, social influence, and compliance gaining* (4th ed.). Boston: Allyn & Bacon.

Giles, H. (2008). Communication Accommodation Theory. In L. A. Baxter & D. O. Braithwaite (Eds.), *Engaging theories in interpersonal communication: Multiple perspectives* (pp. 161–173). Thousand Oaks, CA: Sage.

McCroskey, J. C. (1970). Measures of communication-bound anxiety. *Speech Monographs, 37,* 269–277.

Menzel, K. E., & Carrell, L. J. (1994). The relationship between preparation and performance in public speaking. *Communication Education, 43,* 17–26.

Pearson, J. C., Child, J. T., & Kahl, D. H., Jr. (2006). Preparation meeting opportunity: How do college students prepare for public speeches? *Communication Quarterly, 54,* 351–366.

Smith, T. E., & Frymier, A. B. (2006). Get "real": Does practicing speeches before an audience improve performance? *Communication Quarterly, 54,* 111–125.

Wallechinsky, D., & Wallace, A. (1995). *The book of lists* (Reprint ed.). New York: Lb Books.

15

Interviewing

This chapter is dedicated to something that will be of great importance throughout your professional life—interviews. An **interview** is a goal-driven transaction characterized by questions and answers, clear structure, control, and imbalance. An interview is usually a dyadic transaction, meaning that it takes place between two people. A talk show host asking questions of a celebrity would be one example of a dyadic interview. Sometimes, however, a person may be interviewed by two or more people or in a panel situation. Consider, for instance, when someone testifies before Congress and is asked a series of questions by a panel of senators. We introduce various types of interviews in this chapter, but we primarily focus on employment interviews, since those are the types of interviews the majority of people reading this book are most concerned about at this point in their lives.

Interviews share many characteristics with other types of communication. Certainly, all of the properties of communication discussed throughout the book remain intact. Communication within an interview is transactional and symbolic (both verbal and nonverbal), requires meaning, is both presentational and representational, and takes much for granted. An interview requires effective listening (engaged, relational, and critical) on the part of everyone involved in order to be successful. Furthermore, identity, relational, and cultural work are all being conducted during an interview. There are certain characteristics, though, that make interviews very unique types of communication, and we will examine those later.

This chapter ultimately focuses on how to conduct and participate in employment interviews. We begin by discussing the preparation for an interview. We then examine what must take place during the beginning of an interview. Next, we explore what happens during the question-and-answer portion of an interview. From an interviewer standpoint, we discuss developing different types of questions, sequencing the questions, directive and nondirective questioning, and avoiding illegal questions. From an interviewee standpoint, we discuss adjusting the interview frame for greater success, learning from successful and unsuccessful interviews, answering common interview questions, and handling illegal questions. We then examine what must take place during the conclusion of an interview. We next discuss the responsibilities of interviewers and interviewees following an interview. Finally, since most people will not be invited to interview with an organization without an effective cover letter and résumé, we discuss the construction of these vital application tools.

Focus Questions

1. What are the characteristics of an interview?
2. What are the types of interviews?
3. What are the preinterview responsibilities of interviewers and interviewees?
4. How should a person begin an employment interview?
5. What types of questions and questioning styles may an interviewer use?
6. How should interviewees respond to questions during an interview?
7. How should a person conclude an employment interview?
8. What are the postinterview responsibilities of interviewers and interviewees?
9. What are a cover letter and résumé?

Characteristics of an Interview

Interviews encompass unique characteristics that distinguish them from other types of communication. In what follows, we examine five characteristics of interviews: (1) goal-driven, (2) question–answer, (3) structured, (4) controlled, and (5) unbalanced.

Goal-Driven

Interviews are generally more *goal-driven* than other types of communication, especially those taking place between two people. All communication achieves something beyond the simple exchange of symbols, but these achievements and creations are not always purposeful and intended. Interviews have a clear purpose, a goal to be achieved. Information may be desired, a problem may need to be resolved, persuasion may be desired, someone may need assistance with a personal problem, or an employer may be seeking the best person for a job opening and a potential employee may be looking for a good employer.

Question–Answer

Another characteristic of interviews is the *question–answer* nature of the transaction. The majority of an interview consists of one person (sometimes more than one) asking questions and another person answering those questions. Everyday communication includes occasional questions and answers—especially if people are getting to know one another—but not to the extent of an interview. Furthermore, in most everyday communication, it is not usually the case that one person is in charge of asking the questions while the other person is in charge of answering them.

Structured

Interviews also tend to be more *structured* than other types of communication. Whereas a casual interaction between two people may happen spontaneously and have no clear focus, interviews involve planning and preparation and also tend to have a clear sequence. Certain actions are expected during an interview in order to reach the clearly defined goal discussed previously. We write more about the planning and sequence of interviews later in the chapter.

Controlled

Interviews are generally *controlled* by an interviewer, who is responsible for moving the interview toward its intended goal. The amount of control exerted during an interview depends on this goal, which is achieved in part by the questions asked and the communication environment established. Once again, this—specifically whether an interview is characterized as *directive* or *nondirective*—is a topic we discuss in more detail later in the chapter.

Unbalanced

A final characteristic of interviews is that the time spent talking by an interviewee and an interviewer is usually *unbalanced*. Typically, an interviewer will speak for 30% of the time, and an interviewee will speak for 70% of the time. Of course, the type of interview will dictate exactly how much time each party spends talking, but more often than not, an interviewee will talk more and an interviewer will talk less.

Types of Interviews

Now that we have discussed the characteristics of an interview, we can examine various types of interviews. You may have already experienced some of these interviews in the past and will likely encounter them many times throughout both your personal life and your professional life in the future. We will begin with the employment interview, since this type of interview will receive the most attention in the remainder of the chapter. Note that the first three types of interviews discussed encompass the workplace. Initial employment is not the only place you will come across interviews in your professional life.

Employment Interviews

When people think of interviews, an employment interview is probably what comes immediately to mind. **Employment interviews** are those in which a potential employer interviews a potential employee. Both parties have a great deal riding on the success of an interview. The potential employee is not only seeking employment but also determining whether the job is one that would be accepted if offered. The potential employer is searching not only for a qualified applicant but also for someone who would actually benefit the organization. Potential employers also want to convince potential employees that the position is one they should accept if offered.

Performance Interviews

Also known as *performance reviews,* **performance interviews** are those in which an individual's activities and work are discussed. These interviews are most often conducted between employees and supervisors, but you may also experience them in educational and other settings. For instance, students frequently discuss their progress toward a degree with an advisor or perhaps even a committee of professors. In both situations, a person's strengths and weaknesses are discussed with the ultimate goal being to improve his or her performance. Naturally such interviews can be stressful, but they can also provide people with valuable information that can be used to strengthen their performance and to help them achieve personal and professional goals. These interviews are also an opportunity for the goals and culture of an organization to be reinforced.

Exit Interviews

Exit interviews are those that occur when a person chooses to leave a place of employment. The conventional wisdom is that someone who is leaving may be more likely to provide honest answers about organizational cultures, policies, supervisors, compensation, and other aspects of the workplace. If used correctly, these interviews can provide employers with valuable insight that can be incorporated to improve employee satisfaction and thus the productivity and success of an organization. These interviews are also increasingly common in education and among multiple types of groups, such as volunteer organizations.

Make Your Case

Do exit interviews provide accurate and useful information to employers? Or will employees leaving an organization still hesitate to provide full disclosure of the positive and negative aspects of the organization? What factors may determine whether an exit interview will be worthwhile?

Information-Gaining Interviews

You may have previously experienced an information-gaining interview and not even realized it as such. **Information-gaining interviews** are those in which a person solicits information from another person. You have likely responded to surveys, which is one form of information-gaining interview. A doctor asking you about your symptoms during an office visit would be another example of this form of interview. You may conduct information-gaining interviews when preparing speeches and papers for school or work. These sorts of interviews are also frequently seen on webcasts and included in newspapers, magazines, and blogs.

Persuasive Interviews

Persuasive interviews are those that have influence as the ultimate goal. The interviewer may appear to be gaining information but is actually attempting to influence the thoughts or actions of the interviewee. This form of interview may sound a bit manipulative and perhaps underhanded, but it is quite common. When salespeople ask your opinion about a product or service, they often do so in a way that attempts to sway you toward what they want you to purchase. At other times, what appears to be a survey is in reality an attempt to persuade. Political workers have frequently been accused of dirty tricks under the guise of conducting straightforward surveys. They attempt to plant a seed of doubt or concern in the mind of the interviewee. For instance, imagine being asked, "If the incumbent were convicted of running a cock-fighting ring, would this influence your vote in the upcoming election?" Depending on your opinion of roosters or animal cruelty in general, it would or would not affect your vote, but such questions often influence voter perceptions of candidates and result in rumors being circulated.

Problem-Solving Interviews

When experiencing difficulties or facing an unknown challenge, people may engage in **problem-solving interviews**, those in which a problem is isolated and solutions are generated. These types of interviews may be conducted by someone with greater experience or insight than the person being interviewed. Students, for example, may be questioned by their professors in order to determine why they may be experiencing difficulties in a class. Sometimes problem-solving interviews are conducted by someone with general knowledge of a situation but whose fresh approach can be beneficial. For instance, a colleague may be asked to engage in a problem-solving interview when difficulties are encountered with a project at work. Someone not involved with a situation will often provide alternative approaches to solving a problem.

Photo 15.1 What is the difference between information-gathering interviews like the one pictured here and persuasive interviews? Is the difference always obvious to the person being interviewed? (See page 404.)

Helping Interviews

Unlike problem-solving interviews, **helping interviews** are always conducted by someone with expertise in a given area and whose services are engaged by someone in need of advice. The most obvious example of a helping interview would be a psychologist asking questions of a client. However, other helping interviews include those conducted by credit card counselors with people facing a heavy debt load or attorneys advising clients on legal matters.

Preinterview Responsibilities

Having examined the characteristics of interviews and different types of interviews, we now focus our attention fully on employment interviews. Although other types of interviews are important, as mentioned previously employment interviews are likely the most important for people reading this book. The entire employment interview process will be discussed, from preinterview responsibilities of both an interviewer and an interviewee to postinterview responsibilities of both an interviewer and an interviewee. Along the way, we will explore the beginning of an interview, how interviewers should ask questions, how interviewees should answer questions, and how an interview should come to a close. So, let's get started by discussing what should be done in preparation for an interview.

Interviewer Responsibilities

We will begin our discussion of preinterview responsibilities by focusing on the duties of an interviewer. There are four primary responsibilities of the interviewer prior to the interview: (1) reviewing application material, (2) preparing questions and an interview outline, (3) gathering materials, and (4) beginning on time.

Review Application Material

The interviewer should review a job candidate's application material prior to the interview. Accordingly, you should not use the interview itself to review the application material. Doing so conveys a lack of preparation and respect, and it wastes valuable time that should be used to conduct the interview. Furthermore, as we next discuss, reviewing a job candidate's application material should be done beforehand in order to develop specific questions to ask each individual interviewee.

Prepare Questions and an Interview Outline

The interviewer should prepare a list of questions in advance of the interview. (Various types of interview questions are discussed later in the chapter.) Preparing questions in advance helps ensure that the information desired from the job candidate is elicited. It also helps ensure that the interview will be conducted within the proper time constraints. If multiple job candidates are being interviewed, using common questions will make it easier to compare and contrast them. However, each interview will demand the inclusion of unique questions adapted to each individual interviewee.

These questions should be included in an interview outline, which reminds the interviewer of his or her duties during the various parts of an interview. For instance, as we discuss later, an interviewer should provide the interviewee with a purpose and an agenda at the beginning of an interview and summarize the interview, ask for questions, and preview future action and the schedule among other tasks in the conclusion. Including these tasks in an interview outline will help make sure they are included during the interview. We urge you to be diligent in your creation of interview questions and interview outlines. This task can be the difference between conducting a successful interview and conducting a poor interview.

Gather Materials

The interviewer should gather materials needed for the interview before the interviewee arrives rather than after he or she arrives. Searching for the application material, interview outline, and writing materials for notes—even if these things are close by—indicates a lack of preparation and, consequently, a lack of respect for the interviewee. It also takes up valuable time that should be dedicated to conducting the interview.

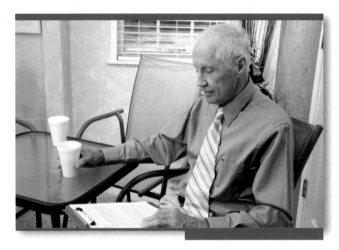

Begin on Time

The interviewer should strive to begin the interview on schedule rather than causing a delay. As with failing to gather materials beforehand, making the interviewee wait past the scheduled time is unprofessional and conveys a lack of respect for the interviewee. Avoid scheduling a meeting or another activity that may run long immediately before an interview. If multiple interviews are being conducted during a single day or period, make sure some time is scheduled between them and maintain adherence to the schedules of the interviews themselves. Ideally, there will be enough time prior to an interview to gather materials and review the application material and enough time following an interview to review your performance and evaluate the interviewee.

Photo 15.2 The person in this picture is reviewing application material prior to interviewing a job candidate. What are the other responsibilities of an interviewer prior to the interview? (See page 404.)

Interviewee Responsibilities

An interviewee also has responsibilities prior to the interview. There are a total of seven duties that must be conducted by the interviewee: (1) gathering information, (2) preparing questions, (3) practicing, (4) ensuring a professional personal appearance, (5) bringing materials, (6) arriving on time, and (7) turning off the cell phone.

Gather Information

Prior to an employment interview, an interviewee must gather information about the organization, about the profession, and about himself or herself. Communication professionals have traditionally focused on the need to gather information about the organization, but the latter two areas are just as significant.

Exhibiting knowledge about the organization during the interview will convey proper preparation, enthusiasm for the position, and a desire to become part of the organization. As we discuss later in the chapter, exhibiting knowledge about the organization is a distinguishing characteristic of successful interviewees. Such information may include the organization's history, future plans, challenges, accomplishments, and other characteristics. Exhibiting knowledge about the profession during the interview will also be beneficial. A job candidate will most likely possess knowledge about the profession before gathering information. However, it is especially important that interviewees appear knowledgeable of the latest developments within the profession. Furthermore, addressing such developments in relation to the organization's needs and goals will be especially impressive.

An interviewee should also gather information about himself or herself. Perhaps *gather* is not as appropriate as the term *formulate*. People already possess knowledge and information about themselves, but this information is not necessarily composed in a way that can be clearly articulated. It may not even be clear to them. When it comes to the interview, though, this information needs to be conveyed in a clear and supportive manner. Accordingly, gathering *or* formulating information about oneself must be done in preparation for an interview. Table 15.1 offers some questions to help guide this formulation.

Table 15.1 Formulating Information About Oneself
What are my long-term professional goals? How will they be achieved?
What are my short-term professional goals? How will they be achieved?
What are my greatest achievements? What did I learn from them?
What are my greatest failures? What did I learn from them?
What are my greatest strengths? How am I using them and developing them?
What are my greatest weaknesses? How am I overcoming them?
Why did I choose this profession?
Why do I want this position? How does this position fit with my professional goals?
Why do I want to work for this organization? How does this organization fit with my professional goals?
What professional experiences have made me an ideal candidate for this position?
What education and training have made me an ideal candidate for this position?
What skills make me an ideal candidate for this position?

Prepare Questions

An interviewee should also prepare a list of questions to ask the interviewer concerning the organization and the position. Questions about the organization could surround future goals, organizational structure, perceived challenges and strengths of the organization, organizational culture, and management style. Questions concerning the position could include such topics as experiences of previous employees, history of the position, evaluation of performance, percentage of time devoted to various responsibilities of the position, perceived challenges and opportunities of the position, amount of supervision, and why the position is now available.

There are a few lines of questioning that should be avoided by an interviewee. Questions deemed illegal when asked by an interviewer should not be asked by an interviewee. Asking these questions would not result in legal consequences, but they are just as discriminatory and inappropriate when asked by an interviewee as when asked by an interviewer. (We discuss illegal questions later in this chapter.) Also, an interviewee should not ask questions with answers available on an organization's website or in material already provided by the organization. Asking such questions would suggest, appropriately, a lack of preparation on the part of an interviewee. An interviewee should also avoid asking about salary or benefits. If you are like us, answers to questions about salary and benefits would seem helpful in determining whether or not the position would be accepted if offered. However, most professional cultures deem such questions inappropriate, so it is advisable to not ask them.

Practice

An interviewee should also practice the interview as part of his or her preparation. Compile a list of questions that you might be asked during an interview. (Some of the most common interview questions are discussed later in this chapter.) Once these questions have been compiled, practice answering them aloud. Having an idea about what you might say is not sufficient. Actually articulating your thoughts and hearing the words come out of your mouth will better prepare you for the actual interview. If possible, have someone else play the role of the interviewer and ask you questions (some of which may come from your list and some of which may not). Make the interview situation as complete and as realistic as possible, including arrival at the interview setting, initiating the interview, answering the questions, concluding the interview, and leaving the interview setting. You may even want to dress as you will at the actual interview. Practicing will also enable you to diminish some of those unknown elements of interviewing that often lead to nervousness and anxiety.

College Experience

Many schools have career centers, or similarly named offices, that provide assistance for students when seeking employment. Among their many services, some even conduct mock interviews for practice. We strongly encourage you to seek out such opportunities on your campus.

Professional Personal Appearance

Personal appearance—including clothing, hairstyles, tattoos, jewelry, makeup, and hygiene—is a reflection of how you perceive yourself, how you wish to be perceived by others, and your relationship with others. People make judgments, accurately or not, based on the appearance of others. Accordingly, interviewees should strive to convey credibility and professionalism through their personal appearance, and should appear in a manner consistent with expectations of the interviewer in order to establish relational connections with him or her. Rather than developing a one-size-fits-all model of interview appearance, it is best to dress according to the position for which you are interviewing. The general rule of thumb is dressing one step above how you would generally dress for the position if hired. And, when in doubt, it is always better to be overdressed rather than underdressed.

Photo 15.3 If an interviewee arrives early for an interview, is it a good idea for him or her to catch up on rest while waiting? (See page 404.)

Arrive on Time

Few other behaviors make a worse impression than arriving late to an interview. Arriving late not only is unprofessional and disrespectful but also may result in decreasing the amount of time available for the interview. Of course, arriving too early might make an interviewee seem overeager. So, we are not suggesting you arrive 2 hours before the interview is scheduled. Planning to arrive 15 minutes early will enable you to be punctual without appearing overly enthusiastic or nervous. If you do happen to arrive early, use that time to freshen up and review your materials.

Bring Materials

Speaking of materials, an interviewee should bring some to the interview. You should plan on bringing (1) additional copies of your résumé, (2) paper and writing utensils, and (3) a list of questions to ask the interviewer. In most situations, these items should be housed within a briefcase or professional-looking folder. Copies of your résumé will allow you to provide the interviewer with an additional copy if necessary and to review specific items with the interviewer if he or she so desires. The paper and writing utensils will allow you to take notes during the interview. The list of questions exhibits preparation and will enable you to remember specific questions you want to ask.

For some people, asking them to bring paper and writing utensils might be like asking them to bring a stone tablet, chisel, and hammer. In other words, it may seem outdated since these people (perhaps you) primarily record items using a laptop computer or PDA (personal digital assistant). At this point, in the majority of workplaces, technological expectations would not include the use of a laptop computer or PDA during an interview. Accordingly, the interviewer may find its use strange and perhaps even unprofessional. However, perceptions of technology are continuously changing (Chapter 9), and the use of these items may be more acceptable in the near future. Furthermore, there may be some organizations and industries in which they are acceptable now. The use of these items may also make you appear technologically savvy and progressive, which could be seen as a bonus by some interviewers. Use your best judgment as to whether a laptop computer or PDA would be appropriate, given the expectations of the interviewer and the identity you wish to convey during the interview.

Turn Off the Cell Phone

Perceptions of technology are continuously changing, but it will be a long time before the ringing of a cell phone is deemed an appropriate occurrence during an employment interview. You should turn off your cell phone completely and keep it out of sight during an interview. Your sole focus should be on the interviewer and the discussion at

Much of what is discussed in this chapter involves face-to-face interviews, but you may also be asked to interview by telephone or webcam. Here are some tips for these types of interviews.

Telephone Interviews

1. Select a quiet place that is free of potential distractions.
2. Do not eat, drink, or chew gum.
3. Even though the interviewer will not see you smile, doing so will come though in your voice.
4. Stand or sit up straight in order to strengthen your voice.
5. Avoid nonfluencies such as *um* and *uh*, since these are even more obvious over the telephone.
6. Have your résumé, notes, and other materials available should you need them.

Webcam Interviews

1. Select a quiet place that is free of potential distractions.
2. Test the camera and speaker prior to the interview.
3. Be aware of what appears in the background and remove anything that could be distracting.
4. Your personal appearance should mirror your appearance for a face-to-face interview.
5. Look directly at the camera, but avoid staring at it, much like you would avoid staring at someone with whom you are talking face-to-face.
6. Remember that the interviewer may be able to see and hear you prior to and immediately following the interview.

hand. We sincerely hope it never happens to you, but if you do forget to turn off your cell phone during an interview and it happens to ring, quickly apologize to the interviewer and turn it off at that time. Do not answer the call—even to tell the person you will call him or her back. Certainly do not carry on a conversation with the person who called. Your professionalism and respect for the interviewer (along with yourself) will be called into question by a ringing cell phone.

Beginning an Employment Interview

Now that the preinterview responsibilities have been accomplished, it is time to begin the interview. When beginning an interview, the participants must (1) greet one another and establish proxemics, (2) negotiate the relational connection and tone of the interview, and (3) establish the purpose and agenda of the interview.

Greeting and Establishing Proxemics

Initial impressions have a tremendous impact on perceptions of another person and whether additional contact is desired. Accordingly, the opening moments are crucial to the success of an interview, especially for an interviewee.

As an interviewee, you must convey respect for an interviewer's space (Chapter 3). If the interview takes place in an office, always knock and wait for permission to enter prior to entering, even if the door is open. Unless directed to do otherwise, address the interviewer using his or her last name and a formal or professional title (Dr., Mr., Ms., Your Holiness). Exchange greetings and introduce yourself, if necessary, while initiating a professional handshake with the interviewer to establish a positive relational connection and to suggest confidence. Shaking hands with a firm grip while looking the other person in the eye has been shown to increase ratings of employment suitability by interviewers (G. L. Stewart, Dustin, Barrick, & Darnold, 2008). Fist bumps or high fives are never appropriate, unless the interviewer is a Wonder Twin or has just completed an incredible athletic feat! Wait for the interviewer to direct you to where you will be positioned during the interview, rather than moving to an area or being seated beforehand.

As an interviewer, strive to make the interviewee feel welcomed and appreciated through your greeting. Initiate a handshake, if the interviewee has not already done so. Prepare in advance where the interviewee will be positioned for the interview and direct him or her to that space accordingly. As we discuss, where you and the interviewee are positioned will impact the relational connection and tone of the interview.

Listen in on Your Life

Recall employment interviews in which you have been either the interviewee or the interviewer. Assess which aspects of the interview went well and which aspects of the interview needed improvement. As you read this chapter, consider how your entire performance could be improved. If you have never participated in an employment interview, ask someone you know who has done so to describe his or her interview experiences to you.

Negotiating Relational Connection and Tone

During most employment interviews, the interviewer possesses more power than the interviewee. The extent of that power distance and the tone of the interview (formal, relaxed, humorous, serious) will be negotiated by the interviewer and interviewee. This negotiation will take place throughout the course of an interview but is often established during its opening moments. Although interviewees are free to attempt to develop whatever relational connection and tone they desire, it is generally best for them to follow the verbal and nonverbal cues of the interviewer, especially if they want the job.

The guidelines offered here are most appropriate in Western cultures. Be certain to keep cultural differences involving space and touch in mind when considering interviews in other cultural contexts.

Verbal cues from an interviewer will inform an interviewee of the desired tone and relationship. If an interviewer asks to be called by his or her first name, that could be an indication of a relatively relaxed interview context and a sense of equality with the interviewee. If an interviewer makes a joke at the beginning of an interview, that might also be an indication of a generally relaxed interview context. Self-disclosure, or perhaps even self-deprecation, may be an indication of a desire for equality. An interviewer may very well verbally announce a desire for a relaxed interview context. If an interviewer does none of these things or does not verbally indicate informality or equality in other ways, he or she probably expects a formal, traditional interview context.

Accompanying nonverbal cues from an interviewer will also inform an interviewee of the desired tone and relationship. Smiling along with other positive nonverbal behaviors will certainly indicate a different tone than would frowning and other negative nonverbal behaviors. Beyond these cues, however, the placement of an interviewee in relation to the interviewer may indicate the degree of formality of the interview and the relational connection the interviewer wishes to develop. For instance, an interviewer seated on one side of a desk and an interviewee seated on the other side would indicate a more formal interview and a less equal relationship. On the other hand, an interviewer seated next to an interviewee, perhaps on chairs positioned at right angles with one another, would indicate a more relaxed interview and a more equal relationship.

Establishing Purpose and Agenda

Establishing the purpose and agenda is the responsibility of the interviewer. The purpose of an employment interview is fairly obvious, but establishing the agenda is especially important. As an interviewer, you should inform the interviewee how long the interview will take place. You may also want to preview the areas of questioning or other features to make an interviewee more comfortable through the partial removal of unknown variables. Doing so also establishes your expectations as an interviewer of how the interview will be conducted.

Don't forget to genuinely smile during your next employment interview. Interviewees with genuine dynamic smiles are evaluated more favorably by interviewers than those with fake smiles or neutral facial expressions (Krumhuber, Manstead, Cosker, Marshall, & Rosin, 2009).

Asking the Questions During an Employment Interview

Now that the interview has begun, it is time to address the matter of questions and answers. We first examine the types of questions that an interviewer can ask during the interview and then examine different styles of questioning. You may be at the point in your professional life where you are more concerned about being an interviewee than an interviewer. However, even if this is the case, you may very well be conducting interviews in the future. Further, knowing what the interviewer is doing will help you immensely as an interviewee.

There are three pairs of question types that may be asked during an interview: (1) primary and secondary, (2) open and closed, and (3) neutral and leading. There also exist different styles of questioning involving the amount of control exerted by the interviewer. As an interviewer, you must also be aware of illegal lines of questioning that must be avoided. We begin our exploration of asking the questions by examining the different types of questions that can be asked.

Primary and Secondary Questions

Prior to an interview, an interviewer will likely have compiled a list of questions covering the primary topics that he or she wishes to discuss with an interviewee. Questions that introduce new topics during an interview are known as **primary questions**. Examples of primary questions include the following:

- What led to your interest in digital storytelling?
- What responsibilities did you have at your last job?
- What experience do you have working with flux capacitors?
- In what ways has your major prepared you for a position like this one?

Interviewee responses to questions will likely lead an interviewer to ask follow-up questions to seek elaboration or further information. These types of questions are known as **secondary questions**, of which there are two main types: probing questions and mirror questions. **Probing questions** are brief statements or words that urge an interviewee to continue or to elaborate on a response such as "Go on," "Uh-huh," and "What else?" **Mirror questions** paraphrase an interviewee's previous response to ensure clarification and to elicit elaboration. For instance, an interviewer may ask, "From what you said, it seems you have previous experience with this product line, but have you had direct experience working in this market?" Additional examples of secondary questions include the following:

- What other aspects did you find most rewarding?
- In what ways?
- Which of those did you most dislike?
- Is that correct?

The best way to distinguish primary and secondary questions is that secondary questions only make sense when preceded by a primary question and subsequent response. Beginning a series of questions with any of the preceding examples would not make any sense.

Open and Closed Questions

The questions asked during an interview will be either open or closed. **Open questions** are those that enable and prompt interviewees to answer in a wide range of ways. Examples of open questions include the following:

- Tell me about your decision to become a Foley artist.
- What led you to volunteer with the Retired Professors Fund?
- Describe a time when you had to work with a group.
- How would you describe your work ethic?

Open questions serve three important functions. First, and most obvious, open questions enable interviewers to gather information about an interviewee. Second, these questions enable an interviewer to assess the communication skills of an interviewee. Third, open questions provide valuable insight into the worldview of an interviewee. Recalling both the presentational nature of communication discussed in Chapter 1 and Kenneth Burke's pentad discussed in Chapter 2, words and stories have meaning beyond that which appears on the surface and provide a glimpse into how people perceive situations, themselves, and others.

Contrary to open questions, **closed questions** are those that limit the range of an interviewee's response. Examples of closed questions include the following:

- Where did you attend college?
- What positions did you hold at your previous company?
- Are you willing to work weekends?
- What was the most difficult aspect of your past job?

Closed questions serve important functions during an interview. Closed questions do not take up as much time as open questions, so they can be especially valuable when time is limited. These questions can also be used to gather specific information about an interviewee. Finally, the answers to closed questions make it relatively easy to compare and contrast candidates for a position. Such evaluations are especially easy to make when dealing with **bipolar questions**, a type of closed question that forces an interviewee to select one of two responses. The answers to bipolar questions are frequently either yes or no. The third example in the preceding list is considered a bipolar question that would be answered with either an affirmative or a negative. Some bipolar questions ask interviewees to select between two presented choices. For instance, an interviewer might ask, "Which do you believe is most important to success at work—hard work or talent?"

Neutral and Leading Questions

When developing questions for an interview, it is best to include neutral questions and to avoid leading questions. **Neutral questions** provide an interviewee with no indication of a preferred way to respond. Examples of neutral questions include the following:

- Why did you select communication studies as a major?
- What do you think of our new product line?
- What are your thoughts on labor unions?
- Describe the qualities of your previous supervisor.

Notice that these examples do not direct an interviewee toward a specific response or one that is obviously preferred by the interviewer. Some people might believe that the second example involving a "new product line" would direct an interviewee toward a favorable response. However, an interviewer may want to determine whether the interviewee is someone who would not be afraid to express opinions and who would be able to improve and enhance the company's products.

Leading questions are those that suggest to an interviewee a preferred way to respond. Examples of these types of questions include the following and are based on those in the preceding list:

- What influenced your incredibly wise decision to major in communication studies?
- You do approve of our new product line, don't you?
- What are some of the problems you see with labor unions?
- What did you like most about your previous supervisor?

In these examples, an interviewer would be guiding an interviewee toward a specific type of answer. (We know that the decision to major in communication studies is obviously incredibly wise, but the first one still counts!) Generally, it is best to avoid leading questions during interviews and not to give interviewees an indication about how they should answer. Still, leading questions are sometimes used to determine whether an interviewee is someone who would hold his or her ground. Once again, the production line example could be a test to determine an interviewee's confidence and ability to voice concerns.

Directive and Nondirective Questioning

The fact that interviews are controlled is one of their characteristics mentioned earlier in this chapter. However, the amount of control exerted during an interview will vary, based especially on the specific goal of an interview. Some types of interviews require great control by the interviewer, while other types of interviews require little control and more flexibility by the interviewer.

Directive interviews are those that are greatly controlled by an interviewer. Questions tend to be closed and perhaps leading (C. J. Stewart & Cash, 2000). A directive interviewer tends to follow a clear line of questioning, deviating only to guide an interviewee back on topic or when wanting an interviewee to elaborate. Watch an attorney cross-examining a witness on *Law & Order* for a good example of a directive interview. The questions are certainly leading, and many tend to be closed. Further, the person being questioned on the stand is not allowed to deviate from the line of questioning, with the attorney being fully in control.

Nondirective interviews, on the other hand, are those in which the direction of the interview is primarily given to the interviewee. A nondirective interviewer generally introduces fairly broad topic areas and then allows an interviewee to "take off" in whatever direction desired. Accordingly, the questions asked tend to be open and neutral (Stewart & Cash, 2000). For an example of a nondirective interview, watch a talk show host interviewing a celebrity. A preinterview of sorts has occurred prior to the program

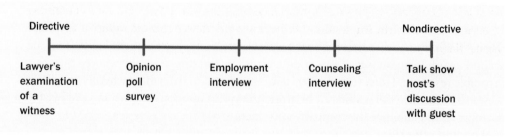

Figure 15.1 A continuum of interviewer control

in which members of the staff have asked what the celebrity would like to talk about and have discussed possible questions the host might ask. During the actual program, the host will ask a general question ("How's the weather?"), knowing the celebrity will take it from there. The examples featured in Figure 15.1 are those offered by Gouran, Wiethoff, and Doelger (1994) and exhibit the range of directive and nondirective interviews.

Avoiding Illegal Questions

When seeking the best candidate for a job, it may seem like a good idea to ask as many questions as possible and to learn as much as possible about someone, including many intricate details of his or her life. However, there are some questions that cannot be asked and for good reason—they are potentially discriminatory. Equal employment opportunity (EEO) laws have been established, in part, to prevent possible discrimination during the hiring process, whether it is done intentionally or unintentionally. Even the most well-intentioned comment or question can be discriminatory; therefore, you should be aware of questions that must be avoided.

Common areas that cannot be discussed with potential employees include age, marital/family status, ethnicity/national origin, religion, affiliations, and disabilities. In some cases, however, otherwise illegal areas of questioning are allowed. Some jobs demand certain abilities or requirements, known as *bona fide occupational qualifications*. For instance, it is illegal to inquire about the age of an applicant unless there is a minimum age requirement for a job or unless the job is one where a retirement age is enforced, such as a commercial airline pilot. Working for a religious organization may require affiliation with that religion. Furthermore, some occupations require certain physical abilities. However, bona fide occupational qualifications that counter discriminatory questions are not as common as you might think, and it is best to avoid areas of potential discrimination. Table 15.2 presents areas to avoid along with examples of illegal and legal questions.

Contrarian Challenge

We—along with the federal government—encourage you to avoid asking illegal questions as part of the interview process. However, aside from instances of bona fide occupational qualifications, are there instances during which asking such questions would be beneficial? Should they be allowed during the interview process?

You can learn more about illegal questions and workers' rights by visiting the Equal Employment Opportunity Commission website at www.eeoc.gov/.

Answering the Questions During an Employment Interview

Having examined the asking of questions during an interview, we can now explore the answering of questions. We first discuss how adjusting the interview frame can greatly

Table 15.2 Avoiding Illegal Questions

Age

Illegal questions

- How old are you?
- What year were you born?

Legal questions

- Are you 21 years old or older, and thereby legally allowed to accept this position if offered?
- Are you under the age of 60 years old, and thereby legally allowed to accept this position if offered?

Marital/family status

Illegal questions

- Are you married or living with a partner?
- Are you pregnant?
- Do you have any children or plan on having children?

Legal questions

- There is a great deal of travel involved with this position. Do you foresee any problems with this requirement?
- Will the long hours required of this job pose any problems for you?
- Would you be willing to relocate if necessary?
- Do you have any responsibilities that may prevent you from meeting the requirements of this position?

Ethnicity/national origin

Illegal questions

- What is your ethnicity?
- Where is your family from?
- Were you born in the United States?
- What is your native language?

Legal questions

- Do you have any language abilities that would be helpful in this position?
- Are you authorized to work in the United States?

Religion

Illegal questions

- Are you religious?
- What religion are you?
- Do you worship regularly at a church/mosque/temple?
- Do you believe in God?

Legal questions

- Are you able to work on Saturday evenings/Sunday mornings, if needed?

Affiliations

Illegal questions

- What clubs or social organizations do you belong to?
- Are you a Republican or a Democrat?
- Are you now or have you ever been a member of the Communist Party?

Legal questions
- Do you belong to any professional organizations that would benefit your ability to perform this job?

Disabilities

Illegal questions
- What is your medical history?
- Do you have any disabilities?
- How would you describe your family's health?
- What resulted in your disability?

Legal questions
- This job requires that a person be able to lift 100 pounds. Would you have any problems fulfilling that requirement?

benefit interviewees. Next, we investigate some of the lessons learned from both successful and unsuccessful interviewees. Then, methods for answering some of the most common interview questions are offered. Finally, we discuss how to answer illegal questions should they be asked during an interview.

Adjusting the Interview Frame

Before you began reading this chapter, you probably had a good idea about what happens during an interview. It is possible that you have been through at least one before. Yet, even if you have not personally experienced an interview, you have likely seen them depicted in movies or television programs and you have likely talked about interviews with people who have experienced them. Therefore, you are well aware of the *frames* surrounding interviews. Frames were introduced in Chapter 1, and we even included interviews as an example. They are basic forms of knowledge that enable people to define a scenario, which in turn helps them determine meaning and understand the roles and expectations of the participants. In the interview frame, one person generally asks a lot of questions and the other one answers them, but you are hopefully recognizing that it is more complex than this description.

How a person frames a situation often dictates what will happen. If a person frames a situation as one in which he or she will play the role of bumbling fool, then the person will likely act like a bumbling fool. Coined by Robert Merton (1957), a **self-fulfilling prophecy** maintains that if someone believes a particular outcome will take place, his or her actions will often lead to its fruition. Accordingly, if you think you will succeed (or fail) at a task, you are more likely to do so, because your actions will likely be those that lead to success (or failure). Therefore, you should always expect to perform well during an interview. Naturally, just because you expect to perform well and end up doing so does not mean that you will get the position you seek. However, it will certainly improve your chances.

We can go a bit deeper with this notion of framing an interview, though. Many interviewees frame an interview as a situation in which they are on trial to determine whether they are capable or worthy of a position and must defend themselves. Anderson and Killenberg (2009, p. 229) have suggested that an interviewee instead frame the interview less threateningly as (1) *an opportunity rather than a test*, (2) *a learning experience rather than a demonstration*, and (3) *a dialogue rather than a monologue*.

You should strive to avoid viewing the interview as a test through which your worthiness as a potential employee, your skills, and your knowledge, along with your value as a human being, are all being called into question. Instead, view the interview as an opportunity to discuss the many ways you could contribute to an organization, to display the skills and knowledge that make you qualified for the position, and, of course, to confirm your value as a human being. In most instances, you would not be asked to interview unless an employer already viewed you as capable of performing the duties of a position and doing so successfully.

Furthermore, do not view the interview merely as a performance in which the above attributes are displayed. Rather, view the interview as an opportunity to learn about yourself. Preparation for and participation in an interview require determining your strengths, weaknesses, and goals, as well as reviewing how your past experiences have brought you to your current place in this world. It is an opportunity to establish personal and professional goals.

Finally, do not view the interview as something that is dominated by one person, while the other person is relegated to a subordinate or immaterial position. Instead, an interview should be viewed as something that is created (transacted) by all participants, who are equally responsible and necessary for its development and who can all potentially gain from the experience. Both an interviewee and an interviewer gain personally and professionally from the interview. They are able to learn about themselves and others; an interviewee has an opportunity to acquire a potentially fulfilling work position, and an interviewer has an opportunity to acquire the services of someone who could potentially improve an organization.

You are hopefully engaged in critical analysis and evaluation as discussed in Chapter 4. If so, you might find the use of a study (Einhorn, 1981) that is roughly 30 years old a bit suspect. We would be the first to tell you to be cautious when coming across apparently dated sources. In this case, however, the age of the source has not diminished the value of its findings. Still, maintain a critical stance when reading this or any book.

Learning From Successful and Unsuccessful Interviewees

Reframing the interview means that an interview can be successful even if you are not offered a position. After all, each interview can be a learning experience that allows you to grow personally and professionally. However, we recognize that such growth does not matter to someone whose primary goals are simply being offered a job and not living out of his or her vehicle. So, for the moment, let's focus on success as being offered a position following an interview.

A great deal can be learned about such success from the people doing the hiring, and this is exactly what was done in a study conducted by Lois Einhorn (1981). As part of this study, the communicative choices of successful and unsuccessful interviewees were examined and categorized. Table 15.3 outlines six key differences between successful and unsuccessful interviewee communication.

Table 15.3 Learning From Successful and Unsuccessful Interviewees

Clear career goals

Successful interviewees are able to clearly articulate their career goals and explain how those goals relate with the position for which they are interviewing.

Unsuccessful interviewees, on the other hand, provide no clear indication of career goals or how those goals might relate to the position for which they are interviewing.

Identification with employers

Successful interviewees mention the organization by name often and exhibit knowledge of the organization.

Unsuccessful interviewees rarely mention the organization by name and demonstrate little to no previous knowledge of the organization.

Support for arguments

Successful interviewees provide illustrations, comparisons and contrasts, statistics, and even testimony from colleagues, supervisors, and instructors.

Unsuccessful interviewees provide little evidence or support material when answering questions.

Participation

Successful interviewees are actively involved in the development of the interview throughout the entire process and spend a great deal of the interview talking.

Unsuccessful interviewees play a passive role in the development of the interview and talk very little during the interview.

Language

Successful interviewees use active, concrete, and positive words along with technical jargon associated with the position.

Unsuccessful interviewees use passive, ambiguous, and negative words while using little or no technical jargon.

Nonverbal delivery

Successful interviewees speak loudly and confidently while also using vocal variety and avoiding nonfluencies. They incorporate meaningful gestures and support interviewer comments with positive nonverbal feedback such as nodding and smiling.

Unsuccessful interviewees speak softly and provide little vocal variety while including longer-than-appropriate pauses. They use few gestures and engage in distracting mannerisms such as rubbing their hands or shaking their legs. They also engage in little or no eye contact with the interviewer.

Answering Common Questions

There are many questions you might be asked during an interview, so it is impossible to cover them all. At the same time, there are a few questions (in various forms and

Photo 15.4 Would keeping her hands clasped throughout the interview improve or diminish this interviewee's chances of being offered the position? (See page 404.)

phrases) that come up more than others. In what follows, we address 10 of the most common questions and discuss some of the best ways to answer them during your interview.

Tell Me a Little About Yourself

When asking you to describe yourself during an interview, the interviewer could not care less about such items as your astrological sign, favorite restaurants, achievements in youth sports, or high school prom theme. An interviewer wants to know how you could benefit the organization, and you should answer accordingly. You should discuss your education, previous work experience, career highlights, and achievements, being sure to emphasize how this information fits the position and would benefit the organization.

What Are Your Greatest Strengths?

This sort of question will almost always arise during an interview in some form or another. Going into the interview, you should have a ready-made list of three or four strengths that you can discuss. Be sure to have concrete examples to support each one and show how these strengths will enable you to succeed at the position.

What Are Your Greatest Weaknesses?

If you say, when asked the preceding question, "Well, I'm pretty lazy, and things would probably start disappearing from around the office if you hired me," you probably will not get the job. It is a responsibility of the interviewee to answer all questions honestly. That being said, you can certainly phrase your responses in a way that minimizes any weaknesses you might mention. Communication professionals often suggest the time-honored tactic of offering a weakness that sounds more like a strength. ("I am such a hard worker that I often get drained by the end of the day. And, I tend to work too many weekends.") However, such responses sound misleading, have become a bit cliché, and do not indicate a genuine ability or interest in recognizing and addressing areas in need of improvement. You may instead want to offer a genuine weakness along with what you are doing to overcome it. ("My Excel skills are in need of development, so I have been taking a night class devoted to the program.") This tactic is especially helpful if there is an obvious skill or ability that you are lacking but that is required for the position or would benefit the position.

What Do You Know About This Organization?

When asked this question, you should exhibit an awareness of such items as the organization's mission, history, growth, and future plans, and perhaps its key personnel. It is a prime opportunity to underscore your enthusiasm for the position and demonstrate how you could benefit the organization based on its present and future endeavors.

Why Do You Want to Work Here?

This question provides another opportunity to reinforce your knowledge of the organization. Likewise, it is another chance for you to discuss your enthusiasm for the position and the organization. Finally, it is a chance to show how your abilities suit the organization and how hiring you would be mutually beneficial. In doing so, you must provide clear, explicit explanations and support for your assertions. For instance, it is not enough to say you could help the organization expand; rather, you must fully explain how you could do so. Remember, the extent of support for arguments is one of the distinguishing characteristics of successful and unsuccessful interviewees.

What Is Your Ideal Job?

This is a tricky question, because you should not necessarily say, "This one"—unless that is true, in which case you should discuss why. At the same time, if you mention a job other than the position for which you are applying, it may appear as if you are uninterested or you plan to move on as soon as something better comes along. Accordingly, you should play it safe and simply *describe* attributes of an ideal position (i.e., meaningful, challenging, fulfilling) while also discussing how the present position meets that description.

Why Do You Want to Leave Your Current Job?

Your current employer may be an idiotic, unprofessional, and unethical ogre who treats you like dirt and may very well eat small children, but you should probably not be that descriptive during an interview. If there were major problems, you may want to address but not dwell on them, taking partial responsibility while discussing what you have learned from the situation. Doing so may be especially wise if the interviewer is possibly aware of these problems. More often than not, however, it is best to focus on the positive attributes of your current (or previous) job, discussing how you have developed professionally and offering legitimate reasons for wanting to leave (i.e., moving to new location, desire for professional growth). One of the reasons interviewers ask this question is to determine whether you will be happy and likely to stay if offered the position in their organization. Therefore, it is wise to discuss how this position better fits your professional goals and desires when compared to your current position.

What Are Your Expectations in Terms of Salary?

This is another very tricky question, because you do not want to put yourself out of reach and you do not want to sell yourself short. Some people suggest placing the question back on the interviewer ("What do people with my experience usually earn here?"), but the question asks for *your* expectations for salary, not his or her expectations. A good way to address this question is by conducting research beforehand to learn the average salaries for a particular position in a particular area. ("Based on the research I have conducted, I would expect the salary to be between $40,000 and $48,000 each year in addition to incentive bonuses.")

Where Do You See Yourself in 5 Years?

This question is usually asked to gauge a person's ambitions, sense of reality, and fit with the company. Your answer will depend, of course, on where you actually want to be in your professional life 5 years from that moment. If you anticipate holding the very position for which you are interviewing, you should say so while also talking about the professional growth that will have taken place and your plans to enhance the organization through that position. If you anticipate moving through the ranks of the organization, your rise to the top should be properly ambitious and realistic. Further, you should stress your plans for professional growth and anticipated contributions to the organization that would justify such advancement. If you anticipate not being with the organization in 5 years, indicating as much may be justifiable if the position is considered short-term. However, you should stress how your time at the organization would be mutually beneficial.

Why Should We Hire You?

When asked this question, you should have a very good answer. If you do not know why the organization should hire you, the interviewer will surely not know either. It may sound as if the interviewer is questioning your abilities, but he or she simply wants to know how you would benefit the organization. Accordingly, this is a perfect opportunity to reinforce your strengths and abilities by discussing how they will benefit the organization.

Dealing With Illegal Questions

We previously discussed illegal questions that should not be asked during an interview, but just because they *should not be* asked does not mean that they *will not be* asked. Sometimes this violation is intentional, while at other times it is unintentional. Whichever the case, you may very well be asked an illegal question while being interviewed for a position. How you deal with such a violation depends on such factors as your perception of its intentionality and, in all honesty, how badly you want the job. However, when it comes to the latter, if such violations occur in the interview process, you may need to seriously question whether the position and the employer are right for you. C. J. Stewart and Cash (2000, pp. 294–295) have offered strategies, outlined in Table 15.4, that can be utilized if you are asked an illegal question during an interview and choose to continue the meeting.

Concluding an Employment Interview

When concluding an employment interview, it is important that positive relational connections among the participants be maintained. Important information needs to be offered during the conclusion of an interview, and certain functions must take place.

Table 15.4 Strategies for Answering Illegal Questions	
Tactful refusal	
Question:	Where are your parents from?
Response:	I don't believe my parents' places of origin matter for this position.
Direct but brief answer	
Question:	How did you injure your leg?
Response:	It was injured while jogging.
Tactful inquiry	
Question:	Where do you go to church?
Response:	How does that question pertain to this position?
Neutralize concern	
Question:	Do you have any children?
Response	Yes, but they would in no way interfere with my work here.
Exploit the question	
Question:	Is English your native language?
Response:	No. My native language is Ket, which would be beneficial for this company since it plans on opening offices in central Siberia next year.

So, let's explore the responsibilities of both interviewers and interviewees during the conclusion of an employment interview.

Interviewer Responsibilities

We will begin with the responsibilities of an interviewer. There are six things an interviewer must do during the conclusion of an interview: (1) provide a wrap-up signal, (2) summarize the interview, (3) ask for questions, (4) preview future actions and schedule, (5) offer thanks, and (6) engage in farewells.

Wrap-Up Signal

Responsibility for controlling an interview rests with the interviewer. Therefore, the interviewer should initiate the conclusion of the interview through a **wrap-up signal**, a phrase indicating the beginning of the conclusion (e.g., "As we near the end of the interview," "As we begin to conclude our discussion"). An interviewer should always allow enough time for both parties to adequately perform their responsibilities of the conclusion, rather than trying to cram everything into the final moments of the interview.

Summarize the Interview

The interviewer should provide a straightforward, relatively brief summary of the information provided by the interviewee during the interview. Doing so will make the interviewee feel understood and will allow him or her to make any necessary clarifications. Interviewers should be careful not to sound either overly enthusiastic or overly dismissive when summarizing this information. This approach will prevent giving the interviewee either false hope or the feeling of failure.

Ask for Questions

The interviewer should always ask the interviewee for questions about the position and about the organization. The answers to these questions should be truthful and provide an accurate reflection of the position and organization. Hiring someone who has been given false impressions may lead to negative feelings and the need to conduct another search should that person decide that the position and organization are not the good fit he or she was led to believe. The questions asked by an interviewee will also provide additional information about that person, including knowledge and motivations.

Photo 15.5 Is it the responsibility of the interviewer or the interviewee to bring a formal end to the interview? (See page 404.)

Preview Future Actions and Schedule

The interviewer should also provide the interviewee with information pertaining to what will happen next and the schedule for decisions about the position. Interviewers are not required to provide any guarantees or odds of employment, nor do they have to disclose how many other job candidates are being interviewed for the position.

Offer Thanks

It is common to erroneously perceive an employment interview as something an interviewer is doing as a favor or because of some grand benevolence. However, the interview is being conducted, in part, because an interviewer (representing an organization) is in need of someone's professional services. Furthermore, the interviewee has invested time, energy, and emotion into the interview process. Accordingly, sincere thanks for participation in the interview should be offered.

Farewells

Finally, it is the responsibility of an interviewer to formally end the interview by offering a handshake and expressing a professional farewell remark to the interviewee. There is certainly no reason to prolong the formal ending of the interview, but you should avoid making it seem as if you are rushing an interviewee out of the office. Otherwise, positive relational connections that may have been established will be diminished, and an otherwise constructive interview may be viewed negatively.

Interviewee Responsibilities

Along with the interviewer, the interviewee also has responsibilities during the conclusion of an interview. There are five things an interviewee must do during this part of an interview: (1) ask questions, (2) reinforce qualifications and enthusiasm, (3) inquire about the future schedule, (4) offer thanks, and (5) engage in farewells.

Ask Questions

Interviewees should have questions prepared and written out during their preinterview preparations. As part of most interviews, an interviewer will ask whether an interviewee has any questions he or she would like to ask. Not asking any questions would indicate a lack of preparation and enthusiasm, so it is a good idea to have some developed. An interviewer may occasionally fail to provide an interviewer an opportunity to ask questions. If it is clear that the interview is ready to end and that the interviewer does not plan on asking for questions, it is acceptable to politely ask if you may pose a few questions. Remember, an interview is not just about whether an interviewee will be offered a position but also about whether an interviewee will accept the position, if offered.

Reinforce Qualifications and Enthusiasm

An interviewee should also briefly summarize the qualifications that make him or her an ideal candidate, along with underscoring his or her enthusiasm for the position. Doing so will help reinforce strengths and abilities while ensuring that key experiences, education, training, and other information have been conveyed. It may also assist the interviewer in remembering and documenting these items.

Inquire About Schedule (If Not Provided)

The interviewer is responsible for providing an interviewee with a schedule of future contact and decision making. However, it is perfectly acceptable to inquire about this information should an interviewer fail to provide it.

Offer Thanks

As mentioned earlier, an interviewer should be grateful for the time, energy, and emotion that an interviewee has put into the interview process. Likewise, an interviewee should be grateful for the work of an interviewer. As this chapter indicates, there is a lot more work involved when interviewing people for a position, and items such as searching for job candidates (constructing the job announcement, gaining approval through human resources, advertising, reviewing applications) and completing the hiring process (deciding who gets the offer, negotiating compensation, dealing with human resources) are not even addressed. Accordingly, sincere thanks should be offered to the interviewer.

Farewells

The interviewer should initiate the formal end of the interview. An interviewee should follow the lead of the interviewer and not unnecessarily prolong the departure. A smile and professional handshake will help maintain a positive relational connection with the interviewer. As an interviewee, you should keep the Strategic Communication box in mind when making an exit, and remember that your evaluation as a job candidate will continue until you completely leave the interview location.

Postinterview Responsibilities

Just because the interview has been concluded does not mean that the work is done. Both interviewers and interviewees have postinterview responsibilities that are vital to their professional development and that will improve interviewees' chances of being offered the position and help interviewers determine the best candidate for the organization. We begin our discussion with the responsibilities of an interviewer.

Interviewer Responsibilities

Following the interview, an interviewer must complete the following three tasks: (1) review the job candidate, (2) assess his or her personal performance, and (3) contact the interviewee with a final decision about the position.

Assess the Job Candidate

An interviewer should record his or her evaluation of the interviewee along with any additional thoughts or information as soon as possible following the interview. Recording impressions and other relevant information is especially important if many interviews are being conducted, and doing so as soon as possible will reduce the amount of information that is lost with time. Contact with references, documented experience, training, and other background information will be used when making final employment decisions, but information gleaned from the interview is also very important when making such decisions and should be properly documented. Table 15.5 provides areas that can be addressed when evaluating a job candidate following the interview.

Strategic Communication

Remember that both an interviewer and an interviewee are being evaluated at all times, not just when questions are being asked and answered. An interviewee's behaviors prior to and following a meeting can be used when forming judgments about his or her overall character and professionalism. When interviewing, you should avoid any odd behaviors while waiting for the interview to take place or when leaving the interview location, while also remembering to be respectful of the office staff—they generally deserve such respect regardless of whether you are attempting to make a good impression. Also, interview sessions occasionally include tours of buildings, introductions to members of the organization, meals, and transportation to or from the interview location. An interviewee will be evaluated throughout all of these situations, so make sure you remain aware that assessments are being made. Such occasions and activities are also a good opportunity to evaluate the interviewer and determine whether the position or organization is right for you.

Table 15.5 Assessing a Job Candidate

- What are the candidate's strengths?
- What are the candidate's weaknesses?
- How does this candidate compare with other candidates?
- How personable does the candidate seem?
- How would the candidate fit with the organization's climate?
- How knowledgeable about the position and the organization does the candidate seem?
- Are there any concerns about whether the candidate would be successful in this position?
- What additional questions or information about the candidate need to be addressed?

Assess Personal Performance

The interviewer should also assess his or her performance in order to improve both personally and professionally. Focus equally on the positive and negative aspects of the interview performance. Regardless of how much interviewing experience you may possess, there is always room for improvement. Table 15.6 provides a few questions you may pose when evaluating your performance as an interviewer.

Table 15.6 Assessing Performance as Interviewer

- Did I make the interviewee comfortable and establish the desired tone of the interview? How can I improve these aspects of the interview?
- Did my questions elicit the information needed to fully evaluate the job candidate? How can I improve these questions to enhance the quality of the information gained?
- Did I avoid illegal questions?
- What nonverbal communication most benefited my performance? How can I improve my nonverbal communication?
- How well did I listen during the interview? How can I improve my listening?
- Were my responses to the questions posed by the interviewee complete and accurate? In what ways can I improve my responses?
- Did I provide the interviewee with information about future contact and a realistic timetable for decisions about the position?
- Was the interview conducted within the time constraints? Did all portions of the interview receive the appropriate amount of attention? How can I improve my use of time?

Contact Interviewee

The interviewer should ensure that *all* interviewees are contacted about the final decision. This contact should come either personally or through whatever method is used by the organization. Contacting interviewees is a professional courtesy that, unfortunately, is increasingly absent during many job searches. There exists no legitimate excuse for not contacting and acknowledging a job candidate who did not receive an offer. Not contacting job candidates is not only unprofessional but also cruel! Additionally, a person may not have been suited for this position, but he or she may be ideal for a future position. A lack of contact may prevent a well-suited candidate from applying for a future position—for good reason. A person who is mistreated during the interview process may eventually be in a position that could negatively influence the organization. Ultimately, interviewers should simply contact all interviewees because it is the humane thing to do.

Interviewee Responsibilities

An interviewee has three responsibilities following an interview: (1) assess the interview, (2) send a follow-up letter, and (3) avoid irritating the interviewer.

Assess the Interview

Following the interview, an interviewee should develop a candid assessment of his or her performance. The sooner this assessment can be conducted, the fresher the information and the more accurate the recollection. Strive to give equal attention to the aspects of the interview that went well and those that need improvement. Regardless of how you might feel about the interview, even the best interview can be improved, and an awful interview is never as bad as it seems. The best way to improve as an interviewee is through an honest assessment of your performance.

An interviewee should also develop an honest assessment of the position and organization. Developing this assessment will help determine whether the position is something you will accept if offered. It will also increase your understanding about careers and industries for which you are interviewing. Tables 15.7 and 15.8 provide questions to assess your performance, the position, and the organization.

Table 15.7 Assessing Performance as Interviewee

- Which questions were answered well? What made these good answers?
- What questions were not answered well? How can I improve these answers?
- Were my questions appropriate? How can I improve these questions?
- What nonverbal communication most benefited my performance? How can I improve my nonverbal communication?
- How well did I listen during the interview? How can I improve my listening?

Table 15.8 Assessing Position and Organization

- What are the pros and cons of the position?
- What are the pros and cons of the organization?
- How does this position compare with other available positions?
- How does this organization compare with other organizations?
- How has my understanding and evaluation of this career/profession changed?

Send Follow-Up Letter

An interviewee should also send a letter of thanks following the interview. In addition to thanking the interviewer for his or her time, it is an opportunity to reinforce interest in the position and remind the interviewer of qualifications and experience. If something was not mentioned during the interview, this letter is a good opportunity to add that information. Interviewers occasionally ask for additional information or materials. These items can be included with the letter as well. Do not appear overly confident about the interview, nor should you apologize for a less-than-stellar interview. The letter should also be viewed as a professional correspondence. Accordingly, it should be respectful, well written, and free of grammatical errors. The letter can be handwritten, typed, or e-mailed, although some people disagree about which of these is most appropriate. People and organizations view technology in different ways (Chapter 9), so use your best judgment as to whether it will be deemed an appropriate method of correspondence.

Avoid Irritating the Interviewer

This postinterview requirement may seem obvious, but you should avoid irritating the interviewer by inquiring about the progress of a job search. Do not send the interviewer numerous letters, leave phone messages every hour on the hour, or send the interviewer a Facebook friendship request. We understand that waiting for an employment decision can be excruciatingly painful, but waiting is something that must be done. Irritating the interviewer will in no way increase your chances of being offered the position and will likely hinder those chances. If you have not heard from the interviewer by the time he or she indicated you would be contacted, however, it is acceptable to politely inquire about the status of the position. A number of variables can lead to a delay in the search process, so it is not uncommon, nor is it necessarily a personal affront against you. The organization may very well be busy renting a truck to dump a load of money on your doorstep.

Cover Letters and Résumés

As mentioned at the beginning of the chapter, you will not be invited to an employment interview without a quality cover letter and résumé. Accordingly, we now address some key elements in the construction of these essential items. We begin by discussing the cover letter, which is the tool used to get a potential employer to actually review your résumé.

Cover Letters

A **cover letter** has four purposes: (1) declare interest in the position, (2) provide a summary of qualifications, (3) compel the person to read your résumé, and (4) request an interview. Employers often receive numerous applications for a single position, and quite often application materials are given only slight attention. Therefore, hopeful employees should do everything possible to ensure that their materials stand out from the rest and receive adequate attention. In what follows, we present the key elements of effective cover letters.

Address Letter to Specific Person

Many applicants do not take the time to confirm who will be reading their materials and consequently do not address their cover letter to a specific person. Simply addressing the letter "To Whom It May Concern" will not make your cover letter stand out from the rest and will elicit *little* concern from the receiver. A quick phone call to the organization will likely provide you with the name of the person to whom the letter should be addressed, if it is unavailable in the job announcement/advertisement. Be certain to use the person's last name only and to address the person using his or her proper title.

Case in Point

Evaluate your most recent cover letter and résumé using the guidelines and suggestions offered in this chapter. In what ways could they be improved? If you have never written a cover letter and résumé, prepare them for a fictional position in your career field or for an actual position you wish to obtain. Even if you are not currently seeking employment, it is never too early to develop or update these important career tools.

Identify the Position

Identify the position for which you are applying in the first paragraph of the letter. An organization may have multiple positions available, and you want to ensure that you are being considered for the one you intend. You should also indicate how you discovered the position's availability. Finally, you should display knowledge about and positive regard for the organization. Including this information shows that you have taken the time to learn about the organization and that you view it favorably. Some applicants—especially those applying for hundreds of positions—use form cover letters and change nothing but the name and address of the company. Such form letters will generate less interest than letters in which the applicant appears clearly knowledgeable about the organization and interested in working there.

Summarize Qualifications and Promote Résumé

Summarize the qualifications that make you an ideal fit for the position in the second paragraph. You may discuss such items as your education and training, experiences, special skills, and activities that have prepared you for the position and that will enable you to successfully fulfill the duties of the position. Be sure to emphasize what you can provide for the organization. At the end of this paragraph, you should encourage the reader to refer to your résumé. You can do this by mentioning specific information that can be discovered there or by simply mentioning the additional information that can be discovered through its examination.

Reaffirm Interest and Request an Interview

Reaffirm your interest in the position and request an interview in the final paragraph of the cover letter. You may want to indicate your intention to contact this person in the future ("I will contact you in two weeks to see if you require additional information about my credentials or desire any additional materials"). Another option in the final paragraph is to request a date to meet with the employer. This might be especially appropriate if you are presently located in an area other than the organization and will happen to be visiting that area ("I will be in the Keynsham area June 30–July 5 and would appreciate the opportunity to meet with you during that time to discuss my qualifications in more detail").

Sign Off With Respect and Professionalism

When ending the letter, you should use the term *Sincerely* or *Respectfully* or *Cordially* rather than *Yours Truly* or *Yours Faithfully,* which is too personal when corresponding with someone you likely do not know, and rather than *Best Wishes* or *Cheers,* which is too informal for a professional letter. Use your full name and do not use a nickname. Sign the letter using dark ink in a legible and professional manner, avoiding unnecessary flourish (i.e., no swirly lines at the end or hearts/smiley faces dotting an *i*). You should end the letter properly to ensure the quality of the letter established thus far is maintained.

Résumés

The purpose of a **résumé** is to present your credentials for a position in a clear and concise manner. Employers may spend less than a minute looking at your résumé, so the information included should be not only clear and concise but also positive and obviously appropriate to the position for which you are applying. In what follows, we discuss the key elements of effective résumés.

Name and Contact Information

As with your cover letter, you should use your full name when constructing a résumé and avoid using nicknames. Include the following contact information: (1) address, (2) telephone number, and (3) e-mail address. Include a personal website address only if it is solely professional or academic. If you are a student, you may have both a campus address and telephone number and a permanent address and telephone number. If this is the case, include both your campus contact information and your permanent contact information. As mentioned in Chapter 9, make sure that your e-mail

Cover letters and résumés should be easy for the employer to read. They should be sent flat rather than folded and printed on light-colored paper rather than dark-colored paper. Of course, some employers prefer to receive application material digitally (Schullery, Ickes, & Schullery, 2009). Furthermore, many career networking sites enable applicants to post video résumés. Be sure to read position announcements carefully to determine an employer's preferred method of delivery.

address adheres to professional standards. Someone whose e-mail address begins *Lazy-drunk93* will not receive many interview offers!

Career Objective

Next, you must include your career objective. This objective should be one sentence and never over two sentences. It should also be explicitly tailored to meet the needs of the organization and the position for which you are applying. The employer will be asking himself or herself what you can do for the organization, not what the organization can do for you. A vague statement of interests and a lack of commitment to the organization will not suffice.

Education and Training

Education and training should follow your career objective. List your degrees or training in reverse chronological order so that your most recent (and likely most relevant) information appears first. Listing your high school degree is not necessary if you are presently enrolled in or have completed college. This section should include the following information: (1) degree completion (or expected completion) date along with all majors or minors, (2) college name and location, and (3) awards, honors, or certificates. Use your own best judgment as to whether you should include your grade point average. Some fields may place more importance on this number than others.

Experiences

The experiences section of your résumé will include your employment history and other endeavors such as volunteer work if they happen to be relevant to the position for which you are applying. As with your education history, list your experiences in reverse chronological order. This section should include the following information: (1) position, (2) name of the organization along with location (city and state), (3) dates of employment or service (month and year), and (4) responsibilities and accomplishments. Your responsibilities and accomplishments are especially important in this section, and you should emphasize those that are most applicable to the position you are hoping to receive. These responsibilities and accomplishments are usually not written in complete sentences. Instead, begin each phrase with a verb that implies action (e.g., *spearheaded, updated, developed, increased*).

It has traditionally been suggested that résumés be confined to one page. However, two pages are acceptable if warranted by your credentials. Place the most important information on the front page, because many employers will still not read beyond the first one. Staple the pages together but include your name and a page number on the second page in case they get separated. Even people with many years of experience should be able to synthesize their credentials into two pages, so we suggest never going beyond a two-page limit.

Skills

Next, include the skills that are most relevant to the position for which you are applying. These skills could include abilities in such areas as computer programs, languages, laboratory protocol, machinery, tools, or whatever areas most fit the position. If you possess multiple skills within a particular category, you may wish to use that category as a heading. For instance, you may possess skills in multiple computer programs and include these under a header titled *Computer Skills.*

Activities

When listing activities on your résumé, you should include those most relevant to the position first. However, in this case, feel free to also list activities that are not necessarily related to the position. Of course, you should only include those activities that reflect favorably on you, but listing activities can indicate a well-rounded person with many life experiences from which to draw when dealing with people and participating in organizational life.

FOCUS QUESTIONS REVISITED

1. What are the characteristics of an interview?
Interviews are goal-driven, structured, controlled, and unbalanced and feature questions and answers.

2. What are the types of interviews?
The following are the most common types of interviews: (1) employment interviews, (2) performance interviews, (3) exit interviews, (4) information-gaining interviews, (5) persuasive interviews, (6) problem-solving interviews, and (7) helping interviews.

3. What are the preinterview responsibilities of interviewers and interviewees?
Prior to an interview, an interviewer must review application material, prepare questions and an interview outline, gather material, and ensure the interview begins on time. An interviewee must gather information, prepare questions, practice, bring materials, form a professional personal appearance, and arrive on time.

4. How should a person begin an employment interview?
During the beginning of an interview, participants must greet one another and establish proxemics, begin to negotiate the desired relational connection and tone of the interview, and establish the purpose and agenda of the interview.

5. What types of questions and questioning styles may an interviewer use?
The different types of questions that an interviewer may ask include the following: (1) primary and secondary, (2) open and closed, and (3) neutral and leading. The interviewer may not ask questions that are potentially discriminatory. The type of control exerted by the interview can be either directive or nondirective.

6. How should interviewees respond to questions during an interview?

When answering the questions, interviewees should attempt to adjust the interview frame in order to view the interview as an opportunity, a learning experience, and a dialogue rather than a test, a demonstration, or a monologue. They should also learn from successful interviewees, who articulate clear goals; identify with employers; provide support for arguments; participate in the development of the interview; use active, concrete words; and display dynamic nonverbal communication. Interviewees should be prepared to answer common questions asked during employment interviews and also be prepared should they be asked an illegal question.

7. How should a person conclude an employment interview?

When concluding an employment interview as an interviewer, you should provide a wrap-up signal, summarize the interview, ask for questions, preview future actions and schedule, extend thanks, and offer farewells. When concluding an employment interview as an interviewee, you should ask questions, reinforce qualifications and enthusiasm, inquire about the schedule if it has not been offered, extend thanks, and offer farewells.

8. What are the postinterview responsibilities of interviewers and interviewees?

Following an interview, an interviewer must review the job candidate, assess his or her performance, and contact the interviewee with a final decision about the position. An interviewee must assess the interview, develop a follow-up letter, and avoid irritating the interviewer.

9. What are a cover letter and résumé?

A cover letter declares interest in a position, summarizes qualification, focuses attention on the résumé, and requests an interview. The key features of a cover letter include (1) a focus on a specific person, (2) identification of the position, (3) a summary of qualifications and the promotion of the résumé, (4) a reaffirmation of interest and a request for an interview, and (5) a professional and respectful sign-off. The purpose of a résumé is to present your credentials for a position in a clear and concise manner. The key elements of a résumé include (1) name and contact information, (2) career objective, (3) education and training, (4) experiences, (5) skills, and (6) activities.

KEY CONCEPTS

bipolar questions 381
closed questions 381
cover letter 398
directive interviews 382
employment interviews 369
exit interviews 370

helping interviews 371
information-gaining interviews 370
interview 367
leading questions 381
mirror questions 380
neutral questions 381

QUESTIONS TO ASK YOUR FRIENDS

1. Ask a friend to describe his or her most recent employment interview. What aspects of the interview went well? What aspects of the interview needed improvement? Having read this chapter, provide your friend with advice about how to improve his or her performance during interviews.

2. Ask a friend to participate in mock interviews with you. You should alternate between being an interviewer and being an interviewee. Evaluate your performances and pinpoint areas for improvement and development.

3. Ask a friend to review your cover letter and résumé. What suggestions for improvement does he or she make?

MEDIA LINKS

1. Watch an interview conducted on television or available online. What open and closed questions are included? Are the questions mostly neutral or mostly leading? Are secondary questions included? Is this a directive or a nondirective interview?

2. Watch an interview conducted on television or available online with the sound muted. What does the nonverbal communication of the interviewer and interviewee suggest in terms of their relational connection and the tone of the interview? Next, watch the interview with the sound turned on. Does the verbal communication of the interviewer and interviewee match your perceptions of their relational connection and the tone of the interview conveyed nonverbally?

3. Find a clip from *Law & Order* or another fictional program featuring a lawyer questioning a witness. Next, find a clip from a television news program in which someone is being interviewed. Finally, find a clip from a late-night talk show in which a celebrity is being interviewed about his or her latest project. How would you rank these examples in terms of being directive or nondirective? What features caused you to rank them in that order?

ETHICAL ISSUES

1. If an interviewee is not interested in a position and simply desires interview experience, is it ethical for him or her to take part in an interview? If an interviewer already has a job candidate selected for the position, is it ethical for him or her to interview other candidates for the position in order to simply fulfill legal or other requirements?

2. Is it ethical for an interviewee to embellish his or her accomplishments during an interview? Where is the line drawn between describing accomplishments in a positive manner and fabricating these accomplishments?

3. If an interviewer inadvertently asks an illegal question, should he or she be reported to the proper authorities? Is it possible to distinguish purposeful and inadvertent behavior in such situations? Should the consequences be different?

ANSWERS TO PHOTO CAPTIONS

Photo 15.1 ▪ Information-gaining interviews are those through which an interviewer gains information from an interviewee, whereas persuasive interviews are those through which an interviewer attempts to influence the interviewee. The differences between them are not always obvious to the individual being interviewed.

Photo 15.2 ▪ In addition to reviewing a job candidate's application material prior to an interview, an interviewer must also prepare questions and an interview outline, gather materials, and ensure that the interview begins on time—so the person in the photo had better hurry up and finish that coffee!

Photo 15.3 ▪ No. It would not be a good idea for an interviewee to close his or her eyes and nap. Hopefully, you got this one correct. If not, we are glad you now know, and you may want to read closely the Strategic Communication box about interviewees always being evaluated.

Photo 15.4 ▪ Keeping her hands clasped during the interview will likely hinder this interviewee's chances of being offered the position. Successful interviewees tend to incorporate meaningful gestures, whereas unsuccessful interviewees tend to use few gestures, or they engage in distracting mannerisms such as rubbing hands or playing with watches and jewelry.

Photo 15.5 ▪ It is the responsibility of the interviewer to bring a formal end to the interview.

STUDENT STUDY SITE

Visit the study site at **www.sagepub.com/boc2e** for e-flashcards, practice quizzes, journal articles and additional study resources.

REFERENCES

Anderson, R., & Killenberg, G. M. (2009). *Interviewing: Speaking, listening, and learning for professional life.* New York: Oxford University Press.

Einhorn, L. J. (1981). An inner view of the job interview: An investigation of successful communicative behaviors. *Communication Education, 30,* 217–228.

Gouran, D. S., Wiethoff, W. E., & Doelger, J. A. (1994). *Mastering communication* (2nd ed.). Boston: Allyn & Bacon.

Krumhuber, E., Manstead, A. S. R., Cosker, D., Marshall, D., & Rosin, P. L. (2009). Effects of dynamic attributes of smiles in human and synthetic faces: A simulated job interview setting. *Journal of Nonverbal Behavior, 33,* 1–16.

Merton, R. K. (1957). *Social theory and social structure.* Glencoe, IL: Free Press.

Schullery, N. M., Ickes, L., & Schullery, S. E. (2009). Employer preferences for résumés and cover letters. *Business Communication Quarterly, 72,* 153–176.

Stewart, C. J., & Cash, W. B., Jr. (2000). *Interviewing: Principles and practices* (9th ed.). New York: McGraw-Hill.

Stewart, G. L., Dustin, S. L., Barrick, M R., & Darnold, T. C. (2008). Exploring the handshake in employment interviews. *Journal of Applied Psychology, 93,* 1139–1146.

Glossary

accommodation: when people change their accent, their rate of speech, and even the words they use to indicate a relational connection with the person to whom they are talking

accountable self: the aspect of self that allows other people to morally judge a person's performance

accounts: forms of communication that go beyond the facts and offer justifications, excuses, exonerations, explanations, or accusations

altercasting: how language can impose a certain identity on people (e.g., "Only a *fool* would . . ."; "The *brightest students* will get this chapter without any trouble") and then burden them with the duty to live up to the description, whether positive or negative

anchor position (social judgment theory): represents the preferred or most acceptable position in an argument

appeal to authority (fallacious argument): when a person's authority or credibility in one area is used to support another area

appeal to people (fallacious argument): claims that something is good or beneficial because everyone else agrees with this evaluation (also called *bandwagon appeal*)

appeal to relationships (fallacious argument): when relationships are used to justify certain behaviors and to convince others of their appropriateness

argument against the source (fallacious argument): when the source of a message, rather than the message itself, is attacked (also called *ad hominem* argument)

assimilation effect (social judgment theory): maintains that if someone advocates a position within a person's latitude of acceptance, he or she will view it as closer to his or her anchor position than it really is

asynchronous–communication: communication in which there is a slight or prolonged delay between the message and the response; the interactants must alternate between sending and receiving messages

attending: the second step in the listening process when stimuli are perceived and focused on

attention getter: a device used to draw the audience into a presentation

attitude of reflection (symbolic interactionism): thinking about how you look in other people's eyes, or reflecting on the fact that other people can see you as a social object from their point of view

attitudes: learned predispositions to evaluate something in a positive or negative way that guide people's thinking and behavior

audience involvement (social judgment theory): audience members' recognition of a topic's significance and importance in their lives

autonomy–connectedness: dialectic tension caused by one's desire to retain some independence yet be connected to another person in a relationship

back region: a frame where a social interaction is regarded as not under public scrutiny, so people do not have to present their public face (e.g., when servers are in the kitchen or when there are no customers in a restaurant, the servers do not have to behave with dignity or with respect toward customers—and often do not)

backchannel communication: vocalizations by a listener that give feedback to the speaker to show interest, attention, and/or a willingness to keep listening

balance principle: a principle of speech organization and development that maintains the points of the body of a speech must be relatively equal in scope and importance

base: the number of people, objects, or things included in a study

beliefs: what a person holds to be true or false

bipolar question: a type of closed question that forces an interviewee to select one of two responses

body: part of a speech where an argument is developed and presented and where a relational connection with an audience is maintained

body buffer zone: a kind of imaginary aura around you that you regard as part of yourself and your personal space

brainstorming: a method of gathering and generating ideas, without immediate evaluation; for example, by writing down or calling out everything that comes to mind for a specific (generally brief) period

Burke's pentad: five elements common to all stories and situations: scene, agent, act, agency, and purpose

captive audience: an audience that is required to listen to a presentation

causal pattern: the main points of a speech are arranged according to cause and effect

chronemics: the study of use and evaluation of time in interactions

chronological pattern: the main points of a speech are arranged according to their position in a time sequence

claim of conjecture: a claim that something will be true or false in the future

claim of fact: a claim maintaining that something is true or false

claim of policy: a claim maintaining that a course of action should or should not be taken

claim of value: a claim maintaining that something is good or bad, beneficial or detrimental, or another evaluative criterion

clincher statement: a phrase that allows a speaker to end a speech strongly and smoothly

closed questions: questions that limit the range of an interviewee's response (contrast with *open questions*)

co-culture: a smaller group of culture within a larger cultural mass

coded system of meaning: a set of beliefs, a heritage, and a way of being that is transacted in communication

cohesiveness: working in unison

collectivist (culture): subscribing to a belief system that stresses group benefit and the overriding value of working harmoniously rather than individual personal advancement

common purpose: sharing goals and objectives; working toward the same end to achieve a particular result

communication apprehension: fear or anxiety about speaking in public

communication as action: the act of sending messages—whether or not they are received

communication as interaction: an exchange of information between two (or more) individuals

communication as transaction: the construction of shared meanings or understandings between two (or more) individuals

comparison: demonstrating or revealing how things are similar

composition fallacy (fallacious argument): argues that the parts are the same as the whole

composure: the ability to appear calm under pressure

conclusion: part of a speech that reinforces and completes a speech while also reinforcing a relationship with an audience

concrete words: represent tangible objects that can be experienced through sensory channels (touch, taste, smell, hearing, seeing); include real people, objects, actions, and locations

concurrent media use: use of two or more media systems simultaneously

conflict: real or perceived incompatibilities of processes, understandings, and viewpoints between people

conflict-as-destructive culture: a culture based on four assumptions: that conflict is a destructive disturbance of the peace; that the social system should not be adjusted to meet the needs of members, but members should adapt to established values; that confrontations are destructive and ineffective; and that disputants should be disciplined

conflict-as-opportunity culture: a culture based on four assumptions: that conflict is a normal, useful process; that all issues are subject to change through negotiation; that direct confrontation and conciliation are valued; and that conflict is a necessary renegotiation of an implied contract—a redistribution of opportunity, a release of tensions, and a renewal of relationships

connotative meaning: the overtones, implications, or additional meanings associated with a word or an object

consistency: a message is free of internal contradiction and is in harmony with information known to be true

constitutive approach to communication: communication can create or bring into existence something that has not been there before, such as an agreement, a contract, or an identity

content creation: the creation of online material such as social networking pages and blogs as well as the online posting of original pictures, videos, reviews, and comments that serves in the construction of identity

content (representational) listening: obstacle to listening when people focus on the content level of meaning, or literal meaning, rather than the social or relational level of meaning

contrast: demonstrating or revealing how things are different

contrast effect (social judgment theory): maintains that if someone advocates a position within a person's latitude of rejection, he or she will view it as farther from his or her anchor position than it really is

convergence: a person moves toward the style of talk used by the other speaker

conversational hypertext: coded messages within conversation that an informed listener will effortlessly understand

counteractive communication: gets the group back on track by reminding group members of the purposes they are there to serve

cover letter: a letter sent when seeking employment, which has four purposes: (1) declare interest in the position, (2) provide a summary of qualifications, (3) compel the person to read your résumé, and (4) request an interview

critical listening: the process of analyzing and evaluating the accuracy, legitimacy, and value of messages

cross-cultural communication: compares the communication styles and patterns of people from very different cultural/social structures, such as nation-states

cultural persuadables: the cultural premises and norms that delineate a range of what may and what must be persuaded (as opposed to certain topics in a society that require no persuasive appeal because the matters are taken for granted)

cum hoc ergo propter hoc (fallacious argument): argues that if one thing happens at the same time as another, it was caused by the thing with which it coincides; Latin for "with this; therefore, because of this"

decoding: drawing meaning from something you observe

deductive reasoning: using general conclusions, premises, or principles to reach a conclusion about a specific example or instance

definition: the meaning of a word or phrase

demographics: characteristics of a person or an audience that can provide insight into one's knowledge, experiences, interests, needs, attitudes, beliefs, and values

denotative meaning: the identification of something by pointing it out ("That is a cat")

descriptive language: provides the audience with a clearer picture of what is discussed by *describing* it in more detail

Devil terms: powerfully evocative terms viewed negatively in a society (see *God terms*)

dialectic tension: occurs whenever one is in two minds about something because one feels a simultaneous pull in two directions

directive interviews: interviews that are greatly controlled by an interviewer

disruptive communication: diverts a group from its goals and takes it down side alleys

distracting mannerisms: bodily movements that allow a person to discharge nervous energy but that serve no actual purpose in a presentation and often divert attention away from the message

divergence: a talker moves away from another's style of speech to make a relational point, such as establishing dislike or superiority

division fallacy (fallacious argument): argues the whole is the same as its parts

dyadic process: part of the process of breakdown of relationships that involves a confrontation with a partner and the open discussion of a problem with a relationship

dynamic: elements of nonverbal communication that are changeable during interaction (e.g., facial expression, posture, gesturing; contrast with *static*)

dynamism: a secondary dimension of credibility referring to being energetic and enthusiastic

egocentric listening: obstacle to listening when people focus more on their message and self-presentation than on the message of the other person involved in an interaction

elimination pattern: offers a series of solutions to a problem and then systematically eliminates each one until the solution remaining is the one that the speaker supports

emoticons: text-based symbols used to express emotions online, often to alleviate problems associated with a lack of nonverbal cues

employment interviews: interviews in which a potential employer interviews a potential employee

encoding: putting feelings into behavior through nonverbal communication

engaged listening: making a personal relational connection with the source of a message that results from the source and the receiver actively working together to create shared meaning and understanding

enthymeme: a syllogism that excludes one or two of its three components (see *syllogism*)

environmental distraction: obstacle to listening that results from the physical location where listening takes place

equivocation (fallacious argument): relies on the ambiguousness of language to make an argument

essential function of talk: a function of talk that makes the relationship real and talks it into being, often by using coupling references or making assumptions that the relationship exists

ethnocentric bias: believing that the way one's own culture does things is the right and only way to do them

ethos: the use of speaker credibility to impact an audience

evoke (purpose): to generate an emotion from the audience

examples: specific cases used to represent a larger whole to clarify or explain something

exit interviews: interviews that occur when a person chooses to leave a place of employment

experiential superiority: obstacle to listening when people fail to fully listen to someone else because they believe that they possess more or superior knowledge and experience than the other person

expert testimony: testimony that comes from someone with special training, instruction, or knowledge in a particular area

expository speech: a speech providing the audience with a detailed or in-depth review or analysis of an object, a creation, a place, a person, a concept, or an event

extemporaneous delivery: the use of minimal notes, generally recommended as the way to achieve a natural and conversational delivery while ensuring the accuracy of ideas

facework: the management of people's dignity or self-respect, known as "face"

facts: provable or documented truths that can be used as evidence to support claims

factual diversion: obstacle to listening that occurs when so much emphasis is placed on attending to every detail of a message that the main point becomes lost

fallacious argument: an argument that appears legitimate but is actually based on faulty reasoning or insufficient evidence

false alternatives (fallacious argument): occurs when only two options are provided, one of which is generally presented as the poor choice or one that should be avoided

formal power: that which is formally allocated by a system or group to particular people (e.g., bosses, the police, school principals; compare with *informal power*)

frames: basic forms of knowledge that provide a definition of a scenario, either because both people agree on the nature of the situation or because the cultural assumptions built into the interaction and the previous relational context of talk give them a clue

front region: a place where a social interaction is regarded as under public scrutiny, so people have to be on their best behavior or acting out their professional roles or intended "face" (e.g., the restaurant, where servers have to behave with dignity and with respect toward customers)

general purpose: the basic objective a speaker wishes to achieve

given belief: a belief that the majority of people in an audience will view as either true or false

God terms: powerfully evocative terms that are viewed positively in a society (see *Devil terms*)

grave dressing process: part of the breakdown of relationships that consists of creating the story of why a relationship died and erecting a metaphorical tombstone that summarizes its main events and features from its birth to its death

group culture: the set of expectations and practices that a group develops to make itself distinctive from other groups and to give its members a sense of exclusive membership (e.g., dress code, specialized language, particular rituals)

group norms: rules and procedures that occur in a group but not necessarily outside it and that are enforced by the use of power or rules for behavior

group sanctions: punishments for "stepping out of line," speaking out of turn, or failing to accept the ruling of the chair or leader

guidance principle: a principle of speech organization and development that maintains a speaker must guide and direct the audience throughout the entire speech

haptics: the study of the specific nonverbal behaviors involving touch

hasty generalization (fallacious argument): when a conclusion is based on a single occurrence or insufficient data or sample size

hearing: the passive physiological act of receiving sound that takes place when sound waves hit a person's eardrums

helping interviews: interviews conducted by someone with expertise in a given area and whose services are engaged by someone in need of advice

high code: a formal, grammatical, and very correct—often "official"—way of talking

high-context culture: a culture that places a great deal of emphasis on the total environment (context) where speech and interaction take place, especially on the relationships between the speakers rather than just on what they say (see *low-context culture*)

how-to speech: describes the procedure or methods through which something is accomplished with the expectation that the audience will be able to perform the process

hypothetical illustrations: fabricated illustrations using typical characteristics to describe particular situations, objects, or people, as well as illustrations describing what could happen in the future

identity: a person's uniqueness, represented by descriptions, a self-concept, inner thoughts, and performances, that is symbolized in interactions with other people and presented for their assessment and moral evaluation

illustrations: examples offered in an extended narrative form

immediacy: linguistic inclusion (e.g., *let's*, *we*, *us*)

indexical function of talk: demonstrates or indicates the nature of the relationship between speakers

individual inventory: a listing of a person's preferences, likes, dislikes, and experiences that can be used when selecting a topic

individualist: one who subscribes to a belief system that focuses on the individual person and his or her personal dreams, goals and achievements, and right to make choices

inductive reasoning: deriving a general conclusion based on specific evidence, examples, or instances

inform (purpose): to develop audience understanding of a topic through definition, clarification, demonstration, or explanation of a process

informal power: operates through relationships and individual reputations without formal status (e.g., someone may not actually be the boss but might exert more influence on other workers by being highly respected; compare with *formal power*)

information-gaining interviews: interviews in which a person solicits information from another person

inspiring: a secondary dimension of credibility referring to the ability to instill enthusiasm in others

instrumental function of talk: when what is said brings about a goal that you have in mind for the relationship, and talk is the means or instrument by which it is accomplished (e.g., asking someone on a date or to come with you to a party)

intentionality: a basic assumption in communication studies that messages indicate somebody's intentions or that they are produced intentionally or in a way that gives insight, at the very least, into the sender's mental processes

intercultural communication: examines how people from different cultural/social structures speak to one another and what difficulties or conflicts they encounter, over and above the different languages they speak

interdependence: the reliance of each member of a team or group on the other members, making their outcomes dependent on the collaboration and interrelated performance of all members (e.g., a football team dividing up the jobs of throwing, catching, and blocking)

interpreting: the third step in the listening process when meaning is assigned to sounds and symbolic activity

interview: a goal-driven transaction characterized by questions and answers, clear structure, control, and imbalance

intrapsychic process: part of the process of breakdown of a relationship where an individual reflects on the strengths and weaknesses of a relationship and begins to consider the possibility of ending it

introduction: part of a speech that lays the foundation for the body and establishes a positive relational connection with an audience

kinesics: the study of movements that take place during the course of an interaction

labeling: naming an object or person with a label that the object or person has to live up to

langue: the formal grammatical structure of language (contrast with *parole*)

latitude of acceptance (social judgment theory): positions in an argument that an audience deems acceptable

latitude of noncommitment (social judgment theory): positions in an argument that an audience neither wholly accepts nor wholly rejects

latitude of rejection (social judgment theory): positions in an argument that an audience deems unacceptable

lay testimony: testimony that comes from someone without expertise in a particular area but who possesses experience in that area

leadership: the formal position where a specific person has power over the others in the group and is given the responsibility of leading its activities

leading questions: questions that suggest to an interviewee a preferred way to respond (contrast with *neutral questions*)

leakage: unintentional betrayal of internal feelings through nonverbal communication

listening: the active process of receiving, attending to, interpreting, and responding to symbolic activity

logos: the use of logic or reasoning to impact an audience

low code: an informal and often ungrammatical way of talking

low-context culture: assumes that the message itself means everything, and it is much more important to have a well-structured argument or a well-delivered presentation than it is to be a member of the royal family or a cousin of the person listening (see *high-context culture*)

main points: statements that directly support or develop a thesis

manuscript delivery: reading from a complete manuscript of a speech

mean: the average number (i.e., the *total* of scores divided by the *number* of scores that were added together to make the total)

meaning: what a symbol represents

media equation: people use the same social rules and expectations when interacting with technology as they do with other people

media generations: generations that are differentiated by unique media grammar and media consciousness based on the technological environment in which they are born

media literacy: the learned ability to access, interpret, and evaluate media products

media profile: a compilation of a person's media preferences and general use of media

median: the number that rests in the middle of all the other numbers, where half of the numbers are less than this number, and the other half are more than this number

medium: means through which a message is conveyed

medium distraction: obstacle to listening that results from limitations or problems inherent in certain media and technology, such as mobile phones or Internet connections

memorized delivery: a speech that has been committed to memory and is delivered without the use of a manuscript or any notes whatsoever

message complexity: obstacle to listening when a person finds a message so complex or confusing that he or she stops listening

microcoordination: the unique management of social interaction made possible through cell phones

mirror questions (secondary questions): questions that paraphrase an interviewee's previous response to ensure clarification and to elicit elaboration

mode: the number that occurs most often in a set of numbers

monochronic culture: a culture that views time as a valuable commodity and punctuality as very important

moral accountability: people are held morally accountable for their actions, statements, or claims and have to explain them as legitimate or reasonable to other people

naming: distinguishing items from other items for which people also have (different) words

narrative: any organized story, report, or talk that has a plot, an argument, or a theme and in which speakers both relate facts and arrange the story in a way that provides an account, an explanation, or a conclusion

narrowcasting: tendency to focus media products on specific audience members connected by a common bond

negative face wants: the desire not to be imposed upon or treated as inferior (contrast with *positive face wants*)

neutral questions: questions that provide an interviewee with no indication of a preferred way to respond (contrast with *leading questions*)

nondirective interviews: interviews in which the direction of the interview is primarily given to the interviewee

nonfluencies: meaningless vocal fillers that distract from a presentation

norm of reciprocity: if one person says something self-disclosing to another person in everyday life, that person should tell the first person something self-disclosing in return

open brainstorming: type of brainstorming in groups where each person generates a list of ideas with no topic boundary

open questions: questions that enable and prompt interviewees to answer in a wide range of ways (contrast with *closed questions*)

openness–privacy: a dialectic tension caused by people's need to be honest and open yet to retain some privacy and control over information others have about them

operational definition: a concrete explanation of meaning that is more specific, original, or personal than what a dictionary might provide

opinions: personal beliefs or speculations that, while perhaps based on facts, have not been proven or verified

oral citations: references to the source of the evidence and support material used during a presentation

organizational pattern: an arrangement of the main points of a speech that best enables audience comprehension

orientation phase: the part of a speech in which a speaker provides the audience members with information that allows them to better understand and appreciate the material presented in the body of a speech

parasocial relationships: "relationships" established with media characters and personalities

parole: how people actually use language: where they often speak using informal and ungrammatical language structure that carries meaning to us all the same (contrast with *langue*)

pauses: breaks in the vocal flow

past experience with the source: obstacle to listening when previous encounters with a person lead people to dismiss or fail to critically examine a message because the person has generally been right (or wrong) in the past

pathos: the use of emotional appeals to impact an audience

pentad: five components of narratives that explain the motivation of symbolic action

perception: process of actively selecting, organizing, and evaluating information, activities, situations, people, and essentially all the things that make up your world

performance interviews: interviews in which an individual's activities and work are discussed

performative self: a self that is a creative performance based on the social demands and norms of a given situation

personal constructs: bipolar dimensions used to measure and evaluate things

personal relationships: relationships that only specified and irreplaceable individuals (such as your mother, father, brother, sister, or very best friend) can have with you

personal space: space legitimately claimed or occupied by a person for the time being; the area around a person that is regarded as part of the person and in which only informal and close relationships are conducted

personal testimony: testimony that comes from oneself

persuade (purpose): desire to change audience beliefs, enhance existing beliefs, or convince the audience to enact a particular behavior or perform a particular action

persuasive interviews: interviews that have influence as the ultimate goal

pitch: the highness or lowness of a speaker's voice

plausibility: the extent to which a message seems legitimate

points principle: a principle of speech organization and development that highlights the basic building blocks of an argument: the main points and subpoints

polychronic culture: a culture that sees time not as linear and simple but as complex and made up of many strands, none of which is more important than any other—hence such culture's relaxed attitude toward time

polysemy: multiple meanings for the same word or symbol

population: refers to whom or what a study included (e.g., people, number of TV shows, types of foods)

positive face wants: the need to be seen and accepted as a worthwhile and reasonable person (contrast with *negative face wants*)

post hoc ergo propter hoc: argues that something is caused by whatever happens before it; Latin for "after this; therefore, because of this"

presentation: one person's particular version of, or "take" on, the facts or events (contrast with *representation*)

presentation aids: audio and visual tools used by a speaker to enhance audience understanding, appreciation, and retention that also impact a speaker's credibility and audience attention

primary questions: questions that introduce new topics during an interview (contrast with *secondary questions*)

probing questions (secondary questions): brief statements or words that urge an interviewee to continue or to elaborate on a response

problem–solution pattern: divides the body of the speech by first addressing a problem and then offering a solution to that problem

problem-solving interviews: interviews in which a problem is isolated and solutions are generated

process speech: describes the procedure or method through which something is accomplished *without* the expectation that the audience will actually perform the process

promotive communication: works toward moving the agenda along and keeping people on track

prototype: best-case example of something

provisions of relationships: the deep and important psychological and supportive benefits that relationships provide

proxemics: the study of space and distance in communication

question–answer pattern: posing questions an audience may have about a subject and then answering them in a manner that favors a speaker's position

rate (of speech): how fast or slowly a person speaks, generally determined by how many words are spoken per minute

receiving: the initial step in the listening process where hearing and listening connect

red herring (fallacious argument): the use of another issue to divert attention away from the real issue

reflecting (paraphrasing): summarizing what another person has said to convey understanding of the message

regulators: nonverbal actions that indicate to others how you want them to behave or what you want them to do

relational continuity constructional units (RCCUs): small-talk ways of demonstrating that the relationship persists during absence of face-to-face contact

relational listening: recognizing, understanding, and addressing the interconnection of relationships and communication during the listening process

relational technologies: such technologies as cell phones, iPods, and PDAs whose use has relational functions and implications in society and within specific groups

representation: describes facts or conveys information (contrast with *presentation*)

responding: final step in the listening process that entails reacting to the message of another person

résumé: document used when seeking employment that presents credentials for a position in a clear and concise manner

resurrection process: part of the breakdown of relationships that deals with how people prepare themselves for new relationships after ending an old one

richness: the characteristics of a message determined by the number of verbal and nonverbal cues available through a medium or technology

Sapir/Whorf hypothesis: the idea that it is the names of objects and ideas that make verbal distinctions and help you make conceptual distinctions rather than the other way around

schemata: mental structures that are used to organize information in part by clustering or linking associated material

scripts: guides for behavior developed from our system of knowledge

secondary questions: follow-up questions asked when seeking elaboration or further information (see *probing questions* and *mirror questions;* contrast with *primary questions*)

selective listening: obstacle to listening when people focus on the points of a message that correspond with their views and interests and pay less attention to those that do not

self-concept: a personal, private, and essential core, covered with layers of secrecy, privacy, and convention

self-disclosure: the revelation of personal information that others could not know unless the person *made* it known

self-fulfilling prophecy: principle maintaining if someone believes a particular outcome will take place, his or her actions will often lead to its fruition

semantic diversion: obstacle to listening that occurs when people are distracted by words or phrases used in a message through negative response or unfamiliarity

sign: a consequence or an indicator of something specific, which cannot be changed by arbitrary actions or labels (e.g., "Wet streets are a sign of rain")

sociability: a secondary dimension of credibility referring to the "friendliness or likeableness" that enables a speaker to appear personable

social construction (of meaning): the way in which symbols take on meaning in a social context or society as they are used over time

social judgment theory: explains how people may respond to a range of positions surrounding a particular topic or issue

social process: part of the process of breakdown in a relationship that involves telling other people in the network about the problems and either seeking their help to keep the relationship together or seeking support for one's own version of the story of why it has come apart

social relationships: relationships in which the specific people in a given role can be changed and the relationship would still occur (e.g., customer–client relationships are the same irrespective of who is the customer and who is the client on a particular occasion; compare with *personal relationships*)

socialization impact of media: depictions of relationships in media provide models of behavior that inform people about how to engage in relationships

socioemotional (leadership style): style of leadership through which members are made to feel comfortable, satisfied, valued, and understood (compare with *task (leadership style)*)

source distraction: obstacle to listening that results from auditory and visual characteristics of the message source

spatial pattern: main points of a speech are arranged according to their physical relation

specific purpose: exactly what a speaker wants to achieve through a presentation

speech (communication) codes: sets of communication patterns that are the norm for that culture, and only that culture, hence defining it as different from others around it

speech communities: sets of people whose speech codes and practices identify them as a cultural unit, sharing characteristic values through their equally characteristic speech

speech of definition and description: a speech providing an extended explanation or depiction of an object, a creation, a place, a person, a concept, or an event

speech to actuate: a speech delivered in an attempt to impact audience behavior

speech to convince: a speech delivered in an attempt to impact audience thinking; encompasses a primary claim, or essentially what the speaker is trying to convince the audience to believe

static: elements of nonverbal communication that are fixed during interaction (e.g., shape of the room where an interaction takes place, color of eyes, clothes worn during an interview; contrast with *dynamic*)

statistics: numbers that demonstrate or establish size, trends, associations, and categories

status of the source: an obstacle to listening when a person's rank, reputation, or social position leads people to dismiss or fail to critically examine a message

subpoints: statements that support and explain the main points of a speech

syllogism: a form of argumentation consisting of a major premise, a minor premise, and a conclusion (see *enthymeme*)

symbol: an arbitrary representation of ideas, objects, people, relationships, cultures, genders, races, and so forth

symbolic interactionism: how broad social forces affect or even transact an individual person's view of who he or she is

symbolic self: the self that is transacted in interaction with other people; that arises out of social interaction, not vice versa; and hence that does not just "belong to you"

synchronous communication: communication in which people interact in real time and can at once both send and receive messages

task (leadership style): style of leadership through which proper group procedures and goals are emphasized (compare with *socioemotional (leadership style)*)

testimony: declarations or statements of a person's findings, opinions, conclusions, or experience

thesis statement: encapsulates the entire speech and is what will be maintained or argued throughout the presentation

topic-specific brainstorming: type of brainstorming in which a person generates a list of items dealing with one specific topic or idea

topical pattern: arranges support material in a speech according to specific categories, groupings, or grounds

transitions: phrases or statements that serve to connect the major parts or sections of a speech and to guide the audience through the presentation

turn taking: when one speaker hands over speaking to another person

unity principle: a principle of speech organization and development that maintains a speaker should stay focused and provide only information that supports the speech's thesis and main points

uses and gratifications: research that has attempted to determine why media systems are used and what audience members gain from their use

values: deeply held and enduring judgments of significance or importance that often provide the basis for both beliefs and attitudes

verifiability: an indication that the material being provided can be confirmed by other sources or means

vocalics (paralanguage): vocal characteristics that provide information about how verbal communication should be interpreted and how the speaker is feeling

volume: how loudly or quietly a person speaks

voluntary audience: an audience of people who are listening to a speech because they have personally chosen to be there

wandering thoughts: an obstacle to listening involving daydreams or thoughts about things other than the message being presented

wrap-up signal: indicates to the audience both verbally and nonverbally that the speaker has reached the conclusion of a public presentation; also a phrase, usually uttered by the interviewer, that signals the beginning of an interview's conclusion

Photo Credits

Chapter 1

Chapter Opening Photo: © Steve Duck.
Photo 1.1: © Creatas/ThinkStock.
Photo 1.2: © iStockphoto.com/macfoto80.
Photo 1.3: © Jupiterimages/Pixland/ThinkStock.
Photo 1.4: © Comstock Images/ThinkStock.
Photo 1.5: © Comstock Images/ThinkStock

Chapter 2

Chapter Opening Photo: © iStockphoto.com/
    knape.
Photo 2.1: © iStockphoto.com/llhoward.
Photo 2.2: © iStockphoto.com/Brosa.
Photo 2.3: © iStockphoto.com/Tina Lorien.
Photo 2.4: © iStockphoto.com/duncan1890.
Photo 2.5: © BananaStock/ThinkStock.

Chapter 3

Chapter Opening Photo: © iStockphoto.com/
    gemenacom.
Photo 3.1: © iStockphoto.com/paulprescott72.
Photo 3.2: © iStockphoto.com/MaxFX.
Photo 3.3: ©iStockphoto.com/webphotographeer.
Photo 3.4a: © Keith Brofsky/Photodisc/
    ThinkStock.
Photo 3.4b: © Michael Jenner/Robert Harding
    World Imagery/Getty Images.
Photo 3.5: © iStockphoto.com/Elenathewise.

Chapter 4

Chapter Opening Photo: © Stockbyte/
    ThinkStock.
Photo 4.1: © Can Stock Photo Inc./
    Monkeybusiness.
Photo 4.2: © Jupiterimages/Comstock/
    ThinkStock.
Photo 4.3: © Getty Images/AbleStock.com/
    ThinkStock.
Photo 4.4: © Digital Vision./ThinkStock.
Photo 4.5: © Dave & Les Jacobs/Getty Images.

Chapter 5

Chapter Opening Photo: © iStockphoto.com/
    SensorSpot.
Photo 5.1: © iStockphoto.com/killerb10.
Photo 5.2: © iStockphoto.com/parema.
Photo 5.3: © iStockphoto.com/NoDerog.
Photo 5.4: © iStockphoto.com/ranplett.
Photo 5.5: © iStockphoto.com/crazychristina.

Chapter 6

Chapter Opening Photo: © iStockphoto.com/
    deanm1974.
Photo 6.1: © iStockphoto.com/diane39.
Photo 6.2: © iStockphoto.com/Claudiad.
Photo 6.3: © iStockphoto.com/Slobo Mitic.
Photo 6.4: © iStockphoto.com/Brad Killer.
Photo 6.5: © iStockphoto.com/Deadair.

Chapter 7

Chapter Opening Photo: © iStockphoto.com/
    leezsnow.
Photo 7.1: © iStockphoto.com/nickfree.
Photo 7.2: © iStockphoto.com/wynnter.
Photo 7.3: © iStockphoto.com/claylib.
Photo 7.4: © iStockphoto.com/photosbyjim.
Photo 7.5: © iStockphoto.com/belknap.

Chapter 8

Chapter Opening Photo: © iStockphoto.com/
    summersetretrievers.
Photo 8.1: © Digital Vision./ThinkStock.
Photo 8.2: © Stockbyte/ThinkStock.
Photo 8.3: © Fuse/Getty Images.
Photo 8.4: © Peter Turnley/Corbis.
Photo 8.5: © Can Stock Photo Inc./monkeybusiness.

Chapter 9

Chapter Opening Photo: © iStockphoto.com/
    Sophia Tsibikaki.
Photo 9.1: © Fancy/Jupiter Images.

Photo 9.2: © Getty Images/ Photos.com/
ThinkStock.
Photo 9.3: © Chris Jackson/Getty Images
Entertainment/Getty.
Photo 9.4: © Rayes/Digital Vision/ThinkStock.
Photo 9.5: © Comstock/ThinkStock.

Chapter 10

Chapter Opening Photo: © Dave J. Anthony/
Getty.
Photo 10.1: © Hemera Technologies/Ablestock/
ThinkStock.
Photo 10.2: © iStockphoto.com/
monkeybusinessimages.
Photo 10.3: © Bob D'Amico /ABC via Getty
Images.
Photo 10.4: © Business Wire/Getty.
Photo:10.5: © Can Stock Photo Inc./
SmallTownStudio.

Chapter 11

Chapter Opening Photo: © Getty Images/ Photos.
com/ThinkStock.
Photo 11.1: © Tami Chappell/Reuters/Corbis.
Photo 11.2: © Somos/Veer.
Photo 11.3: © Creatas/ThinkStock.
Photo 11.4: © Simon Jarratt/Corbis.
Photo 11.5: © iStockphoto.com/BartCo.

Chapter 12

Chapter Opening Photo: © gulfimages/Getty
Images.

Photo 12.1: © iStockphoto.com/dlewis33.
Photo 12.2: © Stockbyte/ThinkStock.
Photo12.3: © Will & Deni McIntyre/Getty Images.
Photo 12.4: © iStockphoto.com/Blue_Cutler.
Photo 12.5: © iStockphoto.com/pixdeluxe.

Chapter 13

Chapter Opening Photo: © iStockphoto.com/
Kativ.
Photo 13.1: © iStockphoto.com/kcline.
Photo 13.2: © iStockphoto.com/MotoEd.
Photo 13.3: © BananaStock/ThinkStock.
Photo 13.4: © Bernhard Lang.
Photo 13.5: © Win McNamee/Getty Images.

Chapter 14

Chapter Opening Photo: © Photodisc/
ThinkStock.
Photo 14.1: © Polka Dot Images/ThinkStock.
Photo 14.2: © Stockbyte.
Photo 14.3: © Jupiterimages/Photos.com.
Photo 14.4: © Comstock.
Photo 14.5: © Mel Yates.

Chapter 15

Chapter Opening Photo: © iStockphoto.com/
AlexRaths.
Photo 15.1: © iStockphoto.com/wdstock.
Photo 15.2: © iStockphoto.com/fstop123.
Photo 15.3: © iStockphoto.com/jsmith.
Photo 15.4: © iStockphoto.com/matzaball.
Photo 15.5: © iStockphoto.com/jsmith.

Author Index

Subject Index